# THE LITTLE, BROWN READER

Irene Mc Sorley
June 13th 1990

# THE LITTLE, BROWN READER

*Fifth Edition*

*Edited by*

**MARCIA STUBBS**
*Wellesley College*

**SYLVAN BARNET**
*Tufts University*

**Scott, Foresman and Company**
*Glenview, Illinois   Boston   London*

**Library of Congress Cataloging-in-Publication Data**

The Little, Brown reader / edited by Marcia Stubbs, Sylvan Barnet. —
   5th ed.
      p.   cm.
   Includes index.
   ISBN 0-673-39680-0
   1. College readers.   I. Stubbs, Marcia.   II. Barnet, Sylvan.
   PE1122.L56,  1989
808'.0427—dc19                                                88–39265
                                                                CIP

Copyright © 1989 by Marcia Stubbs and Sylvan Barnet

3  4  5  6  7  8  9  10 — RRC — 94  93  92  91  90  89

**Cover art:** *"A Day at the Race," Richard Diebenkorn, 1953. The Carnegie Museum of Art, Pittsburgh; Patrons Art Fund, 1953.*

Printed in the United States of America

Acknowledgments begin on page 1154.

# PREFACE

Books have been put to all sorts of unexpected uses. Tolstoy used Tatishef's dictionaries as a test of physical endurance, holding them in his outstretched hand for five minutes, enduring "terrible pain." Books (especially pocket-sized Bibles) have served as armor by deflecting bullets. And they have served as weapons: two hundred years ago the formidable Dr. Johnson knocked a man down with a large book.

In a course in writing, what is the proper use of the book in hand? This anthology contains some one hundred and thirty essays, together with a few poems, stories, and fables, and numerous paragraphs and aphorisms. But these readings are not the subject matter of the course; the subject matter of a writing course is writing, particularly the writing the students themselves produce. The responsibilities we felt as editors, then, were to include selections that encourage and enable students to write well, and to exclude selections that do not.

To talk of "enabling" first: Students, like all other writers, write best when they write on fairly specific topics that can come within their experience and within their command in the time that they have available to write. A glance at the first four thematic sections of our table of contents—these follow Chapter 1, which offers an overview of "Reading (and Writing About) Essays"—will reveal the general areas within which, we believe, students can find topics they have already given some thought to and are likely to be encountering in other courses as well: family relationships, love and courtship; food and diet, clothing, buildings and neighborhoods; schools; work, sports, and play. Although the next three sections ("Open for Business," "Messages," and "Networks") are also on familiar subjects—entrepreneurship, language, and popular culture—the selections themselves offer ways of thinking about these subjects that may be less familiar. Television commercials and films, for example, can be thought of as networks that articulate and transmit values implicit in a culture. The last four sections are about areas of experience that, while hardly remote from students' interest, are perhaps more difficult for all of us to grasp concretely: the tension between civil rights and liberties and the need for law and order; the nature of scientific inquiry; the memories and passions that shape or embody our personal values, our identities, and our being; and, finally, the nature of religious faith—Hebrew, Christian, and Muslim. In these last sections, therefore, we have taken particular care to exclude writing that is, for our purposes, too abstract, or too technical, or too elaborate.

This returns us to the need we felt as editors to think carefully about whether selections we were inclined to use—because they were beautifully written or on a stimulating topic—would encourage students to write. Such encouragement does not come, we feel, solely from the subject of an essay or from its excellence; it comes when the essay engenders in the reader a confidence in the writing process itself. No one quality in essays automatically teaches such confidence: not length or brevity, not difficulty or simplicity, not necessarily clarity, and almost certainly not brilliance. But essays that teach writing demonstrate, in some way, that the writers had some stake in what they were saying, took some pains to say what they meant, and took pleasure in having said it. The selections we include vary in length, complexity, subtlety, tone, and purpose. Most were written by our contemporaries, but not all. The authors include historians, sociologists, architects, scientists, saints, and philosophers, as well as journalists and other professional writers. And we have included some pictures in each section. But we hope that everything here will allow students, including those who have previously read very little, to establish helpful connections between the activities that produced the words (and pictures) in these pages and their own work in putting critical responses to them on paper.

Although any arrangement of the selections—thematic, rhetorical, alphabetical, chronological, or random—would have suited our purposes, we preferred the thematic arrangement. For one thing, by narrowing our choices it helped us to make decisions. But more important, we know that in the real world what people write about is subjects, and we didn't want to miss any opportunity to suggest that what goes on in writing courses is something like what goes on outside. The thematic categories are not intended to be rigid, however, and they do not pretend to be comprehensive; some of the questions following the selections suggest that leaping across boundaries is permitted, even encouraged. And, for instructors who prefer to organize their writing courses rhetorically, we have added a selective table of contents organized rhetorically. Finally, we append a glossary of terms for students of writing and a brief essay on looking at and writing about pictures. The pictures (beautiful things in themselves, we think), like the essays, stories, and poems, suggest or provide immediate or nearly immediate experiences for students to write about.

As usual, we are indebted to readers-in-residence. Morton Berman, William Burto, and Judith Stubbs have often read our material and then told us what we wanted to hear.

While we were selecting the essays, we received helpful advice from Eric D. Brown, Kenneth Cooney, William Devlin, George D. Haich, Ruth C. Hege, William E. Lucas, William Lutz, Mary Shesgreen, Judith Stanford, Michael West, and Harvey Vetstein.

We thank those instructors who generously offered suggestions based on their classroom experience with the first four editions: Bonnie Alexander, Kenneth Alrutz, Marianne Antczack, Norman Sidney Ashbridge, Andrew Aung, Donald Babcock, James Barcus, Lloyd Becker, Frank Bidart, Joseph Blimm, Frank Bliss, Beverly Boone, Grant Boswell, George Branam, Lillian Broderick, Ruth Brown, Jean Young Brunk, Beth Burch, Debra L. Burguaet, Anne Burley, Carol Burns, D. G. Campbell, J. V. Chambers, John Clifford, Ann Connor, Anne Cooney, Marion Copeland, Robert Cosgrove, Helene Davis, Donald DeSulis, John A. R. Dick, Fiona Emde, Robert Erickson, Richard Fahey, Evelyn Farbman, Michael Feehan, Linda Feldmeier, Gretchen Fillmore, Sister Jeremy Finnegan, Kathleen P. Flint, Martha Flint, William Ford, Joseph S. Frany, James French, Charles Frey, Yvonne Frey, David Gadziola, George Griffith, Steve Hamelman, Bettina Hanlon, Brian O. Hannon, Hymen H. Hart, Pat Hart, Steven Harvey, Mal Haslett, Stephen Hathaway, Mark Hawkins, George Hayhoe, Zelda Hedden-Sellman, Kathryn Hellerstein, Dr. Elbert R. Hill, Maureen Hoal, David Hoddeson, Kathryn Holms, John Howe, William Howrath, Morris Husted, Lois B. Janzer, Johanna Jung, F. A. Kachur, Michael Kalter, Robert D. Keohan, Richard Kirchoffer, Walt Klarner, Robert Knox, Karl Kumm, Sandra M. Lee, Dorinda Lemaire, Claudia Limbert, Joyce D. Lipkis, Marie M. McAllister, Anne McCormick, Charles McLaughlin, Garry Merritt, George Miller, John Milstead, Mary F. Minton, Chris M. Mott, Abigail Mulcahy, John Nesselhof, Robert Ohafson, Terry Otten, Jewyl Pallette, Linda Pelzer, Richard Price, Richard Priebe, Phyllis Reed, Karyn Riedell, Leo Rockas, Duncan Rollo, Harriet Rosenblum, Ronald Ruland, Ralph St. Louis, Jack Seltzer, Emerson

Shuck, Carol Sicherman, James Smith, Larry Smith, Mark Smith, Harry Solomon, John Stahl, Judith Stanford, Carol Starikoff, Petra Steele, William B. Stone, Mary Lee Strode, William L. Stull, Tereatha Taylor, David Templeman, Elizabeth Tentarelli, Robert Thompson, Leatrice Timmons, Pamela Topping, Marilyn Valention, J. Keith Veizer, Brother Roland Vigeant, Lorraine Viscardi, Anthony Vital, Carolyn Wall, Don Wall, Doug Watson, Mary Weinkauf, Mark Wenz, Richard Whitworth, Lyn Yonack, Lee Yosha, and Thomas Young.

We owe a special debt to Professor John Harwood and other teachers in the composition program at Pennsylvania State University for suggesting ways in which *The Little, Brown Reader* can be used in a course that emphasizes persuasive writing.

We are grateful to colleagues at Wellesley College—Michael David Coogan, Katheryn H. Doran, Lidwien Kapteijns, Louise Marlow, Robert Umans, Winifred Jane Wood, and Teresa Amott—who suggested materials for the new sections on science and religion, or who otherwise assisted us with this new edition.

People at Little, Brown have been unfailingly helpful; we would especially like to thank Cynthia Chapin and Joseph Opiela.

## A Note on the Fifth Edition

"Never read a book that is not old." Thus Emerson. It's good advice, but we are of course pleased that when *The Little, Brown Reader* was published it immediately found a receptive audience. Second, third, and fourth editions allowed us to strengthen the book by adding some recent essays, and now the publisher has asked for a fifth edition in order to meet the needs of instructors who wish to continue to use the book but who also want something new. William Hazlitt, Emerson's older contemporary, said that he always read an old book when a new one was published. We hope that this new edition allows instructors to read both at once, for although we have now (1) provided an introductory chapter on reading and writing essays, (2) substituted many essays within the thematic chapters—for instance six new essays in "Networks," including one by Woody Allen on colorizing film—and (3) added three new thematic sections ("Open for Business," "Science or Pseudoscience?" and "Articles of Faith"), we have also tried to preserve the original character of the book.

# CONTENTS

## 1  READING (AND WRITING ABOUT) ESSAYS

## 2   ALL IN THE FAMILY

\* Denotes fiction.
\*\* Denotes poetry.

# 3  FOOD, CLOTHING, SHELTER

# 4 TEACHING AND LEARNING

## 5   WORK AND PLAY

## 6   OPEN FOR BUSINESS

## 8  NETWORKS

# 10   SCIENCE OR PSEUDOSCIENCE?

# 11   THE DEEP HEART'S CORE

# 12  ARTICLES OF FAITH

# RHETORICAL GUIDE

## Analogy

## Analysis or Classification

## Argument
(See *Persuasion*)

## Autobiography
(see *Journal and Personal Report*)

## Cause and Effect

## Comparison and Contrast

# Definition

# Description

# Diction

# Evaluation

## Examples, Illustrations

## Exposition

# Irony
(See also *Persuasion*)

# Journal and Personal Report

# Narration

# Persuasion

# Style

# 1
## READING
## (AND WRITING ABOUT)
## ESSAYS

# Getting Started: Skimming and Reading

"Some books are to be tasted, others to be swallowed, and some few to be chewed and digested." You may already have encountered this wise remark by Francis Bacon, a very good reader (and a good writer too, though he did not write Shakespeare's plays). Bacon puts his finger on an important truth: not all books (or essays) are to be read in the same way. We occasionally see advertisements for courses in speed reading; one ad claimed that President Kennedy took such a course and learned to read a couple of hundred pages in an hour. That's about the right speed for most of the stuff that crossed his desk. But (despite the advertisements) he wasn't reading, he was skimming. The art of skimming is essential if we are to survive the daily deluge of paper loosed upon us, and most of us develop the art satisfactorily: we get through junk mail in a matter of seconds, the newspaper and *Time* or *Newsweek* in a matter of minutes. We skim, perhaps taking in only the captions, and then, when an item catches our interest, we stop skimming and really read; possibly we even go back and reread the opening paragraphs that we had skimmed.

Skimming has its place in academic life too; in studying for an examination or in doing a research paper you probably will skim many pages to find the material that is relevant and that will require close reading. Even if you know at the outset that an article or book is important, you may skim it first, to get the gist, so that you can then more easily read it a second time (really a first time) and take notes on it. Skimming may reveal, for instance, that each chapter ends with a summary, and so even before you begin to read closely you know that you will not have to take very general notes later when you inch through each page.

Inevitably, however, and especially in a composition course, much of the assigned reading and every essay that you intend to write about must be read slowly and with all of your powers of attention. Only by reading attentively do we hear in the mind's ear the writer's *tone*— whether it is ironic or earnestly straightforward, indignant or genial. Perhaps you know the line from Owen Wister's novel *The Virginian*: "When you call me that, smile." Words spoken with a smile mean something different from the same words forced through clenched teeth. But while speakers can communicate by body language and by gestures, by facial expressions and by changes in tone of voice, writers have only words in ink on paper. As a writer, you are learning control of tone as you learn to take pains in your choice of words, in the way you arrange sentences, and even in the punctuation marks you may find yourself changing in your final draft. These skills will pay off doubly if you apply them to your reading, by putting yourself in the place of the writer whose work you are reading. As a reader—a thoughtful reader—you must also make some effort to "hear" the writer's tone as part of the meaning the words communicate. Skimming is not adequate to that task.

Close reading begins with reading the title, and thinking about it, at least briefly. If we pick up an essay called "Do-It-Yourself Brain Surgery" we ought to know at once that we can prepare to be amused. Such a title must be ironic; it simply cannot be taken straight by a thoughtful reader. What about Judy Syfers's "Why I Want a Wife"? That title on an essay by a woman demands at least a double take and, very likely, a glance at the biographical note at the bottom of the page. There, as it happens (page 41 in this book), you'll find the information that the essay first appeared in the premier issue of *Ms.* magazine. If that means nothing to you, reading the first paragraph, just three brief sentences, should confirm your hunch that Syfers's title is not exactly straightforward and it should prepare you for the essay's ironic content.

We say "should" because a surprising number of college students persist, despite these clues, in reading this and other essays containing irony as if the essays were perfectly straightforward or even solemn. Perhaps such students have been conditioned to expect only "fact" in a printed text, and thus miss what is more usually there—a particular writer's opinions, beliefs, and attitudes, which may or may not be based on facts or supported by facts. Or, it may be that such students, whose own conversation and even writing are often richly ironic, fail to detect irony in what they read because they have come to expect that anything in a textbook, certainly anything in a textbook for an English class, is solemn and boring, and that a safe tack is to fake a kind of pious interest in it, whatever it is. If you have fallen into that trap yourself, we recommend two remedies: first, consciously question your own assumptions about what you read; and second, at least in reading this book, be prepared for some surprises.

Many titles in this anthology *are* perfectly straightforward and informative. Paul Goodman's "A Proposal to Abolish Grading" is one, and Paul Robinson's "TV Can't Educate" is a terse summary of the essay's argument, or thesis. But some titles convey very little: E. B. White's "Education" hardly prepares us for his rather genial comparison of a public elementary school with a private school, or for the argumentative edge of the comparison. We will have to read further to get even the faintest idea of what he is up to. Orwell's "Shooting an Elephant" deliberately misleads us, for the title suggests some sort of hunting tale, though if we know that Orwell is fundamentally a social critic we suspect he is not really going to give us a yarn about an Englishman's pleasure in shooting big game.

## Identifying the Topic and Thesis

If the writer's *thesis* is not stated or implied in the title, it ought to become increasingly evident as you work your way into the essay. This thesis is a point, an argument; and a point or argument implies an *attitude* toward a *topic*. In reading, then, try to identify the topic (not really do-it-yourself brain surgery, but do-it-yourself books) and the attitude (amused contempt for such books). Even an essay that is largely narrative, recounting a personal experience or a bit of history, will usually include an attitude toward the event being narrated, and it is the attitude—the interpretation of the event—rather than the event itself that is usually the richest part of the essay. "Shooting an Elephant" does in fact recount an episode in which Orwell shot an elephant, but the essay is really about *why* he shot the elephant, and what the experience revealed. His analysis of the episode brought him, he says, to an understanding of "the real nature of imperialism—the real motives for which despotic governments act."

Here is Orwell's essay.

George Orwell

# Shooting an Elephant

In Moulmein, in Lower Burma, I was hated by large num- 1
bers of people—the only time in my life that I have been important
enough for this to happen to me. I was sub-divisional police officer of
the town, and in an aimless, petty kind of way anti-European feeling
was very bitter. No one had the guts to raise a riot, but if a European
woman went through the bazaars alone somebody would probably
spit betel juice over her dress. As a police officer I was an obvious
target and was baited whenever it seemed safe to do so. When a nimble
Burman tripped me up on the football field and the referee (another
Burman) looked the other way, the crowd yelled with hideous laughter. This happened more than once. In the end the sneering yellow
faces of young men that met me everywhere, the insults hooted after
me when I was at a safe distance, got badly on my nerves. The young
Buddhist priests were the worst of all. There were several thousands
of them in the town and none of them seemed to have anything to do
except stand on street corners and jeer at Europeans.

All this was perplexing and upsetting. For at that time I had already 2
made up my mind that imperialism was an evil thing and the sooner
I chucked up my job and got out of it the better. Theoretically—and
secretly, of course—I was all for the Burmese and all against their
oppressors, the British. As for the job I was doing, I hated it more
bitterly than I can perhaps make clear. In a job like that you see the
dirty work of Empire at close quarters. The wretched prisoners huddling in the stinking cages of the lock-ups, the grey, cowed faces of
the long-term convicts, the scarred buttocks of the men who had been
flogged with bamboos—all these oppressed me with an intolerable
sense of guilt. But I could get nothing into perspective. I was young
and ill-educated and I had had to think out my problems in the utter

---

George Orwell (1903–1950) was the pen name adopted by Eric Blair, an Englishman born in India. Orwell was educated at Eton, in England, but in 1921 he went
back to the East and served for five years as a police officer in Burma. He then
returned to Europe, doing odd jobs while writing novels and stories. In 1936 he
fought in the Spanish Civil War on the side of the Republicans, an experience
reported in *Homage to Catalonia* (1938). His last years were spent writing in
England.

---

silence that is imposed on every Englishman in the East. I did not even know that the British Empire is dying, still less did I know that it is a great deal better than the younger empires that are going to supplant it. All I knew was that I was stuck between my hatred of the empire I served and my rage against the evil-spirited little beasts who tried to make my job impossible. With one part of my mind I thought of the British Raj as an unbreakable tyranny, as something clamped down, in *saecula saeculorum*,[1] upon the will of the prostrate peoples; with another part I thought that the greatest joy in the world would be to drive a bayonet into a Buddhist priest's guts. Feelings like these are normal by-products of imperialism; ask any Anglo-Indian official, if you can catch him off duty.

One day something happened which in a roundabout way was  3
enlightening. It was a tiny incident in itself, but it gave me a better glimpse than I had had before of the real nature of imperialism—the real motives for which despotic governments act. Early one morning the sub-inspector at a police station the other end of town rang me up on the 'phone and said that an elephant was ravaging the bazaar. Would I please come and do something about it? I did not know what I could do, but I wanted to see what was happening and I got on to a pony and started out. I took my rifle, an old .44 Winchester and much too small to kill an elephant, but I thought the noise might be useful *in terrorem*.[2] Various Burmans stopped me on the way and told me about the elephant's doings. It was not, of course, a wild elephant, but a tame one which had gone "must." It had been chained up, as tame elephants always are when their attack of "must" is due, but on the previous night it had broken its chain and escaped. Its mahout, the only person who could manage it when it was in that state, had set out in pursuit, but had taken the wrong direction and was now twelve hours' journey away, and in the morning the elephant had suddenly reappeared in the town. The Burmese population had no weapons and were quite helpless against it. It had already destroyed somebody's bamboo hut, killed a cow and raided some fruit-stalls and devoured the stock; also it had met the municipal rubbish van and, when the driver jumped out and took to his heels, had turned the van over and inflicted violences upon it.

The Burmese sub-inspector and some Indian constables were wait-  4
ing for me in the quarter where the elephant had been seen. It was a

[1] For world without end. (Editors' note)
[2] As a warning. (Editors' note)

very poor quarter, a labyrinth of squalid bamboo huts, thatched with palmleaf, winding all over a steep hillside. I remember that it was a cloudy, stuffy morning at the beginning of the rains. We began questioning the people as to where the elephant had gone and, as usual, failed to get any definite information. That is invariably the case in the East; a story always sounds clear enough at a distance, but the nearer you get to the scene of events the vaguer it becomes. Some of the people said that the elephant had gone in one direction, some said that he had gone in another, some professed not even to have heard of any elephant. I had almost made up my mind that the whole story was a pack of lies, when we heard yells a little distance away. There was a loud, scandalized cry of "Go away, child! Go away this instant!" and an old woman with a switch in her hand came round the corner of a hut, violently shooing away a crowd of naked children. Some more women followed, clicking their tongues and exclaiming; evidently there was something that the children ought not to have seen. I rounded the hut and saw a man's dead body sprawling in the mud. He was an Indian, a black Dravidian coolie, almost naked, and he could not have been dead many minutes. The people said that the elephant had come suddenly upon him round the corner of the hut, caught him with its trunk, put its foot on his back and ground him into the earth. This was the rainy season and the ground was soft, and his face had scored a trench a foot deep and a couple of yards long. He was lying on his belly with arms crucified and head sharply twisted to one side. His face was coated with mud, the eyes wide open, the teeth bared and grinning with an expression of unendurable agony. (Never tell me, by the way, that the dead look peaceful. Most of the corpses I have seen looked devilish.) The friction of the great beast's foot had stripped the skin from his back as neatly as one skins a rabbit. As soon as I saw the dead man I sent an orderly to a friend's house nearby to borrow an elephant rifle. I had already sent back the pony, not wanting it to go mad with fright and throw me if it smelt the elephant.

The orderly came back in a few minutes with a rifle and five cartridges, and meanwhile some Burmans had arrived and told us that the elephant was in the paddy fields below, only a few hundred yards away. As I started forward practically the whole population of the quarter flocked out of the houses and followed me. They had seen the rifle and were all shouting excitedly that I was going to shoot the elephant. They had not shown much interest in the elephant when he was merely ravaging their homes, but it was different now that he was going to be shot. It was a bit of fun to them, as it would be to an

English crowd; besides they wanted the meat. It made me vaguely uneasy. I had no intention of shooting the elephant—I had merely sent for the rifle to defend myself if necessary—and it is always un-nerving to have a crowd following you. I marched down the hill, look-ing and feeling a fool, with the rifle over my shoulder and an ever-growing army of people jostling at my heels. At the bottom, when you got away from the huts, there was a metalled road and beyond that a miry waste of paddy fields a thousand yards across, not yet ploughed but soggy from the first rains and dotted with coarse grass. The ele-phant was standing eight yards from the road, his left side towards us. He took not the slightest notice of the crowd's approach. He was tearing up bunches of grass, beating them against his knees to clean them and stuffing them into his mouth.

I had halted on the road. As soon as I saw the elephant I knew    6
with perfect certainty that I ought not to shoot him. It is a serious matter to shoot a working elephant—it is comparable to destroying a huge and costly piece of machinery—and obviously one ought not to do it if it can possibly be avoided. And at that distance, peacefully eating, the elephant looked no more dangerous than a cow. I thought then and I think now that his attack of "must" was already passing off; in which case he would merely wander harmlessly about until the mahout came back and caught him. Moreover, I did not in the least want to shoot him. I decided that I would watch him for a little while to make sure that he did not turn savage again, and then go home.

But at that moment, I glanced round at the crowd that had followed    7
me. It was an immense crowd, two thousand at the least and growing every minute. It blocked the road for a long distance on either side. I looked at the sea of yellow faces above the garish clothes—faces all happy and excited over this bit of fun, all certain that the elephant was going to be shot. They were watching me as they would watch a con-juror about to perform a trick. They did not like me, but with the magical rifle in my hands I was momentarily worth watching. And suddenly I realized that I should have to shoot the elephant after all. The people expected it of me and I had got to do it; I could feel their two thousand wills pressing me forward, irresistibly. And it was at this moment, as I stood there with the rifle in my hands, that I first grasped the hollowness, the futility of the white man's dominion in the East. Here was I, the white man with his gun, standing in front of the unarmed native crowd—seemingly the leading actor of the piece; but in reality I was only an absurd puppet pushed to and fro by the will of those yellow faces behind. I perceived in this moment that when

the white man turns tyrant it is his own freedom that he destroys. He becomes a sort of hollow, posing dummy, the conventionalized figure of a sahib. For it is the condition of his rule that he shall spend his life in trying to impress the "natives," and so in every crisis he has got to do what the "natives" expect of him. He wears a mask, and his face grows to fit it. I had got to shoot the elephant. I had committed myself to doing it when I sent for the rifle. A sahib has got to act like a sahib; he has got to appear resolute, to know his own mind and do definite things. To come all that way, rifle in hand, with two thousand people marching at my heels, and then to trail feebly away, having done nothing—no, that was impossible. The crowd would laugh at me. And my whole life, every white man's life in the East, was one long struggle not to be laughed at.

But I did not want to shoot the elephant. I watched him beating    8 his bunch of grass against his knees, with that preoccupied grandmotherly air that elephants have. It seemed to me that it would be murder to shoot him. At that age I was not squeamish about killing animals, but I had never shot an elephant and never wanted to. (Somehow it always seems worse to kill a *large* animal.) Besides, there was the beast's owner to be considered. Alive, the elephant was worth at least a hundred pounds; dead, he would only be worth the value of his tusks, five pounds, possibly. But I had got to act quickly. I turned to some experienced-looking Burmans who had been there when we arrived, and asked them how the elephant had been behaving. They all said the same thing: he took no notice of you if you left him alone, but he might charge if you went too close to him.

It was perfectly clear to me what I ought to do. I ought to walk    9 up to within, say, twenty-five yards of the elephant and test his behavior. If he charged, I could shoot; if he took no notice of me, it would be safe to leave him until the mahout came back. But also I knew that I was going to do no such thing. I was a poor shot with a rifle and the ground was soft mud into which one would sink at every step. If the elephant charged and I missed him, I should have about as much chance as a toad under a steam-roller. But even then I was not thinking particularly of my own skin, only of the watchful yellow faces behind. For at that moment, with the crowd watching me, I was not afraid in the ordinary sense, as I would have been if I had been alone. A white man mustn't be frightened in front of "natives"; and so, in general, he isn't frightened. The sole thought in my mind was that if anything went wrong those two thousand Burmans would see me pursued, caught, trampled on and reduced to a grinning corpse like that Indian up the hill. And if that happened it was quite probable that some of them would laugh. That would never do. There was only one alternative. I shoved the cartridges into the magazine and lay down on the road to get a better aim.

The crowd grew very still, and a deep, low, happy sigh, as of  10 people who see the theatre curtain go up at last, breathed from innumerable throats. They were going to have their bit of fun after all. The rifle was a beautiful German thing with cross-hair sights. I did not then know that in shooting an elephant one would shoot to cut an imaginary bar running from ear-hole to ear-hole. I ought, therefore, as the elephant was sideways on, to have aimed straight at his earhole; actually I aimed several inches in front of this, thinking the brain would be further forward.

When I pulled the trigger I did not hear the bang or feel the kick—  11 one never does when a shot goes home—but I heard the devilish roar of glee that went up from the crowd. In that instant, in too short a time, one would have thought, even for the bullet to get there, a mysterious, terrible change had come over the elephant. He neither stirred nor fell, but every line of his body had altered. He looked suddenly stricken, shrunken, immensely old, as though the frightful impact of the bullet had paralysed him without knocking him down. At last, after what seemed a long time—it might have been five seconds, I dare say—he sagged flabbily to his knees. His mouth slobbered. An enormous senility seemed to have settled upon him. One could have imagined him thousands of years old. I fired again into the same spot. At the second shot he did not collapse but climbed with desperate slowness to his feet and stood weakly upright, with legs sagging and head drooping. I fired a third time. That was the shot that did for him. You could see the agony of it jolt his whole body and knock the last remnant of strength from his legs. But in falling he seemed for a moment to rise, for as his hind legs collapsed beneath him he seemed to tower upward like a huge rock toppling, his trunk reaching skywards like a tree. He trumpeted, for the first and only time. And then down he came, his belly towards me, with a crash that seemed to shake the ground even where I lay.

I got up. The Burmans were already racing past me across the  12 mud. It was obvious that the elephant would never rise again, but he was not dead. He was breathing very rhythmically with long rattling gasps, his great mound of a side painfully rising and falling. His mouth was wide open. I could see far down into caverns of pale pink throat. I waited a long time for him to die, but his breathing did not weaken. Finally I fired my two remaining shots into the spot where I thought his heart must be. The thick blood welled out of him like red velvet, but still he did not die. His body did not even jerk when the shots hit him, the tortured breathing continued without a pause. He was dying, very slowly and in great agony, but in some world remote from me where not even a bullet could damage him further. I felt I had to put an end to that dreadful noise. It seemed dreadful to see the great beast lying there, powerless to move and yet powerless to die, and not even to be able to finish him. I sent back for my small rifle and poured shot after shot into his heart and down his throat. They seemed to make no impression. The tortured gasps continued as steadily as the ticking of a clock.

In the end I could not stand it any longer and went away. I heard 13 later that it took him half an hour to die. Burmans were bringing dahs and baskets even before I left, and I was told they had stripped his body almost to the bones by the afternoon.

Afterwards, of course, there were endless discussions about the 14 shooting of the elephant. The owner was furious, but he was only an Indian and could do nothing. Besides, legally I had done the right thing, for a mad elephant has to be killed, like a mad dog, if its owner fails to control it. Among the Europeans opinion was divided. The older men said I was right, the younger men said it was a damn shame to shoot an elephant for killing a coolie, because the elephant was worth more than any damn Coringhee coolie. And afterwards I was very glad that the coolie had been killed; it put me legally in the right and it gave me sufficient pretext for shooting the elephant. I often wondered whether any of the others grasped that I had done it solely to avoid looking a fool.

---

## Underlining, Highlighting, Summarizing

Reading with a pencil in hand is a great aid to thinking. As you read, underline or highlight key expressions and those sentences that strike you as especially important, for instance topic sentences or sentences that seem to summarize. But beware of underlining and highlighting so much material that you merely make the text unreadable. For an especially complex or detailed essay, you probably will find it helpful to jot down a sentence summarizing each paragraph, or each group of closely related paragraphs, thus giving yourself a sort of outline of the essay you are reading.

Orwell's first two paragraphs, for instance, might be summarized thus:

1. Orwell, a police officer in Lower Burma, like other Europeans was assaulted in minor ways (unfairly tripped during a game) by the Burmans.
2. He was upset because he was anti-imperialist and pro-Burmese, but he was not educated enough to understand how to reconcile his hatred of empire with his hatred of the Burmese who made his life difficult.

Whether you will want—or need—to make an outline-summary of Orwell's essay depends on how difficult you found it. If you found "Shooting an Elephant" difficult to follow, you will get a better grasp of it by rereading it and making summaries of this sort. The act of summarizing each paragraph will, of course, help you grasp the meaning of the paragraphs. You won't want to write so much for an essay that strikes you as extremely easy, but at the very least you will want to jot down some key words and phrases. Making a list of key phrases or ideas or making an outline and writing a summary are laborious activities, but they are worth the effort; you will gain a closer knowledge of the material than can be gained by merely letting your eye run over the page, or even than can be gained by underlining or highlighting.

## Asking Questions, Taking Notes

"It is thinking," the philosopher John Locke wrote, "that makes what we read ours." But when do you start writing about what you have read? And how do you begin? The answer is that if you have been reading closely you have already begun writing. You have had a pen or pencil in hand, a notebook or sheets of paper beside your book, probably a dictionary within arm's reach, perhaps a handbook, and, of course, a wastebasket. You have read with pen in hand not simply to record what you think, but to help you think. Assuming that you are reading a book that you own, as you read begin making discreet marks in the margins of the text. Not broad yellow lines through every other sentence—those will only distract you later and impede thoughtful rereading—but little checks, or brackets, or question marks next to passages that you find especially interesting, or puzzling, or quotable. On rereading, paying special attention to those passages, you may begin to detect a pattern that will disclose a topic and may eventually lead you to formulate a thesis.

Suppose you are going to write on "Shooting an Elephant." Possibly at this stage of the course your instructor is concerned with teaching a particular topic—let's say organization, or narration, or description, or the uses of foreshadowing—and therefore he or she limits the scope of your study of Orwell's essay to an examination of this topic. Perhaps the topic is organization. In reading or rereading the essay you notice that from the third paragraph through the next-to-last paragraph, Orwell is telling a story, but in the middle—not the end—he tells us the significance of the story. And so you mark the passage, perhaps with a question mark, perhaps with a pair of square brackets:

> And it was at this moment, as I stood there with the rifle in my hands, that I first grasped the hollowness, the futility of the white man's dominion in the East. . . . I perceived in this moment that when the white man turns tyrant it is his own freedom that he destroys. He becomes a sort of hollow, posing dummy, the conventionalized figure of a sahib.

You might even jot down some questions in your notebook. Why does Orwell spill the beans here, and why—pages later—does he describe at length the death throes of the elephant, since even without the elephant's lingering death he had come to his insight? Answers will vary (perhaps good reasons can be offered, or perhaps Orwell bungled the essay), but in noting and questioning this apparently unusual organization you may come to a fuller understanding of Orwell's essay (and you may also learn something about strategies of organization that you can apply to your own writing in other courses and after you leave college).

Of course, the passages that you mark, in one way or another, will depend largely on the assigned topic. For example, if your instructor's assignment includes words such as "summarize," "compare," "define," "evaluate," you will be alerted to think in particular directions. It's important to read the assignment carefully before you begin to work. It's equally important to consult and reread the assignment at various stages in your work to be sure you haven't wandered off the track—into summarizing or into writing a personal narrative, for example, when an analysis—a careful examination—was called for. If you don't understand the assignment, you should not hesitate to ask your instructor or a peer advisor for help. And you should start early enough so that you have time to know what your questions about the assignment are and get help with them.

Let's say, however, that the instructor has not assigned a topic but has left the choice up to you. Again, your jottings of various sorts (lists of key phrases, underlinings, formulation of Orwell's thesis, and perhaps a summary) should suggest various possibilities. Perhaps you were puzzled by Orwell's depiction of the Burmese, which doesn't seem terribly sympathetic for someone who claims to be on their side. "Sneering yellow faces," "no one had the guts to raise a riot"—such passages may be worth thinking about and writing about. Looking at the essay again you notice that although Orwell begins with more or less the conventional attitudes of the white oppressor, he increasingly reveals his sympathy for the Burmese without sentimentalizing them. An essay on Orwell's way of depicting the Burmese (and therefore to some extent on his way of depicting his own changing attitudes) as it develops in his essay is a possibility. At this point you might try writing a few sentences in your notebook.

Let's assume that on thinking further about "Shooting an Elephant" you come to feel that your greatest interest is in Orwell's political interpretation of his action. Now, in other words, you are *settling on a topic*. You keep coming back to that passage, in the middle, about his recognition of the nature of imperialism, and somehow you don't quite feel that Orwell has correctly interpreted his own experience. For one thing, you are bothered by what seems to you to be an act of cowardice on his part. Yes, the pressure on him was great—that mob at his back, his fear of losing face—and you see that Orwell has from the beginning of the essay carefully depicted the plight of the white man in Burma. But you still think that a person of greater moral fiber would have resisted the pressure and would not have shot the elephant. That is to say (and this is crucial in feeling your way toward your essay), you are beginning to *formulate a thesis statement*.

## Free Writing

Perhaps now is the time to engage in what is called "free writing," or "free associating," or "pre-writing," scribbling away so that one idea on paper will help to call up another. What you produce at this stage is not so much a first draft as a zero draft, but it is invaluable as a means of developing your thoughts. Free writing is especially easy if you use a word processor; you can enter material with much less physical effort than is expended in pushing a pen across paper, and you will thus find that you can put down a good many ideas, some of which really will turn out to be good. Orwell, you may come to feel, is explaining away his own failure by giving it a grand significance, by inflating it with political meaning. And so now you are *refining the thesis*. (Almost surely, however, you will want to refine it further, when your ideas become somewhat clarified during the process of writing your first draft.)

The step after this will be to work out, at least tentatively, *strategies for putting forth this thesis*. How will you begin? With a quotation from Orwell? With a statement of your initial reaction to the essay? Which passages will you quote? What tone will you adopt? Will a comparison be useful? How personal should you get? You can't hope to settle all of these questions at once, and it will almost certainly be impossible for you to write an introductory paragraph. Fortunately, the only thing you need to do at this point is to *start writing*. With a topic in mind, an idea about it (your tentative thesis), and some rough notes, you start getting as many of your ideas on paper as you can.

## Listing and Outlining

At this point it might be useful to sketch a very rough outline, a sort of shopping list of the points you want to make. Here is the outline with which one student began. Notice, by the way, how one idea gave rise to another. Making a list is not so much a matter of putting down ideas that you already have as a matter of *generating* ideas that you didn't know you had.

```
Sympathy for Orwell—how he creates it
His interpretation of shooting ("the system")
Why I don't buy it
Was he a "tyrant"?
Was he a "dummy"?
Maybe a (coward?)
How I interpret shooting: guilt
Why he misinterprets: Guilt
(End with something good?)
```

## The First Draft

With some such rough outline in front of you, simply begin writing sentences. Don't worry about mechanical matters, such as spelling, or getting every word exactly right. Leave gaps in your sentences if you need to. What you are doing is writing a *rough draft* that no one else need ever see and that even you must not regard as sacred. You can always add or delete, or change a word, or even your mind. If you have written a rough outline you will probably tinker with that too as your ideas take clearer shape because you find more and more evidence to support or to modify the thesis.

When you reach this point, you are probably ready to try writing your introductory paragraph. If you own a word processor, you'll probably be ready now to open a file for your first draft. But if you share a word processor with many others, at a computer center, for example, it's probably more efficient, and certainly more courteous, to work through at least one draft by hand, or on your own typewriter. If you don't compose on a word processor, take a fresh sheet of paper for this job. If you find that your first effort is a false start, crumple the page and throw it away. Your next attempt, or your next after your next, will be better and will show you what parts of your draft can be used, what must be added, deleted, or rearranged.

## Imagining Your Audience

When you reread your draft, try to imagine someone else reading it. You may have received, with your assignment, instructions about the audience your essay should address. If not, you must define for yourself the reader you intend to persuade, and then you must keep that reader in mind as you compose and revise. We suggest that you imagine your reader to be someone like you, a classmate perhaps. But it's helpful to imagine that your reader has *not* read the essay you're writing about; it is essential to imagine that your reader knows and understands the essay less well than you do. Your reader certainly does not know what assignment you are fulfilling, and could not have arrived, unassisted, at the thesis you are prepared to argue.

With such a reader in mind—obviously not your instructor—you will be careful to be clear and to be consistent. You will take care, for example, probably in your first paragraph, to identify, at least by author and title, the essay you are analyzing. A footnote following your first quotation from the essay will usually suffice to give your reader further details of where and when the essay was published.

Keeping your reader in mind will also help you to decide how much summary to include, where the summary is needed, how much detail it should contain, and at what points in your analysis—your examination of the essay you are responding to—an additional sentence or two of summary would be helpful. Imagining a real reader may also help to remind you that it is your job to analyze and to persuade, that is, to set forth a thoughtful response to the essay and not offer a mere synopsis. Summarize only enough to keep your real reader with you, following you step by step and, we hope, agreeing with each point you make.

## Reading Your Draft

To write a good essay you must be a good reader not only of the essay you are writing about but also of the essay you yourself are writing. We're not talking about proofreading or correcting spelling errors, though of course you must engage also in those activities.

As you read your draft, keep in mind the fact that your essay should contain two theses and two voices—Orwell's thesis and voice, and your own thesis and voice. That is, the reader should be told, early and fairly, what Orwell's point is, and should get some sense of the way Orwell makes the point. The reader should also perceive *your* point, and be able to take some pleasure in the way in which you make your point. Note, too, that the point or thesis and the voice that predominates in the essay are yours (unless the assignment has been merely to summarize a published essay). That is, your essay is, finally, *your* essay—a thoughtful *response* to someone else's essay. It probably will begin with an introductory comment, and will then give a brief summary of the essay you are responding to, but chiefly it will set forth your own views.

## Revising and Editing Your Draft

And then, of course, you revise (preferably after giving the manuscript a day's rest) and revise again, perhaps adding or deleting some quotations, and checking the quotations for accuracy. Perhaps now you are ready to give your essay a title. Your title may prompt you to make still further changes: substituting one quotation for another, finding more exact verbs for your draft, perhaps even adding new material, and almost certainly revising your conclusion.

At this point, try reading your essay aloud, preferably to a roommate, friend, or classmate. But if it is 3:00 A.M. and you alone are awake, read it aloud anyway (quietly). Again, imagine a real reader, or listener. You'll almost certainly find yourself deleting unnecessary repetitions and adding necessary transitions such as "but," "furthermore," and "on the other hand."

Finally, check spellings of words you're not sure of in a dictionary, and check doubtful constructions in a handbook. In short, you laboriously do all the things that will make your essay seem effortless to your reader. This includes typing (or writing legibly) and, after giving yourself and your manuscript as much rest as time allows, proofreading (and making final corrections as necessary).

## Sample Essay

We have just described (partly by imagining them) the thought processes and the work of a student who wrote the following essay. We suggest that first you reread Orwell's essay. Then read the student's essay. Finally, reread her essay, this time glancing back at her rough outline and our marginal notes.

| | |
|---|---|
| Title is provocative, and implies the thesis | **Is Orwell's Elephant Big Enough to Hold Orwell's Interpretation?** |
| Essay begins by identifying Orwell and showing appreciation of Orwell, i.e., shows fair-mindedness | George Orwell's "Shooting an Elephant" is a memorable essay about his experience as a British police officer in Burma, and it is almost the exciting story the title seems to promise. The beginning of the first sentence compels our attention: "In Moulmein, in Lower Burma, I was hated by large numbers of people." And, so |
| Correctly identifies Orwell's tone | that on second thought this will not seem egotistical to the reader, Orwell wryly adds that this was "the only time in my life that I have been important enough for this to happen to |
| Reference to note citing source | me."[1] We can hardly fail to like the writer of this sentence. The next paragraph, too, with its sympathy for |
| Citation of source, and explanation of subsequent references | 1. In *The Little, Brown Reader,* 5th ed., Marcia Stubbs and Sylvan Barnet, eds. (Glenview, Ill.: Scott, Foresman, 1989), p. 5. Subsequent references will be made parenthetically within the text. |

Summary in which brief, relevant quotations let us hear Orwell's voice

Transition ("But") lets us know that essayist will now take a somewhat different view

Student's thesis statement

Repetition of "interpretation" provides transition

Relevant summary

Student clearly sets forth Orwell's thesis

Relevant summary

Page reference given

"the wretched prisoners huddling in the stinking cages of the lock-ups" presents us with a man who, because of his sympathy for the oppressed and because of his "intolerable sense of guilt," gains our sympathy. But to say that we sympathize with Orwell is not to say that we have to share all of his opinions. Although we have to take his word for what happened when he shot the elephant, and we recognize that he has first-hand experience of imperialism, we do not have to believe that his interpretation of his experience gives us the truth about the nature of imperialism.

He first presents his interpretation just beyond the middle of the essay—just as Orwell is about to shoot the elephant (page 8). He explains not one but two things. He explains why he shot the elephant, and he also explains, or claims to explain, the contradiction of imperialism: "When the white man turns tyrant it is his own freedom that he destroys. He becomes a sort of hollow, posing dummy." Now, in "Shooting an Elephant" Orwell admits that he became a sort of dummy. He felt that he was forced to shoot the elephant because the Burmese wanted him to shoot it, and he was afraid not to live up to their expectations. He was afraid, he says, that if he didn't shoot the elephant "the crowd would laugh at me" (p. 9). Orwell has effectively prepared us for the terrible power of contemptuous laughter when, in his first paragraph, he says, "The crowd yelled with hideous laughter." Nevertheless the generalization about what happens "when the white man turns tyrant" is not really supported. In the first place, Orwell does not give us any reason to believe that he was a tyrant. True, he was a British police officer in Burma, and thus he was a representative of imperial England, but nothing in the essay suggests that he was cruel or even unfair. We do know, however, that his work as a policeman produced in him "an intolerable sense of guilt" (page 5), and this, I think, is a clue to Orwell's interpretation of his act.

First sentence of new paragraph offers a clear transition

What was his act? Under pressure from a crowd, he needlessly killed an elephant. He certainly should feel guilt for killing a harmless beast, and also for depriving the owner of valuable property. And he should feel guilt, I think, for yielding to the pressure of the crowd. I am not saying that I wouldn't have yielded too,

Student does not overstate her criticism

but I am saying that it was wrong to yield and that a stronger person would have said to himself or herself, "Never mind what all of these people think; the elephant is harmless and I won't shoot it." Perhaps if he had refused to shoot the elephant the malicious jeers would soon have turned into cheers for the brave sahib who dared to face a crazy elephant and then walked calmly away.

Clarification of student's thesis

But Orwell did yield to the mob, and he felt guilty for doing so. It is probably this guilt, this awareness of his weakness, rather than the guilt about being a policeman in Burma, that is at the heart of the essay. But apparently he couldn't face it. Despite his modesty and his no doubt genuine sympathy for the victims of imperialism, he shifts the blame from himself to, as we now say, "the system." It isn't really his fault, Orwell says in effect, that he was a coward; it is the nature of imperialism to turn the imperialist into a coward, a "dummy."

Again essayist tries to be fair and not seem superior to author she is analyzing; good tone

Let me say again that, judging from this essay, Orwell was in many ways a decent person, and we can admire his honesty when he admits, in the last line, that he killed the elephant "solely to avoid looking a fool." This humble confession certainly gains our sympathy, and if the essay were entirely about his deed and his awareness of his weakness there would be nothing to complain about. But Orwell tries to explain away his failure by seeing himself as (no less than the Burmese) the victim of imperialism. Finally, then for all of his good nature and his modesty and his confession of weakness, he presents himself as innocent. He <u>had</u> to shoot the elephant, he wants us to believe, because imperialists <u>have</u> to do what their victims want them to do. His comments about the nature of imperialism may or may not be true. But it seems clear, even from his own essay, that Orwell's action in the last analysis resulted not from "the nature of imperialism," as he claims, but from Orwell's own failure of nerve.

Forceful ending

Restatement of student's thesis

Our marginal comments offer our chief views, but a brief restatement and amplification may be useful:

1.  Although the title may be a trifle strained, it at least provides the reader with a focus, and thus it is far better than such an unhelpful title as "George Orwell's 'Shooting an Elephant' " or "On 'Shooting an Elephant.' "
2.  Keeping her audience in mind, the student helpfully identifies and summarizes Orwell's essay.

3.  The writer's tone is satisfactory. She is critical of Orwell, but she avoids overstating her case or condescending to him.

## Using Quotations

Our marginal comments call your attention to some of the essay's strengths as well as to some of the conventions of editing your final draft. Here we remind you of procedures for using quotations (covered in detail in most handbooks). These procedures are not noteworthy when handled properly, but they become noticeable and even ruinous to your essay when bungled. Read the following reminders over, check them against the student's essay you just read, and consult them again the first few times you write about an essay.

1.  *Quote.* Quotations from the work under discussion provide indispensable support for your thesis.
2.  *Don't overquote.* Most of the essay should consist of your own words.
3.  *Quote briefly.* Use quotations as evidence, not as padding.
4.  *Comment on what you quote,* immediately before or immediately after the quotation. Make sure your reader understands why you find the quotation relevant. Don't count on the quotation to make your point for you.
5.  *Take care with embedded quotations* (quotations within a sentence of your own). A quotation must fit grammatically into the sentence of which it is a part.

Incorrect:

> The first sentence does not sound egotistical because "the only time in my life that I have been important enough for this to happen to me."

Correct:

> The first sentence does not sound egotistical because Orwell adds that this was "the only time in my life that I have been important enough for this to happen to me."

Don't try to fit a long quotation into the middle of one of your own sentences. It is almost impossible for the reader to come out of the quotation and pick up the thread of your sentence. It is better to lead into a long quotation with "Orwell says," and then, after quoting, to begin a new sentence of your own.

6. *Quote exactly.* Any material that you add (to make the quotation coherent with your sentence) must be in square brackets. Thus:

> Orwell says the torture of prisoners "oppressed [him] with an intolerable sense of guilt."

An ellipsis (any material that you omit from within a quotation) must be indicated by three spaced periods:

> He knew that "a sahib has got to . . . know his own mind and do definite things."

If a quotation ends before the end of the author's sentence, add a period and then three spaced periods to indicate the omission:

> As Orwell claims, "it was a tiny incident in itself. . . ."

(Orwell's sentence followed the word "itself" with "but it gave me a better glimpse than I had had before of the real nature of imperialism—the real motives for which despotic governments act.")

7. *Quote fairly.* It would not be fair, for example, to say "Orwell claims he 'had done the right thing' " when in fact he says "legally I had done the right thing." His qualification "legally" is important, and it would be unfair to omit it.

8. *Identify the quotation* clearly for your reader. Notice in this essay such helpful expressions as "Orwell . . . adds," and "The next paragraph . . . represents," as well as references to pages.

9. *Identify the source of quotations in a footnote,* or in a list of Works Cited if you are using more than one source.

10. *Check your punctuation.* Remember: Periods and commas go inside of quotation marks, semicolons and colons go outside. Question marks and exclamation points go inside if they are part of the quotation, outside if they are your own.

## A Checklist for Analyzing and Evaluating an Essay That You Are Writing About

When you read, try to read sympathetically, opening yourself to the writer's vision of things. But when you have finished a sympathetic reading, and an attentive reading, and you have made various sorts of notes, probably including an outline and a summary of the essay you are reading, you are ready to *analyze* the writer's methods and to *evaluate* the piece.

In analyzing, you will examine the relationships between the parts; that is, you will ask such questions as:

What is the *topic* of the essay (see page 4). Try to state it, preferably in writing, as specifically as possible. For example, broadly speaking one might say that the subject of Orwell's "Shooting an Elephant" is British imperialism in India, but within this subject his topic, more specifically, is the effects of imperialism on the imperialists themselves.

What is the essay's *thesis* (either stated or implied)? If you have located a *thesis sentence* in the essay, underline it and write *thesis* in the margin. If the thesis is implied, try to formulate it in a sentence of your own.

What does the title do? What *purpose* does it suggest the writer holds?

What is the function of the opening paragraph (or paragraphs)? What claim on our attention or beliefs does it make?

What speaker or *persona* (see page 1149) does the writer create, and how does the writer create it?

Does the tone (page 2) shift as the essay progresses? If so, why does it shift?

What *audience* is the writer addressing? The general, literate public, or a more specialized group?

How is the argument set forth? By logic? By drawing on personal experience? What evidence is there that the writer is an authority on the topic? Are there other appeals to authority? What other kinds of evidence support the essay's claim? What are the author's underlying assumptions? Are they stated or implied, and are they acceptable to you, or can you challenge them?

If there is a formal, explicit conclusion, underline or restate it. If the conclusion is not stated, but is implied, what does the writer want us to conclude?

In evaluating, you will ask such questions as:

Is the essay as clear as it can be, given the complexity of the material? For example, do specific examples help to make the generalizations clear? Are crucial terms adequately defined? If the thesis is not explicitly stated, is the essay unclear or is it perhaps better because of the indirectness?

If the conclusion is not stated but implied, why does the writer not state it?

Is the argument (if the essay is chiefly an argument) convincing, or is it marred by faulty thinking? If statistics are used, are they sound and relevant? If authorities are quoted, are they indeed authorities (rather than just big names) on this topic?

Is the essay interesting? If so, in what ways, and if not, why not?—which gets us back to analysis. If there are passages of undisguised argument, for instance, are they clear without being repetitious and boring? Do specific examples clarify and enliven general assertions?

If the essay includes narrative or descriptive passages, are they pertinent? Should they have been amplified, or should they have been reduced or even deleted?

How is the essay organized? Is the organization effective? Does the essay build to a climax?

Another way of thinking about the criteria for evaluating an essay is this:

Is the essay persuasive (whether because of its logic or because of the power of the speaker's personality)? and,

Does the essay give pleasure?

Don't hesitate to demand that an essay give you pleasure. The author probably thought that he or she was writing well, and certainly hoped to hold your interest throughout the essay and to make you feel that you were learning something of interest. In short, the author hoped that you would like the essay. You have every right to evaluate the essay partly by considering the degree of pleasure that it affords. Of course, in *your* essay you cannot simply say that you enjoyed an essay or that you were bored by it. You will have to support your assertions with reasons based on evidence. To support your assertions you must have read the writer's words carefully, so we are back to an earlier point: the first thing to do if you are going to write about a piece of writing is to read it attentively, pen or pencil in hand.

As you read and reread the material that you are writing about, subjecting it to the kinds of questions we have mentioned, your understanding of it will almost surely deepen. You will probably come to feel that it is better—or worse—than you had thought at first, or in any case somewhat different.

As you prepare to write your own essay, and as you draft it, you are learning, feeling your way toward a considered analysis. All writers are in the position of the little girl who, told by an adult that she should think before she spoke, replied, "How do I know what I think until I say it?" But once having said something—whether in a mental question to yourself or in a note or a draft—you have to evaluate your thought, and improve it if it doesn't stand up under further scrutiny.

# 2
## ALL IN THE FAMILY

"*While we're at supper, Billy, you'd make Daddy and Mommy very happy
if you'd remove your hat, your sunglasses, and your earring.*"

Drawing by Ziegler; © 1985 The New Yorker Magazine, Inc.

*Sonia*
**Joanne Leonard, 1966**

Courtesy of the Göteborgs Konstmuseum

*Feeding Time*
**Paul Martin, 1892**

# Short Views

After a certain age, the more one becomes oneself, the more obvious one's family traits become.
Marcel Proust

All happy families resemble one another; every unhappy family is unhappy in its own fashion.
Leo Tolstoy, *Anna Karenina*

On Tuesday, March 31, he and I dined at General Paoli's. A question was started, whether the state of marriage was natural to man. Johnson. "Sir, it is so far from being natural for a man and woman to live in a state of marriage, that we find all the motives which they have for remaining in that connection, and the restraints which civilized society imposes to prevent separation, are hardly sufficient to keep them together." The General said, that in a state of nature a man and woman uniting together would form a strong and constant affection, by the mutual pleasure each would receive; and that the same causes of dissension would not arise between them, as occur between husband and wife in a civilized state. Johnson. "Sir, they would have dissensions enough, though of another kind. One would choose to go a hunting in this wood, the other in that; one would choose to go a fishing in this lake, the other in that; or, perhaps, one would choose to go a hunting, when the other would choose to go a fishing; and so they would part. Besides, Sir, a savage man and a savage woman meet by chance; and when the man sees another woman that pleases him better, he will leave the first."
James Boswell

Marriage is the best of human statuses and the worst, and it will continue to be. And that is why, though its future in some form or other is as assured as anything can be, this future is as equivocal as its past. The demands that men and women make on marriage will never be fully met; they cannot be.
Jessie Bernard

The basis of the family is, of course, the fact that parents feel a special kind of affection towards their own children, different from that which they feel towards each other or towards other children. It is true that some parents feel little or no parental affection, and it is also true that some women are capable of feeling an affection for children not their own almost as strong as that which they could feel for their own. Nevertheless the broad fact remains, that parental affection is a special kind of feeling which the normal human being experiences towards his or her own children, but not towards any other human being. This emotion is one which we inherit from our animal ancestors. In this respect Freud seems to me not sufficiently biological in his outlook, for anyone who will observe an animal mother with her young can see that her behavior towards them follows an entirely different pattern from her behavior towards the male with whom she has sex relations. And this same different and instinctive pattern, though in a modified and less definite form, exists among human beings. If it were not for this special emotion there would be almost nothing to be said for the family as an institution, since children might equally well be left to the care of professionals. As things are, however, the special affection which parents have for children, provided their instincts are not atrophied, is of value both to the parents themselves and to the children. The value of parental affection to children lies largely in the fact that it is more reliable than any other affection. One's friends like one for one's merits, one's lovers for one's charms; if the merits or the charms diminish, friends and lovers may vanish. But it is in times of misfortune that parents are most to be relied upon, in illness, and even in disgrace if the parents are of the right sort. We all feel pleasure when we are admired for our merits, but most of us are sufficiently modest at heart to feel that such admiration is precarious. Our parents love us because we are their children and this is an unalterable fact, so that we feel more safe with them than with anyone else. In times of success this may seem unimportant, but in times of failure it affords a consolation and a security not to be found elsewhere.
    **Bertrand Russell**


A slavish bondage to parents cramps every faculty of the mind; and Mr. Locke very judiciously observes, that "if the mind be curbed and humbled too much in children, if their spirits be abased and broken much by too strict an hand over them, they lose all their

vigour and industry." This strict hand may in some degree account for the weakness of women; for girls, from various causes, are more kept down by their parents, in every sense of the word, than boys. The duty expected from them is, like all the duties arbitrarily imposed on women, more from a sense of propriety, more out of respect for decorum, than reason; and thus taught slavishly to submit to their parents, they are prepared for the slavery of marriage. I may be told that a number of women are not slaves in the marriage state. True, but they then become tyrants; for it is not rational freedom, but a lawless kind of power resembling the authority exercised by the favourites of absolute monarchs, which they obtain by debasing means.
        **Mary Wollstonecraft**


Twenty years from now humanity will be in the midst of one of its most painful and difficult social changes. This century will be the last in which families of more than two children can be tolerated; everyone knows this, and the only argument is over the means of achieving the goal. But there is another aspect of the matter which is seldom given much serious consideration.

   The two-child family is not large enough to generate the interactions that develop a good personality; this is why single children are often monsters. Probably the optimum number of siblings is four or five—twice the permissible quota. This means that, somehow, several families must be psychologically fused together for the health of the child, and of society. Working out ways of doing this will raise the blood pressure of a whole generation of lawyers and moralists.
        **Arthur C. Clarke**


Nobody who has not been in the interior of a family can say what the difficulties of any individual of that family may be.
        **Jane Austen,** *Emma*


When I was young enough to still spend a long time buttoning my shoes in the morning, I'd listen toward the hall: Daddy upstairs was shaving in the bathroom and Mother downstairs was frying the bacon. They would begin whistling back and forth to each other up and down the stairwell. My father would whistle his phrase, my mother would try to whistle, then hum hers back. It was their duet. I drew my buttonhook in and out and listened to it—I knew it was

"The Merry Widow." The difference was, their song almost floated with laughter: how different from the record, which growled from the beginning, as if the Victrola were only slowly being wound up. They kept it running between them, up and down the stairs where I was now just about ready to run clattering down and show them my shoes.

Eudora Welty

## Lewis Coser

# The Family

Following the French anthropologist Claude Lévi-Strauss,     1
we can define the family as a group manifesting these characteristics: it finds its origin in marriage; it consists of husband, wife and children born in their wedlock—though other relatives may find their place close to that nuclear group; and the members of the group are united by moral, legal, economic, religious, and social rights and obligations. These include a network of sexual rights and prohibitions and a variety of socially patterned feelings such as love, attraction, piety, awe, and so on.

The family is among the few universal institutions of mankind.     2
No known society lacks small kinship groups of parents and children related through the process of reproduction. But recognition of the universality of this institution must immediately be followed by the acknowledgment that its forms are exceedingly varied. The fact that many family organizations are not monogamic, as in the West, led many nineteenth-century observers to the erroneous conclusion that in "early" stages of evolution there existed no families, and that "group

Lewis Coser, born in Berlin, in 1913, was educated at the Sorbonne in Paris and at Columbia University, where he received a Ph.D. in sociology in 1954. He now teaches at the State University of New York, Stony Brook, and holds the title Distinguished Professor.

marriage," institutionalized promiscuity, prevailed. This is emphatically not the case; even though patterned wife-lending shocked the sensibilities of Victorian anthropologists, such an institution is evidently predicated on the fact that men have wives in the first place. No matter what their specific forms, families in all known societies have performed major social functions—reproduction, maintenance, socialization, and social placement of the young.

Families may be monogamous or polygamous—there are systems    3 where one man is entitled to several wives and others where several husbands share one wife. A society may recognize primarily the small nuclear conjugal unit of husband and wife with their immediate descendants or it may institutionalize the large extended family linking several generations and emphasizing consanguinity more than the conjugal bond. Residence after marriage may be matrilocal, patrilocal or neolocal; exchanges of goods and services between families at the time of marriage may be based on bride price, groom price or an equal exchange; endogamous or exogamous regulations may indicate who is and who is not eligible for marriage; the choice of a mate may be controlled by parents or it may be left in large measure to the young persons concerned. These are but a few of the many differences which characterize family structures in variant societies.

# Questions

1. At the end of paragraph 2, Coser writes: "No matter what their specific forms, families in all known societies have performed major social functions—reproduction, maintenance, socialization, and social placement of the young." What does "socialization" mean? How does it differ from "social placement of the young"? What specific forms does each take in our society?
2. Can you give examples of "moral, legal, economic, religious, and social rights and obligations" (paragraph 1) that unite members of a family?
3. Compare Coser and Plumb (pages 37–41) on the social functions of the family. According to Plumb, what responsibility does the family in our society have in performing the social functions Coser lists? How do other institutions compete with the family in performing some of these functions?

## J. H. Plumb

# The Dying Family

I was rather astonished when a minibus drove up to my 1
house and out poured ten children. They had with them two parents,
but not one child had them both in common as mother and father,
and two of them belonged to neither parent, but to a former husband
of the wife who had died. Both parents, well into middle age, had just
embarked, one on his fourth, the other on her third marriage. The
children, who came in all sizes, and ranged from blonde nordic to jet-
haired Greek, bounded around the garden, young and old as happy
as any children that I have seen. To them, as Californians, their situation was not particularly odd; most of their friends had multiple
parents. Indeed to them perhaps the odd family was the one which
Western culture has held up as a model for two thousand years or
more—the lifelong union of man and wife. But it took me a very long
time to believe that they could be either happy or adjusted. And yet,
were they a sign of the future, a way the world was going?

Unlike anthropologists or sociologists, historians have not studied 2
family life very closely. Until recently we knew very little of the age
at which people married in Western Europe in the centuries earlier
than the nineteenth or how many children they had, or what the rates
of illegitimacy might be or whether, newly wed, they lived with their
parents or set up a house of their own. Few of these questions can be
answered with exactitude even now, but we can make better guesses.
We know even less, however, of the detailed sexual practices that
marriage covered: indeed this is a subject to which historians are only
just turning their attention. But we do know much more of the function
of family life—its social role—particularly if we turn from the centuries
to the millennia and pay attention to the broad similarities rather than
the fascinating differences between one region and another: and, if we
do, we realize that the family has changed far more profoundly than
even the bus load of Californians might lead us to expect.

Basically the family has fulfilled three social functions—to provide 3

J[ohn] H[arold] Plumb, born in England in 1911, was professor of modern English
history at the University of Cambridge until his retirement. He also taught at
universities in the United States.

a basic labor force, to transmit property and to educate and train children not only into an accepted social pattern, but also in the work skills upon which their future subsistence would depend. Until very recent times, the vast majority of children never went to any school: their school was the family, where they learned to dig and sow and reap and herd their animals, or they learned their father's craft of smith or carpenter or potter. The unitary family was particularly good at coping with the small peasant holdings which covered most of the world's fertile regions from China to Peru. In the primitive peasant world a child of four or five could begin to earn its keep in the fields, as they still can in India and Africa: and whether Moslem, Hindu, Inca or Christian, one wife at a time was all that the bulk of the world's population could support, even though their religion permitted them more. Indeed, it was the primitive nature of peasant economy which gave the family, as we know it, its wide diffusion and its remarkable continuity.

Whether or not it existed before the neolithic revolution we shall 4 never know, but certainly it must have gained in strength as families became rooted to the soil. Many very primitive people who live in a pre-agrarian society of hunting and food-gathering often tend to have a looser structure of marriage and the women a far greater freedom of choice and easier divorce, as with the Esquimaux, than is permitted in peasant societies. There can be little doubt that the neolithic revolution created new opportunities for the family as we know it, partly because this revolution created new property relations. More importantly it created great masses of property, beyond anything earlier societies had known. True, there were a few hunting peoples, such as the Kwakiutl Indians, who had considerable possessions—complex lodges, great pieces of copper and piles of fibre blankets, which periodically they destroyed in great battles of raging pride—but the property, personal or communal, of most primitive hunting people is usually trivial.

After the revolution in agriculture, property and its transmission 5 lay at the very heart of social relations and possessed an actuality which we find hard to grasp. Although we are much richer, possessions are more anonymous, often little more than marks in a ledger, and what we own constantly changes. Whereas for the majority of mankind over this last seven thousand years property has been deeply personal and familial: a plot of land, if not absolute ownership over it, then valuable rights in it; sometimes a house, even though it be a hovel by our standards; perhaps no more than the tools and materials of a craft, yet these possessions were the route both to survival and to betterment. Hence they were endowed with manna, bound up with the deepest roots of personality. In all societies the question of property became embedded in every aspect of family life, particularly marriage and the succession and rights of children. Because of property's vital importance, subservience of women and children to the will of the father, limited only by social custom, became the pattern of most great peasant societies. Marriage was sanctified not only by the rites of religion, but by the transmission of property. Few societies could tolerate freedom of choice in marriage—too much vital to the success or failure of a family depended on it: an ugly girl with five cows was a far fairer prospect than a pretty girl with one. And because of the sexual drives of frail human nature, the customs of marriage and of family relationships needed to be rigorously enforced. Tradition sanctified them; religion blessed them. Some societies reversed the sexually restrictive nature of permanent marriage and permitted additional wives, but such permission was meaningless to the mass of the peasantry who fought a desperate battle to support a single family. And, as we shall see, the patterns of family life were always looser for the rich and the favored.

But a family was always more than property expressed clearly and visibly in real goods; it was for thousands of years both a school and a tribunal, the basic unit of social organization whose function in modern society has been very largely taken over by the state. In most peasant societies, life is regulated by the village community, by the patriarchs of the village, and the only officer of the central government these villagers see with any regularity is the tax-gatherer; but in societies that have grown more complex, and this is particularly true of the West during the last four hundred years, life has become regulated by the nation state or by the growth in power and importance of more generalized local communities—the town or county. 6

This has naturally weakened the authority of heads of families, a fact that can be symbolically illustrated by change in social custom. No child in Western Europe would sit unbidden in the presence of its parents until the eighteenth century: if it did it could be sure of rebuke and punishment. No head of a household would have thought twice about beating a recalcitrant young servant or apprentice before the end of the nineteenth century. For a younger brother to marry without the consent of his eldest brother would have been regarded as a social enormity; and sisters were disposable property. All of this power has vanished. Indeed the family ties of all of us have been so loosened that 7 we find it hard to grasp the intensity of family relationships or their complexity, they have disintegrated so rapidly this last hundred years. Now nearly every child in the Western world, male or female, is educated outside the family from five years of age. The skills they learn are rarely, if ever, transmitted by parents: and what is more they learn about the nature of their own world, its social structure and its relationships in time outside the family. For millennia the family was the great transmitter and formulator of social custom; but it now only retains a shadow of this function, usually for very young children only.

Although the economic and education functions of the family have 8 declined, most of us feel that it provides the most satisfactory emotional basis for human beings; that a secure family life breeds stability, a capacity not only for happiness, but also to adjust to society's demands. This, too, may be based on misjudgment, for family life in the past was not remarkable for its happiness. We get few glimpses into the private lives of men and women long dead, but when we do we often find strain, frustration, petty tyranny. For so many human beings family life was a prison from which they could not escape. And although it might create deep satisfactions here and there, the majority of the rich and affluent classes of the last four hundred years in Western Europe created for themselves a double standard, particularly as far as sex was concerned. In a few cities such as Calvin's Geneva, the purity of family life might be maintained, but the aristocracies of France, Italy and Britain tolerated, without undue concern, adultery, homosexuality and that sexual freedom which, for better or worse, we consider the hallmark of modern life. Indeed the family as the basic social group began firstly to fail, except in its property relations, amongst the aristocracy.

But what we think of as a social crisis of this generation—the rapid 9 growth of divorce, the emancipation of women and adolescents, the sexual and educational revolutions, even the revolution in eating which is undermining the family as the basis of nourishment, for over a hundred years ago the majority of Europeans never ate in public in their lives—all of these things, which are steadily making the family weaker and weaker, are the inexorable result of the changes in society itself. The family as a unit of social organization was remarkably appropriate for a less complex world of agriculture and craftsmanship, a world which stretches back some seven thousand years, but ever since industry and highly urbanized societies began to take its place, the social functions of the family have steadily weakened—and this is a process that is unlikely to be halted. And there is no historical reason to believe that human beings could be less or more happy, less or more stable. Like any other human institution the family has always been molded by the changing needs of society, sometimes slowly, sometimes fast. And that bus load of children does no more than symbolize the failure, not of marriage, but of the role of the old-fashioned family unit in a modern, urbanized, scientific and affluent society.

## Questions

1. In paragraph 3 Plumb uses the term "unitary family," but he does not define it. How might it be defined? Explain how you arrived at your definition.
2. Paraphrase the sentence (in paragraph 5) "Hence they were endowed with manna, bound up with the deepest roots of personality."
3. Plumb says (paragraph 9) that "the revolution in eating" is "undermining the family as the basis of nourishment." Explain. To what extent do you agree that a family's eating habits reveal its stability?

Judy Syfers

# Why I Want a Wife

I belong to that classification of people known as wives. I    1
am A Wife. And, not altogether incidentally, I am a mother.

Not too long ago a male friend of mine appeared on the scene    2
fresh from a recent divorce. He had one child, who is, of course, with his ex-wife. He is looking for another wife. As I thought about him while I was ironing one evening, it suddenly occurred to me that I, too, would like to have a wife. Why do I want a wife?

Judy Syfers was born in San Francisco in 1937. She received a bachelor's degree from the University of Iowa in 1960 and wanted to do the graduate work that would qualify her for teaching in a university, but she was dissuaded by her male teachers. "Why I Want a Wife" originally appeared in the first issue of *Ms*.

I would like to go back to school so that I can become economically  3
independent, support myself, and, if need be, support those dependent upon me. I want a wife who will work and send me to school.
And while I am going to school I want a wife to take care of my children. I want a wife to keep track of the children's doctor and dentist
appointments. And to keep track of mine, too. I want a wife to make
sure my children eat properly and are kept clean. I want a wife who
will wash the children's clothes and keep them mended. I want a wife
who is a good nurturant attendant to my children, who arranges for
their schooling, makes sure that they have an adequate social life with
their peers, takes them to the park, the zoo, etc. I want a wife who
takes care of the children when they are sick, a wife who arranges to
be around when the children need special care, because, of course I
cannot miss classes at school. My wife must arrange to lose time at
work and not lose the job. It may mean a small cut in my wife's income
from time to time, but I guess I can tolerate that. Needless to say, my
wife will arrange and pay for the care of the children while my wife
is working.

I want a wife who will take care of *my* physical needs. I want a  4
wife who will keep my house clean. A wife who will pick up after my
children, a wife who will pick up after me. I want a wife who will keep
my clothes clean, ironed, mended, replaced when need be, and who
will see to it that my personal things are kept in their proper place so
that I can find what I need the minute I need it. I want a wife who
cooks the meals, a wife who is a *good* cook. I want a wife who will
plan the menus, do the necessary grocery shopping, prepare the meals,
serve them pleasantly, and then do the cleaning up while I do my
studying. I want a wife who will care for me when I am sick and
sympathize with my pain and loss of time from school. I want a wife
to go along when our family takes a vacation so that someone can
continue to care for me and my children when I need a rest and a
change of scene.

I want a wife who will not bother me with rambling complaints  5
about a wife's duties. But I want a wife who will listen to me when I
feel the need to explain a rather difficult point I have come across in
my course of studies. And I want a wife who will type my papers for
me when I have written them.

I want a wife who will take care of the details of my social life.  6
When my wife and I are invited out by my friends, I want a wife who
will take care of the babysitting arrangements. When I meet people at
school that I like and want to entertain, I want a wife who will have

the house clean, will prepare a special meal, serve it to me and my friends, and not interrupt when I talk about things that interest me and my friends. I want a wife who will have arranged that the children are fed and ready for bed before my guests arrive so that the children do not bother us. I want a wife who takes care of the needs of my guests so that they feel comfortable, who makes sure that they have an ashtray, that they are passed the hors d'oeuvres, that they are offered a second helping of the food, that their wine glasses are replenished when necessary, that their coffee is served to them as they like it. And I want a wife who knows that sometimes I need a night out by myself.

I want a wife who is sensitive to my sexual needs, a wife who 7 makes love passionately and eagerly when I feel like it, a wife who makes sure that I am satisfied. And, of course, I want a wife who will not demand sexual attention when I am not in the mood for it. I want a wife who assumes the complete responsibility for birth control, because I do not want more children. I want a wife who will remain sexually faithful to me so that I do not have to clutter up my intellectual life with jealousies. And I want a wife who understands that *my* sexual needs may entail more than strict adherence to monogamy. I must, after all, be able to relate to people as fully as possible.

If, by chance, I find another person more suitable as a wife than 8 the wife I already have, I want the liberty to replace my present wife with another one. Naturally, I will expect a fresh, new life; my wife will take the children and be solely responsible for them so that I am left free.

When I am through with school and have a job, I want my wife 9 to quit working and remain at home so that my wife can more fully and completely take care of a wife's duties.

My God, who *wouldn't* want a wife?                    10

# Questions

1. Does the second sentence of the essay mean anything different from the first? If so, what? If not, why is it there?
2. Describing a recently divorced man, Syfers says in paragraph 2: "He had one child, who is, of course, with his ex-wife." What information does "of course" convey? What attitude or tone?
3. If the constant repetition of "I want a wife who . . ." is not boring, what keeps it from being boring?

4.  Syfers is attacking sexual stereotyping. Do you find in her essay any assumptions or details that limit the stereotyping to an economic class, or to an ethnic or racial group? Explain.

Julie Matthaei

# Political Economy and Family Policy

**O**ur current, "natural" family system, based on biological similarities and differences, is in crisis. Not only are its institutions breaking down, they are also under attack as unjust, unequal, and unfree. The "natural" family system needs to be replaced by a consciously social family system; this means socializing parenting costs and pursuing policies which attack the sexual division of labor and better integrate economic and family life.     1

The family plays a central role in the distribution of income and wealth in our society, reproducing class, race, and gender inequalities. This paper will 1) present a radical and feminist analysis of the "traditional" family system, 2) discuss the recent breakdown of this system, 3) present a radical and feminist critique of the traditional family system, and 4) indicate social policies which would build a family system more consistent with the principles of equality, freedom, and social justice.     2

## The "Natural" Family

The development of capitalism and wage labor in the nineteenth-century U.S. brought with it new familial institutions. The family con-     3

Julie Matthaei teaches economics at Wellesley College and is active with the Economic Literacy Project of Women for Economic Justice of Boston. She is the author of *An Economic History of Women in America* and is working on a book entitled *Beyond Sex and Blood: Economy, Family, and the Breakdown of the "Natural" Family.*

tinued to be patriarchal—ruled by the husband/father—but was less defined by and involved in commodity production, either as a family firm, or as a family enslaved to producing for others. The family emerged as an increasingly personal and feminine sphere, physically separate and distinct from the competitive and masculine economy (Matthaei 1982). Since, in the nineteenth century, "scientific" explanations of social life were replacing the former religious ones, the new familial institutions were viewed as "natural," and stress was placed on their determination by biological similarities and differences. This "natural"[1] family system has three, interconnected parts:

1. *"Natural" Marriage.* Marriage is seen as a union of naturally different and complementary beings: men/males and women/females (biological sex and social gender are equated). Men and women are believed to be instinctually heterosexual; those who form homosexual liaisons are viewed as unnatural and perverted.[2] Men are seen as natural bread-winners, competing in the economy, and women as natural homemakers, caring for their husbands and children in the home, and segregated into dead-end, low paid "women's jobs." Forced into this sexual division of labor, men and women need one another to be socially complete, and in order to undertake the essential function of marriage, which is seen as . . .

2. *"Natural" Parenting.* Parenting is seen as the biological production of offspring, a process in which adults pass on their identities and wealth to their children, to "their own flesh and blood." Children are seen as the responsibility and property of their parents. Women/females are seen as naturally endowed with special maternal instincts which make them more qualified than men/males for parenting.

3. *"Natural" Community.* Connected to the view of family life as natural is a white racist view of society which divides people into races and views whites as the biologically superior race. Whites rationalize their political and economic domination of people of color not only as natural but also as part of "white man's burden to civilize the savages."[3] Races and white supremacy are perpetuated as social entities

---

[1] Natural is in quotes because the "natural" family system is actually a social product.

[2] In contrast, previous times viewed homosexual attractions as natural (and shared by all) but immoral and not to be acted on (Weeks 1979).

[3] Similarly, whites in the Eugenics movement argued that poor whites had inferior genes, and worked to limit their reproduction (Gould 1981).

by the prohibition of racial intermarriage; by the passing down of wealth or poverty, language and culture to one's children; and by racially segregated institutions such as housing and job markets.

## The Breakdown of the "Natural" Family System

In the last fifteen years, the "natural" family system has been breaking down and coming under increasing attack by feminists and others.     4

1. *Married women have entered the labor force and "men's jobs" in growing numbers, challenging the "natural" sexual division of labor.* Now over half of married women are in paid jobs at any one time. Women are demanding entry into the better-paid "men's jobs," and pressing their husbands to do "women's work" in the home. The "natural" marriage union between a bread-winning husband and a homemaking wife has become the exception rather than the rule, characterizing only 29% of husband/wife couples in 1985 (Current Population Reports March 1985).     5

2. *Married women's labor force participation has created a crisis in day care: there is a severe shortage of day care facilities, especially affordable ones.* In New York, for example, between 830,000 and 1.2 million preschool and school-age children vie for the fewer than 135,000 available licensed child care placements (Select Committee on Children 1987). The shortage of day care, combined with the absence of flexible jobs, forces parents to use make-shift arrangements: 2.1 million or 7% of 5–13 year olds whose mothers work outside the home are admittedly left unsupervised; actual numbers are much higher (Children's Defense Fund 1987).     6

3. *Growing numbers are not living in husband/wife families;* only 57% of all households include married couples. Adults are marrying later, spending more time living alone (23.4% of all households) or with friends or lovers. Homosexuality appears to be on the rise, and gays are coming out of the closet and demanding their rights. Marriages have become very unstable; divorce rates more than tripled between 1960 and 1982, more than doubling the number of female-headed households (1986 and 1987 Statistical Abstracts).     7

4. *"Natural" parenting is on the wane.* Divorces create "unnatural" female-headed households, most with dependent children. Unwed mothering has increased to comprise 1 in 5 births and over half of all births among blacks (1987 Statistical Abstract). Remarriages create "unnatural" families, with step-parents and -siblings. More "unnatural" is the trend for sterile couples, gays, and singles to obtain children     8

through artificial insemination, surrogate mothers, and inter-country inter-racial adoptions.

What do these trends mean? Members of the so-called Moral Ma-    9
jority interpret them as the breakdown of *the* family; their solution, embodied in the Family Protection Act of the late 1970s and early 1980s, is to put the "natural" family back together: encourage marriage; discourage divorce, unwed mothering, homosexuality; and get married women out of men's jobs and back into the home. The radical perspective is the opposite; the "natural" family is only one of many possible family systems, a very oppressive and ineffective one at that, as the next section will show. Growing numbers are rejecting the "natural" family system, and trying to create alternative family structures. What society needs is a radical family policy to focus and facilitate this process of dismantling of the old family system and constructing a new and more liberated one.

## The Radical Critique of the "Natural" Family

The radical critique of the "natural" family has many prongs. All of    10
these are underlain by a common claim—the "natural" family is not natural, necessary, or optimal, and a more adequate family system needs to be developed.

1. *The "natural" family system is not natural.* Biological differences    11
in skin color or sex organs, and biological similarities between parent and child, do not necessitate a particular family form, or hierarchy and difference between the sexes and races. Past family systems have been very different from the "natural" family.[4] It is not nature but our society which is producing and reproducing the "natural" family, and its associated institutions of gender and race difference and inequality, through parenting practices, laws, labor market structures, and culture.

2. *The "natural" family system is classist and racist.* The conception    12

---

[4] Among the Rangiroa, adopted children were given equal status and rights as biological offspring, and considered "one belly" (from the same mother) with one another and with their other siblings (Sahlins 1976). In the New England and Southern colonies, mothering among the wealthy was essentially biological, producing one's husband's children, who were then nursed and cared for by poor white or slave women. Mead (1935) found societies where men and women shared the early care of children. Many societies see polygamy as the norm for marriage; others have allowed females to live as men and take wives after having cross-sex dreams (Blackwood 1984). Among the ancient Greeks, the highest form of love for an adult man was homosexual love for a younger man.

of the "natural" family is generated by the dominant culture of upper-class, native-born whites, who then claim it applies to all. Since being a man means bread-winning and supporting a homebound home-maker and children, men without "family wage" jobs due to unem-ployment, class, or race discrimination are seen (and often see them-selves) as less than manly. Black women, forced into the labor force to compensate for their husbands' lack of economic opportunity, are viewed as unfeminine, castrating "matriarchs," and the extended and chosen family system which blacks have developed to combat poverty and economic insecurity is condemned as deviant (Stack 1974). The inability of the poor to properly parent their children because of their meager resources is seen as a fault in their characters, and they are criticized for having children at all, as if the poor do not have a right to parent.

3. *The "natural" family system impoverishes female-headed households.* 13 Women and children face high risks of poverty. Married women are to specialize in unpaid homemaking and mothering, complementing their husbands' bread-winning. Divorce or widowhood leaves women with little access to income, but with major if not full emotional and financial responsibility for the children.[5] "Women's jobs" do not pay enough to cover child care and keep female households with young children out of poverty. The present welfare system (Aid to Families with Dependent Children), structured to support the "natural" family system, does not even provide female-headed families with poverty-level income. The result: the majority of black and Hispanic female-headed families (50 and 53%, respectively), and 27% of white female-headed families, are poor. Children are penalized the most: 54% of children in such families are poor (Current Population Reports 1985).

4. *"Natural" marriage creates inequality between the sexes.* Since wives 14 are relegated to unpaid housework and low paid jobs, they are eco-nomically dependent upon their husbands. Fear of losing this financial support can force women into subservience to their husbands, and into staying in unsatisfying marriages. Indeed, some feminists see "natural" marriage as a struggle in which men have gained the upper hand by monopolizing the higher-paid jobs (Hartmann 1981). What-ever its origins, "natural" marriage is clearly unequal, making mutual love and respect difficult.

---

[5] In 1983, only 35% of mothers caring for their children with absent fathers received any child-support, and the average yearly payment was only $2,341; only 6% of separated or divorced women received any alimony (1987 Statistical Abstract).

5. *"Natural" parenting is oppressive and unjust.* Along with financial    15
responsibility, parents are given almost total power over children. Children have no rights, and no system through which they can complain
about mistreatment or find alternative parents (Rodham 1976). In a
society where most men are under the power of bosses, and women
under that of their husbands, parenting provides an arena where
adults have total power and authority. It is easy to forget one's children's needs and use or abuse them to fill one's own needs. What
results is not only an epidemic of child physical and sexual abuse,[6]
but also the training of each child to accept and participate in hierarchical and authoritarian systems, from schools to workplaces to politics
(Miller 1981).

6. *The "natural" family perpetuates inequality between families* through    16
the generations, because parents pass down their economic position
to their children. Inheritance keeps ownership of the means of production in the hands of a few, mostly white, families.[7] Children born
into higher-income families receive better nutrition, housing, health
care, and schooling than their poor counterparts, have the "insurance"
of wealthy relatives to back them up and encourage risk-taking, and
can expect to inherit wealth. On the other hand, 11 million children
(one in five) must live without even the most basic goods and services
(Current Population Reports 1985). This is not only unjust but also
irrational: it is in society's interest to guarantee quality health care and
education to its future workers and citizens.

7. *The "natural" family system discourages the formation of alternative*    17
*families, while forcing many into unwanted "natural" families.* Its broad
and virulent anti-gay discrimination—from education, employment,
housing, and marriage laws to media images—makes it very difficult
for people to love and share their lives with people of the same sex.
It discriminates against couples who are unable to have children biologically by treating adoption and artificial insemination as "unnatural" and undesirable options. On the other hand, the "natural" family's equation of sex, reproduction, and marriage creates unwanted
children by creating opposition to sex education, birth control for unmarried teens, and abortion. Forty percent of all births are mistimed
or unwanted—for those under 24, a disastrous 53%—forcing millions

[6] The media have focussed on child abuse by strangers—on day care scandals and
missing children—whereas the vast majority of children are abused by their parents
or relatives (Eliasoph 1986).
[7] The wealthiest 2.4% of households owns 65% of the income-producing wealth
(Edwards, Reich, Weisskopf 1986).

of women into premature or unwanted motherhood and/or marriages (1987 Statistical Abstract).

## Conceptualizing a Social Family System

The "natural" family system is inadequate, oppressive, and is coming  18
apart at the seams. At the same time, all need the love and warmth and sharing and parenting which family relationships provide.[8] Hence criticism is not enough; an *alternative* and better vision of family life needs to be delineated, along with a set of concrete policies to bring such a new family system into being.

The oppressiveness of the "natural" family system was accepted  19
because its institutions were seen as natural and inevitable. Our new family system would be a *consciously* social one, its institutions developed through study, discussion, struggle and compromise, and continually criticized and improved so as to maximize freedom, equality, self-fulfillment, democracy, and justice. Here are some of the central principles of such a system; while it may appear utopian, many are living out parts of this vision now.

*Social Marriage.* Marriage would become a *symmetrical* relationship  20
between whole, equal, and socially independent human beings, each participating in a similar range of familial, economic and political activities.[9] Its basis would be mutual love of the other, i.e., liking of, respect for, and sexual attraction to the person the other is, as providing the reason for intimate sharing of lives and living spaces and, if desired, parenting. Couples would not be expected to stay together "for better or for worse . . . as long as ye both shall live"; nor would they need to, since each would have earnings.

*Social Parenting.* Parenting would be recognized as a quintessen-  21
tially *social* activity which, by shaping our unconsciousnesses, bodies, and minds, shapes the future of our society. Society would ensure that each child is well cared for and educated, since the upbringing of children as physically and psychologically healthy, creative, educated, and socially-conscious citizens is essential both to society's well-being, and

[8] Some feminists and gays have taken an "anti-family" position, as if the "natural" family is the only family form (Barrett and McIntosh 1982); however they usually advocate some alternative, family-like institutions.
[9] If this seems far-fetched, an October 1977 CBS–*New York Times* National Survey found that 50% of 30–44 year olds, and 67% of 18–29 year olds, preferred a symmetrical marriage (of a man and woman who both had jobs, did housework, and cared for the children) over the traditional, complementary one.

to our belief in equal opportunity. This would include providing children and their parents with economic and institutional support, as well as seeking out optimal parenting practices and educating prospective parents in them.

*Social Community.* Cultural and economic differences between 22 groups of people would be acknowledged to be social rather than natural products. All human beings would be recognized as equally human citizens of the world, and a concept of basic human rights, both political and economic, developed. Intercultural marriages would be encouraged to further social understanding.

## Bringing the Social Family into Being: A Policy Check-list

Although the "natural" family system is in decline, the social family 23 system cannot replace it unless there are many changes in our economic and social institutions. Here are some of the policies which will help bring about these changes; many are now in place in other countries.

1. *Policies which socialize parenting*                                              24

a. *Policies which establish the right of all adults to choose when and if they wish to parent.* Universal sex education and parenting training for adolescents, as well as access of all to free, safe, 100% effective birth control, abortions, and adoption placement, are needed to make every child a wanted child. At the same time, society must recognize the right of those who are infertile, gay, or single to parent, and support the development of alternative modes of obtaining children from adoption to artificial insemination and in-vitro fertilization.[10] The right to parent must also be protected by programs to help low-income parents with the costs of child-rearing (see 1b). Finally, the right to parent must be seen as socially established, rather than inhering in the genetic connection between a parent and a child; parenting rights must be revocable if a parent neglects or abuses a child, and society should seek to prevent child abuse through an effective system of child advocates and parenting support and training.

b. *Policies which ensure a basic, social inheritance for every child.* The

[10] Most doctors refuse to artificially inseminate single or lesbian women. The developing practice of surrogate mothering is very controversial among feminists and radicals. Since eggs can be fertilized outside of a womb, and embryos can be raised in incubators from the age of a few months, there are many other possibilities, including impregnating men, or even producing infants entirely outside of human bodies, as Marge Piercy (1976) and Shulamith Firestone (1970) have envisioned.

best way to ensure healthy and provided-for children is to ensure this health and income to all families through a system of national health insurance and a combination of anti-poverty measures, from full employment, to comparable worth, to a guaranteed annual income. In addition, since having children does increase a family's poverty risk, family allowances should be provided to parents according to need.[11] Furthermore, all children need to have access to high quality, free or sliding-scale education, from preschool day care when their parents are at work, to elementary and secondary school and college. This "social inheritance" program would be paid for by high inheritance taxes and very progressive income and/or luxury taxes. Such taxes would, in themselves, help reduce the present gross inequalities of opportunity among children.[12]

c. *Policies which socialize child-care costs: government- and business-subsidized day care.* Making quality child care available and affordable to all should be the joint financial responsibility of business and government, since it benefits both employers and society at large. A few trend-setting employers now provide child-care benefits to their workers, having found that these more than pay for themselves by decreasing worker absenteeism, increasing productivity, and attracting top workers (Blau and Ferber 1986). Current federal funding through Title 20 is woefully inadequate; many states are serving less than 30% of their eligible populations (Select Committee on Children 1987). One survey found that ¼ of all full-time homemakers, and ½ of all single parents, were kept from employment and training programs by the unavailability of child care (Cal. Governor's Task Force on Child Care 1986). Again, Sweden provides the example to follow: the government pays 90% of the child-care costs of public day care centers, which are used by over half of children with employed mothers (Blau and Ferber 1986).

On the other hand, to permit parents with job commitments to spend more time with their children, especially their infants, a system of paid leaves from work without loss of one's job or seniority must

25

---

[11] Sweden and France give housing allowances to parents (Kamerman and Kahn 1979); many European countries have national health insurance and family allowances. Swedish policy is to guarantee all citizens a minimum standard of living (Ibid.); in the U.S., the needy only receive support through "entitlement" programs, which require certain qualifications (such as being a female household head with children) other than being poor, and which do not, in any event, raise incomes up to the poverty level.

[12] See Chester (1982) for a review of Western thought on inheritance.

be established. The U.S. does not even have laws guaranteeing prospective parents an *unpaid* leave when they have or adopt a child.[13] In a few states, women can use their temporary disability insurance to pay for 4 to 10 weeks of pregnancy/infant care leave (Kamerman et al. 1983). Again, Sweden is the model in this area, with 1) paid, year-long parental leaves, 2) up to 60 days a year paid leave to care for sick children, and 3) the right for all full-time employed parents with children under 8 to reduce their work weeks (with reduced pay) to 30 hours a week (Ginsberg 1983). Radicals have advocated a shorter work week without reduction in pay as a solution to unemployment and low productivity, for it would create more jobs, reduce unemployment, and increase output (Bowles, Gordon, and Weisskopf 1983); a consideration of the needs of parents makes such policies even more desirable. Other innovations which allow adults to combine work with parenting are flex-time and flex-place (working at home); the extension of health, pension, and other benefits to part-time workers; and the cafeteria benefit plan, which allows dual-career couples to eliminate doubly-covered benefits in favor of more of other benefits, such as leaves or child-care support (Farley 1983; Kamerman and Hayes 1982).

2. *Policies to support egalitarian, symmetrical marriages* in which partners participate equally in parenting, housework, the labor force, and political life.[14]

a. *Comparable worth, affirmative action, increased unionization.* Comparable worth would increase the pay of women's jobs to that of men's jobs requiring comparable skill, effort, and responsibility. Affirmative action encourages women to enter into traditionally masculine jobs. Women need to organize in unions to fight for the above, and for general wage increases; one platform is "solidarity wages," again practiced in Sweden, in which workers agree to take part of their wage increase to reduce inequalities among them. Together these policies would stop the segregation of women into low-paid, dead end, less-satisfying jobs, reduce women's economic dependence upon men, and encourage more similar work and family participation by the sexes.

b. *Socialization of parenting* (see #1 above) would support sym-

---

[13] Kamerman and Kingston (in Kamerman and Hayes 1982) found that paid maternity leave was available to fewer than one-third of all employed women in 1978, and averaged only about six weeks of benefits.
[14] Cuba encourages such marriages through its "Family Code," adopted in 1975 (Randall 1981); however, it still discriminates against gay couples.

metrical marriage, for it would allow adults to combine parenting with labor force commitments, reducing the pressure to specialize as in "natural" marriage.

c. *Repeal of the laws that discourage formation of "unnatural" marriages and non-traditional households.* This includes repealing sodomy laws and advocating legislation prohibiting discrimination against gays in employment, housing, insurance, foster parenting, adoption, and other areas.[15] Gay relationships must be legitimized in marriage laws, to give spouses health insurance, pension, inheritance, and other benefits and rights enjoyed by heterosexual spouses.[16] The repeal of co-residence laws, which in many states prohibit the cohabitation of more than two unrelated adults, is needed to allow the formation of non-biologically–based extended families.

d. *Individual rather than joint taxation of married couples.* Our present income tax system is progressive and married couples are taxed on the basis of their combined incomes. This discourages wives from entering the labor force since, when a woman's earnings raise the household's tax bracket, much of her earnings are paid to the government in taxes.[17] Taxing adults individually (as is currently done in Sweden), rather than jointly, would instead encourage both members of a couple to participate in the labor force.

e. *Policies to aid the casualties of the "natural" marriage system.* Until the above changes are achieved, women and children will continue to face high poverty risks when they live in female-headed households. Many feminists advocate the strengthening of alimony and child-support laws; however, this both reinforces the "natural" marriage notion that husbands should be the main providers, and reproduces class and race inequality, because wives' and children's incomes depend on that

---

[15] Sodomy laws, which outlaw forms of "unnatural sex" (e.g., anal intercourse and oral/genital sex, either heterosexual or homosexual), still exist in many states, and were recently upheld by the Supreme Court, although they are seldom enforced. Many cities and a few states have passed gay rights legislation, and more and more employers have extended their non-discrimination policy to include sexual preference or orientation.

[16] In June 1987, the Swedish Parliament approved a bill which gave gay couples the same rights as heterosexuals married by common law; it will allow couples to sign housing leases as couples, regulate the division of property after a break-up, and grant lovers the right to inherit property in the absence of a will (*Gay Community News*, June 14–20, 1987).

[17] Even though the recent tax reform reduced the progressivity of the tax system, and a 1983 reform exempted 10% of the income of the lower-earning partner from taxation, the "marriage penalty" persists (Blau and Ferber 1986).

of their husbands/fathers. Extensive welfare reform, combined with the policies above, is a better solution.

3. *Policies to create social community*. Labor market reforms (2a) must [27] always aim at eliminating both race and sex segregation and discrimination. These, along with social inheritance policies, will go far in stopping the economic reproduction of racial inequality in the U.S. The decline of "natural" parenting views of children as "one's own flesh and blood" will foster, and in turn be fostered by, the decline of conceptions of race, as both are replaced by a view of a human community reproduced through social parenting.

## Bibliography

Barrett, Michele, and McIntosh, Mary. 1982. *The Anti-Social Family*. London: New Left Books.

Blackwood, Evelyn. 1984. Sexuality and Gender in Certain Native Tribes: The Case of Cross-Gender Females. *Signs* 10(1):27–42.

Blau, Francine, and Ferber, Marianne. 1986. *The Economics of Women, Men, and Work*. Englewood Cliffs, N.J.: Prentice-Hall.

Bowles, Samuel, David M. Gordon, and Thomas E. Weisskopf. 1983. *Beyond the Wasteland: A Democratic Alternative to Economic Decline*. New York: Anchor/Doubleday.

Chester, Ronald. 1982. *Inheritance, Wealth, and Society*. Bloomington: Indiana University Press.

Children's Defense Fund. 1987. Unpublished paper.

Edwards, Richard, Reich, Michael, and Weisskopf, Thomas. 1986. *The Capitalist System*. Englewood Cliffs, N.J.: Prentice-Hall. Third Edition.

Eliasoph, Nina. 1986. Drive-In Mortality, Child Abuse, and the Media. *Socialist Review* #90, 16(6):7–31.

Farley, Jennie, ed. 1983. *The Woman in Management*. New York: ILR Press.

Firestone, Shulamith. 1970. *The Dialectic of Sex*. New York: Morrow.

Ginsberg, Helen. 1983. *Full Employment and Public Policy: The United States and Sweden*. Lexington, Mass.: D.C. Heath and Co.

Gould, Steven J. 1981. *The Mismeasure of Men*. New York: Norton.

Hartmann, Heidi. 1981. The Unhappy Marriage of Marxism and Feminism. In *Women and Revolution: A Discussion of the Unhappy Marriage of Marxism and Feminism*, Lydia Sargent (ed.), pp. 1–41. Boston: South End Press.

Kamerman, Sheila, and Kahn, Alfred. 1979. *Family Policy: Government and Families in Fourteen Countries*. New York: Columbia University Press.

Kamerman, Sheila, and Hayes, Cheryl, eds. 1982. *Families that Work: Children in a Changing World*. Washington: National Academy Press.

Kamerman, Sheila, et al., eds. 1983. *Maternity Policies and Working Women*. New York: Columbia University Press.

Matthaei, Julie. 1982. *An Economic History of Women in America: Women's Work, the Sexual Division of Labor, and the Development of Capitalism*. New York: Schocken Books.

Mead, Margaret. 1935. *Sex and Temperament in Three Primitive Societies*. New York: William Morrow and Co.

Miller, Alice. 1981. *The Drama of the Gifted Child*. trans. by Ruth Ward. New York: Basic Books.

Piercy, Marge. 1976. *Woman on the Edge of Time*. New York: Fawcett.

Randall, Margaret. 1981. *Women in Cuba: Twenty Years Later*. New York: Smyrna Press.

Rodham, Hilary. 1976. Children under the Law. In *Rethinking Childhood* Arlene Skolnick (ed.). Boston: Little, Brown and Co.

Sahlins, Marshall. 1976. *The Use and Abuse of Biology: An Anthropological Critique of Sociobiology*. Ann Arbor: University of Michigan Press.

Select Committee on Children, Youth and Families, U.S. House of Representatives. 1987. Fact Sheet: Hearing on Child Care, Key to Employment in a Changing Economy. March 10.

Stack, Carol. 1974. *All Our Kin*. New York: Harper & Row.

U.S. Bureau of the Census, Current Population Reports. 1985. Household and Family Characteristics: March 1985.

——. 1985. Money Income and Poverty Status of Families and Persons in the United States.

——. 1986. 1987. Statistical Abstract of the United States.

Weeks, Jeffrey. 1979. *Coming Out: Homosexual Politics in Britain, from the Nineteenth Century to the Present*. London: Quartet Books.

# Questions

1. What, if anything, strikes you as "radical" in Matthaei's "radical analysis" of the "'natural' family" (paragraph 3)? Do any parts of this analysis strike you as unfair, misleading, or wrong? If so, which parts, and what do you find wrong with them?

2. In paragraph 7 Matthaei says that "adults are marrying later." Assuming this statement to be true, what do you think are the causes? What do you think may be the consequences, good and bad? (For an argument deploring this trend, see the essay by McFarlane, pages 58–61.)

3. In paragraph 10 Matthaei denies that the "natural" family is natural. Do you think she proves her case? If not, in what way(s) does she fail?

4. Matthaei argues (paragraph 15) that the idea of the "natural" family

can lead easily to child abuse. Can one argue, in response, that the "natural" family is better suited to assist children in growing into healthy, responsible, happy adults than is any conceivable alternative arrangement? If you think so, what arguments might you offer? (For an interesting argument that children should be granted legal rights to escape impossible families, see "Confessions of an Erstwhile Child," pages 103–108.)

5. In paragraph 17 Matthaei argues that the idea of the "natural" family "discriminates against couples who are unable to have children biologically." Is she saying that all adults—including the sterile, the infertile, and those who do not wish to engage in heterosexual sex—have a right to have children? If she is saying this, on what might she base this right? (In her next paragraph she says, "All need the love and warmth and sharing and parenting which family relationships provide." Is this need perhaps the basis for a right—possessed by all adults—to have children? (See also the discussion in paragraph 24.)

6. Much of the essay is devoted to arguing on behalf of various kinds of equality. For example, in paragraph 20, in discussing "social marriage," Matthaei says that "marriage would become a symmetrical relationship between whole, equal, and socially independent human beings." The two persons involved would participate "in a similar range of familial, economic and political activities." But what if both persons do not share an interest in, for example, political activities? Should they therefore not marry? (For an argument that it is better for a couple *not* to share their interests around the clock and seven days a week, see the essay by Perrin, pages 80–83.) Or suppose that one person enjoyed the world of paid work and the other preferred to engage, at least for a while, chiefly in the role of parenting and housekeeping. Do you think such a marriage would be inherently unstable?

7. In point 1b of paragraph 24, Matthaei argues for programs and policies that would redistribute wealth—for example, a guaranteed annual income. Suppose someone argued (or at least asserted) that he or she saw no reason to support the families of the poor. What reply might you make?

8. Matthaei apparently sees marriage as involving only two adults. Do you assume that she rejects polygamy (a practice not unknown in the United States and elsewhere)? And what about polyandry (one woman with two or more husbands)? If you accept Matthaei's arguments, or most of them, how do *you* feel about polygamy and polyandry? Arguments for polygamy can be found in the essay by B. Aisha Lemu (pages 73–76). What argument(s) for polyandry can you imagine?

Jonda McFarlane

# The Meaning of Marriage

I know I'm on dangerous ground; my own children say 1
I'm a victim of my consuming desire to be a grandparent. But I think
American men and women are waiting too long to get married. Instead
of waiting until all the graduate degrees are earned, the BMW is parked
in front of the condo, the invitation to become a partner has arrived
and foreign lands have been explored, young people should be going
for the gold—ring, that is—at a younger age.

How can I suggest something so obviously retrogressive? How can 2
I dismiss all the liberating changes of the last 25 years? The answer
lies in what I see when I look at young people today: too often unhappy
creatures who seem, in spite of all their liberty and all their achievements, to be desperately searching for meaning in their lives.

Having reached adulthood at the very last moment before the 3
youth revolution of the 1960s, I have watched the erasure of old rules
and their replacement by unsettling new ones. And I have tried to be
open-minded about the results. Would life be better in this brave new
world? Although these changes took place after I myself was already
married, I watched as the effects washed over the younger siblings of
my friends and then held my breath as my own children threaded their
way through the forest of new mores. As parents, those of us in my
peer group *had* to pay attention; we were completely unprepared for
these challenges because society was operating by a totally new set of
rules. We were confused and not a little frightened, but we struggled
to help our children learn what they needed to know to be happy
adults.

The changes weren't all for the worse. The political demonstrations 4
of the '60s and '70s awakened our youth to the need to be involved
in the shaping of local and national policy. Feminism opened doors
for our daughters and helped our sons to re-evaluate some pretty firmly
held notions about the roles of both men and women. And the sexual
revolution—really the toughest one for us parents to deal with—did

Jonda McFarlane teaches English at Bethesda–Chevy Chase (Maryland) High
School. This essay originally appeared in *Newsweek* in 1987.

mean that fewer adolescents took on marriage when all they really wanted was sex.

Unfortunately, our young people didn't always know how to handle all this freedom. Like many new Russian émigrés, they often found it confusing and difficult to suddenly have control over their lives. When decisions concerning *limits* arose, they had no guidelines to help them. In some cases feminism produced young women who—free to "have it all"—nearly killed themselves trying to do just that. Dramatically higher abortion and teenage pregnancy rates, as well as enormous increases in social diseases (and now AIDS) resulted from the inability to set limits on sexual freedom. And now we have a generation so committed to success in the marketplace, or to "fun," that it puts off for years the commitment to marriage.

As parents, however, we can see that many of our children are not, in fact, happier. What is often missing in their lives, it seems, is a sense of values—and here we parents must share the responsibility. Acquiescing in their demands for a less rule-oriented society, we somehow neglected to hand down the fundamental values we had learned in an earlier time. Now they have plenty of freedom but too little meaning in their lives.

Well, then, how does one go about this business of finding meaning in life? The basic tenet is what it has been since civilization began: "think of others." That means avoiding actions that could harm another (ponder the ramifications of *that* in your professional and private lives). It means thinking of your work as something that makes a contribution to society, not just as the way to pay the bills. It means doing things that make other people's lives better.

## Challenges of Life

Marriage both illustrates and reinforces the importance of thinking of others. For as long as there has been human society, men and women have recognized their need to mate—to establish a lifelong bond that provides the essence of the support that each human being needs as he struggles to face the challenges of life. Throughout history, it has been this union—in which each partner is concerned with the good of the other—which above all other forces has made it possible for men and women to experience their greatest joy. It is this built-in support system that enables them to be the best that they can be. It is this sharing of life's best *and worst* times that exponentially increases our ability to find meaning in life. A sunset watched in solitude on a foreign shore only increases your loneliness; the same sight shared with a loved one is a special moment. When we think back on our sorrows and our joys, we realize that in both cases the first thing we do is reach out for the person we are closest to. As happy as we feel when the baby is born or the promotion arrives, our true joy comes from watching that person's face when we share the news. When our twins were born, my husband was in Vietnam. He didn't see them or hold them until they were seven months old. It wasn't easy to care for them and their three-year-old sister by myself during those long months. But the truth is that the most difficult part was not being able to share them with their father. Until his return, my experience of childbirth was never quite complete.

Those who fear the commitment of marriage, who avoid the trou-  9 ble and the responsibility in the name of more time, more money or more pleasure, cheat only themselves. Those who wait until they reach all their other goals before presenting themselves to a deserving mate often find their success empty. How much better to struggle *with* someone to reach a common goal, to be able to say, "We did it together," than to strive for one's own good.

Several caveats here: first, I am not speaking about teenagers or  10 those just out of college. Second, I am aware that some people are single through no choice of their own—though I think that the mind-set of the times has something to do with that, too. But the rest of you should take heed. And now that we've got *that* settled, can we talk about grandchildren?

# Questions

1.  In paragraph 2 McFarlane says that her remarks in favor of earlier marriage are prompted by seeing many "unhappy creatures who seem, in spite of all their liberty and all their achievements, to be desperately searching for meaning in their lives." Do you see what she sees? Or, on the other hand, do you see many "unhappy creatures" whose marriages—made in early adulthood—ended in divorce? By the way, what are the connotations of "creatures" instead of, say, "men and women"? Or does she mean only "women"?

2.  In paragraph 6 McFarlane says that "a sense of values" seems to be missing from the lives of many people. In the next two paragraphs she goes on to specify some of these values. Do you subscribe to them? Are you under the impression that many people do

not, and that their failure to subscribe to these values is the cause
of their unhappiness?

3. McFarlane suggests (paragraph 8) that the need "to establish a
   lifelong bond" with a mate has been recognized "for as long as
   there has been human society." What evidence does she offer? Or
   is the point so obvious that she need not provide any evidence to
   support it? What evidence, if any, can you offer to dispute her assertion?

4. This essay appeared in *Newsweek*. Sketch, from this article alone,
   a profile of the readers of *Newsweek*. Age? Sex? Race? Economic
   bracket? Do you think the profile you have just constructed—a profile based only on this article—is an accurate profile of the readers
   of *Newsweek?* Or do some of McFarlane's assumptions exclude
   from your profile some of the magazine's readers?

Richard John Neuhaus

# Renting Women,
# Buying Babies
# and Class Struggles

Quite suddenly, it seems, we have a new form of trade in   1
human beings. It is called surrogate motherhood, and several states
have already declared it legitimate by establishing regulations for the
trade. Voices have been raised to oppose the baby traders before their
business becomes a fait accompli.[1] It may already be too late for that.

Richard John Neuhaus, a Lutheran clergyman who for seventeen years served
as senior pastor in a black and Hispanic parish in Brooklyn, New York, is now
director of the Rockford Institute Center on Religion and Society in New York
City. He is editor of *Religion and Society Report* and editor-in-chief of *This World:
A Journal of Religion and Public Life.* He is also the author of several books,
including *The Naked Public Square: Religion and Democracy in America.*

[1] Fait accompli: thing already done, so that opposition is useless (French). (Editors'
note).

The *New York Times* has editorially pronounced that regulation is the only way to go since, after all, "the business is probably here to stay." Numerous objections of a moral, legal, and commonsensical nature have been raised to surrogate motherhood. One aspect that has not been sufficiently explored is the way in which the baby trade so rudely rips the veil off class divisions and hostilities in American life.

## Surrogating Today and Yesterday

The most celebrated, or notorious, case of surrogate motherhood is the    2
one that has swirled around "Baby M" in a New Jersey courtroom. Some of the details are by now well known. Mr. William Stern, a biochemist married to Dr. Elizabeth Stern, a pediatrician who thought pregnancy might be bad for her health, contracted with Mrs. Mary Beth Whitehead to have his baby in return for $10,000 plus an equal amount in expenses. Mrs. Whitehead and her husband Richard, a sanitation worker, agreed. The surrogate contract is not uninteresting, including as it does provisions for amniocentesis and obligatory abortion if Mr. Stern did not like the results of the test. Also, Mrs. Whitehead would not receive the $10,000 but only a small payment for her troubles "in the event the child is miscarried, dies, or is stillborn." The Sterns were taking no chances. But they could not prevent Mary Beth Whitehead from changing her mind. "It's such a miracle to see a child born," she said. "The feeling is overwhelming. All the pain and suffering you've gone through is all gone." Within five minutes she is breastfeeding the baby, the bonding is effected, she runs away to avoid having to turn the baby over to the Sterns, the Sterns hire detectives to snatch the baby, and it all ends up in a court trying to decide who gets to keep the baby.

The liberal Catholic journal, *Commonweal*, observes: "Surrogate    3
motherhood is a simple idea. It has become a critical issue today not because of the breakthrough in technology but because of a breakdown in moral understanding—namely, the understanding that human reproduction should be firmly placed in the matrix of personal sexuality, marital love, and family bonds." The point is an important one. Also in religious circles today, there is much prattle about changing moral rules because of technological advances and new discoveries about sexuality. It is highly doubtful that we know anything very significant about sexuality that, say, Saint Augustine did not know. As to surrogate motherhood, long before the dawn of modern science human males had mastered the technique of impregnating women other than

their wives. Genesis 16 tells how Sarah and Abraham chose Hagar to be the surrogate mother of Ishmael. That too turned out badly, although Hagar did get to keep the child. Hagar, of course, was a slave.

Today it is at least gauche to speak of buying or renting women. 4 The Sterns got over that awkwardness by hiring a Manhattan clinical psychologist who testified, "In both structural and functional terms, Mr. and Mrs. Stern's role as parents to Baby M was achieved by a surrogate uterus and not a surrogate mother." The contract did not call for Mrs. Whitehead to get involved. In fact *she* was supposed to stay out of this deal altogether. Mary Beth's problem, it would seem, is that she was not able to disaggregate herself from her uterus. She did not understand that she could rent out her uterus just as the Manhattan doctor could rent out his certified expertise. The capable lawyers hired by the Sterns had made it all very clear, and for a while she thought she understood, but then somehow the whole thing began to seem surreal. (Not being an educated person, she did not say it seemed surreal. She said it just seemed wrong.)

## Taking Advantage

True, there are those who argue that there is nothing new in the rich 5 renting the nonrich, whether in whole or in part. A servant or employee, they say, is in effect a rented person. It is hard to argue with people who say such things. More often than not, they are the kind of people who also say that property is theft and tolerance is oppression. One can point out that the employee is free to quit, that a person's work "belongs" to him even if he is paid to do it, that the worker may find fulfillment in the work, and so forth. But such wrongheaded people do have one undeniable point: with respect to the negotiation of worldly affairs, rich people do generally have the advantage of nonrich people. That said, one can only hope it will be acknowledged that there is something singular about the connections between a woman, her sexuality, and her procreative capacity. It is not the kind of acknowledgment people can be argued into, and those to whom it must be explained probably cannot understand. Proabortion proponents of a woman's "reproductive rights" regularly appeal to the uniquely intimate relationship between a woman and her body. Strangely enough, many of them also approve surrogate motherhood as a further step in rationalizing sexual relationships and liberating society from the oppression of traditional mores. The recently discovered constitutional doctrine of "privacy," it would seem, is absolute—unless you have accepted money to have it violated. The inviolably intimate sphere of sexuality is one thing, but a deal is a deal.

As with abortion, there is another party involved. As is not the  6 case with abortion, everyone here recognizes the other party involved. Baby M, having passed the quality-control tests, is certified as a Class-A member of the species. The question is who owns this valuable product. Presumably ownership is fifty-fifty between Mrs. Whitehead and Mr. Stern. Mr. Stern's case is that Mrs. Whitehead had agreed to sell her share of the baby for $10,000 and then reneged on the deal. A Solomonic decision may be required, except Solomon's proposed solution would likely be found unconstitutional. Mary Beth is perplexed by the ownership conundrum. The following is from a taped telephone conversation admitted in evidence: "WHITEHEAD: I gave her life. I did. I had the right during the whole pregnancy to terminate it, didn't I? STERN: It was your body. WHITEHEAD: That's right. It was my body and now you're telling me that I have no right. STERN: Because you made an agreement . . . you signed an agreement." It is not that nothing is sacred anymore. It is simply that the sacred has been relocated, away from realities such as life and motherhood and placed in a contract signed and sealed by money. Some simplistic types who have not kept up with the demands of cultural change find this repugnant. For example, William Pierce, president of the National Committee for Adoption, flatly says: "If you regulate surrogate motherhood, that is making a public statement that it's all right. We decided a hundred years ago we didn't want people bought and sold in this country."

That is not the question, says the judge in the Baby M case. The  7 question, the only question, is what is "in the best interest" of Baby M. In other words, who can offer Baby M the better prospect for the good things in life, the Whiteheads or the Sterns? Here, although the word is never used, the question of class takes center stage in the courtroom drama. The relative stability of American society is due in part to our kindly veiling of class distinctions and hostilities. People making $20,000 and people making $100,000 or more have tacitly agreed to say they are middle class. In fact, some are rich and some are not rich and some are poor. In terms of income, the Sterns are upper-middle or upper class, the Whiteheads are low–low-middle class and have at times been poor. Perhaps more important than the criterion of income, the Sterns and their allies in the New Jersey courtroom represent the new knowledge class. The disputes are over symbolic knowledge; that is to say, over how to establish the "meaning" of ideas such as parenthood, love, stability, life opportunity, and psychological well-being. In the symbolic knowledge showdown, Mary Beth Whitehead is pitifully outgunned. She has never even heard of the transvaluation of values, which is what the Baby M trial is all about.

## Class Struggle

It is not simply that the Sterns can hire a battery of lawyers, detectives, psychological experts and social workers, while Mary Beth must get along with a lawyer three years out of school whose main experience has been in liability cases. No, the greater disparity is that the Sterns, their hired experts, the judge, and almost everyone else involved represents the new class arrayed against the world of the Whiteheads who represent the bottom side of the working class. In the class war being waged in the courtroom, the chief weapon of the new class is contempt for the world of their cultural inferiors, a world so blatantly represented by the Whiteheads. Mrs. Whitehead must be criticized for her decision to enter into the agreement in the first place. But that is not a criticism employed in the courtroom to discredit Mrs. Whitehead, for it might reflect unfavorably on the other party to the agreement, even suggesting that perhaps Mr. Stern took advantage.

Rather, Mary Beth Whitehead is to be discredited and declared an unfit mother because the world of which she is part is unfit for Mr. Stern's baby, or at least not nearly so fit as the world of the Sterns. So extensive evidence is presented that the Whiteheads have had a hard time of it financially, even living in a house trailer for a time. More than that, Mrs. Whitehead received welfare payments for a few months and her husband underwent a bout with alcoholism some years ago. The mandatory new class attitude under usual circumstances is that there is absolutely no stigma whatsoever attached to welfare or alcoholism. But that is under usual circumstances. In the class war being fought in the New Jersey courtroom such things are sure evidence of moral turpitude and the Whiteheads' "unsuitability" as parents for the 50 percent wellborn Baby M. In addition, a team of mental health experts has testified that Mrs. Whitehead shows definite signs of "distress," and one psychiatrist bluntly says she is suffering from "mixed personality disorder." That presumed illness is defined as "traits from several personality disorders but not all the criteria of any one disorder." It is a kind of catchall category in which, one fears, most human beings might be caught. Yet another psychiatrist in the new class alliance attempts to come up with harder evidence. Dr. Judith Brown Greif said that Mrs. Whitehead "often is unable to separate out her own needs from the needs of the baby." Well, there you have it. Mary Beth, in her pathetic ignorance, probably thought that was a sign of being a good mother. Little does she know about the need-fulfilling autonomy of the psychologically mature.

In order to get empirical support for their class biases, a group of        10
mental health and child development experts visited "for several hours" in the Whitehead and Stern homes to observe firsthand how Baby M "related" to the respective parties. At the Whiteheads, Baby M seemed very happy, but their other two children, ages eleven and twelve, were vying for her attention and Mrs. Whitehead exhibited "an inflated sense of self." This, according to Dr. Marshall Schechter, psychiatrist at the University of Pennsylvania, was revealed in her making "an assumption that because she is the mother, the child, Baby M, belongs to her. This gives no credence to or value to the genetic contribution of the birth father." Things were different at the quiet and spacious Stern home. There were no other children to interrupt and, as Dr. and Mrs. Stern sat on the living room floor chatting with their mental health visitors, Baby M gave every sign of relating very well to Mr. Stern. Of Mr. Stern one psychiatrist reported. "He is a thoughtful, sensitive man with a deep sense of responsibility and a respect for privacy." He did not need to add that none of those nice things could be said of Mrs. Whitehead.

Another expert (the one who contributed the distinction between        11
renting the woman and renting the uterus), unequivocally declared that the Sterns are "far and away more capable of meeting the baby's needs than the Whiteheads." This includes of course his professional evaluation of Dr. Elizabeth, the wife. She is also, the experts told the court, very good at relating. In Dr. Stern's extensive court testimony, according to the *Times*, "she spoke of her delights at home with the baby and her disdain for Mrs. Whitehead." Often, she testified, she takes the baby shopping. "She's the cutest thing around. She's always pulling at the clothes in Bloomingdale's, trying to get them off the rack." At Bloomies, of course. You can bet that Mary Beth Whitehead probably doesn't even know where it is.

We Americans have a way of declaring something outrageous,        12
repugnant, odious, and beyond the pale—and then concluding that we should regulate it. Surrogate motherhood should not be regulated, it should be outlawed. Some think the buying and selling of human beings was outlawed with the abolition of slavery, and the renting of women with laws against prostitution. But those big questions are

bypassed if one agrees with the court that the only question is, "What is in the best interest of the child?" Then enters the ugly factor of naked class advantage. If "interest" is defined by material wellbeing, life opportunities, professionally certified mental and emotional health, and a "lifestyle" approved by the new knowledge class, then clearly the baby must go to the Sterns. By the criteria by which Mary Beth Whitehead is declared an unsuitable mother, millions of (dare we use the term?) lower-class women are unsuitable mothers. (One waits to see whether the court would take her other two children into custody.) By the criteria by which the Sterns are found to be "far and away more capable of meeting the baby's needs," people of recognized achievement and approved attitudes have a right to the best babies that money can buy.

# Questions

1.  In paragraph 2 what words or phrases convey Neuhaus's antipathy for the Sterns?
2.  What words, phrases, or sentences in paragraph 4 are examples of verbal (conscious) irony, or even of sarcasm? (On irony, see page 1147 in the glossary.) Do you consider the paragraph effective? Why, or why not? As you reread the essay, what other striking instances of verbal irony do you note?
3.  In paragraph 5 Neuhaus finds it strange that many people who approve of abortion "also approve surrogate motherhood as a further step in rationalizing sexual relationships and liberating society from the oppression of traditional mores." If you do *not* find it strange, explain why. (For instance, you might try to argue that if a woman has a right to abort a fetus, she also has the right to rent out her uterus, on the grounds that it is *her* body. Do you imagine that Neuhaus would find this explanation acceptable? Why, or why not?)
4.  In paragraph 6 Neuhaus quotes Stern as reminding Mary Beth Whitehead that she "made an agreement." Does Neuhaus believe that the agreement—the contract—settles the issue? Do you?
5.  In his opening paragraph Neuhaus claims that "the baby trade" exposes class conflict in American life. How does he support this point? If you agree that his main point is that surrogacy arrangements are immoral, does this secondary point support his thesis or dilute it?
6.  In his final paragraph Neuhaus bluntly states: "Surrogate motherhood should not be regulated, it should be outlawed." Do you agree or disagree? Why?

7.  In the week after the birth of the baby, the Whiteheads and the Sterns passed the baby back and forth. Later the Whiteheads kept the baby for four months, until, on March 31, 1987, a court awarded custody of the child to the Sterns and terminated Ms. Whitehead's custody rights. Ten months later the New Jersey Supreme Court declared the surrogacy contract illegal and voided, and also voided the adoption of the baby by Dr. Stern, allowing her no parental rights. Ms. Whitehead was given visitation rights. The child is now legally the daughter of Ms. Whitehead and Mr. Stern, who must negotiate visitation rights, as a divorced couple must. What do you think of the court's decision?

Lionel Tiger

# Omnigamy
## The New Kinship System

A hapless British cabinet minister responsible for the hapless UK telephone system once complained that the more phones installed in his country, the more there were to call, and so the demand for phones increased: supply creates demand. Somewhat the same thing is happening with marriage in America. The more divorces there are, the more experienced marriers exist, ready to remarry—and many do. The divorce rate has jumped 250 percent in the past 21 years; about 80 percent of the formerly married remarry. With each new marriage, the parents and children involved acquire a whole new set of relatives, friends, and associations—in effect, they stretch their kinship system. Many people are married to people who have been married to other people who are now married to still others to whom the first parties may not have been married, but to whom somebody has likely been married. Our society, once based on the principle of solid monogamy until death do us part, has shifted toward a pattern of serial polygamy, in which people experience more than one spouse, if only one at a

Lionel Tiger, born in 1937, is the director of graduate programs in anthropology at Rutgers University. His most recent book is *Optimism: The Biology of Hope.*

time. Thus we appear to be moving to a new and imprecise system we might call omnigamy, in which each will be married to all.

People keep marrying, even though happy marriages are regarded  2 as surprising and much-envied occurrences. The not-so-stately pageant of marriage goes on, heedless of the cautionary cries of pain and the clenched question: Why? Various responsible estimators expect that from a third to a half of the marriages formed in this decade will end in divorce sometime. This is astonishing. It is also astonishing that, under the circumstances, marriage is still legally allowed. If nearly half of anything else ended so disastrously, the government would surely ban it immediately. If half the tacos served in restaurants caused dysentery, if half the people learning karate broke their palms, if only 6 percent of people who went on roller-coasters damaged their middle ears, the public would be clamoring for action. Yet the most intimate of disasters—with consequences that may last a lifetime for both adults and children—happens over and over again. Marriage has not yet gone underground.

To an anthropologist, the emergence of a new kinship system  3 should be as exciting as the discovery of a new comet to an astronomer. But in the case of omnigamy, the developing pattern is still unclear, the forces shaping it unanalyzed, the final structure difficult to predict. We know the numbers of marriages and remarriages, but what about the apparent acceleration of the process? The new system permits— perhaps even demands—that its members repair themselves quickly after crises of vast personal proportion. In the slap-dash, overpraised, and sentimental film *An Unmarried Woman,* Jill Clayburgh explains to her (quite nauseating) therapist how agonizing and lonely it was when her husband of umpteen years left her, and how she has been without sexual congress for such a long, long time. When the therapist hears this dreadful fact, she earnestly recommends that this casualty of a massive private accident return immediately to the sexual fray. It has, after all, been *seven weeks.*

The heroine subsequently decides to reject an offer to join an at-  4 tractive and apparently quite suitable artist. Instead she chooses to lead an independent life as a part-time secretary in a SoHo art gallery, which makes her somewhat radical with respect to the omnigamous system. For her obligation seems clear: she must form some sturdy response, one way or the other, to the ambient fact of marriage and remarriage. To remain haunted by grief and inhibited by a sense of failure is taken as a mere expression of cowardice or restlessness. When anthropology first started out, the difficult trick in studying any culture was to discover just what the kinship system was—who was married to whom, and why, and what connections counted for inheritance, status, and authority. We found that marriage was the instrument for creating the extended family, which provided for most human needs in the tribal societies. If an anthropologist from the Trobriand Islands came here now, he or she could well conclude that by stimulating further marriages, divorce has come to be an important organizing principle in our society, since kinship alliances among divorced people are so extensive and complex.

When parents divorce and remarry, the new family connections 5 extend the reach of family life to dimensions a Baganda or Trobriander or Hopi could well understand. Take an example: after the divorce of A and B, siblings A1 and B1 live with A and her new husband, C, but visit B and his new wife, D, on weekends. C's children, C1, C2, and C3, like to go to basketball games with A1 and B1. D's children by her first marriage also enjoy the company of A1 and B1, and take them along on visits to their father, E, a former star athlete who becomes an important hero and role model to the children of A, who has never met him and probably never will.

Nor is it only marriage that binds. In a world where all Mom and 6 Dad's companions are potential mates, Dad's live-in girl friend may turn up for parents' night at school when he's out of town. She also may have a brother—a kind of stepuncle to the kids—with a 40-foot sloop. (The spreading network can put children in touch with a dislocating variety of styles.)

What this means for children, and how it affects their sense of 7 what is stable, what is optional, what is fast, slow, brisk, or stately, is, of course, difficult to say. The generation of children spawned by the Age of Omnigamy has not yet made its mark on the social system in any clear way; we cannot know whether they are immune, immunized, or carriers of the bug across generational lines. In the old days, people were titillated by the polygamous habits of Hollywood celebrities, but few were tempted to emulate them. Parents, grandparents, aunts, and uncles seem to be more important role models for children. When they keep changing partners, it will likely increase the child's sense of the tentativeness in all relations that the new system reflects.

While I am not implying that omnigamous parents set a bad ex- 8 ample, they surely set some example. The consequences for their own children and for those others with whom they come in contact must be considerable. Divorce as a recurrent aspect of life may make it relatively easier for children to accept when they are young, but harder to avoid when they become adults. And who has calculated the effect of omnigamy on grandparents, whose connections with their grand-children suddenly come to be mediated by strangers—stepparents who might even move them to some distant city?

I do not mean to be alarmist and implacably negative about all 9 this. The existence of relatively civilized divorced options is as much a sign of human freedom as it is of sanctioned personal confusion and pain. Who, after all, would wish to confirm in their desperate plight the countless, real-world descendants of Madame Bovary?

Surely, too, there is a value in the extension of personal experience 10 to wider circles of people than strict and permanent monogamy permits. And there is presumably an enhancement of personal vividness, which the new, relatively unstructured world permits—if not coerces.

Omnigamy may have interesting economic implications as well. 11 Adrienne Harris of York University in Toronto has pointed out that each marital separation stimulates the repurchase of those items left in one household and needed in the next. Like amoebas splitting, one dishwasher becomes two, one vacuum cleaner becomes two, one television becomes two; domestic purchases even become impetuous ("Why shouldn't I have my Cuisinart to do my fish mousse when he/she has *our* Cuisinart for hers/his?"). One can't help speculating that the rapid increase in retail outlets selling cooking equipment reflects the doubled demands of the new kinship system.

And where would the real estate market be without house sales 12 to accommodate people who can no longer accommodate each other? And has anyone wondered why the garage sale has recently become so common? The economic shifts that depend on the breakup and reforming of marital units are a form of internal colonialism: at the same time that the United States can no longer control foreign markets, it is expanding its internal ones. The family system, which both Engels and Marx saw as the stimulus for the development of capitalism, may even, in the new form, turn out to be one of its props. As with all colonialisms, however, many people come to be exploited. Taking up the options omnigamy offers strains the financial and emotional resources both.

Can it be said that these comments apply mostly to a small group 13 of self-involved persons inhabiting the Upper East and West Sides of Manhattan, where the production of novels and articles about marriage and anguished personal failure is a major cottage industry? No. If the divorce rates persist and cities continue to export their social patterns, as in the past, other communities still complacently conventional and relatively monogamous will make a gradual but perceptual shift to omnigamy. The pattern will broaden unless there is soon—and there could be—a renewed commitment to monogamous fidelity, and possibly even to the importance of virginity as a factor in marital choice (this possibility seems rather remote). What does seem clear is that many changes will derive from these many changes, perhaps even a return to notions of marriage based on economic convenience and an agreement to mount a common assault on loneliness. Marriage could be on its way to becoming a generalized corporate, if small-scale, experience capable of providing some sense of community and some prospect of continuity. But it may also become a relatively planless arrangement and rearrangement of fickle magnets inexplicably and episodically drawn into each other's orbits for varying purposes and periods.

# Questions

1. In the first sentence, speaking of the United Kingdom, Tiger uses the adjective "hapless" twice. What does "hapless" mean? Why does he repeat the word? Does the analogy that Tiger makes between telephones and marriages have a point? If so, what is it? Where else does Tiger use comparisons? How effective are they? Do you see any patterns in his use of them?
2. Describe the construction of the sentence, in paragraph 1, beginning "Many people are married to people who have been married. . . ." How would you characterize the tone of this sentence? And how would you characterize the tone of the last sentence in paragraph 1?
3. In paragraph 2 Tiger says, "People keep marrying." Does he suggest why they do? Or why they should not?
4. At the end of paragraph 3, why does Tiger italicize *seven weeks?*
5. In paragraph 7 Tiger claims that it is "difficult to say" what effect the spreading network of kinship alliances will have on children. Perhaps it is. In the course of his essay he does nevertheless imply some effects. What are they? How does he imply them?
6. Tiger begins paragraph 9 by saying: "I do not mean to be alarmist and implacably negative about all this." In the next few paragraphs what benefits from "omnigamy" does he foresee? Are they in fact benefits? To whom?
7. On the whole is "Omnigamy: The New Kinship System" more persuasive about the benefits or about the harms of "serial polygamy"?

8.  If you have read Plumb's "The Dying Family" (pages 37–41), do you think that Plumb would agree with Tiger about a trend toward "omnigamy"? Does either essayist suggest a cause behind this trend? Can you explain it?

## B. Aisha Lemu

# In Defense of Polygamy

$P$erhaps the aspect of Islam in respect of women which is most prominent in the Western mind is that of polygamy. Firstly let me clarify that Islam does not impose polygamy as a universal practice. The Prophet himself was a monogamist for the greater part of his married life, from the age of twenty-five when he married Khadija until he was fifty when she died.    1

One should therefore regard monogamy as the norm and polygamy as the exception.    2

One may observe that, although it has been abused in some times and some places, polygamy has under certain circumstances a valuable function. In some situations it may be considered as the lesser of two evils, and in other situations it may even be a positively beneficial arrangement.    3

The most obvious example of this occurs in times of war when there are inevitably large numbers of widows and girls whose fiances and husbands have been killed in the fighting. One has only to recall the figures of the dead in the first and second world wars to be aware that literally millions of women and girls lost their husbands and fiances and were left alone without any income or care or protection for themselves or their children. If it is still maintained that under these circumstances a man may marry only one wife, what options are left to the millions of other women who have no hope of getting a husband? Their choice, bluntly stated, is between a chaste and childless old maid-    4

---

B. Aisha Lemu comes from an English background. She is now a Muslim. We print here part of a talk she gave (and part of the discussion that followed) at the International Islamic Conference held in London in April 1976.

enhood, or becoming somebody's mistress—that is, an unofficial second wife with no legal rights for herself or for her children. Most women would not welcome either of these since most women have always wanted and still do want the security of a legal husband and family.

The compromise therefore is for women under these circumstances 5 to face the fact that if given the alternative many of them would rather share a husband than have none at all. And there is no doubt that it is easier to share a husband when it is an established and publicly recognised practice than when it is carried on secretly along with attempts to deceive the first wife.

And it is no secret that polygamy of a sort is widely carried on in 6 Europe and America. The difference is that while the Western man has no legal obligations to his second, third or fourth mistresses and their children, the Muslim husband has complete legal obligations towards his second, third or fourth wife and their children.

There may be other circumstances unrelated to war—individual 7 circumstances, where marriage to more than one wife may be preferable to other available alternatives—for example, where the first wife is chronically sick or disabled. There are of course some husbands who can manage this situation, but no one would deny its potential hazards. A second marriage in some cases could be a solution acceptable to all three parties.

Again there are cases in which a wife is unable to have children, 8 while the husband very much wants them. Under Western laws a man must either accept his wife's childlessness if he can, or if he cannot he must find a means of divorce in order to marry again. This could be avoided in some cases if the parties agreed on a second marriage.

There are other cases where a marriage has not been very suc- 9 cessful and the husband loves another woman. This situation is so familiar that it is known as the Eternal Triangle. Under Western laws the husband cannot marry the second woman without divorcing the first one. But the first wife may not wish to be divorced. She may no longer love her husband, but she may still respect him and wish to stay with him for the security of marriage, for herself and their children. Similarly the second woman may not wish to break up the man's first family. There are certain cases such as this where both women could accept a polygamous marriage rather than face divorce on the one hand or an extra-marital affair on the other.

I have mentioned some of these examples because to the majority 10 of Westerners polygamy is only thought of in the context of a harem of glamorous young girls, not as a possible solution to some of the problems of Western society itself. I have given some time to it not in order to advocate its indiscriminate use, but in an attempt to show that it is a practice not to be condemned without thinking of its uses and possible benefits in any community.

[A slightly edited version of the discussion that followed Lemu's talk 11 is given below.]

## Discussion

*Question:* I would like to ask a question in relation to polygamy. 12 If one concedes the arguments you have given in support of a man having more than one wife in certain circumstances, would the same arguments be extended to the situation of a woman in relation to her husband/husbands? To be more precise, if a woman becomes invalid and sexually incapacitated and because of that the husband is allowed to have a second wife, why should not the same hold good in respect of men? If a husband becomes invalid, would it be permitted for the wife to have a second husband?

*B. Aisha Lemu:* The instances which I quoted were examples of 13 human circumstances where there is a genuine problem and I mentioned that in the Western world the options are limited. That is, either you stay with it or you obtain divorce, you cannot bring the third alternative of another wife. Now the question of a woman having more than one husband raises a number of other problems. One of them is the question of inheritance. If a woman has more than one husband, there is no certainty of the paternity of the child, and I think this is something which will be very disturbing to men, not to be sure that a certain child is their own, that it might be the child of another husband. Another problem that one could foresee here is that for a woman to look after one husband is, generally speaking, considered to be quite enough trouble (laughter and applause) without bringing upon herself more than one.

# Questions

1. Lemu says that polygamy is sometimes the lesser of two evils, and sometimes "a positively beneficial arrangement." What are some examples she gives of each category? Does polygamy strike you as a practical solution to the circumstances she describes?

2.  In paragraph 10 Lemu suggests that polygamy is a possible solution
    to some problems of *Western* society itself. To what problems does
    she refer? Does polygamy strike you as a practical solution to these
    problems? Whether or not you think polygamy practical, do you
    think it should be a legal option in our society? Why, or why not?
3.  In her response to a question about polyandry, Lemu does not an-
    swer the specific question she was asked. What question does she
    answer, and how does she answer it? What objection might be
    made to her answer?

Barbara Ehrenreich

# The "Playboy" Man and the American Family

As a scapegoat for social pathology, feminism ranks with    1
creeping socialism, godless atheism, and other well-known historic
threats to public order. We have, in the last decade alone, been accused
of causing male impotence, encouraging sexual perversity, and undermining our colorful national tradition of sex roles. In most cases,
we're happy to take the credit, but there's one charge that can still
make strong women cringe: the accusation that feminism "destroyed
the family" or is deeply and wickedly "antifamily" even when we are
talking about wholesome domestic issues like child care for working
parents or who folds the clothes.

The real issue in the debate over the family, it turns out, is *marriage*    2
(heterosexual, monogamous, and so on), and when the critics charge
feminists with being "antifamily," they mean we are responsible for
"broken" homes, the 50 percent divorce rate, unwed mothers, and
sometimes the entire "me generation."

The notion that women, and feminists in particular, have been    3
waging war on matrimony departs so far from common experience

Barbara Ehrenreich is the co-author of *Remaking Love* and the author of *The
Hearts of Men: American Dreams and the Flight from Commitment.* This essay
originally appeared in *Ms.* in June 1983.

and cultural memory as to deserve the status of whimsy. True, many women initiate divorces, and not only because their husbands are drunks and batterers. True, too, that a few brave women, from Emma Goldman on, have taken a principled stand against marriage as an unwelcome intrusion of government into their private lives. But the truth is that if either sex has been in revolt against marriage, it is men, and that the male revolt against marriage started long before our own rebellion as feminists.

When I was growing up in the 1950s, male hostility to marriage  4 and the responsibilities of breadwinning was an accepted fact of life. In the comics, Daisy Mae kept in training all year to catch L'il Abner on Sadie Hawkins Day, and poor, beaten-down Dagwood slaved away at the office to keep Blondie supplied with new hats. From a male perspective, which was pretty much the only one around, marriage was a "trap" for men and a lifelong sinecure for women. Even after they were "caught," men tried to escape in minor ways—into baseball, golf, hunting, bowling, poker games, or the ideal, female-free world of Westerns.

This flight from "maturity," as concerned psychiatrists dubbed it,  5 is one of the most venerable themes in American literary culture. In American mythic tradition, women are the civilizers and entrappers; men the footloose adventurers. Our heroes chase across the sea after great white whales, raft down the Mississippi, or ride off into the sunset on horseback. Cooper's *Deerslayer* traveled light; Davy Crockett didn't fuss over mortgage payments; and Rip Van Winkle, not quite so enterprising, went to sleep for 20 years to escape a nagging wife.

But it was in the 1950s that male hostility to marriage began to  6 take a more urgent and articulate tone. There were low rumblings against gray-flannel "conformity"—a code word for male acquiescence to marriage and breadwinning—but in an America that was busily purging itself of Communists, bohemians, and similar deviants, no viable alternative was offered. Until Hugh Hefner's *Playboy,* which began publication in 1953. From the first feature article in the very first issue, *Playboy*'s writers railed against "gold-digging women"—wives, ex-wives, and would-be wives—all of them bent on crushing "man's adventurous, freedom-loving spirit." Marriage was an "estate in which the sexes . . . live half-slave and half-free," the slave-half being, of course, the husbands who toiled away while their wives spent their time "relaxing, reading, watching TV, playing cards, socializing. . . ." No man had to put up with this, *Playboy* told its readers: Why sign on for a life contract with one woman when there were so many Bunnies to sample? Why settle for "conformity, togetherness . . . and slow death" when you could have a bachelor apartment, a stereo, and a life of sybaritic thrills? By 1956, nearly a million loyal male readers were getting this manifesto of the male revolt.

All this, I emphasize, was going on at a time when there were 7 fewer open feminists in the entire land than there are today in, say, the executive ranks of the Mormon Church. Married women by the thousands felt trapped and desperate too, but they weren't seething with a subversive zeal to "destroy the family" or smash the institution of marriage. In fact, when it came to marriage, Hefner was the radical; Friedan the conservative. Her manifesto of female discontent (*The Feminine Mystique,* published a full 10 years after the first issue of *Playboy*) argued that wider opportunities for women would strengthen marriage, since divorce reflected "the growing aversion and hostility that men have for the feminine millstones hanging around their necks. . . ." Friedan, and most of the feminists who followed, wanted a more equal, companionate marriage; Hefner and his followers simply wanted *out.*

There should be no mystery why, over the years, women have 8 had a disproportionate investment in marriage. Women's earnings average out to a little more than $10,000 a year each—nowhere near enough to support a single in a swinging lifestyle, much less a single mother and her children. For most women, the obvious survival strategy has been to establish a claim on some man's more generous wage, i.e., to marry him. For men, on the other hand, as *Playboy*'s writers clearly saw, the reverse is true: not counting love, home-cooked meals, or other benefits of the married state, it makes more sense for a man to keep his paycheck for himself, rather than sharing it with an underpaid or unemployed woman and her no doubt unemployed children. A recent study by Stanford University sociologist Lenore J. Weitzman suggests the magnitude of men and women's divergent interests: upon divorce, a woman's standard of living falls, on the average, by 73 percent for the first year, while the standard of living of her ex-husband *rises* by 42 percent. For men, the alternative to marriage might be loneliness and TV dinners; for women it is, all too often, poverty.

By the standards of the 1950s, today's men are in many respects 9 "free" at last: 7.3 million of them live alone (nearly half of them in the "never married" category) compared to 3.5 million in 1970. (The number of women living alone has also increased, but at a much lower rate, because single women are far more likely to live with children than single men.) If a man remains single until he is 28 or even 38, he may be criticized by girlfriends for his "fear of commitment," but he will no longer be suspected of an unhealthy attachment to his mother or a latent tendency to you-know-what. If he divorces his middle-aged wife for some sweet young thing, he may be viewed not as a traitor to the American way, but as a man who has a demonstrated capacity for "growth."

At the risk of sounding "antifamily," I must say that I do not think these changes, and the male revolt that inspired them, are an altogether bad thing. As feminists, we have always stood for men's as well as for women's liberation, which includes their right to be something other than husbands and breadwinners. As my son's mother, I know that I want him to grow up to be a loving and responsible adult, but I also know that it would be heartbreaking to see him "tied down," as the expression goes, to a lifetime of meaningless, uncreative jobs in order to support a family. So my purpose in recalling the recent history of men's revolt is not to say, "So there, blame *them!*" 10

The problem, and it is a big one, is that men may have won their freedom before we win our battle against sexism. Women might like to be free-spirited adventurers too, but the female equivalent of "playboy" does not work well in a culture still riddled with misogyny. We still earn less than men, whether or not we have men to help support us. Which is only to say that the feminist agenda is as urgent as ever, and those who are concerned about "the family" should remember that we—and our sisters and daughters and mothers—are members of it also. 11

# Questions

1. To whom does "we" refer in paragraph 1? *Ms.*, in which this essay originally appeared, addresses primarily women's issues, but is Ehrenreich's tone hospitable to male readers as well? Or is she likely to offend them?

2. Ehrenreich calls attention to the hostility to marriage displayed in comic strips and in *Playboy.* Do you think that such writings are to be taken seriously, or are they merely harmless jests? On what do you base your response?

3. Find the fragmentary sentence in paragraph 6. How can its use be justified?

4. Reread the essay closely, and jot down some brief notes concerning the precautions Ehrenreich takes to make her position appear reasonable.

5.  How does Ehrenreich rate the relative "investment in marriage"
    (paragraph 8) of men and of women? If you have read Perrin's "A
    Part-time Marriage" (see below), do you find Perrin generally agree-
    ing or disagreeing with Ehrenreich's assessment?

Noel Perrin

# A Part-time Marriage

When my wife told me she wanted a divorce, I responded    1
like any normal college professor. I hurried to the college library. I
wanted to get hold of some books on divorce and find out what was
happening to me.

Over the next week (my wife meanwhile having left), I read or    2
skimmed about 20. Nineteen of them were no help at all. They offered
advice on financial settlements. They told me my wife and I should
have been in counseling. A bit late for *that* advice.

What I sought was insight. I especially wanted to understand what    3
was wrong with me that my wife had left, and not even for someone
else, but just to be rid of *me*. College professors think they can learn
that sort of thing from books.

As it turned out, I could. Or at least I got a start. The 20th book    4
was a collection of essays by various sociologists, and one of the pieces
took my breath away. It was like reading my own horoscope.

The two authors had studied a large group of divorced people    5
much like my wife and me. That is, they focused on middle-class Americans of the straight-arrow persuasion. Serious types, believers in marriage for life. Likely to be parents—and, on the whole, good parents.
Likely to have pillar-of-the-community potential. But, nevertheless, all
divorced.

---

Noel Perrin (b. 1927) was educated at Williams College, Duke University, and
Cambridge University. He has written on a wide variety of subjects, for instance
on Thomas Bowdler (the editor of an expurgated edition of Shakespeare, and
hence the source of the word *bowdlerize*, "to expurgate prudishly") and on the
introduction of guns to Japan in the sixteenth century. Since 1959 he has taught
English at Dartmouth College.

Naturally there were many different reasons why all these people 6
had divorced, and many different ways they behaved after divorce.
But there was a dominant pattern, and I instantly recognized myself
in it. Recognized my wife, too. Reading the essay told me not only
what was wrong with me, but also with her. It was the same flaw in
both of us. It even gave me a hint as to what my postdivorce behavior
was likely to be, and how I might find happiness in the future.

This is the story the essay told me. Or, rather, this is the story the 7
essay hinted at, and that I have since pieced together with much observation, a number of embarrassingly personal questions put to divorced friends, and to some extent from my own life.

Somewhere in some suburb or town or small city, a middle-class 8
couple separate. They are probably between 30 and 40 years old. They
own a house and have children. The conscious or official reason for
their separation is quite different from what it would have been in
their parents' generation. Then, it would have been a man leaving his
wife for another, and usually younger, woman. Now it's a woman
leaving her husband in order to find herself.

When they separate, the wife normally stays in the house they 9
occupied as a married couple. Neither wants to uproot the children.
The husband moves to an apartment, which is nearly always going to
be closer to his place of employment than the house was. The ex-wife
will almost certainly never see that apartment. The husband, however,
sees his former house all the time. Not only is he coming by to pick
up the children for visits; if he and his ex-wife are on reasonably good
terms, he is apt to visit them right there, while she makes use of the
time to do errands or to see a friend.

Back when these two were married, they had an informal labor 10
division. She did inside work, he did outside. Naturally there were
exceptions: She gardened, and he did his share of the dishes, maybe
even baked bread. But mostly he mowed the lawn and fixed the lawn
mower; she put up any new curtains, often enough ones she had made
herself.

One Saturday, six months or a year after they separated, he comes 11
to see the kids. He plans also to mow the lawn. Before she leaves, she
says, "That damn overhead garage door you got is off the track again.
Do you think you'd have time to fix it?" Apartment life makes him
restless. He jumps at the chance.

She, just as honorable and straight-arrow as he, has no idea of 12
asking for this as a favor. She invites him to stay for an early dinner.
She may put it indirectly—"Michael and Sally want their daddy to

have supper with them"—but he is clear that the invitation also proceeds from her.

Provided neither of them has met a really attractive other person 13 yet, they now move into a routine. He comes regularly to do the outside chores, and always stays for dinner. If the children are young enough, he may read to them before bedtime. She may wash his shirts.

One such evening, they both happen to be stirred not only by 14 physical desire but by loneliness. "Oh, you might as well come upstairs," she says with a certain self-contempt. He needs no second invitation; they are upstairs in a flash. It is a delightful end to the evening. More delightful than anything they remember from their marriage, or at least from the later part of it.

That, too, now becomes part of the pattern. He never stays the 15 full night, because, good parents that they are, they don't want the children to get any false hopes up—as they would, seeing their father at breakfast.

Such a relation may go on for several years, may even be inter- 16 rupted by a romance on one side or the other and then resume. It may even grow to the point where she's mending as well as washing his shirts, and he is advising her on her tax returns and fixing her car.

What they have achieved postdivorce is what their marriage 17 should have been like in the first place. Part-time. Seven days a week of marriage was too much. One afternoon and two evenings is just right.

Although our society is even now witnessing de facto part-time 18 arrangements, such as the couple who work in different cities and meet only on weekends, we have no theory of part-time marriage, at least no theory that has reached the general public. The romantic notion still dominates that if you love someone, you obviously want to be with them all the time.

To me it's clear we need such a theory. There are certainly people 19 who thrive on seven-day-a-week marriages. They have a high level of intimacy and they may be better, warmer people than the rest of us. But there are millions and millions of us with medium or low levels of intimacy. We find full-time family membership a strain. If we could enter marriage with more realistic expectations of what closeness means for us, I suspect the divorce rate might permanently turn downward. It's too bad there isn't a sort of glucose tolerance test for intimacy.

As for me personally, I still do want to get married again. About 20 four days a week.

## Questions

1. In the model that Perrin discusses, what is the cause for divorce?
2. Judging from what you have seen around you, do you think many divorces proceed from the cause Perrin cites?
3. Does Perrin's behavior (and that of his wife) strike you as immoral? As bad for themselves, bad for the children, and bad for society? Or, on the other hand, should this sort of arrangement be recognized as a type of satisfactory family arrangement?
4. In paragraph 19 Perrin argues that a need exists for part-time marriages. Does he persuade you, or do you think he is rationalizing his own shortcomings or sense of failure?
5. Did you enjoy reading the essay? Why, or why not? If some passages especially pleased you—perhaps because they were amusing, or notably insightful—examine them to see why they impressed you.
6. Perrin begins his essay as a first-person narrative: "When my wife told me she wanted a divorce . . ." Beginning with paragraph 8 he shifts into a third-person narrative: "Somewhere in some suburb or town or small city, a middle-class couple separate." Can you suggest reasons for this shift? Does it work—that is, does the shift retain or heighten your interest? If you have first-hand knowledge of divorce, try telling about it through a third-person narrative.

Jane Howard

# All Happy Clans Are Alike

### In Search of the Good Family

Call it a clan, call it a network, call it a tribe, call it a   1
family. Whatever you call it, whoever you are, you need one. You
need one because you are human. You didn't come from nowhere.

Jane Howard, born in Springfield, Illinois, in 1935, was educated at the University of Michigan. She served as reporter, writer, and editor for *Life* magazine, and she is the author of several books.

Before you, around you, and presumably after you, too, there are others. Some of these others must matter a lot—to you, and if you are very lucky, to one another. Their welfare must be nearly as important to you as your own. Even if you live alone, even if your solitude is elected and ebullient, you still cannot do without a clan or a tribe.

The trouble with the clans and tribes many of us were born into 2 is not that they consist of meddlesome ogres but that they are too far away. In emergencies we rush across continents and if need be oceans to their sides, as they do to ours. Maybe we even make a habit of seeing them, once or twice a year, for the sheer pleasure of it. But blood ties seldom dictate our addresses. Our blood kin are often too remote to ease us from our Tuesdays to our Wednesdays. For this we must rely on our families of friends. If our relatives are not, do not wish to be, or for whatever reasons cannot be our friends, then by some complex alchemy we must try to transform our friends into our relatives. If blood and roots don't do the job, then we must look to water and branches, and sort ourselves into new constellations, new families.

These new families, to borrow the terminology of an African tribe 3 (the Bangwa of the Cameroons), may consist either of friends of the road, ascribed by chance, or friends of the heart, achieved by choice. Ascribed friends are those we happen to go to school with, work with, or live near. They know where we went last weekend and whether we still have a cold. Just being around gives them a provisional importance in our lives, and us in theirs. Maybe they will still matter to us when we or they move away; quite likely they won't. Six months or two years will probably erase us from each other's thoughts, unless by some chance they and we have become friends of the heart.

Wishing to be friends, as Aristotle, wrote, is quick work, but 4 friendship is a slowly ripening fruit. An ancient proverb he quotes in his *Ethics* had it that you cannot know a man until you and he together have eaten a peck of salt. Now a peck, a quarter of a bushel, is quite a lot of salt—more, perhaps, than most pairs of people ever have occasion to share. We must try though. We must sit together at as many tables as we can. We must steer each other through enough seasons and weathers so that sooner or later it crosses our minds that one of us, God knows which or with what sorrow, must one day mourn the other.

We must devise new ways, or revive old ones, to equip ourselves 5 with kinfolk. Maybe such an impulse prompted whoever ordered the cake I saw in my neighborhood bakery to have it frosted to say "HAPPY BIRTHDAY SURROGATE." I like to think that this cake was decorated not for a judge but for someone's surrogate mother or surrogate brother: Loathsome jargon, but admirable sentiment. If you didn't conceive me or if we didn't grow up in the same house, we can still be related, if we decide we ought to be. It is never too late, I like to hope, to augment our families in ways nature neglected to do. It is never too late to choose new clans.

The best-chosen clans, like the best friendships and the best blood families, endure by accumulating a history solid enough to suggest a future. But clans that don't last have merit too. We can lament them but we shouldn't deride them. Better an ephemeral clan or tribe than none at all. A few of my life's most tribally joyous times, in fact, have been spent with people whom I have yet to see again. This saddens me, as it may them too, but dwelling overlong on such sadness does no good. A more fertile exercise is to think back on those times and try to figure out what made them, for all their brevity, so stirring. What can such times teach us about forming new and more lasting tribes in the future? 6

New tribes and clans can no more be willed into existence, of course, than any other good thing can. We keep trying, though. To try, with gritted teeth and girded loins, is after all American. That is what the two Helens and I were talking about the day we had lunch in a room up in a high-rise motel near the Kansas City airport. We had lunch there at the end of a two-day conference on families. The two Helens were social scientists, but I liked them even so, among other reasons because they both objected to that motel's coffee shop even more than I did. One of the Helens, from Virginia, disliked it so much that she had brought along homemade whole wheat bread, sesame butter, and honey from her parents' farm in South Dakota, where she had visited before the conference. Her picnic was the best thing that happened, to me at least, those whole two days. 7

"If you're voluntarily childless and alone," said the other Helen, who was from Pennsylvania by way of Puerto Rico, "it gets harder and harder with the passage of time. It's stressful. That's why you need support systems." I had been hearing quite a bit of talk about "support systems." The term is not among my favorites, but I can understand its currency. Whatever "support systems" may be, the need for them is clearly urgent, and not just in this country. Are there not thriving "megafamilies" of as many as three hundred people in Scandinavia? Have not the Japanese for years had an honored, en- 8 during—if perhaps by our standards rather rigid—custom of adopting nonrelatives to fill gaps in their families? Should we not applaud and maybe imitate such ingenuity?

And consider our own Unitarians. From Santa Barbara to Boston 9 they have been earnestly dividing their congregations into arbitrary "extended families" whose members are bound to act like each other's relatives. Kurt Vonnegut, Jr., plays with a similar train of thought in his fictional *Slapstick*. In that book every newborn baby is assigned a randomly chosen middle name, like Uranium or Daffodil or Raspberry. These middle names are connected with hyphens to numbers between one and twenty, and any two people who have the same middle name are automatically related. This is all to the good, the author thinks, because "human beings need all the relatives they can get—as possible donors or receivers not of love but of common decency." He envisions these extended families as "one of the four greatest inventions by Americans," the others being *Robert's Rules of Order*, the Bill of Rights, and the principles of Alcoholics Anonymous.

This charming notion might even work, if it weren't so arbitrary. 10 Already each of us is born into one family not of our choosing. If we're going to devise new ones, we might as well have the luxury of picking the members ourselves. Clever picking might result in new families whose benefits would surpass or at least equal those of the old. As a member in reasonable standing of six or seven tribes in addition to the one I was born to, I have been trying to figure which characteristics are common to both kinds of families.

1. Good families have a chief, or a heroine, or a founder—someone 11 around whom others cluster, whose achievements, as the Yiddish word has it, let them *kvell*, and whose example spurs them on to like feats. Some blood dynasties produce such figures regularly; others languish for as many as five generations between demigods, wondering with each new pregnancy whether this, at last, might be the messianic baby who will redeem them. Look, is there not something gubernatorial about her footstep, or musical about the way he bangs with his spoon on his cup? All clans, of all kinds, need such a figure now and then. Sometimes clans based on water rather than blood harbor several such personages at one time. The Bloomsbury Group in London six decades ago was not much hampered by its lack of a temporal history.

2. Good families have a switchboard operator—someone who can- 12 not help but keep track of what all the others are up to, who plays Houston Mission Control to everyone else's Apollo. This role is as-

sumed rather than assigned. The person who volunteers for it often has the instincts of an archivist, and feels driven to keep scrapbooks and photograph albums up to date, so that the clan can see proof of its own continuity.

3. Good families are much to all their members, but everything to 13 none. Good families are fortresses with many windows and doors to the outer world. The blood clans I feel most drawn to were founded by parents who are nearly as devoted to what they do outside as they are to each other and their children. Their curiosity and passion are contagious. Everybody, where they live, is busy. Paint is spattered on eyeglasses. Mud lurks under fingernails. Person-to-person calls come in the middle of the night from Tokyo and Brussels. Catcher's mitts, ballet slippers, overdue library books, and other signs of extrafamilial concerns are everywhere.

4. Good families are hospitable. Knowing that hosts need guests 14 as much as guests need hosts, they are generous with honorary memberships for friends, whom they urge to come early and often and to stay late. Such clans exude a vivid sense of surrounding rings of relatives, neighbors, teachers, students, and godparents, any of whom at any time might break or slide into the inner circle. Inside that circle a wholesome, tacit emotional feudalism develops: you give me protection, I'll give you fealty. Such pacts begin with, but soon go far beyond, the jolly exchange of pie at Thanksgiving or cake on a birthday. They mean that you can ask me to supervise your children for the fortnight you will be in the hospital, and that however inconvenient this might be for me, I shall manage to do so. It means I can phone you on what for me is a dreary, wretched Sunday afternoon and for you is the eve of a deadline, knowing you will tell me to come right over, if only to watch you type. It means we need not dissemble. ("To yield to seeming," as Martin Buber wrote, "is man's essential cowardice, to resist it is his essential courage . . . one must at times pay dearly for life lived from the being, but it is never too dear.")

5. Good families deal squarely with direness. Pity the tribe that 15 doesn't have, and cherish, at least one flamboyant eccentric. Pity too the one that supposes it can avoid for long the woes to which all flesh is heir. Lunacy, bankruptcy, suicide, and other unthinkable fates sooner or later afflict the noblest of clans with an undertow of gloom. Family life is a set of givens, someone once told me, and it takes courage to see certain givens as blessings rather than as curses. It surely does. Contradictions and inconsistencies are givens, too. So is the battle against what the Oregon patriarch Kenneth Babbs calls malarkey.

"There's always malarkey lurking, bubbles in the cesspool, fetid bubbles that pop and smell. But I don't put up with malarkey, between my stepkids and my natural ones or anywhere else in the family."

6. Good families prize their rituals. Nothing welds a family more 16 than these. Rituals are vital especially for clans without histories, because they evoke a past, imply a future, and hint at continuity. No line in the seder service at Passover reassures more than the last: "Next year in Jerusalem!" A clan becomes more of a clan each time it gathers to observe a fixed ritual (Christmas, birthdays, Thanksgiving, and so on), grieves at a funeral (anyone may come to most funerals; those who do declare their tribalness), and devises a new rite of its own. Equinox breakfasts can be at least as welding as Memorial Day parades. Several of my colleagues and I used to meet for lunch every Pearl Harbor Day, preferably to eat some politically neutral fare like smorgasbord, to "forgive" our only ancestrally Japanese friend, Irene Kubota Neves. For that and other things we became, and remain, a sort of family.

"Rituals," a California friend of mine said, "aren't just externals 17 and holidays. They are the performances of our lives. They are a kind of shorthand. They can't be decreed. My mother used to try to decree them. She'd make such a goddamn fuss over what we talked about at dinner, aiming at Topics of Common Interest, topics that celebrated our cohesion as a family. These performances were always hollow, because the phenomenology of the moment got sacrificed for the *idea* of the moment. Real rituals are discovered in retrospect. They emerge around constitutive moments, moments that only happen once, around whose memory meanings cluster. You don't choose those moments. They choose themselves." A lucky clan includes a born mythologizer, like my blood sister, who has the gift for apprehending such a moment when she sees it, and who cannot help but invent new rituals everywhere she goes.

7. Good families are affectionate. This of course is a matter of style. 18 I know clans whose members greet each other with gingerly handshakes or, in what pass for kisses, with hurried brushes of jawbones, as if the object were to touch not the lips but the ears. I don't see how such people manage. "The tribe that does not hug," as someone who has been part of many *ad hoc* families recently wrote to me, "is no tribe at all. More and more I realize that everybody, regardless of age, needs to be hugged and comforted in a brotherly or sisterly way now and then. Preferably now."

8. Good families have a sense of place, which these days is not 19

achieved easily. As Susanne Langer wrote in 1957, "Most people have no home that is a symbol of their childhood, not even a definite memory of one place to serve that purpose . . . all the old symbols are gone." Once I asked a roomful of supper guests if anyone felt a strong pull to any certain spot on the face of the earth. Everyone was silent, except for a visitor from Bavaria. The rest of us seemed to know all too well what Walker Percy means in *The Moviegoer* when he tells of the "genie-soul of a place, which every place has or else is not a place [and which] wherever you go, you must meet and master or else be met and mastered." All that meeting and mastering saps plenty of strength. It also underscores our need for tribal bases of the sort which soaring real estate taxes and splintering families have made all but obsolete.

So what are we to do, those of us whose habit and pleasure and    20
doom is our tendency, as a Georgia lady put it, to "fly off at every other whipstitch?" Think in terms of movable feasts, that's what. Live here, wherever here may be, as if we were going to belong here for the rest of our lives. Learn to hallow whatever ground we happen to stand on or land on. Like medieval knights who took their tapestries along on Crusades, like modern Afghanis with their yurts, we must pack such totems and icons as we can to make short-term quarters feel like home. Pillows, small rugs, watercolors can dispel much of the chilling anonymity of a motel room or sublet apartment. When we can, we should live in rooms with stoves or fireplaces or at least candlelight. The ancient saying is still true: Extinguished hearth, extinguished family.

Round tables help too, and as a friend of mine once put it, so do    21
"too many comfortable chairs, with surfaces to put feet on, arranged so as to encourage a maximum of eye contact." Such rooms inspire good talk, of which good clans can never have enough.

9. Good families, not just the blood kind, find some way to connect    22
with posterity. "To forge a link in the humble chain of being, encircling heirs to ancestors," as Michael Novak has written, "is to walk within a circle of magic as primitive as humans knew in caves." He is talking of course about babies, feeling them leap in wombs, giving them suck. Parenthood, however, is a state which some miss by chance and others by design, and a vocation to which not all are called. Some of us, like the novelist Richard P. Brickner, look on as others "name their children and their children in turn name their own lives, devising their own flags from their parents' cloth." What are we who lack children to do? Build houses? Plant trees? Write books or symphonies or laws? Per-

haps, but even if we do these things, there should be children on the sidelines if not at the center of our lives.

It is a sadly impoverished tribe that does not allow access to, and    23 make much of, some children. Not too much, of course; it has truly been said that never in history have so many educated people devoted so much attention to so few children. Attention, in excess, can turn to fawning, which isn't much better than neglect. Still, if we don't regularly see and talk to and laugh with people who can expect to outlive us by twenty years or so, we had better get busy and find some.

10. Good families also honor their elders. The wider the age range,    24 the stronger the tribe. Jean-Paul Sartre and Margaret Mead, to name two spectacularly confident former children, have both remarked on the central importance of grandparents in their own early lives. Grandparents are now in much more abundant supply than they were a generation or two ago, when old age was more rare. If actual grandparents are not at hand, no family should have too hard a time finding substitute ones to whom to pay unfeigned homage. The Soviet Union's enchantment with day-care centers, I have heard, stems at least in part from the state's eagerness to keep children away from their presumably subversive grandparents. Let that be a lesson to clans based on interest as well as to those based on genes.

Of course there are elders and elders. Most people in America, as    25 David T. Bazelon has written, haven't the slightest idea of what to do with the extra thirty years they have been given to live. Few are as briskly secure as Alice Roosevelt Longworth, who once, when I visited her for tea, showed a recent photograph and asked whether I didn't think it made her look like "a malevolent Eurasian concubine—an *aged* malevolent Eurasian concubine." I admitted that it did, which was just what she wanted to hear. But those of us whose fathers weren't Presidents may not grow old, if at all, with such style.

Sad stories abound. The mother of one friend of mine languished    26 for years, never far from a coma, in a nursing home. Only when her husband and children sang one of her favorite old songs, such as "Lord Jeffrey Amherst," would a smile fleet across her face. But a man I know of in New Jersey, who couldn't stand the state of Iowa or babies, changed his mind on both counts when his daughter, who lived in Iowa, had a baby. Suddenly he took to inventing business trips to St. Louis, by way of Cedar Rapids, phoning to say he would be at the airport there at 11:31 P.M. and "Be sure to bring Jake!" That cheers me. So did part of a talk I had with a woman in Albuquerque, whom I hadn't seen since a trip some years before to the Soviet Union.

"Honey," she said when I phoned her during a short stopover  27
and asked how she was, "if I were any better I'd blow up and *bust!* I
can't *tell* you how *neat* it is to put some age on! A lot of it, of course,
has to do with going to the shrink, getting uncorked, and of course it
doesn't hurt to have money—no, we *don't* have a ranch; it's only 900
acres, so we call it a farm. But every year, as far as age is concerned,
I seem to get better, doing more and more stuff I love to do. The only
thing I've ever wanted and don't have is a good marriage. Nothing I
do ever pleases the men I marry. The only reason I'm still married
now is it's too much trouble not to be. But my girls are growing up
to be just *neat* humans, and the men they're sharing their lives with
are too. They pick nice guys, my girls. I wish I could say the same.
But I'm a lot better off than many women my age. I go to parties where
sixty-year-olds with blue bouffant hairdos are still telling the same
jokes they told twenty-five or thirty years ago. Complacent? No, that's
not it, exactly. What they are is sad—sad as the dickens. They don't
seem to be *connected*."

Some days my handwriting resembles my mother's, slanting hope-  28
fully and a bit extravagantly eastward. Other days it looks more like
my father's: resolute, vertical, guardedly free of loops. Both my parents
will remain in my nerves and muscles and mind until the day I die,
and so will my sister, but they aren't the only ones. If I were to die
tomorrow, the obituary would note that my father and sister survived
me. True, but not true enough. Like most official lists of survivors,
this one would be incomplete.

Several of the most affecting relationships I have ever known of,  29
or been part of, have sprung not from genes or contracts but from
serendipitous, uncanny bonds of choice. I don't think enough can be
said for the fierce tenderness such bonds can generate. Maybe the best
thing to say is nothing at all, or very little. Midwestern preachers used
to hold that "a heavy rain doesn't seep into the ground but rolls off—
when you preach to farmers, your sermon should be a drizzle instead
of a downpour." So too with any cause that matters: shouting and
lapel-grabbing and institutionalizing can do more harm than good. A
quiet approach works better.

"I wish it would hurry up and get colder," I said one warm af-  30
ternoon several Octobers ago to a black man with whom I was walking
in a park.

"Don't worry," he told me. "Like my grandmother used to say  31
when I was a boy, 'Hawk'll be here soon enough.' "

"What did she mean by 'hawk'?"  32

"Hawk meant winter, cold, trouble. And she was right: the hawk 33
always came."

With regard to families, many would say that the hawk has long 34
been here, hovering. "I'd rather put up with being lonely now than
have to put up with being still more lonely in the future," says a character in Natsume Soseki's novel *Kokoro*. "We live in an age of freedom,
independence, and the self, and I imagine this loneliness is the price
we have to pay for it." Seven decades earlier, in *Either/Or*, Sören Kierkegaard had written, "Our age has lost all the substantial categories
of family, state, and race. It must leave the individual entirely to himself, so that in a stricter sense he becomes his own creator."

If it is true that we must create ourselves, maybe while we are 35
about it we can also devise some new kinds of families, new connections to supplement the old ones. The second verse of a hymn by James
Russell Lowell says,

> New occasions bring new duties;
> Time makes ancient good uncouth.

Surely one outworn "good" is the maxim that blood relatives are the
only ones who can or should greatly matter. Or look at it another way:
go back six generations, and each one of us has sixty-four direct ancestors. Go back twenty—only four or five centuries, not such a big chunk
of human history—and we each have more than a million. Does it not
stand to reason, since the world population was then so much smaller,
that we all have a lot more cousins—though admittedly distant ones—
than we were brought up to suspect? And don't these cousins deserve
our attention?

One day after lunch at a friend's apartment I waited in his lobby 36
while he collected his mail. Out of the elevator came two nurses supporting a wizened, staring woman who couldn't have weighed much
more than seventy pounds. It was all the woman could do to make
her way down the three steps to the sidewalk and the curb where a
car was waiting. Those steps must have been to that woman what a
steep mountain trail would be to me. The nurses guided her down
them with infinite patience.

"Easy, darlin'," one nurse said to the woman. 37

"That's a good girl," said the other. The woman, my friend's door- 38
man told us, was ninety. That morning she had fallen and hurt herself.
On her forehead was something which, had it not been a bruise, we

might have thought beautiful: a marvel of mauve and lavender and magenta. This woman, who was then being taken to a nursing home, had lived in my friend's apartment building for forty years. All her relatives were dead, and her few surviving friends no longer chose to see her.

"But how can that be?" I asked my friend. "*We* could never be   39
that alone, could we?"

"Don't be so sure," said my friend, who knows more of such   40
matters than I do. "Even if we were to end up in the same nursing home, if I was in markedly worse shape than you were, you might not want to see me, either."

"But I can't imagine not wanting to see you."   41

"It happens," my friend said.   42

Maybe we can keep it from happening. Maybe the hawk can be   43
kept at bay, if we give more thought to our tribes and our clans and our several kinds of families. No aim seems to me more urgent, nor any achievement more worthy of a psalm. So *hosanna in excelsis*, and blest be the tie that binds. And please pass the salt.

# Questions

1.   Howard begins paragraph 7 by saying: "New tribes and clans can no more be willed into existence, of course, than any other good thing can." What other passages in the essay support this view? What passages contradict it? Does Howard succeed in reconciling the contradiction?

2.   In her last paragraph Howard suggests that we might prevent loneliness by giving "more thought to our tribes and our clans and our several kinds of families." How might Lionel Tiger (pages 68–72) respond to her suggestion? Did either Howard's or Tiger's essay stimulate your thoughts on families? Which did you find more useful in thinking about family relationships?

Laura Cunningham

# The Girls' Room

**W**hen I heard she was coming to stay with us I was   1
pleased. At age eight I thought of "grandmother" as a generic brand.
My friends had grandmothers who seemed permanently bent over
cookie racks. They were a source of constant treats and sweets. They
were pinchers of cheeks, huggers and kissers. My own grandmother
had always lived in a distant state; I had no memory of her when she
decided to join the household recently established for me by my two
uncles.

But with the example of my friends' grandmothers before me, I   2
could hardly wait to have a grandmother of my own—and the cookies
would be nice too. For while my uncles provided a cuisine that ranged
from tuna croquettes to Swedish meatballs, they showed no signs of
baking anything more elegant than a potato.

My main concern on the day of my grandmother's arrival was:   3
How soon would she start the cookies? I remember her arrival, my
uncles flanking her as they walked down the apartment corridor. She
wore a hat, a tailored navy blue suit, an ermine stole. She held, tucked
under her arm, the purple leather folder that contained her work in
progress, a manuscript entitled "Philosophy for Women." She was
preceded by her custom-made white trunk packed with purses, necklaces, earrings, dresses and more purple-inked pages that stress "the
spiritual above the material."

She was small—at 5 feet 1 inch not much taller than I was—thin   4
and straight, with a pug nose, one brown eye (the good eye) and one
blue eye (the bad eye, frosted by cataracts). Her name was "Esther in
Hebrew, Edna in English, and Etka in Russian." She preferred the
Russian, referring to herself as "Etka from Minsk." It was not at once
apparent that she was deaf in her left ear (the bad ear) but could hear
with the right (the good ear). Because her good ear happened to be

---

Laura Cunningham was born in 1947. Orphaned at the age of eight, she was
brought up by two unmarried uncles, both of whom were writers. She says that
she became a writer because she didn't know that one could become anything
else. Had she known of other possibilities, she says, she would have become a
ballerina.

on the opposite side from the good eye, anyone who spoke to her had to run around her in circles, or sway to and fro, if eye contact and audibility were to be achieved simultaneously.

Etka from Minsk had arrived not directly from Minsk, as the black- 5 eyed ermine stole seemed to suggest, but after many moves. She entered with the draft of family scandal at her back, blown out of her daughter's home after assaults upon her dignity. She held the evidence: an empty-socketed peacock pin. My cousin, an eleven-year-old boy, had surgically plucked out the rhinestone eyes. She could not be expected to stay where such acts occurred. She had to be among "human beings," among "real people" who could understand. We seemed to understand. We—my two uncles and I—encircled her, studied her vandalized peacock pin and vowed that such things would never happen with "us."

She patted my head—a good sign—and asked me to sing the Is- 6 raeli national anthem. I did, and she handed me a dollar. My uncles went off to their jobs, leaving me alone with my grandmother for the first time. I looked at her, expecting her to start rolling out the cookie dough. Instead she suggested: "Now maybe you could fix me some lunch?"

It wasn't supposed to be this way, I thought, as I took her order: 7 "toasted cheese and a sliced orange." Neither was she supposed to share my pink and orange bedroom, but she did. The bedroom soon exhibited a dual character—stuffed animals on one side, a hospital bed on the other. Within the household this chamber was soon referred to as "the girls' room." The name, given by Uncle Abe, who saw no incongruity, only the affinity of sex, turned out to be apt, for what went on in the girls' room could easily have been labeled sibling rivalry if she had not been eighty and I eight. I soon found that I had acquired not a traditional grandmother but an aged kid sister.

The theft and rivalry began within days. My grandmother had 8 given me her most cherished possession, a violet beaded bag. In return I gave her my heart-shaped "ivory" pin and matching earrings. That night she stole back the purse but insisted on keeping the pin and earrings. I turned to my uncles for mediation and ran up against unforeseen resistance. They thought my grandmother should keep the beaded bag; they didn't want to upset her.

I burned at the injustice of it and felt the heat of an uncomfortable 9 truth: where I once had my uncles' undivided indulgence, they were now split as my grandmother and I vied for their attention. The household, formerly geared to my little-girl needs, was rearranged to accommodate hers. I suffered serious affronts—my grandmother, in a fit of frugality, scissored all the household blankets, including what a psychiatrist would have dubbed my "security" blanket, in half. "Now," she said, her good eye gleaming, "we have twice as many." I lay under my narrow slice of blanket and stared hopelessly up at the ceiling. I thought evilly of ways of getting my grandmother out of the apartment.

Matters worsened, as more and more of my trinkets disappeared. 10 One afternoon I came home from school to find her squeezed into my unbuttoned favorite blouse. Rouged and beribboned, she insisted that the size 3 blouse was hers. Meanwhile, I was forced to adapt to her idiosyncrasies: she covered everything black—from the dog to the telephone—with white doilies. She left saucers balanced on top of glasses. She sang nonstop. She tried to lock my dog out of the apartment.

The word that explained her behavior was "arteriosclerosis." She 11 had forgotten so much that sometimes she would greet me with "You look familiar." At other times she'd ask, "What hotel is this?" My answer, shouted in her good ear, was: "We're not in a hotel! This is our apartment!" The response would be a hoot of laughter: "Then why are we in the ballroom?"

Finally we fought: arm-to-arm combat. I was shocked at her grip, 12 steely as the bars that locked her into bed at night. Her good eye burned into mine and she said, "I'll tell." And she did. For the first time I was scolded. She had turned their love to disapproval, I thought, and how it chafed.

Eventually our rivalry mellowed into conspiracy. Within months 13 we found we had uses for each other. I provided the lunches and secret, forbidden ice cream sundaes. She rewarded me with cold cash. She continued to take my clothes; I charged her competitive prices. I hated school; she paid me not to go. When I came home for lunch I usually stayed.

Our household endured the status quo for eight years: my uncles, 14 my grandmother and I. Within the foursome rivalries and alliances shifted. I became my grandmother's friend and she became mine. We were the source of all the family comedy. When she said she wanted a college diploma we gave her one—with tinfoil stars and a "magna magna summa summa cum laude" inscription. We sang and performed skits. We talcum-powdered hair and wearing one of her old dresses, I would appear as her "long-lost friend." We had other themes, including a pen pal, "The Professor."

Of course, living with an elderly person had its raw aspects. When 15
she was ill our girls' room took on the stark aura of a geriatrics ward.
I imagined, to my shame, that neighbors could stare in through cur-
tainless windows as I tended to my grandmother's most personal
needs.

Yet, in these times of age segregation, with grandmothers sent off 16
to impersonal places, I wonder if the love and the comedy weren't
worth the intermittent difficulties? Certainly I learned what it might
be to become old. And I took as much comfort as my grandmother did
in a nightly exchange of Russian endearments—"Ya tebya lyublyu,"
"Ya tebya tozhe lyublyu—"I love you," "I love you, too."

If I sold my grandmother blouses and baubles, maybe she gave 17
me the truth in exchange. Once, when we were alone in the girls'
room, she turned to me, suddenly lucid, her good eye as bright as it
would ever be—a look I somehow recognized as her "real" gaze—and
said, "My life passes like a dream."

# Questions

1.  In the second sentence, what does Cunningham mean by "a generic
    brand"?
2.  What is the title of Esther's manuscript? What is it about? Do you
    detect any irony in the way Cunningham conveys this information?
    Explain.
3.  In the second sentence of paragraph 4, what is conveyed by putting
    the names within quotation marks?
4.  Is paragraph 4—about Esther's physical disabilities—in bad taste?
    Explain.
5.  In her last paragraph Cunningham says that perhaps her grand-
    mother gave her "the truth." What does she mean?
6.  "I burned at the injustice of it and felt the heat of an uncomfortable
    truth." Where in the narrative does Cunningham say this? What was
    the "truth"? If you remember a similar experience, write a narrative
    that discloses both the experience and the truth on which it was
    based. Or, write an essay of 500 words on your own most potent
    experience of living with or near an elderly person.

## Black Elk

# High Horse's Courting

You know, in the old days, it was not very easy to get  1
a girl when you wanted to be married. Sometimes it was hard work
for a young man and he had to stand a great deal. Say I am a young
man and I have seen a young girl who looks so beautiful to me that
I feel all sick when I think about her. I cannot just go and tell her about
it and then get married if she is willing. I have to be a very sneaky
fellow to talk to her at all, and after I have managed to talk to her,
that is only the beginning.

Probably for a long time I have been feeling sick about a certain  2
girl because I love her so much, but she will not even look at me, and
her parents keep a good watch over her. But I keep feeling worse and
worse all the time; so maybe I sneak up to her tepee in the dark and
wait until she comes out. Maybe I just wait there all night and don't
get any sleep at all and she does not come out. Then I feel sicker than
ever about her.

Maybe I hide in the brush by a spring where she sometimes goes  3
to get water, and when she comes by, if nobody is looking, then I jump
out and hold her and just make her listen to me. If she likes me too,
I can tell that from the way she acts, for she is very bashful and maybe
will not say a word or even look at me the first time. So I let her go,
and then maybe I sneak around until I can see her father alone, and
I tell him how many horses I can give him for his beautiful girl, and
by now I am feeling so sick that maybe I would give him all the horses
in the world if I had them.

Well, this young man I am telling about was called High Horse,  4
and there was a girl in the village who looked so beautiful to him that
he was just sick all over from thinking about her so much and he was
getting sicker all the time. The girl was very shy, and her parents

---

Black Elk, a *wichasha wakon* (holy man) of the Oglala Sioux, as a small boy
witnessed the battle of the Little Bighorn (1876). He lived to see his people all
but annihilated and his hopes for them extinguished. In 1931, toward the end
of his life, he told his life story to the poet and scholar John G. Neihardt to
preserve a sacred vision given him.

"High Horses Courting" is a comic interlude in *Black Elk Speaks*, a predominantly tragic memoir.

thought a great deal of her because they were not young any more
and this was the only child they had. So they watched her all day long,
and they fixed it so that she would be safe at night too when they were
asleep. They thought so much of her that they had made a rawhide
bed for her to sleep in, and after they knew that High Horse was
sneaking around after her, they took rawhide thongs and tied the girl
in bed at night so that nobody could steal her when they were asleep,
for they were not sure but that their girl might really want to be stolen.

Well, after High Horse had been sneaking around a good while     5
and hiding and waiting for the girl and getting sicker all the time, he
finally caught her alone and made her talk to him. Then he found out
that she liked him maybe a little. Of course this did not make him feel
well. It made him sicker than ever, but now he felt as brave as a bison
bull, and so he went right to her father and said he loved the girl so
much that he would give two good horses for her—one of them young
and the other one not so very old.

But the old man just waved his hand, meaning for High Horse to     6
go away and quit talking foolishness like that.

High Horse was feeling sicker than ever about it; but there was     7
another young fellow who said he would loan High Horse two ponies
and when he got some more horses, why, he could just give them
back for the ones he had borrowed.

Then High Horse went back to the old man and said he would     8
give four horses for the girl—two of them young and the other two
not hardly old at all. But the old man just waved his hand and would
not say anything.

So High Horse sneaked around until he could talk to the girl again,     9
and he asked her to run away with him. He told her he thought he
would just fall over and die if she did not. But she said she would not
do that; she wanted to be bought like a fine woman. You see she
thought a great deal of herself too.

That made High Horse feel so very sick that he could not eat a     10
bite, and he went around with his head hanging down as though he
might just fall down and die any time.

Red Deer was another young fellow, and he and High Horse were     11
great comrades, always doing things together. Red Deer saw how High
Horse was acting, and he said: "Cousin, what is the matter? Are you
sick in the belly? You look as though you were going to die."

Then High Horse told Red Deer how it was, and said he thought     12
he could not stay alive much longer if he could not marry the girl pretty
quick.

Red Deer thought awhile about it, and then he said: "Cousin, I  13
have a plan, and if you are man enough to do as I tell you, then
everything will be all right. She will not run away with you; her old
man will not take four horses; and four horses are all you can get. You
must steal her and run away with her. Then afterwhile you can come
back and the old man cannot do anything because she will be your
woman. Probably she wants you to steal her anyway."

So they planned what High Horse had to do, and he said he loved  14
the girl so much that he was man enough to do anything Red Deer or
anybody else could think up. So this is what they did.

That night late they sneaked up to the girl's tepee and waited until  15
it sounded inside as though the old man and the old woman and the
girl were sound asleep. Then High Horse crawled under the tepee with
a knife. He had to cut the rawhide thongs first, and then Red Deer,
who was pulling up the stakes around that side of the tepee, was going
to help drag the girl outside and gag her. After that, High Horse could
put her across his pony in front of him and hurry out of there and be
happy all the rest of his life.

When High Horse had crawled inside, he felt so nervous that he  16
could hear his heart drumming, and it seemed so loud he felt sure it
would 'waken the old folks. But it did not, and afterwhile he began
cutting the thongs. Every time he cut one it made a pop and nearly
scared him to death. But he was getting along all right and all the
thongs were cut down as far as the girl's thighs, when he became so
nervous that his knife slipped and stuck the girl. She gave a big, loud
yell. Then the old folks jumped up and yelled too. By this time High
Horse was outside, and he and Red Deer were running away like
antelope. The old man and some other people chased the young men
but they got away in the dark and nobody knew who it was.

Well, if you ever wanted a beautiful girl you will know how sick  17
High Horse was now. It was very bad the way he felt, and it looked
as though he would starve even if he did not drop over dead sometime.

Red Deer kept thinking about this, and after a few days he went  18
to High Horse and said: "Cousin, take courage! I have another plan,
and I am sure, if you are man enough, we can steal her this time."
And High Horse said: "I am man enough to do anything anybody can
think up, if I can only get that girl."

So this is what they did.  19

They went away from the village alone, and Red Deer made High  20
Horse strip naked. Then he painted High Horse solid white all over,
and after that he painted black stripes all over the white and put black

rings around High Horse's eyes. High Horse looked terrible. He looked so terrible that when Red Deer was through painting and took a good look at what he had done, he said it scared even him a little.

"Now," Red Deer said, "if you get caught again, everybody will    21
be so scared they will think you are a bad spirit and will be afraid to chase you."

So when the night was getting old and everybody was sound    22
asleep, they sneaked back to the girl's tepee. High Horse crawled in with his knife, as before, and Red Deer waited outside, ready to drag the girl out and gag her when High Horse had all the thongs cut.

High Horse crept up by the girl's bed and began cutting at the    23
thongs. But he kept thinking, "If they see me they will shoot me be- cause I look so terrible." The girl was restless and kept squirming around in bed, and when a thong was cut, it popped. So High Horse worked very slowly and carefully.

But he must have made some noise, for suddenly the old woman    24
awoke and said to her old man: "Old Man, wake up! There is somebody in this tepee!" But the old man was sleepy and didn't want to be both- ered. He said: "Of course there is somebody in this tepee. Go to sleep and don't bother me." Then he snored some more.

But High Horse was so scared by now that he lay very still and    25
as flat to the ground as he could. Now, you see, he had not been sleeping very well for a long time because he was so sick about the girl. And while he was lying there waiting for the old woman to snore, he just forgot everything, even how beautiful the girl was. Red Deer who was lying outside ready to do his part, wondered and wondered what had happened in there, but he did not dare call out to High Horse.

Afterwhile the day began to break and Red Deer had to leave with    26
the two ponies he had staked there for his comrade and girl, or some- body would see him.

So he left.    27

Now when it was getting light in the tepee, the girl awoke and    28
the first thing she saw was a terrible animal, all white with black stripes on it, lying asleep beside her bed. So she screamed, and then the old woman screamed and the old man yelled. High Horse jumped up, scared almost to death, and he nearly knocked the tepee down getting out of there.

People were coming running from all over the village with guns    29
and bows and axes, and everybody was yelling.

By now High Horse was running so fast that he hardly touched    30
the ground at all, and he looked so terrible that the people fled from

him and let him run. Some braves wanted to shoot at him, but the others said he might be some sacred being and it would bring bad trouble to kill him.

High Horse made for the river that was near, and in among the   31
brush he found a hollow tree and dived into it. Afterwhile some braves came there and he could hear them saying that it was some bad spirit that had come out of the water and gone back in again.

That morning the people were ordered to break camp and move   32
away from there. So they did, while High Horse was hiding in his hollow tree.

Now Red Deer had been watching all this from his own tepee and   33
trying to look as though he were as much surprised and scared as all the others. So when the camp moved, he sneaked back to where he had seen his comrade disappear. When he was down there in the brush, he called, and High Horse answered, because he knew his friend's voice. They washed off the paint from High Horse and sat down on the river bank to talk about their troubles.

High Horse said he never would go back to the village as long as   34
he lived and he did not care what happened to him now. He said he was going to go on the war-path all by himself. Red Deer said: "No, cousin, you are not going on the war-path alone, because I am going with you."

So Red Deer got everything ready, and at night they started out   35
on the war-path all alone. After several days they came to a Crow camp just about sundown, and when it was dark they sneaked up to where the Crow horses were grazing, killed the horse guard, who was not thinking about enemies because he thought all the Lakotas were far away, and drove off about a hundred horses.

They got a big start because all the Crow horses stampeded and   36
it was probably morning before the Crow warriors could catch any horses to ride. Red Deer and High Horse fled with their herd three days and nights before they reached the village of their people. Then they drove the whole herd right into the village and up in front of the girl's tepee. The old man was there, and High Horse called out to him and asked if he thought maybe that would be enough horses for his girl. The old man did not wave him away that time. It was not the horses that he wanted. What he wanted was a son who was a real man and good for something.

So High Horse got his girl after all, and I think he deserved   37
her.

# Questions

Although High Horse's behavior is amusing and at times ridiculous, how does Black Elk make it clear that he is not ridiculing the young man, but is instead in sympathy with him? Consider the following questions:

1. What is the effect of the first three paragraphs? Think about the first two sentences, and then the passage beginning "Say I am a young man . . ." and ending ". . . I would give him all the horses in the world if I had them."
2. Describe the behavior of the young girl, and of her father and mother. How do they contribute to the comedy? How does their behavior affect your understanding of Black Elk's attitude toward High Horse?
3. What is the function of Red Deer?
4. The narrative consists of several episodes. List them in the order in which they occur, and then describe the narrative's structure. How does this structure affect the tone?

Anonymous

# Confessions of an Erstwhile Child

Some years ago I attempted to introduce a class of Upward  1
Bound students to political theory via More's *Utopia*. It was a mistake: I taught precious little theory and earned More a class full of undying enemies on account of two of his ideas. The first, that all members of a Utopian family were subject to the lifelong authority of its eldest male. The second, the Utopian provision that should a child wish to follow a profession different from that of his family, he could be transferred by adoption to a family that practiced the desired trade. My students were not impressed with my claim that the one provision softened the other and made for a fair compromise—for what causes most of our quarrels with our parents but our choice of life-patterns,

The anonymous author of this essay has revealed only that he was forty when he wrote it, is married, and is the father of three children.

of occupation? In objecting to the first provision my students were picturing themselves as children, subject to an unyielding authority. But on the second provision they surprised me by taking the parents' role and arguing that this form of ad lib adoption denied them a fundamental right of ownership over their children. It occurred to me that these reactions were two parts of the same pathology: having suffered the discipline of unreasonable parents, one has earned the right to be unreasonable in turn to one's children. The phenomenon has well-known parallels, such as frantic martinets who have risen from the ranks. Having served time as property, my Upward Bound students wanted theirs back as proprietors. I shuddered. It hardly takes an advanced course in Freudian psychology to realize that the perpetuation, generation after generation, of psychic lesions must go right to this source, the philosophically dubious notion that children are the property of their biological parents, compounded with the unphilosophic certitude so many parents harbor, that their children must serve an apprenticeship as like their own as they can manage.

The idea of the child as property has always bothered me, for 2 personal reasons I shall outline. I lack the feeling that I own my children and I have always scoffed at the idea that what they are and do is a continuation or a rejection of my being. I like them, I sympathize with them, I acknowledge the obligation to support them for a term of years—but I am not so fond or foolish as to regard a biological tie as a lien on their loyalty or respect, nor to imagine that I am equipped with preternatural powers of guidance as to their success and happiness. Beyond inculcating some of the obvious social protocols required in civilized life, who am I to pronounce on what makes for a happy or successful life? How many of us can say that we have successfully managed our own lives? Can we do better with our children? I am unimpressed, to say no more, with parents who have no great track record, presuming to oracular powers in regard to their children's lives.

The current debate over the Equal Rights Amendment frequently 3 turns to custody questions. Opponents of ERA have made the horrifying discovery that ERA will spell the end of the mother's presumed rights of custody in divorce or separation cases, and that fathers may begin custody rights. Indeed a few odd cases have been so settled recently in anticipation of the ratification of ERA. If ratified, ERA would be an extremely blunt instrument for calling the whole idea of custody into question, but I for one will applaud anything that serves to begin debate. As important as equal rights between adults may be, I think that the rights of children are a far more serious and unattended need. To me, custody by natural parents, far from being a presumed right only re-examined in case of collapsing marriages, should be viewed as a privilege.

At this point I have to explain why I can so calmly contemplate 4 the denial of so-called parental rights.

I am the only child of two harsh and combative personalities who 5 married, seemingly, in order to have a sparring partner always at hand. My parents have had no other consistent or lasting aim in life but to win out over each other in a contest of wills. They still live, vigorous and angry septuagenarians, their ferocity little blunted by age or human respect. My earliest memories—almost my sole memories— are of unending combat, in which I was sometimes an appalled spectator, more often a hopeless negotiator in a war of no quarter, and most often a bystander accused of covert belligerency on behalf of one side or the other, and frequently of both! I grew up with two supposed adults who were absorbed in their hatreds and recriminations to the exclusion of almost all other reality. Not only did I pass by almost unnoticed in their struggle, the Depression and World War II passed them by equally unnoticed. I figured mainly as a practice target for sarcasm and invective, and occasionally as the ultimate culprit responsible for their unhappiness. ("If it weren't for you," my mother would sometimes say, "I could leave that SOB," a remark belied by her refusal to leave the SOB during these 20 long years since I left their "shelter.")

The reader may ask, "How did you survive if your parents' house 6 was all that bad?" I have three answers. First, I survived by the moral equivalent of running away to sea or the circus, i.e., by burying myself in books and study, especially in the history of faraway and (I thought) more idealistic times than our own, and by consciously shaping my life and tastes to be as different as possible from those of my parents (this was a reproach to them, they knew, and it formed the basis of a whole secondary area of conflict and misunderstanding). Second, I survived because statistically most people "survive" horrible families, but survival can be a qualified term, as it is in my case by a permanently impaired digestive system and an unnatural sensitivity to raised voices. And third, though I found solace in schooling and the rationality, cooperation and basic fairness in teachers that I missed in my parents, I must now question whether it is healthy for a child to count so heavily on schooling for the love and approval that he deserves from his home and family. Even if schooling can do this well, in later life it means that one is loyal and affectionate toward schooling, not toward parents, who may in some sense need affection even if they don't "deserve" it. I am not unaware that however fair and rational I may be in reaction to my parents' counter-examples, I am a very cold-hearted man. I might have done better transferred to a new family, not just by receiving love, but through learning to give it—a lack I mourn as much or more than my failure to receive.

It is little wonder then that I have an acquired immunity to the notion that parental custody is by and large a preferable thing. In my case, almost anything else would have been preferable, including even a rather callously run orphanage—anything for a little peace and quiet. Some people are simply unfit, under any conditions, to be parents, even if, indeed especially if, they maintain the charade of a viable marriage. My parents had no moral right to custody of children, and I cannot believe that my experience is unique or particularly isolated. There are all too many such marriages, in which some form of horror, congenial enough to adults too sick or crazed to recognize it, works its daily ruination on children. Surely thousands of children conclude at age 10 or 11, as I did, that marriage is simply an institution in which people are free to be as beastly as they have a mind to, which may lead either to a rejection of marriage or to a decision to reduplicate a sick marriage a second time, with another generation of victims. It is time to consider the rights of the victims. 7

How to implement a nascent theory of justice for children is difficult to say. One cannot imagine taking the word of a five-year-old against his parents, but what about a 10- or 12-year-old? At *some* point, children should have the right to escape the dominance of impossible parents. The matter used to be easier than it has been since World War I. The time-honored solution—for boys—of running away from home has been made infeasible by economic conditions, fingerprints, social security and minimum wage laws. No apprenticeship system exists any more, much less its upper-class medieval version—with required exchange of boys at puberty among noble families to serve as pages and so forth. The adoption system contemplated in More's *Utopia* is a half-remembered echo of a medieval life, in which society, wiser than its theory, decreed a general exchange of children at or just before puberty, whether through apprenticeship or page-service, or more informal arrangements, like going to a university at 14 or running away with troubadors or gypsies. 8

Exchanging children is a wisely conceived safety valve against a 9 too traumatic involvement between the biological parent and the child. Children need an alternative to living all their formative life in the same biological unit. They should have the right to petition for release from some sorts of families, to join other families, or to engage in other sorts of relationships that may provide equivalent service but may not be organized as a family. The nuclear family, after all, is not such an old or proven vehicle. Phillippe Aries' book, *Centuries of Childhood*, made the important point that the idea of helpless childhood is itself a notion of recent origin, that grew up simultaneously in the 16th and 17th centuries with the small and tight-knit nuclear family, sealed off from the world by another recent invention, "privacy." The older *extended* family (which is the kind More knew about) was probably more authoritarian on paper but much less productive of dependency in actual operation. There ought to be more than one way a youngster can enter adult society with more than half of his sanity left. At least no one should be forced to remain in a no-win game against a couple of crazy parents for 15–18 years. At 10 or 12, children in really messy situations should have the legal right to petition for removal from impossible families, and those rights should be reasonably easy to exercise. (This goes on de facto among the poor, of course, but it is not legal, and usually carries both stigma and danger.) The minimum wage laws should be modified to exempt such persons, especially if they wish to continue their education, working perhaps for public agencies, if they have no other means of support. If their parents can support them, then the equivalent of child support should be charged them to maintain their children, not in luxury, but adequately. Adoption of older children should be facilitated by easing of legal procedures (designed mainly to govern the adoption of *infants*) plus tax advantages for those willing to adopt older children on grounds of goodwill. Indeed children wishing to escape impossible family situations should be allowed a fair degree of initiative in finding and negotiating with possible future families.

Obviously the risk of rackets would be very high unless the exact 10 terms of such provisions were framed very carefully, but the possibility of rackets is less frightening to anyone who thinks about it for long than the dangers of the present situation, which are evident and unrelieved by any signs of improvement. In barely a century this country has changed from a relatively loose society in which Huckleberry Finns were not uncommon, to a society of tense, airless nuclear families in which unhealthy and neurotic tendencies, once spawned in a family, tend to repeat themselves at a magnifying and accelerating rate. We may soon gain the distinction of being the only nation on earth to need not just medicare but "psychi-care." We have invested far too heavily in the unproved "equity" called the nuclear family; that stock is about to crash and we ought to begin finding escape options. In colonial days many New England colonies passed laws imposing fines or extra taxes on parents who kept their children under their own roofs after age 15 or 16, on the sensible notion that a person of that age ought to be out and doing on his own, whether going to Yale or apprenticing in a foundry. Even without the benefit of Freud, the colonial fathers had a good sense of what was wrong with a closely bound and centripetal family structure—it concentrates craziness like compound interest, and so they hit it with monetary penalties, a proper Protestant response, intolerant at once of both mystery and excuses. But this was the last gasp of a medieval and fundamentally Catholic idea that children, God help them, while they may be the children of *these* particular parents biologically, spiritually are the children of God, and more appositely are the children of the entire community, for which the entire community takes responsibility. The unguessed secret of the middle ages was not that monasteries relieved parents of unwanted children; more frequently, they relieved children of unwanted parents!

# Questions

1. What is the author's thesis? (Quote the thesis sentence.) Apart from his own experience, what evidence or other means does he offer to persuade you to accept his thesis?

2. What part does the *tone* of his article play in persuading you to agree with him, or in alienating you? Does his tone strike you, perhaps, as vigorous or belligerent, as ironic or bitter, as reasonable or hysterical?

3. The author admits (paragraph 6) that he is "a very cold-hearted man." Do you remember your initial reaction to that sentence? What was it? Overall, does the author strengthen or jeopardize his argument by this admission? Explain.

4. If you did not find the article persuasive, did you find it interesting? Can you explain why?

Jonathan Swift

# A Modest Proposal
### For Preventing the Children of Poor People in Ireland from Being a Burden to Their Parents or Country, and for Making Them Beneficial to the Public

It is a melancholy object to those who walk through this 1
great town or travel in the country, when they see the streets, the
roads, and cabin doors, crowded with beggars of the female sex, followed by three, four, or six children, all in rags and importuning every
passenger for an alms. These mothers, instead of being able to work
for their honest livelihood, are forced to employ all their time in stroll-
ing to beg sustenance for their helpless infants: who as they grow up
either turn thieves for want of work, or leave their dear native country
to fight for the pretender in Spain, or sell themselves to the Barbadoes.

I think it is agreed by all parties that this prodigious number of 2
children in the arms, or on the backs, or at the heels of their mothers,
and frequently of their fathers, is in the present deplorable state of the
kingdom a very great additional grievance; and, therefore, whoever
could find out a fair, cheap, and easy method of making these children
sound, useful members of the commonwealth, would deserve so well
of the public as to have his statue set up for a preserver of the nation.

But my intention is very far from being confined to provide only 3
for the children of professed beggars; it is of a much greater extent,
and shall take in the whole number of infants at a certain age who are

Jonathan Swift (1667–1745) was born in Ireland of an English family. He was
ordained in the Church of Ireland in 1694, and in 1714 he became dean of St.
Patrick's Cathedral, Dublin. He wrote abundantly on political and religious topics, often motivated (in his own words) by "savage indignation." It is ironic that
*Gulliver's Travels*, the masterpiece by this master of irony, is most widely thought
of as a book for children.

From the middle of the sixteenth century the English regulated the Irish
economy so that it would enrich England. Heavy taxes and other repressive
legislation impoverished Ireland, and in 1728, the year before Swift wrote "A
Modest Proposal," Ireland was further weakened by a severe famine. Swift,
deeply moved by the injustice, the stupidity, and the suffering that he found in
Ireland, adopts the disguise or persona of an economist and offers an ironic
suggestion on how Irish families may improve their conditions.

born of parents in effect as little able to support them as those who demand our charity in the streets.

As to my own part, having turned my thoughts for many years 4 upon this important subject, and maturely weighed the several schemes of our projectors, I have always found them grossly mistaken in their computation. It is true, a child just dropped from its dam may be supported by her milk for a solar year, with little other nourishment; at most not above the value of 2s.,[1] which the mother may certainly get, or the value in scraps, by her lawful occupation of begging; and it is exactly at one year old that I propose to provide for them in such a manner as instead of being a charge upon their parents or the parish, or wanting food and raiment for the rest of their lives, they shall on the contrary contribute to the feeding, and partly to the clothing, of many thousands.

There is likewise another great advantage in my scheme, that it 5 will prevent those voluntary abortions, and that horrid practice of women murdering their bastard children, alas! too frequent among us! sacrificing the poor innocent babes I doubt more to avoid the expense than the shame, which would move tears and pity in the most savage and inhuman breast.

The number of souls in this kingdom being usually reckoned one 6 million and a half, of these I calculate there may be about 200,000 couple whose wives are breeders; from which number I subtract 30,000 couple who are able to maintain their own children (although I apprehend there cannot be so many, under the present distress of the kingdom); but this being granted, there will remain 170,000 breeders. I again subtract 50,000 for those women who miscarry, or whose children die by accident or disease within the year. There only remain 120,000 children of poor parents annually born. The question therefore is, how this number shall be reared and provided for? which, as I have already said, under the present situation of affairs, is utterly impossible by all the methods hitherto proposed. For we can neither employ them in handicraft or agriculture; we neither build houses (I mean in the country) nor cultivate land; they can very seldom pick up a livelihood by stealing, till they arrive at six years old, except where they are of towardly parts; although I confess they learn the rudiments much earlier; during which time they can, however, be properly looked upon only as probationers; as I have been informed by a principal gentleman in

---

[1] 2s. = two shillings. Later in the essay, "£" and "l" stand for pounds and "d" for pence (Editors' note)

the county of Cavan, who protested to me that he never knew above one or two instances under the age of six, even in a part of the kingdom so renowned for the quickest proficiency in that art.

I am assured by our merchants, that a boy or a girl before twelve 7 years old is no saleable commodity; and even when they come to this age they will not yield above 3l. or 3l. 2s. 6d. at most on the exchange; which cannot turn to account either to the parents or kingdom, the charge of nutriment and rags having been at least four times that value.

I shall now therefore humbly propose my own thoughts, which I 8 hope will not be liable to the least objection.

I have been assured by a very knowing American of my acquaint- 9 ance in London, that a young healthy child well nursed is at a year old a most delicious, nourishing, and wholesome food, whether stewed, roasted, baked, or broiled; and I make no doubt that it will equally serve in a fricassee or a ragout.

I do therefore humbly offer it to public consideration that of the 10 120,000 children already computed, 20,000 may be reserved for breed, whereof only one-fourth part to be males; which is more than we allow to sheep, black cattle, or swine; and my reason is, that these children are seldom the fruits of marriage, a circumstance not much regarded by our savages; therefore one male will be sufficient to serve four fe- males. That the remaining 100,000 may, at a year old, be offered in sale to the persons of quality and fortune through the kingdom; always advising the mother to let them suck plentifully in the last month, so as to render them plump and fat for a good table. A child will make two dishes at an entertainment for friends; and when the family dines alone, the fore or hind quarter will make a reasonable dish, and sea- soned with a little pepper or salt will be very good boiled on the fourth day, especially in winter.

I have reckoned upon a medium that a child just born will weigh 11 12 pounds, and in a solar year, if tolerably nursed, will increase to 28 pounds.

I grant this food will be somewhat dear, and therefore very proper 12 for landlords, who, as they have already devoured most of the parents, seem to have the best title to the children.

Infant's flesh will be in season throughout the year, but more plen- 13 tiful in March, and a little before and after: for we are told by a grave author, an eminent French physician, that fish being a prolific diet, there are more children born in Roman Catholic countries about nine months after Lent than at any other season; therefore, reckoning a year after Lent, the markets will be more glutted than usual, because the number of popish infants is at least three to one in this kingdom: and therefore it will have one other collateral advantage, by lessening the number of papists among us.

I have already computed the charge of nursing a beggar's child (in which list I reckon all cottagers, laborers, and four-fifths of the farmers) to be about 2s. per annum, rags included; and I believe no gentleman would repine to give 10s. for the carcass of a good fat child, which, as I have said, will make four dishes of excellent nutritive meat, when he has only some particular friend or his own family to dine with him. Thus the squire will learn to be a good landlord, and grow popular among the tenants; the mother will have 8s. net profit, and be fit for work till she produces another child. 14

Those who are more thrifty (as I must confess the times require) may flay the carcass; the skin of which artificially dressed will make admirable gloves for ladies, and summer boots for fine gentlemen. 15

As to our city of Dublin, shambles may be appointed for this purpose in the most convenient parts of it, and butchers we may be assured will not be wanting: although I rather recommend buying the children alive, and dressing them hot from the knife as we do roasting pigs. 16

A very worthy person, a true lover of his country, and whose virtues I highly esteem, was lately pleased in discoursing on this matter to offer a refinement upon my scheme. He said that many gentlemen of this kingdom, having of late destroyed their deer, he conceived that the want of venison might be well supplied by the bodies of young lads and maidens, not exceeding fourteen years of age nor under twelve; so great a number of both sexes in every country being now ready to starve for want of work and service; and these to be disposed of by their parents, if alive, or otherwise by their nearest relations. But with due deference to so excellent a friend and so deserving a patriot, I cannot be altogether in his sentiments; for as to the males, my American acquaintance assured me from frequent experience that their flesh was generally tough and lean, like that of our schoolboys by continual exercise, and their taste disagreeable; and to fatten them would not answer the charge. Then as to the females, it would, I think, with humble submission be a loss to the public, because they soon would become breeders themselves: and besides, it is not improbable that some scrupulous people might be apt to censure such a practice (although indeed very unjustly), as a little bordering upon cruelty; which, I confess, has always been with me the strongest objection against any project, how well soever intended. 17

But in order to justify my friend, he confessed that this expedient 18
was put into his head by the famous Psalmanazar, a native of the island
Formosa, who came from thence to London about twenty years ago:
and in conversation told my friend, that in his country when any young
person happened to be put to death, the executioner sold the carcass
to persons of quality as a prime dainty; and that in his time the body
of a plump girl of fifteen, who was crucified for an attempt to poison
the emperor, was sold to his imperial majesty's prime minister of state,
and other great mandarins of the court, in joints from the gibbet, at
400 crowns. Neither indeed can I deny, that if the same use were made
of several plump young girls in this town, who without one single
groat to their fortunes cannot stir abroad without a chair, and appear
at the playhouse and assemblies in foreign fineries which they never
will pay for, the kingdom would not be the worse.

Some persons of a desponding spirit are in great concern about 19
that vast number of poor people, who are aged, diseased, or maimed,
and I have been desired to employ my thoughts what course may be
taken to ease the nation of so grievous an encumbrance. But I am not
in the least pain upon that matter, because it is very well known that
they are every day dying and rotting by cold and famine, and filth and
vermin, as fast as can be reasonably expected. And as to the young
laborers, they are now in as hopeful a condition: they cannot get work,
and consequently pine away for want of nourishment, to a degree that
if at any time they are accidentally hired to common labor, they have
not strength to perform it; and thus the country and themselves are
happily delivered from the evils to come.

I have too long digressed, and therefore shall return to my subject. 20
I think the advantages by the proposal which I have made are obvious
and many, as well as of the highest importance.

For first, as I have already observed, it would greatly lessen the 21
number of papists, with whom we are yearly overrun, being the principal breeders of the nation as well as our most dangerous enemies;
and who stay at home on purpose to deliver the kingdom to the Pretender, hoping to take their advantage by the absence of so many good
Protestants, who have chosen rather to leave their country than stay
at home and pay tithes against their conscience to an Episcopal curate.

Secondly, The poor tenants will have something valuable of their 22
own, which by law may be made liable to distress and help to pay
their landlord's rent, their corn and cattle being already seized, and
money a thing unknown.

Thirdly, Whereas the maintenance of 100,000 children from two 23 years old and upward, cannot be computed at less than 10s. a-piece per annum, the nation's stock will be thereby increased £50,000 per annum, beside the profit of a new dish introduced to the tables of all gentlemen of fortune in the kingdom who have any refinement in taste. And the money will circulate among ourselves, the goods being entirely of our own growth and manufacture.

Fourthly, The constant breeders beside the gain of 8s. sterling per  24
annum by the sale of their children, will be rid of the charge of maintaining them after the first year.

Fifthly, This food would likewise bring great custom to taverns,  25
where the vintners will certainly be so prudent as to procure the best receipts for dressing it to perfection, and consequently have their houses frequented by all the fine gentlemen, who justly value themselves upon their knowledge in good eating; and a skilful cook who understands how to oblige his guests, will contrive to make it as expensive as they please.

Sixthly, This would be a great inducement to marriage, which all  26
wise nations have either encouraged by rewards or enforced by laws and penalties. It would increase the care and tenderness of mothers toward their children, when they were sure of a settlement for life to the poor babes, provided in some sort by the public, to their annual profit instead of expense. We should see an honest emulation among the married women, which of them would bring the fattest child to the market. Men would become as fond of their wives during the time of their pregnancy as they are now of their mares in foal, their cows in calf, their sows when they are ready to farrow; nor offer to beat or kick them (as is too frequent a practice) for fear of a miscarriage.

Many other advantages might be enumerated. For instance, the  27
addition of some thousand carcasses in our exportation of barreled beef, the propagation of swine's flesh, and improvement in the art of making good bacon, so much wanted among us by the great destruction of pigs, too frequent at our table; which are no way comparable in taste or magnificence to a well-grown, fat, yearling child, which roasted whole will make a considerable figure at a lord mayor's feast or any other public entertainment. But this and many others I omit, being studious of brevity.

Supposing that 1,000 families in this city would be constant cus-  28
tomers for infants' flesh, besides others who might have it at merry-meetings, particularly at weddings and christenings, I compute that Dublin would take off annually about 20,000 carcasses; and the rest of

the kingdom (where probably they will be sold somewhat cheaper) the remaining 80,000.

I can think of no one objection that will possibly be raised against this proposal, unless it should be urged that the number of people will be thereby much lessened in the kingdom. This I freely own, and it was indeed one principal design in offering it to the world. I desire the reader will observe, that I calculate my remedy for this one individual kingdom of Ireland and for no other that ever was, is, or I think ever can be upon earth. Therefore let no man talk to me of other expedients: of taxing our absentees at 5s. a pound: of using neither clothes nor household furniture except what is of our own growth and manufacture: of utterly rejecting the materials and instruments that promote foreign luxury: of curing the expensiveness of pride, vanity, idleness, and gaming in our women: of introducing a vein of parsimony, prudence, and temperance: of learning to love our country, in the want of which we differ even from Laplanders and the inhabitants of Topinamboo: of quitting our animosities and factions, nor acting any longer like the Jews, who were murdering one another at the very moment their city was taken: of being a little cautious not to sell our country and conscience for nothing: of teaching landlords to have at least one degree of mercy toward their tenants: lastly, of putting a spirit of honesty, industry, and skill into our shopkeepers; who, if a resolution could now be taken to buy only our native goods, would immediately unite to cheat and exact upon us in the price, the measure, and the goodness, nor could ever yet be brought to make one fair proposal of just dealing, though often and earnestly invited to it. 29

Therefore, I repeat, let no man talk to me of these and the like expedients, till he has at least some glimpse of hope that there will be ever some hearty and sincere attempt to put them in practice. 30

But as to myself, having been wearied out for many years with offering vain, idle, visionary thoughts, and at length utterly despairing of success, I fortunately fell upon this proposal; which, as it is wholly new, so it has something solid and real, of no expense and little trouble, full in our own power, and whereby we can incur no danger in disobliging England. For this kind of commodity will not bear exportation, the flesh being of too tender a consistence to admit a long continuance in salt, although perhaps I could name a country which would be glad to eat up our whole nation without it. 31

After all, I am not so violently bent upon my own opinion as to reject any offer proposed by wise men, which shall be found equally 32 innocent, cheap, easy, and effectual. But before something of that kind shall be advanced in contradiction to my scheme, and offering a better, I desire the author or authors will be pleased maturely to consider two points. First, as things now stand, how they will be able to find food and raiment for 100,000 useless mouths and backs. And secondly, there being a round million of creatures in human figure throughout this kingdom, whose subsistence put into a common stock would leave them in debt 200,000,000*l.* sterling, adding those who are beggars by profession to the bulk of farmers, cottagers, and laborers, with the wives and children who are beggars in effect; I desire those politicians who dislike my overture, and may perhaps be so bold as to attempt an answer, that they will first ask the parents of these mortals, whether they would not at this day think it a great happiness to have been sold for food at a year old in the manner I prescribe, and thereby have avoided such a perpetual scene of misfortunes as they have since gone through by the oppression of landlords, the impossibility of paying rent without money or trade, the want of common sustenance, with neither house nor clothes to cover them from the inclemencies of the weather, and the most inevitable prospect of entailing the like or greater miseries upon their breed for ever.

I profess, in the sincerity of my heart, that I have not the least  33 personal interest in endeavoring to promote this necessary work, having no other motive than the public good of my country, by advancing our trade, providing for infants, relieving the poor, and giving some pleasure to the rich. I have no children by which I can propose to get a single penny; the youngest being nine years old, and my wife past child-bearing.

# Questions

1.  In paragraph 4, Swift speaks of "projectors." Check the *Oxford English Dictionary* to see the implications of this word in the eighteenth century. Keeping these implications in mind, characterize the pamphleteer (not Swift but his persona, an invented "projector") who offers his "modest proposal." What sort of man does he think he is? What sort of man do we regard him as? Support your assertions with evidence.
2.  In the first paragraph the speaker says that the sight of mothers begging is "melancholy." In this paragraph what assumption does the speaker make about women that in part gives rise to this mel-

ancholy? Now that you are familiar with the entire essay, explain
Swift's strategy in his first paragraph.
3.  Explain the function of the "other expedients" (listed in paragraph
    29).
4.  How might you argue that although this satire is primarily ferocious,
    it also contains some playful touches? What specific passages
    might support your argument?
5.  In the speaker's view, what underlies good family relationships?

Peter Singer

# Animal Liberation

## I

We are familiar with Black Liberation, Gay Liberation,    1
and a variety of other movements. With Women's Liberation some
thought we had come to the end of the road. Discrimination on the
basis of sex, it has been said, is the last form of discrimination that is
universally accepted and practiced without pretense, even in those
liberal circles which have long prided themselves on their freedom
from racial discrimination. But one should always be wary of talking
of "the last remaining form of discrimination." If we have learned
anything from the liberation movements, we should have learned how
difficult it is to be aware of the ways in which we discriminate until
they are forcefully pointed out to us. A liberation movement demands
an expansion of our moral horizons, so that practices that were previously regarded as natural and inevitable are now seen as intolerable.

*Animals, Men and Morals* is a manifesto for an Animal Liberation    2
movement. The contributors to the book may not all see the issue this
way. They are a varied group. Philosophers, ranging from professors
to graduate students, make up the largest contingent. There are five
of them, including the three editors, and there is also an extract from

Peter Singer teaches philosophy at Monash University in Melbourne, Australia.
This essay originally appeared, in 1973, as a review of *Animals, Men and Morals*,
edited by Stanley and Roslind Godlovitch and John Harris.

the unjustly neglected German philosopher with an English name, Leonard Nelson, who died in 1927. There are essays by two novelist/ critics, Brigid Brophy and Maureen Duffy, and another by Muriel the Lady Dowding, widow of Dowding of Battle of Britain fame and the founder of "Beauty Without Cruelty," a movement that campaigns against the use of animals for furs and cosmetics. The other pieces are by a psychologist, a botanist, a sociologist, and Ruth Harrison, who is probably best described as a professional campaigner for animal welfare.

Whether or not these people, as individuals, would all agree that    3
they are launching a liberation movement for animals, the book as a whole amounts to no less. It is a demand for a complete change in our attitudes to nonhumans. It is a demand that we cease to regard the exploitation of other species as natural and inevitable, and that, instead, we see it as a continuing moral outrage. Patrick Corbett, Professor of Philosophy at Sussex University, captures the spirit of the book in his closing words:

> . . . We require now to extend the great principles of liberty, equality and fraternity over the lives of animals. Let animal slavery join human slavery in the graveyard of the past.

The reader is likely to be skeptical. "Animal Liberation" sounds    4
more like a parody of liberation movements than a serious objective. The reader may think: We support the claims of blacks and women for equality because blacks and women really are equal to whites and males—equal in intelligence and in abilities, capacity for leadership, rationality, and so on. Humans and nonhumans obviously are not equal in these respects. Since justice demands only that we treat equals equally, unequal treatment of humans and nonhumans cannot be an injustice.

This is a tempting reply, but a dangerous one. It commits the non-    5
racist and non-sexist to a dogmatic belief that blacks and women really are just as intelligent, able, etc., as whites and males—and no more. Quite possibly this happens to be the case. Certainly attempts to prove that racial or sexual differences in these respects have a genetic origin have not been conclusive. But do we really want to stake our demand for equality on the assumption that there are no genetic differences of this kind between the different races or sexes? Surely the appropriate response to those who claim to have found evidence for such genetic differences is not to stick to the belief that there are no differences,

whatever the evidence to the contrary; rather one should be clear that the claim to equality does not depend on IQ. Moral equality is distinct from factual equality. Otherwise it would be nonsense to talk of the equality of human beings, since humans, as individuals, obviously differ in intelligence and almost any ability one cares to name. If possessing greater intelligence does not entitle one human to exploit another, why should it entitle humans to exploit nonhumans?

Jeremy Bentham expressed the essential basis of equality in his 6 famous formula: "Each to count for one and none for more than one." In other words, the interests of every being that has interests are to be taken into account and treated equally with the like interests of any other being. Other moral philosophers, before and after Bentham, have made the same point in different ways. Our concern for others must not depend on whether they possess certain characteristics, though just what that concern involves may, of course, vary according to such characteristics.

Bentham, incidentally, was well aware that the logic of the demand 7 for racial equality did not stop at the equality of humans. He wrote:

> The day *may* come when the rest of the animal creation may acquire those rights which never could have been withholden from them but by the hand of tyranny. The French have already discovered that the blackness of the skin is no reason why a human being should be abandoned without redress to the caprice of a tormentor. It may one day come to be recognized that the number of the legs, the villosity of the skin, or the termination of the *os sacrum*, are reasons equally insufficient for abandoning a sensitive being to the same fate. What else is it that should trace the insuperable line? Is it the faculty of reason, or perhaps the faculty of discourse? But a full-grown horse or dog is beyond comparison a more rational, as well as a more conversable animal, than an infant of a day, or a week, or even a month, old. But suppose they were otherwise, what would it avail? The question is not, Can they *reason?* nor Can they *talk?* but, Can they *suffer?*[1]

Surely Bentham was right. If a being suffers, there can be no moral justification for refusing to take that suffering into consideration, and, indeed, to count it equally with the like suffering (if rough comparisons can be made) of any other being.

So the only question is: Do animals other than man suffer? Most 8 people agree unhesitatingly that animals like cats and dogs can and

[1] *The Principles of Morals and Legislation*, ch. XVII, sec. 1, footnote to paragraph 4.

do suffer, and this seems also to be assumed by those laws that prohibit wanton cruelty to such animals. Personally, I have no doubt at all about this and find it hard to take seriously the doubts that a few people apparently do have. The editors and contributors of *Animals, Men and Morals* seem to feel the same way, for although the question is raised more than once, doubts are quickly dismissed each time. Nevertheless, because this is such a fundamental point, it is worth asking what grounds we have for attributing suffering to other animals.

It is best to begin by asking what grounds any individual human   9 has for supposing that other humans feel pain. Since pain is a state of consciousness, a "mental event," it can never be directly observed. No observations, whether behavioral signs such as writhing or screaming or physiological or neurological recordings, are observations of pain itself. Pain is something one feels, and one can only infer that others are feeling it from various external indications. The fact that only philosophers are ever skeptical about whether other humans feel pain shows that we regard such inference as justifiable in the case of humans.

Is there any reason why the same inference should be unjustifiable   10 for other animals? Nearly all the external signs which lead us to infer pain in other humans can be seen in other species, especially "higher" animals such as mammals and birds. Behavioral signs—writhing, yelping, or other forms of calling, attempts to avoid the source of pain, and many others—are present. We know, too, that these animals are biologically similar in the relevant respects, having nervous systems like ours which can be observed to function as ours do.

So the grounds for inferring that these animals can feel pain are   11 nearly as good as the grounds for inferring other humans do. Only nearly, for there is one behavioral sign that humans have but non-humans, with the exception of one or two specially raised chimpanzees, do not have. This, of course, is a developed language. As the quotation from Bentham indicates, this has long been regarded as an important distinction between man and other animals. Other animals may communicate with each other, but not in the way we do. Following Chomsky, many people now mark this distinction by saying that only humans communicate in a form that is governed by rules of syntax. (For the purposes of this argument, linguists allow those chimpanzees who have learned a syntactic sign language to rank as honorary humans.) Nevertheless, as Bentham pointed out, this distinction is not relevant to the question of how animals ought to be treated, unless it can be linked to the issue of whether animals suffer.

This link may be attempted in two ways. First, there is a hazy line   12 of philosophical thought, stemming perhaps from some doctrines associated with Wittgenstein, which maintains that we cannot meaningfully attribute states of consciousness to beings without language. I have not seen this argument made explicit in print, though I have come across it in conversation. This position seems to me very implausible, and I doubt that it would be held at all if it were not thought to be a consequence of a broader view of the significance of language. It may be that the use of a public, rule-governed language is a precondition of conceptual thought. It may even be, although personally I doubt it, that we cannot meaningfully speak of a creature having an intention unless that creature can use a language. But states like pain, surely, are more primitive than either of these, and seem to have nothing to do with language.

Indeed, as Jane Goodall points out in her study of chimpanzees,   13
when it comes to the expression of feelings and emotions, humans tend to fall back on non-linguistic modes of communication which are often found among apes, such as a cheering pat on the back, an exuberant embrace, a clasp of hands, and so on.[2] Michael Peters makes a similar point in his contribution to *Animals, Men and Morals* when he notes that the basic signals we use to convey pain, fear, sexual arousal, and so on are not specific to our species. So there seems to be no reason at all to believe that a creature without language cannot suffer.

The second, and more easily appreciated way of linking language   14
and the existence of pain is to say that the best evidence that we can have that another creature is in pain is when he tells us that he is. This is a distinct line of argument, for it is not being denied that a non-language-user conceivably could suffer, but only that we could know that he is suffering. Still, this line of argument seems to me to fail, and for reasons similar to those just given. "I am in pain" is not the best possible evidence that the speaker is in pain (he might be lying) and it is certainly not the only possible evidence. Behavioral signs and knowledge of the animal's biological similarity to ourselves together provide adequate evidence that animals do suffer. After all, we would not accept linguistic evidence if it contradicted the rest of the evidence. If a man was severely burned, and behaved as if he were in pain, writhing, groaning, being very careful not to let his burned skin touch anything, and so on, but later said he had not been in pain at all, we would be more likely to conclude that he was lying or suffering from amnesia than that he had not been in pain.

Even if there were stronger grounds for refusing to attribute pain   15

[2] Jane van Lawick-Goodall, *In the Shadow of Man* (Houghton Mifflin, 1971), p. 225.

to those who do not have a language, the consequences of this refusal might lead us to examine these grounds unusually critically. Human infants, as well as some adults, are unable to use language. Are we to deny that a year-old infant can suffer? If not, how can language be crucial? Of course, most parents can understand the responses of even very young infants better than they understand the responses of other animals, and sometimes infant responses can be understood in the light of later development.

This, however, is just a fact about the relative knowledge we have    16
of our own species and other species, and most of this knowledge is simply derived from closer contact. Those who have studied the behavior of other animals soon learn to understand their responses at least as well as we understand those of an infant. (I am not referring to Jane Goodall's and other well-known studies of apes. Consider, for example, the degree of understanding achieved by Tinbergen from watching herring gulls.[3] Just as we can understand infant human behavior in the light of adult human behavior, so we can understand the behavior of other species in the light of our own behavior (and sometimes we can understand our own behavior better in the light of the behavior of other species).

The grounds we have for believing that other mammals and birds    17
suffer are, then, closely analogous to the grounds we have for believing that other humans suffer. It remains to consider how far down the evolutionary scale this analogy holds. Obviously it becomes poorer when we get further away from man. To be more precise would require a detailed examination of all that we know about other forms of life. With fish, reptiles, and other vertebrates the analogy still seems strong, with molluscs like oysters it is much weaker. Insects are more difficult, and it may be that in our present state of knowledge we must be agnostic about whether they are capable of suffering.

If there is no moral justification for ignoring suffering when it    18
occurs, and it does occur in other species, what are we to say of our attitudes toward these other species? Richard Ryder, one of the contributors to *Animals, Men and Morals*, uses the term "speciesism" to describe the belief that we are entitled to treat members of other species in a way in which it would be wrong to treat members of our own species. The term is not euphonious, but it neatly makes the analogy with racism. The non-racist would do well to bear the analogy in mind when he is inclined to defend human behavior toward nonhumans. "Shouldn't we worry about improving the lot of our own species before

---

[3] N. Tinbergen, *The Herring Gull's World* (Basic Books, 1961).

we concern ourselves with other species?" he may ask. If we substitute "race" for "species" we shall see that the question is better not asked. "Is a vegetarian diet nutritionally adequate?" resembles the slave-owner's claim that he and the whole economy of the South would be ruined without slave labor. There is even a parallel with skeptical doubts about whether animals suffer, for some defenders of slavery professed to doubt whether blacks really suffer in the way whites do.

I do not want to give the impression, however, that the case for    19
Animal Liberation is based on the analogy with racism and no more. On the contrary, *Animals, Men and Morals* describes the various ways in which humans exploit nonhumans, and several contributors consider the defenses that have been offered, including the defense of meat-eating mentioned in the last paragraph. Sometimes the rebuttals are scornfully dismissive, rather than carefully designed to convince the detached critic. This may be a fault, but it is a fault that is inevitable, given the kind of book this is. The issue is not one on which one can remain detached. As the editors state in their Introduction:

> Once the full force of moral assessment has been made explicit there can be no rational excuse left for killing animals, be they killed for food, science, or sheer personal indulgence. We have not assembled this book to provide the reader with yet another manual on how to make brutalities less brutal. Compromise, in the traditional sense of the term, is simple unthinking weakness when one considers the actual reasons for our crude relationships with the other animals.

The point is that on this issue there are few critics who are gen-    20
uinely detached. People who eat pieces of slaughtered nonhumans every day find it hard to believe that they are doing wrong; and they also find it hard to imagine what else they could eat. So for those who do not place nonhumans beyond the pale of morality, there comes a stage when further argument seems pointless, a stage at which one can only accuse one's opponent of hypocrisy and reach for the sort of sociological account of our practices and the way we defend them that is attempted by David Wood in his contribution to this book. On the other hand, to those unconvinced by the arguments, and unable to accept that they are merely rationalizing their dietary preferences and their fear of being thought peculiar, such sociological explanations can only seem insultingly arrogant.

## II

The logic of speciesism is most apparent in the practice of exper-    21
imenting on nonhumans in order to benefit humans. This is because

the issue is rarely obscured by allegations that nonhumans are so different from humans that we cannot know anything about whether they suffer. The defender of vivisection cannot use this argument because he needs to stress the similarities between man and other animals in order to justify the usefulness to the former of experiments on the latter. The researcher who makes rats choose between starvation and electric shocks to see if they develop ulcers (they do) does so because he knows that the rat has a nervous system very similar to man's, and presumably feels an electric shock in a similar way.

Richard Ryder's restrained account of experiments on animals 22 made me angrier with my fellow men than anything else in this book. Ryder, a clinical psychologist by profession, himself experimented on animals before he came to hold the view he puts forward in his essay. Experimenting on animals is now a large industry, both academic and commercial. In 1969, more than 5 million experiments were performed in Britain, the vast majority without anesthetic (though how many of these involved pain is not known). There are no accurate U.S. figures, since there is no federal law on the subject, and in many cases no state law either. Estimates vary from 20 million to 200 million. Ryder suggests that 80 million may be the best guess. We tend to think that this is all for vital medical research, but of course it is not. Huge numbers of animals are used in university departments from Forestry to Psychology, and even more are used for commercial purposes, to test whether cosmetics can cause skin damage, or shampoos eye damage, or to test food additives or laxatives or sleeping pills or anything else.

A standard test for foodstuffs is the "LD50." The object of this test 23 is to find the dosage level at which 50 percent of the test animals will die. This means that nearly all of them will become very sick before finally succumbing or surviving. When the substance is a harmless one, it may be necessary to force huge doses down the animals, until in some cases sheer volume or concentration causes death.

Ryder gives a selection of experiments, taken from recent scientific 24 journals. I will quote two, not for the sake of indulging in gory details, but in order to give an idea of what normal researchers think they may legitimately do to other species. The point is not that the individual researchers are cruel men, but that they are behaving in a way that is allowed by our speciesist attitudes. As Ryder points out, even if only 1 percent of the experiments involve severe pain, that is 50,000 experiments in Britain each year, or nearly 150 every day (and about fifteen times as many in the United States, if Ryder's guess is right). Here then are two experiments.

O. S. Ray and R. J. Barrett of Pittsburgh gave electric shocks to the feet of 1,042 mice. They then caused convulsions by giving more intense shocks through cup-shaped electrodes applied to the animals' eyes or through pressure spring clips attached to their ears. Unfortunately some of the mice who "successfully completed Day One training were found sick or dead prior to testing on Day Two." [*Journal of Comparative and Physiological Psychology*, 1969, vol. 67, pp. 110–116]

At the National Institute for Medical Research, Mill Hill, London, W. Feldberg and S. L. Sherwood injected chemicals into the brains of cats—"with a number of widely different substances, recurrent patterns of reaction were obtained. Retching, vomiting, defaecation, increased salivation and greatly accelerated respiration leading to panting were common features." . . .

The injection into the brain of a large dose of Tubocuraine caused the cat to jump "from the table to the floor and then straight into its cage, where it started calling more and more noisily whilst moving about restlessly and jerkily . . . finally the cat fell with legs and neck flexed, jerking in rapid clonic movements, the condition being that of a major [epileptic] convulsion . . . within a few seconds the cat got up, ran for a few yards at high speed and fell in another fit. The whole process was repeated several times within the next ten minutes, during which the cat lost faeces and foamed at the mouth."

This animal finally died thirty-five minutes after the brain injection. [*Journal of Physiology*, 1954, vol. 123, pp. 148–167]

There is nothing secret about these experiments. One has only to open any recent volume of a learned journal, such as the *Journal of Comparative and Physiological Psychology*, to find full descriptions of experiments of this sort, together with the results obtained—results that are frequently trivial and obvious. The experiments are often supported by public funds.

It is a significant indication of the level of acceptability of these practices that, although these experiments are taking place at this moment on university campuses throughout the country, there has, so far as I know, not been the slightest protest from the student movement. Students have been rightly concerned that their universities should not discriminate on grounds of race or sex, and that they should not serve the purposes of the military or big business. Speciesism continues undisturbed, and many students participate in it. There may be a few qualms at first, but since everyone regards it as normal, and it may even be a required part of a course, the student soon becomes hardened and, dismissing his earlier feelings as "mere sentient," comes to regard animals as statistics rather than sentiment beings with interests that warrant consideration.

Argument about vivisection has often missed the point because it   27 has been put in absolutist terms: Would the abolitionist be prepared to let thousands die if they could be saved by experimenting on a single animal? The way to reply to this purely hypothetical question is to pose another: Would the experimenter be prepared to experiment on a human orphan under six months old, if it were the only way to save many lives? (I say "orphan" to avoid the complication of parental feelings, although in doing so I am being overfair to the experimenter, since the nonhuman subjects of experiments are not orphans.) A negative answer to this question indicates that the experimenter's readiness to use nonhumans is simple discrimination, for adult apes, cats, mice, and other mammals are more conscious of what is happening to them, more self-directing, and, so far as we can tell, just as sensitive to pain as a human infant. There is no characteristic that human infants possess that adult mammals do not have to the same or a higher degree.

(It might be possible to hold that what makes it wrong to exper-   28 iment on a human infant is that the infant will in time develop into more than the nonhuman, but one would then, to be consistent, have to oppose abortion, and perhaps contraception, too, for the fetus and the egg and sperm have the same potential as the infant. Moreover, one would still have no reason for experimenting on a nonhuman rather than a human with brain damage severe enough to make it impossible for him to rise above infant level.)

The experimenter, then, shows a bias for his own species when-   29 ever he carries out an experiment on a nonhuman for a purpose that he would not think justified him in using a human being at an equal or lower level of sentience, awareness, ability to be self-directing, etc. No one familiar with the kind of results yielded by these experiments can have the slightest doubt that if this bias were eliminated the number of experiments performed would be zero or very close to it.

### III

If it is vivisection that shows the logic of speciesism most clearly, it is   30 the use of other species for food that is at the heart of our attitudes toward them. Most of *Animals, Men and Morals* is an attack on meat-eating—an attack which is based solely on concern for nonhumans, without reference to arguments derived from considerations of ecology, macrobiotics, health, or religion.

The idea that nonhumans are utilities, means to our ends, per- 31
vades our thought. Even conservationists who are concerned about
the slaughter of wild fowl but not about the vastly greater slaughter
of chickens for our tables are thinking in this way—they are worried
about what we would lose if there were less wildlife. Stanley Godlovitch, pursuing the Marxist idea that our thinking is formed by the
activities we undertake in satisfying our needs, suggests that man's
first classification of his environment was into Edibles and Inedibles.
Most animals came into the first category, and there they have remained.

Man may always have killed other species for food, but he has 32
never exploited them so ruthlessly as he does today. Farming has suc-
cumbed to business methods, the objective being to get the highest
possible ratio of output (meat, eggs, milk) to input (fodder, labor costs,
etc.). Ruth Harrison's essay "On Factory Farming" gives an account
of some aspects of modern methods, and of the unsuccessful British
campaign for effective controls, a campaign which was sparked off by
her *Animal Machines* (Stuart: London, 1964).

Her article is in no way a substitute for her earlier book. This is a 33
pity since, as she says, "Farm produce is still associated with mental
pictures of animals browsing in the fields . . . of hens having a last
forage before going to roost. . . ." Yet neither in her article nor elsewhere in *Animals, Men and Morals* is this false image replaced by a clear
idea of the nature and extent of factory farming. We learn of this only
indirectly, when we hear of the code of reform proposed by an advisory
committee set up by the British government.

Among the proposals, which the government refused to imple- 34
ment on the grounds that they were too idealistic, were: *"Any animals
should at least have room to turn around freely."*

Factory farm animals need liberation in the most literal sense. Veal 35
calves are kept in stalls five feet by two feet. They are usually slaughtered when about four months old, and have been too big to turn in
their stalls for at least a month. Intensive beef herds, kept in stalls only
proportionally larger for much longer periods, account for a growing
percentage of beef production. Sows are often similarly confined when
pregnant, which, because of artifical methods of increasing fertility,
can be most of the time. Animals confined in this way do not waste
food by exercising, nor do they develop unpalatable muscle.

*"A dry bedded area should be provided for all stock."* Intensively kept 36
animals usually have to stand and sleep on slatted floors without straw,
because this makes cleaning easier.

*"Palatable roughage must be readily available to all calves after one week 37 of age."* In order to produce the pale veal housewives are said to prefer, calves are fed on an all-liquid diet until slaughter, even though they are long past the age at which they would normally eat grass. They develop a craving for roughage, evidenced by attempts to gnaw wood from their stalls. (For the same reason, their diet is deficient in iron.)

*"Battery cages for poultry should be large enough for a bird to be able to 38 stretch one wing at a time."* Under current British practice, a cage for four or five laying hens has a floor area of twenty inches by eighteen inches, scarcely larger than a double page of the *New York Review of Books*. In this space, on a sloping wire floor (sloping so the eggs roll down, wire so the dung drops through) the birds live for a year or eighteen months while artificial lighting and temperature conditions combine with drugs in their food to squeeze the maximum number of eggs out of them. Table birds are also sometimes kept in cages. More often they are reared in sheds, no less crowded. Under these conditions all the birds' natural activities are frustrated, and they develop "vices" such as pecking each other to death. To prevent this, beaks are often cut off, and the sheds kept dark.

How many of those who support factory farming by buying its 39 produce know anything about the way it is produced? How many have heard something about it, but are reluctant to check up for fear that it will make them uncomfortable? To non-speciesists, the typical consumer's mixture of ignorance, reluctance to find out the truth, and vague belief that nothing really bad could be allowed seems analogous to the attitudes of "decent Germans" to the death camps.

There are, of course, some defenders of factory farming. Their 40 arguments are considered, though again rather sketchily, by John Harris. Among the most common: "Since they have never known anything else, they don't suffer." This argument will not be put by anyone who knows anything about animal behavior, since he will know that not all behavior has to be learned. Chickens attempt to stretch wings, walk around, scratch, and even dustbathe or build a nest, even though they have never lived under conditions that allowed these activities. Calves can suffer from maternal deprivation no matter at what age they were taken from their mothers. "We need these intensive methods to provide protein for a growing population." As ecologists and famine relief organizations know, we can produce far more protein per acre if we grow the right vegetable crop, soy beans for instance, than if we use the land to grow crops to be converted into protein by animals who use nearly 90 percent of the protein themselves, even when unable to exercise.

There will be many readers of this book who will agree that factory 41
farming involves an unjustifiable degree of exploitation of sentient
creatures, and yet will want to say that there is nothing wrong with
rearing animals for food, provided it is done "humanely." These people are saying, in effect, that although we should not cause animals
to suffer, there is nothing wrong with killing them.

There are two possible replies to this view. One is to attempt to 42
show that this combination of attitudes is absurd. Roslind Godlovitch
takes this course in her essay, which is an examination of some common attitudes to animals. She argues that from the combination of
"animal suffering is to be avoided" and "there is nothing wrong with
killing animals" it follows that all animal life ought to be exterminated
(since all sentient creatures will suffer to some degree at some point
in their lives). Euthanasia is a contentious issue only because we place
some value on living. If we did not, the least amount of suffering would
justify it. Accordingly, if we deny that we have a duty to exterminate
all animal life, we must concede that we are placing some value on
animal life.

This argument seems to me valid, although one could still reply 43
that the value of animal life is to be derived from the pleasures that
life can have for them, so that, provided their lives have a balance of
pleasure over pain, we are justified in rearing them. But this would
imply that we ought to produce animals and let them live as pleasantly
as possible, without suffering.

At this point, one can make the second of the two possible replies 44
to the view that rearing and killing animals for food is all right so long
as it is done humanely. This second reply is that so long as we think
that a nonhuman may be killed simply so that a human can satisfy his
taste for meat, we are still thinking of nonhumans as means rather
than as ends in themselves. The factory farm is nothing more than the
application of technology to this concept. Even traditional methods
involve castration, the separation of mothers and their young, the
breaking up of herds, branding or ear-punching, and of course transportation to the abattoirs and the final moments of terror when the
animal smells blood and senses danger. If we were to try rearing animals so that they lived and died without suffering, we should find
that to do so on anything like the scale of today's meat industry would
be a sheer impossibility. Meat would become the prerogative of the
rich.

I have been able to discuss only some of the contributions to this 45
book, saying nothing about, for instance, the essays on killing for furs
and for sport. Nor have I considered all the detailed questions that

need to be asked once we start thinking about other species in the radically different way presented by this book. What, for instance, are we to do about genuine conflicts of interest like rats biting slum children? I am not sure of the answer, but the essential point is just that we *do* see this as a conflict of interests, that we recognize that rats have interests too. Then we may begin to think about other ways of resolving the conflict—perhaps by leaving out rat baits that sterilize the rats instead of killing them.

I have not discussed such problems because they are side issues   46
compared with the exploitation of other species for food and for experimental purposes. On these central matters, I hope that I have said enough to show that this book, despite its flaws, is a challenge to every human to recognize his attitudes to nonhumans as a form of prejudice no less objectionable than racism or sexism. It is a challenge that demands not just a change of attitudes, but a change in our way of life, for it requires us to become vegetarians.

Can a purely moral demand of this kind succeed? The odds are   47
certainly against it. The book holds out no inducements. It does not tell us that we will become healthier, or enjoy life more, if we cease exploiting animals. Animal Liberation will require greater altruism on the part of mankind than any other liberation movement, since animals are incapable of demanding it for themselves, or of protesting against their exploitation by votes, demonstrations, or bombs. Is man capable of such genuine altruism? Who knows? If this book does have a significant effect, however, it will be a vindication of all those who have believed that man has within himself the potential for more than cruelty and selfishness.

# Questions

1.  Reread Singer's first seven paragraphs carefully, observing how he leads us to see that "animal liberation" is not a joke. It will help you to understand his strategy if for each of his paragraphs you write one sentence either summarizing the paragraph or commenting on what it accomplishes in his argument.
2.  What grounds does Singer find for attributing suffering to nonhumans? List the arguments he offers to dismiss the relevance of a developed language. Why does he find it necessary to offer these arguments?
3.  Does Singer attribute the capacity to feel pain to all species? Explain.

4.  How does Singer define speciesism? To what extent does he use the analogy of speciesism to racism?
5.  What is vivisection? Why, according to Singer, *must* defenders of vivisection also defend speciesism? Why do many of us who would not be willing to defend speciesism tolerate or even participate in experiments on animals?
6.  What use of animals does Singer analyze beginning with paragraph 30? Why does he reserve this discussion for the last part of his essay? Why does he offer more detailed and more concrete examples in this section than in the second part, beginning with paragraph 21?

## Jamaica Kincaid

# Girl

Wash the white clothes on Monday and put them on      1
the stone heap; wash the color clothes on Tuesday and put them on the clothesline to dry; don't walk barehead in the hot sun; cook pumpkin fritters in very hot sweet oil; soak your little cloths right after you take them off; when buying cotton to make yourself a nice blouse, be sure that it doesn't have gum in it, because that way it won't hold up well after a wash; soak salt fish overnight before you cook it; is it true that you sing benna in Sunday school?; always eat your food in such a way that it won't turn someone else's stomach; on Sundays try to walk like a lady and not like the slut you are so bent on becoming; don't sing benna in Sunday school; you mustn't speak to wharf-rat boys, not even to give directions; don't eat fruits on the street—flies will follow you; *but I don't sing benna on Sundays at all and never in Sunday school;* this is how to sew on a button; this is how to make a buttonhole for the button you have just sewed on; this is how to hem a dress when you see the hem coming down and so to prevent yourself from

---

Jamaica Kincaid, born in St. Johns, Antigua, in 1949 and educated there at the Princess Margaret School, is a writer for *The New Yorker.* Ms. Kincaid informs us that "benna," mentioned early in this piece, refers to "songs of the sort your parents didn't want you to sing, at first calypso and later rock and roll."

looking like the slut I know you are so bent on becoming; this is how you iron your father's khaki shirt so that it doesn't have a crease; this is how you iron your father's khaki pants so that they don't have a crease; this is how you grow okra—far from the house, because okra tree harbors red ants; when you are growing dasheen, make sure it gets plenty of water or else it makes your throat itch when you are eating it; this is how you sweep a corner; this is how you sweep a whole house; this is how you sweep a yard; this is how you smile to someone you don't like too much; this is how you smile to someone you don't like at all; this is how you smile to someone you like completely; this is how you set a table for tea; this is how you set a table for dinner; this is how you set a table for dinner with an important guest; this is how you set a table for lunch; this is how you set a table for breakfast; this is how to behave in the presence of men who don't know you very well, and this way they won't recognize immediately the slut I have warned you against becoming; be sure to wash every day, even if it is with your own spit; don't squat down to play marbles—you are not a boy, you know; don't pick people's flowers—you might catch something; don't throw stones at blackbirds, because it might not be a blackbird at all; this is how to make a bread pudding; this is how to make doukona; this is how to make pepper pot; this is how to make a good medicine for a cold; this is how to make a good medicine to throw away a child before it even becomes a child; this is how to catch a fish; this is how to throw back a fish you don't like, and that way something bad won't fall on you; this is how to bully a man; this is how a man bullies you; this is how to love a man, and if this doesn't work there are other ways, and if they don't work don't feel too bad about giving up; this is how to spit up in the air if you feel like it, and this is how to move quick so that it doesn't fall on you; this is how to make ends meet; always squeeze bread to make sure it's fresh; *but what if the baker won't let me feel the bread?;* you mean to say that after all you are really going to be the kind of woman who the baker won't let near the bread?

# Question

In a paragraph, identify the two characters whose voices we hear in this story. Explain what we know about them (their circumstances and their relationship). Cite specific evidence from the text. For example, what is the effect of the frequent repetition of "this is how"? Are there other words or phrases frequently repeated?

Italo Calvino

# The Aquatic Uncle

*The first vertebrates who, in the Carboniferous period, aban-* 1
*doned aquatic life for terrestrial, descended from the osseous, pulmonate fish whose fins were capable of rotation beneath their bodies and thus could be used as paws on the earth.*

By then it was clear that the water period was coming to an end,—*old Qfwfq recalled,*—those who decided to make the great move were growing more and more numerous, there wasn't a family that didn't have some loved one up on dry land, and everybody told fabulous tales of the things that could be done there, and they called back to their relatives to join them. There was no holding the young fish; they slapped their fins on the muddy banks to see if they would work as paws, as the more talented ones had already discovered. But just at that time the differences among us were becoming accentuated: there might be a family that had been living on land, say, for several generations, whose young people acted in a way that wasn't even amphibious but almost reptilian already; and there were others who lingered, still living like fish, those who, in fact, became even more fishy than they had been before.

Our family, I must say, including grandparents, was all up on the shore, padding about as if we had never known how to do anything else. If it hadn't been for the obstinacy of our great-uncle N'ba N'ga, we would have long since lost all contact with the aquatic world.

Italo Calvino (1923–1985) was of Italian descent, but he was born in Cuba, where his father was engaged in agricultural research. Soon after his birth, the family returned to Italy, where Calvino was educated. During World War II he was a member of the Anti-Fascist Resistance; later he edited an intellectual journal and wrote stories, novels, and essays.

We print here one of the twelve fanciful stories that constitute *Cosmicomics*.

Yes, we had a great-uncle who was a fish, on my paternal grand-mother's side, to be precise, of the Coelacanthus family of the De-vonian period (the fresh-water branch: who are, for that matter, cous-ins of the others—but I don't want to go into all these questions of kinship, nobody can ever follow them anyhow). So as I was saying, this great-uncle lived in certain muddy shallows, among the roots of some protoconifers, in that inlet of the lagoon where all our ancestors had been born. He never stirred from there: at any season of the year all we had to do was push ourselves over the softer layers of vegetation until we could feel ourselves sinking into the dampness, and there below, a few palms' lengths from the edge, we could see the column of little bubbles he sent up, breathing heavily the way old folk do, or the little cloud of mud scraped up by his sharp snout, always rum-maging around, more out of habit than out of the need to hunt for anything.

"Uncle N'ba N'ga! We've come to pay you a visit! Were you ex-   5 pecting us?" we would shout, slapping our paws and tails in the water to attract his attention. "We've brought you some insects that grow where we live! Uncle N'ba N'ga! Have you ever seen such fat cock-roaches? Taste one and see if you like it. . . ."

"You can clean those revolting warts you've got with your stinking cockroaches!" Our great-uncle's answer was always some remark of this sort, or perhaps even ruder: this is how he welcomed us every time, but we paid no attention because we knew he would mellow after a little while, accept our presents gladly, and converse in politer tones.

"What do you mean, Uncle? Warts? When did you ever see any warts on us?"

This business about warts was a widespread prejudice among the old fish: a notion that, from living on dry land, we would develop warts all over our bodies, exuding liquid matter: this was true enough for the toads, but we had nothing in common with them; on the con-trary, our skin, smooth and slippery, was such as no fish had ever had; and our great-uncle knew this perfectly well, but he still couldn't stop larding his talk with all the slanders and intolerance he had grown up in the midst of.

We went to visit our great-uncle once a year, the whole family together. It also gave us an opportunity to have a reunion, since we were scattered all over the continent; we could exchange bits of news, trade edible insects, and discuss old questions that were still unsettled.

Our great-uncle spoke his mind even on questions that were re-   10 moved from him by miles and miles of dry land, such as the division of territory for dragonfly hunting; and he would side with this one or that one, according to his own reasoning, which was always aquatic. "But don't you know that it's always better to hunt on the bottom and not on the water's surface? So what are you getting all upset over?"

"But, Uncle, you see: it isn't a question of hunting on the bottom or on the surface. I live at the foot of a hill, and he lives halfway up the slope. . . . You know what I mean by hill, Uncle. . . ."

And he said: "You always find the best crayfish at the foot of the cliffs." It just wasn't possible to make him accept a reality different from his own.

And yet, his opinions continued to exert an authority over all of us; in the end we asked his advice about matters he didn't begin to understand, though we knew he could be dead wrong. Perhaps his authority stemmed from the fact that he was a leftover from the past, from his way of using old figures of speech, like: "Lower your fins there, youngster!," whose meaning we didn't grasp very clearly.

We had made various attempts to get him up on land with us, and we went on making them; indeed, on this score, the rivalry among the various branches of the family never died out, because whoever managed to take our great-uncle home with him would achieve a position of pre-eminence over the rest of our relatives. But the rivalry was pointless, because our uncle wouldn't dream of leaving the lagoon.

"Uncle, if you only knew how sorry we feel leaving you all alone, at your age, in the midst of all that dampness. . . . We've had a wonderful idea . . ." someone would begin.  15

"I was expecting the lot of you to catch on finally," the old fish interrupted, "now you've got over the whim of scraping around in that drought, so it's time you came back to live like normal beings. Here there's plenty of water for all, and when it comes to food, there's never been a better season for worms. You can all dive right in, and we won't have to discuss it any further."

"No, no, Uncle N'ba N'ga, you've got it all wrong. We wanted to take you to live with us, in a lovely little meadow. . . . You'll be nice and snug; we'll dig you a little damp hole. You'll be able to turn and toss in it, just like here. And you might even try taking a few steps around the place: you'll be very good at it, just wait and see. And besides, at your time of life, the climate on land is much more suitable. So come now, Uncle N'ba N'ga, don't wait to be coaxed. Won't you come home with us?"

"No!" was our great-uncle's sharp reply, and taking a nose dive into the water, he vanished from our sight.

"But why, Uncle? What have you got against the idea? We simply don't understand. Anyone as broad-minded as you ought to be above certain prejudices. . . ."

From an angry huff of water at the surface, before the final plunge 20 with a still-agile jerk of his tail fin, came our uncle's final answer: "He who has fleas in his scales swims with his belly in the mud!" which must have been an idiomatic expression (similar to our own, much more concise proverb: "If you itch, scratch"), with that term "mud" which he insisted on using where we would say "land."

That was about the time when I fell in love. Lll and I spent our days together, chasing each other; no one as quick as she had ever been seen before; in the ferns, which were as tall as trees in those days, she would climb to the top in one burst, and the tops would bend almost to the ground, then she would jump down and run off again; I, with slower and somewhat clumsier movements, followed her. We ventured into zones of the interior where no print had ever marked the dry and crusty terrain; at times I stopped, frightened at having come so far from the expanse of the lagoons. But nothing seemed so far from aquatic life as she, Lll, did: the deserts of sand and stones, the prairies, the thick forests, the rocky hillocks, the quartz mountains: this was her world, a world that seemed made especially to be scanned by her oblong eyes, to be trod by her darting steps. When you looked at her smooth skin, you felt that scales had never existed.

Her relatives made me a bit ill at ease; hers was one of those families who had become established on Earth in the earliest period and had finally become convinced they had never lived anywhere else, one of those families who, by now, even laid their eggs on dry terrain, protected by a hard shell, and Lll, if you looked at her when she jumped, at her flashing movements, you could tell she had been born the way she was now, from one of those eggs warmed by sand and sun, having completely skipped the swimming, wriggling phase of the tadpole, which was still obligatory in our less evolved families.

The time had come for Lll to meet my family: and since its oldest and most authoritative member was Great-Uncle N'ba N'ga, I couldn't avoid a visit to him, to introduce my fiancée. But every time an opportunity occurred, I postponed it, out of embarrassment; knowing the prejudices among which she had been brought up, I hadn't yet dared tell Lll that my great-uncle was a fish.

One day we had wandered off to one of those damp promontories that girdle the lagoon, where the ground is made not so much of sand

as of tangled roots and rotting vegetation. And Lll came out with one
of her usual dares, her challenges to feats: "Qfwfq, how long can you
keep your balance? Let's see who can run closest to the edge here!"
And she darted forward with her Earth-creature's leap, now slightly
hesitant, however.

This time I not only felt I could follow her, but also that I could     25
win, because my paws got a better grip on damp surfaces. "As close
to the edge as you like!" I cried. "And even beyond it!"

"Don't talk nonsense!" she said. "How can you run beyond the
edge? It's all water there!"

Perhaps this was the opportune moment to bring up the subject
of my great-uncle. "What of that?" I said to her. "There are those who
run on this side of the edge, and those who run on the other."

"You're saying things that make no sense at all!"

"I'm saying that my great-uncle N'ba N'ga lives in the water the
way we live on the land, and he's never come out of it!"

"Ha! I'd like to meet this N'ba N'ga of yours!"     30

She had no sooner finished saying this than the muddied surface
of the lagoon gurgled with bubbles, moved in a little eddy, and allowed
a nose, all covered with spiky scales, to appear.

"Well, here I am. What's the trouble?" Great-Uncle said, staring
at Lll with eyes as round and inexpressive as stones, flapping the gills
at either side of his enormous throat. Never before had my great-uncle
seemed so different from the rest of us: a real monster.

"Uncle, if you don't mind . . . this is . . . I mean, I have the pleasure to present to you my future bride, Lll," and I pointed to my
fiancée, who for some unknown reason had stood erect on her hind
paws, in one of her most exotic poses, certainly the least likely to be
appreciated by that boorish old relative.

"And so, young lady, you've come to wet your tail a bit, eh?" my
great-uncle said: a remark that in his day no doubt had been considered
courtly, but to us sounded downright indecent.

I looked at Lll, convinced I would see her turn and run off with     35
a shocked twitter. But I hadn't considered how strong her training
was, her habit of ignoring all vulgarity in the world around her. "Tell
me something: those little plants there . . ." she said, nonchalantly,
pointing to some rushes growing tall in the midst of the lagoon, "where
do they put down their roots?"

One of those questions you ask just to make conversation: as if
she cared about those rushes! But it seemed Uncle had been waiting
only for that moment to start explaining the why and the wherefore

of the roots of floating trees and how you could swim among them and, indeed, how they were the very best places for hunting.

I thought he would never stop. I huffed impatiently, I tried to interrupt him. But what did that saucy Lll do? She encouraged him! "Oh, so you go hunting among those underwater roots? How interesting!"

I could have sunk into the ground from shame.

And he said: "I'm not fooling! The worms you find there! You can fill your belly, all right!" And without giving it a second thought, he dived. An agile dive such as I'd never seen him make before. Or rather, he made a leap into the air—his whole length out of the water, all dotted with scales—spreading the spiky fans of his fins; then, when he had completed a fine half-circle in the air, he plunged back, head-first, and disappeared quickly with a kind of screw-motion of his crescentshaped tail.

At this sight, I recalled the little speech I had prepared hastily to    40 apologize to Lll, taking advantage of my uncle's departure ("You really have to understand him, you know, this mania for living like a fish has finally even made him look like a fish"), but the words died in my throat. Not even I had ever realized the full extent of my grandmother's brother's fishiness. So I just said: "It's late, Lll, let's go . . ." and already my great-uncle was re-emerging, holding in his shark's lips a garland of worms and muddy seaweed.

It seemed too good to be true, when we finally took our leave; but as I trotted along silently behind Lll, I was thinking that now she would begin to make her comments, that the worst was still to come. But then Lll, without stopping, turned slightly toward me: "He's very nice, your uncle," and that was all she said. More than once in the past her irony had disarmed me; but the icy sensation that filled me at this remark was so awful that I would rather not have seen her any more than to have to face the subject again.

Instead, we went on seeing each other, going together, and the lagoon episode was never mentioned. I was still uneasy: it was no use my trying to persuade myself she had forgotten; every now and then I suspected she was remaining silent in order to embarrass me later in some spectacular way, in front of her family, or else—and, for me, this was an even worse hypothesis—she was making an effort to talk about other things only because she felt sorry for me. Then, out of a clear sky, one morning she said curtly: "See here, aren't you going to take me to visit your uncle any more?"

In a faint voice I asked: "Are you joking?"

Not at all; she was in earnest, she couldn't wait to go back and have a little chat with old N'ba N'ga. I was all mixed up.

That time our visit to the lagoon lasted longer. We lay on a sloping   45
bank, all three of us: my great-uncle was nearest the water, but the two of us were half in and half out, too, so anyone seeing us from the distance, all close together, wouldn't have known who was terrestrial and who was aquatic.

The fish started in with one of his usual tirades: the superiority of water respiration to air breathing, and all his repertory of denigration. "Now Lll will jump up and give him what for!" I thought. Instead, that day Lll was apparently using a different tactic: she argued seriously, defending our point of view, but as if she were also taking old N'ba N'ga's notions into consideration.

According to my great-uncle, the lands that had emerged were a limited phenomenon: they were going to disappear just as they had cropped up or, in any event, they would be subject to constant changes: volcanoes, glaciations, earthquakes, upheavals, changes of climate and of vegetation. And our life in the midst of all this would have to face constant transformations, in the course of which whole races would disappear, and the only survivors would be those who were prepared to change the bases of their existence so radically that the reasons why living was beautiful would be completely overwhelmed and forgotten.

This prospect was in absolute contradiction to the optimism in which we children of the coast had been brought up, and I opposed the idea with shocked protests. But for me the true, living confutation of those arguments was Lll: in her I saw the perfect, definitive form, born from the conquest of the land that had emerged; she was the sum of the new boundless possibilities that had opened. How could my great-uncle try to deny the incarnate reality of Lll? I was aflame with polemical passion, and I thought that my fiancée was being all too patient and too understanding with our opponent.

True, even for me—used as I was to hearing only grumblings and abuse from my great-uncle's mouth—this logically arranged argumentation of his came as a novelty, though it was still spiced with antiquated and bombastic expressions and was made comical by his peculiar accent. It was also amazing to hear him display a detailed familiarity—though entirely external—with the continental lands.

But Lll, with her questions, tried to make him talk as much as   50
possible about life under water: and, to be sure, this was the theme that elicited the most tightly knit, even emotional discourse from my

great-uncle. Compared to the uncertainties of earth and air, lagoons and seas and oceans represented a future with security. Down there, changes would be very few, space and provender were unlimited, the temperature would always be steady; in short, life would be maintained as it had gone on till then, in its achieved, perfect forms, without metamorphoses or additions with dubious outcome, and every individual would be able to develop his own nature, to arrive at the essence of himself and of all things. My great-uncle spoke of the aquatic future without embellishments or illusions, he didn't conceal the problems, even serious ones, that would arise (most worrying of all, the increase of saline content); but they were problems that wouldn't upset the values and the proportions in which he believed.

"But now we gallop over valleys and mountains, Uncle!" I cried, speaking for myself but especially for Lll, who remained silent.

"Go on with you, tadpole, when you're wet again, you'll be back home!" he apostrophized, to me, resuming the tone I had always heard him use with us.

"Don't you think, Uncle, that if we wanted to learn to breathe under water, it would be too late?" Lll asked earnestly, and I didn't know whether to feel flattered because she had called my old relative uncle or confused because certain questions (at least, so I was accustomed to think) shouldn't even be asked.

"If you're game, sweetie," the fish said, "I can teach you in a minute!"

Lll came out with an odd laugh, then finally began to run away, to run on and on beyond all pursuit. 55

I hunted for her across plains and hills, I reached the top of a basalt spur which dominated the surrounding landscape of deserts and forests surrounded by the waters. Lll was there. What she had wanted to tell me—I had understood her!—by listening to N'ba N'ga and then by fleeing and taking refuge up here was surely this: we had to live in our world thoroughly, as the old fish lived in his.

"I'll live here, the way Uncle does down there," I shouted, stammering a bit; then I corrected myself: "The two of us will live here, together!" because it was true that without her I didn't feel secure.

But what did Lll answer me then? I blush when I remember it even now, after all these geological eras. She answered: "Get along with you, tadpole; it takes more than that!" And I didn't know whether she was imitating my great-uncle, to mock him and me at once, or whether she had really assumed the old nut's attitude toward his nephew, and either hypothesis was equally discouraging, because both meant she considered me at a halfway stage, a creature not at home in the one world or in the other.

Had I lost her? Suspecting this, I hastened to woo her back. I took to performing all sorts of feats: hunting flying insects, leaping, digging underground dens, wrestling with the strongest of our group. I was proud of myself, but unfortunately whenever I did something brave, she wasn't there to see me: she kept disappearing, and no one knew where she had gone off to hide.

Finally I understood: she went to the lagoon, where my great-uncle 60 was teaching her to swim under water. I saw them surface together: they were moving along at the same speed, like brother and sister.

"You know?" she said, gaily, "my paws work beautifully as fins!"

"Good for you! That's a big step forward," I couldn't help remarking, sarcastically.

It was a game, for her: I understood. But a game I didn't like. I had to recall her to reality, to the future that was awaiting her.

One day I waited for her in the midst of a woods of tall ferns which sloped to the water.

"Lll, I have to talk to you," I said as soon as I saw her, "you've 65 been amusing yourself long enough. We have more important things ahead of us. I've discovered a passage in the mountains: beyond it stretches an immense stone plain, just abandoned by the water. We'll be the first to settle there, we'll populate unknown lands, you and I, and our children."

"The sea is immense," Lll said.

"Stop repeating that old fool's nonsense. The world belongs to those with legs, not to fish, and you know it."

"I know that he's somebody who is somebody," Lll said.

"And what about me?"

"There's nobody with legs who is like him."                    70

"And your family?"

"We've quarreled. They don't understand anything."

"Why, you're crazy! Nobody can turn back!"

"I can."

"And what do you think you'll do, all alone with an old fish?"    75

"Marry him. Be a fish again with him. And bring still more fish into the world. Good-by."

And with one of those rapid climbs of hers, the last, she reached the top of a fern frond, bent it toward the lagoon, and let go in a dive. She surfaced, but she wasn't alone: the sturdy, curved tail of Great-Uncle N'ba N'ga rose near hers and, together, they cleft the waters.

It was a hard blow for me. But, after all, what could I do about it? I went on my way, in the midst of the world's transformations, being transformed myself. Every now and then, among the many forms of living beings, I encountered one who "was somebody" more than I was: one who announced the future, the duck-billed platypus who nurses its young, just hatched from the egg; or I might encounter another who bore witness to a past beyond all return, a dinosaur who had survived into the beginning of the Cenozoic, or else—a crocodile— part of the past that had discovered a way to remain immobile through the centuries. They all had something, I know, that made them some- how superior to me, sublime, something that made me, compared to them, mediocre. And yet I wouldn't have traded places with any of them.

# Questions

1.  In paragraph 2 Old Qfwfq recalls "the great move." What is the great move, and who (or what) is old Qfwfq?
2.  What is the conflict between Qfwfq and Uncle N'ba N'ga? In what ways does it strike you as realistic?
3.  About midway through the story Qfwfq reports: "That was about the time when I fell in love" (paragraph 21). Reread the paragraph and jot down the details that convince you that Qfwfq was indeed in love.
4.  The uncle predicts that the land will be subject to terrible changes and that "the only survivors would be those who were prepared to change the bases of their existence so radically that the reasons why living was beautiful would be completely overwhelmed and forgotten." What are "the reasons why living was beautiful"?
5.  At what point do you become aware that N'ba N'ga and Lll are flirt- ing with each other? When does Qfwfq become aware of this? How do you feel when Lll gives him the brush-off?
6.  If the story has a hero, would you say the hero is N'ba N'ga or Qfwfq? Explain.
7.  At the end of the story Qfwfq compares himself to others he meets as he goes on his way and confesses his mediocrity. In terms of the story, what does "mediocrity" mean? Why does Qfwfq say, referring to those others, that he wouldn't trade places with any of them?

## Theodore Roethke

# My Papa's Waltz

The whiskey on your breath
Could make a small boy dizzy;
But I hung on like death:
Such waltzing was not easy.                                          4

We romped until the pans
Slid from the kitchen shelf;
My mother's countenance
Could not unfrown itself.                                            8

The hand that held my wrist
Was battered on one knuckle;
At every step you missed
My right ear scraped a buckle.                                      12

You beat time on my head
With a palm caked hard by dirt,
Then waltzed me off to bed
Still clinging to your shirt.                                        16

## Questions

1. Who is the speaker?
2. Summarize the scene presented. Which details suggest what has happened before the waltz began? Do any details suggest that there have been similar scenes before?
3. How does the speaker feel about his father?
4. Describe the rhythm of the poem. Is it appropriate to a waltz?

---

Theodore Roethke (1908–1963), author of eight volumes of poetry, was born in Saginaw, Michigan. Roethke's father ran a greenhouse, but the son earned his living by teaching English literature, chiefly at the University of Washington, in Seattle.

# 3
## FOOD, CLOTHING, SHELTER

*Mr. and Mrs. A. B., on Their Farm, near Kersey, Colorado*
**Arthur Rothstein, 1939**

Oil on beaver board, 76 × 63.3 cm. Friends of American Art Collection, 1930. © 1988 The Art Institute of Chicago. All Rights Reserved.

*A Graveyard and Steel Mill in Bethlehem, Pennsylvania*
**Walker Evans, 1936**

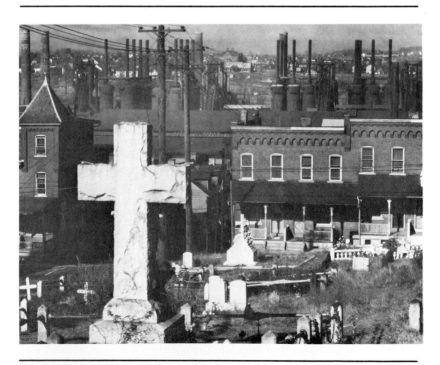

Gelatin-silver print, 7⅞″ × 9⅝″. Collection, The Museum of Modern Art, New York. Gift of the Farm Security Administration.

# Short Views

The discovery of a new dish does more for human happiness than the discovery of a new star.
### Anthelme Brillat-Savarin

The great secret of vegetarianism is never to eat vegetables.
### George Bernard Shaw

What is patriotism but the love of the good things we ate in our childhood?
### Lin Yutang

Man ist was man isst (German saying: We are what we eat)
### Anonymous

Coffee drunk out of wine glasses is really miserable stuff, as is meat cut at the table with a pair of scissors.
### G. C. Lichtenberg

It is hard to provide and cook so simple and clean a diet as will not offend the imagination; but this, I think, is to be fed when we feed the body; they should both sit down at the same table. Yet perhaps this may be done. The fruits eaten temperately need not make us ashamed of our appetites, nor interrupt the worthiest pursuits. But put an extra condiment into your dish, and it will poison you. It is not worth the while to live by rich cookery. Most men would feel shame if caught preparing with their own hands precisely such a dinner, whether of animal or vegetable food, as is every day prepared for them by others. Yet till this is otherwise we are not civilized, and, if gentlemen and ladies, are not true men and women. This certainly suggests what change is to be made. It may be vain to ask why the imagination will not be reconciled to flesh and fat. I am satisfied that it is not. It is not a reproach that man is a carnivorous animal? True, he can and does live, in a great measure, by preying on other animals; but this is a miserable way— as any one who will go to snaring rabbits, or slaughtering lambs, may learn—and he will be regarded as a benefactor of his race who shall teach man to confine himself to a more innocent and wholesome diet. Whatever my own practice may be, I have no doubt that it is a part of the destiny of the human race, in its gradual improvement, to leave off eating animals, as surely as the savage tribes have left off eating each other when they came in contact with the more civilized.

**Henry David Thoreau**

This seems to be an era of gratuitous inventions and negative improvements. Consider the beer can. It was beautiful—as beautiful as the clothespin, as inevitable as the wine bottle, as dignified and reassuring as the fire hydrant. A tranquil cylinder of delightfully resonant metal, it could be opened in an instant, requiring only the application of a handy gadget freely dispensed by every grocer. Who can forget the small symmetrical thrill of those two triangular punctures, the dainty *pffff*, the little crest of suds that foamed eagerly in the exultation of release? Now we are given, instead, a top beetling with an ugly, shmoo-shaped "tab," which, after fiercely resisting the tugging, bleeding fingers of the thirsty man, threatens his lips with a dangerous and hideous hole. However, we have discovered a way to thwart Progress, usually so unthwartable. *Turn the beer can upside down and open the bottom.* The bottom is still the way the top used to be. True, this operation gives the beer an unsettling jolt, and the sight of a consistently inverted beer can might make people edgy, not to say queasy. But the latter difficulty could be eliminated if manufacturers would design cans that looked the same whichever end was up, like playing cards. What we need is Progress with an escape hatch.

**John Updike**

A man is in general better pleased when he has a good dinner upon his table than when his wife talks Greek.

**Samuel Johnson**

Better is a dinner of herbs where love is, than a stalled ox and hatred therewith.

**Proverbs 15:17**

I can't help thinking that the decline in table manners has something to do with fast food. There are no rules of etiquette for eating a Big Mac and a side of fries. The whole idea of fast food is

to get eating out of the way as quickly as possible so you can get to
something else. It's difficult, too, to have respect for a fast food
cheeseburger. And if you don't have respect for what you're eating
how can you have any respect for yourself or the people you're
eating with?
        **Diane White**


The fashion wears out more apparel than the man.
        **William Shakespeare,** *Much Ado About Nothing*


The more I think of it, the more it appears to me that dress is the
foundation of society.
        **Thomas Carlyle**


What would a man be—what would *any* man be—without his
clothes? As soon as one stops and thinks over that proposition, one
realizes that without his clothes a man would be nothing at all; that
the clothes do not merely make the man, the clothes *are* the man;
that without them he is a cipher, a vacancy, a nobody, a nothing.
        Titles—another . . . artificiality—are a part of his clothing. They
and the dry-goods conceal the wearer's inferiority and make him
seem great and a wonder, when at bottom there is nothing
remarkable about him. They can move a nation to fall on its knees
and sincerely worship an Emperor who, without the clothes and the
title, would drop to the rank of the cobbler and be swallowed up
and lost sight of in the massed multitude of the inconsequentials. . . .
        A policeman in plain clothes is one man; in his uniform he is
ten. Clothes and title are the most potent thing, the most
formidable influence, in the earth. They move the human race to
willing and spontaneous respect for the judge, the general, the
admiral, the bishop, the ambassador, the frivolous earl, the idiot
duke, the sultan, the king, the emperor. No great title is efficient
without clothes to support it.
        . . . Is the human race a joke? Was it devised and patched
together in a dull time when there was nothing important to do?
Has it no respect for itself? . . . I think my respect of it is drooping,
sinking—and my respect for myself along with it. . . . There is but
one restorative—*clothes!* respect-reviving, spirit-uplifting clothes!
heaven's kindliest gift to man, his only protection against finding
himself out: they deceive him, they confer dignity upon him;
without them he has none. How charitable are clothes, how

beneficent, how puissant, how inestimably precious! Mine are able to expand a human cipher into a globe-shadowing portent; they can command the respect of the whole world—including my own, which is fading. I will put them on.
     **Mark Twain**

Put on the costume of the country you visit, but keep the clothes you will need to go home in.
     **Denis Diderot**

No one finds difficulty in assenting to the commonplace that the greater part of the expenditure incurred by all classes for apparel is incurred for the sake of respectable appearance rather than for the protection of the person. And probably at no other point is the sense of shabbiness so keenly felt as it is if we fall short of the standard set by social usage in this matter of dress. It is true of dress in even a higher degree than of most other items of consumption, that people will undergo a very considerable degree of privation in the comforts or the necessaries of life in order to afford what is considered a decent amount of wasteful consumption; so that it is by no means an uncommon occurrence, in an inclement climate, for people to go ill clad in order to appear well dressed. And the commercial value of the goods used for clothing in any modern community is made up to a much larger extent of the fashionableness, the reputability of the goods than of the mechanical service which they render in clothing the person or the wearer. The need of dress is eminently a "higher" or spiritual need.
     **Thorstein Veblen**

Long before I am near enough to talk to you on the street, in a meeting, or at a party, you announce your sex, age and class to me through what you are wearing—and very possibly give me important information (or misinformation) as to your occupation, origin, personality, opinions, tastes, sexual desires and current mood. . . . By the time we meet and converse we have already spoken to each other in an older and more universal tongue.
     **Alison Lurie**

We currently have very different gut feelings about male and female cross-dressing. Women's wearing of male clothes—pants with front

flies, button-down shirts, ties, even tuxedos—goes unremarked or at most, is 'cute' in paradoxically accentuating the femininity of the wearer. A woman wearing such clothes remains a woman. She is not 'passing for a man' or engaging in transvestism. But consider a man in a skirt. For one thing, men who want to be thought of as masculine do not wear female clothing in public, except occasionally to costume parties—where the very fact of cross-dressing is hilarious (rather than adorable). He is seen as imitating, if not becoming, a woman, with very different audience response depending on the verisimilitude of the imitation. A man who is too good at it creates nervousness; a man who leaves traces of his masculinity (beard, chest hair) is seen as only kidding, and that is funny. But men do not ever casually adopt female fashions as women do men's. Similarly, in part as a badge of togetherness, women often appropriate 'their' men's pajama tops, old shirts, sweaters. The reverse never occurs.
                    **Robin Lakoff and Raquel Scherr**

Tradition in clothes may well outlast tradition in occupation. When Sandra Day O'Connor was sworn in as the first woman to serve on the United States Supreme Court, there was no mistaking which one she was in the formal group picture. Eight smiling justices wore trousers and long black judicial robes that came to the ankles and one smiling justice wore a specially hemmed robe that came to the knees. Justice O'Connor was the one in nylon stockings.
                    **Susan Brownmiller**

Skin, if it is attractive, can be part of the design.
                    **Rudi Gernreich**

Architecture is to be regarded by us with the most serious thought. We may live without her, and worship without her, but we cannot remember without her. How cold is all history, how lifeless all imagery, compared to that which the living nation writes, and the uncorrupted marble bears!—how many pages of doubtful record might we not often spare, for a few stones left one upon another! The ambition of the old Babel builders was well directed for this world: there are but two strong conquerors of the forgetfulness of men. Poetry and Architecture; and the latter in some sort includes the former, and is mightier in its reality: it is well to have, not only what men have thought and felt, but what their hands have

handled, and their strength wrought, and their eyes beheld, all the days of their life.
**John Ruskin**

We shall live to see the day, I trust, when no man shall build his house for posterity. . . . He might just as reasonably order a durable suit of clothes . . . so that his great-grandchildren should cut precisely the same figure in the world. . . . I doubt whether even one public edifice . . . should be built of such permanent materials. . . . Better that they should crumble to ruin, once in twenty years or thereabouts, as a hint to the people to reform the institutions which they symbolize.
**Nathaniel Hawthorne,** *The House of the Seven Gables*

If I had to say which was telling the truth about society, a speech by a Minister of Housing or the actual buildings put up in his time, I should believe the buildings.
**Kenneth Clark**

A house is a machine for living.
**Le Corbusier**

I like a man who likes to see a fine barn as well as a good tragedy.
**Ralph Waldo Emerson**

## Roger B. Swain

# Firewood

Grandfather holds up his pants with a piece of string. He  1
has a belt somewhere, but he has lots more string—from bakery boxes,
packages that came in the mail, bales of hay. It is all unknotted, rolled
up, saved, and eventually reused to lengthen a clothesline, to splint
a cracked chair rung, even to gather up firewood.

Fascinated by a man who is knotted instead of buckled, his grand-  2
son follows him across the broad side lawn of the farm into the maple
woods. There the two of them collect dead branches, breaking them
into short, even lengths. When they have a pile, they tie the sticks into
a tight bundle with a piece of string, and carry the bundle back to the
house, down the kitchen stairs, and add it to the pile of firewood
behind the fruit-room door.

Years later, as the boy learns to use a hatchet and then an axe, he  3
cuts thicker firewood, chopping up branches that are too thick to break
just by stepping on them. Sometimes he chops down small trees,
shouting, "Timber!" when they fall. The small sticks his grandfather
still gathers have become kindling, not real firewood.

Today he owns a chain saw and in a few noisy, smoky, vibration-  4
filled minutes, he can cut down a tree two feet in diameter. A tree that
big contains a cord and a half of wood—a good part of the winter's
wood supply. And he cuts it in a fraction of the time it takes his grandfather to pick up an equal amount of sticks.

All his friends have chain saws. Even those who have discovered  5
that it doesn't take a 24-inch-long blade to cut down a 24-inch-diameter
tree are buying bigger chain saws to speed up their firewood cutting.
There is no place for an old man and his used string in a modern forest,
where men safely swaddled in earmuffs, face shields, and cut-proof
pants rip down trees, their two-cycle engines shattering the Sunday
silence.

Cutting down a big tree has become easy, but a tree two feet in  6

Roger Swain was born in Cambridge, Massachusetts, in 1949. He is the science
editor for *Horticulture* magazine and a regular contributor to other publications,
including *The New York Times* and *Technology Illustrated*. Swain lives outside
Boston and on a small farm in New Hampshire.

diameter, even when it is sawn into short lengths, won't fit into a wood stove. It must be split. Driving steel wedges with a sledgehammer takes the build of a blacksmith, the spirit of a gandy dancer. No one likes splitting wood for very long. Those who have split the most are the ones who crowd around demonstrations of mechanical wood splitters at county fairs, watching the fat, shiny, hydraulic piston advance and retreat, each time easily dividing a log in two. Mesmerized by a machine that does so easily what each of them has struggled with, the spectators have only two questions: "How much does it cost?" they ask the demonstrator, and "Couldn't I build one like that myself?" they ask themselves.

None of them question whether the logs need to be split, for logs   7
that size can't be burned otherwise. But do the logs need to be split, or rather, should we be splitting logs? Foresters are alarmed when they see a truckload of cordwood cut from large trees. In the northeastern United States, foresters warn us, there won't be any trees left for lumber if all the prime sawlogs are thoughtlessly butchered into 16-inch lengths. The big trees, with straight, sound boles, should be sawn into boards—made into steaks, not ground beef.

Even if splitting logs isn't squandering board feet of lumber, it is   8
wasting energy when you consider how difficult it is to pass a huge log through the door of a wood stove. Splitting wood with sledges and wedges, with a splitting maul, or with (heaven forbid) an axe is good exercise that quickly becomes exhausting. If you have a mechanical log splitter, you must count not only the cost of the gasoline, but the energy used in the manufacture of the machine itself, the steel, the aluminum, the rubber.

By the time you have reduced a log to firewood, the firewood   9
gathered by grandfather looks pretty good. The so-called kindling looks as if it might serve as a main course for a fire, not just the appetizer. Gathering up sticks may take a little more time, but it takes a lot less energy and hardly any strength.

In New England, where the pastures have grown up to trees,   10
where stone walls now lead off into the forest, there is such an abundance of wood that it is easy to understand how people get lost in it and end up wishing they could afford a mechanical log splitter. There is simply so much vegetation that people can't see clear to the economies.

In the rest of the world, however, where the forests are still being   11
converted to pastures, if not deserts, wood is in short supply. The scarcity is a lot more serious than a lack of bean poles for the garden.

There is not enough wood to cook food and keep warm. The problem is most serious in the countries of the Indian subcontinent, central Africa south of the Sahara, the Andes of South America, Central America, and the Caribbean. Firewood is now more than a day's walk from Katmandu if you gather it yourself, and a quarter of a family's yearly income if you buy it in town in Niger. Industrial nations dominate the world news with concern over the oil and coal supply, but scarcely any printer's ink is used to chronicle a much more serious energy shortage: the daily concern of the two billion people who do 90 percent of their cooking and heating with wood or charcoal.

The late Mao Zedong said, "Forestry supports agriculture." What      12
he meant was that an adequate food supply without a means to cook it is a tin can without a can opener. A shortage of wood not only makes it difficult to digest what food there is, but it may reduce the harvest itself. In India, Pakistan, Bangladesh, and a great many countries where firewood is scarce or nonexistent, people are burning dried dung. This generates heat but at the same time it deprives cropland of essential nutrients and organic matter. India's National Commission on Agriculture has gone so far as to declare that the use of cow dung as a source of noncommercial fuel is virtually a crime.

In an effort to conserve existing supplies of firewood, stove de-      13
signers everywhere are experimenting with more efficient cooking stoves. These stoves, simple in design and built from locally abundant materials like sand, clay, and old beer cans, focus the flames on the cooking surface. The pots are arranged to fit tightly, and in such a way that hot gases flow around them. The aim of the designers is to produce an inexpensive stove with an overall fuel efficiency of 20 to 30 percent, reducing the current wood requirement five- to tenfold.

With an increasing global population, however, conservation will      14
not be enough. More firewood needs to be grown, and this means both better management of existing forests and the planting of new ones. Massive reforestation programs are easy to design and difficult to implement. The obstacles that must be overcome range from politics to herds of cattle, sheep, and goats that will destroy any newly planted seedlings. But firewood can be grown as a crop, and on land that is too rocky, too wet, or too steep for conventional agriculture.

The choice of which kind of trees to grow for firewood will depend      15
on the site, but, in general, the trees will be pioneer species, the kind that grow up following a forest fire or landslide. Since the bare expanses of land created by man and his animals are as desolate as any

created by a natural disaster, the colonists need to be as vigorous and adaptable as possible. Some of the trees, like alder and various legumes, will be ones that can fix their own nitrogen. Others, like ailanthus, will be trees that grow so vigorously we call them weeds. Most important, they will be species that regenerate rapidly and spontaneously after they are cut for firewood.

Anyone who has tried to get rid of a red maple by cutting it down  16 knows that it won't work. You can cut the tree down to the ground and mow over it repeatedly, and the tree keeps sending up sprouts from the stump. When you are trying to make a clearing in the woods, this endless sprouting can drive you to herbicide. Ignore the sprouts and in a few years you have woods again, a dense thicket of many small trunks.

Nineteenth-century Victorian novels are full of such thickets, or  17 coppices, as they were called. Since then, most people have forgotten exactly what the word means, but it is coming back into common usage. In the last year both the National Academy of Sciences and the *Next Whole Earth Catalog* have expounded on the virtues of coppicing as a way to solve the world's energy crisis.

If you want to grow trees for firewood, they should be ones that  18 coppice well; that is, they should grow rapidly from stump sprouts or root suckers once the original tree has been cut down.

Given enough time, say, sixty to one hundred years, a coppice  19 will come to resemble an ordinary wood, most of the trunks having been shaded out and killed by a few especially vigorous ones. Traditionally, however, a coppice is harvested every five to twenty years, at a time when the cutting yields a lot of small poles. While it takes only one tree, 21 inches in diameter at breast height, to supply a cord of firewood, it takes ninety trees if each measures only 3 inches. Nevertheless, a coppice of aspen after ten years of growth may contain five thousand such poles in an acre, or about fifty cords of firewood.

Many tree species coppice well: among northern temperate spe-  20 cies, white ash, aspen, basswood (*Tilia*), black locust, chestnut, maple, oak, and tulip tree (*Liriodendron*). How often the trees are cut depends in part on the species. Willows for basketmaking are cut annually. For other trees, ten years is a common rotation. Some living trees have been cut down every decade for more than three centuries.

Coppice regrowth is harvested in the dormant season if possible,  21 from three weeks after leaf fall to six weeks before bud break. Cuts are sloping and made close to the ground because a smooth, slanted cut sheds water, and the sprouts that arise from the root collar at or below the ground surface are the most vigorous and the least susceptible to rot.

In places where grazing animals might devour the new shoots, a  22 modified cutting technique called pollarding is used. Here the original trunk is cut 4 to 12 feet above the ground and a cluster of sprouts develops at that height. These, in turn, are cut every fifteen years or less to prevent their becoming so thick that they break off and damage the pollard head. The trunks that remain can be used as living fence posts.

Coppicing is an ancient method of tree management going back  23 in Europe some three thousand years to the Neolithic Age. In Great Britain, woodsmen managed coppices for the production of poles, firewood, and small wood for fences. Foresters, on the other hand, managed large trees for lumber. At a time when "by hook or by crook" referred to the right to gather whatever dead wood could be pulled down with a stick, the woodsman was more important than the forester. In the United States, oak and chestnut were once coppiced to produce charcoal. Before the widespread use of coal, whole hillsides were cut, or "coaled," for making iron and steel.

There are three advantages to coppicing. First, it eliminates the  24 need to plant a new seedling for each tree that is cut down. At the time a trunk is cut, there is a well-established root system that will hold the soil on steep slopes and thus prevent erosion, and will also feed the new sprouts, permitting their rapid growth.

Second, by concentrating the crop in that period of the tree's life  25 cycle when growth is most rapid, the annual production of wood from a given area reaches a maximum. Whereas an unmanaged forest may produce as little as a ton of dry firewood per acre per year, a well-managed coppice will produce ten times that. A family of four needs about 0.9 tons of firewood for cooking each year, and in a well-managed coppice that much firewood can be grown in an area 65 feet on a side. Some tree species have given even higher yields. Chestnut coppices in England have yielded 18 tons per acre per year, and the tropical legume tree *Leucaena leucocephala* has yielded 40 tons.

Finally, wood that is harvested after no more than a couple of  26 decades is conveniently small. Critics will claim that much of it is brushwood, too small to burn. But they are the kind of people who own log splitters and advocate using giant machines to chop up whole trees to burn in power plants. Small wood is convenient. It doesn't require a chain saw to cut it down or cut it up. It doesn't need splitting. It dries rapidly. And you can tie up bundles of it with string.

Coppicing is sure to become an established practice wherever fire- 27 wood plantations are established. But as long as half the wood being cut is still being used for cooking and heating, why should coppicing be relegated to Timbuktu? Even in the industrialized countries, people are returning to wood as a source of heat. The advantages of coppicing are the same in everyone's backyard, temperate or tropical, under-developed or overdeveloped. Grandfather, of course, must have known this all along: neatly tied bundles of firewood economize on more than string.

## Questions

1.  Paragraph 1 is engaging, but it is also functional. How does this descriptive paragraph relate to Swain's thesis?
2.  If we assume that the "grandson" referred to in paragraphs 2, 3, and 4 is Swain himself, why does Swain use the third person instead of the first person?
3.  Swain begins paragraph 18 by saying, "If you want to grow trees for firewood. . . ." He has nowhere explicitly said that we *should* grow trees for firewood, but he has been quietly arguing in that direction. Trace his argument up to this point.
4.  In a paragraph summarize Swain's essay, making explicit his thesis.
5.  Write an opening paragraph describing a person (as Swain does), and then in a second paragraph explain how your first paragraph, apparently descriptive, could be used to introduce and support a thesis. Note that this second paragraph, unlike the first, is not part of an imagined essay, but is an explanation of where you would go, and why.

Peter Farb and George Armelagos

# The Patterns of Eating

$A$mong the important societal rules that represent one    1
component of cuisine are table manners. As a socially instilled form
of conduct, they reveal the attitudes typical of a society. Changes in
table manners through time, as they have been documented for western Europe, likewise reflect fundamental changes in human relationships. Medieval courtiers saw their table manners as distinguishing
them from crude peasants; but by modern standards, the manners
were not exactly refined. Feudal lords used their unwashed hands to
scoop food from a common bowl and they passed around a single
goblet from which all drank. A finger or two would be extended while
eating, so as to be kept free of grease and thus available for the next
course, or for dipping into spices and condiments—possibly accounting for today's "polite" custom of extending the finger while holding
a spoon or small fork. Soups and sauces were commonly drunk by
lifting the bowl to the mouth; several diners frequently ate from the
same bread trencher. Even lords and nobles would toss gnawed bones
back into the common dish, wolf down their food, spit onto the table
(preferred conduct called for spitting under it), and blew their noses
into the tablecloth.

By about the beginning of the sixteenth century, table manners    2
began to move in the direction of today's standards. The importance
attached to them is indicated by the phenomenal success of a treatise,
*On Civility in Children,* by the philosopher Erasmus, which appeared
in 1530; reprinted more than thirty times in the next six years, it also
appeared in numerous translations. Erasmus' idea of good table manners was far from modern, but it did represent an advance. He believed, for example, that an upper class diner was distinguished by
putting only three fingers of one hand into the bowl, instead of the
entire hand in the manner of the lower class. Wait a few moments
after being seated before you dip into it, he advises. Do not poke
around in your dish, but take the first piece you touch. Do not put

Peter Farb (1929–1980) was a naturalist, linguist, anthropologist, and spokesman
for conservation. George Armelagos is a professor of anthropology at the University of Massachusetts, Amherst.

chewed food from the mouth back on your plate; instead, throw it under the table or behind your chair.

By the time of Erasmus, the changing table manners reveal a fundamental shift in society. People no longer ate from the same dish or drank from the same goblet, but were divided from one another by a new wall of constraint. Once the spontaneous, direct, and informal manners of the Middle Ages had been repressed, people began to feel shame. Defecation and urination were now regarded as private activities; handkerchiefs came into use for blowing the nose; nightclothes were now worn, and bedrooms were set apart as private areas. Before the sixteenth century, even nobles ate in their vast kitchens; only then did a special room designated for eating come into use away from the bloody sides of meat, the animals about to be slaughtered, and the bustling servants. These new inhibitions became the essence of "civilized" behavior, distinguishing adults from children, the upper classes from the lower, and Europeans from the "savages" then being discovered around the world. Restraint in eating habits became more marked in the centuries that followed. By about 1800, napkins were in common use, and before long they were placed on the thighs rather than wrapped around the neck; coffee and tea were no longer slurped out of the saucer; bread was genteelly broken into small pieces with the fingers rather than cut into large chunks with a knife.   3

Numerous paintings that depict meals—with subjects such as the Last Supper, the wedding at Cana, or Herod's feast—show what dining tables looked like before the seventeenth century. Forks were not depicted until about 1600 (when Jacopo Bassano painted one in a Last Supper), and very few spoons were shown. At least one knife is always depicted—an especially large one when it is the only one available for all the guests—but small individual knives were often at each place. Tin disks or oval pieces of wood had already replaced the bread trenchers. This change in eating utensils typified the new table manners in Europe. (In many other parts of the world, no utensils at all were used. In the Near East, for example, it was traditional to bring food to the mouth with the fingers of the right hand, the left being unacceptable because it was reserved for wiping the buttocks.) Utensils were employed in part because of a change in the attitude toward meat. During the Middle Ages, whole sides of meat, or even an entire dead animal, had been brought to the table and then carved in view of the diners. Beginning in the seventeenth century, at first in France but later elsewhere, the practice began to go out of fashion. One reason was that the family was ceasing to be a production unit that did its own slaugh-   4 tering; as that function was transferred to specialists outside the home, the family became essentially a consumption unit. In addition, the size of the family was decreasing, and consequently whole animals, or even large parts of them, were uneconomical. The cuisines of Europe reflected these social and economic changes. The animal origin of meat dishes was concealed by the arts of preparation. Meat itself became distasteful to look upon, and carving was moved out of sight to the kitchen. Comparable changes had already taken place in Chinese cuisine, with meat being cut up beforehand, unobserved by the diners. England was an exception to the change in Europe, and in its former colonies—the United States, Canada, Australia, and South Africa— the custom has persisted of bringing a joint of meat to the table to be carved.

Once carving was no longer considered a necessary skill among   5 the well-bred, changes inevitably took place in the use of the knife, unquestionably the earliest utensil used for manipulating food. (In fact, the earliest English cookbooks were not so much guides to recipes as guides to carving meat.) The attitude of diners toward the knife, going back to the Middle Ages and the Renaissance, had always been ambivalent. The knife served as a utensil, but it offered a potential threat because it was also a weapon. Thus taboos were increasingly placed upon its use: It was to be held by the point with the blunt handle presented; it was not to be placed anywhere near the face; and most important, the uses to which it was put were sharply restricted. It was not to be used for cutting soft foods such as boiled eggs or fish, or round ones such as potatoes, or to be lifted from the table for courses that did not need it. In short, good table manners in Europe gradually removed the threatening aspect of the knife from social occasions. A similar change had taken place much earlier in China when the warrior was supplanted by the scholar as a cultural model. The knife was banished completely from the table in favor of chopsticks, which is why the Chinese came to regard Europeans as barbarians at their table who "eat with swords."

The fork in particular enabled Europeans to separate themselves   6 from the eating process, even avoiding manual contact with their food. When the fork first appeared in Europe, toward the end of the Middle Ages, it was used solely as an instrument for lifting chunks from the common bowl. Beginning in the sixteenth century, the fork was increasingly used by members of the upper classes—first in Italy, then in France, and finally in Germany and England. By then, social relations in western Europe had so changed that a utensil was needed to spare diners from the "uncivilized" and distasteful necessity of picking up food and putting it into the mouth with the fingers. The addition of the fork to the table was once said to be for reasons of hygiene, but this cannot be true. By the sixteenth century people were no longer eating from a common bowl but from their own plates, and since they also washed their hands before meals, their fingers were now every bit as hygienic as a fork would have been. Nor can the reason for the adoption of the fork be connected with the wish not to soil the long ruff that was worn on the sleeve at the time, since the fork was also adopted in various countries where ruffs were not then in fashion.

Along with the appearance of the fork, all table utensils began to   7
change and proliferate from the sixteenth century onward. Soup was no longer eaten directly from the dish, but each diner used an individual spoon for that purpose. When a diner wanted a second helping from the serving dish, a ladle or a fresh spoon was used. More and more special utensils were developed for each kind of food: soup spoons, oyster forks, salad forks, two-tined fondue forks, blunt butter knives, special utensils for various desserts and kinds of fruit, each one differently shaped, of a different size, with differently numbered prongs and with blunt or serrated edges. The present European pattern eventually emerged, in which each person is provided with a table setting of as many as a dozen utensils at a full-course meal. With that, the separation of the human body from the taking of food became virtually complete. Good table manners dictated that even the cobs of maize were to be held by prongs inserted in each end, and the bones of lamb chops covered by ruffled paper pantalettes. Only under special conditions—as when Western people consciously imitate an earlier stage in culture at a picnic, fish fry, cookout, or campfire—do they still tear food apart with their fingers and their teeth, in a nostalgic reenactment of eating behaviors long vanished.

Today's neighborhood barbecue recreates a world of sharing and   8
hospitality that becomes rarer each year. We regard as a curiosity the behavior of hunters in exotic regions. But every year millions of North Americans take to the woods and lakes to kill a wide variety of animals—with a difference, of course: What hunters do for survival we do for sport (and also for proof of masculinity, for male bonding, and for various psychological rewards). Like hunters, too, we stuff ourselves almost whenever food is available. Nibbling on a roasted ear of maize gives us, in addition to nutrients, the satisfaction of participating in culturally simpler ways. A festive meal, however, is still thought of in Victorian terms, with the dominant male officiating over the roast,

the dominant female apportioning vegetables, the extended family gathered around the table, with everything in its proper place—a revered picture, as indeed it was so painted by Norman Rockwell, yet one that becomes less accurate with each year that passes.

# Questions

1. Reverse the first sentence (begin with "Table manners" and end with "cuisine"). Which order is more usual? Why did the authors choose the order they did?
2. If your library has a copy of *On Civility in Children*, cull three other examples of Erasmus's recommendations.
3. Find the first edition (or at least an early edition) of Emily Post's book of etiquette. What rules of etiquette strike you as being quaint?
4. How do Farb and Armelagos account for feelings of shame associated with urination and defecation? Does their reasoning strike you as plausible?
5. Study a reproduction of a pre-seventeenth century painting that depicts a meal (for instance, da Vinci's *The Last Supper*). Then describe and analyze the food, the table utensils, and the postures and manners of the diners.
6. Describe and analyze a contemporary meal: a church or fraternal picnic, a family holiday meal, or a dormitory breakfast. What social attitudes or values does it embody and reveal?
7. "Parents are often irritated by their childrens' table manners; equally often children are revulsed by the eating habits of their parents or other adults." Write a brief essay (approximately 500 words) using this sentence as your thesis.

Michael J. Arlen

# Ode to Thanksgiving

It is time, at last, to speak the truth about Thanksgiving,   1
and the truth is this. Thanksgiving is really not such a terrific holiday.
Consider the traditional symbols of the event: Dried cornhusks hanging on the door! Terrible wine! Cranberry jelly in little bowls of extremely doubtful provenance which everyone is required to handle with the greatest of care! Consider the participants, the merrymakers: men and women (also children) who have survived passably well throughout the years, mainly as a result of living at considerable distances from their dear parents and beloved siblings, who on this feast of feasts must apparently forgather (as if beckoned by an aberrant Fairy Godmother), usually by circuitous routes, through heavy traffic, at a common meeting place, where the very moods, distempers, and obtrusive personal habits that have kept them all happily apart since adulthood are then and there encouraged to slowly ferment beneath the cornhusks, and gradually rise with the aid of the terrible wine, and finally burst forth out of control under the stimulus of the cranberry jelly! No, it is a mockery of a holiday. For instance: *Thank you, O Lord, for what we are about to receive.* This is surely not a gala concept. There are no presents, unless one counts Aunt Bertha's sweet rolls a present, which no one does. There is precious little in the way of costumery: miniature plastic turkeys and those witless Pilgrim hats. There is no sex. Indeed, Thanksgiving is the one day of the year (a fact known to everybody) when all thoughts of sex completely vanish, evaporating from apartments, houses, condominiums, and mobile homes like steam from a bathroom mirror.

Consider also the nowhereness of the time of year: the last week   2
or so in November. It is obviously not yet winter: winter, with its death-dealing blizzards and its girls in tiny skirts pirouetting on the ice. On the other hand, it is certainly not much use to anyone as fall; no golden leaves or Oktoberfests, and so forth. Instead, it is a no-man's land between the seasons. In the cold and sobersides northern half of the country, it is a vaguely unsettling interregnum of long, mournful walks

Michael Arlen was born in London in 1930. He came to the United States in 1940, and in time became a reporter and then an essayist.

beneath leafless trees: the long, mournful walks following the midday repast with the dread inevitability of pie following turkey, and the leafless trees looming or standing about like eyesores, and the ground either as hard as iron or slightly mushy, and the light snow always beginning to fall when one is halfway to the old green gate—flecks of cold, watery stuff plopping between neck and collar, for the reason that, it being not yet winter, one has forgotten or not chosen to bring along a muffler. It is a corollary to the long, mournful Thanksgiving walk that the absence of this muffler is quickly noticed and that four weeks or so later, at Christmastime, instead of the Sony Betamax one had secretly hoped the children might have chipped in to purchase, one receives another muffler: by then the thirty-third. Thirty-three mufflers! Some walk! Of course, things are more fun in the warm and loony southern part of the country. No snow there of any kind. No need of mufflers. Also, no long, mournful walks, because in the warm and loony southern part of the country everybody drives. So everybody drives over to Uncle Jasper's house to watch the Cougars play the Gators, a not entirely unimportant conflict which will determine whether the Gators get a Bowl bid or must take another post-season exhibition tour of North Korea. But no sooner do the Cougars kick off (an astonishing end-over-end squiggly thing that floats lazily above the arena before plummeting down toward K. C. McCoy and catching him on the helmet) than Auntie Em starts hustling turkey. Soon Cousin May is slamming around the bowls and platters, and Cousin Bernice is oohing and ahing about "all the fixin's," and Uncle Bob is making low, insincere sounds of appreciation: "Yummy, yummy, Auntie Em, I'll have me some more of these delicious yams!" Delicious yams? Uncle Bob's eyes roll wildly in his head. Billy Joe Quaglino throws his long bomb in the middle of Grandpa Morris saying grace, Grandpa Morris speaking so low nobody can hear him, which is just as well, since he is reciting what he can remember of his last union contract. And then, just as J. B. (Speedy) Snood begins his ninety-two-yard punt return, Auntie Em starts dealing everyone second helpings of her famous stuffing, as if she were pushing a controlled substance, which it well might be, since there are no easily recognizable ingredients visible to the naked eye.

Consider for a moment the Thanksgiving meal itself. It has become a sort of refuge for endangered species of starch: cauliflower, turnips, pumpkin, mince (whatever "mince" is), those blessed yams. Bowls of luridly colored yams, with no taste at all, lying torpid under a lava flow of marshmallow! And then the sacred turkey. One might as well

3

try to construct a holiday repast around a fish—say, a nice piece of boiled haddock. After all, turkey tastes very similar to haddock: same consistency, same quite remarkable absence of flavor. But then, if the Thanksgiving *pièce de résistance* were a nice piece of boiled haddock instead of turkey, there wouldn't be all that fun for Dad when Mom hands him the sterling-silver, bone-handled carving set (a wedding present from her parents and not sharpened since) and then everyone sits around pretending not to watch while he saws and tears away at the bird as if he were trying to burrow his way into or out of some grotesque, fowllike prison.

What of the good side to Thanksgiving, you ask. There is always 4 a good side to everything. Not to Thanksgiving. There is only a bad side and then a worse side. For instance, Grandmother's best linen tablecloth is a bad side: the fact that it is produced each year, in the manner of a red flag being produced before a bull, and then is always spilled upon by whichever child is doing poorest at school that term and so is in need of greatest reassurance. Thus: "Oh, my God, *Veronica*, you just spilled grape juice (or plum wine or tar) on Grandmother's best linen tablecloth!" But now comes worse. For at this point Cousin Bill, the one who lost all Cousin Edwina's money on the car dealership three years ago and has apparently been drinking steadily since Halloween, bizarrely chooses to say: "Seems to me those old glasses are always falling over." To which Auntie Meg is heard to add: "Somehow I don't remember receivin' any of those old glasses." To which Uncle Fred replies: "That's because you and George decided to go on vacation to Hawaii the summer Grandpa Sam was dying." Now Grandmother is sobbing, though not so uncontrollably that she can refrain from murmuring: "I think that volcano painting I threw away by mistake got sent me from Hawaii, heaven knows why." But the gods are merciful, even the Pilgrim-hatted god of cornhusks and soggy stuffing, and there is an end to everything, even to Thanksgiving. Indeed, there is a grandeur to the feelings of finality and doom which usually settle on a house after the Thanksgiving celebration is over, for with the completion of Thanksgiving Day the year itself has been properly terminated: shot through the cranium with a high-velocity candied yam. At this calendrical nadir, all energy on the planet has gone, all fun has fled, all the terrible wine has been drunk.

But then, overnight, life once again begins to stir, emerging, even 5 by the next morning, in the form of Japanese window displays and Taiwanese Christmas lighting, from the primeval ooze of the nation's department stores. Thus, a new year dawns, bringing with it immediate and cheering possibilities of extended consumer debt, office-party flirtations, good—or, at least mediocre—wine and visions of Supersaver excursion fares to Montego Bay. It is worth noting, perhaps, that this true new year always starts with the same mute, powerful mythic ceremony: the surreptitious tossing out, in the early morning, of all those horrid aluminum-foil packages of yams and cauliflower and stuffing and red, gummy cranberry substance which have been squeezed into the refrigerator as if a reenactment of the siege of Paris were shortly expected. Soon afterward, the phoenix of Christmas can be observed as it slowly rises, beating its drumsticks, once again goggle-eyed with hope and unrealistic expectations.

# Questions

1. Judging from paragraph 1 alone do you think Arlen is entirely serious? Support your view with evidence.
2. Let's assume that at least some of Arlen's sentences strike you as interesting. Analyze a few such sentences, accounting for their effect.

**Paul Goldberger**

---

# Quick! Before It Crumbles!

**An Architecture Critic Looks at Cookie Architecture**

*Sugar Wafer (Nabisco)*

There is no attempt to imitate the ancient forms of traditional, indi-   1
vidually baked cookies here—this is a modern cookie through and
through. Its simple rectangular form, clean and pure, just reeks of mass
production and modern technological methods. The two wafers, held
together by the sugar-cream filling, appear to float, and the Nabisco
trademark, stamped repeatedly across the top, confirms that this is a
machine-age object. Clearly the Sugar Wafer is the Mies van der Rohe
of cookies.

*Fig Newton (Nabisco)*

This, too, is a sandwich but different in every way from the Sugar   2
Wafer. Here the imagery is more traditional, more sensual even; a
rounded form of cookie dough arcs over the fig concoction inside, and

---

Paul Goldberger is the architecture critic for *The New York Times.* He has also
contributed articles to various magazines, and is the author of *The City Observed*,
a book about the architecture of Manhattan.

the whole is soft and pliable. Like all good pieces of design, it has an appropriate form for its use, since the insides of Fig Newtons can ooze and would not be held in place by a more rigid form. The thing could have had a somewhat different shape, but the rounded top is a comfortable, familiar image, and it's easy to hold. Not a revolutionary object but an intelligent one.

## Milano (Pepperidge Farms)

This long, chocolate-filled cookie summons up contradictory associations. Its rounded ends suggest both the traditional image of stodgy ladyfingers and the curves of Art Deco, while the subtle yet forceful "V" embossed onto the surface creates an abstract image of force and movement. The "V" is the kind of ornament that wishes to appear modern without really being modern, which would have meant banning ornament altogether. That romantic symbolism of the modern was an Art Deco characteristic, of course; come to think of it the Milano is rather Art Deco in spirit.

## Mallomar (Nabisco)

This marshmallow, chocolate and cracker combination is the ultimate sensual cookie—indeed, its resemblance to the female breast has been cited so often as to sound rather trite. But the cookie's imagery need not be read so literally—the voluptuousness of the form, which with its nipped waist rather resembles the New Orleans Superdome, is enough. Like all good pieces of design, the form of the cookie is primarily derived from functional needs, but with just enough distinction to make it instantly identifiable. The result is a cultural icon—the cookie equivalent, surely, of the Coke bottle.

*Lorna Doone (Nabisco)*

Like the Las Vegas casino that is overwhelmed by its sign, image is all   5
in the Lorna Doone. It is a plain, simple cookie (of shortbread, in fact), but a cookie like all other cookies—except for its sign. The Lorna Doone logo, a four-pointed star with the cookie's name and a pair of fleur-de-lis-like decorations, covers the entire surface of the cookie in low relief. Cleverly, the designers of this cookie have placed the logo so that the points of the star align with the corners of the square, forcing one to pivot the cookie forty-five degrees, so that its shape appears instead to be a diamond. It is a superb example of the ordinary made extraordinary.

*Oatmeal Peanut Sandwich (Sunshine)*

If the Sugar Wafer is the Mies van der Rohe of cookies, this is the   6
Robert Venturi—not pretentiously modern but, rather, eager to prove

its ordinariness, its lack of real design, and in so zealous a way that it ends up looking far dowdier than a *really* ordinary cookie like your basic gingersnap. The Oatmeal Peanut Sandwich is frumpy, like a plump matron in a flower-print dress, or an old piece of linoleum. But it is frumpy in an intentional way and not by accident—one senses that the designers of this cookie knew the Venturi principle that the average user of architecture (read eater of cookies) is far more comfortable with plain, ordinary forms that do not require him to adjust radically any of his perceptions.

# Questions

1.  How seriously do you take these descriptions? Do they have any point, or are they sheer fooling around?
2.  Explain—to someone who does not understand them—the references, in context, to Mies van der Rohe, Art Deco, the New Orleans Superdome, and Robert Venturi. If you had to do some research, explain what sources you used and how you located the sources. What difficulties, if any, did you encounter?
3.  Explicate Goldberger's final sentence on the Mallomar: "The result is a cultural icon—the cookie equivalent, surely, of the Coke bottle."
4.  Write a similar description of some cookie not discussed by Goldberger. Or write a description, along these lines, of a McDonald's hamburger, a BLT, and a hero sandwich. Other possibilities: a pizza, a bagel, and a taco.

Henry David Thoreau

# As for Clothing

As for Clothing, to come at once to the practical part of    1
the question, perhaps we are led oftener by the love of novelty and a
regard for the opinions of men, in procuring it, than by a true utility.
Let him who has work to do recollect that the object of clothing is,
first, to retain the vital heat, and secondly, in this state of society, to
cover nakedness, and he may judge how much of any necessary or
important work may be accomplished without adding to his wardrobe.
Kings and queens who wear a suit but once, though made by some
tailor or dressmaker to their majesties, cannot know the comfort of
wearing a suit that fits. They are no better than wooden horses to hang
the clean clothes on. Every day our garments become more assimilated
to ourselves, receiving the impress of the wearer's character, until we
hesitate to lay them aside, without such delay and medical appliances
and some such solemnity even as our bodies. No man ever stood the
lower in my estimation for having a patch in his clothes; yet I am sure
that there is greater anxiety, commonly, to have fashionable, or at least
clean and unpatched clothes, than to have a sound conscience. But
even if the rent is not mended, perhaps the worst vice betrayed is
improvidence. I sometimes try my acquaintances by such tests as
these,—Who could wear a patch, or two extra seams only, over the
knee? Most have as if they believed that their prospects for life would
be ruined if they should do it. It would be easier for them to hobble
to town with a broken leg than with a broken pantaloon. Often if an
accident happens to a gentleman's legs, they can be mended; but if a
similar accident happens to the legs of his pantaloons, there is no help
for it; for he considers, not what is truly respectable, but what is respected. We know but few men, a great many coats and breeches.
Dress a scarecrow in your last shift, you standing shiftless by, who

---

Henry David Thoreau (1817–1862) was born in Concord, Massachusetts, where
he spent most of his life ("I have travelled a good deal in Concord"). He taught
and lectured, but chiefly he observed, thought, and wrote. From July 5, 1845, to
September 6, 1847, he lived near Concord in a cabin at Walden Pond, an experience recorded in *Walden* (1854).

"As for Clothing" (editors' title) comes from *Walden*, Chapter 1.

would not soonest salute the scarecrow? Passing a cornfield the other day, close by a hat and coat on a stake, I recognized the owner of the farm. He was only a little more weather-beaten than when I saw him last. I have heard of a dog that barked at every stranger who approached his master's premises with clothes on, but was easily quieted by a naked thief. It is an interesting question how far men would retain their relative rank if they were divested of their clothes. Could you, in such a case, tell surely of any company of civilized men which belonged to the most respected class? When Madam Pfeiffer, in her adventurous travels round the world, from east to west, had got so near home as Asiatic Russia, she says that she felt the necessity of wearing other than a traveling dress, when she went to meet the authorities, for she "was now in a civilized country, where . . . people are judged of by their clothes." Even in our democratic New England towns the accidental possession of wealth, and its manifestation in dress and equipage alone, obtain for the possessor almost universal respect. But they who yield such respect, numerous as they are, are so far heathen, and need to have a missionary sent to them. Beside, clothes introduced sewing, a kind of work which you may call endless; a woman's dress, at least, is never done.

A man who has at length found something to do will not need to get a new suit to do it in; for him the old will do, that has lain dusty in the garret for an indeterminate period. Old shoes will serve a hero longer than they have served his valet,—if a hero even has a valet,— bare feet are older than shoes, and he can make them do. Only they who go to soirées and legislative halls must have new coats, coats to change as often as the man changes in them. But if my jacket and trousers, my hat and shoes, are fit to worship God in, they will do; will they not? Who ever saw his old clothes—his old coat, actually worn out, resolved into its primitive elements, so that it was not a deed of charity to bestow it on some poor boy, by him perchance to be bestowed on some poorer still, or shall we say richer, who could do with less? I say, beware of all enterprises that require new clothes, and not rather a new wearer of clothes. If there is not a new man, how can the new clothes be made to fit? If you have any enterprise before you, try it in your old clothes. All men want, not something to *do with*, but something to *do*, or rather something to *be*. Perhaps we should never procure a new suit, however ragged or dirty the old, until we have so conducted, so enterprised or sailed in some way, that we feel like new men in the old, and that to retain it would be like keeping new wine in old bottles. Our moulting season, like that of the fowls must be a crisis in our lives. The loon retires to solitary ponds to spend it. Thus also the snake casts its slough, and the caterpillar its wormy coat, by an internal industry and expansion; for clothes are but our outmost cuticle and mortal coil. Otherwise we shall be found sailing under false colors, and be inevitably cashiered at last by our own opinion, as well as that of mankind.

We don garment after garment, as if we grew like exogenous plants 3 by addition without. Our outside and often thin and fanciful clothes are our epidermis, or false skin, which partakes not of our life, and may be stripped off here and there without fatal injury; our thicker garments, constantly worn, are our cellular integument, or cortex; but our shirts are our liber,[1] or true bark, which cannot be removed without girdling and so destroying the man. I believe that all races at some seasons wear something equivalent to the shirt. It is desirable that a man be clad so simply that he can lay his hands on himself in the dark, and that he live in all respects so compactly and preparedly, that, if an enemy take the town, he can, like the old philosopher, walk out the gate empty-handed without anxiety. While one thick garment is, for most purposes, as good as three thin ones, and cheap clothing can be obtained at prices really to suit customers; while a thick coat can be bought for five dollars, which will last as many years, thick pantaloons for two dollars, cowhide boots for a dollar and a half a pair, a summer hat for a quarter of a dollar, and a winter cap for sixty-two and a half cents, or a better be made at home at a nominal cost, where is he so poor that, clad in such a suit, *of his own earning*, there will not be found wise men to do him reverence?

When I ask for a garment of a particular form, my tailoress tells 4 me gravely, "They do not make them so now," not emphasizing the "They" at all, as if she quoted an authority as impersonal as the Fates, and I find it difficult to get made what I want, simply because she cannot believe that I mean what I say, that I am so rash. When I hear this oracular sentence, I am for a moment absorbed in thought, emphasizing to myself each word separately that I may come at the meaning of it, that I may find out by what degree of consanguinity *They* are related to *me*, and what authority they may have in an affair which affects me so nearly; and finally, I am inclined to answer her with equal mystery, and without any more emphasis of the "they"—"It is true, they did not make them so recently, but they do now." Of what use this measuring of me if she does not measure my character, but only

[1] Inner bark of a tree. (Editors' note)

the breadth of my shoulders, as it were a peg to hang the coat on? We worship not the Graces, nor the Parcæ, but Fashion. She spins and weaves and cuts with full authority. The head monkey at Paris puts on a traveller's cap, and all the monkeys in America do the same. I sometimes despair of getting anything quite simple and honest done in this world by the help of men. They would have to be passed through a powerful press first, to squeeze their old notions out of them, so that they would not soon get upon their legs again; and then there would be some one in the company with a maggot in his head, hatched from an egg deposited there nobody knows when, for not even fire kills these things, and you would have lost your labor. Nevertheless, we will not forget that some Egyptian wheat was handed down to us by a mummy.

On the whole, I think that it cannot be maintained that dressing    5 has in this or any country risen to the dignity of an art. At present men make shift to wear what they can get. Like shipwrecked sailors, they put on what they can find on the beach, and at a little distance, whether of space or time, laugh at each other's masquerade. Every generation laughs at the old fashions, but follows religiously the new. We are amused at beholding the costume of Henry VIII, or Queen Elizabeth, as much as if it was that of the King and Queen of the Cannibal Islands. All costume off a man is pitiful or grotesque. It is only the serious eye peering from and the sincere life passed within it which restrain laughter and consecrate the costume of any people. Let Harlequin be taken with a fit of the colic and his trappings will have to serve that mood too. When the soldier is hit by a cannon ball rags are as becoming as purple.

The childish and savage taste of men and women for new patterns    6 keeps how many shaking and squinting through kaleidoscopes that they may discover the particular figure which this generation requires today. The manufacturers have learned that this taste is merely whim- sical. Of two patterns which differ only by a few threads more or less of a particular color, the one will be sold readily, the other lie on the shelf, though it frequently happens that after the lapse of a season the latter becomes the most fashionable. Comparatively, tattooing is not the hideous custom which it is called. It is not barbarous merely be- cause the printing is skin-deep and unalterable.

I cannot believe that our factory system is the best mode by which    7 men may get clothing. The condition of the operatives is becoming every day more like that of the English; and it cannot be wondered at, since, as far as I have heard or observed, the principal object is, not that mankind may be well and honestly clad, but, unquestionably, that the corporations may be enriched. In the long run men hit only what they aim at. Therefore, though they should fail immediately, they had better aim at something high.

# Questions

1. What, according to Thoreau, are the legitimate functions of clothing? What other functions does he reject, or fail to consider?
2. In paragraph 7, Thoreau criticizes the factory system. Is the criticism mild or severe? Explain. Point out some of the earlier passages in which he touches on the relation of clothes to a faulty economic system.
3. Many of Thoreau's sentences mean both what they say literally and something more; often, like proverbs, they express abstract or general truths in concrete, homely language. How might these sentences be interpreted?
   a. We know but few men, a great many coats and breeches.
   b. Dress a scarecrow in your last shift, you standing shiftless by, who would not soonest salute the scarecrow?
   c. If you have any enterprise before you, try it in your old clothes.
   d. Every generation laughs at the old fashions, but follows religiously the new.
   e. When the soldier is hit by a cannon ball rags are as becoming as purple.

## Melvin Konner

# Kick Off Your Heels

**A** friend of mine, a sedate historian, allows how he used   1
to sit in the library as a graduate student at Princeton trying to bury his thoughts in some thick tome. In those bad old days, when Princeton

Melvin Konner, an anthropologist at Emory University and a nonpracticing physician, writes a column entitled "Body and Mind" for the *New York Times Magazine*.

was all-male, the appearance of a female visitor would sometimes be signaled by a sound outside the window in the summer evening: the unmistakable click, click of high heels on the garden walk. Like the bell that made Pavlov's dog salivate, the mere sound of the walk triggered a physiological cascade. Such is the drift of the male brain that it can be drawn off course, for at least minutes, by the sound of a symbol of sexuality.

Yet consider what those heels do with the female form. The legs are slimmed and lengthened; this makes them what students of animal behavior call a supernormal stimulus—recalling, yet exaggerating the lengthening that occurs at puberty. (Pin-up drawings always exaggerate length.) At the same time, the feet are shortened—daintier? For some reason, both men and women seem to prefer smaller feet. Heels tighten the calves and make them prominent. The buttocks are thrown up and out (a distant echo, perhaps, of the sexual "presenting" of female mammals) and the bosom thrust forward, producing the S-curve for which women bustled and corseted brutally in time past. That certain something—not a ponytail—that sways when she walks (because women's hips are wider and not poised over the knees) sways more than usual. And she is hobbled. She is charmingly (to him) off-balance on her pedestal, and unable to flee. (A convicted mugger has said, "We would wait under a stairwell in the subway station and, when we heard the click of the wobbly spiked heel, we knew we had one.")

The message is not unambiguous helplessness. The heels just about abolish the average male advantage in height. The points of the heels and the toes are suitable weapons. But regardless of ambiguity, they convey a message: Look at me; get close if you can—or, if you haven't the courage, try to go back to your book.

Courting creatures signal sex in myriad ways. Often the males do the strutting. The peacock spreads his magnificent eyed feathers, and antelope like the Uganda kob prance and clang great antlers against each other. Other species leave some posing to the female. In the 10-spined stickleback, a little fresh-water fish of the British Isles, the female flashes a bit of swollen silver belly and triggers the male's courtship dance. The female zebra finch, an Australian perching bird, sits on a branch and stretches in a horizontal posture. While the male watches nearby, she bends her legs, sleeks her gray feathers and flutters her black-and-white tail. The female great crested grebe, ordinarily a graceful diving waterbird, assumes an even more awkward posture, sitting on the water with her wings spread and shoulders pointing down.

Humans are no slouches when it comes to sexual signaling. On 5 the contrary, we take the signals nature has given us—an arched brow, a descending eyelid, a smile—and embellish them with every conceivable cultural brush stroke. Draping or painting or piercing or molding the body has gone on for millenniums. New Guinea men paint themselves dramatically for dancing, and marriageable Papuan maidens bear elegant tatoos. Extensive, patterned scars variously signified femininity and manliness in many African cultures. Lip plugs, head molding, circumcision, ear stretching, tooth filing—the list goes on.

Fewer than a hundred years ago, Western women tied themselves 6 in corsets that damaged abdominal organs and made them respiratory wrecks. At the same time, the Chinese were still practicing the extraordinary 1,000-year-old tradition of foot-binding. The resulting foot was shortened, with all toes but the first curled under and the arch drastically raised—essentially, high heels made of bone. This distortion was a matter of pride, a sign of nobility and allure.

How close do our own artificial high heels come to that old Chinese 7 ideal? Not very, but there are similarities. Both signify sex and class, and achieve femininity. And both, to different degrees, result in impairment.

Orthopedists and chiropractors see the consequences in backache 8 and knee problems. One orthopedics textbook describes the gait in such shoes as "ungainly" and "mincing," and notes that the normal cushioning is lost. Authorities agree that the toes and balls of the feet in high heels must bear too much weight in striking the ground, and that they transmit the shock upward. After prolonged wearing of high heels, the calf muscles and the Achilles' tendon may permanently contract. Robert Donatelli, a physical therapist, says shortened calf muscles may cause the knees to be slightly flexed; this in turn may cause chronic flection of hips. The ultimate result may produce a shape of buttocks suggestive to the male, but at the cost of increased lumbar lordosis, harmful pressure on the lumbar discs that can cause low-back pain.

Richard Benjamin, a podiatrist at the Greater Southeastern Hos- 9 pital in Washington, says, too, that throwing the weight on the ball of the foot diminishes the normal roles of both heel and big toe. Incorrect turning of the foot throws the knee out, affecting the hip and back. Like the S-shaped stance, the exaggerated pelvic sway provides allure at a cost in physical damage.

Podiatrists do see several times more women than men, primarily 10 because of high-heeled shoes with pointed toes. Pain in foot bones is almost inevitable, but this is only the beginning. Abrasions, calluses, bunions (*hallux valgus*), tendinitis, ingrown toenails and serious bone deformities such as hammer toes and "pump bump"—a bony enlargement of the heel where the shoe rim bites into it—are frequent. Bunions can be serious; they can force the joint between the big toe and the adjacent metatarsal bone to become so bent for so long that calcium buildup renders it permanently and painfully deviated. The ratio of women to men who have this disorder is estimated to be 40-to-1. High heels also cause abnormal thickening of skin and bone at the ball of the foot, and this can force the small toes under the foot, crushing them, in some rare cases. Sheldon Flaxman, a foot surgeon, concludes: "These shoes should be worn for special occasions only." Even then, he says, they should not be pointed and the heels should be as low as possible.

High heels are, after all, relatively new in Western tradition. In 11 the 16th century, the elegant—men and women alike—began to like upward-tilting footwear. Before the Elizabethan period in England, flatness in shoes was consistent with both elegance and sex. One will search in vain in earlier paintings and sculpture for evidence of shoes that lever people off the ground. By the mid-18th century, men's shoes had returned to normalcy, but women were stuck on their awkward platforms, and there they have remained. The most extreme form— the stiletto of the 1950's—was often banned, to prevent damage to floors. No laws, written or unwritten, prevent damage to feet—or to women's sense of freedom.

Why do we have such an attachment to this hurtful fashion? The 12 Freudians have had a field day with it, likening it to a mild version of the condition in which a fetishist (always a man) can be aroused only by a shoe. They even invoke sadomasochism as well, and in this explanation the pain and harm are no longer incidental. As I get older, the pain is what I most often see. But I have to admit that a woman will sometimes take me by surprise—dressed to the nines, high-heeled shoes and all.

I'm fighting it though, the part of it that comes from bad shoes. 13 I expect to win. I think of adjectives that apply to women in flat shoes: lithe, graceful, earthy, athletic, sensible, fleet, dancing, practical, fresh, nimble, strong—and sexy, definitely sexy. (Don't look for logic here,

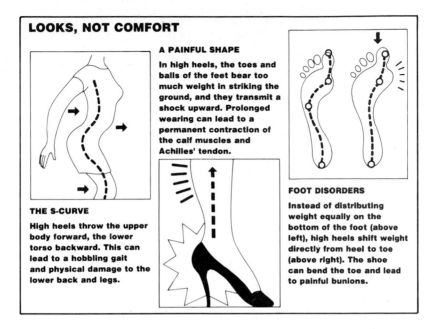

**LOOKS, NOT COMFORT**

**A PAINFUL SHAPE**

In high heels, the toes and balls of the feet bear too much weight in striking the ground, and they transmit a shock upward. Prolonged wearing can lead to a permanent contraction of the calf muscles and Achilles' tendon.

**THE S-CURVE**

High heels throw the upper body forward, the lower torso backward. This can lead to a hobbling gait and physical damage to the lower back and legs.

**FOOT DISORDERS**

Instead of distributing weight equally on the bottom of the foot (above left), high heels shift weight directly from heel to toe (above right). The shoe can bend the toe and lead to painful bunions.

we're talking about hormones.) I think of the women depicted by Greek and Roman art—they didn't need to be hobbled to interest men. I think of the polka and the hora instead of the waltz and the tango— and as for whatever it is we do to rock music, that works just as well in flats.

Still, it's hard to visualize a great formal party without stylish 14 women kicking up their high heels. Like some of the other indulgences of that and like occasions, they're probably O.K. in moderation. But for everyday wear they make as little sense as a three-martini lunch. They're a relatively recent innovation. They've wormed their way into our sexual imagery. But it's hard to see why they have to stay there.

# Questions

1. In paragraph 11 Konner points out that from the sixteenth through the mid-eighteenth century both men and women wore "upward-tilting footwear." Does Konner suggest, or can you explain, why men abandoned footwear that, if nothing else, allowed them to add inches to their height, while women remained "stuck on their awkward platforms"?

2.  What other fashions can you think of that can be described as potentially unhealthy or hurtful. Are they primarily men's or women's fashions?

3.  In his concluding sentence Konner suggests that high heels might go out of fashion. Do you see any evidence that they are losing ground?

4.  Do you consider an essay on high-heeled shoes too frivolous to appear in a composition text? Why, or why not? Try to offer *reasons* that support your assertion.

Garrison Keillor

# Something from the Sixties

A friend writes: 1

About five o'clock last Sunday evening, my son burst into the 2
kitchen and said, "I didn't know it was so late!" He was due at a party
immediately—a sixties party, he said—and he needed something from
the sixties to wear. My son is almost fifteen years old, the size of a
grown man, and when he bursts into a room glassware rattles and the
cat on your lap grabs on to your knees and leaps from the starting
block. I used to think the phrase "burst into the room" was only for
detective fiction, until my son got his growth. He can burst in a way
that, done by an older fellow, would mean that angels had descended
into the front yard and were eating apples off the tree, and he does it
whenever he's late—as being my son, he often is. I have so little sense
of time that when he said he needed something from the sixties it took
me a moment to place that decade. It's the one he was born toward
the end of.

I asked, "What sort of stuff you want to wear?" 3

He said, "I don't know. Whatever they wore then." 4

We went up to the attic, into a long, low room under the eaves 5
where I've squirreled away some boxes of old stuff; I dug into one
box, and the first thing I hauled out was the very thing he wanted. A
thigh-length leather vest covered with fringe and studded with silver,
it dates from around 1967, a fanciful time in college-boy fashions. Like
many boys, I grew up in nice clothes my mother bought, but was
meanwhile admiring Roy Rogers, Sergeant Rock, the Cisco Kid, and
other sharp dressers, so when I left home I was ready to step out and

This short essay, which we have entitled "Something from the Sixties," comes
from "The Talk of the Town," a heading used over several short, anonymous
essays published weekly in *The New Yorker*. The essay purports to be a letter
from a friend, except for the first line ("A friend writes"), but one may conjecture
that the piece was composed by Garrison Keillor, who, following a convention
used in "The Talk of the Town," does not use the first person singular pronoun.
Keillor is the author of several books, including *Lake Wobegon Days*, and was
the host of a popular radio show, "A Prairie Home Companion."

be somebody. Military Surplus was the basic style then—olive drab, and navy-blue pea jackets—with a touch of Common Man in the work boots and blue work shirts, but if you showed up in Riverboat Gambler or Spanish Peasant or Rodeo King nobody blinked, nobody laughed. I haven't worn the vest in ten years, but a few weeks ago, seeing a picture of Michael Jackson wearing a fancy band jacket like the ones the Beatles wore on the cover of "Sgt. Pepper," I missed the fun I used to have getting dressed in the morning. Pull on the jeans, a shirt with brilliant-red roses, a pair of Red Wing boots. A denim jacket. Rose-tinted glasses. A cowboy hat. Or an engineer's cap. Or, instead of jeans, bib overalls. Or white trousers with blue stripes. Take off the denim jacket, take off the rose shirt, try the neon-green bowling shirt with "Moose" stitched on the pocket, the black dinner jacket. Now the dark-green Chinese Army cap. And an orange tie with hula dancers and palm trees.

Then—presto!—I pulled the rose shirt out. He put it on, and the vest, which weighs about fifteen pounds, and by then I had found him a hat—a broad-brimmed panama that ought to make you think of a cotton planter enjoying a Sazerac[1] on a veranda in New Orleans. I followed him down to his bedroom, where he admired himself in a full-length mirror. 6

"Who wore this?" he asked. 7

I said that I did. 8

"Did you really? This? You?" 9

Yes, I really did. After he was born, in 1969, I wore it less and less, finally settling down with what I think of as the Dad look, and now I would no sooner wear my old fringed vest in public than walk around in a taffeta tutu. I loved the fact that it fitted him so well, though, and his pleasure at the heft and extravagance of the thing, the poses he struck in front of the mirror. Later, when he got home and reported that his costume was a big hit and that all his friends had tried on the vest, it made me happy again. You squirrel away old stuff on the principle of its being useful and interesting someday; it's wonderful when the day finally arrives. That vest was waiting for a boy to come along—a boy who has a flair for the dramatic, who bursts into rooms—and to jump right into the part. I'm happy to be the audience. 10

---

[1] A bourbon cocktail flavored with a bitter liqueur. (Editors' note)

# Questions

1. In the second line of this essay we are told that the action begins "About five o'clock last Sunday evening." Does it matter that we know what time it was, or what day of the week? Explain.
2. Much of paragraph 1 is used to describe the way the son enters the room. How does the description characterize the son? How does it relate to the point of the narrative?
3. Toward the end of paragraph 5 Keillor writes a string of fragments. Try to describe the effect of this rhetorical device.
4. In the next-to-last paragraph, what feelings toward his father does the son communicate in "Did you really? This? You?" What feelings does the father have for his son, and how do you know?
5. In the last paragraph Keillor says he settled down with "what I think of as the Dad look." When you read that, what picture of him comes to mind? Try to describe the clothes, the body stance, the expression of a man wearing "the Dad look." Be as specific as you can.
6. The conclusion to the piece is: "I'm happy to be the audience." What details in the account make the word "audience" especially fitting? And what other details persuade you that "happy" is the precise word to summarize the tone of the essay?
7. In the last paragraph the writer says: "You squirrel away old stuff on the principle of its being useful and interesting some day." What do you (or members of your family) "squirrel away"? Why? Explain, in two or three paragraphs.

## Robert Sommer

# Hard Architecture

Prison fixtures are being installed in the restrooms of city 1
parks. According to the manufacturers' statements, they are supposed
to be vandal-proof. One advertisement shows a man attacking a toilet

Robert Sommer teaches psychology and environmental studies at the University of California at Davis. Our selection comes from *Tight Spaces*, a study of the "New Brutalism" manifested in windowless concrete buildings and in uncomfortable parks and airports.

with a sledgehammer. According to Sacramento, California, Recreation Director Solon Wishmam, Jr., "There is no exposed plumbing in the new buildings. The external fixtures are made of cast aluminum covered with hard epoxy. The buildings themselves are made of concrete blocks rather than wood or brick."[1] This same trend toward hard buildings is evident in public facilities across the country. Picnic tables are being cast of concrete rather than built of wood and are embedded several feet into the ground. It isn't possible to move these tables to a shady place or combine two tables to accommodate a large group, but that is an inconvenience for the users rather than the park officials. The older wood and metal tables remaining from a happier era are chained to blocks of concrete or steel posts.

The original inspiration for the park restroom, the prison cell, illustrates the hard facts of hard architecture. Human beings are enclosed in steel cages with the bare minimum of furnishings or amenities. In some cells there may be no furniture whatever except for the furthest advance in the field of vandal-proof plumbing, the hole in the concrete floor, otherwise known as a Chinese toilet. Because nothing is provided that the inmate might destroy, he may have to sleep on a bare concrete floor without mattress or blanket. I am not talking about the Middle Ages or some backward part of the nation. I have a clear image of an isolation cell circa 1973 with a man in a steel cage for 23 hours a day with nothing to do but pace the floor and curse the guard watching him through the slit in a steel door. The architecture of the isolation cell is based on a variant of Murphy's Law—if something can be destroyed, it will be destroyed.[2] In mental hospitals of the early 1950s, the line was, "If you give the patients anything nice, they won't take care of it." For public housing tenants it went "If you provide good architecture they won't appreciate it." There is the same denigrating we/they dichotomy in all these assessments of people's response to their surroundings. We know what's best for them and they don't. Even if we provide what they say they'd like, they won't take care of it and will probably destroy it. Ergo, it is best for everyone, especially the taxpayers who foot the bill, to design things that cannot be destroyed.

The result is that architecture is designed to be strong and resistant to human imprint. To the inhabitants it seems impervious, impersonal,

2

3

---

[1] Jeff Raimundo, "Park Facilities Are Still Vulnerable," Sacramento *Bee*, February 8, 1973, p. B1.
[2] Murphy's Law No. 1: If something can go wrong, it will. Law No. 2: The toast always falls butter side down.

and inorganic. Lady Allen, who pioneered the adventure playground in Great Britain, was appalled at American play yards which she described as "an administrator's heaven and a child's hell . . . asphalt barracks yards behind wire mesh screen barriers" built primarily for ease and economy of maintenance.[3] There is a whole industry built around supplying steel cages for prisons, wire mesh fences for city parks, and graffiti-resistant paint for public buildings. On a larger scale, the hardening of the landscape is evident in the ever-growing freeway system, the residential and second-home subdivisions pushing aside orchards and forests, the straightening and cementing of river beds, the walled and guarded cities of suburbia, and the TV cameras in banks and apartment buildings.

Another characteristic of hard architecture is a lack of permeability   4
between inside and out. Often this means an absence of windows, a style referred to in Berkeley as post-revolutionary architecture. At first glance the Bank of America on Berkeley's Telegraph Avenue seems to have windows but these are really reflecting metal surfaces. The new postal center in Oakland, with its tiny slit windows, looks as if it were intended for urban guerrilla warfare. Older buildings that still have plate glass use steel shutters and gates that can be drawn across the exterior in a matter of minutes. Some corporations are moving their data-processing machinery underground where they are less vulnerable to attack. The fact that employees must work underground forty hours a week is a minor cost borne by the employees rather than the architect.

Hard architecture means wall surfaces that resist human imprint.   5
Dark colors and rough cement were satisfactory prior to the advent of the aerosol can. The counter response of the hard-line designers has taken two forms. The first is the legal effort to remove aerosol cans from the hands of potential graffitists. Ordinances have been proposed to make it illegal to carry open aerosol cans on city streets. A New York State Senator has proposed a bill to make it illegal for people under eighteen to purchase cans of spray paint. The other approach is to develop vandal-resistant surfaces and stronger kinds of paint remover. In a six-month period New York City purchased 7,000 gallons of a yellow jelly called DWR (dirty word remover) from a Moorestown, N.J., manufacturer of industrial chemicals. The remover comes in two strengths and the heavier duty version is optimistically called Enzitall.[4]

[3] Lady Allen of Hurtwood, *Planning for Play* (Cambridge: M.I.T. Press, 1968).
[4] "Help Arrives," Cincinnati *Enquirer*, April 23, 1972.

Planners of President Nixon's inauguration sprayed the trees alongside
the motorcade route with a material that prevented birds from roosting
there. They didn't want the president being embarrassed by an occasional bird-dropping. The two-year interval during which the birds
would be unable to roost on these trees is a minor inconvenience again
borne by the users.

Most of these efforts to harden the environment have had the  6
avowed purpose of increasing security. Frequently this reason is a cov-
erup for a desire to maintain order, discipline, or control. Although
these motives are related to security, there are important differences
between security and control that must be recognized and heeded if
a democratic society is to continue. . . .

## Ideological Supports for Hard Buildings

Any effort to soften hard buildings and improve the lot of the public  7
housing tenant, the prisoner, or the park user will encounter the popular prejudice against "frills" in public facilities. As they say about
army buildings, "It doesn't have to be cheap, it just has to look cheap."
The taxpayer doesn't want to believe that people living in public housing are better off than he is. Almost every prison official advocates
individual cells for prisoners. The logic behind single cells is compelling; it includes the physical protection of weaker inmates, reduces
homosexual relationships, enables better control of inmates in single
cells, as well as increased privacy and personal dignity. However,
whenever prison officials argue for single cells, they are accused of
coddling convicts. The apocryphal question from the state legislature
is how single rooms can be justified for people who have broken the
law when army recruits are compelled to live in open barracks. Is it
reasonable to provide more amenities for lawbreakers than for draf-
tees?

There are several good answers to this question. First we can turn  8
to Florence Nightingale's dictum that the first requisite of a hospital
is that it do the patients no harm. The minimum criterion of a prison
should be that an inmate emerges no worse than when he entered.
At present this is not the case and prisons are accurately described as
breeding grounds for criminal behavior. When someone is hurt and
angry, there is no reason to believe that putting him in a degrading
and dehumanizing environment will improve his outlook or behavior.
Indeed there is every reason to suppose that this will worsen whatever
antisocial attitudes presently exist.

The logic of subjecting the poor, the criminal, and the deviant to  9
degrading conditions is also based on a puritanical attitude toward
comfort. A belief in the redemptive value of hard work and frugality
pervades much of our thinking about people who are public charges.
The first American prison was developed in Pennsylvania in response
to demands for the humane treatment of criminals by the Quaker sect,
a group characterized both by its humane impulses and a disdain for
anything beyond the minimum in personal comfort. Following Quaker
precepts, lawbreakers were confined in solitary cells with ample time
to consider their transgressions and become penitent. The cells were
quite large and the inmate remained in his cell most of the day apart
from a one-hour exercise period. Later, when large-scale workshops
proved more efficient than individual craft work performed in a single
cell, the solitary system of the Pennsylvania prison was replaced by
the silent system of the Auburn Prison, in which inmates also lived in
single cells but came together to work and eat but had to remain silent.
The idea that an ascetic life would help to rehabilitate prisoners was
used against any effort to humanize the institutions.

Even today, efforts to improve the drab conditions of army life,  10
to permit recruits to personalize their sleeping quarters or choose their
own hair styles, are regarded by many senior officers as responsible
for breakdowns in order and discipline. Not too long ago architects
who planned college classrooms and dormitories were advised against
making the furnishings too pleasant or comfortable lest the students
become distracted or fall asleep. Guidebooks for undergraduate students still warn against too many amenities in the student's room. Here
is a sampling of advice on dormitory furnishing: "Choose a straight
backed chair rather than a very comfortable one. . . ." "All of the votes
are in favor of a simple, rugged, straightbacked chair with no cushion.
You study best when you are not too comfortable or relaxed. . . ."
"For obvious reasons, avoid studying on a couch, easy chair, or in bed.
. . ." "A bed is no place to study. Neither is a sofa, nor a foam rubber
lounge chair. When you are too relaxed and comfortable physically,
your concentration also relaxes. A straight-backed wooden chair is best
for most students; it allows them to work at maximum concentration
for longer periods." Before analyzing the attitudes behind these recommendations, let me state emphatically that there is no evidence that
people work better when they are uncomfortable. Let the reader examine his or her own circumstances while reading this book. Are you
sitting bolt upright in a straight-backed chair or lying on a couch with
your head against a cushion? My own observations of the way students

read suggest that when a couch or easy chair is available, it will be chosen almost every time over the rugged, virtuous, and uncomfortable straight-backed chair.

Another ideological prop behind hard architecture is neo-behaviorism. Providing decent housing for public charges would be "rewarding" poverty or criminal behavior. The argument goes beyond the accusation of simply coddling convicts to the idea that improved conditions will actually "reinforce" criminal tendencies. Neo-behaviorism maintains that people won't be deterred from crime if the consequences are not sufficiently dire. This requires some form of punishment—if not actual torture then at least confinement without amenity. The critical question is whether confinement and removal from society constitute sufficient punishment or whether the transgressor must be punished still further during confinement. There is no evidence to indicate that such punishment exerts any positive influences on an inmate's character. Instead it increases his alienation from and his bitterness toward society. There is not much basis for believing that dehumanizing public housing will help to reduce welfare rolls, juvenile delinquency, or anything else society considers bad. Poor housing lowers the self-image of the tenant and helps to convince him how little society cares about his plight. This is not a terribly important consideration to a philosophy that is unabashedly beyond freedom and dignity. Hard, hard, hard, ain't it hard? Yes it is. But does it work? No, it doesn't. City officials across the country will testify that there is no such thing as a vandal-proof restroom or picnic bench. If restrooms are built out of concrete they will be dynamited and have concrete poured down the toilet holes. Vandals, thousands of helmeted Huns riding out of the East, have managed to dig out concrete blocks and haul away picnic tables weighing hundreds of pounds. Bolt cutters and wire snippers can sever any chain-link fence manufactured today. In the People's Park disturbance of 1972, the metal poles for the fence were used to break up the macadam of the parking lot. Local police were very cooperative in carting away the broken macadam pieces lest they in turn be used to break the windows of local stores. The harder the architecture, the greater its potential as a weapon if it is used against the authorities. Prison inmates have learned how to make deadly knives from steel bedsprings. Hard architecture also costs more to adapt or remove. Pennsylvania's Eastern Penitentiary, built in 1829, was closed down in 1966, but has yet to be removed from the site because of the high razing expense. The extra costs of hard architecture are manifold; first in the initial purchase price because it costs twice as much as ordinary items, second in its potential for abuse once it is destroyed as well as the greater cost in repairing or removing a heavy and rigid item designed to be installed permanently, and finally the human costs resulting from being in cold, ugly, and impersonal buildings.

Challenge people to destroy something and they will find a way    12
to do it. Many people prefer to ignore the great amount of technological ingenuity released in wartime. Although only sketchy accounts of the automated battlefield have been made public, it is evident that the Vietnam War has produced the most sophisticated gadgetry in the history of warfare. If city agencies use remote sensors and infrared photography to detect the presence of people in parks after closing time, it is likely that such methods will have the same success in New York parks that they had in Vietnam. Authorities who go the route of vandal-proof facilities are deluding themselves. They are short-range thinkers who cost everyone money in the long run. Adversity puts human ingenuity to the test and the prison inmate naked in his strip cell is tested more severely. By law the California authorities are required to provide even strip-cell inmates with their own Bibles. The result is that the Bible has become a weapon in a manner unintended by the most ardent missionary. Inmates stuff the pages into the ventilator shaft and use the covers to stop up the Chinese toilet. Think of what the inmate could do if he had a table and chair to work with! An advisory committee on dental hygiene ran into problems when it suggested to the California Department of Corrections that inmates should be allowed to use dental floss. Prison officials pointed out that dental floss "when coated with an abrasive substance, could be as effective as metal blades in cutting through iron bars."[5]

The major defects of hard architecture are that it is costly, dehu-    13
manizing, and it isn't effective. Besides that, it doesn't look very nice. The prototype of hard architecture is the strip cell in the maximum security prison containing nothing but reinforced concrete poured over a steel cage without any amenities. If we can develop ways of humanizing the prison cell, perhaps we can also do so for schools, parks, and other public facilities.

The rationale of the hard prison is that the inmate will destroy    14
anything that is provided for him. It is easy to prove the correctness of this view by giving a wooden chair to an inmate in a strip cell. It is likely that he will bang the chair against the wall until the legs have

[5] Sacramento *Bee*, May 8, 1973, p. B2.

come loose and he has several clubs in his possession. Give him a mattress and sooner or later the authorities will have a fire or smoke problem on their hands. Just what does this prove? One can also supply numerous examples of maximum security cells that are equally secure and full of amenities including rugs, tables, desks, television sets, and stereo systems. In prison disturbances, where inmates are rampaging against virtually every part of the prison building, television sets purchased with inmate welfare funds remain undisturbed. Nor do inmates destroy the paintings made by their fellow prisoners.

The arguments against providing amenities for inmates do not 15 discuss the costs of denying a human existence to the lawbreakers. I have never heard anyone maintain that the inmate's mental or physical health is improved by a bare, unheated cell with no exercise yard or outside stimulation. This experience does not teach him a greater respect for the law or the society that maintains him under such dehumanizing conditions. However, guards legitimately object to providing chairs for inmates who are going to break them apart and fashion clubs from the pieces. The typical solution has been to harden prison furnishings with indestructible materials and attach them to the walls. But human ingenuity can always find a way to destroy things that are physically or spiritually oppressive.

Another assumption behind hard architecture is that security 16 through steel, concrete, and electronic surveillance is cheaper and more effective than security through public access. Stated another way, security can be gained through technological control of the environment. This is perhaps valid when one is working *with* people rather than against them. To design a highway to minimize ambiguity, error, and accidents increases everyone's sense of security. I feel more comfortable riding my bike on a well-planned bicycle path than on a street or highway that was designed with automobiles in mind. However, we have not been discussing situations in which everyone gains from good design, but rather those in which hard architecture is used by one group to exclude or oppress another.

The emulation of the prison as a security environment is the more 17 ironic because the prison is a failing institution from everyone's standpoint. It provides no security for inmates, guards, wardens, and visitors. It does provide a short-run protection to outside society by segregating offenders for brief periods, but this must be weighed against the corrosive effects of incarceration in an oppressive and unnatural environment.

## Soft Architecture

If experience has shown that hard architecture isn't working from the  18
standpoint of economics, aesthetics, or human dignity, what then is
the answer? The solution, I believe, is to reverse course and make
buildings more rather than less responsive to their users. Instead of
hardening things to resist human imprint, let us design buildings,
parks, and cities to welcome and reflect the presence of human
beings—let us abandon the fruitless and costly search for ever more
secure cell furnishings. There is another alternative to the completely
empty cell. This would involve materials such as foam and inflatables
as well as other types of plastics. Provided one selects materials that
are fire proof, the security implications of an inexpensive air mattress
or styrofoam chair are virtually zero, or at least they are considerably
less than with ordinary prison furnishings. There is no justification for
inmates in maximum security cells sleeping on hard concrete floors
when the wholesale cost of an air mattress is twenty cents. At least
an inmate should be offered a choice between the bare concrete floor
and an air mattress which he can destroy if he chooses. If he elects to
destroy the air mattress, the security implications to the guard as well
as the cost to the taxpayers are minimal. However, if he does not
destroy it, an equally inexpensive foam chair might be tried next. In
this way a valid transaction between the inmate and the authorities
regarding cell furnishings could be established.

Soft architecture can change the relationship between keeper and  19
inmate. New Jersey State Penitentiary in Leesburg was deliberately
built by the architects to include breakable materials; a necessary adjunct to a humane environment. Glass abounds and each cell has natural light with an exterior window in addition to the glazed walls separating cells from courtyards. Locally some people refer to this medium
security facility as "the glass house." All windows face the interior
courtyards and exterior security is provided by the back wall of the
residential units, a deep overhang of the roof to prevent climbing, and
a cyclone fence surrounding the entire site. However the interior of
the prison contains a great amount of breakable material requiring inmates and guards to reach a mutually satisfactory accommodation,
because any burst of anger would result in shattered glass.[6] It would
indeed be difficult to run a repressive prison in "the glass house." On

[6] Suzanne Stephens, "Pushing Prisons Aside," *The Architectural Forum* (March 1973),
pp. 28–51.

the other hand, it requires tremendous tact, patience, and sensitivity to run such a prison. Let the reader answer whether he or she would prefer to work (or be confined) in Leesburg or in a traditional institution.

Several years ago, the dormitories on my campus had strict rules against students hanging pictures or posters on the walls. There were constant inspections by university officials who removed illegal posters and fined the offenders. The basis for these regulations was that the tacks or tape used to mount these posters would scratch the walls. The prohibition against decorating dormitory rooms continued for years even though it was a constant irritant as well as being costly and ineffective. Besides the inspections there was the annual repainting bill, which mounted steadily over the years. Eventually the administration decided that it would be cheaper and happier for everyone to let students hang anything they wanted on their walls. The housing office now provides paint at the beginning of the year so that students can erase anything done by the previous occupants and have the colors they want. Students living on the same floor can decide jointly how the corridors and stairwells are to be painted. New dormitories now contain soft wall materials such as cork or burlap on wood so that students can hang pictures, mobiles, or macramé without marring the surface. They are built to be largely maintained by the users. This has proven cheaper and more satisfying than the previous arrangement of bare walls accompanied by constant inspections, fines, and reprimands, as well as periodic repainting by the maintenance staff. It costs $15 per room to allow students to do the painting themselves, compared to $75 charged by the physical plant office. In 1970, the repaint rate was 10 percent—that is, only one out of ten rooms was repainted by the subsequent occupant.[7]

On any college campus there is always a shortage of study space, particularly around exam time. There is also a great deal of unused space in the evenings, in the form of academic offices, laboratories, and even cafeterias, but it is difficult to get these opened for student use. I don't know of a single campus where faculty offices are available in the evenings as study space—the territorial feelings of the faculty toward their offices are too strong. However on a number of campuses there have been successful campaigns to open up the cafeterias in the evenings. These campaigns have been successful only sporadically and

20

21

[7] Robbie Hart, "Room Painting in the Residence Halls," Unpublished report, University of California, Davis Housing Office, 1970.

probably less than one-third of university cafeterias are routinely opened for evening studiers, another third are opened during examination periods, and the remainder are locked and available only during specified meal hours. The arguments against opening up cafeterias are custodial and security-oriented—the students will disturb the table arrangements and will steal the utensils and perhaps even the chairs and tables themselves. At a large university in Los Angeles where the silverware is automatically returned to the locked kitchen after meals, the explanation for closing the cafeteria in the evenings is that the students would steal the salt and pepper shakers. Like the belief that mental patients will flush magazines down the toilets, prisoners will destroy decent furnishings if they have them, or park users will chop up wooden benches, a few instances can always be cited, but the trade-offs in social utility and aesthetics are rarely considered. The best counterargument for opening up college cafeterias for evening studiers is that the system works on scores of campuses across the nation. The loss of twenty salt and pepper shakers and perhaps an extra $10 per evening in janitorial services to open up two cafeterias for around-the-clock use might provide the campus with an additional 15,000 feet of prime study space already equipped with tables and chairs. If need be, the student government or some dormitory organization can provide proctors or monitors in the late evening hours.

In all such illustrations—magazines for mental patients, amenities 22 for prisoners, and study space for college students—the security and custodial opposition is largely specious, but this is obvious only to someone knowledgeable about the situation elsewhere. The argument that mental patients will immediately tear up magazines and flush them down the toilet has at least minimal logic *unless* one has worked on a psychiatric ward where magazines and newspapers are freely available. The arguments against amenity for prisoners seem equally ridiculous if one has seen maximum security cells equipped with carpets, stereos, green plants, and tropical fish. To the criticism that inmates will hide knives and drugs in flower pots and stereos, one can cite the fact that inmates presently secrete weapons and contraband even in the barest cells and sometimes as suppositories. It is also true that the majority of stabbings and other serious injuries have occurred at the most security-conscious institutions. The explanation always returns to the "type of inmate" and never to the type of place. The mental patients who had free access to newspapers and magazines and didn't flush them down the toilets were presumably a "better class of patients." Similarly, students at University *A* who have access to cafeterias for evening study and leave the salt and pepper shakers undisturbed are a "better class of students." This "class logic" treats people apart from their surroundings, as if there is some intrinsic self independent of the environment. This is a false model of any natural process, including person/environment transactions. There is no behavior apart from environment even *in utero*. People adapt themselves to their surroundings in diverse and complex ways. When those surroundings are cold and oppressive, people who can will avoid them. Unfortunately many people, for economic, social, or statutory reasons, cannot avoid places that oppress them. The result may be somatic disorders, anxiety, and irritation, but the probable outcome will be numbness to one's surroundings, with psychological withdrawal substituting for physical avoidance. . . .

The dream of a society in which people who share common goals 23 will trust and respect one another is being suffocated in a torrent of concrete, steel, and sophisticated security equipment. I would feel less strongly if windowless buildings, barbed-wire fences, and electronic surveillance equipment were infrequent aberrations of paranoid homeowners and public officials, but they are not. Housing projects, schools, playgrounds, courtrooms, and commercial buildings reveal the hardening process at an advanced stage. If there is truth to Churchill's dictum that the buildings we shape will eventually shape us, then the inevitable result of hard buildings will be withdrawn, callous, and indifferent people. A security emphasis is being poured into concrete that will harden our children's children fifty years from now. . . .

## Personalization

There is no single best arrangement of office furniture and no way for 24 a designer, building manager, or psychologist to intuit someone's space needs without meeting the person, seeing the sort of job he or she has to do, and how he or she does it. Every faculty office on my campus comes equipped with a standard complement of furniture—a desk, filing cabinet, table, two or three bookcases, coat rack, and so on. Because all these people have the same job title (professor) and the size and shape of all office pieces are identical, one could conceive of standardized office arrangements. However a walk down the hallways reveals a great diversity of arrangements. One man has placed his bookcase between his desk and the door for maximum privacy. Another has joined together his desk and table to yield a large work area and writing surface as well as considerable distance from any visitor, and a third has placed all furniture against the walls to remove any barriers between himself and the students. Numerous attempts at personalization are evident. Out of their own pocket, faculty purchased rugs, drapes, wall-hangings, and pictures of every description, as well as artifacts and symbols of their respective professions. The same diversity of arrangements is evident in the student dormitories, which also come equipped with a standardized complement of similar furniture. Sometimes I think I have seen every conceivable arrangement of two desks, two beds, two chairs, and two dressers, but invariably I am surprised to find a novel pattern.

Instead of guessing "user needs" one should aim at providing  25 access to a pool or selection of furnishings and allow people to arrange their office areas as they see fit. During the occupation of the administration building during Berkeley's Free Speech Movement crisis in 1964, it was reported that the students had broken into and ransacked the office of President Emeritus Robert Gordon Sproul. When the police had removed the demonstrators, they found Sproul's office in disarray with papers strewn about the floor. The situation was resolved when Sproul's secretary reported that her employer often worked on the floor and left papers strewn about.

The idea that people should be able to control and personalize  26 their work spaces is well within the technical capability of the building industry. It does call for a reversal of the tendency to centralize services and decision-making regarding the physical environment. In the short run it may be cheaper to omit the light switches in an office building, but this makes it difficult to show slides and it is also terribly wasteful of electric power. The same point applies to heating, air conditioning, and humidity controls. There is something tragic about an employee who is officially reprimanded for placing cardboard over her air conditioning vent or a poster on the wall to brighten an otherwise drab office. There is no contradiction between central design and local control provided one develops an overall design scheme that makes allowance for local inputs. One can design a soft building in which each occupant controls his own temperature—hotels and motels do this routinely—or one can design a hard building in which the custodian controls everyone's temperature. In the work on classroom seating . . . it was found that janitors arranged chairs in accordance with their educational philosophies. They also followed their own standards of temperature, humidity, and illumination. The custodian in my building has a clear conception of where my desk and chair belong. Every morning I move my chair over to the side of the room and every evening he returns it to my desk. He arranges the room according to his scheme and I to mine. Fortunately the rules allow me to move my chair. I visited a conference room in one government agency and found taped to the wall under the President's picture a diagram specifying how every item of furniture in the room was to be arranged.

Pleas for personalizing offices and work spaces are academic and 27 even precious until one sees the drab and impersonal conditions under which many people work. At the offices of a large insurance company I found hundreds of clerk's desks in straight rows in a large open room with phones ringing, people scurrying about, and no one having any control over the thermal, acoustical, or visual environment. A federal agency building is liable to be a maze of offices of identical size, shape, and decor. All the furniture, including desks and bookcases, is government-issue grey and on every wall there is a framed photograph of the President and the agency director. A few executives are able to place maps on the walls for visual relief, but that is all. The quest for stimulating and attractive work places, the right to personalize one's own spaces and control temperature and illumination and noise are not academic issues to people who must spend eight hours a day in these settings. I don't feel it is necessary to "prove" that people in colorful offices will type more accurately, stay healthier, or buy more government bonds than people in drab offices. People should have the right to attractive and humane working conditions. Somehow the onus of the argument for a decent environment always falls upon the person who wants to improve things; the custodians and the rest of the grey wall crowd never have to defend drab and unresponsive buildings. This is a curious double standard. If an employee hangs up a poster by his desk, he is imposing his values and artistic tastes on the other employees, but if the management paints all the walls in the building grey or institutional green, that is part of the natural order. We eventually tune them out and thereby become alienated from the very buildings in which we spend our daylight hours.

Ugly and drab furnishings cannot be justified economically. For a 28 corporation or government agency, colored items would cost only slightly more than grey ones and on a large order the difference would disappear entirely. There is some poetic justice that many of the drab furnishings of state office buildings are manufactured by the state prison system. In private corporations, which buy their furniture in the free market where a wide variety of styles and colors is available, standardization is less a result of economics or efficiency than of insensitivity and deliberate unconcern. There is also more than a hint of authoritarianism in the idea that each employee must accept the specific furniture arrangement provided by the company. In a large corporation or agency it would be feasible to give each employee a choice of desk, chair, file cabinet, table, and waste basket from a central furniture pool, not only at the time of employment, but every six months if the person felt like changing things around. This may sound utopian but it isn't. It doesn't take all that long to move furniture. The main objective is not so much to keep the furniture moving as it is to sensitize people to the connection between themselves and their surroundings and counteract the pervasive numbness and apathy. The idea of so many millions of people singlemindedly going to dingy little work stations in large skyscrapers, completely turned off to other people and places, is profoundly disturbing. This kind of numbness to one's surroundings can become a life style.

# Questions

1. List the chief characteristics of hard architecture. If any buildings on your campus or in its neighborhood embody some of the characteristics, specify the buildings in your list.

2. Among the common assumptions that Sommer challenges are these: public facilities should not have frills (paragraph 7); a prisoner should not have the luxury of living in a single room (paragraph 7); students study best when not too comfortable (paragraph 10); decent public housing rewards poverty or criminal behavior (paragraph 11). If you held any of these views, has Sommer persuaded you to drop them? If so, how? If not, why has he failed? Next, list three or four other assumptions that Sommer himself makes about human behavior and evaluate them.

3. In paragraph 26 Sommer says that "janitors arranged chairs [in a classroom] in accordance with their educational philosophies." What do you think the arrangement was? What philosophy is implied in this arrangement?

4. Amplify Sommer's last sentence, showing how "numbness to one's surroundings can become a life style." (Many people find the words "life style" faddish and imprecise. Can you think of a better expression?)

John Steinbeck

# Mobile Homes

 $I$ can only suspect that the lonely man peoples his driving  1
dreams with friends, that the loveless man surrounds himself with
lovely loving women, and that children climb through the dreaming
of the childless driver. And how about the areas of regrets? If only I
had done so-and-so, or had not said such-and-such—my God, the
damn thing might not have happened. Finding this potential in my
own mind, I can suspect it in others, but I will never know, for no
one ever tells. And this is why, on my journey which was designed
for observation, I stayed as much as possible on secondary roads where
there was much to see and hear and smell, and avoided the great wide
traffic slashes which promote the self by fostering daydreams. . . .

On these roads out of the manufacturing centers there moved  2
many mobile homes, pulled by specially designed trucks, and since
these mobile homes comprise one of my generalities, I may as well get
to them now. Early in my travels I had become aware of these new
things under the sun, of their great numbers, and since they occur in
increasing numbers all over the nation, observation of them and perhaps some speculation is in order. They are not trailers to be pulled
by one's own car but shining cars long as pullmans. From the beginning of my travels I had noticed the sale lots where they were sold
and traded, but then I began to be aware of the parks where they sit
down in uneasy permanence. In Maine I took to stopping the night
in these parks, talking to the managers and to the dwellers in this new
kind of housing, for they gather in groups of like to like.

John Steinbeck (1902–1968) was born in Salinas, California, and much of his
writing concerns the Salinas Valley. In 1919 he entered Stanford University, but
he left without a degree. He was determined to become a writer, yet for some
ten years he had little success and supported himself by odd jobs. Between 1935
and 1939, however, he achieved fame with several important books, including
*Tortilla Flat* (1935), *In Dubious Battle* (1936), *Of Mice and Men* (1937), and *The
Grapes of Wrath* (1939).

In addition to writing novels and short stories Steinbeck wrote some non-
fiction, notably *Travels with Charlie* (1962), a record of his automobile tour—
with his poodle, Charley—of forty states. The passage we print here comes from
*Travels*; the title of the selection is our own.

They are wonderfully built homes, aluminum skins, double- 3
walled, with insulation, and often paneled with veneer of hardwood.
Sometimes as much as forty feet long, they have two to five rooms,
and are complete with air-conditioners, toilets, baths, and invariably
television. The parks where they sit are sometimes landscaped and
equipped with every facility. I talked with the park men, who were
enthusiastic. A mobile home is drawn to the trailer park and installed
on a ramp, a heavy rubber sewer pipe is bolted underneath, water and
electricity power connected, the television antenna raised, and the family is in residence. Several park managers agreed that last year one in
four new housing units in the whole country was a mobile home. The
park men charge a small ground rent plus fees for water and electricity.
Telephones are connected in nearly all of them simply by plugging in
a jack. Sometimes the park has a general store for supplies, but if not
the supermarkets which dot the countryside are available. Parking difficulties in the towns have caused these markets to move to the open
country where they are immune from town taxes. This is also true of
the trailer parks. The fact that these homes can be moved does not
mean that they do move. Sometimes their owners stay for years in one
place, plant gardens, build little walls of cinder blocks, put out awnings
and garden furniture. It is a whole way of life that was new to me.
These homes are never cheap and often are quite expensive and lavish.
I have seen some that cost $20,000 and contained all the thousand
appliances we live by—dishwashers, automatic clothes washers and
driers, refrigerators and deep freezes.

The owners were not only willing but glad and proud to show 4
their homes to me. The rooms, while small, were well proportioned.
Every conceivable unit was built in. Wide windows, some even called
picture windows, destroyed any sense of being closed in; the bedrooms
and beds were spacious and the storage space unbelievable. It seemed
to me a revolution in living and on a rapid increase. Why did a family
choose to live in such a home? Well, it was comfortable, compact, easy
to keep clean, easy to heat.

In Maine: "I'm tired of living in a cold barn with the wind whistling 5
through, tired of the torment of little taxes and payments for this and
that. It's warm and cozy and in the summer the air-conditioner keeps
us cool."

"What is the usual income bracket of the mobiles?" 6

"That is variable but a goodly number are in the ten-thousand- to 7
twenty-thousand-dollar class."

"Has job uncertainty anything to do with the rapid increase of 8
these units?"

"Well perhaps there may be some of that. Who knows what is in     9
store tomorrow? Mechanics, plant engineers, architects, accountants,
and even here and there a doctor or a dentist live in the mobile. If a
plant or a factory closes down, you're not trapped with property you
can't sell. Suppose the husband has a job and is buying a house and
there's a layoff. The value goes out of his house. But if he has a mobile
home he rents a trucking service and moves on and he hasn't lost
anything. He may never have to do it, but the fact that he can is a
comfort to him."

"How are they purchased?"     10

"On time, just like an automobile. It's like paying rent."     11

And then I discovered the greatest selling appeal of all—one that     12
crawls through nearly all American life. Improvements are made
on these mobile homes every year. If you are doing well you turn
yours in on a new model just as you do with an automobile if you can
possibly afford to. There's status to that. And the turn-in value is
higher than that of automobiles because there's a ready market for
used homes. And after a few years the once expensive home may
have a poorer family. They are easy to maintain, no need to paint
since they are usually of aluminum, and are not tied to fluctuating
land values.

"How about schools?"     13

The school buses pick the children up right at the park and bring     14
them back. The family car takes the head of the house to work and
the family to a drive-in movie at night. It's a healthy life out in the
country air. The payments, even if high and festooned with interest,
are no worse then renting an apartment and fighting the owner for
heat. And where could you rent such a comfortable ground-floor apartment with a place for your car outside the door? Where else could the
kids have a dog? Nearly every mobile home has a dog, as Charley
discovered to his delight. Twice I was invited to dinner in a mobile
home and several times watched a football game on television. A manager told me that one of the first considerations in his business was
to find and buy a place where television reception is good. Since I did
not require any facilities, sewer, water, or electricity, the price to me
for stopping the night was one dollar.

The first impression forced on me was that permanence is neither     15
achieved nor desired by mobile people. They do not buy for the generations, but only until a new model they can afford comes out. The
mobile units are by no means limited to the park communities.
Hundreds of them will be found sitting beside a farm house, and this

was explained to me. There was a time when, on the occasion of a son's marriage and the addition of a wife and later of children to the farm, it was customary to add a wing or at least a lean-to on the home place. Now in many cases a mobile unit takes the place of additional building. A farmer from whom I bought eggs and home-smoked bacon told me of the advantages. Each family has a privacy it never had before. The old folks are not irritated by crying babies. The mother-in-law problem is abated because the new daughter has a privacy she never had and a place of her own in which to build the structure of a family. When they move away, and nearly all Americans move away, or want to, they do not leave unused and therefore useless rooms. Relations between the generations are greatly improved. The son is a guest when he visits the parents' house, and the parents are guests in the son's house.

Then there are the loners, and I have talked with them also. Driv- 16 ing along, you see high on a hill a single mobile home placed to command a great view. Others nestle under trees fringing a river or a lake. These loners have rented a tiny piece of land from the owner. They need only enough for the unit and the right of passage to get to it. Sometimes the loner digs a well and a cesspool, and plants a garden, but others transport their water in fifty-gallon oil drums. Enormous ingenuity is apparent with some of the loners in placing the water supply higher than the unit and connecting it with plastic pipe so that a gravity flow is insured.

One of the dinners that I shared in a mobile home was cooked in 17 an immaculate kitchen, walled in plastic tile, with stainless-steel sinks and ovens and stoves flush with the wall. The fuel is butane or some other bottled gas which can be picked up anywhere. We ate in a dining alcove paneled in mahogany veneer. I've never had a better or a more comfortable dinner. I had brought a bottle of whisky as my contribution, and afterward we sat in deep comfortable chairs cushioned in foam rubber. This family liked the way they lived and wouldn't think of going back to the old way. The husband worked as a garage mechanic about four miles away and made good pay. Two children walked to the highway every morning and were picked up by a yellow school bus.

Sipping a highball after dinner, hearing the rushing of water in 18 the electric dishwasher in the kitchen, I brought up a question that had puzzled me. These were good, thoughtful, intelligent people. I said, "One of our most treasured feelings concerns roots, growing up rooted in some soil or some community." How did they feel about raising their children without roots? Was it good or bad? Would they miss it or not?

The father, a good-looking, fair-skinned man with dark eyes, an-    19
swered me. "How many people today have what you are talking about? What roots are there in an apartment twelve floors up? What roots are in a housing development of hundreds and thousands of small dwellings almost exactly alike? My father came from Italy," he said. "He grew up in Tuscany in a house where his family had lived maybe a thousand years. That's roots for you, no running water, no toilet, and they cooked with charcoal or vine clippings. They had just two rooms, a kitchen and a bedroom where everybody slept, grandpa, father and all the kids, no place to read, no place to be alone, and never had had. Was that better? I bet if you gave my old man the choice he'd cut his roots and live like this." He waved his hands at the comfortable room. "Fact is, he cut his roots away and came to America. Then he lived in a tenement in New York—just one room, walk-up, cold water and no heat. That's where I was born and I lived in the streets as a kid until my old man got a job upstate in New York in the grape country. You see, he knew about vines, that's about all he knew. Now you take my wife. She's Irish descent. Her people had roots too."

"In a peat bog," the wife said. "And lived on potatoes." She gazed    20
fondly through the door at her fine kitchen.

"Don't you miss some kind of permanence?"    21

"Who's got permanence? Factory closes down, you move on.    22
Good times and things opening up, you move on where it's better. You got roots you sit and starve. You take the pioneers in the history books. They were movers. Take up land, sell it, move on. I read in a book how Lincoln's family came to Illinois on a raft. They had some barrels of whisky for a bank account. How many kids in America stay in the place where they were born, if they can get out?"

"You've thought about it a lot."    23

"Don't have to think about it. There it is. I've got a good trade.    24
Long as there's automobiles I can get work, but suppose the place I work goes broke. I got to move where there's a job. I get to my job in three minutes. You want I should drive twenty miles because I got roots?"

Later they showed me magazines designed exclusively for mobile    25
dwellers, stories and poems and hints for successful mobile living. How to stop a leak. How to choose a place for sun or coolness. And there were advertisements for gadgets, fascinating things, for cooking,

cleaning, washing clothes, furniture and beds and cribs. Also there were full-page pictures of new models, each one grander and more shiny than the next.

"There's thousands of them," said the father, "and there's going to be millions." 26

"Joe's quite a dreamer," the wife said. "He's always figuring something out. Tell him your ideas, Joe." 27

"Maybe he wouldn't be interested." 28

"Sure I would." 29

"Well, it's not a dream like she said, it's for real, and I'm going to do it pretty soon. Take a little capital, but it would pay off. I been looking around the used lots for the unit I want at the price I want to pay. Going to rip out the guts and set it up for a repair shop. I got enough tools nearly already, and I'll stock little things like windshield wipers and fan belts and cylinder rings and inner tubes, stuff like that. You take these courts are getting bigger and bigger. Some of the mobile people got two cars. I'll rent me a hundred feet of ground right near and I'll be in business. There's one thing you can say about cars, there's nearly always something wrong with them that's got to be fixed. And I'll have my house, this here one right beside my shop. That way I would have a bell and give twenty-four-hour service." 30

"Sounds like a good deal," I said. And it does. 31

"Best thing about it," Joe went on, "if business fell off, why, I'd just move on where it was good." 32

His wife said, "Joe's got it all worked out on paper where everything's going to go, every wrench and drill, even an electric welder. Joe's a wonderful welder." 33

I said, "I take back what I said, Joe. I guess you've got your roots in a grease pit." 34

"You could do worse. I even worked that out. And you know, when the kids grow up, we can even work our way south in the winter and north in the summer." 35

"Joe does good work," said his wife. "He's got his own steady customers where he works. Some men come fifty miles to get Joe to work on their cars because he does good work." 36

"I'm a real good mechanic," said Joe. 37

Driving the big highway near Toledo I had a conversation with Charley on the subject of roots. He listened but he didn't reply. In the pattern-thinking about roots I and most other people have left two things out of consideration. Could it be that Americans are a restless people, a mobile people, never satisfied with where they are as a matter 38 of selection? The pioneers, the immigrants who peopled the continent, were the restless ones in Europe. The steady rooted ones stayed home and are still there. But every one of us, except the Negroes forced here as slaves, are descended from the restless ones, the wayward ones who were not content to stay at home. Wouldn't it be unusual if we had not inherited this tendency? And the fact is that we have. But that's the short view. What are roots and how long have we had them? If our species has existed for a couple of million years, what is its history? Our remote ancestors followed the game, moved with the food supply, and fled from evil weather, from ice and the changing seasons. Then after millennia beyond thinking they domesticated some animals so that they lived with their food supply. Then of necessity they followed the grass that fed their flocks in endless wanderings. Only when agriculture came into practice—and that's not very long ago in terms of the whole history—did a place achieve meaning and value and permanence. But land is a tangible, and tangibles have a way of getting into few hands. Thus it was that one man wanted ownership of land and at the same time wanted servitude because someone had to work it. Roots were in ownership of land, in tangible and immovable possessions. In this view we are a restless species with a very short history of roots, and those not widely distributed. Perhaps we have overrated roots as a psychic need. Maybe the greater the urge, the deeper and more ancient is the need, the will, the hunger to be somewhere else.

# Questions

1. In paragraph 1 Steinbeck explains why he preferred secondary roads to heavily used roads. Explain his reason, in your own words. Exactly what does he mean when he says that "the great wide traffic slashes . . . promote the self by fostering daydreams"?
2. If you have ever lived in a mobile home, what do you consider its advantages? Its disadvantages? If you have never lived in one, on the basis of this essay do you think someday you might give it a try? Why, or why not?
3. In paragraphs 18–22 Steinbeck raises the question of whether the residents of mobile homes may be "without roots." The father, in paragraph 19, suggests that people who live in apartments, or in housing developments, also probably lack roots. Do you find his argument compelling? Why, or why not?
4. In paragraph 34 Steinbeck says, "I take back what I said, Joe. I guess

you've got your roots in a grease pit." What does he mean? Does his response have any relevance to other members of Joe's family?

5.  In the last paragraph Steinbeck writes, "We are a restless species with a very short history of roots." What can you add to his meditation? If you have read Calvino's "The Aquatic Uncle" (pages 133–144), how does that story add to Steinbeck's meditation?

Jane Jacobs

# A Good Neighborhood

Anthropologist Elena Padilla, author of *Up from Puerto*        1
*Rico,* describing Puerto Rican life in a poor and squalid district of New York, tells how much people know about each other—who is to be trusted and who not, who is defiant of the law and who upholds it, who is competent and well informed and who is inept and ignorant—and how these things are known from the public life of the sidewalk and its associated enterprises. These are matters of public character. But she also tells how select are those permitted to drop into the kitchen for a cup of coffee, how strong are the ties, and how limited the number of a person's genuine confidants, those who share in a person's private life and private affairs. She tells how it is not considered dignified for everyone to know one's affairs. Nor is it considered dignified to snoop on others beyond the face presented in public. It does violence to a person's privacy and rights. In this, the people she describes are essentially the same as the people of the mixed, Americanized city street on which I live, and essentially the same as the people who live in high-income apartments or fine town houses, too.

A good city street neighborhood achieves a marvel of balance be-        2
tween its people's determination to have essential privacy and their simultaneous wishes for differing degrees of contact, enjoyment or

Jane Jacobs was born in Scranton, Pennsylvania, in 1916. From 1952 until 1962 she served as an associate editor of *Architectural Forum.* In addition to *The Death and Life of Great American Cities,* from which "A Good Neighborhood" (editors' title) comes, she has written *The Economy of Cities.*

help from the people around. This balance is largely made up of small, sensitively managed details, practiced and accepted so casually that they are normally taken for granted.

Perhaps I can best explain this subtle but all-important balance in   3
terms of the stores where people leave keys for their friends, a common custom in New York. In our family, for example, when a friend wants to use our place while we are away for a weekend or everyone happens to be out during the day, or a visitor for whom we do not wish to wait up is spending the night, we tell such a friend that he can pick up the key at the delicatessen across the street. Joe Cornacchia, who keeps the delicatessen, usually has a dozen or so keys at a time for handing out like this. He has a special drawer for them.

Now why do I, and many others, select Joe as a logical custodian   4
for keys? Because we trust him, first, to be a responsible custodian, but equally important because we know that he combines a feeling of good will with a feeling of no personal responsibility about our private affairs. Joe considers it no concern of his whom we choose to permit in our places and why.

Around on the other side of our block, people leave their keys at   5
a Spanish grocery. On the other side of Joe's block, people leave them at the candy store. Down a block they leave them at the coffee shop, and a few hundred feet around the corner from that, in a barber shop. Around one corner from two fashionable blocks of town houses and apartments in the Upper East Side, people leave their keys in a butcher shop and a bookshop; around another corner they leave them in a cleaner's and a drug store. In unfashionable East Harlem keys are left with at least one florist, in bakeries, in luncheonettes, in Spanish and Italian groceries.

The point, wherever they are left, is not the kind of ostensible   6
service that the enterprise offers, but the kind of proprietor it has.

A service like this cannot be formalized. Identifications . . . ques-   7
tions . . . insurance against mishaps. The all-essential line between public service and privacy would be transgressed by institutionaliza-tion. Nobody in his right mind would leave his key in such a place. The service must be given as a favor by someone with an unshakable understanding of the difference between a person's key and a person's private life, or it cannot be given at all.

Or consider the line drawn by Mr. Jaffe at the candy store around   8
our corner—a line so well understood by his customers and by other storekeepers too that they can spend their whole lives in its presence and never think about it consciously. One ordinary morning last win-

ter, Mr. Jaffe, whose formal business name is Bernie, and his wife, whose formal business name is Ann, supervised the small children crossing at the corner on the way to P.S. 41, as Bernie always does because he sees the need; lent an umbrella to one customer and a dollar to another; took custody of two keys; took in some packages for people in the next building who were away; lectured two youngsters who asked for cigarettes; gave street directions; took custody of a watch to give the repair man across the street when he opened later; gave out information on the range of rents in the neighborhood to an apartment seeker; listened to a tale of domestic difficulty and offered reassurance; told some rowdies they could not come in unless they behaved and then defined (and got) good behavior; provided an incidental forum for half a dozen conversations among customers who dropped in for oddments; set aside certain newly arrived papers and magazines for regular customers who would depend on getting them; advised a mother who came for a birthday present not to get the ship-model kit because another child going to the same birthday party was giving that; and got a back copy (this was for me) of the previous day's newspaper out of the deliverer's surplus returns when he came by.

After considering this multiplicity of extra-merchandising services 9 I asked Bernie, "Do you ever introduce your customers to each other?"

He looked startled at the idea, even dismayed. "No," he said 10 thoughtfully. "That would just not be advisable. Sometimes, if I know two customers who are in at the same time have an interest in common, I bring up the subject in conversation and let them carry it on from there if they want to. But oh no, I wouldn't introduce them."

When I told this to an acquaintance in a suburb, she promptly 11 assumed that Mr. Jaffe felt that to make an introduction would be to step above his social class. Not at all. In our neighborhood, storekeepers like the Jaffes enjoy an excellent social status, that of businessmen. In income they are apt to be the peers of the general run of customers and in independence they are the superiors. Their advice, as men or women of common sense and experience, is sought and respected. They are well known as individuals, rather than unknown as class symbols. No; this is that almost unconsciously enforced, well-balanced line showing, the line between the city public world and the world of privacy.

This line can be maintained, without awkwardness to anyone, be- 12 cause of the great plenty of opportunities for public contact in the enterprises along the sidewalks, or on the sidewalks themselves as people move to and fro or deliberately loiter when they feel like it, and also because of the presence of many public hosts, so to speak, proprietors of meeting places like Bernie's where one is free to hang around or dash in and out, no strings attached.

Under this system, it is possible in a city street neighborhood to know all kinds of people without unwelcome entanglements, without boredom, necessity for excuses, explanations, fears of giving offense, embarrassments respecting impositions or commitments, and all such paraphernalia of obligations which can accompany less limited relationships. It is possible to be on excellent sidewalk terms with people who are very different from oneself, and even, as time passes, on familiar public terms with them. Such relationships can, and do, endure for many years, for decades; they could never have formed without that line, much less endured. They form precisely because they are by-the-way to people's normal public sorties. 13

# Questions

1. In paragraphs 1 and 2 Jacobs defines "a good city street neighborhood." Are her standards applicable to suburban or rural neighborhoods? If not, how might they be adapted?
2. What other qualities define a good neighborhood for you? What makes for a bad neighborhood?
3. Jacobs doesn't speak here of how good neighborhoods, or bad, come into existence. What forces, in your opinion, create good or bad neighborhoods? Can the evolution of neighborhoods be predicted, or controlled?
4. If you reread the first paragraph, you will notice that the first sentence is unusually long and that the second is unusually short; the third is fairly long and the fourth fairly short. What is the effect of these two shorter sentences, beyond mere variety? Elsewhere in the essay, too, Jacob's prose includes some very long sentences, but they probably did not confuse you. Why?

# E. B. White

# The Door

Everything (he kept saying) is something it isn't. And everybody is always somewhere else. Maybe it was the city, being in the city, that made him feel how queer everything was and that it was something else. Maybe (he kept thinking) it was the names of the things. The names were tex and frequently koid. Or they were flex and oid or they were duroid (sani) or flexsan (duro), but everything was glass (but not quite glass) and the thing that you touched (the surface, washable, crease-resistant) was rubber, only it wasn't quite rubber and you didn't quite touch it but almost. The wall, which was glass but thrutex, turned out on being approached not to be a wall, it was something else, it was an opening or doorway—and the doorway (through which he saw himself approaching) turned out to be something else, it was a wall. And what he had eaten not having agreed with him.

He was in a washable house, but he wasn't sure. Now about those rats, he kept saying to himself. He meant the rats that the Professor had driven crazy by forcing them to deal with problems which were beyond the scope of rats, the insoluble problems. He meant the rats that had been trained to jump at the square card with the circle in the middle, and the card (because it was something it wasn't) would give way and let the rat into a place where the food was, but then one day it would be a trick played on the rat, and the card would be changed, and the rat would jump but the card wouldn't give way, and it was an impossible situation (for a rat) and the rat would go insane and into its eyes would come the unspeakably bright imploring look of the frustrated, and after the convulsions were over and the frantic racing around, then the passive stage would set in and the willingness to let anything be done to it, even if it was something else.

He didn't know which door (or wall) or opening in the house to jump at, to get through, because one was an opening that wasn't a

E[lwyn] B[rooks] White (1899–1985) wrote poetry and fiction, but he is most widely known as an essayist and as the coauthor (with William Strunk, Jr.) of *Elements of Style.* After a long career at *The New Yorker* he retired to Maine, but he continued to write until the year before his death at the age of 86.

door (it was a void, or koid) and the other was a wall that wasn't opening, it was a sanitary cupboard of the same color. He caught a glimpse of his eyes staring into his eyes, in the thrutex, and in them was the expression he had seen in the picture of the rats—weary after convulsions and the frantic racing around, when they were willing and did not mind having anything done to them. More and more (he kept saying) I am confronted by a problem which is incapable of solution (for this time even if he chose the right door, there would be no food behind it) and that is what madness is, and things seeming different from what they are. He heard, in the house where he was, in the city to which he had gone (as toward a door which might, or might not, give way), a noise—not a loud noise but more of a low prefabricated humming. It came from a place in the base of the wall (or stat) where the flue carrying the filterable air was, and not far from the Minipiano, which was made of the same material nailbrushes are made of, and which was under the stairs. "This, too, has been tested," she said, pointing, but not at it, "and found viable." It wasn't a loud noise, he kept thinking, sorry that he had seen his eyes, even though it was through his own eyes that he had seen them.

First will come the convulsions (he said), then the exhaustion, then 4 the willingness to let anything be done. "And you better believe it *will* be."

All his life he had been confronted by situations which were in- 5 capable of being solved, and there was a deliberateness behind all this, behind this changing of the card (or door), because they would always wait till you had learned to jump at the certain card (or door)—the one with the circle—and then they would change it on you. There have been so many doors changed on me, he said, in the last twenty years, but it is now becoming clear that it is an impossible situation, and the question is whether to jump again, even though they ruffle you in the rump with a blast of air—to make you jump. He wished he wasn't standing by the Minipiano. First they would teach you the prayers and the Psalms, and that would be the right door (the one with the circle) and the long sweet words with the holy sound, and that would be the one to jump at to get where the food was. Then one day you jumped and it didn't give way, so that all you got was the bump on the nose, and the first bewilderment, the first young bewilderment.

I don't know whether to tell her about the door they substituted 6 or not, he said, the one with the equation on it and the picture of the amoeba reproducing itself by division. Or the one with the photostatic copy of the check for thirty-two dollars and fifty cents. But the jumping was so long ago, although the bump is . . . how those old wounds hurt! Being crazy this way wouldn't be so bad if only, if only. If only when you put your foot forward to take a step, the ground wouldn't come up to meet your foot the way it does. And the same way in the street (only I may never get back to the street unless I jump at the right door), the curb coming up to meet your foot, anticipating ever so delicately the weight of the body, which is somewhere else. "We could take your name," she said, "and send it to you." And it wouldn't be so bad if only you could read a sentence all the way through without jumping (your eye) to something else on the same page; and then (he kept thinking) there was that man out in Jersey, the one who started to chop his trees down, one by one, the man who began talking about how he would take his house to pieces, brick by brick, because he faced a problem incapable of solution, probably, so he began to hack at the trees in the yard, began to pluck with trembling fingers at the bricks in the house. Even if a house is not washable, it is worth taking down. It is not till later that the exhaustion sets in.

But it is inevitable that they will keep changing the doors on you, he said, because that is what they are for; and the thing is to get used to it and not let it unsettle the mind. But that would mean not jumping, and you can't. Nobody can not jump. There will be no not-jumping. Among rats, perhaps, but among people never. Everybody has to keep jumping at a door (the one with the circle on it) because that is the way everybody is, especially some people. You wouldn't want me, standing here, to tell you, would you, about my friend the poet (deceased) who said, "My heart has followed all my days something I cannot name"? (It had the circle on it.) And like many poets, although few so beloved, he is gone. It killed him, the jumping. First, of course, there were the preliminary bouts, the convulsions, and the calm and the willingness.

I remember the door with the picture of the girl on it (only it was spring), her arms outstretched in loveliness, her dress (it was the one with the circle on it) uncaught, beginning the slow, clear, blinding cascade—and I guess we would all like to try that door again, for it seemed like the way and for a while it was the way, the door would open and you would go through winged and exalted (like any rat) and the food would be there, the way the Professor had it arranged, everything O.K., and you had chosen the right door for the world was young. The time they changed that door on me, my nose bled for a hundred hours—how do you like that, Madam? Or would you prefer to show me further through this so strange house, or you could take my name and send it to me, for although my heart has followed all my days something I cannot name, I am tired of the jumping and I do not know which way to go, Madam, and I am not even sure that I am not tried beyond the endurance of man (rat, if you will) and have taken leave of sanity. What are you following these days, old friend, after your recovery from the last bump? What is the name, or is it something you cannot name? The rats have a name for it by this time, perhaps, but I don't know what they call it. I call it plexikoid and it comes in sheets, something like insulating board, unattainable and ugli-proof.

And there was the man out in Jersey, because I keep thinking about 9 his terrible necessity and the passion and trouble he had gone to all those years in the indescribable abundance of a householder's detail, building the estate and the planting of the trees and in spring the lawn-dressing and in fall the bulbs for the spring burgeoning, and the watering of the grass on the long light evenings in summer and the gravel for the driveway (all had to be thought out, planned) and the decorative borders, probably, the perennials and the bug spray, and the building of the house from plans of the architect, first the sills, then the studs, then the full corn in the ear, the floors laid on the floor timbers, smoothed, and then the carpets upon the smooth floors and the curtains and the rods therefor. And then, almost without warning, he would be jumping at the same old door and it wouldn't give: they had changed it on him, making life no longer supportable under the elms in the elm shade, under the maples in the maple shade.

"Here you have the maximum of openness in a small room."        10

It was impossible to say (maybe it was the city) what made him 11 feel the way he did, and I am not the only one either, he kept thinking—ask any doctor if I am. The doctors, they know how many there are, they even know where the trouble is only they don't like to tell you about the prefrontal lobe because that means making a hole in your skull and removing the work of centuries. It took so long coming, this lobe, so many, many years. (Is it something you read in the paper, perhaps?) And now, the strain being so great, the door having been changed by the Professor once too often . . . but it only means a whiff of ether, a few deft strokes, and the higher animal becomes a little easier in his mind and more like the lower one. From now on, you see, that's the way it will be, the ones with the small prefrontal lobes will win because the other ones are hurt too much by this incessant bumping. They can stand just so much, eh, Doctor? (And what is that, pray, that you have in your hand?) Still, you never can tell, eh, Madam?

He crossed (carefully) the room, the thick carpet under him softly, 12 and went toward the door carefully, which was glass and he could see himself in it, and which, at his approach, opened to allow him to pass through; and beyond he half expected to find one of the old doors that he had known, perhaps the one with the circle, the one with the girl her arms outstretched in loveliness and beauty before him. But he saw instead a moving stairway, and descended in light (he kept thinking) to the street below and to the other people. As he stepped off, the ground came up slightly, to meet his foot.

# Questions

1.  What information does the first paragraph give us about the story's setting and about the main character? What is the effect of all the parenthetical interruptions? How can White's use of a fragmentary sentence at the end of the paragraph be defended?
2.  In paragraph 2 the man recalls an account of a psychologist's experiment. What was the experiment's purpose? Why does the man recall it?
3.  Beginning with paragraph 5 the man reflects on the last twenty years of his life and on the "doors" that were constantly changed on him. What do the doors and their constant changing symbolize? He gives four examples. What are they, and what does each represent? Do the examples suggest that the man's problem is unique, or that it is shared by many of us?
4.  What do the "man out in Jersey," the "poet (deceased)," and the man have in common? How are they dissimilar?
5.  In paragraph 11 the doctor offers the man a solution of a kind. What is it? What does White think of this solution?
6.  Does the story have a happy ending? Explain.

## William Carlos Williams

# The Poor

It's the anarchy of poverty
delights me, the old
yellow wooden house indented
among the new brick tenements                    4

Or a cast iron balcony
with panels showing oak branches
in full leaf. It fits
the dress of the children                        8

reflecting every stage and
custom of necessity—
Chimneys, roofs, fences of
wood and metal in an unfenced                    12

age and enclosing next to
nothing at all: the old man
in a sweater and soft black
hat who sweeps the sidewalk—                     16

his own ten feet of it—
in a wind that fitfully
turning his corner has
overwhelmed the entire city                      20

# Questions

1.  In the context of the poem, how would you define "anarchy"?
2.  Poverty does not usually inspire delight. How does the poem support the opening statement?

William Carlos Williams (1883–1963) was a pediatrician with a wide practice among the industrial population in and around Rutherford, New Jersey. He was also a prolific writer. His works include short stories, novels, essays, plays, poems, and an autobiography.

# 4
## TEACHING AND LEARNING

*Doonesbury*
**Gary Trudeau**

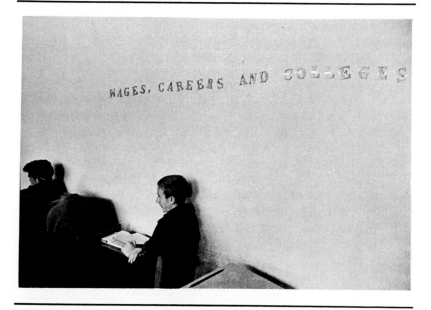

*Washoe Makes the Sign for "Drink"*
**T. J. Kaminski**

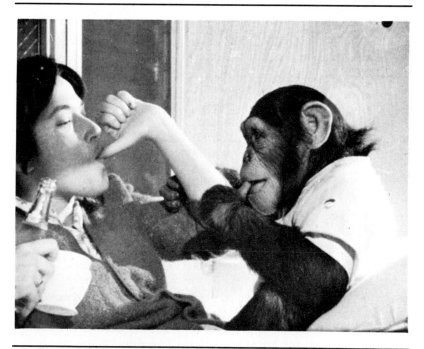

Courtesy R. A. and B. T. Gardner

# Short Views

Knowledge is power.
**Francis Bacon**

Hard students are commonly troubled with gouts, catarrahs, rheums, cachexia, bradypepsia, bad eyes, stone, and collick, crudities, oppilations, vertigo, winds, consumptions, and all such diseases as come by over-much sitting: they are most part lean, dry, ill-colored . . . and all through immoderate pains and extraordinary studies.
**Robert Burton**

In my opinion, the only justification for high schools is as therapeutic halfway houses for the deranged. Normal adolescents can find themselves and grow further only by coping with the jobs, sex, and chances of the real world—it is useless to feed them curricular imitations. I would simply abolish the high schools, substituting apprenticeships and other alternatives and protecting the young from gross exploitation by putting the school money directly in their pockets. The very few who have authentic scholarly interests will gravitate to their own libraries, teachers, and academies, as they always did in the past, when they could afford it. In organic communities, adolescents cluster together in their own youth houses, for their fun and games and loud music, without bothering sober folk. I see no reason whatsoever for adults to set up or direct such nests or to be there at all unless invited.
**Paul Goodman**

I can judge one of the main effects of personal grading by the attitudes of students who land in my remedial course in college. They hate and fear writing more than anything else they have had to do in school. If they see a blank sheet of paper on which they are expected to write something, they look as though they want to scream. Apparently they have never written anything that anyone thought was good. At least, no one ever *told* them that anything in their writing was good. All their teachers looked for were mistakes, and there are so many kinds of mistakes in writing that their students despair of ever learning to avoid them.

The attitude toward writing that these students have developed is well illustrated by a story told by the Russian writer Chekhov about a kitten that was given to his uncle. The uncle wanted to make the kitten a champion killer of mice, so while it was still very young, he showed it a live mouse in a cage. Since the kitten's hunting instinct had not yet developed, it examined the mouse curiously but without any hostility. The uncle wanted to teach it that such fraternizing with the enemy was wrong, so he slapped the kitten, scolded it, and sent it away in disgrace. The next day the same mouse was shown to the kitten again. This time the kitten regarded it rather fearfully but without any aggressive intent. Again the uncle slapped it, scolded it, and sent it away. This treatment went on day after day. After some time, as soon as the kitten saw or smelled that mouse, it screamed and tried to climb up the walls. At that point the uncle lost patience and gave the kitten away, saying that it was stupid and would never learn. Of course the kitten had learned perfectly, and had learned exactly what it had been taught, but unfortunately not what the uncle intended to teach. "I can sympathize with that kitten," says Chekhov, "because that same uncle tried to teach me Latin."
        **Paul B. Diederich**

A woman came to Rabbi Israel, the great maggid or teacher in Koznitz, and told him, with many tears, that she had been married a dozen years and still had not borne a son. "What are you willing to do about it?" he asked her. She did not know what to say. "My mother," so the maggid told her, "was aging and still had no child. Then she heard that the holy Baal Shem was stopping over in Apt in the course of a journey. She hurried to his inn and begged him to pray she might bear a son. 'What are you willing to do about it?' he asked. 'My husband is a poor book-binder,' she replied, 'but I do have one fine thing that I shall give to the rabbi.' She went home as fast as she could and fetched her good cape, her 'Katinka,' which was carefully stowed away in a chest. But when she returned to the inn with it, she heard that the Baal Shem had already left for Mezbizh. She immediately set out after him and since she had no money to ride, she walked from town to town with her 'Katinka' until she came to Mezbizh. The Baal Shem took the cape and hung it on the wall. 'It is well,' he said. My mother walked all the way back, from town to town, until she reached Apt. A year later, I was born."

"I, too," cried the woman, "will bring you a cape of mine so that I may get a son."

"That won't work," said the maggid. "You heard the story. My mother had no story to go by."
**Hasidic Tale**

You go to a great school not for knowledge so much as for arts and habits; for the habit of attention, for the art of expression, for the art of assuming at a moment's notice a new intellectual posture, for the art of entering quickly into another person's thought, for the habit of submitting to censure and refutation, for the art of indicating assent or dissent in graduated terms, for the habit of regarding minute points of accuracy, for the habit of working out what is possible in a given time, for taste, for discrimination, for mental courage and mental soberness. Above all, you go to a great school for self-knowledge.
**William Cory**

How people keep correcting us when we are young! There's always some bad habit or other they tell us we ought to get over. Yet most bad habits are tools to help us through life.
**Johann Wolfgang von Goethe**

Supposing anyone were to suggest that the best results for the individual and society could be derived through compulsory feeding. Would not the most ignorant rebel against such a stupid procedure? And yet the stomach has far greater adaptability to almost any situation than the brain. With all that, we find it quite natural to have compulsory mental feeding.

Indeed, we actually consider ourselves superior to other nations, because we have evolved a compulsory brain tube through which, for a certain number of hours every day, and for so many years, we can force into the child's mind a large quantity of mental nutrition.

. . . The great harm done by our system of education is not so much that it teaches nothing worth knowing, that it helps to perpetuate privileged classes, that it assists them in the criminal procedure of robbing and exploiting the masses; the harm of the system lies in its boastful proclamation that it stands for true education, thereby enslaving the masses a great deal more than could an absolute ruler.
**Emma Goldman**

The education of women should always be relative to that of men. To please, to be useful to us, to make us love and esteem them, to educate us when young, to take care of us when grown up; to advise, to console us, to render our lives easy and agreeable. These are the duties of women at all times, and what they should be taught in their infancy.
**Jean Jacques Rousseau,** *Emile*

If Johnny can't learn because he is hungry, that's the fault of poverty. But if Johnny can't pay attention because he is sleepy, that's the fault of parents.

What does it matter if we have a new book or an old book, if we open neither?
**Jesse Jackson**

*Education.* An education in things is not. We all are involved in the condemnation of words, an age of words. We are shut up in schools and college recitation rooms for ten or fifteen years, and come out at last with a bellyfull of words and do not know a thing. We cannot use our hands, or our legs, or our eyes, or our arms. We do not know an edible root in the woods. We cannot tell our course by the stars, nor the hour of the day by the sun. It is well if we can swim and skate. We are afraid of a horse, of a cow, of a dog, of a cat, of a spider. Far better was the Roman rule to teach a boy nothing that he could not learn standing. Now here are my wise young neighbors who, instead of getting, like the woodmen, into a railroad-car, where they have not even the activity of holding the reins, have got into a boat which they have built with their own hands, with sails which they have contrived to serve as a tent by night, and gone up the Merrimack to live by their wits on the fish of the stream and the berries of the wood. My worthy neighbor Dr. Bartlett expressed a true parental instinct when he desired to send his boy with them to learn something. The farm, the farm, is the right school. The reason of my deep respect for the farmer is that he is a realist, and not a dictionary. The farm is a piece of the world, the school-house is not. The farm, by training the physical, rectifies and invigorates the metaphysical and moral nature.
**Ralph Waldo Emerson**

Universities are, of course, hostile to geniuses.
**Ralph Waldo Emerson**

The man who can make hard things easy is the educator.
   **Ralph Waldo Emerson**


It is perhaps idle to wonder what, from my present point of view,
would have been an ideal education. If I could provide such a
curriculum for my own children they, in their turn, might find it all
a bore. But the fantasy of what I would have liked to learn as a
child may be revealing, since I feel unequipped by education for
problems that lie outside the cloistered, literary domain in which I
am competent and at home. Looking back, then, I would have
arranged for myself to be taught survival techniques for both
natural and urban wildernesses. I would want to have been
instructed in self-hypnosis, in *aikido* (the esoteric and purely self-
defensive style of judo), in elementary medicine, in sexual hygiene,
in vegetable gardening, in astronomy, navigation, and sailing; in
cookery and clothesmaking, in metalwork and carpentry, in
drawing and painting, in printing and typography, in botany and
biology, in optics and acoustics, in semantics and psychology, in
mysticism and yoga, in electronics and mathematical fantasy, in
drama and dancing, in singing and in playing an instrument by ear;
in wandering, in advanced daydreaming, in prestidigitation, in
techniques of escape from bondage, in disguise, in conversation
with birds and beasts, in ventriloquism, in French and German
conversation, in planetary history, in morphology, and in classical
Chinese. Actually, the main thing left out of my education was a
proper love for my own body, because one feared to cherish
anything so obviously mortal and prone to sickness.
   **Alan Watts**


If then a practical end must be assigned to a University course, I say
it is that of training good members of society. Its art is the art of
social life, and its end is fitness for the world. It neither confines its
views to particular professions on the one hand, nor creates heroes
or inspires genius on the other. Works indeed of genius fall under
no art; heroic minds come under no rule; a University is not a
birthplace of poets or of immortal authors, of founders of schools,
leaders of colonies, or conquerors of nations. It does not promise a
generation of Aristotles or Newtons, of Napoleons or Washingtons,
of Raphaels or Shakespeares, though such miracles of nature it has
before now contained within its precincts. Nor is it content on the
other hand with forming the critic or the experimentalist, the

economist or the engineer, though such too it includes within its
scope. But a University training is the great ordinary means to a
great but ordinary end; it aims at raising the intellectual tone of
society, at cultivating the public mind, at purifying the national
taste, at supplying true principles to popular enthusiasm and fixed
aims to popular aspiration, at giving enlargement and sobriety to
the ideas of the age, at facilitating the exercise of political power,
and refining the intercourse of private life. It is the education which
gives a man a clear conscious view of his own opinions and
judgments, a truth in developing them, an eloquence in expressing
them, and a force in urging them. It teaches him to see things as
they are, to go right to the point, to disentangle a skein of thought,
to detect what is sophistical, and to discard what is irrelevant. It
prepares him to fill any post with credit, and to master any subject
with facility. It shows him how to accommodate himself to others,
how to throw himself into their state of mind, how to bring before
them his own, how to influence them, how to come to an
understanding with them, how to bear with them.
          John Henry Newman


Education! Which of the various me's do you propose to educate,
and which do you propose to suppress?
          D. H. Lawrence


Think about the kind of world you want to live and work in. What
do you need to know to build the world? Demand that your
teachers teach you that.
          Prince Kropotkin


The entire object of true education is to make people not merely *do*
the right things, but *enjoy* the right things.
          John Ruskin


Nan-in, a Japanese master during the Meiji era (1868–1912),
received a university professor who came to inquire about Zen.
     Nan-in served tea. He poured his visitor's cup full, and then
kept on pouring.
     The professor watched the overflow until he no longer could
restrain himself. "It is overfull. No more will go in!"
     "Like this cup," Nan-in said, "you are full of your own

opinions and speculations. How can I show you Zen unless you first empty your cup?"
**Anonymous Zen Anecdote**

I think [Raymond Weaver] first attracted my attention as someone worth watching when, while we were both new instructors, I heard from a bewildered freshman about the quiz he had just given. The first question written on the blackboard was, "Which of the required readings in this course did you find least interesting?" Then, after members of the class had had ten minutes in which to expatiate on what was certainly to many a congenial topic, he wrote the second question: "To what defect in yourself do you attribute this lack of interest?"
**Joseph Wood Krutch**

## Plato

# The Myth of the Cave

**A**nd now, I said, let me show in a figure how far our nature    1 is enlightened or unenlightened—Behold! human beings living in an underground den, which has a mouth open toward the light and reaching all along the den; here they have been from their childhood, and have their legs and necks chained so that they cannot move, and can

---

Plato (427–347 B.C.), born in Athens, the son of an aristocratic family, wrote thirty dialogues in which Socrates is the chief speaker. Socrates, about twenty-five years older than Plato, was a philosopher who called himself a gadfly to Athenians. For his efforts at stinging them into thought, the Athenians executed him in 399 B.C. "The Myth of the Cave" is the beginning of Book VII of Plato's dialogue entitled *The Republic*. Socrates is talking with Glaucon.

For Plato, true knowledge is philosophic insight or awareness of the Good, not mere opinion or the knack of getting along in this world by remembering how things have usually worked in the past. To illustrate his idea that awareness of the Good is different from the ability to recognize the things of this shabby world, Plato (through his spokesman Socrates) resorts to an allegory: men imprisoned in a cave see on a wall in front of them the shadows or images of objects that are really behind them, and they hear echoes, not real voices. (The shadows are caused by the light from a fire behind the objects, and the echoes

only see before them, being prevented by the chains from turning round their heads. Above and behind them a fire is blazing at a distance, and between the fire and the prisoners there is a raised way; and you will see, if you look, a low wall built along the way, like the screen which marionette players have in front of them, over which they show the puppets.

I see.

And do you see, I said, men passing along the wall carrying all sorts of vessels, and statutes and figures of animals made of wood and stone and various materials, which appear over the wall? Some of them are talking, others silent.

You have shown me a strange image, and they are strange prisoners.

Like ourselves, I replied; and they see only their own shadows,     5 or the shadows of one another, which the fire throws on the opposite wall of the cave?

True, he said; how could they see anything but the shadows if they were never allowed to move their heads?

And of the objects which are being carried in like manner they would only see the shadows?

Yes, he said.

And if they were able to converse with one another, would they not suppose that they were naming what was actually before them?

by the cave's acoustical properties.) The prisoners, unable to perceive the real objects and the real voices, mistakenly think that the shadows and the echoes are real, and some of them grow highly adept at dealing with this illusory world. Were Plato writing today, he might have made the cave a movie theater: we see on the screen in front of us images caused by an object (film, passing in front of light) that is behind us. Moreover, the film itself is an illusory image, for it bears only the traces of a yet more real world—the world that was photographed—outside of the movie theater. And when we leave the theater to go into the real world, our eyes have become so accustomed to the illusory world that we at first blink with discomfort—just as Plato's freed prisoners do when they move out of the cave—at the real world of bright day, and we long for the familiar darkness. So too, Plato suggests, dwellers in ignorance may prefer the familiar shadows of their unenlightened world ("the world of becoming") to the bright world of the eternal Good ("the world of being") that education reveals.

We have just used the word "education." You will notice that the first sentence in the translation (by Benjamin Jowett) says that the myth will show "how far our nature is enlightened or unenlightened." In the original Greek the words here translated "enlightened" and "unenlightened" are *paideia* and *apaideusia*. No translation can fully catch the exact meanings of these elusive words. Depending on the context, *paideia* may be translated as "enlightenment," "education," "civilization," "culture," "knowledge of the good."

Very true.                                                                                    10

And suppose further that the prison had an echo which came from the other side, would they not be sure when one of the passersby spoke that the voice which they heard came from the passing shadow?

No question, he replied.

To them, I said, the truth would be literally nothing but the shadows of the images.

That is certain.

And now look again, and see what will naturally follow if the    15 prisoners are released and disabused of their error. At first, when any of them is liberated and compelled suddenly to stand up and turn his neck round and walk and look toward the light, he will suffer sharp pains; the glare will distress him, and he will be unable to see the realities of which in his former state he had seen the shadows; and then conceive some one saying to him, that what he saw before was an illusion, but that now, when he is approaching nearer to being and his eye is turned toward more real existence, he has a clearer vision—what will be his reply? And you may further imagine that his instructor is pointing to the objects as they pass and requiring him to name them—will he not be perplexed? Will he not fancy that the shadows which he formerly saw are truer than the objects which are now shown to him?

Far truer.

And if he is compelled to look straight at the light, will he not have a pain in his eyes which will make him turn away to take refuge in the objects of vision which he can see, and which he will conceive to be in reality clearer than the things which are now being shown to him?

True, he said.

And suppose once more, that he is reluctantly dragged up a steep and rugged ascent, and held fast until he is forced into the presence of the sun himself, is he not likely to be pained and irritated? When he approaches the light his eyes will be dazzled, and he will not be able to see anything at all of what are now called realities.

Not all in a moment, he said.                                                    20

He will require to grow accustomed to the sight of the upper world. And first he will see the shadows best, next the reflections of men and other objects in the water, and then the objects themselves; then he will gaze upon the light of the moon and the stars and the spangled heaven; and he will see the sky and the stars by night better than the sun or the light of the sun by day?

Certainly.

Last of all he will be able to see the sun, and not mere reflections of him in the water, but he will see him in his own proper place, and not in another; and he will contemplate him as he is.

Certainly.

He will then proceed to argue that this is he who gives the season  25
and the years, and is the guardian of all that is in the visible world, and in a certain way the cause of all things which he and his fellows have been accustomed to behold?

Clearly, he said, he would first see the sun and then reason about him.

And when he remembered his old habitation, and the wisdom of the den and his fellow-prisoners, do you not suppose that he would felicitate himself on the change, and pity them?

Certainly, he would.

And if they were in the habit of conferring honors among themselves on those who were quickest to observe the passing shadows and to remark which of them went before, and which followed after, and which were together; and who were therefore best able to draw conclusions as to the future, do you think that he would care for such honors and glories, or envy the possessors of them? Would he not say with Homer,

Better to be the poor servant of a poor master,

and to endure anything, rather than think as they do and live after their manner?

Yes, he said, I think that he would rather suffer anything than  30
entertain these false notions and live in this miserable manner.

Imagine once more, I said, such an one coming suddenly out of the sun to be replaced in his old situation; would he not be certain to have his eyes full of darkness?

To be sure, he said.

And if there were a contest, and he had to compete in measuring the shadows with the prisoners who had never moved out of the den, while his sight was still weak, and before his eyes had become steady (and the time which would be needed to acquire this new habit of sight might be very considerable), would he not be ridiculous? Men would say of him that up he went and down he came without his eyes; and that it was better not even to think of ascending; and if any one tried to loose another and lead him up to the light, let them only catch the offender, and they would put him to death.

No question, he said.

This entire allegory, I said, you may now append, dear Glaucon,  35
to the previous argument; the prison-house is the world of sight, the
light of the fire is the sun, and you will not misapprehend me if you
interpret the journey upwards to be the ascent of the soul into the
intellectual world according to my poor belief, which, at your desire,
I have expressed—whether rightly or wrongly God knows. But,
whether true or false, my opinion is that in the world of knowledge
the idea of good appears last of all, and is seen only with an effort;
and, when seen, is also inferred to be the universal author of all things
beautiful and right, parent of light and of the lord of light in this visible
world, and the immediate source of reason and truth in the intellectual;
and that this is the power upon which he who would act rationally
either in public or private life must have his eye fixed.

I agree, he said, as far as I am able to understand you.

Moreover, I said, you must not wonder that those who attain to
this beatific vision are unwilling to descend to human affairs; for their
souls are ever hastening into the upper world where they desire to
dwell; which desire of theirs is very natural, if our allegory may be
trusted.

Yes, very natural.

And is there anything surprising in one who passes from divine
contemplations to the evil state of man, misbehaving himself in a ridiculous manner; if, while his eyes are blinking and before he has
become accustomed to the surrounding darkness, he is compelled to
fight in courts of law, or in other places, about the images or the shadows of images of justice, and is endeavoring to meet the conceptions
of those who have never yet seen absolute justice?

Anything but surprising, he replied.                              40

Any one who has common sense will remember that the bewil-
derments of the eyes are of two kinds, and arise from two causes,
either from coming out of the light or from going into the light, which
is true of the mind's eye, quite as much as of the bodily eye; and he
who remembers this when he sees any one whose vision is perplexed
and weak, will not be too ready to laugh; he will first ask whether that
soul of man has come out of the brighter life, and is unable to see
because unaccustomed to the dark, or having turned from darkness
to the day is dazzled by excess of light. And he will count the one
happy in his condition and state of being, and he will pity the other;
or, if he have a mind to laugh at the soul which comes from below
into the light, there will be more reason in this than in the laugh which
greets him who returns from above out of the light into the den.

That, he said, is a very just distinction.

But then, if I am right, certain professors of education must be wrong when they say that they can put a knowledge into the soul which was not there before, like sight into blind eyes.

They undoubtedly say this, he replied.

Whereas, our argument shows that the power and capacity of 45 learning exists in the soul already; and that just as the eye was unable to turn from darkness to light without the whole body, so too the instrument of knowledge can only by the movement of the whole soul be turned from the world of becoming into that of being, and learn by degrees to endure the sight of being, and of the brightest and best of being, or in other words, of the good.

Very true.

And must there not be some art which will effect conversion in the easiest and quickest manner; not implanting the faculty of sight, for that exists already, but has been turned in the wrong direction, and is looking away from the truth?

Yes, he said, such an art may be presumed.

And whereas the other so-called virtues of the soul seem to be akin to bodily qualities, for even when they are not originally innate they can be implanted later by habit and exercise, the virtue of wisdom more than anything else contains a divine element which always remains, and by this conversion is rendered useful and profitable; or, on the other hand, hurtful and useless. Did you never observe the narrow intelligence flashing from the keen eye of a clever rogue—how eager he is, how clearly his paltry soul sees the way to his end; he is the reverse of blind, but his keen eyesight is forced into the service of evil, and he is mischievous in proportion to his cleverness?

Very true, he said.                                                                          50

But what if there had been a circumcision of such natures in the days of their youth; and they had been severed from those sensual pleasures, such as eating and drinking, which, like leaden weights, were attached to them at their birth, and which drag them down and turn the vision of their souls upon the things that are below—if, I say, they had been released from these impediments and turned in the opposite direction, the very same faculty in them would have seen the truth as keenly as they see what their eyes are turned to now.

Very likely.

Yes, I said; and there is another thing which is likely, or rather a necessary inference from what has preceded, that neither the uneducated and uninformed of the truth, nor yet those who never make an end of their education, will be able ministers of State; not the former, because they have no single aim of duty which is the rule of all their actions, private as well as public; nor the latter, because they will not act at all except upon compulsion, fancying that they are already dwelling apart in the islands of the blest.

Very true, he replied.

Then, I said, the business of us who are the founders of the State 55 will be to compel the best minds to attain that knowledge which we have already shown to be the greatest of all—they must continue to ascend until they arrive at the good; but when they have ascended and seen enough we must not allow them to do as they do now.

What do you mean?

I mean that they remain in the upper world: but this must not be allowed; they must be made to descend again among the prisoners in the den, and partake of their labors and honors, whether they are worth having or not.

But is not this unjust? he said; ought we to give them a worse life, when they might have a better?

You have again forgotten, my friend, I said, the intention of the legislator, who did not aim at making any one class in the State happy above the rest; the happiness was to be in the whole State, and he held the citizens together by persuasion and necessity, making them benefactors of the State, and therefore benefactors of one another; to this end he created them, not to please themselves, but to be his instruments in binding up the State.

True, he said, I had forgotten.                                                    60

Observe, Glaucon, that there will be no injustice in compelling our philosophers to have a care and providence of others; we shall explain to them that in other States, men of their class are not obliged to share in the toils of politics: and this is reasonable, for they grow up at their own sweet will, and the government would rather not have them. Being self-taught, they cannot be expected to show any gratitude for a culture which they have never received. But we have brought you into the world to be rulers of the hive, kings of yourselves and of the other citizens, and have educated you far better and more perfectly than they have been educated, and you are better able to share in the double duty. Wherefore each of you, when his turn comes, must go down to the general underground abode, and get the habit of seeing in the dark. When you have acquired the habit, you will see ten thousand times better than the inhabitants of the den, and you will know what the several images are, and what they represent, because you have seen the beautiful and just and good in their truth. And thus our State which is also yours will be a reality, and not a dream only, and will be administered in a spirit unlike that of other States, in which men fight with one another about shadows only and are distracted in the struggle for power, which in their eyes is a great good. Whereas the truth is that the State in which the rulers are most reluctant to govern is always the best and most quietly governed, and the State in which they are most eager, the worst.

Quite true, he replied.

And will our pupils, when they hear this, refuse to take their turn at the toils of State, when they are allowed to spend the greater part of their time with one another in the heavenly light?

Impossible, he answered; for they are just men, and the commands which we impose upon them are just; there can be no doubt that every one of them will take office as a stern necessity, and not after the fashion of our present rulers of State.

Yes, my friend, I said; and there lies the point. You must contrive 65 for your future rulers another and a better life than that of a ruler, and then you may have a well-ordered State; for only in the State which offers this, will they rule who are truly rich, not in silver and gold, but in virtue and wisdom, which are the true blessings of life. Whereas if they go to the administration of public affairs, poor and hungering after their own private advantage, thinking that hence they are to snatch the chief good, order there can never be; for they will be fighting about office, and the civil and domestic broils which thus arise will be the ruin of the rulers themselves and of the whole State.

Most true, he replied.

And the only life which looks down upon the life of political ambition is that of true philosophy. Do you know of any other?

Indeed, I do not, he said.

And those who govern ought not to be lovers of the task? For, if they are, there will be rival lovers, and they will fight.

No question. 70

Who then are those whom we shall compel to be guardians? Surely they will be the men who are wisest about affairs of State, and by whom the State is best administered, and who at the same time have other honors and another and a better life than that of politics?

They are the men, and I will choose them, he replied.

And now shall we consider in what way such guardians will be produced, and how they are to be brought from darkness to light— as some are said to have ascended from the world below to the gods?

By all means, he replied.

The process, I said, is not the turning over of an oyster-shell,[1] but   75
the turning round of a soul passing from a day which is little better
than night to the true day of being, that is, the ascent from below
which we affirm to be true philosophy?

Quite so.

# Questions

1.  Plato is not merely reporting one of Socrates' conversations; he is
    teaching. What advantages does a dialogue have over a narrative
    or an essay as a way of teaching philosophy? How is the form of a
    dialogue especially suited to solving a problem?
2.  If you don't know the etymology of the word "conversion," look it
    up in a dictionary. How is the etymology appropriate to Plato's idea
    about education.
3.  In paragraph 19, describing the prisoner as "reluctantly dragged"
    upward and "forced" to look at the sun, Socrates asks: "Is he not
    likely to be pained and irritated?" Can you recall experiencing pain
    and irritation while learning something you later were glad to have
    learned? Can you recall learning something new *without* experi-
    encing pain and irritation?
4.  "The State in which the rulers are most reluctant to govern is always
    the best and most quietly governed, and the State in which they
    are most eager, the worst" (paragraph 61). What does Socrates
    mean? Using examples from contemporary politics, defend this
    proposition, or argue against it.
5.  Can you account for the power of this myth or fable? In our intro-
    ductory comment (page 231) we tried to clarify the message by
    saying that a movie theater might serve as well as a cave, but in
    fact if the story were recast using a movie theater, would the emo-
    tional power be the same? Why or why not?
6.  The metaphors of education as conversion and ascent are linked
    by the metaphor of light. Consider such expressions as "I see"
    (meaning "I understand") and "Let me give an illustration" (from
    the Latin *in* = in, and *lustrare* = to make bright). What other expres-
    sions about light are used metaphorically to describe intellectual
    comprehension?

---

[1] An allusion to a game in which two parties fled or pursued according as an oyster-
shell which was thrown into the air fell with the dark or light side uppermost.

Ernesto Galarza

# Growing into Manhood

Up to the time a boy was between five and six years old, 1
Jalcocotán was for the most part an easy place in which to live. The
neighbors and *compadres* and *comadres* who scolded you for your bad
manners or sent you on errands did not interfere much if you were
respectful and stayed out of the way. With my two cousins and other
boys of my own age I always had something to watch or to do.

The near side of the pond was shallow and fringed with reeds and 2
tall clumps of grass that blossomed with plumes of cream-colored fluff.
Around them the pond was always muddy and cool. In your bare feet
you sank up to the ankles and by wriggling your toes you could raise
oozy, iridescent bubbles. Trampling and squishing the mud, we made
plopping hollow sounds and pretended we had gas on our stomachs.
Pulling your foot out of the soft gumbo while your friends listened
closely made noise remarkably like the mules in the corrals when they
dropped manure.

Although we never collected polliwogs or frogs or lizards we 3
chased them along the mud flat until they hopped into deep water or
slithered away in the grass. Water snakes were everywhere, which we
imagined were poisonous *víboras* or copperheads, like those the *jalcocotecanos* found in the forest. We spiced our play with a legend about
an alligator that had crawled all the way up from Miramar and lay in
wait for us somewhere in a deep pool of the arroyo—a monster no
less real because he lived only in our imagination.

When the older boys of the village came to the pond on Sunday 4
afternoons we watched them swim and dive. From a high branch of
the big *nogal* they dropped a swing made of bush vines we called *liana*,
braided like the women of the pueblo did their hair. The boy who was
to dive next waited up in the *nogal*. Another handed him the end of
the *liana*. The diver kicked off and let go as high as he could swing,
his naked brown body twisting through the air like a split string bean.

Ernesto Galarza, a teacher, writer, and lecturer, lives in San Jose, California.
"Growing into Manhood" (editors' title) is from Part One of *Barrio Boy*, a book
that began, Galarza says, "as anecdotes I told my family about Jalcocotán, the
mountain village in western Mexico where I was born."

On our side of the swimming hole the smaller boys stripped and paddled while the divers yelled instructions on strokes and kicks.

Once in a great while the older boys would also allow us to join 5 them in the bullfights they organized in one corner of the pasture. The bulls, the matadores, and the picadores were the ten- to twelve-year-olds, and the master of the fight was the oldest of the gang. We were permitted to take part only as fans or *aficionados*, to provide the yelling, the catcalls and the cheers. The master of the *corrida* directed us to sit on the ground on the upper slope of the bullring, which was entirely imaginary.

From behind a tree a trumpeter stepped to the edge of the ring. 6 Blowing on a make-believe bugle he sounded a call and the bull rushed in—a boy with a plain sarape over his shoulders, holding with both hands in front of his chest the bleached skull of a steer complete with horns. Between the horns a large, thick cactus leaf from which the thorns had been removed, was tied. It was at the cactus pad that the matadores and picadores aimed their wooden swords and bamboo spears.

If the fight went according to the rules, the master declared the 7 bull dead after a few rushes, by counting the stabs into the cactus, and the dead bull was replaced by a live one. Sometimes a sword or a spear missed the cactus pad and poked the bull in the stomach or some more sensitive spot. If the bull suspected that the miss was on purpose and dropped his skull to charge the torero with his fists, there was a free-for-all. We *aficionados* fell on one another with grunts and kicks, wrestling on the ground to increase the bedlam. If the commotion got out of the hands of the master of the *corrida*, there was always an adult watching from the village across the arroyo, who would walk over to the ring to scatter the rioters and send them home.

The girls of the village, needless to say, did not take part in the 8 swimming parties or in the action of the bullfights. Neither did we, the boys who were under seven years of age.

This by no means put us in the same class. Up to his third year, 9 a boy could still be led by the hand or undressed by an older sister. He was a *chilpayate*, a toddler who could play on the street naked without anybody noticing it. Little by little the *chilpayates* became men of sorts. They noticed that only girls had their earlobes pierced, wearing bits of string until their parents could afford genuine rings. They had to sit for hours to have their hair braided. At five years of age girls began to learn to carry water up from the arroyo in *ollas*, holding them on top of their heads with both hands, something that no man in Jalco would think of doing. They played silly games like La Ronda, hopping around and around, we thought, like *zopilotes*. Boys did girls' chores only if, and everybody knew that it was only if, there were no girls in the family—like shaking and sunning the bed mats or sprinkling the street in front of your cottage.

Between five and six, the fact that girls belonged to a lower class became even more obvious. Boys went into the forest to gather firewood. If their father's *milpa* or banana patch was not too far away they would be sent off before noon with a hot lunch in the haversack. They picked coffee beans on the lower branches of the bushes. They were taught to halter the burros and water them at the arroyo. They cut and bundled weeds in the *milpa* to feed the hens and the stock.   10

When a Jalco boy was passing six years of age and had become used to such jobs, he spent more and more of his day with the men and less time with the women. He was given more important tasks, which had a great deal to do with his becoming a man: "para que se vaya haciendo hombre." At six, a boy stood about as tall as a machete, but he would not be able to use one for several years. By the time he was fourteen he would be a man, complete with a machete of his own, working the *milpa* or the coffee patch or the banana stand by the side of his father, and able to do it by himself, if necessary.   11

Somewhere between seven and fourteen the village noticed other signs of his coming manhood. The surest of these was his watching the girls when they went to the arroyo to scrub clothes and bathe. We under-sixers could do this anyway without anyone paying attention or chasing us off. Sitting high on a boulder just above the pond I could see them, with a white skirt pulled up and pinned over one shoulder, slapping the clothes on the rocks, dipping them in the water and wringing them. When the washing was over they slipped off the skirt and slid into a pool, dunking themselves, chattering and laughing above the noise of the current. That was how I found out, without my folks making any particular fuss, that there were at least two important differences between boys and girls besides the braids and the perforated ears.   12

That was not, however, real girl watching. Around twelve years, boys stood away, behind a tree or a bush. If someone noticed, they pretended that they were going into the forest or to the *milpa* to work.   13

After you picked out a girl you began watching her in the village, coming closer step by step until everybody knew it. In this way the girl was staked out and every other young man in the pueblo was on notice. Any other watcher would have to fight for it sooner or later.   14

All this took time; if you began watching when you were around twelve by the time you were sixteen you could propose, asking your parents to ask hers for permission to get married.

All this happened only if the parents of the girl liked you. If they  15 didn't, her father would let you know. Jalco was a small, tight town and you could easily be caught shadowing the girl or even speaking to her. She would most likely get a beating, and you might be chased away by her father or brothers.

But you were not ready to take the risks of going steady in Jalco  16 until you had proved yourself a man at work. At six years of age or thereabouts you stopped being a playmate and became an apprentice. Jacinto and his father were a good example of this.

Chinto, as we called him, became an apprentice *campesino* when  17 he was only a little older than I. I saw them pass in front of our cottage in the early dawn, Chinto following his *jefe* to their cornpatch down the mountain. The man walked ahead, his cotton pants cinched tightly to his waist, one side of the fly crossed over the other and tucked into the waistband. The legs of the *calzones* were wound snug to the ankles, like puttees. At this time of the day the grass along the path to the *milpa* would be heavy with dew; the puttees soaked up less moisture than the bell-bottoms of the pants legs when they were loose. The soles and leather thongs of the huaraches the father wore were the soiled brown color of his ankles and toes. The hat was the usual ice cream cone of straw set on a wide brim curving down over the eyes and upward above the neck. He carried a machete in a sheath with the rawhide loop over one shoulder, and over the other the lunch bag.

Jacinto walked behind, dressed exactly like his father, except that  18 he did not carry a machete. Several paces behind, he trotted to keep up with the steady gait of the man, learning the first lesson of his life as a *campesino:* that he would spend the rest of his life walking, walking, walking. "Ay va Jacinto con su papá," someone said in the gloom of our kitchen. It was the end of another boy and the beginning of another man.

They came back at nightfall in the same way, the man leading the  19 boy. Both had rolled their pants legs above the knees, their white cotton shirts open in front, their hats tilted back. The man carried his huaraches over his shoulder. When the trail had roughened and cal-loused the feet of the boy, he would do the same.

The daily rounds that Jacinto and his father made were either to  20 the cornpatch, the *platanar* where they cultivated banana trees or to the few rows of peppers and *jitomate* they tended. We knew the day that Jacinto went to pick coffee berries with his father, because they both carried wicker baskets, the man a large one, Jacinto a small one. When they left the village for several days to herd cattle for a *patrón*, father and son carried rawhide slings, the father a long sling, the boy a short one. Rounding up heifers and calves, the father taught the boy to whirl the sling and let one end go, timing it so the pebble would strike the target. Jacinto showed us how, when he was practicing in the pasture.

Jacinto and the other seven-year-olds who were growing into man-   21
hood lost no time in making it clear to the rest of us that we were nothing but stay-at-homes. As we felt more important than girls, so Jacinto and his fellow apprentices felt more important than us. It took courage to walk toward the *milpa* through the forest where you could step on a rattler any moment, if you didn't see it coiled in the path or hear its tail buzzing. It took stamina to weed the corn hills and the banana trees under the broiling sun. Only a boy with manstuff in him could walk down the mountain and up the next ridge to spend the night tending heaps of burning wood to make charcoal that the burros carried to Tepic and San Blas. At night from Jalco we could see the orange bonfires high up on the mountain to the east. We saw Jacinto come back with his father from such work—jaunty *carboneros* with rolled-up pants legs, hats tilted back, face and legs and arms smeared with charcoal, dust, and sweat.

It was in the cultivated patches in the forest that boys grew into   22
men. With machetes they cleared the steep slopes and the hollows, setting fire to the brush and the stumps. In the ashes they planted corn, beans, peppers, *jitomate,* and bananas. Under the shade of a tall tree they grew coffee bushes. The forest provided the rest of Jalcotán's living—timber, charcoal, wild fruit, herbs, bears, deer, and hides from alligators and cougars.

Out of the forest a man took out only what he and his family could   23
use. Not all the *campesinos* in Jalcocotán, or in all the pueblos on the mountain together took out so much that the *monte* and the arroyo could not replenish themselves. In the conversation of the townspeople they were ancient sayings—*dichos*—that showed how long the people and the forest had lived together: "Agua que no has de beber, déjala correr"—at the arroyo drink your fill, let the rest run down the hill. "El que a buen árbol se arrima buena sombra le da"—the shade beneath a goodly tree is good for you and good for me.

Other than the stone walls of their corrals, the *jalcocotecanos* did   24
not build fences to separate one man's property from another's. When

the soil wore out in a *milpa* and another one was cleared, there were
no old fences to take down or new ones to put up.

The world of work into which Jacinto and the other seven-year-   25
olds were apprenticed was within sight and sound of the pueblo. It
was work under the blazing sun, in rainstorms, in pitch-black nights.
It was work that you were always walking to or walking from, work
without wages and work without end. It was work that gave you a
bone-tired feeling at the end of the day, so you learned to swing a
machete, to tighten a cinch, and to walk without lost motion. Between
seven and twelve you learned all this, each lesson driven home when
your *jefe* said with a scowl: "Así no, hombre; así." And he showed
you how.

But he knew that there was another world of work beyond Jalco.   26
Over in Miramar, Los Cocos, Puga and such places there were haciendas where peasants from the pueblos could work for money. Some
*jalcocotecanos* did this kind of hiring out. They cut sugarcane, herded
cattle, butchered steers, tended the crops, gathered coconuts for the
soap works, and cleared land *a puro machetazo*—with your bare hands
and a machete.

Boys who went with their fathers to the haciendas soon learned   27
the differences between making a living on the mountain and working
for the *patrones*. One was that on the mountain you took home corn,
bananas, peppers, coffee, and anything else you had raised, but never
money. From the hacienda, when your contract ended, you never took
anything to eat or wear except what you paid for at the *tienda de raya*,
the company store. A peon could make as much as ten pesos a month
at hard labor working from dawn to dusk, seven days a week, four
weeks every month. It came to about two or three centavos per hour,
plus your meals and a place to spread your straw sleeping mat.

The most important difference, however, was the *capataz*, the rid-   28
ing boss who watched the laborers all day long, just as the *guardia*
watched them throughout the night. The business of the *capataz* was
to keep the *peonanda,* as the crews of field hands were called, hustling
at the assigned tasks. He carried a machete slung from his saddle, a
whip, and often a pistol: the equipment of a top sergeant of the hacienda. The captain was the *Administrador*, who in turn took his orders
from the *patrón* who probably lived in Tepic or Guadalajara or perhaps
even in La Capital, as everyone called Mexico City.

The men who had worked on haciendas knew of these matters.   29
We heard snatches of firsthand reports from them but mostly we
learned from Don Catarino, José, Don Cleofas, and the muleteers who
passed through Jalco. Whoever had been there came back cursing it.

The riding boss was the Devil on horseback; in the company store every centavo you earned was taken back by a clerk who kept numbers in a book that proved you always owed him something. If a peon left the hacienda before his contract was over and his debts were paid, he became a fugitive. He either returned to his pueblo, his *compadres* and his *milpa* in some far-off place in the mountains, or he scratched for a living, lost in the forest. Old men in the village talked of the time they had worked on a hacienda as if they had served a sentence in prison or on a chain gang. They remembered capataces who had whipped them or cursed them fifty years before, and they still murmured a phrase: "Algún día me la pagan." There were a hundred blood debts of this kind in Jalcocotán, Doña Esther said, thousands of them in all the villages of the Sierra Madre, and millions in all the pueblos of Mexico.

"Algún día me la pagan."        30

"Tía, what does that mean?" I asked her more than once. She        31 always sent me to my mother with the question. Her answer was: "It means that somebody owes him something."

"But what does somebody owe him?"        32

The anger and the foreboding in "algún día me la pagan" was in        33 my mother's voice: "Something that hurts." She did not explain, just as she would not tell me why Catalino the bandit hated the *rurales* and shot so many of them.

Guessing at what people meant, I came to *feel* certain words rather        34 than to *know* them. They were words which came from the lips of the *jalcocotecanos* with an accent of suspicion, of fear, and of hatred. These words were *los rurales*, the *jefe politico*, the *señor gobernador*, *las autoridades*, *el gobierno*. When a stranger rode into Jalco, people stopped talking. Every detail about him and his horse was observed for a clue as to whether he was one of the *autoridades*.

It was the same with all outsiders. They always came asking ques-        35 tions, which the *jalcocotecanos* answered politely but roundabout. For me the world began to divide itself into two kinds of people—the men on horseback and the men who walked.

# Questions

1. Summarize the contents of paragraphs 1 through 7. How has Galarza organized his materials in these paragraphs? What other ways of organizing them can you imagine? What is the function of paragraph 8?

2.  In this chapter from *Barrio Boy* Galarza reflects on several distinct areas in the education and indoctrination of the child into the world of the adult. What are they? Could you outline, with comparable distinctness, parts of your own education and indoctrination? If not, why not?

## E. B. White

# Education

I have an increasing admiration for the teacher in the country school where we have a third-grade scholar in attendance. She not only undertakes to instruct her charges in all the subjects of the first three grades, but she manages to function quietly and effectively as a guardian of their health, their clothes, their habits, their mothers, and their snowball engagements. She has been doing this sort of Augean task for twenty years, and is both kind and wise. She cooks for the children on the stove that heats the room, and she can cool their passions or warm their soup with equal competence. She conceives their costumes, cleans up their messes, and shares their confidences. My boy already regards his teacher as his great friend, and I think tells her a great deal more than he tells us.

The shift from city school to country school was something we worried about quietly all last summer. I have always rather favored public school over private school, if only because in public school you meet a greater variety of children. This bias of mine, I suspect, is partly an attempt to justify my own past (I never knew anything but public schools) and partly an involuntary defense against getting kicked in the shins by a young ceramist on his way to the kiln. My wife was unacquainted with public schools, never having been exposed (in her early life) to anything more public than the washroom of Miss Win-

E[lwyn] B[rooks] White (1899–1985) wrote poetry and fiction, but he is most widely known as an essayist and as the coauthor (with William Strunk, Jr.) of *Elements of Style*. After a long career at *The New Yorker* he retired to Maine, but he continued to write until the year before his death at the age of 86.

sor's. Regardless of our backgrounds, we both knew that the change in schools was something that concerned not us but the scholar himself. We hoped it would work out all right. In New York our son went to a medium-priced private institution with semi-progressive ideas of education, and modern plumbing. He learned fast, kept well, and we were satisfied. It was an electric, colorful, regimented existence with moments of pleasurable pause and giddy incident. The day the Christmas angel fainted and had to be carried out by one of the Wise Men was educational in the highest sense of the term. Our scholar gave imitations of it around the house for weeks afterward, and I doubt if it ever goes completely out of his mind.

His days were rich in formal experience. Wearing overalls and an  3
old sweater (the accepted uniform of the private seminary), he sallied forth at morn accompanied by a nurse or a parent and walked (or was pulled) two blocks to a corner where the school bus made a flag stop. This flashy vehicle was as punctual as death: seeing us waiting at the cold curb, it would sweep to a halt, open its mouth, suck the boy in, and spring away with an angry growl. It was a good deal like a train picking up a bag of mail. At school the scholar was worked on for six or seven hours by half a dozen teachers and a nurse, and was revived on orange juice in mid-morning. In a cinder court he played games supervised by an athletic instructor, and in a cafeteria he ate lunch worked out by a dietitian. He soon learned to read with gratifying facility and discernment and to make Indian weapons of a semi-deadly nature. Whenever one of his classmates fell low of a fever the news was put on the wires and there were breathless phone calls to physicians, discussing periods of incubation and allied magic.

In the country all one can say is that the situation is different, and  4
somehow more casual. Dressed in corduroys, sweatshirt, and short rubber boots, and carrying a tin dinner-pail pail, our scholar departs at the crack of dawn for the village school, two and a half miles down the road, next to the cemetery. When the road is open and the car will start, he makes the journey by motor, courtesy of his old man. When the snow is deep or the motor is dead or both, he makes it on the hoof. In the afternoons he walks or hitches all or part of the way home in fair weather, gets transported in foul. The schoolhouse is a two-room frame building, bungalow type, shingles stained a burnt brown with weather-resistant stain. It has a chemical toilet in the basement and two teachers above the stairs. One takes the first three grades, the other the fourth, fifth, and sixth. They have little or no time for individual instruction, and no time at all for the esoteric. They teach

what they know themselves, just as fast and as hard as they can manage. The pupils sit still at their desks in class, and do their milling around outdoors during recess.

There is no supervised play. They play cops and robbers (only 5 they call it "Jail") and throw things at one another—snowballs in winter, rose hips in fall. It seems to satisfy them. They also construct darts, pinwheels, and "pick-up sticks" (jackstraws), and the school itself does a brisk trade in penny candy, which is for sale right in the classroom and which contains "surprises." The most highly prized surprise is a fake cigarette, made of cardboard, fiendishly lifelike.

The memory of how apprehensive we were at the beginning is 6 still strong. The boy was nervous about the change too. The tension, on that first fair morning in September when we drove him to school, almost blew the windows out of the sedan. And when later we picked him up on the road, wandering along with his little blue lunch-pail, and got his laconic report "All right" in answer to our inquiry about how the day had gone, our relief was vast. Now, after almost a year of it, the only difference we can discover in the two school experiences is that in the country he sleeps better at night—and *that* probably is more the air than the education. When grilled on the subject of school-in-country vs. school-in-city, he replied that the chief difference is that the day seems to go so much quicker in the country. "Just like lightning," he reported.

# Questions

1. Which school, public or private, does White prefer? Since White doesn't state his preference outright, from what evidence were you able to infer it?
2. In the first half of paragraph 2 White admits to a bias in favor of public schools, and he speculates, half-seriously, about the origins of his bias. If his intention here is not simply to amuse us, what is it?
3. What is White's strongest argument in favor of the school he prefers? Where in the essay do you find it?

## Maya Angelou

# Graduation

The children in Stamps trembled visibly with anticipation. 1
Some adults were excited too, but to be certain the whole young population had come down with graduation epidemic. Large classes were
graduating from both the grammar school and the high school. Even
those who were years removed from their own day of glorious release
were anxious to help with preparations as a kind of dry run. The junior
students who were moving into the vacating classes' chairs were tra-
dition-bound to show their talents for leadership and management.
They strutted through the school and around the campus exerting pressure on the lower grades. Their authority was so new that occasionally
if they pressed a little too hard it had to be overlooked. After all, next
term was coming, and it never hurt a sixth grader to have a play sister
in the eighth grade, or a tenth-year student to be able to call a twelfth
grader Bubba. So all was endured in a spirit of shared understanding.
But the graduating classes themselves were the nobility. Like travelers
with exotic destinations on their minds, the graduates were remarkably
forgetful. They came to school without their books, or tablets or even
pencils. Volunteers fell over themselves to secure replacements for the
missing equipment. When accepted, the willing workers might or
might not be thanked, and it was of no importance to the pregraduation
rites. Even teachers were respectful of the now quiet and aging seniors,
and tended to speak to them, if not as equals, as beings only slightly
lower than themselves. After tests were returned and grades given,
the student body, which acted like an extended family, knew who did
well, who excelled, and what piteous ones had failed.

Unlike the white high school, Lafayette County Training School 2
distinguished itself by having neither lawn, nor hedges, nor tennis
court, nor climbing ivy. Its two buildings (main classrooms, the grade
school and home economics) were set on a dirt hill with no fence to
limit either its boundaries or those of bordering farms. There was a
large expanse to the left of the school which was used alternately as

---

Maya Angelou was born in St. Louis in 1928. She has written books of poetry
and three autobiographic books.

"Graduation" (editors' title) is from her first autobiography, *I Know Why the
Caged Bird Sings*, Chapter 23.

a baseball diamond or a basketball court. Rusty hoops on the swaying poles represented the permanent recreational equipment, although bats and balls could be borrowed from the P.E. teacher if the borrower was qualified and if the diamond wasn't occupied.

Over this rocky area relieved by a few shady tall persimmon trees 3 the graduating class walked. The girls often held hands and no longer bothered to speak to the lower students. There was a sadness about them, as if this old world was not their home and they were bound for higher ground. The boys, on the other hand, had become more friendly, more outgoing. A decided change from the closed attitude they projected while studying for finals. Now they seemed not ready to give up the old school, the familiar paths and classrooms. Only a small percentage would be continuing on to college—one of the South's A & M (agricultural and mechanical) schools, which trained Negro youths to be carpenters, farmers, handymen, masons, maids, cooks and baby nurses. Their future rode heavily on their shoulders, and blinded them to the collective joy that had pervaded the lives of the boys and girls in the grammar school graduating class.

Parents who could afford it had ordered new shoes and ready- 4 made clothes for themselves from Sears and Roebuck or Montgomery Ward. They also engaged the best seamstresses to make the floating graduating dresses and to cut down secondhand pants which would be pressed to a military slickness for the important event.

Oh, it was important, all right. Whitefolks would attend the cer- 5 emony, and two or three would speak of God and home, and the Southern way of life, and Mrs. Parsons, the principal's wife, would play the graduation march while the lower-grade graduates paraded down the aisles and took their seats below the platform. The high school seniors would wait in empty classrooms to make their dramatic entrance.

In the Store I was the person of the moment. The birthday girl. 6 The center. Bailey had graduated the year before, although to do so he had had to forfeit all pleasures to make up for his time lost in Baton Rouge.

My class was wearing butter-yellow piqué dresses, and Momma 7 launched out on mine. She smocked the yoke into tiny crisscrossing puckers, then shirred the rest of the bodice. Her dark fingers ducked in and out of the lemony cloth as she embroidered raised daisies around the hem. Before she considered herself finished she had added a crocheted cuff on the puff sleeves, and a pointy crocheted collar.

I was going to be lovely. A walking model of all the various styles   8
of fine hand sewing and it didn't worry me that I was only twelve
years old and merely graduating from the eighth grade. Besides, many
teachers in Arkansas Negro schools had only that diploma and were
licensed to impart wisdom.

The days had become longer and more noticeable. The faded beige   9
of former times had been replaced with strong and sure colors. I began
to see my classmates' clothes, their skin tones, and the dust that waved
off pussy willows. Clouds that lazed across the sky were objects of
great concern to me. Their shiftier shapes might have held a message
that in my new happiness and with a little bit of time I'd soon decipher.
During that period I looked at the arch of heaven so religiously my
neck kept a steady ache. I had taken to smiling more often, and my
jaws hurt from the unaccustomed activity. Between the two physical
sore spots, I suppose I could have been uncomfortable, but that was
not the case. As a member of the winning team (the graduating class
of 1940) I had outdistanced unpleasant sensations by miles. I was
headed for the freedom of open fields.

Youth and social approval allied themselves with me and we tram-   10
meled memories of slights and insults. The wind of our swift passage
remodeled my features. Lost tears were pounded to mud and then to
dust. Years of withdrawal were brushed aside and left behind, as hanging ropes of parasitic moss.

My work alone had awarded me a top place and I was going to   11
be one of the first called in the graduating ceremonies. On the classroom blackboard, as well as on the bulletin board in the auditorium,
there were blue stars and white stars and red stars. No absences, no
tardinesses, and my academic work was among the best of the year.
I could say the preamble to the Constitution even faster than Bailey.
We timed ourselves often: "WethepeopleoftheUnitedStatesinorder-
toformamoreperfectunion . . ." I had memorized the Presidents of the
United States from Washington to Roosevelt in chronological as well
as alphabetical order.

My hair pleased me too. Gradually the black mass had lengthened   12
and thickened, so that it kept at last to its braided pattern, and I didn't
have to yank my scalp off when I tried to comb it.

Louise and I had rehearsed the exercises until we tired out our-   13
selves. Henry Reed was class valedictorian. He was a small, very black
boy with hooded eyes, a long, broad nose and an oddly shaped head.
I had admired him for years because each term he and I vied for the
best grades in our class. Most often he bested me, but instead of being

disappointed I was pleased that we shared top places between us. Like many Southern Black children, he lived with his grandmother, who was as strict as Momma and as kind as she knew how to be. He was courteous, respectful and soft-spoken to elders, but on the play-ground he chose to play the roughest games. I admired him. Anyone, I reckoned, sufficiently afraid or sufficiently dull could be polite. But to be able to operate at a top level with both adults and children was admirable.

His valedictory speech was entitled "To Be or Not to Be." The 14 rigid tenth-grade teacher had helped him to write it. He'd been working on the dramatic stresses for months.

The weeks until graduation were filled with heady activities. A 15 group of small children were to be presented in a play about buttercups and daisies and bunny rabbits. They could be heard throughout the building practicing their hops and their little songs that sounded like silver bells. The older girls (non-graduates, of course) were assigned the task of making refreshments for the night's festivities. A tangy scent of ginger, cinnamon, nutmeg and chocolate wafted around the home economics building as the budding cooks made samples for themselves and their teachers.

In every corner of the workshop, axes and saws split fresh timber 16 as the woodshop boys made sets and stage scenery. Only the graduates were left out of the general bustle. We were free to sit in the library at the back of the building or look in quite detachedly, naturally, on the measures being taken for our event.

Even the minister preached on graduation the Sunday before. His 17 subject was, "Let your light so shine that men will see your good works and praise your father, Who is in Heaven." Although the sermon was purported to be addressed to us, he used the occasion to speak to backsliders, gamblers, and general ne'er-do-wells. But since he had called our names at the beginning of the service we were mollified.

Among Negroes the tradition was to give presents to children 18 going only from one grade to another. How much more important this was when the person was graduating at the top of the class. Uncle Willie and Momma had sent away for a Mickey Mouse watch like Bailey's. Louise gave me four embroidered handkerchiefs. (I gave her three crocheted doilies.) Mrs. Sneed, the minister's wife, made me an underskirt to wear for graduation, and nearly every customer gave me a nickel or maybe even a dime with the instruction "Keep on moving to higher ground," or some such encouragement.

Amazingly the great day finally dawned and I was out of bed 19 before I knew it. I threw open the back door to see it more clearly, but Momma said, "Sister, come away from that door and put your robe on."

I hoped the memory of that morning would never leave me. Sun- 20
light was itself still young, and the day had none of the insistence maturity would bring it in a few hours. In my robe and barefoot in the backyard, under cover of going to see about my new beans, I gave myself up to the gentle warmth and thanked God that no matter what evil I had done in my life He had allowed me to live to see this day. Somewhere in my fatalism I had expected to die, accidentally, and never have the chance to walk up the stairs in the auditorium and gracefully receive my hard-earned diploma. Out of God's merciful bosom I had won reprieve.

Bailey came out in his robe and gave me a box wrapped in Christ- 21
mas paper. He said he had saved his money for months to pay for it. It felt like a box of chocolates, but I knew Bailey wouldn't save money to buy candy when we had all we could want under our noses.

He was as proud of the gift as I. It was a soft-leather-bound copy 22
of a collection of poems by Edgar Allan Poe, or, as Bailey and I called him, "Eap." I turned to "Annabel Lee" and we walked up and down the garden rows, the cool dirt between our toes, reciting the beautifully sad lines.

Momma made a Sunday breakfast although it was only Friday. 23
After we finished the blessing, I opened by eyes to find the watch on my plate. It was a dream of a day. Everything went smoothly and to my credit. I didn't have to be reminded or scolded for anything. Near evening I was too jittery to attend to chores, so Bailey volunteered to do all before his bath.

Days before, we had made a sign for the Store and as we turned 24
out the lights Momma hung the cardboard over the doorknob. It read clearly: CLOSED. GRADUATION.

My dress fitted perfectly and everyone said that I looked like a 25
sunbeam in it. On the hill, going toward the school, Bailey walked behind with Uncle Willie, who muttered, "Go on, Ju." He wanted him to walk ahead with us because it embarrassed him to have to walk so slowly. Bailey said he'd let the ladies walk together, and the men would bring up the rear. We all laughed, nicely.

Little children dashed by out of the dark like fireflies. Their crepe- 26
paper dresses and butterfly wings were not made for running and we heard more than one rip, dryly, and the regretful "uh uh" that fol-lowed.

The school blazed without gaiety. The windows seemed cold and   27
unfriendly from the lower hill. A sense of ill-fated timing crept over
me, and if Momma hadn't reached for my hand I would have drifted
back to Bailey and Uncle Willie, and possibly beyond. She made a few
slow jokes about my feet getting cold, and tugged me along to the
now-strange building.

Around the front steps, assurance came back. There were my fel-   28
low "greats," the graduating class. Hair brushed back, legs oiled, new
dresses and pressed pleats, fresh pocket handkerchiefs and little hand-
bags, all homesewn. Oh, we were up to snuff, all right. I joined my
comrades and didn't even see my family go in to find seats in the
crowded auditorium.

The school band struck up a march and all classes filed in as had   29
been rehearsed. We stood in front of our seats, as assigned, and on a
signal from the choir director, we sat. No sooner had this been accomplished that the band started to play the national anthem. We rose
again and sang the song, after which we recited the pledge of allegiance. We remained standing for a brief minute before the choir director and the principal signaled to us, rather desperately I thought,
to take our seats. The command was so unusual that our carefully
rehearsed and smooth-running machine was thrown off. For a full
minute we fumbled for our chairs and bumped into each other awk-
wardly. Habits change or solidify under pressure, so in our state of
nervous tension we had been ready to follow our usual assembly pattern: the American National Anthem, then the pledge of allegiance,
then the song every Black person I knew called the Negro National
Anthem. All done in the same key, with the same passion and most
often standing on the same foot.

Finding my seat at last, I was overcome with a presentiment of   30
worse things to come. Something unrehearsed, unplanned, was going
to happen, and we were going to be made to look bad. I distinctly
remember being explicit in the choice of pronoun. It was "we," the
graduating class, the unit, that concerned me then.

The principal welcomed "parents and friends" and asked the Bap-   31
tist minister to lead us in prayer. His invocation was brief and punchy,
and for a second I thought we were getting back on the high road to
right action. When the principal came back to the dais, however, his
voice had changed. Sounds always affected me profoundly and the
principal's voice was one of my favorites. During assembly it melted
and lowed weakly into the audience. It had not been in my plan to

listen to him, but my curiosity was piqued and I straightened up to give him my attention.

He was talking about Booker T. Washington, our "late great 32 leader," who said we can be as close as the fingers on the hand, etc. . . . Then he said a few vague things about friendship and the friendship of kindly people to those less fortunate than themselves. With that his voice nearly faded, thin, away. Like a river diminishing to a stream and then to a trickle. But he cleared his throat and said, "Our speaker tonight, who is also our friend, came from Texarkana to deliver the commencement address, but due to the irregularity of the train schedule, he's going to, as they say, 'speak and run.' " He said that we understood and wanted the man to know that we were most grateful for the time he was able to give us and then something about how we were willing always to adjust to another's program, and without more ado—"I give you Mr. Edward Donleavy."

Not one but two white men came through the door offstage. The 33 shorter one walked to the speaker's platform, and the tall one moved over to the center seat and sat down. But that was our principal's seat, and already occupied. The dislodged gentleman bounced around for a long breath or two before the Baptist minister gave him his chair, then with more dignity than the situation deserved, the minister walked off the stage.

Donleavy looked at the audience once (on reflection, I'm sure that 34 he wanted only to reassure himself that we were really there), adjusted his glasses and began to read from a sheaf of papers.

He was glad "to be here and to see the work going on just as it 35 was in the other schools."

At the first "Amen" from the audience I willed the offender to 36 immediate death by choking on the word. But Amen's and Yes, sir's began to fall around the room like rain through a ragged umbrella.

He told us of the wonderful changes we children in Stamps had 37 in store. The Central School (naturally, the white school was Central) had already been granted improvements that would be in use in the fall. A well-known artist was coming from Little Rock to teach art to them. They were going to have the newest microscopes and chemistry equipment for their laboratory. Mr. Donleavy didn't leave us long in the dark over who made these improvements available to Central High. Nor were we to be ignored in the general betterment scheme he had in mind.

He said that he had pointed out to people at a very high level that 38

one of the first-line football tacklers at Arkansas Agricultural and Mechanical College had graduated from good old Lafayette County Training School. Here fewer Amen's were heard. Those few that did break through lay dully in the air with the heaviness of habit.

He went on to praise us. He went on to say how he had bragged  39
that "one of the best basketball players at Fisk sank his first ball right here at Lafayette County Training School."

The white kids were going to have a chance to become Galileos  40
and Madame Curies and Edisons and Gauguins, and our boys (the girls weren't even in on it) would try to be Jesse Owenses and Joe Louises.

Owens and the Brown Bomber were great heroes in our world,  41
but what school official in the white-goddom of Little Rock had the right to decide that those two men must be our only heroes? Who decided that for Henry Reed to become a scientist he had to work like George Washington Carver, as a bootblack, to buy a lousy microscope? Bailey was obviously always going to be small to be an athlete, so which concrete angel glued to what country seat had decided that if my brother wanted to become a lawyer he had to first pay penance for his skin by picking cotton and hoeing corn and studying correspondence books at night for twenty years?

The man's dead words fell like bricks around the auditorium and  42
too many settled in my belly. Constrained by hard-learned manners I couldn't look behind me, but to my left and right the proud graduating class of 1940 had dropped their heads. Every girl in my row had found something new to do with her handkerchief. Some folded the tiny squares into love knots, some into triangles, but most were wadding them, then pressing them flat on their yellow laps.

On the dais, the ancient tragedy was being replayed. Professor  43
Parsons sat, a sculptor's reject, rigid. His large, heavy body seemed devoid of will or willingness, and his eyes said he was no longer with us. The other teachers examined the flag (which was draped stage right) or their notes, or the windows which opened on our now-famous playing diamond.

Graduation, the hush-hush magic time of frills and gifts and con-  44
gratulations and diplomas, was finished for me before my name was called. The accomplishment was nothing. The meticulous maps, drawn in three colors of ink, learning and spelling decasyllabic words, memorizing the whole of *The Rape of Lucrece*—it was nothing. Donleavy had exposed us.

We were maids and farmers, handymen and washerwomen, and    45
anything higher that we aspired to was farcical and presumptuous.
Then I wished that Gabriel Prosser and Nat Turner had killed all whitefolks in their beds and that Abraham Lincoln had been assassinated
before the signing of the Emancipation Proclamation, and that Harriet
Tubman had been killed by that blow on her head and Christopher
Columbus had drowned in the *Santa Maria*.

It was awful to be Negro and have no control over my life. It was    46
brutal to be young and already trained to sit quietly and listen to
charges brought against my color with no chance of defense. We
should all be dead. I thought I should like to see us all dead, one on
top of the other. A pyramid of flesh with the whitefolks on the bottom,
as the broad base, then the Indians with their silly tomahawks and
teepees and wigwams and treaties, the Negroes with their mops and
recipes and cotton sacks and spirituals sticking out of their mouths.
The Dutch children should all stumble in their wooden shoes and break
their necks. The French should choke to death on the Louisiana Purchase (1803) while silkworms ate all the Chinese with their stupid pig-
tails. As a species, we were an abomination. All of us.

Donleavy was running for election, and assured our parents that    47
if he won we could count on having the only colored paved playing
field in that part of Arkansas. Also—he never looked up to acknowledge the grunts of acceptance—also, we were bound to get some new
equipment for the home economics building and the workshop.

He finished, and since there was no need to give any more than    48
the most perfunctory thank-you's, he nodded to the men on the stage,
and the tall white man who was never introduced joined him at the
door. They left with the attitude that now they were off to something
really important. (The graduation ceremonies at Lafayette County
Training School had been a mere preliminary.)

The ugliness they left was palpable. An uninvited guest who    49
wouldn't leave. The choir was summoned and sang a modern arrangement of "Onward, Christian Soldiers," with new words pertaining to graduates seeking their place in the world. But it didn't work.
Elouise, the daughter of the Baptist minister, recited "Invictus," and
I could have cried at the impertinence of "I am the master of my fate,
I am the captain of my soul."

My name had lost its ring of familiarity and I had to be nudged    50
to go and receive my diploma. All my preparations had fled. I neither
marched up to the stage like a conquering Amazon, nor did I look in

the audience for Bailey's nod of approval. Marguerite Johnson, I heard the name again, my honors were read, there were noises in the audience of appreciation, and I took my place on the stage as rehearsed.

I thought about colors I hated: ecru, puce, lavender, beige and  51
black.

There was shuffling and rustling around me, then Henry Reed  52
was giving his valedictory address, "To Be or Not to Be." Hadn't he heard the whitefolks? We couldn't *be,* so the question was a waste of time. Henry's voice came out clear and strong. I feared to look at him. Hadn't he got the message? There was no "nobler in the mind" for Negroes because the world didn't think we had minds, and they let us know it. "Outrageous fortune"? Now, that was a joke. When the ceremony was over I had to tell Henry Reed some things. That is, if I still cared. Not "rub," Henry, "erase." "Ah, there's the erase." Us.

Henry had been a good student in elocution. His voice rose on  53
tides of promise and fell on waves of warnings. The English teacher had helped him to create a sermon winging through Hamlet's soliloquy. To be a man, a doer, a builder, a leader, or to be a tool, an unfunny joke, a crusher of funky toadstools. I marveled that Henry could go through with the speech as if we had a choice.

I had been listening and silently rebutting each sentence with my  54
eyes closed; then there was a hush, which in an audience warns that something unplanned is happening. I looked up and saw Henry Reed, the conservative, the proper, the A student, turn his back to the audience and turn to us (the proud graduating class of 1940) and sing, nearly speaking,

> Lift ev'ry voice and sing
> Till earth and heaven ring
> Ring with the harmonies of Liberty . . .

It was the poem written by James Weldon Johnson. It was the music composed by J. Rosamond Johnson. It was the Negro National Anthem. Out of habit we were singing it.

Our mothers and fathers stood in the dark hall and joined the  55
hymn of encouragement. A kindergarten teacher led the small children onto the stage and the buttercups and daisies and bunny rabbits marked time and tried to follow:

> Stony the road we trod
> Bitter the chastening rod

Felt in the days when hope, unborn, had died.
Yet with a steady beat
Have not our weary feet
Come to the place for which our fathers sighed?

Every child I knew had learned that song with his ABC's and along 56
with "Jesus Loves Me This I Know." But I personally had never heard
it before. Never heard the words, despite the thousands of times I had
sung them. Never thought they had anything to do with me.

On the other hand, the words of Patrick Henry had made such 57
an impression on me that I had been able to stretch myself tall and
trembling and say, "I know not what course others may take, but as
for me, give me liberty or give me death."

And now I heard, really for the first time: 58

We have come over a way that with tears has been watered,
We have come, trading our path through the blood of the slaughtered.

While echoes of the song shivered in the air, Henry Reed bowed 59
his head, said "Thank you," and returned to his place in the line. The
tears that slipped down many faces were not wiped away in shame.

We were on top again. As always, again. We survived. The depths 60
had been icy and dark, but now a bright sun spoke to our souls. I was
no longer simply a member of the proud graduating class of 1940; I
was a proud member of the wonderful, beautiful Negro race.

Oh, Black known and unknown poets, how often have your auc- 61
tioned pains sustained us? Who will compute the lonely nights made
less lonely by your songs, or the empty pots made less tragic by your
tales?

If we were a people much given to revealing secrets, we might 62
raise monuments and sacrifice to the memories of our poets, but slavery cured us of that weakness. It may be enough, however, to have
it said that we survive in exact relationship to the dedication of our
poets (include preachers, musicians and blues singers).

# Questions

1. In paragraph 1 notice such overstatements as "glorious release,"
   "the graduating classes themselves were the nobility," and "exotic
   destinations." Find further examples in the next few pages. What
   is the function of this diction?

2. Characterize the writer as you perceive her up through paragraph 28. Support your characterization with references to specific passages. Next, characterize her in paragraph 46, which begins "It was awful to be Negro." Next, characterize her on the basis of the entire essay. Finally, in a sentence, try to describe the change, telling the main attitudes or moods that she goes through.

3. How would you define "poets" as Angelou uses the word in the last sentence?

Pauline Kael

# High School and Other Forms of Madness

Many of us grow to hate documentaries in school, because the use of movies to teach us something seems a cheat—a pill disguised as candy—and documentaries always seem to be about something we're not interested in. But Wiseman's documentaries show what is left out of both fictional movies and standard documentaries that simplify for a purpose, and his films deal with the primary institutions of our lives: *Titicut Follies* (Bridgewater, an institution in which we lock away the criminally insane), *High School* (a high school in a large Eastern city), and *Law and Order* (the Kansas City police force). Television has been accustoming us to a horrible false kind of "involvement"; sometimes it seems that the only thing the news shows can think of is to get close to emotion. They shove a camera and a microphone in front of people in moments of stress and disaster and grief, and ram their equipment into any pores and cavities they can reach. Wiseman made comparable mistakes in *Titicut Follies*, but he learned better fast.

*High School* is so familiar and so extraordinarily evocative that a feeling of empathy with the students floods over us. How did we live

Pauline Kael, born in 1919 in Petaluma, California, grew up in San Francisco and attended the University of California at Berkeley. She regularly writes film criticism for *The New Yorker*.

through it? How did we keep any spirit? When you see a kid trying to make a phone call and being interrupted with "Do you have a pass to use the phone?" it all floods back—the low ceilings and pale-green walls of the basement where the lockers were, the constant defensiveness, that sense of always being in danger of breaking some pointless, petty rule. When since that time has one ever needed a pass to make a phone call? This movie takes one back to where, one discovers, time has stood still. Here is the girl humiliated for having worn a short dress to the Senior Prom, being told it was "offensive" to the whole class. Here it is all over again—the insistence that you be "respectful"; and the teachers' incredible instinct for "disrespect," their antennae always extended for that little bit of reservation or irony in your tone, the tiny spark that you desperately need to preserve your *self*-respect. One can barely hear it in the way a boy says "Yes, sir" to the dean, but the dean, ever on the alert, snaps, "Don't give me that 'Yes, sir' business!. . . . There's no sincereness behind it." Here, all over again, is the dullness of high-school education:

> *Teacher:* What on the horizon or what existed that forced labor to turn to collective bargaining? What was there a lack of?
> *Girl:* Communications?
> *Teacher:* Security, yes, communications, lack of security, concern for the job. The important thing is this, let's get to the beginning. First of all, there was the lack of security; second of all, there was a lack of communication. . . .

The same old pseudo-knowledge is used to support what the 3 schools think is moral. The visiting gynecologist in a sex-education class lectures the boys:

> The more a fellow gets into bed with more different girls, the more insecure he is, and this shows up actually later in all the divorce statistics in America. . . . You can graph right on a graph, the more girls fellows got into bed with or vice-versa the higher the divorce rate, the greater the sexual inadequacy. . . .

And there's the beautiful military doubletalk when it's a question 4 of a teacher's incompetence or unfairness. A boy protests a disciplinary action against him by a teacher, and after he has explained his innocence, the dean talks him into accepting the punishment "to establish that you can be a man and that you can take orders." The teachers are masters here; they're in a superior position for the only time in their lives, probably, and most of the petty tyrannies—like laying on the homework—aren't fully conscious. They justify each other's actions as a matter of course, and put the students in the wrong in the same indifferent way. They put a student down with "It's nice to be individualistic, but there are certain places to be individualistic," yet they never tell you where. How can one stand up against such bland authoritarianism? The teachers, crushing and processing, are the most insidious kind of enemy, the enemy with corrupt values who means well. The counsellor advising on college plans who says "You can have all your dream schools, but at the bottom you ought to have some college of last resort where you could be sure that you would go, if none of your dreams came through" certainly means to be realistic and helpful. But one can imagine what it must feel like to be a kid trudging off to the bottom college of last resort. There's a jolly good Joe of a teacher staging a fashion show who tells the girls, "Your legs are all too heavy. . . . Don't wear it too short; it looks miserable." And she's not wrong. But, given the beauty norms set up in this society, what are they to do? Cut off their legs? Emigrate? They're defeated from the legs up. Mediocrity and defeat sit in the offices and classrooms, and in those oppressive monitored halls.

We went through it all in order to graduate and be rid of passes 5 forever, and once it was over we put it out of our minds, and here are the students still serving time until graduation, still sitting in class staring out the windows or watching the crawling hands of those ugly school clocks. So much of this education is part of an obsolete system of authority that broke down long ago, yet the teachers and administrators are still out there, persevering, "building character." *High School* seems an obvious kind of film to make, but as far as I know no one before has gone into an ordinary, middle-class, "good" (most of the students go to college) high school with a camera and looked around to see what it's like. The students are even more apathetic than we were. Probably the conflicts over the restrictions come earlier now—in junior high—and by high school the kids either are trying to cool it and get through to college or are just beaten down and sitting it out. We may have had a few teachers who really got us interested in something—it was one of the disappointments of the movie *Up the Down Staircase* that, treating this theme, it failed to be convincing—and, remembering our good luck, we could always say that even if a school was rotten, there were bound to be a few great teachers in it. This movie shows competent teachers and teachers who are trying their best but not one teacher who really makes contact in the way that means a difference in your life. The students are as apathetic toward the young English teacher playing and analyzing a Simon & Garfunkel record as toward the English teacher reciting "Casey at the Bat," and, even granted that as poetry there might not be much to choose between them—and perhaps Casey has the edge—still, one might think the students would, just as a *courtesy*, respond to the young teacher's attempt, the way one always gave the ingénue in the stock company a special round of applause. But it's very likely that high schools no longer *are* saved by live teachers, if hostility and cynicism and apathy set in right after children learn their basic skills. The students here sit on their hands even when a teacher tries. That's the only visible difference between this school and mine. I think we would have responded appreciatively to obvious effort, even if we thought the teacher was a jerk; these kids are beyond that. So the teachers are trapped, too. The teachers come off much worse than the police do in *Law and Order*. *High School* is a revelation because now that we see school from the outside, the teachers seem to give themselves away every time they open their mouths—and to be unaware of it.

At the end, the principal—a fine-looking woman—holds up a let-  6
ter from a former student, on stationery marked "U.S.S. Okinawa," and reads it to the faculty:

> I have only a few hours before I go. Today I will take a plane trip from this ship. I pray that I'll make it back but it's all in God's hands now. You see, I am going with three other men. We are going to be dropped behind the D.M.Z. (the Demilitarized Zone). The reason for telling you this is that all my insurance money will be given for that scholarship I once started but never finished, if I don't make it back. I am only insured for $10,000. Maybe it could help someone. I have been trying to become a Big Brother in Vietnam, but it is very hard to do. I have to write back and forth to San Diego, California, and that takes time. I only hope that I am good enough to become one. God only knows. My personal family usually doesn't understand me. . . . They say: "Don't you value life? Are you crazy?" My answer is: "Yes. But I value all the lives of South Vietnam and the free world so that they and all of us can live in peace." Am I wrong? If I do my best and believe in what I do, believe that what I do is right—that is all I can do. . . . Please don't say anything to Mrs. C. She would only worry over me. I am not worth it. I am only a body doing a job. In closing I thank everyone for what they all have done for me.

And the principal comments, "Now, when you get a letter like this, to me it means that we are very successful at [this] high school. I think you will agree with me."

It's a great scene—a consummation of the educational process 7 we've been watching: They are successful at turning out bodies to do a job. Yet it's also painfully clear that the school must have given this soldier more kindness and affection than he'd ever had before. There must be other students who respond to the genuine benevolence behind the cant and who are grateful to those who labor to turn them into men. For those students, this schooling in conformity is successful.

Wiseman extends our understanding of our common life the way 8 novelists used to—a way largely abandoned by the modern novel and left to the journalists but not often picked up by them. What he's doing is so simple and so basic that it's like a rediscovery of what we knew, or should know. We often want more information about the people and their predicaments than he gives, but this is perhaps less a criticism of Wiseman's method than it is a testimonial to his success in making us care about his subjects. With fictional movies using so little of our shared experience, and the big TV news "specials" increasingly using that idiot "McLuhanite" fragmentation technique that scrambles all experience—as if the deliberate purpose were to make us indifferent to the life around us—it's a good sign when a movie sends us out wanting to know more and feeling that there is more to know. Wiseman is probably the most sophisticated intelligence to enter the documentary field in recent years.

# Questions

1. In paragraph 2 Kael assumes that her readers share with her the view, based on experience, that high school is dull, dispiriting, and even humiliating. Is the assumption warranted?
2. At the end of paragraph 2 Kael quotes a bit of dialogue. Pinpoint examples of dullness in the dialogue.
3. The language of paragraph 4 suggests that high school is a battleground between teachers and students. Are the hostilities Kael cites familiar? If not, do you find them nevertheless convincing? With what weapons is each side armed?
4. In paragraph 1 Kael writes: "Many of us grow to hate documentaries in school." Did you? If so, why? What reasons might you offer to argue that the documentary films you saw in school were educational or anti-educational?

Nathan Glazer

# Some Very Modest
# Proposals for the
# Improvement of
# American Education

$T$hat we can do a great deal for the sorry state of American   1
education with more money is generally accepted. Even apparently
modest proposals will, however, cost a great deal of money. Consider
something as simple as increasing the average compensation of American teachers—who are generally considered underpaid—by $2,000 a
year each. The bill would come to five billion dollars a year. A similar
figure is reached by the report of the highly qualified Twentieth Century Fund Task Force on Federal, Elementary, and Secondary Educational Policy, which proposes fellowships and additional compensation for master teachers. Reducing class size 10 percent, or increasing the number of teachers by the same percentage, would cost another
five billion dollars: With present-day federal deficits, these look like
small sums, but since education is paid for almost entirely by states
and local government, these modest proposals would lead to substantial and painful tax increases. (I leave aside for the moment the
views of skeptics who believe that none of these changes would
matter.)

But the occasional visitor to American schools will note some   2
changes that would cost much less, nothing at all, or even save
money—and yet would improve at least the educational *environment*
in American schools (once again, we ignore those skeptics who would
insist that even a better educational environment cannot be guaranteed
to improve educational achievement). In the spirit of evoking further
cheap proposals, here is a small list of suggestions that, to my mind
at least—and the mind I believe of any adult who visits American
public schools—would mean a clear plus for American education:

Nathan Glazer, born in 1923 in New York City, is a professor of education and
sociology at Harvard University. He is co-editor of *The Public Interest* magazine
and the co-author of *The Lonely Crowd* and *Beyond the Melting Pot*.

1. *Disconnect all loudspeaker systems in American schools—or at least* 3
*reserve them, like the hotline between Moscow and Washington, for only the*
*gravest emergencies.* The American classroom—and the American
teacher and his or her charges—is continually interrupted by announcements from central headquarters over the loudspeaker system.
These remind teachers to bring in some form or other; or students to
bring in some form or other; or students engaged in some activity to
remember to come to practice or rehearsal; or they announce a change
of time for some activity. There is nothing so unnerving to a teacher
engaged in trying to explain something, or a student engaged in trying
to understand something, as the crackle of the loudspeaker prepared
to issue an announcement, and the harsh and gravelly voice (the systems are not obviously of the highest grade) of the announcement
itself.

Aside from questions of personal taste, why would this be a good 4
idea? As I have suggested, one reason is that the loudspeaker interrupts efforts to communicate complicated material that requires undivided attention. Second, it demeans the teacher as professional:
every announcement tells her whatever she is doing is not very important and can be interrupted at any time. Third, it accentuates the
notion of hierarchy in education—the principal and assistant principal
are the important people, and command time and attention even in
the midst of instruction. Perhaps I have been softened by too many
years as a college teacher, but it would be unimaginable that a loudspeaker, if one existed, would ever interrupt a college class except
under conditions of the gravest and most immediate threat to life and
limb. One way of showing students that education is important is not
to interrupt it for band-rehearsal announcements.

2. *Disarm the school.* One of the most depressing aspects of the 5
urban school in the United States is the degree of security manifest
within it, and that seems to me quite contradictory to what a school
should be. Outer doors are locked. Security guards are present in the
corridors. Internal doors are locked. Passes are necessary to enter the
school or move within it, for outsiders and for students. Students are
marched in groups from classroom to classroom, under the eye of the
teachers. It is understandable that given the conditions in lower-class
areas in our large cities—and not only lower-class areas—some degree
of security-mindedness is necessary. There is valuable equipment—
typewriters, computers, audio-visual equipment—that can be stolen;
vandalism is a serious concern; marauders can enter the school in

search for equipment, or teachers' pocketbooks, or to threaten directly personal safety in search of money or sex, and so on. School integration and busing, at least in their initial stages, have contributed to increased interracial tensions in schools and have in part severed the link between community and school. The difference in ethnic and racial composition of faculty, other staff, administrators, and students contributes to the same end.

Having acknowledged all this, I still believe the school should feel    6 less like a prison than it does. One should examine to what extent outside doors must be closed; to what extent the security guard cannot be replaced by local parents, volunteer or paid; the degree to which the endless bells indicating "stop" and "go" are really necessary. I suspect that now that the most difficult period of school integration has passed, now that teachers and administrators and staff more closely parallel in race and ethnic background students and community owing to the increase in black and Hispanic teachers and administrators, we may be saddled with more security than we need. Here we come to the sticky problem of *removing* security measures whose need has decreased. What school board will open itself to suit or to public criticism by deliberately providing *less* security? And yet one must consider the atmosphere of the school and a school's primary objective as a teaching agent: can this be reconciled with a condition of maximum security? Perhaps there are lessons to be learned from colleges and community colleges in older urban areas, which in my experience do seem to manage with less security. One reason is that there are more adults around in such institutions. Is that a hint as to how we could manage better in our public schools?

3. *Enlist the children in keeping the school clean.* Occasionally we see    7 a practice abroad that suggests possible transfer to the American scene. In Japan, the children clean the school. There is a time of day when mops and pails and brooms come out, and the children sweep up and wash up. This does, I am sure, suggest to the children that this is *their* school, that it is not simply a matter of being forced to go to a foreign institution that imposes alien demands upon them. I can imagine some obstacles in the way of instituting regular student clean-up in American schools—custodians' unions, for example, might object. But they can be reassured that children don't do that good a job, and they will still be needed. Once again, as in the case of the security problem, one wants to create in the school, if at all possible, a common enterprise of teachers and students, without the latter being bored and resistant,

the former, in response, becoming equally indifferent. The school should be seen as everyone's workplace—and participation in cleaning the school will help.

4. *Save old schools.* Build fewer new ones. It has often surprised me 8 that while in schools such as Eton and Oxford—and indeed well-known private schools and colleges in the United States—old buildings are prized, in so many communities older public schools are torn down when to the naked eye they have many virtues that would warrant their maintenance and use. Only a few blocks from where I live, an excellent example of late nineteenth-century fine brickwork and carved stonework that served as the Cambridge Latin School came down for a remodeling. The carved elements are still displayed about the re-modeled school, but why a building of such character should have deserved demolition escaped my understanding, particularly since one can take it almost as a given that a school building put up before the 1940s will be built of heavier and sturdier materials than one con-structed today. Even the inconveniences of the old can possess a charm that makes them worthwhile. And indeed many of the reforms that seemed to require new buildings (for example, classrooms without walls, concentrated around activities centers in large open rooms) have turned out, on use, to be not so desirable. Our aim should be to give each school a history, a character, something that at least some stu-dents respond to. The pressures for new buildings are enormous, and sometimes perfectly legitimate (as when communities expand), but often illegitimate, as when builders and building-trades workers and contract-givers seek an opportunity or when state aid makes it appear as if a new building won't cost anything.

5. *Look on new hardware with a skeptical eye.* I think it likely that the 9 passion for the new in the way of teaching-hardware not only does not contribute to higher educational achievement but may well serve as a temporary means to evade the real and hard tasks of teaching—which really require almost no hardware at all, besides textbooks, blackboard, and chalk. Admittedly, when one comes to high-school science, something more is called for. And yet our tendency is to al-ways find cover behind new hardware. It's *fun* to get new audio-visual equipment, new rooms equipped with them in which all kinds of things can be done by flicking a switch or twisting a dial, or, as is now the case, to decide what kind of personal computers and software are necessary for a good educational program. Once again, foreign ex-perience can be enlightening. When Japanese education was already well ahead of American, most Japanese schools were in prewar

wooden buildings. (They are now as up-to-date as ours, but neither their age nor up-to-dateness has much to do with their good record of achievement.) Resisting the appeal of new hardware not only saves money, and provides less in the way of saleable goods to burglarize, but it also prevents distraction from the principal tasks of reading, writing, and calculating. When it turns out that computers and new software are shown to do a better job at these key tasks—I am skeptical as to whether this will ever be the case—there will be time enough to splurge on new equipment. The teacher, alone, up front, explaining, encouraging, guiding, is the heart of the matter—the rest is fun, and very helpful to corporate income, and gives an inflated headquarters staff something new to do. But students will have time enough to learn about computers when they get to college, and getting there will depend almost not at all on what they can do with computers, but how well they understand words and sentences, and how well they do at simple mathematics.

There is nothing wrong with old textbooks, too. Recently, review- 10 ing some recent high-school American history texts, I was astonished to discover they come out in new editions every two years or so, and not because the main body of the text is improved, but because the textbook wants to be able to claim it covers the very last presidential campaign, and the events of the last few years. This is a waste of time and energy and money. There is enough to teach in American history up to 1950 or 1960 not to worry about whether the text includes Reagan's tax cuts. I suspect many new texts in other areas also offer little advantage over the older ones. There is also a virtue in a teacher becoming acquainted with a particular textbook. When I read that a school is disadvantaged because its textbooks are old, I am always mystified. Even the newest advances in physics and biology might well be reserved for college.

6. *Expand the pool from which we draw good teachers.* This general 11 heading covers a number of simple and concrete things, such as: if a teacher is considered qualified to teach at a good private school, that teacher should be considered qualified to teach at a public school. It has always seemed to me ridiculous that teachers accepted at the best private schools in New York City or top preparatory schools in the country would not be allowed to teach in the public school system of New York or Boston. Often, they are willing—after all, the pay is better in public schools and there are greater fringe benefits. They might, it is true, be driven out of those schools by the challenge of lower- and working-class children. But when they are willing, it seems unbeliev-

able that the teacher qualified (or so Brearley thinks) for Brearley will not be allowed to teach at P.S. 122. Greater use of part-time teachers might also be able to draw upon people with qualities that we are told the average teacher unfortunately doesn't possess—such as a higher level of competence in writing and mathematics.

Our recurrent concern with foreign-language teaching should lead    12
us to recruit foreign-born teachers. There are problems in getting teaching jobs today in Germany and France—yet teachers there are typically drawn from pools of students with higher academic skills than is the case in this country. Paradoxically, we make it easy for teachers of Spanish-language background to get jobs owing to the expansion of bilingual programs—but then their teaching is confined to children whose Spanish accent doesn't need improvement. It would make more sense to expose children of foreign-language background more to teachers with native English—and children from English-speaking families to teachers who speak French, German, Spanish, and, why not, Japanese, and Chinese natively. This would mean that rules requiring that a teacher must be a citizen, or must speak English without an accent, should be lifted for special teachers with special tasks. Perhaps we could make the most of the oversupply of teachers in some foreign countries by using them to teach mathematics—a subject where accent doesn't count. The school system in Georgia is already recruiting from Germany. Colleges often use teaching assistants whose English is not native and far from perfect, including Asians from Korea and China, to assist in science and mathematics courses. (There are many state laws which would not permit them to teach in elementary and secondary schools.)

All the suggestions above eschew any involvement with some    13
great issues of education—tradition or reform, the teaching of values, the role of religion in the schools—that have in the past dominated arguments over education and still do today. But I add one more proposal that is still, I am afraid, somewhat controversial:

7. *Let students, within reason, pick their schools, or let parents choose*    14
*them for them.* All those informed on school issues will sense the heaving depths of controversy under this apparently modest proposal. Does this mean they might choose parochial schools, without being required to pay tuition out of their own pockets? Or does this mean black children would be allowed to attend schools in black areas, and whites in white areas, or the reverse if each is so inclined? As we all know, the two great issues of religion and race stand in the way of any such simple and commonsensical arrangement. Students are reg-

ularly bused from one section of a city to another because of their race, and students cannot without financial penalty attend that substantial sector of schools—30 percent or so in most Northern and Midwestern cities—that are called "private." I ignore the question of whether, holding all factors constant, students do "better" in private or public schools, in racially well-mixed or hardly mixed schools. The evidence will always be uncertain. What is perhaps less arguable is that students will do better in a school that forms a community, in which teachers, parents, and students all agree that *that* is the school they want to teach in, to attend, to send their children to. I would guess that this is the kind of school most of the readers of this article have attended; it is the kind of school, alas, that our complex racial and religious history makes it harder and harder for those of minority race or of lower- and working-class status to attend.

I have eschewed the grand proposals—for curriculum change, for   15 improving the quality of entering teachers, for checking on the competence of teachers in service, for establishing national standards for achievement in different levels of education—all of which now form the agenda for many state commissions of educational reform and all of which seem reasonable to me. Rather, I have concentrated on a variety of other things that serve to remove distraction, to open the school to those of quality who would be willing to enter it to improve it, to concentrate on the essentials of teaching and learning as I (and many others) have experienced it. It would be possible to propose larger changes in the same direction: for example, reduce the size of the bureaucracies in urban school systems. Some of my modest proposals are insidiously intended to do this—if there were less effort devoted to building new schools, buying new equipment, evaluating new textbooks, or busing children, there would be no need to maintain quite so many people at headquarters. Or so I would hope.

In the meantime, why not disconnect the loudspeakers?   16

# Questions

1.  What does "modest" mean in Glazer's second sentence?
2.  Glazer's third proposal is to have children clean their schools. How do you imagine high school students would respond to this proposal? How would you and your friends have responded?

3. Analyze the arrangement of Glazer's proposals. Do you discern any order or pattern in them?
4. If you disagree with one of Glazer's proposals, set forth your disagreement in a paragraph or two.
5. What proposals can you add to Glazer's list of "modest proposals"? Take one of your proposals and argue for it, in a paragraph or two.

Neil Postman

# Order in the Classroom

William O'Connor, who is unknown to me in a personal way, was once a member of the Boston School Committee, in which capacity he made the following remark: "We have no inferior education in our schools. What we have been getting is an inferior type of student."

The remark is easy to ridicule, and I have had some fun with it in the past. But there are a couple of senses in which it is perfectly sound.

In the first place, a classroom is a technique for the achievement of certain kinds of learning. It is a workable technique provided that both the teacher and the student have the skill and, particularly, the attitudes that are fundamental to it. Among these, from the student's point of view, are tolerance for delayed gratification, a certain measure of respect for and fear of authority, and a willingness to accommodate one's individual desires to the interests of group cohesion and purpose. These attitudes cannot be taught easily in school because they are a necessary component of the teaching situation itself. The problem is not unlike trying to find out how to spell a word by looking it up in the dictionary. If you do not know how a word is spelled, it is hard to look it up. In the same way, little can be taught in school unless

Neil Postman, born in New York City in 1931, has taught in elementary and secondary schools and is now a professor of communication arts and sciences at New York University.

these attitudes are present. And if they are not, to teach them is difficult.

Obviously, such attitudes must be learned during the years before  4
a child starts school; that is, in the home. This is the real meaning of
the phrase "preschool education." If a child is not made ready at home
for the classroom experience, he or she usually cannot benefit from
any normal school program. Just as important, the school is defenseless
against such a child, who, typically, is a source of disorder in a situation
that requires order. I raise this issue because education reform is impossible without order in the classroom. Without the attitudes that
lead to order, the classroom is an entirely impotent technique. Therefore, one possible translation of Mr. O'Connor's remark is, "We have
a useful technique for educating youth but too many of them have not
been provided at home with the attitudes necessary for the technique
to work."

In still another way Mr. O'Connor's remark makes plain sense.  5
The electronic media, with their emphasis on visual imagery, immediacy, non-linearity, and fragmentation, do not give support to the
attitudes that are fundamental to the classroom; that is, Mr. O'Connor's remark can be translated as, "We would not have an inferior
education if it were the nineteenth century. Our problem is that we
have been getting students who are products of the twentieth century." But there is nothing nonsensical about this, either. The nineteenth century had much to recommend it, and we certainly may be
permitted to allow it to exert an influence on the twentieth. The classroom is a nineteenth-century invention, and we ought to prize what
it has to offer. It is one of the few social organizations left to us in
which sequence, social order, hierarchy, continuity, and deferred
pleasure are important.

The problem of disorder in the classroom is created largely by two  6
factors: a dissolving family structure, out of which come youngsters
who are "unfit" for the presuppositions of a classroom; and a radically
altered information environment, which undermines the foundation
of school. The question, then, is, What should be done about the increasing tendency toward disorder in the classroom?

Liberal reformers, such as Kenneth Keniston, have answers, of a  7
sort. Keniston argues that economic reforms should be made so that
the integrity and authority of the family can be restored. He believes
that poverty is the main cause of family dissolution, and that by im-

proving the economic situation of families, we may kindle a sense of order and aspiration in the lives of children. Some of the reforms he suggests in his book *All Our Children* seem practical, although they are long-range and offer no immediate response to the problem of present disorder. Some Utopians, such as Ivan Illich, have offered other solutions; for example, dissolving the schools altogether, or so completely restructuring the school environment that its traditional assumptions are rendered irrelevant. To paraphrase Karl Kraus's epigram about psychoanalysis, these proposals are the Utopian disease of which they consider themselves the cure.

One of the best answers comes from Dr. Howard Hurwitz, who 8 is neither a liberal reformer nor a Utopian. It is a good solution, I believe, because it tries to respond to the needs not only of children who are unprepared for school because of parental failure but of children of all backgrounds who are being made strangers to the assumptions of school by the biases of the electronic media.

During the eleven years Dr. Hurwitz was principal at Long Island 9 City High School, the average number of suspensions each year was three, while in many New York City high schools the average runs close to one hundred. Also, during his tenure, not one instance of an assault on a teacher was reported, and daily student attendance averaged better than 90 percent, which in the context of the New York City school scene represents a riot of devotion.

Although I consider some of Dr. Hurwitz's curriculum ideas un- 10 inspired and even wrong-headed, he understands a few things of overriding importance that many educators of more expansive imagination do not. The first is that educators must devote at least as much attention to the immediate consequences of disorder as to its abstract causes. Whatever the causes of disorder and alienation, the consequences are severe and, if not curbed, result in making the school impotent. At the risk of becoming a symbol of reaction, Hurwitz ran "a tight ship." He holds to the belief, for example, that a child's right to an education is terminated at the point where the child interferes with the right of other children to have one.

Dr. Hurwitz also understands that disorder expands proportion- 11 ately to the tolerance for it, and that children of all kinds of home backgrounds can learn, in varying degrees, to function in situations where disorder is not tolerated at all. He does not believe that it is inevitably or only the children of the poor who are disorderly. In spite of what the "revisionist" education historians may say, poor people still regard school as an avenue of social and economic advancement for their children, and do not object in the least to its being an orderly and structured experience.

All this adds up to the common sense view that the school ought 12 not to accommodate itself to disorder, or to the biases of other communication systems. The children of the poor are likely to continue to be with us. Some parents will fail to assume competent responsibility for the preschool education of their children. The media will increase the intensity of their fragmenting influence. Educators must live with these facts. But Dr. Hurwitz believes that as a technique for learning, the classroom can work if students are oriented toward its assumptions, not the other way around. William O'Connor, wherever he is, would probably agree. And so do I. The school is not an extension of the street, the movie theater, a rock concert, or a playground. And it is certainly not an extension of the psychiatric clinic. It is a special environment that requires the enforcement of certain traditional rules of controlled group interaction. The school may be the only remaining public situation in which such rules have any meaning, and it would be a grave mistake to change those rules because some children find them hard or cannot function within them. Children who cannot ought to be removed from the environment in the interests of those who can.

Wholesale suspensions, however, are a symptom of disorder, not 13 a cure for it. And what makes Hurwitz's school noteworthy is the small number of suspensions that have been necessary. This is not the result of his having "good" students or "bad" students. It is the result of his having created an unambiguous, rigorous, and serious attitude—a nineteenth-century attitude, if you will—toward what constitutes acceptable school behavior. In other words, Dr. Hurwitz's school turns out to be a place where children of all backgrounds—fit and unfit—can function, or can learn to function, and where the biases of our information environment are emphatically opposed.

At this point I should like to leave the particulars of Dr. Hurwitz's 14 solution and, retaining their spirit, indicate some particulars of my own.

Let us start, for instance, with the idea of a dress code. A dress 15 code signifies that school is a special place in which special kinds of behavior are required. The way one dresses is an indication of an attitude toward a situation. And the way one is *expected* to dress indicates what that attitude ought to be. You would not wear dungarees and a T-shirt that says "Feel Me" when attending a church wedding. That would be considered an outrage against the tone and meaning of the situation. The school has every right and reason, I believe, to expect the same sort of consideration.

Those who are inclined to think this is a superficial point are prob- 16 ably forgetting that symbols not only reflect our feelings but to some extent create them. One's kneeling in church, for example, reflects a sense of reverence but also engenders reverence. If we want school to *feel* like a special place, we can find no better way to begin than by requiring students to dress in a manner befitting the seriousness of the enterprise and the institution. I should include teachers in this requirement. I know of one high school in which the principal has put forward a dress code of sorts for teachers. (He has not, apparently, had the courage to propose one for the students.) For males the requirement is merely a jacket and tie. One of his teachers bitterly complained to me that such a regulation infringed upon his civil rights. And yet, this teacher will accept without complaint the same regulation when it is enforced by an elegant restaurant. His complaint and his acquiescence tell a great deal about how he values schools and how he values restaurants.

I do not have in mind, for students, uniforms of the type some- 17 times worn in parochial schools. I am referring here to some reasonable standard of dress which would mark school as a place of dignity and seriousness. And I might add that I do not believe for one moment the argument that poor people would be unable to clothe their children properly if such a code were in force. Furthermore, I do not believe that poor people have advanced that argument. It is an argument that middle-class education critics have made on behalf of the poor.

Another argument advanced in behalf of the poor and oppressed 18 is the students' right to their own language. I have never heard this argument come from parents whose children are not competent to use Standard English. It is an argument, once again, put forward by "liberal" education critics whose children *are* competent in Standard English but who in some curious way wish to express their solidarity with and charity for those who are less capable. It is a case of pure condescension, and I do not think teachers should be taken in by it. Like the mode of dress, the mode of language in school ought to be relatively formal and exemplary, and therefore markedly different from the custom in less rigorous places. It is particularly important that teachers should avoid trying to win their students' affection by adopting the language of youth. Such teachers frequently win only the contempt of their students, who sense that the language of teachers and the language of students ought to be different; that is to say, the world of adults is different from the world of children.

In this connection, it is worth saying that the modern conception 19 of childhood is a product of the sixteenth century, as Philippe Aries has documented in his *The Centuries of Childhood*. Prior to that century, children as young as six and seven were treated in all important respects as if they were adults. Their language, their dress, their legal status, their responsibilities, their labor, were much the same as those of adults. The concept of childhood as an identifiable stage in human growth began to develop in the sixteenth century and has continued into our own times. However, with the emergence of electronic media of communication, a reversal of this trend seems to be taking place. In a culture in which the distribution of information is almost wholly undifferentiated, age categories begin to disappear. Television, in itself, may bring an end to childhood. In truth, there is no such thing as "children's programming," at least not for children over the age of eight or nine. Everyone sees and hears the same things. We have already reached a point where crimes of youth are indistinguishable from those of adults, and we may soon reach a point where the punishments will be the same.

I raise this point because the school is one of our few remaining 20 institutions based on firm distinctions between childhood and adulthood, and on the assumption that adults have something of value to teach the young. That is why teachers must avoid emulating in dress and speech the style of the young. It is also why the school ought to be a place for what we might call "manners education": the adults in school ought to be concerned with teaching youth a standard of civilized interaction.

Again those who are inclined to regard this as superficial may be 21 underestimating the power of media such as television and radio to teach how one is to conduct oneself in public. In a general sense, the media "unprepare" the young for behavior in groups. A young man who goes through the day with a radio affixed to his ear is learning to be indifferent to any shared sound. A young woman who can turn off a television program that does not suit her needs at the moment is learning impatience with any stimulus that is not responsive to her interests.

But school is not a radio station or a television program. It is a 22 social situation requiring the subordination of one's own impulses and interests to those of the group. In a word, manners. As a rule, elementary school teachers will exert considerable effort in teaching manners. I believe they refer to this effort as "socializing the child." But it is astonishing how precipitously this effort is diminished at higher levels. It is certainly neglected in the high schools, and where it is not, there is usually an excessive concern for "bad habits," such as smoking, drinking, and in some nineteenth-century schools, swearing. But, as William James noted, our virtues are as habitual as our vices. Where is the attention given to the "Good morning" habit, to the "I beg your pardon" habit, to the "Please forgive the interruption" habit?

The most civilized high school class I have ever seen was one in    23
which students and teacher said "Good morning" to each other and in which the students stood up when they had something to say. The teacher, moreover, thanked each student for any contribution made to the class, did not sit with his feet on the desk, and did not interrupt a student unless he had asked permission to do so. The students, in turn, did not interrupt each other, or chew gum, or read comic books when they were bored. To avoid being a burden to others when one is bored is the essence of civilized behavior.

Of this teacher, I might also say that he made no attempt to en-    24
tertain his students or model his classroom along the lines of a TV program. He was concerned not only to teach his students manners but to teach them how to attend in a classroom, which is partly a matter of manners but also necessary to their intellectual development. One of the more serious difficulties teachers now face in the classroom results from the fact that their students suffer media-shortened attention spans and have become accustomed, also through intense media exposure, to novelty, variety, and entertainment. Some teachers have made desperate attempts to keep their students "tuned in" by fashioning their classes along the lines of *Sesame Street* or the *Tonight* show. They tell jokes. They change the pace. They show films, play records, and avoid *anything* that would take more than eight minutes. Although their motivation is understandable, this is what their students least need. However difficult it may be, the teacher must try to achieve student attention and even enthusiasm through the attraction of ideas, not razzmatazz. Those who think I am speaking here in favor of "dull" classes may themselves, through media exposure, have lost an understanding of the potential for excitement contained in an idea. The media (one prays) are not so powerful that they can obliterate in the young, particularly in the adolescent, what William James referred to as a "theoretic instinct," a need to know reasons, causes, abstract conceptions. Such an "instinct" can be seen in its earliest stages in what

he calls the "sporadic metaphysical inquiries of children as to who made God, and why they have five fingers. . . ."

I trust that the reader is not misled by what I have been saying.  25
As I see it, nothing in any of the above leads to the conclusion that I favor a classroom that is authoritarian or coldhearted, or dominated by a teacher insensitive to students and how they learn. I merely want to affirm the importance of the classroom as a special place, aloof from the biases of the media; a place in which the uses of the intellect are given prominence in a setting of elevated language, civilized manners, and respect for social symbols.

# Questions

1. In paragraph 3 what does Postman mean by "tolerance for delayed gratification"? By the way, two paragraphs later Postman uses an expression that is approximately synonymous with "delayed gratification." What is this expression?

2. Postman in part blames "the electronic media," because (he says in paragraph 5) they emphasize "fragmentation." Does he give any examples in his essay? Do you think you know what he means? And do you think he is right?

3. Who is Postman's audience? High school students? Parents and teachers? Professors of education? And who is Postman—that is, putting aside the biographical note on page 272, what sort of person does the author of the essay reveal himself to be? A frustrated high school teacher? A professor of education? An intelligent layperson? Does he seem to know what he is talking about?

4. In paragraph 10 we are told, with approval, that a principal named Dr. Howard Hurwitz "ran 'a tight ship.' " First, make sure that you know what the phrase means, and then write an essay of 500 words evaluating the degree of success of some instructor or administrator who ran a tight ship in your school. Your essay will, of course, have to give us a sense of what the instructor or administrator did, as well as your evaluation of the results of his or her teaching or administrating.

5. If you disagree with Postman on the value of a dress code, set forth your disagreement in a persuasive essay of 500 words.

6. Write an editorial—as an alumnus or alumna—for your high school newspaper, summarizing Postman's essay in a paragraph, and then comparing your school with Postman's idea of a good school, and, finally, evaluating your school and Postman's essay. You may, for example, conclude that, thank heavens, your school was nothing like Postman's ideal school.

Merry White

# Japanese Education
## How Do They Do It?

Japan has become the new reference point for the devel- 1
oping nations and the West, and comparisons with Japan cause increasing wonder and sometimes envy. Travel agents continue to profit
from the curiosity of Americans, particularly businessmen, who take
regular tours of Japan seeking the secrets of Japanese industry. They
come back with photographs and full notebooks, convinced they have
learned secrets that can be transplanted to their own companies.

Even the Japanese have entered the pop-sociological search for the 2
secrets of their own success, their journalists suggest that they emphasize problem *prevention* while Americans make up for their lack of
prescience and care through *remediation* (in the case of cars, recalls for
flawed models). The explanation given by a European Economic Community report—that the Japanese are workaholics willing, masochist-
ically, to live in "rabbit hutches" without complaint—was met with
amused derision in Japan. But it seems that those who do not look for
transportable "secrets" are nonetheless willing to believe that the
source of Japanese success is genetic, and thus completely untrans-
ferable. There are alternatives to these positions, and an examination
of Japanese education provides us with a backdrop for considering
them.

## The Social Consensus

The attention given to the decline of both American industry and Amer- 3
ican education has not yet led to an awareness here of the close relationship between the development of people and the development
of society, an awareness we see everywhere in Japanese thought and
institutions, and whose effects we can see in the individual achievements of Japanese children. If Americans realized how powerful the
relationship is between Japanese school achievement and social and

Merry White is the author of *The Japanese Educational Challenge* (1987). She
is also the author of a book on noodles. White, who has served as an administrator of Harvard's East Asian Studies Program, now teaches sociology at Boston University.

economic successes we might see the same kind of protectionist language aimed at the Japanese educational system that we see directed at their automobile industry. ("The Japanese must stop producing such able and committed students because *it isn't fair*.")

The Japanese understand how important it is to have not just a  4 high level of literacy (which they have had since well before modernization), but also a high level of education in the whole population. It has been said that the Japanese high school graduate is as well educated as an American college graduate, and indeed it is impressive that any worker on the factory floor can be expected to understand statistical material, work from complex graphs and charts, and perform sophisticated mathematical operations. This consensus that education is important, however simple it may sound, is the single most important contributor to the success of Japanese schools. Across the population, among parents, at all institutional and bureaucratic levels, and highest on the list of national priorities, is the stress on excellence in education. This is not just rhetoric. If the consensus, societal mobilization, and personal commitment—all focused on education—are not available to Americans, the reason is not genetic, nor are we locked in an immutable cultural pattern. We simply have not mobilized around our children.

There are clear advantages to being a Japanese child: a homoge-  5 neous population focused on perpetuating its cultural identity; an occupational system where selection and promotion are based on educational credentials; a relatively equal distribution of educational opportunities; a universal core curriculum; highly trained and rewarded teachers; and families, especially mothers, devoted to enhancing the life chances of children and working cooperatively with the educational system. Finally, there are high standards for performance in every sector, and a carefully graded series of performance expectations in the school curriculum.

It is clear from these assertions that the measurable cognitive  6 achievements of Japanese education represent only part of the picture. The American press stresses these achievements and accounts for them in terms of government expenditures, longer school years, and early use of homework. While the International Association for the Evaluation of Educational Achievement (IEA) test scores certainly indicate that Japanese children are testing higher than any children in the world (especially in math and science), and while some researchers have even claimed that Japanese children on average score 11 points more than American children on IQ tests, the social and psychological dimensions of Japanese education are similarly impressive and are primary contributors to cognitive achievement. The support given by family and teachers to the emotional and behavioral development of the child provides a base for the child's acquisition of knowledge and problem-solving skills. But beyond this, the Japanese think a major function of education is the development of a happy, engaged, and secure child, able to work hard and cooperate with others.

## *Inside the Japanese School*

In order to understand the context of the Japanese educational system, 7 some basic information is necessary:

1. Education is compulsory for ages six to 15, or through lower 8 secondary school. (Age is almost always correlated with grade level, by the way, because only rarely is a child "kept back" and almost never "put ahead.") Non-compulsory high school attendance (both public and private) is nearly universal, at 98 percent.

2. There is extensive "non-official" private education. Increasing 9 numbers of children attend pre-schools. Currently, about 95 percent of the five-year olds are in kindergarten or nursery school, 70 percent of the four-year olds and 10 percent of three-year olds. Many older children attend *juku* (after school classes) as well. These are private classes in a great variety of subjects, but most enhance and reinforce the material to be learned for high school or college entrance examinations. There are also *yobiko* (cram schools) for those taking an extra year between high school and college to prepare for the exams.

3. While competition for entrance to the most prestigious uni- 10 versities is very stiff, nearly 40 percent of the college-age group attend college or university. (The rates are slightly higher for women, since many attend two-year junior colleges.)

4. Japanese children attend school 240 days a year, compared to 11 180 in the U.S. Many children spend Sundays in study or tutoring, and vacation classes are also available. Children do not necessarily see this as oppressive, and younger children often ask their parents to send them to *juku* as a way of being with their friends after school. Homework starts in first grade, and children in Japan spend more time in home study than children in any other country except Taiwan. In Japan, 8 percent of the high school seniors spend less than five hours per week on homework, compared to 65 percent of American seniors.[1]

---

[1] Thomas Rohlen, *Japan's High Schools* (Berkeley: University of California Press, 1983), p. 277.

5. Primary and lower secondary schools provide what we would 12 call a core curriculum: a required and comprehensive course of study progressing along a logical path, with attention given to children's developmental levels. In elementary and lower secondary school, language learning dominates the school curriculum, and takes up the greatest number of classroom hours, particularly from second to fourth grade. The large number of characters to be learned requires an emphasis on memorization and drill that is not exhibited in the rest of the curriculum. Arithmetic and math are next in number of class hours, followed by social studies. The curriculum includes regular physical education and morning exercise as part of a "whole-child" program. In high school all students take Japanese, English, math, science, and social studies each year, and all students have had courses in chemistry, biology, physics, and earth sciences. All high school students take calculus.

6. Computers and other technology do not play a large role in 13 schools. The calculator is used, but has not replaced mental calculations or, for that matter, the abacus. There is no national program to develop high technology skills in children. Americans spend much more money on science and technology in the schools; the Japanese spend more on teacher training and salaries.

These features should be seen in the context of a history of emphasis on education in Japan. To begin with, an interest in mass (or at least widespread) education greatly antedated the introduction of Western schools to Japan. Literacy, numeracy, and a moral education were considered important for people of all classes. When Western style universal compulsory schooling was introduced in 1872, it was after a deliberate and wide-ranging search throughout the world that resulted in a selection of features from German, French, and American educational systems that would advance Japan's modernization and complement her culture. While uniform, centralized schooling was an import, it eventually brought out Japan's already refined powers of adaptation—not the ability to adapt to a new mode as much as *the ability to adapt the foreign mode to Japanese needs and conditions.*

Also striking was the rapidity with which Japan developed a mod- 15 ern educational system and made it truly universal. In 1873, one year after the Education Act, there was 28 percent enrollment in primary schools, but by 1904 enrollment had already reached 98 percent—one percent less than the current rate. The rush to educate children was buttressed both by the wish to catch up with the West and by a cultural interest in schooling.

## A Truly National System

Tradition, ideology, and international competition are not, however,  16
the only motive forces in Japanese education: other factors are as significant. First, Japan has a relatively homogeneous population. Racially
and economically there is little variety. Minority groups, such as Ko-
reans and the former out-castes, exist and do suffer some discrimination, but all children have equal access to good schooling. Income
is more evenly distributed in Japan than in America and most people
(96 percent in a recent Prime Minister's Office poll) consider themselves middle class. There are few remaining regional differences that
affect the educational system, except perhaps local accents.

Second, educational financing and planning are centralized. While  17
American educational policy sees the responsibility for schooling as a
local matter, Japanese planners can rely on a centralized source of
funding, curriculum guidance, and textbook selection. In terms of educational spending as a percentage of total GNP, the U.S. and Japan
are not so far apart: The U.S. devotes 6.8 percent of its GNP to education, and Japan devotes 8.6 percent. But in Japan about 50 percent
of this is national funding, while in the U.S. the federal government
provides only 8 percent of the total expenditure on education, most
of which is applied to special education, not to core schooling. Moreover, in the U.S. there exist no national institutions to build a consensus on what and how our children are taught. The most significant
outcome of centralization in Japan is the even distribution of resources
and quality instruction across the country. National planners and pol-
icymakers can mobilize a highly qualified teaching force and offer incentives that make even the most remote areas attractive to good teachers.

Third (but perhaps most important in the comparison with the  18
United States), teachers enjoy respect and high status, job security,
and good pay. More than in any other country, teachers in Japan are
highly qualified: Their mastery of their fields is the major job qualification, and all have at least a bachelor's degree in their specialty.
Moreover, they have a high degree of professional involvement as
teachers: 74 percent are said to belong to some professional teachers'
association in which teaching methods and curriculum are actively discussed.[2]

Teachers are hired for life, at starting salaries equivalent to starting  19

[2] William Cummings, *Education and Equality in Japan* (Princeton: Princeton University Press, 1980), p. 159.

salaries for college graduates in the corporate world. Elementary and junior high school teachers earn $18,200 per year on the average, high school teachers $19,000. Compared to other Japanese public sector workers, who earn an average of $16,800, this is a high salary, but it is less than that of managers in large companies or bureaucrats in prestigious ministries. In comparison with American teachers, whose salaries average $17,600, it is an absolutely higher wage. The difference is especially striking when one considers that over all professions, salaries are lower in Japan than in the U.S. In fact, American teachers' salaries are near the bottom of the scale of jobs requiring a college degree. Relative status and prestige correlate with salary in both countries. Japanese teachers' pay increases, as elsewhere in Japan, are tied to a seniority ladder, and older "master teachers" are given extra pay as teacher supervisors in each subject.[3]

Japanese teachers see their work as permanent: Teaching is not a   20
waystation on a path to other careers. Teachers work hard at improving their skills and knowledge of their subject, and attend refresher courses and upgrading programs provided by the Ministry of Education. While there are tendencies, encouraged by the Teachers' Union, to downplay the traditional image of the "devoted, selfless teacher" (since this is seen as exploitative), and to redefine the teacher as a wage laborer with regular hours, rather than as a member of a "sacred" profession, teachers still regularly work overtime and see their job's sphere extending beyond classroom instruction. Classes are large: The average is about 40 students to one teacher. Teachers feel responsible for their students' discipline, behavior, morality, and for their general social adjustment as well as for their cognitive development. They are "on duty" after school hours and during vacations, and supervise vacation play and study. They visit their students' families at home, and are available to parents with questions and anxieties about their children. The Teachers' Union protests strongly against this extensive role, but both teachers and parents reinforce this role, tied as it is to the high status of the teacher.

Fourth, there is strong ideological and institutional support for   21
education because the occupational system relies on schools to select the right person for the right organization. Note that this is not the same as the "right job" or "slot": A new company recruit, almost

---

[3] There is a debate in Japan today concerning rewarding good teachers with higher pay: Professor Sumiko Iwao, of Keio University, reports that when quality is measured in yen, the commitment of teachers to good teaching declines.

always a recent graduate, is not expected to have a skill or special identity, but to be appropriate in general educational background and character for a company. The company then trains recruits in the skills they will need, as well as in the company style. Of course, the basic skill level of the population of high school and college graduates is extremely high. But the important fact is that the social consensus supports an educational system that creates a committed, productive labor force. And although the emphasis seems to be on educational credentials, the quality of graduates possessing these credentials is indisputably high.

## Mom

The background I have presented—of national consensus, institutional     22
centralization, and fiscal support—alone does not explain the successes of Japanese education. There are other, less tangible factors that derive from cultural conceptions of development and learning, the valued role of maternal support, and psychological factors in Japanese pedagogy, and which distinguish it from American schooling.

The role of mothers is especially important. The average Japanese     23
mother feels her child has the potential for success: Children are believed to be born with no distinguishing abilities (or disabilities) and can be mobilized to achieve and perform at high levels. Effort and commitment are required, and, at least at the beginning, it is the mother's job to engage the child. One way of looking at Japanese child development is to look at the words and concepts related to parental goals for their children. A "good child" has the following, frequently invoked characteristics: He is *otonashii* (mild or gentle), *sunao* (compliant, obedient, and cooperative), *akarui* (bright, alert), and *genki* (energetic and spirited). *Sunao* has frequently been translated as "obedient," but it would be more appropriate to use "open minded," "nonresistant," or "authentic in intent and cooperative in spirit." The English word "obedience" implies subordination and lack of self-determination, but *sunao* assumes that what we call compliance (with a negative connotation) is really cooperation, an act of affirmation of the self. A child who is *sunao* has not yielded his personal autonomy for the sake of cooperation; cooperation does not imply giving up the self, but in fact implies that working with others is the appropriate setting for expressing and enhancing the self.

One encourages a *sunao* child through the technique, especially     24
used by mothers and elementary school teachers, of *wakaraseru*, or

"getting the child to understand." The basic principle of child rearing seems to be: Never go against the child. *Wakaraseru* is often a long-term process that ultimately engages the child in the mother's goals, and makes her goals the child's own, thus producing an authentic cooperation, as in *sunao*. The distinction between external, social expectations and the child's own personal goals becomes blurred from this point on. An American might see this manipulation of the child through what we would call "indulgence" as preventing him from having a strong will of his own, but the Japanese mother sees long term benefits of self-motivated cooperation and real commitment.

Japanese mothers are active teachers as well, and have a real curriculum for their pre-school children: Games, teaching aids, ordinary activities are all focused on the child's development. There are counting games for very small babies, songs to help children learn new words, devices to focus the child's concentration. Parents buy an average of two or three new books every month for their preschoolers, and there are about 40 monthly activity magazines for preschoolers, very highly subscribed. The result is that most, at least most urban children, can read and write the phonetic syllabary before they enter school, and can do simple computations. 25

Maternal involvement becomes much more extensive and "serious" once she and the child enter the elementary school community. In addition to formal involvement in frequent ceremonies and school events, PTA meetings and visiting days, the mother spends much time each day helping the child with homework (sometimes to the point at which the teachers joke that they are really grading the mothers by proxy). There are classes for mothers, called *mamajuku*, that prepare mothers in subjects their children are studying. Homework is considered above all a means for developing a sense of responsibility in the child, and like much in early childhood education, it is seen as a device to train character. 26

The Japanese phenomenon of maternal involvement recently surfaced in Riverdale, New York, where many Japanese families have settled. School teachers and principals there noted that each Japanese family was purchasing two sets of textbooks. On inquiring, they found that the second set was for the mother, who could better coach her child if she worked during the day to keep up with his lessons. These teachers said that children entering in September with no English ability finished in June at the top of their classes in every subject. 27

The effort mothers put into their children's examinations has been given a high profile by the press. This is called the *kyoiku mama* syn- 28 drome—the mother invested in her children's progress. In contrast to Western theories of achievement, which emphasize individual effort and ability, the Japanese consider academic achievement to be an outgrowth of an interdependent network of cooperative effort and planning. The caricature of the mother's over-investment, however, portrays a woman who has totally identified with her child's success or failure, and who has no separate identity of her own. The press emphasizes the negative aspects of this involvement with accounts of maternal nervous breakdowns, reporting a murder by a mother of the child next-door, who made too much noise while her child was studying. But the press also feeds the mother's investment by exhorting her to prepare a good work environment for the studying child, to subscribe to special exam-preparation magazines, to hire tutors, and to prepare a nutritious and exam-appropriate diet.

High-schoolers from outlying areas taking entrance exams in 29
Tokyo come with their mothers to stay in special rooms put aside by hotels. They are provided with special food, study rooms, counselors, and tension-release rooms, all meant to supply home-care away from home. The home study-desk bought by most parents for their smaller children symbolizes the hovering care and intensity of the mother's involvement: All models have a high front and half-sides, cutting out distractions and enclosing the workspace in womb-like protection. There is a built-in study light, shelves, a clock, electric pencil sharpener, and built-in calculator. The most popular model includes a push-button connecting to a buzzer in the kitchen to summon mother for help or for a snack.

## "How Do You Feel About Cubing?"

Not much work has been done yet to analyze the relationship between 30
the strongly supportive learning atmosphere and high achievement in Japan. In the home, mothers train small children in a disciplined, committed use of energy through what Takeo Doi has called the encouragement of "positive dependency"; in the schools as well there is a recognition that attention to the child's emotional relationship to his work, peers, and teachers is necessary for learning.

A look at a Japanese classroom yields some concrete examples of 31
this. Many Westerners believe that Japanese educational successes are due to an emphasis on rote learning and memorization, that the classroom is rigidly disciplined. This is far from reality. An American teacher walking into a fourth grade science class in Japan would be

horrified: children all talking at once, leaping and calling for the teacher's attention. The typical American's response is to wonder, "who's in control of this room?" But if one understands the content of the lively chatter, it is clear that all the noise and movement is focused on the work itself—children are shouting out answers, suggesting other methods, exclaiming in excitement over results, and not gossiping, teasing, or planning games for recess. As long as it is the result of this engagement, the teacher is not concerned over the noise, which may measure a teacher's success. (It has been estimated that American teachers spend about 60 percent of class time on organizing, controlling, and disciplining the class, while Japanese teachers spend only 10 percent.)

A fifth grade math class I observed reveals some elements of this pedagogy. The day I visited, the class was presented with a general statement about cubing. Before any concrete facts, formulae, or even drawings were displayed, the teacher asked the class to take out their math diaries and spend a few minutes writing down their feelings and anticipations over this new concept. It is hard for me to imagine an American math teacher beginning a lesson with an exhortation to examine one's emotional predispositions about cubing (but that may be only because my own math training was antediluvian). 32

After that, the teacher asked for conjectures from the children about the surface and volume of a cube and asked for some ideas about formulae for calculation. The teacher asked the class to cluster into its component *han* (working groups) of four or five children each, and gave out materials for measurement and construction. One group left the room with large pieces of cardboard, to construct a model of a cubic meter. The groups worked internally on solutions to problems set by the teacher and competed with each other to finish first. After a while, the cubic meter group returned, groaning under the bulk of its model, and everyone gasped over its size. (There were many comments and guesses as to how many children could fit inside.) The teacher then set the whole class a very challenging problem, well over their heads, and gave them the rest of the class time to work on it. The class ended without a solution, but the teacher made no particular effort to get or give an answer, although she exhorted them to be energetic. (It was several days before the class got the answer—there was no deadline but the excitement did not flag.) 33

Several characteristics of this class deserve highlighting. First, there was attention to feelings and predispositions, provision of facts, and opportunities for discovery. The teacher preferred to focus on pro- 34 cess, engagement, commitment, and performance rather than on discipline (in our sense) and production. Second, the *han:* Assignments are made to groups, not to individuals (this is also true at the workplace) although individual progress and achievement are closely monitored. Children are supported, praised, and allowed to make mistakes through trial and error within the group. The group is also pitted against other groups, and the group's success is each person's triumph, and vice versa. Groups are made up by the teacher and are designed to include a mixture of skill levels—there is a *hancho* (leader) whose job it is to choreograph the group's work, to encourage the slower members, and to act as a reporter to the class at large.

Japanese teachers seem to recognize the emotional as well as the intellectual aspects of engagement. Japanese pedagogy (and maternal socialization) are based on the belief that effort is the most important factor in achievement, and that the teacher's job is to get the child to commit himself positively and energetically to hard work. This emphasis is most explicit in elementary school, but persists later as a prerequisite for the self-discipline and effort children exhibit in high school. 35

American educational rhetoric does invoke "the whole child," does seek "self-expression," and does promote emotional engagement in "discovery learning." But Japanese teaching style, at least in primary schools, effectively employs an engaging, challenging teaching style that surpasses most American attempts. In the cubing class, I was struck by the spontaneity, excitement, and (to American eyes) "unruly" dedication of the children to the new idea, and impressed with the teacher's ability to create this positive mood. It could be a cultural difference: We usually separate cognition and emotional affect, and then devise artificial means of reintroducing "feeling" into learning. It is rather like the way canned fruit juices are produced—first denatured by the preserving process and then topped up with chemical vitamins to replace what was lost. 36

## The Role of Competition

The frequent accusation that Japanese education involves children in hellish competition must also be examined. In the elementary school classroom, competition is negotiated by means of the *han.* The educational system tries to accommodate both the ideology of harmony and the interest in hierarchy and ranking. The introduction of graded, competitive Western modes of education into societies where mini- 37 mizing differences between people is valued has often produced severe social and psychological dislocation (as in Africa and other parts of the Third World). In Japan, the importance of the modern educational system as a talent selector and the need to preserve harmony and homogeneity have produced complementary rather than conflicting forces. The regular classroom is a place where the individual does not stick out, but where individual needs are met and goals are set. Children are not held back nor advanced by ability: the cohesion of the age group is said to be more important. Teachers focus on pulling up the slower learners, rather than tracking the class to suit different abilities. For the most part, teachers and the school system refuse to engage in examination preparation hysteria. Part of the reason for this is pressure from the Teachers' Union, a very large and powerful labor union which consistently resists any moves away from the egalitarian and undifferentiating mode of learning. Turning teachers into drill instructors is said to be dehumanizing, and the process of cramming a poor substitute for education.

So where is the competitive selection principle served? In the *juku*.  38 *Juku* are tough competitive classes, often with up to 500 in one lecture hall. The most prestigious are themselves very selective and there are examinations (and preparation courses for these) to enter the *juku*. Some *juku* specialize in particular universities' entrance exams, and they will boast of their rate of admission into their universities. It is estimated that one third of all primary school students and one half of all secondary school students attend *juku*, but in Tokyo the rate rises to 86 percent of junior high school students. The "king of *juku*," Furukawa Noboru, the creator of a vast chain of such classes, says that *juku* are necessary to bridge the gap of present realities in Japan. He says that public schools do not face the fact of competition, and that ignoring the reality does not help children. The Ministry of Education usually ignores this non-accredited alternative and complementary system, and permits this functional division to take the pressure off the public schools. While there is considerable grumbling by parents, and while it is clear that the *juku* introduce an inegalitarian element into the process of schooling (since they do cost money), they do, by their separation from the regular school, permit the persistence of more traditional modes of learning, while allowing for a fast track in the examinations.

It is important to note that in Japan there really is only one moment  39 of critical importance to one's career chances—the entrance examination to college. There are few opportunities to change paths or retool.

Americans' belief that one can be recreated at any time in life, that the self-made person can get ahead, simply is not possible in Japan—thus the intense focus on examinations.

## The Problems—in Context

This rapid tour through the Japanese educational system cannot neglect 40 the problems. However, two things must be kept in mind when considering these well-publicized difficulties: One is that although problems do exist, the statistical reality is that, compared to the West, Japan still looks very good indeed. The other is that the Japanese themselves tend to be quite critical, and educational problems are given attention. But this attention should be seen in context: Not that people are not truly concerned about real problems, but that the anxiety seems related to a sense of national insecurity. The Japanese focus on educational issues may emanate from a sense of the importance of intellectual development in a society where there are few other resources. Any educational problem seems to put the nation truly at risk.

Japanese parents are critical and watchful of the schools and are 41 not complacent about their children's successes. There was a telling example of this in a recent comparative study of American and Japanese education. Mothers in Minneapolis and in Sendai, roughly comparable cities, were asked to evaluate their children's school experiences. The Minneapolis mothers consistently answered that the schools were fine and that their children were doing well, while the Sendai mothers were very critical of their schools and worried that their children were not performing up to potential. Whose children were, in objective tests, doing better? The Sendai group—in fact so much better that the poorest performer in the Japanese group was well ahead of the best in the American group. Mothers in Japan and the U.S. have very different perspectives on performance: Japanese mothers attribute failure to lack of effort while American mothers explain it as lack of ability. Japanese children have an external standard of excellence to which they can aspire, while an American child normally can only say he will "do his best."

Problems have surfaced, of course. Psychotherapists report a syn- 42 drome among children related to school and examination pressure. School phobia, psychosomatic symptoms, and juvenile suicide are most frequently reported. Japan does lead the world in school-related suicides for the 15- to 19-year old age group, at about 300 per year. Recently, the "battered teacher" and "battered parent" syndromes have received much attention. There are cases where teenagers have attacked or killed parents and teachers, and these have been related to examination pressure. The numbers involved in these cases are very small—at least in comparison with American delinquency patterns and other juvenile pathologies. Dropouts, drug use, and violent juvenile crimes are almost non-existent in Japan. The crimes reported in one year among school-age children in Osaka, for example, are equal to those reported in one day in New York.

Criticism leveled at Japanese education by Western observers focuses on what they regard as a suppression of genius and individuality, and a lack of attention to the development of creativity in children. The first may indeed be a problem—for the geniuses—because there is little provision for tracking them to their best advantage. There has been discussion of introducing tracking so that individual ability can be better served, but this has not been implemented. The superbright may indeed be disadvantaged.  43

On the other hand, creativity and innovation *are* encouraged, but their manifestations may be different from those an American observer would expect. We must look at our own assumptions, to see if they are too limited. Americans see creativity in children as a fragile blossom that is stifled by rigid educational systems or adult standards. Creativity involves a necessary break with traditional content and methods, and implies the creation of a new idea or artifact. Whether creativity is in the child or in the teaching, and how it is to be measured, are questions no one has answered satisfactorily. Why we emphasize it is another question, probably related to our theories of progress and the importance we attach to unique accomplishments that push society forward. The fact is that, if anything, our schools do less to encourage creativity than do the Japanese, especially in the arts. All children in Japan learn two instruments and how to read music in elementary school, have regular drawing and painting classes, and work in small groups to create projects they themselves devise. It is true, though, that if everyone must be a soloist or composer to be considered creative, then most Japanese are not encouraged to be creative.  44

It is not enough to claim that the Japanese have been successful in training children to take exams at the expense of a broader education. And it is not at all appropriate to say that they are unable to develop children's individuality and create the geniuses who make scientific breakthroughs. The first is untrue and the second remains to be shown as false by the Japanese themselves, who are now mobilizing to produce more scientists and technologists. In fact, the scales  45 are tipped in favor of Japan, and to represent it otherwise would be a distortion.

The success of the Japanese model has led to its use in other rapidly 46 developing countries, including South Korea, Taiwan, and Singapore. There, education is seen as the linchpin for development, and attention to children has meant the allocation of considerable resources to schools. The results are similar to those seen in Japanese schools: highly motivated, hard-working students who like school and who have achieved very high scores on international achievement tests.

## Seeing Ourselves Through Japanese Eyes

What *America* can learn from Japan is rather an open question. We can, 47 to begin with, learn more *about* Japan, and in doing so, learn more about ourselves. Japanese advancements of the past 20 years were based on American principles of productivity (such as "quality control"), not on samurai management skills and zen austerities. Looking for Japanese secrets, or worse, protesting that they are inhuman or unfair, will not get us very far. They have shown they can adjust programs and policies to the needs and resources of the times; we must do the same. We need to regain the scientific literacy we lost and reacquire the concrete skills and participatory techniques we need. We should see Japan as establishing a new standard, not as a model to be emulated. To match that standard we have to aim at general excellence, develop a long-term view, and act consistently over time with regard to our children's education.

# Questions

1. In paragraph 4 White contrasts Japanese commitment to education with our own. Where in our society might one look for evidence of commitment or lack of commitment to education?

2. In paragraph 5 White lists many "clear advantages to being a Japanese child." Considering your education, or any other grounds you choose, which of these "advantages" would you like to have? Are there any you would gladly do without? Can you explain why? How many of the Japanese advantages appear to be dependent on the first that White lists, "a homogeneous population"? Are you aware of advantages to growing up in a heterogeneous population? (For an explanation of Japanese homogeneity, see paragraph 16.)

3. At the end of paragraph 6 White says that "the Japanese think a

major function of education is the development of a happy, engaged, and secure child, able to work hard and cooperate with others." Complete the following sentence: "Americans think a major function of education is . . .''

4. In paragraph 11 White discusses the amount of time Japanese students spend on homework. What were your own experiences with homework? Did homework contribute significantly to your education? Were there assignments you now regard as counterproductive?

5. In paragraph 13 White says that computers do not play a large role in Japanese schools. If computers played a fairly large role in your education, what do you think you learned from them, aside from how to operate them?

6. In paragraph 18 White reports that Japanese teachers are highly qualified. Do you think that, on the whole, your high school teachers were highly qualified? If you were able to do so, what measures would you take to insure well-qualified teachers in *all* American high schools? (White's paragraph 19 may provide some ideas.)

7. In paragraph 32 White briefly describes a math class about to study cubing. Does the procedure followed in the class strike you as being of any value? Why, or why not? And what about the procedure described in the next paragraph? (In thinking about this, consider also White's comments in paragraphs 34–35.) Looking back at a class in which you learned a good deal, what "elements of pedagogy" (White's words, paragraph 32) made the class successful?

8. In paragraph 37 White says that children in Japanese schools are almost never held back or advanced because of ability, and there is no tracking system. What do you think of this system? (Consider also paragraphs 43 and 44.)

9. In paragraph 39 White writes of the belief of Americans that "one can be recreated at any time in life, that the self-made person can get ahead." To what extent do you share these beliefs? To what extent did the schools you attended promote them?

10. Japan has produced relatively few winners of the Nobel Prize. Did White's essay help you to understand why this might be so? Do you take the lack of Nobel Prize winners to be a significant criticism of the Japanese educational system?

11. Given the great differences between our societies, what, if anything, do you think our educational system can learn from the Japanese system? (For example, we are far less homogeneous. And the mothers in our society often hold paying jobs, whereas few Japanese mothers do. Further, two thirds of our teenagers hold part-time jobs, whereas almost no Japanese teenagers hold jobs.)

Theodore Sizer

# Principals' Questions

$\mathbf{A}$s I traveled among schools, their principals pressed me with questions, many of which were practical, specific.

*What's your curriculum . . . What subjects should be offered?* they asked.

I replied: Let's not start with subjects; that usually leads us into the swamp called "coverage." What counts are positive answers to three questions: Can graduates of this high school teach themselves? Are they decent people? Can they effectively use the principal ways of looking at the world, ways represented by the major and traditional academic disciplines?

*What do you mean, "teach themselves"?*

Learning how to observe and analyze a situation or problem and being able to make sense of it, use it, criticize it, reject or accept it. This is more than simple "problem-solving," since many of the enriching things in life are not, in fact, problems. "Teaching oneself" is nothing more than knowing how to inform and enrich oneself. Ideally a school would like not only to equip a student with those skills, but also to inspire him or her to use them.

*How is this done?*

By directly giving students the task of teaching themselves and helping them with it. It means providing fewer answers and insisting that students find the right (or at least defensible) answers themselves. It means that teachers must focus more on *how* kids think than on what they think.

*This will take lots of time.*

Yes, indeed. There will be far less opportunity for teachers to tell things, and, as a result, less coverage, of fewer subject areas. Of course, ultimately it means more coverage because the student is able to learn on his or her own.

Theodore Sizer, born in New Haven in 1937, was educated at Yale and Harvard. After serving from 1964 to 1972 as dean of the Harvard Graduate School of Education, he served as headmaster of Phillips Academy, Andover. In 1981 and 1982 he visited some fifty secondary schools, preparing to write *Horace's Compromise*, the book from which our selection is taken. (The title refers to an imaginary or composite teacher named Horace, who finds that he must compromise on his job.)

*Which fewer areas? Be specific.*     10

I will, but with the clear understanding that there is no One Best     11
Curriculum for all schools. While we all have to agree on some general
outcomes that give meaning to the high school diploma, the means to
these outcomes must be kept flexible. No two schools will or should
have precisely the same characteristics; wise diversity is *essential* for
quality. Furthermore, top-down edicts about "what" and "how" demonstrably do not work. Each school must find its own way, and in
so doing gain the energy that such a search provides.

Let me give you the beginnings of one model. I would organize     12
a high school into four areas or large departments:

1. Inquiry and Expression
2. Mathematics and Science
3. Literature and the Arts
4. Philosophy and History

You will immediately note that "English," that pivotally important but
often misconstrued or even unconstrued "subject," would disappear.
By "expression," I mean all kinds of communication, but above all
writing, the litmus paper of thought. Some of "communication" is
brute skill, such as the use of a keyboard (that sine qua non for the
modern citizen) and clear, if rudimentary handwriting. Visual communication is included, as are gesture and physical nuance and tone,
those tools used so powerfully by such masters as Winston Churchill
and Ronald Reagan. A teacher cannot ascertain a student's thought
processes unless they are expressed.

Mathematics is the language of science, the language of certainties.     13
Science, of course, is full of uncertainty, as is much of higher mathematics, but for beginners it is the certainties that dominate. Number
systems work in certain ways. Axioms hold. The pituitary gland se-
cretes certain hormones; if it fails to do so, predictable consequences
ensue. The world around us has its share of certainties, and we should
learn about them, learn to be masters of them. Basic arithmetic, al-
gebra, some geometry and statistics, physics and biology, are the keys.
I would merge the traditional departments of mathematics and science,
thus forcing coordination of the real and abstract worlds of certainty.
The fresh, modern necessity for study in computer science can be the
first bit of glue in this process of collaboration; that subject nicely strad-
dles both areas.

Human expression cuts across written and spoken languages, the-     14
ater, song, and visual art. There is much common ground in these

attempts of man and woman to explain their predicament, yet English, music, and art usually proceed in as much splendid isolation as do mathematics and science. This is wasteful, as aesthetic expression and learning from others' attempts to find meaning are of a piece. All need representation and benefit from an alliance.

History, if it is responsibly taught, is perhaps the most difficult    15
subject for most high school students, because it involves the abstraction of time past. One often can engage it well first through autobiography and then through biography, proceeding finally to the "biographies" of communities, which make up most conventional history. Things were as they were for reasons, and from these incidents evolve concepts in geography, economics, and sociology. For most students at this stage, these disciplines should remain the handmaidens of history. The exception is philosophy, particularly moral and political philosophy. A political philosophy, essentially that associated with American constitutionalism, is the bedrock of enlightened democratic citizenship, and adolescence, more than any other stage of life, is filled with a search for values. The study of elementary ethics, for example, not only provides excellent opportunities for learning intellectual skills, but also powerfully engages students' interest.

*Why so few subjects?*    16

There are several reasons. One is to lessen the splintered view of    17
knowledge that usually confronts high school students. Their world rarely uses the fine distinctions between academic disciplines; insisting on them confuses young scholars. A second serves teachers: strict specialization hobbles much skill training. Good coaching cuts across academic specializations. The current organization is very wasteful. A third reason: a few areas, taught in large time blocks, greatly reduce both the scheduling problems and the frenetic quality of the school day. Finally, more broadly and sensibly construed subject areas allow greater scope for teachers.

*Won't students want electives?*    18

Yes, in that they will want opportunities to study what interests    19
them and what helps them. However, this personalization can be well accommodated *within* each broad area, rather than through a smorgasbord of unrelated courses.

*This sounds deadly, very academic and removed from kids' lives.*    20

It sounds deadly because it has often been taught in deadly ways.    21
I am regularly assaulted for being an "elitist" for proposing this program, yet no critic will argue, when I press him, that any of the objectives I put forward is inappropriate for every adolescent. A teacher

must start where the students are—and this may *not* be chapter one in the textbook. One works to engage each student, to get him or her to experience some aspect of an area, and to feel that experience to be successful. It takes time, ingenuity, patience. Most difficult to reach will be the demoralized youngsters, the ones who see school as a hostile place. Many of these students come from low-income families. They will need special attention and classes that use extensive coaching—not only to help them gain the skills they often lack but also to promote some fresh self-assurance in them. Vast classes heavy with lecturing must be avoided.

*You've left out physical education and vocational education.*        22

Let's start with physical education. Much of what happens in        23
schools today under that rubric is neither education (or at best is disconnected applied biology) nor very physical (thirty minutes once a week playing volleyball does not mean much, except perhaps as a useful vent for built-up adolescent steam). Citizens should know about their bodies and be taught that the need for exercise is a good thing. These are worthy topics for a good science-mathematics area to present.

The same kind of argument can be made for vocational education.        24
Specific job training is a good thing, but not at the expense of a school's core. The best place to learn most jobs is on site. The common exception is business education, most prominently training for secretarial positions. The important points are ability to type and, beyond that, being well informed, literate, and able to handle numbers. If typing is a schoolwide requirement, and the other skills the inevitable consequence of the student's taking the core topics, the exception is moot.

Two more points about vocational education: tomorrow's economy        25
will be volatile and dependent on flexible workers with a high level of intellectual skills. Thus, the best vocational education will be one in general education in the use of one's mind. Second, we must remember that most of today's high school students are or wish to be in the labor market. As the age cohort shrinks, the demand for its labor in most communities will grow. Educators are not going to reverse this trend; it will be better if they seize it, and adapt schools in demanding, sensible ways to the reality of adolescent employment. Working per se can be good for adolescents.

*All that may be true in the abstract. But the fact remains that you'll lose*        26
*a lot of kids if you cut out voc ed and athletics.*

No, not necessarily. Remember that but a small minority of high        27
school students are significantly involved in vocational education and

interscholastic athletics. Furthermore, to the extent that these activities form a bridge to the central subjects, I'm for them. Unfortunately, today in many schools they have a life of their own, at the expense of an education in mind and character.

*What of foreign language?*                                                    28

The cry for its requirement in schooling is abroad in the land as a    29
cure for American isolation and chauvinism. For many adolescents, such study has merit; for others, little sense. If you cannot master your own language, it is inefficient to start another. If you have little immediate need to use a second language, the time spent in learning it is largely wasted—unless that "foreign" language is English. An absolute requirement for study of a foreign tongue can divert from other topics time that is crucial for a particularly needy student. The issue of ethnocentrism is more important than language study and must be addressed through the history courses.

*What of bilingual education?*                                                 30

Ideally, all Americans should enjoy it—but the real problem is that   31
of non-English speaking students. They should be immersed in English intensively. Their nonlinguistic studies should continue—for no longer than necessary—in their mother tongues. Their self-confidence, often associated with their facility in language, should be reinforced. Empathy and patience are crucial here; rigid formulae passed down from central authorities *guarantee* inefficiency and frustration. The goal is confident youngsters, adept and effectively fluent in two languages.

*I'm still skeptical about your overall plan. You can pull this off only if*    32
*you had none but highly motivated students in your school. What of tracking*
*and the turned-off student?*

Just as now, some kids won't hook in; I know that. If they've          33
shown themselves competent in the minima of literacy, numeracy, and civic understanding, let them leave high school—with the promise that they can come back in the future. The community college system in many regions makes this an easy alternative.

In addition, there are the troublemakers, the kids who don't want    34
necessarily to leave school, but want just to stay there because it's fun, where their friends are. Of course, good teachers can work with them to try to change their attitudes. However, if they disrupt, they should be expelled, with the same opportunities to return later as all dropouts have. As long as they have met the state's requirements, no one should force them into school. Ideally, too, they should have a variety of programs from which to choose. Highly personalized alternative programs have frequently worked for this sort of student.

As to tracking: there would be none and there would be a great ³⁵
deal. Every student would be enrolled in each subject area all the time.
There would therefore be none of the current tracks, usually called
honors, college preparatory, general, technical, and so forth. But
within each subject area, the students would progress at their own
pace. This would create multiple tracks, ones that are flexible and that
put no child in any dead end.

*That will be very messy.* ³⁶

Yes, it will. Learning is messy. It can be handled if the units (sep- ³⁷
arate high schools, or "houses" within high schools) are kept small
enough to allow a particular group of teachers to know particular students well and develop a track for each. Class patterns will vary by
need, some larger for telling, some smaller for coaching and questioning. Students will be working much more on their own than they
do now; there will be no strict age grading. One learns how to learn
by experience, not by being told things.

*Won't this add financial cost?* ³⁸

Some, perhaps. It need not, as long as schools retreat from the ³⁹
objective of "comprehensiveness" and concentrate on classroom teaching. There are models of "zero-based budgets" which demonstrate that
schools, if simply organized, can have well-paid faculty and fewer than
eighty students per teacher, without increasing current per-pupil expenditure.

*You haven't mentioned guidance counselors.* ⁴⁰

Counselors today act either as administrators, arranging schedules ⁴¹
and job and college interviews and the like, or as teachers, coaching
and questioning young people about their personal concerns. Good
teachers *are* good counselors, in that second sense; students turn to
them for help, whether or not their titles identify them as "guidance"
people. Most high school guidance departments are overloaded with
obligations, many of which are contradictory—for example, serving
both as a place where students can obtain confidential personal counsel
and as a disciplinary arm of the school (perhaps running the "inschool
suspension" program for students who have repeatedly broken rules).

A decentralized school with small academic units has less need ⁴²
for specialized counseling offices; improved faculty-student ratios
make this possible. The administrative obligations now traditionally
handled by such offices can be placed directly under the principal.
Staff members who are well trained in counseling and testing skills
can support the teachers in each small academic unit.

*We are being asked often these days about "computer literacy" and the* ⁴³ *needs of a "new technological society." How does your plan address these areas?*

Computers, like calculators, books, and other familiar products of 44 technology, should be welcomed by schools. Well used, they might significantly extend teachers' coaching efforts as well as help students learn. While we should learn to employ the products of the new technologies, we should keep in mind two critical points: it is up to us to select the data to be put into them, and we must choose with care the uses we put them to.

*Should public schools formally provide time for voluntary prayer?*    45

No. There is ample time and opportunity outside school for reli- 46 gious observances. Furthermore, the fact that public schools would not set time aside for prayer does not imply rejection of its importance. Schools should *not* claim to be comprehensive, arrogating to their routines every consequential aspect of an adolescent's life. High schools are limited to helping adolescents use their minds well—and this includes becoming thoughtful and decent people.

*What of standards?*    47

The existence of final "exhibitions" by students as a condition to 48 receiving their diplomas will give teachers a much greater control of standards than they currently have. These standards, combined with a variety of external examinations, such as the Advanced Placement Examinations of the College Board, Regents' Examinations in some states, and, it is hoped, a growing list of other instruments that a school or an individual student could adopt or take voluntarily, would give outside authorities, like regional accrediting agencies, a good sense of the quality of work being done.

*A lot turns on those teachers. Are they good enough?*    49

They've got to be.    50

Remedies like all these are neat, but abstractions, castles in the 51 air. Seeing adolescents in classrooms reminds one that, in substantial measure, school is *their* castle, that they have to want to build it.

I arrived by car at the school at 7:15 A.M., thirty minutes before 52 the first bell. It was a cool day, and the first arrivals to the large high school I was visiting were gathered in clots in the sun outside, around the low, meandering structures that housed their classrooms. Parking lots and hard-used lawns encircled the buildings. There were no sidewalks in this neighborhood, even though it was quite built up; the school property was ringed by small houses and business establishments. Everyone came to school by bus or by private car.

I turned into one of the driveways leading toward what appeared   53
to be the school's central building and was immediately bounced out
of the seat of my rented Datsun by the first of a series of asphalt bumps
in the road. These barriers, it was painfully obvious, were there to
slow down the dozens of vehicles that used the driveway and were
already lined up in the lots next to the school, row on row of loyal
steel beasts tethered by this pedagogical water hole. I found a place
and parked.

It was immediately clear from the stares I received from nearby   54
students that I picked a student lot, not one for staff or for visitors.
Since it seemed to me large enough to accommodate one more little
car, I left the Datsun where it was. It was ridiculously out of place,
surrounded by pickup trucks, high on their springs and mud spattered,
and by jalopies, late sixties' Chevrolets, old Ford Mustangs, Plymouth
Satellites, each cumbrously settled upon great oversize rear tires. While
all appeared poised, snouts down, to roar purposefully off to God
knows where, for the moment they simply cowered here, submissive.
Their masters and mistresses leaned against them or sat on them, chatting. Many drank coffee out of paper cups. Some smoked furtively as
I drew near; though unfamiliar to them, I was wearing the drab coat-
tie-slacks uniform of the school administrator who might admonish
them.

My first instinct was to snicker at the parking lot scene. It was an   55
eighties' version of an *American Graffiti* strip, indeed an overdrawn one,
because the dusty trucks and drag-equipped cars were grotesquely
numerous. My condescension disappeared, however, when I paid
more attention to the students gathered around these vehicles, kids
observing the visitor who had taken a space on their turf. Their attitude
was in no way menacing, but it was freighted with an absence of interest. I was an object to be observed and, if they were smoking, to
be mildly reacted to. Beyond that, I might have been a bird in the vast
aviary of a boring zoo; I was a piece of the scenery, glimpsed as part
of hanging out before school. None of these kids was playing principal's pet by coming up and asking me whether I needed help or
directions to the office, but no one hassled me, either. The human
confrontation was neutral, nearly nonexistent.

These were older students, drivers. In their easy chatting among   56
themselves, in their self-absorption and nonchalance, they showed
self-assurance bordering on truculence. They had their own world.

My reaction was nervousness. I tried to smile a sorry-fellas-but-I-   57
didn't-know-where-the-visitors'-parking-lot-was message, but it did

not come off. I felt the awkward outsider, at distance from these composed young people. Even as I knew that at the bell they would enter the buildings and engage in the rituals of dutiful school-going and that they would get more boisterous and engaging as the early morning mist over their spirits parted, I also knew that these were considerable people, ones who would play the game adult educators asked them to play only when and how they wanted to. The fact that many of them, for a host of reasons, chose to go along with the structures of the school did not lessen the force of the observation: they possessed the autonomous power not to.

In this sense, kids run schools. Their apparent acquiescence to     58
what their elders want them to do is always provisional. Their ability to undermine even the illusions of certain adult authority and of an expectation of deference was admirably if benignly displayed by the students on the parking lot. A less benign challenge can be made by students in any classroom when, for whatever reason, they collectively, quietly, but assuredly decide to say no. The fact that most go along with the system masks the nascent power that students hold. Few adults outside the teaching profession understand this.

The evening before, I had met the superintendent of this school     59
district. He was a man of great force and national reputation. His administration ran the district with efficiency and closely centralized authority. In talking of his work, we had both used the ready metaphors of schoolkeeping, most turning around an image of old folk (the teachers) passing something of self-evident importance to young folk (the students). This morning all of these metaphors seemed naïve. All assumed the young student to be a passive receptacle or, at the least, a supplicant for knowledge. The adolescents in that parking lot were neither passive nor suppliant. However much we adults may want them to be eagerly receptive and respectful of our agenda for their schooling, the choice to be that or something else—neutral, hostile, inattentive—was unequivocally theirs. If we want our well-intentioned plans to succeed, we'll have to *inspire* the adolescents to join in them— inspire even the sullen, uninterested kids one sees in parking lots at the start of a school day.

The vision of school as an uncomplicated place where teachers     60
pass along the torch of knowledge to eager students is sadly innocent.

# Questions

1. Sizer's essay seems to be divided into two parts, the second part beginning with paragraph 51. What is the connection between the second part and the first? Why do you think Sizer included the second part?

2. In paragraph 5, Sizer asserts that a good high school education teaches students "to observe and analyze a situation or problem" and "to make sense of it, use it, criticize it, reject or accept it." Do you think that your high school had such goals? Did some or all of your courses seek to produce such students? If at least one course or one instructor had such goals, discuss the methods of the course or of the instructor, or both. Sizer himself gives his ideas about how these skills can be taught. Does his formula apply to your experience?

3. Sizer says in paragraph 11 that "there is no One Best Curriculum for all schools." Why can't it be argued that since all students will face the responsibility of being informed citizens, a single curriculum (for instance, so many years of American history, so many years of other history, so many years of science, or literature, and so forth) makes sense for all—for males and females, farmers and city dwellers—in short, at least for all who speak English and who are not mentally handicapped?

4. Sizer, in paragraph 12, characterizes writing as "the litmus paper of thought." What does this mean?

5. In paragraph 13 Sizer proposes merging "the traditional departments of mathematics and science, thus forcing coordination of the real and abstract worlds of certainty." Drawing on your experience of science and mathematics in high school, write an essay of 750–1000 words imagining and evaluating the results of such a merger in your high school. Or, thinking of Sizer's remark (paragraph 14) that "English, music, and art usually proceed in . . . splendid isolation," imagine and evaluate a course in which two or perhaps all three of these were combined.

6. Taking into account Sizer's remarks on history (paragraph 15), evaluate the study of history in your high school.

Robert Coles

# Student Volunteers, Academic Credit

Despite the enticements of our competitive, consumerist 1
culture, a growing number of high school, undergraduate and graduate
students are finding time to do local volunteer work. We applaud such
evidence of idealism put into daily or weekly practice in what amounts
to a national service program. As one Middle Western college dean
said, it is "exactly the kind of constructive extra-curricular activity this
school values."

I have heard many students sharply, and properly, challenge such 2
use of the phrase "extra-curricular." They object to this false distinction
between their intellectual life and their work in, say, a ghetto neighborhood. After all, isn't the mind kept busy in many important ways
when one leaves a campus to work in a neighborhood where people
live constantly in great jeopardy?

When a student crosses the ocean to study French or Spanish for 3
a year, or to assist in a social scientist's "field work," we have no
reluctance to consider such an effort intellectual and worthy of academic credit.

But when that same student spends time working with people 4
who, after all, live in a world as different in certain respects as some
of those studied by anthropologists and sociologists, they are pursuing
an "extra-curricular" activity.

Is this the right way to respond to the substantial amount of per- 5
sonal commitment involved in tutoring needy children, feeding the
homeless in soup kitchens and reaching out to vulnerable families to
provide medical or legal assistance?

When I listen to my students describe what they see and hear in 6

Robert Coles received his M.D. degree in 1954 and later became a psychiatrist.
He now teaches psychiatry at Harvard, and has written several prizewinning
books on classes and cultures in the United States. He has also written about
literature.

voluntary "extra-curricular" activities, I realize how much they are learning.

For example, listen to an undergraduate—he has tutored and 7 played basketball in a ghetto neighborhood—trying to educate his teacher:

> I never knew people live like that until I started going there. I'd read a book or two [about ghetto problems] and mostly forgotten what I read, but you don't forget the kids when you see them every week. Now I know a little of what those families are like. I know about their history, the story of their past: They'll talk with you and take you back a few generations—from the rural South to up here.

He went on: 8

> I know about the anthropology and sociology—what the people eat, and what they say and what they do with their time. I know about the psychology—what's troubling them, and what they want and what scares them to death. I know about the politics of that neighborhood, and the economics—where the power is, and how the people make their living. It's not only tutoring I'm doing, it's learning—the kids teach me, and their parents do, too.

He contrasted the vivid, enduring education he was getting out- 9 side of school with what occasionally takes place inside—when he sits in class or prepares in his room for tests. "I cram stuff in, and forget it right after the exam," he said. "I sit and take notes automatically, and lots of times I doze off." But he was not suggesting that he deserved academic credit for the acquisition of outsidé learning.

A bright, able student, successful by most standards, he craves 10 intellectual and moral challenges, and has found them in the volunteer work he has done for several years. An able writer, he found time to contribute several articles to a local paper—descriptions of the children he teaches, of the lives they live, of the points about life they have made to him.

He wishes more would come of his volunteer work. He wants to 11 study carefully and discuss books by novelists, social scientists and essayists that delineate and sort out the complexities, ironies, ambiguities, confusions and apprehensions he witnesses—and those in himself as an outsider who, trying to understand and change a particular world, achieves successes but also encounters obstacles and contends with failures.

He would like to compare his own observations, goals, hopes, 12 disappointments, discouragements, and his sense of burn-out with similar experiences described in books of the documentary tradition that have mattered over time.

Put differently, he wants to learn from what he does. He wants 13 a chance to talk and write about his volunteer work while also discussing significant books, films and collections of photographs that would give that work a broader perspective.

Surely, we who teach in universities can develop courses that will 14 respond to the challenge of student voluntarism—that connect its moral energy with the life of the mind.

# Questions

1. If you speak of one of your activities, or of an activity of another student, as "extra-curricular," what do you mean by the word? What activities do you include? Do you think that Coles would agree that these activities were properly labeled extra-curricular?

2. Do you think Coles is right (paragraphs 1–2) in suggesting that it is improper to call "extra-curricular" an activity such as a student's voluntary "work in, say, a ghetto neighborhood"?

3. In paragraph 3 Coles gives examples of two kinds of activities for which schools regularly award credit. But *why* do such activities merit credit (if they do)? What are the assumptions behind giving credit to them?

4. In paragraph 4 Coles suggests that the student who volunteers to work "with people who . . . live in a world as different in certain respects as some of those studied by anthropologists and sociologists" is engaged in an activity comparable to studying a language or doing sociological fieldwork. Do you agree? Why, or why not?

5. In paragraphs 7 and 8 Coles reports a student's summary of what he or she learned by tutoring and playing basketball in a ghetto neighborhood. The student learned, for instance, "about the anthropology and sociology . . . what they say and what they do with their time." Coles goes on, quoting the student: "I know about the psychology—what's troubling them, and what they want and what scares them to death. I know about the politics of that neighborhood, and the economics—where the power is, and how the people make their living."

   Doubtless this student learned a good deal, and it is clear that

Coles is enthusiastic about the student's "acquisition of outside learning" (paragraph 9). Do you imagine—judging from the whole essay—that Coles would be equally enthusiastic if the student had learned about the anthropology, sociology, and economics of persons who work on the Chicago Stock Exchange? On what do you base your answer? Would *you* be equally enthusiastic about the acquisition of such knowledge? Why, or why not?

6. How might one of the courses you are taking, or have taken, be altered to satisfy the challenge that Coles presents in his final paragraph?

John Holt

# The Right to Control One's Learning

Young people should have the right to control and direct  1
their own learning, that is, to decide what they want to learn, and when, where, how, how much, how fast, and with what help they want to learn it. To be still more specific, I want them to have the right to decide if, when, how much, and by whom they want to be *taught* and the right to decide whether they want to learn in a school and if so which one and for how much of the time.

No human right, except the right to life itself, is more fundamental  2
than this. A person's freedom of learning is part of his freedom of thought, even more basic than his freedom of speech. If we take from someone his right to decide what he will be curious about, we destroy his freedom of thought. We say, in effect, you must think not about what interests and concerns *you*, but about what interests and concerns *us*.

We might call this the right of curiosity, the right to ask whatever  3
questions are most important to us. As adults, we assume that we

John Holt (1923–1985) taught in schools and colleges and wrote numerous books on education.

have the right to decide what does or does not interest us, what we will look into and what we will leave alone. We take this right for granted, cannot imagine that it might be taken away from us. Indeed, as far as I know, it has never been written into any body of law. Even the writers of our Constitution did not mention it. They thought it was enough to guarantee citizens the freedom of speech and the freedom to spread their ideas as widely as they wished and could. It did not occur to them that even the most tyrannical government would try to control people's minds, what they thought and knew. That idea was to come later, under the benevolent guise of compulsory universal education.

This right of each of us to control our own learning is now in 4 danger. When we put into our laws the highly authoritarian notion that someone should and could decide what all young people were to learn and beyond that, could do whatever might seem necessary (which now includes dosing them with drugs) to compel them to learn it, we took a long step down a very steep and dangerous path. The requirement that a child go to school, for about six hours a day, 180 days a year, for about ten years, whether or not he learns anything there, whether or not he already knows it or could learn it faster or better somewhere else, is such a gross violation of civil liberties that few adults would stand for it. But the child who resists is treated as a criminal. With this requirement we created an industry, an army of people whose whole work was to tell young people what they had to learn and to try to make them learn it. Some of these people, wanting to exercise even more power over others, to be even more "helpful," or simply because the industry is not growing fast enough to hold all the people who want to get into it, are now beginning to say, "If it is good for children for us to decide what they shall learn and to make them learn it, why wouldn't it be good for everyone? If compulsory education is a good thing, how can there be too much of it? Why should we allow anyone, of any age, to decide that he has had enough of it? Why should we allow older people, any more than young, not to know what we know when their ignorance may have bad consequences for all of us? Why should we not *make* them know what they *ought* to know?"

They are beginning to talk, as one man did on a nationwide TV 5 show, about "womb-to-tomb" schooling. If hours of homework every night are good for the young, why wouldn't they be good for us all— they would keep us away from the TV set and other frivolous pursuits. Some group of experts, somewhere, would be glad to decide what we all ought to know and then every so often check up on us to make sure we knew it—with, of course, appropriate penalties if we did not.

I am very serious in saying that I think this is coming unless we prepare against it and take steps to prevent it. The right I ask for the young is a right that I want to preserve for the rest of us, the right *to decide what goes into our minds.* This is much more than the right to decide whether or when or how much to go to school or what school you want to go to. That right is important, but it is only part of a much larger and more fundamental right, which I might call the right to Learn, as opposed to being Educated, *i.e.,* made to learn what someone else thinks would be good for you. It is not just compulsory schooling but compulsory Education that I oppose and want to do away with.

That children might have the control of their own learning, including the right to decide if, when, how much, and where they wanted to go to school, frightens and angers many people. They ask me, "Are you saying that if the parents wanted the child to go to school, and the child didn't want to go, that he wouldn't have to go? Are you saying that if the parents wanted the child to go to one school, and the child wanted to go to another, that the child would have the right to decide?" Yes, that is what I say. Some people ask, "If school wasn't compulsory, wouldn't many parents take their children out of school to exploit their labor in one way or another?" Such questions are often both snobbish and hypocritical. The questioner assumes and implies (though rarely says) that these bad parents are people poorer and less schooled than he. Also, though he appears to be defending the right of children to go to school, what he really is defending is the right of the state to compel them to go whether they want to or not. What he wants, in short, is that children should be in school, not that they should have any choice about going.

But saying that children should have the right to choose to go or not to go to school does not mean that the ideas and wishes of the parents would have no weight. Unless he is estranged from his parents and rebelling against them, a child cares very much about what they think and want. Most of the time, he doesn't want to anger or worry or disappoint them. Right now, in families where the parents feel that they have some choice about their children's schooling, there is much bargaining about schools. Such parents, when their children are little, often ask them whether they want to go to nursery school or kindergarten. Or they may take them to school for a while to try it out. Or, if they have a choice of schools, they may take them to several to see which they think they will like the best. Later, they care whether the

6

7

8

child likes his school. If he does not, they try to do something about it, get him out of it, find a school he will like.

I know some parents who for years had a running bargain with their children, "If on a given day you just can't stand the thought of school, you don't feel well, you are afraid of something that may happen, you have something of your own that you very much want to do—well, you can stay home." Needless to say, the schools, with their supporting experts, fight it with all their might—Don't Give in to Your Child, Make Him Go to School, He's Got to Learn. Some parents, when their own plans make it possible for them to take an interesting trip, take their children with them. They don't ask the school's permission, they just go. If the child doesn't want to make the trip and would rather stay in school, they work out a way for him to do that. Some parents, when their child is frightened, unhappy, and suffering in school, as many children are, just take him out. Hal Bennett, in his excellent book *No More Public School*, talks about ways to do this.

A friend of mine told me that when her boy was in third grade, he had a bad teacher, bullying, contemptuous, sarcastic, cruel. Many of the class switched to another section, but this eight-year-old, being tough, defiant, and stubborn, hung on. One day—his parents did not learn this until about two years later—having had enough of the teacher's meanness, he just got up from his desk and without saying a word, walked out of the room and went home. But for all his toughness and resiliency of spirit, the experience was hard on him. He grew more timid and quarrelsome, less outgoing and confident. He lost his ordinary good humor. Even his handwriting began to go to pieces—was much worse in the spring of the school year than in the previous fall. One spring day he sat at breakfast, eating his cereal. After a while he stopped eating and sat silently thinking about the day ahead. His eyes filled up with tears, and two big ones slowly rolled down his cheeks. His mother, who ordinarily stays out of the school life of her children, saw this and knew what it was about. "Listen," she said to him, "we don't have to go on with this. If you've had enough of that teacher, if she's making school so bad for you that you don't want to go any more, I'll be perfectly happy just to pull you right out. We can manage it. Just say the word." He was horrified and indignant. "No!" he said, "I couldn't do that." "Okay," she said, "whatever you want is fine. Just let me know." And so they left it. He had decided that he was going to tough it out, and he did. But I am sure knowing that he had the support of his mother and the chance to give it up if it got too much for him gave him the strength he needed to go on.

To say that children should have the right to control and direct 11
their own learning, to go to school or not as they chose, does not mean
that the law would forbid the parents to express an opinion or wish
or strong desire on the matter. It only means that if their natural authority is not strong enough the parents can't call in the cops to make
the child do what they are not able to persuade him to do. And the
law may say that there is a limit to the amount of pressure or coercion
the parents can apply to the child to deny him a choice that he has a
legal right to make.

When I urge that children should control their learning there is 12
one argument that people bring up so often that I feel I must anticipate
and meet it here. It says that schools are a place where children can
for a while be protected against the bad influences of the world outside,
particularly from its greed, dishonesty, and commercialism. It says that
in school children may have a glimpse of a higher way of life, of people
acting from other and better motives than greed and fear. People say,
"We know that society is bad enough as it is and that children will be
exposed to it and corrupted by it soon enough. But if we let children
go out into the larger world as soon as they wanted, they would be
tempted and corrupted just that much sooner."

They seem to believe that schools are better, more honorable places 13
than the world outside—what a friend of mine at Harvard once called
"museums of virtue." Or that people in school, both children and
adults, act from higher and better motives than people outside. In this
they are mistaken. There are, of course, some good schools. But on
the whole, far from being the opposite of, or an antidote to, the world
outside, with all its envy, fear, greed, and obsessive competitiveness,
the schools are very much like it. If anything, they are worse, a terrible,
abstract, simplified caricature of it. In the world outside the school,
some work, at least, is done honestly and well, for its own sake, not
just to get ahead of others; people are not everywhere and always being
set in competition against each other; people are not (or not yet) in
every minute of their lives subject to the arbitrary, irrevocable orders
and judgment of others. But in most schools, a student is every minute
doing what others tell him, subject to their judgment, in situations in
which he can only win at the expense of other students.

This is a harsh judgment. Let me say again, as I have before, that 14
schools are worse than most of the people in them and that many of
these people do many harmful things they would rather not do, and
a great many other harmful things that they do not even see as harmful.
The whole of school is much worse than the sum of its parts. There

are very few people in the U.S. today (or perhaps anywhere, any time) in *any* occupation, who could be trusted with the kind of power that schools give most teachers over their students. Schools seem to me among the most anti-democratic, most authoritarian, most destructive, and most dangerous institutions of modern society. No other institution does more harm or more lasting harm to more people or destroys so much of their curiosity, independence, trust, dignity, and sense of identity and worth. Even quite kindly schools are inhibited and corrupted by the knowledge of children and teachers alike that they are *performing* for the judgment and approval of others—the children for the teachers; the teachers for the parents, supervisors, school board, or the state. No one is ever free from feeling that he is being judged all the time, or soon may be. Even after the best class experiences teachers must ask themselves, "Were we right to do that? Can we prove we were right? Will it get us in trouble?"

What corrupts the school, and makes it so much worse than most    15
of the people in it, or than they would like it to be, is its power—just as their powerlessness corrupts the students. The school is corrupted by the endless anxious demand of the parents to know how their child is doing—meaning is he ahead of the other kids—and their demand that he be kept ahead. Schools do not protect children from the badness of the world outside. They are at least as bad as the world outside, and the harm they do to the children in their power creates much of the badness of the world outside. The sickness of the modern world is in many ways a school-induced sickness. It is in school that most people learn to expect and accept that some expert can always place them in some sort of rank or hierarchy. It is in school that we meet, become used to, and learn to believe in the totally controlled society. We do not learn much science, but we learn to worship "scientists" and to believe that anything we might conceivably need or want can only come, and someday will come, from them. The school is the closest we have yet been able to come to Huxley's *Brave New World*, with its alphas and betas, deltas and epsilons—and now it even has its soma. Everyone, including children, should have the right to say "No!" to it.[1]

[1] Aldous Huxley's *Brave New World* (1932) depicts a totalitarian society that scientifically controls the populace. Babies are created in laboratories and are conditioned; adults are given *soma* pills to prevent depression. John Holt, following Huxley, plays on the Greek letters for A, B, D, and E, suggesting that the grading system of our schools turns into a doping system. (Editors' note)

# Questions

1. Holt's opening sentence pretty much dismisses the idea of compulsory education. What arguments can be offered on behalf of compulsory education? How can you defend the requirement that children be schooled—even if the children and their parents don't wish them to go to school?

2. In paragraph 4, Holt refers to "an industry, an army of people." To whom does he refer? What is the effect of describing them as an "industry" and an "army"?

3. Read paragraphs 12 and 13, and then write an essay of 500 words evaluating your high school in the light of Holt's comment that most schools encourage morally destructive competition.

4. If you have read Postman's essay (pages 272–279), write an essay of 500–750 words comparing and evaluating the two essays as examples of persuasive writing. Note: your topic is not "Which of the Two Essays I Subscribe to"; rather, it is an analysis and an evaluation of the essays as *persuasion.*

5. If you have read Anonymous, "Confessions of an Erstwhile Child" (pages 103–108), what ideas do you find there that are similar to Holt's? In a paragraph or two, point out the similarities, citing specific passages in each essay.

Paul Goodman

# A Proposal to Abolish Grading

Let half a dozen of the prestigious Universities—Chicago, 1
Stanford, the Ivy League—abolish grading, and use testing only and
entirely for pedagogic purposes as teachers see fit.

Anyone who knows the frantic temper of the present schools will 2
understand the transvaluation of values that would be effected by this
modest innovation. For most of the students, the competitive grade
has come to be the essence. The naïve teacher points to the beauty of
the subject and the ingenuity of the research; the shrewd student asks
if he is responsible for that on the final exam.

Let me at once dispose of an objection whose unanimity is quite 3
fascinating. I think that the great majority of professors agree that
grading hinders teaching and creates a bad spirit, going as far as cheating and plagiarizing. I have before me the collection of essays, *Examining in Harvard College,* and this is the consensus. It is uniformly
asserted, however, that the grading is inevitable; for how else will the
graduate schools, the foundations the corporations *know* whom to accept, reward, hire? How will the talent scouts know whom to tap?

By testing the applicants, of course, according to the specific task- 4
requirements of the inducting institution, just as applicants for the
Civil Service or for licenses in medicine, law, and architecture are
tested. Why should Harvard professors do the testing *for* corporations
and graduate-schools?

The objection is ludicrous. Dean Whitla, of the Harvard Office of 5
Tests, points out that the scholastic-aptitude and achievement tests
used for *admission* to Harvard are a super-excellent index for all-around

Paul Goodman (1911–1972) received his bachelor's degree from City College in
New York and his Ph.D. from the University of Chicago. He taught in several
colleges and universities, and he wrote prolifically on literature, politics, and
education. Goodman's view that students were victims of a corrupt society made
him especially popular on campuses, even in the 1960s when students tended
to distrust anyone over thirty. "A Proposal to Abolish Grading" (editors' title) is
an extract from *Compulsory Miseducation and the Community of Scholars*
(1966).

Harvard performance, better than high-school grades or particular Harvard course-grades. Presumably, these college-entrance tests are tailored for what Harvard and similar institutions want. By the same logic, would not an employer do far better to apply his own job-aptitude test rather than to rely on the vagaries of Harvard sectionmen. Indeed, I doubt that many employers bother to look at such grades; they are more likely to be interested merely in the fact of a Harvard diploma, whatever that connotes to them. The grades have most of their weight with the graduate schools—here, as elsewhere, the system runs mainly for its own sake.

It is really necessary to remind our academics of the ancient history 6 of Examination. In the medieval university, the whole point of the gruelling trial of the candidate was whether or not to accept him as a peer. His disputation and lecture for the Master's was just that, a master-piece to enter the guild. It was not to make comparative evaluations. It was not to weed out and select for an extra-mural licensor or employer. It was certainly not to pit one young fellow against another in an ugly competition. My philosophic impression is that the medievals thought they knew what a good job of work was and that we are competitive because we do not know. But the more status is achieved by largely irrelevant competitive evaluation, the less will we ever know.

(Of course, our American examinations never did have this purely 7 guild orientation, just as our faculties have rarely had absolute autonomy; the examining was to satisfy Overseers, Elders, distant Regents— and they as paternal superiors have always doted on giving grades, rather than accepting peers. But I submit that this set-up itself makes it impossible for the student to *become* a master, to *have* grown up, and to commence on his own. He will always be making A or B for some overseer. And in the present atmosphere, he will always be climbing on his friend's neck.)

Perhaps the chief objectors to abolishing grading would be the 8 students and their parents. The parents should be simply disregarded; their anxiety has done enough damage already. For the students, it seems to me that a primary duty of the university is to deprive them of their props, their dependence on extrinsic valuation and motivation, and to force them to confront the difficult enterprise itself and finally lose themselves in it.

A miserable effect of grading is to nullify the various uses of test- 9 ing. Testing, for both student and teacher, is a means of structuring, and also of finding out what is blank or wrong and what has been assimilated and can be taken for granted. Review—including high-pressure review—is a means of bringing together the fragments, so that there are flashes of synoptic insight.

There are several good reasons for testing, and kinds of test. But   10
if the aim is to discover weakness, what is the point of down-grading and punishing it, and thereby inviting the student to conceal his weakness, by faking and bulling, if not cheating? The natural conclusion of synthesis is the insight itself, not a grade for having had it. For the important purpose of placement, if one can establish in the student the belief that one is testing *not* to grade and make invidious comparisons but for his own advantage, the student should normally seek his own level, where he is challenged and yet capable, rather than trying to get by. If the student dares to accept himself as he is, a teacher's grade is a crude instrument compared with a student's self-awareness. But it is rare in our universities that students are encouraged to notice objectively their vast confusion. Unlike Socrates, our teachers rely on power-drives rather than shame and ingenuous idealism.

Many students are lazy, so teachers try to goad or threaten them   11
by grading. In the long run this must do more harm than good. Laziness is a character-defense. It may be a way of avoiding learning, in order to protect the conceit that one is already perfect (deeper, the despair that one *never* can). It may be a way of avoiding just the risk of failing and being down-graded. Sometimes it is a way of politely saying, "I won't." But since it is the authoritarian grown-up demands that have created such attitudes in the first place, why repeat the trauma? There comes a time when we must treat people as adult, laziness and all. It is one thing courageously to fire a do-nothing out of your class; it is quite another thing to evaluate him with a lordly F.

Most important of all, it is often obvious that balking in doing the   12
work, especially among bright young people who get to great universities, means exactly what it says: The work does not suit me, not this subject, or not at this time, or not in this school, or not in school altogether. The student might not be bookish; he might be school-tired; perhaps his development ought now to take another direction. Yet unfortunately, if such a student is intelligent and is not sure of himself, he *can* be bullied into passing, and this obscures everything. My hunch is that I am describing a common situation. What a grim waste of young life and teacherly effort! Such a student will retain nothing of what he has "passed" in. Sometimes he must get mononucleosis to tell his story and be believed.

And ironically, the converse is also probably commonly true. A   13 student flunks and is mechanically weeded out, who is really ready and eager to learn in a scholastic setting, but he has not quite caught on. A good teacher can recognize the situation, but the computer wreaks its will.

## Questions

1. In his opening paragraph Goodman limits his suggestion about grading and testing to "half a dozen of the prestigious Universities." Does he offer any reason for this limitation? Can you?
2. In paragraph 3 Goodman says that "the great majority of professors agree that grading hinders teaching." What evidence does he offer to support this claim? What arguments might be made that grading assists teaching? Should Goodman have made them?
3. As a student, have grades helped you to learn, or have grades hindered you? Explain.

Mary Field Belenky, Blythe McVicker Clinchy, Nancy Rule Goldberger, and Jill Mattuck Tarule

# Toward an Education for Women

We begin with the reminiscences of two ordinary women,  1 each recalling an hour during her first year at college. One of them, now middle aged, remembered the first meeting of an introductory

Mary Belenky is an assistant research professor at the University of Vermont, Blythe Clinchy is a professor of psychology at Wellesley College, Nancy Goldberger is a visiting scholar in psychology at New York University, and Jill Tarule is an associate professor at Lesley College Graduate School. The essay printed here is part of Chapter 9 of their book, *Women's Ways of Knowing*, a study of how women's intellectual abilities develop. The chapter's title, which we have borrowed, is "Toward an Education for Women."

science course. The professor marched into the lecture hall, placed upon his desk a large jar filled with dried beans, and invited the students to guess how many beans the jar contained. After listening to an enthusiastic chorus of wildly inaccurate estimates the professor smiled a thin, dry smile, revealed the correct answer, and announced, "You have just learned an important lesson about science. Never trust the evidence of your own senses."

Thirty years later, the woman could guess what the professor had 2 in mind. He saw himself, perhaps, as inviting his students to embark upon an exciting voyage into a mysterious underworld invisible to the naked eye, accessible only through scientific method and scientific instruments. But the seventeen-year-old girl could not accept or even hear the invitation. Her sense of herself as a knower was shaky, and it was based on the belief that she could use her own firsthand experience as a source of truth. This man was saying that this belief was fallacious. He was taking away her only tool for knowing and providing her with no substitute. "I remember feeling small and scared," the woman says, "and I did the only thing I could do. I dropped the course that afternoon, and I haven't gone near science since."

The second woman, in her first year at college, told a superficially 3 similar but profoundly different story about a philosophy class she had attended just a month or two before the interview. The teacher came into class carrying a large cardboard cube. She placed it on the desk in front of her and asked the class what it was. They said it was a cube. She asked what a cube was, and they said a cube contained six equal square sides. She asked how they knew that this object contained six equal square sides. By looking at it, they said. "But how do you know?" the teacher asked again. She pointed to the side facing her and, therefore, invisible to the students; then she lifted the cube and pointed to the side that had been face down on the desk, and, therefore, also invisible. "We can't look at all six sides of a cube at once, can we? So we can't exactly *see* a cube. And yet, you're right. You know it's a cube. But you know it not just because you have eyes but because you have intelligence. You invent the sides you cannot see. You use your intelligence to create the 'truth' about cubes."

The student said to the interviewer,                                    4

> It blew my mind. You'll think I'm nuts, but I ran back to the dorm and I called my boyfriend and I said, "Listen, this is just incredible," and I told him all about it. I'm not sure he could see why I was so excited. I'm not sure I understand it myself. But I really felt, for the

first time, like I was really in college, like I was—I don't know—sort of *grown up*.

Both stories are about the limitations of firsthand experience as a    5
source of knowledge—we cannot simply see the truth about either the
jar of beans or the cube—but there is a difference. We can know the
truth about cubes. Indeed, the students did know it. As the science
professor pointed out, the students were wrong about the beans; their
senses had deceived them. But, as the philosophy teacher pointed out,
the students were right about the cube; their minds had served them
well.

The science professor was the only person in the room who knew    6
how many beans were in that jar. Theoretically, the knowledge was
available to the students; they could have counted the beans. But faced
with that tedious prospect, most would doubtless take the professor's
word for it. He is authority. They had to rely upon his knowledge
rather than their own. On the other hand, every member of the philosophy class knew that the cube had six sides. They were all colleagues.

The science professor exercised his authority in a benign fashion,    7
promising the students that he would provide them with the tools they
needed to excavate invisible truths. Similarly, the philosophy teacher
planned to teach her students the skills of philosophical analysis, but
she was at pains to assure them that they already possessed the tools
to construct some powerful truths. They had built cubes on their own,
using only their own powers of inference, without the aid of elaborate
procedures or fancy apparatus or even a teacher. Although a teacher
might have told them once that a cube contained six equal square sides,
they did not have to take the teacher's word for it; they could have
easily verified it for themselves.

The lesson the science professor wanted to teach is that experience    8
is a source of error. Taught in isolation, this lesson diminished the
student, rendering her dumb and dependent. The philosophy teacher's lesson was that although raw experience is insufficient, by reflecting upon it the student could arrive at truth. It was a lesson that made
the student feel more powerful ("sort of grown up").

No doubt it is true that, as the professor in May Sarton's novel    9
*The Small Room* says, the "art" of being a student requires humility.
But the woman we interviewed did not find the science lesson hum-
bling; she found it humiliating. Arrogance was not then and is not
now her natural habitat. Like most of the women in our sample she

lacked confidence in herself as a thinker; and the kind of learning the science teacher demanded was not only painful but crippling.

In thinking about the education of women, Adrienne Rich writes,     10
"Suppose we were to ask ourselves, simply: What does a woman need to know?" A woman, like any other human being, does need to know that the mind makes mistakes; but our interviews have convinced us that every woman, regardless of age, social class, ethnicity, and academic achievement, needs to know that she is capable of intelligent thought, and she needs to know it right away. Perhaps men learn this lesson before going to college, or perhaps they can wait until they have proved themselves to hear it; we do not know. We do know that many of the women we interviewed had not yet learned it.

# Questions

1.   How is the professor in the first anecdote characterized? Look particularly at the words used in paragraphs 1 and 2 to describe him. How is the student characterized? Look back at the first sentence: Why do the writers use the word "ordinary" to describe both students? Why did they not simply say, "We begin with the reminiscences of two women"?

2.   In paragraph 5 the writers say, "Both stories are about the limitations of firsthand experience as a source of knowledge." What else do the stories have in common? What are the important differences? What particular difference is most relevant to the main point of the essay?

3.   Look again at paragraph 6. The science teacher is described as being "authority." The students "had to rely upon his knowledge rather than their own." Is this relationship between teacher and students more likely in science courses than in philosophy or literature courses? Is it inevitable in sciences courses? If so, why?

4.   What is the main point of the concluding paragraph? Do the two anecdotes support this point? To what extent does your own experience confirm it, or not confirm it?

Paul Robinson

# TV Can't Educate

On July 20 [1978] NBC aired a documentary on life in Marin    1
County, a bedroom community just across the Golden Gate Bridge
from San Francisco. The program was called "I Want It All Now" and
its single theme was the predominance of narcissism in Marin. The
program's host, Edwin Newman, introduced viewers, in his studied
casual manner, to a variety of "consciousness raising" groups en-
sconced in Marin and insinuated that this new narcissistic manner was
leading to a breakdown not only of the family (a divorce rate of 75
percent was mentioned three times) but also of traditional civic virtue.
The following day the *San Francisco Chronicle* carried a long, front-page
article on the outraged reaction of Marin's respectable citizenry to what
it considered a grossly distorted portrait of itself. Several residents
argued, persuasively, that Marin was in fact a highly political suburb—
that it had been a hot spot of the anti-Vietnam war movement, and
that only last year it had responded dramatically to the water crisis in
California, cutting back on water use much more than was required
by law. Television journalism appeared to be up to its old tricks: producers saw what they wanted to see, and they were not about to pass
up the chance to show a woman being massaged by two nude men
and chirping about how delightful it was to "receive" without having
to "give."

I was reminded, however improbably, of an experience in Berlin,    2
where I had spent the previous six months teaching. The Germans are
all exercised over a recent movie about Adolf Hitler (*Hitler: Eine Kar-
riere*), which is based on a biography by the journalist Joachim Fest.
The charge leveled against the film is that it glorifies Hitler (though it
uses nothing but documentary footage; there are no actors), and it has
been linked with a supposed resurgence of Nazism in Germany, particularly among the young. I saw only parts of the film and therefore
can't speak to the justice of the charge. What I wish to report on—
and what the Marin program brought to mind—is a lecture I attended
by a young German historian from the Free University of Berlin, in

Paul Robinson was born in San Diego in 1940. He teaches history at Stanford
University, specializing in modern European intellectual history.

which he took issue with the film because it had failed to treat Hitler's relations with the German industrialists, who were crucial in supporting the Nazi Party before it came to power and apparently benefited from its success.

The critics of the Newman program and my young scholar friend 3 in Berlin were guilty of the same error. They both bought the assumption that television and movies can be a source of knowledge, that one can "learn" from them. By knowledge and learning I obviously don't mean an assortment of facts. Rather I have in mind the analytic process that locates pieces of information within a larger context of argument and meaning. Movies and TV are structurally unsuited to that process.

There is no great mystery here. It's a simple matter of time. Learn- 4 ing requires one kind of time, visual media are bound to another. In learning one must be able to freeze the absorption of fact or proposition at any moment in order to make mental comparisons, to test the fact or proposition against known facts and propositions, to measure it against the formal rules of logic and evidence—in short, to carry on a mental debate. Television is a matter of seconds, minutes and hours, it moves inexorably forward, and thus even with the best will in the world (a utopian assumption), it can never teach. In the last analysis there is only one way to learn: by reading. That's how you'll find out about Hitler's relations with the German industrialists, if you can find out about them at all. Such a complex, many-layered phenomenon simply cannot be reduced to a scene (which would presumably meet my scholar-friend's objection) in which Hitler has dinner with Baron Krupp. Similarly, you will not find out about life in Marin County from an hour-long TV program or, for that matter, from a 24-hour-long one. What are the control populations? What statistical methods are being used? Is there more consciousness raising going on in Marin than in Cambridge? What is the correlation between narcissism and income level, educational background, employment, religious affiliation, marital status, sexual inclination and so forth? If these questions have answers, they are to be found in the books and articles of sociologists, not on TV.

I am prepared, indeed eager, to follow my argument to its logical 5 conclusion: the worst thing on TV is educational TV (and not just on educational stations). By comparison the gratuitous violence of most commercial shows is a mere peccadillo. Educational TV corrupts the very notion of education and renders its victims uneducable. I hear grown-ups launching conversations with, "Mike Wallace says that . . ." as if Mike Wallace actually knew something. Viewers hold forth authoritatively about South Africa, or DNA, or black holes, or whatever because they have watched a segment about them on "60 Minutes" or some such program. Complete ignorance really would be preferable, because ignorance at least preserves a mental space that might someday be filled with real knowledge, or some approximation of it.

There is a new form of slumming popular among intellectuals: 6 watching "bad" (i.e. commercial) TV and even writing books about it (as Dan Wakefield has about the afternoon soap opera "All My Children"). I would like to think that the motive behind this development is revulsion against the intellectual pretensions of "good" TV. But, as often happens with academics, the reaction has been dressed up in phony theoretical garb. "All My Children," we're supposed to believe, is the great American novel, heir to the tradition of Dickens and Trollope. Of course it's nothing of the sort. But it *is* very good entertainment. And that is precisely what TV is prepared to do: to entertain, to divert, above all to amuse. It is superbly amusing, ironically, for the same reason that it can't educate: it is tied to the clock, which has enormous comic potential. It is not accidental that one speaks of a comedian's "timing." Jack Benny would not be funny in print. He must wait just the right length of time after the robber threatens, "Your money or your life," before responding. (Imagine the situation in a novel: "The robber said, 'Your money or your life.' Jack took ten seconds trying to make up his mind.") Nor can you do a double-take in print, only on the screen. The brilliant manipulation of time made "The Honeymooners" so funny: Art Carney squandered it while Jackie Gleason, whose clock ran at double-time, burned. Audrey Meadows stood immobile, producing a magnificently sustained and silent obligato to Gleason's frantic buffo patter.

Television, then, is superbly fit to amuse. And amusement is not 7 to be despised. At the very least it provides an escape from the world and from ourselves. It is pleasurable (by definition, one might say), and it gives us a sense of union with humanity, if only in its foibles. Herbert Marcuse might even contend that it keeps alive the image of an unrepressed existence. Television can provide all this. But it can't educate.

Movies are faced with the same dilemma. The desire to educate 8 accounts, I believe, for the increasingly deliberate pace of movies. It is as if the director were trying to provide room within his time-bound narrative for the kind of reflection associated with analysis. This was brought home to me recently when, during the same week, I saw the movie *Julia* in the theater and *Jezebel* on TV. The latter, made in 1938, portrays the tragedy of a strong-willed southern girl who refuses to conform to the rules of antebellum New Orleans society. The most striking difference between the two movies is their pace. *Jezebel* moves along swiftly (there is probably more dialogue in the first 15 minutes than in all of *Julia*), treats its theme with appropriate superficiality and entertains effortlessly. *Julia*, on the other hand, is lugubrious and obviously beyond its depth. It succeeds only with the character of Julia herself, who, like Jezebel, is powerful, beautiful, virtuous and unburdened by intellectual or psychological complexity. By way of contrast, the narrative figure, Lilli, tries vainly to deal with issues that movies can't manage: the difficulty of writing, a relationship with an older man who is at once lover, mentor, and patient-to-be, the tension between literary success and political commitment. All of these are wonderfully captured in Lillian Hellman's memoir, but not even two fine actors like Jane Fonda and Jason Robards can bring such uncinematic matters to life on the screen. The "issue" of the memoir—despite all those meaningful silences—inevitably eluded the movie.

Let us, then, not ask more of movies and TV than they can deliver.  9 In fact, let us discourage them from trying to "educate" us.

# Questions

1. The first paragraph speaks of the "new narcissistic manner." What is narcissism? How is the etymology of the word (like "narcotic," it derives ultimately from the Greek *narkē*, "numbness") relevant to the meaning of narcissism?

2. In paragraph 4 Robinson argues that one can't learn from television because television doesn't allow the viewer time "to make mental comparisons, to test the fact or proposition against known facts and propositions, . . . in short, to carry on a mental debate." If this is true, does it follow that the lecture method of teaching is also inherently ineffective? Is Robinson defining teaching and learning (see especially paragraph 3) too narrowly?

Patricia Nelson Limerick

# The Phenomenon of Phantom Students

## Diagnosis and Treatment

On any number of occasions, students have told me that  1
I am the first and only professor they have spoken to. This was, at
first, flattering. Then curiosity began to replace vanity. How had conversation between teacher and student become, for many students, a
novelty? These students conducted themselves as if the University
were a museum: the professors on display, the students at a distance,
directing any questions to the museum's guides and guards—the graduate students.

The museum model is not University policy. No "guide for in-  2
structors" tells professors to cultivate aloofness and keep students in
their place. No "guide for undergraduates" tells them to speak to graduate students, and only approach professors on extremely solemn and
serious business.

This is not University policy, and it is by no means the experience  3
of all Harvard students. Many confidently talk to their professors; in
occasional cases, introducing a measure of shyness and humility would
not be altogether unfortunate. I have no notion what the actual statistics are, but it is my impression that the disengaged are no insig-
nificant minority. Harvard has an abundance of factors creating phantoms—my term for the radically disengaged, those staying resolutely
on the academic periphery, taking large lecture classes, writing survivalist papers and exams. Phantomhood—even in its milder versions—is a significant problem and deserves the University's attention.

What creates phantoms? They tell remarkably similar stories. In  4
the basic narrative, the freshman arrives with the familiar doubt: did

Patricia Nelson Limerick was born in Banning, California, in 1951, and educated
at the Universities of California at Santa Cruz and Yale. She has taught history
at Yale, Harvard, and the University of Colorado (her special interests are Western
history, American Indian history, and environmental history), but she is also interested in the teaching of writing and in (as this essay reveals) students. "The
Phenomenon of Phantom Students" was originally published in the *Harvard
Gazette*, a weekly publication for the university community.

Admissions make a mistake? Paradoxically, the doubt coexists with vanity; high school was easy, and Harvard won't be much worse for an individual of such certified achievement. Then, in the basic phantom story, a paper comes back with a devastating grade. Since a direct nerve connects the student's prose to his self-respect and dignity, and since the Expository Writing Program stands as the Ellis Island of Harvard, many of these initial injuries involve Expos.

## Crucial Fork

The crucial fork in the road comes here: the paper, more than likely 5 produced in good faith, is a disaster; the student has been judged by standards he doesn't understand. The split outcome really cannot be overdramatized: one route goes direct to defeat, resignation, and cynicism; the other offers a struggle, rewriting, and very probably, the learning of new skills.

Some of those new skills involve writing, but for this subject, the 6 significant skill involves conversation—direct, productive—in which the grader of the paper says precisely and clearly how the paper went wrong, and how the author can make it better. (On the instructor's side, if there is any more intellectually demanding exercise in the academic world than this, I don't know what it is.) One successful round of this kind of dialogue has, I think, an immunizing effect; on the occasion of the next disastrous paper, the precedent set makes another collapse unlikely.

For the representative phantom, though, any number of things go 7 wrong. Even if the instructor clearly explains the paper's problems, panic keeps the phantom from hearing. Conversation with instructors becomes an unhappy experience, avoided by anyone with any sense, in which papers are picked on to no particular result.

The essential groundwork completed, the phantom can become a 8 part of a community in which groups of the radically disengaged make their unfortunate academic status a matter of pride or, alternatively, the phantom can think of himself as uniquely and distinctively cut off from the University. In either case, the crucial transition is complete: from thinking, "I *may* be the fluke in Admissions," the student has moved on to certainty: "I *am* the fluke." From here on, the prospect for positive student/faculty contact meets the unpassable obstacle: the student's own fatalism.

I draw here a portrait of extreme cases—with academic under- 9 performance part of the package. There are a substantial number of individuals doing perfectly competent academic work who still would choose a visit to the dentist over a visit to a professor. Usually, no particular unhappy event explains their shyness, and one could certainly argue that their situation is not particularly unfortunate. They are doing the reading, and writing their papers, and getting solid educations. But they are missing something. Recently, my course assistant arranged for me to have lunch with a recently graduated student who had been in my class; four years of a good academic performance, and she had never spoken to a professor. She was a remarkable person, involved over a long time in volunteer work for the homeless. I think both she and Harvard would have profited had she been comfortable talking with professors.

## Student/Faculty Contact

I address myself here to the problem of student/faculty contact in the 10 case of students both with and without academic problems. Reading and writing with both ease and intensity are fundamental goals; speaking with ease and intensity should be in the package.

How are students to be persuaded to talk to professors? This en- 11 couragement should not offer false advertising. One simply cannot say that all professors are at heart accessible and friendly. Some of them are certifiably grumpy, and many of them are shy. They are still worth talking to.

With a major interest in Indian/White relations, I cannot resist 12 thinking anthropologically. White people and Indian people still confront each other through a fog of stereotypes (all Indians are noble and in touch with nature, or, alternatively, all Indians are demoralized and in touch with alcohol), and the impulse to provide a comparable analysis for student/professor relations is irresistible. Images have equal powers in both situations.

## Commonly Held Student Myths about Professors

1a. *Professors Must Be Asked Specific, Better Yet, Bibliographic Questions.* 13 Professors do not converse like ordinary people. To speak their language, you must address them in this fashion: "Professor X, I was very interested in your remarks about the unification of the Northwest Company and the Hudson's Bay Company in 1821, and I wondered if you might direct me to further reading." If you do not have a specific question like this, then you have no business troubling a professor.

1b. *Professors Only Like to Talk about Senior Theses*. This proposition 14
was brought home to me at a Quincy House gathering. A number of
students and I were speaking on a general, humane topic (sports?)
when they discovered my hidden identity. The truth out, they began
to tell me about their senior theses. The evening, I felt, became something of a busman's holiday.

2. *Professors Only Want to Talk with Other Elegant, Learned and Bril-* 15
*liant Conversationalists.* (Numbers 1 and 2 may appear to be contradictory, but they often coexist.) Living in the intellectual equivalent of
Mt. McKinley or Mt. Whitney, professors do not like to descend the
mountain to talk to the lowlanders. They are used to sophisticated,
erudite conversation, in contrast to which normal speech sounds embarrassingly flat and pedestrian. Even if they seem to tolerate the
speech of mortals, professors are inwardly thinking how stupid it
sounds. They have, in their distinguished careers, heard nearly every
insight there is. If a new idea seems to occur to a student in 1983, it
can be assumed that the professor first heard that idea sometime in
the 1950s. Having a memory built on the order of a steel trap, the
professor does not need to hear it again.

3. *If I Speak to a Professor, He Will Probably (and Maybe Rightly) Assume* 16
*That I Am a Grade-grubbing Toady.* (The students, of course, use a more
vivid term.) This belief actually concerns attitudes to other students:
dependent, hypocritical drudges hang around professors, asking insincere questions, and seeking recommendation letters; students with
integrity keep their distance and avoid the dishonor of visibly trying
to make an impression.

Countering these three assumptions does not require a debasing 17
of professional status; respect for achievement and authority, and excessive deference and fear are two different matters. Number 1 and
#2 are both extremely widespread, and #3 has, I think, the greatest
power over phantoms. In the further reaches of phantomhood, these
assumptions rest on considerable hostility toward the institution, a
basic act of self-defense in which the individual reasons (if that's the
word): "Harvard has ignored and injured me; well, Harvard is stupid
anyway." We are dealing here, in other words, with wounded dignity,
a condition not known for bringing out the finest in human behavior.

In the last eight years, I have seen many phantoms emerge from 18
hiding; I have enormous faith in their potential for recovery. Nothing
encouraged me more than the Committee on College Life meeting last
spring. I had promised to bring expert witnesses—verifiable phan-

toms. Having made the promise, I began to regret it. If these individuals barely had the courage to talk to me, how would they face a panel of five professors, two deans and five students? Would any consent to appear? The first five I called said yes—without reluctance. At the committee, they spoke with frankness and energy. To be equally frank, that amazed me—I evidently expected that I would have to act as their interpreter. They were, instead, perfectly capable of speaking for themselves.

There is a fairly reliable personal solution to the problem of phantomhood for faculty to follow:     19

1. *Discover the phantoms* (midterm grade sheets locate the ones with     20 academic problems; reports from course assistants and from professorial visits to sections identify the others).

2. *Contact them.*     21

3. *Get an acknowledgment of the condition of phantomhood, directly and*     22 *briefly.* (Don't milk it for its misery, which is often at a pretty high level.)

4. *Engage them in a specific project—ideally, rewriting a paper.* Here,     23 the instructor is most productive when she uses her own enthusiasm for the subject to launch a discussion of the ideas in the paper, so that the student slides, without perceiving it, into what was hitherto unimaginable—"an intellectual conversation with a professor."

5. *Keep a careful eye out for achievement on the part of the student, during*     24 *the conversation, and comment on it.* This is only in part "encouragement"—the primary goal is to help the individual penetrate the mysterious standards of what constitutes "insight" or a "a solid point."

6. *Hold out for concrete evidence of recovery—a successfully rewritten*     25 *paper, for instance.* These second drafts are almost without exception much better papers—primarily because the student now has what was wholly lacking before—faith in a living, actual audience.

7. *Encourage a wide application of the new principles.* The student's     26 logical next step is to say to the instructor, "I can work with you because you are different from the others." Resist this. The sports analogy is the best: you may need a coach at the start of learning a sport, but you do not need to coach at your elbow for the rest of your career in that sport. Professors, like most other individuals, like snowflakes, are all different. That, surely, is part of their charm.

Phantoms are not beyond understanding, and certainly not be-     27 yond recovery. But there is another, equally complex party to the basic transactions of student/faculty contact. We might now take up the question of the genesis of shyness, harriedness and grumpiness in professors.

How nice to lead a leisured life in a book-lined office, I used to think, chatting, reading and (if *real* work meant actually teaching classes) working only a few hours a week. Cross the line into professorhood, and the plot thickens considerably. Those few minutes a week in class rest on hours of preparation. Reading exams and papers closely eats up time. Then, of course, there is "one's own work"— research and writing for promised articles and books. Add to this, participation in professional organizations and department and University committees, and one's leisured time in the book-lined office often comes down to checking the datebook to see where one is due next. **28**

That is in part why professors can seem grumpy and aloof, even when they are genuinely committed to teaching. Phantoms, and prospective phantoms, should be advised not to take personal injury when cut short by an individual who will have to stay up most of the night revising the next day's lecture and writing recommendation letters. Schedule a meeting for a time when the universe at least gives the illusion of being a bit more in the professor's control, and try not to resent any accidental rudeness. **29**

More important, phantoms should be encouraged to use empathy in understanding the professors. Phantoms are, after all, experts in shyness; shyness, while not universal in the professorial population, is no stranger. Consider the pattern: the individual is initially drawn to the world of books and private contemplation, communicating more often through writing than through speech. How nice, the susceptible individual thinks, that there is a profession that encourages and supports this retreat to private intellectual exertion. And that promise seems to hold for the initial years of graduate school, and then, abruptly, the treachery stands exposed. One has to walk into a classroom, cause everyone else to fall silent, and become the center of attention. It is a shy person's nightmare, and individuals evolve the best mechanisms for dealing with it that they can. Once the mechanisms are in place, the individual holds on to them. It is undeniably more dignified to seem aloof and uncaring than to seem scared and shy. **30**

I write as a reformed phantom myself—one, happily, in the category in which academic problems did not play a part. My papers carried me through college and graduate school; I was a veritable sphinx in classes. Occupying—initially to my horror—the teacher's chair, phantomhood became a luxury I could not afford. **31**

A few years ago, when I had just started teaching, an old professor    32
of mine from Santa Cruz came to Yale for the year. "We're so frag-
mented at Santa Cruz," he said, "I am really looking forward to having
hard-hitting intellectual conversations again."

"Hard-hitting intellectual conversations?" I didn't seem to have    33
ever had one. It was a concept beyond the reach of an only partially
recovered phantom.

Seven or eight years later, I am thoroughly addicted to the kind    34
of conversations I thought I would never have. They provide the core
of vitality for the university, the only real cement that makes such a
collection of disparate individuals into a community. I want the phantoms included in the community.

# Questions

1. In paragraph 3 Limerick says: "This is not University policy, and it
   is by no means the experience of all Harvard students. Many confidently talk to their professors; in occasional cases, introducing a
   measure of shyness and humility would not be altogether unfortunate." Rewrite the second of these two sentences, putting the
   basic idea more directly. Next, compare your version with Limerick's. Which is better, and why? (By the way, the rhetorical device
   used in "would not be altogether unfortunate" is called *litotes.* If
   you don't know this word, look it up in a dictionary to see exactly
   what it means.)
2. Limerick mentions that after receiving an essay with a "devastating
   grade," a student finds that "conversation with instructors becomes
   an unhappy experience, avoided by anyone with any sense." If on
   some occasion your good sense deserted you and you therefore
   engaged in conversation with an instructor, was the conversation
   profitable? Why, or why not?
3. Let's assume that you find this essay interesting, and not simply
   because of the subject matter. *Why* is it interesting? What are some
   of the rhetorical devices that the author uses to engage your attention?
4. In paragraph 4 Limerick refers to the Expository Writing Program
   as "the Ellis Island of Harvard." Explain the metaphor. In the same
   paragraph she says: "A direct nerve connects the student's prose
   to his self-respect." Again, explain the metaphor and then try to
   explain why, for most of us, it rings true.
5. In paragraph 3 Limerick mentions, but does not define or explain,
   something she labels "survivalist papers and exams." In a para-

graph invent a definition for this term, using both Limerick's essay
and your own experience as sources.

6. Without naming or in any other way clearly identifying the instructor, write an essay of 500 words in which you explain why—at least
for that instructor—you are a phantom student. Or, on the other
hand, write an essay explaining why you have enjoyed conversing
with an instructor. Hint: a few bits of dialogue will probably be effective.

7. Write a dialogue of an imaginary conference between a composition teacher and a phantom. (Even though this is an exercise in
writing pure fiction, you may use one of your own essays as a prop.)

## Toni Cade Bambara

# The Lesson

$B$ack in the days when everyone was old and stupid or   1
young and foolish and me and Sugar were the only ones just right,
this lady moved on our block with nappy hair and proper speech and
no makeup. And quite naturally we laughed at her, laughed the way
we did at the junk man who went about his business like he was some
big-time president and his sorry-ass horse his secretary. And we kinda
hated her too, hated the way we did the winos who cluttered up our
parks and pissed on our handball walls and stank up our hallways and
stairs so you couldn't halfway play hide-and-seek without a goddamn
gas mask. Miss Moore was her name. The only woman on the block
with no first name. And she was black as hell, cept for her feet, which
were fish-white and spooky. And she was always planning these bor-
ing-ass things for us to do, us being my cousin, mostly, who lived on
the block cause we all moved North the same time and to the same

Toni Cade Bambara, born in New York City in 1939, received her B.A. from
Queens College in 1959 and her M.A. from City College in 1964. Both schools
are part of the City University of New York. She has studied mime and dance,
has taught at Livingston College of Rutgers University, and has worked for the
New York State Department of Welfare.

apartment then spread out gradual to breathe. And our parents would yank our heads into some kinda shape and crisp up our clothes so we'd be presentable for travel with Miss Moore, who always looked like she was going to church, though she never did. Which is just one of things the grownups talked about when they talked behind her back like a dog. But when she came calling with some sachet she'd sewed up or some gingerbread she'd made or some book, why then they'd all be too embarrassed to turn her down and we'd get handed over all spruced up. She'd been to college and said it was only right that she should take responsibility for the young ones' education, and she not even related by marriage or blood. So they'd go for it. Specially Aunt Gretchen. She was the main gofer in the family. You got some ole dumb shit foolishness you want somebody to go for, you send for Aunt Gretchen. She been screwed into the go-along for so long, it's a blood-deep natural thing with her. Which is how she got saddled with me and Sugar and Junior in the first place while our mothers were in a la-de-da apartment up the block having a good ole time.

So this one day Miss Moore rounds us all up at the mailbox and it's puredee hot and she's knockin herself out about arithmetic. And school suppose to let up in summer I heard, but she don't never let up. And the starch in my pinafore scratching the shit outta me and I'm really hating this nappy-head bitch and her goddamn college degree. I'd much rather go to the pool or to the show where it's cool. So me and Sugar leaning on the mailbox being surly, which is a Miss Moore word. And Flyboy checking out what everybody brought for lunch. And Fat Butt already wasting his peanut-butter-and-jelly sandwich like the pig he is. And Junebug punchin on Q.T.'s arm for potato chips. And Rosie Giraffe shifting from one hip to the other waiting for somebody to step on her foot or ask her if she from Georgia so she can kick ass, preferably Mercedes'. And Miss Moore asking us do we know what money is, like we a bunch of retards. I mean real money, she say, like it's only poker chips or monopoly papers we lay on the grocer. So right away I'm tired of this and say so. And would much rather snatch Sugar and go to the Sunset and terrorize the West Indian kids and take their hair ribbons and their money too. And Miss Moore files that remark away for next week's lesson on brotherhood, I can tell. And finally I say we oughta get to the subway cause it's cooler and besides we might meet some cute boys. Sugar done swiped her mama's lipstick, so we ready.

So we heading down the street and she's boring us silly about what things cost and what our parents make and how much goes for rent and how money ain't divided up right in this country. And then she gets to the part about we all poor and live in the slums, which I don't feature. And I'm ready to speak on that, but she steps out in the street and hails two cabs just like that. Then she hustles half the crew in with her and hands me a five-dollar bill and tells me to calculate 10 percent tip for the driver. And we're off. Me and Sugar and Junebug and Flyboy hanging out the window and hollering to everybody, putting lipstick on each other cause Flyboy a faggot anyway, and making farts with our sweaty armpits. But I'm mostly trying to figure how to spend this money. But they all fascinated with the meter ticking and Junebug starts laying bets as to how much it'll read when Flyboy can't hold his breath no more. Then Sugar lay bets as to how much it'll be when we get there. So I'm stuck. Don't nobody want to go for my plan, which is to jump out at the next light and run off to the first bar-b-que we can find. Then the driver tells us to get the hell out cause we there already. And the meter reads eight-five cents. And I'm stalling to figure out the tip and Sugar say give him a dime. And I decide he don't need it bad as I do, so later for him. But then he tries to take off with Junebug's foot still in the door so we talk about his mama something ferocious. Then we check out that we on Fifth Avenue and everybody dressed up in stockings. One lady in a fur coat, hot as it is. White folks crazy.

"This is the place," Miss Moore say, presenting it to us in the voice she uses at the museum. "Let's look in the windows before we go in." 4

"Can we steal?" Sugar asks very serious like she's getting the ground rules squared away before she plays. "I beg your pardon," say Miss Moore, and we fall out. So she leads us around the windows of the toy store and me and Sugar screamin, "This is mine, that's mine, I gotta have that, that was made for me, I was born for that," till Big Butt drowns us out. 5

"Hey, I'm goin to buy that there." 6

"That there? You don't even know what it is, stupid." 7

"I do so," he say punchin on Rosie Giraffe. "It's a microscope." 8

"Whatcha gonna do with a microscope, fool?" 9

"Look at things." 10

"Like what, Ronald?" ask Miss Moore. And Big Butt ain't got the first notion. So here go Miss Moore gabbing about the thousands of bacteria in a drop of water and the somethinorother in a speck of blood and the million and one living things in the air around us is invisible to the naked eye. And what she say that for? Junebug go to town on that "naked" and we rolling. Then Miss Moore ask what it cost. So 11 we all jam into the window smudgin it up and the price tag say $300. So then she ask how long'd take for Big Butt and Junebug to save up their allowances. "Too long," I say. "Yeh," adds Sugar, "outgrown it by that time." And Miss Moore say no, you never outgrow learning instruments. "Why, even medical students and interns and," blah, blah, blah. And we ready to choke Big Butt for bringing it up in the first damn place.

"This here costs four hundred eighty dollars," say Rosie Giraffe. 12 So we pile up all over her to see what she pointin out. My eyes tell me it's a chunk of glass cracked with something heavy, and different-color inks dripped into the splits, then the whole thing put into a oven or something. But for $480 it don't make sense.

"That's a paperweight made of semi-precious stones fused to- 13 gether under tremendous pressure," she explains slowly, with her hands doing the mining and all the factory work.

"So what's a paperweight?" asks Rosie Giraffe. 14

"To weigh paper with, dumbbell," say Flyboy, the wise man from 15 the East.

"Not exactly," say Miss Moore, which is what she say when you 16 warm or way off too. "It's to weigh paper down so it won't scatter and make your desk untidy." So right away me and Sugar curtsy to each other and then to Mercedes who is more the tidy type.

"We don't keep paper on top of the desk in my class," say Junebug, 17 figuring Miss Moore crazy or lyin one.

"At home, then," she say. "Don't you have a calendar and a pencil 18 case and a blotter and a letter-opener on your desk at home where you do your homework?" And she know damn well what our homes look like cause she nosys around in them every chance she gets.

"I don't even have a desk," say Junebug. "Do we?" 19

"No. And I don't get no homework neither," says Big Butt. 20

"And I don't even have a home," say Flyboy like he do at school 21 to keep the white folks off his back and sorry for him. Send this poor kid to camp posters, is his specialty.

"I do," says Mercedes. "I have a box of stationery on my desk 22 and a picture of my cat. My godmother bought the stationery and the desk. There's a big rose on each sheet and the envelopes smell like roses."

"Who wants to know about your smelly-ass stationery," say Rosie 23 Giraffe fore I can get my two cents in.

"It's important to have a work area all your own so that. . . ." 24

"Will you look at this sailboat, please," say Flyboy, cuttin her off 25 and pointin to the thing like it was his. So once again we tumble all over each other to gaze at this magnificent thing in the toy store which is just big enough to maybe sail two kittens across the pond if you strap them to the posts tight. We all start reciting the price tag like we in assembly. "Handcrafted sailboat of fiberglass at one thousand one hundred ninety-five dollars."

"Unbelievable," I hear myself say and am really stunned. I read 26 it again for myself just in case the group recitation put me in a trance. Same thing. For some reason this pisses me off. We look at Miss Moore and she lookin at us, waiting for I dunno what.

"Who'd pay all that when you can buy a sailboat set for a quarter 27 at Pop's, a tube of glue for a dime, and a ball of string for eight cents? It must have a motor and a whole lot else besides," I say. "My sailboat cost me about fifty cents."

"But will it take water?" say Mercedes with her smart ass.     28

"Took mine to Alley Pond Park once," say Flyboy. "String broke. 29 Lost it. Pity."

"Sailed mine in Central Park and it keeled over and sank. Had to 30 ask my father for another dollar."

"And you got the strap," laugh Big Butt. "The jerk didn't even 31 have a string on it. My old man wailed on his behind."

Little Q.T. was staring hard at the sailboat and you could see he 32 wanted it bad. But he too little and somebody'd just take it from him. So what the hell. "This boat for kids, Miss Moore?"

"Parents silly to buy something like that just to get all broke up," 33 say Rosie Giraffe.

"That much money it should last forever," I figure.     34

"My father'd buy it for me if I wanted it."     35

"Your father, my ass," say Rosie Giraffe getting a chance to finally 36 push Mercedes.

"Must be rich people shop here," say Q.T.     37

"You are a very bright boy," say Flyboy. "What was your first 38 clue?" And he rap him on the head with the back of his knuckles, since Q.T. the only one he could get away with. Though Q.T. liable to come up behind you years later and get his licks in when you half expect it.

"What I want to know is," I says to Miss Moore though I never 39 talk to her, I wouldn't give the bitch that satisfaction, "is how much a real boat costs? I figure a thousand'd get you a yacht any day."

"Why don't you check that out," she says, "and report back to 40 the group?" Which really pains my ass. If you gonna mess up a perfectly good swim day least you could do is have some answers. "Let's go in," she say like she got something up her sleeve. Only she don't lead the way. So me and Sugar turn the corner to where the entrance is, but when we get there I kinda hang back. Not that I'm scared, what's there to be afraid of, just a toy store. But I feel funny, shame. But what I got to be shamed about? Got as much right to go in as anybody. But somehow I can't seem to get hold of the door, so I step away for Sugar to lead. But she hangs back too. And I look at her and she looks at me and this is ridiculous. I mean, damn, I have never ever been shy about doing nothing or going nowhere. But then Mercedes steps up and then Rosie Giraffe and Big Butt crowd in behind and shove, and next thing we all stuffed into the doorway with only Mercedes squeezing past us, smoothing out her jumper and walking right down the aisle. Then the rest of us tumble in like a glued-together jigsaw done all wrong. And people lookin at us. And it's like the time me and Sugar crashed into the Catholic church on a dare. But once we got in there and everything so hushed and holy and the candles and the bowin and the handkerchiefs on all the drooping heads, I just couldn't go through with the plan. Which was for me to run up to the altar and do a tap dance while Sugar played the nose flute and messed around in the holy water. And Sugar kept givin me the elbow. Then later teased me so bad I tied her up in the shower and turned it on and locked her in. And she'd be there till this day if Aunt Gretchen hadn't finally figured I was lyin about the boarder takin a shower.

Same thing in the store. We all walkin on tiptoe and hardly touchin 41 the games and puzzles and things. And I watched Miss Moore who is steady watchin us like she waiting for a sign. Like Mama Drewery watches the sky and sniffs the air and takes note of just how much slant is in the bird formation. Then me and Sugar bump smack into each other, so busy gazing at the toys, 'specially the sailboat. But we don't laugh and go into our fat-lady bump-stomach routine. We just stare at the price tag. Then Sugar run a finger over the whole boat. And I'm jealous and want to hit her. Maybe not her, but I sure want to punch somebody in the mouth.

"Watcha bring us here for, Miss Moore?" 42

"You sound angry, Sylvia. Are you mad about something?" Givin 43 me one of them grins like she tellin a grown-up joke that never turns out to be funny. And she's lookin very closely at me like maybe she plannin to do my portrait from memory. I'm mad, but I won't give her that satisfaction. So I slouch around the store bein very bored and say, "Let's go."

Me and Sugar at the back of the train watchin the tracks whizzin    44
by large then small then gettin gobbled up in the dark. I'm thinkin
about this tricky toy I saw in the store. A clown that somersaults on
a bar then does chin-ups just cause you yank lightly at his leg. Cost
$35. I could see me askin my mother for a $35 birthday clown. "You
wanna who that costs what?" she'd say, cocking her head to the side
to get a better view of the hole in my head. Thirty-five dollars and the
whole household could go visit Grandaddy Nelson in the country.
Thirty-five dollars would pay for the rent and the piano bill too. Who
are these people that spend that much for performing clowns and $1000
for toy sailboats? What kinda work they do and how they live and
how come we ain't in on it? Where we are is who we are, Miss Moore
always pointin out. But it don't necessarily have to be that way, she
always adds then waits for somebody to say that poor people have to
wake up and demand their share of the pie and don't none of us know
what kind of pie she talkin about in the first damn place. But she ain't
so smart cause I still got her four dollars from the taxi and she sure
ain't gettin it. Messin up my day with this shit. Sugar nudges me in
my pocket and winks.

Miss Moore lines us up in front of the mailbox where we started    45
from, seem like years ago, and I got a headache for thinkin so hard.
And we lean all over each other so we can hold up under the draggy-
ass lecture she always finishes us off with at the end before we thank
her for borin us to tears. But she just looks at us like she readin
tea leaves. Finally she say, "Well, what did you think of F.A.O.
Schwartz?"

Rosie Giraffe mumbles, "White folks crazy."    46

"I'd like to go there again when I get my birthday money," says    47
Mercedes, and we shove her out the pack so she has to lean on the
mailbox by herself.

"I'd like a shower. Tiring day," say Flyboy.    48

Then Sugar surprises me by sayin, "You know, Miss Moore, I    49
don't think all of us here put together eat in a year what that sailboat
costs." And Miss Moore lights up like somebody goosed her. "And?"
she say, urging Sugar on. Only I'm standin on her foot so she don't
continue.

"Imagine for a minute what kind of society it is in which some    50
people can spend on a toy what it would cost to feed a family of six
or seven. What do you think?"

"I think," say Sugar pushing me off her feet like she never done    51
before, cause I whip her ass in a minute, "that this is not much of a

democracy if you ask me. Equal chance to pursue happiness means an equal crack at the dough, don't it?" Miss Moore is besides herself and I am disgusted with Sugar's treachery. So I stand on her foot one more time to see if she'll shove me. She shuts up, and Miss Moore looks at me, sorrowfully I'm thinkin. And somethin weird is goin on. I can feel it in my chest.

"Anybody else learn anything today?" lookin dead at me. I walk away and Sugar has to run to catch up and don't even seem to notice when I shrug her arm off my shoulder.                                    52

"Well, we got four dollars anyway," she says.                          53

"Uh hunh."                                                              54

"We could go to Hascombs and get half a chocolate layer and then to the Sunset and still have plenty money for potato chips and ice cream sodas."                                                               55

"Uh hunh."                                                              56

"Race you to Hascombs," she say.                                        57

We start down the block and she gets ahead which is O.K. by me cause I'm goin to the West End and then over to the Drive to think this day through. She can run if she want to and even run faster. But ain't nobody gonna beat me at nuthin.                                     58

# Questions

1. What is the point of Miss Moore's lesson? Why does Sylvia resist it?
2. Describe the relationship between Sugar and Sylvia. What is Sugar's function in the story?
3. What does the last line of the story suggest?

Wu-tsu Fa-yen

# Zen and the Art of Burglary

If people ask me what Zen is like, I will say that it is like  1
learning the art of burglary. The son of a burglar saw his father growing
older and thought, "If he is unable to carry on his profession, who
will be the breadwinner of the family, except myself? I must learn the
trade." He intimated the idea to his father, who approved of it.

One night the father took the son to a big house, broke through  2
the fence, entered the house, and, opening one of the large chests,
told the son to go in and pick out the clothing. As soon as the son got
into it, the father dropped the lid and securely applied the lock. The
father now came out to the courtyard and loudly knocked at the door,
waking up the whole family; then he quietly slipped away by the hole
in the fence. The residents got excited and lighted candles, but they
found that the burglar had already gone.

The son, who remained all the time securely confined in the chest,  3
thought of his cruel father. He was greatly mortified, then a fine idea
flashed upon him. He made a noise like the gnawing of a rat. The
family told the maid to take a candle and examine the chest. When
the lid was unlocked, out came the prisoner, who blew out the light,
pushed away the maid, and fled. The people ran after him. Noticing
a well by the road, he picked up a large stone and threw it into the
water. The pursuers all gathered around the well trying to find the
burglar drowning himself in the dark hole.

In the meantime he went safely back to his father's house. He  4

---

Wu-tsu Fa-yen (1025–1104) was a Chinese Zen Buddhist priest. More exactly, he
was a Ch'an priest; *Zen* is Japanese for the Chinese *Ch'an*.

The practitioner of Zen (to use the more common name) seeks *satori*, "enlightenment" or "awakening." The awakening is from a world of blind strivings
(including those of reason and of morality). The awakened being, free from a
sense of the self in opposition to all other things, perceives the unity of all things.
Wu-tsu belonged to the branch of Zen that uses "shock therapy, the purpose of
which is to jolt the student out of his analytical and conceptual way of thinking
and lead him back to his natural and spontaneous faculty" (Kenneth Ch'en,
*Buddhism in China* [1964, rptd. 1972], p. 359).

The title of this story, from *The Sayings of Goso Hōyen*, is the editors'.

---

blamed his father deeply for his narrow escape. Said the father, "Be not offended, my son. Just tell me how you got out of it." When the son told him all about his adventures, the father remarked, "There you are, you have learned the art."

# Questions

1. What assumptions about knowledge did the father make? Can you think of any of your own experiences that substantiate these assumptions?
2. Is there anything you have studied or are studying to which Zen pedagogical methods would be applicable? If so, explain by setting forth a sample lesson.

# 5
## WORK AND PLAY

*Lettuce Cutters, Salinas Valley*
**Dorothea Lange, 1935**

Farm Security Administration Photo, Library of Congress

*High School Football*
**Edward Hausner, 1967**

Courtesy NYT Pictures

# Short Views

Work and play are words used to describe the same thing under differing conditions.
**Mark Twain**

The Battle of Waterloo was won on the playing fields of Eton.
**Attributed to the Duke of Wellington**

The competitive spirit goes by many names. Most simply and directly, it is called "the work ethic." As the name implies, the work ethic holds that labor is good in itself; that a man or woman at work not only makes a contribution to his fellow man, but becomes a better person by virtue of the act of working. That work ethic is ingrained in the American character. That is why most of us consider it immoral to be lazy or slothful—even if a person is well off enough not to have to work or deliberately avoids work by going on welfare.
**Richard Milhous Nixon**

In the laws of political economy, the alienation of the worker from his product is expressed as follows: the more the worker produces, the less he has to consume; the more value he creates, the more valueless, the more unworthy he becomes; the better formed is his product, the more deformed becomes the worker; the more civilized his product, the more brutalized becomes the worker; the mightier the work, the more powerless the worker; the more ingenious the work, the duller becomes the worker and the more he becomes nature's bondsman.

Political economy conceals the alienation inherent in labor by avoiding any mention of the evil effects of work on those who work. Thus, whereas labor produces miracles for the rich, for the worker it produces destitution. Labor produces palaces, but for the worker, hovels. It produces beauty, but it cripples the worker. It replaces labor by machines, but how does it treat the worker? By throwing some workers back into a barbarous kind of work, and by turning the rest into machines. It produces intelligence, but for the worker, stupidity and cretinism.
**Karl Marx**

My young men shall never work. Men who work cannot dream, and wisdom comes in dreams.
**Smohalla, of the Nez Perce**

Everyone who is prosperous or successful must have dreamed of something. It is not because he is a good worker that he is prosperous, but because he dreamed.
**Lost Star, of the Maricopa**

The possible quantity of play depends on the possible quantity of pay.
**John Ruskin**

It can't be just a job. It's not worth playing just for money. It's a way of life. When we were kids there was the release in playing, the sweetness in being able to move and control your body. This is what play is. Beating somebody is secondary. When I was a kid, to really *move* was my delight. I felt released because I could move around anybody. I was free.
**Eric Nesterenko, Professional Hockey Player**

Winning is not the most important thing; it's everything.
**Vince Lombardi**

Serious sport has nothing to do with fair play. It is bound up with hatred, jealousy, boastfulness, disregard of all rules and sadistic pleasure in witnessing violence: in other words, it is war minus the shooting.
**George Orwell**

The maturity of man—that means, to have reacquired the seriousness that one has as a child at play.
**Friedrich Nietzsche**

The boys throw stones at the frogs in sport, but the frogs die not in sport but in earnest.
**Bion**

## Bertrand Russell

# Work

Whether work should be placed among the causes of happiness or among the causes of unhappiness may perhaps be regarded as a doubtful question. There is certainly much work which is exceedingly irksome, and an excess of work is always very painful. I think, however, that, provided work is not excessive in amount, even the dullest work is to most people less painful than idleness. There are in work all grades, from mere relief of tedium up to the profoundest delights, according to the nature of the work and the abilities of the worker. Most of the work that most people have to do is not in itself interesting, but even such work has certain great advantages. To begin with, it fills a good many hours of the day without the need of deciding what one shall do. Most people, when they are left free to fill their own time according to their own choice, are at a loss to think of anything sufficiently pleasant to be worth doing. And whatever they decide on, they are troubled by the feeling that something else would have been pleasanter. To be able to fill leisure intelligently is the last product of civilization, and at present very few people have reached this level. Moreover the exercise of choice is in itself tiresome. Except to people with unusual initiative it is positively agreeable to be told what to do at each hour of the day, provided the orders are not too unpleasant. Most of the idle rich suffer unspeakable boredom as the price of their freedom from drudgery. At times, they may find relief by hunting big game in Africa, or by flying round the world, but the

Bertrand Russell (1872–1970) was educated at Trinity College, Cambridge. He published his first book, *The Study of German Social Democracy*, in 1896; subsequent books on mathematics and on philosophy quickly established his international reputation. His pacifist opposition to World War I cost him his appointment at Trinity College, and won him a prison sentence of six months. While serving this sentence he wrote his *Introduction to Mathematical Philosophy*. In 1940 an appointment to teach at the College of the City of New York was withdrawn because of Russell's unorthodox moral views. But he was not always treated shabbily; he won numerous awards, including (in 1950) a Nobel Prize. After World War II he devoted most of his energy to warning the world about the dangers of nuclear war.

In reading the first sentence of the essay that we reprint, you should know that the essay comes from a book called *The Conquest of Happiness*.

number of such sensations is limited, especially after youth is past. Accordingly the more intelligent rich men work nearly as hard as if they were poor, while rich women for the most part keep themselves busy with innumerable trifles of whose earth-shaking importance they are firmly persuaded.

Work therefore is desirable, first and foremost, as a preventive of boredom, for the boredom that a man feels when he is doing necessary though uninteresting work is as nothing in comparison with the boredom that he feels when he has nothing to do with his days. With this advantage of work another is associated, namely that it makes holidays much more delicious when they come. Provided a man does not have to work so hard as to impair his vigor, he is likely to find far more zest in his free time than an idle man could possibly find.    2

The second advantage of most paid work and of some unpaid work is that it gives chances of success and opportunities for ambition. In most work success is measured by income, and while our capitalistic society continues, this is inevitable. It is only where the best work is concerned that this measure ceases to be the natural one to apply. The desire that men feel to increase their income is quite as much a desire for success as for the extra comforts that a higher income can procure. However dull work may be, it becomes bearable if it is a means of building up a reputation, whether in the world at large or only in one's own circle. Continuity of purpose is one of the most essential ingredients of happiness in the long run, and for most men this comes chiefly through their work. In this respect those women whose lives are occupied with housework are much less fortunate than men, or than women who work outside the home. The domesticated wife does not receive wages, has no means of bettering herself, is taken for granted by her husband (who sees practically nothing of what she does), and is valued by him not for her housework but for quite other qualities. Of course this does not apply to those women who are sufficiently well-to-do to make beautiful houses and beautiful gardens and become the envy of their neighbors; but such women are comparatively few, and for the great majority housework cannot bring as much satisfaction as work of other kinds brings to men and to professional women.    3

The satisfaction of killing time and of affording some outlet, however modest, for ambition, belongs to most work, and is sufficient to make even a man whose work is dull happier on the average than a man who has no work at all. But when work is interesting, it is capable of giving satisfaction of a far higher order than mere relief from tedium.    4

The kinds of work in which there is some interest may be arranged in a hierarchy. I shall begin with those which are only mildly interesting and end with those that are worthy to absorb the whole energies of a great man.

Two chief elements make work interesting; first, the exercise of 5 skill, and second, construction.

Every man who has acquired some unusual skill enjoys exercising 6 it until it has become a matter of course, or until he can no longer improve himself. This motive to activity begins in early childhood: a boy who can stand on his head becomes reluctant to stand on his feet. A great deal of work gives the same pleasure that is to be derived from games of skill. The work of a lawyer or a politician must contain in a more delectable form a great deal of the same pleasure that is to be derived from playing bridge. Here of course there is not only the exercise of skill but the outwitting of a skilled opponent. Even where this competitive element is absent, however, the performance of difficult feats is agreeable. A man who can do stunts in an aëroplane finds the pleasure so great that for the sake of it he is willing to risk his life. I imagine that an able surgeon, in spite of the painful circumstances in which his work is done, derives satisfaction from the exquisite precision of his operations. The same kind of pleasure, though in a less intense form, is to be derived from a great deal of work of a humbler kind. All skilled work can be pleasurable, provided the skill required is either variable or capable of indefinite improvement. If these conditions are absent, it will cease to be interesting when a man has acquired his maximum skill. A man who runs three-mile races will cease to find pleasure in this occupation when he passes the age at which he can beat his own previous record. Fortunately there is a very considerable amount of work in which new circumstances call for new skill and a man can go on improving, at any rate until he has reached middle age. In some kinds of skilled work, such as politics, for example, it seems that men are at their best between sixty and seventy, the reason being that in such occupations a wide experience of other men is essential. For this reason successful politicians are apt to be happier at the age of seventy than any other men of equal age. Their only competitors in this respect are the men who are the heads of big businesses.

There is, however, another element possessed by the best work, 7 which is even more important as a source of happiness than is the exercise of skill. This is the element of constructiveness. In some work, though by no means in most, something is built up which remains as a monument when the work is completed. We may distinguish construction from destruction by the following criterion. In construction the initial state of affairs is comparatively haphazard, while the final state of affairs embodies a purpose: in destruction the reverse is the case; the initial state of affairs embodies a purpose, while the final state of affairs is haphazard, that is to say, all that is intended by the destroyer is to produce a state of affairs which does not embody a certain purpose. This criterion applies in the most literal and obvious case, namely the construction and destruction of buildings. In constructing a building a previously made plan is carried out, whereas in destroying it no one decides exactly how the materials are to lie when the demolition is complete. Destruction is of course necessary very often as a preliminary to subsequent construction; in that case it is part of a whole which is constructive. But not infrequently a man will engage in activities of which the purpose is destructive without regard to any construction that may come after. Frequently he will conceal this from himself by the belief that he is only sweeping away in order to build afresh, but it is generally possible to unmask this pretense, when it is a pretense, by asking him what the subsequent construction is to be. On this subject it will be found that he will speak vaguely and without enthusiasm, whereas on the preliminary destruction he has spoken precisely and with zest. This applies to not a few revolutionaries and militarists and other apostles of violence. They are actuated, usually without their own knowledge, by hatred: the destruction of what they hate is their real purpose, and they are comparatively indifferent to the question what is to come after it. Now I cannot deny that in the work of destruction as in the work of construction there may be joy. It is a fiercer joy, perhaps at moments more intense, but it is less profoundly satisfying, since the result is one in which little satisfaction is to be found. You kill your enemy, and when he is dead your occupation is gone, and the satisfaction that you derive from victory quickly fades. The work of construction, on the other hand, when completed is delightful to contemplate, and moreover is never so fully completed that there is nothing further to do about it. The most satisfactory purposes are those that lead on indefinitely from one success to another without ever coming to a dead end; and in this respect it will be found that construction is a greater source of happiness than destruction. Perhaps it would be more correct to say that those who find satisfaction in construction find in it greater satisfaction than the lovers of destruction can find in destruction, for if once you have become filled with hate you will not easily derive from construction the pleasure which another man would derive from it.

At the same time few things are so likely to cure the habit of hatred 8 as the opportunity to do constructive work of an important kind.

The satisfaction to be derived from success in a great constructive 9 enterprise is one of the most massive that life has to offer, although unfortunately in its highest forms it is open only to men of exceptional ability. Nothing can rob a man of the happiness of successful achievement in an important piece of work, unless it be the proof that after all his work was bad. There are many forms of such satisfaction. The man who by a scheme of irrigation has caused the wilderness to blossom like the rose enjoys it in one of its most tangible forms. The creation of an organization may be a work of supreme importance. So is the work of those few statesmen who have devoted their lives to producing order out of chaos, of whom Lenin is the supreme type in our day. The most obvious examples are artists and men of science. Shakespeare says of his verse: "So long as men can breathe, or eyes can see, so long lives this." And it cannot be doubted that the thought consoled him for misfortune. In his sonnets he maintains that the thought of his friend reconciled him to life, but I cannot help suspecting that the sonnets he wrote to his friend were even more effective for this purpose than the friend himself. Great artists and great men of science do work which is in itself delightful; while they are doing it, it secures them the respect of those whose respect is worth having, which gives them the most fundamental kind of power, namely power over men's thoughts and feelings. They have also the most solid reasons for thinking well of themselves. This combination of fortunate circumstances ought, one would think, to be enough to make any man happy. Nevertheless it is not so. Michael Angelo, for example, was a profoundly unhappy man, and maintained (not, I am sure, with truth) that he would not have troubled to produce works of art if he had not had to pay the debts of his impecunious relations. The power to produce great art is very often, though by no means always, associated with a temperamental unhappiness, so great that but for the joy which the artist derives from his work, he would be driven to suicide. We cannot, therefore, maintain that even the greatest work must make a man happy; we can only maintain that it must make him less unhappy. Men of science, however, are far less often temperamentally unhappy than artists are, and in the main the men who do great work in science are happy men, whose happiness is derived primarily from their work.

One of the causes of unhappiness among intellectuals in the 10 present day is that so many of them, especially those whose skill is literary, find no opportunity for the independent exercise of their talents, but have to hire themselves out to rich corporations directed by Philistines, who insist upon their producing what they themselves regard as pernicious nonsense. If you were to inquire among journalists in either England or America whether they believed in the policy of the newspaper for which they worked, you would find, I believe, that only a small minority do so; the rest, for the sake of a livelihood, prostitute their skill to purposes which they believe to be harmful. Such work cannot bring any real satisfaction, and in the course of reconciling himself to the doing of it, a man has to make himself so cynical that he can no longer derive whole-hearted satisfaction from anything whatever. I cannot condemn men who undertake work of this sort, since starvation is too serious an alternative, but I think that where it is possible to do work that is satisfactory to a man's constructive impulses without entirely starving, he will be well advised from the point of view of his own happiness if he chooses it in preference to work much more highly paid but not seeming to him worth doing on its own account. Without self-respect genuine happiness is scarcely possible. And the man who is ashamed of his work can hardly achieve self-respect.

The satisfaction of constructive work, though it may, as things are, 11 be the privilege of a minority, can nevertheless be the privilege of a quite large minority. Any man who is his own master in his work can feel it; so can any man whose work appears to him useful and requires considerable skill. The production of satisfactory children is a difficult constructive work capable of affording profound satisfaction. Any woman who has achieved this can feel that as a result of her labor the world contains something of value which it would not otherwise contain.

Human beings differ profoundly in regard to the tendency to regard 12 their lives as a whole. To some men it is natural to do so, and essential to happiness to be able to do so with some satisfaction. To others life is a series of detached incidents without directed movement and without unity. I think the former sort are more likely to achieve happiness than the latter, since they will gradually build up those circumstances from which they can derive contentment and self-respect, whereas the others will be blown about by the winds of circumstances now this way, now that, without ever arriving at any haven. The habit of viewing life as a whole is an essential part both of wisdom and of true morality, and is one of the things which ought to be encouraged in education. Consistent purpose is not enough to make life happy, but it is an almost indispensable condition of a happy life. And consistent purpose embodies itself mainly in work.

## Questions

1. Russell is generally admired for his exceptionally clear prose. List some of the devices that make for clarity in this essay.
2. Russell is thought of as a left-winger. Aside from the casual reference to Lenin in paragraph 9, is there anything in "Work" to which Barry Goldwater, Ronald Reagan, or William Buckley might object? Of which statements might they especially approve?
3. Russell says (paragraph 3): "The desire that men feel to increase their income is quite as much a desire for success as for the extra comforts that a higher income can procure." In its context, what does "success" mean? In your experience, do Russell's words ring true? Why, or why not?

W. H. Auden

# Work, Labor, and Play

So far as I know, Miss Hannah Arendt was the first person    1
to define the essential difference between work and labor. To be happy, a man must feel, firstly, free and, secondly, important. He cannot be really happy if he is compelled by society to do what he does not enjoy

---

W[ystan] H[ugh] Auden (1907–1973) was born and educated in England. In 1939 he came to the United States and he became an American citizen. In 1972, however, he returned to England to live. Although Auden established his reputation chiefly with his poetry, he also wrote plays, libretti, and essays, all of high quality.

One of Auden's most unusual books is *A Certain World: A Commonplace Book*. It is an anthology of some of his favorite passages from other people's books, along with brief reflections on his reading. The passage we print here begins with a reference to Hannah Arendt's *The Human Condition*.

doing, or if what he enjoys doing is ignored by society as of no value or importance. In a society where slavery in the strict sense has been abolished, the sign that what a man does is of social value is that he is paid money to do it, but a laborer today can rightly be called a wage slave. A man is a laborer if the job society offers him is of no interest to himself but he is compelled to take it by the necessity of earning a living and supporting his family.

The antithesis to labor is play. When we play a game, we enjoy 2 what we are doing, otherwise we should not play it, but it is a purely private activity; society could not care less whether we play it or not.

Between labor and play stands work. A man is a worker if he is 3 personally interested in the job which society pays him to do; what from the point of view of society is necessary labor is from his own point of view voluntary play. Whether a job is to be classified as labor or work depends, not on the job itself, but on the tastes of the individual who undertakes it. The difference does not, for example, coincide with the difference between a manual and a mental job; a gardener or a cobbler may be a worker, a bank clerk a laborer. Which a man is can be seen from his attitude toward leisure. To a worker, leisure means simply the hours he needs to relax and rest in order to work efficiently. He is therefore more likely to take too little leisure than too much; workers die of coronaries and forget their wives' birthdays. To the laborer, on the other hand, leisure means freedom from compulsion, so that it is natural for him to imagine that the fewer hours he has to spend laboring, and the more hours he is free to play, the better.

What percentage of the population in a modern technological soci- 4 ety are, like myself, in the fortunate position of being workers? At a guess I would say sixteen per cent, and I do not think that figure is likely to get bigger in the future.

Technology and the division of labor have done two things: by 5 eliminating in many fields the need for special strength or skill; they have made a very large number of paid occupations which formerly were enjoyable work into boring labor, and by increasing productivity they have reduced the number of necessary laboring hours. It is already possible to imagine a society in which the majority of the population, that is to say, its laborers, will have almost as much leisure as in earlier times was enjoyed by the aristocracy. When one recalls how aristocracies in the past actually behaved, the prospect is not cheerful. Indeed, the problem of dealing with boredom may be even more difficult for such a future mass society than it was for aristocracies. The latter, for example, ritualized their time; there was a season to shoot grouse, a season to spend in town, etc. The masses are more likely to replace an unchanging ritual by fashion which it will be in the economic interest of certain people to change as often as possible. Again, the masses cannot go in for hunting, for very soon there would be no animals left to hunt. For other aristocratic amusements like gambling, dueling, and warfare, it may be only too easy to find equivalents in dangerous driving, drug-taking, and senseless acts of violence. Workers seldom commit acts of violence, because they can put their aggression into their work, be it physical like the work of a smith, or mental like the work of a scientist or an artist. The role of aggression in mental work is aptly expressed by the phrase "getting one's teeth into a problem."

# Question

Some readers have had trouble following Auden in his first three paragraphs, although by the end of the third paragraph the difficulties have disappeared. Can you summarize the first paragraph in a sentence? If you think that the development of the idea in these first three paragraphs could be clearer, insert the necessary phrases or sentences, or with arrows indicate the places to which sentences should be moved.

# Malcolm X

# The Shoeshine Boy

When I got home, Ella said there had been a telephone 1
call from somebody named Shorty. He had left a message that over at
the Roseland State Ballroom, the shoeshine boy was quitting that night,
and Shorty had told him to hold the job for me.

"Malcolm, you haven't had any experience shining shoes," Ella 2
said. Her expression and tone of voice told me she wasn't happy about
my taking that job. I didn't particularly care, because I was already
speechless thinking about being somewhere close to the greatest bands
in the world. I didn't even wait to eat any dinner.

The ballroom was all lighted when I got there. A man at the front 3
door was letting in members of Benny Goodman's band. I told him I
wanted to see the shoeshine boy, Freddie.

"You're going to be the new one?" he asked. I said I thought I 4
was, and he laughed, "Well, maybe you'll hit the numbers and get a
Cadillac, too." He told me that I'd find Freddie upstairs in the men's
room on the second floor.

But downstairs before I went up, I stepped over and snatched a 5
glimpse inside the ballroom. I just couldn't believe the size of that
waxed floor! At the far end, under the soft, rose-colored lights, was
the bandstand with the Benny Goodman musicians moving around,
laughing and talking, arranging their horns and stands.

A wiry, brown-skinned, conked fellow upstairs in the men's room 6

---

Malcolm X, born Malcolm Little in Nebraska in 1925, was the son of a Baptist
minister. He completed the eighth grade, but then he got into trouble and was
sent to a reformatory. After his release he became a thief, dope peddler, and
pimp. In 1944 he was sent to jail, where he spent six and a half years. During
his years in jail he became a convert to the Black Muslim faith. Paroled in 1950,
he served as a minister and founded Muslim temples throughout the United
States. In 1964, however, he broke with Elijah Muhammad, leader of the Black
Muslims and a powerful advocate of separation of whites and blacks. Malcolm
X formed a new group, the Organization of Afro-American Unity, but a year later
he was assassinated in New York. His *Autobiography*, written with Alex Haley,
was published in 1964. Haley (b. 1921) is also the author of *Roots*, a study tracing
a black family back through seven generations.

"The Shoeshine Boy" (editors' title) is from *The Autobiography of Malcolm
X*, chapter 3.

greeted me. "You Shorty's homeboy?" I said I was, and he said he was Freddie. "Good old boy," he said. "He called me, he just heard I hit the big number, and he figured right I'd be quitting." I told Freddie what the man at the front door had said about a Cadillac. He laughed and said, "Burns them white cats up when you get yourself something. Yeah, I told them I was going to get me one—just to bug them."

Freddie then said for me to pay close attention, that he was going 7 to be busy and for me to watch but not get in the way, and he'd try to get me ready to take over at the next dance, a couple of nights later.

As Freddie busied himself setting up the shoeshine stand, he told 8 me, "Get here early . . . your shoeshine rags and brushes by this footstand . . . your polish bottles, paste wax, suede brushes over here . . . everything in place, you get rushed, you never need to waste motion. . . ."

While you shined shoes, I learned, you also kept watch on cus- 9 tomers inside, leaving the urinals. You darted over and offered a small white hand towel. "A lot of cats who ain't planning to wash their hands, sometimes you can run up with a towel and shame them. Your towels are really your best hustle in here. Cost you a penny apiece to launder—you always get at least a nickel tip."

The shoeshine customers, and any from the inside rest room who 10 took a towel, you whiskbroomed a couple of licks. "A nickel or a dime tip, just give 'em that," Freddie said. "But for two bits, Uncle Tom a little—white cats especially like that. I've had them to come back two, three times a dance."

From down below, the sound of the music had begun floating up. 11 I guess I stood transfixed. "You never seen a big dance?" asked Freddie. "Run on awhile, and watch."

There were a few couples already dancing under the rose-covered 12 lights. But even more exciting to me was the crowd thronging in. The most glamorous-looking white women I'd ever seen—young ones, old ones, white cats buying tickets at the window, sticking big wads of green bills back into their pockets, checking the women's coats, and taking their arms and squiring them inside.

Freddie had some early customers when I got back upstairs. Be- 13 tween the shoeshine stand and thrusting towels to me just as they approached the wash basin, Freddie seemed to be doing four things at once. "Here, you can take over the whiskbroom," he said, "just two or three licks—but let 'em feel it."

When things slowed a little, he said, "You ain't seen nothing to- 14 night. You wait until you see a spooks' dance! Man, our own people carry *on!*" Whenever he had a moment, he kept schooling me. "Shoe-laces, this drawer here. You just starting out, I'm going to make these to you as a present. Buy them for a nickel a pair, tell cats they need laces if they do, and charge two bits."

Every Benny Goodman record I'd ever heard in my life, it seemed, 15 was filtering faintly into where we were. During another customer lull, Freddie let me slip back outside again to listen. Peggy Lee was at the mike singing. Beautiful! She had just joined the band and she was from North Dakota and had been singing with a group in Chicago when Mrs. Benny Goodman discovered her, we had heard some customers say. She finished the song and the crowd burst into applause. She was a big hit.

"It knocked me out, too, when I first broke in here," Freddie said, 16 grinning, when I went back in there. "But, look, you ever shined any shoes?" He laughed when I said I hadn't, excepting my own. "Well, let's get to work. I never had neither." Freddie got on the stand and went to work on his own shoes. Brush, liquid polish, brush, paste wax, shine rag, lacquer sole dressing . . . step by step, Freddie showed me what to do.

"But you got to get a whole lot faster. You can't waste time!" 17 Freddie showed me how fast on my own shoes. Then, because business was tapering off, he had time to give me a demonstration of how to make the shine rag pop like a firecracker. "Dig the action?" he asked. He did it in slow motion. I got down and tried it on his shoes. I had the principle of it. "Just got to do it faster," Freddie said. "It's a jive noise, that's all. Cats tip better, they figure you're knocking yourself out!"

# Questions

1.  In this selection Malcolm X is more concerned with Benny Goodman than with learning about shining shoes. Freddie is concerned with teaching Malcolm the trade. What are *we* concerned with in this selection?
2.  How would you characterize Freddie's attitude toward his job? Compare it with Maggie Holmes's attitude (pages 383–390) toward her job.
3.  In paragraph 17 Freddie demonstrates a "jive noise." Using evidence from this selection, the library, mother wit, or what you will, define "jive."
4.  On what date did Malcolm begin his apprenticeship as a shoeshine boy? How did you arrive at that date?

Studs Terkel

# Three Workers

## I. Terry Mason, Airline Stewardess

*She has been an airline stewardess for six years. She is twenty-* 1
*six-years old, recently married. "The majority of airline stewardesses are from*
*small towns. I myself am from Nebraska. It's supposed to be one of the nicest*
*professions for a woman—if she can't be a model or in the movies. All the*
*great benefits: flying around the world, meeting all those people. It is a nice*
*status symbol.*

*"I have five older sisters and they were all married before they were twenty.* 2
*The minute they got out of high school, they would end up getting married.*
*That was the thing everybody did, was get married. When I told my parents*
*I was going to the airlines, they got excited. They were so happy that one of*
*the girls could go out and see the world and spend some time being single. I*
*didn't get married until I was almost twenty-five. My mother especially*
*thought it would be great that I could have the ambition, the nerve to go to*
*the big city on my own and try to accomplish being a stewardess."*

When people ask you what you're doing and you say stewardess, 3
you're really proud, you think it's great. It's like a stepping stone. The
first two months I started flying I had already been to London, Paris,
and Rome. And me from Broken Bow, Nebraska. But after you start
working, it's not as glamorous as you thought it was going to be.

They like girls that have a nice personality and that are pleasant 4
to look at. If a woman has a problem with blemishes, they take her
off. Until the appearance counselor thinks she's ready to go back on.
One day this girl showed up, she had a very slight black eye. They
took her off. Little things like that.

We had to go to stew school for five weeks. We'd go through a 5

---

Studs Terkel was born Louis Terkel in New York City in 1912. He was brought
up in Chicago and graduated from the University of Chicago. Terkel has been
an actor, playwright, columnist, and disc jockey, but he is best known as the
man who makes books out of tape recordings of people he gets to talk. These
oral histories are *Division Street: America* (1966), *Hard Times* (1970), and *Working* (1974).

"Three Workers" (editors' title) is from the last of these books.

whole week of makeup and poise. I didn't like this. They make you feel like you've never been out in public. They showed you how to smoke a cigarette, when to smoke a cigarette, how to look at a man's eyes. Our teacher, she had this idea we had to be sexy. One day in class she was showing us how to accept a light for a cigarette from a man and never blow it out. When he lights it, just look in his eyes. It was really funny, all the girls laughed.

It's never proper for a woman to light her own cigarette. You hold 6 it up and of course you're out with a guy who knows the right way to light the cigarette. You look into their eyes as they're lighting your cigarette and you're cupping his hand, but holding it just very light, so that he can feel your touch and your warmth. (Laughs.) You do not blow the match out. It used to be really great for a woman to blow the match out when she looked in his eyes, but she said now the man blows the match out.

The idea is not to be too obvious about it. They don't want you 7 to look too forward. That's the whole thing, being a lady but still giving out that womanly appeal, like the body movement and the lips and the eyes. The guy's supposed to look in your eyes. You could be a real mean woman. You're a lady and doing all these evil things with your eyes.

She did try to promote people smoking. She said smoking can be 8 part of your conversation. If you don't know what to say, you can always pull out a cigarette. She says it makes you more comfortable. I started smoking when I was on the airlines.

Our airline picks the girl-next-door type. At one time they 9 wouldn't let us wear false eyelashes and false fingernails. Now it's required that you wear false eyelashes, and if you do not have the right length nails, you wear false nails. Everything is supposed to be becoming to the passenger.

That's the whole thing: meeting all these great men that either 10 have great business backgrounds or are good looking or different. You do meet a lot of movie stars and a lot of political people, but you don't get to really visit with them that much. You never really get to go out with these men. Stewardesses are impressed only by name people. But a normal millionaire that you don't know you're not impressed about. The only thing that really thrills a stewardess is a passenger like Kennedy or movie stars or somebody political. Celebrities.

I think our average age is twenty-six. But our supervisors tell us 11 what kind of make-up to wear, what kind of lipstick to wear, if our hair is not the right style for us, if we're not smiling enough. They even tell us how to act when you're on a pass. Like last night I met my husband. I was in plain clothes. I wanted to kiss him. But I'm not supposed to kiss anybody at the terminal. You're not supposed to walk off with a passenger, hand in hand. After you get out of the terminal, that's all yours.

The majority of passengers do make passes. The ones that do make 12 passes are married and are business people. When I tell them I'm married, they say, "I'm married and you're married and you're away from home and so am I and nobody's gonna find out." The majority of those who make passes at you, you wouldn't accept a date if they were friends of yours at home.

After I was a stewardess for a year, and I was single, I came down 13 to the near North Side of Chicago, which is the swinging place for singles. Stewardess, that was a dirty name. In a big city, it's an easy woman. I didn't like this at all. All these books—*Coffee, Tea and Me.*

I lived in an apartment complex where the majority there were 14 stewardesses.[1] The other women were secretaries and teachers. They would go to our parties and they would end up being among the worst. They never had stories about these secretaries and nurses, but they sure had good ones about stewardesses.

I meet a lot of other wives or single women. The first minute they 15 start talking to me, they're really cold. They think the majority of stewardesses are snobs or they may be jealous. These women think we have a great time, that we are playgirls, that we have the advantage to go out with every type of man we want. So when they first meet us, they really turn off on us.

When you first start flying, the majority of girls do live in apart- 16 ment complexes by the airport. The men they meet are airport employees: ramp rats, cleaning airplanes and things like that, mechanics, and young pilots, not married, ones just coming in fresh.

After a year we get tired of that, so we move into the city to get 17 involved with men that are usually young executives, like at Xerox or something. Young businessmen in the early thirties and late twenties, they really think stewardesses are the gals to go out with if they want to get so far. They wear their hats and their suits and in the winter their black gloves. The women are getting older, they're getting twenty-four, twenty-five. They get involved with bartenders too. Stewardesses and bartenders are a pair. (Laughs.)

---

[1]"In New York, stewardesses live five or six girls to one apartment. They think they can get by because they're in and out so much. But there's gonna be a few nights they're all gonna be home at once and a couple of 'em will have to sleep on the floor."

One time I went down into the area of swinging bars with two   18
other girls. We just didn't want anybody to know that we were stewardesses, so we had this story made up that we were going to a
women's college in Colorado. That went over. We had people that
were talking to us, being nice to us, being polite. Down there, they
wouldn't even be polite. They'd buy you drinks but then they'd steal
your stool if you got up to go to the restroom. But when they knew
you weren't stewardesses, just young ladies that were going to a
women's college, they were really nice to us.

They say you can spot a stewardess by the way she wears her   19
makeup. At that time we all had short hair and everybody had it cut
in stew school exactly alike. If there's two blondes they have their hair
cut very short, wearing the same shade of makeup, and they get into
uniform, people say, "Oh, you look like sisters." Wonder why?
(Laughs.)

The majority of us were against it because they wouldn't let you   20
say how *you'd* like your hair cut, they wouldn't let you have your own
personality, *your* makeup, *your* clothes. They'd tell you what length
skirts to wear. At one time they told us we couldn't wear anything
one inch above the knees. And no pants at that time. It's different
now.

Wigs used to be forbidden. Now it's the style. Now it's permissible   21
for nice women to wear wigs, eyelashes, and false fingernails. Before
it was the harder looking women that wore them. Women showing
up in pants, it wasn't ladylike. Hot pants are in now. Most airlines
change styles every year.

*She describes stewardess schools in the past as being like college dorms: it was*   22
*forbidden to go out during the week; signing in and out on Friday and Saturday*
*nights. "They've cut down stewardess school quite a bit. Cut down on how-*
*to-serve meal classes and paperwork. A lot of girls get on aircraft these days*
*and don't know where a magazine is, where the tray tables are for passen-*
*gers. . . . Every day we used to have an examination. If you missed over two*
*questions, that was a failure. They'd ask us ten questions. If you failed two*
*tests out of the whole five weeks, you would have to leave. Now they don't*
*have any exams at all. Usually we get a raise every year. We haven't been*
*getting that lately."*

We have long duty hours. We can be on duty for thirteen hours.   23
But we're not supposed to fly over eight hours. This is in a twenty-
four-hour period. During the eight hours, you could be flying from
Chicago to Flint, to Moline, short runs. You stop twenty minutes. So

you get to New York finally, after five stops, let's say. You have an hour on your own. But you have to be on the plane thirty minutes before departure time. How many restaurants can serve you food in thirty minutes? So you've gone thirteen hours, off and on duty, having half-hours and no time to eat. This is the normal thing. If we have only thirty minutes and we don't have time to eat, it's our hard luck.

Pilots have the same thing too. They end up grabbing a sandwich    24
and eating in the cockpit. When I first started flying we were not supposed to eat at all on the aircraft, even though there was an extra meal left over. Now we can eat in the buffet. We have to stand there with all those dirty dishes and eat our meals—if there's one left over. We cannot eat in the public eye. We cannot bring it out if there's an extra seat. You can smoke in the cockpit, in the restrooms, but not in the public's eye.

*"We have a union. It's a division of the pilot's union. It helps us out on*    25
*duty time and working privileges. It makes sure that if we're in Cleveland and stuck because of weather and thirteen hours have gone by, we can go to bed. Before we had a union the stew office would call and say, 'You're working another seven.' I worked one time thirty-six hours straight."*

The other day I had fifty-five minutes to serve 101 coach passen-    26
gers, a cocktail and full-meal service. You do it fast and terrible. You're very rude. You don't mean to be rude, you just don't have time to answer questions. You smile and you just ignore it. You get three drink orders in a hurry. There's been many times when you miss the glass, pouring, and you pour it in the man's lap. You just don't say I'm sorry. You give him a cloth and you keep going. That's the bad part of the job.

Sometimes I get tired of working first class. These people think    27
they're great, paying for more, and want more. Also I get tired of coach passengers asking for something that he thinks he's a first-class passenger. We get this attitude of difference from our airlines. They're just dividing the class of people. If we're on a first-class pass, the women are to wear a dress or a nice pants suit that has a matching jacket, and the men are to dress with suit jacket and tie and white shirt. And yet so many types of first-class passengers: some have grubby clothes, jeans and moccasins and everything. They can afford to dress the way they feel. . . .

If I want to fly first class, I pay the five dollars difference. I like    28
the idea of getting free drinks, free champagne, free wine. In a coach,

you don't. A coach passenger might say, "Could I have a pillow?" So you give him a pillow. Then he'll say, "Could you bring me a glass of water?" A step behind him there's the water fountain. In first class, if the guy says, "I want a glass of water," even if the water fountain is right by his arm, you'd bring it for him. We give him all this extra because he's first class. Which isn't fair. . . .

When you're in a coach, you feel like there's just heads and heads and heads of people. That's all you can see. In first class, being less people, you're more relaxed, you have more time. When you get on a 727, we have one coatroom. Our airline tells us you hang up first-class coats only. When a coach passenger says, "Could you hang up my coat?" most of the time I'll hang it up. Why should I hang up first class and not coach? 29

One girl is for first class only and there's two girls for coach. The senior girl will be first class. That first-class girl gets used to working first class. If she happens to walk through the coach, if someone asks her for something, she'll make the other girls do it. The first stew always stays at the door and welcomes everybody aboard and says good-by to everybody when they leave. That's why a lot of girls don't like to be first class. 30

There's an old story on the airline. The stewardess asks if he'd like something to drink, him and his wife. He says, "I'd like a martini." The stewardess asks the wife, "Would you like a drink?" She doesn't say anything, and the husband says, "I'm sorry, she's not used to talking to the help." (Laughs.) When I started flying, that was the first story I heard. 31

I've never had the nerve to speak up to anybody that's pinched me or said something dirty. Because I've always been afraid of these onion letters. These are bad letters. If you get a certain amount of bad letters, you're fired. When you get a bad letter you have to go in and talk to the supervisor. Other girls now, there are many of 'em that are coming around and telling them what they feel. The passenger reacts: She's telling me off! He doesn't believe it. Sometimes the passenger needs it. 32

One guy got his steak and he said, "This is too medium, I want mine rarer." The girl said, "I'm sorry, I don't cook the food, it's pre-cooked." He picked up the meal and threw it on the floor. She says, "If you don't pick the meal up right now, I'll make sure the crew members come back here and make you pick it up." (With awe) She's talking right back at him and loud, right in front of everybody. He really didn't think she would yell at him. Man, he picked up the 33 meal. . . . The younger girls don't take that guff any more, like we used to. When the passenger is giving you a bad time, you talk back to him.

It's always: the passenger is right. When a passenger says something mean, we're supposed to smile and say, "I understand." We're supposed to *really* smile because stewardesses' supervisors have been getting reports that the girls have been back-talking passengers. Even when they pinch us or say dirty things, we're supposed to smile at them. That's one thing they taught us at stew school. Like he's rubbing your body somewhere, you're supposed to just put his hand down and not say anything and smile at him. That's the main thing, smile. 34

When I first went to class, they told me I had a crooked smile. She showed me how to smile. She said, "Kinda press a little smile on"— which I did. "Oh, that's great," she said, "that's a *good* smile." But I couldn't do it. I didn't feel like I was doing it on my own. Even if we're sad, we're supposed to have a smile on our face. 35

I came in after a flight one day, my grandfather had died. Usually they call you up or meet you at the flight and say, "We have some bad news for you." I pick up this piece of paper in my mailbox and it says, "Mother called in. Your grandfather died today." It was written like, say, two cups of sugar. Was I mad! They wouldn't give me time off for the funeral. You can only have time off for your parents or somebody you have lived with. I have never lived with my grandparents. I went anyway. 36

A lot of our girls are teachers, nurses, everything. They do this part-time, 'cause you have enough time off for another kind of job. I personally work for conventions. I work electronic and auto shows. Companies hire me to stay in their booth and talk about products. I have this speech to tell. At others, all I do is pass out matches or candy. Nowadays every booth has a young girl in it. 37

People just love to drink on airplanes. They feel adventurous. So you're serving drinks and meals and there's very few times that you can sit down. If she does sit down, she's forgotten how to sit down and talk to passengers. I used to play bridge with passengers. But that doesn't happen any more. We're not supposed to be sitting down, or have a magazine or read a newspaper. If it's a flight from Boston to Los Angeles, you're supposed to have a half an hour talking to passengers. But the only time we can sit down is when we go to the cockpit. You're not supposed to spend any more than five minutes up there for a cigarette. 38

We could be sitting down on our jump seat and if you had a su- 39 pervisor on board, she would write you up—for not mixing with the crowd. We're supposed to be told when she walks on board. Many times you don't know. They do have personnel that ride the flights that don't give their names—checking, and they don't tell you about it. Sometimes a girl gets caught smoking in the cabin. Say it's a long flight, maybe a night flight. You're playing cards with a passenger and you say, "Would it bother you if I smoke?" And he says no. She would write you up and get you fired for smoking in the airplane.

They have a limit on how far you can mix. They want you to be sociable, but if he offers you a cigarette, not to take it. When you're outside, they encourage you to take cigarettes. 40

You give your time to everybody, you share it, not too much with one passenger. Everybody else may be snoring away and there's three guys, maybe military, and they're awake 'cause they're going home and excited. So you're playing cards with 'em. If you have a supervisor on, that would be a no-no. They call a lot of things no-no's. 41

They call us professional people but they talk to us as very young, childishly. They check us all the time on appearance. They check our weight every month. Even though you've been flying twenty years, they check you and say that's a no-no. If you're not spreading yourself around passengers enough, that's a no-no. Not hanging up first-class passenger's coats, that's a no-no, even though there's no room in the coatroom. You're supposed to somehow make room. If you're a pound over, they can take you off flight until you get under. 42

Accidents? I've never yet been so scared that I didn't want to get in the airplane. But there've been times at take-offs, there's been something funny. Here I am thinking, What if I die today? I've got too much to do. I can't die today. I use it as a joke. 43

I've had emergencies where I've had to evacuate the aircraft. I was coming back from Las Vegas and being a lively stewardess I stayed up all night, gambled. We had a load full of passengers. The captain tells me we're going to have an emergency landing in Chicago because we lost a pin out of the nose gear. When we land, the nose gear is gonna collapse. He wants me to prepare the whole cabin for the landing, but not for two more hours. And not to tell the other stewardesses, because they were new girls and would get all excited. So I had to keep this in me for two more hours, wondering, Am I gonna die today? And this is Easter Sunday. And I was serving the passengers drinks and food and this guy got mad at me because his omelet was too cold. And I was gonna say, "You just wait, buddy, you're not gonna worry about that omelet." But I was nice about it, because I didn't want to 44 have trouble with a passenger, especially when I have to prepare him for an emergency.

I told the passengers over the intercom: "The captain says it's just  45 a precaution, there's nothing to worry about." I'm just gonna explain how to get out of the airplane fast, how to be in a braced position. They can't wear glasses or high heels, purses, things out of aisles, under the seats. And make sure everybody's pretty quiet. We had a blind woman on with a dog. We had to get people to help her off and all this stuff.

They were fantastic. Nobody screamed, cried, or hollered. When  46 we got on the ground, everything was fine. The captain landed perfect. But there was a little jolt, and the passengers started screaming and hollering: They held it all back and all of a sudden we got on the ground, blah.

I was great. (Laughs.) That's what was funny. I thought, I have  47 a husband now. I don't know how he would take it, my dying on an airplane. So I thought, I can't die. When I got on the intercom, I was so calm. Also we're supposed to keep a smile on our face. Even during an emergency, you're supposed to walk through the cabin and make everybody feel comfortable with a smile. When you're on the jump seat everybody's looking at you. You're supposed to sit there, holding your ankles, in a position to get out of that airplane fast with a big fat smile on your face.

Doctors tell stewardesses two bad things about them. They're  48 gonna get wrinkles all over their face because they smile with their mouth and their eyes. And also with the pressurization on the airplane, we're not supposed to get up while we're climbing because it causes varicose veins in our legs. So they say being a stewardess ruins your looks.

A lot of stewardesses wanted to be models. The Tanya girl used  49 to be a stewardess on our airline. A stewardess is what they could get and a model is what they couldn't get. They weren't the type of person, they weren't that beautiful, they weren't that thin. So their second choice would be stewardess.

*What did you want to be?* I wanted to get out of Broken Bow, Nebraska.  50 (Laughs.)

POSTSCRIPT: *"Everytime I go home, they all meet me at the airplane. Not one*  51 *of my sisters has been on an airplane. All their children think that Terry is just fantastic, because their mom and dad—my sisters and their husbands—*

*feel so stupid. 'Look at us. I wish I could have done that.' I know they feel bad, that they never had the chance. But they're happy I can come home and tell them about things. I send them things from Europe. They get to tell all their friends that their sister's a stewardess. They get real excited about that. The first thing they come out and say, 'One of my sisters is a stewardess.'*

"My father got a promotion with his company and they wrote in their     52
business news that he had a family of seven, six girls and a boy, and one girl
is a stewardess in Chicago. And went on to say what I did, and didn't say a
word about anything else."[2]

## II. Roberta Victor, Hooker

*She had been a prostitute, starting at the age of fifteen. During*     53
*the first five or six years, she worked as a high-priced call girl in Manhattan.*
*Later she was a streetwalker. . . .*

You never used your own name in hustling. I used a different     54
name practically every week. If you got busted, it was more difficult
for them to find out who you really were. The role one plays when
hustling had nothing to do with who you are. It's only fitting and
proper you take another name.

There were certain names that were in great demand. Every second     55
hustler had the name Kim or Tracy or Stacy and a couple others that
were in vogue. These were all young women from seventeen to twenty-
five, and we picked these very non-ethnic-oriented WASP names, rich
names.

A hustler is any woman in American society. I was the kind of     56
hustler who received money for favors granted rather than the type
of hustler who signs a lifetime contract for her trick. Or the kind of
hustler who carefully reads women's magazines and learns what it is
proper to give for each date, depending on how much money her date
or trick spends on her.

The favors I granted were not always sexual. When I was a call     57
girl, men were not paying for sex. They were paying for something
else. They were either paying to act out a fantasy or they were paying
for companionship or they were paying to be seen with a well-dressed
young woman. Or they were paying for somebody to listen to them.
They were paying for a *lot* of things. Some men were paying for sex
that *they* felt was deviant. They were paying so that nobody would

[2]Questions on this selection appear on pages 390–391.

accuse them of being perverted or dirty or nasty. A large proportion of these guys asked things that were not at all deviant. Many of them wanted oral sex. They felt they couldn't ask their wives or girl friends because they'd be repulsed. Many of them wanted somebody to talk dirty to them. Every good call girl in New York used to share her book and we all knew the same tricks.

We know a guy who used to lie in a coffin in the middle of his  58 bedroom and he would see the girl only once. He got his kicks when the door would be open, the lights would be out, and there would be candles in the living room, and all you could see was his coffin on wheels. As you walked into the living room, he'd suddenly sit up. Of course, you screamed. He got his kicks when you screamed. Or the guy who set a table like the Last Supper and sat in a robe and sandals and wanted you to play Mary Magdalene. (Laughs.)

I was about fifteen, going on sixteen. I was sitting in a coffee shop  59 in the Village, and a friend of mine came by. She said: "I've got a cab waiting. Hurry up. You can make fifty dollars in twenty minutes." Looking back, I wonder why I was so willing to run out of the coffee shop, get in a cab, and turn a trick. It wasn't traumatic because my training had been in how to be a hustler anyway.

I learned it from the society around me, just as a woman. We're  60 taught how to hustle, how to attract, hold a man, and give sexual favors in return. The language that you hear all the time, "Don't sell yourself cheap." "Hold out for the highest bidder." "Is it proper to kiss a man good night on the first date?" The implication is it may not be proper on the first date, but if he takes you out to dinner on the second date, it's proper. If he brings you a bottle of perfume on the third date, you should let him touch you above the waist. And go on from here. It's a market place transaction.

Somehow I managed to absorb that when I was quite young. So  61 it wasn't even a moment of truth when this woman came into the coffee shop and said; "Come on." I was back in twenty-five minutes and I felt no guilt.

*She was a virgin until she was fourteen. A jazz musician, with whom she had*  62 *fallen in love, avoided her. "So I went out to have sex with somebody to present him with an accomplished fact. I found it nonpleasurable. I did a lot of sleeping around before I ever took money."*

*A precocious child, she was already attending a high school of demanding*  63 *academic standards. "I was very lonely. I didn't experience myself as being attractive. I had always felt I was too big, too fat, too awkward, didn't look like a Pepsi-Cola ad, was not anywhere near the American Dream. Guys were* *mostly scared of me. I was athletic, I was bright, and I didn't know how to* *keep my mouth shut. I didn't know how to play the games right.*

"*I understood very clearly they were not attracted to me for what I was,* 64 *but as a sexual object. I was attractive. The year before I started hustling there* *were a lot of guys that wanted to go to bed with me. They didn't want to get* *involved emotionally, but they did want to ball. For a while I was willing to* *accept that. It was feeling intimacy, feeling close, feeling warm.*

"*The time spent in bed wasn't unpleasant. It just wasn't terribly pleasant.* 65 *It was a way of feeling somebody cared about me, at least for a moment. And* *it mattered that I was there, that I was important. I discovered that in bed it* *was possible. It was one skill that I had and I was proud of my reputation as* *an amateur.*

"*I viewed all girls as being threats. That's what we were all taught. You* 66 *can't be friends with another woman, she might take your man. If you tell her* *anything about how you really feel, she'll use it against you. You smile at* *other girls and you spend time with them when there's nothing better to do,* *but you'd leave any girl sitting anywhere if you had an opportunity to go* *somewhere with a man. Because the most important thing in life is the way* *men feel about you.*"

How could you forget your first trick? (Laughs.) We took a cab to 67 midtown Manhattan, we went to a penthouse. The guy up there was quite well known. What he really wanted to do was watch two women make love, and then he wanted to have sex with me. It was barely sex. He was almost finished by the time we started. He barely touched me and we were finished.

Of course, we faked it, the woman and me. The ethic was: You 68 don't participate in a sexual act with another woman if a trick is watching. You always fake it. You're putting something over on him and he's paying for something he didn't really get. That's the only way you can keep any sense of self-respect.

The call girl ethic is very strong. You were the lowest of the low 69 if you allowed yourself to feel anything with a trick. The bed puts you on their level. The way you maintain your integrity is by acting all the way through. It's not too far removed from what most American women do—which is to put on a big smile and act.

It was a tremendous kick. Here I was doing absolutely nothing, 70 *feeling* nothing, and in twenty minutes I was going to walk out with fifty dollars in my pocket. That just made me feel absolutely marvelous. I came downtown. I can't believe this! I'm not changed, I'm the same as I was twenty minutes ago, except that now I have fifty dollars in my pocket. It really was tremendous status. How many people could make fifty dollars for twenty minutes' work? Folks work for eighty dollars take-home pay. I worked twenty minutes for fifty dollars clear, no taxes, nothing! I was still in school, I was smoking grass, I was shooting heroin, I wasn't hooked yet, and I had money. It was terrific.

After that, I made it my business to let my friend know that I was available for more of these situations. (Laughs.) She had good connections. Very shortly I linked up with a couple of others who had a good call book. 71

Books of phone numbers are passed around from call girl to call girl. They're numbers of folks who are quite respectable and with whom there is little risk. They're not liable to pull a knife on you, they're not going to cheat you out of money. Businessmen and society figures. There's three or four groups. The wealthy executive, who makes periodic trips into the city and is known to several girls. There's the social figure, whose name appears quite regularly in the society pages and who's a regular once-a-week John. Or there's the quiet, independently wealthy type. Nobody knows how they got their money. I know one of them made his money off munitions in World War II. Then there's the entertainer. There's another crowd that runs around the night spots, the 21 Club. . . . 72

These were the people whose names you saw in the paper almost every day. But I knew what they were really like. Any John who was obnoxious or aggressive was just crossed out of your book. You passed the word around that this person was not somebody other people should call. 73

We used to share numbers—standard procedure. The book I had I got from a guy who got it from a very good call girl. We kept a copy of that book in a safe deposit box. The standard procedure was that somebody new gave half of what they got the first time for each number. You'd tell them: "Call so-and-so, that's a fifty-dollar trick." They would give you twenty-five dollars. Then the number was theirs. My first book, I paid half of each trick to the person who gave it to me. After that, it was my book. 74

The book had the name and phone number coded, the price, what the person wants, and the contact name. For four years I didn't turn a trick for less than fifty dollars. They were all fifty to one hundred dollars and up for twenty minutes, an hour. The understanding is: it doesn't get conducted as a business transaction. The myth is that it's a social occasion. 75

You're expected to be well dressed, well made up, appear glad 76 to see the man. I would get a book from somebody and I would call and say, "I'm a friend of so-and-so's, and she thought it would be nice if we got together." The next move was his. Invariably he'd say, "Why don't we do that? Tonight or tomorrow night. Why don't you come over for a drink?" I would get very carefully dressed and made up. . . .

There's a given way of dressing in that league—that's to dress 77 well but not ostentatiously. You have to pass doormen, cabdrivers. You have to look as if you belong in those buildings on Park Avenue or Central Park West. You're expected not to look cheap, not to look hard. Youth is the premium. I was quite young, but I looked older, so I had to work very hard at looking my age. Most men want girls who are eighteen. They really want girls who are younger, but they're afraid of trouble.

Preparations are very elaborate. It has to do with beauty parlors 78 and shopping for clothes and taking long baths and spending money on preserving the kind of front that gives you a respectable address and telephone and being seen at the right clubs and drinking at the right bars. And being able to read the newspapers faithfully, so that not only can you talk about current events, you can talk about the society columns as well.

It's a social ritual. Being able to talk about what is happening and 79 learn from this great master, and be properly respectful and know the names that he mentions. They always drop names of their friends, their contacts, and their clients. You should recognize these. Playing a role. . . .

At the beginning I was very excited. But in order to continue I had 80 to turn myself off. I had to disassociate who I was from what I was doing.

It's a process of numbing yourself. I couldn't associate with people 81 who were not in the life—either the drug life or the hustling life. I found I couldn't turn myself back on when I finished working. When I turned myself off, I was numb—emotionally, sexually numb.

At first I felt like I was putting one over on all the other poor slobs 82 that would go to work at eight-thirty in the morning and come home at five. I was coming home at four in the morning and I could sleep all day. I really thought a lot of people would change places with me because of the romantic image: being able to spend two hours out, riding cabs, and coming home with a hundred dollars. I could spend my mornings doing my nails, going to the beauty parlor, taking long baths, going shopping. . . .

It was usually two tricks a night. That was easily a hundred, a 83 hundred and a quarter. I always had money in my pocket. I didn't know what the inside of a subway smelled like. Nobody traveled any other way except by cab. I ate in all the best restaurants and I drank in all the best clubs. A lot of people wanted you to go out to dinner with them. All you had to do was be an ornament.

Almost all the call girls I knew were involved in drugs. The fast   84 life, the night hours. At after-hours clubs, if you're not a big drinker, you usually find somebody who has cocaine, 'cause that's the big drug in those places. You wake up at noon, there's not very much to do till nine or ten that night. Everybody else is at work, so you shoot heroin. After a while the work became a means of supplying drugs, rather than drugs being something we took when we were bored.

The work becomes boring because you're not part of the life.   85 You're the part that's always hidden. The doormen smirk when you come in, 'cause they know what's going on. The cabdriver, when you give him a certain address—he knows exactly where you're going when you're riding up Park Avenue at ten o'clock at night, for Christ sake. You leave there and go back—to what? Really, to what? To an emptiness. You've got all this money in your pocket and nobody you care about.

When I was a call girl I looked down on streetwalkers. I couldn't   86 understand why anybody would put themselves in that position. It seemed to me to be hard work and very dangerous. What I was doing was basically riskless. You never had to worry about disease. These were folks who you know took care of themselves and saw the doctor regularly. Their apartments were always immaculate and the liquor was always good. They were always polite. You didn't have to ask them for money first. It was always implicit: when you were ready to leave, there would be an envelope under the lamp or there'd be something in your pocketbook. It never had to be discussed.

I had to work an awful lot harder for the same money when I was   87 a streetwalker. I remember having knives pulled on me, broken bottles held over my head, being raped, having my money stolen back from me, having to jump out of a second-story window, having a gun pointed at me.

As a call girl, I had lunch at the same places society women had   88 lunch. There was no way of telling me apart from anybody else in the upper tax bracket. I made my own hours, no more than three or so hours of work an evening. I didn't have to accept calls. All I had to do was play a role.

As a streetwalker, I didn't have to act. I let myself show the con-   89 tempt I felt for the tricks. They weren't paying enough to make it worth performing for them. As a call girl, I pretended I enjoyed it sexually. You have to act as if you had an orgasm. As a streetwalker, I didn't. I used to lie there with my hands behind my head and do mathematics equations in my head or memorize the keyboard typewriter.

It was strictly a transaction. No conversation, no acting, no myth 90 around it, no romanticism. It was purely a business transaction. You always asked for your money in front. If you could get away without undressing totally, you did that.

It's not too different than the distinction between an executive 91 secretary and somebody in the typing pool. As an executive secretary you really identify with your boss. When you're part of the typing pool, you're a body, you're hired labor, a set of hands on the type-writer. You have nothing to do with whoever is passing the work down to you. You do it as quickly as you can.

*What led you to the streets?* 92

My drug habit. It got a lot larger. I started looking bad. All my money 93 was going for drugs. I didn't have any money to spend on keeping myself up and going to beauty parlors and having a decent address and telephone.

If you can't keep yourself up, you can't call on your old tricks. 94 You drop out of circulation. As a call girl, you have to maintain a whole image. The trick wants to know he can call you at a certain number and you have to have a stable address. You must look presentable, not like death on a soda cracker.

I looked terrible. When I hit the streets, I tried to stick to at least 95 twenty dollars and folks would laugh. I needed a hundred dollars a night to maintain a drug habit and keep a room somewhere. It meant turning seven or eight tricks a night. I was out on the street from nine o'clock at night till four in the morning. I was taking subways and eating in hamburger stands.

For the first time I ran the risk of being busted. I was never arrested 96 as a call girl. Every once in a while a cop would get hold of somebody's book. They would call one of the girls and say, "I'm a friend of so-and-so's." They would try to trap them. I never took calls from people I didn't know. But on the streets, how do you know who you're gonna pick up?

As a call girl, some of my tricks were upper echelon cops, not 97 patrolmen. Priests, financiers, garment industry folks, bigtimers. On the street, they ranged from *junior* executive types, blue-collar workers, upwardly striving postal workers, college kids, suburban white collars who were in the city for the big night, restaurant workers. . . .

You walk a certain area, usually five or six blocks. It has a couple    98
of restaurants, a couple of bars. There's the step in-between: hanging out in a given bar, where people come to you. I did that briefly.

You'd walk very slowly, you'd stop and look in the window. Some-    99
body would come up to you. There was a ritual here too. The law says in order to arrest a woman for prostitution, she has to mention money and she has to tell you what she'll do for the money. We would keep within the letter of the law, even though the cops never did.

Somebody would come up and say, "It's a nice night, isn't it?"    100
"Yes." They'd say, "Are you busy?" I'd say, "Not particularly." "Would you like to come with me and have a drink?" You start walking and they say, "I have fifteen dollars or twelve dollars and I'm very lonely." Something to preserve the myth. Then they want you to spell out exactly what you're willing to do for the money.

I never approached anybody on the street. That was the ultimate    101
risk. Even if he weren't a cop, he could be some kind of supersquare, who would call a cop. I was trapped by cops several times.

The first one didn't even trap me as a trick. It was three in the    102
morning. I was in Chinatown. I ran into a trick I knew. We made contact in a restaurant. He went home and I followed him a few minutes later. I knew the address. I remember passing a banana truck. It didn't dawn on me that it was strange for somebody to be selling bananas at three in the morning. I spent about twenty minutes with my friend. He paid me. I put the money in my shoe. I opened the door and got thrown back against the wall. The banana salesman was a vice squad cop. He'd stood on the garbage can to peer in the window. I got three years for that one.

I was under age. I was four months short of twenty-one. They sent    103
me to what was then called Girls' Term Court. They wouldn't allow me a lawyer because I wasn't an adult, so it wasn't really a criminal charge. The judge said I was rehabilitable. Instead of giving me thirty days, he gave me three years in the reformatory. It was very friendly of him. I was out on parole a couple of times before I'd get caught and sent back.

I once really got trapped. It was about midnight and a guy came    104
down the street. He said he was a postal worker who just got off the shift. He told me how much money he had and what he wanted. I took him to my room. The cop isn't supposed to undress. If you can

describe the color of his shorts, it's an invalid arrest. Not only did he show me the color of his shorts, he went to bed with me. Then he pulled a badge and a gun and busted me.

He lied to me. He told me he was a narc and didn't want to bust    105
me for hustling. If I would tell him who was dealing in the neighborhood, he'd cut me loose. I lied to him, but he won. He got me to walk out of the building past all my friends and when we got to the car, he threw me in. (Laughs.) It was great fun. I did time for that—close to four years.

*What's the status of the streetwalker in prison?*    106

It's fine. Everybody there has been hustling. It's status in reverse.    107
Anybody who comes in saying things like they could never hustle is looked down on as being somewhat crazy.

*She speaks of a profound love she had for a woman who she's met in prison;*    108
*of her nursing her lover after the woman had become blind.*
   *"I was out of the country for a couple of years. I worked a house in Mexico.*    109
*It had heavy velour curtains—a Mexican version of a French whorehouse.*
*There was a reception area, where the men would come and we'd parade in*
*front of them.*
   *"The Mexicans wanted American girls. The Americans wanted Mexican*    110
*girls. So I didn't get any American tricks. I had to give a certain amount to*
*the house for each trick I turned and anything I negotiated over that amount*
*was mine. It was far less than anything I had taken in the States.*
   *"I was in great demand even though I wasn't a blonde. A girl friend of*    111
*mine worked there two nights. She was Norwegian and very blonde. Every*
*trick who came in wanted her. Her head couldn't handle it all. She quit after*
*two nights. So I was the only American.*
   *"That was really hard work. The Mexicans would play* macho. *American*    112
*tricks will come as quickly as they can. Mexicans will hold back and make me*
*work for my money. I swear to God they were doing multiplication tables in*
*their heads to keep from having an orgasm. I would use every trick I knew to*
*get them to finish. It was crazy!*
   *"I was teaching school at the same time. I used* Alice in Wonderland    113
*as the text in my English class. During the day I tutored English for fifth-*
*and sixth-grade kids. In the evening, I worked in the call house.*
   *"The junk down there was quite cheap and quite good. My habit was quite*    114
*large. I loved dope more than anything else around. After a while I couldn't*

*differentiate between working and not working. All men were tricks, all re-
lationships were acting. I was completely turned off."*

*She quit shooting dope the moment she was slugged, brutally beaten by* 115
*a dealer who wanted her. This was her revelatory experience. "It was the final
indignity. I'd had tricks pulling broken bottles on me, I'd been in razor fights,
but nobody had ever* hit *me." It was a threat to her status. "I was strong. I
could handle myself. A tough broad. This was threatened, so . . ."*

I can't talk for women who were involved with pimps. That was 116
where I always drew the line. I always thought pimps were lower than
pregnant cockroaches. I didn't want anything to do with them. I was
involved from time to time with some men. They were either selling
dope or stealing, but they were not depending on my income. Nor
were they telling me to get my ass out on the street. I never supported
a man.

As a call girl I got satisfaction, an unbelievable joy—perhaps per- 117
verted—in knowing what these reputable folks were really like. Being
able to open a newspaper every morning, read about this pillar of
society, and know what a pig he really was. The tremendous kick in
knowing that I didn't feel anything, that I was acting and they weren't.
It's sick, but no sicker than what every woman is taught, all right?

I was in *control* with every one of those relationships. You're vul- 118
nerable if you allow yourself to be involved sexually. I wasn't. They
were. I called it. Being able to manipulate somebody sexually, I could
determine when I wanted that particular transaction to end. 'Cause I
could make the guy come. I could play all kinds of games. See? It was
a tremendous sense of power.

What I did was no different from what ninety-nine percent of 119
American women are taught to do. I took the money from under the
lamp instead of in Arpege. What would I do with 150 bottles of Arpege
a week?

You become your job. I became what I did. I became a hustler. I 120
became cold, I became hard, I became turned off, I became numb.
Even when I wasn't hustling, I was a hustler. I don't think it's terribly
different from somebody who works on the assembly line forty hours
a week and comes home cut off, numb, dehumanized. People aren't
built to switch on and off like water faucets.

What was really horrifying about jail is that it really isn't horrifying. 121
You adjust very easily. The same thing with hustling. It became my
life. It was too much of an effort to try to make contact with another
human being, to force myself to care, to feel.

I didn't care about me. It didn't matter whether I got up or didn't    122
get up. I got high as soon as I awoke. The first thing I'd reach for,
with my eyes half-closed, was my dope. I didn't like my work. It was
messy. That was the biggest feeling about it. Here's all these guys
slobbering over you all night long. I'm lying there, doing math or
conjugations or Spanish poetry in my head. (Laughs.) And they're
slobbering. God! God! What enabled me to do it was being high—
high and numb.

The overt hustling society is the microcosm of the rest of the soci-    123
ety. The power relationships are the same and the games are the same.
Only this one I was in control of. The greater one I wasn't. In the
outside society, if I tried to be me, I wasn't in control of anything. As
a bright, assertive woman, I had no power. As a cold, manipulative
hustler, I had a lot. I knew I was playing a role. Most women are
taught to become what they act. All I did was act out the reality of
American womanhood.[3]

## III. Maggie Holmes, Domestic

What bugs me now, since I'm on welfare, is people saying    124
they give you the money for nothin'. When I think back what we had
to come through, up from the South, comin' here. The hard work we
had to do. It really gets me, when I hear people . . . It do somethin'
to me. I think violence.

I think what we had to work for. I used to work for $1.50 a week.    125
This is five days a week, sometimes six. If you live in the servant
quarter, your time is never off, because if they decide to have a party
at night, you gotta come out. My grandmother, I remember when she
used to work, we'd get milk and a pound of butter. I mean this was
pay. I'm thinkin' about what my poor parents worked for, gettin' nothing. What do the white think about when they think? Do they ever
think about what *they* would do?

*She had worked as a domestic, hotel chambermaid, and as "kitchen help in*    126
*cafés" for the past twenty-five years, up North and down South. She lives*
*with her four children.*

When it come to housework, I can't do it now. I can't stand it,    127
cause it do somethin' to my mind. They want you to clean the house,

[3]Questions on this selection appear on page 390.

want you to wash, even the windows, want you to iron. You not
supposed to wash no dishes. You ain't supposed to make no beds up.
Lots of 'em try to sneak it in on you, think you don't know that. So
the doorbell rings and I didn't answer to. The bell's ringin' and I'm
still doin' my work. She ask me why I don't answer the bell, I say;
"Do I come here to be a butler?" And I don't see myself to be no
doormaid. I came to do some work, and I'm gonna do my work. When
you end up, you's nursemaid, you's cook. They puts all this on you.
If you want a job to cleanin', you ask for just cleanin'. She wants you
to do in one day what she hasn't did all year.

Now this bug me: the first thing she gonna do is pull out this damn    128
rubber thing—just fittin' for your knees. Knee pads—like you're workin' in the fields, like people pickin' cotton. No mop or nothin'. That's
why you find so many black women here got rheumatism in their legs,
knees. When you get on that cold floor, I don't care how warm the
house is, you can feel the cold on the floor, the water and stuff. I never
see nobody on their knees until I come North. In the South, they had
mops. Most times, if they had real heavy work, they always had a
man to come in. Washin' windows, that's a man's job. They don't
think nothin' about askin' you to do that here. They don't have no
feeling that that's what bothers you. I think to myself; My God, if I
had somebody come and do my floors, clean up for me, I'd appreciate
it. They don't say nothin' about it. Act like you haven't even done
anything. They has no feelin's.

I worked for one old hen on Lake Shore Drive. You remember that    129
big snow they had there?[4] Remember when you couldn't get there?
When I gets to work she says: "Call the office." She complained to
the lady where I got the job, said I was late to work. So I called. So I
said, in the phone (Shouts), *What do you want with me? I got home*
four black, beautiful kids. Before I go to anybody's job in the morning
I see that my kids are at school. I gonna see that they have warm clothes
on and they fed." I'm lookin' right at the woman I'm workin' for.
(Laughs.) When I get through the phone I tell this employer: "That
goes for you too. The only thing I live for is my kids. There's nothin',
you and nobody else." The expression on her face: What is this?
(Laughs.) She thought I was gonna be like (mimics "Aunt Jemima"):

[4]It was the week of Chicago's Big Snow-In, beginning January 25, 1967. Traffic was
hopelessly snarled. Scores of thousands couldn't get to work.

"Yes ma'am, I'll try to get here a little early." But it wasn't like that. (Laughs.)

When I come in the door that day she told me pull my shoes off. 130 I said, "For what? I can wipe my feet at the door here, but I'm not gettin' out of my shoes, it's cold." She look at me like she said: Oh my God, what I got here? (Laughs.) I'm knowin' I ain't gonna make no eight hours here. I can't take it.

She had everything in there snow white. And that means work, 131 believe me. In the dining room she had a blue set, she had sky-blue chairs. They had a bedroom with pink and blue. I look and say, "I know what this means." It means sho' 'nough—knees. I said, "I'm gonna try and make it today, *if* I can make it." Usually when they're so bad, you have to leave.

I ask her where the mop is. She say she don't have no mop. I said, 132 "Don't tell me you mop the floor on your knees. I know you don't." They usually hid these mops in the clothes closet. I go out behind all these clothes and get the mop out. (Laughs.) They don't get on their knees, but they don't think nothin' about askin' a black woman. She says, "All you—you girls. . . ." She stop. I say, "All you *niggers,* is that what you want to say?" She give me this stupid look. I say, "I'm glad you tellin' me that there's more like me." (Laughs.) I told her, "You better give me my money and let me go, 'cause I'm gettin' angry. So I made her give me my carfare and what I had worked that day.

Most when you find decent work is when you find one that work 133 themselves. They know what it's like to get up in the morning and go to work. In the suburbs they ain't got nothin' to do. They has nothin' else to think about. Their mind's just about blowed.

It's just like they're talkin' about mental health. Poor people's men- 134 tal health is different than the rich white. Mine could come from a job or not havin' enough money for my kids. Mine is from me being poor. That don't mean you're sick. His sickness is from money, graftin' where he want more. I don't have *any.* You live like that day to day, penny to penny.

I worked for a woman, her husband's a judge. I cleaned the whole 135 house. When it was time for me to go home, she decided she wants some ironing. She goes in the basement, she turn on the air condi- tioner. She said, "I think you can go down in the basement and finish your day out. It's air conditioned." I said, "I don't care what you got down there, I'm not ironing. You look at that slip, it says cleanin'. Don't say no ironin'. She wanted me to wash the walls in the bathroom.

I said, "If you look at that telephone book they got all kinds of ads there under house cleanin'." She said the same thing as the other one, "All you girls—" I said same thing I said to the other one; "You mean niggers." (Laughs.)

*They ever call you by your last name?*     136

Oh God, they wouldn't do that. (Laughs.)     137

*Do you call her by her last name?*     138

Most time I don't call her, period. I don't say anything to her. I don't     139
talk nasty to nobody, but when I go to work I don't talk to people.
Most time they don't like what you're gonna say. So I keeps quiet.

*Most of her jobs were "way out in the suburbs. You get a bus and you ride     140
till you get a subway. After you gets to Howard,[5] you gets the El. If you get
to the end of the line and there's no bus, they pick you up. I don't like to work
in the city, 'cause they don't pay you nothin'. And these old buildings are so
nasty. It takes so much time to clean 'em. They are not kept up so good, like
suburbs. Most of the new homes out there, it's easier to clean."*

*A commonly observed phenomenon: during the early evening hour, trains,     141
crowded, predominantly by young white men carrying attaché cases, pass
trains headed in the opposite direction, crowded, predominantly by middle-
aged black women carrying brown paper bags. Neither group, it appears,
glances at the other.*

"We spend most of the time ridin'. You get caught goin' out from the     142
suburbs at nighttime, man, you're really sittin' there for hours. There's nothin'
movin'. You got a certain hour to meet trains. You get a transfer, you have
to get that train. It's a shuffle to get in and out of the job. If you miss that
train at five o'clock, what time you gonna get out that end? Sometime you
don't get home till eight o'clock. . . ."

You don't feel like washin' your own window when you come     143
from out there, scrubbin'. If you work in one of them houses eight
hours, you gotta come home do the same thing over . . . you don't
feel like . . . (sighs softly) . . . tired. You gotta come home, take care

[5]The boundary line separating Chicago from the North Shore suburb, Evanston.

of your kids, you gotta cook, you gotta wash. Most of the time, you gotta wash for the kids for somethin' to wear to school. You gotta clean up, 'cause you didn't have time in the morning. You gotta wash and iron and whatever you do, nights. You be so tired, until you don't feel like even doin' nothin'.

You get up at six, you fix breakfast for the kids, you get them ready  144
to go on to school. Leave home about eight. Most of the time I make biscuits for my kids, cornbread you gotta make. I don't mean the canned kind. This I don't call cookin', when you go in that refrigerator and get some beans and drop 'em in a pot. And TV dinners, they go stick 'em in the stove and she say she cooked. This is not cookin'.

And *she's* tired. Tired from doin' what? You got a washing dryer,  145
you got an electric sweeper, anything at fingertips. All she gotta do is unfroze 'em, dump 'em in the pot, and she's tired! I go to the store, I get my vegetables, greens, I wash 'em. I gotta pick 'em first. I don't eat none of that stuff, like in the cans. She don't do that, and she says she's tired.

When you work for them, when you get in that house in the morn-  146
ing, boy, they got one arm in their coat and a scarf on their head. And when you open that door, she shoots by you, she's gone. Know what I mean? They want you to come there and keep the kids and let them get out. What she think about how am I gonna do? Like I gets tired of my kids too. I'd like to go out too. It bugs you to think that they don't have no feelin's about that.

Most of the time I work for them and they be out. I don't like to  147
work for 'em when they be in the house so much. They don't have no work to do. All they do is get on the telephone and talk about one another. Make you sick. I'll go and close the door. They're all the same, everybody's house is the same. You think they rehearse it . . .

When I work, only thing I be worryin' about is my kids. I just  148
don't like to leave 'em too long. When they get out of school, you wonder if they out on the street. The only thing I worry is if they had a place to play in easy. I always call two, three times. When she don't like you to call, I'm in a hurry to get out of there. (Laughs.) My mind is gettin' home, what are you gonna find to cook before the stores close.

This Nixon was sayin' he don't see nothin' wrong with people  149
doin' scrubbin'. For generations that's all we done. He should know we wants to be doctors and teachers and lawyers like him. I don't want my kids to come up and do domestic work. It's degrading. You can't

see no tomorrow there. We done this for generation and generation—cooks and butlers all your life. They want their kids to be lawyers, doctors, and things. You don't want 'em in no cafés workin'. . . .

When they say about the neighborhood we live in is dirty, why do they ask me to come and clean their house? We, the people in the slums, the same nasty women they have come to their house in the suburbs every day. If these women are so filthy, why you want them to clean for you? They don't go and clean for us. We go and clean for them. 150

I worked one day where this white person did some housework. I'm lookin' at the difference how she with me and her. She had a guilt feeling towards that lady. They feel they shouldn't ask them to do this type of work, but they don't mind askin' me. 151

They want you to get in a uniform. You take me and my mother, she work in what she wear. She tells you, "If that place so dirty where I can't wear my dress, I won't do the job." You can't go to work dressed like they do, 'cause they think you're not working—like you should get dirty, at least. They don't say what kind of uniform, just say uniform. This is in case anybody come in, the black be workin'. They don't want you walkin' around dressed up, lookin' like them. They asks you sometimes, "Don't you have somethin' else to put on?" I say, "No, 'cause I'm not gettin' on my knees." 152

They move with caution now, believe me. They want to know, "What should I call you?" I say, "Don't call me a Negro, I'm black." So they say, "Okay, I don't want to make you angry with me." (Laughs.) The old-timers, a lot of 'em was real religious. "Lord'll make a way." I say, "I'm makin' my own way." I'm not anti-Bible or anti-God, but I just let 'em know I don't think thataway. 153

The younger women, they don't pay you too much attention. Most of 'em work. The older women, they behind you, wiping. I don't like nobody checkin' behind me. When you go to work, they want to show you how to clean. That really gets me, somebody showin' me how to clean. I been doin' it all my life. They come and get the rag and show you how to do it. (Laughs.) I stand there, look at 'em. Lotta times I ask her, "You finished?" I say, "If there's anything you gotta go and do, I wish you'd go." I don't need nobody to show me how to clean. 154

I had them put money down and pretend they can't find it and have me look for it. I worked for one, she had dropped ten dollars on the floor, and I was sweepin' and I'm glad I seen it, because if I had put that sweeper on it, she coulda said I got it. I had to push the couch 155 back and the ten dollars was there. Oh, I had 'em, when you go to dust, they put something . . . to test you.

I worked at a hotel. A hotel's the same thing. You makin' beds, scrubbin' toilets, and things. You gotta put in linens and towels. You still cleanin'. When people come in the room—that's what bugs me—they give you that look: You just a maid. It do somethin' to me. It really gets into me.                                                          156

Some of the guests are nice. The only thing you try to do is to hurry up and get this bed made and get outa here, 'cause they'll get you to do somethin' else. If they take that room, they want everything they paid for. (Laughs.) They get so many towels, they can't use 'em all. But you gotta put up all those towels. They want that pillow, they want that blanket. You gotta be trottin' back and forth and gettin' all those things.                                                          157

In the meantime, when they have the hotel full, we put in extra beds—the little foldin' things. They say they didn't order the bed. They stand and look at you like you crazy. Now you gotta take this bed back all the way from the twelfth floor to the second. The guy at the desk, he got the wrong room. He don't say, "I made a mistake." You take the blame.                                                          158

And you get some guys . . . you can't work with afightin' 'em. He'll call down and say he wants some towels. When you knock, he says, "Come in." He's standing there without a stitch of clothes on, buck naked. You're not goin' in there. You only throw those towels and go back. Most of the time you wait till he got out of there.                                                          159

When somethin's missin', it's always the maid took it. If we find one of those type people, we tell the house lady, "You have to go in there and clean it yourself." If I crack that door, and nobody's in, I wouldn't go in there. If a girl had been in there, they would call and tell you, "Did you see something?" They won't say you got it. It's the same thing. You say no. They say, "It *musta* been in there."                                                          160

Last summer I worked at a place and she missed a purse. I didn't work on that floor that day. She called the office, "Did you see that lady's purse?" I said, "No, I haven't been in the room." He asked me again, Did I . . .? I had to stay till twelve o'clock. She found it. It was under some papers. I quit, 'cause they end up sayin' you stole somethin'.                                                          161

You know what I wanted to do all my life? I wanted to play piano. And I'd want to write songs and things, that's what I really wanted to do. If I could just get myself enough to buy a piano. . . . And I'd                                                          162 like to write about my life, if I could sit long enough: How I growed up in the South and my grandparents and my father—I'd like to do that. I would like to dig up more of black history, too. I would love to for my kids.

Lotta times I'm tellin' 'em about things, they'll be sayin', "Mom, that's olden days." (Laughs.) They don't understand, because it's so far from what happening now. Mighty few young black women are doin' domestic work. And I'm glad. That's why I want my kids to go to school. This one lady told me, "All you people are gettin' like that." I said, "I'm glad." There's no more gettin' on their knees.    163

# Questions

*Terry Mason, Airline Stewardess*
1. How satisfied is Terry Mason with her job? What are the sources of her satisfactions? Her dissatisfactions? Try to sketch her values, and to characterize her.
2. Using Mason's remarks as evidence, evaluate the training program for stewardesses (now called flight attendants). Is it intelligent? Is it immoral? Do you think that after stew school the airlines deal fairly with the stewardesses?
3. Has this selection changed your idea of the job of a stewardess? If so, in what ways?

*Roberta Victor, Hooker*
1. In paragraph 55 Victor lists some desirable ("very non-ethnic-oriented WASP") names: Kim, Tracy, Stacy. Why are such names considered desirable?
2. In the first paragraph of her interview Victor says: "The role one plays when hustling had nothing to do with who you are." Judging from the interview as a whole, is she deceiving herself? In paragraph 56 she says that all women in America are hustlers, and she returns to this notion, especially in the final paragraph. Again, is she deceiving herself, or has she put her finger on a truth, or at least a partial truth? Terkel tells us (paragraph 63) that she was a bright child. During the interview does Victor say anything that strikes you as especially perceptive? Does her language occasionally show unusual vitality? Are there touches of wit?

*Maggie Holmes, Domestic*
1. How do you account for the difference in treatment (paragraph 128) of domestic help in the North and the South?

2. What evidence is there that Holmes is witty? resourceful? insightful?

3. How would you describe Holmes's attitude toward suburban house-wives? Does it make sense?

Virginia Woolf

# Professions for Women

When your secretary invited me to come here, she told    1
me that your Society is concerned with the employment of women and she suggested that I might tell you something about my own profes-sional experiences. It is true I am a woman; it is true I am employed, but what professional experiences have I had? It is difficult to say. My profession is literature; and in that profession there are fewer expe-riences for women than in any other, with the exception of the stage—fewer, I mean, that are peculiar to women. For the road was cut many years ago—by Fanny Burney, by Aphra Behn, by Harriet Martineau, by Jane Austen, by George Eliot—many famous women, and many more unknown and forgotten, have been before me, making the path smooth, and regulating my steps. Thus, when I came to write, there were very few material obstacles in my way. Writing was a reputable and harmless occupation. The family peace was not broken by the scratching of a pen. No demand was made upon the family purse. For ten and sixpence one can buy paper enough to write all the plays of Shakespeare—if one has a mind that way. Pianos and models, Paris, Vienna and Berlin, masters and mistresses, are not needed by a writer. The cheapness of writing paper is, of course, the reason why women

Virginia Woolf (1882–1941) was born in London into an upper-middle-class lit-erary family. In 1912 she married a writer, and with him she founded the Hogarth Press, whose important publications included not only books by T. S. Eliot but her own novels.

This essay was originally a talk delivered in 1931 to The Women's Service League.

have succeeded as writers before they have succeeded in the other professions.

But to tell you my story—it is a simple one. You have only got to   2
figure to yourselves a girl in a bedroom with a pen in her hand. She had only to move that pen from left to right—from ten o'clock to one. Then it occurred to her to do what is simple and cheap enough after all—to slip a few of those pages into an envelope, fix a penny stamp in the corner, and drop the envelope in the red box at the corner. It was thus that I became a journalist; and my effort was rewarded on the first day of the following month—a very glorious day it was for me—by a letter from an editor containing a check for one pound ten shillings and sixpence. But to show you how little I deserve to be called a professional woman, how little I know of the struggles and difficulties of such lives, I have to admit that instead of spending that sum upon bread and butter, rent, shoes and stockings, or butcher's bills, I went out and bought a cat—a beautiful cat, a Persian cat, which very soon involved me in bitter disputes with my neighbors.

What could be easier than to write articles and to buy Persian cats   3
with the profits? But wait a moment. Articles have to be about something. Mine, I seem to remember, was about a novel by a famous man. And while I was writing this review, I discovered that if I were going to review books I should need to do battle with a certain phantom. And the phantom was a woman, and when I came to know her better I called her after the heroine of a famous poem, The Angel in the House. It was she who used to come between me and my paper when I was writing reviews. It was she who bothered me and wasted my time and so tormented me that at last I killed her. You who come of a younger and happier generation may not have heard of her—you may not know what I mean by the Angel in the House. I will describe her as shortly as I can. She was intensely sympathetic. She was immensely charming. She was utterly unselfish. She excelled in the difficult arts of family life. She sacrificed herself daily. If there was chicken, she took the leg; if there was a draught she sat in it—in short she was so constituted that she never had a mind or a wish of her own, but preferred to sympathize always with the minds and wishes of others. Above all—I need not say it—she was pure. Her purity was supposed to be her chief beauty—her blushes, her great grace. In those days—the last of Queen Victoria—every house had its Angel. And when I came to write I encountered her with the very first words. The shadow of her wings fell on my page; I heard the rustling of her skirts

in the room. Directly, that is to say, I took my pen in hand to review that novel by a famous man, she slipped behind me and whispered: "My dear, you are a young woman. You are writing about a book that has been written by a man. Be sympathetic; be tender; flatter; deceive; use all the arts and wiles of our sex. Never let anybody guess that you have a mind of your own. Above all, be pure." And she made as if to guide my pen. I now record the one act for which I take some credit to myself, though the credit rightly belongs to some excellent ancestors of mine who left me a certain sum of money—shall we say five hundred pounds a year?—so that it was not necessary for me to depend solely on charm for my living. I turned upon her and caught her by the throat. I did my best to kill her. My excuse, if I were to be had up in a court of law, would be that I acted in self-defense. Had I not killed her she would have killed me. She would have plucked the heart out of my writing. For, as I found, directly I put pen to paper, you cannot review even a novel without having a mind of your own, without expressing what you think to be the truth about human relations, morality, sex. And all these questions, according to the Angel in the House, cannot be dealt with freely and openly by women; they must charm, they must conciliate, they must—to put it bluntly—tell lies if they are to succeed. Thus, whenever I felt the shadow of her wing or the radiance of her halo upon my page, I took up the inkpot and flung it at her. She died hard. Her fictitious nature was of great assistance to her. It is far harder to kill a phantom than a reality. She was always creeping back when I thought I had despatched her. Though I flatter myself that I killed her in the end, the struggle was severe; it took much time that had better have been spent upon learning Greek grammar; or in roaming the world in search of adventures. But it was a real experience; it was an experience that was bound to befall all women writers at that time. Killing the Angel in the House was part of the occupation of a woman writer.

But to continue my story. The Angel was dead; what then remained? You may say that what remained was a simple and common object—a young woman in a bedroom with an inkpot. In other words, now that she had rid herself of falsehood, that young woman had only to be herself. Ah, but what is "herself"? I mean, what is a woman? I assure you, I do not know. I do not believe that you know. I do not believe that anybody can know until she has expressed herself in all the arts and professions open to human skill. That indeed is one of the reasons why I have come here—out of respect for you, who are 4 in process of showing us by your experiments what a woman is, who are in process of providing us, by your failures and successes, with that extremely important piece of information.

But to continue the story of my professional experiences. I made one pound ten and six by my first review; and I bought a Persian cat with the proceeds. Then I grew ambitious. A Persian cat is all very well, I said; but a Persian cat is not enough. I must have a motor car. And it was thus that I became a novelist—for it is a very strange thing that people will give you a motor car if you will tell them a story. It is a still stranger thing that there is nothing so delightful in the world as telling stories. It is far pleasanter than writing reviews of famous novels. And yet, if I am to obey your secretary and tell you my professional experiences as a novelist, I must tell you about a very strange experience that befell me as a novelist. And to understand it you must try first to imagine a novelist's state of mind. I hope I am not giving away professional secrets if I say that a novelist's chief desire is to be as unconscious as possible. He has to induce in himself a state of perpetual lethargy. He wants life to proceed with the utmost quiet and regularity. He wants to see the same faces, to read the same books, to do the same things day after day, month after month, while he is writing, so that nothing may break the illusion in which he is living— so that nothing may disturb or disquiet the mysterious nosings about, feelings round, darts, dashes and sudden discoveries of that very shy and illusive spirit, the imagination. I suspect that this state is the same both for men and women. Be that as it may, I want you to imagine me writing a novel in a state of trance. I want you to figure to yourselves a girl sitting with a pen in her hand, which for minutes, and indeed for hours, she never dips into the inkpot. The image that comes to my mind when I think of this girl is the image of a fisherman lying sunk in dreams on the verge of a deep lake with a rod held out over the water. She was letting her imagination sweep unchecked round every rock and cranny of the world that lies submerged in the depths of our unconscious being. Now came the experience, the experience that I believe to be far commoner with women writers than with men. The line raced through the girl's fingers. Her imagination had rushed away. It had sought the pools, the depths, the dark places where the largest fish slumber. And then there was a smash. There was an explosion. There was foam and confusion. The imagination had dashed itself against something hard. The girl was roused from her dream. She was indeed in a state of the most acute and difficult distress. To speak without figure she had thought of something, something about the

5

body, about the passions which it was unfitting for her as a woman to say. Men, her reason told her, would be shocked. The consciousness of what men will say of a woman who speaks the truth about her passions had roused her from her artist's state of unconsciousness. She could write no more. The trance was over. Her imagination could work no longer. This I believe to be a very common experience with women writers—they are impeded by the extreme conventionality of the other sex. For though men sensibly allow themselves great freedom in these respects, I doubt that they realize or can control the extreme severity with which they condemn such freedom in women.

These then were two very genuine experiences of my own. These 6 were two of the adventures of my professional life. The first—killing the Angel in the House—I think I solved. She died. But the second, telling the truth about my own experiences as a body, I do not think I solved. I doubt that any woman has solved it yet. The obstacles against her are still immensely powerful—and yet they are very difficult to define. Outwardly, what is simpler than to write books? Outwardly, what obstacles are there for a woman rather than for a man? Inwardly, I think, the case is very different; she has still many ghosts to fight, many prejudices to overcome. Indeed it will be a long time still, I think, before a woman can sit down to write a book without finding a phantom to be slain, a rock to be dashed against. And if this is so in literature, the freest of all professions for women, how is it in the new professions which you are now for the first time entering?

Those are the questions that I should like, had I time, to ask you. 7 And indeed, if I have laid stress upon these professional experiences of mine, it is because I believe that they are, though in different forms, yours also. Even when the path is nominally open—when there is nothing to prevent a woman from being a doctor, a lawyer, a civil servant—there are many phantoms and obstacles, as I believe, looming in her way. To discuss and define them is I think of great value and importance; for thus only can the labor be shared, the difficulties be solved. But besides this, it is necessary also to discuss the ends and the aims for which we are fighting, for which we are doing battle with these formidable obstacles. Those aims cannot be taken for granted; they must be perpetually questioned and examined. The whole position, as I see it—here in this hall surrounded by women practising for the first time in history I know not how many different professions—is one of extraordinary interest and importance. You have won rooms of your own in the house hitherto exclusively owned by men. You are able, though not without great labor and effort, to pay the rent. You are earning your five hundred pounds a year. But this freedom is only a beginning; the room is your own, but it is still bare. It has to be furnished; it has to be decorated; it has to be shared. How are you going to furnish it, how are you going to decorate it? With whom are you going to share it, and upon what terms? These, I think, are questions of the utmost importance and interest. For the first time in history you are able to ask them; for the first time you are able to decide for yourselves what the answers should be. Willingly would I stay and discuss those questions and answers—but not tonight. My time is up; and I must cease.

# Questions

1. How would you characterize Woolf's tone, especially her attitude toward her subject and herself, in the first paragraph?
2. What do you think Woolf means when she says (paragraph 3): "It is far harder to kill a phantom than a reality"?
3. Woolf conjectures (paragraph 6) that she has not solved the problem of "telling the truth about my own experiences as a body." Is there any reason to believe that today a woman has more difficulty than a man in telling the truth about the experiences of the body?
4. In paragraph 7 Woolf suggests that phantoms as well as obstacles impede women from becoming doctors and lawyers. What might some of these phantoms be?
5. This essay is highly metaphoric. Speaking roughly (or, rather, as precisely as possible), what is the meaning of the metaphor of "rooms" in the final paragraph? What does Woolf mean when she says: "The room is your own, but it is still bare. . . . With whom are you going to share it, and upon what terms?"
6. Evaluate the last two sentences. Are they too abrupt and mechanical? Or do they provide a fitting conclusion to the speech?

Gloria Steinem

# The Importance of Work

Toward the end of the 1970s, *The Wall Street Journal* de-  1
voted an eight-part, front-page series to "the working woman"—that
is, the influx of women into the paid-labor force—as the greatest
change in American life since the Industrial Revolution.

Many women readers greeted both the news and the definition  2
with cynicism. After all, women have always worked. If all the productive work of human maintenance that women do in the home were
valued at its replacement cost, the gross national product of the United
States would go up by 26 percent. It's just that we are now more likely
than ever before to leave our poorly rewarded, low-security, high-risk
job of homemaking (though we're still trying to explain that it's a perfectly good one and that the problem is male society's refusal both to
do it and to give it an economic value) for more secure, independent,
and better-paid jobs outside the home.

Obviously, the real work revolution won't come until all produc-  3
tive work is rewarded—including child rearing and other jobs done
in the home—and men are integrated into so-called women's work as
well as vice versa. But the radical change being touted by the *Journal*
and other media is one part of that long integration process: the unprecedented flood of women into salaried jobs, that is, into the labor
force as it has been male-defined and previously occupied by men. We
are already more than 41 percent of it—the highest proportion in history. Given the fact that women also make up a whopping 69 percent
of the "discouraged labor force" (that is, people who need jobs but
don't get counted in the unemployment statistics because they've
given up looking), plus an official female unemployment rate that is
substantially higher than men's, it's clear that we could expand to
become fully half of the national work force by 1990.

Faced with this determination of women to find a little independ-  4

Gloria Steinem was born in Toledo in 1934 and educated at Smith College. An
active figure in politics, civil rights affairs, and feminist issues, she was a co-
founder of the Women's Action Alliance and a co-founder and editor of *Ms.*
magazine. We reprint an essay from her most recent book, *Outrageous Acts and
Everyday Rebellions* (1983).

ence and to be paid and honored for our work, experts have rushed to ask: "Why?" It's a question rarely directed at male workers. Their basic motivations of survival and personal satisfaction are taken for granted. Indeed, men are regarded as "odd" and therefore subjects for sociological study and journalistic reports only when they *don't* have work, even if they are rich and don't need jobs or are poor and can't find them. Nonetheless, pollsters and sociologists have gone to great expense to prove that women work outside the home because of dire financial need, or if we persist despite the presence of a wage-earning male, out of some desire to buy "little extras" for our families, or even out of good old-fashioned penis envy.

Job interviewers and even our own families may still ask salaried     5
women the big "Why?" If we have small children at home or are in some job regarded as "men's work," the incidence of such questions increases. Condescending or accusatory versions of "What's a nice girl like you doing in a place like this?" have not disappeared from the workplace.

How do we answer these assumptions that we are "working" out     6
of some pressing or peculiar need? Do we feel okay about arguing that it's as natural for us to have salaried jobs as for our husbands—whether or not we have young children at home? Can we enjoy strong career ambitions without worrying about being thought "unfeminine"? When we confront men's growing resentment of women competing in the work force (often in the form of such guilt-producing accusations as "You're taking men's jobs away" or "You're damaging your children"), do we simply state that a decent job is a basic human right for everybody?

I'm afraid the answer is often no. As individuals and as a move-     7
ment, we tend to retreat into some version of a tactically questionable defense: "Womenworkbecausewehaveto." The phrase has become one word, one key on the typewriter—an economic form of the socially "feminine" stance of passivity and self-sacrifice. Under attack, we still tend to present ourselves as creatures of economic necessity and familial devotion. "Womenworkbecausewehaveto" has become the easiest thing to say.

Like most truisms, this one is easy to prove with statistics. Eco-     8
nomic need *is* the most consistent work motive—for women as well as men. In 1976, for instance, 43 percent of all women in the paid-labor force were single, widowed, separated, or divorced, and working to support themselves and their dependents. An additional 21 percent were married to men who had earned less than ten thousand dollars

in the previous year, the minimum then required to support a family of four. In fact, if you take men's pensions, stocks, real estate, and various forms of accumulated wealth into account, a good statistical case can be made that there are more women who "have" to work (that is, who have neither the accumulated wealth, nor husbands whose work or wealth can support them for the rest of their lives) than there are men with the same need. If we were going to ask one group "Do you really need this job?" we should ask men.

But the first weakness of the whole "have to work" defense is its 9 deceptiveness. Anyone who has ever experienced dehumanized life on welfare or any other confidence-shaking dependency knows that a paid job may be preferable to the dole, even when the handout is coming from a family member. Yet the will and self-confidence to work on one's own can diminish as dependency and fear increase. That may explain why—contrary to the "have to" rationale—wives of men who earn less than three thousand dollars a year are actually *less* likely to be employed than wives whose husbands make ten thousand dollars a year or more.

Furthermore, the greatest proportion of employed wives is found 10 among families with a total household income of twenty-five to fifty thousand dollars a year. This is the statistical underpinning used by some sociologists to prove that women's work is mainly important for boosting families into the middle or upper middle class. Thus, women's incomes are largely used for buying "luxuries" and "little extras": a neat double-whammy that renders us secondary within our families, and makes our jobs expendable in hard times. We may even go along with this interpretation (at least, up to the point of getting fired so a male can have our job). It preserves a husbandly ego-need to be seen as the primary breadwinner, and still allows us a safe "feminine" excuse for working.

But there are often rewards that we're not confessing. As noted 11 in *The Two-Career Couple,* by Francine and Douglas Hall: "Women who hold jobs by choice, even blue-collar routine jobs, are more satisfied with their lives than are the full-time housewives."

In addition to personal satisfaction, there is also society's need for 12 all its members' talents. Suppose that jobs were given out on only a "have to work" basis to both women and men—one job per household. It would be unthinkable to lose the unique abilities of, for instance, Eleanor Holmes Norton, the distinguished chair of the Equal Employment Opportunity Commission. But would we then be forced to question the important work of her husband, Edward Norton, who is also a distinguished lawyer? Since men earn more than twice as much as women on the average, the wife in most households would be more likely to give up her job. Does that mean the nation could do as well without millions of its nurses, teachers, and secretaries? Or that the rare man who earns less than his wife should give up his job?

It was this kind of waste of human talents on a society-wide scale 13 that traumatized millions of unemployed or underemployed Americans during the Depression. Then, a one-job-per-household rule seemed somewhat justified, yet the concept was used to displace women workers only, create intolerable dependencies, and waste female talent that the country needed. That Depression experience, plus the energy and example of women who were finally allowed to work during the manpower shortage created by World War II, led Congress to reinterpret the meaning of the country's full-employment goal in its Economic Act of 1946. Full employment was officially defined as "the employment of those who want to work, without regard to whether their employment is, by some definition, necessary. This goal applies equally to men and to women." Since bad economic times are again creating a resentment of employed women—as well as creating more need for women to be employed—we need such a goal more than ever. Women are again being caught in a tragic double bind: We are required to be strong and then punished for our strength.

Clearly, anything less than government and popular commitment 14 to this 1946 definition of full employment will leave the less powerful groups, whoever they may be, in danger. Almost as important as the financial penalty paid by the powerless is the suffering that comes from being shut out of paid and recognized work. Without it, we lose much of our self-respect and our ability to prove that we are alive by making some difference in the world. That's just as true for the suburban woman as it is for the unemployed steel worker.

But it won't be easy to give up the passive defense of "wework- 15 becausewehaveto."

When a woman who is struggling to support her children and 16 grandchildren on welfare sees her neighbor working as a waitress, even though that neighbor's husband has a job, she may feel resentful; and the waitress (of course, not the waitress's husband) may feel guilty. Yet unless we establish the obligation to provide a job for everyone who is willing and able to work, that welfare woman may herself be penalized by policies that give out only one public-service job per household. She and her daughter will have to make a painful and divisive decision about which of them gets that precious job, and the whole household will have to survive on only one salary.

A job as a human right is a principle that applies to men as well 17 as women. But women have more cause to fight for it. The phenomenon of the "working woman" has been held responsible for everything from an increase in male impotence (which turned out, incidentally, to be attributable to medication for high blood pressure) to the rising cost of steak (which was due to high energy costs and beef import restrictions, not women's refusal to prepare the cheaper, slower-cooking cuts). Unless we see a job as part of every citizen's right to autonomy and personal fulfillment, we will continue to be vulnerable to someone else's idea of what "need" is, and whose "need" counts the most.

In many ways, women who do not have to work for simple sur- 18 vival, but who choose to do so nonetheless, are on the frontier of asserting this right for all women. Those with well-to-do husbands are dangerously easy for us to resent and put down. It's easier still to resent women from families of inherited wealth, even though men generally control and benefit from that wealth. (There is no Rockefeller Sisters Fund, no J. P. Morgan & Daughters, and sons-in-law may be the ones who really sleep their way to power.) But to prevent a woman whose husband or father is wealthy from earning her own living, and from gaining the self-confidence that comes with that ability, is to keep her needful of that unearned power and less willing to disperse it. Moreover, it is to lose forever her unique talents.

Perhaps modern feminists have been guilty of a kind of reverse 19 snobbism that keeps us from reaching out to the wives and daughters of wealthy men; yet it was exactly such women who refused the restrictions of class and financed the first wave of feminist revolution.

For most of us, however, "womenworkbecausewehaveto" is just 20 true enough to be seductive as a personal defense.

If we use it without also staking out the larger human right to a 21 job, however, we will never achieve that right. And we will always be subject to the false argument that independence for women is a luxury affordable only in good economic times. Alternatives to layoffs will not be explored, acceptable unemployment will always be used to frighten those with jobs into accepting low wages, and we will never remedy the real cost, both to families and to the country, of dependent women and a massive loss of talent.

Worst of all, we may never learn to find productive, honored work    22
as a natural part of ourselves and as one of life's basic pleasures.

# Questions

1. In a sentence or two, state Gloria Steinem's thesis.
2. In paragraph 2 Steinem characterizes homemaking as a "poorly rewarded, low-security, high-risk job." How might she justify each of these descriptions of homemaking? Do you agree that home-making is rightly classified as a job? If so, do you agree with her description of it?
3. If you are a female reading Steinem's article, have you ever heard a version of the question, "What's a nice girl like you doing in a place like this?" If you are a male, have you ever been asked a male version of this question about a job you were doing or applying for? Describe your experience in a paragraph or two.
4. Restate in your own words Steinem's explanation (paragraph 9) of why "wives of men who earn less than three thousand dollars a year are actually *less* likely to be employed than wives whose husbands make ten thousand dollars a year or more." What is your reaction to the fact and to this explanation of it? Surprise, disbelief, acceptance, or what?
5. To whom does Steinem appear to address her remarks? Cite evidence for your answer. In your opinion, is this audience likely to find her argument persuasive? Would a different audience find it more or less persuasive? Explain.
6. In addition to arguments, what persuasive devices does Steinem use? How, for example, does she persuade you that she speaks with authority? What other authorities does she cite? How would you characterize her diction and tone, for instance in paragraph 18? (On diction, see page 1144; on tone, see page 1153.)
7. Steinem suggests two reasons for working: "personal satisfaction" and "society's need for all its members' talents." Suppose that you had no financial need to work. Do you imagine that you would choose to work in order to gain "personal satisfaction"? Or, again if you had no need to work, would you assume that you are morally obligated to contribute to society by engaging in paid work?
8. Summarize, in a paragraph of about 100–150 words, Steinem's argument that it is entirely proper for wealthy women to work for pay. In the course of your paragraph you may quote briefly from the essay.

Charles Krauthammer

# The Just Wage
## From Bad to Worth

The latest entry on the list of sacred democratic causes is   1
comparable worth. According to that doctrine, it is demonstrable that
low-paying female-dominated jobs, like nursing, are worth as much
(to employers or society) as "comparable" male-dominated jobs, like
plumbing, and that therefore by right and by law they should be paid
the same. Comparable worth has become not only *the* women's issue
of the 1980s, but also the most prominent civil rights issue not specifically directed at blacks. The Democratic Party has warmly embraced
it. Every one of its presidential candidates has endorsed it. In the 1984
platform, that sea of well-intended ambiguity and evasion, there are
few islands of certainty. Comparable worth is one of them.

Comparable worth is advancing in the courts, too. In 1981 the   2
Supreme Court opened the door a crack by ruling that female prison
guards could sue for violation of the equal-pay provisions of the 1964
Civil Rights Act, even though they did not do precisely the same work
as the better-paid male prison guards. That narrow ruling was broken
open in December 1983 in a sweeping victory for comparable worth
in Washington State. A federal district judge found the state guilty of
massive discrimination because its female-dominated jobs were paying
less than "comparable" male-dominated jobs. He ordered an immediate increase in the women's wages and restitution for past injury.
The back pay alone will run into the hundreds of millions of dollars.

Comparable worth may indeed be an idea whose time has come.   3
Where does it come from? When the plumber makes a house call and
charges forty dollars an hour to fix a leak, the instinct of most people
is to suspect that the plumber is overpaid—the beneficiary of some
combination of scarce skills, powerful unions, and dumb luck. The
instinct of comparable worth advocates is to see the plumber's wage
as a standard of fairness, to conclude that the rest of us (meaning:
women) are underpaid, and to identify discrimination as the source

Charles Krauthammer holds a medical degree and has served as chief resident
in psychiatry at Harvard Medical School. In 1983 he became a contributing essayist for *Time*, and in 1984 he began a weekly column for the *Washington Post*.

of that underpayment. But since overt discrimination on the basis of sex has been legally forbidden for twenty years, to make that charge stick nowadays requires a bit of subtlety.

One claim is that women's wages are depressed today because of 4 a legacy of past discrimination: namely, the "crowding" of women into certain fields (like nursing, teaching, secretarial work), thus artificially depressing their wages. Did sexual stereotyping really "crowd" women into their jobs? Sexual stereotyping worked both ways: it kept women in, but it also kept men out, thus artificially excluding potential wage competition from half the population, and, more important, from about two-thirds to three-quarters of the labor force (because of the higher participation rate of men). Sex-segregation is obviously unfair, but it is hard to see how it caused downward pressure on women's wages when, at the same time, through the socially enforced exclusion of men, it sheltered "women's work" from a vast pool of competitors. Moreover, as the social barriers that kept men and women from entering each other's traditional fields have fallen during the last twenty years, there has been much more movement of women into men's fields than vice versa. "Women's work" is less crowded than ever.

If the crowding argument is weak, then one is forced to resort to 5 the "grand conspiracy" theory. "The system of wages was set up by a grand conspiracy, so to speak, that has held down the wages of women to minimize labor costs," explained the business agent of the union that in 1981 struck for and won a famous comparable-worth settlement in San Jose. But since to minimize labor costs employers try to hold down the wages of everyone, the thrust of the argument must be that there is a particular desire to do so additionally in the case of women. In other words, the market is inherently discriminatory. Women nurses are paid less than they deserve, simply because they are women. How to prove it? Comparing their wages to that of male nurses won't do, since their pay is, by law, equal. So one must compare nurses' wages to that of, say, plumbers, show that nurses make less, and claim that nurses are discriminated against because they deserve—they are worth—the same.

What is the basis of that claim? In San Jose, Washington State, 6 and other comparable worth cases, the basis is a "study." A consultant is called in to set up a committee to rank every job according to certain criteria. In Washington State, the Willis scale gives marks for "knowledge and skills," "mental demands," "accountability," and "working conditions." The committee then awards points in each category to every job, tallies them up, and declares those with equal totals to have—*voilà!*—comparable worth.

There is no need to belabor the absurdity of this system, so I'll stick to the high points. It is, above all, a mandate for arbitrariness: every subjective determination, no matter how whimsically arrived at, is first enshrined in a number to give it an entirely specious solidity, then added to another number no less insubstantial, to yield a total entirely meaningless. (An exercise: compare, with numbers, the "mental demands" on a truck driver and a secretary.) Everything is arbitrary: the categories, the rankings, even the choice of judges. And even if none of this were true, even if every category were ontologically self-evident, every ranking mathematically precise, every judge Solomonic, there remains one factor wholly unaccounted for which permits the system to be skewed in any direction one wishes: the *weight* assigned to each category. In the Willis scale, points for "knowledge and skills" are worth as much as points for "working conditions." But does ten points in knowledge and skills make up for ten points in hazardous working conditions? Who is to say that a secretary's two years of college are equal in worth to—and not half or double the worth of—the trucker's risk of getting killed on the highways? Mr. Willis, that's who.

Conclusions based on such "studies" are not a whit less capricious than the simple assertion, "secretaries are worth as much as truck drivers." Trotting out Willis, of course, allows you to dress up a feeling in scientific trappings. It allows H.R. 4599, Representative Mary Rose Oakar's bill legislating comparable worth in federal employment, to dispose of the arbitrariness problem in the *definitions.* "Job evaluation technique" is defined as "an objective method of determining the comparable value of different jobs." Next problem.

Some advocates of comparable worth, aware of this objectivity conundrum and perhaps less confident that it can be defined out of existence, propose an alternate solution. Instead of ranking the intrinsic worth of the job (by admittedly arbitrary criteria), they propose ranking the worth of the worker. Barbara Bergmann, an economist at the University of Maryland, believes that people with similar qualifications, training and experience should be receiving the same return on their "human capital." Breaking new ground in discrimination theory, she claims that "in a nondiscriminatory setup, identical people should be paid identically." And what makes people identical? Their credentials: qualifications, training, experience. This is not just credentialism gone wild, and highly disadvantageous to non-yuppy workers with poor résumés, who need the help of the women's movement the most; it leads to the logical absurdity that people should be paid not for the actual work they do, but for the work they *could* do. We've gone from equal pay for equal work to equal pay for comparable work, to equal pay for potential work. Summarizing the Bergmann position, the Center for Philosophy in Public Policy at the University of Maryland explains helpfully that "if a nursing supervisor could do the work of a higher-paid hospital purchasing agent, then her wages should be the same as his." But why stop there? What if her credentials are the same as those of the hospital administrator, or her city councillor, or her U.S. Senator? And what about the starving actress, waiting on tables for a living? If she can act as well as Bo Derek (to set a standard anyone can meet), shouldn't she be getting a million dollars a year— that is, if the "setup" is to deserve the adjective "nondiscriminatory"?

Now, even if there were a shred of merit in any of these systems  10 for determining comparable worth, we should be wary of implementing them if only because of the sheer social chaos they would create. The only sure consequence of comparable worth one can foresee was described by the winning attorney in the Washington State case: "This decision . . . should stimulate an avalanche of private litigation on behalf of the victims of discrimination." The judicial and bureaucratic monster comparable worth will call into being—a whole new layer of judges, court-appointed "masters" (there already is one in the Washington State suit), lawyers, and consultants—will not just sit once to fix wages and then retire. The process will be endless. Fairness will require constant readjustment. There will still exist such a thing as supply and demand. Even if comparable worth advocates succeed in abolishing it for women's work (remember, Washington State was found to have broken the law for paying women market wages rather than comparable worth wages), it will still operate for men's wages, the standard by which women's (comparable worth) wages will be set. Now, what if nurses are awarded plumbers' pay, and there develops a housing slowdown and a plumber surplus, and plumbers' wages fall? Will nurses' salaries have to be ratcheted down? And if not, what is to prevent the plumbers from suing, alleging they are underpaid relative to comparably equal nurses?

Which brings us to the equity problem. Almost everyone feels he  11 or she is underpaid. Moreover, even a plumber can point to at least one person or group of persons who are getting more than they are "worth." Why can't he claim that class of people as the equitable standard, and march to court demanding restitution? If comparable worth is simple justice, as its advocates claim, why should only women be entitled to it? Why not comparable worth for everyone?

The whole search for the "just wage," which is what comparable  12 worth is all about, is, like the search for the "just price," inherently elusive in a capitalist system. It is not that justice has nothing to say about wages and prices in a market economy, but that what it does say it says negatively. For example, it declares that whatever the wage, it must be the same for people regardless of sex, race or other characteristics; but it doesn't say what the wage should be. Even the minimum-wage law says merely that a wage may not be below a certain floor. (Even capitalism has a notion of exploitative labor.) Beyond that, the law is silent. The reason it is silent, the reason we decide to let the market decide, is no great mystery. It was first elaborated by Adam Smith, and amplified by the experience of the Soviet Union and other command economies. Market economies are agnostic on the question of a just wage or a just price not simply because of a philosophical belief that the question, if it is a question, is unanswerable, but also because of the belief, and the experience, that attempts to answer it have a habit of leaving everyone worse off than before.

Finally, even granting that women in traditionally female jobs are  13 underpaid, it is not as if we live in a fixed economy which blocks off all avenues of redress. If secretaries are indeed paid less than they are "worth," they have several options. One is suggested by Coleman Young, the mayor of Detroit, a former labor leader and no conservative: "If a painter makes more than a secretary, then let more women be painters. Equal opportunity and affirmative action is how you do that." A woman entering the labor force today has no claim that she has been crowded into low-paying professions because of discrimination. She has choices.

Older women, of course, who have already invested much in their  14 professions, are more constrained. But they have the same avenues open to them—such as organizing—as other similarly constrained (predominantly male) workers who struggle for higher wages in other settings. In Denver, for example, nurses sought comparable worth wage gains in court and lost; they then went on strike and won. True, in some occupations, even strong unions can't raise wages very much. But as the president of the International Ladies Garment Workers Union (85 percent female) explained in objecting to a highfalutin AFL-CIO endorsement of comparable worth, the problem is not discrimination but the market. His workers have low wages because they compete with workers overseas who are paid thirty cents an hour. Comparable worth doctrine may declare that garment workers ought to be making as much as truck drivers. But if the theory ever became practice, garment workers would be free of more than discrimination. They would be free of their jobs.

Why is the obvious about comparable worth so rarely heard? Why     15
is it for Democrats the ultimate motherhood issue? Because here again the party of the big heart identifies a class of people who feel they aren't getting their just due, blames that condition on a single cause (discrimination), then offers a "rational" solution, on whose messy details it prefers not to dwell. But those details add up to a swamp of mindless arbitrariness and bureaucratic inefficiency, shrouded in a fine mist of pseudo-scientific objectivity. And the surest results will be unending litigation and an entirely new generation of inequities. These inequities, moreover, will be frozen in place by force of law, and thus that much more difficult to dislodge.

Comparable worth asks the question: How many nurses would it     16
take to screw in a lightbulb? The joke is that, having not the faintest idea, it demands that a committee invent an answer, that the answer become law and that the law supplant the market. Even Karl Marx, who also had legitimate complaints about the equity of wages set by the market, had a more plausible alternative.

# Questions

1. Explain the pun in the title. Is it simply a joke, or is it relevant to Krauthammer's thesis?
2. What information is advanced in paragraph 1? What attitude? (Barbara Bergmann, whose essay on comparable worth follows, speaks of the "raucous, mocking tone" of critics. Do you notice that tone here?)
3. In paragraph 3 Krauthammer says, "Comparable worth may indeed be an idea whose time has come." But he does not go on, as one might expect, to argue in favor of comparable worth. What does he do in the rest of the paragraph? On the question of the plumber's wage that he poses in this paragraph, do you identify yourself with "the instinct of most people" or with "the instinct of comparable worth advocates"? Is it possible to take both positions simultaneously?
4. In paragraph 4 Krauthammer suggests that "sexual stereotyping worked both ways: it kept women in, but it also kept men out, thus

artificially excluding potential wage competition from half the population." He mentions nursing, teaching, and secretarial work as female-dominated jobs, but of course other fields, such as child care and domestic work, could be added to his list. Do you think that if more men enter these fields the wages will (as Krauthammer implies) decline? Why, or why not?

5. In paragraph 7 Krauthammer challenges the reader to "compare, with numbers, the 'mental demands' on a truck driver and a secretary." Take up the challenge. Can you make this comparison? If so, make it; if not, explain why it cannot be made.

6. In paragraph 9 Krauthammer compares a starving actress with Bo Derek. Do you agree with the point he makes? If not, what argument can you make? (Even if you agree with his point, you may find it irrelevant to the argument, or so exceptional a case that perhaps it can be ignored.)

7. Krauthammer several times refers to the Washington State case in which the state was found guilty of "massive discrimination" (paragraph 2). In paragraph 10 he predicts that comparable worth will create "a judicial and bureaucratic monster" and an endless process of suits and readjustments not only of women's wages but of men's. Does he expect this monster to emerge from the Washington State case? If the judgment in the case were to inspire a multitude of suits and readjustments of wages, would that discredit the judgment or the case for comparable worth?

8. In paragraph 11 Krauthammer writes, "Even a plumber can point to at least one person or group of persons who are getting more than they are 'worth.' Why can't he claim that class of people as the equitable standard, and march to court demanding restitution?" How would you answer that question? Under what circumstances *could* a plumber demand equitable pay? From whom would he (or she) demand it?

9. On the basis of this article, how would you define "comparable worth"? (If you have trouble coming up with a definition, read Barbara Bergmann's essay on page 410, and try again.)

Barbara R. Bergmann

# Pay Equity—How to
# Argue Back

$T$hanks to the pay equity campaign, state and local gov-     1
ernments around the country are taking steps to raise the pay scales
in the traditionally female occupations. The drumbeat of criticism continues, however, with that raucous, mocking tone that we are used to
hearing in response to any proposal to improve women's status. Some
of it comes from the same folks who oppose shelters for battered
women—they are against anything that would make women more
uppity. But some of the criticism is serious and needs answering.

The first count of the indictment is that pay equity adjustments     2
tamper with "wage scales set in the marketplace." Of course they do.
The pay that the market decrees for women's labor is badly depressed
by discrimination. Pay equity adjustments, along with affirmative action for hiring and promoting women, are attempts to get away from
the sex discrimination that most employers practice, and that now
dominates the "market." The real question is, what harm would be
done?

If women's wages are raised, then employers will want to employ     3
fewer of them, say pay equity's critics. For a response we can point
to the example of Australia, where government pay boards handed
out equity raises in the traditional women's occupations amounting to
about 30 percent. Australian economists fully expected to see women's
unemployment rates rise significantly as a result. After thorough
study, they had to report that the bad effects hadn't materialized. In
Sweden, Britain, West Germany, Holland, and Denmark, women
workers have had significant gains in pay. In terms of equity with men,
they are way ahead of American women. In none of these countries
are there reports of special unemployment problems for women. There
is no reason to think that American women will experience such problems either.

Another complaint against pay equity is that, apart from the mar-     4

Barbara R. Bergmann, a professor of economics at the American University,
has written a book entitled *The Economic Emergence of American Women.*

ket, there is no really good way to compare men's and women's occupations, so how could we decide which ones should have comparable pay? "How can you compare a secretary to a truck driver, or a
nurse to a tree trimmer?" the opponents of pay equity ask plaintively
in mock anguish. The answer is that employers do have a method that
they rely on to make comparisons between very different occupations.
It is called "job evaluation."

Many large employers already use job evaluation techniques in    5
setting pay, and well-respected consulting firms help in the implementation. These employers use job evaluation because the idea of a
"market" that will tell them the wage for each of hundreds of job titles
is sheer fantasy. However, these firms have wanted to avoid paying
male-level salaries to women, so they never directly compared the
qualities of traditional women's jobs and traditional men's jobs. They
set up a job evaluation system for the jobs labeled "clerical" and an
entirely different one for the jobs labeled "administrative." It is as if
they were doing job evaluations on blue paper for the men and on
pink paper for the women, taking care not to compare the pink and
blue sheets. The idea of pay equity is that men's and women's jobs
should be evaluated by a unified system, and then pay scales adjusted
accordingly. The basic methodology already exists, and already is in
widespread use in business and in government. It just needs to be
cleaned up a bit.

Another allegation about pay equity is that the costs will be huge—    6
billions of dollars. That's true, but since there are millions of women
involved, billions of dollars are needed to make a dent in the problem.
Where can we get the billions for pay equity? They will come out of
the billions that are handed out every year as wage increases to workers. At most, for a few years, women will get larger-than-average increases, and for a few years men will get smaller-than-average increases. Nobody's pay need go down. Nor will profits or budgets be
wiped out.

The silliest argument the pay equity critics have come up with is    7
that women will be so satisfied with their pay in the traditional female
jobs that they will stop trying to get into the better jobs reserved for
men. That argument is an insult to every secretary who has been
passed over for a promotion to a job she could do better than the man
who got it. Better pay has never prevented men or women from wanting promotions.

Pay equity is going forward for the women employees of state and    8
local governments because a combination of political and union pres-

sure is being exerted behind it. For it to spread to the private sector, unions must confront the issue at the bargaining table. Where there is no union, or where the union is indifferent to women's issues, women employees must organize on their own. Whether pay equity lawsuits will be worthwhile depends on the Supreme Court.

One of the economic effects of pay equity that seldom gets men-  9 tioned is its effect on poverty. A healthy boost in the pay of the traditional women's occupations is the best and may be the only way that we have of reducing poverty among women in the near future. It might rescue from poverty some of the millions of children dependent on those women. When you come to think about it, it's women's current salaries that make poor economic sense. Pay equity makes good economic sense.

# Questions

1. From the title and first paragraph of this essay, would you say that Bergmann is addressing proponents or opponents of pay equity? Considering that the article was published in *Ms.*, does she strike an appropriate opening note. Does she risk alienating readers?

2. What Bergmann and many other people call "pay equity" is called, by still others, "comparable worth." If you advocate the idea, which term do you prefer? Why?

3. In paragraph 4 Bergmann mentions the opposition's belief that the only way to compare the value of a secretary with the value of a tree trimmer is to see what the market offers. Bergmann says there is an alternative, "job evaluation." In her next paragraph she offers a comment on job evaluations. If you were evaluating the two jobs she mentions in paragraph 4—secretary and tree trimmer—which job would you find deserving of higher pay? Why? What criteria would you use? Possible criteria might be the amount of education or training, or the skill level, required; the degree of responsibility; the amount of initiative (or intelligence?) required; and work conditions (e.g., congenial or uncongenial).

4. Why is the choice of criteria important in establishing pay equity? Try to explain your answer by again comparing the jobs of the secretary and the tree trimmer, this time using criteria other than those listed in question 3.

5. In paragraph 7 Bergmann speaks of certain "better jobs [that are] reserved for men." What are some examples of such jobs? What makes them "better"? Money, and nothing else?

6. In rejecting the request of Denver nurses that they be paid as much

as Denver tree trimmers, a federal judge noted that such a change in pay involved "the possibility of disrupting the entire economic system in the United States." Is the possibility of such disruption a sound reason for rejecting the change? Why, or why not?

7. If you have ever been underpaid, or overpaid, because of sexual or racial discrimination, explain the circumstances and then argue the case that might have been made for pay equity.

Lester C. Thurow

# Why Women Are Paid Less Than Men

In the 40 years from 1939 to 1979 white women who work  1
full time have with monotonous regularity made slightly less than 60 percent as much as white men. Why?

Over the same time period, minorities have made substantial  2
progress in catching up with whites, with minority women making even more progress than minority men. Black men now earn 72 percent as much as white men (up 16 percentage points since the mid-1950's) but black women earn 92 percent as much as white women. Hispanic men make 71 percent of what their white counterparts do, but Hispanic women make 82 percent as much as white women. As a result of their faster progress, fully employed black women make 75 percent as much as fully employed black men while Hispanic women earn 68 percent as much as Hispanic men.

This faster progress may, however, end when minority women  3
finally catch up with white women. In the bible of the New Right, George Gilder's *Wealth and Poverty*, the 60 percent is just one of Mother Nature's constants like the speed of light or the force of gravity. Men

Lester C. Thurow, born in Montana in 1938, is dean of the Sloan School of Management at the Massachusetts Institute of Technology. Among his books are *Poverty and Discrimination* and *The Political Economy of Income Redistribution Policies*.

are programmed to provide for their families economically while women are programmed to take care of their families emotionally and physically. As a result men put more effort into their jobs than women. The net result is a difference in work intensity that leads to that 40 percent gap in earnings. But there is no discrimination against women—only the biological facts of life.

The problem with this assertion is just that. It is an assertion with 4 no evidence for it other than the fact that white women have made 60 percent as much as men for a long period of time.

"Discrimination against women" is an easy answer but it also has 5 its problems as an adequate explanation. Why is discrimination against women not declining under the same social forces that are leading to a lessening of discrimination against minorities? In recent years women have made more use of the enforcement provisions of the Equal Employment Opportunities Commission and the courts than minorities. Why do the laws that prohibit discrimination against women and minorities work for minorities but not for women?

When men discriminate against women, they run into a problem. 6 To discriminate against women is to discriminate against your own wife and to lower your own family income. To prevent women from working is to force men to work more.

When whites discriminate against blacks, they can at least think 7 that they are raising their own incomes. When men discriminate against women they have to know that they are lowering their own family income and increasing their own work effort.

While discrimination undoubtedly explains part of the male-female 8 earnings differential, one has to believe that men are monumentally stupid or irrational to explain all of the earnings gap in terms of discrimination. There must be something else going on.

Back in 1939 it was possible to attribute the earnings gap to large 9 differences in educational attainments. But the educational gap between men and women has been eliminated since World War II. It is no longer possible to use education as an explanation for the lower earnings of women. Some observers have argued that women earn less money since they are less reliable workers who are more apt to leave the labor force. But it is difficult to maintain this position since women are less apt to quit one job to take another and as a result they tend to work as long, or longer, for any one employer. From any employer's perspective they are more reliable, not less reliable, than men.

Part of the answer is visible if you look at the lifetime earnings 10 profile of men. Suppose that you were asked to predict which men in a group of 25-year-olds would become economically successful. At age 25 it is difficult to tell who will be economically successful and your predictions are apt to be highly inaccurate. But suppose that you were asked to predict which men in a group of 35-year-olds would become economically successful. If you are successful at age 35, you are very likely to remain successful for the rest of your life. If you have not become economically successful by age 35, you are very unlikely to do so later.

The decade between 25 and 35 is when men either succeed or fail.   11
It is the decade when lawyers become partners in the good firms, when business managers make it onto the "fast track," when academics get tenure at good universities, and when blue collar workers find the job opportunities that will lead to training opportunities and the skills that will generate high earnings. If there is any one decade when it pays to work hard and to be consistently in the labor force, it is the decade between 25 and 35. For those who succeed, earnings will rise rapidly. For those who fail, earnings will remain flat for the rest of their lives.

But the decade between 25 and 35 is precisely the decade when   12
women are most apt to leave the labor force or become part-time workers to have children. When they do, the current system of promotion and skill acquisition will extract an enormous lifetime price.

This leaves essentially two avenues for equalizing male and female   13
earnings. Families where women who wish to have successful careers, compete with men, and achieve the same earnings should alter their family plans and have their children either before 25 or after 35. Or society can attempt to alter the existing promotion and skill acquisition system so that there is a longer time period in which both men and women can attempt to successfully enter the labor force. Without some combination of these two factors, a substantial fraction of the male-female earnings differentials are apt to persist for the next 40 years, even if discrimination against women is eliminated.

# Questions

1. Thurow assumes that discrimination against women can't possibly be the whole explanation for their lower earnings. On what does he base this assumption? Do you agree with his assumption?
2. Evaluate Thurow's opening paragraph, explaining why you find it effective or ineffective.
3. After giving his analysis, Thurow ends the essay by suggesting two

ways in which the differential in earnings may be decreased. Does he convey enthusiasm? Optimism? Is the tone of the ending consistent with the tone of the rest of the essay?

4. If you have read Bergmann's "Pay Equity—How to Answer Back" (page 410), set forth what you think would be Bergmann's response to Thurow's analysis of the problem and her response to his two proposals for equalizing male and female earnings.

Barbara Ehrenreich

# A Step Back to the Workhouse?

The commentators are calling it a "remarkable consensus."    1
Workfare, as programs to force welfare recipients to work are known, was once abhorred by liberals as a step back toward the 17th-century workhouse or—worse—slavery. But today no political candidate dares step outdoors without some plan for curing "welfare dependency" by putting its hapless victims to work—if necessary, at the nearest Burger King. It is as if the men who run things, or who aspire to run things (and we are, unfortunately, talking mostly about men when we talk about candidates), had gone off and caucused for a while and decided on the one constituency that could be safely sacrificed in the name of political expediency and "new ideas," and that constituency is poor women.

Most of the arguments for workfare are simply the same indes-    2
tructible stereotypes that have been around, in one form or another, since the first public relief program in England 400 years ago: that the poor are poor because they are lazy and dissolute, and that they are lazy and dissolute because they are suffering from "welfare dependency." Add a touch of modern race and gender stereotypes and you have the image that haunts the workfare advocates: a slovenly, over-

Barbara Ehrenreich, author of *The Economic Emergence of Women* (1986), writes regularly for the *New York Times* and for *Ms.*

weight, black woman who produces a baby a year in order to augment her welfare checks.

But there is a new twist to this season's spurt of welfare-bashing: 3 workfare is being presented as a kind of *feminist* alternative to welfare. As Senator Daniel Patrick Moynihan (D.-N.Y.) has put it, "A program that was designed to pay mothers to stay at home with their children [i.e., welfare, or Aid to Families with Dependent Children] cannot succeed when we now observe most mothers going out to work." Never mind the startling illogic of this argument, which is on a par with saying that no woman should stay home with her children because other women do not, or that a laid-off male worker should not receive unemployment compensation because most men have been observed holding jobs. We are being asked to believe that pushing destitute mothers into the work force (in some versions of workfare, for no other compensation than the welfare payments they would have received anyway) is consistent with women's strivings toward self-determination.

Now I will acknowledge that most women on welfare—like most 4 unemployed women in general—would rather have jobs. And I will further acknowledge that many of the proponents of workfare, possibly including Senator Moynihan and the Democratic Presidential candidates, have mounted the bandwagon with the best of intentions. Welfare surely needs reform. But workfare is not the solution, because "dependency"—with all its implications of laziness and depravity—is not the problem. The problem is poverty, which most women enter in a uniquely devastating way—with their children in tow.

Let me introduce a real person, if only because real people, as 5 opposed to imaginative stereotypes, never seem to make an appearance in the current rhetoric on welfare. "Lynn," as I will call her, is a friend and onetime neighbor who has been on welfare for two years. She is also about as unlike the stereotypical "welfare mother" as one can get—which is to say that she is a fairly typical welfare recipient. She has only one child, which puts her among the 74 percent of welfare recipients who have only one or two children. She is white (not that that should matter), as are almost half of welfare recipients. Like most welfare recipients, she is not herself the daughter of a welfare recipient, and hence not part of anything that could be called an "intergenerational cycle of dependency." And like every woman on welfare I have ever talked to, she resents the bureaucratic hassles that are the psychic price of welfare. But, for now, there are no alternatives.

When I first met Lynn, she seemed withdrawn and disoriented. 6

She had just taken the biggest step of her 25 years; she had left an abusive husband and she was scared: scared about whether she could survive on her own and scared of her estranged husband. He owned a small restaurant; she was a high school dropout who had been a waitress when she met him. During their three years of marriage he had beaten her repeatedly. Only after he threw her down a flight of stairs had she realized that her life was in danger and moved out. I don't think I fully grasped the terror she had lived in until one summer day when he chased Lynn to the door of my house with a drawn gun.

Gradually Lynn began to put her life together. She got a divorce   7 and went on welfare; she found a pediatrician who would accept Medicaid and a supermarket that would take food stamps. She fixed up her apartment with second-hand furniture and flea market curtains. She was, by my admittedly low standards, a compulsive housekeeper and an overprotective mother; and when she wasn't waxing her floors or ironing her two-year-old's playsuits, she was studying the help-wanted ads. She spent a lot of her time struggling with details that most of us barely notice—the price of cigarettes, mittens, or of a bus ticket to the welfare office—yet, somehow, she regained her sense of humor. In fact, most of the time we spent together was probably spent laughing—over the foibles of the neighbors, the conceits of men, and the snares of welfare and the rest of "the system."

Yet for all its inadequacies, Lynn was grateful for welfare. Maybe   8 if she had been more intellectually inclined she would have found out that she was suffering from "welfare dependency," a condition that is supposed to sap the will and demolish the work ethic. But "dependency" is not an issue when it is a choice between an abusive husband and an impersonal government. Welfare had given Lynn a brief shelter in a hostile world, and as far as she was concerned, it was her ticket to *independence*.

Suppose there had been no welfare at the time when Lynn finally   9 summoned the courage to leave her husband. Suppose she had gone for help and been told she would have to "work off" her benefits in some menial government job (restocking the toilet paper in rest rooms is one such "job" assigned to New York women in a current workfare program). Or suppose, as in some versions of workfare, she had been told she would have to take the first available private sector job, which (for a non–high school graduate like Lynn) would have paid near the minimum wage, or $3.35 an hour. How would she have been able to afford child care? What would she have done for health insurance (as a welfare recipient she had Medicaid, but most low-paying jobs offer little or no coverage)? Would she have ever made the decision to leave her husband in the first place?

As Ruth Sidel points out in *Women and Children Last* (Viking), most    10
women who are or have been on welfare have stories like Lynn's. They go onto welfare in response to a crisis—divorce, illness, loss of a job, the birth of an additional child to feed—and they remain on welfare for two years or less. They are not victims of any "welfare culture," but of a society that increasingly expects women to both raise and support children—and often on wages that would barely support a woman alone. In fact, even some of the most vociferous advocates of replacing welfare with workfare admit that, in their own estimation, only about 15 percent of welfare recipients fit the stereotype associated with "welfare dependency": demoralization, long-term welfare use, lack of drive, and so on.

But workfare will not help anyone, not even the presumed 15 per-    11
cent of "bad apples" for whose sake the majority will be penalized. First, it will not help because it does not solve the problem that drives most women into poverty in the first place: how to hold a job *and* care for children. Child care in a licensed, professionally run center can easily cost as much as $100 a week per child—more than most states now pay in welfare benefits and (for two children) more than most welfare recipients could expect to earn in the work force. Any serious effort to get welfare recipients into the work force would require child-care provisions at a price that would probably end up higher than the current budget for AFDC. But none of the workfare advocates are pro- posing that sort of massive public commitment to child care.

Then there is the problem of jobs. So far, studies show that existing    12
state workfare programs have had virtually no success in improving their participants' incomes or employment rates. Small wonder: nearly half the new jobs generated in recent years pay poverty-level wages; and most welfare recipients will enter jobs that pay near the minimum wage, which is $6,900 a year—26 percent less than the poverty level for a family of three. A menial, low-wage job may be character-building (from a middle-class vantage point), but it will not lift anyone out of poverty.

Some of my feminist activist friends argue that it is too late to stop    13
the workfare juggernaut. The best we can do, they say, is to try to defeat the more pernicious proposals: those that are over-coercive, that do not offer funds for child care, or that would relegate workfare clients to a "subemployee" status unprotected by federal labor and civil rights legislation. Our goal, the pragmatists argue, should be to harness the

current enthusiasm for workfare to push for services welfare recipients genuinely need, such as child care and job training and counseling.

I wish the pragmatists well, but for me, it would be a betrayal of 14 women like Lynn to encourage the workfare bandwagon in any way. Most women, like Lynn, do not take up welfare as a career, but as an emergency measure in a time of personal trauma and dire need. At such times, the last thing they need is to be hustled into a low-wage job, and left to piece together child care, health insurance, transportation, and all the other ingredients of survival. In fact, the main effect of workfare may be to discourage needy women from seeking any help at all—a disastrous result in a nation already suffering from a child poverty rate of nearly 25 percent. Public policy should be aimed at giving impoverished mothers (and, I would add, fathers) the help they so urgently need—not only in the form of job opportunities, but sufficient income support to live on until a job worth taking comes along.

Besides, there is an ancient feminist principle at stake. The premise 15 of all the workfare proposals—the more humane as well as the nasty— is that single mothers on welfare are *not working*. But, to quote the old feminist bumper sticker, EVERY MOTHER IS A WORKING MOTHER. And those who labor to raise their children in poverty—to feed and clothe them on meager budgets and to nurture them in an uncaring world—are working the hardest. The feminist position has never been that all women must pack off their children and enter the work force, but that all women's work—in the home or on the job—should be valued and respected.

*Barbara Ehrenreich's essay stimulated a lively response from Ms. readers. The following letters were published in the February 1988 issue.*

I was absolutely thrilled when I read Barbara Ehrenreich's article on 16 workfare ("A Step Back to the Workhouse?" November 1987). As a single mother who received welfare for several years (with no child support) I'm against everything that workfare stands for. I belong to an organization called Women, Work, and Welfare, a group of current and former welfare recipients trying to empower ourselves and become a part of the decisions that affect our lives as poor women. It seems as if everybody but the welfare recipient herself has a hand in the decisions that are made.

CHERI HONKALA
*Minneapolis, Minn.*

I arrived in Chicago in 1952 with a husband and two children from a 17
camp in Europe. I had another child in 1953, lost a newborn in 1954,
had a miscarriage, a hysterectomy, and a divorce in 1955. I *never* received child support. My ex-husband was remarried within two
months.

I *never* received welfare. I worked in another culture, while in very 18
bad health. I found a two-room flat, had no furniture and slept for
years on the floor. I even went back to school at night and had to
contend with companies like Gulf Oil Corp., which did not believe in
promoting women. But I just slugged on.

By the end of the sixties, I had two daughters in college, and I 19
had bought a house. My total earnings for 1970 from three jobs came
to a whopping $8,000.

A full-time minimum wage job *can* support one adult and one 20
child. One just has to learn how to do it.

URSULA SCHRAMM
*Hurley, Wis.*


I found myself agreeing with the problems that Barbara Ehrenreich 21
outlines in the present workfare program.

Yet deep inside a protesting rumbling exploded when I read that 22
impoverished mothers should receive sufficient income support to live
on "until a job worth taking comes along." *Bullshit!* Sure, we all should
have the right to only work a job we love, but how many of us can
afford to wait for it? That we are often forced to work at jobs that are
not fulfilling says a lot about our society in which more needs to be
changed than just the welfare system!

My mother was forced to go to work when I was nine years old. 23
Our family was in dire financial straits and at the age of 50 she took
a job in a factory. Was that job "worth taking"? Did it utilize her unique
talents? *No!* Did it bring her personal fulfillment? *No!* Did it prevent
the bank from foreclosing on our home? *Yes!* Did it give my mother
the power to overcome our financial crisis and maintain her autonomy?
*Yes!* You tell me if it was "worth taking." That depends on what your
self-respect is worth to you.

GAIL FREI
*Newtown Square, Pa.*


Barbara Ehrenreich omitted a major element in her discussion of the 24
victimization of welfare families: the inability or unwillingness of the
legal system to award *and enforce* realistic child support. Until it stops

being easier to abandon your children than to default on that car loan, women and those who depend on them will be welfare/workfare victims.

SUSAN MARTIN RYNARD
*Durham, N.C.*

I went on welfare when my daughter was three, when I left my husband. I had a high school education, but had always wanted to go to college. I was 25.    25

So, with the help of the government, I got my B.S. in nursing. I worked for several years as an R.N. and then returned to school for my master's degree. For graduate school, I lived on savings, loans, and grants. The loans ($19,000 for undergrad and graduate in all) will be paid off in less than a year, in time for my daughter to begin college!    26

KATHRYN REID
*Silverado, Calif.*

Although I share Barbara Ehrenreich's concerns about workfare and the plight of her friend Lynn, the conclusions she draws strike me as misguided. We live in a society where the myths of the work ethic and self-help are deeply embedded in the popular culture; where resort to the dole is frowned upon unless the need is temporary or arises from disability; where the middle-class majority feels inequitably taxed, as compared to the wealthy, to support a system that directly benefits few of its members.    27

Feminists and other liberals should acknowledge the swelling demand for welfare reform. Our support should be conditional upon the incorporation in any welfare reform plan of provision for *quality* childcare facilities; upon the minimization of coercion; and upon further efforts to compel ex-spouses to pay their fair share of support. Nothing in this approach rules out our going ahead simultaneously with other, parallel efforts to question the mystique of work or to expose the links between welfare and poverty, on the one hand, and capitalism and the subordination of women, on the other.    28

DAVID G. BECKER
*Hanover, N.H.*

California *is* serious about workfare, but we call it GAIN (Greater Avenues for Independence). It offers welfare recipients vocational counseling, up to two years of vocational training, and workshops in how to get and hold a job.    29

GAIN also pays for child care and transportation. No job need be  30
accepted by the recipient unless she/he will *net* at least as much as their
AFCD grant, *including* child care, transportation, and medical insurance. And even then, they will receive funds to cover these costs for
three months after they begin working to help them make the transition to the work force.

JANE KIRCHMAN
*Guerneville, Calif.*

# Questions

1. List the objections Ehrenreich makes to workfare, and pose an answer for each. Your answers may attempt to rebut her objections,
on grounds either of their logic or of information she neglects to
consider (for example, provisions in workfare programs you know
of). Where her objections seem reasonable, propose improvements
to workfare that you would like to see embodied in a program in
your community. The letters answering Ehrenreich may provide
some assistance. If so, quote, summarize, or paraphrase useful
parts of the letters, giving appropriate acknowledgment to the writers.
2. Gloria Steinem in "The Importance of Work" (page 397) does not
address the issue of welfare versus workfare, but a careful reading
of her essay will suggest ideas and arguments on both sides of the
question. Read her essay and report on the two or three ideas that
struck you as interesting contributions to a discussion of workfare.

Ian Buruma

# Work as a Form of Beauty

**D**o the Japanese really work harder than everybody else?  1
They, as well as most experts trying to explain the Japanese phenomenon, certainly think so. Myself, I sometimes wonder. The Japanese
do have a work ethic, not unlike the Protestant one, expressed in such
clichés as: we Japanese don't work to live, we live to work, unlike
foreigners who . . . But ethics in Japan can seldom—if ever—be separated from aesthetics. Work is a form of beauty, in the sense that it
matters less what one does than how one is seen to do it. Japanese,
more than any other people I know, have made work into a spectacle,
if not a fine art.

There is a yearly festival that clearly illustrates this. Among the  2
most celebrated heroes of the common man in Edo were the firemen.
Flamboyantly tattooed with dragons—a beast associated with water
in Japan and thus with firefighting—these noble tough guys were sent
to put out the "Flowers of Edo"[1] by displays of derring-do. They would
climb to impossible heights on bamboo ladders, passing heavy buckets
of water along a human chain with great acrobatic skill. These once
indispensable skills have since been replaced by more modern methods, but they are still practiced every year at the firemen's festival in
Tokyo. The ladder-climbing, bucket-juggling, death-defying acts are
literally a circus of work.

The aesthetic approach to work, exemplified by the brave firemen,  3
is still a feature of the factory floor, too. Factory—and office—walls
are usually festooned with gracefully written Chinese characters po-
etically expressing the company philosophy. Typical would be something like: Work is the essence of the human spirit; spirit is the essence
of harmony. But such slogans aside, it is in the ways of the workers
themselves that a traditional aesthetic can be seen.

The president of a Japanese ball bearing company once said in an  4

Ian Buruma, cultural editor of the *Far Eastern Economic Review* in Hong Kong,
is the author of *Behind the Mask*, a study of contemporary Japanese culture.

[1] Edo is the old name for Tokyo; "Flowers of Edo" are fires. (Editors' note)

*Fire Brigade Performance at Yoshida Bridge, Yokohama*
**Anonymous, c. 1890**

interview that in his factory it took exactly four seconds to grind a ball bearing fifteen millimeters in diameter. He was not joking: watching a Japanese assembly line is like watching a ballet performance: every body movement has been worked out to achieve utmost efficiency; every tool can be reached with minimum effort. Not just that: everything is calculated to allow the worker to accomplish the maximum amount of work in one continuous movement. (Anyone who has seen a sushi chef in action, putting rice and fish together with the utmost speed, grace and economy of movement, will know what I mean. It is a perfect illustration of how function and beauty merge in Japan, to become indistinguishable.)

This does not mean that the Japanese work harder than other peo- 5 ple. Despite the often rather theatrical insistence on working overtime—to show dedication rather than for any practical reason—time wasting is endemic to Japan's vastly overmanned companies. People will spend hours reading comic books rather than break the taboo of leaving before the boss. But there does seem to be an attention to detail and good workmanship, which is often lost in the West. While nineteenth-century methods and a remarkable degree of inefficiency still persist in such institutions as banks or the construction business, industries geared to export are models of productivity. So, while on one hand it takes an army of carpenters and roof builders an endless amount of time to build an ordinary house, motorcycles, TV sets and cameras roll off assembly lines at almost unbelievable speeds. What is more, they are likely to have fewer flaws than similar products elsewhere.

Traditional approaches to work partly explain why. Company loy- 6 alty, discipline and, that magic word, consensus—all these qualities have been fostered in Japan for centuries. Military discipline and loyalty were part of the samurai ethic; the necessity for consultation and consensus-forming was part of village life.

Some of these attitudes can be seen in modern companies, often 7 under a Western guise. Perhaps the most celebrated attitude toward the Japanese working system—seen especially in such books on the "economic miracle" as Ezra Vogel's *Japan as Number One*—is "quality control," actually based on an American idea, imported in the 1950s. Workers are encouraged to participate in the process, not just by checking, but through constantly improving the quality of products and the efficiency with which they are produced. A type of letterbox is to be found at the end of all assembly lines, in which workers are asked to deposit suggestions and criticisms, which are discussed weekly at "quality control meetings." Bright ideas do sometimes make their way to the top and are even occasionally implemented. During the early 1970s it was still common to find slips of paper attached to Japanese products with the names of the workers and controllers responsible for that particular camera or gadget. Thus, a note of humanity was introduced in an otherwise rather faceless production process.

The advantage of such participation is that it makes a dull job more   8 interesting; instead of a sulky work force agitating for longer teabreaks, Japanese workers, ideally, feel that they are involved in the achievements of their companies and take pride in them. There is a tradition in Japan—and in China—of mass-production craftsmen, not on the scale of modern factories, of course, but of large potteries, printing firms or kimono makers. Japanese have always excelled at highly skilled crafts aimed at a huge market.

Worker participation also appeals to the traditional ideal of con-   9 sensus: decisions are not made by one man at the top, but as a result of long consultations in which everybody's voice is heard. Of course it does not always work this way in reality, especially in so-called "one-man" companies led by tough self-made entrepreneurs. But the important thing is that people have the feeling they are not just nuts, bolts or, more to the point these days, digits.

The Japanese love for uniforms is another aspect of the aesthetic   10 work ethic. Uniforms help to foster a collective identity. But apart from that, the work one does ought to be visibly identifiable. Filmmakers wear sunglasses; artists wear berets—the sort of thing painters sported in Montmartre; salarymen wear suits. Even leisure—so often a form of work—has its uniforms: Sunday afternoon hikers wear alpine gear; photo enthusiasts wear safari jackets. All this, so there can be no mistake about what people are up to; it is also an expression of the Japanese belief that once form has been established, substance will follow. The best, most extreme, and thus not entirely typical example of this aesthetic approach in industry is Fanuc Ltd., the world's largest maker of digital machine tools. Company management has the idea that yellow is the color most conducive to high performance. Consequently, everything in the factory, from the machines to the workers' uniforms, is bright yellow.

This aesthetic approach to work is the strongest continuous tra-   11 dition linking old Japan and the world of high technology. A crucial element is the way work aesthetics is taught. The most common Japanese methods are both old and surprisingly uniform. They are based on a Zen-like ideal of cultivated intuition, honed by endless repetition.

This ideal is most romantically expressed in the example of Zen archery. To master the "Way of Archery," said the monks of the Edo period (1603–1868), one had to become one with one's bow. The arrow thus shot would automatically hit the target. What was meant is that the discursive mind, rambling and random, gets in the way of total concentration. To reach the ideal state of readiness one must empty the mind: in other words, stop thinking and you shall find.

The process of acquiring this intuitive technique is based upon a   12
special relationship between master and pupil, a relationship Westerners—and many modern Japanese—like to call "feudal." Whether this is apt or not, such relationships are still very common in Japan, especially in arts and crafts.

Rather than theory, however, I would like to offer some examples.   13
They are imaginary examples and so, to put the ideas across, somewhat caricatural. But each in its own way represents the aesthetic ideal. I shall start with a modern craftsman: a photographer.

Since childhood, Kazuo Ito had wanted to be a photographer.   14
Through a friend's introduction he was taken on as a second assistant by a famous fashion photographer, whom Ito calls *sensei* (master). Professional photographers, like painters, writers or anybody else successful enough to have apprentices (*deshi*) are usually called *sensei*.

Ito lives in a small room at the master's studio. As an apprentice,   15
his duties are without limit. The first thing he does in the morning is make coffee for the first assistant, who comes in at eight. He then polishes lenses, gets the equipment ready, tests the light batteries, anything, as long as he looks busy when the master comes in. Like the daughter-in-law in a traditional household, Ito gets up before everyone else and goes to bed after everybody is asleep.

The assistant is rarely told directly what to do. He has to anticipate   16
the wishes of his superiors. If an order has to be given, it means Ito is already too late. If he guesses wrongly, he is yelled at, not by the master himself, but by the first assistant. This is part of the learning process. Nothing is explained, nothing is explicit. Ito is taught the ropes like a circus monkey, by watching his trainer carefully: right merits a pat on the head (if he's lucky), wrong elicits a humiliating scolding. A slight shake of the head means he has to light the photographer's cigarette; a short grunt means adjust the umbrella on the top light.

Ito is paid the equivalent of one hundred dollars a month, but   17
stays at the studio rent free. His meals, wolfed down during work,

are also paid for by the master. His own money goes toward drinking on Saturday nights with other photographers' assistants. He has been known to get into scrapes, but the master always takes care of the damage. The master has taken the place of Ito's father, in a way, and his indulgence has to be paid for by total obedience during working hours. Ito does not enjoy himself especially, but realizes that his present hardship is a necessary initiation into the life of a photographer. He is proud of his capacity to suffer through it, and consoles himself with the idea that one day he will be called master too.

Such methods do not foster the kind of individual initiative 18 thought to be indispensable to creative work in the West. Indeed, the Japanese have a reputation for being imitators, technically polished imitators, but copycats nonetheless. Of course, mimicry is the essence of learning everywhere, but Japanese appear to carry it to extremes. Leaving the romantic matter of unique individuality aside, this stereotypical view of the Japanese is not entirely accurate. A wise Japanese—I forget who—once put it this way: only when everybody wears exactly the same kimono can one detect true individual differences. Acting in the Kabuki theater comes about as close as one can get to this aesthetic.

Becoming an actor of female roles (*onnagata*) in Kabuki had not 19 been a matter of choice for Ayame. He was born into a Kabuki actor's family, and he learned the rudimentary steps of traditional dance as soon as he could walk. His grandfather would move his hands and feet for him, over and over again, until he could do it himself. In his early teens his slender build, graceful movement and high-pitched voice made the specialization in female roles an obvious choice. The only male roles he subsequently played were those of effeminate young lovers, the type Japanese matrons, for some reason, have always idolized.

Ayame was preparing for his grand entrance as an Edo-period 20 courtesan. He had applied his makeup in a style unchanged since the play was written. While waiting for his cue, he sipped from a cup of green tea, supplied by one of his apprentices, who watched his every move. As with the photographer's assistant, a Kabuki apprentice is rarely told anything directly. He must learn intuitively, as it were. To get it wrong, in the olden days, meant a severe beating.

When he stepped onto the stage, the audience applauded loudly 21 and members of a professional claque, seated in various parts of the auditorium, called out his stage name. His gracefully stylized walk and the coquettish movement of the eyes reminded connoisseurs of his grandfather, also a famous *onnagata*, who acted in the style of his father, a celebrated nineteenth-century actor.

Ayame's disciples were looking at him intently from backstage. 22 One day the best of them might, with luck and hard work, emulate his master's technique to perfection. He would have to be so much like him that he could wear his style like a skin. That would not be enough, however. True mastery lies in the way one's own skin comes almost imperceptibly peeping through the master's. Only then can one be said to control the style and not vice versa. There are only a few people left who could recognize the new skin, but that does not in any way diminish its greatness.

The repetitive zeal with which Japanese go about honing their 23 skills makes them seem obsessed with form, with mechanics rather than content. A rather touching example of this is the first reaction of Japanese audiences to moving pictures: they turned round their chairs to watch the projector, a source of much more fascination than the images flickering on the screen. Added to their reputation as copycats is their image as robots. This, too, is missing the point. The preoccupation with style does not necessarily mean the lack of a soul; just as Japanese do not feel that good manners make a human being less "real," "himself," "natural" or whatever term one wishes to use for that elusive inner core of man. Style, in the post-romantic West, is largely an extension of man's ego; traditional style in Japan—and China, for that matter—is more a transformation of the ego: to acquire a perfect technique, one eliminates, as it were, one's individuality, only to regain it by transcending the skill. This new individuality is not the expression of one's real private life, but an individual interpretation of something already there and thus in the public domain.

Private life in Japan is just that: private. An artist or, for that matter, 24 a waitress is not expected to reveal his—or her—private "self," but his public one. The borderline between public and private worlds is much clearer in Japan than it is in the West (as in China, many Japanese houses have walls around them). Thus, the public self is not seen as a humiliating infringement on the "real" self. Of course, in certain periods, Japanese artists have rebelled against this division and the rigidity of style by going to the opposite extreme: writers of the "natural" school saw it as their vocation to burden the reader with the minutest details of their private lives. One key, I think, to the public aesthetic is the skill of an elevator girl.

Yoko Sato is nineteen and she is being trained to be an elevator 25 girl in a department store. She lives at home with her parents but needs the extra money she earns to buy clothes and go to discos on Saturday nights. It's hard being an elevator girl for, as Yoko is ceaselessly told, she is the face of the store. If she does something wrong or displeases a customer, the company loses face.

Yoko does not much enjoy the lectures on company loyalty or  26 philosophy written in fussy Chinese characters by the owner of the store, who likes to expound at length on the uniqueness of his firm. Still, Yoko learned all the lines by heart and recites them every morning with her colleagues. It may be a lot of boring nonsense, but this is the way things are done, and Yoko wants to do a good job.

The voice and bowing lessons are a little more interesting. Yoko  27 always prides herself on being a good mimic—her imitations of the pompous section chief make her friends laugh. The perfect elevator girl's voice is high-pitched, on the verge of falsetto, and seeming to bubble over into merry laughter, without actually doing so. This is not an easy effect to achieve and it takes hours of drilling. Yoko's name was called out by the teacher, asking her to come forward. She was told to speak the following lines: this lift is going up, this lift is going down; and again: this lift is going up . . . and again. Her pitch was too low and her delivery not quite sprightly enough. The teacher told her to practice at home.

Bowing lessons are a more mechanical exercise. An inventive  28 young engineer in the design department devised a bowing machine. It is a steel contraption a bit like those metal detectors through which one must pass at international airports. An electronic eye, built into the machine, registers exactly the angle of the bow and lights flicker on at fifteen degrees, thirty degrees and forty-five degrees. The teacher of the bowing class explained that the "fifteen bow" was for an informal greeting to colleagues. The "thirty bow" was appropriate for meeting senior members of the store, and the deepest bow essential when welcoming clients, shoppers and other visitors. Much of the average day of an elevator girl is spent at a perfect forty-five degree angle.

Yoko does not find this in the least humiliating, or even dull.  29 Learning a skill like this is a challenge, and she is eager to get it just right. The girls were lined up in front of the machine and one by one, like pupils at a gymnastics class, they walked up to make three bows. Yoko missed the first one by several degrees; the disapproving noise of an electronic buzzer told her so. She blushed. The second, thirty degrees, she got wrong again, by inches. Determined to get it right the next time, she bent down, back straight, fingers together and eyes trained on the floor about three feet from her toes—the light flashed, she did it, a smile of contentment spread across her face.

This is an extreme—though in Japan by no means despised—ex-  30 ample of the insistence on form and of the way it is taught. The training of elevator girls also points to another constant factor in Japanese attitudes to work: form in human relations. The importance of etiquette and ritual in Japanese work is vital. When male bosses tell their female staff that serving tea, bowing to clients and other such ceremonial functions are as necessary as the jobs usually reserved for men, they are only being partly hypocritical. To be sure, many men would feel threatened if too many women encroached on their traditional domains. It is much safer to insist that women should stick to the home after marriage or, in the case of unmarried "office ladies" (OLs), stick to making tea or other ceremonies. But, at the same time, Japanese do attach far more importance to such decorative functions than Westerners tend to do; and they genuinely feel that women do them best. Although some Western tourists might find the artificial ways of elevator girls grating, humiliating or, at best, quaint, Japanese feel comfortable with them and indeed miss such service when it is not provided.

Men, too, spend much of their time on the rites of human relations.  31 Although Japanese have a strong sense of hierarchy, decisions are based upon at least a show of consensus. This makes it difficult to take individual initiatives, and passing the buck is therefore a national sport. Consensus, as indeed all forms of Japanese business, is built on personal relations. These relations are based on mutual obligations: if I do this for you, you do that for me. Such favors are rarely expressed directly and relations take much time and effort to cement. This is where most salarymen—the middle-ranking samurai of today—come in. Because there are so many salarymen and so many relations to cement, many hours are spent in coffee shops during the day and bars and restaurants at night. This may seem inconsequential or even parasitic to the Western mind. It certainly does not make for efficiency. But just as the trade of rugs in the Middle East cannot proceed without endless cups of tea, the coffee shop workers are the backbone of the Japanese miracle. Let us turn again to an example.

Every table at the Café L'Etoile, a coffee shop in the Ginza, was  32 occupied. Through the thick screen of cigarette smoke one could just discern Kazuo Sasaki, a young employee of one of the largest advertising companies. He was exchanging *meishi* (name cards) with three men from a small public relations firm. All four of them studied the cards carefully, made polite hissing noises and sat down. Sasaki ordered his tenth cup of coffee and lit his thirteenth filter-tipped cigarette.

His order was taken by a uniformed young waiter who yelled out 33 the command to another waiter, who shouted it to another link in the chain. The effect was highly theatrical—a spectacle of work, as it were. This particular gimmick was unique to L'Etoile and new waiters were drilled endlessly until they got it just right.

So much of Sasaki's day was spent meeting people in coffee shops 34 that it was easier to reach him at Café L'Etoile than at his office. He has been working for his company for four years. His main job is to delegate commissions taken by his company to smaller companies, who then often delegate them to even smaller firms.

Business was not much discussed at Café L'Etoile. It would be 35 indelicate to come directly to the point. Instead, Sasaki had become expert at discussing golf handicaps—the nearest he got to a golf course himself was one of those practicing ranges where one spent hours hitting balls into a giant net. He also had an endless supply of jokes about last night's hangover, or jocular comments on his client's sexual prowess. He always knew the latest baseball results and could talk for hours about television programs. On those rare occasions when an eccentric client insisted on talking about politics or books, Sasaki was at least a good listener. He has, in short, the social graces of a very superior barber.

In a country where so much depends on social graces, this is not 36 to be despised. It is, I think rightly, argued that human relationships in Japan transcend abstract ideals of right and wrong. This is not true, for instance, in the Judeo-Christian tradition, where God is the final arbiter, in whose eyes we shall be judged. To commit perjury in a Japanese court, to protect one's boss, is the moral thing to do. Loyalty transcends a mere law. (This was proven several times during the long case against former Prime Minister Kakuei Tanaka.)

This principle permeates working relationships at every level of 37 Japanese society. It explains, for example, the workings of the Japanese underworld. The underworld in Japan, though not necessarily respectable, is in many ways an overworld. Gangsters have their jobs to do, just like milkmen or prime ministers. Their roles in society, though, again, not respectable, are acknowledged. An often told story is about a man who woke up one night to find a *dorobō* (thief) going through his wallet. According to this tale, the man let him be, for a thief has to make a living too.

Tetsu Yamazaki is a *yakuza* (gangster). He prefers another term for 38 his trade, however: *ninkyōdō* (The Way of Chivalry). This sounds more traditional, more in keeping with Yamazaki's image of himself. Like many of his colleagues, Yamazaki likes to dissociate himself from the common criminal who, alas, has begun to predominate in the Japanese underworld.

Yamazaki, *oyabun* (boss, or literally father figure) of his gang, Ya- 39 mazakigumi, was expecting the local police chief for tea. This official had a habit of dropping in at the Yamazakigumi headquarters for afternoon chats. He kept abreast this way of the latest underworld gossip and in exchange for a good tip, he let Yamazaki carry on with his operations—within traditionally and mutually understood limits, of course. Extortion, protection rackets, prostitution were all right (somebody had to do those jobs), but physical violence against innocent people was not. Extortion, to name one occupation, does not always work without at least the threat of violence; but that fine line could always be worked out between gangster boss and policeman. The police chief was a reasonable man and Yamazaki, when necessary, a generous one.

The policeman arrived. He took his shoes off at the door and was 40 loudly greeted by bowing young mobsters with crew cuts. He was ushered into the main room, where he made an informal bow to Yamazaki who bowed in return. The boss, dressed in a green, pin-striped suit, a yellow shirt, red tie and diamond clip, barked an order. A young mobster bowed, and slipped noiselessly into the kitchen, from where he emerged five minutes later with two cups of tea.

The police chief, after discussing the weather and inquiring after 41 Yamazaki's golf handicap, asked a question about a recent murder case. He knew which gang was involved. He also knew that the boss of that gang was in debt to Yamazaki. Yamazaki himself was in some trouble over an amphetamine bust. So the police chief asked if perhaps Yamazaki could persuade his fellow boss to hand over the murderer, and then the amphetamine case could be forgotten.

Yamazaki thought this was a reasonable proposition and called up 42 his friend. He told him what was up and asked him to hand over the man as a personal favor. Now, the "murderer" did not have to be the man who actually did it. It is an old Japanese—and Chinese—tradition that underlings take the full rap for crimes committed by their superiors. Unlike plea bargaining in the United States, where offenders get lesser punishments for cooperating, the Japanese system actually allows innocent people to substitute for the real culprits. These "innocents" are obliged to do this out of loyalty to their bosses. It is, in short, their duty.

There is something in it for the substitute, however, for after he 43 gets out of jail there will be certain promotion waiting for him. The man will be happy, the murderer—a senior in the gang hierarchy—even happier. The police will have done their duty and Yamazaki will be off the amphetamine hook.

Their work concluded, the two men promised to meet again soon 44 and the police chief took his leave. Next, Yamazaki received a magazine reporter who wanted to know about traditional customs of the yakuza world. The boss was in his element here, as he liked to hold forth on the noble traditions he upheld. He was the heir of Kunisada Chuji (a legendary nineteenth-century Robin Hood type of gangster). If it weren't for men like him, who took care of their boys and taught them the ways of chivalry, the streets of Japan would no longer be safe. The good yakuza still understood the Japanese code of honor, forgotten by the young who were corrupted by communist schoolteachers and foreign fashions. Leftists were selling Japan out to the foreigners and it was his duty, as a *yakuza* of the old school, to stop this from happening. When asked about the nobility of extortion, violence and amphetamine trafficking, Yamazaki got quite indignant: only bad mobsters engage in such practices; good *yakuza* had nothing to do with it; he was a protector of the poor, just like Kunisada Chuji; why, if the reporter wanted to have proof of this, he could call the local police chief: he knew all about it.

Human relations based on hierarchy are a comfort to many, es- 45 pecially in a highly competitive world. In most Japanese companies seniority counts for more than competence and, ideally, one's job is forever assured. This works best for mediocrity—which, for face-saving reasons, is rarely exposed—and worst for talented mavericks.

Talent, being highly individualistic and thus socially troublesome, 46 is not always highly regarded in Japan. Hard work and skill, especially in the sense of dexterity (*kiyō*), are the two qualities Japanese pride themselves on as a people. The traditional Japanese stress on refining and miniaturizing everything—the Korean critic Yi O Ryong argues that this is the key to Japanese culture—may explain the modern success in transistor, microchip or camera making. But although manual dexterity, the appearance of consensus and the discipline—not to say docility—of the Japanese rank and file account for some of Japan's success story, no country can succeed without talented mavericks. Despite the Japanese saying that nails that stick out must be hammered in, there are those odd, talented exceptions, even in Japan, who refuse to be hammered in. Though sometimes respected, such people are rarely liked. The great Japanese filmmaker Akira Kurosawa, known in Japan as The Emperor, is a case in point. He is undoubtedly one of the greatest artists of the century, but Japanese critics have consistently tried to pull him off his pedestal, often in snide personal attacks. He has consistently refused to toe the social line; he has neither masters nor pupils; the ritual of human relations is less important to him than his talent. He is, in short, a loner, as is almost every truly gifted man or woman in this collectivist society.

But the creative force in Japan comes from these loners. They tend   47 to come to the fore mostly in periods of social instability. The immediate aftermath of World War II seems to have been especially congenial to nonconformist entrepreneurs. Akio Morita, founder of Sony, Konosuke Matsushita of Matsushita and Soichirō Honda, the grand old man behind the motor cars, immediately come to mind. The interesting thing about such creative oddballs is that once they make it to the top, they almost invariably become traditional masters, laying down the rules for the young to follow. They are more than teachers of technical skills or business methods, in the manner of such figures as Lee Iacocca. In fact, they conform more closely to the image of the classical Confucian sage, concerned with ethics and moral philosophy rather than technique. Matsushita wrote a kind of bible, expounding his philosophy; and Honda's autobiography has an equally lofty tone.

Recently the enormous success of high technology industries has   48 spawned a new generation of mavericks—whiz kids, laying the paths to Japanese versions of Silicon Valley. Such people are especially interesting as they combine the old Japanese penchant for miniature refinement and uncommon individualism. They often get their start in research and development departments of large companies, but proceed to break with the time-honored tradition of company loyalty to start their own firms. According to an official at the Ministry of International Trade and Industry there are now about five thousand "highly innovative" small companies with the potential to emerge as future Sonys or Hondas. No doubt their leaders, too, will one day write their books and become masters.

Although the difference between artists and craftsmen has never   49 been as clear in Japan as in the post-romantic West, there have always been mavericks in the arts as well. But those who do not follow masters often pay a heavy price. The number of suicides among Japanese writers in this century cannot be a mere romantic aberration. Such artists, like the gung-ho entrepreneurs, also thrive in times of unrest. The turbulent early nineteenth century produced such highly eccentric playwrights as Tsuruya Namboku and artists such as Ekin, who rejected every traditional school and persisted in a highly individualistic style. Two famous eccentric geniuses of our own time are Kurosawa and the author Yukio Mishima (1925–1970), Japan's most celebrated twentieth-century novelist, who ended his life at forty-five in a dramatic suicide.

Creative loners are by no means limited to men. In some periods   50 of Japanese history women had more freedom to express themselves than men, paradoxically because they had less freedom to engage in other public pursuits. Perhaps the greatest period for Japanese literature was the Heian (794–1185), particularly the tenth century, when the *kana* syllabary, a truly indigenous script, was developed. While educated men—virtually restricted to the aristocracy—still wrote in literary Chinese, talented women expressed themselves in the vernacular; the obvious example being Murasaki Shikibu (978–1015/31?), the author of *Genji monogatari (The Tale of Genji)*. One of the greatest writers of modern Japan was also a woman: Higuchi Ichiyō (1872–1896), who lived and died—very young—at the end of the nineteenth century. Both women wrote mostly about loneliness—a common theme in literature and a usual fate of writers anywhere, to be sure, but especially in Japan, where isolation from the common herd is particularly keenly felt.

So originality and creativity do exist in Japan. But they are all too   51 often stifled by the pressure to conform. It takes tremendous courage to continue on in one's individual course. Let us be thankful for those few who do. But while such gifted eccentrics are rarer than in countries where individualism is fostered, there is an advantage to the Japanese preference for skill over originality. In places where everyone wants to be a star, but mediocrity necessarily prevails, there is a disturbing lack of pride in an ordinary job well done. In Western Europe there is even a perverse tendency to be proud of sloppiness. Japan may have fewer Nobel Prize winners than, say, Britain, but to see a shop girl wrap a package or a factoryworker assemble a bike is to see routine work developed to a fine art. This, the lack of Nobel Prizes not withstanding, may be Japan's grandest tradition.

# Questions

1.  In paragraph 1 Buruma says (and he then develops the idea in later paragraphs) that in Japan work can seldom be separated from aesthetics: "It matters less what one does than how one is seen to do it." Does such a conception play any role in the United States? If so, what examples can you give?

2.  In paragraph 18 Buruma quotes a wise Japanese as saying, "Only when everybody wears exactly the same kimono can one detect true individual differences." What does this mean, and do you agree with it? Whether or not you agree, explain the idea to someone who doesn't grasp the sentence. And while you are at it, explain the relevance of the idea to the topic of the essay—work.

3.  Explain in your own words the contrasting notions of style in the East and West, referred to in paragraph 23.

4.  In paragraphs 26–30 Buruma discusses the training an elevator girl participates in. He says that "Yoko does not find [her training] in the least humiliating, or even dull." You probably have not been trained to operate an elevator in a department store, but have you ever gone through training that is at least somewhat similar to Yoko's? If so, how did you respond to such training? Did the culture in which you grew up prepare you to accept such training, or did it instill in you values that conflict with it?

5.  Explain Buruma's final sentence, taking into account the entire essay.

6.  What do you think of this essay as a piece of expository writing? What is skillful or unskilled about it? (You might devote your analysis to one paragraph, or to a group of paragraphs such as 32–36, on Mr. Sasaki's day at the cafe, or 37–44, on the gangster Yamazaki.)

## Sir Thomas More

# Work and Play in Utopia

### Their Occupations

Agriculture is the one occupation at which everyone 1
works, men and women alike, with no exceptions. They are trained
in it from childhood, partly in the schools where they learn theory,
and partly through field trips to nearby farms, which make something
like a game of practical instruction. On these trips they not only watch
the work being done, but frequently pitch in and get a workout by
doing the jobs themselves.

Besides farm work (which, as I said, everybody performs), each 2
person is taught a particular trade of his own, such as wool-working,
linen-making, masonry, metal-work, or carpentry. There is no other
craft that is practiced by any considerable number of them. Throughout
the island people wear, and down through the centuries they have
always worn, the same style of clothing, except for the distinction
between the sexes, and between married and unmarried persons. Their
clothing is attractive, does not hamper bodily movement, and serves
for warm as well as cold weather; what is more, each household can
make its own.

Every person (and this includes women as well as men) learns a 3
second trade, besides agriculture. As the weaker sex, women practice
the lighter crafts, such as working in wool or linen; the heavier crafts
are assigned to the men. As a rule, the son is trained to his father's
craft; for which most feel a natural inclination. But if anyone is attracted

Sir Thomas More (1478–1535) was an extremely able English administrator and
diplomat who rose to high rank in the government of King Henry VIII, but when
he opposed the King's break with Roman Catholicism (Henry demanded that his
subjects recognize him as Supreme Head of the Church), More was beheaded.
Four hundred years later, in 1935, he was canonized.

More wrote *Utopia* in Latin (the international language of the Renaissance)
in 1516. The word is Greek for "no place," but the Greek-sounding names for
officials in this imaginary land—a syphogrant is elected by a group of thirty
households, and a tranibor governs a group of ten syphogrants—have no meaning. Though the book is fictional, setting forth a playful vision of an ideal society,
there is no story; it is not a novel but a sort of essay.

"Work and Play" (editors' title) is about a tenth of the book.

to another occupation, he is transferred by adoption into a family practicing the trade he prefers. When anyone makes such a change, both
his father and the authorities make sure that he is assigned to a grave
and responsible householder. After a man has learned one trade, if he
wants to learn another, he gets the same permission. When he has
learned both, he pursues whichever he likes better, unless the city
needs one more than the other.

The chief and almost the only business of the syphogrants is to 4
manage matters so that no one sits around in idleness, and assure that
everyone works hard at his trade. But no one has to exhaust himself
with endless toil from early morning to late at night, as if he were a
beast of burden. Such wretchedness, really worse than slavery, is the
common lot of workmen in all countries, except Utopia. Of the day's
twenty-four hours, the Utopians devote only six to work. They work
three hours before noon, when they go to dinner. After dinner they
rest for a couple of hours, then go to work for another three hours.
Then they have supper, and at eight o'clock (counting the first hour
after noon as one), they go to bed and sleep eight hours.

The other hours of the day, when they are not working, eating, 5
or sleeping, are left to each man's individual discretion, provided he
does not waste them in roistering or sloth, but uses them busily in
some occupation that pleases him. Generally these periods are devoted
to intellectual activity. For they have an established custom of giving
public lectures before daybreak; attendance at these lectures is required
only of those who have been specially chosen to devote themselves to
learning, but a great many other people, both men and women, choose
voluntarily to attend. Depending on their interests, some go to one
lecture, some to another. But if anyone would rather devote his spare
time to his trade, as many do who don't care for the intellectual life,
this is not discouraged; in fact, such persons are commended as especially useful to the commonwealth.

After supper, they devote an hour to recreation, in their gardens 6
when the weather is fine, or during winter weather in the common
halls where they have their meals. There they either play music or
amuse themselves with conversation. They know nothing about gambling with dice, or other such foolish and ruinous games. They do play
two games not unlike our own chess. One is a battle of numbers, in
which one number captures another. The other is a game in which the
vices fight a battle against the virtues. The game is set up to show how
the vices oppose one another, yet readily combine against the virtues;
then, what vices oppose what virtues, how they try to assault them

openly or undermine them in secret; how the virtues can break the strength of the vices or turn their purposes to good; and finally, by what means one side or the other gains the victory.

But in all this, you may get a wrong impression, if we don't go back and consider one point more carefully. Because they allot only six hours to work, you might think the necessities of life would be in scant supply. This is far from the case. Their working hours are ample to provide not only enough but more than enough of the necessities and even the conveniences of life. You will easily appreciate this if you consider how large a part of the population in other countries exists without doing any work at all. In the first place, hardly any of the women, who are a full half of the population, work; or, if they do, then as a rule their husbands lie snoring in the bed. Then there is a great lazy gang of priests and so-called religious men. Add to them all the rich, especially the landlords, who are commonly called gentlemen and nobility. Include with them their retainers, that mob of swaggering bullies. Finally, reckon in with these the sturdy and lusty beggars, who go about feigning some disease as an excuse for their idleness. You will certainly find that the things which satisfy our needs are produced by far fewer hands than you had supposed.

And now consider how few of those who do work are doing really essential things. For where money is the standard of everything, many superfluous trades are bound to be carried on simply to satisfy luxury and licentiousness. Suppose the multitude of those who now work were limited to a few trades, and set to producing more and more of those conveniences and commodities that nature really requires. They would be bound to produce so much that the prices would drop, and the workmen would be unable to gain a living. But suppose again that all the workers in useless trades were put to useful ones, and that all the idlers (who now guzzle twice as much as the workingmen who make what they consume) were assigned to productive tasks—well, you can easily see how little time each man would have to spend working, in order to produce all the goods that human needs and conveniences require—yes, and human pleasure too, as long as it's true and natural pleasure.

The experience of Utopia makes this perfectly apparent. In each city and its surrounding countryside barely five hundred of those men and women whose age and strength make them fit for work are exempted from it. Among these are the syphogrants, who by law are free not to work; yet they don't take advantage of the privilege, preferring to set a good example to their fellow-citizens. Some others are permanently exempted from work so that they may devote themselves to study, but only on the recommendation of the priests and through a secret vote of the syphogrants. If any of these scholars disappoints their hopes, he becomes a workman again. On the other hand, it happens from time to time that a craftsman devotes his leisure so earnestly to study, and makes such progress as a result, that he is relieved of manual labor, and promoted to the class of learned men. From this class of scholars are chosen ambassadors, priests, tranibors, and the prince himself, who used to be called Barzanes, but in their modern tongue is known as Ademus. Since all the rest of the population is neither idle nor occupied in useless trades, it is easy to see why they produce so much in so short a working day.

Apart from all this, in several of the necessary crafts their way of    10 life requires less total labor than does that of people elsewhere. In other countries, building and repairing houses requires the constant work of many men, because what a father has built, his thriftless heir lets fall into ruin; and then his successor has to repair, at great expense, what could easily have been maintained at a very small charge. Further, even when a man has built a splendid house at large cost, someone else may think he has finer taste, let the first house fall to ruin, and then build another one somewhere else for just as much money. But among the Utopians, where everything has been established, and the commonwealth is carefully regulated, building a brand-new home on a new site is a rare event. They are not only quick to repair damage, but foresighted in preventing it. The result is that their buildings last for a very long time with minimum repairs; and the carpenters and masons sometimes have so little to do, that they are set to hewing timber and cutting stone in case some future need for it should arise.

Consider, too, how little labor their clothing requires. Their work    11 clothes are loose garments made of leather which last as long as seven years. When they go out in public, they cover these rough working-clothes with a cloak. Throughout the entire island, everyone wears the same colored cloak, which is the color of natural wool. As a result, they not only need less wool than people in other countries, but what they do need is less expensive. They use linen cloth most, because it requires least labor. They like linen cloth to be white and wool cloth to be clean; but they put no price on fineness of texture. Elsewhere a man is not satisfied with four or five woolen cloaks of different colors and as many silk shirts, or if he's a show-off, even ten of each are not enough. But a Utopian is content with a single cloak, and generally wears it for two seasons. There is no reason at all why he should want any others, for if he had them, he would not be better protected against the cold, nor would he appear in any way better dressed.

When there is an abundance of everything, as a result of everyone   12
working at useful trades, and nobody consuming to excess, then great numbers of the people often go out to work on the roads, if any of them need repairing. And when there is no need even for this sort of public work, then the officials very often proclaim a short work day, since they never force their citizens to perform useless labor. The chief aim of their constitution and government is that, whenever public needs permit, all citizens should be free, so far as possible, to withdraw their time and energy from the service of the body, and devote themselves to the freedom and culture of the mind. For that, they think, is the real happiness of life. . . .

## Their Moral Philosophy

They conclude, after carefully considering and weighing the   13
matter, that all our actions and the virtues exercised within them look toward pleasure and happiness at their ultimate end.

By pleasure they understand every state or movement of body or   14
mind in which man naturally finds delight. They are right in considering man's appetites natural. By simply following his senses and his right reason a man may discover what is pleasant by nature—it is a delight which does not injure others, which does not preclude a greater pleasure, and which is not followed by pain. But a pleasure which is against nature, and which men call "delightful" only by the emptiest of fictions (as if one could change the real nature of things just by changing their names), does not really make for happiness; in fact they say, it destroys happiness. And the reason is that men whose minds are filled with false ideas of pleasure have no room left for true and genuine delight. As a matter of fact, there are a great many things which have no sweetness in them, but are mainly or entirely bitter— yet which through the perverse enticements of evil lusts are considered very great pleasures, and even the supreme goals of life.

Among those who pursue this false pleasure the Utopians include   15
those whom I mentioned before, the men who think themselves finer fellows because they wear finer clothes. These people are twice mistaken: first in thinking their clothes better than anyone else's, and then in thinking themselves better because of their clothes. As far as a coat's usefulness goes, what does it matter if it was woven of thin thread or

thick? Yet they act as if they were set apart by nature herself, rather than their own fantasies; they strut about, and put on airs. Because they have a fancy suit, they think themselves entitled to honors they would never have expected if they were poorly dressed, and they get very angry if someone passes them by without showing special respect.

It is the same kind of absurdity to be pleased by empty, ceremonial 16 honors. What true and natural pleasure can you get from someone's bent knee or bared head? Will the creaks in your own knees be eased thereby, or the madness in your head? The phantom of false pleasure is illustrated by other men who run mad with delight over their own blue blood, plume themselves on their nobility, and applaud themselves for all their rich ancestors (the only ancestors worth having nowadays), and all their ancient family estates. Even if they don't have the shred of an estate themselves, or if they've squandered every penny of their inheritance, they don't consider themselves a bit less noble.

In the same class the Utopians put those people I described before, 17 who are mad for jewelry and gems, and think themselves divinely happy if they find a good specimen, especially of the sort which happens to be fashionable in their country at the time—for stones vary in value from one market to another. The collector will not make an offer for the stone till it's taken out of its setting, and even then he will not buy unless the dealer guarantees and gives security that it is a true and genuine stone. What he fears is that his eyes will be deceived by a counterfeit. But if you consider the matter, why should a counterfeit give any less pleasure when your eyes cannot distinguish it from a real gem? Both should be of equal value to you, as they would be, in fact, to a blind man.

Speaking of false pleasure, what about those who pile up money, 18 not because they want to do anything with the heap, but so they can sit and look at it? Is that true pleasure they experience, or aren't they simply cheated by a show of pleasure? Or what of those with the opposite vice, the men who hide away money they will never use and perhaps never even see again? In their anxiety to hold onto their money, they actually lose it. For what else happens when you deprive yourself, and perhaps other people too, of a chance to use money, by burying it in the ground? And yet when the miser has hidden his treasure, he exults over it as if his mind were now free to rejoice. Suppose someone stole it, and the miser died ten years later, knowing nothing of the theft. During all those ten years, what did it matter whether the money was stolen or not? In either case, it was equally useless to the owner.

To these false and foolish pleasures they add gambling, which they 19 have heard about, though they've never tried it, as well as hunting and hawking. What pleasure can there be, they wonder, in throwing dice on a table? If there were any pleasure in the action, wouldn't doing it over and over again quickly make one tired of it? What pleasure can there be in listening to the barking and yelping of dogs—isn't that rather a disgusting noise? Is there any more real pleasure when a dog chases a rabbit than there is when a dog chases a dog? If what you like is fast running, there's plenty of that in both cases; they're just about the same. But if what you really want is slaughter, if you want to see a living creature torn apart under your eyes, then the whole thing is wrong. You ought to feel nothing but pity when you see the hare fleeing from the hound, the weak creature tormented by the stronger, the fearful and timid beast brutalized by the savage one, the harmless hare killed by the cruel dog. The Utopians, who regard this whole activity of hunting as unworthy of free men, have assigned it, accordingly, to their butchers, who as I said before, are all slaves. In their eyes, hunting is the lowest thing even butchers can do. In the slaughterhouse, their work is more useful and honest—besides which, they kill animals only from necessity; but in hunting they seek merely their own pleasure from the killing and mutilating of some poor little creature. Taking such relish in the sight of death, even if it's only beasts, reveals, in the opinion of the Utopians, a cruel disposition. Or if he isn't cruel to start with, the hunter quickly becomes so through the constant practice of such brutal pleasures.

Most men consider these activities, and countless others like them, to be pleasures; but the Utopians say flatly they have nothing at all to do with real pleasure since there's nothing naturally pleasant about them. They often please the senses, and in this they are like pleasure, but that does not alter their basic nature. The enjoyment doesn't arise from the experience itself, but only from the perverse mind of the individual, as a result of which he mistakes the bitter for the sweet, just as pregnant women, whose taste has been turned awry, sometimes think pitch and tallow taste sweeter than honey. A man's taste may be similarly depraved, by disease or by custom, but that does not change the nature of pleasure, or of anything else.

# Questions

1.  What does More assume are the only functions of clothing? Do you agree with More, or do you find other important reasons why people wear the clothes that they wear?

2.  The "work ethic" assumes that labor is good in itself—that there is some sort of virtue in work. Further, many people assume that work, at least certain kinds of work done under certain conditions, affords happiness to the worker. What does More's attitude seem to be on these two related points?

3.  What is More's opinion of hunting? What arguments in support of hunting are commonly offered? In your opinion, does More successfully counter those arguments?

4.  In approximately 500 words set forth More's assumptions about the sources of happiness.

5.  More says that each Utopian is free to do what he wishes with leisure hours, "provided he does not waste them in roistering or sloth." (By the way, since the Utopians work six hours a day, if they sleep eight hours they have ten hours of free time.) In 500 words develop an argument for or against this proviso concerning the pursuit of happiness. (You may want to recall that our own government to some degree regulates our pleasure, for instance by outlawing bullfights.)

6.  Note the passage (paragraph 6) in which More describes two games enjoyed by Utopians. Imitating More's style in describing the second game, write a paragraph describing a video game as a Utopian, or anti-Utopian, recreation.

Marie Winn

# The End of Play

Of all the changes that have altered the topography of    1
childhood, the most dramatic has been the disappearance of childhood
play. Whereas a decade or two ago children were easily distinguished
from the adult world by the very nature of their play, today children's
occupations do not differ greatly from adult diversions.

Marie Winn, born in Czechoslovakia in 1936, came to New York when she was still a child. She later graduated from Radcliffe College and then did further academic work at Columbia University. Our selection comes from *Childhood Without Children* (1983), a book based in part on interviews with hundreds of children and parents.

Infants and toddlers, to be sure, continue to follow certain timeless 2
patterns of manipulation and exploration; adolescents, too, have not
changed their free-time habits so very much, turning as they ever have
towards adult pastimes and amusements in their drive for autonomy,
self-mastery, and sexual discovery. It is among the ranks of school-
age children, those six-to-twelve-year-olds who once avidly filled their
free moments with childhood play, that the greatest change is evident.
In the place of traditional, sometimes ancient childhood games that
were still popular a generation ago, in the place of fantasy and make-
believe play—"You be the mommy and I'll be the daddy"—doll play
or toy-soldier play, jump-rope play, ball-bouncing play, today's children have substituted television viewing and, most recently, video
games.

Many parents have misgivings about the influence of television. 3
They sense that a steady and time-consuming exposure to passive entertainment might damage the ability to play imaginatively and re-
sourcefully, or prevent this ability from developing in the first place.
A mother of two school-age children recalls: "When I was growing
up, we used to go out into the vacant lots and make up week-long
dramas and sagas. This was during third, fourth, fifth grades. But my
own kids have never done that sort of thing, and somehow it bothers
me. I wish we had cut down on the TV years ago, and maybe the kids
would have learned how to play."

The testimony of parents who eliminate television for periods of 4
time strengthens the connection between children's television watching and changed play patterns. Many parents discover that when their
children don't have television to fill their free time, they resort to the
old kinds of imaginative, traditional "children's play." Moreover, these
parents often observe that under such circumstances "they begin to
seem more like children" or "they act more childlike." Clearly, a part
of the definition of childhood, in adults' minds, resides in the nature
of children's play.

Children themselves sometimes recognize the link between play 5
and their own special definition as children. In an interview about
children's books with four ten-year-old girls, one of them said: "I read
this story about a girl my age growing up twenty years ago—you
know, in 1960 or so—and she seemed so much younger than me in
her behavior. Like she might be playing with dolls, or playing all sorts
of children's games, or jump-roping or something." The other girls all
agreed that they had noticed a similar discrepancy between themselves
and fictional children in books of the past: those children seemed more
like children. "So what do *you* do in your spare time, if you don't play

with dolls or play make-believe games or jump rope or do things kids did twenty years ago?" they were asked. They laughed and answered, "We watch TV."

But perhaps other societal factors have caused children to give up 6 play. Children's greater exposure to adult realities, their knowledge of adult sexuality, for instance, might make them more sophisticated, less likely to play like children. Evidence from the counterculture communes of the sixties and seventies adds weight to the argument that it is television above all that has eliminated children's play. Studies of children raised in a variety of such communes, all television-free, showed the little communards continuing to fill their time with those forms of play that have all but vanished from the lives of conventionally reared American children. And yet these counterculture kids were casually exposed to all sorts of adult matters—drug taking, sexual intercourse. Indeed, they sometimes incorporated these matters into their play: "We're mating," a pair of six-year-olds told a reporter to explain their curious bumps and grinds. Nevertheless, to all observers the commune children preserved a distinctly childlike and even innocent demeanor, an impression that was produced mainly by the fact that they spent most of their time playing. Their play defined them as belonging to a special world of childhood.

Not all children have lost the desire to engage in the old-style 7 childhood play. But so long as the most popular, most dominant members of the peer group, who are often the most socially precocious, are "beyond" playing, then a common desire to conform makes it harder for those children who still have the drive to play to go ahead and do so. Parents often report that their children seem ashamed of previously common forms of play and hide their involvement with such play from their peers. "My fifth-grader still plays with dolls," a mother tells, "but she keeps them hidden in the basement where nobody will see them." This social check on the play instinct serves to hasten the end of childhood for even the least advanced children.

What seems to have replaced play in the lives of great numbers 8 of preadolescents these days, starting as early as fourth grade, is a burgeoning interest in boy-girl interactions—"going out" or "going together." These activities do not necessarily involve going anywhere or doing anything sexual, but nevertheless are the first stage of a sexual process that used to commence at puberty or even later. Those more sophisticated children who are already involved in such manifestly unchildlike interest make plain their low opinion of their peers who still *play*. "Some of the kids in the class are real weird," a fifth-grade boy states. "They're not interested in going out, just in trucks and stuff, or games pretending they're monsters. Some of them don't even *try* to be cool."

## Video Games Versus Marbles

Is there really any great difference, one might ask, between that gang     9
of kids playing video games by the hour at their local candy store these days and those small fry who used to hang around together spending equal amounts of time playing marbles? It is easy to see a similarity between the two activities: each requires a certain amount of manual dexterity, each is almost as much fun to watch as to play, each is simple and yet challenging enough for that middle-childhood age group for whom time can be so oppressive if unfilled.

One significant difference between the modern pre-teen fad of     10
video games and the once popular but now almost extinct pastime of marbles is economic: playing video games costs twenty-five cents for approximately three minutes of play; playing marbles, after a small initial investment, is free. The children who frequent video-game machines require a considerable outlay of quarters to subsidize their fun; two, three, or four dollars is not an unusual expenditure for an eight- or nine-year-old spending an hour or two with his friends playing Asteroids or Pac-Man or Space Invaders. For most of the children the money comes from their weekly allowance. Some augment this amount by enterprising commercial ventures—trading and selling comic books, or doing chores around the house for extra money.

But what difference does it make *where* the money comes from?     11
Why should that make video games any less satisfactory as an amusement for children? In fact, having to pay for the entertainment, whatever the source of the money, and having its duration limited by one's financial resources changes the nature of the game, in a subtle way diminishing the satisfactions it offers. Money and time become intertwined, as they so often are in the adult world and as, in the past, they almost never were in the child's world. For the child playing marbles, meanwhile, time has a far more carefree quality, bounded only by the requirements to be home by suppertime or by dark.

But the video-game-playing child has an additional burden—a burden     12
den of choice, of knowing that the money used for playing Pac-Man could have been saved for Christmas, could have been used to buy something tangible, perhaps something "worthwhile," as his parents might say, rather than being "wasted" on video games. There is a

certain sense of adultness that spending money imparts, a feeling of being a consumer, which distinguishes a game with a price from its counterparts among the traditional childhood games children once played at no cost.

There are other differences as well. Unlike child-initiated and child-organized games such as marbles, video games are adult-created mechanisms not entirely within the child's control, and thus less likely to impart a sense of mastery and fulfillment: the coin may get jammed, the machine may go haywire, the little blobs may stop eating the funny little dots. Then the child must go to the storekeeper to complain, to get his money back. He may be "ripped off" and simply lose his quarter, much as his parents are when they buy a faulty appliance. This possibility of disaster gives the child's play a certain weight that marbles never imposed on its light-hearted players. [13]

Even if a child has a video game at home requiring no coin outlay, the play it provides is less than optimal. The noise level of the machine is high—too high, usually, for the child to conduct a conversation easily with another child. And yet, according to its enthusiasts, this very noisiness is a part of the game's attraction. The loud whizzes, crashes, and whirrs of the video-game machine "blow the mind" and create an excitement that is quite apart from the excitement generated simply by trying to win a game. A traditional childhood game such as marbles, on the other hand, has little built-in stimulation; the excitement of playing is generated entirely by the players' own actions. And while the pace of a game of marbles is close to the child's natural physiological rhythms, the frenzied activities of video games serve to "rev up" the child in an artificial way, almost in the way a stimulant or an amphetamine might. Meanwhile the perceptual impact of a video game is similar to that of watching television—the action, after all, takes place on a television screen—causing the eye to defocus slightly and creating a certain alteration in the child's natural state of consciousness. [14]

Parents' instinctive reaction to their children's involvement with video games provides another clue to the difference between this contemporary form of play and the more traditional pastimes such as marbles. While parents, indeed most adults, derive open pleasure from watching children at play, most parents today are not delighted to watch their kids flicking away at the Pac-Man machine. This does not seem to them to be real play. As a mother of two school-age children anxiously explains, "We used to do real childhood sorts of things when I was a kid. We'd build forts and put on crazy plays and make up new [15] languages, and just generally we *played*. But today my kids don't play that way at all. They like video games and of course they still go in for sports outdoors. They go roller skating and ice skating and skiing and all. But they don't seem to really *play*."

Some of this feeling may represent a certain nostalgia for the past 16 and the old generation's resistance to the different ways of the new. But it is more likely that most adults have an instinctive understanding of the importance of play in their own childhood. This feeling stokes their fears that their children are being deprived of something irreplaceable when they flip the levers on the video machines to manipulate the electronic images rather than flick their fingers to send a marble shooting towards another marble.

## *Play Deprivation*

In addition to television's influence, some parents and teachers ascribe 17 children's diminished drive to play to recent changes in the school curriculum, especially in the early grades.

"Kindergarten, traditionally a playful port of entry into formal 18 school, is becoming more academic, with children being taught specific skills, taking tests, and occasionally even having homework," begins a report on new directions in early childhood education. Since 1970, according to the United States census, the proportion of three- and four-year-olds enrolled in school has risen dramatically, from 20.5 percent to 36.7 percent in 1980, and these nursery schools have largely joined the push towards academic acceleration in the early grades. Moreover, middle-class nursery schools in recent years have introduced substantial doses of academic material into their daily programs, often using those particular devices originally intended to help culturally deprived preschoolers in compensatory programs such as Headstart to catch up with their middle-class peers. Indeed, some of the increased focus on academic skills in nursery schools and kindergartens is related to the widespread popularity among young children and their parents of *Sesame Street*, a program originally intended to help deprived children attain academic skills, but universally watched by middle-class toddlers as well.

Parents of the *Sesame Street* generation often demand a "serious," 19 skill-centered program for their preschoolers in school, afraid that the old-fashioned, play-centered curriculum will bore their alphabet-spouting, number-chanting four- and five-year-olds. A few parents, especially those whose children have not attended television classes or nursery school, complain of the high-powered pace of kindergarten these days. A father whose five-year-old daughter attends a public kindergarten declares: "There's a lot more pressure put on little kids these days than when we were kids, that's for sure. My daughter never went to nursery school and never watched *Sesame,* and she had a lot of trouble when she entered kindergarten this fall. By October, just a month and a half into the program, she was already flunking. The teacher told us our daughter couldn't keep up with the other kids. And believe me, she's a bright kid! All the other kids were getting gold stars and smiley faces for their work, and every day Emily would come home in tears because she didn't get a gold star. Remember when we were in kindergarten? We were *children* then. We were allowed just to play!"

A kindergarten teacher confirms the trend towards early academic pressure. "We're expected by the dictates of the school system to push a lot of curriculum," she explains. "Kids in our kindergarten can't sit around playing with blocks any more. We've just managed to squeeze in one hour of free play a week, on Fridays." 20

The diminished emphasis on fantasy and play and imaginative activities in early childhood education and the increased focus on early academic-skill acquisition have helped to change childhood from a play-centered time of life to one more closely resembling the style of adulthood: purposeful, success-centered, competitive. The likelihood is that these preschool "workers" will not metamorphose back into players when they move on to grade school. This decline in play is surely one of the reasons why so many teachers today comment that their third- or fourth-graders act like tired businessmen instead of like children. 21

What might be the consequences of this change in children's play? Children's propensity to engage in that extraordinary series of behaviors characterized as "play" is perhaps the single great dividing line between childhood and adulthood, and has probably been so throughout history. The make-believe games anthropologists have recorded of children in primitive societies around the world attest to the universality of play and to the uniqueness of this activity to the immature members of each society. But in those societies, and probably in Western society before the middle or late eighteenth century, there was always a certain similarity between children's play and adult work. The child's imaginative play took the form of imitation of various aspects of adult life, culminating in the gradual transformation of the child's play from make-believe work to *real* work. At this point, in primitive societies or in our own society of the past, the child took her 22 or his place in the adult work world and the distinctions between adulthood and childhood virtually vanished. But in today's technologically advanced society there is no place for the child in the adult work world. There are not enough jobs, even of the most menial kind, to go around for adults, much less for children. The child must continue to be dependent on adults for many years while gaining the knowledge and skills necessary to become a working member of society.

This is not a new situation for children. For centuries children have endured a prolonged period of dependence long after the helplessness of early childhood is over. But until recent years children remained childlike and playful far longer than they do today. Kept isolated from the adult world as a result of deliberate secrecy and protectiveness, they continued to find pleasure in socially sanctioned childish activities until the imperatives of adolescence led them to strike out for independence and self-sufficiency.     23

Today, however, with children's inclusion in the adult world both through the instrument of television and as a result of a deliberately preparatory, integrative style of child rearing, the old forms of play no longer seem to provide children with enough excitement and stimulation. What then are these so-called children to do for fulfillment if their desire to play has been vitiated and yet their entry into the working world of adulthood must be delayed for many years? The answer is precisely to get involved in those areas that cause contemporary parents so much distress: addictive television viewing during the school years followed, in adolescence or even before, by a search for similar oblivion via alcohol and drugs; exploration of the world of sensuality and sexuality before achieving the emotional maturity necessary for altruistic relationships.     24

Psychiatrists have observed among children in recent years a marked increase in the occurrence of depression, a state long considered antithetical to the nature of childhood. Perhaps this phenomenon is at least somewhat connected with the current sense of uselessness and alienation that children feel, a sense that play may once upon a time have kept in abeyance.     25

# Questions

1. In a sentence or two sum up Winn's thesis.
2. When you were a child, what did you do in your "spare time"? Judging from your own experience, is Winn's first paragraph true, or at least roughly true?

3.  Assuming that children today do indeed spend many hours watching television and playing video games, is it true that these activities "do not differ greatly from adult diversions"? To test Winn's assertion, list the diversions of adults and of children that you know of from your own experience. Are the two lists indeed strikingly similar? Or do the lists reveal important differences? Explain.

4.  Winn's argument is largely composed of a series of comparisons between the play of children before access to TV and after; between traditional and contemporary kindergarten; between childhood in primitive (and our own pre-industrial) society and in technologically advanced societies. List the points she makes to develop each of these comparisons. How well does each comparison support her thesis?

5.  Winn obviously prefers that children in play make up stories rather than watch television. What reasons can be given to prefer making up stories, or reading stories in a book, to watching stories on television? Winn does not mention being read to by an adult as an activity of childhood. Draw your own comparison between traditional bedtime story-reading and nighttime TV-watching. Would such a comparison have strengthened or weakened Winn's argument?

6.  Speaking of video games (paragraph 11), Winn argues that "having to pay for the entertainment . . . changes the nature of the game, in a subtle way diminishing the satisfactions it offers." Can one reply that having to pay helps a child to appreciate the value of money? In short, can it be argued that paying for one's pleasure is a way of becoming mature?

**Black Elk**

# War Games

When it was summer again we were camping on the 1
Rosebud, and I did not feel so much afraid, because the Wasichus
seemed farther away and there was peace there in the valley and there
was plenty of meat. But all the boys from five or six years up were
playing war. The little boys would gather together from the different
bands of the tribe and fight each other with mud balls that they threw
with willow sticks. And the big boys played the game called Throwing-
Them-Off-Their-Horses, which is a battle all but the killing; and sometimes they got hurt. The horsebacks from the different bands would
line up and charge upon each other, yelling; and when the ponies came
together on the run, they would rear and flounder and scream in a
big dust, and the riders would seize each other, wrestling until one
side had lost all its men, for those who fell upon the ground were
counted dead.

When I was older, I, too, often played this game. We were always 2
naked when we played it, just as warriors are when they go into battle
if it is not too cold, because they are swifter without clothes. Once I
fell off on my back right in the middle of a bed of prickly pears, and
it took my mother a long while to pick all the stickers out of me. I was
still too little to play war that summer, but I can remember watching
the other boys, and I thought that when we all grew up and were big
together, maybe we could kill all the Wasichus or drive them far away
from our country. . . .

There was a war game that we little boys played after a big hunt. 3
We went out a little way from the village and built some grass tepees,
playing we were enemies and this was our village. We had an adviser,
and when it got dark he would order us to go and steal some dried
meat from the big people. He would hold a stick up to us and we had

---

Black Elk, a *wichasha wakon* (holy man) of the Oglala Sioux as a small boy
witnessed the battle of the Little Bighorn (1876). He lived to see his people all
but annihilated and his hopes for them extinguished. In 1931, toward the end
of his life, he told his life story to the poet and scholar John G. Neihardt to
preserve a sacred vision given him.

"War Games" (editors' title) is from *Black Elk Speaks*.

---

to bite off a piece of it. If we bit a big piece we had to get a big piece of meat, and if we bit a little piece, we did not have to get so much. Then we started for the big people's village, crawling on our bellies, and when we got back without getting caught, we would have a big feast and a dance and make kill talks, telling of our brave deeds like warriors. Once, I remember, I had no brave deed to tell. I crawled up to a leaning tree beside a tepee and there was meat hanging on the limbs. I wanted a tongue I saw up there in the moonlight, so I climbed up. But just as I was about to reach it, the man in the tepee yelled "Ye-a-a!" He was saying this to his dog, who was stealing some meat too, but I thought the man had seen me, and I was so scared I fell out of the tree and ran away crying.

Then we used to have what we called a chapped breast dance.    4 Our adviser would look us over to see whose breast was burned most from not having it covered with the robe we wore; and the boy chosen would lead the dance while we all sang like this:

> I have a chapped breast.
> My breast is red.
> My breast is yellow.

And we practiced endurance too. Our adviser would put dry sunflower seeds on our wrists. These were lit at the top, and we had to let them burn clear down to the skin. They hurt and made sores, but if we knocked them off or cried Owh!, we would be called women.

# Questions

1. Notice the subjective passages in Black Elk's descriptions of the games he played as a child. What do they reveal about Black Elk as a child and as an adult? How appropriate are these revelations to his topic?

2. The Duke of Wellington is reported to have said that the battle of Waterloo was won on the playing fields of Eton. Try to describe a game that is a small version of an adult activity that teaches adult habits, good or bad. As an experiment, write the description as objectively as you can. Then rewrite it, allowing your description to reveal your attitudes, as a child and now, to the game, to other children, and to the adult world.

Joseph Epstein

# Obsessed with Sport

I cannot remember when I was not surrounded by sports, 1
when talk of sports was not in the air, when I did not care passionately
about sports. As a boy in Chicago in the late Forties, I lived in the
same building as the sister and brother-in-law of Barney Ross, the
welterweight champion. Half a block away, down near the lake, the
Sullivan High School football team worked out in the spring and autumn. Summers the same field was given over to baseball and men's
softball on Sundays. A few blocks to the north was the Touhy Avenue
Fieldhouse, where basketball was played, and lifeguards trained, and
behind which, in a softball field frozen over in winter, crack-the-whip,
hockey, and speed skating took over. To the west, a block or so up
Morse Avenue, was the Morse Avenue "L" Recreations, a combined
pool hall and bowling alley. Life, in short, was games.

My father had no interest in sports. He had grown up, one of the 2
ten children of Russian Jewish immigrant parents, on tough Notre
Dame Street in Montreal, where the major sports were craps, poker,
and petty larceny. He left Montreal at seventeen to come to Chicago,
where he worked hard and successfully so that his sons might play.
Two of his boyhood friends from Notre Dame Street, who had the
comic-book names of Sammy and Danny Spunt, had also come to Chicago, where they bought the Ringside Gym on Dearborn Street in the
Loop. All the big names worked out at Ringside for their Chicago
fights: Willie Pep, Tony Zale, Joe Louis. At eight or nine I would take
the El downtown to the Ringside, be introduced around by Danny
Spunt ("Tony Zale, I'd like you to meet the son of an old friend of
mine. Kid, I'd like you to meet the middleweight champion of the
world"), and return home with an envelope filled with autographed
8-by-10 glossies of Gus Lesnevich, Tammy Mauriello, Kid Gavilan, and
the wondrous Sugar Ray.

I lived on, off, and in sports. *Sport* magazine had recently begun 3

---

Joseph Epstein was born in Chicago in 1937. He is the author of several books
on American culture, the editor of *American Scholar* (a quarterly review published by Phi Beta Kappa), and an occasional teacher of English at Northwestern
University.

publication, and I gobbled up its issues cover to cover, soon becoming knowledgeable not only about the major sports—baseball, football, and basketball—but about golf, hockey, tennis, and horse racing, so that I scored reputably on the Sport Quiz, a regular department at the front of the magazine. Another regular department was the Sport Classic, which featured longish profiles of the legendary figures in the history of sports: Ty Cobb, Jim Thorpe, Bobby Jones, Big Bill Tilden, Red Grange, Man o' War. I next moved on to the sports novels of John R. Tunis—*All-American, The Iron Duke, The Kid from Tomkinsville, The Kid Comes Back, World Series*, the lot—which I read with as much excitement as any books I have read since.

The time was, as is now apparent, a splendid era in sports. Ted 4 Williams, Joe DiMaggio, and Stan Musial were afield; first Jack Kramer, then Pancho Gonzales, dominated tennis; George Mikan led the Minneapolis Lakers, and the Harlem Globetrotters could still be taken seriously; Doc Blanchard and Glen Davis, Mr. Inside and Mr. Outside, were playing for Army, Johnny Lujack was at Notre Dame; in the pros Sammy Baugh, Bob Waterfield, and Sid Luckman were the major T-formation quarterbacks; Joe Louis and Sugar Ray Robinson fought frequently; the two Willies, Mosconi and Hoppe, put in regular appearances at Bensinger's in the Loop; Eddie Arcaro seemed to ride three, four winners a day. Giants, it truly seemed, walked the earth.

All learning of craft—which sport, like writing, most assuredly 5 is—involves imitation, especially in the early stages; and I was an excellent mimic. By the time I was ten years old I had mastery over all the big-time moves: the spit in the mitt, the fluid infield chatter, the knocking of dirt from the spikes; the rhythmic barking out of signals, hands high under the center's crotch to take the ball; the three bounces and deep breath before shooting the free throw (on this last, I regretted not being a Catholic, so that I might be able to make the sign of the cross before shooting, as was then the fashion among Catholic high-school and college players). I went in for athletic haberdashery in a big way, often going beyond mimicry to the point of flat-out phoniness— wearing, for example, a knee pad while playing basketball, though my knees were always, exasperatingly, intact.

I always looked good, which was important, because form is in- 6 trinsic to sports; but in my case it was doubly important, because the truth is that I wasn't really very good. Or at any rate not good enough. Two factors accounted for this. The first was that, without being shy about body contact, I lacked a certain indispensable aggressiveness; the second, connected closely to the first, was that, when it came right down to it, I did not care enough about winning. I would rather lose a point attempting a slashing cross-court backhand than play for an easier winner down the side; the long jump shot always had more allure for me than the safer drive to the basket. Given a choice between the two vanities of winning and looking good, I almost always preferred looking good.

I shall never forget the afternoon, sometime along about my thir- 7 teenth year, when, shooting baskets alone, I came upon the technique for shooting the hook. Although today it has nowhere near the consequence of the jump shot—an innovation that has been to basketball what the jet has been to air travel—the hook is still the single most beautiful shot in the game. The rhythm and grace of it, the sway of the body off the pivot, the release of the ball behind the head and off the fingertips, the touch and instinct involved in its execution, make the hook altogether a balletic thing, and to achieve it is to feel one of the most delectable sensations in sports. That afternoon, on a deserted side street, shooting on a rickety wooden backboard and a black rim without a net, I felt it and grew nearly drunk on the feeling. Rain came down, dirt washed in the gutters, flecks of it spattering my clothes and arms and face, but, soaked and cold though I was, I do not think I would have left that basket on that afternoon for anything. I threw up hook after hook, from every angle, from farther and farther out, off the board, without the board, and hook after hook went in. Only pitch darkness drove me home.

I do not say that not to have shot the hook is never to have lived, 8 but only that, once having done so, the pleasure it gives is not so easily forgotten. Every sport offers similar pleasures, the pleasures taken differing by temperament: the canter into the end zone to meet a floating touchdown pass, or the clean, crisp feel of a perfect block or tackle; the long straight drive or the precisely played approach shot to the green; the solid overhead; the pickup on the tricky short hop or the long ball down one of the power alleys. Different sports, different pleasures. But so keen are these pleasures—pleasures of execution, of craft completed—that, along with being unforgettable, they are also worth recapturing in any available way, and the most available way, when reflexes have slowed, when muscle no longer responds so readily to brain, is from the grandstand or, perhaps more often nowadays, from the chair before the television.

*Pleasures of the Spectator*

I have put in days on the bench, but years in my chair before the     9
television set. Recently it has occurred to me that over the years I have
heard more hours of talk from the announcer Curt Gowdy than from
my own father, who is not a reticent man. I have been thoroughly
Schenkeled, Mussbergered, Summeralled, Cosselled, DeRogotissed,
and Garagiolaed. How many hundreds—thousands?—of hours have
I spent watching sports of all sorts, either at parks or stadiums or over
television? I am glad I shall never have a precise answer. Yet neither
apparently can I get enough. What is the fascination? Why is it that,
with the prospect of a game to watch in the evening or on the weekend,
the day seems lighter and brighter? What do I get out of it?

What I get out of it, according to one fairly prominent view, is an     10
outlet for my violent emotions. Knee-wrenching, rib-cracking, head-
busting, this view has it, is what sports are really about, with sports
fans being essentially sadists, and cowardly sadists at that, for they
take their violence not at firsthand but at second remove. Enthusiasm
for sports among Americans is little more than a reflection of the national penchant for violence. Military men talk about game plans; the
long touchdown pass is called the bomb. The average pro-football fan,
seeing a quarterback writhing on the ground at midfield as a result of
the ministrations of Joe Green, Carl Eller, or Lyle Alzado, twitters with
glee, finds his ultimate reward, and declares a little holiday in the
blackest corner of his heart.

But this is a criticism that comes at sports by way of politics. To     11
believe it one has to believe that the history of the United States is
chiefly one of rape, expropriation, and aggressive imperialism. To dismiss it, however, one need only know something about sports. Violence is indubitably a part of some sports; in some—hockey is an example—it sometimes comes close to being featured. But in no sport—
not even boxing, that most rudimentary of sports—is it the main item,
and in many other sports it plays no part at all. A distinction worth
insisting on is that between violence and roughness. Roughness, a
willingness to mix it up, to take if need be an elbow in the jaw, is part
of rebounding in basketball, yet violence is not. Even in pro football,
most maligned of modern American sports, more of roughness than
of violence is involved. Roughness raises the stakes, provides the pressure, behind execution. A splendid because true phrase has come
about in pro football to cover the situation in which a pass receiver,
certain that he will be tackled upon the instant he makes his reception,

drops a ball he should otherwise have caught easily—the phrase, best delivered in a Southern accent such as Don Meredith's, is "He heard footsteps on that one, Howard." Although a part of the attraction, it is not so much those footsteps that fill the stands and the den chairs on Sunday afternoons as it is those men who elude them: the Lynn Swanns, the Fran Tarkentons, the O. J. Simpsons. The American love of violence theory really will not wash. Dick Butkus did not get us into Vietnam.

Many who would not argue that sports reflect American violence 12 nevertheless claim that they imbue one with the competitive spirit. In some who are already amply endowed with it, sports doubtless do tend to refine (or possibly brutalize) the desire to win. Yet sports also teach a serious respect for craft. Competition, though it flourishes as always, is in bad odor nowadays; but craft, officially respected, does not flourish greatly outside the boutique.

If the love of violence or the competitive urge does not put me in 13 my chair for the countless games I watch, is it, then, nostalgia, a yearning to regain the more glowing moments of adolescence? Many argue that this is precisely so, that American men exist in a state of perpetual immaturity, suspended between boy- and manhood. "The difference between men and boys," says Liberace, "is the price of their toys." (I have paid more than $300 for two half-season tickets to the Chicago Bulls games, parking fees not included.) Such unending enthusiasm for games may have something to do with adolescence, but little, I suspect, with regaining anything whatever. Instead, it has more to do with watching men do regularly and surpassingly what, as an adolescent, one did often bumblingly though with an occasional flash of genius. To have played these games oneself as a boy or a young man helps immeasurably the appreciation that in watching a sport played at professional caliber one is witnessing the extraordinary made to look ordinary. That a game may have no consequence outside itself—no effect on history, on one's own life, on anything really—does not make it trivial but only makes the enjoyment of it all the purer.

The notion that men watch sports to regain their adolescence pic- 14 tures them sitting in the stands or at home watching a game and, within their psyches, muttering, "There, but for the lack of grace of God, go I." And it is true that a number of contemporary authors who are taken seriously have indeed written about sports with a strong overlay of yearning. In the men's softball games described in the fiction of Philip Roth, center field is a place akin to Arcady. Arcadian, too, is the outfield in Willie Morris's memoir of growing up in the South, *North Toward Home*. In the first half of *Rabbit Run* John Updike takes up the life of a man whose days are downhill all the way after hitting his peak as a high-school basketball star—and in the writing Updike himself evinces a nice soft touch of undisguised longing. In *A Fan's Notes*, a book combining yearning and self-disgust in roughly equal measure, Frederick Exley makes plain that he would much prefer to have been born into the skin of Frank Gifford rather than into his own.

But most men who are enraptured by sports do not think any such     15
thing. I should like to have Kareem Abdul-Jabbar's sky hook, but not, especially for civilian life, the excessive height that is necessary to its execution. I should like to have Jimmy Connors's ground strokes, but no part of his mind. These are men born with certain gifts, gifts honed by practice and determination, that I, and millions along with me, enjoy seeing on display. But the reality principle is too deeply ingrained, at least in a man of my years, for me to even imagine exchanging places with them. One might as well imagine oneself in the winner's circle at Churchill Downs as the horse.

Fantasy is an element in sports when they are played in adoles-     16
cence—an alley basket becomes the glass backboard at Madison Square Garden, a concrete park district tennis court with grass creeping out of the service line becomes center court at Wimbledon—but fantasy of this kind is hard to come by. Part of this has to do with age; but as large a part has to do with the age in which we live. Sport has always been a business but never more so than currently, and nothing lends itself less to fantasy than business. Reading the sports section has become rather like reading the business section—mergers, trades, salary negotiations, contract disputes, options, and strikes fill the columns. Along with the details of business, those of the psychological and social problems of athletes have come to the fore. The old *Sport* magazine concentrated on play on the field, with only an occasional digressive reference to personal life. ("Yogi likes plenty of pizza in the off-season and spends a lot of his time at his teammate Phil Rizzuto's bowling alley" is a rough facsimile of a sentence from its pages that I recall.) But the magazine in its current version, as well as the now more popular *Sports Illustrated*, expends much space on the private lives of athletes—their divorces, hang-ups, race relations, need for approval, concern for security, potted philosophies—with the result that the grand is made to seem small.

On the other side of the ledger, there is a view that finds a shim-     17
mering significance in everything having to do with sports. Literary

men in general are notoriously to be distrusted on the subject. They dig around everywhere, and can be depended upon to find much treasure where none is buried. Norman Mailer mining metaphysical ore in every jab of Muhammad Ali, an existential nugget in each of his various and profuse utterances, is a particularly horrendous example. Even the sensible William Carlos Williams was not above this sort of temptation. In a poem entitled "At the Ball Game," we find the lines "It is the Inquisition, the/Revolution." Dr. Williams could not have been much fun at the ball park.

## The Real Thing

If enthusiasm for sports has little to do with providing an outlet for violent emotions, regaining adolescence, discovering metaphysical truths, the Inquisition or the Revolution, then what, I ask myself, am I doing past midnight, when I have to be up at 5:30 the next morning, watching on television what will turn out to be a seventeen-inning game between the New York Mets and the St. Louis Cardinals? The conversation coming out of my television set is of a very low grade, even for sports announcing. But even the dreary talk cannot put me off—the rehash of statistics, the advice to youngsters to keep their gloves low when in the field, the thin jokes. Neither the Mets nor the Cards figure to be contenders this year. The only possible effect that this game can have on my life is to make me dog-tired the next day. Yet I cannot pull myself away. I want to know how it is going to end. True, the score will be available in the morning paper. But that is not the same thing. What is going on here?  18

One thing that is going on is the practice of craft of a very high order, which is intrinsically interesting. But something as important is involved, something rarer in contemporary life, the spectacle of which gives enormous satisfaction. To define this satisfaction negatively, it is the absence of fraudulence and fakery. No small item, this, when one stops to think that in nearly every realm of contemporary life fraud and fakery have an established—some would say a preponderant—place. Advertising, politics, business, and journalism are only the most obvious examples. Fraud seems similarly pervasive in modern art: in painters whose reputations rest on press agentry; in writers who write one way and live quite another; in composers who are taken seriously but whose work cannot be seriously listened to. At a time when *image* is one of the most frequently used words in American speech and writing, one does not too often come upon the real thing.  19

Sport may be the toy department of life, but one of its abiding   20
compensations is that, at least on the field, it is the real thing. Much
has been done in recent years in the attempt to ruin sport—the ruth-
lessness of owners, the greed of players, the general exploitation of
fans. But even all this cannot destroy it. On the court, down on the
field, sport is fraud-free and fakeproof. With a full count, two men on,
his team down by one run in the last of the eighth, a batter (as well
as a pitcher) is beyond the aid of public relations. At match point at
Forest Hills a player's press clippings are of no help. Last year's earnings will not sink a twelve-foot putt on the eighteenth at Augusta.
Alan Page, galloping up along a quarterback's blind side, figures to be
neglectful of that quarterback's image as a swinger. In all these situations, and hundreds of others, a man either comes through or he
doesn't. He is alone out there, naked but for his ability, which counts
for everything. Something there is that is elemental about this, and
something greatly satisfying.

Another part of the satisfaction to be got from sports—from play-   21
ing them, but also from watching them being played—derives from
their special clarity. Sports offer clarity of a kind sufficient to engage
the most serious minds. That the Cambridge mathematician G. H.
Hardy closely followed cricket and avidly read cricket scores is not
altogether surprising. Numbers in sports are ubiquitous. Scores, stand-
ings, averages, times, records—comfort is found in such numbers.
ERA, RBI, FGP, pass completions, turnovers, category upon category
of statistics are kept for nearly every aspect of athletic activity. (Why,
I recently heard someone ask, are records not kept for catchers throwing out runners attempting to steal? Because, the answer is, often runners steal on pitchers, and so it would be unfair to charge these stolen
bases against catchers.) As perhaps in no other sphere, numbers in
sports tell one where things stand. No loopholes here, where figures,
for once, do not lie. Nowhere else is such specificity of result available.

Clarity about character is also available in sports. "You Americans   22
hold to the proposition that it is self-evident that all men are created
equal," I not long ago heard an Englishman say, adding, "it had better
be self-evident, for no other evidence for it exists." Sport coldly demonstrates physical inequalities—there are the larger, the faster, the
stronger, the more graceful athletes—but it also throws up human
types who have devised ways to redress these inequalities. One such
type is the hustler. In every realm but that of sports the word *hustle*
is pejorative, whereas in sports it is approbative. Two of the hustler
breed, Pete Rose of the Cincinnati Reds and Jerry Sloan of the Chicago

Bulls, are men who supplement reasonably high levels of ability with unreasonably high levels of courage and desire. Other athletes—Joe Morgan and Oscar Robertson come to mind—bring superior athletic intelligence to bear upon their play. And Bill Russell, late of the Boston Celtics, who if the truth be known was not an inherently superior athlete, blended hustle and intelligence with what abilities he did have and through force of character established supremacy.

Whence do hustle, intelligence, and character in sports derive, 23 especially since they apparently do not necessarily carry over into life? Joe DiMaggio and Sugar Ray Robinson, two of the most instinctively intelligent and physically elegant athletes, brought little of either of these qualities over into their business or personal activities. Some athletes can do all but one important thing well: Wilt Chamberlain at the free-throw line, for those who recall his misery there, leaves a permanent picture of a mental block in action. Other athletes—Connie Hawkins, Ilie Nastase, Dick Allen—have all the physical gifts in superabundance, yet, because of some insufficiency of character, some searing flaw, never come near to fulfilling their promise. Coaches supply yet another gallery of human types, from the fanatical Vince Lombardi to the comical Casey Stengel to the measured and aptly named John Wooden. The cast of characters in sport, the variety of situations, the complexity of behavior it puts on display, the overall human exhibit it offers—together these supply an enjoyment akin to that once provided by reading interminably long but inexhaustibly rich nineteenth-century novels.

In a wider sense, sport is culture. For many American men it rep- 24 resents a common background, a shared interest. It has a binding power that transcends social class and education. Some years ago I found myself working in the South among men with whom I shared nothing in the way of region, religion, education, politics, or general views; we shared nothing, in fact, but sports, which was enough for us to get along and grow to become friends, in the process showing how superficial all the things that might have kept us apart in fact were. More recently, in Chicago, at a time when race relations were in a particularly jagged state, I recall emerging from an NBA game, in which the Chicago Bulls in overtime beat the Milwaukee Bucks, into a snowy night and an aura of common good feeling that, for a time, submerged the enmity between races; laughing, throwing snowballs, exuberant generally, the crowd leaving the Chicago Stadium that night was not divided by being black and white but unified by being Bull

fans. Last year's Boston-Cincinnati World Series, one of the most gratifying in memory, coming hard upon a year of extreme political div-
isiveness, performed, however briefly, something of the same function. How much better it felt to agree about the mastery of Luis Tiant
than to argue about the wretchedness of Richard Nixon.

In sports as in life, character does not much change. I have recently   25
begun to play a game called racquet ball, and I find I would still rather
look good than win, which is what I usually do: look good and lose.
I beat the rum-dums but go down before quality players. I get compliments in defeat. Men who beat me admire the whip of my strokes,
my wrist action, my anticipation, the power I get behind the ball. When
this occurs I feel like a woman who is complimented for the shape of
her bottom when it is her mind she craves admiration for, though of
course she will take what praise she can get.

R. H. Tawney, the great historian of religion and capitalism, once   26
remarked that the only progress he could note during the course of
his lifetime was in the deportment of dogs. For myself, I would say
that the chief progress in the course of my lifetime has been in the
quality and variety of athletic gear. Racquets made of metal, aluminum,
wood, and fiberglass, balls of different colors, sneakers of all materials
and designs, posh warm-up suits, tube socks, sweatbands for the head
and wrist in various colors and pipings; only the athletic supporter,
the old jockstrap, remains unornamented, but perhaps even now Vera
or Peter Max is at the drawing board. In any event, with all this elegant
plumage available, it is a nice time to be playing ball again.

Sports can be impervious to age. My father-in-law, a man of style,   27
seriousness, and great good humor who died a year ago in his late
sixties, was born in South Bend, Indiana, and in his early manhood
left the Catholic Church—two facts that conjoined to give him an intense interest in the fortunes of the teams from Notre Dame. He loved
to see them lose. The torch has been passed on. I now love to see Notre
Dame lose, and when it does I think of him and remember his smile.

When I was a boy I had a neighbor, a man who, after retirement,   28
had a number of strokes. An old man and a young boy, we had in
common a love of sports, which, when we met on the street, was our
only topic of conversation. He once inspected a new glove of mine,
and instructed me to rub it down with neat's-foot-oil, place a ball firmly
in the pocket, wrap string tightly around the glove, and leave it like
that for the winter. I did, and it worked. After his last stroke but one,
he seldom left his house. Afternoons he spent in a chair in his bedroom,
a blanket over his lap, listening to Cub games over the radio. It was

while listening to a ball game that he quietly died. I cannot imagine a better way.

# Questions

1. In his first two paragraphs Epstein writes of the opportunities he had when growing up in Chicago in the 1940s to live "on, off, and in sports." Compare or contrast those opportunities with your own. How do you account for the differences? (Were there some similarities?)

2. In paragraph 4 Epstein writes of the 1940s: "The time was, as is now apparent, a splendid era in sports." Looking back at the decade in your life (which can be the current decade) in which you have been most engaged as a sports fan, would you characterize it also as "a splendid era"? If not, how would you characterize it—disillusioning, mediocre, uneven? Try to support your characterization concretely, as Epstein does in paragraph 4.

3. In paragraph 5 Epstein writes: "All learning of craft—which sport, like writing, most assuredly is—involves imitation, especially in the early stages." Did you learn sports by imitation? Explain. What about writing? Why, or why not?

4. In paragraph 13 Epstein points out that having played a game as a boy or young man (presumably also as a girl or young woman) helps one to appreciate the performance of professionals. Do you think the same principle holds true for literature, music, dance, art? Should all children have a chance to learn to play musical instruments, to paint, and to write, not in the expectation that they will all practice those arts as adults, but to enhance their later enjoyment and support of concerts, museums, books, and theater?

5. What makes spectator sports appealing? After dismissing violence and the spectator's nostalgia for adolescence as the source of their appeal, Epstein cites three or four reasons why spectator sports appeal to him. Why does your favorite spectator sport appeal to you?

6. If you are not a sports fan, is there an area of your experience in which you feel close to being obsessed? Music? food? clothes? dogs? sex? If you were to write about this obsession, how might outlining Epstein's essay help you to find ideas?

## John Updike

# A & P

In walks these three girls in nothing but bathing suits. I'm    1
in the third checkout slot, with my back to the door, so I don't see
them until they're over by the bread. The one that caught my eye first
was the one in the plaid green two-piece. She was a chunky kid, with
a good tan and a sweet broad soft-looking can with those two crescents
of white just under it, where the sun never seems to hit, at the top of
the backs of her legs. I stood there with my hand on a box of HiHo
crackers trying to remember if I rang it up or not. I ring it up again
and the customer starts giving me hell. She's one of these cash-register-
watchers, a witch about fifty with rouge on her cheekbones and no
eyebrows, and I know it made her day to trip me up. She'd been
watching cash registers for fifty years and probably never seen a mistake before.

By the time I got her feathers smoothed and her goodies into a    2
bag—she gives me a little snort in passing, if she'd been born at the
right time they would have burned her over in Salem—by the time I
get her on her way the girls had circled around the bread and were
coming back, without a pushcart, back my way along the counters, in
the aisle between the checkouts and the Special bins. They didn't even
have shoes on. There was this chunky one, with the two-piece—it was
bright green and the seams on the bra were still sharp and her belly
was still pretty pale so I guessed she just got it (the suit)—there was
this one, with one of those chubby berry-faces, the lips all bunched
together under her nose, this one, and a tall one, with black hair that
hadn't quite frizzed right, and one of these sunburns right across under
the eyes, and a chin that was too long—you know, the kind of girl
other girls think is very "striking" and "attractive" but never quite
makes it, as they very well know, which is why they like her so much—

John Updike was born in 1932 in Shillington, Pennsylvania. After graduating
from college he studied art for a year in England, but he then returned to the
United States and began working as a staff reporter for the *New Yorker.* He soon
published stories in the magazine, and he continues to do so. He has also written
novels (including *Rabbit, Run* and *The Witches of Eastwick*), essays, and light
verse. The story we print here, "A & P," was published in 1961, but many readers
find that except for the prices mentioned there is nothing dated about it.

and then the third one, that wasn't quite so tall. She was the queen. She kind of led them, the other two peeking around and making their shoulders round. She didn't look around, not this queen, she just walked straight on slowly, on these long white prima-donna legs. She came down a little hard on her heels, as if she didn't walk in her bare feet that much, putting down her heels and then letting the weight move along to her toes as if she was testing the floor with every step, putting a little deliberate extra action into it. You never know for sure how girls' minds work (do you really think it's a mind in there or just a little buzz like a bee in a glass jar?) but you got the idea she had talked the other two into coming in here with her, and now she was showing them how to do it, walk slow and hold yourself straight.

She had on a kind of dirty-pink—beige maybe, I don't know— 3 bathing suit with a little nubble all over it and, what got me, the straps were down. They were off her shoulders looped loose around the cool tops of her arms, and I guess as a result the suit had slipped a little on her, so all around the top of the cloth there was this shining rim. If it hadn't been there you wouldn't have known there could have been anything whiter than those shoulders. With the straps pushed off, there was nothing between the top of the suit and the top of her head except just *her*, this clean bare plane of the top of her chest down from the shoulder bones like a dented sheet of metal tilted in the light. I mean, it was more than pretty.

She had sort of oaky hair that the sun and salt had bleached, done 4 up in a bun that was unravelling, and a kind of prim face. Walking into the A & P with your straps down, I suppose it's the only kind of face you *can* have. She held her head so high her neck, coming up out of those white shoulders, looked kind of stretched, but I didn't mind. The longer her neck was, the more of her there was.

She must have felt in the corner of her eye me and over my shoul- 5 der Stokesie in the second slot watching, but she didn't tip. Not this queen. She kept her eyes moving across the racks, and stopped, and turned so slow it made my stomach rub the inside of my apron, and buzzed to the other two, who kind of huddled against her for relief, and then they all three of them went up the cat and dog food-breakfast cereal-macaroni-rice-raisins-seasonings-spreads-spaghetti-soft drinks-crackers-and-cookies aisle. From the third slot I look straight up this aisle to the meat counter, and I watched them all the way. The fat one with the tan sort of fumbled with the cookies, but on second thought she put the package back. The sheep pushing their carts down the aisle—the girls were walking against the usual traffic (not that we have one-way signs or anything)—were pretty hilarious. You could see them, when Queenie's white shoulders dawned on them, kind of jerk, or hop, or hiccup, but their eyes snapped back to their own baskets and on they pushed. I bet you could set off dynamite in an A & P and the people would by and large keep reaching and checking oatmeal off their lists and muttering "Let me see, there was a third thing, began with A, asparagus, no, ah, yes, applesauce!" or whatever it is they do mutter. But there was no doubt, this jiggled them. A few house slaves in pin curlers even look around after pushing their carts past to make sure what they had seen was correct.

You know, it's one thing to have a girl in a bathing suit down on  6
the beach, where what with the glare nobody can look at each other much anyway, and another thing in the cool of the A & P, under the fluorescent lights, against all those stacked packages, with her feet paddling along naked over our checker-board green-and-cream rubber-tile floor.

"Oh, Daddy," Stokesie said beside me. "I feel so faint."  7

"Darling," I said. "Hold me tight." Stokesie's married, with two  8
babies chalked up on his fuselage already, but as far as I can tell that's the only difference. He's twenty-two, and I was nineteen this April.

"Is it done?" he asks, the responsible married man finding his  9
voice. I forgot to say he thinks he's going to be manager some sunny day, maybe in 1990 when it's called the Great Alexandrov and Petrooshki Tea Company or something.

What he meant was, our town is five miles from a beach, with a  10
big summer colony out on the Point, but we're right in the middle of town, and the women generally put on a shirt or shorts or something before they get out of the car into the street. And anyway these are usually women with six children and varicose veins mapping their legs and nobody, including them, could care less. As I say, we're right in the middle of town, and if you stand at our front doors you can see two banks and the Congregational church and the newspaper store and three real estate offices and about twenty-seven old freeloaders tearing up Central Street because the sewer broke again. It's not as if we're on the Cape; we're north of Boston and there's people in this town haven't seen the ocean for twenty years.

The girls had reached the meat counter and were asking McMahon  11
something. He pointed, they pointed, and they shuffled out of sight behind a pyramid of Diet Delight peaches. All that was left for us to see was old McMahon patting his mouth and looking after them sizing

up their joints. Poor kids, I began to feel sorry for them, they couldn't help it.

Now here comes the sad part of the story, at least my family says it's sad, but I don't think it's so sad myself. The store's pretty empty, it being Thursday afternoon, so there was nothing much to do except lean on the register and wait for the girls to show up again. The whole store was like a pinball machine and I didn't know which tunnel they'd come out of. After a while they come around out of the far aisle, around the light bulbs, records at discount of the Caribbean Six or Tony Martin Sings or some such gunk you wonder they waste the wax on, sixpacks of candy bars, and plastic toys done up in cellophane that fall apart when a kid looks at them anyway. Around they come, Queenie still leading the way, and holding a little gray jar in her hand. Slots Three through Seven are unmanned and I could see her wondering between Stokes and me, but Stokesie with his usual luck draws an old party in baggy gray pants who stumbles up with four giant cans of pineapple juice (what do these bums *do* with all that pineapple juice? I've often asked myself) so the girls come to me. Queenie puts down the jar and I take it into my fingers icy cold. Kingfish Fancy Herring Snacks in Pure Sour Cream: 49¢. Now her hands are empty, not a ring or a bracelet, bare as God made them, and I wonder where the money's coming from. Still with that prim look she lifts a folded dollar bill out of the hollow at the center of her nubbled pink top. The jar went heavy in my hand. Really, I thought that was so cute. 12

Then everybody's luck begins to run out. Lengel comes in from haggling with a truck full of cabbages on the lot and is about to scuttle into the door marked MANAGER behind which he hides all day when the girls touch his eye. Lengel's pretty dreary, teaches Sunday school and the rest, but he doesn't miss that much. He comes over and says, "Girls, this isn't the beach." 13

Queenie blushes, though maybe it's just a brush of sunburn I was noticing for the first time, now that she was so close. "My mother asked me to pick up a jar of herring snacks." Her voice kind of startled me, the way voices do when you see the people first, coming out so flat and dumb yet kind of tony, too, the way it ticked over "pick up" and "snacks." All of a sudden I slid right down her voice into her living room. Her father and the other men were standing around in ice-cream coats and bow ties and the women were in sandals picking up herring snacks on toothpicks off a big glass plate and they were all holding drinks the color of water with olives and sprigs of mint in 14 them. When my parents have somebody over they get lemonade and if it's a real racy affair Schlitz in tall glasses with "They'll Do It Every Time" cartoons stencilled on.

"That's all right," Lengel said. "But this isn't the beach." His repeating this struck me as funny, as if it had just occurred to him, and he had been thinking all these years the A & P was a great big dune and he was the head lifeguard. He didn't like my smiling—as I say he doesn't miss much—but he concentrates on giving the girls that sad Sunday-school-superintendent stare.    15

Queenie's blush is no sunburn now, and the plump one in plaid, that I liked better from the back—a really sweet can—pipes up, "We weren't doing any shopping. We just came in for the one thing."    16

"That makes no difference," Lengel tells her, and I could see from the way his eyes went that he hadn't noticed she was wearing a two-piece before. "We want you decently dressed when you come in here."    17

"We *are* decent," Queenie says suddenly, her lower lip pushing, getting sore now that she remembers her place, a place from which the crowd that runs the A & P must look pretty crummy. Fancy Herring Snacks flashed in her very blue eyes.    18

"Girls, I don't want to argue with you. After this come in here with your shoulders covered. It's our policy." He turns his back. That's policy for you. Policy is what the kingpins want. What the others want is juvenile delinquency.    19

All this while, the customers had been showing up with their carts but, you know, sheep, seeing a scene, they had all bunched up on Stokesie, who shook open a paper bag as gently as peeling a peach, not wanting to miss a word. I could feel in the silence everybody getting nervous, most of all Lengel, who asks me, "Sammy, have you rung up this purchase?"    20

I thought and said "No" but it wasn't about that I was thinking. I go through the punches, 4, 9, GROC, TOT—it's more complicated than you think and after you do it often enough, it begins to make a little song, that you hear words to, in my case "Hello (*bing*) there, you (*gung*) hap-py *peepul* (*splat*)!"—the *splat* being the drawer flying out. I uncrease the bill, tenderly as you may imagine, it just having come from between the two smoothest scoops of vanilla I had ever known were there, and pass a half and a penny into her narrow pink palm, and nestle the herrings in a bag and twist its neck and hand it over, all the time thinking.    21

The girls, and who'd blame them, are in a hurry to get out, so I    22 say "I quit" to Lengel quick enough for them to hear, hoping they'll stop and watch me, their unsuspected hero. They keep right on going, into the electric eye; the door flies open and they flicker across the lot to their car, Queenie and Plaid and Big Tall Goony-Goony (not that as raw material she was so bad), leaving me with Lengel and a kink in his eyebrow.

"Did you say something, Sammy?"    23

"I said I quit."    24

"I thought you did."    25

"You didn't have to embarrass them."    26

"It was they who were embarrassing us."    27

I started to say something that came out "Fiddle-de-doo." It's a    28
saying of my grandmother's, and I know she would have been pleased.

"I don't think you know what you're saying," Lengel said.    29

"I know you don't," I said. "But I do." I pull the bow at the back    30
of my apron and start shrugging it off my shoulders. A couple customers that had been heading for my slot begin to knock against each other, like scared pigs in a chute.

Lengel sighs and begins to look very patient and old and gray.    31
He's been a friend of my parents for years. "Sammy, you don't want to do this to your Mom and Dad," he tells me. It's true, I don't. But it seems to me that once you begin a gesture it's fatal not to go through with it. I fold the apron, "Sammy" stitched in red on the pocket, and put it on the counter, and drop the bow tie on top of it. The bow tie is theirs, if you've ever wondered. "You'll feel this for the rest of your life," Lengel says, and I know that's true, too, but remembering how he made that pretty girl blush makes me so scrunchy inside I punch the No Sale tab and the machine whirs "pee-pul" and the drawer splats out. One advantage to this scene taking place in summer, I can follow this up with a clean exit, there's no fumbling around getting your coat and galoshes, I just saunter into the electric eye in my white shirt that my mother ironed the night before, and the door heaves itself open, and outside the sunshine is skating around on the asphalt.

I look around for my girls, but they're gone, of course. There    32
wasn't anybody but some young married screaming with her children about some candy they didn't get by the door of a powder-blue Falcon station wagon. Looking back in the big windows, over the bags of peat moss and aluminum lawn furniture stacked on the pavement, I could see Lengel in my place in the slot, checking the sheep through. His face was dark gray and his back stiff, as if he'd just had an injection

of iron, and my stomach kind of fell as I felt how hard the world was going to be to me hereafter.

# Questions

1. Have you ever quit a job on a matter of principle? If so, explain the circumstances, and the short- and long-term consequences.
2. If you have ever thought of quitting a job on a matter of principle but then did not do so, explain the circumstances and your present analysis of your behavior.
3. Some students regard Sammy as a sexist, and say that the failure of the girls to notice his gesture is a fitting punishment for his sexism. Evaluate this view.

## Theodore Roethke

# Child on Top of a Greenhouse

The wind billowing out the seat of my britches,
My feet crackling splinters of glass and dried putty,
The half-grown chrysanthemums staring up like
    accusers,
Up through the streaked glass, flashing with sunlight,
A few white clouds all rushing eastward,
A line of elms plunging and tossing like horses,
And everyone, everyone pointing up and shouting!

Theodore Roethke (1908–1963), author of eight volumes of poetry, was born in Saginaw, Michigan. Roethke's father ran a greenhouse, but the son earned his living by teaching English literature, chiefly at the University of Washington, in Seattle.

# Questions

1.  What must have happened just before the scene described in the poem? What details serve as clues?
2.  How does the child feel about being on top of the greenhouse? How do you know?
3.  The poem is an incomplete or fragmentary sentence. By changing the present participles (from "billowing" in the first line to "shouting" in the last line) to verbs, convert the fragment to a sentence. Read the "revised" poem through, then explain what has been lost.

# 6
## OPEN FOR BUSINESS

Museu Nacional de Arte Antiga, Lisbon, Portugal

*A Portuguese Ship Leaving Goa for Japan*
**Anonymous**

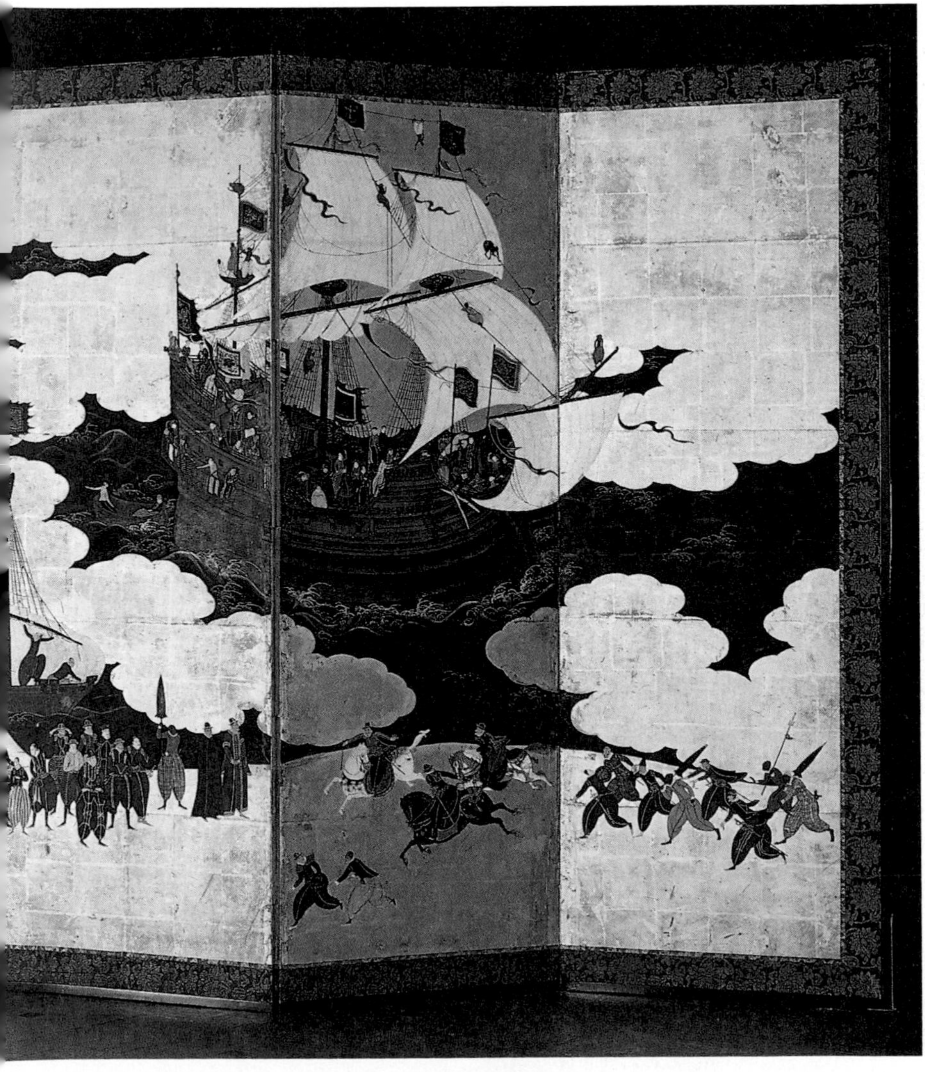

*Georg Giesze, Merchant*
**Hans Holbein the Younger, 1532**

*John Pierpont Morgan*
**Edward Steichen, 1903**

# Short Views

The chief business of the American people is business.
**Calvin Coolidge**


The business of business is business.
**Anonymous**


Business underlies everything in our national life, including our spiritual life. Witness the fact that in the Lord's Prayer the first petition is for daily bread. No one can worship God or love his neighbor on an empty stomach.
**Woodrow Wilson**


We demand that big business give the people a square deal; in return we must insist that when anyone engaged in big business honestly endeavors to do right he shall himself be given a square deal.
**Theodore Roosevelt**


Entrepreneurial profit . . . is the expression of the value of what the entrepreneur contributes to production in exactly the same sense that wages are the value expression of what the worker "produces." It is not a profit of exploitation any more than are wages.
**Joseph Alois Schumpeter**


Every individual necessarily labors to render the annual revenue of the society as great as he can. He generally indeed neither intends to promote the public interest, nor knows how much he is promoting it.. . . . He intends only his own gain, and he is in this, as in many other cases, led by an invisible hand to promote an end which was no part of his intention. . . . By pursuing his own interest he frequently promotes that of the society more effectually than when he really intends to promote it. I have never known much good done by those who affected to trade for the public good.
**Adam Smith**

482

All systems either of preference or of restraint, therefore, being thus completely taken away, the obvious and simple system of natural liberty establishes itself of its own accord. Every man, as long as he does not violate the laws of justice, is left perfectly free to pursue his own interest in his own way, and to bring both his industry and capital into competition with those of any other man or order of men. The sovereign is completely discharged from a duty, in the attempting to perform which he must always be exposed to innumerable delusions, and for the proper performance of which no human wisdom or knowledge could ever be sufficient: the duty of superintending the industry of private people.
**Adam Smith**

Don't gamble. Take all your savings and buy some good stock and hold it till it goes up. If it don't go up, don't buy it.
**Will Rogers**

Men of business must not break their word twice.
**Thomas Fuller**

A corporation cannot blush.
**attributed to Howel Walsh**

All business sagacity reduces itself in the last analysis to a judicious use of sabotage.
**Thorstein Veblen**

I talked of the little attachment which subsisted between near relations in London. "Sir," said Johnson, "in a country so commercial as ours, where every man can do for himself, there is not so much occasion for that attachment. No man is thought the worse of here, whose brother was hanged. In uncommercial countries, many of the branches of a family must depend on the stock; so, in order to make the head of the family take care of them, they are represented as connected with his reputation, that, self-love being interested, he may exert himself to promote their interest. You have first large circles, or clans; as commerce increases, the connection is confined to families. By degrees, that too goes off, as having become unnecessary, and there being few opportunities of intercourse. One brother is a merchant in the city, and another is an officer in the guards. How little intercourse can these two have!"
**James Boswell**

Still we live meanly, like ants; though the fable tells us that we were long ago changed into men; like pygmies we fight with cranes; it is error upon error, and clout upon clout, and our best virtue has for its occasion a superfluous and evitable wretchedness. Our life is frittered away by detail. An honest man has hardly need to count more than his ten fingers, or in extreme cases he may add his ten toes, and lump the rest. Simplicity, simplicity, simplicity! I say, let your affairs be as two or three, and not a hundred or a thousand; instead of a million count half a dozen, and keep your accounts on your thumb nail. In the midst of this chopping sea of civilized life, such are the clouds and storms and quicksands and thousand-and-one items to be allowed for, that a man has to live, if he would not founder and go to the bottom and not make his port at all, by dead reckoning, and he must be a great calculator indeed who succeeds. Simplify, simplify. Instead of three meals a day, if it be necessary eat but one; instead of a hundred dishes, five; and reduce other things in proportion. Our life is like a German Confederacy, made up of petty states, with its boundary forever fluctuating, so that even a German cannot tell you how it is bounded at any moment. The nation itself, with all its so-called internal improvements, which, by the way are all external and superficial, is just such an unwieldy and overgrown establishment, cluttered with furniture and tripped up by its own traps, ruined by luxury and heedless expense, by want of calculation and a worthy aim, as the million households in the land; and the only cure for it as for them is in a rigid economy, a stern and more than Spartan simplicity of life and elevation of purpose. It lives too fast. Men think that it is essential that the *Nation* have commerce, and export ice, and talk through a telegraph, and ride thirty miles an hour, without a doubt, whether *they* do or not; but whether we should live like baboons or like men, is a little uncertain. If we do not get out sleepers, and forge rails, and devote days and nights to the work, but go to tinkering upon our *lives* to improve *them,* who will build railroads? And if railroads are not built, how shall we get to heaven in season? But if we stay at home and mind our business, who will want railroads? We do not ride on the railroad; it rides upon us. Did you ever think what those sleepers are that underlie the railroad? Each one is a man, an Irishman, or a Yankee man. The rails are laid on them, and they are covered with sand, and the cars run smoothly over them. They are sound sleepers, I assure you. And every few years a new lot is laid down and run over; so that, if some have the pleasure of riding on a rail, others have the misfortune to be ridden upon. And when they run over a man that is walking in his sleep, a supernumerary sleeper in the wrong position, and wake him up, they suddenly stop the cars, and make a hue and cry about it, as if this were an exception. I am glad to know that it takes a gang of men for every five miles to keep the sleepers down and level in their beds as it is, for this is a sign that they may sometime get up again.

Henry David Thoreau

Alexis de Tocqueville

# That Aristocracy May Be Engendered by Manufactures

I have shown that democracy is favourable to the growth  1
of manufactures, and that it increases without limit the numbers of the manufacturing classes: we shall now see by what side-road manufacturers may possibly in their turn bring men back to aristocracy. It is acknowledged that when a workman is engaged every day upon the same detail, the whole commodity is produced with greater ease, promptitude, and economy. It is likewise acknowledged that the cost

Alexis de Tocqueville (1805-1859), French politician and writer, is best known in this country as the author of *Democracy in America*, though in France he is esteemed also for his other writings and for his political activity just before and after the Revolution of 1848.

In 1831—when he was not quite twenty-six—Tocqueville arrived in the United States in order to study the penal system. After landing at Newport, Rhode Island, he set out on a journey of nine months and some 7,000 miles, traveling by steamer, stage coach, and horseback, and visiting such places as Buffalo, Boston, New Orleans, and Green Bay. In 1835 he published *De la démocratie en Amérique*. Translated into English and published in four volumes (1835-1840), the book soon became a classic of political literature.

of the production of manufactured goods is diminished by the extent of the establishment in which they are made, and by the amount of capital employed or of credit. These truths had long been imperfectly discerned, but in our time they have been demonstrated. They have been already applied to many very important kinds of manufactures, and the humblest will gradually be governed by them. I know of nothing in politics which deserves to fix the attention of the legislator more closely than these two new axioms of the science of manufactures.

When a workman is unceasingly and exclusively engaged in the fabrication of one thing, he ultimately does his work with singular dexterity; but at the same time he loses the general faculty of applying his mind to the direction of the work. He every day becomes more adroit and less industrious; so that it may be said of him, that in proportion as the workman improves the man is degraded. What can be expected of a man who has spent twenty years of his life in making heads for pins? and to what can that mighty human intelligence, which has so often stirred the world, be applied in him, except it be to investigate the best method of making pins' heads? When a workman has spent a considerable portion of his existence in this manner, his thoughts are for ever set upon the object of his daily toil; his body has contracted certain fixed habits, which it can never shake off: in a word, he no longer belongs to himself, but to the calling which he has chosen. It is in vain that laws and manners have been at the pains to level all barriers round such a man, and to open to him on every side a thousand different paths to fortune; a theory of manufactures more powerful than manners and laws binds him to a craft, and frequently to a spot, which he cannot leave: it assigns to him a certain place in society, beyond which he cannot go: in the midst of universal movement it has rendered him stationary. 2

In proportion as the principle of the division of labour is more extensively applied, the workman becomes more weak, more narrow-minded, and more dependent. The art advances, the artisan recedes. On the other hand, in proportion as it becomes more manifest that the productions of manufactures are by so much the cheaper and better as the manufacture is larger and the amount of capital employed more considerable, wealthy and educated men come forward to embark in manufactures which were heretofore abandoned to poor or ignorant handicraftsmen. The magnitude of the efforts required, and the importance of the results to be obtained, attract them. Thus at the very time at which the science of manufactures lowers the class of workmen, it raises the class of masters. 3

Whereas the workman concentrates his faculties more and more 4 upon the study of a single detail, the master surveys a more extensive whole, and the mind of the latter is enlarged in proportion as that of the former is narrowed. In a short time the one will require nothing but physical strength without intelligence; the other stands in need of science, and almost of genius, to ensure success. This man resembles more and more the administrator of a vast empire—that man, a brute. The master and the workman have then here no similarity, and their differences increase every day. They are only connected as the two rings at the extremities of a long chain. Each of them fills the station which is made for him, and out of which he does not get: the one is continually, closely, and necessarily dependent upon the other, and seems as much born to obey as that other is to command. What is this but aristocracy?

As the conditions of men constituting the nation become more and 5 more equal, the demand for manufactured commodities becomes more general and more extensive; and the cheapness which places these objects within the reach of slender fortunes becomes a great element of success. Hence there are every day more men of great opulence and education who devote their wealth and knowledge to manufactures; and who seek, by opening large establishments, and by a strict division of labour, to meet the fresh demands which are made on all sides. Thus, in proportion as the mass of the nation turns to democracy, that particular class which is engaged in manufactures becomes more aristocratic. Men grow more alike in the one—more different in the other; and inequality increases in the less numerous class in the same ratio in which it decreases in the community. Hence it would appear, on searching to the bottom, that aristocracy should naturally spring out of the bosom of democracy.

But this kind of aristocracy by no means resembles those kinds 6 which preceded it. It will be observed at once, that as it applies exclusively to manufactures and to some manufacturing callings, it is a monstrous exception in the general aspect of society. The small aristocratic societies which are formed by some manufacturers in the midst of the immense democracy of our age, contain, like the great aristocratic societies of former ages, some men who are very opulent, and a multitude who are wretchedly poor. The poor have few means of escaping from their condition and becoming rich; but the rich are constantly becoming poor, or they give up business when they have realised a fortune. Thus the elements of which the class of the poor is composed are fixed; but the elements of which the class of the rich is composed are not so. To say the truth, though there are rich men, the class of rich men does not exist; for these rich individuals have no feelings or purposes in common, no mutual traditions or mutual hopes; there are therefore members, but no body.

Not only are the rich not compactly united amongst themselves,   7 but there is no real bond between them and the poor. Their relative position is not a permanent one; they are constantly drawn together or separated by their interests. The workman is generally dependent on the master, but not on any particular master; these two men meet in the factory, but know not each other elsewhere; and whilst they come into contact on one point, they stand very wide apart on all others. The manufacturer asks nothing of the workman but his labour; the workman expects nothing from him but his wages. The one contracts no obligation to protect, nor the other to defend; and they are not permanently connected either by habit or by duty. The aristocracy created by business rarely settles in the midst of the manufacturing population which it directs: the object is not to govern that population, but to use it. An aristocracy thus constituted can have no great hold upon these whom it employs; and even if it succeed in retaining them at one moment, they escape the next: it knows not how to will, and it cannot act. The territorial aristocracy of former ages was either bound by law, or thought itself bound by usage, to come to the relief of its serving-men, and to succour their distresses. But the manufacturing aristocracy of our age first impoverishes and debases the men who serve it, and then abandons them to be supported by the charity of the public. This is a natural consequence of what has been said before. Between the workman and the master there are frequent relations, but no real partnership.

I am of opinion, upon the whole, that the manufacturing aristoc-   8 racy which is growing up under our eyes, is one of the harshest which ever existed in the world; but at the same time it is one of the most confined and least dangerous. Nevertheless the friends of democracy should keep their eyes anxiously fixed in this direction; for if ever a permanent inequality of conditions and aristocracy again penetrate into the world, it may be predicted that this is the channel by which they will enter.

# Questions

1. Tocqueville argues that the growth of manufacturing business creates a new aristocratic class. Explain how he reaches that conclusion.

2. Does Tocqueville favor the rise of the new aristocracy? Where do you find support for your answer?
3. Nearly two centuries have passed since Tocqueville wrote, and his style may strike us as unfamiliar, even unnecessarily difficult. If you agree, explain what features of his style account for the difficulty. Then try rewriting paragraph 2 of this essay in your own style and voice.
4. If you have ever had a job making or selling any product, argue that Tocqueville is right—or is wrong—in his assertions about what the job does to the individual.
5. Try applying Tocqueville's argument to the automobile industry as it now exists. Do you think the industry has produced the sorts of people Tocqueville anticipated?

### W. H. Auden

# The Almighty Dollar

$P$olitical and technological developments are rapidly ob-   1
literating all cultural differences and it is possible that, in a not remote future, it will be impossible to distinguish human beings living on one area of the earth's surface from those living on any other, but our different pasts have not yet been completely erased and cultural differences are still perceptible. The most striking difference between an American and a European is the difference in their attitudes towards money. Every European knows, as a matter of historical fact, that in Europe wealth could only be acquired at the expense of other human beings, either by conquering them or by exploiting their labor in factories. Further, even after the Industrial Revolution began, the number of persons who could rise from poverty to wealth was small; the vast majority took it for granted that they would not be much richer nor

W. H. Auden (1907–1973) was born and educated in England, but in 1939 he emigrated to the United States, and in 1946 he became a naturalized citizen. Although Auden is known chiefly as a poet—indeed, as one of the chief poets of the period—he also wrote plays, libretti, and essays.

poorer than their fathers. In consequence, no European associates wealth with personal merit or poverty with personal failure.

To a European, money means power, the freedom to do as he 2 likes, which also means that, consciously or unconsciously, he says: "I want to have as much money as possible myself and others to have as little money as possible."

In the United States, wealth was also acquired by stealing, but the 3 real exploited victim was not a human being but poor Mother Earth and her creatures who were ruthlessly plundered. It is true that the Indians were expropriated or exterminated, but this was not, as it had always been in Europe, a matter of the conquerer seizing the wealth of the conquered, for the Indian had never realized the potential riches of his country. It is also true that, in the Southern states, men lived on the labor of slaves, but slave labor did not make them fortunes; what made slavery in the South all the more inexcusable was that, in addition to being morally wicked, it didn't even pay off handsomely.

Thanks to the natural resources of the country, every American, 4 until quite recently, could reasonably look forward to making more money than his father, so that, if he made less, the fault must be his; he was either lazy or inefficient. What an American values, therefore, is not the possession of money as such, but his power to make it as proof of his manhood; once he has proved himself by making it, it has served its function and can be lost or given away. In no society in history have rich men given away so large a part of their fortunes. A poor American feels guilty at being poor, but less guilty than an American *rentier*[1] who had inherited wealth but is doing nothing to increase it; what can the latter do but take to drink and psychoanalysis?

In the Fifth Circle on the Mount of Purgatory,[2] I do not think that 5 many Americans will be found among the Avaricious; but I suspect that the Prodigals may be almost an American colony. The great vice of Americans is not materialism but a lack of respect for matter.

## Questions

1. Do you think that Auden's generalizations (in the first three paragraphs) about European versus American wealth are fundamentally accurate? If not, what are your objections?

---

[1] A *rentier* (French) is one who derives income from property or investments. (Editors' note)
[2] A reference to Dante's *Divine Comedy*, part of which describes repentant souls being purged by suffering on various levels of a mountain. (Editors' note)

2.  In paragraph 4 Auden writes, "What an American values, therefore, is not the possession of money as such, but his power to make it as proof of his manhood. . . ." Leaving aside, for the moment, the obvious sexism of this observation, do you find any truth in it? How do you think Auden might explain why *women* want money? (Or, in your experience, do women want money to the same extent and for the same reasons men do?)
3.  If you have some knowledge of an Asian, African, or Latin American country, what generalization can you offer about its citizens' attitude toward wealth?
4.  Do you agree with Auden's final sentence? Why, or why not?

## Elbert Hubbard

# A Message to Garcia

In all this Cuban business[1] there is one man stands out on   1
my memory like Mars at perihelion.[2]

When war broke out between Spain and the United States, it was   2
very necessary to communicate quickly with the leader of the Insur-
gents. Garcia was somewhere in the mountain fastnesses of Cuba—
no one knew where. No mail nor telegraph message could reach him.
The President must secure his cooperation, and quickly.

What to do!   3

Some one said to the President, "There is a fellow by the name   4
of Rowan will find Garcia for you, if anybody can."

Elbert Hubbard (1856–1915), born in Bloomington, Illinois, settled in East Aurora, New York, where he founded an artist colony and established the Roycroft Press. The stated ideals of the press were high, but the products were rather shoddy imitations of fine books. Hubbard also edited a magazine, *The Philistine* (1895–1915), to which he was the chief contributor.

[1] Hubbard wrote the essay in 1899, hence "all this Cuban business" refers to the Spanish-American War (1898) and to the peace settlement. Calixto Garcia y Iñigues (1839–1898) was a Cuban revolutionary whose advice was sought by President McKinley. Andrew S. Rowan located Garcia, who then conferred with McKinley in Washington, D.C., where Garcia died. (Editors' note)

[2] Mars at perihelion, i.e., Mars when it is nearest to the sun. (Editors' note)

Rowan was sent for and given a letter to be delivered to Garcia.   5

How "the fellow by the name of Rowan" took the letter, sealed   6
it up in an oil-skin pouch, strapped it over his heart, in four days landed
by night off the coast of Cuba from an open boat, disappeared into
the jungle, and in three weeks came out on the other side of the Island,
having traversed a hostile country on foot, and delivered his letter to
Garcia, are things I have no special desire now to tell in detail. The
point I wish to make is this: McKinley gave Rowan a letter to be delivered to Garcia; Rowan took the letter and did not ask "Where is he
at?"

By the Eternal! there is a man whose form should be cast in death-   7
less bronze and the statue placed in every college of the land. It is not
book-learning young men need, nor instruction about this and that,
but a stiffening of the vertebræ which will cause them to be loyal to
a trust, to act promptly, concentrate their energies: do the thing—
"Carry a message to Garcia."

General Garcia is dead now, but there are other Garcias. No man   8
who has endeavored to carry out an enterprise where many hands
were needed but has been well-nigh appalled at times by the imbecility
of the average man—the inability or unwillingness to concentrate on
a thing and do it. Slip-shod assistance, foolish inattention, dowdy indifference, & half-hearted work seem the rule; and no man succeeds,
unless by hook or crook, or threat, he forces or bribes other men to
assist him; or mayhap, God in his goodness performs a miracle, and
sends him an Angel of Light for an assistant. You, reader, put this
matter to a test: You are sitting now in your office—six clerks are within
call. Summon any one and make this request: "Please look in the encyclopedia and make a brief memorandum for me concerning the life
of Correggio."

Will the clerk quietly say, "Yes sir," and go do the task?   9

On your life he will not. He will look at you out of a fishy eye and   10
ask one or more of the following questions:

Who was he?

Which encyclopedia?

Where is the encyclopedia?

Was I hired for that?

Don't you mean Bismarck?   15

What's the matter with Charlie doing it?

Is he dead?

Is there any hurry?

Shan't I bring you the book and let you look it up yourself?

What do you want to know for?    20

And I will lay you ten to one that after you have answered the questions, & explained how to find the information, and why you want it, the clerk will go off and get one of the other clerks to help him try to find Garcia—and then come back and tell you there is no such man. Of course I may lose my bet, but according to the Law of Average I will not.

Now if you are wise you will not bother to explain to your "assistant" that Correggio is indexed under the C's, not in the K's, but you will smile sweetly and say, "Never mind," and go look it up yourself.

And this incapacity for independent action, this moral stupidity, this infirmity of the will, this unwillingness to cheerfully catch hold and lift, are the things that put pure Socialism so far into the future. If men will not act for themselves, what will they do when the benefit of their effort is for all? A first-mate with knotted club seems necessary; and the dread of getting "the bounce" Saturday night, holds many a worker to his place. Advertise for a stenographer, and nine out of ten who apply can neither spell nor punctuate—and do not think it necessary to.

Can such a one write a letter to Garcia?

"You see that book-keeper," said the foreman to me in a large    25 factory.

"Yes, what about him?"

"Well, he's a fine accountant, but if I'd send him up town on an errand, he might accomplish the errand all right, and on the other hand, might stop at four saloons on the way, and when he got to Main Street, would forget what he had been sent for."

Can such a man be entrusted to carry a message to Garcia?

We have recently been hearing much maudlin sympathy expressed for the "down-trodden denizen of the sweatshop" and the "homeless wanderer searching for honest employment," and with it all often go many hard words for the men in power.

Nothing is said about the employer who grows old before his time    30 in a vain attempt to get frowsy ne'er-do-wells to do intelligent work; and his long, patient striving with "help" that does nothing but loaf when his back is turned. In every store and factory there is a constant weeding-out process going on. The employer is constantly sending away "help" that have shown their incapacity to further the interests of the business, and others are being taken on. No matter how good times are, this sorting continues, only if times are hard and work is scarce, the sorting is done finer—but out and forever out the incompetent and unworthy go. It is the survival of the fittest. Self-interest prompts every employer to keep the best—those who can carry a message to Garcia.

I know one man of really brilliant parts who has not the ability to 31 manage a business of his own, and yet who is absolutely worthless to any one else, because he carries with him constantly the insane suspicion that his employer is oppressing, or intending to oppress him. He cannot give orders; and he will not receive them. Should a message be given him to take to Garcia, he would probably at once refer to you as a greedy, grasping Shylock, and tell you to "Take it yourself!" He regards all business men as rogues, and constantly uses the term "commercial" as an epithet. To-night this man walks the streets looking for work, the wind whistling through his thread-bare coat. No one who knows him dare employ him, for he is a regular fire-brand of discontent. He is impervious to reason, and the only thing that can impress him is the toe of a thick-soled No. 9 boot.

Of course I know that one so morally deformed is no less to be 32 pitied than a physical cripple: but in our pitying, let us drop a tear, too, for the men who are striving to carry on a great enterprise, whose working hours are not limited by the whistle, and whose hair is fast turning white through the struggle to hold in line dowdy indifference, slip-shod imbecility, and the heartless ingratitude, which, but for their enterprise, would be both hungry and homeless.

Have I put the matter too strongly? Possibly I have; but when all 33 the world has gone a-slumming I wish to speak a word of sympathy for the man who succeeds—the man who, against great odds, has directed the efforts of others, and having succeeded, finds there's nothing in it: nothing but bare board and clothes. I have carried a dinner pail and worked for day's wages, and I have also been an employer of labor, and I know there is something to be said on both sides. There is no excellence, per se, in poverty; rags are no recommendation; and all employers are not rapacious and high handed, any more than all poor men are virtuous. My heart goes out to the man who does his work when the "boss" is away, as well as when he is at home. And the man, who, when given a letter for Garcia, quietly takes the missive, without asking any idiotic questions, and with no lurking intention of chucking it into the nearest sewer, or of doing aught else but deliver it, never gets "laid off," nor has to go on a strike for higher wages. Civilization is one long anxious search for just such individuals. Anything such a man asks shall be granted. He is wanted in every city, town and village—in every office, shop, store and factory. The world cries out for such: he is needed, and is needed badly—the man who can carry a message to Garcia.

## Questions

1. In paragraph 30 Hubbard invokes the phrase "survival of the fittest." Why? What does he mean?
2. In the first third of the twentieth century employers distributed to their employees millions of copies of this essay. The essay is apparently almost unknown today. Why?
3. If you did not know who Correggio was when you began this essay, did you look him up while reading the essay or immediately after finishing it? Why, or why not? If you didn't look him up, do you plan to? If you do look him up, you might think about whether Hubbard would offer him a job.
4. Under what circumstances would you go to work for Hubbard? Would you hire him to work for you? Why?

Alexandra Armstrong

# Starting a Business

$M$arian Strong, a 33-year-old married woman with two    1
children, ages six and eight, worked at a bank until her first child was born. Her husband, Edward, has worked for the same corporation for the past 10 years. Paid $50,000 annually, he feels that his job is stable. Their expenses are moderate, both mortgage on their home and the car loan payments are low. Although they live on Edward's salary, three years ago Marian went to work for H & R Block preparing tax returns. While there, she managed to save $5,000 of her earnings.

Alexandra Armstrong, president of an independent financial planning firm, has appeared on such television programs as *Good Morning America* and *Wall Street Week*. In 1987 *Money* magazine called her one of the "most qualified Financial Planners in the U.S." The essay reprinted here appeared in *Ms.* magazine.

In addition to enjoying the work, Marian discovered that many of 2
the company's clients needed to know how to set up and maintain
financial records. A number were willing to pay a fee to have this done
and some even wanted her to pay their monthly bills. As a result,
Marian, who recently inherited $5,000 from an aunt, would like to use
this windfall to start her own home-based business to organize and
maintain financial records for clients.

I recommended Marian prepare a business plan describing the 3
nature of her business, and why she believes there's a need for it.
Estimates of her start-up costs, as well as projected expenses and income for the first year, must also be included. I also reminded her that
people in home-based offices often find excuses not to work, and that
a wise move would be to have a separate room devoted exclusively to
business.

Having decided to give one room totally to her work, Marian 4
needed a computer, a copying machine, some furniture and stationery.
Her savings, which she estimates at $5,000, will cover these expenses.
I told her not to expect to be profitable in the first year, but to plan
for the worst case. Marian has her inheritance to fall back on, as well
as an untapped $5,000 line of credit that she shares with her husband.

Marian wasn't sure whether her business should be a sole pro- 5
prietorship, partnership, or a corporation. As a rule one should achieve
$100,000 in revenues before incorporation is worthwhile. I recom-
mended a sole proprietorship until her revenues become substantial,
because it is less encumbering than a partnership.

We then discussed her marketing strategy. She needs to make sure 6
that people find out about her business, while keeping her costs minimal. I suggested that she write letters introducing herself to estate
planners and CPAs who don't want to be involved in record keeping;
use personal contacts for referrals, like her former colleagues at H &
R Block; and also make contact with organizations that cater to women
over the age of 60, since they usually have little experience handling
their own financial affairs.

It is important that Marian regularly review her situation to see 7
how her sales and profits are progressing in line with projections and
whether more marketing should be done or cost reduction techniques
be employed.

Last, but not least, I stressed the importance when starting a busi- 8
ness of getting good advisers: a lawyer to help determine potential
liabilities that might be involved; an insurance agent to make sure of
sufficient liability coverage; and a tax adviser who specializes in small
businesses. This is not an area where one should try to save money,

but on the other hand, one good initial conversation with a business lawyer or consultant at an hourly rate is often sufficient, and the same holds true for a tax adviser. Then one can continue to consult on a need-to-know basis.

There are also a number of organizations that Marian can turn to   9 for advice and valuable information. The National Association of Women Business Owners, 600 South Federal Street, Suite 400, Chicago, Illinois 60605, is an excellent resource for women in sole proprietorships and has many local chapters. The National Alliance of Homebased Businesswomen, P.O. Box 306, Midland Park, New Jersey 07432, and the Small Business Administration are also useful.

## Questions

1. This essay is fundamentally an essay on a process—in this case, how to start a business. Reread it, and see whether (within the severe limitations of the space allowed) it covers all the main points. And does it waste space on irrelevant matters?
2. Do you think the essay is well organized? What *is* the organization?
3. What do you think of Marian Strong's idea for a business, and why?

Thomas P. Rohlen

# For the Manager's Bookshelf

### Why Japanese Education Works

**The Japanese School: Lessons for Industrial America** by Benjamin Duke. New York: Praeger, 1986. 265 pages. $32.95 hardbound, $12.95 paper.

**The Japanese Educational Challenge: A Commitment to Children** by Merry White. New York: Free Press, 1987. 250 pages. $18.95 hardbound.

Thomas P. Rohlen, a professor of anthropology at Stanford University, is the author of *Japan's High Schools* and the co-editor of *Inside the Japanese System*, a book on Japanese political economy. This essay was originally published as a book review in the *Harvard Business Review*.

Japan's trade prowess has given rise to a peculiar media syndrome— 1
let's call it Japan daze. In this syndrome, praise for Japan's accomplishments leads to insistence that we learn from the Japanese. Others,
in reaction, then disparage Japan or attribute its success to government
intervention or national character. Finally, confusion about facts and
contradictory interpretations fill the public mind and a kind of daze
sets in. This result shouldn't be surprising since Japan is so important
and distinctive and our preoccupation so new. But it disguises some
important changes already on the books, changes managers are the
most likely to recognize.

Much that has happened in management in the last ten years stems 2
from the need to cope with the Japanese challenge. In manufacturing,
the Japanese example has given rise or momentum to a new emphasis
on quality, more attention to inventory control, an effort to build cooperative supplier relationships, encouragement of worker participation, new patterns of union-management relations, and much more.
Strategy and finance, while less deeply affected, have also reflected
new ways of thinking based on Japanese practice. Nor has management been the only area affected: unions, industrial policy, even the
conduct of police work have been changed in directions pointed out
by the Japanese.

In none of these instances, however, have the changes been mat- 3
ters of simple emulation. Americans abhor a copycat, but we will respond to a competitive challenge. And this is how Japan has been
influencing us. We have been forced to ask hard questions, ones that
left on our own we would have resisted and would still be resisting if
it weren't for the pressure of the marketplace. Japan daze disguises a
more fundamental truth: under Japan's stimulus, America is definitely
changing.

Signs of this adaptive learning process have lately been appearing 4
in education. For most of this century, the public schools were our
pride and joy. Visitors from around the world crowded into our classrooms to observe our philosophy in action. We taught others. There
was very little they taught us. We promised educational opportunity.
We emphasized practical learning. And our economic success confirmed the virtue of our approach.

Such confidence and intellectual isolation are no longer warranted. 5
The floundering state of U.S. manufacturing and the unfilled academic
requirements of emerging high-tech industries highlight the problems
of American schools—poor overall results, disorder, lack of standards,
and great disparity in quality. Now two books, *The Japanese School:*

*Lessons for Industrial America,* by Benjamin Duke, and *The Japanese Educational Challenge: A Commitment to Children,* by Merry White, introduce us to the Japanese case and the challenge it represents.

Both Duke and White come to the same basic conclusion: superb   6
human resources are the foundation of Japan's success, and they come from an educational system superior to our own. Remember all the advantages the United States started off with after World War II? Scale, low-cost capital, a superior infrastructure, cheap resources, the most advanced technology, the largest domestic market, an outstanding global market share. The only advantages the Japanese could claim were government policies that protected and developed industries, an absence of international burdens, and a talented population.

Government policies alone create nothing industrial. So Japan's   7
new prowess, we must conclude, has sprung from the nation's basic capacities—skilled workers, strong management, a will to succeed, and a talent for learning. Certainly, people and management show up time and again in studies that compare the efficiencies of our manufacturing and theirs.

Benjamin Duke, a professor of education at International Christian   8
University in Tokyo and a longtime resident of Japan, presents his case in a straightforward manner. He notes that the Japanese government has placed education among its highest priorities for more than a century, viewing it as key in the effort to catch and overtake Western industrial leaders. This has meant four things: national standards, adequate resources evenly allocated, high status for teachers, and a drive for continuous improvement.

Turning to the schools themselves, Duke shows how they create   9
loyal workers by teaching the importance of cooperation and responsibility to peers. Whereas in America schools tend to encourage individualism and independent choice, in Japan the classroom group occupies center stage in virtually every aspect of school life. This, Duke argues, helps explain such things as the low absenteeism, the teamwork, and the responsiveness to company needs that characterize the Japanese work force. Sharing the same social values, schools anticipate the needs of the workplace.

Similarly, Duke credits the schools with creating a highly literate   10
work force armed with superb math and science skills. This takes some explaining. First, while a quarter of the U.S. student population drops out before the end of high school, the comparable proportion in Japan is less than 10%. Second, by the time they graduate from high school, Japanese students will have attended classes $2\frac{1}{2}$ years more than their

American counterparts thanks to longer school years and Saturday classes. The Japanese curriculum also moves at a faster pace, so much so that the math high school students are required to take is taught in the United States at the college level. Further, weekly teaching time is about a quarter longer because of fewer disturbances and extraneous events.

The results speak for themselves. Japan has almost no illiteracy, 11 whereas functional illiteracy is estimated at around 20% in the United States. Japanese students earn top scores on international math and science tests, while U.S. students score below the mean. The range of variation for Japanese scores is narrow (implying equality of training), whereas it is large for the American sample. In virtually every subject from music to world history, Japanese children learn more, much more, than their American counterparts during the first 12 years of school.

Focusing next on diligence, Duke shows how exam competition, 12 which can begin at the kindergarten level and is nearly universal by the time students enter high school, instills habits of hard work, concentration, and persistence. Half of the nation's middle-school population attends cram schools (further evidence that competition is intense). The result is that the typical Japanese student spends twice as much time doing homework as the typical American.

Reading Duke's account, you can't help feeling jealous of Japanese 13 managers, who are given such skilled and disciplined workers to lead. In fact, were it not for their recent successes with American workers at places like Honda's Marysville plant and the GM-Toyota Fremont joint venture, we might be inclined to discount the praise heaped on Japanese managers.

More to the point, however, is how readily education and man- 14 agement fit together in Japan, encompassing not just skills but also a work ethic and a philosophy of organization. Higher levels of delegation, the notion that line operators can regularly improve process technology, the de-emphasis of monetary incentives, the use of teams, the encouragement of crosstraining and continuous learning, the egalitarian spirit, the sense of trust among levels—all begin with the assumption of a willing, compliant, and socialized work force accustomed to hard work, discipline, and cooperation.

Japanese managers in this country either seek out such a work 15 force (as in the many greenfield startups far from our big cities) or carefully select and intensively train U.S. workers to reach Japanese standards. The once-militant head of the union at the Toyota-run plant in Fremont told me recently that he has learned more in the last 2 years than he had in the previous 20 under GM management in the same plant. Clearly, the Toyota managers have decided they can remedy years of performance problems through their own educational efforts.

The commitment to learning that fosters this belief is a key theme in Merry White's book. Whereas Duke deals almost exclusively with the schools, White also examines the family, the psychology of learning, and the culture. Formerly a researcher at Harvard's Graduate School of Education and now a professor of Japanese sociology at Boston University, she seeks explanations for Japan's educational success in the attitudes that underlie the process. This exploration is more subtle and speculative than a simple recitation of the virtues of Japanese schools and also more difficult to summarize. But in essence White argues that Japan is a society devoted to children and to learning. 16

This devotion begins with mothers who focus on child rearing as a valued occupation and continues with teachers who have learned how to guide children toward social goals without alienating them. Without preaching social morality, Japanese teachers continuously demonstrate the commonsense wisdom of cooperative living. They also share certain attitudes that are tied to important differences in the teaching and learning process. 17

A good example is the Japanese teacher's faith in the potential of all children. Less emphasis on each child's inherent ability reinforces the Japanese tendency to view effort as the crucial determinant of success. What does this mean concretely? In U.S. schools, we tend to look for disabilities and to single out slow learners, which in turn leads to ability groupings, special programs, fast and slow tracks, and self-fulfilling prophecies about each child's future. The results are great differentiation in outcomes, help for those with learning handicaps, classroom patterns that discourage teamwork, and a convenient explanation for poor results that takes the onus off the child, the teacher, and the family. 18

The Japanese approach, on the other hand, starts with the assumption that all children, with only the most obvious exceptions, can learn at the same pace. This leads to classrooms in which the whole class stays together, class unity and cooperation are the norm, and children, especially slower ones, are pushed harder and harder to make their best effort. 19

Which approach is better depends on context. In Japan, certain 20 factors minimize differences among students. There is much less disparity in family and ethnic background, as well as less divorce and poverty. Further, students have less difficulty beginning to read Japanese, while American elementary classrooms inevitably divide into distinct reading-level groups. The point, therefore, is not that we should adopt the Japanese approach wholesale but rather that we must be on guard against the excesses of our approach—unnecessary differentiation, demotivating excuses, and low expectations and standards.

In education, as in manufacturing, Japan is useful as a mirror, not 21 a model. Japanese practice reveals the problems in our approach and challenges us to improve, but it offers few off-the-shelf solutions. Both authors agree on this point, despite their obvious admiration for Japan's accomplishments and their belief that we have much to learn. We don't need a shopping list; we do need a deeper commitment to education from parents, teachers, government, and business. Our performance is so markedly inferior that only a fool would imagine we can catch up easily or discover a single approach that will fix the problem. Japan has traveled a long road in building its system, and the pivotal factor has not been technique or organization or even philosophy. Rather, it has been the general agreement, decade after decade, that education is a crucial national priority and that better and better results are possible if a society and its leaders maintain a commitment to it.

Numerous reports, most notably *A Nation at Risk* (put out by the 22 National Commission on Excellence in Education), have urged us to reform our public schools to better compete with the Japanese. Businesspeople, once disinterested observers, have begun to link education to the competitiveness of their companies, their local economies, and the nation as a whole.

But if Japan is the competitive standard, our efforts are just be- 23 ginning. Changing public education is a much harder task than turning GM around, and we know how difficult that is proving to be. As we learned from the Sputnik-inspired reforms 25 years ago, it takes more than brief flurries of public outcry and frantic change to make a dent in educational problems. And with the federal government essentially a bystander, the job of setting progressively higher standards and strengthening the schools is falling on states and localities, where debate usually falters on the specious issues of money and equity.

In this respect, the Japanese example can help us do some fresh 24 thinking. Japan's success has little to comfort ideologues of either the left or the right. Curricular standards and much of the money come from the central government. The teachers' union is powerful. A voucher system would be anathema to most Japanese parents because it would imply an abdication of responsibility by the government and the loss of a common focus. Teachers' salaries are somewhat more attractive than in the United States, but then teachers work 12 months a year. Class size is large by our standards and physical plants are Spartan, but large sums of money are spent on equalizing the resources available in each district. Few special programs exist. Teachers have tenure almost from the start, and salaries are based on seniority. With so many characteristics we would fault, how do the Japanese do so well?

Certainly they begin with a different kind of population, one that 25 is homogeneous and middle-class in character. Very few Japanese children come from impoverished or broken homes or begin school not speaking Japanese or have parents who cannot read. Yet many U.S. schoolchildren have these problems, and meeting the challenge they represent requires a dedication and an educational response unrelated to what the Japanese are doing. But if our failure is most conspicuous with the students who never learn to read or who drop out of school, in some ways we fail even more seriously with the students whose family backgrounds are no different from the average Japanese and who graduate from high school with knowledge and skills the Japanese would expect of an eighth or a ninth grader.

Our failure is not primarily the fault of teachers. Duke and White 26 make it clear that they see no difference in the quality of the teachers in the two countries. Rather, the failure comes from a lack of clear public standards reinforced by parents, future employers, and school authorities themselves. Lacking initiative from the federal government, we have been spending money, blaming teachers, and wringing our hands without the confidence or leadership to set high graduation requirements and stick with them. A commitment to excellence, the current catchphrase, means little if there is no quality-control system in place and if everyone is inclined to blame someone else.

Of course, a set of basic standards will neither represent the high- 27 est ideals of education nor measure many of the most important aspects of what we want to teach. But without a set of enforced standards, gradually raised over many years, there is no reality quotient in the system. Our schools will simply continue to drift from one intellectually satisfying and politically easy fix to another.

Since schools are local problems in America, local leaders are cru- 28 cial. It is here that business has most to contribute. Quite simply, no group of parents is likely to make as much difference in giving backbone to real, sustained reform. The business community can allocate jobs. It can provide the rationale. It is in a position to give teachers recognition and respect. It can wage the political battles. It can provide a sense of urgency and vision to the community as a whole.

If we are to avoid Japan daze in education, we must acknowledge 29 squarely the challenge Japanese education presents: except for our universities and elite schools, we are producing second-rate products. Then, rather than getting bogged down in debate about the pros and cons of this or that Japanese practice, communities need to agree that the status quo is unsatisfactory. Perhaps community leaders and parents could follow the example business has set and visit Japanese schools to see firsthand the high standards that are being achieved and reassure themselves that no cultural magic is involved in achieving them.

Next we must agree on a strategy for raising standards. This is an 30 American problem with no obvious Japanese equivalent. Finally, our most complex and lasting task is to discover what education's real needs are. The very fact that Japanese educational practice contains so little that we would immediately embrace only underscores our need to rethink the issues and get away from the interest-group and ideology-ridden debates in which we are caught. It's time to tackle fundamental questions about how to support schools and teachers in their job of meeting the Japanese challenge.

# Questions

1. In paragraph 6 Rohlen says, "Superb human resources are the foundation of Japan's success, and they come from an educational system superior to our own." Judging from Rohlen's essay, how do you think he would describe "superb human resources"? Do you share his enthusiasm for these qualities? If not, why not?
2. According to Rohlen, what are some of the changes in American business practices resulting from Japan's "trade prowess"? *How* have these changes been the result of Japanese influence?
3. What connection does Rohlen point to between Japanese business and Japanese education? Does he see a parallel connection between business and education in the United States? If so, what is it?
4. In paragraph 14 Rohlen speaks of a "socialized work force." What does he mean by that? Is the work force "socialized" in the United States?

5.  In paragraph 17 Rohlen says, "Without preaching social morality, Japanese teachers continuously demonstrate the commonsense wisdom of cooperative living." (He might have mentioned, for example, that in Japanese schools the students serve the lunches and then do the cleaning up; indeed, they do all the cleaning in the school, including scrubbing floors and dusting.) If possible, give examples of demonstrations of "the commonsense wisdom of cooperative living" that you have experienced in school. Could such demonstrations be amplified? If so, how?

6.  Rohlen's review appeared in the *Harvard Business Review,* so his audience consists of persons—chiefly managers—in business. Why does he call attention to demonstrations of "cooperative living" (paragraph 17) rather than to demonstrations of competitiveness?

7.  What distinction does Rohlen (and Merry White, apparently) make between a child's inherent ability and the same child's potential? What is the implied contrast between Japanese and American schools on this point? Does Rohlen believe that one emphasis is better than the other? If not, what does he recommend?

8.  What contrast does Rohlen make or imply between Japan and the United States in the role of government in education? Does he recommend a more active role for our federal government?

9.  What role does the author see for business in improving American education? If you have read Milton Friedman's essay (page 513), do you think Friedman would agree that the role is appropriate for business?

## Robert W. Keidel

# A New Game for Managers to Play

As the football season gradually gives way to basketball, 1 corporate managers would do well to consider the differences between these games. For just as football mirrors industrial structures of the

Robert W. Keidel, a graduate of Williams College and the Wharton School of the University of Pennsylvania, directs a consulting firm. He is the author of *Game Plans: Sports Strategies for Business* (1985) and *Corporate Players: Designs for Working and Winning Together* (1988).

past, basketball points the way to the corporate structure of the future.

It's the difference between the former chief executive officer of I. 2
T. T., Harold Geneen, the master football coach who dictates his players' roles and actions, and Donald Burr, the People Express Airlines chief executive officer, who puts his players on the floor and lets them manage themselves.

Football is, metaphorically, a way of life in work today—the cor- 3
porate sport. This is reflected in the language many managers use:

"It's taken my staff and me a sizable chunk of time, but we now 4
have a solid game plan for the XYZ job. Jack, I want you to quarterback this thing all the way into the end zone. Of course, a lot of it will be making the proper assignments—getting the right people to run interference and the right ones to run with the ball. But my main concern is that we avoid mistakes. No fumbles, no interceptions, no sacks, no penalties. I don't want us to have to play catch-up; no two-minute drills at the end. I want the game plan executed exactly the way it's drawn. When we're done we want to look back with pride at a win— and not have to Monday-morning-quarterback a loss."

Does this football language represent more than just a convenient 5
shorthand? Almost certainly it does, because the metaphors we use routinely are the means by which we structure experience. Thus, football metaphors may well reflect—and reinforce—underlying organizational dynamics. But football, despite its pervasiveness, is the wrong model for most corporations.

Consider the scenario above. Planning has been neatly separated 6
from implementation; those expected to carry out the game plan had no part in creating it. Also, the communication flow is one-way: from the head coach (speaker) to the quarterback (Jack)—and, presumably, from the quarterback to the other players. And the thrust of the message is risk-averse; the real name of the game is control—minimizing mistakes. But perhaps most significant is the assumption of stability— that nothing will change to invalidate the corporate game plan. "No surprises!" as Mr. Geneen likes to say.

Stability is a realistic assumption in football, even given the sport's 7
enormous complexity, because of the time available to coaches—between games and between plays. A pro football game can very nearly be programmed. Carl Peterson, formerly with the Philadelphia Eagles and now president of the United States Football League's champions, the Baltimore Stars, has estimated that managing a game is 75 percent preparation and only 25 percent adjustment.

Thus, football truly is the realm of the coach—the head coach, he 8 who calls the shots. (Most pro quarterbacks do not call their own plays.) As Bum Phillips has said in tribute to the head coach of the Miami Dolphins, Don Shula, "He can take his'n and beat your'n, or he can take your'n and beat his'n."

But football is not an appropriate model for most businesses pre- 9 cisely because instability is an overwhelming fact of life. Market competition grows ever more spastic, product life-cycles shrink unimaginably and technology courses on paths of its own.

In this milieu, corporate "players" simply cannot perform effec- 10 tively if they must wait for each play to be called for them, and remain in fixed positions—or in narrowly defined roles—like football players; increasingly, they need to deploy themselves flexibly, in novel combinations.

Thirty years ago it may have been possible to regard core business 11 functions—R&D, manufacturing and marketing—as separate worlds, with little need for interaction. R&D would design the product and then lob it over the wall to manufacturing; manufacturing would make the product and lob it over another wall to the customer.

No need to worry about problems that do not fit neatly into the 12 standard departments; these are inconsequential and infrequent. And when they do arise, they are simply bumped up the hierarchy to senior management—the head coach and his staff.

In effect, performance is roughly the sum of the functions—just 13 as a football team's performance is the sum of the performances of its platoons—offense, defense and special teams. Clearly, this view of the corporation is anachronistic. Yet it remains all too common.

Business's "season" is changing, and a new metaphor is needed. 14 While football will continue to be a useful model for pursuing machinelike efficiency and consistency—that is, for minimizing redundancies, bottlenecks and errors—this design favors stability at the expense of change. Since now more than ever businesses must continuously innovate and adapt, a more promising model is basketball.

To begin with, basketball is too dynamic a sport to permit the rigid 15 separation of planning and execution that characterizes football. Unlike football teams, basketball teams do not pause and regroup after each play. As the former star player and coach Bill Russell has noted, "Your game plan may be wiped out by what happens in the first minute of play." Success in basketball depends on the ability of the coach and players to plan and adjust while in motion. Such behavior requires all-around communication—just as basketball demands all-around passing, as opposed to football's linear sequence of "forward," one-way passing.

Basketball also puts a premium on generalist skills. Although dif-    16
ferent players will assume somewhat different roles on the court, all must be able to dribble, pass, shoot, rebound and play defense. Everyone handles the ball—a far cry from what happens on the gridiron. Indeed, basketball is much more player-oriented than football—a sport in which players tend to be viewed as interchangeable parts.

If football is a risk-averse game, basketball is risk-accepting. In    17
basketball, change is seen as normal, not exceptional; hence, change is regarded more as the source of opportunities than of threats. Mr. Geneen has claimed that "Ninety-nine percent of all surprises in business are negative."

Mr. Geneen's perspective is classic football and is tenable in stable,    18
"controllable" environments. But such environments are becoming rare. The future increasingly belongs to managers like Mr. Burr or James Treybig, the founder of Tandem Computers, who thrive on change rather than flee from it.

We need fewer head coaches and more player-coaches, less    19
scripted teamwork and more spontaneous teamwork. We need to integrate planning and doing—managing and working—far more than we have to date. Are you playing yesterday's game—or tomorrow's?

# Questions

1. In his first paragraph Keidel says that "football mirrors industrial structures of the past" whereas "basketball points the way to the corporate structure of the future." He several times makes similar assertions—for instance, in paragraph 5 he says "football . . . is the wrong model for most corporations." Does he support his view with evidence? If so, call attention to the evidence he offers. Are you convinced by his argument?

2. Keidel says (paragraph 5) that "the metaphors we use routinely are the means by which we structure experience." Consider metaphors drawn from the world of business but used in the context of education. An administrator, for instance, may say, "Last year we *produced* 1,000 majors in business administration; next year we hope to *turn out* twelve hundred; the *bottom line* is, the *supply still falls short of the demand*." What do such metaphors tell us about the

ways in which the speaker sees education (or, to use Keidel's words, the ways in which he or she "structure[s] experience")?

3.  As the preceding question indicates, business itself can provide metaphors, such as "producing" or "turning out" students. In the next few days jot down examples that you encounter in newspapers, television ads, political speeches, or whatever and analyze their implications. (You may even find businesses that use metaphors drawn from business.)

4.  In paragraph 2 Keidel refers to People Express Airlines. What point does he hope to make? Is People Express still in business? (If you don't know, how would you go about finding out?) Does the current status of People Express affect the status of his argument?

Warren Bennis

# Time to Hang Up the Old Sports Clichés

Americans are, on the whole, simple and direct people.     1
We do not incline toward nuances or subtleties, in either our lives or our work. We opt inevitably for the concrete over the abstract. We are also extremely competitive, relishing opponents' losses as we boast of our own victories. For these reasons, sports are not only our favorite form of entertainment but the principal model and metaphor for our own lives.

At home and at work, we talk often of winning and losing, scoring     2
touchdowns, carrying the ball, close calls, going down to the wire, batting a thousand, hitting paydirt and going into extra innings, and while we may like movie, TV and music stars, we admire sports stars. Every father wants his sons to shine on the playing fields, which is

Warren Bennis, born in New York City in 1925, was educated at Antioch College and the Massachusetts Institute of Technology. From 1971 to 1977 he served as the president of the University of Cincinnati. The author of several important books on management, he now teaches at the School of Business in the University of Southern California.

why Little League games frequently have all the carefree air of the London blitz.

Preachers and politicians, among others, see this national obses- 3 sion as healthy, portray us as good people interested in good, clean fun. Universities, including mine, celebrate and reward their athletes as heroes. When the Super Bowl rolls around, the country focuses on The Game.

I am admittedly as obsessed as anyone. I seem to remember forever 4 great plays, great players and even the scores of great games, though I sometimes cannot recall whom I sat next to at dinner three nights ago. But I am also convinced that it is time to find a new model.

Life is not a baseball game. It's never called on account of darkness, 5 much less canceled because of inclement weather. And while major sports are big business now, business is not a sport, and never was. Indeed, thinking of business as a kind of game or sport was always simplistic. Now it's downright dangerous.

Games are of limited duration, take place on or in fixed and finite 6 sites and are governed by openly promulgated rules that are enforced on the spot by neutral professionals. Moreover, they are performed by relatively evenly matched teams that are counseled and led through every move by seasoned hands. Scores are kept, and at the end of the game, a winner is declared.

Business is usually a little different. In fact, if there is anyone out 7 there who can say that his business is of limited duration, takes place on a fixed site, is governed by openly promulgated rules that are enforced on the spot by neutral professionals, competes only on relatively even terms and performs in a way that can be measured in runs or points, then he is either extraordinarily lucky or seriously deluded.

The risks in thinking of business in sports terms are numerous. 8 First, to measure a business on the basis of wins and losses is to misunderstand both the purposes of a specific business and the nature of business itself. No business—whether it sells insurance or manufactures cars—can or should be designed to win. Rather, it should be designed to grow, both quantitatively and qualitatively. In this sense, it vies more with itself than with its competition. This is not to say there are never winners or losers—in head-to-head contests, as when two ad agencies are competing for the same account, someone will win and someone will lose. It is to say, to paraphrase Vince Lombardi's legendary dictum, winning isn't everything, it's one of many things a business must accomplish.

Thus, a company designed merely to win, will probably lose in 9 the long run. For example, the John Doe Insurance Company could win the auto market overnight by offering comprehensive coverage for $100 a year. However, the company would fail when the claims began coming in.

Second, it is perilous to think of limits, rules and absolutes in business. Athletes compete for a given number of hours in a given number of games over a given period of weeks or months. Businesses are in the arena for decades, sometimes centuries. Though the action may rise and subside, it never stops. It does not offer any timeouts, much less neatly defined beginnings and endings. 10

American business has traditionally been schizophrenic about rules. When it is flourishing, it wants no rules or regulations. When it is failing, it wants a plethora of rules. For example, Detroit saw Washington as its nemesis until foreign cars flooded the market. Then, Chrysler went to the Feds for a loan, and now Detroit begs Washington to regulate imports while lobbying against Federal safety and quality controls. 11

Athletes perform in a static environment—the size of the field, the length of the contest, even the wardrobes of the players remain the same, day after month after year. Businesses function in a volatile universe, which changes from moment to moment, and hardly ever repeats. It is affected by droughts half a world away, a new gizmo down the street, consumer attitudes and needs, a million things. Given this mercurial context, any business that is not at least as dynamic and flexible as the world in which it functions will soon be out of step or out of business. 12

Clearly, then, there are far more differences between sports and business than similarities. But the danger is that many people will continue to imagine that success in business is like success in sports— flat-out, total victory; a world championship. But the best-run and most successful companies in America do not think in terms of victories and defeats, coming from behind, last-minute saves or shining moments, and they do not count on regulations or referees. Instead, they think in terms of staying power, dedication to quality and an endless effort to do better than they have done. They see change as the only constant, and they try to adapt to the world rather than expect the world to adapt to them. Indeed, it is a business's ability to adapt to an ever-changing world that is the basis for both its success and progress. 13

I should emphasize that I am not criticizing the management of professional sports teams, which are themselves businesses. Some 14 teams are poorly run but others, like the Boston Celtics or Los Angeles Lakers, operate on the same principles that other successful businesses do. They change, they plan for the long-term and they strive ceaselessly for quality. What I object to is comparing the playing field to the marketplace.

The truth is that there is no workable or appropriate metaphor for 15 business except business itself, and that should be sufficient. Like a well-played game, a well-run business is something to see, but, unlike a well-played game, it is not a diversion. Rather, it is life itself—complex, difficult, susceptible to both success and failure, sometimes unruly, always challenging and, often, joyful.

So let's leave the home runs to the Phillies' Mike Schmidt and the 16 touchdowns to the Bears' Walter Payton, and get down to business.

# Questions

1.  In paragraph 5 Bennis suggests that "it's downright dangerous" to see business in terms of metaphors drawn from the world of sports. On the other hand, presumably those who use metaphors believe that the metaphors help them see things freshly and clearly. If you have read Robert Keidel's essay (page 505), do you think that Keidel's use of metaphor clarifies your understanding of business or, on the contrary, does it lead to dangerous misapprehensions? Be as specific as possible.

2.  In paragraph 8, when Bennis says that a business "should be designed to *grow*," he is using a metaphor, for he is comparing a business to a living organism. And in paragraph 11, when he says that American business is "schizophrenic," he uses a metaphor from psychiatry. Reread his essay closely and jot down a list of the metaphors he uses. Do you think his metaphors are useful, or are they (to quote paragraph 5) "dangerous"?

3.  Evaluate Bennis's final paragraph as a final paragraph. What makes it effective or ineffective? Now look at Bennis's opening paragraph. Does his description of Americans largely exclude some groups? Are there readers his opening paragraph might unintentionally "exclude" or turn away?

Milton Friedman

# The Social Responsibility
# of Business Is to Increase
# Its Profits

When I hear businessmen speak eloquently about the "so-  1
cial responsibilities of business in a free-enterprise system," I am reminded of the wonderful line about the Frenchman who discovered
at the age of 70 that he had been speaking prose all his life. The businessmen believe that they are defending free enterprise when they
declaim that business is not concerned "merely" with profit but also
with promoting desirable "social" ends; that business has a "social
conscience" and takes seriously its responsibilities for providing employment, eliminating discrimination, avoiding pollution and whatever else may be the catchwords of the contemporary crop of reformers. In fact they are—or would be if they or anyone else took them
seriously—preaching pure and unadulterated socialism. Businessmen
who talk this way are unwitting puppets of the intellectual forces that
have been undermining the basis of a free society these past decades.

The discussions of the "social responsibilities of business" are no-  2
table for their analytical looseness and lack of rigor. What does it mean
to say that "business" has responsibilities? Only people can have responsibilities. A corporation is an artificial person and in this sense
may have artificial responsibilities, but "business" as a whole cannot
be said to have responsibilities, even in this vague sense. The first step
toward clarity in examining the doctrine of the social responsibility of
business is to ask precisely what it implies for whom.

Presumably, the individuals who are to be responsible are busi-  3
nessmen, which means individual proprietors or corporate executives.
Most of the discussion of social responsibility is directed at corpora-

Milton Friedman, born in Brooklyn in 1912, is a graduate of Rutgers University,
the University of Chicago, and Columbia University. Since 1946 he has taught
economics at the University of Chicago. A leading conservative economist, Friedman has had considerable influence on economic thought in America, through
his popular writings (he wrote a regular column in *Newsweek*), his numerous
scholarly writings, and his presence on national committees.

tions, so in what follows I shall mostly neglect the individual proprietors and speak of corporate executives.

In a free-enterprise, private-property system, a corporate executive  4
is an employee of the owners of the business. He has direct responsibility to his employers. That responsibility is to conduct the business
in accordance with their desires, which generally will be to make as
much money as possible while conforming to the basic rules of the
society, both those embodied in law and those embodied in ethical
custom. Of course, in some cases his employers may have a different
objective. A group of persons might establish a corporation for an
eleemosynary purpose—for example, a hospital or a school. The manager of such a corporation will not have money profit as his objectives
but the rendering of certain services.

In either case, the key point is that, in his capacity as a corporate  5
executive, the manager is the agent of the individuals who own the
corporation or establish the eleemosynary institution, and his primary
responsibility is to them.

Needless to say, this does not mean that it is easy to judge how  6
well he is performing his task. But at least the criterion of performance
is straightforward, and the persons among whom a voluntary con-
tractual arrangement exists are clearly defined.

Of course, the corporate executive is also a person in his own right.  7
As a person, he may have many other responsibilities that he recognizes or assumes voluntarily—to his family, his conscience, his feelings
of charity, his church, his clubs, his city, his country. He may feel
impelled by these responsibilities to devote part of his income to causes
he regards as worthy, to refuse to work for particular corporations,
even to leave his job, for example, to join his country's armed forces.
If we wish, we may refer to some of these responsibilities as "social
responsibilities." But in these respects he is acting as a principal, not
an agent; he is spending his own money or time or energy, not the
money of his employers or the time or energy he has contracted to
devote to their purposes. If these are "social responsibilities," they are
the social responsibilities of individuals, not of business.

What does it mean to say that the corporate executive has a "social  8
responsibility" in his capacity as businessman? If this statement is not
pure rhetoric, it must mean that he is to act in some way that is not
in the interest of his employers. For example, that he is to refrain from
increasing the price of the product in order to contribute to the social
objective of preventing inflation, even though a price increase would
be in the best interests of the corporation. Or that he is to make ex-

penditures on reducing pollution beyond the amount that is in the best interests of the corporation or that is required by law in order to contribute to the social objective of improving the environment. Or that, at the expense of corporate profits, he is to hire "hardcore" unemployed instead of better qualified available workmen to contribute to the social objective of reducing poverty.

In each of these cases, the corporate executive would be spending   9
someone else's money for a general social interest. Insofar as his actions in accord with his "social responsibility" reduce returns to stockholders, he is spending their money. Insofar as his actions raise the price to customers, he is spending the customers' money. Insofar as his actions lower the wages of some employees, he is spending their money.

The stockholders or the customers or the employees could sepa-   10
rately spend their own money on the particular action if they wished to do so. The executive is exercising a distinct "social responsibility," rather than serving as an agent of the stockholders or the customers or the employees, only if he spends the money in a different way than they would have spent it.

But if he does this, he is in effect imposing taxes, on the one hand,   11
and deciding how the tax proceeds shall be spent, on the other.

This process raises political questions on two levels: principle and   12
consequences. On the level of political principle, the imposition of taxes and the expenditure of tax proceeds are governmental functions. We have established elaborate constitutional, parliamentary and judicial provisions to control these functions, to assure that taxes are imposed so far as possible in accordance with the preferences and desires of the public—after all, "taxation without representation" was one of the battle cries of the American Revolution. We have a system of checks and balances to separate the legislative function of imposing taxes and enacting expenditures from the executive function of collecting taxes and administering expenditure programs and from the judicial function of mediating disputes and interpreting the law.

Here the businessman—self-selected or appointed directly or in-   13
directly by stockholders—is to be simultaneously legislator, executive and jurist. He is to decide whom to tax by how much and for what purpose, and he is to spend the proceeds—all this guided only by general exhortations from on high to restrain inflation, improve the environment, fight poverty and so on and on.

The whole justification for permitting the corporate executive to   14
be selected by the stockholders is that the executive is an agent serving

the interests of his principal. This justification disappears when the corporate executive imposes taxes and spends the proceeds for "social" purposes. He becomes in effect a public employee, a civil servant, even though he remains in name an employee of a private enterprise. On grounds of political principle, it is intolerable that such civil servants—insofar as their actions in the name of social responsibility are real and not just window-dressing—should be selected as they are now. If they are to be civil servants, then they must be elected through a political process. If they are to impose taxes and make expenditures to foster "social" objectives, then political machinery must be set up to make the assessment of taxes and to determine through a political process the objectives to be served.

This is the basic reason why the doctrine of "social responsibility" 15 involves the acceptance of the socialist view that political mechanisms, not market mechanisms, are the appropriate way to determine the allocation of scarce resources to alternative uses.

On the grounds of consequences, can the corporate executive in 16 fact discharge his alleged "social responsibilities"? On the other hand, suppose he could get away with spending the stockholders' or customers' or employees' money. How is he to know how to spend it? He is told that he must contribute to fighting inflation. How is he to know what action of his will contribute to that end? He is presumably an expert in running his company—in producing a product or selling it or financing it. But nothing about his selection makes him an expert on inflation. Will his holding down the price of his product reduce inflationary pressure? Or, by leaving more spending power in the hands of his customers, simply divert it elsewhere? Or, by forcing him to produce less because of the lower price, will it simply contribute to shortages? Even if he could answer these questions, how much cost is he justified in imposing on his stockholders, customers and employees for this social purpose? What is his appropriate share and what is the appropriate share of others?

And, whether he wants to or not, can he get away with spending 17 his stockholders', customers' or employees' money? Will not the stockholders fire him? (Either the present ones or those who take over when his actions in the name of social responsibility have reduced the corporation's profits and the price of its stock.) His customers and his employees can desert him for other producers and employers less scrupulous in exercising their social responsibilities.

This facet of "social responsibility" doctrine is brought into sharp 18 relief when the doctrine is used to justify wage restraint by trade unions. The conflict of interest is naked and clear when union officials are asked to subordinate the interest of their members to some more general purpose. If the union officials try to enforce wage restraint, the consequence is likely to be wildcat strikes, rank-and-file revolts and the emergence of strong competitors for their jobs. We thus have the ironic phenomenon that union leaders—at least in the U.S.—have objected to Government interference with the market far more consistently and courageously than have business leaders.

The difficulty of exercising "social responsibility" illustrates, of   19 course, the great virtue of private competitive enterprise—it forces people to be responsible for their own actions and makes it difficult for them to "exploit" other people for either selfish or unselfish purposes. They can do good—but only at their own expense.

Many a reader who has followed the argument this far may be   20 tempted to remonstrate that it is all well and good to speak of Government's having the responsibility to impose taxes and determine expenditures for such "social" purposes as controlling pollution or training the hard-core unemployed, but that the problems are too urgent to wait on the slow course of political processes, that the exercise of social responsibility by businessmen is a quicker and surer way to solve pressing current problems.

Aside from the question of fact—I share Adam Smith's skepticism   21 about the benefits that can be expected from "those who affected to trade for the public good"—this argument must be rejected on grounds of principle. What it amounts to is an assertion that those who favor the taxes and expenditures in question have failed to persuade a majority of their fellow citizens to be of like mind and that they are seeking to attain by undemocratic procedures what they cannot attain by democratic procedures. In a free society, it is hard for "evil" people to do "evil," especially since one man's good is another's evil.

I have, for simplicity, concentrated on the special case of the cor-   22 porate executive, except only for the brief digression on trade unions. But precisely the same argument applies to the newer phenomenon of calling upon stockholders to require corporations to exercise social responsibility (the recent G.M. crusade for example). In most of these cases, what is in effect involved is some stockholders trying to get other stockholders (or customers or employees) to contribute against their will to "social" causes favored by the activists. Insofar as they succeed, they are again imposing taxes and spending the proceeds.

The situation of the individual proprietor is somewhat different.   23 If he acts to reduce the returns of his enterprise in order to exercise

his "social responsibility," he is spending his own money, not someone else's. If he wishes to spend his money on such purposes, that is
his right, and I cannot see that there is any objection to his doing so.
In the process, he, too, may impose costs on employees and customers.
However, because he is far less likely than a large corporation or union
to have monopolistic power, any such side effects will tend to be minor.

Of course, in practice the doctrine of social responsibility is fre-   24
quently a cloak for actions that are justified on other grounds rather
than a reason for those actions.

To illustrate, it may well be in the long-run interest of a corporation   25
that is a major employer in a small community to devote resources to
providing amenities to that community or to improving its government. That may make it easier to attract desirable employees, it may
reduce the wage bill or lessen losses from pilferage and sabotage or
have other worthwhile effects. Or it may be that, given the laws about
the deductibility of corporate charitable contributions, the stockholders
can contribute more to charities they favor by having the corporation
make the gift than by doing it themselves, since they can in that way
contribute an amount that would otherwise have been paid as corporate taxes.

In each of these—and many similar—cases, there is a strong temp-   26
tation to rationalize these actions as an exercise of "social responsibility." In the present climate of opinion, with its widespread aversion
to "capitalism," "profits," the "soulless corporation" and so on, this
is one way for a corporation to generate goodwill as a byproduct of
expenditures that are entirely justified in its own self-interest.

It would be inconsistent of me to call on corporate executives to   27
refrain from this hypocritical window-dressing because it harms the
foundations of a free society. That would be to call on them to exercise
a "social responsibility"! If our institutions and the attitudes of the
public make it in their self-interest to cloak their actions in this way,
I cannot summon much indignation to denounce them. At the same
time, I can express admiration for those individual proprietors or owners of closely held corporations or stockholders of more broadly held
corporations who disdain such tactics as approaching fraud.

Whether blameworthy or not, the use of the cloak of social re-   28
sponsibility, and the nonsense spoken in its name by influential and
prestigious businessmen, does clearly harm the foundations of a free
society. I have been impressed time and again by the schizophrenic
character of many businessmen. They are capable of being extremely
far-sighted and clear-headed in matters that are internal to their busi-

nesses. They are incredibly short-sighted and muddle-headed in matters that are outside their businesses but affect the possible survival of business in general. This short-sightedness is strikingly exemplified in the calls from many businessmen for wage and price guidelines or controls or income policies. There is nothing that could do more in a brief period to destroy a market system and replace it by a centrally controlled system than effective governmental control of prices and wages.

The short-sightedness is also exemplified in speeches by busi- 29 nessmen on social responsibility. This may gain them kudos in the short run. But it helps to strengthen the already too prevalent view that the pursuit of profits is wicked and immoral and must be curbed and controlled by external forces. Once this view is adopted, the external forces that curb the market will not be the social consciences, however highly developed, of the pontificating executives; it will be the iron fist of Government bureaucrats. Here, as with price and wage controls, businessmen seem to me to reveal a suicidal impulse.

The political principle that underlies the market mechanism is una- 30 nimity. In an ideal free market resting on private property, no individual can coerce any other, all cooperation is voluntary, all parties to such cooperation benefit or they need not participate. There are no values, no "social" responsibilities in any sense other than the shared values and responsibilities of individuals. Society is a collection of individuals and of the various groups they voluntarily form.

The political principle that underlies the political mechanism is 31 conformity. The individual must serve a more general social interest— whether that be determined by a church or a dictator or a majority. The individual may have a vote and say in what is to be done, but if he is overruled, he must conform. It is appropriate for some to require others to contribute to a general social purpose whether they wish to or not.

Unfortunately, unanimity is not always feasible. There are some 32 respects in which conformity appears unavoidable, so I do not see how one can avoid the use of the political mechanism altogether.

But the doctrine of "social responsibility" taken seriously would 33 extend the scope of the political mechanism to every human activity. It does not differ in philosophy from the most explicitly collectivist doctrine. It differs only by professing to believe that collectivist ends can be attained without collectivist means. That is why, in my book "Capitalism and Freedom," I have called it a "fundamentally subversive doctrine" in a free society, and have said that in such a society, "there is one and only one social responsibility of business—to use its resources and engage in activities designed to increase its profits so long as it stays within the rules of the game, which is to say, engages in open and free competition without deception or fraud."

# Questions

1. Friedman says that corporate executives who spend the corporation's money "for a general social interest" are "in effect imposing taxes . . . and deciding how the tax proceeds shall be spent . . ." (paragraphs 9 and 11). Is the use of the word "tax" effective? Is it fair? (Notice that paragraphs 12, 13, and 14, as well as some later paragraphs, also speak of taxes.)

2. "The socialist view," Friedman says in paragraph 15, is "that political mechanisms, not market mechanisms, are the appropriate way to determine the allocation of scarce resources to alternative uses." Suppose a fellow student told you that he or she found this passage puzzling. How would you clarify it?

3. Some persons in business have replied to Friedman by arguing that because the owners of today's corporations are rarely involved in running them, the corporations can properly be viewed not as private property but as social institutions able to formulate goals of their own. These people argue that the managers of a corporation are public trustees of a multipurpose organization, and their job is to use their power to promote the interests not only of stockholders but of employees and of the general public. What do you think are the strengths and the weaknesses of this reply?

4. Does Friedman argue that corporations have no responsibilities?

5. In *Religion and the Rise of Capitalism* R. H. Tawney said that "economic organization must allow for the fact that, unless industry is to be paralyzed by recurrent revolts on the part of outraged human nature, it must satisfy criteria which are not purely economic." Do you think Friedman would agree? Why, or why not?

Barbara Ehrenreich and Annette Fuentes

# Life on the Global Assembly Line

In Ciudad Juárez, Mexico, Anna M. rises at 5 A.M. to feed her 1
son before starting on the two-hour bus trip to the maquiladora (factory). He
will spend the day along with four other children in a neighbor's one-room
home. Anna's husband, frustrated by being unable to find work for himself,
left for the United States six months ago. She wonders, as she carefully applies
her new lip gloss, whether she ought to consider herself still married. It might
be good to take a night course, become a secretary. But she seldom gets home
before eight at night, and the factory, where she stitches brassieres that will
be sold in the United States through J. C. Penney, pays only $48 a week.

In Penang, Malaysia, Julie K. is up before the three other young women 2
with whom she shares a room, and starts heating the leftover rice from last
night's supper. She looks good in the company's green-trimmed uniform, and
she's proud to work in a modern, American-owned factory. Only not quite so
proud as when she started working three years ago—she thinks as she squints
out the door at a passing group of women. Her job involves peering all day
through a microscope, bonding hair-thin gold wires to a silicon chip destined
to end up inside a pocket calculator, and at 21, she is afraid she can no longer
see very clearly.

Every morning, between four and seven, thousands of women like 3
Anna and Julie head out for the day shift. In Ciudad Juárez, they crowd
into *ruteras* (rundown vans) for the trip from the slum neighborhoods
to the industrial parks on the outskirts of the city. In Penang they
squeeze, 60 or more at a time, into buses for the trip from the village
to the low, modern factory buildings of the Bayan Lepas free trade
zone. In Taiwan, they walk from the dormitories—where the night
shift is already asleep in the still-warm beds—through the checkpoints
in the high fence surrounding the factory zone.

This is the world's new industrial proletariat: young, female, Third 4
World. Viewed from the "first world," they are still faceless, gender-

Barbara Ehrenreich writes regularly for the *New York Times* and for *Ms.* Annette
Fuentes, the editor of *Sisterhood Is Global*, has also written for *Ms.*

less "cheap labor," signaling their existence only through a label or tiny imprint—"made in Hong Kong," or Taiwan, Korea, the Dominican Republic, Mexico, the Philippines. But they may be one of the most strategic blocs of womanpower in the world of the 1980s. Conservatively, there are 2 million Third World female industrial workers employed now, millions more looking for work, and their numbers are rising every year. Anyone whose image of Third World women features picturesque peasants with babies slung on their backs should be prepared to update it. Just in the last decade, Third World women have become a critical element in the global economy and a key "resource" for expanding multinational corporations.

It doesn't take more than second-grade arithmetic to understand 5 what's happening. In the United States, an assembly-line worker is likely to earn, depending on her length of employment, between $3.10 and $5 an hour. In many Third World countries, a woman doing the same work will earn $3 to $5 a *day*. According to the magazine *Business Asia*, in 1976 the average hourly wage for unskilled work (male or female) was 55 cents in Hong Kong, 52 cents in South Korea, 32 cents in the Philippines, and 17 cents in Indonesia. The logic of the situation is compelling: why pay someone in Massachusetts $5 an hour to do what someone in Manila will do for $2.50 a day? Or, as a corollary, why pay a male worker anywhere to do what a female worker will do for 40 to 60 percent less?

And so, almost everything that can be packed up is being moved 6 out to the Third World; not heavy industry, but just about anything light enough to travel—garment manufacture, textiles, toys, footwear, pharmaceuticals, wigs, appliance parts, tape decks, computer components, plastic goods. In some industries, like garment and textile, American jobs are lost in the process, and the biggest losers are women, often black and Hispanic. But what's going on is much more than a matter of runaway shops. Economists are talking about a "new international division of labor," in which the process of production is broken down and the fragments are dispersed to different parts of the world. In general, the low-skilled jobs are farmed out to the Third World, where labor costs are minuscule, while control over the overall process and technology remains safely at company headquarters in "first world" countries like the United States and Japan.

The American electronics industry provides a classic example: cir- 7 cuits are printed on silicon wafers and tested in California; then the wafers are shipped to Asia for the labor-intensive process by which they are cut into tiny chips and bonded to circuit boards; final assembly into products such as calculators or military equipment usually takes place in the United States. Garment manufacture too is often broken into geographically separated steps, with the most repetitive, labor-intensive jobs going to the poor countries of the southern hemisphere. Most Third World countries welcome whatever jobs come their way in the new division of labor, and the major international development agencies—like the World Bank and the United States Agency for International Development (AID)—encourage them to take what they can get.

So much any economist could tell you. What is less often noted 8 is the *gender* breakdown of the emerging international division of labor. Eighty to 90 percent of the low-skilled assembly jobs that go to the Third World are performed by women—in a remarkable switch from earlier patterns of foreign-dominated industrialization. Until now, "development" under the aegis of foreign corporations has usually meant more jobs for men and—compared to traditional agricultural society— a diminished economic status for women. But multinational corporations and Third World governments alike consider assembly-line work—whether the product is Barbie dolls or missile parts—to be "women's work."

One reason is that women can, in many countries, still be legally 9 paid less than men. But the sheer tedium of the jobs adds to the multinationals' preference for women workers—a preference made clear, for example, by this ad from a Mexican newspaper: *We need female workers; older than 17, younger than 30; single and without children; minimum education primary school, maximum education one year of preparatory school [high school]: available for all shifts.*

It's an article of faith with management that only women can do, 10 or will do, the monotonous, painstaking work that American business is exporting to the Third World. Bill Mitchell, whose job is to attract United States businesses to the Bermudez Industrial Park in Ciudad Juárez told us with a certain macho pride: "A man just won't stay in this tedious kind of work. He'd walk out in a couple of hours." The personnel manager of a light assembly plant in Taiwan told anthropologist Linda Gail Arrigo: "Young male workers are too restless and impatient to do monotonous work with no career value. If displeased, they sabotage the machines and even threaten the foreman. But girls? At most, they cry a little."

In fact, the American businessmen we talked to claimed that Third 11 World women genuinely enjoy doing the very things that would drive a man to assault and sabotage. "You should watch these kids going into work," Bill Mitchell told us. "You don't have any sullenness here. They smile." A top-level management consultant who specializes in advising American companies on where to relocate their factories gave us this global generalization: "The [factory] girls genuinely enjoy themselves. They're away from their families. They have spending money. They can buy motorbikes, whatever. Of course it's a regulated experience too—with dormitories to live in—so it's a healthful experience."

What is the real experience of the women in the emerging Third  12
World industrial work force? The conventional Western stereotypes leap to mind: You can't really compare, the standards are so different. . . . Everything's easier in warm countries. . . . They really don't have any alternatives. . . . Commenting on the low wages his company pays its women workers in Singapore, a Hewlett-Packard vice-president said, "They live much differently here than we do. . . ." But the differences are ultimately very simple. To start with, they have less money.

The great majority of the women in the new Third World work  13
force live at or near the subsistence level for one person, whether they work for a multinational corporation or a locally owned factory. In the Philippines, for example, starting wages in U.S.-owned electronics plants are between $34 to $46 a month, compared to a cost of living of $37 a month; in Indonesia the starting wages are actually about $7 a month less than the cost of living. "Living," in these cases, should be interpreted minimally: a diet of rice, dried fish, and water—a Coke might cost a half-day's wages—lodging in a room occupied by four or more other people. Rachael Grossman, a researcher with the Southeast Asia Resource Center, found women employees of U.S. multinational firms in Malaysia and the Philippines living four to eight in a room in boardinghouses, or squeezing into tiny extensions built onto squatter huts near the factory. Where companies do provide dormitories for their employees, they are not of the "healthful," collegiate variety implied by our corporate informant. Staff from the American Friends Service Committee report that dormitory space is "likely to be crowded, with bed rotation paralleling shift rotation—while one shift works, another sleeps, as many as twenty to a room." In one case in Thailand, they found the dormitory "filthy," with workers forced to find their own place to sleep among "splintered floorboards, rusting sheets of metal, and scraps of dirty cloth."

Wages do increase with seniority, but the money does not go to  14
pay for studio apartments or, very likely, motorbikes. A 1970 study of

young women factory workers in Hong Kong found that 88 percent of them were turning more than half their earnings over to their parents. In areas that are still largely agricultural (such as parts of the Philippines and Malaysia), or places where male unemployment runs high (such as northern Mexico), a woman factory worker may be the sole source of cash income for an entire extended family.

But wages on a par with what an 11-year-old American could earn   15
on a paper route, and living conditions resembling what Engels found in nineteenth-century Manchester are only part of the story. The rest begins at the factory gate. The work that multinational corporations export to the Third World is not only the most tedious, but often the most hazardous part of the production process. The countries they go to are, for the most part, those that will guarantee no interference from health and safety inspectors, trade unions, or even free-lance reformers. As a result, most Third World factory women work under conditions that already have broken or will break their health—or their nerves—within a few years, and often before they've worked long enough to earn any more than a subsistence wage.

Consider first the electronics industry, which is generally thought   16
to be the safest and cleanest of the exported industries. The factory buildings are low and modern, like those one might find in a suburban American industrial park. Inside, rows of young women, neatly dressed in the company uniform or T-shirt, work quietly at their stations. There is air conditioning (not for the women's comfort, but to protect the delicate semiconductor parts they work with), and high-volume piped-in Bee Gees hits (not so much for entertainment, as to prevent talking).

For many Third World women, electronics is a prestige occupation,   17
at least compared to other kinds of factory work. They are unlikely to know that in the United States the National Institute on Occupational Safety and Health (NIOSH) has placed electronics on its select list of "high health-risk industries using the greatest number of toxic substances." If electronics assembly work is risky here, it is doubly so in countries where there is no equivalent of NIOSH to even issue warnings. In many plants toxic chemicals and solvents sit in open containers, filling the work area with fumes that can literally knock you out. "We have been told of cases where ten to twelve women passed out at once," an AFSC field worker in northern Mexico told us, "and the newspapers report this as 'mass hysteria.' "

In one stage of the electronics assembly process, the workers have   18
to dip the circuits into open vats of acid. According to Irene Johnson

and Carol Bragg, who toured the National Semiconductor plant in Penang, Malaysia, the women who do the dipping "wear rubber gloves
and boots, but these sometimes leak, and burns are common." Occasionally, whole fingers are lost. More commonly, what electronics
workers lose is the 20/20 vision they are required to have when they
are hired. Most electronics workers spend seven to nine hours a day
peering through microscopes, straining to meet their quotas.

One study in South Korea found that most electronics assembly     19
workers developed severe eye problems after only one year of employment: 88 percent had chronic conjunctivitis; 44 percent became
nearsighted; and 19 percent developed astigmatism. A manager for
Hewlett-Packard's Malaysia plant, in an interview with Rachael Grossman, denied that there were any eye problems: "These girls are used
to working with 'scopes.' We've found no eye problems. But it sure
makes me dizzy to look through those things."

Electronics, recall, is the "cleanest" of the exported industries.     20
Conditions in the garment and textile industry rival those of any nineteenth-century sweatshop. The firms, generally local subcontractors to
large American chains such as J. C. Penney and Sears, as well as
smaller manufacturers, are usually even more indifferent to the health
of their employees than the multinationals. Some of the worst conditions have been documented in South Korea, where the garment and
textile industries have helped spark that country's "economic miracle."
Workers are packed into poorly lit rooms, where summer temperatures
rise above 100 degrees. Textile dust, which can cause permanent lung
damage, fills the air. When there are rush orders, management may
require forced overtime of as much as 48 hours at a stretch, and if that
seems to go beyond the limits of human endurance, pep pills and
amphetamine injections are thoughtfully provided. In her diary (originally published in a magazine now banned by the South Korean government) Min Chong Suk, 30, a sewing-machine operator, wrote of
working from 7 A.M. to 11:30 P.M. in a garment factory: "When [the
apprentices] shake the waste threads from the clothes, the whole room
fills with dust, and it is hard to breathe. Since we've been working in
such dusty air, there have been increasing numbers of people getting
tuberculosis, bronchitis, and eye diseases. Since we are women, it
makes us so sad when we have pale, unhealthy, wrinkled faces like
dried-up spinach. . . . It seems to me that no one knows our blood
dissolves into the threads and seams, with sighs and sorrow."

In all the exported industries, the most invidious, inescapable     21
health hazard is stress. On their home ground United States corpo-

rations are not likely to sacrifice productivity for human comfort. On someone else's home ground, however, anything goes. Lunch breaks may be barely long enough for a woman to stand in line at the canteen or hawkers' stalls. Visits to the bathroom are treated as privilege; in some cases, workers must raise their hands for permission to use the toilet, and waits up to a half hour are common. Rotating shifts—the day shift one week, the night shift the next—wreak havoc with sleep patterns. Because inaccuracies or failure to meet production quotas can mean substantial pay losses, the pressures are quickly internalized; stomach ailments and nervous problems are not unusual in the multinationals' Third World female work force. In some situations, good work is as likely to be punished as slow or shoddy work. Correspondent Michael Flannery, writing for the AFL-CIO's *American Federationist*, tells the story of 23-year-old Basilia Altagracia, a seamstress who stitched collars onto ladies' blouses in the La Romana (Dominican Republic) free trade zone (a heavily guarded industrial zone owned by Gulf & Western Industries, Inc.):

"A nimble veteran seamstress, Miss Altagracia eventually began 22 to earn as much as $5.75 a day. . . . 'I was exceeding my piecework quota by a lot.' . . . But then, Altagracia said, her plant supervisor, a Cuban emigré, called her into his office. 'He said I was doing a fine job, but that I and some other of the women were making too much money, and he was being forced to lower what we earned for each piece we sewed.' On the best days, she now can clear barely $3, she said. 'I was earning less, so I started working six and seven days a week. But I was tired and I could not work as fast as before.' " Within a few months, she was too ill to work at all.

As if poor health and the stress of factory life weren't enough to 23 drive women into early retirement, management actually encourages a high turnover in many industries. "As you know, when seniority rises, wages rise," the management consultant to U.S. multinationals told us. He explained that it's cheaper to train a fresh supply of teenagers than to pay experienced women higher wages. "Older" women, aged 23 or 24, are likely to be laid off and not rehired.

We estimate, based on fragmentary data from several sources, that 24 the multinational corporations may already have used up (cast off) as many as 6 million Third World workers—women who are too ill, too old (30 is over the hill in most industries), or too exhausted to be useful any more. Few "retire" with any transferable skills or savings. The lucky ones find husbands.

The unlucky ones find themselves at the margins of society—as 25 bar girls, "hostesses," or prostitutes.

*At 21, Julie's greatest fear is that she will never be able to find a husband.*   26
*She knows that just being a "factory girl" is enough to give anyone a bad*
*reputation. When she first started working at the electronics company, her*
*father refused to speak to her for three months. Now every time she leaves*
*Penang to go back to visit her home village she has to put up with a lecture*
*on morality from her older brother—not to mention a barrage of lewd remarks*
*from men outside her family. If they knew that she had actually gone out on*
*a few dates, that she had been to a discotheque, that she had once kissed a*
*young man who said he was a student . . . Julie's stomach tightens as she*
*imagines her family's reaction. She tries to concentrate on the kind of man she*
*would like to marry: an engineer or technician of some sort, someone who had*
*been to California, where the company headquarters are located and where even*
*the grandmothers wear tight pants and lipstick—someone who had a good*
*attitude about women. But if she ends up having to wear glasses, like her*
*cousin who worked three years at the "scopes," she might as well forget about*
*finding anyone to marry her.*

One of the most serious occupational hazards that Julie and mil-   27
lions of women like her may face is the lifelong stigma of having been
a "factory girl." Most of the cultures favored by multinational corporations in their search for cheap labor are patriarchal in the grand
old style: any young woman who is not under the wing of a father,
husband, or older brother must be "loose." High levels of unemployment among men, as in Mexico, contribute to male resentment of working women. (Ironically, in some places the multinationals have increased male unemployment—for example, by paving over fishing and
farming villages to make way for industrial parks.) Add to all this the
fact that certain companies—American electronics firms are in the
lead—actively promote Western-style sexual objectification as a means
of insuring employee loyalty: there are company-sponsored cosmetics
classes, "guess whose legs these are" contests, and swim-suit-style
beauty contests where the prize might be a free night *for two* in a fancy
hotel. Corporate-promoted Westernization only heightens the hostility
many men feel toward any independent working women—having a
job is bad enough, wearing jeans and mascara to work is going too
far.

Anthropologist Patricia Fernandez, who has worked in a *maqui-*   28
*ladora* herself, believes that the stigmatization of working women
serves, indirectly, to keep them in line. "You have to think of the kind
of socialization that girls experience in a very Catholic—or, for that

matter, Muslim—society. The fear of having a 'reputation' is enough to make a lot of women bend over backward to be 'respectable' and ladylike, which is just what management wants." She points out that in northern Mexico, the tabloids delight in playing up stories of alleged vice in the *maquiladoras*—indiscriminate sex on the job, epidemics of venereal disease, fetuses found in factory rest rooms. "I worry about this because there are those who treat you differently as soon as they know you have a job at a *maquiladora*," one woman told Fernandez. "Maybe they think that if you have to work, there is a chance you're a whore."

And there is always a chance you'll wind up as one. Probably only 29 a small minority of Third World factory workers turn to prostitution when their working days come to an end. But it is, as for women everywhere, the employment of last resort, the only thing to do when the factories don't need you and traditional society won't—or, for economic reasons, can't—take you back. In the Philippines, the brothel business is expanding as fast as the factory system. If they can't use you one way, they can use you another.

# Questions

1.  Consider the title of the essay. Before reading the essay, what connotations are immediately suggested by "global assembly line"? Now that you have finished reading the essay, evaluate the title.
2.  Before you read this essay, what was your image of the multinational corporation? Was it mostly positive, or negative, or neutral? To what extent has the article affected the way you think about multinational corporations? If, for example, you were offered a managerial job in a multinational, would you be inclined to ask questions about their employment practices abroad that you might not have asked before reading this article?
3.  Paragraph 1, which gives us a quick portrait of Anna, tells us that "Anna's husband, frustrated by being unable to find work for himself, left for the United States six months ago." Why do the authors bother to include this detail? Is it in any way relevant to their thesis, or is it simply for human interest?
4.  According to paragraph 10, management believes "that only women can do, or will do, the monotonous, painstaking work that American business is exporting to the Third World." Do the authors

of the essay believe this? Do *you* believe that women by nature—
or by training—are more suited than men "to do monotonous work
with no career value"?

5. Paragraph 11 reports some statements businessmen offer as reasons why Third World women supposedly enjoy their jobs. Do you
think these reasons (or some of them) have any merit? Do paragraphs 12–14 and 17–21 adequately refute these reasons?

6. In paragraph 14 we learn that 88 percent of the young female workers in Hong Kong turned more than half of their wages over to their
parents. What conclusions can one reasonably draw from this assertion?

7. Why do you suppose that Julie (paragraphs 2 and 26) works in a
factory?

8. In paragraph 27 the author tells us that "high levels of unemployment among men, as in Mexico, contribute to male resentment of
working women." Does this analysis strike you as probably true?
If so, what do you think American business can do about the Mexican economy?

9. Given what you have read about the working conditions of women
in Third World countries, when you buy your next sweater (or tennis
racquet or calculator or whatever) will you reject products made in
Third World countries?

## Bowen H. McCoy

# The Parable of the Sadhu

Last year, as the first participant in the new six-month sab- 1
batical program that Morgan Stanley has adopted, I enjoyed a rare
opportunity to collect my thoughts as well as do some traveling. I spent
the first three months in Nepal, walking 600 miles through 200 villages

Bowen H. McCoy, a graduate of Stanford University and the Harvard Business
School, has worked at Morgan Stanley and Co. since 1962. His essay on "The
Problem of the Sadhu" was awarded the *Harvard Business Review* Ethics Prize
in 1983. McCoy has also published essays in *Management Review, Urban Land,*
and *Theology Today.*

in the Himalayas and climbing some 120,000 vertical feet. On the trip my sole Western companion was an anthropologist who shed light on the cultural patterns of the villages we passed through.

During the Nepal hike, something occurred that has had a pow- 2 erful impact on my thinking about corporate ethics. Although some might argue that the experience has no relevance to business, it was a situation in which a basic ethical dilemma suddenly intruded into the lives of a group of individuals. How the group responded I think holds a lesson for all organizations no matter how defined.

The Nepal experience was more rugged and adventuresome than 3 I had anticipated. Most commercial treks last two or three weeks and cover a quarter of the distance we traveled.

My friend Stephen, the anthropologist, and I were halfway 4 through the 60-day Himalayan part of the trip when we reached the high point, an 18,000-foot pass over a crest that we'd have to traverse to reach to the village of Muktinath, an ancient holy place for pilgrims.

Six years earlier I had suffered pulmonary edema, an acute form 5 of altitude sickness, at 16,500 feet in the vicinity of Everest base camp, so we were understandably concerned about what would happen at 18,000 feet. Moreover, the Himalayas were having their wettest spring in 20 years; hip-deep powder and ice had already driven us off one ridge. If we failed to cross the pass, I feared that the last half of our "once in a lifetime" trip would be ruined.

The night before we would try the pass, we camped at a hut at 6 14,500 feet. In the photos taken at that camp, my face appears wan. The last village we'd passed through was a sturdy two-day walk below us, and I was tired.

During the late afternoon, four backpackers from New Zealand 7 joined us, and we spent most of the night awake, anticipating the climb. Below we could see the fires of two other parties, which turned out to be two Swiss couples and a Japanese hiking club.

To get over the steep part of the climb before the sun melted the 8 steps cut in the ice, we departed at 3:30 A.M. The New Zealanders left first, followed by Stephen and myself, our porters and Sherpas, and then the Swiss. The Japanese lingered in their camp. The sky was clear, and we were confident that no spring storm would erupt that day to close the pass.

At 15,500 feet, it looked to me as if Stephen were shuffling and 9 staggering a bit, which are symptoms of altitude sickness. (The initial stage of altitude sickness brings a headache and nausea. As the condition worsens, a climber may encounter difficult breathing, disorientation, aphasia, and paralysis.) I felt strong, my adrenaline was flowing, but I was very concerned about my ultimate ability to get across. A couple of our porters were also suffering from the height, and Pasang, our Sherpa sirdar (leader), was worried.

Just after daybreak, while we rested at 15,500 feet, one of the New   10
Zealanders, who had gone ahead, came staggering down toward us with a body slung across his shoulders. He dumped the almost naked, barefoot body of an Indian holy man—a sadhu—at my feet. He had found the pilgrim lying on the ice, shivering and suffering from hypothermia. I cradled the sadhu's head and laid him out on the rocks. The New Zealander was angry. He wanted to get across the pass before the bright sun melted the snow. He said, "Look, I've done what I can. You have porters and Sherpa guides. You care for him. We're going on!" He turned and went back up the mountain to join his friends.

I took a carotid pulse and found that the sadhu was still alive. We   11
figured he had probably visited the holy shrines at Muktinath and was on his way home. It was fruitless to question why he had chosen this desperately high route instead of the safe, heavily traveled caravan route through the Kali Gandaki gorge. Or why he was almost naked and with no shoes, or how long he had been lying in the pass. The answers weren't going to solve our problem.

Stephen and the four Swiss began stripping off outer clothing and   12
opening their packs. The sadhu was soon clothed from head to foot. He was not able to walk, but he was very much alive. I looked down the mountain and spotted below the Japanese climbers marching up with a horse.

Without a great deal of thought, I told Stephen and Pasang that   13
I was concerned about withstanding the heights to come and wanted to get over the pass. I took off after several of our porters who had gone ahead.

On the steep part of the ascent where, if the ice steps had given   14
way, I would have slid down about 3,000 feet, I felt vertigo. I stopped for a breather, allowing the Swiss to catch up with me. I inquired about the sadhu and Stephen. They said that the sadhu was fine and that Stephen was just behind. I set off again for the summit.

Stephen arrived at the summit an hour after I did. Still exhilarated   15
by victory, I ran down the snow slope to congratulate him. He was suffering from altitude sickness, walking 15 steps, then stopping, walking 15 steps, then stopping. Pasang accompanied him all the way up. When I reached them, Stephen glared at me and said: "How do you feel about contributing to the death of a fellow man?"

I did not fully comprehend what he meant.                                    16

"Is the sadhu dead?" I inquired.                                              17

"No," replied Stephen, "but he surely will be!"                              18

· After I had gone, and the Swiss had departed not long after, Ste-        19
phen had remained with the sadhu. When the Japanese had arrived,
Stephen had asked to use their horse to transport the sadhu down to
the hut. They had refused. He had then asked Pasang to have a group
of our porters carry the sadhu. Pasang had resisted the idea, saying
that the porters would have to exert all their energy to get themselves
over the pass. He had thought they could not carry a man down 1,000
feet to the hut, reclimb the slope, and get across safely before the snow
melted. Pasang had pressed Stephen not to delay any longer.

The Sherpas had carried the sadhu down to a rock in the sun at       20
about 15,000 feet and had pointed out the hut another 500 feet below.
The Japanese had given him food and drink. When they had last seen
him he was listlessly throwing rocks at the Japanese party's dog, which
had frightened him.

We do not know if the sadhu lived or died.                                   21

For many of the following days and evenings Stephen and I dis-      22
cussed and debated our behavior toward the sadhu. Stephen is a committed Quaker with deep moral vision. He said, "I feel that what happened with the sadhu is a good example of the breakdown between
the individual ethic and the corporate ethic. No one person was willing
to assume ultimate responsibility for the sadhu. Each was willing to
do his bit just so long as it was not too inconvenient. When it got to
be a bother, everyone just passed the buck to someone else and took
off. Jesus was relevant to a more individualistic stage of society, but
how do we interpret his teaching today in a world filled with large,
impersonal organizations and groups?"

I defended the larger group, saying, "Look, we all cared. We all       23
stopped and gave aid and comfort. Everyone did his bit. The New
Zealander carried him down below the snow line. I took his pulse and
suggested we treat him for hypothermia. You and the Swiss gave him
clothing and got him warmed up. The Japanese gave him food and
water. The Sherpas carried him down to the sun and pointed out the
easy trail toward the hut. He was well enough to throw rocks at a dog.
What more could we do?"

"You have just described the typical affluent Westerner's response    24
to a problem. Throwing money—in this case food and sweaters—at
it, but not solving the fundamentals!" Stephen retorted.

"What would satisfy you?" I said. "Here we are, a group of New      25

Zealanders, Swiss, Americans, and Japanese who have never met before and who are at the apex of one of the most powerful experiences of our lives. Some years the pass is so bad no one gets over it. What right does an almost naked pilgrim who chooses the wrong trail have to disrupt our lives? Even the Sherpas had no interest in risking the trip to help him beyond a certain point."

Stephen calmly rebutted, "I wonder what the Sherpas would have done if the sadhu had been a well-dressed Nepali, or what the Japanese would have done if the sadhu had been a well-dressed Asian, or what you would have done, Buzz, if the sadhu had been a well-dressed Western woman?"    26

"Where, in your opinion," I asked instead, "is the limit of our responsibility in a situation like this? We had our own well-being to worry about. Our Sherpa guides were unwilling to jeopardize us or the porters for the sadhu. No one else on the mountain was willing to commit himself beyond certain self-imposed limits."    27

Stephen said, "As individual Christians or people with a Western ethical tradition, we can fulfill our obligations in such a situation only if (1) the sadhu dies in our care, (2) the sadhu demonstrates to us that he could undertake the two-day walk down to the village, or (3) we carry the sadhu for two days down to the village and convince someone there to care for him."    28

"Leaving the sadhu in the sun with food and clothing, while he demonstrated hand-eye coordination by throwing a rock at a dog, comes close to fulfilling items one and two," I answered. "And it wouldn't have made sense to take him to the village where the people appeared to be far less caring than the Sherpas, so the third condition is impractical. Are you really saying that, no matter what the implications, we should, at the drop of a hat, have changed our entire plan?"    29

Despite my arguments, I felt and continue to feel guilt about the sadhu. I had literally walked through a classic moral dilemma without fully thinking through the consequences. My excuses for my actions include a high adrenaline flow, a superordinate goal, and a once-in-a-lifetime opportunity—factors in the usual corporate situation, especially when one is under stress.    30

Real moral dilemmas are ambiguous, and many of us hike right through them, unaware that they exist. When, usually after the fact, someone makes an issue of them, we tend to resent his or her bringing it up. Often, when the full import of what we have done (or not done) falls on us, we dig into a defensive position from which it is very    31 difficult to emerge. In rare circumstances we may contemplate what we have done from inside a prison.

Had we mountaineers been free of physical and mental stress 32 caused by the effort and the high altitude, we might have treated the sadhu differently. Yet isn't stress the real test of personal and corporate values? The instant decisions executives make under pressure reveal the most about personal and corporate character.

Among the many questions that occur to me when pondering my 33 experience are: What are the practical limits of moral imagination and vision? Is there a collective or institutional ethic beyond the ethics of the individual? At what level of effort or commitment can one discharge one's ethical responsibilities?

Not every ethical dilemma has a right solution. Reasonable people 34 often disagree; otherwise there would be no dilemma. In a business context, however, it is essential that managers agree on a process for dealing with dilemmas.

The sadhu experience offers an interesting parallel to business sit- 35 uations. An immediate response was mandatory. Failure to act was a decision in itself. Up on the mountain we could not resign and submit our résumés to a headhunter. In contrast to philosophy, business involves action and implementation—getting things done. Managers must come up with answers to problems based on what they see and what they allow to influence their decision-making processes. On the mountain, none of us but Stephen realized the true dimensions of the situation we were facing.

One of our problems was that as a group we had no process for 36 developing a consensus. We had no sense of purpose or plan. The difficulties of dealing with the sadhu were so complex that no one person could handle it. Because it did not have a set of preconditions that could guide its action to an acceptable resolution, the group reacted instinctively as individuals. The cross-cultural nature of the group added a further layer of complexity. We had no leader with whom we could all identify and in whose purpose we believed. Only Stephen was willing to take charge, but he could not gain adequate support to care for the sadhu.

Some organizations do have a value system that transcends the 37 personal values of the managers. Such values, which go beyond profitability, are usually revealed when the organization is under stress. People throughout the organization generally accept its values, which, because they are not presented as a rigid list of commandments, may be somewhat ambiguous. The stories people tell, rather than printed materials, transmit these conceptions of what is proper behavior.

For 20 years I have been exposed at senior levels to a variety of 38 corporations and organizations. It is amazing how quickly an outsider can sense the tone and style of an organization and the degree of tolerated openness and freedom to challenge management.

Organizations that do not have a heritage of mutually accepted, 39 shared values tend to become unhinged during stress, with each individual bailing out for himself. In the great takeover battles we have witnessed during past years, companies that had strong cultures drew the wagons around them and fought it out, while other companies saw executives supported by their golden parachutes, bail out of the struggles.

Because corporations and their members are interdependent, for 40 the corporation to be strong the members need to share a preconceived notion of what is correct behavior, a "business ethic," and think of it as a positive force, not a constraint.

As an investment banker I am continually warned by well-meaning 41 lawyers, clients, and associates to be wary of conflicts of interest. Yet if I were to run away from every difficult situation, I wouldn't be an effective investment banker. I have to feel my way through conflicts. An effective manager can't run from risk either; he or she has to confront and deal with risk. To feel "safe" in doing this, managers need the guidelines of an agreed-on process and set of values within the organization.

After my three months in Nepal, I spent three months as an ex- 42 ecutive-in-residence at both Stanford Business School and the Center for Ethics and Social Policy at the Graduate Theological Union at Berkeley. These six months away from my job gave me time to assimilate 20 years of business experience. My thoughts turned often to the meaning of the leadership role in any large organization. Students at the seminary thought of themselves as antibusiness. But when I questioned them they agreed that they distrusted all large organizations, including the church. They perceived all large organizations as impersonal and opposed to individual values and needs. Yet we all know of organizations where peoples' values and beliefs are respected and their expressions encouraged. What makes the difference? Can we identify the difference and, as a result, manage more effectively?

The word "ethics" turns off many and confuses more. Yet the 43 notions of shared values and an agreed-on process for dealing with adversity and change—what many people mean when they talk about corporate culture—seem to be at the heart of the ethical issue. People who are in touch with their own core beliefs and the beliefs of others and are sustained by them can be more comfortable living on the cutting edge. At times, taking a tough line or a decisive stand in a muddle of ambiguity is the only ethical thing to do. If a manager is indecisive and spends time trying to figure out the "good" thing to do, the enterprise may be lost.

Business ethics, then, has to do with the authenticity and integrity 44 of the enterprise. To be ethical is to follow the business as well as the cultural goals of the corporation, its owners, its employees, and its customers. Those who cannot serve the corporate vision are not authentic business people and, therefore, are not ethical in the business sense.

At this stage of my own business experience I have a strong interest 45 in organizational behavior. Sociologists are keenly studying what they call corporate stories, legends, and heroes as a way organizations have of transmitting the value system. Corporations such as Arco have even hired consultants to perform an audit of their corporate culture. In a company, the leader is the person who understands, interprets, and manages the corporate value system. Effective managers are then action-oriented people who resolve conflict, are tolerant of ambiguity, stress, and change, and have a strong sense of purpose for themselves and their organizations.

If all this is true, I wonder about the role of the professional man- 46 ager who moves from company to company. How can he or she quickly absorb the values and culture of different organizations? Or is there, indeed, an art of management that is totally transportable? Assuming such fungible managers do exist, is it proper for them to manipulate the values of others?

What would have happened had Stephen and I carried the sadhu 47 for two days back to the village and become involved with the villagers in his care? In four trips to Nepal my most interesting experiences occurred in 1975 when I lived in a Sherpa home in the Khumbu for five days recovering from altitude sickness. The high point of Stephen's trip was an invitation to participate in a family funeral ceremony in Manang. Neither experience had to do with climbing the high passes of the Himalayas. Why were we so reluctant to try the lower path, the ambiguous trail? Perhaps because we did not have a leader who could reveal the greater purpose of the trip to us.

Why didn't Stephen with his moral vision opt to take the sadhu 48 under his personal care? The answer is because, in part, Stephen was hard-stressed physically himself, and because, in part, without some support system that involved our involuntary and episodic community on the mountain, it was beyond his individual capacity to do so.

I see the current interest in corporate culture and corporate value 49 systems as a positive response to Stephen's pessimism about the decline of the role of the individual in large organizations. Individuals who operate from a thoughtful set of personal values provide the foundation for a corporate culture. A corporate tradition that encourages freedom of inquiry, supports personal values, and reinforces a focused sense of direction can fulfill the need for individuality along with the prosperity and success of the group. Without such corporate support, the individual is lost.

That is the lesson of the sadhu. In a complex corporate situation, 50 the individual requires and deserves the support of the group. If people cannot find such support from their organization, they don't know how to act. If such support is forthcoming, a person has a stake in the success of the group, and can add much to the process of establishing and maintaining a corporate culture. It is management's challenge to be sensitive to individual needs, to shape them, and to direct and focus them for the benefit of the group as a whole.

For each of us the sadhu lives. Should we stop what we are doing 51 and comfort him; or should we keep trudging up toward the high pass? Should I pause to help the derelict I pass on the street each night as I walk by the Yale Club en route to Grand Central Station? Am I his brother? What is the nature of our responsibility if we consider ourselves to be ethical persons? Perhaps it is to change the values of the group so that it can, with all its resources, take the other road.

# Questions

1.  In paragraph 26 Stephen says:

    I wonder what the Sherpas would have done if the sadhu had been a well-dressed Nepali, or what the Japanese would have done if the sadhu had been a well-dressed Asian, or what you would have done, Buzz, if the sadhu had been a well-dressed Western woman?

    First, what would *you* have done if you had met the sadhu? Second, do you think your response would have been different if instead of the sadhu you had met a well-dressed person of your own culture.

(By the way, notice that for Westerners McCoy adds the complication of changing the sex of the person met. Would the sex affect your response? Why?)

2. In paragraph 30 McCoy offers excuses for his action—"a high adrenaline flow, a superordinate goal, and a once-in-a-lifetime opportunity." Two paragraphs later he emphasizes the "physical and mental stress caused by the effort and the high altitude." Does he suggest that these factors justified his behavior? Do you think they do?

3. In paragraph 37 McCoy mentions that "some organizations do have a value system that transcends the personal values of the managers. Such values, which go beyond profitability, are usually revealed when the organization is under stress." If you have read Milton Friedman's essay (page 513), what do you think Friedman's response to this point would be?

4. Set forth in one paragraph what you take to be McCoy's view of how managers *should* act and what conditions are necessary to enable them to act in this way.

5. Many people believe that the only responsibility of businesspersons—or of anyone else—is to obey the law of the land. How adequate do you find this principle?

6. In his conclusion McCoy says, "For each of us the sadhu lives." What does he mean by this?

## John S. Fielden

# "What Do You Mean You Don't Like My Style"

In large corporations all over the country, people are playing a game of paddleball—with drafts of letters instead of balls. Volley after volley goes back and forth between those who sign the letters

John S. Fielden, formerly an associate editor of the *Harvard Business Review*—the journal in which this essay first appeared—is now University Professor of Management at the University of Alabama.

and those who actually write them. It's a game nobody likes, but it continues, and we pay for it. The workday has no extra time for such unproductiveness. What causes this round robin of revision?

Typos? Factual misstatements? Poor format? No. *Style* does. Ask 2 yourself how often you hear statements like these:

"It takes new assistants about a year to learn my style. Until they do, I have no choice but to bounce letters back for revision. I won't sign a letter if it doesn't sound like me."
"I find it difficult, almost impossible, to write letters for my boss's signature. The boss's style is different from mine."

In companies where managers primarily write their own letters, 3 confusion about style also reigns. Someone sends out a letter and hears later that the reaction was not at all the one desired. It is reported that the reader doesn't like the writer's "tone." A colleague looks over a copy of the letter and says, "No wonder the reader doesn't like this letter. You shouldn't have said things the way you did. You used the wrong style for a letter like this." "Style?" the writer says. "What's wrong with my style?" "I don't know" is the response. "I just don't like the way you said things."

Everybody talks about style, but almost nobody understands the 4 meaning of the word in the business environment. And this lack of understanding hurts both those who write letters for another's signature and those who write for themselves. Neither knows where to turn for help. Strunk and White's marvelous book *The Elements of Style* devotes only a few pages to a discussion of style, and that concerns only literary style.[1] Books like the Chicago *Manual of Style*[2] seem to define style as all the technical points they cover, from abbreviations and capitalizations to footnotes and bibliographies. And dictionary definitions are usually too vague to be helpful.

Even such a general definition as this offers scant help, although 5 perhaps it comes closest to how business people use the word:

Style is "the way something is said or done, as distinguished from its substance."[3]

[1] William Strunk, Jr., and E. B. White, *The Elements of Style* (New York: Macmillan, 1979).
[2] *A Manual of Style* (Chicago: University of Chicago Press, 1969).
[3] *The American Heritage Dictionary of the English Language* (Boston: American Heritage and Houghton Mifflin, 1969).

Managers signing drafts written by subordinates, and the subor- 6
dinates themselves, already know that they have trouble agreeing on
"the way things should be said." What, for instance, is meant by
"way"? In trying to find that way, both managers and subordinates
are chasing a will-o'-the-wisp. There *is* no magical way, no perfect,
universal way of writing things that will fend off criticism of style.
There is no one style of writing in business that is appropriate in all
situations and for all readers, even though managers and subordinates
usually talk and behave as if there were.

But why all the confusion? Isn't style really the way we say things? 7
Certainly it is. Then writing style must be made up of the particular
words we select to express our ideas and the types of sentences and
paragraphs we put together to convey those ideas. What else could it
be? Writing has no tone of voice or body gesture to impart additional
meanings. In written communication, tone comes from what a reader
reads into the words and sentences used.

Words express more than *denotations*, the definitions found in dic- 8
tionaries. They also carry *connotations*. In the feelings and images associated with each word lies the capacity a writing style has for producing an emotional reaction in a reader. And in that capacity lies the
tone of a piece of writing. Style is largely a matter of tone. The writer
uses a style; the reader infers a communication's tone. Tone comes
from what a reader reads into the words and sentences a writer uses.

In the business environment, tone is especially important. Busi- 9
ness writing is not literary writing. Literary artists use unique styles
to "express" themselves to a general audience. Business people write
to particular persons in particular situations, not so much to express
themselves as to accomplish particular purposes, "to get a job done."
If a reader doesn't like a novelist's tone, nothing much can happen to
the writer short of failing to sell some books. In the business situation,
however, an offensive style may not only prevent a sale but may also
turn away a customer, work against a promotion, or even cost you a
job.

While style can be distinguished from substance, it cannot be di- 10
vorced from substance. In business writing, style cannot be divorced
from the circumstances under which something is written or from the
likes, dislikes, position, and power of the reader.

A workable definition of style in business writing would be some- 11
thing like this:

Style is that choice of words, sentences, and paragraph format which
by virtue of being appropriate to the situation and to the power po-

sitions of both writer and reader produces the desired reaction and
result.

Let's take a case and see what we can learn from it. Assume that   12
you are an executive in a very large information-processing company.
You receive the following letter:

Mr. (Ms.) Leslie J. Cash
XYZ Corporation
Main Street
Anytown, U.S.A.

Dear Leslie:
As you know, I respect your professional opinion highly. The advice
your people have given us at ABC Corporation as we have moved
into a comprehensive information system over the past three years
has been very helpful. I'm writing to you now, however, in my role
as chairman of the executive committee of the trustees of our hospital.
We at Community General Hospital have decided to establish a skilled
volunteer data processing evaluation team to assess proposals to automate our hospital's information flow.

I have suggested your name to my committee. I know you could get
real satisfaction from helping your community as a member of this
evaluation team. Please say yes. I look forward to being able to count
on your advice. Let me hear from you soon.

Frank J. Scalpel
Chairman
Executive Committee
Community General Hospital
Anytown, U.S.A.

If you accepted the appointment mentioned in this letter, you   13
would have a conflict of interest. You are an executive at XYZ, Inc.
You know that XYZ will submit a proposal to install a comprehensive
information system for the hospital. Mr. Scalpel is the vice president
of finance at ABC Corp., a very good customer of yours. You know
him well since you have worked with him on community programs
as well as in the business world.

I can think of four typical responses to Scalpel's letter. Each says   14
essentially the same thing, but each is written in a different business
style:

## Response 1

Mr. Frank J. Scalpel
Chairman, Executive Committee
Community General Hospital
Anytown, U.S.A.

Dear Frank,
As you realize, this litigious age often makes it necessary for large companies to take stringent measures not only to avoid conflicts of interest on the part of their employees but also to preclude even the very suggestion of conflict. And, since my company intends to submit a proposal with reference to automating the hospital's information flow, it would not appear seemly for me to be part of an evaluation team assessing competitors' proposals. Even if I were to excuse myself from consideration of the XYZ proposal, I would still be vulnerable to charges that I gave short shrift to competitors' offerings.

If there is any other way that I can serve the committee that will not raise this conflict-of-interest specter, you know that I would find it pleasurable to be of service, as always.

Sincerely,

## Response 2

Dear Frank,
Your comments relative to your respect for my professional opinion are most appreciated. Moreover, your invitation to serve on the hospital's data processing evaluation team is received with gratitude, albeit with some concern.

The evaluation team must be composed of persons free of alliance with any of the vendors submitting proposals. For that reason, it is felt that my services on the team could be construed as a conflict of interest.

Perhaps help can be given in some other way. Again, please be assured that your invitation has been appreciated.

Sincerely,

## Response 3

Dear Frank,
Thank you for suggesting my name as a possible member of your data processing evaluation team. I wish I could serve, but I cannot.

XYZ intends, naturally, to submit a proposal to automate the hospital's information flow. You can see the position of conflict I would be in if I were on the evaluation team.

Just let me know of any other way I can be of help. You know I would be more than willing. Thanks again for the invitation.

Cordially,

**Response 4**

Dear Frank,
Thanks for the kind words and the invitation. Sure wish I could say yes. Can't, though.

XYZ intends to submit a sure-fire proposal on automating the hospital's information. Shouldn't be judge and advocate at the same time!

Any other way I can help, Frank—just ask. Thanks again.

Cordially,

## *What Do You Think of These Letters?*

Which letter has the style you like best? Check off the response you prefer. 15

Response        1        2        3        4
                □        □        □        □

Which letter has the style resembling the one you customarily use? 16
Again, check off your choice.

Response        1        2        3        4
                □        □        □        □

Which terms best describe the style of each letter? Check the appropriate boxes. 17

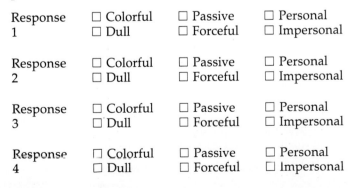

| Response 1 | □ Colorful | □ Passive | □ Personal |
|---|---|---|---|
| | □ Dull | □ Forceful | □ Impersonal |

| Response 2 | □ Colorful | □ Passive | □ Personal |
|---|---|---|---|
| | □ Dull | □ Forceful | □ Impersonal |

| Response 3 | □ Colorful | □ Passive | □ Personal |
|---|---|---|---|
| | □ Dull | □ Forceful | □ Impersonal |

| Response 4 | □ Colorful | □ Passive | □ Personal |
|---|---|---|---|
| | □ Dull | □ Forceful | □ Impersonal |

*Let's Compare Reactions*

Now that you've given your reactions, let's compare them with some of mine. 18

Response 1 seems cold, impersonal, complex. Most business peo- 19 ple would, I think, react somewhat negatively to this style because it seems to push the reader away from the writer. Its word choice has a cerebral quality that, while flattering to the reader's intelligence, also parades the writer's.

Response 2 is fairly cool, quite impersonal, and somewhat com- 20 plex. Readers' reactions will probably be neither strongly positive nor strongly negative. This style of writing is "blah" because it is heavily passive. Instead of saying "I appreciate your comments," it says "Your comments are most appreciated"; instead of "I think that my service could be construed as a conflict of interest," it says "It is felt that my service could be construed. . . ." The use of the passive voice subordinates writers modestly to the back of sentences or causes them to disappear.

This is the impersonal, passive style of writing that many with 21 engineering, mathematics, or scientific backgrounds feel most comfortable using. It is harmless, but it is certainly not colorful; nor is it forceful or interesting.

Response 3 illustrates the style of writing that most high-level 22 executives use. It is simple; it is personal; it is warm without being syrupy; it is forceful, like a firm handshake. Almost everybody in business likes this style, although lower-level managers often find themselves afraid to write so forthrightly (and, as a result, often find themselves retreating into the styles of responses 1 and 2—the style of 1 to make themselves look "smart" to superiors and the style of 2 to appear unbossy and fairly impersonal). Persons who find response 2 congenial may feel a bit dubious about the appropriateness of response 3. (Although I have no way of proving this judgment, I would guess that more readers in high positions—perhaps more owner-managers—would like response 3 than would readers who are still in lower positions.)

Response 4 goes beyond being forceful; it is annoyingly self-con- 23 fident and breezy. It is colorful and conversational to an extreme, and it is so intensely personal and warm that many business people would be offended, even if they were very close acquaintances of Frank Scalpel's. "It sounds like an advertising person's chitchat," some would probably say.

As you compared your responses with mine, did you say, "What 24 difference does it make which style *I* like or which most resembles *my* customary style? What matters is which style will go over best with Mr. Scalpel in this situation"? If you did, we're getting somewhere.

Earlier, when we defined business writing style, some may have 25 wanted to add, "And that style should sound like me." This was left out for a good reason. Circumstances not only alter cases; they alter the "you" that it is wise for your style to project. Sometimes it's wise to be forceful; at other times it's suicidal. Sometimes being sprightly and colorful is appropriate; at other times it's ludicrous. There are times to be personal and times to be impersonal.

Not understanding this matter of style and tone is why the big 26 corporation game of paddleball between managers and subordinates goes on and on. The subordinate tries to imitate the boss's style, but in actuality—unless the boss is extremely insensitive—he or she has no single style for all circumstances and for all readers. What usually happens is that after several tries, the subordinate writes a letter that the boss signs. "Aha!" the subordinate says. "So that's what the boss wants!" And then the subordinate tries to use that style for all situations and readers. Later, the superior begins rejecting drafts written in the very style he or she professed liking before. Both parties throw up their hands.

This volleying is foolish and wasteful. Both superior and subor- 27 dinate have to recognize that in business writing, style cannot be considered apart from the given situation or from the person to whom the writing is directed. Expert writers select the style that fits a particular reader and the type of writing situation with which they are faced. In business, people often face the following writing situations:

**Positive situations.**
Saying yes or conveying good news.

**Situations where some action is asked of the reader.**
Giving orders or persuading someone to do as requested.

**Information-conveying situations.**
Giving the price of ten widgets, for example.

**Negative situations.**
Saying no or relaying bad news.

In each of these situations, the choice of style is of strategic im- 28 portance.

In positive situations, a writer can relax on all fronts. Readers are 29 usually so pleased to hear the good news that they pay little attention to anything else. Yet it is possible for someone to communicate good news in such a cold, impersonal, roundabout, and almost begrudging way that the reader becomes upset.

Action-request situations involve a form of bargaining. In a situ- 30 ation where the writer holds all the power, he or she can use a forceful commanding style. When the writer holds no power over the reader, though, actions have to be asked for and the reader persuaded, not ordered. In such cases, a forceful style will not be suitable at all.

In information-conveying situations, getting the message across 31 forcefully and straightforwardly is best. Such situations are not usually charged emotionally.

In negative situations, diplomacy becomes very important. The 32 right style depends on the relative positions of the person saying no and the person being told no.

For instance, if you were Leslie Cash, the person in the example 33 at the beginning of the article whom Frank Scalpel was inviting to serve on a hospital's evaluation team, you would be in a situation of having to say no to a very important customer of your company. You would also be in a doubly sensitive situation because it is unlikely that Mr. Scalpel would fail to recognize that he is asking you to enter a conflict-of-interest situation. He is probably asking you *anyway*. Therefore, you would not only have to tell him no, but you would have to avoid telling him that he has asked you to do something that is highly unethical. In this instance, you would be faced with communicating two negative messages at once or else not giving Scalpel any sensible reason for refusing to serve.

Now that we've thought about the strategic implications of style, 34 let's go back to look at each of the responses to Scalpel's request and ask ourselves which is best.

Do we *want* to be personal and warm? Usually yes. But in this 35 situation? Do we want to communicate clearly and directly and force-fully? Usually yes. But here? Do we want to appear as if we're brushing aside the conflict, as the third response does? Or do we want to ap-proach that issue long-windedly, as in the first response, or passively, as in the second? What is the strategically appropriate style?

In the abstract, we have no way of knowing which of these re- 36 sponses will go over best with Mr. Scalpel. The choice is a matter of judgment in a concrete situation. Judging the situation accurately is what separates successful from unsuccessful executive communica-tors.

Looking at the situation with strategy in mind, we note that in the  37
first response, the writer draws back from being close, knowing that
it is necessary to reject not only one but two of the reader's requests.
By using legalistic phraseology and Latinate vocabulary, the writer
lowers the personal nature of the communication and transforms it
into a formal statement. It gives an abstract, textbooklike response that
removes the tone of personal rejection.

The very fact that response 1 is difficult to read and dull in impact  38
may be a strategic asset in this type of negative situation. But if in this
situation a subordinate presented response 1 to you for your signature,
would it be appropriate for you to reject it because it is not written in
the style *you* happen to *like* best in the abstract—say, the style of response 3?

Now let's look at response 2. Again, we see that a lack of personal  39
warmth may be quite appropriate to the situation at hand. Almost
immediately, the letter draws back into impersonality. And by using
the passive constantly, the writer avoids the need to say "I must say
no." Furthermore, the term *construed* reinforces the passive in the second paragraph. This term is a very weak but possibly a strategically
wise way of implying that *some* persons (*other* people, not the writer)
could interpret Scalpel's request as an invitation to participate in an
improper action. Now we can see that, instead of seeming dull and
lacking in personal warmth as it did in the abstract, response 2 may
be the type of letter we would be wise to send out, that is, when we
have taken the whole situation into careful consideration and not just
our personal likes and dislikes.

The third response, and to even greater extent the fourth, have  40
styles that are strategically inappropriate for this situation. In fact, Scalpel might well regard the colorful style of the fourth response as highly
offensive. Both responses directly and forcefully point out the obvious
conflict, but by being so direct each runs the risk of subtly offending
him. (The third response is "you can see the position of conflict I'd be
in if I were on the evaluation team," and the fourth is "Shouldn't be
judge and advocate at the same time!") We could make a pretty strong
argument that the direct, forceful, candid style of the third response
and the breezy, warm, colorful, intensely personal "advertising" style
of the fourth response may both prove ineffectual in a delicate, negative situation such as this.

At this point, readers may say, "All right. I'm convinced. I need  41
to adjust my style to what is appropriate in each situation. And I also
need to give directions to others to let them know how to adjust their
styles. But I haven't the foggiest notion of how to do either!" Some

suggestions for varying your writing style follow. I am not implying that a communication must be written in one style only. A letter to be read aloud at a colleague's retirement party, for instance, may call not only for a warm, personal style but for colorfulness as well. A long analytic report may require a passive, impersonal style, but the persuasive cover letter may call for recommendations being presented in a very forceful style.

## For a Forceful Style

This style is usually appropriate only in situations where the writer 42 has the power, such as in action requests in the form of orders or when you are saying no firmly but politely to a subordinate.

Use the active voice. Have your sentences do something to people and to objects, not just lie there having things done to them; have them give orders: "Correct this error immediately" (you-understood is the subject) instead of "A correction should be made" (which leaves the reader wondering, made by whom).

Step up front and be counted: "I have decided not to recommend you for promotion" instead of "Unfortunately, a positive recommendation for your promotion is not forthcoming."

Do not beat around the bush or act like a politician. If something needs to be said, say it directly.

Write most of your sentences in subject-verb-object order. Do not weaken them by putting namby-pamby phrases before the subject: "I have decided to fund your project" instead of "After much deliberation and weighing of the pros and cons, I have decided to fund your project."

Do not weaken sentences by relegating the point or the action to a subordinate clause: If your point is that your company has won a contract, say "Acme won the contract, although the bidding was intense and highly competitive," not "Although Acme won the contract, the bidding was intense and highly competitive."

Adopt a tone of confidence and surety about what you say by avoiding weasel words like: "Possibly," "maybe," "perhaps." "It could be concluded that. . . ." "Some might conclude that. . . ."

## For a Passive Style

This style is often appropriate in negative situations and in situations 43 where the writer is in a lower position than the reader.

Avoid the imperative—never give an order: Say "A more effective and time-conserving presentation of ideas should be devised before our next meeting" as opposed to "Do a better job of presenting your ideas at our next meeting. Respect my time and get right to the point."

Use the passive voice heavily because it subordinates the subject to the end of the sentence or buries the subject entirely. The passive is especially handy when you are in a low-power position and need to convey negative information to a reader who is in a higher position (an important customer, for instance): Say "Valuable resources are being wasted" instead of "Valuable resources are being wasted by your company" or, even worse, "You are wasting valuable resources."

Avoid taking responsibility for negative statements by attributing them to faceless, impersonal "others": Say "It is more than possible that several objections to your proposed plans might be raised by some observers" or "Several objections might be raised by those hostile to your plans" instead of "I have several objections to your plans."

Use weasel words, especially if the reader is in a high-power position and will not like what you are saying.

Use long sentences and heavy paragraphs to slow down the reader's comprehension of sensitive or negative information.

## For a Personal Style

This style is usually appropriate in good-news and persuasive action-request situations. 44

Use the active voice, which puts you, as the writer, at the front of sentences: "Thank you very much for your comments" or "I appreciated your comments" instead of "Your comments were very much appreciated by me" or the even more impersonal "Your comments were very much appreciated."

Use persons' names (first names, when appropriate) instead of referring to them by title: "Bill James attended the meeting" instead of "Acme's director attended the meeting."

Use personal pronouns—especially "you" and "I"—when you are saying positive things: "I so much appreciate the work you've done" as opposed to "The work you've done is appreciated."

Use short sentences that capture the rhythm of ordinary conversation: "I discussed your proposal with Frank. He's all for it!" as opposed to "This is to inform you that your proposal was taken up at Friday's meeting and that it was regarded with favor."

Use contractions ("can't," "won't," "shouldn't") to sound informal and conversational.

Direct questions to the reader: "Just ask yourself, how would your company like to save $10,000?"

Interject positive personal thoughts and references that will make the reader know that this letter is really to him or her and not some type of form letter sent to just anyone.

## For an Impersonal Style

This style is usually appropriate in negative and information-conveying     45
situations. It's always appropriate in technical and scientific writing and usually when you are writing to technical readers.

Avoid using persons' names, especially first names. Refer to people, if at all, by title or job description: "I would like to know what you think of this plan" instead of "What do you think of this, Herb?" "Our vice president of finance" or "the finance department," not "Ms. Jones."

Avoid using personal pronouns, especially "you" and "I" ("we" may be all right because the corporate we is faceless and impersonal): "The logistics are difficult, and the idea may not work" instead of "I think you have planned things so that the logistics are difficult and your idea may not work." "We wonder if the idea will work" rather than "I don't think the idea will work."

Use the passive voice to make yourself conveniently disappear when desirable: "An error in the calculations has been made" instead of "I think your calculations are wrong."

Make some of your sentences complex and some paragraphs long; avoid the brisk, direct, simple-sentence style of conversation.

## For a Colorful Style

Sometimes a lively style is appropriate in good-news situations. It is     46
most commonly found in the highly persuasive writing of advertisements and sales letters.

Insert some adjectives and adverbs: Instead of "This proposal will save corporate resources," write "This (hard-hitting) (productivity-building) (money-saving) proposal will (easily) (surely) (quickly) (immediately) save our (hard-earned) (increasingly scarce) (carefully guarded) corporate resources."

If appropriate, use a metaphor (A is B) or a simile (A is like B) to make a point: "Truly this program is a *miracle* of logical design." "Our solution strikes at the very *root* of Acme's problems." "This program is like *magic* in its ability to. . . ."

## For a Less Colorful Style

By avoiding adjectives, adverbs, metaphors, and figures of speech, you    47
can make your style less colorful. Such a style is appropriate for ordinary business writing and also results from:

Blending the impersonal style with the passive style.
Employing words that remove any semblance of wit, liveliness, and
    vigor from the writing.

Please bear in mind that these six styles are not mutually exclusive.    48
There is some overlap. A passive style is usually far more impersonal than personal and also not very colorful. A forceful style is likely to be more personal than impersonal, and a colorful style is likely to be fairly forceful. Nevertheless, these styles are distinct enough to justify talking about them. If we fail to make such distinctions, style becomes a catchall term that means nothing specific. Even if not precise, these distinctions enable us to talk about style and its elements and to learn to write appropriately for each situation.

What conclusions can we draw from this discussion? Simply that,    49
whether you write your own letters or have to manage the writing of subordinates, to be an effective communicator, you must realize that:

1.  Each style has an impact on the reader.
2.  Style communicates to readers almost as much as the content of a message.
3.  Style cannot be isolated from a situation.
4.  Generalizing about which style is the best in all situations is impossible.
5.  Style must be altered to suit the circumstances.
6.  Style must be discussed sensibly in the work situation.

These conclusions will be of obvious help to managers who write    50
their own letters. But what help will these conclusions be to managers

who direct assistants in the writing of letters? In many instances, writing assignments go directly to subordinates for handling. Often, manager and assistant have no chance to discuss style strategy together. In such cases, rather than merely submitting a response for a signature, the subordinate would be wise to append a note: e.g., "This is a very sensitive situation, I think. Therefore, I deliberately drew back into a largely impersonal and passive style." At least, the boss will not jump to the conclusion that the assistant has written a letter of low impact by accident.

When they do route writing assignments to assistants, superiors 51 could save much valuable time and prevent mutual distress if they told the subordinates what style seemed strategically wise in each situation. Playing guessing games also wastes money.

And if, as is often the case, neither superior nor subordinate has 52 a clear sense of what style is best, the two can agree to draft a response in one style first, and if that doesn't sound right, to adjust the style appropriately.

Those who write their own letters can try drafting several re- 53 sponses to tough but important situations, each in a different style. It's wise to sleep on them and then decide which sounds best.

Whether you write for yourself or for someone else, it is extremely 54 unlikely that in difficult situations a first draft will be signed by you or anyone else. Only the amateur expects writing perfection on the first try. By learning to control your style and to engineer the tone of your communications, you can make your writing effective.

# Questions

1. Characterize the style of Fielden's first two paragraphs. (His essay, of course, says much about style, but for a brief additional discussion of style you may wish to consult p. 1151 in the glossary.)
2. In paragraph 11 Fielden offers what he calls a "workable definition of style in business writing." Do you find this definition workable for other forms of writing as well—for example, term papers, editorials in the school newspaper, love letters? Why, or why not?
3. If you disagree with Fielden's analysis of any of the four letters Leslie Cash drafts to send to Frank Scalpel, explain the basis of your disagreement.
4. Many textbooks urge students to avoid using the passive voice, but in paragraph 43 Fielden says that the passive "is often appropriate

in negative situations and in situations where the writer is in a lower position than the reader." Look at his examples and then evaluate his advice.

5. This essay appeared in the *Harvard Business Review* and has been one of its most popular reprints. Explain why, in your opinion, it has been popular, or why you find its popularity surprising.

6. Let's assume that Cash sent Scalpel the third letter. You are Scalpel; write a letter to Cash acknowledging receipt of Cash's letter. In fact, write two letters, one a poor letter and one a good letter.

7. In discussing "strategy," Fielden writes in paragraph 25: "Sometimes it's wise to be forceful; at other times it's suicidal. Sometimes being sprightly and colorful is appropriate; at other times it's ludicrous. There are times to be personal and times to be impersonal." Try to recall examples from your own experience (whether writing or speaking) that illustrate one or more of these circumstances. Then write a paragraph combining Fielden's sentence (which you should feel free to modify) with your illustration of it.

## Sherwood Anderson

# The Egg

My father was, I am sure, intended by nature to be a cheer-     1
ful, kindly man. Until he was thirty-four years old he worked as a farmhand for a man named Thomas Butterworth whose place lay near the town of Bidwell, Ohio. He had then a horse of his own, and on Saturday evenings drove into town to spend a few hours in social

Sherwood Anderson (1876–1941) was born in Camden, Ohio. He dropped out of school at fourteen—his attendance had already been irregular—worked at odd jobs, and in 1898 served briefly in the Spanish-American War. He then turned to advertising and business, and by 1904 was a fairly prosperous manager of paint factories. In 1912, however, in the midst of dictating a business letter, he walked out of the office and disappeared for several days. Soon after he began writing poems, stories, and novels, and in 1919 he published the book still regarded as his chief work, *Winesburg, Ohio*. "The Egg" was first published in 1920.

intercourse with other farmhands. In town he drank several glasses of beer and stood about in Ben Head's saloon—crowded on Saturday evenings with visiting farmhands. Songs were sung and glasses thumped on the bar. At ten o'clock father drove home along a lonely country road, made his horse comfortable for the night, and himself went to bed, quite happy in his position in life. He had at that time no notion of trying to rise in the world.

It was in the spring of his thirty-fifth year that father married my mother, then a country school-teacher, and in the following spring I came wriggling and crying into the world. Something happened to the two people. They became ambitious. The American passion for getting up in the world took possession of them.

It may have been that mother was responsible. Being a school-teacher she had no doubt read books and magazines. She had, I presume, read of how Garfield, Lincoln, and other Americans rose from poverty to fame and greatness, and as I lay beside her—in the days of her lying-in—she may have dreamed that I would some day rule men and cities. At any rate she induced father to give up his place as a farmhand, sell his horse, and embark on an independent enterprise of his own. She was a tall silent woman with a long nose and troubled gray eyes. For herself she wanted nothing. For father and myself she was incurably ambitious.

The first venture into which the two people went turned out badly. They rented ten acres of poor stony land on Grigg's road, eight miles from Bidwell, and launched into chicken-raising. I grew into boyhood on the place and got my first impressions of life there. From the beginning they were impressions of disaster, and if, in my turn, I am a gloomy man inclined to see the darker side of life, I attribute it to the fact that what should have been for me the happy joyous days of childhood were spent on a chicken farm.

One unversed in such matters can have no notion of the many and tragic things that can happen to a chicken. It is born out of an egg, lives for a few weeks as a tiny fluffy thing such as you will see pictured on Easter cards, then becomes hideously naked, eats quantities of corn and meal bought by the sweat of your father's brow, gets diseases called pip, cholera, and other names, stands looking with stupid eyes at the sun, becomes sick and dies. A few hens and now and then a rooster, intended to serve God's mysterious ends, struggle through to maturity. The hens lay eggs out of which come other chickens and the dreadful cycle is thus made complete. It is all unbelievably complex. Most philosophers must have been raised on chicken farms.

One hopes for so much from a chicken and is so dreadfully disillusioned. Small chickens, just setting out on the journey of life, look so bright and alert and they are in fact so dreadfully stupid. They are so much like people they mix one up in one's judgments of life. If disease does not kill them, they wait until your expectations are thoroughly aroused and then walk under the wheels of a wagon—to go squashed and dead back to their maker. Vermin infest their youth, and fortunes must be spent for curative powders. In later life I have seen how a literature has been built up on the subject of fortunes to be made out of the raising of chickens. It is intended to be read by the gods who have just eaten of the tree of the knowledge of good and evil. It is a hopeful literature and declares that much may be done by simple ambitious people who own a few hens. Do not be led astray by it. It was not written for you. Go hunt for gold on the frozen hills of Alaska, put your faith in the honesty of a politician, believe if you will that the world is daily growing better and that good will triumph over evil, but do not read and believe the literature that is written concerning the hen. It was not written for you.

I, however, digress. My tale does not primarily concern itself with the hen. If correctly told it will center on the egg. For ten years my father and mother struggled to make our chicken farm pay and then they gave up their struggle and began another. They moved into the town of Bidwell, Ohio, and embarked in the restaurant business. After ten years of worry with incubators that did not hatch, and with tiny— and in their own way lovely—balls of fluff that passed on into seminaked pullethood and from that into dead henhood, we threw all aside and, packing our belongings on a wagon, drove down Grigg's Road toward Bidwell, a tiny caravan of hope looking for a new place from which to start on our upward journey through life. 6

We must have been a sad-looking lot, not, I fancy, unlike refugees fleeing from a battlefield. Mother and I walked in the road. The wagon that contained our goods had been borrowed for the day from Mr. Albert Griggs, a neighbor. Out of its side stuck the legs of cheap chairs, and at the back of the pile of beds, tables, and boxes filled with kitchen utensils was a crate of live chickens, and on top of that the baby carriage in which I had been wheeled about in my infancy. Why we stuck to the baby carriage I don't know. It was unlikely other children would be born and the wheels were broken. People who have few possessions cling tightly to those they have. That is one of the facts that make life so discouraging. 7

Father rode on top of the wagon. He was then a bald-headed man of forty-five, a little fat, and from long association with mother and 8 the chickens he had become habitually silent and discouraged. All during our ten years on the chicken farm he had worked as a laborer on neighboring farms and most of the money he had earned had been spent for remedies to cure chicken diseases, on Wilmer's White Wonder Cholera Cure or Professor Bidlow's Egg Producer or some other preparations that mother found advertised in the poultry papers. There were two little patches of hair on father's head just above his ears. I remember that as a child I used to sit looking at him when he had gone to sleep in a chair before the stove on Sunday afternoons in the winter. I had at that time already begun to read books and have notions of my own, and the bald path that led over the top of his head was, I fancied, something like a broad road, such a road as Caesar might have made on which to lead his legions out of Rome and into the wonders of an unknown world. The tufts of hair that grew above father's ears were, I thought, like forests. I fell into a half-sleeping, half-waking state and dreamed I was a tiny thing going along the road into a far beautiful place where there were no chicken farms and where life was a happy eggless affair.

One might write a book concerning our flight from the chicken farm into town. Mother and I walked the entire eight miles—she to be sure that nothing fell from the wagon and I to see the wonders of the world. On the seat of the wagon beside father was his greatest treasure. I will tell you of that. 9

On a chicken farm, where hundreds and even thousands of chickens come out of eggs, surprising things sometimes happen. Grotesques are born out of eggs as out of people. The accident does not often occur—perhaps once in a thousand births. A chicken is, you see, born that has four legs, two pairs of wings, two heads, or what not. The things do not live. They go quickly back to the hand of their maker that has for a moment trembled. The fact that the poor little things could not live was one of the tragedies of life to father. He had some sort of notion that if he could but bring into henhood or roosterhood a five-legged hen or a two-headed rooster his fortune would be made. He dreamed of taking the wonder about the county fairs and of growing rich by exhibiting it to other farmhands. 10

At any rate, he saved all the little monstrous things that had been born on our chicken farm. They were preserved in alcohol and put each in its own glass bottle. These he had carefully put into a box, and on our journey into town it was carried on the wagon seat beside him. He drove the horses with one hand and with the other clung to the box. When we got to our destination, the box was taken down at once and the bottles removed. All during our days as keepers of a restaurant 11 in the town of Bidwell, Ohio, the grotesques in their little glass bottles sat on a shelf back of the counter. Mother sometimes protested, but father was a rock on the subject of his treasure. The grotesques were, he declared, valuable. People, he said, liked to look at strange and wonderful things.

Did I say that we embarked in the restaurant business in the town    12 of Bidwell, Ohio? I exaggerated a little. The town itself lay at the foot of a low hill and on the shore of a small river. The railroad did not run through the town and the station was a mile away to the north at a place called Pickleville. There had been a cider mill and pickle factory at the station, but before the time of our coming they had both gone out of business. In the morning and in the evening busses came down to the station along a road called Turner's Pike from the hotel on the main street of Bidwell. Our going to the out-of-the-way place to embark in the restaurant business was mother's idea. She talked of it for a year and then one day went off and rented an empty store building opposite the railroad station. It was her idea that the restaurant would be profitable. Traveling men, she said, would be always waiting around to take trains out of town and town people would come to the station to await incoming trains. They would come to the restaurant to buy pieces of pie and drink coffee. Now that I am older I know that she had another motive in going. She was ambitious for me. She wanted me to rise in the world, to get into a town school and become a man of the towns.

At Pickleville father and mother worked hard, as they always had    13 done. At first there was the necessity of putting our place into shape to be a restaurant. That took a month. Father built a shelf on which he put tins of vegetables. He painted a sign on which he put his name in large red letters. Below his name was the sharp command—"EAT HERE"—that was so seldom obeyed. A showcase was bought and filled with cigars and tobacco. Mother scrubbed the floors and the walls of the room. I went to school in the town and was glad to be away from the farm, from the presence of the discouraged, sad-looking chickens. Still I was not very joyous. In the evening I walked home from school along Turner's Pike and remembered the children I had seen playing in the town school yard. A troop of little girls had gone hopping about and singing. I tried that. Down along the frozen road I went hopping solemnly on one leg. "Hippity Hop To The Barber Shop," I sang shrilly. Then I stopped and looked doubtfully about. I was afraid of being seen in my gay mood. It must have seemed to me that I was doing a thing that should not be done by one who, like myself, had been raised on a chicken farm where death was a daily visitor.

Mother decided that our restaurant should remain open at night. 14 At ten in the evening a passenger train went north past our door followed by a local freight. The freight crew had switching to do in Pickleville, and when the work was done they came to our restaurant for hot coffee and food. Sometimes one of them ordered a fried egg. In the morning at four they returned north-bound and again visited us. A little trade began to grow up. Mother slept at night and during the day tended the restaurant and fed our boarders while father slept. He slept in the same bed mother had occupied during the night and I went off to the town of Bidwell and to school. During the long nights, while mother and I slept, father cooked meats that were to go into sandwiches for the lunch baskets of our boarders. Then an idea in regard to getting up in the world came into his head. The American spirit took hold of him. He also became ambitious.

In the long nights when there was little to do, father had time to 15 think. That was his undoing. He decided that he had in the past been an unsuccessful man because he had not been cheerful enough and that in the future he would adopt a cheerful outlook on life. In the early morning he came upstairs and got into bed with mother. She woke and the two talked. From my bed in the corner I listened.

It was father's idea that both he and mother should try to entertain 16 the people who came to eat at our restaurant. I cannot now remember his words, but he gave the impression of one about to become in some obscure way a kind of public entertainer. When people, particularly young people from the town of Bidwell, came into our place, as on very rare occasions they did, bright entertaining conversation was to be made. From father's words I gathered that something of the jolly innkeeper effect was to be sought. Mother must have been doubtful from the first, but she said nothing discouraging. It was father's notion that a passion for the company of himself and mother would spring up in the breasts of the younger people of the town of Bidwell. In the evening bright happy groups would come singing down Turner's Pike. They would troop shouting with joy and laughter into our place. There would be song and festivity. I do not mean to give the impression that father spoke so elaborately of the matter. He was, as I have said, an uncommunicative man. "They want some place to go. I tell you they want some place to go," he said over and over. That was as far as he got. My own imagination has filled in the blanks.

For two or three weeks this notion of father's invaded our house. 17

We did not talk much, but in our daily lives tried earnestly to make smiles take the place of glum looks. Mother smiled at the boarders and I, catching the infection, smiled at our cat. Father became a little feverish in his anxiety to please. There was, no doubt, lurking somewhere in him, a touch of the spirit of the showman. He did not waste much of his ammunition on the railroad men he served at night, but seemed to be waiting for a young man or woman from Bidwell to come in to show what he could do. On the counter in the restaurant there was a wire basket kept always filled with eggs, and it must have been before his eyes when the idea of being entertaining was born in his brain. There was something pre-natal about the way eggs kept themselves connected with the development of his idea. At any rate, an egg ruined his new impulse in life. Late one night I was awakened by a roar of anger coming from father's throat. Both mother and I sat upright in our beds. With trembling hands she lighted a lamp that stood on a table by her head. Downstairs the front door of our restaurant went shut with a bang and in a few minutes father tramped up the stairs. He held an egg in his hand and his hand trembled as though he were having a chill. There was a half-insane light in his eyes. As he stood glaring at us I was sure he intended throwing the egg at either mother or me. Then he laid it gently on the table beside the lamp and dropped on his knees beside mother's bed. He began to cry like a boy, and I, carried away by his grief, cried with him. The two of us filled the little upstairs room with our wailing voices. It is ridiculous, but of the picture we made I can remember only the fact that mother's hand continually stroked the bald path that ran across the top of his head. I have forgotten what mother said to him and how she induced him to tell her of what had happened downstairs. His explanation also has gone out of my mind. I remember only my own grief and fright and the shiny path over father's head glowing in the lamplight as he knelt by the bed.

As to what happened downstairs. For some unexplainable reason 18 I know the story as well as though I had been a witness to my father's discomfiture. One in time gets to know many unexplainable things. On that evening young Joe Kane, son of a merchant of Bidwell, came to Pickleville to meet his father, who was expected on the ten-o'clock evening train from the South. The train was three hours late and Joe came into our place to loaf about and to wait for its arrival. The local freight train came in and the freight crew were fed. Joe was left alone in the restaurant with father.

From the moment he came into our place the Bidwell young man 19 must have been puzzled by my father's actions. It was his notion that father was angry at him for hanging around. He noticed that the restaurant-keeper was apparently disturbed by his presence and he thought of going out. However, it began to rain and he did not fancy the long walk to town and back. He bought a five-cent cigar and ordered a cup of coffee. He had a newspaper in his pocket and took it out and began to read. "I'm waiting for the evening train. It's late," he said apologetically.

For a long time father, whom Joe Kane had never seen before, remained silently gazing at his visitor. He was no doubt suffering from an attack of stage fright. As so often happens in life he had thought so much and so often of the situation that now confronted him that he was somewhat nervous in its presence. 20

For one thing, he did not know what to do with his hands. He thrust one of them nervously over the counter and shook hands with Joe Kane. "How-de-do," he said. Joe Kane put his newspaper down and stared at him. Father's eyes lighted on the basket of eggs that sat on the counter and he began to talk. "Well," he began hesitatingly, "well, you have heard of Christopher Columbus, eh?" He seemed to be angry. "That Christopher Columbus was a cheat," he declared emphatically. "He talked of making an egg stand on its end. He talked, he did, and then he went and broke the end of the egg." 21

My father seemed to his visitor to be beside himself at the duplicity of Christopher Columbus. He muttered and swore. He declared it was wrong to teach children that Christopher Columbus was a great man when, after all, he cheated at the critical moment. He had declared he would make an egg stand on end and then, when his bluff had been called, he had done a trick. Still grumbling at Columbus, father took an egg from the basket on the counter and began to walk up and down. He rolled the egg between the palms of his hands. He smiled genially. He began to mumble words regarding the effect to be produced on an egg by the electricity that comes out of the human body. He declared that, without breaking its shell and by virtue of rolling it back and forth in his hands, he could stand the egg on its end. He explained that the warmth of his hands and the gentle rolling movement he gave the egg created a new center of gravity, and Joe Kane was mildly interested. "I have handled thousands of eggs," father said. "No one knows more about eggs than I do." 22

He stood the egg on the counter and it fell on its side. He tried the trick again and again, each time rolling the egg between the palms of his hands and saying the words regarding the wonders of electricity 23 and the laws of gravity. When after a half-hour's effort he did succeed in making the egg stand for a moment, he looked up to find that his visitor was no longer watching. By the time he had succeeded in calling Joe Kane's attention to the success of his effort, the egg had again rolled over and lay on its side.

Afire with the showman's passion and at the same time a good 24 deal disconcerted by the failure of his first effort, father now took the bottles containing the poultry monstrosities down from their place on the shelf and began to show them to his visitor. "How would you like to have seven legs and two heads like this fellow?" he asked, exhibiting the most remarkable of his treasures. A cheerful smile played over his face. He reached over the counter and tried to slap Joe Kane on the shoulder as he had seen men do in Ben Head's saloon when he was a young farmhand and drove to town on Saturday evenings. His visitor was made a little ill by the sight of the body of the terribly deformed bird floating in the alcohol in the bottle and got up to go. Coming from behind the counter, father took hold of the young man's arm and led him back to his seat. He grew a little angry and for a moment had to turn his face away and force himself to smile. Then he put the bottles back on the shelf. In an outburst of generosity he fairly compelled Joe Kane to have a fresh cup of coffee and another cigar at his expense. Then he took a pan and filling it with vinegar, taken from a jug that sat beneath the counter, he declared himself about to do a new trick. "I will heat this egg in this pan of vinegar," he said. "Then I will put it through the neck of a bottle without breaking the shell. When the egg is inside the bottle it will resume its normal shape and the shell will become hard again. Then I will give the bottle with the egg in it to you. You can take it about with you wherever you go. People will want to know how you got the egg in the bottle. Don't tell them. Keep them guessing. That is the way to have fun with this trick."

Father grinned and winked at his visitor. Joe Kane decided that 25 the man who confronted him was mildly insane but harmless. He drank the cup of coffee that had been given him and began to read his paper again. When the egg had been heated in vinegar, father carried it on a spoon to the counter and going into a back room got an empty bottle. He was angry because his visitor did not watch him as he began to do his trick, but nevertheless went cheerfully to work. For a long time he struggled, trying to get the egg to go through the neck of the bottle. He put the pan of vinegar back on the stove, intending to reheat the egg, then picked it up and burned his fingers. After a second bath in the hot vinegar, the shell of the egg had been softened a little, but not enough for his purpose. He worked and worked and a spirit of desperate determination took possession of him. When he thought that at last the trick was about to be consummated, the delayed train came in at the station and Joe Kane started to go nonchalantly out at the door. Father made a last desperate effort to conquer the egg and make it do the thing that would establish his reputation as one who knew how to entertain guests who came into his restaurant. He worried the egg. He attempted to be somewhat rough with it. He swore and the sweat stood out on his forehead. The egg broke under his hand. When the contents spurted over his clothes, Joe Kane, who had stopped at the door, turned and laughed.

A roar of anger rose from my father's throat. He danced and shouted a string of inarticulate words. Grabbing another egg from the basket on the counter, he threw it, just missing the head of the young man as he dodged through the door and escaped.    26

Father came upstairs to mother and me with an egg in his hand.    27
I do not know what he intended to do. I imagine he had some idea of destroying it, of destroying all eggs, and that he intended to let mother and me see him begin. When, however, he got into the presence of mother, something happened to him. He laid the egg gently on the table and dropped on his knees by the bed as I have already explained. He later decided to close the restaurant for the night and to come upstairs and get into bed. When he did so, he blew out the light and after much muttered conversation both he and mother went to sleep. I suppose I went to sleep also, but my sleep was troubled. I awoke at dawn and for a long time looked at the egg that lay on the table. I wondered why eggs had to be and why from the egg came the hen who again laid the egg. The question got into my blood. It has stayed there, I imagine, because I am the son of my father. At any rate, the problem remains unsolved in my mind. And that, I conclude, is but another evidence of the complete and final triumph of the egg— at least as far as my family is concerned.

# Questions

1. In a paragraph or two characterize the father, including in your discussion a comment on whether or not he is hypocritical. Then discuss, in an additional paragraph or two, whether his failure is based on his own inadequacies.

2. What do you make out of the narrator's statement that the story "if correctly told . . . will center on the egg"?
3. In a sentence state the theme of the story. Then in the remainder of the paragraph, offer support for your view of the theme.
4. Characterize the narrator.
5. In 250–500 words, recount a story of some businessperson you know. The story should reveal the person's character, and convey to the reader a sense of the character's view of life. Your own view— for example, admiration, amusement, or sorrow—should be implicit, but do not state this view explicitly.

# 7
## MESSAGES

*The Argument*
**Leonard Freed, 1965**

Magnum Photos

*The Computer Operator*
**Arthur Tress, 1976**

# Short Views

We must be as clear as our natural reticence allows us to be.
**Marianne Moore**


To talk too much about oneself may also be a means of
concealment.
**Freidrich Nietzsche**


Darling Laura, sweet whiskers, do try to write me better letters.
Your last, dated 19 December received today, so eagerly expected,
was a bitter disappointment. Do realize that a letter need not be a
bald chronicle of events; I know you lead a dull life now, my heart
bleeds for it, though I believe you could make it more interesting if
you had the will. But that is no reason to make your letters as dull
as your life. I simply am not interested in Bridget's children. Do
grasp that. A letter should be a form of conversation; write as
though you were talking to me.
**Evelyn Waugh**


[From the dedication of Robert Louis Stevenson's *Travels with a
Donkey*] Every book is, in an intimate sense, a circular letter to the
friends of him who writes it. They alone take his meaning; they find
private messages, assurances of love, and expressions of gratitude
dropped for them in every corner. The public is but a generous
patron who defrays the postage. Yet, though the letter is directed to
all, we have an old and kindly custom of addressing it on the
outside to one. Of what shall a man be proud, if he is not proud of
his friends? And so, my dear Sidney Colvin, it is with pride that I
sign myself affectionately yours,
**Robert Louis Stevenson**


While I am thinking about metaphor, a flock of purple finches
arrives on the lawn. Since I haven't seen these birds for some years,
I am only fairly sure of their being in fact purple finches, so I get
down Peterson's *Field Guide* and read his description: "Male: About
size of House Sparrow, rosy-red, brightest on head and rump."
That checks quite well, but his next remark—"a sparrow dipped in

raspberry juice,"—is decisive: it fits. I look out the window again, and now I know that I am seeing purple finches.
**Howard Nemerov**

We will understand the world, and preserve ourselves and our values in it, only insofar as we have a language that is alert and responsive to it, and careful of it. I mean that literally. When we give our plows such brand names as "Sod Blaster," we are imposing on their use conceptual limits which raise the likelihood that they will be used destructively. When we speak of man's "war against nature," or of a "peace offensive," we are accepting the limitations of a metaphor that suggests, and even proposes, violent solutions. When students ask for the right of "participatory input" at the meetings of a faculty organization, they are thinking of democratic process, but they are *speaking* of a convocation of robots, and are thus devaluing the very traditions that they invoke.
**Wendell Berry**

Because it deals with struggle, sports writing is required to be vigorous, and because it scorns formality it must be slangy and colloquial. But slang is particularly unfitted for frequent repetition and sports writing is, above any other type of contemporary writing, repetitious, laden with clichés. The wretched sports writer, with slight material and often (one suspects) even slighter interest, is compelled to assume concern he does not feel and to conceal his yawns under forced shouts of simulated excitement. A tyrannical convention of his dreary craft prevents him from repeating his verbs; yet there are only a certain number of synonyms for win and lose. He has done what he can with *win, top, upset, pace, defeat, trounce, decision* (verb), *crush, sock, blitz, spank, clobber, whip, wallop, down, spill,* and the like, but the demand far exceeds the capacity of the language. No one, apparently, using only the normal resources of the richest language known, can make sports interesting.

The strained variation is interspersed with the strained periphrasis. An injured thumb is *the dislocated digit* and the backfield is *a bevy of backs.* Alliteration is freely employed. Not since *Widsith* has its artful aid been so assiduously sought.
**Bergen and Cornelia Evans**

A man is known by the books he reads, by the company he keeps, by the praise he gives, by his dress, by his tastes, by his distastes,

by the stories he tells, by his gait, by the motion of his eye, by the look of his house, of his chamber; for nothing on earth is solitary, but everything hath affinities infinite. . . .
        **Ralph Waldo Emerson**

Gifts from parents to children always carry the most meaningful messages. The way parents think about presents goes one step beyond the objects themselves—the ties, dolls, sleds, record players, kerchiefs, bicycles and model airplanes that wait by the Christmas tree. The gifts are, in effect, one way of telling boys and girls, "We love you even though you have been a bad boy all month" or, "We love having a daughter" or, "We treat all our children alike" or, "It is all right for girls to have some toys made for boys" or, "This alarm clock will help you get started in the morning all by yourself." Throughout all the centuries since the invention of a Santa Claus figure who represented a special recognition of children's behavior, good and bad, presents have given parents a way of telling children about their love and hopes and expectations for them.
        **Margaret Mead**

A good painter is to paint two main things, namely, man and the working of man's mind. The first is easy, the second difficult, for it is to be represented through the gestures and movements of the limbs.
        **Leonardo da Vinci**

If you saw a bullet hit a bird, and he told you he wasn't shot, you might weep at his courtesy, but you would certainly doubt his word.
        **Emily Dickinson**

Edward T. Hall

# Proxemics in the
# Arab World

In spite of over two thousand years of contact, Westerners 1
and Arabs still do not understand each other. Proxemic research reveals some insights into this difficulty. Americans in the Middle East
are immediately struck by two conflicting sensations. In public they
are compressed and overwhelmed by smells, crowding, and high noise
levels; in Arab homes Americans are apt to rattle around, feeling exposed and often somewhat inadequate because of too much space! (The
Arab houses and apartments of the middle and upper classes which
Americans stationed abroad commonly occupy are much larger than
the dwellings such Americans usually inhabit.) Both the high sensory
stimulation which is experienced in public places and the basic insecurity which comes from being in a dwelling that is too large provide
Americans with an introduction to the sensory world of the Arab.

## Behavior in Public

Pushing and shoving in public places is characteristic of Middle Eastern 2
culture. Yet it is not entirely what Americans think it is (being pushy
and rude) but stems from a different set of assumptions concerning
not only the relations between people but how one experiences the
body as well. Paradoxically, Arabs consider northern Europeans and
Americans pushy, too. This was very puzzling to me when I started
investigating these two views. How could Americans who stand aside

Edward T. Hall was born in Missouri in 1914. He is a professor of anthropology
at Northwestern University.

Hall is especially concerned with "proxemics," a word derived from the Latin
*proximus,* "nearest." Proxemics is the study of people's responses to spatial
relationships—for example, their ways of marking out their territory in public
places, and their responses to what they consider to be crowding. In these pages
from his book *The Hidden Dimension* (1966), Hall suggests that Arabs and Westerners must understand the proxemic customs of each other's culture; without
such understanding, other communications between them are likely to be mis-
understood.

and avoid touching be considered pushy? I used to ask Arabs to explain this paradox. None of my subjects was able to tell me specifically what particulars of American behavior were responsible, yet they all agreed that the impression was widespread among Arabs. After repeated unsuccessful attempts to gain insight into the cognitive world of the Arab on this particular point, I filed it away as a question that only time would answer. When the answer came, it was because of a seemingly inconsequential annoyance.

While waiting for a friend in a Washington, D.C., hotel lobby and 3 wanting to be both visible and alone, I had seated myself in a solitary chair outside the normal stream of traffic. In such a setting most Americans follow a rule, which is all the more binding because we seldom think about it, that can be stated as follows: as soon as a person stops or is seated in a public place, there balloons around him a small sphere of privacy which is considered inviolate. The size of the sphere varies with the degree of crowding, the age, sex, and the importance of the person, as well as the general surroundings. Anyone who enters this zone and stays there is intruding. In fact, a stranger who intrudes, even for a specific purpose, acknowledges the fact that he has intruded by beginning his request with "Pardon me, but can you tell me . . . ?"

To continue, as I waited in the deserted lobby, a stranger walked 4 up to where I was sitting and stood close enough so that not only could I easily touch him but I could even hear him breathing. In addition, the dark mass of his body filled the peripheral field of vision on my left side. If the lobby had been crowded with people, I would have understood his behavior, but in an empty lobby his presence made me exceedingly uncomfortable. Feeling annoyed by this intrusion, I moved my body in such a way as to communicate annoyance. Strangely enough, instead of moving away, my actions seemed only to encourage him, because he moved even closer. In spite of the temptation to escape the annoyance, I put aside thoughts of abandoning my post, thinking, "To hell with it. Why should I move? I was here first and I'm not going to let this fellow drive me out even if he is a boor." Fortunately, a group of people soon arrived whom my tormentor immediately joined. Their mannerisms explained his behavior, for I knew from both speech and gestures that they were Arabs. I had not been able to make this crucial identification by looking at my subject when he was alone because he wasn't talking and he was wearing American clothes.

In describing the scene later to an Arab colleague, two contrasting 5 patterns emerged. My concept and my feelings about my own circle of privacy in a "public" place immediately struck my Arab friend as strange and puzzling. He said, "After all, it's a public place, isn't it?" Pursuing this line of inquiry, I found that an Arab thought I had no rights whatsoever by virtue of occupying a given spot; neither my place nor my body was inviolate! For the Arab, there is no such thing as an intrusion in public. Public means public. With this insight, a great range of Arab behavior that had been puzzling, annoying, and sometimes even frightening began to make sense. I learned, for example, that if *A* is standing on a street corner and *B* wants his spot, *B* is within his rights if he does what he can to make *A* uncomfortable enough to move. In Beirut only the hardy sit in the last row in a movie theater, because there are usually standees who want seats and who push and shove and make such a nuisance that most people give up and leave. Seen in this light, the Arab who "intruded" on my space in the hotel lobby had apparently selected it for the very reason I had: it was a good place to watch two doors and the elevator. My show of annoyance, instead of driving him away, had only encouraged him. He thought he was about to get me to move.

Another silent source of friction between Americans and Arabs is  6 in an area that Americans treat very informally—the manners and rights of the road. In general, in the United States we tend to defer to the vehicle that is bigger, more powerful, faster, and heavily laden. While a pedestrian walking along a road may feel annoyed he will not think it unusual to step aside for a fast-moving automobile. He knows that because he is moving he does not have the right to the space around him that he has when he is standing still (as I was in the hotel lobby). It appears that the reverse is true with the Arabs who apparently *take on rights to space as they move.* For someone else to move into a space an Arab is also moving into is a violation of his rights. It is infuriating to an Arab to have someone else cut in front of him on the highway. It is the American's cavalier treatment of moving space that makes the Arab call him aggressive and pushy.

## Concepts of Privacy

The experience described above and many others suggested to me that  7 Arabs might actually have a wholly contrasting set of assumptions concerning the body and the rights associated with it. Certainly the Arab tendency to shove and push each other in public and to feel and pinch women in public conveyances would not be tolerated by Westerners. It appeared to me that they must not have any concept of a private zone outside the body. This proved to be precisely the case.

In the Western world, the person is synonymous with an indi-    8
vidual inside a skin. And in northern Europe generally, the skin and
even the clothes may be inviolate. You need permission to touch either
if you are a stranger. This rule applies in some parts of France, where
the mere touching of another person during an argument used to be
legally defined as assault. For the Arab the location of the person in
relation to the body is quite different. The person exists somewhere
down inside the body. The ego is not completely hidden, however,
because it can be reached very easily with an insult. It is protected
from touch but not from words. The dissociation of the body and the
ego may explain why the public amputation of a thief's hand is tolerated as standard punishment in Saudi Arabia. It also sheds light on
why an Arab employer living in a modern apartment can provide his
servant with a room that is a boxlike cubicle approximately 5 by 10 by
4 feet in size that is not only hung from the ceiling to conserve floor
space but has an opening so that the servant can be spied on.

As one might suspect, deep orientations toward the self such as    9
the one just described are also reflected in the language. This was
brought to my attention one afternoon when an Arab colleague who
is the author of an Arab-English dictionary arrived in my office and
threw himself into a chair in a state of obvious exhaustion. When I
asked him what had been going on, he said: "I have spent the entire
afternoon trying to find the Arab equivalent of the English word 'rape.'
There is no such word in Arabic. All my sources, both written and
spoken, can come up with no more than an approximation, such as
'He took her against her will.' There is nothing in Arabic approaching
your meaning as it is expressed in that one word."

Differing concepts of the placement of the ego in relation to the    10
body are not easily grasped. Once an idea like this is accepted, however, it is possible to understand many other facets of Arab life that
would otherwise be difficult to explain. One of these is the high population density of Arab cities like Cairo, Beirut, and Damascus. According to the animal studies described [elsewhere], the Arabs should
be living in a perpetual behavioral sink. While it is probable that Arabs
are suffering from population pressures, it is also just as possible that
continued pressure from the desert has resulted in a cultural adaptation
to high density which takes the form described above. Tucking the
ego down inside the body shell not only would permit higher population densities but would explain why it is that Arab communications
are stepped up as much as they are when compared to northern European communication patterns. Not only is the sheer noise level much

higher, but the piercing look of the eyes, the touch of the hands, and the mutual bathing in the warm moist breath during conversation represent stepped-up sensory inputs to a level which many Europeans find unbearably intense.

The Arab dream is for lots of space in the home, which unfortu-  11
nately many Arabs cannot afford. Yet when he has space, it is very different from what one finds in most American homes. Arab spaces inside their upper middle-class homes are tremendous by our standards. They avoid partitions because Arabs *do not like to be alone.* The form of the home is such as to hold the family together inside a single protective shell, because Arabs are deeply involved with each other. Their personalities are intermingled and take nourishment from each other like the roots and soil. If one is not with people and actively involved in some way, one is deprived of life. An old Arab saying reflects this value: "Paradise without people should not be entered because it is Hell." Therefore, Arabs in the United States often feel socially and sensorially deprived and long to be back where there is human warmth and contact.

Since there is no physical privacy as we know it in the Arab family,  12
not even a word for privacy, one could expect that the Arabs might use some other means to be alone. Their way to be alone is to stop talking. Like the English, an Arab who shuts himself off in this way is not indicating that anything is wrong or that he is withdrawing, only that he wants to be alone with his own thoughts or does not want to be intruded upon. One subject said that her father would come and go for days at a time without saying a word, and no one in the family thought anything of it. Yet for this very reason, an Arab exchange student visiting a Kansas farm failed to pick up the cue that his American hosts were mad at him when they gave him the "silent treatment." He only discovered something was wrong when they took him to town and tried forcibly to put him on a bus to Washington, D.C., the headquarters of the exchange program responsible for his presence in the U.S.

## Arab Personal Distances

Like everyone else in the world, Arabs are unable to formulate specific  13
rules for their informal behavior patterns. In fact, they often deny that there are any rules, and they are made anxious by suggestions that such is the case. Therefore, in order to determine how the Arab sets

distances, I investigated the use of each sense separately. Gradually, definite and distinctive behavioral patterns began to emerge.

Olfaction occupies a prominent place in the Arab life. Not only is   14
it one of the distance-setting mechanisms, but it is a vital part of a complex system of behavior. Arabs consistently breathe on people when they talk. However, this habit is more than a matter of different manners. To the Arab good smells are pleasing and a way of being involved with each other. To smell one's friend is not only nice but desirable, for to deny him your breath is to act ashamed. Americans, on the other hand, trained as they are not to breathe in people's faces, automatically communicate shame in trying to be polite. Who would expect that when our highest diplomats are putting on their best manners they are also communicating shame? Yet this is what occurs constantly, because diplomacy is not only "eyeball to eyeball" but breath to breath.

By stressing olfaction, Arabs do not try to eliminate all the body's   15
odors, only to enhance them and use them in building human relationships. Nor are they self-conscious about telling others when they don't like the way they smell. A man leaving his house in the morning may be told by his uncle, "Habib, your stomach is sour and your breath doesn't smell too good. Better not talk too close to people today." Smell is even considered in the choice of a mate. When couples are being matched for marriage, the man's go-between will sometimes ask to smell the girl, who may be turned down if she doesn't "smell nice." Arabs recognize that smell and disposition may be linked.

In a word, the olfactory boundary performs two roles in Arab life.   16
It enfolds those who want to relate and separates those who don't. The Arab finds it essential to stay inside the olfactory zone as a means of keeping tab on changes in emotion. What is more, he may feel crowded as soon as he smells something unpleasant. While not much is known about "olfactory crowding," this may prove to be as significant as any other variable in the crowding complex because it is tied directly to the body chemistry and hence to the state of health and emotions. It is not surprising, therefore, that the olfactory boundary constitutes for the Arabs an informal distance-setting mechanism in contrast to the visual mechanisms of the Westerner.

## Facing and Not Facing

One of my earliest discoveries in the field of intercultural communi-   17
cation was that the position of the bodies of people in conversation

varies with the culture. Even so, it is used to puzzle me that a special Arab friend seemed unable to walk and talk at the same time. After years in the United States, he could not bring himself to stroll along, facing forward while talking. Our progress would be arrested while he edged ahead, cutting slightly in front of me and turning sideways so we could see each other. Once in this position, he would stop. His behavior was explained when I learned that for the Arabs to view the other person peripherally is regarded as impolite, and to sit or stand back-to-back is considered very rude. You must be involved when interacting with Arabs who are friends.

One mistaken American notion is that Arabs conduct all conver-  18 sations at close distances. This is not the case at all. On social occasions, they may sit on opposite sides of the room and talk across the room to each other. They are, however, apt to take offense when Americans use what are to them ambiguous distances, such as the four- to seven-foot social-consultative distance. They frequently complain that Americans are cold or aloof or "don't care." This was what an elderly Arab diplomat in an American hospital thought when the American nurses used "professional" distance. He had the feeling that he was being ignored, that they might not take good care of him. Another Arab subject remarked, referring to American behavior, "What's the matter? Do I smell bad? Or are they afraid of me?"

Arabs who interact with Americans report experiencing a certain  19 flatness traceable in part to a very different use of the eyes in private and in public as well as between friends and strangers. Even though it is rude for a guest to walk around the Arab home eying things, Arabs look at each other in ways which seem hostile or challenging to the American. One Arab informant said that he was in constant hot water with Americans because of the way he looked at them without the slightest intention of offending. In fact, he had on several occasions barely avoided fights with American men who apparently thought their masculinity was being challenged because of the way he was looking at them. As noted earlier, Arabs look each other in the eye when talking with an intensity that makes most Americans highly uncomfortable.

## Involvement

As the reader must gather by now, Arabs are involved with each other  20 on many different levels simultaneously. Privacy in a public place is foreign to them. Business transactions in the bazaar, for example, are not just between buyer and seller, but are participated in by everyone. Anyone who is standing around may join in. If a grownup sees a boy breaking a window, he must stop him even if he doesn't know him. Involvement and participation are expressed in other ways as well. If two men are fighting, the crowd must intervene. On the political level, *to fail to intervene* when trouble is brewing is to take sides, which is what our State Department always seems to be doing. Given the fact that few people in the world today are even remotely aware of the cultural mold that forms their thoughts, it is normal for Arabs to view *our* behavior as though it stemmed from *their* own hidden set of assumptions.

## Feelings About Enclosed Spaces

In the course of my interviews with Arabs the term "tomb" kept crop-  21
ping up in conjunction with enclosed space. In a word, Arabs don't mind being crowded by people but hate to be hemmed in by walls. They show a much greater overt sensitivity to architectural crowding than we do. Enclosed space must meet at least three requirements that I know of if it is to satisfy the Arabs: there must be plenty of unobstructed space in which to move around (possibly as much as a thousand square feet); very high ceilings—so high in fact that they do not normally impinge on the visual field; and, in addition, there must be an unobstructed view. It was spaces such as these in which the Americans referred to earlier felt so uncomfortable. One sees the Arab's need for a view expressed in many ways, even negatively, for to cut off a neighbor's view is one of the most effective ways of spiting him. In Beirut one can see what is known locally as the "spite house." It is nothing more than a thick, four-story wall, built at the end of a long fight between neighbors, on a narrow strip of land, for the express purpose of denying a view of the Mediterranean to any house built on the land behind. According to one of my informants, there is also a house on a small plot of land between Beirut and Damascus which is completely surrounded by a neighbor's wall built high enough to cut off the view from all windows!

## Boundaries

Proxemic patterns tell us other things about Arab culture. For example,  22
the whole concept of the boundary as an abstraction is almost impossible to pin down. In one sense, there are no boundaries. "Edges" of

towns, yes, but permanent boundaries out in the country (hidden lines), no. In the course of my work with Arab subjects I had a difficult time translating our concept of a boundary into terms which could be equated with theirs. In order to clarify the distinctions between the two very different definitions, I thought it might be helpful to pinpoint acts which constituted trespass. To date, I have been unable to discover anything even remotely resembling our own legal concept of trespass.

Arab behavior in regard to their own real estate is apparently an extension of, and therefore consistent with, their approach to the body. My subjects simply failed to respond whenever trespass was mentioned. They didn't seem to understand what I meant by this term. This may be explained by the fact that they organize relationships with each other according to closed social systems rather than spatially. For thousands of years Moslems, Marinites, Druses, and Jews have lived in their own villages, each with strong kin affiliations. Their hierarchy of loyalties is: first to one's self, then to kinsman, townsman, or tribesman, co-religionist and/or countryman. Anyone not in these categories is a stranger. Strangers and enemies are very closely linked, if not synonymous, in Arab thought. Trespass in this context is a matter of who you are, rather than a piece of land or a space with a boundary that can be denied to anyone and everyone, friend and foe alike. 23

In summary, proxemic patterns differ. By examining them it is possible to reveal hidden cultural frames that determine the structure of a given people's perceptual world. Perceiving the world differently leads to differential definitions of what constitutes crowded living, different interpersonal relations, and a different approach to both local and international politics. 24

# Questions

1. According to Hall, why do Arabs think Americans are pushy? And, again according to Hall, why do Arabs not consider themselves pushy?
2. Explain what Hall means by "cognitive world" (paragraph 2); by "ego" (paragraph 10); by "behavioral sink" (in the same paragraph). Then explain, for the benefit of someone who did not understand the terms, how you know what Hall means by each.
3. In paragraph 9 Hall points out that there is no Arabic equivalent of the English word "rape." Can you provide an example of a similar gap in English or in another language? Does a cultural difference account for the linguistic difference?

4.  In paragraph 3 Hall says of a rule that it "is all the more binding because we seldom think about it." Is this generally true of rules? What examples or counter-examples support your view?

Keith H. Basso

# "Stalking with Stories"
Names, Places, and Moral Narratives Among the Western Apache

Shortly before his death in 1960, Clyde Kluckhohn made    1
the following observation in a course he gave at Harvard University
on the history of anthropological thought: "The most interesting claims
people make are those they make about themselves. Cultural anthropologists should keep this in mind, especially when they are doing
fieldwork." This essay focuses on a small set of spoken texts in which
members of a contemporary American Indian society express claims
about themselves, their language, and the lands on which they live.
Specifically, I shall be concerned here with a set of statements that
were made by men and women from the Western Apache community
at Cibecue, a dispersed settlement of 1100 people that has been inhabited by Apaches for centuries and is located near the center of Fort
Apache Indian Reservation in east-central Arizona (see Figure 1). The
statements that interest me, which could be supplemented by a large
number of others, are the following.

1.  The land is always stalking people. The land makes people live
    right. The land looks after us. The land looks after people. [Mrs.
    Annie Peaches, age 77, 1977]

Keith H. Basso has taught at the University of Arizona, Yale University, and the
University of New Mexico. He has conducted linguistic and ethnographic research in the Western Apache community at Cibecue, in Arizona, since 1959.

**Figure 1.**  *Map showing location of the community of Cibecue on the Fort Apache Indian Reservation, Arizona.*

2.  Our children are losing the land. It doesn't go to work on them anymore. They don't know the stories about what happened at these places. That's why some get into trouble. [Mr. Ronnie Lupe, age 42; Chairman, White Mountain Apache Tribe, 1978]

3.  We used to survive only off the land. Now it's no longer that way. Now we live only with money, so we need jobs. But the land still looks after us. We know the names of the places where everything happened. So we stay away from badness. [Mr. Nick Thompson, age 64, 1980]

4.  I think of that mountain called "white rocks lie above in a compact cluster" as if it were my maternal grandmother. I recall stories of how it once was at that mountain. The stories told to me were like arrows. Elsewhere, hearing that mountain's name, I see it. Its name is like a picture. Stories go to work on you like arrows. Stories make you live right. Stories make you replace yourself. [Mr. Benson Lewis, age 64, 1979]

5.  One time I went to L.A., training for mechanic. It was no good, sure no good. I start drinking, hang around bars all the time. I start getting into trouble with my wife, fight sometimes with her. It was *bad*. I forget about this country here around Cibecue. I

forget all the names and stories. I don't hear them in my mind anymore. I forget how to live right, forget how to be strong. [Mr. Wilson Lavender, age 52, 1975]

If the texts of these statements resist quick and easy interpretation, it is not because the people who made them are confused or cloudy thinkers. Neither is it because, as one unfortunate commentator would have us believe, the Western Apache are "mystically inclined and correspondingly inarticulate." The problem we face is a semiotic* one, a barrier to constructing appropriate sense and significance. It arises from the obvious circumstance that all views articulated by Apache people are informed by their experience in a culturally constituted world of objects and events with which most of us are unfamiliar. What sort of world is it? Or, to draw the question into somewhat sharper focus, what is the cultural context in which Apache statements such as those presented above find acceptance as valid claims about reality?

More specifically, what is required to interpret Annie Peaches's claim that the land occupied by the Western Apache is "always stalking people" and that because of this they know how to "live right"? And how should we understand Chairman Lupe's assertion that Apache children sometimes misbehave because the land "doesn't go to work on them anymore"? Why does Nick Thompson claim that his knowledge of place-names and historical events enables him to "stay away from badness"? And why does Benson Lewis liken place-names to pictures, stories to arrows, and a mountain near the community of Cibecue to his maternal grandmother? What should we make of Wilson Lavender's recollection of an unhappy time in California when forgetting place-names and stories caused him to forget "how to be strong"? Are these claims structured in metaphorical terms, or, given Western Apache assumptions about the physical universe and the place of people within it, are they somehow to be interpreted literally? In any case, what is the reasoning that lies behind the claims, the informal logic of which they are simultaneously products and expressions? Above all, what makes the claims make sense?

I address these and other questions through an investigation of how Western Apaches talk about the natural landscape and the importance they attach to named locations within it. Accordingly, my discussion focuses on elements of language and patterns of speech,

---

* "Semiotics" is the science of signs—not merely of language (verbal signs), traffic signals, and semaphor but also of other things that make "statements," such as gestures, clothing, posture, houses. (Editors' note)

my purpose being to discover from these elements and patterns something of how Apache people construe their land and render it intelligible. Whenever Apaches describe the land—or, as happens more frequently, whenever they tell stories about incidents that have occurred at particular points upon it—they take steps to constitute it in relation to themselves. Which is simply to say that in acts of speech, mundane and otherwise, Apaches negotiate images and understandings of the land which are accepted as credible accounts of what it actually is, why it is significant, and how it impinges on the daily lives of men and women.

## "Learn the Names"

Nick Thompson is, by his own admission, an old man. It is possible,    5
he told me once, that he was born in 1918. Beneath snow-white hair cut short, his face is round and compact, his features small and sharply molded. His large, black, and very bright eyes move quickly, and when he smiles he acquires an expression that is at once mischievous and intimidating. I have known him for more than 20 years, and he has instructed me often on matters pertaining to Western Apache language and culture. A man who delights in play, he has also teased me unmercifully, concocted humorous stories about me that are thoroughly apocryphal, and embarrassed me before large numbers of incredulous Apaches by inquiring publicly into the most intimate details of my private life. Described by many people in Cibecue as a true "Slim Coyote" (*ma' ts'ósé*), Nick Thompson is outspoken, incorrigible, and unabashed.[1] He is also generous, thoughtful, and highly intelligent. I value his friendship immensely.

As I bring my Jeep to a halt on the road beside the old man's camp,    6
I hear Nick complaining loudly to his wife about the changing character of life in Cibecue and its regrettable effects on younger members of the community. I have heard these complaints before and I know they are deeply felt. But still, on this sunny morning in June 1977, it is hard to suppress a smile, for the image Nick presents, a striking example of what can be achieved with sartorial *bricolage,* is hardly what one would expect of a staunch tribal conservative. Crippled since childhood

---

[1] A prominent figure in Western Apache oral literature, Slim Coyote is appreciated by Apache people for his keen and crafty intelligence, his complex and unpredictable personality, and his penchant for getting himself into difficult situations from which he always manages to extract himself, usually with humorous and embarrassing results.

and partially paralyzed by a recent stroke, the old man is seated in the shade of a cottonwood tree a few yards from the modest wooden cabin where he lives with his wife and two small grandchildren. He is smoking a mentholated Salem cigarette and is studying with undisguised approval the shoes on his feet—a new pair of bright blue Nike running shoes trimmed in incandescent orange. He is also wearing a pair of faded green trousers, a battered brown cowboy hat, and a white T-shirt with "Disneyland" printed in large red letters across the front. Within easy reach of his chair, resting on the base of an upended washtub, is a copy of the *National Enquirer*, a mug of hot coffee, and an open box of chocolate-covered doughnuts. If Nick Thompson is an opponent of social change, it is certainly not evident from his appearance. But appearances can be deceiving, and Nick, who is an accomplished singer and a medicine man of substantial reputation, would be the first to point this out.

The old man greets me with his eyes. Nothing is said for a minute 7 or two, but then we begin to talk, exchanging bits of local news until enough time has passed for me to politely announce the purpose of my visit. I explain that I am puzzled by certain statements that Apaches have made about the country surrounding Cibecue and that I am anxious to know how to interpret them. To my surprise, Nick does not ask what I have been told or by whom. He responds instead by swinging out his arm in a wide arc. "Learn the names," he says. "Learn the names of all these places." Unprepared for such a firm and unequivocal suggestion (it sounds to me like nothing less than an order), I retreat into silence. "Start with the names," the old man continues. "I will teach you like before. Come back tomorrow morning." Nodding in agreement, I thank Nick for his willingness to help and tell him what I will be able to pay him. He says the wage is fair.

A few moments later, as I stand to take my leave, Nick's face breaks 8 suddenly into a broad smile and his eyes begin to dance. I know that look very well and brace myself for the farewell joke that almost always accompanies it. The old man wastes no time. He says I look lonely. He urges me to have prolonged and abundant sex with very old women. He says it prevents nosebleeds. He says that someday I can write a book about it. Flustered and at a loss for words, I smile weakly and shake my head. Delighted with this reaction, Nick laughs heartily and reaches for his coffee and a chocolate-covered doughnut. Our encounter has come to an end.

I return to the old man's camp the following day and start to learn 9 Western Apache place names. My lessons, which are interrupted by mapping trips with more mobile Apache consultants, continue for the next ten weeks. In late August, shortly before I must leave Cibecue, Nick asks to see the maps. He is not impressed. "White men need paper maps," he observes. "We have maps in our minds."

Located in a narrow valley at an elevation of 1507 m, the settlement 10 at Cibecue (from *deeschii' bikoh,* "valley with elongated red bluffs") is bisected by a shallow stream emanating from springs that rise in low-lying mountains to the north. Apache homes, separated by horse pastures, agricultural plots, and ceremonial dancegrounds, are located on both sides of the stream for a distance of approximately 8 km. The valley itself, which is bounded on the east and west by a broken series of red sandstone bluffs, displays marked topographic diversity in the form of heavily dissected canyons and arroyos, broad alluvial flood plains, and several clusters of prominent peaks. Vegetation ranges from a mixed Ponderosa Pine–Douglas Fir association near the headwaters of Cibecue Creek to a chaparral community, consisting of scrub oak, cat's-claw, agave, and a variety of cactus species, at the confluence of the creek with the Salt River. In between, numerous other floral associations occur, including dense riparian communities and heavy stands of cottonwood, oak, walnut, and pine.

Together with Michael W. Graves, I have mapped nearly 104 km² 11 in and around the community at Cibecue and within this area have recorded the Western Apache names of 296 locations; it is, to say the least, a region densely packed with place-names. But large numbers alone do not account for the high frequency with which place-names typically appear in Western Apache discourse. In part, this pattern of regular and recurrent use results from the fact that Apaches, who travel a great deal to and from their homes, habitually call on each other to describe their trips in detail. Almost invariably, and in sharp contrast to comparable reports delivered by Anglos living at Cibecue, these descriptions focus as much on *where* events occurred as on the nature and consequences of the events themselves. This practice has been observed in other Apachean groups as well, including, as Harry Hoijer (personal communication, 1973) notes, the Navajo: "Even the most minute occurrences are described by Navajos in close conjunction with their physical settings, suggesting that unless narrated events are *spatially anchored* their significance is somehow reduced and cannot be properly assessed." Hoijer could just as well be speaking of the Western Apache.

Something else contributes to the common use of place-names in 12

Western Apache communities, however, and that, quite simply, is that Apaches enjoy using them. For example, several years ago, when I was stringing a barbed-wire fence with two Apache cowboys from Cibecue, I noticed that one of them was talking quietly to himself. When I listened carefully, I discovered that he was reciting a list of place-names—a long list, punctuated only by spurts of tobacco juice, that went on for nearly ten minutes. Later, when I ventured to ask him about it, he said he frequently "talked names" to himself. Why? "I like to," he said. "I ride that way in my mind." And on dozens of other occasions when I have been working or traveling with Apaches, they have taken satisfaction in pointing out particular locations and pronouncing their names—once, twice, three times or more. Why? "Because we like to," or "Because those names are good to say." More often, however, Apaches account for their enthusiastic use of place-names by commenting on the precision with which the names depict their referents. "That place looks just like its name," someone will explain, or "That name makes me see that place like it really is." Or, as Benson Lewis (example 4) states so succinctly, "Its name is like a picture."

Statements such as these may be interpreted in light of certain facts about the linguistic structure of Western Apache place-names. To begin with, it is essential to understand that all but a very few Apache place-names take the form of complete sentences. This is made possible by one of the most prominent components of the Western Apache language: an elaborate system of prefixes that operates most extensively and productively to modify the stems of verbs. Thus, well-formed sentences can be constructed that are extremely compact yet semantically very rich. It is this combination of brevity and expressiveness, I believe, that appeals to Apaches and makes the mere pronunciation of place-names a satisfying experience.

## "All These Places Have Stories"

When I return to Cibecue in the spring of 1978, Nick Thompson is recovering from a bad case of the flu. He is weak, despondent, and uncomfortable. We speak very little and no mention is made of place-names. His wife is worried about him and so am I. Within a week, however, Nick's eldest son comes to my camp with a message: I am to visit his father and bring with me two packs of Salem cigarettes and a dozen chocolate-covered doughnuts. This is good news.

When I arrive at the old man's camp, he is sitting under the cottonwood tree by his house. A blanket is draped across his knees and he is wearing a heavy plaid jacket and a red vinyl cap with white fur-lined earflaps. There is color in his cheeks and the sparkle is back in his eyes. Shortly after we start to converse, and apropos of nothing I can discern, Nick announces that in 1931 he had sexual intercourse eight times in one night. He wants to know if I have ever been so fortunate. His wife, who has brought us each a cup of coffee, hears this remark and tells him that he is a crazy old man. Nick laughs loudly. Plainly, he is feeling better.

Eventually, I ask Nick if he is ready to resume our work together. "Yes," he says, "but no more on names." What then? "Stories," is his reply. "All these places have stories. We shoot each other with them, like arrows. Come back tomorrow morning." Puzzled once again, but suspecting that the old man has a plan he wants to follow, I tell him I will return. We then discuss Nick's wages. He insists that I pay him more than the year before as it is necessary to keep up with inflation. I agree and we settle on a larger sum. Then comes the predictable farewell joke: a fine piece of nonsense in which Nick, speaking English and imitating certain mannerisms he has come to associate with Anglo physicians, diagnoses my badly sunburned nose as an advanced case of venereal disease.[2] This time it is Nick's wife who laughs loudest.

The next day Nick begins to instruct me on aspects of Western Apache storytelling. Consulting on a regular basis with other Apaches from Cibecue as well, I pursue this topic throughout the summer of 1978.

## Western Apache Historical Tales

If place-names appear frequently in ordinary forms of Western Apache discourse, their use is equally conspicuous in oral narratives. It is here, in conjunction with stories Apaches tell, that we can move closer to an interpretation of native claims about the symbolic importance of geographical features and the personalized relationships that individuals may have with them. The people of Cibecue classify "speech" (*yat'i'*) into three major forms: "ordinary talk" (*yat'i'*), "prayer" (*'okąąhí*), and "narratives" or "stories" (*nagoldi'é*). Narratives are further classified into four major and two minor genres. The major genres include "myths" (*godiyįhgo nagoldi'*; literally, "to tell the holiness"),

16

17

18

---

[2] Jokes of this type are intended to poke fun at the butt of the joke and, at the same time, to comment negatively on the interactional practices of Anglo-Americans.

| Narrative Category | Temporal Locus of Events | Purposes |
|---|---|---|
| *godiyįhgo nagoldi'* ("myth") | *godiyaaná'* ("in the beginning") | to enlighten; to instruct |
| *'ágodzaahí* ("historical tale") | *doo 'áníiná'* ("long ago") | to criticize; to warn; to "shoot" |
| *nlt'éégo nagoldi'* ("saga") | *dííjįįgo* ("modern times") | to entertain; to engross |
| *ch'idii* ("gossip") | *k'ad* ("now") | to inform; to malign |

**Figure 2.** *Major categories of Western Apache narrative distinguished by temporal locus of events and primary purposes for narration.*

"historical tales" (*'ágod-zaahí* or *'ágodzaahí nagoldi'*; literally, "that which has happened" or "to tell of that which has happened"), "sagas" (*nlt'éégo nagoldi'*; literally, "to tell of pleasantness"), and stories that arise in the context of "gossip" (*ch'idii*). The minor genres, which do not concern us here, are "Coyote stories" (*ma' highaalyú' nagoldi'*; literally "to tell of Coyote's travels") and "seduction tales" (*biníima' nagoldi'*; literally, "to tell of sexual desires").

Western Apaches distinguish among the major narrative genres 19 on two basic semantic dimensions: time and purpose. Values on the temporal dimension identify in general terms when the events recounted in narratives took place, while values on the purposive dimension describe the objectives that Apache narrators typically have in recounting them (see Figure 2). Accordingly, "myths" deal with events that occurred "in the beginning" (*'godiyaaná'*), a time when the universe and all things within it were achieving their present form and location. Performed only by the medicine men and medicine women, myths are presented for the primary purpose of enlightenment and instruction: to explain and reaffirm the complex processes by which the known world came into existence. "Historical tales" recount events that took place "long ago" (*doo 'áníiná*) when the Western Apache people, having emerged from below the surface of the earth, were developing their own distinctive ways and customs. Most historical tales describe incidents that occurred prior to the coming of the white man, but some of these stories are set in postreservation times, which began for the Western Apache in 1872. Like myths, historical tales are intended to edify, but their main purpose is to alarm and criticize social delinquents (or, as the Apache say, to "shoot" them), thereby impressing such individuals with the undesirability of improper behavior and alerting them to the punitive consequences of further misconduct.

Although sagas deal with historical themes, these narratives are 20 chiefly concerned with events that have taken place in "modern times" (*dííjįįgo*), usually within the last 60 or 70 years. In contrast to historical tales, which always focus on serious and disturbing matters, sagas are largely devoid of them. Rather than serving as vehicles of personal criticism, the primary purpose of sagas is to provide their listeners with relaxation and entertainment. Stories of the kind associated with gossip consist of reports in which persons relate and interpret events involving other members of the Western Apache community. These stories, which embrace incidents that have occurred "now" or "at present" (*k'ad*), are often told for no other reason than to keep people informed of local developments. Not uncommonly, however, narratives in gossip are also used to ridicule and malign the character of their subjects.

Nowhere do place-names serve more important communicative 21 functions than in the context of historical tales. As if to accentuate this fact, stories of the *'ágodzaahí* genre are stylistically quite simple. Historical tales require no specialized lexicon, display no unusual syntactical constructions, and involve no irregular morphophonemic alternations; neither are they characterized by unique patterns of stress, pitch, volume, or intonation. In these ways *'agodzaahí* narratives contrast sharply with myths and sagas, which entail the use of a variety of genre-specific stylistic devices. Historical tales also differ from myths and sagas by virtue of their brevity. Whereas myths and sagas may take hours to complete, historical tales can usually be delivered in less than five minutes. Western Apache storytellers point out that this is both fitting and effective, because *'ágodzaahí* stories, like the "arrows" (*k'aa*) they are commonly said to represent, work best when they move swiftly. Finally, and most significant of all, historical tales are distinguished from all other forms of Apache narrative by an opening and closing line that identifies with a place-name where the events in the narrative occurred. These lines frame the narrative, mark it unmistakably as belonging to the *'agodzaahí* genre, and evoke a particular physical setting in which listeners can imaginatively situate everything that happens. It is hardly surprising, then, that while Apache storytellers agree that historical tales are "about" the events recounted in the tales, they also emphasize that the tales are "about" the sites at which the events took place.

If the style of Western Apache historical tales is relatively unre- 22 markable, their content is just the opposite. Without exception, and usually in very graphic terms, historical tales focus on persons who suffer misfortune as the consequence of actions that violate Apache standards for acceptable social behavior. More specifically, 'ágodzaahí stories tell of persons who have acted unthinkingly and impulsively in open disregard for "Apache custom" (*ndee bi 'at'ee'*) and who pay for their transgressions by being humiliated, ostracized, or killed. Stories of the 'agodzaahí variety are morality tales pure and simple. When viewed as such by the Apaches—as compact commentaries on what should be avoided so as to deal successfully and effectively with other people—they are highly informative. For what these narratives assert—tacitly, perhaps, but with dozens of compelling examples—is that immoral behavior is irrevocably a community affair and that persons who behave badly will be punished sooner or later. Thus, just as 'ágodzaahí stories are "about" historical events and their geographical locations, they are also "about" the system of rules and values according to which Apaches expect each other to organize and regulate their lives. In an even more fundamental sense, then, historical tales are "about" what it means to *be* a Western Apache, or, to make the point less dramatically, what it is that being an Apache should normally and properly entail.

To see how this is so, let us consider the texts of three historical 23 tales and examine the manner in which they have been interpreted by their Apache narrators.

1.  It happened at "big cottonwood trees stand spreading here and there."

    Long ago, the Pimas and Apaches were fighting. The Pimas were carrying long clubs made from mesquite wood; they were also heavy and hard. Before dawn the Pimas arrived at Cibecue and attacked the Apaches there. The Pimas attacked while the Apaches were still asleep. The Pimas killed the Apaches with their clubs. An old woman woke up; she heard the Apaches crying out. The old woman thought it was her son-in-law because he often picked on her daughter. The old woman cried out: "You pick on my child a lot. You should act pleasantly toward her." Because the old woman cried out, the Pimas learned where she was. The Pimas came running to the old woman's camp and killed her with their clubs. A young girl ran away from there and hid beneath some bushes. She alone survived.

    It happened at "big cottonwood trees stand spreading here and there."

Narrated by Mrs. Annie Peaches, this historical tale deals with the    24
harmful consequences that may come to persons who overstep traditional role boundaries. During the first year of marriage it is customary for young Apache couples to live in the camp of the bride's
parents. At this time, the bride's mother may request that her son-in-
law perform different tasks and she may also instruct and criticize him.
Later, however, when the couple establishes a separate residence, the
bride's mother forfeits this right and may properly interfere in her son-
in-law's affairs only at the request of her daughter. Mrs. Peaches explains that women who do not abide by this arrangement imply that
their sons-in-law are immature and irresponsible, which is a source of
acute embarrassment for the young men and their wives. Thus, even
when meddling might seem to serve a useful purpose, it should be
scrupulously avoided. The woman on whom this story centers failed
to remember this—and was instantly killed.

2.  It happened at "coarse-textured rocks lie above in a compact clus-
    ter."
        Long ago, a man became sexually attracted to his stepdaugh-
    ter. He was living below "coarse-textured rocks lie above in a
    compact cluster" with his stepdaughter and her mother. Waiting
    until no one else was present, and sitting alone with her, he
    started to molest her. The girl's maternal uncle happened to come
    by and he killed the man with a rock. The man's skull was cracked
    open. It was raining. The girl's maternal uncle dragged the man's
    body up above to "coarse-textured rocks lie above in a compact
    cluster" and placed it there in a storage pit. The girl's mother
    came home and was told by her daughter of all that had hap-
    pened. The people who owned the storage pit removed the man's
    body and put it somewhere else. The people never had a wake
    for the dead man's body.
        It happened at "coarse-textured rocks lie above in a compact
    cluster."

Narrated by Mr. Benson Lewis, this historical tale deals with the    25
theme of incest, for sexual contact with stepchildren is considered by
Western Apaches to be an incestuous act. According to Mr. Lewis, the
key line in the story is the penultimate one in which he observes, "The
people never had a wake for the dead man's body." We may assume,
Mr. Lewis says, that because the dead man's camp was located near
the storage pit in which his body was placed, the people who owned
the pit were also his relatives. This makes the neglect with which his

corpse was treated all the more profound, since kinsmen are bound by the strongest of obligations to care for each other when they die. That the dead man's relatives chose to dispense with customary mortuary ritual shows with devastating clarity that they wished to disown him completely.

3.  It happened at "men stand above here and there."
    Long ago, a man killed a cow off the reservation. The cow belonged to a Whiteman. The man was arrested by a policeman living at Cibecue at "men stand above here and there." The policeman was an Apache. The policeman took the man to the head Army officer at Fort Apache. There, at Fort Apache, the head Army officer questioned him. "What do you want?" he said. The policeman said, "I need cartridges and food." The policeman said nothing about the man who had killed the Whiteman's cow. That night some people spoke to the policeman. "It is best to report on him," they said to him. The next day the policeman returned to the head Army officer. "Now what do you want?" he said. The policeman said, "Yesterday I was going to say HELLO and GOOD-BYE but I forgot to do it." Again he said nothing about the man he arrested. Someone was working with words on his mind. The policeman returned with the man to Cibecue. He released him at "men stand above here and there."
    It happened at "men stand above here and there."

This story, narrated by Nick Thompson, describes what happened 26 to a man who acted too much like a white man. Between 1872 and 1895, when the Western Apache were strictly confined to their reservations by U.S. military forces, disease and malnutrition took the lives of many people. Consequently, Apaches who listen to this historical tale find it perfectly acceptable that the man who lived at "men stand above here and there" should have killed and butchered a white man's cow. What is not acceptable is that the policeman, another Apache from the same settlement, should have arrested the rustler and contemplated taking him to jail. But the policeman's plans were thwarted. Someone used witchcraft on him and made him stupid and forgetful. He never informed the military officer at Fort Apache of the real purpose of his visit, and his second encounter with the officer—in which he apologized for neglecting to say "hello" and "good-bye" the previous day—revealed him to be an absurd and laughable figure. Although Western Apaches find portions of this story amusing, Nick Thompson explains that they understand it first and foremost as a harsh indictment of persons who join with outsiders against members of their own community and who, as if to flaunt their lack of allegiance, parade the attitudes and mannerisms of white men.

Thus far, my remarks on what Western Apache historical tales are "about" have centered on features of textual content. This is a familiar strategy and certainly a necessary one, but it is also incomplete. In addition to everything else—places, events, moral standards, conceptions of cultural identity—every historical tale is also "about" the person at whom it is directed. This is because the telling of a historical tale is always prompted by an individual having committed one or more social offenses to which the act of narration, together with the tale itself, is intended as a critical and remedial response. Thus, on those occasions when 'agodzaahí stories are actually told—by real Apache storytellers, in real interpersonal contexts, to real social offenders—these narratives are understood to be accompanied by an unstated message from the storyteller that may be phrased something like this: "I know that you have acted in a way similar or analogous to the way in which someone acted in the story I am telling you. If you continue to act in this way, something similar or analogous to what happened to the character in the story might also happen to you." This metacommunicative message is just as important as any conveyed by the text of the storyteller's tale. For Apaches contend that if the message is taken to heart by the person at whom the tale is aimed— and if, in conjunction with lessons drawn from the tale itself, he or she resolves to improve his or her behavior—a lasting bond will have been created between that individual and the site or sites at which events in the tale took place. The cultural premises that inform this powerful idea will be made explicit presently; but first, in order to understand more clearly what the idea involves, let us examine the circumstances that led to the telling of a historical tale at Cibecue and see how this narrative affected the person for whom it was told. 27

In early June 1977, a 17-year-old Apache woman attended a girls' puberty ceremonial at Cibecue with her hair rolled up in a set of oversized pink plastic curlers. She had returned home two days before from a boarding school in Utah where this sort of ornamentation was considered fashionable by her peers. Something so mundane would have gone unnoticed by others were it not for the fact that Western Apache women of all ages are expected to appear at puberty ceremonials with their hair worn loose. This is one of several ways that women have of showing respect for the ceremonial and also, by implication, for the people who have staged it. The practice of presenting oneself with 28 free-flowing hair is also understood to contribute to the ceremonial's effectiveness, for Apaches hold that the ritual's most basic objectives, which are to invest the pubescent girl with qualities necessary for life as an adult, cannot be achieved unless standard forms of respect are faithfully observed. On this occasion at Cibecue, everyone was following custom except the young woman who arrived wearing curlers. She soon became an object of attention and quiet expressions of disapproval, but no one spoke to her about the large cylindrical objects in her hair.

Two weeks later, the same young woman made a large stack of tortillas and brought them to the camp of her maternal grandmother, a widow in her mid-60s who had organized a small party to celebrate the birthday of her eldest grandson. Eighteen people were on hand, myself included, and all of us were treated to hot coffee and a dinner of boiled beef and potatoes. When the meal was over casual conversation began to flow, and the young woman seated herself on the ground next to her younger sister. And then—quietly, deftly, and totally without warning—her grandmother narrated a version of the historical tale about the forgetful Apache policeman who behaved too much like a white man. Shortly after the story was finished, the young woman stood up, turned away wordlessly, and walked off in the direction of her home. Uncertain of what had happened, I asked her grandmother why she had departed. Had the young woman suddenly become ill? "No," her grandmother replied. "I shot her with an arrow." 29

Approximately two years after this incident occurred, I found myself again in the company of the young woman with the taste for distinctive hairstyles. She had purchased a large carton of groceries at the trading post at Cibecue, and when I offered to drive her home with them she accepted. I inquired on the way if she remembered the time that her grandmother had told us the story about the forgetful policeman. She said she did and then went on, speaking in English, to describe her reactions to it. "I think maybe my grandmother was getting after me, but then I think maybe not, maybe she's working on somebody else. Then I think back on that dance and I know it's me for sure. I sure don't like how she's talking about me, so I quit looking like that. I threw those curlers away." In order to reach the young woman's camp, we had to pass within a few hundred yards of *ndee dah naazįįh* ("men stand above here and there"), the place where the man had lived who was arrested in the story for rustling. I pointed it out to my companion. She said nothing for several moments. Then she 30 smiled and spoke softly in her own language: "I know that place. It stalks me every day."

The comments of this Western Apache woman on her experience  31 as the target of a historical tale are instructive in several respects. To begin with, her statement enables us to imagine something of the sizable psychological impact that historical tales may have on the persons to whom they are presented. Then, too, we can see how '*ágodzaahí* stories may produce quick and palpable effects on the behavior of such individuals, causing them to modify their social conduct in quite specific ways. Lastly, and most revealing of all, the young woman's remarks provide a clear illustration of what Apaches have in mind when they assert that historical tales may establish highly meaningful relationships between individuals and features of the natural landscape.

To appreciate fully the significance of these relationships, as well  32 as their influence on the lives of Western Apache people, we must explore more thoroughly the manner in which the relationships are conceptualized. This can be accomplished through a closer examination of Apache ideas about the activity of storytelling and the acknowledged power of oral narratives, especially historical tales, to promote beneficial changes in people's attitudes toward their responsibilities as members of a moral community. These ideas, which combine to form a native model of how oral narratives work to achieve their intended effects, are expressed in terms of a single dominant metaphor. By now it should come as no surprise to learn that the metaphor draws heavily on the imagery of hunting.

## *"Stalking with Stories"*

Nick Thompson is tired. We have been talking about hunting with  33 stories for two days now and the old man has not had an easy time of it. Yesterday, my uneven control of the Western Apache language prevented him from speaking as rapidly and eloquently as he would have liked, and on too many occasions I was forced to interrupt him with questions. At one point, bored and annoyed with my queries, he told me that I reminded him of a horsefly buzzing around his head. Later, however, when he seemed satisfied that I could follow at least the outline of his thoughts, he recorded on tape a lengthy statement which he said contained everything he wanted me to know. "Take it with you and listen to it," he said. "Tomorrow we put it in English." For the last six hours that is what we have been trying to do. We are finished now and weary of talking. In the weeks to come I will worry about the depth and force of our translation, and twice more I will return to Nick's camp with other questions. But the hardest work is over and both of us know it. Nick has taught me already that hunting with stories is not a simple matter, and as I prepare to leave I say so. "We know," he says, and that is all. Here is Nick Thompson's statement:

> This is what we know about our stories. They go to work on your mind and make you think about your life. Maybe you've not been acting right. Maybe you've been stingy. Maybe you've been chasing after women. Maybe you've been trying to act like a Whiteman. People don't *like* it! So someone goes hunting for you—maybe your grandmother, your grandfather, your uncle. It doesn't matter. Anyone can do it.
>
> So someone stalks you and tells a story about what happened long ago. It doesn't matter if other people are around—you're going to know he's aiming that story at you. All of a sudden it *hits* you! It's like an arrow, they say. Sometimes it just bounces off—it's too soft and you don't think about anything. But when it's strong it goes in *deep* and starts working on your mind right away. No one says anything to you, only that story is all, but now you know that people have been watching you and talking about you. They don't like how you've been acting. So you have to think about your life.
>
> Then you feel weak, real weak, like you are sick. You don't want to eat or talk to anyone. That story is working on you now. You keep thinking about it. That story is changing you now, making you want to live right. That story is making you want to replace yourself. You think only of what you did that was wrong and you don't like it. So you want to live better. After a while, you don't like to think of what you did wrong. So you try to forget that story. You try to pull that arrow out. You think it won't hurt anymore because now you want to live right.
>
> It's hard to keep on living right. Many things jump up at you and block your way. But you won't forget that story. You're going to see the place where it happened, maybe every day if it's nearby and close to Cibecue. If you don't see it, you're going to hear its name and see it in your mind. It doesn't matter if you get old—that place will keep on stalking you like the one who shot you with the story. Maybe that person will die. Even so, that place will keep on stalking you. It's like that person is still alive.
>
> Even if we go far away from here to some big city, places around here keep stalking us. If you live wrong, you will hear the names and see the places in your mind. They keep on stalking you, even if you

go across oceans. The names of all these places are good. They make you remember how to live right, so you want to replace yourself again.

After stories and storytellers have served this beneficial purpose, features of the physical landscape take over and perpetuate it. Mountains and arroyos step in symbolically for grandmothers and uncles. Just as the latter have "stalked" delinquent individuals in the past, so too particular locations continue to "stalk" them in the present. Such surveillance is essential, Apaches maintain, because "living right" requires constant care and attention, and there is always a possibility that old stories and their initial impact, like old arrows and their wounds, will fade and disappear. In other words, there is always a chance that persons who have "replaced themselves" once—or twice, or three times—will relax their guard against "badness" and slip back into undesirable forms of social conduct. Consequently, Apaches explain, individuals need to be continuously reminded of why they were "shot" in the first place and how they reacted to it at the time. Geographical sites, together with the crisp mental "pictures" of them presented by their names, serve admirably in this capacity, inviting people to recall their earlier failings and encouraging them to resolve, once again, to avoid them in the future. Grandmothers and uncles must perish but the landscape endures, and for this the Apache people are deeply grateful. "The land," Nick Thompson observes, "looks after us. The land keeps badness away." 34

It should now be possible for the reader to interpret the Western Apache texts at the beginning of this essay in a manner roughly compatible with the Apache ideas that have shaped them. Moreover, we should be able to appreciate that the claims put forward in the texts are reasonable and appropriate, culturally credible and "correct," the principled expressions of an underlying logic that invests them with internal consistency and coherent conceptual structure. As we have seen, this structure is supplied in large part by the hunting metaphor for Western Apache storytelling. It is chiefly in accordance with this metaphor—or, more exactly, in accordance with the symbolic associations it orders and makes explicit—that the claims presented earlier finally make sense. 35

Thus, the claim of Annie Peaches—that the land occupied by the Western Apache "makes the people live right"—becomes understandable as a proposition about the moral significance of geographical lo- 36 cations as this has been established by historical tales with which the locations are associated. Similarly, Wilson Lavender's claim—that Apaches who fail to remember place-names "forget how to be strong"—rests on an association of place-names with a belief in the power of historical tales to discourage forms of socially unacceptable behavior. Places and their names are also associated by Apaches with the narrators of historical tales, and Benson Lewis's claim—that a certain mountain near Cibecue is his maternal grandmother—can only be interpreted in light of this assumption. The hunting metaphor for storytelling also informs Ronnie Lupe's claim that Western Apache children who are not exposed to historical tales tend to have interpersonal difficulties. As he puts it, "They don't know the stories of what happened at these places. That's why some of them get into trouble." What Mr. Lupe is claiming, of course, is that children who do not learn to associate places and their names with historical tales cannot appreciate the utility of these narratives as guidelines for dealing responsibly and amicably with other people. Consequently, he believes, such individuals are more likely than others to act in ways that run counter to Apache social norms, a sure sign that they are "losing the land." Losing the land is something the Western Apache can ill afford to do, for geographical features have served the people for centuries as indispensable mnemonic pegs on which to hang the moral teachings of their history.

The Apache landscape is full of named locations where time and space have fused and where, through the agency of historical tales, their intersection is made visible for human contemplation. It is also apparent that such locations, charged as they are with personal and social significance, work in important ways to shape the images that Apaches have—or should have—of themselves. Speaking to people like Nick Thompson and Ronnie Lupe, to Annie Peaches and Benson Lewis, one forms the impression that Apaches view the landscape as a repository of distilled wisdom, a stern but benevolent keeper of tradition, an ever-vigilant ally in the efforts of individuals and whole communities to put into practice a set of standards for social living that are uniquely and distinctively their own. In the world that the Western Apache have constituted for themselves, features of the landscape have become symbols of and for this way of living, the symbols of a culture and the enduring moral character of its people.

We may assume that this relationship with the land has been pervasive throughout Western Apache history; but in today's climate of accelerating social change, its importance for Apache people may well be deepening. Communities such as Cibecue, formerly isolated and very much turned inward, were opened up by paved roads less than 20 years ago, and the consequences of improved access and freer travel—including, most noticeably, greatly increased contact with Anglo-Americans—have been pronounced. Younger Apaches, who today complain frequently about the tedium of village life, have started to develop new tastes and ambitions, and some of them are eager to explore the outside world. To the extent that the landscape remains not merely a physical presence but an omnipresent moral force, young Apaches are not likely to forget that the "Whiteman's way" belongs to a different world.

A number of American Indian authors, among them Vine Deloria, Jr. (Sioux), Simon Ortiz (Acoma), Joy Harjo (Creek), and the cultural anthropologist Alfonso Ortiz (San Juan), have written with skill and insight about the moral dimensions of Native American conceptions of the land. No one, however, has addressed the subject with greater sensitivity than N. Scott Momaday (Kiowa). The following passages, taken from his short essay entitled "Native American Attitudes to the Environment" (1974), show clearly what is involved, not only for the Western Apache but for other tribes as well. [39]

> You cannot understand how the Indian thinks of himself in relation to the world around him unless you understand his conception of what is appropriate; particularly what is morally appropriate within the context of that relationship. [1974:82]
>
> The native American ethic with respect to the physical world is a matter of reciprocal appropriation: apropriations in which man invests himself in the landscape, and at the same time incorporates the land-scape into his own most fundamental experience. . . . This appropriation is primarily a matter of imagination which is moral in kind. I mean to say that we are all, I suppose, what we imagine ourselves to be. And that is certainly true of the American Indian. . . . [The Indian] is someone who thinks of himself in a particular way and his idea comprehends his relationship to the physical world. He imagines himself in terms of that relationship and others. And it is that act of imagination, that moral act of imagination, which constitutes his un-derstanding of the physical world. [1974:80]

The summer of 1980 is almost gone and soon I must leave Cibecue. I have walked to Nick's camp to tell him good-bye. This is never easy for me, and we spend most of the time talking about other things. Eventually, I move to thank him for his generosity, his patience, and the things he has taught me. Nick responds by pointing with his lips [40] to a low ridge that runs behind his home in an easterly direction away from Cibecue Creek. "That is a good place," he says. "These are all good places. Goodness is all around."

## Postscript

If the thoughts presented here have a measure of theoretical interest, 41 recent experience has persuaded me that they can have practical value as well. During the last six years, I have authored a number of documents for use in litigation concerning the settlement of Western Apache water rights in the state of Arizona. Until a final decision is reached in the case, I am not permitted to describe the contents of these documents in detail, but one of my assignments has been to write a report dealing with Apache conceptions of the physical environment. That report contains sections on Western Apache place-names, oral narratives, and certain metaphors that Apache people use to formulate aspects of their relationship with the land.

Preliminary hearings resulted in a judgment favorable to Apache 42 interests, and apparently my report was useful, mainly because it helped pave the way for testimony by native witnesses. One of these witnesses was Nick Thompson; and according to attorneys on both sides, the old man's appearance had a decisive impact. After Nick had taken his place on the stand, he was asked by an attorney why he considered water to be important to his people. A man of eminent good sense, Nick replied, "Because we drink it!" And then, without missing a beat, he launched into a historical tale about a large spring not far from Cibecue—*tú nchaa halíí'* ("much water flows up and out")—where long ago a man drowned mysteriously after badly mistreating his wife. When Nick finished the story he went on to say: "We know it happened, so we know not to act like that man who died. It's good we have that water. We need it to live. It's good we have that spring. We need it to live right." Then the old man smiled to himself and his eyes began to dance.

# Questions

1. Basso suggests in paragraph 2 that the five statements by Native Americans in paragraph 1 "resist quick and easy interpretation." When you first read the essay were you puzzled by these statements? Which, if any, did you find especially moving? Why?

2.  In paragraphs 5 through 8 (as well as in later paragraphs) Basso tells us a good deal about Nick Thompson's appearance and personality. What function do you think these descriptions serve?
3.  Judging from this essay, what do cultural anthropologists do? What personal (as distinguished from professional) qualifications should they have, or what "claims" might they make about themselves?
4.  The stories Basso records describe what has happened and also teach moral lessons. Does the lesson taught by the third story (paragraphs 25 and 26) conflict with your own morality? Or do you also find the theft of the cow "perfectly acceptable" under the circumstances?
5.  In paragraph 38 Basso says that in a "climate of accelerating social change" the importance of the Western Apache's relationship with the land "may well be deepening." What evidence does he offer that it is deepening? Might it be argued from the same evidence that it is probably weakening?
6.  If you come from a culture in which landscape is more than inert matter, explain the role of landscape in that culture. ("Landscape" need not be limited to *natural* landscape; it can be urban landscape. Substitute a neighborhood or city block, if appropriate, but the landscape must be a place and not simply individuals associated with it.)
7.  If you come from a culture in which stories are widely regarded as more than casual entertainment, explain the role of stories in that culture.

## C. S. Lewis

# Xmas and Christmas
### A Lost Chapter from Herodotus

And beyond this there lies in the ocean, turned towards 1
the west and north, the island of Niatirb which Hecataeus indeed declares to be the same size and shape as Sicily, but it is larger, though

C[live] S[taples] Lewis (1898–1963) taught medieval and Renaissance literature at Oxford and later at Cambridge. He wrote about literature, and he wrote fiction (including children's books), poetry, and numerous essays and books on Christianity, from the point of view of a believer.

in calling it triangular a man would not miss the mark. It is densely inhabited by men who wear clothes not very different from the other barbarians who occupy the north-western parts of Europe though they do not agree with them in language. These islanders, surpassing all the men of whom we know in patience and endurance, use the following customs.

In the middle of winter when fogs and rains most abound they 2 have a great festival which they call Exmas, and for fifty days they prepare for it in the fashion I shall describe. First of all, every citizen is obliged to send to each of his friends and relations a square piece of hard paper stamped with a picture, which in their speech is called an Exmas-card. But the pictures represent birds sitting on branches, or trees with dark green prickly leaf, or else men in such garments as the Niatirbians believe that their ancestors wore two hundred years ago riding in coaches such as their ancestors used, or houses with snow on their roofs. And the Niatirbians are unwilling to say what these pictures have to do with the festival, guarding (as I suppose) some sacred mystery. And because all men must send these cards the market-place is filled with the crowd of those buying them, so that there is great labour and weariness.

But having bought as many as they suppose to be sufficient, they 3 return to their houses and find there the like cards which others have sent to them. And when they find cards from any to whom they also have sent cards, they throw them away and give thanks to the gods that this labour at least is over for another year. But when they find cards from any to whom they have not sent, then they beat their breasts and wail and utter curses against the sender; and, having sufficiently lamented their misfortune, they put on their boots again and go out into the fog and rain and buy a card for him also. And let this account suffice about Exmas-cards.

They also send gifts to one another, suffering the same things 4 about the gifts as about the cards, or even worse. For every citizen has to guess the value of the gift which every friend will send to him so that he may send one of equal value, whether he can afford it or not. And they buy as gifts for one another such things as no man ever bought for himself. For the sellers, understanding the custom, put forth all kinds of trumpery, and whatever, being useless and ridiculous, they have been unable to sell throughout the year they now sell as an Exmas gift. And though the Niatirbians profess themselves to lack sufficient necessary things, such as metal, leather, wood and paper, yet an incredible quantity of these things is wasted every year, being made into the gifts.

But during these fifty days the oldest, poorest and most miserable 5
of the citizens put on false beards and red robes and walk about the
market-place; being disguised (in my opinion) as *Cronos*. And the sellers of gifts no less than the purchasers become pale and weary, because
of the crowds and the fog, so that any man who came into a Niatirbian
city at this season would think some great public calamity had fallen
on Niatirb. This fifty days of preparation is called in their barbarian
speech the Exmas *Rush*.

But when the day of the festival comes, then most of the citizens, 6
being exhausted with the *Rush*, lie in bed till noon. But in the evening
they eat five times as much supper as on other days and, crowning
themselves with crowns of paper, they become intoxicated. And on
the day after Exmas they are very grave, being internally disordered
by the supper and the drinking and reckoning how much they have
spent on gifts and on the wine. For wine is so dear among the Niatirbians that a man must swallow the worth of a talent before he is
well intoxicated.

Such, then, are their customs about the Exmas. But the few among 7
the Niatirbians have also a festival, separate and to themselves, called
Crissmas, which is on the same day as Exmas. And those who keep
Crissmas, doing the opposite to the majority of the Niatirbians, rise
early on that day with shining faces and go before sunrise to certain
temples where they partake of a sacred feast. And in most of the temples they set out images of a fair woman with a new-born Child on
her knees and certain animals and shepherds adoring the Child. (The
reason of these images is given in a certain sacred story which I know
but do not repeat.)

But I myself conversed with a priest in one of these temples and 8
asked him why they kept Crissmas on the same day as Exmas; for it
appeared to me inconvenient. But the priest replied, It is not lawful,
O Stranger, for us to change the date of Crissmas, but would that Zeus
would put it into the minds of the Niatirbians to keep Exmas at some
other time or not to keep it at all. For Exmas and the *Rush* distract the
minds even of the few from sacred things. And we indeed are glad
that men should make merry at Crissmas; but in Exmas there is no
merriment left. And when I asked him why they endured the *Rush*,
he replied, It is, O Stranger, a *racket*; using (as I suppose) the words
of some oracle and speaking unintelligibly to me (for a *racket* is an
instrument which the barbarians use in a game called *tennis*).

But what Hecataeus says, that Exmas and Crissmas are the same, 9
is not credible. For first, the pictures which are stamped on the Exmas-
cards have nothing to do with the sacred story which the priests tell

about Crissmas. And secondly, the most part of the Niatirbians, not believing the religion of the few, nevertheless send the gifts and cards and participate in the *Rush* and drink, wearing paper caps. But it is not likely that men, even being barbarians, should suffer so many and great things in honour of a god they do not believe in. And now, enough about Niatirb.

# Questions

1. An encyclopedia, or even a dictionary, will give you some information about Herodotus. Check your library for a copy of Herodotus's *History*, read a few pages in it, and then point to two or three places where Lewis has captured something of the flavor of Herodotus.

2. In this semicomic piece, Lewis is making a serious point. What is it?

3. Lewis, an Englishman (let's say a citizen of Great Britain), wrote about Niatirb. Write another lost chapter from Herodotus, describing a custom celebrated in Acirema (or your college, dormitory, or wherever).

4. In an essay of 500 words, compare Lewis's essay with Arlen's "Ode to Thanksgiving" (page 167). What is the main point of each? By what means does each essay make its point? (Explain both the similarities and differences.) Evaluate and compare the success of each essay as (a) persuasion and (b) entertainment.

Abraham Lincoln

# Address at the Dedication of the Gettysburg National Cemetery

$F$our score and seven years ago our fathers brought forth 1
on this continent, a new nation, conceived in Liberty, and dedicated
to the proposition that all men are created equal.

Now we are engaged in a great civil war; testing whether that 2
nation, or any nation so conceived and so dedicated, can long endure.
We are met on a great battlefield of that war. We have come to dedicate
a portion of that field as a final resting-place for those who here gave
their lives that that nation might live. It is altogether fitting and proper
that we should do this.

But, in a larger sense, we cannot dedicate—we cannot conse- 3
crate—we cannot hallow—this ground. The brave men, living and
dead, who struggled here have consecrated it, far above our poor
power to add or detract. The world will little note, nor long remember,
what we say here, but it can never forget what they did here. It is for
us the living, rather, to be dedicated here to the unfinished work which
they who fought here have thus far so nobly advanced. It is rather for
us to be here dedicated to the great task remaining before us—that
from these honored dead we take increased devotion to that cause for
which they gave the last full measure of devotion; that we here highly
resolve that these dead shall not have died in vain; that this nation,
under God, shall have a new birth of freedom; and that government
of the people, by the people, for the people, shall not perish from the
earth.

---

Abraham Lincoln (1809–1865), sixteenth president of the United States, is not usually thought of as a writer, but his published speeches and writings comprise about 1,078,000 words, the equivalent of about 4,000 pages of double-spaced typing. They were all composed without the assistance of a speech writer.

Gilbert Highet

# The Gettysburg Address

Fourscore and seven years ago. . . .                                          1
These five words stand at the entrance to the best-known mon-      2
ument of American prose, one of the finest utterances in the entire
language, and surely one of the greatest speeches in all history. Greatness is like granite: it is molded in fire, and it lasts for many centuries.

Fourscore and seven years ago. . . . It is strange to think that Pres-      3
ident Lincoln was looking back to the 4th of July 1776, and that he and
his speech are now further removed from us than he himself was from
George Washington and the Declaration of Independence. Fourscore
and seven years before the Gettysburg Address, a small group of pa-
triots signed the Declaration. Fourscore and seven years after the Gettysburg Address, it was the year 1950, and that date is already receding
rapidly into our troubled, adventurous, and valiant past.

Inadequately prepared and at first scarcely realized in its full im-      4
portance, the dedication of the graveyard at Gettysburg was one of
the supreme moments of American history. The battle itself had been
a turning point of the war. On the 4th of July 1863, General Meade
repelled Lee's invasion of Pennsylvania. Although he did not follow
up his victory, he had broken one of the most formidable aggressive
enterprises of the Confederate armies. Losses were heavy on both
sides. Thousands of dead were left on the field, and thousands of
wounded died in the hot days following the battle. At first, their burial
was more or less haphazard; but thoughtful men gradually came to
feel that an adequate burying place and memorial were required. These
were established by an interstate commission that autumn, and the
finest speaker in the North was invited to dedicate them. This was the
scholar and statesman Edward Everett of Harvard. He made a good

---

Gilbert Highet (1906–1978) was born in Glasgow, Scotland, and was educated
at Glasgow University and at Oxford University. In 1937 he came to the United
States, and in 1951 he was naturalized. Until his retirement in 1972 he taught
Latin, Greek, and comparative literature at Columbia University. In addition to
writing scholarly studies of classical authors he wrote several general and more
popular books.

---

speech—which is still extant: not at all academic, it is full of close strategic analysis and deep historical understanding.

Lincoln was not invited to speak, at first. Although people knew [5] him as an effective debater, they were not sure whether he was capable of making a serious speech on such a solemn occasion. But one of the impressive things about Lincoln's career is that he constantly strove to *grow*. He was anxious to appear on that occasion and to say something worthy of it. (Also, it has been suggested, he was anxious to remove the impression that he did not know how to behave properly— an impression which had been strengthened by a shocking story about his clowning on the battlefield of Antietam the previous year.) Therefore when he was invited he took considerable care with his speech. He drafted rather more than half of it in the White House before leaving, finished it in the hotel at Gettysburg the night before the ceremony (not in the train, as sometimes reported), and wrote a fair copy next morning.

There are many accounts of the day itself, 19 November 1863. [6] There are many descriptions of Lincoln, all showing the same curious blend of grandeur and awkwardness, or lack of dignity, or—it would be best to call it humility. In the procession he rode horseback: a tall lean man in a high plug hat, straddling a short horse, with his feet too near the ground. He arrived before the chief speaker, and had to wait patiently for half an hour or more. His own speech came right at the end of a long and exhausting ceremony, lasted less than three minutes, and made little impression on the audience. In part this was because they were tired, in part because (as eyewitnesses said) he ended almost before they knew he had begun, and in part because he did not speak the Address, but read it, very slowly, in a thin high voice, with a marked Kentucky accent, pronouncing "to" as "toe" and dropping his final R's.

Some people of course were alert enough to be impressed. Everett [7] congratulated him at once. But most of the newspapers paid little attention to the speech, and some sneered at it. The *Patriot and Union* of Harrisburg wrote, "We pass over the silly remarks of the President; for the credit of the nation we are willing . . . that they shall no more be repeated or thought of"; and the London *Times* said, "The ceremony was rendered ludicrous by some of the sallies of that poor President Lincoln," calling his remarks "dull and commonplace." The first commendation of the Address came in a single sentence of the Chicago *Tribune,* and the first discriminating and detailed praise of it appeared

in the Springfield *Republican*, the Providence *Journal*, and the Philadelphia *Bulletin*. However, three weeks after the ceremony and then
again the following spring, the editor of *Harper's Weekly* published a
sincere and thorough eulogy of the Address, and soon it was attaining
recognition as a masterpiece.

At the time, Lincoln could not care much about the reception of   8
his words. He was exhausted and ill. In the train back to Washington,
he lay down with a wet towel on his head. He had caught smallpox.
At that moment he was incubating it, and he was stricken down soon
after he re-entered the White House. Fortunately it was a mild attack,
and it evoked one of his best jokes: he told his visitors, "At last I have
something I can give to everybody."

He had more than that to give to everybody. He was a unique   9
person, far greater than most people realize until they read his life
with care. The wisdom of his policy, the sources of his statesmanship—
these were things too complex to be discussed in a brief essay. But we
can say something about the Gettysburg Address as a work of art.[1]

A work of art. Yes: for Lincoln was a literary artist, trained both   10
by others and by himself. The textbooks he used as a boy were full of
difficult exercises and skillful devices in formal rhetoric, stressing the
qualities he practiced in his own speaking: antithesis, parallelism, and
verbal harmony. Then he read and reread many admirable models of
thought and expression: the King James Bible, the essays of Bacon,
the best plays of Shakespeare. His favorites were *Hamlet, Lear, Macbeth,
Richard III*, and *Henry VIII*, which he had read dozens of times. He
loved reading aloud, too, and spent hours reading poetry to his friends.
(He told his partner Herndon that he preferred getting the sense of
any document by reading it aloud.) Therefore his serious speeches are
important parts of the long and noble classical tradition of oratory
which begins in Greece, runs through Rome to the modern world, and
is still capable (if we do not neglect it) of producing masterpieces.

The first proof of this is that the Gettysburg Address is full of   11
quotations—or rather of adaptations—which give it strength. It is
partly religious, partly (in the highest sense) political: therefore it is
interwoven with memories of the Bible and memories of American
history. The first and the last words are Biblical cadences. Normally
Lincoln did not say "fourscore" when he meant eighty; but on this

---

[1] For further reference, see W. E. Barton, *Lincoln at Gettysburg* (Bobbs-Merrill, 1930);
R. P. Basler, "Abraham Lincoln's Rhetoric," *American Literature* 11 (1939–40), 167–
182; and L. E. Robinson, *Abraham Lincoln as a Man of Letters* (Chicago, 1918).

solemn occasion he recalled the important dates in the Bible—such as the age of Abraham when his first son was born to him, and he was "fourscore and six years old." Similarly, he did not say there was a chance that democracy might die out: he recalled the somber phrasing in the Book of Job—where Bildad speaks of the destruction of one who shall vanish without a trace, and says that "his branch shall be cut off; his remembrance shall perish from the earth." Then again, the famous description of our State as "government of the people, by the people, for the people" was adumbrated by Daniel Webster in 1830 (he spoke of "the people's government, made for the people, made by the people, and answerable to the people") and then elaborated in 1854 by the abolitionist Theodore Parker (as "government of all the people, by all the people, for all the people"). There is good reason to think that Lincoln took the important phrase "under God" (which he interpolated at the last moment) from Weems, the biographer of Washington; and we know that it had been used at least once by Washington himself.

Analyzing the Address further, we find that it is based on a highly 12 imaginative theme, or group of themes. The subject is—how can we put it so as not to disfigure it?—the subject is the kinship of life and death, that mysterious linkage which we see sometimes as the physical succession of birth and death in our world, sometimes as the contrast, which is perhaps a unity, between death and immortality. The first sentence is concerned with birth:

Our *fathers brought forth a new* nation, *conceived* in liberty.

The final phrase but one expresses the hope that

this nation, under God, shall have a *new birth* of freedom.

And that last phrase of all speaks of continuing life as the triumph over death. Again and again throughout the speech, this mystical contrast and kinship reappear: "those who *gave their lives* that that nation might *live*," "the brave men *living* and *dead*," and so in the central assertion that the dead have already consecrated their own burial place, while "it is for us, the *living*, rather to be dedicated . . . to the great task remaining." The Gettysburg Address is a prose poem; it belongs to the same world as the great elegies, and the adagios of Beethoven.

Its structure, however, is that of a skillfully contrived speech. The 13 oratorical pattern is perfectly clear. Lincoln describes the occasion, dedicates the ground, and then draws a larger conclusion by calling on his hearers to dedicate themselves to the preservation of the Union. But within that, we can trace his constant use of at least two important rhetorical devices.

The first of these is *antithesis:* opposition, contrast. The speech is 14 full of it. Listen:

> The world will little   *note*
> nbsp;       nor long   *remember*   what   *we say* here
> but   it can never   *forget*   what   *they did* here

And so in nearly every sentence: "brave men, *living* and *dead*"; "to *add* or *detract*." There is the antithesis of the Founding Fathers and men of Lincoln's own time:

> Our *fathers brought forth* a new nation . . .
> now *we* are testing whether that nation . . . can *long endure.*

And there is the more terrible antithesis of those who have already died and those who still live to do their duty. Now, antithesis is the figure of contrast and conflict. Lincoln was speaking in the midst of a great civil war.

The other important pattern is different. It is technically called 15 *tricolon*—the division of an idea into three harmonious parts, usually of increasing power. The most famous phrase of the Address is a tricolon:

> government of the people
> nbsp;       by the people
> nbsp;       for the people.

The most solemn sentence is a tricolon:

> we cannot dedicate
> we cannot consecrate
> we cannot hallow      this ground.

And above all, the last sentence (which has sometimes been criticized as too complex) is essentially two parallel phrases, with a tricolon growing out of the second and then producing another tricolon: a trunk, three branches, and a cluster of flowers. Lincoln says that it is for his hearers to be dedicated to the great task remaining before them. Then he goes on.

> that from these honored dead

—apparently he means "in such a way that from these honored dead"—

> we take increased devotion to that cause.

Next, he restates this more briefly:

> that we here highly resolve. . . .

And now the actual resolution follows, in three parts of growing intensity:

> that these dead shall not have died in vain
> that this nation, under God, shall have a new birth
>   of freedom

and that (one more tricolon)

> government of the people
>         by the people
>         for the people
> shall not perish from the earth.

Now, the tricolon is the figure which, through division, emphasizes basic harmony and unity. Lincoln used antithesis because he was speaking to a people at war. He used the tricolon because he was hoping, planning, praying for peace.

No one thinks that when he was drafting the Gettysburg Address, 16 Lincoln deliberately looked up these quotations and consciously chose these particular patterns of thought. No, he chose the theme. From its development and from the emotional tone of the entire occasion, all the rest followed, or grew—by that marvelous process of choice and rejection which is essential to artistic creation. It does not spoil such a work of art to analyze it as closely as we have done; it is altogether fitting and proper that we should do this: for it helps us to penetrate more deeply into the rich meaning of the Gettysburg Address, and it allows us the very rare privilege of watching the workings of a great man's mind.


# Questions

1. At the start of his essay, after quoting the opening words of Lincoln's speech, Highet uses a metaphor and a simile: he says that the words "stand at the entrance to the best-known monument," and that "greatness is like granite: it is molded in fire, and it lasts for many centuries." Are these figures of speech effective? Why or why not? How are the two figures related to each other?
2. Analyze the structure of Highet's essay.
3. This essay was a talk given on the radio, presumably to a large general public. Find passages in the essay that suggest oral delivery to an unspecialized audience. How would you describe Highet's tone?
4. It has been suggested that "government of the people, by the people" is redundant; a government of the people, it is argued, must be the same as a government by the people. Did Lincoln repeat himself merely to get a triad: "of the people, by the people, for the people"? If so, is this a fault? Or can it be argued that "government of the people" really means "government over the people"? If so, what does the entire expression mean?

George Orwell

# Politics and the English Language

Most people who bother with the matter at all would  1
admit that the English language is in a bad way, but it is generally
assumed that we cannot by conscious action do anything about it. Our
civilization is decadent and our language—so the argument runs—
must inevitably share in the general collapse. It follows that any struggle against the abuse of language is a sentimental archaism, like preferring candles to electric light or hansom cabs to aeroplanes. Underneath this lies the half-conscious belief that language is a natural
growth and not an instrument which we shape for our own purposes.

Now, it is clear that the decline of a language must ultimately have  2
political and economic causes: it is not due simply to the bad influence
of this or that individual writer. But an effect can become a cause,
reinforcing the original cause and producing the same effect in an in-
tensified form, and so on indefinitely. A man may take to drink because
he feels himself to be a failure, and then fail all the more completely
because he drinks. It is rather the same thing that is happening to the
English language. It becomes ugly and inaccurate because our thoughts
are foolish, but the slovenliness of our language makes it easier for us
to have foolish thoughts. The point is that the process is reversible.
Modern English, especially written English, is full of bad habits which
spread by imitation and which can be avoided if one is willing to take
the necessary trouble. If one gets rid of these habits one can think more
clearly, and to think clearly is a necessary first step towards political
regeneration: so that the fight against bad English is not frivolous and
is not the exclusive concern of professional writers. I will come back
to this presently, and I hope that by that time the meaning of what I

George Orwell (1903–1950) was the pen name adopted by Eric Blair, an Englishman born in India. Orwell was educated at Eton, in England, but in 1921 he went
back to the East and served for five years as a police officer in Burma. He then
returned to Europe, doing odd jobs while writing novels and stories. In 1936 he
fought in the Spanish Civil War on the side of the Republicans, an experience
reported in *Homage to Catalonia* (1938). His last years were spent writing in
England.

have said here will have become clearer. Meanwhile, here are five specimens of the English language as it is now habitually written.

These five passages have not been picked out because they are ³ especially bad—I could have quoted far worse if I had chosen—but because they illustrate various of the mental vices from which we now suffer. They are a little below the average, but are fairly representative samples. I number them so that I can refer back to them when necessary:

1.  I am not, indeed, sure whether it is not true to say that the Milton who once seemed not unlike a seventeenth-century Shelley had not become, out of an experience ever more bitter in each year, more alien [sic] to the founder of that Jesuit sect which nothing could induce him to tolerate.

    Professor Harold Laski (Essay in *Freedom of Expression*)

2.  Above all, we cannot play ducks and drakes with a native battery of idioms which prescribes such egregious collocations of vocables as the Basic *put up with* for *tolerate* or *put at a loss* for *bewilder*.

    Professor Lancelot Hogben (*Interglossa*)

3.  On the one side we have the free personality: by definition it is not neurotic, for it has neither conflict nor dream. Its desires, such as they are, are transparent, for they are just what institutional approval keeps in the forefront of consciousness; another institutional pattern would alter their number and intensity; there is little in them that is natural, irreducible, or culturally dangerous. But *on the other side,* the social bond itself is noticing but the mutual reflection of these self-secure integrities. Recall the definition of love. Is not this the very picture of a small academic? Where is there a place in this hall of mirrors for either personality or fraternity?

    Essay on Psychology in *Politics* (New York)

4.  All the "best people" from the gentlemen's clubs, and all the frantic fascist captains, united in common hatred of Socialism and bestial horror of the rising tide of the mass revolutionary movement, have turned to acts of provocation, to foul incendiarism, to medieval legends of poisoned wells, to legalize their own destruction of proletarian organizations, and rouse the agitated petty-bourgeoisie to chauvinistic fervor on behalf of the fight against the revolutionary way out of the crisis.

    Communist Pamphlet

5. If a new spirit *is* to be infused into this old country, there is one thorny and contentious reform which must be tackled, and that is the humanization and galvanization of the B.B.C. Timidity here will bespeak canker and atrophy of the soul. The heart of Britain may be sound and of strong beat, for instance, but the British lion's roar at present is like that of Bottom in Shakespeare's *Midsummer Night's Dream*—as gentle as any sucking dove. A virile new Britain cannot continue indefinitely to be traduced in the eyes or rather ears, of the world by the effete languors of Langham Place, brazenly masquerading as "standard English." When the voice of Britain is heard at nine o'clock, better far and infinitely less ludicrous to hear aitches honestly dropped than the present priggish, inflated, inhibited, school-ma'amish arch braying of blameless bashful mewing maidens!

Letter in *Tribune*

Each of these passages has faults of its own, but, quite apart from avoidable ugliness, two qualities are common to all of them. The first is staleness of imagery; the other is lack of precision. The writer either has a meaning and cannot express it, or he inadvertently says something else, or he is almost indifferent as to whether his words mean anything or not. This mixture of vagueness and sheer incompetence is the most marked characteristic of modern English prose, and especially of any kind of political writing. As soon as certain topics are raised, the concrete melts into the abstract and no one seems able to think of turns of speech that are not hackneyed: prose consists less and less of *words* chosen for the sake of their meaning, and more and more of *phrases* tacked together like the sections of a prefabricated henhouse. I list below, with notes and examples, various of the tricks by means of which the work of prose-construction is habitually dodged:

## Dying Metaphors

A newly invented metaphor assists thought by evoking a visual image, while on the other hand a metaphor which is technically "dead" (e.g., *iron resolution*) has in effect reverted to being an ordinary word and can generally be used without loss of vividness. But in between these two classes there is a huge dump of worn-out metaphors which have lost all evocative power and are merely used because they save people the trouble of inventing phrases for themselves. Examples are: *Ring the changes on, take up the cudgels for, toe the line, ride roughshod over, stand shoulder to shoulder with, play into the hands of, no axe to grind, grist to the mill, fishing in troubled waters, on the order of the day, Achilles' heel, swan song, hotbed.* Many of these are used without knowledge of their meaning (what is a "rift," for instance?), and incompatible metaphors are frequently mixed, a sure sign that the writer is not interested in what he is saying. Some metaphors now current have been twisted out of their original meaning without those who use them even being aware of the fact. For example, *toe the line* is sometimes written *tow the line.* Another example is *the hammer and the anvil,* now always used with the implication that the anvil gets the worst of it. In real life it is always the anvil that breaks the hammer, never the other way about: a writer who stopped to think what he was saying would be aware of this, and would avoid perverting the original phrase.

## Operators or Verbal False Limbs

These save the trouble of picking out appropriate verbs and nouns, 6 and at the same time pad each sentence with extra syllables which give it an appearance of symmetry. Characteristic phrases are *render inoperative, militate against, make contact with, be subjected to, give rise to, give grounds for, have the effect of, play a leading part (role) in, make itself felt, take effect, exhibit a tendency to, serve the purpose of, etc., etc.* The keynote is the elimination of simple verbs. Instead of being a single word, such as *break, stop, spoil, mend, kill,* a verb becomes *a phrase,* made up of a noun or adjective tacked on to some general-purpose verb such as *prove, serve, form, play, render.* In addition, the passive voice is wherever possible used in preference to the active, and noun constructions are used instead of gerunds (*by examination of* instead of *by examining*). The range of verbs is further cut down by means of the *-ize* and *de-* formations, and the banal statements are given an appearance of profundity by means of the *not un-* formation. Simple conjunctions and prepositions are replaced by such phrases as *with respect to, having regard to, the fact that, by dint of, in view of, in the interests of, on the hypothesis that;* and the ends of sentences are saved from anticlimax by such resounding common-places as *greatly to be desired, cannot be left out of account, a development to be expected in the near future, deserving of serious consideration, brought to a satisfactory conclusion,* and so on and so forth.

## Pretentious Diction

Words like *phenomenon, element, individual* (as noun), *objective, categorical, effective, virtual, basic, primary, promote, constitute, exhibit, exploit,* 7 *utilize, eliminate, liquidate,* are used to dress up simple statements and give an air of scientific impartiality to biased judgments. Adjectives like *epoch-making, epic, historic, unforgettable, triumphant, age-old, inevitable, inexorable, veritable,* are used to dignify the sordid processes of international politics, while writing that aims at glorifying war usually takes on an archaic color, its characteristic words being: *realm, throne, chariot, mailed fist, trident, sword, shield, buckler, banner, jackboot, clarion.* Foreign words and expressions such as *cul de sac, ancien régime, deus ex machina, mutatis mutandis, status quo, gleichschaltung, weltanschauung,* are used to give an air of culture and elegance. Except for the useful abbreviations *i.e., e.g.,* and *etc.,* there is no real need for any of the hundreds of foreign phrases now current in English. Bad writers, and especially scientific, political and sociological writers, are nearly always haunted by the notion that Latin or Greek words are grander than Saxon ones, and unnecessary words like *expedite, ameliorate, predict, extraneous, deracinated, clandestine, subaqueous* and hundreds of others constantly gain ground from their Anglo-Saxon opposite numbers.[1] The jargon peculiar to Marxist writing (*hyena, hangman, cannibal, petty bourgeois, these gentry, lacquey, flunkey, mad dog, White Guard,* etc.) consists largely of words and phrases translated from Russian, German or French; but the normal way of coining a new word is to use a Latin or Greek root with the appropriate affix and, where necessary, the -*ize* formation. It is often easier to make up words of this kind (*deregionalize, impermissible, extramarital, nonfragmentary* and so forth) than to think up the English words that will cover one's meaning. The result, in general, is an increase in slovenliness and vagueness.

## Meaningless Words

In certain kinds of writing, particularly in art criticism and literary criti-    8
cism, it is normal to come across long passages which are almost completely lacking in meaning.[2] Words like *romantic, plastic, values, human,*

---

[1] An interesting illustration of this is the way in which the English flower names which were in use till very recently are being ousted by Greek ones, *snapdragon* becoming *antirrhinum, forget-me-not* becoming *myosotis,* etc. It is hard to see any practical reason for this change of fashion: it is probably due to an instinctive turning-away from the more homely word and a vague feeling that the Greek word is scientific.

[2] Example: "Comfort's catholicity of perception and image, strangely Whitman-esque in range, almost the exact opposite in aesthetic compulsion, continues to evoke that trembling atmospheric accumulative hinting at a cruel, an inexorably serene timelessness. . . . Wrey Gardiner scores by aiming at simple bull's-eyes with precision. Only they are not simple, and through this contented sadness runs more than the surface bitter-sweet of resignation." (*Poetry Quarterly.*)

*dead, sentimental, natural, vitality,* as used in art criticism, are strictly meaningless, in the sense that they not only do not point to any discoverable object, but are hardly ever expected to do so by the reader. When one critic writes, "The outstanding feature of Mr. X's work is its living quality," while another writes, "the immediately striking thing about Mr. X's work is its peculiar deadness," the reader accepts this as a simple difference of opinion. If words like *black* and *white* were involved, instead of the jargon words *dead* and *living,* he would see at once that language was being used in an improper way. Many political words are similarly abused. The word *Fascism* has now no meaning except in so far as it signifies "something not desirable." The words *democracy, socialism, freedom, patriotic, realistic, justice,* have each of them several different meanings which cannot be reconciled with one another. In the case of a word like *democracy,* not only is there no agreed definition, but the attempt to make one is resisted from all sides. It is almost universally felt that when we call a country democratic we are praising it: consequently the defenders of every kind of régime claim that it is a democracy, and fear that they might have to stop using the word if it were tied down to any one meaning. Words of this kind are often used in a consciously dishonest way. That is, the person who uses them has his own private definition, but allows his hearer to think he means something quite different. Statements like *Marshal Pétain was a true patriot, The Soviet Press is the freest in the world, The Catholic Church is opposed to persecution,* are almost always made with intent to deceive. Other words used in variable meanings, in most cases more or less dishonestly, are: *class, totalitarian, science, progressive, reactionary, bourgeois, equality.*

Now that I have made this catalogue of swindles and perversions, 9 let me give another example of the kind of writing that they lead to. This time it must of its nature be an imaginary one. I am going to translate a passage of good English into modern English of the worst sort. Here is a well-known verse from *Ecclesiastes:*

> I returned and saw under the sun, that the race is not to the swift, nor the battle to the strong, neither yet bread to the wise, nor yet riches to men of understanding, nor yet favour to men of skill; but time and chance happeneth to them all.

Here it is in modern English:    10

> Objective consideration of contemporary phenomena compels the conclusion that success or failure in competitive activities exhibits no

tendency to be commensurate with innate capacity, but that a considerable element of the unpredictable must invariably be taken into account.

This is a parody, but not a very gross one. Exhibit (3), above, for 11 instance, contains several patches of the same kind of English. It will be seen that I have not made a full translation. The beginning and ending of the sentence follow the original meaning fairly closely, but in the middle the concrete illustrations—race, battle, bread—dissolve into the vague phrase "success or failure in competitive activities." This had to be so, because no modern writer of the kind I am discussing—no one capable of using phrases like "objective consideration of contemporary phenomena"—would ever tabulate his thoughts in that precise and detailed way. The whole tendency of modern prose is away from concreteness. Now analyze these two sentences a little more closely. The first contains forty-nine words but only sixty syllables, and all its words are those of everyday life. The second contains thirty-eight words of ninety syllables: eighteen of its words are from Latin roots, and one from Greek. The first sentence contains six vivid images, and only one phrase ("time and chance") that could be called vague. The second contains not a single fresh, arresting phrase, and in spite of its ninety syllables it gives only a shortened version of the meaning contained in the first. Yet without a doubt it is the second kind of sentence that is gaining ground in modern English. I do not want to exaggerate. This kind of writing is not yet universal, and outcrops of simplicity will occur here and there in the worst-written page. Still, if you or I were told to write a few lines on the uncertainty of human fortunes, we should probably come much nearer to my imaginary sentence than to the one from *Ecclesiastes*.

As I have tried to show, modern writing at its worst does not 12 consist in picking out words for the sake of their meaning and inventing images in order to make the meaning clearer. It consists in gumming together long strips of words which have already been set in order by someone else, and making the results presentable by sheer humbug. The attraction of this way of writing is that it is easy. It is easier—even quicker, once you have the habit—to say *In my opinion it is not an unjustifiable assumption that* than to say *I think*. If you use ready-made phrases, you not only don't have to hunt about for words; you also don't have to bother with the rhythms of your sentences, since these phrases are generally so arranged as to be more or less euphonious. When you are composing in a hurry—when you are dictating to a stenographer, for instance, or making a public speech—it is natural to fall into a pretentious, Latinized style. Tags like *a consideration which we should do well to bear in mind* or *a conclusion to which all of us would readily assent* will save many a sentence from coming down with a bump. By using stale metaphors, similes and idioms, you save much mental effort, at the cost of leaving your meaning vague, not only for your reader but for yourself. This is the significance of mixed metaphors. The sole aim of a metaphor is to call up a visual image. When these images clash—as in *The Fascist octopus has sung its swan song, the jackboot is thrown into the melting pot*—it can be taken as certain that the writer is not seeing a mental image of the objects he is naming; in other words he is not really thinking. Look again at the examples I gave at the beginning of this essay. Professor Laski (1) uses five negatives in fifty-three words. One of these is superfluous, making nonsense of the whole passage, and in addition there is the slip *alien* for *akin*, making further nonsense, and several avoidable pieces of clumsiness which increase the general vagueness. Professor Hogben (2) plays ducks and drakes with a battery which is able to write prescriptions, and while, disapproving of the everyday phrase *put up with*, is unwilling to look *egregious* up in the dictionary and see what it means; (3), if one takes an uncharitable attitude towards it, is simply meaningless: probably one could work out its intended meaning by reading the whole of the article in which it occurs. In (4), the writer knows more or less what he wants to say, but an accumulation of stale phrases chokes him like tea leaves blocking a sink. In (5), words and meaning have almost parted company. People who write in this manner usually have a general emotional meaning—they dislike one thing and want to express solidarity with another—but they are not interested in the detail of what they are saying. A scrupulous writer, in every sentence that he writes, will ask himself at least four questions, thus: What am I trying to say? What words will express it? What image or idiom will make it clearer? Is this image fresh enough to have an effect? And he will probably ask himself two more: Could I put it more shortly? Have I said anything that is avoidably ugly? But you are not obliged to go to all this trouble. You can shirk it by simply throwing your mind open and letting the ready-made phrases come crowding in. They will construct your sentences for you—even think your thoughts for you, to a certain extent—and at need they will perform the important service of partially concealing your meaning even from yourself. It is at this point that the special connection between politics and the debasement of language becomes clear.

In our time it is broadly true that political writing is bad writing.    13
Where it is not true, it will generally be found that the writer is some
kind of rebel, expressing his private opinions and not a "party line."
Orthodoxy, of whatever color, seems to demand a lifeless, imitative
style. The political dialects to be found in pamphlets, leading articles,
manifestos, White Papers and the speeches of undersecretaries do, of
course, vary from party to party, but they are all alike in that one almost
never finds in them a fresh, vivid, home-made turn of speech. When
one watches some tired hack on the platform mechanically repeating
the familiar phrases—*bestial atrocities, iron heel, bloodstained tyranny, free
peoples of the world, stand shoulder to shoulder*—one often has a curious
feeling that one is not watching a live human being but some kind of
dummy: a feeling which suddenly becomes stronger at moments when
the light catches the speaker's spectacles and turns them into blank
discs which seem to have no eyes behind them. And this is not altogether fanciful. A speaker who uses that kind of phraseology has
gone some distance towards turning himself into a machine. The appropriate noises are coming out of his larynx, but his brain is not involved as it would be if he were choosing his words for himself. If the
speech he is making is one that he is accustomed to make over and
over again, he may be almost unconscious of what he is saying, as one
is when one utters the responses in church. And this reduced state of
consciousness, if not indispensable, is at any rate favorable to political
conformity.

In our time, political speech and writing are largely the defense    14
of the indefensible. Things like the continuance of British rule in India,
the Russian purges and deportations, the dropping of the atom bombs
on Japan, can indeed be defended, but only by arguments which are
too brutal for most people to face, and which do not square with the
professed aims of political parties. Thus political language has to consist largely of euphemism, question-begging and sheer cloudy vagueness. Defenseless villages are bombarded from the air, the inhabitants
driven out into the countryside, the cattle machine-gunned, the huts
set on fire with incendiary bullets: this is called *pacification*. Millions of
peasants are robbed of their farms and sent trudging along the roads
with no more than they can carry: this is called *transfer of population* or
*rectification of frontiers*. People are imprisoned for years without trial,
or shot in the back of the neck or sent to die of scurvy in Arctic lumber
camps: this is called *elimination of unreliable elements*. Such phraseology
is needed if one wants to name things without calling up mental pictures of them. Consider for instance some comfortable English pro-

fessor defending Russian totalitarianism. He cannot say outright, "I believe in killing off your opponents when you can get good results by doing so." Probably, therefore, he will say something like this:

> While freely conceding that the Soviet regime exhibits certain features which the humanitarian may be inclined to deplore, we must, I think, agree that a certain curtailment of the right to political opposition is an unavoidable concomitant of transitional periods, and that the rigors which the Russian people have been called upon to undergo have been amply justified in the sphere of concrete achievement.

The inflated style is itself a kind of euphemism. A mass of Latin 15 words falls upon the facts like soft snow, blurring the outlines and covering up all the details. The great enemy of clear language is insincerity. When there is a gap between one's real and one's declared aims, one turns as it were instinctively to long words and exhausted idioms, like a cuttlefish squirting out ink. In our age there is no such thing as "keeping out of politics." All issues are political issues, and politics itself is a mass of lies, evasions, folly, hatred and schizophrenia. When the general atmosphere is bad, language must suffer. I should expect to find—this is a guess which I have not sufficient knowledge to verify—that the German, Russian and Italian languages have all deteriorated in the last ten to fifteen years, as a result of dictatorship.

But if thought corrupts language, language can also corrupt 16 thought. A bad usage can spread by tradition and imitation, even among people who should and do know better. The debased language that I have been discussing is in some ways very convenient. Phrases like *a not unjustifiable assumption, leaves much to be desired, would serve no good purpose, a consideration which we should do well to bear in mind,* are a continuous temptation, a packet of aspirins always at one's elbow. Look back through this essay, and for certain you will find that I have again and again committed the very faults I am protesting against. By this morning's post I have received a pamphlet dealing with conditions in Germany. The author tells me that he "felt impelled" to write it. I open it at random, and here is almost the first sentence that I see: "[The Allies] have an opportunity not only of achieving a radical transformation of Germany's social and political structure in such a way as to avoid a nationalistic reaction in Germany itself, but at the same time of laying the foundations of cooperative and unified Europe." You see, he "feels impelled" to write—feels, presumably, that he has something

other way about. In prose, the worst thing one can do with words is to surrender to them. When you think of a concrete object, you think wordlessly, and then, if you want to describe the thing you have been visualizing you probably hunt about till you find the exact words that seem to fit in. When you think of something abstract you are more inclined to use words from the start, and unless you make a conscious effort to prevent it, the existing dialect will come rushing in and do the job for you, at the expense of blurring or even changing your meaning. Probably it is better to put off using words as long as possible and get one's meaning as clear as one can through pictures or sensations. Afterwards one can choose—not simply *accept*—the phrases that will best cover the meaning, and then switch round and decide what impression one's words are likely to make on another person. This last effort of the mind cuts out all stale or mixed images, all prefabricated phrases, needless repetitions, and humbug and vagueness generally. But one can often be in doubt about the effect of a word or a phrase, and one needs rules that one can rely on when instinct fails. I think the following rules will cover most cases:

(i)   Never use a metaphor, simile or other figure of speech which you are used to seeing in print.

(ii)  Never use a long word where a short one will do.

(iii) If it is possible to cut a word out, always cut it out.

(iv)  Never use the passive where you can use the active.

(v)   Never use a foreign phrase, a scientific word or a jargon word if you can think of an everyday English equivalent.

(vi)  Break any of these rules sooner than say anything outright barbarous.

These rules sound elementary, and so they are, but they demand a deep change of attitude in anyone who has grown used to writing in the style now fashionable. One could keep all of them and still write bad English, but one could not write the kind of stuff that I quoted in those five specimens at the beginning of this article.

19     I have not here been considering the literary use of language, but merely language as an instrument for expressing and not for concealing or preventing thought. Stuart Chase and others have come near to claiming that all abstract words are meaningless, and have used this as a pretext for advocating a kind of political quietism. Since you don't know what Fascism is, how can you struggle against Fascism? One need not swallow such absurdities as this, but one ought to recognize

that the present political chaos is connected with the decay of language, and that one can probably bring about some improvement by starting at the verbal end. If you simplify your English, you are freed from the worst follies of orthodoxy. You cannot speak any of the necessary dialects, and when you make a stupid remark its stupidity will be obvious, even to yourself. Political language—and with variations this is true of all political parties, from Conservatives to Anarchists—is designed to make lies sound truthful and murder respectable, and to give an appearance of solidity to pure wind. One cannot change this all in a moment, but one can at least change one's own habits, and from time to time, if one jeers loudly enough, send some worn-out and useless phrase—some *jackboot, Achilles' heel, hotbed, melt-ing pot, acid test, veritable inferno* or other lump of verbal refuse—into the dustbin where it belongs.

## Questions

1. Revise one or two of Orwell's examples of bad writing.
2. Examine Orwell's metaphors. Do they fulfill his requirements for good writing?
3. Look again Orwell's grotesque revision (paragraph 10) of a passage from the Bible. Write a similar version of another passage from the Bible.
4. Can you recall any occasion when you have used words, in writing or speaking, in a consciously dishonest way? If so, can you explain why, or go further and justify your behavior?
5. In paragraph 2 Orwell says, "Written English is full of bad habits which spread by imitation." Are you aware of having acquired any bad writing habits by imitation? If so, imitation of what or whom?

## Robin Lakoff

# You Are What You Say

1   **W**omen's language is that pleasant (dainty?), euphemistic,
never-aggressive way of talking we learned as little girls. Cultural bias
was built into the language we were allowed to speak, the subjects we
were allowed to speak about, and the ways we were spoken of. Having
learned our linguistic lesson well, we go out in the world, only to
discover that we are communicative cripples—damned if we do, and
damned if we don't.

2   If we refuse to talk "like a lady," we are ridiculed and criticized
for being unfeminine. ("She thinks like a man" is, at best, a left-handed
compliment.) If we do learn all the fuzzy-headed, unassertive language
of our sex, we are ridiculed for being unable to think clearly, unable
to take part in a serious discussion, and therefore unfit to hold a position of power.

3   It doesn't take much of this for a woman to begin feeling she deserves such treatment because of inadequacies in her own intelligence
and education.

4   "Women's language" shows up in all levels of English. For example, women are encouraged and allowed to make far more precise
discriminations in naming colors than men do. Words like *mauve, beige,
ecru, aquamarine, lavender,* and so on, are unremarkable in a woman's
active vocabulary, but largely absent from that of most men. I know
of no evidence suggesting that women actually *see* a wider range of
colors than men do. It is simply that fine discriminations of this sort
are relevant to women's vocabularies, but not to men's; to men, who
control most of the interesting affairs of the world, such distinctions
are trivial—irrelevant.

5   In the area of syntax, we find similar gender-related peculiarities
of speech. There is one construction, in particular, that women use
conversationally far more than men: the tag question. A tag is midway

---

Robin Lakoff was born in 1943, and educated at Radcliffe College and Harvard
University. A professor of linguistics at the University of California at Berkeley,
she has been especially interested in the language that women use. The essay
that we give here was first published in *Ms.* magazine in 1974.

between an outright statement and a yes-no question; it is less assertive than the former, but more confident than the latter.

6 A *flat statement* indicates confidence in the speaker's knowledge and is fairly certain to be believed; a *question* indicates a lack of knowledge on some point and implies that the gap in the speaker's knowledge can and will be remedied by an answer. For example, if, at a Little League game, I have had my glasses off, I can legitimately ask someone else: "Was the player out at third?" A *tag question*, being intermediate between statement and question, is used when the speaker is stating a claim, but lacks full confidence in the truth of that claim. So if I say, "Is Joan here?" I will probably not be surprised if my respondent answers "no"; but if I say, "Joan is here, isn't she?" instead, chances are I am already biased in favor of a positive answer, wanting only confirmation. I still want a response, but I have enough knowledge (or think I have) to predict that response. A tag question, then, might be thought of as a statement that doesn't demand to be believed by anyone but the speaker, a way of giving leeway, of not forcing the addressee to go along with the views of the speaker.

7 Another common use of the tag question is in small talk when the speaker is trying to elicit conversation: "Sure is hot here, isn't it?"

8 But in discussing personal feelings or opinions, only the speaker normally has any way of knowing the correct answer. Sentences such as "I have a headache, don't I?" are clearly ridiculous. But there are other examples where it is the speaker's opinions, rather than perceptions, for which corroboration is sought, as in "The situation in Southeast Asia is terrible, isn't it?"

9 While there are, of course, other possible interpretations of a sentence like this, one possibility is that the speaker has a particular answer in mind—"yes," or "no"—but is reluctant to state it badly. This sort of tag question is much more apt to be used by women than by men in conversation. Why is this the case?

10 The tag question allows a speaker to avoid commitment, and thereby avoid conflict with the addressee. The problem is that, by so doing, speakers may also give the impression of not really being sure of themselves, or looking to the addressee for confirmation of their views. This uncertainty is reinforced in more subliminal ways, too. There is a peculiar sentence-intonation pattern, used almost exclusively by women, as far as I know, which changes a declarative answer into a question. The effect of using the rising inflection typical of a yes-no question is to imply that the speaker is seeking confirmation, even

though the speaker is clearly the only one who has the requisite in-formation, which is why the question was put to her in the first place:

(Q)  When will dinner be ready?
(A)  Oh . . . around six o'clock . . . ?

It is as though the second speaker was saying, "Six o'clock—if that's okay with you, if you agree." The person being addressed is put in the position of having to provide confirmation. One likely consequence of this sort of speech pattern in a woman is that, often unbeknownst to herself, the speaker builds a reputation of tentativeness, and others will refrain from taking her seriously or trusting her with any real responsibilities, since she "can't make up her mind," and "isn't sure of herself."

11    Such idiosyncrasies may explain why women's language sounds much more "polite" than men's. It is polite to leave a decision open, not impose your mind, or views, or claims, or anyone else. So a tag question is a kind of polite statement, in that it does not force agree-ment or belief on the addressee. In the same way a request is a polite command, in that it does not force obedience on the addressee, but rather suggests something be done as a favor to the speaker. A clearly stated order implies a threat of certain consequences if it is not fol-lowed, and—even more impolite—implies that the speaker is in a su-perior position and able to enforce the order. By couching wishes in the form of a request, on the other hand, a speaker implies that if the request is not carried out, only the speaker will suffer; noncompliance cannot harm the addressee. So the decision is really left up to the addressee. The distinction becomes clear in these examples:

Close the door.
Please close the door.
Will you close the door?
Will you please close the door?
Won't you close the door?

12    In the same ways as words and speech patterns used by women undermine her image, those used to describe women make matters even worse. Often a word may be used of both men and women (and per-haps of things as well); but when it is applied to women, it assumes a special meaning that, by implication rather than outright assertion, is derogatory to women as a group.

13   The use of euphemisms has this effect. A euphemism is a substitute for a word that has acquired a bad connotation by association with
something unpleasant or embarrassing. But almost as soon as the new
word comes into common usage, it takes on the same old bad connotations, since feelings about the things or people referred to are not
altered by a change of name; thus new euphemisms must be constantly
found.

14   There is one euphemism for *woman* still very much alive. The word,
of course, is *lady. Lady* has a masculine counterpart, namely *gentleman,*
occasionally shortened to *gent.* But for some reason *lady* is very much
commoner than *gent(leman).*

15   The decision to use *lady* rather than *woman,* or vice versa, may
considerably alter the sense of a sentence, as the following examples
show:

(a)   A woman (lady) I know is a dean at Berkeley.

(b)   A woman (lady) I know makes amazing things out of shoelaces
and old boxes.

16   The use of *lady* in (a) imparts a frivolous, or nonserious, tone to
the sentence: the matter under discussion is not one of great moment.
Similarly, in (b), using *lady* here would suggest that the speaker considered the "amazing things" not to be serious art, but merely a hobby
or an aberration. If *woman* is used, she might be a serious sculptor. To
say *lady doctor* is very condescending, since no one ever says *gentleman
doctor* or even *man doctor.* For example, mention in the San Francisco
*Chronicle* of January 31, 1972, of Madalyn Murray O'Hair as the *lady
atheist* reduces her position to that of scatterbrained eccentric. Even
*woman atheist* is scarcely defensible: sex is irrelevant to her philosophical position.

17   Many women argue that, on the other hand, *lady* carries with it
overtones recalling the age of chivalry: conferring exalted stature on
the person so referred to. This makes the term seem polite at first, but
we must also remember that these implications are perilous: they suggest that a "lady" is helpless, and cannot do things by herself.

18   *Lady* can also be used to infer frivolousness, as in titles of organizations. Those that have a serious purpose (not merely that of enabling "the ladies" to spend time with one another) cannot use the
word *lady* in their titles, but less serious ones may. Compare the *Ladies'
Auxiliary* of a men's group, or the *Thursday Evening Ladies' Browning
and Garden Society* with *Ladies' Liberation* or *Ladies' Strike for Peace.*

19    What is curious about this split is that *lady* is in origin a euphemism—a substitute that puts a better face on something people find
uncomfortable—for *woman*. What kind of euphemism is it that subtly
denigrates the people to whom it refers? Perhaps *lady* functions as a
euphemism for *woman* because it does not contain the sexual implications present in *woman*: it is not "embarrassing" in that way. If this
is so, we may expect that, in the future, *lady* will replace *woman* as
the primary word for the human female, since *woman* will have become
too blatantly sexual. That this distinction is already made in some contexts at least is shown in the following examples, where you can try
replacing *woman* with *lady*:

(a)   She's only twelve, but she's already a woman.
(b)   After ten years in jail, Harry wanted to find a woman.
(c)   She's my woman, see, so don't mess around with her.

20    Another common substitute for *woman* is *girl*. One seldom hears
a man past the age of adolescence referred to as a boy, save in expressions like "going out with the boys," which are meant to suggest an
air of adolescent frivolity and irresponsibility. But women of all ages
are "girls": one can have a man—not a boy—Friday, but only a girl—
never a woman or even a lady—Friday; women have girlfriends, but
men do not—in a nonsexual sense—have boyfriends. It may be that
this use of *girl* is euphemistic in the same way the use of *lady* is: in
stressing the idea of immaturity, it removes the sexual connotations
lurking in *woman*. *Girl* brings to mind irresponsibility; you don't send
a girl to do a woman's errand (or even, for that matter, a boy's errand).
She is a person who is both too immature and too far from real life to
be entrusted with responsibilities or with decisions of any serious or
important nature.

21    Now let's take a pair of words which, in terms of the possible
relationships in an earlier society, were simple male-female equivalents, analogous to *bull: cow*. Suppose we find that, for independent
reasons, society has changed in such a way that the original meanings
now are irrelevant. Yet the words have not been discarded, but have
acquired new meanings, metaphorically related to their original
senses. But suppose these new metaphorical uses are no longer parallel
to each other. By seeing where the parallelism breaks down, we discover something about the different roles played by men and women
in this culture. One good example of such a divergence through time
is found in the pair, *master: mistress*. Once used with reference to one's

power over servants, these words have become unusable today in their original master-servant sense as the relationship has become less prevalent in our society. But the words are still common.

22    Unless used with reference to animals, *master* now generally refers to a man who has acquired consummate ability in some field, normally nonsexual. But its feminine counterpart cannot be used this way. It is practically restricted to its sexual sense of "paramour." We start out with two terms, both roughly paraphrasable as "one who has power over another." But the masculine form, once one person is no longer able to have absolute power over another, becomes usable metaphorically in the sense of "having power over *something*." *Master* requires as its object only the name of some activity, something inanimate and abstract. But *mistress* requires a masculine noun in the possessive to precede it. One cannot say: "Rhonda is a mistress." One must be *some-one's* mistress. A man is defined by what he does, a woman by her sexuality, that is, in terms of one particular aspect of her relationship to men. It is one thing to be an *old master* like Hans Holbein,[1] and another to be an *old mistress.*

23    The same is true of the words *spinster* and *bachelor*—gender words for "one who is not married." The resemblance ends with the definition. While *bachelor* is a neuter term, often used as a compliment, *spinster* normally is used pejoratively, with connotations of prissiness, fussiness, and so on. To be a bachelor implies that one has a choice of marrying or not, and this is what makes the idea of a bachelor existence attractive, in the popular literature. He has been pursued and has successfully eluded his pursuers. But a spinster is one who has not been pursued, or at least not seriously. She is old, unwanted goods. The metaphorical connotations of *bachelor* generally suggest sexual freedom; of *spinster*, puritanism or celibacy.

24    These examples could be multiplied. It is generally considered a *faux pas*, in society, to congratulate a woman on her engagement, while it is correct to congratulate her fiancé. Why is this? The reason seems to be that it is impolite to remind people of things that may be uncomfortable to them. To congratulate a woman on her engagement is really to say, "Thank goodness! You had a close call!" For the man, on the other hand, there was no such danger. His choosing to marry is viewed as a good thing, but not something essential.

25    The linguistic double standards holds throughout the life of the relationship. After marriage, bachelor and spinster become man and

---

1 A German painter of the sixteenth century. (Editors' note)

wife, not man and woman. The woman whose husband dies remains "John's widow"; John, however, is never "Mary's widower."

Finally, why is it that salesclerks and others are so quick to call women customers "dear," "honey," and other terms of endearment they really have no business using? A male customer would never put up with it. But women, like children, are supposed to enjoy these endearments, rather than being offended by them.

In more ways than one, it's time to speak up.    27

## Questions

1. Lakoff's first example of "women's language" (paragraph 4) has to do with colors. She says that women are more likely than men to use such words as *mauve, beige,* and *lavender* not because women see a wider range of colors but because men, "who control most of the interesting affairs of the world," regard distinctions of color as trivial and presumably leave them to the women. How adequate does this explanation seem to you?

2. For a day or so try to notice if Lakoff is correct in suggesting that women are more inclined than men to use "tag questions" and to use a "rising inflection" with a declarative sentence. Jot down examples you hear, and write an essay of about 500 words, either supporting or refuting Lakoff.

3. While you are eavesdropping, you might notice, too, whether or not in mixed company women talk more than men. Many men assume that "women talk a lot," but is it true? If, for instance, you spend an evening with an adult couple, try to form an impression about which of the two does more of the talking. Of course this is too small a sample to allow for a generalization; still, it is worth thinking about. If you are at a meeting—perhaps a meeting of a committee with men and women—again try to see whether the males or the females do most of the talking. Try also to see whether one sex interrupts the other more often than the other way around. And try to make some sense out of your findings.

4. In paragraph 11 Lakoff says, "Women's language sounds much more 'polite' than men's," and she implies that this politeness is a way of seeming weak. Do you associate politeness with weakness?

5. The essay originally appeared in *Ms.,* a feminist magazine, rather than in an academic journal devoted to language or to sociology. Why do you suppose she chose *Ms.?* What would you say Lakoff's purpose was in writing and publishing the essay?

**Barbara Lawrence**

# Four-Letter Words Can Hurt You

1   **W**hy should any words be called obscene? Don't they all describe natural human functions? Am I trying to tell them, my students demand, that the "strong, earthy, gut-honest"—or, if they are fans of Norman Mailer, the "rich, liberating, existential"—language they use to describe sexual activity isn't preferable to "phony-sounding, middle-class words like 'intercourse' and 'copulate'?" "Cop you Late!" they say with fancy inflections and gagging grimaces. "Now, what is *that* supposed to mean?"

2   Well, what is it supposed to mean? And why indeed should one group of words describing human functions and human organs be acceptable in ordinary conversation and another, describing presumably the same organs and functions, be tabooed—so much so, in fact, that some of these words still cannot appear in print in many parts of the English-speaking world?

3   The argument that these taboos exist only because of "sexual hang-ups" (middle-class, middle-age, feminist), or even that they are a result of class oppression (the contempt of the Norman conquerors for the language of their Anglo-Saxon serfs), ignores a much more likely explanation, it seems to me, and that is the sources and functions of the words themselves.

4   The best known of the tabooed sexual verbs, for example, comes from the German *ficken*, meaning "to strike"; combined, according to Partridge's etymological dictionary *Origins*, with the Latin sexual verb *futuere*; associated in turn with the Latin *fustis*, "a staff or cudgel"; the Celtic *buc*, "a point, hence to pierce"; the Irish *bot*, "the male member"; the Latin *battuere*, "to beat"; the Gaelic *batair*, "a cudgeller"; the Early Irish *bualaim*, "I strike"; and so forth. It is one of what etymologists

---

Barbara Lawrence was born in Hanover, New Hampshire, and she was educated at Connecticut College and at New York University. She teaches at the State University of New York, at Old Westbury. This essay first appeared in *Ms.* magazine.

sometimes call "the sadistic group of words for the man's part in cop-
ulation."

5    The brutality of this word, then, and its equivalents ("screw,"
"bang," etc.), is not an illusion of the middle class or a crotchet of
Women's Liberation. In their origins and imagery these words carry
undeniably painful, if not sadistic, implications, the object of which is
almost always female. Consider, for example, what a "screw" actually
does to the wood it penetrates; what a painful, even mutilating, activity
this kind of analogy suggests. "Screw" is particularly interesting in
this context, since the noun, according to Partridge, comes from words
meaning "groove," "nut," "ditch," "breeding sow," "scrofula" and
"swelling," while the verb, besides its explicit imagery, has antecedent
associations to "write on," "scratch," "scarify," "and so forth—a revealing fusion of a mechanical or painful action with an obviously
denigrated object.

6    Not all obscene words, of course, are as implicitly sadistic or denigrating to women as these, but all that I know seem to serve a similar
purpose: to reduce the human organism (especially the female organism) and human functions (especially sexual and procreative) to their
least organic, most mechanical dimension; to substitute a trivializing
or deforming resemblance for the complex human reality of what is
being described.

7    Tabooed male descriptives, when they are not openly denigrating
to women, often serve to divorce a male organ or function from any
significant interaction with the female. Take the word "testes," for
example, suggesting "witnesses" (from the Latin testis) to the sexual
and procreative strengths of the male organ; and the obscene counterpart of this word, which suggests little more than a mechanical
shape. Or compare almost any of the "rich," "liberating" sexual verbs,
so fashionable today among male writers, with that much-derided
Latin word "copulate" ("to bind or join together") or even that Anglo-
Saxon phrase (which seems to have had no trouble surviving the Norman Conquest) "make love."

8    How arrogantly self-involved the tabooed words seem in comparison to either of the other terms, and how contemptuous of the
female partner. Understandably so, of course, if she is only a "skirt,"
a "broad," a "chick," a "pussycat" or a "piece." If she is, in other
words, no more than her skirt, or what her skirt conceals; no more
than a breeder, or the broadest part of her; no more than a piece of a
human being or a "piece of tail."

9    The most severely tabooed of all the female descriptives, inciden-

tally, are those like a "piece of tail," which suggest (either explicitly or through antecedents) that there is no significant difference between the female channel through which we are all conceived and born and the anal outlet common to both sexes—a distinction that pornographers have always enjoyed obscuring.

This effort to deny women their biological identity, their individ- [10] uality, their humanness, is such an important aspect of obscene language that one can only marvel at how seldom, in an era preoccupied with definitions of obscenity, this fact is brought to our attention. One problem, of course, is that many of the people in the best position to do this (critics, teachers, writers) are so reluctant today to admit that they are angered or shocked by obscenity. Bored, maybe, unimpressed, aesthetically, displeased, but—no matter how brutal or denigrating the material—never angered, never shocked.

And yet how eloquently angered, how piously shocked many of [11] these same people become if denigrating language is used about any minority group other than women; if the obscenities are racial or ethnic, that is, rather than sexual. Words like "coon," "kike," "spic," "wop," after all, deform identity, deny individuality and humanness in almost exactly the same way that sexual vulgarisms and obscenities do.

No one that I know, least of all my students, would fail to question [12] the values of a society whose literature and entertainment rested heavily on racial or ethnic pejoratives. Are the values of a society whose literature and entertainment rest as heavily as ours on sexual pejoratives any less questionable?

## Question

In addition to giving evidence to support her view, what persuasive devices (such as irony, analogy) does Lawrence use? (On irony, see page 1147; on analogy, see page 1142.)

# Not Waving but
# Drowning

Nobody heard him, the dead man,
But still he lay moaning:
I was much further out than you thought
And not waving but drowning.                                    4

Poor chap, he always loved larking
And now he's dead
It must have been too cold for him his heart gave way,
They said                                                       8

Oh, no no no, it was too cold always
(Still the dead one lay moaning)
I was much too far out all my life
And not waving but drowning.                                    12

## Questions

1.  The first line, "Nobody heard him, the dead man," is, of course,
    literally true. Dead men do not speak. In what other ways is it true?
2.  Who are "they" whose voices we hear in the second stanza? What
    does the punctuation—or lack of it—in line 7 tell us of their feelings
    for the dead man? What effect is produced by the brevity of line 6?
    of line 8?
3.  In the last stanza, does the man reproach himself, or others, or
    simply bemoan his fate? What was the cause of his death?

Stevie Smith (1902–1971) was born Florence Margaret Smith in England. Her
first book was a novel, published in 1936, but she is best known for her several
volumes of poetry.

# 8

## NETWORKS

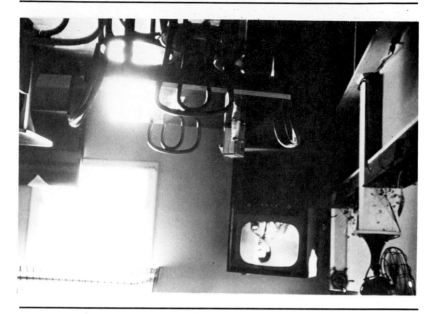

*Restaurant—US 1 Leaving Columbia, South Carolina*
**Robert Frank, 1955**

*Punch and Judy Show at Ilfracombe*
**Paul Martin, 1894**

*Just what is it that makes today's homes so different, so appealing?*
**Richard Hamilton, 1956**

*Sapolio*
**Anonymous, 1909**

# Short Views

Ballads, *bon mots*, anecdotes, give us better insight into the depths of past centuries than grave and voluminous chronicles. "A Straw," says Selden, "thrown up into the air will show how the wind sits, which cannot be learned by casting up a stone."

**Ralph Waldo Emerson**

For a while everybody was laughing at Marvel because we were going after the college crowd. But I've always felt comics were a very valid form of entertainment. There's no reason to look down on telling a good story in the comic book medium. It's just dialogue and illustrations, after all, like film, except that it's a little harder than film because our action is frozen. If Ernest Hemingway had written comic books, they would have been just as good as his novels.

**Stan Lee, of Marvel Comics**

If there is one consistently dishonest element in every situation comedy, no matter how realistic, how bold, how relevant or controversial it may be, it is that no one in a situation comedy is isolated, alone, atomized. In a country where broken marriages are increasing almost geometrically, and where the trend of living alone is becoming an important national fact of life, the world of the situation comedy depicts strong bonds between friends, coworkers, and family. No one sits home at night watching television: the most pervasive habit in American life today usually goes unrecorded in even the most "realistic" comedies because it is not funny. Instead, the sturdiest barriers of isolation vanish under the power of the family bond. The students of Gabe Kotter in *Welcome Back, Kotter* pal around together—an Italian, a black, a Puerto Rican, a Jew, a white eastern European ethnic—in poverty-stricken Brooklyn where, in reality, racial polarization has been at a flash point for a decade or more. And they frequently arrive, alone or together, at the apartment of their teacher, an event which for many New York teachers in such a neighborhood would trigger an emergency call to the police.

**Jeff Greenfield**

Watching television is a habit.
**Martin Meyer**

The medium is the message.
**Marshall McLuhan**

I beheld the wretch—the miserable monster whom I had created.
**Mary Shelley, Frankenstein**

We hear a great deal nowadays about "the importance of communication" and about "improved methods of communication"; but though certain supplementary methods of limited usefulness have recently been invented there are no *improved* methods, because the printed page remains the best and most flexible "means of communication" ever devised.

Even some colleges have joined what seems to be a conspiracy to ignore this fact. A year or two ago I visited a campus where they no longer had an English Department because it had become a Communications Department instead. And I remember saying to one of the professors whom I met on the campus that I thought it a sad day when a professor was seen—as at the moment he was—carrying under his arm, not books, but three film cans.

Just suppose that the radio, the phonograph, the film strip, and all the rest of it had been in existence since the Fifteenth Century but that books had just been invented. What a marvelous advance in communication that would be! And how many advantages the book would be seen to have over any previously known means, including ready availability and the possibility of wide choice. What comes over the air is chosen for you by somebody else and you must receive the communication at a particular moment, or not at all. A book, on the other hand, you can choose for yourself and you can read it at your own convenience. It is always available while a broadcast is gone, usually forever. And how much more economical in time a book is! Deduct from a half-hour broadcast the musical fanfare, the station announcement, the sponsor's commercial, etc., etc., and you can learn by five minutes with a book more than you can get in a half-hour broadcast. "Why," we would say, "this marvelous new invention, the book, just about makes radio obsolete."

But perhaps the greatest of all the advantages of the book as a means of communication is simply that by reading you learn to

read, become more and more capable of receiving more and more
completely more subtle and complicated communications. By
listening to the radio or looking at film strips you become only more
and more passive, less and less capable of giving your attention.
**Joseph Wood Krutch**

## Patricia Meyer Spacks

# What Have 60 Million Readers Found in Nancy Drew?

**I** had quite a lot of trouble managing to reread Nancy Drew. 1
First I went to the New Haven Public Library. They didn't have any
Nancy Drew books; the librarian said that that kind of reading wasn't good
for children. Then I asked my secretary if *she* owned any Nancy Drew.
She said she had had all eighty volumes, she'd read them and her
children read them, but that she'd sold them three weeks before at a garage
sale. She lives in a small town outside New Haven; she thought her
public library might be able to supply me with some books. The next
day she brought me a pile, with copyrights ranging from 1935 to 1985.
Every book in the stack had been taken out consistently about once a
month. If Nancy Drew isn't good for children, it's clear that the children don't realize that.

I started asking people at random whether they'd ever read Nancy 2

---

Patricia Meyer Spacks, a teacher of English literature at Yale University, is a
specialist in eighteenth-century literature, but she has written widely on other
subjects. Among her books are *Gossip* and *The Female Imagination.*
This essay was originally delivered as a talk in conjunction with an exhibition
of the Nancy Drew books at the Wellesley College Library. Harriet Stratemeyer
Adams (mentioned in the final paragraph) used the pseudonym Carolyn Keene
for more than fifty Nancy Drew books.

Drew. Each woman in my arbitrary sample of highly intellectual types said yes; all remembered their childhood experience of Nancy with great pleasure. More surprisingly, several men had also enjoyed Nancy Drew. More surprising still, one of my colleagues reported that his six year old daughter's favorite bedtime reading-aloud books at the moment are Nancy Drew mysteries. And a colleague from another institution revealed that he teaches Nancy Drew in his course on mystery novels.

3    In this context of official disapproval and unofficial enthusiasm, I began my own rereading, feeling rather dutiful about it, expecting to be bored. Not at all: the more I read, the more interested I became in how these reiterative, simple plots and sketchily defined characters worked on their readers. For what it's worth, I concluded that Nancy Drew—the old-fashioned, "out-of-date" version of Nancy Drew—is probably rather good for children.

4    Some of you may remember Bruno Bettelheim's book on fairytales. *The Use of Enchantment.* Analyzing the effect of fairytales on child readers, Bettelheim concludes that such stories provide developmental models. His accounts of individual tales make clear that they offer little boys patterns of mastery. For girls, on the other hand, the most familiar stories reinforce images of passivity and dependence. Sleeping Beauty must await in a state of literal unconsciousness the coming of her prince. Goodness is rewarded in girls—think of Cinderella's domestic virtues!—while courage, independence, and adventurousness (as well as generosity and compassion) win success for boys. Girls are constantly warned (in "Snow White," for instance) of the dangers of their own sexuality. The fairytales, in other words, reinforce cultural stereotypes about male and female roles. Bettelheim doesn't put it this way, but feminist critics after him have repeatedly made the point, often suggesting in what ways women's fairytales might be different. Usually their proposals for useful tales emphasize expression of rage at male domination and of attachment among females.

5    The Nancy Drew stories aren't fairytales or versions of fairytales. Nor do they provide developmental models. On the contrary, Nancy remains staggeringly the same—eighteen years old, "titan-haired," driving her convertible—through one book after another. And no one reads *one* Nancy Drew book: it would be like eating one peanut. (An academic father told me that his eight year old currently has a list of fifty-two more Nancy Drew books she's determined to read.) In an utterly unthreatening way, though, these books generate imaginative power by creating images of female mastery that clearly and directly

address little girls' wishes and fears without encouraging their rage. Let me remind you in some detail of the characters who inhabit these books, the kinds of situations they confront, and the typical outcomes of those situations; then I'll try to say more about how these elements may work to instruct and reassure child readers.

6    Nancy, the perpetual eighteen year old, lives with her father, a prosperous and generous lawyer who has great respect for her abilities and who interferes not at all with her plans. Indeed, if someone steals Nancy's car, her father will promptly provide her with a new and better one (*The Haunted Showboat*, 1957). Her mother having died when Nancy was three, there is no one to come between her and her father; no mother makes restrictive rules or keeps a penetrating eye on Nancy's activities. Nor does she have a cruel stepmother. Instead, a kindly housekeeper (often described as "motherly") exclaims at the girl's cleverness and provides her and her friends with hot cocoa and apple pie. As much of the last two centuries' literature testifies, this is a little girl's dream situation.

7    Nancy has two female allies her own age: Bess, always character-ized either as "a little plump" or as "slightly overweight," with blonde hair and occasional feminine fears; and George, Bess's "spunky cousin," an attractive brunette, who liked athletics and was proud of her boy's name" (*The Clue in the Crumbling Wall*, 1945). Although Nancy origi-nates the most useful tactics for solving mysteries, all solutions result from the combined efforts of the three girls. There is also a boyfriend, Ned Nickerson, who often inhabits the remote peripheries of the nar-ratives. Occasionally someone in the stories will suggest romantic feel-ing between Nancy and Ned; on such occasions, Ned blushes, and Nancy says "Don't be silly."

8    Always competent, Nancy possesses a surprising range of knowl-edge. If a car starts making ominous noises, Nancy will look under-neath and announce "the whole rear housing has given way!" (*The Haunted Showboat*). On the basis of artistic style, she can decide (cor-rectly) that the creator of a given painting was female (*The Strange Message in the Parchment*, 1977). She makes her own travel arrange-ments, checks into hotels by herself with aplomb (*The Eskimo's Secret*, 1985), goes off on airplane trips alone. If one path is blocked, literally or metaphorically, she can always figure out another.

9    Whether she is asked to solve a mystery or simply finds herself in the middle of one, she invariably discovers and analyzes the evi-dence that leads to the solution. Along the way to that solution, she often acquires new funds of knowledge: about the nature of sheep-

raising, for instance, including the realities of slaughter, unsenti-mentally treated; or about how buttons are made; or how you tell good from bad mink pelts. (The reader, of course, learns the same facts.)

10    Each mystery conforms to a single pattern, with variations. Some-one appeals to Nancy for help: an inheritance will be forfeited if the missing heir doesn't show up within a month; a New Orleans family wants to tow an old showboat from a bayou for Mardi Gras, but mys-terious forces prevent the boat's being moved. Alternatively, some-thing happens to Nancy herself: two rosebushes disappear from her yard; a sheepskin coat is stolen from her living room. In either case, she sets out, with paternal approval, to solve the problem, which typi-cally becomes increasingly complicated as she investigates it. Soon she finds a clue, most often a scrap of paper with a cryptic, usually frag-mentary message on it. It takes some time to decipher these messages, but all eventually yield to Nancy's common sense and acumen, with a little help from her friends. And to her dogged persistence. As the housekeeper remarks on one occasion, "I can see why you're a good detective. If you don't find hidden gold under one stone, you turn up another" (*Nancy's Mysterious Letter*, 1968).

11    Each book has its "scary parts," but no threatening situation lasts very long—sometimes only from one sentence to the next. The most common form of menace consists in something being thrown at Nancy. Stones, concrete blocks, bottles come whizzing through the air, from no immediately comprehensible source. Sometimes Nancy is locked up somewhere, but she soon gets away. Sometimes a bridge collapses, or a ladder, or a car tries to run her down. Occasionally cars are tamp-ered with or boats sink; once in a while the heroine faces less definable forms of danger, like the strange sounds that come from the haunted showboat. In the end, always, Nancy discovers the source of every threat and arranges the capture of all threateners. And each book con-cludes with the promise of its successor, in a formulation of this sort: "Nancy was thoughtful for a moment [sometimes, more forthrightly, she is sad] as she realized this mystery was solved. Little did she know that she would soon become involved in the exciting *Mystery of Croc-odile Island*" (*The Strange Message in the Parchment*).

12    All mysteries provide the satisfaction of problems solved and allow their readers vicarious participation in the process of solution. At this level, one can readily explain the appeal of the Nancy Drew books to a young audience. They are just scary enough, just difficult enough, to supply titillation and stimulation without making excessive de-mands on intelligence or endurance. Reading one Nancy Drew book

educates the reader in how to approach the next. Soon a child grows into awareness of the pattern and can almost expect without quite knowing what's going to happen. The combination of familiarity and novelty generates a potent source of pleasure.

13    But the pleasure goes deeper than this, and the meaning of mysteries stated and resolved has special weight for youthful readers. The Nancy Drew stories, over and over, insist that growing up provides no unmanageable difficulties, that adolescence is even for girls a time of freedom and power, not a time of dangerous sexuality, and that young people can play a meaningful part in society. The reassurance of these messages, I suspect, accounts for the enduring popularity of this series—and for the fact that boys as well as girls read them.

14    At no time in the series' history, I suspect, have eighteen year olds read Nancy Drew. The form of identification invited by these books depends on more remote varieties of fantasy than that produced by interaction between a fictional and a literal teen-ager. For eight year olds, on the other hand, the fantasy is utterly satisfying: keeping your loving, approving father all to yourself; not having to endure obscure, troubling rivalries with a mother, yet retaining the forms of maternal comfort; living in conflict-free egalitarian relationship to boys without suspicion or rivalry or teasing from other girls. Lots of love, no overt sex—an ideal situation.

15    The near sexlessness of these narratives must contribute to their appeal for some boys as well. Gender is almost never an explicit issue here. The narrator assumes that girls take care of themselves as boys do, that girls and boys alike face problems and solve them. The freedom of a world in which gender is suppressed as a category manifestly extends to boys as well as girls.

16    So the fables of mastery can apply to both sexes. Over and over, these stories tell child-readers the same thing: if you persist, you can figure it out—"it" being not only the individual mystery that concerns Nancy at any given moment, but the larger mystery of grown-up existence. Nancy never needs to be aggressive and she feels angry only at injustices, but she can rarely be scared. No one succeeds in bullying her. Although she's by no means remarkably articulate, she knows what she thinks and she has a solid sense of self-confidence, presumably based on her repeated successes.

17    The notion of "growing up" that Nancy and her friends epitomize offers all kinds of reassurance to a child. It's a kind of up-to-date version of *Peter Pan*: instead of remaining forever a child, to be taken care of by big dogs and charming female fairies, one can imagine retaining

the innocence of childhood, the father who pays the bills, the house-keeper who worries about you just enough and offers warm cookies when they're needed—but also fulfilling, without undue pain, the re-sponsibilities of adulthood and enjoying some of adulthood's privi-leges. Indeed, Nancy excels most of the literal adults around her. The police, for instance, in these fables turn out to be kindly and helpful, but *they* never solve the crime or find the heiress. Over and over, apparent complexity becomes simple as Nancy works at it. What could be more comforting?

18    Children see around them, and hear about, dangers and difficul-ties of adolescence. In the Nancy Drew stories, they can read about adolescence in which all danger is externalized and objectified. If some-one sneaks into your house while you're giving the poor old mailman a cup of hot cocoa and steals a mailbag containing letters of value, that someone can be found and punished. It's a far easier problem to locate and punish him than it is to deal with internal conflicts or external demands for conformity with troubling norms. Even if the mail-thief interests young readers because at some level they recognize in them-selves fleeting impulses to make off with someone else's letters, such impulses are usually less worrisome to little boys and girls than, say, their fantasies about sex. After all, they already know that they're not supposed to steal mail, so it's satisfying to them to learn that the person who breaks the prohibition gets his comeuppance.

19    The adult reader of Nancy Drew notices a striking contrast in these books between the sparseness of realistic detail and the elaboration of plot. The narrator seems more interested in button-making and mink-raising than in the appearance of people or of the physical world, or in details of what people say, wear, and do in day-to-day contact. But she also has a rather intricate conception of plot. Although no single episode takes long to develop and be resolved, a dizzying sequence of events occurs in virtually all Nancy Drew stories. In the first eight pages of *The Clue in the Crumbling Wall*, a policewoman asks Nancy to find a dancer who has disappeared, two rosebushes vanish from the front yard, a damseller shows up. Nancy finds a pearl, she goes to the jeweler to sell it, encounters an "unpleasant man," and has her purse snatched. (And one of those eight pages is occupied by an il-lustration; and some space is taken up by explanations of Nancy's situation, with housekeeper and father, and her history of successful mystery-solving.) Eventually all these happenings will interlock: for the moment, several seem to promise different directions. And Nan-cy's life continues at a comparable pace. The stories make considerable

demands on a child-reader's attention, moving from one episode to another at breakneck speed and connecting episodes in complicated ways. Although the large outlines of plot, as I've already suggested, remain constant from one book to another, it would be difficult to summarize in adequate detail the intricacies of any individual plot.

20    Perhaps it's my training as an eighteenth-century scholar that makes this conjunction of generalized scene and highly specified plot so interesting to me: it's a very eighteenth-century combination. Dr. Johnson, you may remember, suggested through a fictional character that the poet should not try to describe the streaks on the tulip; he should, instead, evoke the type of the tulip, reminding every reader of his or her own direct knowledge of the flower. I have a hunch that that's how the Nancy Drew books work for children. The sketches of scene, character, and conversation create vague outlines for the reader to fill in from personal experience. Dark hair, blonde hair, titian hair: most readers can identify quite straightforwardly with one or another of the girls, given the lack of detail in their characterizations. The father, the housekeeper, the boyfriend, the houses and gardens, the clothes: they could be *anyone's* father or clothes or whatever. On the other hand, details about sheepshearing or the feeding of minks provide a sense of solid information, imaginably useful in the real world.

21    Those complicated plots also involve the process of working things out: they declare that no matter how fast or how crazily things happen, they always turn out to make sense, given persistent effort to fathom them. When you know that everything *will* eventually make sense, it becomes delightful to indulge in the vicarious experience of utter confusion.

22    It might be argued—I'm sure it has been argued—that the unrealistic aspects of this fiction make it useless if not dangerous for children. After all, if I'm right, these books suggest what is neither psychologically nor literally true. Adolescents do not have so much effectual power as Nancy and her friends wield: they do not lead lives free of familial and of internal conflict; they are not always readily able to figure things out; they often feel troubled by their own and other people's sexuality; they sometimes fight with their friends, they sometimes feel depressed, they rarely get to have their fathers all to themselves (if there's no mother, there's usually a girlfriend). Many recent stories for children are predicated on the assumption that useful fictions provide realistic accounts of dangers to be faced in the world. You tell the little girl about drug dealers and divorce, the theory goes,

and she'll be better prepared to deal with them when she confronts them herself.

23  Maybe so; I don't know. I wouldn't want children to read *only* about the idealized white middle-class harmonies depicted in the Nancy Drew books. But I suspect that it's useful for a white middle-class eight year old—and such, obviously, is the intended audience of the series—to be reassured about what lies ahead, to be told that she can solve problems by using available resources, that cooperative models of accomplishment are meaningful, and that she doesn't have to grow up until she wants to. Nancy Drew as she exists on the page resembles an eight year old's idealized self-image more than a realistic portrayal of an eighteen year old. But it's eight year olds who like to read about her, and I strongly suspect that a more up-to-date, "realistic" version of the character will enjoy less popular success than her implausible predecessor. Harriet Statemeyer Adams took pride in having created an early version of the independent woman. Her achievement—the degree to which she causes young readers to feel deeply involved with that figure of the independent woman—may depend partly on exactly the aspects of her fictions that make them seem unrealistic and uncompelling to adults.

## Questions

1. Spacks offers an explanation of why the Nancy Drew books interest children. If you read such books when you were a child, do you now agree with Spacks's analysis of their appeal?

2. If as a child you read some other sort of book designed for children—for example, the kind Spacks refers to in the last two sentences of paragraph 22—what were its appeals?

3. In paragraph 20 Spacks says that "most readers can identify . . . with" Nancy or one of her friends. But in paragraph 23 she refers to the "white middle-class eight year old" as the "intended audience of the series." Does Spacks contradict herself? Or, though she doesn't address the question directly, does her analysis suggest reasons that the books might also appeal to eight-year-olds of other races and classes?

4. In her first paragraph, and in the next-to-last paragraph, Spacks suggests that some people find the Nancy Drew books not good for children, or even dangerous for them. She clearly disagrees. Whether or not you are convinced by her argument, imagine some

books that might be, in your opinion, "not good" or "dangerous" for children to read. What would they be like? What would you do about them? Would you try to keep them out of children's libraries (as the Nancy Drew books have been kept out of the New Haven library)? Or put pressure on publishers not to publish them? Or what?

5. Spacks does not discuss the illustrations in the Nancy Drew books. Consider (in these books or in some others with which you are familiar) the episodes illustrated and also the style of the illustrations. (You may find it helpful to compare the style with other styles used in other books designed for children.)

## Richard A. Hawley

# Television and Adolescents

### A Teacher's View

1    Ever since its novelty wore off in the fifties, we have all known, really, that television in its commercial form wasn't up to much good. This isn't to say that millions of people don't still depend on it, but dependency is hardly a sign of virtue. Except for Marshall McLuhan's grab-bag theoretics, few claims have been advanced for the improving effects of television. In fact, recently there has been a flurry of publishing activity, most notably Marie Winn's *The Plug-in Drug*, about television as a cause of downright mental erosion. But what I think Marie Winn and others need is a concrete, closely observed, and intensely felt illustration of the larger thesis. That's what I offer here.

2    Television has a way of intruding into our lives, and last year it intruded into my life and into the life of the school where I work in a way that many of us there will never forget. We had all taken our seats for morning assembly. The usual announcements were read, after

Richard A. Hawley is dean of students at University School in Hunting Valley, Ohio.

which the morning's senior speaker was introduced. Like many independent schools, ours requires each senior to address the student body in some manner before he graduates. Since public speaking is not a widely distributed gift these days, the senior speeches are infrequently a source of much interest or intentional amusement.

3   As the curtains parted, we could see that the speaker had opted for a skit. On the stage were a covered table and a number of cooking implements. Out stepped the speaker wearing an apron and chef's hat, which very quickly established that he was going to satirize one of my colleagues who has a national reputation as a gourmet chef. Since this colleague is also a man who can take a joke, the prospects for the skit seemed bright. But not for long.

4   At first, I think almost all of us pretended that we didn't hear, that we were making too much of certain, possibly accidental, double entendres. But then came the direct statements and a few blatant physical gestures. Then it was clear! This boy was standing before five hundred of us making fun of what he suggested at some length was the deviant sexual nature of one of his teachers. The response to this was at first stupefaction, then some outbursts of laughter (the groaning kind of laughter that says, "I don't believe you said that"), then a quieting, as the speech progressed, to periodic oohs (the kind that say, "You *did* say that, and you're in for it").

5   When he had finished, there was a nearly nauseating level of tension afloat. As the students filed off to class, I made my way backstage to find the speaker. It had by now dawned on him that he had done something wrong, even seriously wrong. We met in my office.

6   He expressed remorse at having offended a teacher whom he said he particularly liked. (Before the conference I had checked briefly with the teacher and found him badly flustered and deeply hurt.) The remorse was, I felt, genuine. But something was decidedly missing in the boy's explanation of how he came to think that such a presentation might, under any circumstances, have been appropriate. He hadn't, he admitted, really thought about it, and some of his friends thought the idea was funny, and, well, he didn't know. When it occurred to him that serious school action was in the offing, he protested that in no way had he intended the sexual references to be taken seriously—they were, you know, a joke.

7   I pointed out to him that the objects of such jokes have no way to respond: To ignore the insinuation might affirm its validity; on the other hand, to object vigorously would draw additional attention to the offense and sustain the embarrassment connected with it. I pointed

out further that sometimes innocent parties *never* regain their stature after being offended in this manner, and that the injured party was, at the very least, in for a terrible day of school.

8    The boy became reflective and said, "Was it *that* bad? You can see worse on 'Saturday Night Live.'" I told him I doubted this, but if it were true, and were I in a position to judge, I would be in favor of expelling "Saturday Night Live" from the air. He left the office, and subsequently endured the appropriate consequences.

9    For my part, I resolved to turn on "Saturday Night Live," and when I did, I realized the student had spoken truly. The show's quick-succession, absurdist comedy spots depended for their appeal on establishing an almost dangerous sense of inappropriateness: exactly that sense created by our senior speaker. To me, for some years a lapsed viewer, it seemed that both the variety and specificity of sexual innuendo had developed considerably since, say, the once daring Smothers Brothers show of the sixties. What struck me more, however, was how many punch lines and visual gags depended on suddenly introducing the idea of injury or violent death.

10    I happened to tune in the night a funny caption was put over the documentary shot of Middle Eastern political partisans being dragged to death behind an automobile. Was this funny? I asked my students. They said it was "sick" and laughed. Does this kind of fun trivialize crisis? Trivialize cruelty? Inure us to both? Or is it, you know, a joke?

11    The right things were said, I think, to our students about the boy's speech. But I can't say the situation improved. Not more than a couple of weeks later, a speaker garbed in a woman's tennis dress took the podium and began to talk humorously about the transsexual tennis player Renee Richards. I can't think of a subject harder for an adolescent to discuss before an adolescent audience. Rarely noted for their confidence and breadth of vision in matters of human sexuality, adolescents are unlikely to be objective, sympathetic, or (let me tell you) funny about so disturbing a phenomenon as sex change. This particular boy, whose inflection is very flat and whose normal countenance is especially stony, managed to convey almost a sense of bitterness in making his string of insulting and, in his reference to genitals and to menstruation, awfully tasteless cracks.

12    So there it was again: the inappropriateness, the tension. This time the injured party was remote from our particular world, so the hastily arranged conference with the boy turned on general considerations of taste and judgment. This time, however, the speaker was recalcitrant: We could disapprove of his speech and discipline him if we chose, but we ought to know that we could hear the same thing on television.

new to say—and yet his words, like cavalry horses answering the bugle, group themselves automatically into the familiar dreary pattern. This invasion of one's mind by ready-made phrases (*lay the foundations, achieve a radical transformation*) can only be prevented if one is constantly on guard against them, and every such phrase anaesthetizes a portion of one's brain.

17    I said earlier that the decadence of our language is probably cur-able. Those who deny this would argue, if they produced an argument at all, that language merely reflects existing social conditions, and that we cannot influence its development by any direct tinkering with words and constructions. So far as the general tone or spirit of a lan-guage goes, this may be true, but it is not true in detail. Silly words and expressions have often disappeared, not through any evolutionary process but owing to the conscious action of a minority. Two recent examples were *explore every avenue* and *leave no stone unturned*, which were killed by the jeers of a few journalists. There is a long list of flyblown metaphors which could similarly be got rid of if enough peo-ple would interest themselves in the job; and it should also be possible to laugh the *not un-* formation out of existence,[3] to reduce the amount of Latin and Greek in the average sentence, to drive out foreign phrases and strayed scientific words, and, in general, to make pretentiousness unfashionable. But all these are minor points. The defense of the En-glish language implies more than this, and perhaps it is best to start by saying what it does *not* imply.

18    To begin with it has nothing to do with archaism, with the sal-vaging of obsolete words and turns of speech, or with the setting up of a "standard English" which must never be departed from. On the contrary, it is especially concerned with the scrapping of every word or idiom which has outworn its usefulness. It has nothing to do with correct grammar and syntax, which are of no importance so long as one makes one's meaning clear, or with the avoidance of American-isms, or with having what is called a "good prose style." On the other hand it is not concerned with fake simplicity and the attempt to make written English colloquial. Nor does it even imply in every case pre-ferring the Saxon word to the Latin one, though it does imply using the fewest and shortest words that will cover one's meaning. What is above all needed is to let the meaning choose the word, and not the

3 One can cure oneself of the *not un-* formation by memorizing this sentence: *A not unblack dog was chasing a not unsmall rabbit across a not ungreen field.*

At that moment something clicked for me. Not only did my brief   13
exposure to "Saturday Night Live" convince me that, yes, I would
hear the same thing on television, but I was suddenly struck with the
realization that he was using television as an arbiter of taste—that is,
*as an arbiter of good taste.* I began to see in this premise a common ground
upon which he and I could at least argue. Both of us were in agreement
that what is broadcast over television ought to be acceptable; our point
of disagreement was his feeling that broadcasting something over television *made* it acceptable. Alarming as such a feeling is to me, it is not
hard to see how it has developed over the past few decades.

Until the middle sixties, with the exception of the very earthiest   14
plays and novels, the values of home and school and the values of the
popular culture were fairly continuous; if anything, radio, television,
and motion pictures were more staid than real life. Of course, all this
would change very quickly—not because change was requested or
even consented to, but because it wasn't, perhaps couldn't be, resisted.
And suddenly there it all was at once: the most embarrassing expletives
as common speech; every imaginable kind of sexual coupling depicted
in ever increasing candor; obsessively specific wounds, mutilations.

These formerly unacceptable kinds of stimulation made their way   15
more easily into the relatively insulated world of print and film than
they did into the more communal world of the television set. Television
is typically viewed in homes, and what is communally seen and heard
must be communally integrated, or there will be friction. Since American households—set-holds?—share this communal experience for an
estimated two to seven hours per day, the potential for friction is considerable. This is why, on grounds of taste, criticism of television programming tends to be more bitter and more relentless than criticism
of books and films.

Television foes and partisans alike continue to advise, with some   16
reason, that those who object to certain programs ought not to watch
them. But given the impossibility of monitoring the set at all hours,
control over the amount and quality of viewing is difficult to maintain
even in principled, surveillant households. Too, some viewers will
insist on being their brother's keeper. Not everyone who is convinced
that what is beaming over the national airwaves is inhumane, un-
scrupulous, or scurrilous is going to fight to the death for the networks'
right to be so.

For many people, television is no longer on the polite side of real   17
life. This is an obvious observation about a novel development, one
whose consequences are only just dawning on us. A realist or an ex-

istentialist may argue that the unflappably suburban world of "Father Knows Best" revealed none of the complex, ambivalent, and often irrational forces at work in real families: But it is hard to argue that "Father Knows Best" in any way *contributed* to those dark forces. On the contrary, it is possible to argue—although one hesitates to carry it too far—that the theme of Father Knowing Best serves as a psychologically soothing backdrop to the prickly dynamics of real family life. And while today's most highly rated shows suggest that the prevailing seventies' theme is Nobody Knows Anything, there are still apparently enough viewers who like Father Knowing Best to support series like "The Waltons" and "Little House on the Prairie."

Sometimes the theme is compromised in a typical seventies' man- 18 ner, of which "James at 16" provides a good example: The parents are cast very much in the Robert Young-Jane Wyatt mold, but their son James is, to borrow a phrase, kind of now. By far the most interesting thing he did was to lose his virginity on prime time. The fifteen-going-on-sixteen-year-old boys I work with, many of them at least as sophisticated as James, typically hold on to their virginity a bit longer, until the disposition of their sexual feelings is under surer control. The best clinical evidence maintains that the process of bringing newly emergent sexuality under control is *inherently* delicate and troublesome. James' television plunge planted the anxiety-provoking notion in the mind of the adolescent viewer that he was sexually lagging behind not only the precocious kid down the block, but the Average American Boy character of James. (One was allowed to be less anxious when Father Knew Best.)

Why shouldn't television make people anxious? say the producers 19 of programs that make people anxious. After all, the *world* is anxious. (An awfully self-serving position: Programs that arouse anxiety are relevant; those that don't are enjoyable.) Before long, this line of argument begins to lay claim that programs which bring up irritating subjects in an irritating manner are performing a valuable social mission. Norman Lear, the producer of comedies such as "All in the Family" and "Maude," makes such a claim. According to the Lear formula, a controversial topic will be raised, tossed around for laughs, then either discarded or resolved. Resolution occurs when one of the characters tolerates or forgives the controversial person or practice, while some other character, usually a combination of lovable old coot and ass, does not.

As many critics have pointed out, this is only apparent resolution. 20 Nothing much really happens to a racial or sexual conflict when it is laughed at (a device that is supposed to soften outright slurring and stereotyping), discarded, tolerated, or forgiven. The idea that "if we can joke about it this way, we have taken a humanitarian stride" is mistaken. There is plenty of evidence, particularly among the student population, that, for one thing, race relations are more strained today than they were a decade ago. No one would want to claim that racism among youth disappeared during the politically active sixties; however, a claim can be made that when a student was confronted then with having made a racial slur, he seemed to be aware of having violated a standard.

Who is to say that Archie Bunker hath no sting? More and more 21 television comedians, in the manner of Don Rickles, seek *only* to sting. It is really an empirical question, not a matter of taste, whether or not it is harmless, much less healing, to denigrate everybody, including oneself. A hit song by Randy Newman insults small people: this is no parody of unkindness or bigotry, but the real thing. My students understand it perfectly and parrot it enthusiastically. Rebuked, they grimace in exasperation. Nothing in their youthful experience tells them that bigotry is a sign of cultural regression ("It isn't bigotry; it's, you know, a joke"). They prefer to see whatever wicked delights crop up in the media as a progressive casting off of prudish inhibitions. According to such a view, progress is whatever happens next.

Toleration of the intolerable is always worrying, but it is especially 22 so when it takes place among the young, in whom we want to invest so much hope. Tolerating the intolerable is part of a dynamic, not a static, process; the intolerable, when it is nurtured, grows.

Which brings me back to the senior speeches. Two so thoroughly 23 inappropriate presentations in a single year represented a high count for us, so we were not ready, at least I wasn't, for the third.

This time the talk was about a summer spent working on a ranch, 24 and the format was that of a commentary with slides. No apparent harm in this, but there were a number of factors working against the speech's success. The first was that the speaker was renowned for being a card, a reputation the welcoming ovation insisted he live up to. Second, he had not adequately rehearsed the projection of the slides, so that they tended to appear out of order and askew, the effect of which was to provide a subtextual comedy of visual non sequiturs. Third, he chose to capitalize on the audience's nearly unrestrained hilarity by playing up certain questionable references.

The speaker made a fairly good, not too inappropriate crack about 25 a slide which depicted a bull mounting a cow—"Sometimes the corrals get so crowded we have to stack the cattle on top of one another." But he chose to exploit his references to the gelding of bulls. There were, in all, four jokey and brutal evocations of this process which served to keep the image of bull genitalia before our minds for quite a few minutes. Since laughter had already been spent, the castration jokes were met with a kind of nervous applause. Bolstered by this, the speaker closed with a coda to the effect that he would be available after assembly to anybody who wanted tips on "cutting meat."

Since I happened to be in charge that day, I sent him home. It seemed to me, in light of the various reprisals and forewarnings connected with the previous speeches, that this particular performance, though perhaps less offensive in its specific references than the other two, ought to be the last straw. The speaker had clearly exceeded anything required by either schoolboy or cowboy saltiness. He had created an anything-goes atmosphere, and then he had let it go—for which he was applauded. "That was great!" said the boy next to me on the way out of the auditorium.  26

That morning and afterward scores of students, most, but not all, of them civil, hastened to let me know that they felt it was unfair to have sent the speaker home. Not one of them failed to remind me that I could see worse on television. Had I never seen "Saturday Night Live"? That afternoon an opinion poll went up requesting signatures from those who disapproved of the action I had taken and, in an opposing column, those who approved. Within the hour, hundreds expressed disapproval, only one approved.  27

For a day or two at school there was an animated atmosphere of martyrdom (the speaker's, not mine), but it dissipated rapidly, possibly because the right to make castration jokes from the stage was not, as a cause, very catalytic. The banished speaker, a very likable boy, returned, was received warmly, and apologized not at all cringingly.  28

In the calm that has followed, my colleagues and I have taken pains to stress to our students, especially at the commencement of the new school year, that whenever somebody addresses an assembly, it is a special occasion. Speakers are expected to observe definite standards when they speak or perform; audiences are expected to be courteous and restrained. Humor at someone else's expense is out, unless it is prearranged with the party lampooned, and even then it ought not to be inhumane. Excretory and copulatory humor is out; it's too easy. Preparation is important. Being persuasive is important. Being  29 controversial is important. Being funny is a delight to all, though it is harder than it looks.

Perhaps these expectations are high. However, schools, especially 30 parochial and independent schools, are gloriously unencumbered in setting such standards: Schools are often *chosen* for the standards they set, the difference they represent. One of the things schools have an opportunity to be different from is television, for although we are all wired into it and it feels public, like the law, it is actually private, like a door-to-door salesman. We don't have to buy the goods.

Since children who watch a fair amount of television will quite 31 naturally assume they are being told and shown the truth, it seems to me crucial that they are exposed to models who view it selectively and critically, who judge it by criteria other than its potential to engage. My own experience has been that students are surprised, but not hostile, when television programming is harshly judged. I think they may even come to like the idea that they themselves, at their discriminating best, are in the process of becoming people television ought to measure up to.

# Questions

1. The three speeches that disturbed Hawley all had to do with sex, yet (aside from a few casual references, such as the one to the Smothers Brothers) his references to television are to violence, including verbal violence. Is Hawley muddling things?
2. Hawley begins paragraph 19 by asking: "Why shouldn't television make people anxious?" and he goes on to repeat the word "anxious." What is the meaning of "anxious" in this context?
3. Judging from this essay, what sort of person is Hawley? In a paragraph, try to characterize him. (Don't attempt to summarize his argument; confine your remarks to his personality.)

Tipper Gore

# Curbing the
# Sexploitation Industry

$\mathbf{I}$ can't even count the times in the last three years, since    1
I began to express my concern about violence and sexuality in rock
music, that I have been called a prude, a censor, a music hater, even
a book burner. So let me be perfectly clear: I detest censorship. I'm
not advocating censorship but rather a candid and vigorous debate
about the dangers posed for our children by what I call the "sexploitation industry."

We don't need to put a childproof cap on the world, but we do    2
need to remind the nation that children live in it, too, and deserve
respect and sensitive treatment.

When I launched this campaign in 1985 . . . I went to the source    3
of the problem, sharing my concerns and proposals with the entertainment industry. Many producers were sympathetic. Some coop-
erated with my efforts. But others have been overtly hostile, accusing
me of censorship and suggesting, unfairly, that my motives are political. This resistance and hostility has convinced me of the need for a
two-pronged campaign, with equal effort from the entertainment industry and concerned parents. Entertainment producers must take the
first step, by labeling sexually explicit material.

But the industry cannot be expected to solve the problem on its    4
own. Parents should encourage producers to cooperate and praise
them when they do. Producers need to know that parents are aware
of the issue and are reading their advisory labels. Above all, they need
to know that somebody out there cares, that the community at large
is not apathetic about the deep and lasting damage being done to our
children.

What's at issue is not the occasional sexy rock lyric. What trou-    5
bles—indeed, outrages—me is far more vicious: a celebration of the
most gruesome violence, coupled with the explicit message that sado-

---

Tipper Gore, co-founder of the Parents' Music Resource Center, is the author
of a book about violence and obscenity in the arts. Her husband is a United
States senator from Tennessee.

---

masochism is the essence of sex. We're surrounded by examples—in rock lyrics, on television, at the movies and in rental videos. One major TV network recently aired a preview of a soap opera rape scene during a morning game show.

The newest craze in horror movies is something called the "teen 6 slasher" film, and it typically depicts the killing, torture and sexual mutilation of women in sickening detail. Several rock groups now simulate sexual torture and murder during live performances. Others titillate youthful audiences with strippers confined in cages on stage and with half-naked dancers, who often act out sex with band members. Sexual brutality has become the common currency of America's youth culture and with it the pervasive degradation of women.

Why is this graphic violence dangerous? It's especially damaging 7 for young children because they lack the moral judgment of adults. Many children are only dimly aware of the consequences of their actions, and, as parents know, they are excellent mimics. They often imitate violence they see on TV, without necessarily understanding what they are doing or what the consequences might be. One 5-year-old boy from Boston recently got up from watching a teen-slasher film and stabbed a 2-year-old girl with a butcher knife. He didn't mean to kill her (and luckily he did not). He was just imitating the man in the video.

Nor does the danger end as children grow older. National health 8 officials tell us that children younger than teen-agers are apt to react to excessive violence with suicide, satanism, drug and alcohol abuse. Even grown-ups are not immune. One series of studies by researchers at the University of Wisconsin found that men exposed to films in which women are beaten, butchered, maimed and raped were significantly desensitized to the violence. Not only did they express less sympathy for the victims, they even approved of lesser penalties in hypothetical rape trials.

Sado-masochistic pornography is a kind of poison. Like most poi- 9 sons, it probably cannot be totally eliminated, but it certainly could be labeled for what it is and be kept away from those who are most vulnerable. The largest record companies have agreed to this—in principle at least. In November 1985, the Recording Industry Association of America adopted my proposal to alert parents by having producers either put warning labels on records with explicitly sexual lyrics or display the lyrics on the outside of the record jackets. Since then, some companies have complied in good faith, although others have not complied at all.

This is where we parents must step in. We must let the industry 10 know we're angry. We must press for uniform voluntary compliance with labeling guidelines. And we must take an active interest at home in what our children are watching and listening to. After all, we can hardly expect that the labels or printed lyrics alone will discourage young consumers.

Some parents may want to write to the record companies. Others 11 can give their support to groups like the Parent Teacher Association, which have endorsed the labeling idea. All of us can use our purchasing power. We have more power than we think, and we must use it. For the sake of our children, we simply can't afford to slip back into apathy.

My concern for the health and welfare of children has nothing to 12 do with politics: It is addressed to conservatives and liberals alike. Some civil libertarians believe it is wrong even to raise these questions—just as some conservatives believe that the Government should police popular American culture. I reject both these views. I have no desire to restrain artists or cast a "chill" over popular culture. But I believe parents have First Amendment rights, too.

The fate of the family, the dignity of women, the mental health 13 of children—these concerns belong to everyone. We must protect our children with choice, not censorship. Let's start working in our communities to forge a moral consensus for the 1990's. Children need our help, and we must summon the courage to examine the culture that shapes their lives.

# Questions

1. Analyze and evaluate Gore's opening paragraph.
2. Gore says she is not advocating censorship. In a sentence or two state what she *is* advocating. If you agree with her position, what can you add to it? If you disagree, what are the grounds for your disagreement?
3. Consider the songs of some prominent singer, perhaps Madonna, Sade, Michael Jackson, or Bruce Springsteen. Do you find them offensive in any way? If so, explain. If not, explain why parents should not be distressed by the music of the person you have selected.
4. Gore concentrates on rock lyrics, movies, and soap operas. Where

else in our society are we given images of violence and of the degradation of women? Do you think that parents can protect their children from such images? If so, how?

## Marya Mannes

# Television Advertising
## The Splitting Image

$\mathbf{A}$ bride who looks scarcely fourteen whispers, "Oh, Mom, 1 I'm so *happy!*" while a doting family adjust her gown and veil and a male voice croons softly, "A woman is a harder thing to be than a man. She has more feelings to feel." The mitigation of these excesses, it appears, is a feminine deodorant called Secret, which allows our bride to approach the altar with security as well as emotion.

Eddie Albert, a successful actor turned pitchman, bestows his at- 2 tention on a lady with two suitcases, which prompt him to ask her whether she has been on a journey. "No," she says, or words to that effect, as she opens the suitcases. "My two boys bring back their soiled clothes every weekend from college for me to wash." And she goes into the familiar litany of grease, chocolate, mud, coffee, and fruitjuice stains, which presumably record the life of the average American male from two to fifty. Mr. Albert compliments her on this happy device to bring her boys home every week and hands her a box of Biz, because "Biz *is* better."

Two women with stony faces meet cart to cart in a supermarket 3 as one takes a jar of peanut butter off a shelf. When the other asks her in a voice of nitric acid why she takes that brand, the first snaps, "Because I'm choosy for my family!" The two then break into delighted smiles as Number Two makes Number One taste Jif for "mothers who are choosy."

If you have not come across these dramatic interludes, it is because 4 you are not home during the day and do not watch daytime television.

Marya Mannes has published in many journals, from *TV Guide* to *The New Republic*.

It also means that your intestinal tract is spared from severe assaults, your credibility unstrained. Or, for that matter, you may look at commercials like these every day and manage either to ignore them or find nothing—given the fact of advertising—wrong with them. In that case, you are either so brainwashed or so innocent that you remain unaware of what this daily infusion may have done and is doing to an entire people as the long-accepted adjunct of free enterprise and support of "free" television.

"Given the fact" and "long-accepted" are the key words here.   5
Only socialists, communists, idealists (or the BBC) fail to realize that a mass television system cannot exist without the support of sponsors, that the massive cost of maintaining it as a free service cannot be met without the massive income from selling products. You have only to read of the unending struggle to provide financial support for public, noncommercial television for further evidence.

Besides, aren't commercials in the public interest? Don't they help   6
you choose what to buy? Don't they provide needed breaks from programming? Aren't many of them brilliantly done, and some of them funny? And now, with the new sexual freedom, all those gorgeous chicks with their shining hair and gleaming smiles? And if you didn't have commercials taking up a good part of each hour, how on earth would you find enough program material to fill the endless space/time void?

Tick off the yesses and what have you left? You have, I venture   7
to submit, these intangible but possibly high costs: the diminution of human worth, the infusion and hardening of social attitudes no longer valid or desirable, pervasive discontent, and psychic fragmentation.

Should anyone wonder why deception is not an included detri-   8
ment, I suggest that our public is so conditioned to promotion as a way of life, whether in art or politics or products, that elements of exaggeration or distortion are taken for granted. Nobody really believes that a certain shampoo will get a certain swain, or that an unclogged sinus can make a man a swinger. People are merely prepared to hope it will.

But the diminution of human worth is much more subtle and just   9
as pervasive. In the guise of what they consider comedy, the producers of television commercials have created a loathsome gallery of men and women patterned, presumably, on Mr. and Mrs. America. Women liberationists have a major target in the commercial image of woman flashed hourly and daily to the vast majority. There are, indeed, only four kinds of females in this relentless sales procession: the gorgeous

teen-age swinger with bouncing locks; the young mother teaching her baby girl the right soap for skin care; the middle-aged housewife with a voice like a power saw; and the old lady with dentures and irregularity. All these women, to be sure, exist. But between the swinging sex object and the constipated granny there are millions of females never shown in commercials. These are—married or single—intelligent, sensitive women who bring charm to their homes, who work at jobs as well as lend grace to their marriage, who support themselves, who have talents or hobbies or commitments, or who are skilled at their professions.

To my knowledge, as a frequent if reluctant observer, I know of 10 only one woman on a commercial who has a job; a comic plumber pushing Comet. Funny, heh? Think of a dame with a plunger.

With this one representative of our labor force, which is well over 11 thirty million women, we are left with nothing but the full-time housewife in all her whining glory: obsessed with whiter wash, moister cakes, shinier floors, cleaner children, softer diapers, and greaseless fried chicken. In the rare instances when these ladies are not in the kitchen, at the washing machine, or waiting on hubby, they are buying beauty soaps (fantasy, see?) to take home so that their hair will have more body. Or out at the supermarket being choosy.

If they were attractive in their obsessions, they might be bearable. 12 But they are not. They are pushy, loud-mouthed, stupid, and—of all things now—bereft of sexuality. Presumably, the argument in the tenets of advertising is that once a woman marries she changes overnight from plaything to floor-waxer.

To be fair, men make an equivalent transition in commercials. The 13 swinging male with the mod hair and the beautiful chick turns inevitably into the paunchy slob who chokes on his wife's cake. You will notice, however, that the voice urging the viewer to buy the product is nearly always male: gentle, wise, helpful, seductive. And the visible presence telling the housewife how to get shinier floors and whiter wash and lovelier hair is almost invariably a man: the Svengali in modern dress, the Trilby (if only she were!), his willing object.[1]

Woman, in short, is consumer first and human being fourth. A 14 wife and mother who stays home all day buys a lot more than a woman who lives alone or who—married or single—has a job. The young girl

---

[1] In George Du Maurier's novel, *Trilby* (1894), Svengali mesmerizes Trilby and causes her to become a famous singer; when Svengali dies, Trilby loses her voice, dwindles, and soon dies. (Editors' note)

hell-bent on marriage is the next most susceptible consumer. It is entirely understandable, then, that the potential buyers of detergents, foods, polishes, toothpastes, pills, and housewares are the housewives, and that the sex object spends more of *her* money on cosmetics, hair lotions, soaps, mouthwashes, and soft drinks.

Here we come, of course, to the youngest class of consumers, the   15 swinging teen-agers so beloved by advertisers keen on telling them (and us) that they've "got a lot to live, and Pepsi's got a lot to give." This affords a chance to show a squirming, leaping, jiggling group of beautiful kids having a very loud high on rock and—of all things— soda pop. One of commercial TV's most dubious achievements, in fact, is the reinforcement of the self-adulation characteristic of the young as a group.

As for the aging female citizen, the less shown of her the better.   16 She is useful for ailments, but since she buys very little of anything, not having a husband or any children to feed or house to keep, nor— of course—sex appeal to burnish, society and commercials have little place for her. The same is true, to be sure, of older men, who are handy for Bosses with Bad Breath or Doctors with Remedies. Yet, on the whole, men hold up better than women at any age—in life or on television. Lines on their faces are marks of distinction, while on women they are signatures of decay.

There is no question, in any case, that television commercials (and   17 many of the entertainment programs, notably the soap serials that are part of the selling package) reinforce, like an insistent drill, the assumption that a woman's only valid function is that of wife, mother, and servant of men: the inevitable sequel to her earlier function as sex object and swinger.

At a time when more and more women are at long last learning   18 to reject these assumptions as archaic and demeaning, and to grow into individual human beings with a wide option of lives to live, the sellers of the nation are bent upon reinforcing the ancient pattern. They know only too well that by beaming their message to the Consumer Queen they can justify her existence as the housebound Mrs. America: dumber than dumb, whiter than white.

The conditioning starts very early: with the girl child who wants   19 the skin Ivory soap has reputedly given her mother, with the nine-year-old who brings back a cake of Camay instead of the male deodorant her father wanted. (When she confesses that she bought it so she could be "feminine," her father hugs her, and, with the voice of a child-molester, whispers, "My little girl is growing up on me, huh.")

And then, before long, comes the teen-aged bride who "has feelings to feel." It is the little boys who dream of wings, in an airplane commercial; who grow up (with fewer cavities) into the doers. Their little sisters turn into *Cosmopolitan* girls, who in turn become housewives furious that their neighbors' wash is cleaner than theirs.

There is good reason to suspect that this manic obsession with cleanliness, fostered, quite naturally, by the giant soap and detergent interests, may bear some responsibility for the cultivated sloppiness of so many of the young in their clothing as well as in their chosen hideouts. The compulsive housewife who spends more time washing and vacuuming and polishing her possessions than communicating to, or stimulating her children creates a kind of sterility that the young would instinctively reject. The impeccably tidy home, the impeccably tidy lawn are—in a very real sense—unnatural and confining. Yet the commercials confront us with broods of happy children, some of whom—believe it or not—notice the new fresh smell their clean, white sweatshirts exhale thanks to Mom's new "softener." 20

Some major advertisers, for that matter, can even cast a benign eye on the population explosion. In another Biz commercial, the genial Eddie Albert surveys with surprise a long row of dirty clothes heaped before him by a young matron. She answers his natural query by telling him gaily they are the products of her brood of eleven "with one more to come!" she adds as the twelfth turns up. "That's great!" says Mr. Albert, curdling the soul of Planned Parenthood and the future of this planet. 21

Who are, one cannot help but ask, the writers who manage to combine the sales of products with the selling-out of human dreams and dignity? Who people this cosmos of commercials with dolts and fools and shrews and narcissists? Who know so much about quirks and mannerisms and ailments and so little about life? So much about presumed wants and so little about crying needs? 22

Can women advertisers so demean their own sex? Or are there no women in positions of decision high enough to see that their real selves stand up? Do they not know, these extremely clever creators of commercials, what they could do for their audience even while they exploit and entertain them? How they could raise the levels of manners and attitudes while they sell their wares? Or do they really share the worm's-eye view of mass communication that sees, and addresses, only the lowest common denominator? 23

It can be argued that commercials are taken too seriously, that their function is merely to amuse, engage, and sell, and that they do this 24 brilliantly. If that were all to this wheedling of millions, well and good. But it is not. There are two more fallouts from this chronic sales explosion that cannot be measured but that at least can be expected. One has to do with the continual celebration of youth at the expense of maturity. In commercials only the young have access to beauty, sex, and joy in life. What do older women feel, day after day, when love is the exclusive possession of a teen-age girl with a bobbing mantle of hair? What older man would not covet her in restless impotence?

The constant reminder of what is inaccessible must inevitably produce a subterranean but real discontent, just as the continual sight of things and places beyond reach has eaten deeply into the ghetto soul. If we are constantly presented with what we are not or cannot have, the dislocation deepens, contentment vanishes, and frustration reigns. Even for the substantially secure, there is always a better thing, a better way, to buy. That none of these things makes a better life may be consciously acknowledged, but still the desire lodges in the spirit, nagging and pulling. 25

This kind of fragmentation works in potent ways above and beyond the mere fact of program interruption, which is much of the time more of a blessing than a curse, especially in those rare instances when the commercial is deft and funny: the soft and subtle sell. Its overall curse, due to the large number of commercials in each hour, is that it reduces the attention span of a people already so conditioned to constant change and distraction that they cannot tolerate continuity in print or on the air. 26

Specifically, commercial interruption is most damaging during that 10 per cent of programing (a charitable estimate) most important to the mind and spirit of a people: news and public affairs, and drama. To many (and among these are network news producers), commercials have no place or business during the vital process of informing the public. There is something obscene about a newscaster pausing to introduce a deodorant or shampoo commercial between an airplane crash and a body count. It is more than an interruption; it tends to reduce news to a form of running entertainment, to smudge the edges of reality by treating death or disaster or diplomacy on the same level as household appliances or a new gasoline. 27

The answer to this would presumably be to lump the commercials before and after the news or public affairs broadcasts—an answer unpalatable, needless to say, to the sponsors who support them. 28

The same is doubly true of that most unprofitable sector of television, the original play. Essential to any creative composition, 29 whether drama, music or dance, are mood and continuity, both inseparable from form and meaning. They are shattered by the periodic intrusion of commercials, which have become intolerable to the serious artists who have deserted commercial television in droves because the system allows them no real freedom or autonomy. The selling comes first, the creation must accommodate itself. It is the rare and admirable sponsor who restricts or fashions his commercials so as to provide a minimum of intrusion or damaging inappropriateness.

If all these assumptions and imponderables are true, as many suspect, what is the answer or alleviation? 30

One is in the course of difficult emergence: the establishment of 31 a public television system sufficiently funded so that it can give a maximum number of people an alternate diet of pleasure, enlightenment, and stimulation free from commercial fragmentation. So far, for lack of funds to buy talent and equipment, this effort has been in terms of public attention a distinctly minor operation. Even if public television should greatly increase its scope and impact, it cannot in the nature of things and through long public conditioning equal the impact and reach the size of audience now tuned to commercial television.

Enormous amounts of time, money, and talent go into commer- 32 cials. Technically they are often brilliant and innovative, the product not only of the new skills and devices but of imaginative minds. A few of them are both funny and endearing. Who, for instance, will forget the miserable young man with the appalling cold, or the kids taught to use—as an initiation into manhood—a fork instead of a spoon with a certain spaghetti? Among the enlightened sponsors, moreover, are some who manage to combine an image of their corporation and their products with accuracy and restraint.

What has to happen to mass medium advertisers as a whole, and 33 especially on TV, is a totally new approach to their function not only as sellers but as social influencers. They have the same obligation as the broadcast medium itself: not only to entertain but to reflect, not only to reflect but to enlarge public consciousness and human stature.

This may be a tall order, but it is a vital one at a time when Amer- 34 icans have ceased to know who they are and where they are going, and when all the multiple forces acting upon them are daily diminishing their sense of their own value and purpose in life, when social upheaval and social fragmentation have destroyed old patterns, and when survival depends on new ones.

If we continue to see ourselves as the advertisers see us, we have 35 no place to go. Nor, I might add, has commercial broadcasting itself.

# Questions

1. Spend an hour or two looking at daytime television and see if Mannes's observations about the advertisements are accurate.
2. Compare the image of women in daytime advertisements with the image of women in evening advertisements. Are there differences?
3. Mannes says (paragraph 17) that advertisements assume that "a woman's only valid function is that of wife, mother, and servant of men." What do television advertisers assume about a man's "valid function"?
4. In paragraph 20 Mannes suggests: "There is good reason to suspect that this manic obsession with cleanliness, fostered, quite naturally, by the giant soap and detergent interests, may bear some responsibility for the cultivated sloppiness of so many of the young in their clothing as well as in their chosen hideouts." Is there really good reason to suspect this connection? Does Mannes sometimes make doubtful assumptions? If so, point them out.
5. Examine some of Mannes's metaphors, such as "There are two more fallouts from this chronic sales explosion" (paragraph 24), and evaluate them. Are they effective or strained?

Dolores Hayden

# Advertisements, Pornography, and Public Space

Americans need to look more consciously at the ways in   1
which the public domain is misused for spatial displays of gender
stereotypes: These appear in outdoor advertising, and to a lesser extent
in commercial displays, architectural decoration, and public sculpture.

Dolores Hayden was born in New York City in 1945. She did her undergraduate work at Mount Holyoke, and she earned a master's degree in architecture at Harvard. Hayden has taught architecture at the University of California (Berkeley) and at Massachusetts Institute of Technology. She is especially concerned with the political and social implications of public spaces.

While the commercial tone and violence of the American city is often criticized, there is little analysis of the routine way that crude stereotypes appear in public, urban spaces as the staple themes of commercial art. Most Americans are accustomed to seeing giant females in various states of undress smiling and carressing products such as whiskey, food, and records. Male models also sell goods, but they are usually active and clothed—recent ad campaigns aimed at gay men seem to be the first major exception. Several geographers have established that men are most often shown doing active things, posed in the great outdoors; women are shown in reflective postures responding to male demands in interior spaces. As the nineteenth-century sexual double standard is preserved by the urban advertising, many twentieth-century urban men behave as if good women are at home while bad ones adorn the billboards and travel on their own in urban space; at the same time, many urban women are encouraged to think of emotionless, war-mongering, and sexual inexhaustibility as natural to the Marlboro cowboy, war heroes' statues, and every other male adult.

This double standard is the result of advertising practices, graphic  2
design, and urban design. Sanctioned by the zoning laws, billboards are approved by the same urban planning boards who will not permit child care centers or mother-in-law apartments in many residential districts. But the problem with billboards is not only aesthetic degradation. By presenting gender stereotypes in the form of nonverbal body language, fifty feet long and thirty feet high, billboards turn the public space of the city into a stage set for a drama starring enticing women and stern men.

Let us observe outdoor advertising and other urban design phe-  3
nomena with similar effects, as they are experienced by two women on an urban commuting trip along the Sunset Strip in Los Angeles in June 1981. Standing on a street corner, the two women are waiting for a bus to go to work. The bus arrives, bearing a placard on the side advertising a local night club. It shows strippers doing their act, their headless bodies naked from neck to crotch except for a few blue sequins. The two women get on the bus and find seats for the ride along Sunset Boulevard. They look out the windows. As the bus pulls away, their heads appear incongruously above the voluptuous cardboard female bodies displayed on the side. They ride through a district of record company headquarters and film offices, one of the most prosperous in L.A.

Their first views reveal rows of billboards. Silent Marlboro man  4
rides the range; husky, khaki-clad Camel man stares at green hills;

gigantic, uniformed professional athletes catch passes and hit home runs on behalf of booze. These are the male images. Then, on a billboard for whiskey, a horizontal blonde in a backless black velvet dress, slit to the thigh, invites men to "Try on a little Black Velvet." Next, a billboard shows a well-known actress, reclining with legs spread, who notes that avocadoes are only sixteen calories a slice. "Would this body lie to you?" she asks coyly, emphasizing that the body language which communicates blatant sexual availability is only meant to bring attention to her thin figure. Bo Derek offers a pastoral contrast garbed in nothing but a few bits of fur and leather, as she swings on a vine of green leaves, promoting *Tarzan, the Ape Man.*

Next the bus riders pass a club called the Body Shop that advertises 5 "live, nude girls." Two reclining, realistic nudes, one in blue tones in front of a moonlight cityscape, one in orange sunshine tones, stretch their thirty-foot bodies along the sidewalk. This is the same neighborhood where a billboard advertising a Rolling Stones' record album called "Black and Blue" made news ten years ago. A manacled, spread-legged woman with torn clothes proclaimed "I'm Black and Blue from the Rolling Stones—and I love it!" Members of a group called Women Against Violence Against Women (WAVAW) arrived with cans of spray paint and climbed the scaffolding to make small, uneven letters of protest: "This is a crime against women." Demonstrations and boycotts eventually succeeded in achieving the removal of that image, but not in eliminating the graphic design problem. "Black and Blue" has been replaced by James Bond in a tuxedo, pistol in hand, viewed through the spread legs and buttocks of a giant woman in a bathing suit and improbably high heels, captioned "For Your Eyes Only."

When the two women get off the bus in Hollywood, they expe- 6 rience more gender stereotypes as pedestrians. First, they walk past a department store. In the windows mannequins suggest the prevailing ideals of sartorial elegance. The male torsos lean forward, as if they are about to clinch a deal. The female torsos, pin-headed, tip backward and sideways, at odd angles, as if they are about to be pushed over onto a bed. The themes of gender advertisements are trumpeted here in the mannequins' body language as well as on billboards. Next, the women pass an apartment building. Two neoclassical caryatids support the entablature over the front door. Their breasts are bared, their heads carry the load. They recall the architecture of the Erechtheum on the Acropolis in Athens, dating from the 5th century B.C., where the sculptured stone forms of female slaves were used as support for a porch in place of traditional columns and capitals. This is an ancient image of servitude.

After the neo-classical apartment house, the commuters approach 7
a construction site. Here they are subject to an activity traditionally
called "running the gauntlet," but referred to as "girl watching" by
urban sociologist William H. Whyte. Twelve workers stop whatever
they are doing, whistle, and yell: "Hey, baby!" The women put their
heads down, and walk faster, tense with anger. The construction workers take delight in causing exactly this response: "You're cute when
you're mad!" Whyte regards this type of behavior as charming, pedestrian fun in "Street Life," where he even takes pleasure in tracing
its historic antecedents, but he has never been whistled at, hooted at,
and had the dimensions of his body parts analyzed out loud on a public
street.[1]

Finally, these women get to the office building where they work. 8
It has two statues out front of women. Their bronze breasts culminate
in erect nipples. After they pass this last erotic public display of
women's flesh, sanctioned as fine art, they walk in the door to begin
the day's work. Their journey has taken them through an urban landscape filled with images of men as sexual aggressors and women as
submissive sexual objects.

The transient quality of male and female interaction in public 9
streets makes the behavior provoked by billboards and their public
design images particularly difficult to attack. Psychologist Erving Goffman has analyzed both print ads and billboards as *Gender Advertisements* because art directors use exaggerated body language to suggest
that consumers buy not products but images of masculinity or femininity.[2] If passers-by are driving at fifty miles per hour, these gender
cues cannot be subtle. In *Ways of Seeing*, art historian John Berger describes the cumulative problem that gender stereotypes in advertising
create for woman as "split consciousness."[3] While many women guard
themselves, some men assume that ogling is part of normal public life.
Women are always wary, watching men watch them, and wondering
if and when something is going to happen to them.

---

[1] William H. Whyte, "Street Life," *Urban Open Spaces* (Summer 1980), 2. For a more
detailed critique of hassling: Lindsy Van Gelder, "The International Language of
Street Hassling," *Ms.* 9 (May 1981), 15–20, and letters about this article, *Ms.* (Sept.
1981); and Cheryl Benard and Edith Schlaffer, "The Man in the Street: Why He
Harasses," *Ms.* 9 (May 1981), 18–19.
[2] Erving Goffman, *Gender Advertisements* (New York: Harper Colphon, 1976), 24–
27; Nancy Henley, *Body Politics: Power, Sex, and Nonverbal Communication* (Englewood
Cliffs, N.J.: Prentice-Hall, 1977), 30; Marianne Wex, *Let's Take Back Our Space* (Berlin:
Movimento Druck, 1979).
[3] John Berger, et al., *Ways of Seeing* (Harmondsworth, England: BBC and Penguin,
1972), 45–64.

Urban residents also encounter even more explicit sexual images   10
in urban space. Tawdry strip clubs, X-rated films, "adult" bookstores
and sex shops are not uncommon sights. Pornographic video arcades
are the next wave to come. Pornography is a bigger, more profitable
industry in the United States than all legitimate film and record business combined.[4] It spills over into soft-porn, quasi-porn, and tasteless
public imagery everywhere. In the midst of this sex-exploitation, if one
sees a real prostitute, there is mild surprise. Yet soliciting is still a crime.
Of course, the male customer of an adult prostitute is almost never
arrested, but the graphic designer, the urban designer, and the urban
planner never come under suspicion for their contributions to a commercial public landscape that preserves the sexual double standard in
a brutal and vulgar way.

Feminist Laura Shapiro calls our society a "rape culture."[5] Ad-   11
rienne Rich has written of "a world masculinity made unfit for women
or men."[6] But surely most Americans do not consciously, deliberately
accept public space given over to commercial exploitation, violence and
harassment of women. Indeed, the success of the "Moral Majority"
displays how a few activists were able to tap public concern effectively
about commercialized sexuality, albeit in a narrow, antihumanist way.
In contrast, the example of the Women's Christian Temperance Union
under Frances Willard's leadership, and the parks movement under
Olmsted's,[7] show religious idealism, love of nature, and concern for
female safety can be activated into dynamic urban reform movements
that enlarge domestic values into urban values, instead of diminishing
them into domestic pieties.

# Questions

1. What is Hayden's thesis? Where is it stated? How does she support
   it?
2. How does Hayden organize her material? Note, in particular, the
   narrative of two women traveling to work. What does this device
   add to the essay?

---

[4] Tom Hayden, *The American Future: New Visions Beyond Old Frontiers* (Boston: South
End Press, 1980), 15.
[5] Laura Shapiro, "Violence: The Most Obscene Fantasy," in Freeman, ed., *Women:
A Feminist Perspective*, 469–73.
[6] *Ibid.*, 469.
[7] Frederick Law Olmsted (1822–1903) was an American landscape architect. Among
his noble works are Central Park in Manhattan and Prospect Park in Brooklyn.

3. Does Hayden suggest that displays of gender stereotypes contribute to violence against women? Do you believe that they do?
4. In an essay of two or three pages, describe and analyze two billboards, one featuring a man and one featuring a woman. How do they present the "gender stereotypes" that Hayden talks about? Your essay should respond to this question with a clearly formulated thesis sentence (see page 1152).
5. In paragraph 6, Hayden speaks of two "neo-classical caryatids" (architectural pillars in the form of women) flanking a door. She sees these as "an ancient image of servitude." Consult a book such as Spiro Kostof's *History of Architecture* for information about caryatids and then consider whether or not Hayden's interpretation is sound. Formulate a thesis and defend it in a brief essay (a page or a page-and-a-half). Include a citation to the book you have consulted, and, if possible, a photocopy of a picture of a caryatid.
6. If you are familiar with a sculpture of a female figure in a public space in your neighborhood (perhaps in a plaza or in a public building), in a paragraph set forth what the image "says." Or, compare two sculptures, one of a female and one of a male, and explain what each says.
7. In a paragraph or two, describe and analyze a magazine advertisement that promotes gender stereotypes or one that is aimed at gay men. (See Hayden's first paragraph.)

## X. J. Kennedy

# Who Killed King Kong?

The ordeal and spectacular death of King Kong, the giant 1 ape, undoubtedly have been witnessed by more Americans than have ever seen a performance of *Hamlet, Iphigenia at Aulis,* or even *Tobacco Road*. Since RKO-Radio Pictures first released *King Kong,* a quarter-century has gone by; yet year after year, from prints that grow more rain-beaten, from sound tracks that grow more tinny, ticket-buyers by thousands still pursue Kong's luckless fight against the forces of tech-

X. J. Kennedy was born in 1929 in New Jersey. He has published several books of poetry (including a book for children) and several textbooks.

nology, tabloid journalism, and the DAR. They see him chloroformed to sleep, see him whisked from his jungle isle to New York and placed on show, see him burst his chains to roam the city (lugging a frightened blonde), at last to plunge from the spire of the Empire State Building, machine-gunned by model airplanes.

Though Kong may die, one begins to think his legend unkillable.    2
No clearer proof of his hold upon the popular imagination may be seen than what emerged one catastrophic week in March 1955, when New York WOR-TV programmed *Kong* for seven evenings in a row (a total of sixteen showings). Many a rival network vice-president must have scowled when surveys showed that *Kong*—the 1933 B-picture—had lured away fat segments of the viewing populace from such powerful competitors as Ed Sullivan, Groucho Marx and Bishop Sheen.

But even television has failed to run *King Kong* into oblivion. Cof-    3
fee-in-the-lobby cinemas still show the old hunk of hokum, with the apology that in its use of composite shots and animated models the film remains technically interesting. And no other monster in movie history has won so devoted a popular audience. None of the plodding mummies, the stultified Draculas, the white-coated Lugosis with their shiny pinball-machine laboratories, none of the invisible stranglers, berserk robots, or menaces from Mars has ever enjoyed so many res-urrections.

Why does the American public refuse to let King Kong rest in    4
peace? It is true, I'll admit, that *Kong* outdid every monster movie before or since in sheer carnage. Producers Cooper and Schoedsack crammed into it dinosaurs, headhunters, riots, aerial battles, bullets, bombs, bloodletting. Heroine Fay Wray, whose function is mainly to scream, shuts her mouth for hardly one uninterrupted minute from first reel to last. It is also true that *Kong* is larded with good healthy sadism, for those whose joy it is to see the frantic girl dangled from cliffs and harried by pterodactyls. But it seems to me that the abiding appeal of the giant ape rests on other foundations.

Kong has, first of all, the attraction of being manlike. His simian    5
nature gives him one huge advantage over giant ants and walking vegetables in that an audience may conceivably identify with him. Kong's appeal has the quality that established the Tarzan series as American myth—for what man doesn't secretly image himself a huge hairy howler against whom no other monster has a chance? If Tarzan recalls the ape in us, then Kong may well appeal to that great-grand-daddy primordial brute from whose tribe we have all deteriorated.

Intentionally or not, the producers of *King Kong* encourage this   6
identification by etching the character of Kong with keen sympathy.
For the ape is a figure in a tradition familiar to moviegoers: the tradition
of the pitiable monster. We think of Lon Chaney in the role of Quas-
imodo, of Karloff, in the original *Frankenstein*. As we watch the Frankenstein monster's fumbling and disastrous attempts to befriend a
flower-picking child, our sympathies are enlisted with the monster in
his impenetrable loneliness. And so with Kong. As he roars in his
chains, while barkers sell tickets to boobs who gape at him, we perhaps
feel something more deep than pathos. We begin to sense something
of the problem that engaged Eugene O'Neill in *The Hairy Ape*: the dilemma of a displaced animal spirit forced to live in a jungle built by
machines.

*King Kong*, it is true, had special relevance in 1933. Landscapes of   7
the depression are glimpsed early in the film when an impresario,
seeking some desperate pretty girl to play the lead in a jungle movie,
visits souplines and a Woman's Home Mission. In Fay Wray—who's
been caught snitching an apple from a fruitstand—his search is ended.
When he gives her a big feed and a movie contract, the girl is magic-
carpeted out of the world of the National Recovery Act. And when,
in the film's climax, Kong smashes that very Third Avenue landscape
in which Fay had wandered hungry, audiences of 1933 may well have
felt a personal satisfaction.

What is curious is that audiences of 1960 remain hooked. For in   8
the heart of urban man, one suspects, lurks the impulse to fling a bomb.
Though machines speed him to the scene of his daily grind, though
IBM comptometers ("freeing the human mind from drudgery") enable
him to drudge more efficiently once he arrives, there comes a moment
when he wishes to turn upon his machines and kick hell out of them.
He wants to hurl his combination radio-alarmclock out the bedroom
window and listen to its smash. What subway commuter wouldn't
love—just for once—to see the downtown express smack head-on into
the uptown local? Such a wish is gratified in that memorable scene in
*Kong* that opens with a wide-angle shot: interior of a railway car on
the Third Avenue El. Straphangers are nodding, the literate refold their
newspapers. Unknown to them, Kong has torn away a section of trestle
toward which the train now speeds. The motorman spies Kong up
ahead, jams on the brakes. Passengers hurtle together like so many
peas in a pail. In a window of the car appear Kong's bloodshot eyes.
Women shriek. Kong picks up the railway car as if it were a rat, flips

it to the street and ties knots in it, or something. To any commuter the scene must appear one of the most satisfactory pieces of celluloid ever exposed.

Yet however violent his acts, Kong remains a gentleman. Re-    9 markable is his sense of chivalry. Whenever a fresh boa constrictor threatens Fay, Kong first sees that the lady is safely parked, then manfully thrashes her attacker. (And she, the ingrate, runs away every time his back is turned.) Atop the Empire State Building, ignoring his pursuers, Kong places Fay on a ledge as tenderly as if she were a dozen eggs. He fondles her, then turns to face the Army Air Force. And Kong is perhaps the most disinterested lover since Cyrano: His attentions to the lady are utterly without hope of reward. After all, between a five-foot blonde and fifty-foot ape, love can hardly be more than an intellectual flirtation. In his simian way King Kong is the hopelessly yearning lover of Petrarchan convention. His forced exit from his jungle, in chains, results directly from his single-minded pursuit of Fay. He smashes a Broadway theater when the notion enters his dull brain that the flashbulbs of photographers somehow endanger the lady. His perilous shinnying up a skyscraper to pluck Fay from her boudoir is an act of the kindliest of hearts. He's impossible to discourage even though the love of his life can't lay eyes on him without shrieking murder.

The tragedy of King Kong then, is to be the beast who at the end    10 of the fable fails to turn into the handsome prince. This is the conviction that the scriptwriters would leave with us in the film's closing line. As Kong's corpse lies blocking traffic in the street, the entrepreneur who brought Kong to New York turns to the assembled reporters and proclaims: "That's your story, boys—it was Beauty killed the Beast!" But greater forces than those of the screaming Lady have combined to lay Kong low, if you ask me. Kong lives for a time as one of those persecuted near-animal souls bewildered in the middle of an industrial order, whose simple desires are thwarted at every turn. He climbs the Empire State Building because in all New York it's the closest thing he can find to the clifftop of his jungle isle. He dies, a pitiful dolt, and the army brass and publicity-men cackle over him. His death is the only possible outcome to as neat a tragic dilemma as you can ask for. The machine-guns do him in, while the manicured human hero (a nice clean Dartmouth boy) carries away Kong's sweetheart to the altar. O, the misery of it all. There's far more truth about upper-middle-class American life in *King Kong* than in the last seven dozen novels of John P. Marquand.

A Negro friend from Atlanta tells me that in movie houses in col-  11
ored neighborhoods throughout the South, *Kong* does a constant business. They show the thing in Atlanta at least every year, presumably
to the same audiences. Perhaps this popularity may simply be due to
the fact that Kong is one of the most watchable movies ever constructed, but I wonder whether Negro audiences may not find some
archetypical appeal in this serio-comic tale of a huge black powerful
free spirit whom all the hardworking white policemen are out to kill.

Every day in the week on a screen somewhere in the world, King  12
Kong relives his agony. Again and again he expires on the Empire
State Building, as audiences of the devout assist his sacrifice. We watch
him die, and by extension kill the ape within our bones, but these little
deaths of ours occur in prosaic surroundings. We do not die on a tower,
New York before our feet, nor do we give our lives to smash a few
flying machines. It is not for us to bring to a momentary standstill the
civilization in which we move. King Kong does this for us. And so we
kill him again and again, in much-spliced celluloid, while the ape in
us expires from day to day, obscure, in desperation.

# Questions

1. What is your response to Kennedy's colloquial expressions, such
   as "lugging a frightened blonde," "hunk of hokum," "snitching an
   apple"? Are they used for a purpose?
2. In paragraph 3 Kennedy calls *King Kong* "the old hunk of hokum."
   Does he consistently maintain the attitude implied here?
3. How persuasive do you find Kennedy's analysis? Is any of it useful
   in explaining the appeal of other films you have seen?
4. Kennedy refers to *King Kong* as a "monster movie." Can you think
   of other films you would place in that category? How would you
   define "horror movie" or "disaster film" or "science fiction film"?
   Are these, and "monster movie," distinct or overlapping categories?

Ursula K. Le Guin

# American SF and
# The Other

One of the great early socialists said that the status of 1
women in a society is a pretty reliable index of the degree of civilization
of that society. If this is true, then the very low status of women in
SF should make us ponder about whether SF is civilized at all.

The women's movement has made most of us conscious of the 2
fact that SF has either totally ignored women, or presented them as
squeaking dolls subject to instant rape by monsters—or old-maid scientists desexed by hypertrophy of the intellectual organs—or, at best,
loyal little wives or mistresses of accomplished heroes. Male elitism
has run rampant in SF. But is it only male elitism? Isn't the "subjection
of women" in SF merely a symptom of a whole which is authoritarian,
power-worshiping, and intensely parochial?

The question involved here is the question of The Other—the 3
being who is different from yourself. This being can be different from
you in its sex; or in its annual income; or in its way of speaking and
dressing and doing things; or in the color of its skin, or the number
of its legs and heads. In other words, there is the sexual Alien, and
the social Alien, and the cultural Alien, and finally the racial Alien.

Well, how about the social Alien in SF? How about, in Marxist 4
terms, "the proletariat"? Where are they in SF? Where are the poor,
the people who work hard and go to bed hungry? Are they ever *persons*,
in SF? No. They appear as vast anonymous masses fleeing from giant
slime-globules from the Chicago sewers, or dying off by the billion
from pollution or radiation, or as faceless armies being led to battle by
generals and statesmen. In sword and sorcery they behave like the
walk-on parts in a high-school performance of *The Chocolate Prince*.
Now and then there's a busty lass amongst them who is honored by
the attentions of the Captain of the Supreme Terran Command, or in

Ursula K. Le Guin was born in 1919. She has won Hugo and Nebula awards for
her science fiction. Among her best-known works are the Earthsea Trilogy, *The
Lathe of Heaven*, and *Malafrena*.

a spaceship crew there's a quaint old cook, with a Scots or Swedish accent, representing the Wisdom of the Common Folk.

The people, in SF, are not people. They are masses, existing for one purpose: to be led by their superiors. 5

From a social point of view most SF has been incredibly regressive 6 and unimaginative. All those Galactic Empires, taken straight from the British Empire of 1880. All those planets—with 80 trillion miles between them!—conceived of as warring nation-states, or as colonies to be exploited, or to be nudged by the benevolent Imperium of Earth toward self-development—the White Man's Burden all over again. The Rotary Club on Alpha Centauri, that's the size of it.

What about the cultural and the racial Other? This is the Alien 7 everybody recognizes as alien, supposed to be the special concern of SF. Well, in the old pulp SF, it's very simple. The only good alien is a dead alien—whether he is an Aldebaranian Mantis-Man, or a German dentist. And this tradition still flourishes: witness Larry Niven's story "Inconstant Moon" (in *All the Myriad Ways*, 1971) which has a happy ending—consisting of the fact that America, including Los Angeles, was not hurt by a solar flare. Of course a few million Europeans and Asians were fried, but that doesn't matter, it just makes the world a little safer for democracy, in fact. (It is interesting that the female character in the same story is quite brainless; her only function is to say Oh? and Ooooh! to the clever and resourceful hero.)

Then there's the other side of the same coin. If you hold a thing 8 to be totally different from yourself, your fear of it may come out as hatred, or as awe—reverence. So we get all those wise and kindly beings who deign to rescue Earth from her sins and perils. The Alien ends up on a pedestal in a white nightgown and a virtuous smirk— exactly as the "good woman" did in the Victorian Age.

In America, it seems to have been Stanley Weinbaum who invented 9 the sympathetic alien, in *A Martian Odyssey*. From then on, via people like Cyril Kornbluth, Ted Sturgeon, and Cordwainer Smith, SF began to inch its way out of simple racism. Robots—the alien intelligence— begin to behave nicely. With Smith, interestingly enough, the racial alien is combined with the social alien, in the "Underpeople," and they are allowed to have a revolution. As the aliens got more sympathetic, so did the heroes. They began to have emotions, as well as rayguns. Indeed they began to become almost human.

If you deny any affinity with another person or kind of person, if 10 you declare it to be wholly different from yourself—as men have done

to women, and class has done to class, and nation has done to nation—
you may hate it, or deify it; but in either case you have denied its
spiritual equality, and its human reality. You have made it into a thing,
to which the only possible relationship is a power relationship. And
thus you have fatally impoverished your own reality. You have, in
fact, alienated yourself.

This tendency has been remarkably strong in American SF. The  11
only social change presented by most SF has been toward authoritarianism, the domination of ignorant masses by a powerful elite—sometimes presented as a warning, but often quite complacently. Socialism
is never considered as an alternative, and democracy is quite forgotten.
Military virtues are taken as ethical ones. Wealth is assumed to be a
righteous goal and a personal virtue. Competitive free-enterprise capitalism is the economic destiny of the entire Galaxy. In general, American SF has assumed a permanent hierarchy of superiors and inferiors,
with rich, ambitious, aggressive males at the top, then a great gap,
and then at the bottom the poor, the uneducated, the faceless masses,
and all the women. The whole picture is, if I may say so, curiously
"un-American." It is a perfect baboon patriarchy, with the Alpha Male
on top, being respectfully groomed, from time to time, by his inferiors.

Is this speculation? Is this imagination? Is this extrapolation? I call  12
it brainless regressivism.

I think it's time SF writers—and their readers!—stopped day-  13
dreaming about a return to the age of Queen Victoria, and started
thinking about the future. I would like to see the Baboon Ideal replaced
by a little human idealism, and some serious consideration of such
deeply radical, futuristic concepts as Liberty, Equality, and Fraternity.
And remember that about 53 percent of the Brotherhood of Man is the
Sisterhood of Woman.

# Questions

1. Le Guin, like many others, refers to science fiction as SF. What
   does that tell us about the audience she writes for and her relationship with it?
2. If you have read some science fiction or seen some science-fiction
   films, evaluate the following statements in light of your experiences:
   (a) ". . . the very low status of women in SF should make us pon-
       der about whether SF is civilized at all" (paragraph 1).
   (b) "The people, in SF, are not people. They are masses, existing
       for one purpose: to be led by their superiors" (paragraph 5).

   (c)   "Competitive free-enterprise capitalism is the economic destiny of the entire Galaxy" (paragraph 11).
Or choose another strong statement from Le Guin's essay and either support it or contest it, using the examples of SF with which you are familiar.

3.   Le Guin is highly critical of SF. How might it be defended? Can it be argued, for example, that no work of literature can show the whole of reality? Or can science fiction (such as Le Guin describes) be defended on the grounds that it offers a healthy warning about the dangers of science?

## Stephen King

# Why We Crave Horror Movies

**I** think that we're all mentally ill; those of us outside the asylums only hide it a little better—and maybe not all that much better, after all. We've all known people who talk to themselves, people who sometimes squinch their faces into horrible grimaces when they believe no one is watching, people who have some hysterical fear—of snakes, the dark, the tight place, the long drop . . . and, of course, those final worms and grubs that are waiting so patiently underground.

When we pay our four or five bucks and seat ourselves at tenth-row center in a theater showing a horror movie, we are daring the nightmare.

Why? Some of the reasons are simple and obvious. To show that we can, that we are not afraid, that we can ride this roller coaster. Which is not to say that a really good horror movie may not surprise a scream out of us at some point, the way we may scream when the

Stephen King, with 50 millions copies of his books in print, is one of America's most popular authors. King was born in Portland, Maine, in 1947. After graduating from the University of Maine he taught English in high school until he was able to devote himself full-time to writing. In addition to writing stories and novels—some of which have been made into films—he has written *Danse Macabre*, a book that, like the essay we reprint here, discusses the appeal of horror.

roller coaster twists through a complete 360 or plows through a lake at the bottom of the drop. And horror movies, like roller coasters, have always been the special province of the young; by the time one turns 40 or 50, one's appetite for double twists or 360-degree loops may be considerably depleted.

We also go to re-establish our feelings of essential normality; the 4 horror movie is innately conservative, even reactionary. Freda Jackson as the horrible melting woman in *Die, Monster, Die!* confirms for us that no matter how far we may be removed from the beauty of a Robert Redford or a Diana Ross, we are still light-years from true ugliness.

And we go to have fun.                                                     5

Ah, but this is where the ground starts to slope away, isn't it? 6 Because this is a very peculiar sort of fun, indeed. The fun comes from seeing others menaced—sometimes killed. One critic has suggested that if pro football has become the voyeur's version of combat, then the horror film has become the modern version of the public lynching.

It is true that the mythic, "fairy-tale" horror film intends to take 7 away the shades of gray. . . . It urges us to put away our more civilized and adult penchant for analysis and to become children again, seeing things in pure blacks and whites. It may be that horror movies provide psychic relief on this level because this invitation to lapse into simplicity, irrationality and even outright madness is extended so rarely. We are told we may allow our emotions a free rein . . . or no rein at all.

If we are all insane, then sanity becomes a matter of degree. If 8 your insanity leads you to carve up women like Jack the Ripper or the Cleveland Torso Murderer, we clap you away in the funny farm (but neither of those two amateur-night surgeons was ever caught, heh-heh-heh); if, on the other hand, your insanity leads you only to talk to yourself when you're under stress or to pick your nose on your morning bus, then you are left alone to go about your business . . . though it is doubtful that you will ever be invited to the best parties.

The potential lyncher is in almost all of us (excluding saints, past 9 and present; but then, most saints have been crazy in their own ways), and every now and then, he has to be let loose to scream and roll around in the grass. Our emotions and our fears form their own body, and we recognize that it demands its own exercise to maintain proper muscle tone. Certain of these emotional muscles are accepted—even exalted—in civilized society; they are, of course, the emotions that tend to maintain the status quo of civilization itself. Love, friendship, loyalty, kindness—these are all the emotions that we applaud, emotions that have been immortalized in the couplets of Hallmark cards and in the verses (I don't dare call it poetry) of Leonard Nimoy.

When we exhibit these emotions, society showers us with positive 10 reinforcement; we learn this even before we get out of diapers. When, as children, we hug our rotten little puke of a sister and give her a kiss, all the aunts and uncles smile and twit and cry, "Isn't he the sweetest little thing?" Such coveted treats as chocolate-covered graham crackers often follow. But if we deliberately slam the rotten little puke of a sister's fingers in the door, sanctions follow—angry remonstrance from parents, aunts and uncles; instead of a chocolate-covered graham cracker, a spanking.

But anticivilization emotions don't go away, and they demand pe- 11 riodic exercise. We have such "sick" jokes as, "What's the difference between a truckload of bowling balls and a truckload of dead babies?" (You can't unload a truckload of bowling balls with a pitchfork . . . a joke, by the way, that I heard originally from a ten-year-old). Such a joke may surprise a laugh or a grin out of us even as we recoil, a possibility that confirms the thesis: If we share a brotherhood of man, then we also share an insanity of man. None of which is intended as a defense of either the sick joke or insanity but merely as an explanation of why the best horror films, like the best fairy tales, manage to be reactionary, anarchistic, and revolutionary all at the same time.

The mythic horror movie, like the sick joke, has a dirty job to do. 12 It deliberately appeals to all that is worst in us. It is morbidity unchained, our most base instincts let free, our nastiest fantasies realized . . . and it all happens, fittingly enough, in the dark. For those reasons, good liberals often shy away from horror films. For myself, I like to see the most aggressive of them—*Dawn of the Dead*, for instance—as lifting a trap door in the civilized forebrain and throwing a basket of raw meat to the hungry alligators swimming around in that subterranean river beneath.

Why bother? Because it keeps them from getting out, man. It keeps 13 them down there and me up here. It was Lennon and McCartney who said that all you need is love, and I would agree with that.

As long as you keep the gators fed. 14

# Questions

1. In paragraph 6 King, paraphrasing an unnamed critic, suggests that "the horror film has become the modern version of the public lynching." In your opinion, why did some people find excitement in a

lynching? Does the horror film offer somewhat similar excite-
ment(s)?

2.  King suggests, in paragraph 11, that we have within us a stock of
    "anticivilization emotions [that] don't go away, and they demand
    periodic exercise." What, if any, evidence are you aware of that
    supports this view?

3.  In paragraph 11 King tells a joke about dead babies. He suggests
    that jokes of this sort "may surprise a laugh or a grin out of us even
    as we recoil." Analyze your own response to the joke, or to similar
    jokes. Did you laugh, or grin? Or was your response utterly dif-
    ferent? If so, what was it?

4.  In paragraphs 12 and 13 King says that horror movies serve a val-
    uable social purpose. Do you think he has proved his point? What
    are the strengths (if any) and the weaknesses (if any) of his argu-
    ment?

5.  Read Tipper Gore's essay (page 662). Then respond to King's ar-
    gument as you think she might.

## Woody Allen

# The Colorization of Films Insults Artists and Society

In the world of potent self-annihilation, famine and AIDS,    1
terrorists and dishonest public servants and quack evangelists and con-
tras and Sandinistas and cancer, does it really matter if some kid snaps
on his TV and happens to see *The Maltese Falcon* in color? Especially if
he can simply dial the color out and choose to view it in its original
black and white?

Woody Allen, born in Brooklyn in 1935, began writing comic monologues while
he was in high school. He soon wrote for Sid Caesar and Art Carney, and then
developed a nightclub act of his own. Although he still publishes an occasional
story in *The New Yorker,* he is now engaged chiefly in writing and directing films
and in acting in them.

I think it does make a difference and the ramifications of what's    2
called colorization are not wonderful to contemplate. Simply put, the
owners of thousands of classic American black and white films believe
that there would be a larger public for the movies, and consequently
more money, if they were reissued in color. Since they have computers
that can change such masterpieces as *Citizen Kane* and *City Lights* and
*It's A Wonderful Life* into color, it has become a serious problem for
anyone who cares about these movies and has feelings about our image
of ourselves as a culture.

I won't comment about the quality of the color. It's not good, but    3
probably it will get better. Right now it's like elevator music. It has no
soul. All faces are rendered with the same deadening pleasance. The
choices of what colors people should be wearing or what colors rooms
should be (all crucial artistic decisions in making a film) are left to
caprices and speculations by computer technicians who are not qualified to make those choices.

Probably false, but not worth debating here, is the claim that young    4
people won't watch black and white. I would think they would, judging from the amount of stylish music videos and MTV ads that are
done in black and white, undoubtedly after market research. The fact
that audiences of all ages have been watching Charlie Chaplin, Hum-
phrey Bogart, Jimmy Stewart, Fred Astaire—in fact, all the stars and
films of the so-called Golden Age of Hollywood—in black and white
for decades with no diminution of joy also makes me wonder about
these high claims for color. Another point the coloroids make is that
one can always view the original if one prefers. The truth is, however,
that in practical terms, what will happen is that the color versions will
be aired while token copies of the original black and white will lie
around preserved in a vault, unpromoted and unseen.

Another aspect of the problem that one should mention (although    5
it is not the crucial ground on which I will make my stand) is that
American films are a landmark heritage that do our nation proud all
over the world, and should be seen as they were intended to be. One
would wince at defacing great buildings or paintings, and, in the case
of movies, what began as a popular entertainment has, like jazz music,
developed into a serious art form. Now, someone might ask: "Is an
old Abbott and Costello movie art? Should it be viewed in the same
way as *Citizen Kane?*" The answer is that it should be protected, because
all movies are entitled to their personal integrity and, after all, who
knows what future generations will regard as art works of our epoch?

Yet another question: "Why were directors not up in arms about    6 cutting films for television or breaking them up for commercials, insulting them with any number of technical alterations to accommodate the television format?" The answer is that directors always hated these assaults on their work but were powerless to stop them. As in life, one lives with the first few wounds, because to do battle is an overwhelmingly time-consuming and pessimistic prospect.

Still, when the assaults come too often, there is a revolution. The 7 outrage of seeing one's work transformed into color is so dramatically appalling, so "obvious"—as against stopping sporadically for commercials—that this time all the directors, writers and actors chose to fight.

But let me get to the real heart of the matter and to why I think 8 the issue is not merely one that affronts the parties directly involved but has a larger meaning. What's at stake is a moral issue and how our culture chooses to define itself. No one should be able to alter an artist's work in any way whatsoever, for any reason, without the artist's consent. It's really as simple as that.

John Huston has made it clear that he doesn't want *The Maltese* 9 *Falcon* seen in color. This is his right as an artist and certainly must be his choice alone. Nor would I want to see my film *Manhattan* in color. Not if it would bring in 10 times the revenue. Not if all the audiences in the world begged or demanded to see it that way.

I believe the people who are coloring movies have contempt for 10 the audience by claiming, in effect, that viewers are too stupid and too insensitive to appreciate black and white photography—that they must be given, like infants or monkeys, bright colors to keep them amused. They have contempt for the artsit, caring little for the moral right these directors have over their own creations. And, finally, they have contempt for society because they help define it as one that chooses to milk every last dollar out of its artists' work, even if it means mutilating the work and humiliating the culture's creative talent.

This is how we are viewed around the world and how we will be 11 viewed by future generations. Most civilized governments abroad, realizing that their society is at least as much shaped and identified by its artists as by its businessmen, have laws to protect such things from happening. In our society, merchants are willing to degrade anything or anyone so long as it brings in a financial profit. Allowing the colorization of films is a good example of our country's regard for its artists, and why I think the issue of moral rights requires legislative help and protection.

The recent Federal copyright decision says that if a human being 12 uses a certain minimum amount of creativity in coloring a black and white film, the new color version is a separate work that can be copyrighted. In short, if a man colors *Citizen Kane,* it becomes a new movie that can be copyrighted. This must be changed. How? By making sure that Representative Richard A. Gephardt's film integrity bill is passed. It would legalize the moral rights of film artists and, in the process, make colorization without consent illegal.

It is, after all, a very short step to removing the score from *Gone*  13
*With the Wind* and replacing it with a rock score under the mistaken notion that it will render it more enjoyable to young people.

# Questions

1. We find Allen's argumentative strategy worth analyzing. But first, restate in a sentence or two the point he is arguing and the occasion that prompted it. (Note that Allen reports the occasion in his next-to-last paragraph.)

   Now look at Allen's opening paragraph. What does it assume about his audience? What does Allen imply about himself in relation to his audience?

2. In paragraph 2 Allen contrasts two groups. How does he make sure that you will identify yourself with one group and not with the other?

3. In paragraph 3, what words or phrases strike you as particularly lively or persuasive?

4. In paragraph 4 Allen says that "the claim that young people won't watch black and white" is "not worth debating." What does the rest of the paragraph do? Again, what particularly effective words or phrases underscore the point?

5. To what emotions does Allen appeal in paragraph 5?

6. Now consider the substance of his argument. In paragraph 8 Allen says, "No one should be able to alter an artist's work in any way whatsoever, for any reason, without the artist's consent. It's really as simple as that." Do you agree? If so, would you agree to the following propositions? Why or why not?

   a. Producers should be prohibited from showing on television films intended for the theater, unless the producers have the consent of the film director.

   b. Similarly, filmmakers should be prohibted from filming a novel, play, opera, or ballet without the consent of the author or composer. If the author or composer is dead, well, that's unfortunate, but the work cannot be adapted to a film.

What parallel strictures might govern the display of objects in museums, reproductions of works of art, and the translation of classic works of literature?

7.  Finally, consider some black and white film that you admire. What do you think would be lost (or gained) by colorization? (If you have seen the original black and white film and also a colorized version, of course you are in a good position to make comparisons. But in any case you can make a "thought-experiment." You might, for example, imagine a colorized version of Woody Allen's *Manhattan*.)

Stanley Milgram

# Confessions of a News Addict

Let me begin with a confession. I am a news addict. Upon awakening I flip on the *Today* show to learn what events transpired during the night. On the commuter train which takes me to work, I scour *The New York Times*, and find myself absorbed in tales of earthquakes, diplomacy, and economics. I read the newspaper as religiously as my grandparents read their prayerbooks. The sacramental character of the news extends into the evening. The length of my workday is determined precisely by my need to get home in time for Walter Cronkite. My children understand that my communion with Cronkite is something serious and cannot be interrupted for light and transient causes.

But what is it, precisely, that is happening when I and millions of others scour our newspapers, stare at the tube, and pour over the news magazines that surround us? Does it make sense? What is news, and why does it occupy a place of special significance for so many people?

Let us proceed from a simple definition: news is information about

Stanley Milgram, at the time of his death in 1984, was a professor of social psychology at the Graduate Center of the City University of New York. His best-known work is a book entitled *Obedience to Authority*.

events that are going on outside immediate experience. In this sense, news has always been a part of the human situation. In its earliest form, it took the shape of an account brought by a traveler, or a member of the group who wandered further than the rest and found water, game, or signs of a nearby enemy. The utility of such information is self-evident. News is a social mechanism that extends our own eyes and ears to embrace an ever wider domain of events. A knowledge of remote events allows us to prepare for them and take whatever steps are needed to deal with them. This is the classic function of news.

News is the consciousness of Society. It is the means whereby 4 events in the body politic are brought into awareness. And it is curious that regimes which we call *repressive* tend to exhibit the same characteristic of repressed personalities; they are unable, or unwilling, to allow conflictive material into awareness. The disability stems from deep insecurities. The censoring of the repressed material does not eliminate it, but forces it to fester without anyone's rationally coming to grips with it.

Inevitably news comes to be controlled by the dominant political 5 forces of a society. In a totalitarian regime the government attempts to create the image of a world, and of events, that reflects most favorably on those in power. The democratization of news, which goes hand in hand with the diffusion of political power among those governed, is a relatively recent development whose permanence cannot be assured. Democracies are far better able to cope with the reality of events than are totalitarian regimes. Such regimes promulgate a myth of their omnipotence, and are threatened even by events outside the control of the political process. Thus, typically, the Soviet press does not report air crashes, and even natural disasters such as earthquakes are suppressed, out of the notion—rooted in political insecurity—that the event in some manner reflects badly on the regime.

The question for any society is not whether there shall be news, 6 but rather who shall have access to it. Every political system may be characterized by the proportion of information it has which is shared with the people and the proportion withheld. That is why the growth of secret news-gathering agencies, such as the C.I.A., is a troubling one for a democracy. It appears our government wants to keep some news to itself.

At a deeper historical level we can see that news in its present 7 form is closely tied to the rise of the economy, and specifically to the exploitative and risk elements of capitalism. For the nineteenth-century merchant, news meant reports of his ship, of resources to exploit, and the means of minimizing the risk element inherent in entrepreneurship by gaining as much information as possible before his competitors. News services, such as Reuters, developed to serve business and investment interests, who discovered that getting the news quickly was the first step to financial gain.

In a civilization in which all activities tend toward commercial 8 expression—for example, our own—news becomes a product to manufacture and dispense to the consumer. Thus a large-scale industry for the production and consumption of news has evolved. We ingest it with the same insatiable appetite that moves us to purchase the manifold products of our commercial civilization.

News under such circumstances tends toward decadent use. It no 9 longer serves first the classic function of giving us information on which to act, or even to help us construct a mental model of the larger world. It serves mainly as entertainment. The tales of earthquakes, political assassinations, and bitterly fought elections are the heady stuff of which drama or melodrama is made. Happily, we are able to indulge our taste for thriller, romance, or murder mystery under the guise of a patently respectable pursuit. All enlightened people are supposed to know what is going on in the world. If what is going on also happens to be thrilling and exciting, so much the better.

Another feature of the decadent use of news is its increasing rit- 10 ualization. The information becomes subservient to the form in which it is delivered. News is broadcast every evening, whether or not there is vital information to be conveyed. Indeed, the problem for the news networks is to generate sufficient news to fill a given time period. The time period becomes the fundamental fact, the framework into which events must be fitted. As in any ritual, the form persists even when a meaningful content is missing.

Those groups whose survival and well-being are most affected by 11 remote events will be most persistently attuned to them. For example, Israelis, who view the survival of their state as a day-to-day contingency, are among the most news-oriented people in the world. During periods of crisis, portable radios blare in buses and in the market place. Jews, in general, have felt the need to develop antennae for remote events because of a communal insecurity. Any event, no matter how remote—even a farcical *putsch* in Munich led by a paper hanger—may grow into a formidable threat. Thus, constant monitoring of events is strongly reinforced.

Although I am a news addict, my addiction is strongest for news 12 that in many respects seems most remote from my own life and experience. International news receives top priority, followed by national domestic news, and finally—and of least interest—local news. I feel more concerned reading about a student strike in Paris than a murder in my own neighborhood. I am especially uninterested in those news programs that provide a constant litany of fires and local crimes as their standard fare. Yet there is a paradox in this. Surely a criminal loose in my city is of greater personal consequence than an election outcome in Uruguay. Indeed, I sometimes ask what difference it makes to the actual conduct of my life to know about a fracas in Zaire, or a train wreck in Sweden. The total inconsequence of the news for my life is most strikingly brought home when we return from a vacation of several weeks where we have been without any news. I normally scan the accumulated pile of newspapers, but cannot help noticing how little difference it all made to me. And least consequential of all were those remote international events that so rivet my attention in the normal course of the week.

Why this interest in things far away, with a lesser interest in events 13 close at home? Perhaps it is essentially a romantic impulse in the projection of meaning into remote countries, places, and people. Such a romantic impulse stems from a dissatisfaction with the mundane reality of everyday life. The events and places described in the news are remote, and thus we can more readily fix our imaginative sentiments to them. Moreover, an interest in news reinforces the "cosmopolitan" attitude which characterizes modern life, a desire to focus not only on the immediate community, but on the larger world. It is thus the opposite of the "provincialism" which characterized an earlier rural existence.

Living in the modern world, I cannot help but be shaped by it, 14 suckered by the influence and impact of our great institutions. *The New York Times*, *CBS*, and *Newsweek* have made me into a news addict. In daily life I have come to accept the supposition that if *The New York Times* places a story on the front page, it deserves my attention. I feel obligated to know what is going on. But sometimes, in quieter moments, another voice asks: If the news went away, would the world be any worse for it?

# Questions

1. Why does Milgram describe himself as an "addict" and call his essay "confessions"? How seriously is he using the term? (Consider the connotations of "addict" compared with "reader," "consumer," and "fan.")

2. What reasons does Milgram give for being more interested in "things far away" than in "events close at home"? Do you find his reasons adequate? In answering this question reflect on the three or four items of news that have been of absorbing interest to you. What did those items have in common? Why did they interest you?

James Thurber

# The Secret Life of Walter Mitty

W e're going through!" The Commander's voice was like   1
thin ice breaking. He wore his full-dress uniform, with the heavily braided white cap pulled down rakishly over one cold gray eye. "We can't make it, sir. It's spoiling for a hurricane, if you ask me." "I'm not asking you, Lieutenant Berg," said the Commander. "Throw on the power lights! Rev her up to 8,500! We're going through!" The pounding of the cylinders increased; ta-pocketa-pocketa-pocketa-*pocketa-pocketa*. The Commander stared at the ice forming on the pilot window. He walked over and twisted a row of complicated dials. "Switch on No. 8 auxiliary!" he shouted. "Switch on No. 8 auxiliary!" repeated Lieutenant Berg. "Full strength in No. 3 turret!" shouted the Commander. "Full strength in No. 3 turret!" The crew, bending to their various tasks in the huge, hurtling eight-engined Navy hydroplane, looked at each other and grinned. "The Old Man'll get us through," they said to one another. "The Old Man ain't afraid of Hell!" . . .

"Not so fast! You're driving too fast!" said Mrs. Mitty. "What are   2
you driving so fast for?"

"Hmm?" said Walter Mitty. He looked at his wife, in the seat   3
beside him, with shocked astonishment. She seemed grossly unfamiliar, like a strange woman who had yelled at him in a crowd. "You were up to fifty-five," she said. "You know I don't like to go more

---

James Thurber (1894–1961) published most of his essays, stories, and cartoons in *The New Yorker*.

than forty. You were up to fifty-five." Walter Mitty drove on toward Waterbury in silence, the roaring of the SN202 through the worst storm in twenty years of Navy flying fading in the remote, intimate airways of his mind. "You're tensed up again," said Mrs. Mitty. "It's one of your days. I wish you'd let Dr. Renshaw look you over."

Walter Mitty stopped the car in front of the building where his 4 wife went to have her hair done. "Remember to get those overshoes while I'm having my hair done," she said. "I don't need overshoes," said Mitty. She put her mirror back into her bag. "We've been all through that," she said, getting out of the car. "You're not a young man any longer." He raced the engine a little. "Why don't you wear your gloves? Have you lost your gloves?" Walter Mitty reached in a pocket and brought out the gloves. He put them on, but after she had turned and gone into the building and he had driven on to a red light, he took them off again. "Pick it up, brother," snapped a cop as the light changed, and Mitty hastily pulled on his gloves and lurched ahead. He drove around the streets aimlessly for a time, and then he drove past the hospital on his way to the parking lot.

. . . "It's the millionaire banker, Wellington McMillan," said the 5 pretty nurse. "Yes?" said Walter Mitty, removing his gloves slowly. "Who has the case?" "Dr. Renshaw and Dr. Benbow, but there are two specialists here, Dr. Remington from New York and Dr. Pritchard-Mitford from London. He flew over." A door opened down a long, cool corridor and Dr. Renshaw came out. He looked distraught and haggard. "Hello, Mitty," he said. "We're having the devil's own time with McMillan, the millionaire banker and close personal friend of Roosevelt. Obstreosis of the ductal tract. Tertiary. Wish you'd take a look at him." "Glad to," said Mitty.

In the operating room there were whispered introductions: "Dr. 6 Remington, Dr. Mitty. Dr. Pritchard-Mitford, Dr. Mitty." "I've read your book on streptothricosis," said Pritchard-Mitford, shaking hands. "A brilliant performance, sir." "Thank you," said Walter Mitty. "Didn't know you were in the States, Mitty," grumbled Remington. "Coals to Newcastle, bringing Mitford and me up here for a tertiary." "You are very kind," said Mitty. A huge, complicated machine, connected to the operating table, with many tubes and wires, began at this moment to go pocketa-pocketa-pocketa. "The new anaesthetizer is giving away!" shouted an interne. "There is no one in the East who knows how to fix it!" "Quiet, man!" said Mitty, in a low, cool voice. He sprang to the machine, which was now going pocketa-pocketa-queep-pocketa-queep. He began fingering delicately a row of glistening dials. "Give me a fountain pen!" he snapped. Someone handed him a fountain pen. He pulled a faulty piston out of the machine and inserted the pen in its place. "That will hold for ten minutes," he said. "Get on with the operation." A nurse hurried over and whispered to Renshaw, and Mitty saw the man turn pale. "Coreopsis has set in," said Renshaw nervously. "If you would take over, Mitty?" Mitty looked at him and at the craven figure of Benbow, who drank, and at the grave, uncertain faces of the two great specialists. "If you wish," he said. They slipped a white gown on him; he adjusted a mask and drew on thin gloves; nurses handed him shining . . .

"Back it up, Mac! Look out for that Buick!" Walter Mitty jammed    7 on the brakes. "Wrong lane, Mac," said the parking-lot attendant, looking at Mitty closely. "Gee. Yeh," muttered Mitty. He began cautiously to back out of the lane marked "Exit Only." "Leave her sit there," said the attendant. "I'll put her away." Mitty got out of the car. "Hey, better leave the key." "Oh," said Mitty, handing the man the ignition key. The attendant vaulted into the car, backed it up with insolent skill, and put it where it belonged.

They're so damn cocky, thought Walter Mitty, walking along Main    8 Street; they think they know everything. Once he had tried to take his chains off, outside New Milford, and he had got them wound around the axles. A man had had to come out in a wrecking car and unwind them, a young, grinning garage man. Since then Mrs. Mitty always made him drive to a garage to have the chains taken off. The next time, he thought, I'll wear my right arm in a sling; they won't grin at me then. I'll have my right arm in a sling and they'll see I couldn't possibly take the chains off myself. He kicked at the slush on the sidewalk. "Overshoes," he said to himself, and he began looking for a shoe store.

When he came out into the street again, with the overshoes in a    9 box under his arm, Walter Mitty began to wonder what the other thing was his wife had told him to get. She had told him, twice before they set out from their house for Waterbury. In a way he hated these weekly trips to town—he was always getting something wrong. Kleenex, he thought, Squibb's, razor blades? No. Toothpaste, toothbrush, bicarbonate, carborundum, initiative and referendum? He gave it up. But she would remember it. "Where's the what's-its-name?" She would ask. "Don't tell me you forgot the what's-its-name." A newsboy went by shouting something about the Waterbury trial.

. . . "Perhaps this will refresh your memory." The District Attor-    10 ney suddenly thrust a heavy automatic at the quiet figure on the witness stand. "Have you ever seen this before?" Walter Mitty took the gun and examined it expertly. "This is my Webley-Vickers 50-80," he said calmly. An excited buzz ran around the courtroom. The judge rapped for order. "You are a crack shot with any sort of firearms, I believe?" said the District Attorney, insinuatingly. "Objection!" shouted Mitty's attorney. "We have shown that the defendant could not have fired the shot. We have shown that he wore his right arm in a sling on the night of the fourteenth of July." Walter Mitty raised his hand briefly and the bickering attorneys were stilled. "With any known make of gun," he said evenly, "I could have killed Gregory Fitzhurst at three hundred feet *with my left hand*." Pandemonium broke loose in the courtroom. A woman's scream rose above the bedlam and suddenly a lovely, dark-haired girl was in Walter Mitty's arms. The District Attorney struck at her savagely. Without rising from his chair. Mitty let the man have it on the point of the chin. "You miserable cur!"

"Puppy biscuit," said Walter Mitty. He stopped walking and the  11
buildings of Waterbury rose up out of the misty courtroom and surrounded him again. A woman who was passing laughed. "He said 'Puppy biscuit'," she said to her companion. "That man said 'Puppy biscuit' to himself." Walter Mitty hurried on. He went into an A. & P., not the first one he came to but a smaller one farther up the street. "I want some biscuit for small, young dogs," he said to the clerk. "Any special brand, sir?" The greatest pistol shot in the world thought a moment. "It says 'Puppies Bark for It' on the box," said Walter Mitty.

His wife would be through at the hairdresser's in fifteen minutes,  12
Mitty saw in looking at his watch, unless they had trouble drying it; sometimes they had trouble drying it. She didn't like to get to the hotel first; she would want him to be there waiting for her as usual. He found a big leather chair in the lobby, facing a window, and he put the overshoes and the puppy biscuit on the floor beside it. He picked up an old copy of *Liberty* and sank down into the chair. "Can Germany Conquer the World through the Air?" Walter Mitty looked at the pictures of bombing planes and of ruined streets.

. . . "The cannonading has got the wind up in young Raleigh, sir,"  13
said the sergeant. Captain Mitty looked up at him through tousled hair. "Get him to bed," he said wearily, "with the others. I'll fly alone." "But you can't, sir," said the sergeant anxiously. "It takes two men to handle that bomber and the Archies are pounding hell out of the air. Von Richtman's circus is between here and Saulier." "Somebody's got to get the ammunition dump," said Mitty. "I'm going over. Spot of brandy?" He poured a drink for the sergeant and one for himself. War thundered and whined around the dugout and battered at the

door. There was a rending of wood and splinters flew through the room. "A bit of a near thing," said Captain Mitty carelessly. "The box barrage is closing in," said the sergeant. "We only live once, sergeant," said Mitty, with his faint, fleeting smile. "Or do we?" He poured another brandy and tossed it off. "I never see a man could hold his brandy like you, sir," said the sergeant. "Begging your pardon, sir." Captain Mitty stood up and strapped on his huge Webley-Vickers automatic. "It's forty kilometers through hell, sir," said the sergeant. Mitty finished one last brandy. "After all," he said softly, "what isn't?" The pounding of the cannon increased; there was the rat-tat-tatting of machine guns, and from somewhere came the menacing pocketa-pocketa-pocketa of the new flame-throwers. Walter Mitty walked to the door of the dugout humming "Après de Ma Blonde." He turned and waved to the sergeant. "Cheerio!" he said. . . .

Something struck his shoulder. "I've been looking all over this    14
hotel for you," said Mrs. Mitty. "Why do you have to hide in this old chair? How did you expect me to find you?" "Things close in," said Walter Mitty vaguely. "What?" Mrs. Mitty said. "Did you get the what's-its-name? The puppy biscuit? What's in that box?" "Overshoes," said Mitty. "Couldn't you have put them on in the store?" "I was thinking," said Walter Mitty. "Does it ever occur to you that I am sometimes thinking?" She looked at him. "I'm going to take your temperature when I get you home," she said.

They went out through the revolving doors that made a faintly    15
derisive whistling sound when you pushed them. It was two blocks to the parking lot. At the drugstore on the corner she said, "Wait here for me. I forgot something. I won't be a minute." She was more than a minute. Walter Mitty lighted a cigarette. It began to rain, rain with sleet in it. He stood up against the wall of the drugstore, smoking. . . . He put his shoulders back and his heels together. "To hell with the handkerchief," said Walter Mitty scornfully. He took one last drag on his cigarette and snapped it away. Then, with that faint, fleeting smile playing about his lips, he faced the firing squad; erect and motionless, proud and disdainful, Walter Mitty the Undefeated, inscrutable to the last.

# Questions

1. Why does Mitty have daydreams? From what sources has he derived the substance of his daydreams?

2. We may sympathize with Mitty, but we laugh at him, too. Why do

we find the story primarily comic instead of pathetic? If it were intended to move us deeply, rather than to amuse us, what kinds of changes would have to be made in Mitty's daydreams? What other changes would have to be made in the characterization of Mitty and of his wife?

3. In the last sentence Mitty imagines himself facing a firing squad, "Mitty the Undefeated, inscrutable to the last." To what degree can it be argued that he is undefeated and inscrutable?

# 9
## LAW AND ORDER

*Flower Power*
**Bernie Boston, 1967**

*The Problem We All Live With*
**Norman Rockwell, 1964**

*United States Supreme Court*
**Fred Ward**

Black Star

# Short Views

The trouble for the thief is not how to steal the bugle, but where to blow it.
**African proverb**

Whether there was ever a significant increase in crime and when it might have occurred is puzzling, since the phrase, "the land is full of bloody crimes and the city full of violence," did not appear in a recent Chicago newspaper but in a report on a crime wave in the promised land about 600 B.C. as recorded in Ezekiel VII:23. The logical possibility of an ever-increasing crime wave becomes more doubtful when we consider the biblical origin of humankind: Adam, Eve and Cain committed the worst offenses possible and after Abel was killed, all survivors—or 75 percent of the first four human beings—had criminal records. In spite of all righteous claims to the opposite, this crime wave seems to have subsided, never to reach its biblical heights again. It is simpler and more correct to state that crime has always existed but statistics have not.
**Kurt Weis and Michael F. Milakovich**

And God spake all these words, saying, "I am the LORD thy God, which have brought thee out of the land of Egypt, out of the house of bondage.

"Thou shalt have no other gods before me.

"Thou shalt not make unto thee any graven image, or any likeness of any thing that is in heaven above, or that is in the earth beneath, or that is in the water under the earth: thou shalt not bow down thyself to them, nor serve them: for I the LORD thy God am a jealous God, visiting the iniquity of the fathers upon the children unto the third and fourth generation of them that hate me; and showing mercy unto thousands of them that love me, and keep my commandments.

"Thou shalt not take the name of the LORD thy God in vain; for the LORD will not hold him guiltless that taketh his name in vain.

"Remember the sabbath day, to keep it holy. Six days shalt thou labor, and do all thy work: but the seventh day is the sabbath of the L<small>ORD</small> thy God: in it thou shalt not do any work, thou, nor thy son, nor thy daughter, thy manservant, nor thy maidservant, nor thy cattle, nor thy stranger that is within thy gates: for in six days the L<small>ORD</small> made heaven and earth, the sea, and all that in them is, and rested the seventh day: wherefore the L<small>ORD</small> blessed the sabbath day, and hallowed it.

"Honor thy father and thy mother: that thy days may be long upon the land which the L<small>ORD</small> thy God giveth thee.

"Thou shalt not kill.

"Thou shalt not commit adultery.

"Thou shalt not steal.

"Thou shalt not bear false witness against thy neighbor.

"Thou shalt not covet thy neighbor's house, thou shalt not covet thy neighbor's wife, nor his manservant, nor his maidservant, nor his ox, nor his ass, nor any thing that is thy neighbor's."
**Exodus 20:1–17**

*He Commits Theft with His Companions, Not Urged on by Poverty, but from a Certain Distaste of Well-doing.* Theft is punished by Thy law, O Lord, and by the law written in men's hearts, which iniquity itself cannot blot out. For what thief will suffer a thief? Even a rich thief will not suffer him who is driven to it by want. Yet had I a desire to commit robbery, and did so, compelled neither by hunger, nor poverty, but through a distaste for well-doing, and a lustiness of iniquity. For I pilfered that of which I had already sufficient, and much better. Nor did I desire to enjoy what I pilfered, but the theft and sin itself. There was a pear-tree close to our vinyard, heavily laden with fruit, which was tempting neither for its color nor its flavor. To shake and rob this some of us wanton young fellows went, late one night (having, according to our disgraceful habit, prolonged our games in the streets until then), and carried away great loads, not to eat ourselves, but to fling to the very swine, having only eaten some of them; and to do this pleased us all the more because it was not permitted. Behold my heart, O my God; behold my heart, which Thou hadst pity upon when in the bottomless pit. Behold, now, let my heart tell Thee what it was seeking there, that I should be gratuitously wanton, having no inducement to evil but the evil itself. It was foul, and I loved it. I loved to perish. I loved my own error—not that for which I erred; but the error itself. Base soul, falling from Thy firmament to utter

destruction—not seeking aught through the shame but the shame itself!
**St. Augustine**


Whoever desires to found a state and give it laws, must start with assuming that all men are bad and ever ready to display their vicious nature, whenever they may find occasion for it.
**Niccolò Machiavelli**


Every prince must wish to be thought merciful and not cruel. But he must be careful not to misuse this mercifulness. Cesare Borgia was thought cruel, but his cruelty pacified the Romagna, united it, and reduced it to peace and loyalty. If this is carefully considered, it will be seen that Cesare was really much more merciful than the Florentines, who, to escape the name of cruelty, allowed Pistoia to be destroyed. A prince, therefore, should not mind being called cruel so long as he keeps his subjects united and faithful. With a few examples of cruelty he can be more merciful than those who, through too much tenderness, allow disturbances to arise, from which spring murder and plunder, for lawless acts injure the whole community, but the executions ordered by the prince injure only individuals. And of all princes, the new prince cannot escape a reputation for cruelty, because new states are always full of dangers. Virgil says, through the mouth of Dido: "My cruel fate and the newness of my realm force me to do such things, and to keep guard over all my lands."

Still, he must be cautious in believing and in acting, and he should not be easily frightened. He should proceed temperately, with prudence and humanity, so that overconfidence does not make him incautious, and suspicion does not make him intolerable.
**Niccolò Machiavelli**


It is questionable whether, when we break a murderer on the wheel, we aren't lapsing into precisely the mistake of the child who hits the chair he bumps into.
**G. C. Lichtenberg**


If a man were permitted to make all the ballads, he need not care who should make the laws of a nation.
**Andrew Fletcher**

Nature has given women so much power that the law has very
wisely given them very little.
    Samuel Johnson


I asked him whether, as a moralist, he did not think that the
practice of the law, in some degree, hurt the nice feeling of honesty.
JOHNSON. "Why no, Sir, if you act properly. You are not to deceive
your clients with false representations of your opinion: you are not
to tell lies to a judge." BOSWELL. "But what do you think of
supporting a cause which you know to be bad?" JOHNSON. "Sir, you
do not know it to be good or bad till the Judge determines it. I have
said that you are to state facts fairly; so that your thinking, or what
you call knowing, a cause to be bad, must be from reasoning, must
be from your supposing your arguments to be weak and
inconclusive. But, Sir, that is not enough. An argument which does
not convince yourself, may convince the Judge to whom you urge
it; and if it does convince him, why, then, Sir, you are wrong, and
he is right. It is his business to judge; and you are not to be
confident in your own opinion that a cause is bad, but to say all
you can for your client, and then hear the Judge's opinion."
BOSWELL. "But, Sir, does not affecting a warmth when you have no
warmth, and appearing to be clearly of one opinion when you are
in reality of another opinion, does not such dissimulation impair
one's honesty? Is there not some danger that a lawyer may put on
the same mask in common life, in the intercourse with his friends?"
JOHNSON. "Why no, Sir. Everybody knows you are paid for affecting
warmth for your client; and it is, therefore, properly no
dissimulation: the moment you come from the bar you resume your
usual behaviour. Sir, a man will no more carry the artifice of the bar
into the common intercourse of society, than a man who is paid for
tumbling upon his hands will continue to tumble upon his hands
when he should walk on his feet."
    James Boswell


One law for the ox and the ass is oppression.
    William Blake


The law, in its majestic equality, forbids the rich as well as the poor
to sleep under bridges, to beg in the streets, and to steal bread.
    Anatole France

Decency, security and liberty alike demand that government officials shall be subjected to the same rules of conduct that are commands to the citizen. In a government of laws, existence of the government will be imperilled if it fails to observe the law scrupulously. Our Government is the potent, the omnipresent teacher. For good or for ill, it teaches the whole people by its example. Crime is contagious. If the Government becomes a lawbreaker, it breeds contempt for law; it invites every man to become a law unto himself; it invites anarchy. To declare that in the administration of the criminal law the end justifies the means—to declare that the Government may commit crimes in order to secure the conviction of a private criminal—would bring terrible retribution. Against that pernicious doctrine this Court should resolutely set its face.
**Louis D. Brandeis**


The trouble about fighting for human freedom is that you have to spend much of your life defending sons of bitches; for oppressive laws are always aimed at them originally, and oppression must be stopped in the beginning if it is to be stopped at all.
**H. L. Mencken**


Censorship upholds the dignity of the profession, know what I mean?
**Mae West**

## Martin Luther King, Jr.

# Nonviolent Resistance

Oppressed people deal with their oppression in three char-  1
acteristic ways. One way is acquiescence: the oppressed resign themselves to their doom. They tacitly adjust themselves to oppression,
and thereby become conditioned to it. In every movement toward freedom some of the oppressed prefer to remain oppressed. Almost 2800
years ago Moses set out to lead the children of Israel from the slavery
of Egypt to the freedom of the promised land. He soon discovered that
slaves do not always welcome their deliverers. They become accustomed to being slaves. They would rather bear those ills they have,
as Shakespeare pointed out, than flee to others that they know not of.
They prefer the "fleshpots of Egypt" to the ordeals of emancipation.

There is such a thing as the freedom of exhaustion. Some people  2
are so worn down by the yoke of oppression that they give up. A few
years ago in the slum areas of Atlanta, a Negro guitarist used to sing
almost daily: "Ben down so long that down don't bother me." This is
the type of negative freedom and resignation that often engulfs the
life of the oppressed.

But this is not the way out. To accept passively an unjust system  3
is to coöperate with that system; thereby the oppressed become as evil
as the oppressor. Noncoöperation with evil is as much a moral obligation as is coöperation with good. The oppressed must never allow
the conscience of the oppressor to slumber. Religion reminds every
man that he is his brother's keeper. To accept injustice or segregation
passively is to say to the oppressor that his actions are morally right.
It is a way of allowing his conscience to fall asleep. At this moment
the oppressed fails to be his brother's keeper. So acquiescence—while
often the easier way—is not the moral way. It is the way of the coward.
The Negro cannot win the respect of his oppressor by acquiescing; he

Martin Luther King, Jr. (1929–1968), clergyman and civil rights leader, achieved
national fame in 1955–1956 when he led the boycott against segregated bus
lines in Montgomery, Alabama. His policy of passive resistance succeeded in
Montgomery, and King then organized the Southern Christian Leadership Conference in order to extend his efforts. In 1964 he was awarded the Nobel Peace
Prize, but he continued to encounter strong opposition. On April 4, 1968, while
in Memphis to support striking sanitation workers, he was shot and killed.

merely increases the oppressor's arrogance and contempt. Acquiescence is interpreted as proof of the Negro's inferiority. The Negro cannot win the respect of the white people of the South or the peoples of the world if he is willing to sell the future of his children for his personal and immediate comfort and safety.

A second way that oppressed people sometimes deal with oppression is to resort to physical violence and corroding hatred. Violence often brings about momentary results. Nations have frequently won their independence in battle. But in spite of temporary victories, violence never brings permanent peace. It solves no social problem; it merely creates new and more complicated ones.      4

Violence as a way of achieving racial justice is both impractical and immoral. It is impractical because it is a descending spiral ending in destruction for all. The old law of an eye for an eye leaves everybody blind. It is immoral because it seeks to humiliate the opponent rather than win his understanding; it seeks to annihilate rather than to convert. Violence is immoral because it thrives on hatred rather than love. It destroys community and makes brotherhood impossible. It leaves society in monologue rather than dialogue. Violence ends by defeating itself. It creates bitterness in the survivors and brutality in the destroyers. A voice echoes through time saying to every potential Peter, "Put up your sword." History is cluttered with the wreckage of nations that failed to follow his command.      5

If the American Negro and other victims of oppression succumb to the temptation of using violence in the struggle for freedom, future generations will be the recipients of a desolate night of bitterness, and our chief legacy to them will be an endless reign of meaningless chaos. Violence is not the way.      6

The third way open to oppressed people in their quest for freedom is the way of nonviolent resistance. Like the synthesis in Hegelian philosophy, the principle of nonviolent resistance seeks to reconcile the truths of two opposites—acquiescence and violence—while avoiding the extremes and immoralities of both. The nonviolent resister agrees with the person who acquiesces that one should not be physically aggressive toward his opponent; but he balances the equation by agreeing with the person of violence that evil must be resisted. He avoids the nonresistance of the former and the violent resistance of the latter. With nonviolent resistance, no individual or group need submit to any wrong, nor need anyone resort to violence in order to right a wrong.      7

It seems to me that this is the method that must guide the actions      8 of the Negro in the present crisis in race relations. Through nonviolent resistance the Negro will be able to rise to the noble height of opposing the unjust system while loving the perpetrators of the system. The Negro must work passionately and unrelentingly for full stature as a citizen, but he must not use inferior methods to gain it. He must never come to terms with falsehood, malice, hate, or destruction.

Nonviolent resistance makes it possible for the Negro to remain in the South and struggle for his rights. The Negro's problem will not be solved by running away. He cannot listen to the glib suggestion of those who would urge him to migrate en masse to other sections of the country. By grasping his great opportunity in the South he can make a lasting contribution to the moral strength of the nation and set a sublime example of courage for generations yet unborn. 9

By nonviolent resistance, the Negro can also enlist all men of good will in his struggle for equality. The problem is not a purely racial one, with Negroes set against whites. In the end, it is not a struggle between people at all, but a tension between justice and injustice. Nonviolent resistance is not aimed against oppressors but against oppression. Under its banner consciences, not racial groups, are enlisted. 10

If the Negro is to achieve the goal of integration, he must organize himself into a militant and nonviolent mass movement. All three elements are indispensable. The movement for equality and justice can only be a success if it has both a mass and militant character; the barriers to be overcome require both. Nonviolence is an imperative in order to bring about ultimate community. 11

A mass movement of militant quality that is not at the same time committed to nonviolence tends to generate conflict, which in turn breeds anarchy. The support of the participants and the sympathy of the uncommitted are both inhibited by the threat that bloodshed will engulf the community. This reaction in turn encourages the opposition to threaten and resort to force. When, however, the mass movement repudiates violence while moving resolutely toward its goal, its opponents are revealed as the instigators and practitioners of violence if it occurs. Then public support is magnetically attracted to the advocates of nonviolence, while those who employ violence are literally disarmed by overwhelming sentiment against their stand. 12

Only through a nonviolent approach can the fears of the white community be mitigated. A guilt-ridden white minority lives in fear that if the Negro should ever attain power, he would act without restraint or pity to revenge the injustices and brutality of the years. It is something like a parent who continually mistreats a son. One day that 13 parent raises his hand to strike the son, only to discover that the son is now as tall as he is. The parent is suddenly afraid—fearful that the son will use his new physical power to repay his parent for all the blows of the past.

The Negro, once a helpless child, has now grown up politically, 14 culturally, and economically. Many white men fear retaliation. The job of the Negro is to show them that they have nothing to fear, that the Negro understands and forgives and is ready to forget the past. He must convince the white man that all he seeks is justice, *for both himself and the white man*. A mass movement exercising nonviolence is an object lesson in power under discipline, a demonstration to the white community that if such a movement attained a degree of strength, it would use its power creatively and not vengefully.

Nonviolence can touch men where the law cannot reach them. 15 When the law regulates behavior it plays an indirect part in molding public sentiment. The enforcement of the law is itself a form of peaceful persuasion. But the law needs help. The courts can order desegregation of the public schools. But what can be done to mitigate the fears, to disperse the hatred, violence, and irrationality gathered around school integration, to take the initiative out of the hands of racial demagogues, to release respect for the law? In the end, for laws to be obeyed, men must believe they are right.

Here nonviolence comes in as the ultimate form of persuasion. It 16 is the method which seeks to implement the just law by appealing to the conscience of the great decent majority who through blindness, fear, pride, or irrationality have allowed their consciences to sleep.

The nonviolent resisters can summarize their message in the fol- 17 lowing simple terms: We will take direct action against injustice without waiting for other agencies to act. We will not obey unjust laws or submit to unjust practices. We will do this peacefully, openly, cheerfully because our aim is to persuade. We adopt the means of nonviolence because our end is a community at peace with itself. We will try to persuade with our words, but if our words fail, we will try to persuade with our acts. We will always be willing to talk and seek fair compromise, but we are ready to suffer when necessary and even risk our lives to become witnesses to the truth as we see it.

The way of nonviolence means a willingness to suffer and sacrifice. 18 It may mean going to jail. If such is the case the resister must be willing to fill the jail houses of the South. It may even mean physical death. But if physical death is the price that a man must pay to free his children and his white brethren from a permanent death of the spirit, then nothing could be more redemptive.

## Questions

1.  In the first paragraph, the passage about Moses and the children of Israel is not strictly necessary; the essential idea of the paragraph is stated in the previous sentence. Why, then, does King add this material? And why the quotation from Shakespeare?

2.  Pick out two or three sentences that seem to you to be especially effective and analyze the sources of their power. You can choose either isolated sentences or (because King often effectively links sentences with repetition of words or of constructions) consecutive ones.

3.  In a paragraph set forth your understanding of what nonviolent resistance is. Use whatever examples from your own experience or reading you find useful. In a second paragraph, explain how Maya Angelou's "Graduation" (page 249) offers an example of nonviolent resistance.

Plato

# Crito

*Persons of the Dialogue: Socrates and Crito*

Scene: The Prison of Socrates

*Socrates.* Why have you come at this hour, Crito? It must be quite early?

*Crito.* Yes, certainly.

*Soc.* What is the exact time?

*Cr.* The dawn is breaking.

*Soc.* I wonder that the keeper of the prison would let you in.    5

*Cr.* He knows me, because I often come, Socrates; moreover, I have done him a kindness.

*Soc.* And are you only just arrived?

*Cr.* No, I came some time ago.

*Soc.* Then why did you sit and say nothing, instead of at once awakening me?

*Cr.* I should not have liked myself, Socrates, to be in such great    10 trouble and unrest as you are—indeed I should not: I have been watching with amazement your peaceful slumbers; and for that reason I did not awake you, because I wished to minimize the pain. I have always thought you to be of a happy disposition; but never did I see anything like the easy, tranquil manner in which you bear this calamity.

---

Plato (427–347 B.C.) in his dialogues often uses the Athenian philosopher Socrates as a mouthpiece for ideas that scholars believe are Platonic, but in the dialogue called *Crito* he probably was fairly careful to represent Socrates' own ideas.

In 399 B.C. Socrates was convicted of impiety and was sentenced to death. Behind the charge of impiety was another, that Socrates had "corrupted the young." It seems clear, however, that the trial was a way of getting rid of a man considered by some to be a troublesome questioner of conventional opinions.

About a month intervened between the trial and Socrates' death because the law prohibited execution until a sacred ship had returned to Athens. Socrates could easily have escaped from prison but made no effort to leave, as we see in this dialogue reporting his decision to abide by the unjust decision of a duly constituted group of jurors.

*Soc.* Why, Crito, when a man has reached my age he ought not to be repining at the approach of death.

*Cr.* And yet other old men find themselves in similar misfortunes, and age does not prevent them from repining.

*Soc.* That is true. But you have not told me why you come at this early hour.

*Cr.* I come to bring you a message which is sad and painful; not, as I believe, to yourself, but to all of us who are your friends, and saddest of all to me.

*Soc.* What? Has the ship come from Delos, on the arrival of which   15
I am to die?

*Cr.* No, the ship has not actually arrived, but she will probably be here today, as persons who have come from Sunium tell me that they left her there; and therefore tomorrow, Socrates, will be the last day of your life.

*Soc.* Very well, Crito; if such is the will of God, I am willing; but my belief is that there will be a delay of a day.

*Cr.* Why do you think so?

*Soc.* I will tell you, I am to die on the day after the arrival of the ship.

*Cr.* Yes; that is what the authorities say.   20

*Soc.* But I do not think that the ship will be here until tomorrow; this I infer from a vision which I had last night, or rather only just now, when you fortunately allowed me to sleep.

*Cr.* And what was the nature of the vision?

*Soc.* There appeared to me the likeness of a woman, fair and comely, clothed in bright raiment, who called to me and said: O Socrates,

The third day hence to fertile Phthia shalt thou go.[1]

*Cr.* What a singular dream, Socrates!

*Soc.* There can be no doubt about the meaning, Crito, I think.   25

*Cr.* Yes; the meaning is only too clear. But, oh! my beloved Socrates, let me entreat you once more to take my advice and escape. For if you die I shall not only lose a friend who can never be replaced, but there is another evil: people who do not know you and me will believe that I might have saved you if I had been willing to give money, but that I did not care. Now, can there be a worse disgrace than this—that I should be thought to value money more than the life of a friend?

[1] Homer, *Iliad*, ix. 363.

For the many will not be persuaded that I wanted you to escape, and that you refused.

*Soc.* But why, my dear Crito, should we care about the opinion of the many? Good men, and they are the only persons who are worth considering, will think of these things truly as they occurred.

*Cr.* But you see, Socrates, that the opinion of the many must be regarded, for what is now happening shows that they can do the greatest evil to any one who has lost their good opinion.

*Soc.* I only wish it were so, Crito; and that the many could do the greatest evil; for then they would also be able to do the greatest good— and what a fine thing this would be! But in reality they can do neither; for they cannot make a man either wise or foolish; and whatever they do is the result of chance.

*Cr.* Well, I will not dispute with you; but please to tell me, Socrates, whether you are not acting out of regard to me and your other friends: are you not afraid that if you escape from prison we may get into trouble with the informers for having stolen you away, and lose either the whole or a great part of our property; or that even a worse evil may happen to us? Now, if you fear on our account, be at ease; for in order to save you, we ought surely to run this, or even a greater risk; be persuaded, then, and do as I say.

*Soc.* Yes, Crito, that is one fear which you mention, but by no means the only one.

*Cr.* Fear not—there are persons who are willing to get you out of prison at no great cost; and as for the informers, they are far from being exorbitant in their demands—a little money will satisfy them. My means, which are certainly ample, are at your service, and if you have a scruple about spending all mine, here are strangers who will give you the use of theirs; and one of them, Simmias the Theban, has brought a large sum of money for this very purpose; and Cebes and many others are prepared to spend their money in helping you to escape. I say, therefore, do not hesitate on our account, and do not say, as you did in the court, that you will have a difficulty in knowing what to do with yourself anywhere else. For men will love you in other places to which you may go, and not in Athens only; there are friends of mine in Thessaly, if you like to go to them, who will value and protect you, and no Thessalian will give you any trouble. Nor can I think that you are at all justified, Socrates, in betraying your own life when you might be saved; in acting thus you are playing into the hands of your enemies, who are hurrying on your destruction. And further I should say that you are deserting your own children; for you might bring them up and educate them; instead of which you go away and leave them, and they will have to take their chance; and if they do not meet with the usual fate of orphans, there will be small thanks to you. No man should bring children into the world who is unwilling to persevere to the end in their nurture and education. But you appear to be choosing the easier part, not the better and manlier, which would have been more becoming in one who professes to care for virtue in all his actions, like yourself. And indeed, I am ashamed not only of you, but of us who are your friends, when I reflect that the whole business will be attributed entirely to our want of courage. The trial need never have come on, or might have been managed differently; and this last act, or crowning folly, will seem to have occurred through our negligence and cowardice, who might have saved you, if we had been good for anything; and you might have saved yourself, for there was no difficulty at all. See now, Socrates, how sad and discreditable are the consequences, both to us and you. Make up your mind then, or rather have your mind already made up, for the time of deliberation is over, and there is only one thing to be done, which must be done this very night, and if we delay at all will be no longer practicable or possible; I beseech you therefore, Socrates, be persuaded by me, and do as I say.

*Soc.* Dear Crito, your zeal is invaluable, if a right one; but if wrong, the greater the zeal the greater the danger; and therefore we ought to consider whether I shall or shall not do as you say. For I am and always have been one of those natures who must be guided by reason, whatever the reason may be which upon reflection appears to me to be the best; and now that this chance has befallen me, I cannot repudiate my own words: the principles which I have hitherto honored and revered I still honor, and unless we can at once find other and better principles, I am certain not to agree with you; no, not even if the power of the multitude could inflict many more imprisonments, confiscations, deaths, frightening us like children with hobgoblin terrors. What will be the fairest way of considering the question? Shall I return to your old argument about the opinions of men?—we were saying that some of them are to be regarded, and others not. Now were we right in maintaining this before I was condemned? And has the argument which was once good now proved to be talk for the sake of talking— mere childish nonsense? That is what I want to consider with your help, Crito:—whether, under my present circumstances, the argument appears to be in any way different or not; and is to be allowed by me or disallowed. That argument, which, as I believe, is maintained by many persons of authority, was to the effect, as I was saying, that the opinions of some men are to be regarded, and of other men not to be regarded. Now you, Crito, are not going to die tomorrow—at least, there is no human probability of this—and therefore you are disinterested and not liable to be deceived by the circumstances in which you are placed. Tell me then, whether I am right in saying that some opinions, and the opinions of some men only, are to be valued, and that other opinions, and the opinions of other men, are not to be valued. I ask you whether I was right in maintaining this?

*Cr.* Certainly.

*Soc.* The good are to be regarded, and not the bad?                                35

*Cr.* Yes.

*Soc.* And the opinions of the wise are good, and the opinions of the unwise are evil?

*Cr.* Certainly.

*Soc.* And what was said about another matter? Is the pupil who devotes himself to the practice of gymnastics supposed to attend to the praise and blame and opinion of every man, or of one man only— his physician or trainer, whoever he may be?

*Cr.* Of one man only.                                                             40

*Soc.* And he ought to fear the censure and welcome the praise of that one only, and not of the many?

*Cr.* Clearly so.

*Soc.* And he ought to act and train, and eat and drink in the way which seems good to his single master who has understanding, rather than according to the opinion of all other men put together?

*Cr.* True.

*Soc.* And if he disobeys and disregards the opinion and approval     45 of the one, and regards the opinion of the many who have no understanding, will he not suffer evil?

*Cr.* Certainly he will.

*Soc.* And what will the evil be, whither tending and what affecting, in the disobedient person?

*Cr.* Clearly, affecting the body; that is what is destroyed by the evil.

*Soc.* Very good; and is not this true, Crito, of other things which we need not separately enumerate? In questions of just and unjust, fair and foul, good and evil, which are the subjects of our present consultation, ought we to allow the opinion of the many and to fear them; or the opinion of the one man who has understanding? ought we not to fear and reverence him more than all the rest of the world:

and if we desert him shall we not destroy and injure that principle in us which may be assumed to be improved by justice and deteriorated by injustice;—there is such a principle?

*Cr.* Certainly there is, Socrates.                                                  50

*Soc.* Take a parallel instance—if, acting under the advice of those who have no understanding, we destroy that which is improved by health and is deteriorated by disease, would life be worth having? And that which has been destroyed is—the body?

*Cr.* Yes.

*Soc.* Could we live, having an evil and corrupted body?

*Cr.* Certainly not.

*Soc.* And will life be worth having, if that higher part of man be    55
destroyed, which is improved by justice and depraved by injustice? Do we suppose that principle, whatever it may be in man, which has to do with justice and injustice, to be inferior to the body?

*Cr.* Certainly not.

*Soc.* More honorable than the body?

*Cr.* Far more.

*Soc.* Then, my friend, we must not regard what the many say of us: but what he, the one man who has understanding of just and unjust, will say, and what the truth will say. And therefore you begin in error when you advise that we should regard the opinion of the many about just and unjust, good and evil, honorable and dishonorable—"Well," some one will say, "but the many can kill us."

*Cr.* Yes, Socrates; that will clearly be the answer.                   60

*Soc.* And it is true: but still I find with surprise that the old argument is unshaken as ever. And I should like to know whether I may say the same of another proposition—that not life, but a good life, is to be chiefly valued?

*Cr.* Yes, that also remains unshaken.

*Soc.* And a good life is equivalent to a just, honorable one—that holds also?

*Cr.* Yes, it does.

*Soc.* From these premises I proceed to argue the question whether   65
I ought or ought not to try and escape without the consent of the Athenians: and if I am clearly right in escaping, then I will make the attempt; but if not, I will abstain. The other considerations which you mention, of money and loss of character and duty of educating one's children, are, I fear, only the doctrines of the multitude, who would be as ready to restore people to life, if they were able, as they are to put them to death—and with as little reason. But now, since the ar-

gument has thus far prevailed, the only question which remains to be considered is, whether we shall do rightly either in escaping or in suffering others to aid in our escape and paying them in money and thanks, or whether in reality we shall not do rightly; and if the latter, then death or any other calamity which may ensue on my remaining here must not be allowed to enter into the calculation.

*Cr.* I think that you are right, Socrates; how then shall we proceed?

*Soc.* Let us consider the matter together, and do you either refute me if you can, and I will be convinced; or else cease, my dear friend, from repeating to me that I ought to escape against the wishes of the Athenians: for I highly value your attempts to persuade me to do so, but I may not be persuaded against my own better judgment. And now please to consider my first position, and try how you can best answer me.

*Cr.* I will.

*Soc.* Are we to say that we are never intentionally to do wrong, or that in one way we ought and in another we ought not to do wrong, or is doing wrong always evil and dishonorable, as I was just now saying, and as has been already acknowledged by us? Are all our former admissions which were made within a few days to be thrown away? And have we, at our age, been earnestly discoursing with one another all our life long only to discover that we are no better than children? Or, in spite of the opinion of the many, and in spite of consequences whether better or worse, shall we insist on the truth of what was then said, that injustice is always an evil and dishonor to him who acts unjustly? Shall we say so or not?

*Cr.* Yes.                                                                    70

*Soc.* Then we must do no wrong?

*Cr.* Certainly not.

*Soc.* Nor when injured injure in return, as the many imagine; for we must injure no one at all?

*Cr.* Clearly not.

*Soc.* Again, Crito, may we do evil?                                          75

*Cr.* Surely not, Socrates.

*Soc.* And what of doing evil in return for evil, which is the morality of the many—is that just or not?

*Cr.* Not just.

*Soc.* For doing evil to another is the same as injuring him?

*Cr.* Very true.                                                             80

*Soc.* Then we ought not to retaliate or render evil for evil to any one, whatever evil we may have suffered from him. But I would have you consider, Crito, whether you really mean what you are saying. For this opinion has never been held, and never will be held, by any considerable number of persons; and those who are agreed and those who are not agreed upon this point have no common ground, and can only despise one another when they see how widely they differ. Tell me, then, whether you agree with and assent to my first principle, that neither injury nor retaliation nor warding off evil by evil is ever right. And shall that be the premise of our argument? Or do you decline and dissent from this? For so I have ever thought, and continue to think; but, if you are of another opinion, let me hear what you have to say. If, however, you remain of the same mind as formerly, I will proceed to the next step.

*Cr.* You may proceed, for I have not changed my mind.

*Soc.* Then I will go on to the next point, which may be put in the form of a question:—Ought a man to do what he admits to be right, or ought he to betray the right?

*Cr.* He ought to do what he thinks right.

*Soc.* But if this is true, what is the application? In leaving the prison against the will of the Athenians, do I wrong any? or rather do I not wrong those whom I ought least to wrong? Do I not desert the principles which were acknowledged by us to be just—what do you say?

*Cr.* I cannot tell, Socrates; for I do not know.

*Soc.* Then consider the matter in this way:—Imagine that I am about to play truant (you may call the proceeding by any name which you like), and the laws and the government come and interrogate me: "Tell us, Socrates," they say; "what are you about? are you not going by an act of yours to overturn us—the laws, and the whole state, as far as in you lies? Do you imagine that a state can subsist and not be overthrown, in which the decisions of law have no power, but are set aside and trampled upon by individuals?" What will be our answer, Crito, to these and the like words? Any one, and especially a rhetorician, will have a good deal to say on behalf of the law which requires a sentence to be carried out. He will argue that this law should not be set aside; and shall we reply, "Yes; but the state has injured us and given an unjust sentence." Suppose I say that?

*Cr.* Very good, Socrates.

*Soc.* "And was that our agreement with you?" the law would answer; "or were you to abide by the sentence of the state?" And if I were to express my astonishment at their words, the law would probably add: "Answer, Socrates, instead of opening your eyes—you are in the habit of asking and answering questions. Tell us—What complaint have you to make against us which justifies you in attempting to destroy us and the state? In the first place did we not bring you into existence? Your father married your mother by our aid and begat you. Say whether you have any objection to urge against those of us who regulate marriage?" None, I should reply. "Or against those of us who after birth regulate the nurture and education of children, in which you also were trained? Were not the laws, which have the charge of education, right in commanding your father to train you in music and gymnastic?" Right, I should reply. "Well then, since you were brought into the world and nurtured and educated by us, can you deny in the first place that you are our child and slave, as your fathers were before you? And if this is true you are not on equal terms with us; nor can you think that you have a right to do to us what we are doing to you. Would you have any right to strike or revile or do any other evil to your father or your master, if you had one, because you have been struck or reviled by him, or received some other evil at his hands?— you would not say this? And because we think right to destroy you, do you think that you have any right to destroy us in return, and your country as far as in you lies? Will you, O professor of true virtue, pretend that you are justified in this? Has a philosopher like you failed to discover that our country is more to be valued and higher and holier far than mother or father or any ancestor, and more to be regarded in the eyes of the gods and of men of understanding? also to be soothed, and gently and reverently entreated when angry, even more than a father, and either to be persuaded, or if not persuaded, to be obeyed? And when we are punished by her, whether with imprisonment or stripes, the punishment is to be endured in silence; and if she leads us to wounds or death in battle, thither we follow as is right; neither may any one yield or retreat or leave his rank, but whether in battle or in a court of law, or in any other place, he must do what his city and his country order him; or he must change their view of what is just: and if he may do no violence to his father or mother, much less may he do violence to his country." What answer shall we make to this, Crito? Do the laws speak truly, or do they not?

*Cr.* I think that they do.

*Soc.* Then the laws will say, "Consider, Socrates, if we are speaking truly that in your present attempt you are going to do us an injury. For, having brought you into the world, and nurtured and educated you, and given you and every other citizen a share in every good which we had to give, we further proclaim to any Athenian by the liberty which we allow him, that if he does not like us when he has become of age and has seen the ways of the city, and made our acquaintance, he may go where he pleases and take his goods with him. None of us laws will forbid him or interfere with him. Any one who does not like us and the city, and who wants to emigrate to a colony or to any other city, may go where he likes, retaining his property. But he who has experience of the manner in which we order justice and administer the state, and still remains, has entered into an implied contract that he will do as we command him. And he who disobeys us is, as we maintain, thrice wrong; first, because in disobeying us he is disobeying his parents; secondly, because we are the authors of his education; thirdly, because he has made an agreement with us that he will duly obey our commands; and he neither obeys them nor convinces us that our commands are unjust; and we do not rudely impose them, but give him the alternative of obeying or convincing us;—that is what we offer, and he does neither.

"These are the sort of accusations to which, as we were saying, 92 you, Socrates, will be exposed if you accomplish your intentions; you, above all other Athenians." Suppose now I ask, why I rather than anybody else? they will justly retort upon me that I above all other men have acknowledged the agreement. "There is clear proof," they will say, "Socrates, that we and the city were not displeasing to you. Of all Athenians you have been the most constant resident in the city, which, as you never leave, you may be supposed to love. For you never went out of the city either to see the games, except once when you went to the Isthmus, or to any other place unless when you were on military service; nor did you travel as other men do. Nor had you any curiosity to know other states or their laws: your affections did not go beyond us and our state; we were your special favorites, and you acquiesced in our government of you; and here in this city you begat your children, which is a proof of your satisfaction. Moreover, you might in the course of the trial, if you had liked, have fixed the penalty at banishment; the state which refuses to let you go now would have let you go then. But you pretended that you preferred death to exile, and that you were not unwilling to die. And now you have forgotten these fine sentiments, and pay no respect to us the laws, of whom you are the destroyer; and are doing what only a miserable slave would do, running away and turning your back upon the compacts and agreements which you made as a citizen. And first of all answer this very question: Are we right in saying that you agreed to be governed according to us in deed, and not in word only? Is that true or not?" How shall we answer, Crito? Must we not assent?

*Cr.* We cannot help it, Socrates.                                                93

*Soc.* Then will they not say: "You, Socrates, are breaking the cov-     94
enants and agreements which you made with us at your leisure, not
in any haste or under any compulsion or deception, but after you have
had seventy years to think of them, during which time you were at
liberty to leave the city, if we were not to your mind, or if our covenants
appeared to you to be unfair. You had your choice, and might have
gone either to Lacedaemon or Crete, both which states are often
praised by you for their good government, or to some other Hellenic
or foreign state. Whereas you, above all other Athenians, seemed to
be so fond of the state, or, in other words, of us her laws (and who
would care about a state which has no laws?), that you never stirred
out of her; the halt, the blind, the maimed were not more stationary
in her than you were. And now you run away and forsake your agreements. Not so, Socrates, if you will take our advice; do not make yourself ridiculous by escaping out of the city.

"For just consider, if you transgress and err in this sort of way,     95
what good will you do either to yourself or to your friends? That your
friends will be driven into exile and deprived of citizenship, or will
lose their property, is tolerably certain; and you yourself, if you fly to
one of the neighboring cities, as, for example, Thebes or Megara, both
of which are well governed, will come to them as an enemy, Socrates,
and their government will be against you, and all patriotic citizens will
cast an evil eye upon you as a subverter of the laws, and you will
confirm in the minds of the judges the justice of their own condemnation of you. For he who is a corrupter of the laws is more than likely
to be a corrupter of the young and foolish portion of mankind. Will
you then flee from well-ordered cities and virtuous men? and is existence worth having on these terms? Or will you go to them without
shame, and talk to them, Socrates? And what will you say to them?
What you say here about virtue and justice and institutions and laws
being the best things among men? Would that be decent of you? Surely
not. But if you go away from well-governed states to Crito's friends
in Thessaly, where there is great disorder and license, they will be
charmed to hear the tale of your escape from prison, set off with ludicrous particulars of the manner in which you were wrapped in a
goatskin or some other disguise, and metamorphosed as the manner
is of runaways; but will there be no one to remind you that in your
old age you were not ashamed to violate the most sacred laws for a
miserable desire of a little more life? Perhaps not, if you keep them in
a good temper; but if they are out of temper you will hear many degrading things; you will live, but how?—as the flatterer of all men,

and the servant of all men; and doing what?—eating and drinking in Thessaly, having gone abroad in order that you may get a dinner. And where will be your fine sentiments about justice and virtue? Say that you wish to live for the sake of your children—you want to bring them up and educate them—will you take them into Thessaly and deprive them of Athenian citizenship? Is this the benefit which you will confer upon them? Or are you under the impression that they will be better cared for and educated here if you are still alive, although absent from them; for your friends will take care of them? Do you fancy that if you are an inhabitant of Thessaly they will take care of them, and if you are an inhabitant of the other world that they will not take care of them? Nay; but if they who call themselves friends are good for anything, they will—to be sure they will.

"Listen, then, Socrates, to us who have brought you up. Think 96 not of life and children first, and of justice afterward, but of justice first, that you may be justified before the princes of the world below. For neither will you nor any that belong to you be happier or holier or juster in this life, or happier in another, if you do as Crito bids. Now you depart in innocence, a sufferer and not a doer of evil; a victim, not of the laws but of men. But if you go forth, returning evil for evil, and injury for injury, breaking the covenants and agreements which you have made with us, and wronging those whom you ought least of all to wrong, that is to say, yourself, your friends, your country, and us, we shall be angry with you while you live, and our brethren, the laws in the world below, will receive you as an enemy; for they will know that you have done your best to destroy us. Listen, then, to us and not to Crito."

This, dear Crito, is the voice which I seem to hear murmuring in 97 my ears, like the sound of the flute in the ears of the mystic; that voice, I say, is humming in my ears, and prevents me from hearing any other. And I know that anything more which you may say will be vain. Yet speak, if you have anything to say.

*Cr.* I have nothing to say, Socrates. 98

*Soc.* Leave me then, Crito, to fulfill the will of God, and to follow 99 whither he leads.

# Questions

1. Socrates argues that because throughout his life he lived in Athens, in effect he established a compact with the city to live by its laws and must therefore now accept the judgment—however mis-

taken—of a duly constituted court. How convincing is this argument? Suppose this argument were omitted. Would Socrates' conclusion be affected?

2. Socrates argues that just as in matters of caring for the body we heed only experts and not the multitude, so in moral matters we should heed the expert, not the multitude. How convincing is this analogy between bodily health and moral goodness? Socrates sometimes compared himself to an athletic coach, saying he trained people to think. Judging from the dialogue, how did he train a student to think?

3. The personified figure of the laws does not add much to the essential argument. Why, then, is the passage included?

4. The ancient Chinese teacher Confucius asked one of his pupils, "Do you think of me as a man who knows about things as the result of wide study?" When the pupil replied "Yes," Confucius disagreed: "I have one thing, and upon it all the rest is rooted." Exactly what did Confucius mean? If Socrates had been asked the question, would he have given Confucius's answer?

## Luke, John, and an Anonymous Japanese

# Four Short Narratives

### 1. Luke *Parable of the Prodigal Son*

Then drew near unto [Jesus] all the publicans and sinners for to hear him. And the Pharisees and scribes murmured, saying "This man receiveth sinners, and eateth with them." And he said, "A certain

---

Luke, the author of the third of the four Gospels, was a second-generation Christian. He probably was a Roman, though some early accounts refer to him as a Syrian; in any case, he wrote in Greek. John, the author of the fourth Gospel, is traditionally said to be John, son of Zebedee, one of the twelve apostles of Jesus. Tradition also holds that John is the author of three epistles and of Revelation, though much modern scholarship doubts that the same man could have written these works, which differ in matters of style and doctrine. Our two selections from Luke and our one selection from John are all from the King James Version (1611).

The author of the Japanese anecdote called "Muddy Road" is not known.

man had two sons: and the younger of them said to his father, 'Father, give me the portion of goods that falleth to me.' And he divided unto them his living. And not many days after, the younger son gathered all together, and took his journey into a far country, and there wasted his substance with riotous living. And when he had spent all, there arose a mighty famine in that land, and he began to be in want. And he went and joined himself to a citizen of that country, and he sent him into his fields to feed swine. And he would fain have filled his belly with the husks that the swine did eat: and no man gave unto him. And when he came to himself, he said, 'How many hired servants of my father's have bread enough and to spare, and I perish with hunger? I will arise and go to my father, and will say unto him, "Father, I have sinned against heaven, and before thee. And am no more worthy to be called thy son: make me as one of thy hired servants."' And he arose, and came to his father. But when he was yet a great way off, his father saw him, and had compassion, and ran, and fell on his neck, and kissed him. And the son said unto him, 'Father, I have sinned against heaven, and in thy sight, and am no more worthy to be called thy son.' But the father said to his servants, 'Bring forth the best robe, and put it on him, and put a ring on his hand, and shoes on his feet. And bring hither the fatted calf, and kill it, and let us eat, and be merry. For this my son was dead, and is alive again; he was lost, and is found.' And they began to be merry.

Now his elder son was in the field, and as he came and drew nigh to the house, he heard music and dancing. And he called one of the servants, and asked what these things meant. And he said unto him, 'Thy brother is come, and thy father hath killed the fatted calf, because he hath received him safe and sound.' And he was angry, and would not go in: therefore came his father out, and entreated him. And he answering said to his father, 'Lo, these many years do I serve thee, neither transgressed I at any time thy commandment, and yet thou never gavest me a kid, that I might make merry with my friends: but as soon as this thy son was come, which hath devoured thy living with harlots, thou hast killed for him the fatted calf.' And he said unto him, 'Son, thou art ever with me, and all that I have is thine. It was meet that we should make merry, and be glad: for this thy brother was dead, and is alive again: and was lost, and is found.'"

## 2. Luke *Parable of the Good Samaritan*

But [a certain lawyer], willing to justify himself, said unto Jesus, and who is my neighbor?

And Jesus answering said, "A certain man went down from Jerusalem to Jericho, and fell among thieves, which stripped him of his raiment, and wounded him, and departed, leaving him half dead. And by chance there came down a certain priest that way: and when he saw him, he passed by on the other side. And likewise a Levite,[1] when he was at the place, came and looked on him, and passed by on the other side. But a certain Samaritan, as he journeyed, came where he was: and when he saw him, he had compassion on him, and went to him, and bound up his wounds, pouring in oil and wine, and set him on his own beast, and brought him to an inn, and took care of him. And on the morrow when he departed, he took out two pence, and gave them to the host, and said unto him, 'Take care of him; and whatsoever thou spendest more, when I come again, I will repay thee.' Which now of these three, thinkest thou, was neighbor unto him that fell among the thieves?"

And he said, "He that shewed mercy on him."

Then said Jesus unto him, "Go, and do thou likewise."

### 3. John *The Woman Taken in Adultery*

Jesus went unto the Mount of Olives. And early in the morning he came again into the temple, and all the people came unto him; and he sat down, and taught them.

And the scribes and Pharisees brought unto him a woman taken in adultery; and when they had set her in the midst, they said unto him, "Master, this woman was taken in adultery, in the very act. Now Moses in the law commanded us that such should be stoned: but what sayest thou?" This they said, tempting him, that they might have to accuse him. But Jesus stooped down, and with his finger wrote on the ground, as though he heard them not. So when they continued asking him, he lifted up himself, and said unto them, "He that is without sin among you, let him first cast a stone at her." And again he stooped down, and wrote on the ground. And they which heard it, being convicted by their own conscience, went out one by one, beginning at the eldest, even unto the last: and Jesus was left alone, and the woman standing in the midst.

When Jesus had lifted up himself, and saw none but the woman,

---

[1] The Levites were assistants to the temple priests. The Samaritans (referred to in the next sentence) claimed to be Israelites but were regarded by the Jews as transplanted Assyrians. (Editors' note)

he said unto her, "Woman, where are those thine accusers? Hath no man condemned thee?" She said, "No man, Lord." And Jesus said unto her, "Neither do I condemn thee; go, and sin no more."

## 4. Anonymous Japanese *Muddy Road*

Tanzan and Ekido were once traveling together down a muddy road. A heavy rain was still falling.

Coming around a bend, they met a lovely girl in a silk kimono and sash, unable to cross the intersection.

"Come on, girl," said Tanzan at once. Lifting her in his arms, he carried her over the mud.

Ekido did not speak again until that night when they reached a lodging temple. Then he no longer could restrain himself. "We monks don't go near females," he told Tanzan, "especially not young and lovely ones. It is dangerous. Why did you do that?"

"I left the girl there," said Tanzan. "Are you still carrying her?"

# Questions

1. What is the function of the older brother in the Parable of the Prodigal Son? Characterize him, and compare him with the younger brother.
2. Is the father foolish and sentimental? Do we approve or disapprove of his behavior at the end? Explain.
3. The biblical command is to love one's neighbor. The question put to Jesus, before he recounts the Parable of the Good Samaritan, is, "Who is my neighbor?" In the parable, what is Jesus' interpretation of the question and of the commandment?
4. Do you interpret the episode of the Woman Taken in Adultery to say that crime should go unpunished? Or that a judge cannot punish a crime if he himself is guilty of it? Or what?
5. What is the moral of the Japanese story? Does it bear any resemblance to the moral of the Parable of the Good Samaritan? Explain.

Thomas Jefferson

# The Declaration of Independence

In CONGRESS, July 4, 1776.  1

*The Unanimous Declaration of the Thirteen United States of America.*

**W**hen in the Course of human events, it becomes nec-  2
essary for one people to dissolve the political bands which have connected them with another, and to assume among the powers of the
earth, the separate and equal station to which the Laws of Nature and
of Nature's God entitle them, a decent respect to the opinions of mankind requires that they should declare the causes which impel them
to the separation.

We hold these truths to be self-evident, that all men are created  3
equal, that they are endowed by their Creator with certain unalienable
Rights, that among these are Life, Liberty and the pursuit of Happiness.

That to secure these rights, Governments are instituted among  4
Men, deriving their just powers from the consent of the governed.

That whenever any Form of Government becomes destructive of  5
these ends, it is the Right of the People to alter or to abolish it, and
to institute new Government, laying its foundation on such principles
and organizing its powers in such form, as to them shall seem most
likely to effect their Safety and Happiness. Prudence, indeed, will dictate that Governments long established should not be changed for light
and transient causes; and accordingly all experience hath shewn, that
mankind are more disposed to suffer, while evils are sufferable, than
to right themselves by abolishing the forms to which they are accustomed. But when a long train of abuses and usurpations, pursuing
invariably the same Object evinces a design to reduce them under
absolute Despotism, it is their right, it is their duty, to throw off such
Government, and to provide new Guards for their future security.

Thomas Jefferson (1743–1826), governor of Virginia and the third president of
the United States, devoted most of his adult life, until his retirement, to the service
of Virginia and of the nation. The spirit and the wording of the Declaration are
almost entirely Jefferson's.

Such has been the patient sufferance of these Colonies; and such is now the necessity which constrains them to alter their former Systems of Government. The history of the present King of Great Britain is a history of repeated injuries and usurpations, all having in direct object the establishment of an absolute Tyranny over these States. To prove this, let Facts be submitted to a candid world.

He has refused his Assent to Laws, the most wholesome and necessary for the public good.

He has forbidden his Governors to pass Laws of immediate and pressing importance, unless suspended in their operation till his Assent should be obtained; and when so suspended, he has utterly neglected to attend to them.

He has refused to pass other Laws for the accommodation of large districts of people, unless those people would relinquish the right of Representation in the Legislature, a right inestimable to them and formidable to tyrants only.

He has called together legislative bodies at places unusual, uncomfortable, and distant from the depository of their public Records, for the sole purpose of fatiguing them into compliance with his measures.          10

He has dissolved Representative Houses repeatedly, for opposing with manly firmness his invasions on the rights of people.

He has refused for a long time, after such dissolutions, to cause others to be elected; whereby the Legislative powers, incapable of Annihilation, have returned to the People at large for their exercise; the State remaining in the mean time exposed to all the dangers of invasion from without, and convulsions within.

He has endeavoured to prevent the population of these States; for that purpose obstructing the Laws for Naturalization of Foreigners; refusing to pass others to encourage their migrations hither, and raising the conditions of new Appropriations of Lands.

He has obstructed the Administration of Justice, by refusing his Assent to Laws for establishing Judiciary powers.

He has made Judges dependent on his Will alone, for the tenure of their offices, and the amount and payment of their salaries.          15

He has erected a multitude of New Offices, and sent hither swarms of Officers to harass our people, and eat out their substance.

He has kept among us, in times of peace, Standing Armies without the Consent of our legislatures.

He has affected to render the Military independent of and superior to the Civil power.

He has combined with others to subject us to a jurisdiction foreign to our constitution, and unacknowledged by our laws; giving his Assent to their Acts of pretended Legislation:

For Quartering large bodies of armed troops among us:     20

For Protecting them, by a mock Trial, from punishment for any Murders which they should commit on the Inhabitants of these States:

For cutting off our Trade with all parts of the world:

For imposing Taxes on us without our Consent:

For depriving us in many cases, of the benefits of Trial by Jury:

For transporting us beyond Seas to be tried for pretended offences:     25

For abolishing the free System of English Laws in a neighbouring Province, establishing therein an Arbitrary government, and enlarging its Boundaries so as to render it at once an example and fit instrument for introducing the same absolute rule into these Colonies:

For taking away our Charters, abolishing our most valuable Laws, and altering fundamentally the Forms of our Governments:

For suspending our own Legislatures, and declaring themselves invested with power to legislate for us in all cases whatsoever.

He has abdicated Government here, by declaring us out of his Protection and waging War against us:

He has plundered our seas, ravaged our Coasts, burnt our towns,     30 and destroyed the lives of our people.

He is at this time transporting large Armies of foreign Mercenaries     31 to compleat the works of death, desolation and tyranny, already begun with circumstances of Cruelty & perfidy scarcely paralleled in the most barbarous ages, and totally unworthy the Head of a civilized nation.

He has constrained our fellow Citizens taken Captive on the high     32 Seas to bear Arms against their Country, to become the executioners of their friends and Brethren, or to fall themselves by their Hands.

He has excited domestic insurrections amongst us, and has en-     33 deavoured to bring on the inhabitants of our frontiers, the merciless Indian Savages, whose known rule of warfare, is an undistinguished destruction of all ages, sexes and conditions. In every stage of these Oppressions We have Petitioned for Redress in the most humble terms: Our repeated Petitions have been answered only by repeated injury. A Prince, whose character is thus marked by every act which may define a Tyrant, is unfit to be the ruler of a free people. Nor have We been wanting in attentions to our British brethren. We have warned them from time to time of attempts by their legislature to extend an unwarrantable jurisdiction over us. We have reminded them of the circumstances of our emigration and settlement here. We have appealed to their native justice and magnanimity, and we have conjured them by the ties of our common kindred to disavow these usurpations, which, would inevitably interrupt our connections and correspondence. They too have been deaf to the voice of justice and of consanguinity. We must, therefore, acquiesce in the necessity, which denounces our Separation, and hold them, as we hold the rest of mankind, Enemies in War, in Peace Friends.

We, THEREFORE, the Representatives of the UNITED STATES OF AMER- 34 ICA, in General Congress Assembled, appealing to the Supreme Judge of the world for the rectitude of our intentions, do, in the Name and by Authority of the good People of these Colonies, solemnly publish and declare, That these United Colonies are, and of Right ought to be FREE AND INDEPENDENT STATES; that they are Absolved from all Allegiance to the British Crown, and that all political connection between them and the State of Great Britain, is and ought to be totally dissolved; and that as Free and Independent States, they have full Power to levy War, conclude Peace, contract Alliances, establish Commerce, and to do all other Acts and Things which Independent States may of right do.

And for the support of this Declaration, with a firm reliance on 35 the protection of divine Providence, we mutually pledge to each other our Lives, our Fortunes and our sacred Honor.

# Questions

1. What assumptions lie behind the numerous specific reasons that are given to justify the rebellion? Set forth the gist of that argument of the Declaration using the form of reasoning known as a syllogism, which consists of a major premise (such as "All men are mortal"), a minor premise ("Socrates is a man"), and a conclusion ("Therefore, Socrates is mortal"). For a brief discussion of syllogisms, see pages 1143–1144 (deduction).

2. What audience is being addressed in the Declaration of Independence? Cite passages in the text that support your answer.

3. The Library of Congress has the original manuscript of the rough draft of the Declaration. This manuscript itself includes revisions that are indicated below, but it was later further revised. We print the first part of the second paragraph of the draft, and after it the corresponding part of the final version. Try to account for the changes within the draft, and from the revised draft to the final version.

*self evident*

We hold these truths to be ~~sacred & undeniable~~, that all men are

*they are endowed by their creator*

created equal ~~& independent~~, that ~~from that equal creation they~~ *with*

~~derive equal rights some of which are~~        ~~in rights~~

*rights; that these*

inherent & inalienable among ~~which~~ are ~~the preservation~~

~~of~~ life, liberty, & the pursuit of happiness.

We hold these Truths to be self-evident, that all Men are created equal, that they are endowed by their Creator with certain unalienable Rights, that among these are Life, Liberty, and the Pursuit of Happiness.

In a paragraph evaluate the changes. Try to put yourself into Jefferson's mind and see if you can sense why Jefferson made the changes.

4. In a paragraph define *happiness*, and then in a second paragraph explain why, in your opinion, Jefferson spoke of "the pursuit of happiness" rather than of "happiness."

5. In "We Have No 'Right to Happiness' " (page 968) C. S. Lewis discusses the meaning of "the pursuit of happiness" in the Declaration, and a current misinterpretation of the phrase. How does he explain and define the phrase? How does his interpretation differ from what he considers an erroneous interpretation?

6. In a paragraph argue that the assertion that "all Men are created equal" is nonsense, or, on the other hand, that it makes sense.

7. If every person has an unalienable right to life, how can capital punishment be reconciled with the Declaration of Independence? (You need not in fact be a supporter of capital punishment; simply offer the best defense you can think of, in an effort to make it harmonious with the Declaration.)

Rosika Schwimmer

# Court Record of Petition for Naturalization

$R$osika Schwimmer, the petitioner herein, called as a witness in her own behalf, having been first duly sworn, was examined by Mr. Jordan, and testified as follows:

Q. What is your full name, please?

A. Rosika Schwimmer.

Q. You were born in Hungary?

A. Hungary, Budapest. . . .                                                    5

Q. Is it your intention to remain in the United States permanently?

A. It is.

Q. Is there anything in our form of government that you are not in sympathy with?

A. Nothing.

Q. You have read the oath of allegiance?                                      10

A. I did.

Q. Are you able to take that oath without any reservations?

A. I am.

Q. I would like for you to inform the court that this is the information sheet you filled out in connection with your application for citizenship (*handing document to the witness*).

A. Yes.                                                                        15

Q. And in answer to question 22, "If necessary, are you willing to take up arms in defense of this country?" You have answered, "I would not take up arms personally."

A. Yes.

---

Rosika Schwimmer (1877–1948), a Hungarian feminist and pacifist, achieved international fame during the First World War, when she persuaded Henry Ford to support the Ford Peace Ship. In 1921 she moved to the United States, and six years later she applied for citizenship. The court denied her request, as we see in the part of the transcript given here, because she refused to swear that she would bear arms in the defense of the country. The case was appealed, but the Supreme Court upheld the decision, though Justices Holmes, Brandeis, and Sanford dissented. We print Butler's majority opinion on page 747 and Holmes's dissent on 753.

Q. And that is correct, is it?

A. Yes.

Q. Now, on January 11, 1927, Mr. Schlotfeldt wrote you a letter, 20 didn't he?

A. Yes.

Q. About some statement you had made to Colonel Stone?

A. Well, it wasn't a statement. It was part of a letter. It wasn't a statement at all.

Q. And in that you also reiterated to Mr. Schlotfeldt to this effect: "I am an uncompromising pacifist for whom even Jane Addams is not enough of a pacifist. I am an absolute atheist. I have no sense of nationalism."

A. Yes.                                                                25

Q. Is that correct?

A. Yes, that is correct.

Q. THE COURT: What do you mean by "no sense of nationalism?"

A. I mean that if I had a sense of nationalism I could not want to leave the Hungarian nationality into which I was born.

Q. This has nothing to do with war. I am asking you what you 30 mean when you say you have no sense of nationalism, because nationalism is a very comprehensive term and includes more than war.

A. I didn't speak now of war. Perhaps I didn't express myself well enough, Your Honor. I say I meant when I said this, if I had a feeling of nationalism, then being born a Hungarian, I would have such a feeling of Hungarian nationality that I would not want to leave that nationality, whatever the things are that are displeasing me.

Q. In other words, if something came up between Hungary and the United States, your sympathies would still be with Hungary?

A. No, to the contrary they would not be. I said I have no sense of nationality that would bind me to Hungary.

Q. Of course, I do not believe that time is ever coming when this country, this government is going to send its women to fight. We have not as yet a regiment of Amazons.

A. I hope you don't have.                                              35

Q. But we may have to send them as nurses to look after our fighters. We may have to send them in the various religious organizations, like the Y.M.C.A. or the Knights of Columbus, to give succor and aid to our fighters. Now, are you willing to be sent on missions of that sort by this government to look after the boys that are fighting for this country?

A. I am willing to do everything that an American citizen has to do, except fighting.

Q. Well, our women do not fight. We do not expect you to shoulder a musket.

A. Oh, I am willing to obey every law that the American government compels its citizens to do.

Q. Are you willing to do anything that an American woman is 40 called upon to do? I mean an American citizen, a woman of this country.

A. Yes, I am, because I have not found that anything was asked that was against—I mean it is only the fighting question. That is, if American women would be compelled to do that, I would not do that.

Q. You say you are an uncompromising pacifist?

A. Yes.

Q. How far does that go? Does it refer only to yourself?

A. Yes. 45

Q. That you are not going to use your fists on somebody?

A. Yes.

Q. Or that you disapprove of the government fighting?

A. It means that I disapprove of the government asking me to fight.

Q. You mean fight personally? 50

A. Yes, physically.

Q. Carrying a gun?

A. Yes.

Q. Is that as far as it goes?

A. That is as far as it goes. 55

Q. Or is it more deep-seated?

A. No.

Q. Really, of course, none of us wants war—

A. Yes.

Q. But there are a great many of us when war comes, and our 60 country is in danger who get our backs to the wall—

A. Yes.

Q. And we fight until there is nothing but the wall left.

A. Yes.

Q. Now, are you willing to do that?

A. I am afraid, Your Honor, I did not catch the point of the ques- 65 tion. I am awfully sorry.

Q. I don't mean to bear arms for the country.

A. Yes.

Q. The time will never come, I venture to say, when the women of the United States will have to bear arms.

A. Well, I am not willing to bear arms. In every other single way, civic way, I am ready to follow the law and do everything that the law compels American citizens to do. I am willing to do that. That is why I say I can take the oath of allegiance because as far as I, with the able help of my lawyers, could find out there is nothing that I could be compelled to do that I could not do.

Q. Your lawyer can't search into your heart any more than I can. You are the only one that can answer these questions. 70

A. I am opening my heart very frankly because there is nothing to hide. As I said when the question came up, if it is a question of fighting, as much as I desire American citizenship I would not seek the citizenship.

Q. Now, is it a question of fighting personally?

A. Yes.

Q. You yourself?

A. Myself. 75

Q. You do not care how many other women fight?

A. I don't care because I consider it a question of conscience. If there are women fighters, it is their business.

Q. Do you expect to spread this propaganda throughout this country with other women?

A. Which propaganda, may I ask?

Q. That you are an uncompromising pacifist and will not fight. 80

A. Oh, of course, I am always ready to tell that to anyone who wants to hear it.

Q. What is your occupation, madam?

A. I am a writer and lecturer.

Q. And in your writings and in your lectures you take up this question of war and pacifism?

A. If I am asked for that, I do. 85

Q. You know we have a great deal to give—at least we think so—

A. I think so, too.

Q. —when we confer citizenship upon people of other countries.

A. I think so, too.

Q. And we expect when we do that they come in on an equal 90 footing, and out of regard to the other stockholders in this great united corporation we have to see to it that any partners or stockholders coming in are willing to do what those who are already here are willing to do. Now, it seems that your general views—

Now, I am not at all against people writing. There are a great many American citizens who are now decrying the possibility of the occurrence of war. They are against it. We have a great many pacifists in this country, but when the time comes, and they are called out for the country, they forget all their views, all of the things they have been talking about, and start in on the defense of the home.

Now, you can't come in halfway. You must come in the whole distance, because there you are and under that flag is our country, and you can't get under that flag unless you promise to do every single thing that the citizens of this country not only have permission to do, but are willing to do.

A. Well, I can only repeat what I said: that I am willing to do everything that, to my knowledge to this day, American women are asked to do.

THE COURT: Well, can we ask anything more than that?

MR. JORDAN: I would just like, Your Honor, to bring out a few things in Madame Schwimmer's letter to Mr. Schlotfeldt, and also excerpts from one of her radio speeches.

In the letter here, "My answer to question 22 in my petition for final examination demonstrated that I am an uncompromising pacifist." A little farther down: "Highly as I prize the privilege of American citizenship, I could not compromise my way into it by giving an untrue answer to question 22, though for all practical purposes I might have done so."

Then there are a few little excerpts here from the radio talks I would like the court to hear: "I cannot see that a woman's refusal to take up arms is a contradiction to the oath of allegiance, promising to support and defend the Constitution and laws of the United States of America. I have for the fulfillment of this duty other ways and means in mind."

MRS. RABE: Would you mind reading the rest of that statement right there?

MR. JORDAN: That finishes that paragraph, I believe.

MRS. RABE: Oh, does it? I thought she spoke about having written in favor of our Constitution.

THE COURT: Let me ask you this one question—

A. Yes, sir.

Q. If you were called to the service, and the kind of work that women usually can perform better than the men can—say as a nurse or as someone to give cheer to the soldiers—and you were at some place in a war, which I hope never will come, and you saw someone coming in the headquarters or the barracks, wherever it was, with a pistol in his hand to shoot the back of an officer of our country, and you had a pistol handy by, would you kill him?

A. No, I would not.

THE COURT: The application is denied.

105

MR. GEMMILL: Just a moment, Your Honor. We would like to perfect our record. We expect to go up on this case, Your Honor. . . .

MR. GEMMILL: I would like to ask Mrs. Schwimmer one question.

Q. What do you mean, Mrs. Schwimmer, when you say you can take the oath and you are willing to support and defend the Constitution and the laws of the United States?

A. I mean the things that I have practically already done; that I was in many meetings in which it was said that it would be far better to have a Soviet regime—"that is a far better kind of regime"—and myself having lived under Soviet regime in Hungary, I could get up and tell the people—as I have practically done—"Don't think you change to something better." To this day there is no better form of government than that of the United States, which is by the people, for the people, as the great saying is, and that Sovietism is nothing but tyranny under another name—old fashioned tyranny under a new name; and I wrote these things and I said these things, and I can prove it by writings which I can get from Hungary; so that is what I meant; that there are other means to defend the Constitution and the institutions of this country.

Q. Is it your belief, Mrs. Schwimmer, your own personal belief, that you would not take the life of anyone?

110

A. Yes.

Q. Of any animal?

A. Animals, no. I have no objections against taking the life of animals. I personally wouldn't shoot, but I have no objections against that; but I would not shoot. Even if a pistol was pointed to me, I would not shoot.

Q. Is that what you had in mind when you answered the court's last question—

A. Yes.

115

Q. —relative to the shooting of the officer?

A. Yes, of course, I couldn't.

THE COURT: What do you mean by that?

MR. GEMMILL: I mean to say, Your Honor, I am trying to explain her answer. It wasn't the cold-blooded murder of the United States officer that Mrs. Schwimmer had in mind. It was her feeling against the killing of anyone.

THE WITNESS: Yes.                                                                120

MR. GEMMILL: May I ask one or two more questions?

THE COURT: Yes.

MR. GEMMILL: Under the same case, Mrs. Schwimmer, would you have given the officer any warning, if it was possible?

A. Certainly.

Q. So that he could defend himself?                                             125

A. Certainly.

THE COURT: That is, you would have given him—

A. I would try to hit the pistol out of the man's hand who tries to shoot. That is what I would try to do.

Q. Let me ask you this: Would you have thrown yourself on the assailant?

A. Yes, I might do that.                                                         130

Q. And run the risk of being shot yourself?

A. Yes, I might do that. Yes.

MR. JORDAN: You say you might do that?

A. Well, I speak of a possibility. I can't say I would do that. We speak of hypothetical things. I can't say I "will" do that, because there is no occasion for it.

THE COURT: One never can tell until the occasion arises what will    135
be done.

THE WITNESS: If it would happen this moment I would do it.

THE COURT: But my first question referred not to your trying to stop the man from reaching the American soldier.

THE WITNESS: I understand.

THE COURT: —because he may have been ten feet off—

THE WITNESS: I understand.                                                       140

THE COURT: —and the American soldier would have been killed before you could have reached his assailant.

THE WITNESS: Yes.

THE COURT: I am asking if you had the weapon, if it were handy by—

THE WITNESS: Yes.

THE COURT: —would you have killed the assailant—                            145

THE WITNESS: No.

THE COURT: —before he reached the American soldier?

THE WITNESS: No.

THE COURT: Then I am of the same opinion.

MR. GEMMILL: Supposing that pistol had been pointed at you and    150
you had a pistol?

A. I would not defend myself. I mean I wouldn't take a pistol to defend myself even if you handed it to me; under no circumstances.

THE COURT: That question is not involved at all. This is a very close question, gentlemen, and I am really refusing this because the government, I think has no appeal, but it is an attitude—the attitude of the applicant—that I think is not common with the women of this country.

Is there anything more, gentlemen?

MR. GEMMILL: I just want to be a little careful about this record.

THE COURT: Suppose it is written up and then we will reduce it to    155
an agreed statement of facts?

MR. GEMMILL: That is satisfactory.

MR. JORDAN: Do you care, Your Honor, to take the statements of the witnesses so that they will not be required further?

THE COURT: Oh, yes. Let both witnesses step forward, please. . . .

THE COURT: Both of the witnesses believe that the applicant is a thoroughly good woman.

MR. BIRD: Yes.    160

MISS HOLBROOK: Yes, I do.

THE COURT: That is all. That is what we want to know.

MR. JORDAN: The witnesses may be excused then.

MR. GEMMILL: I suppose in this kind of a case a motion for a new trial first should be made.

THE COURT: No, I think not.    165

MR. GEMMILL: Motion in arrest, or pray an appeal then. . . .

THE COURT: . . . You understand, madam, that while the court may have said some things that shock, perhaps, your views of nationalism, we are here to administer the law as we see it. We have taken an oath for that purpose and we try to live up to it. There is nothing personal about it all.

MADAME SCHWIMMER: I realize that, Your Honor.

Pierce Butler

# Opinion of the Supreme Court, in *The United States of America, Petitioner, v. Rosika Schwimmer*

**R**espondent filed a petition for naturalization in the Dis-   1
trict Court for the Northern District of Illinois. The court found her
unable, without mental reservation, to take the prescribed oath of allegiance and not attached to the principles of the Constitution of the
United States and not well disposed to the good order and happiness
of the same; and it denied her application. The Circuit Court of Appeals
reversed the decree and directed the District Court to grant respondent's petition 27 F. (2d) 742.

The Naturalization Act of June 16, 1906 requires:   2

"He [the applicant for naturalization] shall, before he is admitted   3
to citizenship, declare an oath in open court . . . that he will support
and defend the Constitution and laws of the United States against all
enemies, foreign and domestic, and bear true faith and allegiance to
the same." U.S.C., Tit. 8, § 381.

"It shall be made to appear to the satisfaction of the court . . . that   4
during that time [at least 5 years preceding the application] he has
behaved as a man of good moral character, attached to the principles
of the Constitution of the United States, and we!! disposed to the good
order and happiness of the same. . . ." § 382.

Respondent was born in Hungary in 1877 and is a citizen of that   5
country. She came to the United States in August, 1921, to visit and
lecture, has resided in Illinois since the latter part of that month, declared her intention to become a citizen the following November, and

---

Pierce Butler (1866–1939) practiced law in Minnesota until President Harding
appointed him to the Supreme Court in 1923. Butler, who was generally regarded
as a conservative, delivered the majority opinion in the Schwimmer case. We
print part of the Court record of Schwimmer's petition on page 739, and Holmes's
dissent on page 753.

filed petition for naturalization in September, 1926. On a preliminary form, she stated that she understood the principles of and fully believed in our form of government and that she had read, and in becoming a citizen was willing to take, the oath of allegiance. Question 22 was this: "If necessary, are you willing to take up arms in defense of this country?" She answered: "I would not take up arms personally."

She testified that she did not want to remain subject to Hungary,  6
found the United States nearest her ideals of a democratic republic, and that she could whole-heartedly take the oath of allegiance. She said: "I cannot see that a woman's refusal to take up arms is a contradiction to the oath of allegiance." For the fulfillment of the duty to support and defend the Constitution and laws, she had in mind other ways and means. She referred to her interest in civic life, to her wide reading and attendance at lectures and meetings, mentioned her knowledge of foreign languages and that she occasionally glanced through Hungarian, French, German, Dutch, Scandinavian, and Italian publications and said that she could imagine finding in meetings and publications attacks on the American form of government and she would conceive it her duty to uphold it against such attacks. She expressed steadfast opposition to any undemocratic form of government like proletariat, fascist, white terror, or military dictatorships. "All my past work proves that I have always served democratic ideals and fought—though not with arms—against undemocratic institutions." She stated that before coming to this country she had defended American ideals and had defended America in 1924 during an international pacifist congress in Washington.

She also testified: "If . . . the United States can compel its women  7
citizens to take up arms in the defense of the country—something that no other civilized government has ever attempted—I would not be able to comply with this requirement of American citizenship. In this case I would recognize the right of the Government to deal with me as it is dealing with its male citizens who for conscientious reasons refuse to take up arms."

The district director of naturalization by letter called her attention  8
to a statement made by her in private correspondence: "I am an uncompromising pacifist . . . I have no sense of nationalism, only a cosmic consciousness of belonging to the human family." She answered that the statement in her petition demonstrated that she was an uncompromising pacifist. "Highly as I prize the privilege of American citizenship I could not compromise my way into it by giving an

untrue answer to question 22, though for all practical purposes I might have done so, as even men of my age—I was 49 years old last September—are not called to take up arms. . . . That 'I have no nationalistic feeling' is evident from the fact that I wish to give up the nationality of my birth and to adopt a country which is based on principles and institutions more in harmony with my ideals. My 'cosmic consciousness of belonging to the human family' is shared by all those who believe that all human beings are the children of God."

And at the hearing she reiterated her ability and willingness to take the oath of allegiance without reservation and added: "I am willing to do everything that an American citizen has to do except fighting. If American women would be compelled to do that, I would not do that. I am an uncompromising pacifist. . . . I do not care how many other women fight, because I consider it a question of conscience. I am not willing to bear arms. In every other single way I am ready to follow the law and do everything that the law compels American citizens to do. That is why I can take the oath of allegiance, because, as far as I can find out, there is nothing that I could be compelled to do that I can not do. . . . With reference to spreading propaganda among the women throughout the country about my being an uncompromising pacifist and not willing to fight, I am always ready to tell anyone who wants to hear it that I am an uncompromising pacifist and will not fight. In my writings and in my lectures I take up the question of war and pacifism if I am asked for that." 9

Except for eligibility to the Presidency, naturalized citizens stand on the same footing as do native born citizens. All alike owe allegiance to the Government, and the Government owes to them the duty of protection. These are reciprocal obligations and each is a consideration for the other. *Luria* v. *United States*, 231 U.S. 9, 22. But aliens can acquire such equality only by naturalization according to the uniform rules prescribed by the Congress. They have no natural right to become citizens, but only that which is by statute conferred upon them. Because of the great value of the privileges conferred by naturalization, the statutes prescribing qualifications and governing procedure for admission are to be construed with definite purpose to favor and support the Government. And, in order to safeguard against admission of those who are unworthy or who for any reason fail to measure up to required standards, the law puts the burden upon every applicant to show by satisfactory evidence that he has the specified qualifications. *Tutun* v. *United States*, 270 U.S. 568, 578. And see *United States* v. *Ginsberg*, 243. U.S. 472, 475. 10

Every alien claiming citizenship is given the right to submit his   11
petition and evidence in support of it. And, if the requisite facts are
established, he is entitled as of right to admission. On applications for
naturalization, the court's function is "to receive the testimony, to compare it with the law, and to judge on both law and fact." *Spratt* v.
*Spratt,* 4 Pet. 393, 408. We quite recently declared that: "Citizenship
is a high privilege and when doubts exist concerning a grant of it,
generally at least, they should be resolved in favor of the United States
and against the claimant." *United States* v. *Manzi,* 276 U.S. 463, 467.
And when, upon a fair consideration of the evidence adduced upon
an application for citizenship, doubt remains in the mind of the court
as to any essential matter of fact, the United States is entitled to the
benefit of such doubt and the application should be denied.

That it is the duty of citizens by force of arms to defend our gov-   12
ernment against all enemies whenever necessity arises is a fundamental principle of the Constitution.

The common defense was one of the purposes for which the people   13
ordained and established the Constitution. It empowers Congress to
provide for such defense, to declare war, to raise and support armies,
to maintain a navy, to make rules for the government and regulation
of the land and naval forces, to provide for organizing, arming and
disciplining the militia, and for calling it forth to execute the laws of
the Union, suppress insurrections and repel invasions; it makes the
President commander in chief of the army and navy and of the militia
of the several States when called into the service of the United States;
it declares that a well regulated militia, being necessary to the security
of a free State, the right of the people to keep and bear arms, shall not
be infringed. We need not refer to the numerous statutes that contemplate defense of the United States, its Constitution and laws by armed
citizens. This Court, in the *Selective Draft Laws Cases,* 245 U.S. 366,
speaking through Chief Justice White, said (p. 378) that "the very conception of a just government and its duty to the citizen includes the
reciprocal obligation of the citizen to render military service in case of
need. . . ."

Whatever tends to lessen the willingness of citizens to discharge   14
their duty to bear arms in the country's defense detracts from the
strength and safety of the Government. And their opinions and beliefs
as well as their behavior indicating a disposition to hinder in the performance of that duty are subjects of inquiry under the statutory provisions governing naturalization and are of vital importance, for if all
or a large number of citizens oppose such defense the "good order

and happiness" of the United States can not long endure. And it is evident that the views of applicants for naturalization in respect of such matters may not be disregarded. The influence of conscientious objectors against the use of military force in defense of the principles of our Government is apt to be more detrimental than their mere refusal to bear arms. The fact that, by reason of sex, age or other cause, they may be unfit to serve does not lessen their purpose or power to influence others. It is clear from her own statements that the declared opinions of respondent as to armed defense by citizens against enemies of the country were directly pertinent to the investigation of her application.

The record shows that respondent strongly desires to become a  15 citizen. She is a linguist, lecturer and writer; she is well educated and accustomed to discuss government and civic affairs. Her testimony should be considered having regard to her interest and disclosed ability correctly to express herself. Her claim at the hearing that she possessed the required qualifications and was willing to take the oath was much impaired by other parts of her testimony. Taken as a whole it shows that her objection to military service rests on reasons other than mere inability because of her sex and age personally to bear arms. Her expressed willingness to be treated as the Government dealt with conscientious objectors who refused to take up arms in the recent war indicates that she deemed herself to belong to that class. The fact that she is an uncompromising pacifist with no sense of nationalism but only a cosmic sense of belonging to the human family justifies belief that she may be opposed to the use of military force as contemplated by our Constitution and laws. And her testimony clearly suggests that she is disposed to exert her power to influence others to such opposition.

A pacifist in the general sense of the word is one who seeks to  16 maintain peace and to abolish war. Such purposes are in harmony with the Constitution and policy of our Government. But the word is also used and understood to mean one who refuses or is unwilling for any purpose to bear arms because of conscientious considerations and who is disposed to encourage others in such refusal. And one who is without any sense of nationalism is not well bound or held by the ties of affection to any nation or government. Such persons are liable to be incapable of the attachment for and devotion to the principles of our Constitution that is required for aliens seeking naturalization.

It is shown by official records and everywhere well known that  17 during the recent war there were found among those who described

themselves as pacifists and conscientious objectors many citizens—
though happily a minute part of all—who were unwilling to bear arms
in that crisis and who refused to obey the laws of the United States
and the lawful commands of its officers and encouraged such disobedience in others. Local boards found it necessary to issue a great
number of noncombatant certificates, and several thousand who were
called to camp made claim because of conscience for exemption from
any form of military service. Several hundred were convicted and sentenced to imprisonment for offenses involving disobedience, deser-
tion, propaganda and sedition. It is obvious that the acts of such offenders evidence a want of that attachment to the principles of the
Constitution of which the applicant is required to give affirmative evidence by the Naturalization Act.

The language used by respondent to describe her attitude in re-  18
spect of the principles of the Constitution was vague and ambiguous;
the burden was upon her to show what she meant and that her pacifism
and lack of nationalistic sense did not oppose the principle that it is a
duty of citizenship by force of arms when necessary to defend the
country against all enemies, and that her opinions and beliefs would
not prevent or impair the true faith and allegiance required by the Act.
She failed to do so. The District Court was bound by the law to deny
her application.

*The decree of the Circuit Court of
Appeals is reversed.
The decree of the District Court is
affirmed.*[1]

[1] Questions on this selection appear on page 754.

Oliver Wendell Holmes

# Dissent in the Rosika Schwimmer Case

$T$he applicant seems to be a woman of superior character  1
and intelligence, obviously more than ordinarily desirable as a citizen
of the United States. It is agreed that she is qualified for citizenship
except so far as the views set forth in a statement of facts "may show
that the applicant is not attached to the principles of the Constitution
of the United States and well disposed to the good order and happiness
of the same, and except in so far as the same may show that she cannot
take the oath of allegiance without a mental reservation." The views
referred to are an extreme opinion in favor of pacifism and a statement
that she would not bear arms to defend the Constitution. So far as the
adequacy of her oath is concerned, I hardly can see how it is affected
by the statement, inasmuch as she is a woman over fifty years of age,
and would not be allowed to bear arms if she wanted to. And as to
the opinion the whole examination of the applicant shows that she
holds none of the now-dreaded creeds, but thoroughly believes in organized government and prefers that of the United States to any other
in the world. Surely it cannot show lack of attachment to the principles
of the Constitution that she thinks it can be improved. I suppose that
most intelligent people think that it might be. Her particular improvement looking to the abolition of war seems to me not materially different in its bearing on this case from a wish to establish cabinet government as in England, or a single house, or one term of seven years

Oliver Wendell Holmes (1841–1935) was the son of a distinguished Boston writer
with the same name. After serving with distinction as a soldier in the Civil War,
the younger Holmes began practicing law in 1867. In 1870 he began to teach
law at Harvard, and he soon achieved fame by his lectures and his publications.
In 1882 he was appointed to the Massachusetts supreme judicial court; in 1902
he was appointed to the United States Supreme Court. Holmes preached "judicial restraint"; that is, he frequently dissented from the " strict contructionists,"
who, in his opinion, capriciously thwarted the will of the people as it was expressed in the actions of their elected representatives.
     We give here his dissent in the Schwimmer case. For a transcript of part of
the earlier proceedings in this case, see page 739, and for the Court's majority
opinion see page 747.

for the President. To touch a more burning question, only a judge mad with partisanship would exclude because the applicant thought that the Eighteenth Amendment should be repealed.

Of course the fear is that if a war came the applicant would exert activities such as were dealt with in *Schenck* v. *United States*, 249 U.S. 47. But that seems to me unfounded. Her position and motives are wholly different from those of Schenck. She is an optimist and states in strong and, I do not doubt, sincere words her belief that war will disappear and that the impending destiny of mankind is to unite in peaceful leagues. I do not share that optimism nor do I think that a philosophic view of the world would regard war as absurd. But most people who have known it regard it with horror, as a last resort, and, even if not yet ready for cosmopolitan efforts, would welcome any practicable combination that would increase the power on the side of peace. The notion that the applicant's optimistic anticipations would make her a worse citizen is sufficiently answered by her examination, which seems to me a better argument for her admission than any I can offer. Some of her answers might excite popular prejudice, but if there is any principle of the Constitution that more imperatively calls for attachment than any other it is the principle of free thought—not free thought for those who agree with us but freedom for the thought that we hate. I think that we should adhere to that principle with regard to admission into, as well as to life within, this country. And, recurring to the opinion that bars this applicant's way, I would suggest that the Quakers have done their share to make the country what it is, that many citizens agree with the applicant's belief, and that I had not supposed hitherto that we regretted our inability to expel them because they believe more than some of us do in the teachings of the Sermon on the Mount.

# Questions

1. In Dickens's *Oliver Twist* an irate character exclaims, "The law is a ass." Given Mr. Jordan's questions, in the Schwimmer case, and given the majority decision of the Supreme Court, can we say that at least in this case the law was "a ass"? Explain.
2. In a sentence or two summarize Holmes's views of war.
3. Pick out the one sentence in Holmes's dissent that you think is the most memorable, perhaps for *what* is said, perhaps for the *way* it is said, or perhaps for both.

4. If you found Holmes's opinion easier and more enjoyable to read than Butler's, try to account for the difference.

Byron R. White

# Opinion of the Supreme Court, in *New Jersey* v. *T.L.O.* [On the Right to Search Students]

In determining whether the search at issue in this case vi- 1 olated the Fourth Amendment, we are faced initially with the question whether that amendment's prohibition on unreasonable searches and seizures applies to searches conducted by public school officials. We hold that it does.

It is now beyond dispute that "the Federal Constitution, by virtue 2

---

In January 1985, a majority of the United States Supreme Court, in a case called *New Jersey* v. *T.L.O.* (a student's initials), ruled 6–3 that a school official's search of a student who is suspected of disobeying a school regulation does not violate the Fourth Amendment's protection against unreasonable searches and seizures.

The case originated thus: an assistant principal in a New Jersey high school opened the purse of a fourteen-year-old girl who had been caught violating school rules by smoking in the lavatory. The girl denied that she ever smoked, and the assistant principal thought that the contents of her purse would show whether or not she was lying. The purse was found to contain cigarettes, marijuana, and some notes that seemed to indicate that she sold marijuana to other students. The school then called the police.

The case went through three lower courts; almost five years after the event occurred, the case reached the Supreme Court. Associate Justice Byron R. White wrote the majority opinion, joined by Chief Justice Warren E. Burger and by Associate Justices Lewis F. Powell, Jr., William H. Rehnquist, and Sandra Day O'Connor. Associate Justice Harry A. Blackmun concurred in a separate opinion. Associate Justices William J. Brennan, Jr., John Paul Stevens, and Thurgood Marshall dissented in part.

of the 14th Amendment, prohibits unreasonable searches and seizures by state officers." Equally indisputable is the proposition that the 14th Amendment protects the rights of students against encroachment by public school officials.

On reargument, however, the State of New Jersey has argued that 3 the history of the Fourth Amendment indicates that the amendment was intended to regulate only searches and seizures carried out by law enforcement officers; accordingly, although public school officials are concededly state agents for purposes of the 14th Amendment, the Fourth Amendment creates no rights enforceable against them.

But this Court has never limited the amendment's prohibition on 4 unreasonable searches and seizures to operations conducted by the police. Rather, the Court has long spoken of the Fourth Amendment's strictures as restraints imposed upon "governmental action"—that is, "upon the activities of sovereign authority." Accordingly, we have held the Fourth Amendment applicable to the activities of civil as well as criminal authorities: building inspectors, OSHA inspectors, and even firemen entering privately owned premises to battle a fire, are all subject to the restraints imposed by the Fourth Amendment.

Notwithstanding the general applicability of the Fourth Amend- 5 ment to the activities of civil authorities, a few courts have concluded that school officials are exempt from the dictates of the Fourth Amendment by virtue of the special nature of their authority over school-children. Teachers and school administrators, it is said, act *in loco parentis* [i.e., in place of a parent] in their dealings with students: their authority is that of the parent, not the State, and is therefore not subject to the limits of the Fourth Amendment.

Such reasoning is in tension with contemporary reality and the 6 teachings of this Court. We have held school officials subject to the commands of the First Amendment, and the Due Process Clause of the 14th Amendment. If school authorities are state actors for purposes of the constitutional guarantees of freedom of expression and due process, it is difficult to understand why they should be deemed to be exercising parental rather than public authority when conducting searches of their students.

In carrying out searches and other disciplinary functions pursuant 7 to such policies, school officials act as representatives of the State, not merely as surrogates for the parents, and they cannot claim the parents' immunity from the strictures of the Fourth Amendment.

To hold that the Fourth Amendment applies to searches conducted 8 by school authorities is only to begin the inquiry into the standards governing such searches. Although the underlying command of the Fourth Amendment is always that searches and seizures be reasonable, what is reasonable depends on the context within which a search takes place.

## [*Standard of Reasonableness*]

The determination of the standard of reasonableness governing any  9
specific class of searches requires balancing the need to search against the invasion which the search entails. On one side of the balance are arrayed the individual's legitimate expectations of privacy and personal security; on the other, the government's need for effective methods to deal with breaches of public order.

We have recognized that even a limited search of the person is a  10
substantial invasion of privacy. A search of a child's person or of a closed purse or other bag carried on her person, no less than a similar search carried out on an adult, is undoubtedly a severe violation of subjective expectations of privacy.

Of course, the Fourth Amendment does not protect subjective ex-  11
pectations of privacy that are unreasonable or otherwise "illegitimate." The State of New Jersey has argued that because of the pervasive supervision to which children in the schools are necessarily subject, a child has virtually no legitimate expectation of privacy in articles of personal property "unnecessarily" carried into a school. This argument has two factual premises: (1) the fundamental incompatibility of expectations of privacy with the maintenance of a sound educational environment; and (2) the minimal interest of the child in bringing any items of personal property into the school. Both premises are severely flawed.

Although this Court may take notice of the difficulty of maintain-  12
ing discipline in the public schools today, the situation is not so dire that students in the schools may claim no legitimate expectations of privacy.

## [*Privacy and Discipline*]

Against the child's interest in privacy must be set the substantial in-  13
terest of teachers and administrators in maintaining discipline in the classroom and on school grounds. Maintaining order in the classroom has never been easy, but in recent years, school disorder has often taken particularly ugly forms; drug use and violent crime in the schools

have become major social problems. Accordingly, we have recognized that maintaining security and order in the schools requires a certain degree of flexibility in school disciplinary procedures, and we have respected the value of preserving the informality of the student-teacher relationship.

How, then, should we strike the balance between the school- 14 child's legitimate expectations of privacy and the school's equally legitimate need to maintain an environment in which learning can take place? It is evident that the school setting requires some easing of the restrictions to which searches by public authorities are ordinarily subject. The warrant requirement, in particular, is unsuited to the school environment; requiring a teacher to obtain a warrant before searching a child suspected of an infraction of school rules (or of the criminal law) would unduly interfere with the maintenance of the swift and informal disciplinary procedures needed in the schools. We hold today that school officials need not obtain a warrant before searching a student who is under their authority.

The school setting also requires some modification of the level of 15 suspicion of illicit activity needed to justify a search. Ordinarily, a search—even one that may permissibly be carried out without a warrant—must be based upon "probable cause" to believe that a violation of the law has occurred. However, "probable cause" is not an irreducible requirement of a valid search.

## [Balancing of Interests]

The fundamental command of the Fourth Amendment is that searches 16 and seizures be reasonable, and although "both the concept of probable cause and the requirement of a warrant bear on the reasonableness of a search, . . . in certain limited circumstances neither is required." Thus, we have in a number of cases recognized the legality of searches and seizures based on suspicions that, although "reasonable," do not rise to the level of probable cause. Where a careful balancing of governmental and private interests suggests that the public interest is best served by a Fourth Amendment standard of reasonableness that stops short of probable cause, we have not hesitated to adopt such a standard.

We join the majority of courts that have examined this issue in 17 concluding that the accommodation of the privacy interests of schoolchildren with the substantial need of teachers and administrators for freedom to maintain order in the schools does not require strict adherence to the requirement that searches be based on probable cause to believe that the subject of the search has violated or is violating the law.

Rather, the legality of a search of a student should depend simply on the reasonableness, under all the circumstances, of the search. Determining the reasonableness of any search involves a twofold inquiry; first, one must consider "whether the . . . action was justified at its inception," second, one must determine whether the search as actually conducted "was reasonably related in scope to the circumstances which justified the interference in the first place." 18

Under ordinary circumstances, a search of a student by a teacher or other school official will be "justified at its inception" when there are reasonable grounds for suspecting that the search will turn up evidence that the student has violated or is violating either the law or the rules of the school. Such a search will be permissible in its scope when the measures adopted are reasonably related to the objectives of the search and not excessively intrusive in light of the age and sex of the student and the nature of the infraction. 19

This standard will, we trust, neither unduly burden the efforts of school authorities to maintain order in their schools nor authorize unrestrained intrusions upon the privacy of schoolchildren. By focusing attention on the question of reasonableness, the standard will spare teachers and school administrators the necessity of schooling themselves in the niceties of probable cause and permit them to regulate their conduct according to the dictates of reason and common sense. At the same time, the reasonableness standard should insure that the interests of students will be invaded no more than is necessary to achieve the legitimate end of preserving order in the schools. 20

There remains the question of the legality of the search in this case. We recognize that the "reasonable grounds" standard applied by the New Jersey Supreme Court in its consideration of this question is not substantially different from the standard that we have adopted today. Nonetheless, we believe that the New Jersey court's application of that standard to strike down the search of T.L.O.'s purse reflects a somewhat crabbed notion of reasonableness. Our review of the facts surrounding the search leads us to conclude that the search was in no sense unreasonable for Fourth Amendment purposes. [End of majority opinion][1] 21

---

[1] Questions on this selection appear on page 760.

John Paul Stevens

# Dissent in the Case of
# *New Jersey* v. *T.L.O.*

$T$he majority holds that "a search of a student by a teacher 1
or other school official will be 'justified at its inception' when there are
reasonable grounds for suspecting that the search will turn up evidence
*that the student has violated or is violating either the law or the rules of the
school.*"

This standard will permit teachers and school administrators to 2
search students when they suspect that the search will reveal evidence
of [violation of] even the most trivial school regulation or precatory
guideline for students' behavior. For the Court, a search for curlers
and sunglasses in order to enforce the school dress code is apparently
just as important as a search for evidence of heroin addiction or violent
gang activity.

A standard better attuned to this concern would permit teachers 3
and school administrators to search a student when they have reason
to believe that the search will uncover *evidence that the student is violating
the law or engaging in conduct that is seriously disruptive of school order, or
the educational process.*

A standard that varies the extent of the permissible intrusion with 4
the gravity of the suspected offense is also more consistent with com-
mon-law experience and this Court's precedent. Criminal law has traditionally recognized a distinction between essentially regulatory offenses and serious violations of the peace, and graduated the response
of the criminal justice system depending on the character of the violation.

## Questions

1. The Fourth Amendment specifies that a search may not be "unreasonable," and it indicates that authorities may obtain a search
   warrant only for "probable cause" that something illegal will be
   found. The Fourteenth Amendment extends this protection, saying
   (in part) that "No State shall make or enforce any law which shall
   abridge the privileges or immunities of citizens." (Parents are ex-

empted from these strictures, and school authorities have sometimes argued that they serve *in loco parentis,* but the Court has not accepted this argument.) In a case decided in 1969, sixteen years before the case we are looking at, Associate Justice Abe Fortas stated for the majority of the Supreme Court that neither "students [nor] teachers shed their constitutional rights at the schoolhouse gate." But in *New Jersey* v. *T.L.O.* the Court says that any public school student may be searched by school officials, without a warrant, merely because there are "reasonable grounds for suspecting that the search will turn up evidence that the student has violated or is violating either the law or the rules of the school." Remember, in this case the student was searched not because she was suspected of possessing marijuana—a crime—but merely because she was suspected of violating a school rule by smoking a cigarette. A related point: Even if a student is suspected of violating a school prohibition against smoking, does such a suspicion justify searching her purse for cigarettes? After all, a student might bring in her purse cigarettes which she will smoke on her way home from school rather than in school. Moreover, the discovery of cigarettes in T. L. O.'s purse could scarcely be taken as proof that she had indeed been smoking in the lavatory. It could not even be taken as proof that she lied when she said she was a nonsmoker.

In the majority opinion Justice White says that it is "evident that the school setting requires some easing of the restrictions to which searches by public authorities are ordinarily subject." Does White offer evidence supporting what he says is "evident"? List the evidence, if you can find it in White, or if you can think of any. Does this evidence seem to you to be sufficiently compelling to refute Fortas's view?

2.  Let's admit that maintaining order in schools may be extremely difficult. In your opinion does the difficulty justify diminishing the rights of citizens? Smoking is not an illegal activity, yet in this instance a student suspected of smoking—that is, merely of violating a school rule—was searched. A student reasonably suspected of concealing a gun in her purse might conceivably be searched on the grounds that she posed a danger to the school, but can it be held that T. L. O.'s alleged infraction of a school rule posed a serious danger to the school? Admittedly there were strong reasons for thinking she had been smoking and thus violating the school's rule, but does the maintenance of school discipline in such a matter justify a search?

3.  Could a search undertaken on the principle enunciated by the Court's majority mean that whenever authorities perceive what they choose to call "disorder"—perhaps in the activity of an assembly

of protesters in the streets of a big city—they may justify unlawful searches and seizures?

4.  Some forty years before this case, Justice Robert H. Jackson argued that the schools have a special responsibility for adhering to the Constitution: "That they are educating the young for citizenship is reason for scrupulous protection of constitutional freedoms of the individual, if we are not to strangle the free mind at its source and teach youth to discount important principles of our government as mere platitudes." Similarly, in 1967 in an analogous case involving another female pupil, Justice Brennan argued that "The lesson the school authorities taught her that day will undoubtedly make a greater impression than the one her teacher had hoped to convey. . . . Schools cannot expect their students to learn the lessons of good citizenship when the school authorities themselves disregard the fundamental principles underpinning our constitutional freedoms." Do you find these arguments compelling? Why, or why not?

Edward I. Koch

# Death and Justice: How Capital Punishment Affirms Life

Last December a man named Robert Lee Willie, who had    1 been convicted of raping and murdering an 18-year-old woman, was executed in the Louisiana state prison. In a statement issued several minutes before his death, Mr. Willie said: "Killing people is wrong. . . . It makes no difference whether it's citizens, countries, or governments. Killing is wrong." Two weeks later in South Carolina, an admitted killer named Joseph Carl Shaw was put to death for mur-

Edward I. Koch, born in 1924 in New York City, was educated at City College and at New York University Law School. Active in Democratic politics, Mr. Koch has served as mayor of New York since 1978.

dering two teenagers. In an appeal to the governor for clemency, Mr. Shaw wrote: "Killing is wrong when I did it. Killing is wrong when you do it. I hope you have the courage and moral strength to stop the killing."

It is a curiosity of modern life that we find ourselves being lectured    2 on morality by cold-blooded killers. Mr. Willie previously had been convicted of aggravated rape, aggravated kidnapping, and the murders of a Louisiana deputy and a man from Missouri. Mr. Shaw committed another murder a week before the two for which he was executed, and admitted mutilating the body of the 14-year-old girl he killed. I can't help wondering what prompted these murderers to speak out against killing as they entered the death-house door. Did their newfound reverence for life stem from the realization that they were about to lose their own?

Life is indeed precious, and I believe the death penalty helps to    3 affirm this fact. Had the death penalty been a real possibility in the minds of these murderers, they might well have stayed their hand. They might have shown moral awareness before their victims died, and not after. Consider the tragic death of Rosa Velez, who happened to be home when a man named Luis Vera burglarized her apartment in Brooklyn. "Yeah, I shot her," Vera admitted. "She knew me, and I knew I wouldn't go to the chair."

During my 22 years in public service, I have heard the pros and    4 cons of capital punishment expressed with special intensity. As a district leader, councilman, congressman, and mayor, I have represented constituencies generally thought of as liberal. Because I support the death penalty for heinous crimes of murder, I have sometimes been the subject of emotional and outraged attacks by voters who find my position reprehensible or worse. I have listened to their ideas. I have weighed their objections carefully. I still support the death penalty. The reasons I maintain my position can be best understood by examining the arguments most frequently heard in opposition.

1. *The death penalty is "barbaric."* Sometimes opponents of capital    5 punishment horrify with tales of lingering death on the gallows, of faulty electric chairs, or of agony in the gas chamber. Partly in response to such protests, several states such as North Carolina and Texas switched to execution by lethal injection. The condemned person is put to death painlessly, without ropes, voltage, bullets, or gas. Did this answer the objections of death penalty opponents? Of course not. On June 22, 1984, *The New York Times* published an editorial that sarcastically attacked the new "hygienic" method of death by injection,

and stated that "execution can never be made humane through science." So it's not the method that really troubles opponents. It's the death itself they consider barbaric.

Admittedly, capital punishment is not a pleasant topic. However, one does not have to like the death penalty in order to support it any more than one must like radical surgery, radiation, or chemotherapy in order to find necessary these attempts at curing cancer. Ultimately we may learn how to cure cancer with a simple pill. Unfortunately, that day has not yet arrived. Today we are faced with the choice of letting the cancer spread or trying to cure it with the methods available, methods that one day will almost certainly be considered barbaric. But to give up and do nothing would be far more barbaric and would certainly delay the discovery of an eventual cure. The analogy between cancer and murder is imperfect, because murder is not the "disease" we are trying to cure. The disease is injustice. We may not like the death penalty, but it must be available to punish crimes of cold-blooded murder, cases in which any other form of punishment would be inadequate and, therefore, unjust. If we create a society in which injustice is not tolerated, incidents of murder—the most flagrant form of injustice—will diminish. 6

2. *No other major democracy uses the death penalty.* No other major democracy—in fact, few other countries of any description—are plagued by a murder rate such as that in the United States. Fewer and fewer Americans can remember the days when unlocked doors were the norm and murder was a rare and terrible offense. In America the murder rate climbed 122 percent between 1963 and 1980. During that same period, the murder rate in New York City increased by almost 400 percent, and the statistics are even worse in many other cities. A study at M.I.T. showed that based on 1970 homicide rates a person who lived in a large American city ran a greater risk of being murdered than an American soldier in World War II ran of being killed in combat. It is not surprising that the laws of each country differ according to differing conditions and traditions. If other countries had our murder problem, the cry for capital punishment would be just as loud as it is here. And I daresay that any other major democracy where 75 percent of the people supported the death penalty would soon enact it into law. 7

3. *An innocent person might be executed by mistake.* Consider the work of Hugo Adam Bedau, one of the most implacable foes of capital punishment in this country. According to Mr. Bedau, it is "false senti- 8

mentality to argue that the death penalty should be abolished because of the abstract possibility that an innocent person might be executed." He cites a study of the 7,000 executions in this country from 1893 to 1971, and concludes that the record fails to show that such cases occur. The main point, however, is this. If government functioned only when the possibility of error didn't exist, government wouldn't function at all. Human life deserves special protection, and one of the best ways to guarantee that protection is to assure that convicted murderers do not kill again. Only the death penalty can accomplish this end. In a recent case in New Jersey, a man named Richard Biegenwald was freed from prison after serving 18 years for murder; since his release he has been convicted of committing four murders. A prisoner named Lemuel Smith, who while serving four life sentences for murder (plus two life sentences for kidnapping and robbery) in New York's Green Haven Prison, lured a woman corrections officer into the chaplain's office and strangled her. He then mutilated and dismembered her body. An additional life sentence for Smith is meaningless. Because New York has no death penalty statute, Smith has effectively been given a license to kill.

But the problem of multiple murder is not confined to the nation's penitentiaries. In 1981, 91 police officers were killed in the line of duty in this country. Seven percent of those arrested in the cases that have been solved had a previous arrest for murder. In New York City in 1976 and 1977, 85 persons arrested for homicide had a previous arrest for murder. Six of these individuals had two previous arrests for murder, and one had four previous murder arrests. During those two years the New York police were arresting for murder persons with a previous arrest for murder on the average of one every 8.5 days. This is not surprising when we learn that in 1975, for example, the median time served in Massachusetts for homicide was less than two-and-a-half years. In 1976 a study sponsored by the Twentieth Century Fund found that the average time served in the United States for first-degree murder is ten years. The median time served may be considerably lower.    9

4. *Capital punishment cheapens the value of human life.* On the contrary, it can be easily demonstrated that the death penalty strengthens the value of human life. If the penalty for rape were lowered, clearly it would signal a lessened regard for the victims' suffering, humiliation, and personal integrity. It would cheapen their horrible experience, and expose them to an increased danger of recurrence. When we lower the penalty for murder, it signals a lessened regard for the value of the    10

victim's life. Some critics of capital punishment, such as columnist Jimmy Breslin, have suggested that a life sentence is actually a harsher penalty for murder than death. This is sophistic nonsense. A few killers may decide not to appeal a death sentence, but the overwhelming majority make every effort to stay alive. It is by exacting the highest penalty for the taking of human life that we affirm the highest value of human life.

5. *The death penalty is applied in a discriminatory manner.* This factor    11 no longer seems to be the problem it once was. The appeals process for a condemned prisoner is lengthy and painstaking. Every effort is made to see that the verdict and sentence were fairly arrived at. However, assertions of discrimination are not an argument for ending the death penalty but for extending it. It is not justice to exclude everyone from the penalty of the law if a few are found to be so favored. Justice requires that the law be applied equally to all.

6. *Thou Shalt Not Kill.* The Bible is our greatest source of moral    12 inspiration. Opponents of the death penalty frequently cite the sixth of the Ten Commandments in an attempt to prove that capital punishment is divinely proscribed. In the original Hebrew, however, the Sixth Commandment reads, "Thou Shalt Not Commit Murder," and the Torah specifies capital punishment for a variety of offenses. The biblical viewpoint has been upheld by philosophers throughout history. The greatest thinkers of the 19th century—Kant, Locke, Hobbes, Rousseau, Montesquieu, and Mill—agreed that natural law properly authorizes the sovereign to take life in order to vindicate justice. Only Jeremy Bentham was ambivalent. Washington, Jefferson, and Franklin endorsed it. Abraham Lincoln authorized executions for deserters in wartime. Alexis de Tocqueville, who expressed profound respect for American institutions, believed that the death penalty was indispensable to the support of social order. The United States Constitution, widely admired as one of the seminal achievements in the history of humanity, condemns cruel and inhuman punishment, but does not condemn capital punishment.

7. *The death penalty is state-sanctioned murder.* This is the defense    13 with which Messrs. Willie and Shaw hoped to soften the resolve of those who sentenced them to death. By saying in effect, "You're no better than I am," the murderer seeks to bring his accusers down to his own level. It is also a popular argument among opponents of capital punishment, but a transparently false one. Simply put, the state has rights that the private individual does not. In a democracy, those rights are given to the state by the electorate. The execution of a lawfully

condemned killer is no more an act of murder than is legal imprisonment an act of kidnapping. If an individual forces a neighbor to pay him money under threat of punishment, it's called extortion. If the state does it, it's called taxation. Rights and responsibilities surrendered by the individual are what give the state its power to govern. This contract is the foundation of civilization itself.

Everyone wants his or her rights, and will defend them jealously. 14 Not everyone, however, wants responsibilities, especially the painful responsibilities that come with law enforcement. Twenty-one years ago a woman named Kitty Genovese was assaulted and murdered on a street in New York. Dozens of neighbors heard her cries for help but did nothing to assist her. They didn't even call the police. In such a climate the criminal understandably grows bolder. In the presence of moral cowardice, he lectures us on our supposed failings and tries to equate his crimes with our quest for justice.

The death of anyone—even a convicted killer—diminishes us all. 15 But we are diminished even more by a justice system that fails to function. It is an illusion to let ourselves believe that doing away with capital punishment removes the murderer's deed from our conscience. The rights of society are paramount. When we protect guilty lives, we give up innocent lives in exchange. When opponents of capital punishment say to the state: "I will not let you kill in my name," they are also saying to murderers: "You can kill in your *own* name as long as I have an excuse for not getting involved."

It is hard to imagine anything worse than being murdered while 16 neighbors do nothing. But something worse exists. When those same neighbors shrink back from justly punishing the murderer, the victim dies twice.

# Questions

1. Koch is, of course, writing an argument. He wants to persuade his readers. Beginning with paragraph 5, he states the opposition's arguments and tries to refute them. But why did he include his first four paragraphs? What, as persuasion, does each contribute?
2. In paragraph 6, Koch compares our use of capital punishment to our use of "radical surgery, radiation, or chemotherapy." Do you find this analogy impressive—or not—and why? (Note that in this paragraph Koch goes on to say that "the analogy between cancer and murder is imperfect." Should he, then, not have used it?)

3. At the end of paragraph 6, Koch says: "If we create a society in which injustice is not tolerated, incidents of murder—the most flagrant form of injustice—will diminish." Has the earlier part of the paragraph prepared us for this statement?

4. Why, or why not, are you persuaded by Koch's second argument, about the likelihood that if other countries had high rates of murder they too would enact the death penalty?

5. In paragraph 9, Koch speaks of "murder" and then of "homicide." Are these two the same? If not, *why* is Koch bringing in statistics about homicide?

6. In paragraph 12, Koch lists authorities who supported the death penalty. Some of these, for instance Washington and Jefferson, also supported slavery. What can be said in behalf of, and what can be said against, Koch's use of these authorities?

7. In paragraph 15, Koch puts a sentence into the mouths of his opponents. *Is* this what his opponents are in effect saying or thinking?

8. If you have read Schwarzschild's remarks opposing capital punishment, below, write an essay indicating which essay you think is a better piece of persuasive writing. Note that it is not a matter of which position you subscribe to; in your essay you are concerned only with the essays as examples of persuasive writing.

Henry Schwarzschild

# In Opposition to Death Penalty Legislation

You know the classic arguments about the merits of the death penalty:  1

Its dubious and unproved value as a deterrent to violent crime;

The arbitrariness and mistakes inevitable in any system of justice instituted and administered by fallible human beings;

The persistent and ineradicable discrimination on grounds of race, class, and sex in its administration in our country's history (including the present time);

The degrading and hurtful impulse toward retribution and revenge that it expresses;

The barbarousness of its process (whether by burning at the stake, by hanging from the gallows, by frying in the electric chair, by suffocating in the gas chamber, by shooting at the hands of a firing squad, or by lethal injection with a technology designed to heal and save lives);

Even the deeply distorting and costly effect the death penalty has upon the administration of the courts, upon law enforcement, and upon the penal institutions of the country.

Let me therefore concentrate my remarks upon a few selected is-  2
sues about which much unclarity exists in the public mind, in the media, and even in many legislative chambers.

I want to discuss these issues in the context of the evident support  3
of public opinion for the reintroduction of capital punishment in the country. Let me be candid: For the past few years, public opinion polls, whether national or regional, have tended to reflect a substantial majority of the American people affirming their support for the death

Henry Schwarzschild is the director of the National Coalition Against the Death Penalty. The material that we print is an excerpt from his statement submitted at the hearing in 1978 before the Subcommittee on Criminal Justice of the Committee on the Judiciary, House of Representatives, 95th Congress, 2nd Session.

penalty, to the level of between 65 percent and 75 percent—enough to make many an elected official surrender his or her religious or moral principles against capital punishment. As little as twenty years ago, the polls reflected almost precisely the opposite distribution of views in the country. It is not hard to infer what has turned the American people back toward support of so atavistic and demonstrably useless a criminal sanction. The causes are (a) the rising rate of violent crime in the past two decades, (b) the increasing panic about the rising crime rate, together with a justified (as well as exaggerated) fear for the safety of lives and property, (c) the understandable reaction to a terrible series of assassinations and attempted assassinations of our national leaders and other prominent personalities (President John Kennedy, Senator Robert Kennedy, the Rev. Dr. Martin Luther King Jr., Governor George Wallace, Malcolm X, Medgar Evers, and others), (d) the rise of international terrorism, including aircraft hijackings and the murder of prominent political and business leaders as well as the random political killings of innocent victims, (e) many years of the effective discontinuation of capital punishment and the remoteness from actual experience of its horrors, and finally (f) a largely subliminal but sometimes almost articulated racism that attributes most violent criminality to the minority community, that knows quite well that the poor and the black are most often the subjects of the death penalty, and that thinks that's just the way it ought to be.

What, then, are the rational answers to this series of partly understandable and partly impermissible misconceptions in the American public? 4

True, violent crime has risen sharply in the past two decades, but to begin with it has been abundantly demonstrated by social research that the availability of the death penalty has no effect whatsoever upon the rate of violent crime; to the contrary, there is some scientific evidence that death sentences imposed and carried out may, for peculiar reasons of social and psychic pathology, be an incentive to further acts of violence in the society. Furthermore, while the rates of most major, violent felonies have been rising—most probably by reason of increased urbanization, social mobility, economic distress, and the like—the rate of non-negligent homicide has been rising at a rate *slower* than the other major felonies, and non-negligent homicide is, of course, the only crime for which the death penalty has been declared constitutionally permissible by the Supreme Court. The crisis in violent crime, such as it is, has therefore been least acute in the area of homicide. Indeed, in the past three years, the murder rate in this country has 5 actually been declining. Thirdly, there is an appalling number of about 20,000 non-negligent homicides in this country per year. But we would have to return to the condition of the mid-1950s to execute as many as one hundred persons per year, and even that would constitute only one in every two hundred murderers. In other words, we have always picked quite arbitrarily a tiny handful of people among those convicted of murder to be executed, not those who have committed the most heinous, the most revolting, the most destructive murders, but always the poor, the black, the friendless, the life's losers, those without competent, private attorneys, the illiterate, those despised or ignored by the community for reasons having nothing to do with their crime. Ninety-nine and one-half percent of all murderers were never executed—and the deterrent value (which very likely does not exist at all in any case) is reduced to invisibility by the overwhelming likelihood that one will not be caught, or not be prosecuted, or not be tried on a capital charge, or not be convicted, or not be sentenced to death, or have the conviction or sentence reversed on appeal, or have one's sentence commuted.

And if we took the other course and eliminated those high chances 6 of not being executed, but rather carried out the death penalty for every murder, then we should be executing 400 persons per week, every week of the month, every month of the year—and that, Mr. Chairman, should strike even the most ardent supporters of the death penalty as a bloodbath, not as a civilized system of criminal justice.

Assassinations and terrorism are well known to be undeterrable 7 by the threat of the death penalty. They are acts of political desperation or political insanity, always committed by people who are at least willing, if not eager, to be martyrs to their cause. Nor would executing terrorists be a preventive against the subsequent taking of hostages for the purpose of setting political assassins or terrorists free. There would of course be a considerable interval of time between arrest and execution, at least for the purpose of trial and the accompanying processes of law, and during that time their fellow activists would have a far more urgent incentive for taking hostages, since not only the freedom but the very lives of their arrested and sentenced colleagues would be at stake. Let me only respectfully add that distinguished fellow citizens of ours such as Senator Edward Kennedy and Ms. Coretta King, who have suffered terrible sadness in their lives at the hands of assassins, are committed opponents of the death penalty.

There has been only one execution in the United States since 1967, 8 that of Gary Mark Gilmore, by a volunteer firing squad in Utah on

January 17, 1977. Gilmore's execution troubled the public conscience less than it might have otherwise because of his own determination to die. The public and perhaps the legislators of our states and in the Congress have forgotten in a decade that was virtually without executions what sort of demoralizing and brutalizing spectacle executions are. There are now enough people on death row in the country to stage one execution each and every single day for more than a year, to say nothing of the other people who are liable to be sentenced to death during that time. We will again know the details of men crazed with fear, screaming like wounded animals, being dragged from the cell, against their desperate resistance, strapped into the electric chair, voiding their bowels and bladder, being burned alive, almost breaking the restraints from the impact of the high voltage, with their eyeballs popping out of their sockets, the smell of their burning flesh in the nostrils of the witnesses. The ghastly experience of men being hanged, their heads half torn off their bodies, or of the slow strangulation in the gas chamber, or of the press sticking their fingers into the bloody bullet holes of the chair in which Gilmore sat to be executed by rifles, or the use of forcible injection by a paralyzing agent—these reports will not ennoble the image of the United States of America that wants to be the defender of human rights and decency in a world that has largely given up the death penalty as archaic.

No one in this Committee surely is guilty of that shoddiest of all  9
impulses toward capital punishment, namely the sense that white, middle-class people, irrespective of their crime, in fact hardly ever get sentenced to death and in such an extremely rare case are virtually never executed. You, Mr. Chairman and Members, and I and probably everyone in this hearing room are in fact absolutely immune, no matter what ghastly crime we might commit, from the likelihood of being executed for it. The penalty of death is imposed almost entirely upon members of what the distinguished social psychologist Kenneth B. Clark has referred to as "the lower status elements of American society."

Blacks have always constituted a dramatically disproportionate  10
number of persons executed in the United States, far beyond their share of capital crimes, and even as we sit here today they represent half of the more than 500 persons on the death rows of our state prisons. Indeed, not only the race of the criminal is directly proportional to the likelihood of his being sentenced to death and executed but the race of the victim of the crime as well. The large majority of criminal homicides are still disasters between people who have some previous

connection with each other (as husband and wife, parent and child, lovers, business associates, and the like), and murder is therefore still largely an intra-racial event, i.e. black on black or white on white. Yet while half the people under sentence of death right now are black (showing egregious discrimination on the grounds of the race of the murderer), about 85 percent of their victims were white.

In other words, it is far more likely to get the murderer into the  11 electric chair or the gas chamber if he has killed a white person than if he had killed a black person, quite irrespective of his own race. (I say "he" in this context for good reason: the death penalty is also highly discriminatory on grounds of sex. Of the 380 death-row inmates in the country today, only two are women, and even they are far more likely objects of executive commutation of their death sentences than their male counterparts.)

Let me add here that, to the extent to which fear of crime and  12 greater exposure to it, combined with inadequate police protection and more callous jurisprudence, has made the minority communities also voice increasing support for the death penalty, they have not yet fully realized that the death penalty will not protect them from what they (and all of us) rightly fear but that their support of capital punishment will only put their brothers and husbands and sons in jeopardy of being killed by the same state that has been unable properly to protect their lives, their rights, or their property to begin with.

In sum: The public is deeply uninformed about the real social facts  13 of the death penalty and is responding to the seemingly insoluble prob-lem of crime by a retreat to the hope that an even more severe criminal penalty will stem the tide of violence. But it will not. We do not know what will. Judges and lawyers do not know, philosophers and cri-minologists don't, not even civil libertarians or legislators know the answer—if any of us did, we would have long since accomplished our purpose of reducing crime to the irreducible minimum. But legislators are not therefore entitled to suborn illusory solutions merely because they would garner widespread though uninformed public approval, in order to signal to the electorate that they are "tough on crime." Capital punishment does not deal with crime in any useful fashion and in fact deludes the public into an entirely false sense of greater security about that complex social problem. The death penalty is a legislative way of avoiding rather than dealing with the problem of crime, and the American public will come to learn this very dramat-ically and tragically if the Congress should unwisely enact the bill be-fore you today.

Two final words about public support for the death penalty.        14

There are strong indications that the public in great numbers an-        15
swers in the affirmative when asked whether they support capital punishment because they want a death penalty law on the books in the
hope that this threat will deter criminals from committing violent
crimes. Many, perhaps most, of the people who support the enactment
of the death penalty do not want executions and would be horrified
at being asked to sentence a living human being to a premeditated,
ceremonial, legally sanctioned killing. They want deterrence, not electrocutions; prevention, not lethal injections; safety, not firing squads.
But a re-enactment by this Congress of a federal death penalty statute
will give them at best only electrocutions or lethal injections or firing
squads, but neither deterrence nor crime prevention nor safety from
violence.

The last stand of supporters for the death penalty, when all the        16
other arguments have been rebutted or met, is that of retribution or
revenge, the proposition that a murderer has forfeited his life and that
we should kill him as an act of abstract equity, irrespective of whether
executions serve any social purpose whatsoever. We do not need to
preach to each other here this morning, but it is important to have it
said once more that civilized societies have instituted systems of justice
precisely in order to overcome private acts of retribution and revenge
and that they have done so with the understanding that social necessity
and social usefulness will be the guideposts of their punishments.
Since there has never been and cannot be a showing of social usefulness or social necessity for capital punishment, the virtually unanimous voices of the religious community of our land, our leading thinkers and social analysts, in unison with enlightened opinion for
hundreds, perhaps thousands, of years should guide your actions on
this matter. Whatever the understandable, bitter, vengeful impulses
might be of any of us who suffer the disastrous tragedy of having
someone we love or respect murdered by pathological or cruel killers,
the society's laws are written not to gratify those impulses but to channel them into helpful, healing, and life-sustaining directions. Gratifying the impulse for revenge is not the business of a government that
espouses the humane and liberating ideas expressed in our Declaration
of Independence and Constitution. It would be rather a return to the
darkest instincts of mankind. It would be arrogating unto the state,
unto government, either the god-like wisdom to judge who shall live
and who shall die or else the totalitarian arrogance to make that judg-

ment. We, as a nation, have foresworn that idolatry of the state that would justify either of these grounds for the legally sanctioned killing of our fellow citizens, of any human being, except perhaps in personal or national self-defense.

Mr. Chairman: The question before the country and before the Congress ultimately is whether it is the right of the state, with premeditation, with the long foreknowledge of the victim, under color of law, in the name of all of us, with great ceremony, and to the approval of many angry people in our land, to kill a fellow citizen, a fellow human being, to do that which we utterly condemn, which we utterly abhor in him for having done. What does the penalty, after all, say to the American people and to our children? That killing is all right if the right people do it and think they have a good enough reason for doing it! That is the rationale of every pathological murderer walking the street: he thinks he is the right person to do it and has a good reason for doing his destructive deed. How can a thoughtful and sensible person justify killing people who kill people to teach that killing is wrong? How can you avert your eyes from the obvious: that the death penalty and that executions in all their bloody and terrible reality only aggravate the deplorable atmosphere of violence, the disrespect for life, and brutalization of ourselves that we need to overcome? 17

If the death penalty were shown, or even could be shown, to be socially necessary or even useful, I would personally still have a deep objection to it. But those who argue for its re-enactment have not and cannot meet the burden of proving its necessity or usefulness. At the very least, before you kill a human being under law, do you not have to be absolutely certain that you are doing the right thing? But how can you be sure that the criminal justice system has worked with absolute accuracy in designating this single person to be the guilty one, that this single person is the one that should be killed, that killing him is the absolutely right thing to do? You cannot be sure, because human judgment and human institutions are demonstrably fallible. And you cannot kill a man when you are not absolutely sure. You can (indeed sometimes you must) make sure that he is incapacitated from repeating his crime, and we obviously accomplish that by ways other than killing him. And while there is fallibility there also, death is different: it is final, irreversible, barbarous, brutalizing to all who come into contact with it. That it is a very hurtful model for the United States to play in the world, it is a very hurtful model for a democratic and free government to play for its people. 18

# Questions

1. In the first paragraph, what is Schwarzschild getting at when he says that administration of the death penalty has been discriminatory?

2. In paragraph 5 Schwarzschild points out that even when capital punishment was relatively common, "ninety-nine and one-half percent of all murderers were never executed." Assuming the truth of this statement, is it inherently unjust to execute the remaining half of one percent? Would it be adequate to reply thus, by way of analogy: Most of the people who steal are not caught, but those who *are* caught should be punished; the law cannot excuse known wrongdoers simply on the ground that other wrongdoers escape undetected?

3. In paragraph 8, Schwarzschild briefly describes some of the horrible physical responses of persons about to be executed. If one believes that the death penalty serves a useful purpose as a deterrent, should one argue (against Schwarzschild) that executions ought to be televised, so that they would have a maximum effect as deterrents?

4. Can it be argued that in paragraph 16, Schwarzschild distorts an important point: Capital punishment partly satisfies society's sense of justice; that is, certain crimes are so outrageous that a moral society must exact capital punishment—for instance, to satisfy the legitimate outrage of the friends and family of the murderer's victim?

5. What is Schwarzschild's strategy in his next-to-last paragraph?

6. Evaluate Schwarzschild's final paragraph as a piece of persuasion.

7. If you have read Koch's essay (page 762) supporting the death penalty, indicate which of Koch's arguments, if any, Schwarzschild does not face.

Stephen Chapman

# The Prisoner's Dilemma

> If the punitive laws of Islam were applied for only one year, all the devastating injustices would be uprooted. Misdeeds must be punished by the law of retaliation: cut off the hands of the thief; kill the murderers; flog the adulterous woman or man. Your concerns, your "humanitarian" scruples are more childish than reasonable. Under the terms of Koranic law, any judge fulfilling the seven requirements (that he have reached puberty, be a believer, know the Koranic laws perfectly, be just, and not be affected by amnesia, or be a bastard, or be of the female sex) is qualified to be a judge in any type of case. He can thus judge and dispose of twenty trials in a single day, whereas the Occidental justice might take years to argue them out.
>
> From *Sayings of the Ayatollah Khomeini* (Bantam Books)

One of the amusements of life in the modern West is the opportunity 1 to observe the barbaric rituals of countries that are attached to the customs of the dark ages. Take Pakistan, for example, our newest ally and client state in Asia. Last October President Zia, in harmony with the Islamic fervor that is sweeping his part of the world, revived the traditional Moslem practice of flogging lawbreakers in public. In Pakistan, this qualified as mass entertainment, and no fewer than 10,000 law-abiding Pakistanis turned out to see justice done to 26 convicts. To Western sensibilities the spectacle seemed barbaric—both in the sense of cruel and in the sense of pre-civilized. In keeping with Islamic custom each of the unfortunates—who had been caught in prostitution raids the previous night and summarily convicted and sentenced— was stripped down to a pair of white shorts, which were painted with a red stripe across the buttocks (the target). Then he was shackled against an easel, with pads thoughtfully placed over the kidneys to prevent injury. The floggers were muscular, fierce-looking sorts—convicted murderers, as it happens—who paraded around the flogging platform in colorful loincloths. When the time for the ceremony began, one of the floggers took a running start and brought a five-foot stave

Stephen Chapman was on the staff of *New Republic*, where this essay was first published.

down across the first victim's buttocks, eliciting screams from the convict and murmurs from the audience. Each of the 26 received from five to 15 lashes. One had to be carried from the stage unconscious.

Flogging is one of the punishments stipulated by Koranic law, 2 which has made it a popular penological device in several Moslem countries, including Pakistan, Saudi Arabia, and, most recently, the ayatollah's Iran. Flogging, or *ta'zir*, is the general punishment prescribed for offenses that don't carry an explicit Koranic penalty. Some crimes carry automatic *hadd* punishment—stoning or scourging (a severe whipping) for illicit sex, scourging for drinking alcoholic beverages, amputation of the hands for theft. Other crimes—as varied as murder and abandoning Islam—carry the death penalty (usually carried out in public). Colorful practices like these have given the Islamic world an image in the West, as described by historian G. H. Jansen, "of blood dripping from the stumps of amputated hands and from the striped backs of malefactors, and piles of stones barely concealing the battered bodies of adulterous couples." Jansen, whose book *Militant Islam* is generally effusive in its praise of Islamic practices, grows squeamish when considering devices like flogging, amputation, and stoning. But they are given enthusiastic endorsement by the Koran itself.

Such traditions, we all must agree, are no sign of an advanced 3 civilization. In the West, we have replaced these various punishments (including the death penalty in most cases) with a single device. Our custom is to confine criminals in prison for varying lengths of time. In Illinois, a reasonably typical state, grand theft carries a punishment of three to five years; armed robbery can get you from six to 30. The lowest form of felony theft is punishable by one to three years in prison. Most states impose longer sentences on habitual offenders. In Kentucky, for example, habitual offenders can be sentenced to life in prison. Other states are less brazen, preferring the more genteel sounding "indeterminate sentence," which allows parole boards to keep inmates locked up for as long as life. It was under an indeterminate sentence of one to 14 years that George Jackson served 12 years in California prisons for committing a $70 armed robbery. Under a Texas law imposing an automatic life sentence for a third felony conviction, a man was sent to jail for life last year because of three thefts adding up to less than $300 in property value. Texas also is famous for occasionally imposing extravagantly long sentences, often running into hundreds or thousands of years. This gives Texas a leg up on Maryland, which used to sentence some criminals to life plus a day—a distinctive if superfluous flourish.

The punishment *intended* by Western societies in sending their 4 criminals to prison is the loss of freedom. But, as everyone knows, the actual punishment in most American prisons is of a wholly different order. The February 2 riot at New Mexico's state prison in Santa Fe, one of several bloody prison riots in the nine years since the Attica bloodbath, once again dramatized the conditions of life in an American prison. Four hundred prisoners seized control of the prison before dawn. By sunset the next day 33 inmates had died at the hands of other convicts and another 40 people (including five guards) had been seriously hurt. Macabre stories came out of prisoners being hanged, murdered with blow-torches, decapitated, tortured, and mutilated in a variety of gruesome ways by drug-crazed rioters.

The Santa Fe penitentiary was typical of most maximum-security 5 facilities, with prisoners subject to overcrowding, filthy conditions, and routine violence. It also housed first-time, non-violent offenders, like check forgers and drug dealers, with murderers serving life sentences. In a recent lawsuit, the American Civil Liberties Union called the prison "totally unfit for human habitation." But the ACLU says New Mexico's penitentiary is far from the nation's worst.

That American prisons are a disgrace is taken for granted by ex- 6 perts of every ideological stripe. Conservative James Q. Wilson has criticized our "[c]rowded, antiquated prisons that require men and women to live in fear of one another and to suffer not only deprivation of liberty but a brutalizing regimen." Leftist Jessica Mitford has called our prisons "the ultimate expression of injustice and inhumanity." In 1973 a national commission concluded that "the American correctional system today appears to offer minimum protection to the public and maximum harm to the offender." Federal courts have ruled that confinement in prisons in 16 different states violates the constitutional ban on "cruel and unusual punishment."

What are the advantages of being a convicted criminal in an ad- 7 vanced culture? First there is the overcrowding in prisons. One Tennessee prison, for example, has a capacity of 806, according to accepted space standards, but it houses 2300 inmates. One Louisiana facility has confined four and five prisoners in a single six-foot-by-six-foot cell. Then there is the disease caused by overcrowding, unsanitary conditions, and poor or inadequate medical care. A federal appeals court noted that the Tennessee prison had suffered frequent outbreaks of infectious diseases like hepatitis and tuberculosis. But the most distinctive element of American prison life is its constant violence. In his book *Criminal Violence, Criminal Justice*, Charles Silberman noted that in one Louisiana prison, there were 211 stabbings in only three years, 11 of them fatal. There were 15 slayings in a prison in Massachusetts between 1972 and 1975. According to a federal court, in Alabama's penitentiaries (as in many others), "robbery, rape, extortion, theft and assault are everyday occurrences."

At least in regard to cruelty, it's not at all clear that the system of    8
punishment that has evolved in the West is less barbaric than the grotesque practices of Islam. Skeptical? Ask yourself: would you rather be subjected to a few minutes of intense pain and considerable public humiliation, or to be locked away for two or three years in a prison cell crowded with ill-tempered sociopaths? Would you rather lose a hand or spend 10 years or more in a typical state prison? I have taken my own survey on this matter. I have found no one who does not find the Islamic system hideous. And I have found no one who, given the choices mentioned above, would not prefer its penalties to our own.

The great divergence between Western and Islamic fashions in    9
punishment is relatively recent. Until roughly the end of the 18th century, criminals in Western countries rarely were sent to prison. Instead they were subjected to an ingenious assortment of penalties. Many perpetrators of a variety of crimes simply were executed, usually by some imaginative and extremely unpleasant method involving prolonged torture, such as breaking on the wheel, burning at the stake, or drawing and quartering. Michel Foucault's book *Discipline and Punish: The Birth of the Prison* notes one form of capital punishment in which the condemned man's "belly was opened up, his entrails quickly ripped out, so that he had time to see them, with his own eyes, being thrown on the fire; in which he was finally decapitated and his body quartered." Some criminals were forced to serve on slave galleys. But in most cases various corporal measures such as pillorying, flogging, and branding sufficed.

In time, however, public sentiment recoiled against these mea-    10
sures. They were replaced by imprisonment, which was thought to have two advantages. First, it was considered to be more humane. Second, and more important, prison was supposed to hold out the possibility of rehabilitation—purging the criminal of his criminality—something that less civilized punishments did not even aspire to. An 1854 report by inspectors of the Pennsylvania prison system illustrates the hopes nurtured by humanitarian reformers:

> Depraved tendencies, characteristic of the convict, have been restrained by the absence of vicious association, and in the mild teaching

of Christianity, the unhappy criminal finds a solace for an involuntary exile from the comforts of social life. If hungry, he is fed; if naked, he is clothed; if destitute of the first rudiments of education, he is taught to read and write; and if he has never been blessed with a means of livelihood, he is schooled in a mechanical art, which in after life may be to him the source of profit and respectability. Employment is not his toil nor labor, weariness. He embraces them with alacrity, as contributing to his moral and mental elevation.

Imprisonment is now the universal method of punishing criminals  11
in the United States. It is thought to perform five functions, each of which has been given a label by criminologists. First, there is simple *retribution:* punishing the lawbreaker to serve society's sense of justice and to satisfy the victims' desire for revenge. Second, there is *specific deterrence:* discouraging the offender from misbehaving in the future. Third, *general deterrence:* using the offender as an example to discourage others from turning to crime. Fourth, *prevention:* at least during the time he is kept off the streets, the criminal cannot victimize other members of society. Finally, and most important, there is *rehabilitation:* reforming the criminal so that when he returns to society he will be inclined to obey the laws and able to make an honest living.

How satisfactorily do American prisons perform by these criteria?  12
Well, of course, they do punish. But on the other scores they don't do so well. Their effect in discouraging future criminality by the prisoner or others is the subject of much debate, but the soaring rates of the last 20 years suggest that prisons are not a dramatically effective deterrent to criminal behavior. Prisons do isolate convicted criminals, but only to divert crime from ordinary citizens to prison guards and fellow inmates. Almost no one contends anymore that prisons rehabilitate their inmates. If anything, they probably impede rehabilitation by forcing inmates into prolonged and almost exclusive association with other criminals. And prisons cost a lot of money. Housing a typical prisoner in a typical prison costs far more than a stint at a top university. This cost would be justified if prisons did the job they were intended for. But it is clear to all that prisons fail on the very grounds—humanity and hope of rehabilitation—that caused them to replace earlier, cheaper forms of punishment.

The universal acknowledgment that prisons do not rehabilitate  13
criminals has produced two responses. The first is to retain the hope of rehabilitation but do away with imprisonment as much as possible and replace it with various forms of "alternative treatment," such as psychotherapy, supervised probation, and vocational training. Psy-

chiatrist Karl Menninger, one of the principal critics of American pen-
ology, has suggested even more unconventional approaches, such as
"a new job opportunity or a vacation trip, a course of reducing exercises, a cosmetic surgical operation or a herniotomy, some night school
courses, a wedding in the family (even one for the patient!), an in-
spiring sermon." This starry-eyed approach naturally has produced a
backlash from critics on the right, who think that it's time to abandon
the goal of rehabilitation. They argue that prisons perform an important service just by keeping criminals off the streets, and thus should
be used with that purpose alone in mind.

So the debate continues to rage in all the same old ruts. No one,     14
of course, would think of copying the medieval practices of Islamic
nations and experimenting with punishments such as flogging and
amputation. But let us consider them anyway. How do they compare
with our American prison system in achieving the ostensible objectives
of punishment? First, do they punish? Obviously they do, and in a
uniquely painful and memorable way. Of course any sensible person,
given the choice, would prefer suffering these punishments to years
of incarceration in a typical American prison. But presumably no Western penologist would criticize Islamic punishments on the grounds that
they are not barbaric enough. Do they deter crime? Yes, and probably
more effectively than sending convicts off to prison. Now we read
about a prison sentence in the newspaper, then think no more about
the criminal's payment for his crimes until, perhaps, years later we
read a small item reporting his release. By contrast, one can easily
imagine the vivid impression it would leave to be wandering through
a local shopping center and to stumble onto the scene of some poor
wretch being lustily flogged. And the occasional sight of an habitual
offender walking around with a bloody stump at the end of his arm
no doubt also would serve as a forceful reminder that crime does not
pay.

Do flogging and amputation discourage recidivism? No one knows     15
whether the scars on his back would dissuade a criminal from risking
another crime, but it is hard to imagine that corporal measures could
stimulate a higher rate of recidivism than already exists. Islamic forms
of punishment do not serve the favorite new right goal of simply iso-
lating criminals from the rest of society, but they may achieve the same
purpose of making further crimes impossible. In the movie *Bonnie and
Clyde,* Warren Beatty successfully robs a bank with his arm in a sling,
but this must be dismissed as artistic license. It must be extraordinarily

difficult, at the very least, to perform much violent crime with only one hand.

Do these medieval forms of punishment rehabilitate the criminal? 16 Plainly not. But long prison terms do not rehabilitate either. And it is just as plain that typical Islamic punishments are no crueler to the convict than incarceration in the typical American state prison.

Of course there are other reasons besides its bizarre forms of pun- 17 ishment that the Islamic system of justice seems uncivilized to the Western mind. One is the absence of due process. Another is the long list of offenses—such as drinking, adultery, blasphemy, "profiteering," and so on—that can bring on conviction and punishment. A third is all the ritualistic mumbo-jumbo in pronouncements of Islamic law (like that talk about puberty and amnesia in the ayatollah's quotation at the beginning of this article). Even in these matters, however, a little cultural modesty is called for. The vast majority of American criminals are convicted and sentenced as a result of plea bargaining, in which due process plays almost no role. It has been only half a century since a wave of religious fundamentalism stirred this country to outlaw the consumption of alcoholic beverages. Most states also still have laws imposing austere constraints on sexual conduct. Only two weeks ago the *Washington Post* reported that the FBI had spent two and a half years and untold amounts of money to break up a nationwide pornography ring. Flogging the clients of prostitutes, as the Pakistanis did, does seem silly. But only a few months ago Mayor Koch of New York was proposing that clients caught in his own city have their names broadcast by radio stations. We are not so far advanced on such matters as we often like to think. Finally, my lawyer friends assure me that the rules of jurisdiction for American courts contain plenty of petty requirements and bizarre distinctions that would sound silly enough to foreign ears.

Perhaps it sounds barbaric to talk of flogging and amputation, and 18 perhaps it is. But our system of punishment also is barbaric, and probably more so. Only cultural smugness about their system and willful ignorance about our own make it easy to regard the one as cruel and the other as civilized. We inflict our cruelties away from public view, while nations like Pakistan stage them in front of 10,000 onlookers. Their outrages are visible; ours are not. Most Americans can live their lives for years without having their peace of mind disturbed by the knowledge of what goes on in our prisons. To choose imprisonment over flogging and amputation is not to choose human kindness over cruelty, but merely to prefer that our cruelties be kept out of sight, and out of mind.

Public flogging and amputation may be more barbaric forms of   19
punishment than imprisonment, even if they are not more cruel. Society may pay a higher price for them, even if the particular criminal does not. Revulsion against officially sanctioned violence and infliction of pain derives from something deeply ingrained in the Western conscience, and clearly it is something admirable. Grotesque displays of the sort that occur in Islamic countries probably breed a greater tolerance for physical cruelty, for example, which prisons do not do precisely because they conceal their cruelties. In fact it is our admirable intolerance for calculated violence that makes it necessary for us to conceal what we have not been able to do away with. In a way this is a good thing, since it holds out the hope that we may eventually find a way to do away with it. But in another way it is a bad thing, since it permits us to congratulate ourselves on our civilized humanitarianism while violating its norms in this one area of our national life.

# Questions

1.  What is the effect of juxtaposing the epigraph (the quotation at the top of the essay) with the first paragraph? By the time we finish the first paragraph, do we feel confident that the Ayatollah has been put into his place? Having read the entire essay, how would you explain Chapman's strategy in beginning the way he begins?

2.  Consider the two systems of punishment, and make a list of the pros and cons for each, drawing on Chapman's essay but adding any other points that you can think of.

3.  Despite apparent disclaimers, implied for example by using the word "barbaric" when speaking of Islamic punishments, is Chapman in fact arguing that we adopt a system of punishment more or less similar to the Islamic system? If not, what *is* he arguing? What do you think is the chief message that he wishes to convey?

4.  In paragraph 8, Chapman says that the persons whom he surveyed preferred the Islamic punishments to our own. Ask a dozen or so people to read Chapman's essay, at least up to this point, and find out their preferences. In 500 words report the result of your survey, including some effective quotations.

Joyce Carol Oates

# How I Contemplated the World from the Detroit House of Correction and Began My Life over Again

Notes *for an essay for an English class at Baldwin Country Day*   1
*School; poking around in debris; disgust and curiosity; a revelation of the*
*meaning of life; a happy ending. . . .*

## I. Events

1. The girl (myself) is walking through Branden's, that excellent store.   2
Suburb of a large famous city that is a symbol for large famous American cities. The event sneaks up on the girl, who believes she is herding
it along with a small fixed smile, a girl of fifteen, innocently experienced. She dawdles in a certain style by a counter of costume jewelry.
Rings, earrings, necklaces. Prices from $5 to $50, all within reach. All
ugly. She eases over to the glove counter, where everything is ugly
too. In her close-fitted coat with its black fur collar she contemplates
the luxury of Branden's, which she has known for many years: its many
mild pale lights, easy on the eye and the soul, its elaborate tinkly
decorations, its women shoppers with their excellent shoes and coats
and hairdos, all dawdling gracefully, in no hurry.

Who was ever in a hurry here?   3

2. The girl seated at home. A small library, paneled walls of oak.   4
Someone is talking to me. An earnest husky female voice drives itself

---

Joyce Carol Oates was born in 1938 in Millerport, New York. She won a scholarship to Syracuse University, from which she graduated (Phi Beta Kappa and
valedictorian) in 1960. She went on to do graduate work in English, first at the
University of Wisconsin and then at Rice University, but she withdrew from Rice
in order to devote more time to writing. Her first collection of stories, *By the
North Gate*, was published in 1963. Since then she has published steadily—
stories, poems, essays, and (in twenty years) sixteen novels.

against my ears, nervous, frightened, groping around my heart, saying, "If you wanted gloves why didn't you say so? Why didn't you ask for them?" That store, Branden's, is owned by Raymond Forrest who lives on DuMaurier Drive. We live on Sioux Drive. Raymond Forrest. A handsome man? An ugly man? A man of fifty or sixty, with gray hair, or a man of forty with earnest courteous eyes, a good golf game, who is Raymond Forrest, this man who is my salvation? Father has been talking to him. Father is not his physician; Dr. Berg is his physician. Father and Dr. Berg refer patients to each other. There is a connection. Mother plays bridge with. . . . On Mondays and Wednesdays our maid Billie works at. . . . The strings draw together in a cat's cradle, making a net to save you when you fall. . . .

3. *Harriet Arnold's.* A small shop, better than Branden's. Mother   5 in her black coat, I in my close-fitted blue coat. Shopping. Now look at this, isn't this cute, do you want this, why don't you want this, try this on, take this with you to the fitting room, take this also, what's wrong with you, what can I do for you, why are you so strange . . . ? "I wanted to steal but not to buy," I don't tell her. The girl droops along in her coat and gloves and leather boots, her eyes scan the horizon which is pastel pink and decorated like Branden's, tasteful walls and modern ceilings with graceful glimmering lights.

4. Weeks later, the girl at a bus-stop. Two o'clock in the afternoon,   6 a Tuesday, obviously she has walked out of school.

5. The girl stepping down from a bus. Afternoon, weather chang-   7 ing to colder. Detroit. Pavement and closed-up stores; grillwork over the windows of a pawnshop. What is a pawnshop, exactly?

## II. Characters

1. The girl stands five feet five inches tall. An ordinary height. Baldwin   8 Country Day School draws them up to that height. She dreams along the corridors and presses her face against the Thermoplex glass. No frost or steam can ever form on that glass. A smudge of grease from her forehead . . . could she be boiled down to grease? She wears her hair loose and long and straight in suburban teenage style, 1968. Eyes smudged with pencil, dark brown. Brown hair. Vague green eyes. A pretty girl? An ugly girl? She sings to herself under her breath, idling in the corridor, thinking of her many secrets (the thirty dollars she once took from the purse of a friend's mother, just for fun, the basement window she smashed in her own house just for fun) and thinking of her brother who is at Susquehanna Boys' Academy, an excellent

preparatory school in Maine, remembering him unclearly . . . he has long manic hair and a squeaking voice and he looks like one of the popular teenage singers of 1968, one of those in a group, *The Certain Forces, The Way Out, The Maniacs Responsible.* The girl in her turn looks like one of those fieldsful of girls who listen to the boys' singing, dreaming and mooning restlessly, breaking into high sullen laughter, innocently experienced.

2. The mother. A midwestern woman of Detroit and suburbs. Belongs to the Detroit Athletic Club. Also the Detroit Golf Club. Also the Bloomfield Hills Country Club. The Village Women's Club at which lectures are given each winter on Genet and Sartre and James Baldwin, by the Director of the Adult Education Program at Wayne State University. . . . The Bloomfield Art Association. Also the Founders Society of the Detroit Institute of Arts. Also. . . . Oh, she is in perpetual motion, this lady, hair like blown-up gold and finer than gold, hair and fingers and body of inestimable grace. Heavy weighs the gold on the back of her hairbrush and hand mirror. Heavy heavy the candlesticks in the dining room. Very heavy is the big car, a Lincoln, long and black, that on one cool autumn day split a squirrel's body in two unequal parts. [9]

3. The father, Dr. _____. He belongs to the same club as #2. A player of squash and golf; he has a golfer's umbrella of stripes. Candy stripes. In his mouth nothing turns to sugar, however, saliva works no miracles here. His doctoring is of the slightly sick. The sick are sent elsewhere (to Dr. Berg?), the deathly sick are sent back for more tests and their bills are sent to their homes, the unsick are sent to Dr. Coronet (Isabel, a lady), an excellent psychiatrist for unsick people who angrily believe they are sick and want to do something about it. If they demand a male psychiatrist, the unsick are sent by Dr. _____(my father) to Dr. Lowenstein, a male psychiatrist, excellent and expensive, with a limited practice. [10]

4. Clarita. She is twenty, twenty-five, she is thirty or more? Pretty, ugly, what? She is a woman lounging by the side of a road, in jeans and a sweater, hitch-hiking, or she is slouched on a stool at a counter in some roadside diner. A hard line of jaw. Curious eyes. Amused eyes. Behind her eyes processions move, funeral pageants, cartoons. She says, "I never can figure out why girls like you bum around down here. What are you looking for anyway?" An odor of tobacco about her. Unwashed underclothes, or no underclothes, unwashed skin, gritty toes, hair long and falling into strands, not recently washed. [11]

5. Simon. In this city the weather changes abruptly, so Simon's [12]

weather changes abruptly. He sleeps through the afternoon. He sleeps through the morning. Rising he gropes around for something to get him going, for a cigarette or a pill to drive him out to the street, where the temperature is hovering around 35°. Why doesn't it drop? Why, why doesn't the cold clean air come down from Canada, will he have to go up into Canada to get it, will he have to leave the Country of his Birth and sink into Canada's frosty fields . . . ? Will the F.B.I. (which he dreams about constantly) chase him over the Canadian border on foot, hounded out in a blizzard of broken glass and horns . . . ?

"Once I was Huckleberry Finn," Simon says, "but now I am Roderick Usher." Beset by frenzies and fears, this man who makes my spine go cold, he takes green pills, yellow pills, pills of white and capsules of dark blue and green . . . he takes other things I may not mention, for what if Simon seeks me out and climbs into my girl's bedroom here in Bloomfield Hills and strangles me, what then . . . ? (As I write this I begin to shiver. Why do I shiver? I am now sixteen and sixteen is not an age for shivering.) It comes from Simon, who is always cold.    13

### III. World Events

Nothing.    14

### IV. People & Circumstances Contributing to This Delinquency

Nothing.    15

### V. Sioux Drive

George, Clyde G. 240 Sioux. A manufacturer's representative; children, a dog; a wife. Georgian with the usual columns. You think of the White House, then of Thomas Jefferson, then your mind goes blank on the white pillars and you think of nothing. Norris, Ralph W. 246 Sioux. Public relations. Colonial. Bay window, brick, stone, concrete, wood, green shutters, sidewalk, lantern, grass, trees, blacktop drive, two children, one of them my classmate Esther (Esther Norris) at Baldwin. Wife, cars. Ramsey, Michael D. 250 Sioux. Colonial. Big living room, thirty by twenty-five, fireplaces in living room, library, recreation room, paneled walls wet bar five bathrooms five bedrooms two lav-    16 atories central air conditioning automatic sprinkler automatic garage door three children one wife two cars a breakfast room a patio a large fenced lot fourteen trees a front door with a brass knocker never knocked. Next is our house. Classic contemporary. Traditional modern. Attached garage, attached Florida room, attached patio, attached pool and cabana, attached roof. A front door mailslot through which pour *Time Magazine, Fortune, Life, Business Week, The Wall Street Journal, The New York Times, The New Yorker, The Saturday Review, M.D., Modern Medicine, Disease of the Month* . . . and also. . . . And in addition to all this, a quiet sealed letter from Baldwin saying: *Your daughter is not doing work compatible with her performance on the Stanford-Binet.* . . . And your son is not doing well, not well at all, very sad. Where is your son anyway? Once he stole trick-and-treat candy from some six-year-old kids, he himself being a robust ten. The beginning. Now your daughter steals. In the Village Pharmacy she made off with, yes she did, don't deny it, she made off with a copy of *Pageant Magazine* for no reason, she swiped a roll of lifesavers in a green wrapper and was in no need of saving her life or even in need of sucking candy; when she was no more than eight years old she stole, don't blush, she stole a package of *Tums* only because it was out on the counter and available, and the nice lady behind the counter (now dead) said nothing. . . . Sioux Drive. Maples, oaks, elms. Diseased elms cut down. Sioux Drive runs into Roosevelt Drive. Slow turning lanes, not streets, all drives and lanes and ways and passes. A private police force. Quiet private police, in unmarked cars. Cruising on Saturday evenings with paternal smiles for the residents who are streaming in and out of houses, going to and from parties, a thousand parties, slightly staggering, the women in their furs alighting from automobiles bought of Ford and General Motors and Chrysler, very heavy automobiles. No foreign cars. Detroit. In 275 Sioux, down the block, in that magnificent French Normandy mansion, lives _____himself, who has the C _____account itself, imagine that! Look at where he lives and look at the enormous trees and chimneys, imagine his many fireplaces, imagine his wife and children, imagine his wife's hair, imagine her fingernails, imagine her bathtub of smooth clean glowing pink, imagine their embraces, his trouser pockets filled with odd coins and keys and dust and peanuts, imagine their ecstasy on Sioux Drive, imagine their income tax returns, imagine their little boy's pride in his experimental car, a scaled-down C _____, as he roars around the neighborhood on the sidewalks frightening dogs and Negro maids, oh imagine all these things, imagine everything, let your mind roar out all over Sioux Drive and DuMaurier Drive and Roosevelt Drive and Ticonderoga Pass and Burning Bush Way and Lincolnshire Pass and Lois Lane.

When spring comes, its winds blow nothing to Sioux Drive, no    17
odors of hollyhocks or forsythia, nothing Sioux Drive doesn't already possess, everything is planted and performing. The weather vanes, had they weather vanes, don't have to turn with the wind, don't have to contend with the weather. There is no weather.

## VI. Detroit

There is always weather in Detroit. Detroit's temperature is always 32°.    18
Fast falling temperatures. Slow rising temperatures. Wind from the north-northeast four to forty miles an hour, small craft warnings, partly cloudy today and Wednesday changing to partly sunny through Thursday . . . small warnings of frost, soot warnings, traffic warnings, hazardous lake conditions for small craft and swimmers, restless Negro gangs, restless cloud formations, restless temperatures aching to fall out the very bottom of the thermometer or shoot up over the top and boil everything over in red mercury.

Detroit's temperature is 32°. Fast falling temperatures. Slow rising    19
temperatures. Wind from the north-northeast four to forty miles an hour. . . .

## VII. Events

1. The girl's heart is pounding. In her pocket is a pair of gloves! In a    20
plastic bag! Airproof breathproof plastic bag, gloves selling for twenty-five dollars on Branden's counter! In her pocket! Shoplifted! . . . In her purse is a blue comb, not very clean. In her purse is a leather billfold (a birthday present from her grandmother in Philadelphia) with snapshots of the family in clean plastic windows, in the billfold are bills, she doesn't know how many bills. . . . In her purse is an ominous note from her friend Tykie *What's this about Joe H. and the kids hanging around at Louise's Sat. night? You heard anything?* . . . passed in French class. In her purse is a lot of dirty yellow Kleenex, her mother's heart would break to see such dirty Kleenex, and at the bottom of her purse are brown hairpins and safety pins and a broken pencil and a ballpoint pen (blue) stolen from somewhere forgotten and a purse-size compact of Cover Girl Make-Up, Ivory Rose. . . . Her lipstick is Broken Heart, a corrupt pink; her fingers are trembling like crazy; her teeth are be-

ginning to chatter; her insides are alive; her eyes glow in her head; she is saying to her mother's astonished face *I want to steal but not to buy.*

    2. At Clarita's. Day or night? What room is this? A bed, a regular 21 bed, and a mattress on the floor nearby. Wallpaper hanging in strips. Clarita says she tore it like that with her teeth. She was fighting a barbaric tribe that night, high from some pills she was battling for her life with men wearing helmets of heavy iron and their faces no more than Christian crosses to breathe through, every one of those bastards looking like her lover Simon, who seems to breathe with great difficulty through the slits of mouth and nostrils in his face. Clarita has never heard of Sioux Drive. Raymond Forrest cuts no ice with her, nor does the C _____ account and its millions; Harvard Business School could be at the corner of Vernor and 12th Street for all she cares, and Vietnam might have sunk by now into the Dead Sea under its tons of debris, for all the amazement she could show . . . her face is overworked, overwrought, at the age of twenty (thirty?) it is already exhausted but fanciful and ready for a laugh. Clarita says mournfully to me *Honey somebody is going to turn you out let me give you warning.* In a movie shown on late television Clarita is not a mess like this but a nurse, with short neat hair and a dedicated look, in love with her doctor and her doctor's patients and their diseases, enamored of needles and sponges and rubbing alcohol. . . . Or no: she is a private secretary. Robert Cummings is her boss. She helps him with fantastic plots, the canned audience laughs, no, the audience doesn't laugh because nothing is funny, instead her boss is Robert Taylor and they are not boss and secretary but husband and wife, she is threatened by a young starlet, she is grim, handsome, wifely, a good companion for a good man. . . . She is Claudette Colbert. Her sister too is Claudette Colbert. They are twins, identical. Her husband Charles Boyer is a very rich handsome man and her sister, Claudette Colbert, is plotting her death in order to take her place as the rich man's wife, no one will know because they are *twins.* . . . All these marvelous lives Clarita might have lived, but she fell out the bottom at the age of thirteen. At the age when I was packing my overnight case for a slumber party at Toni Deshield's she was tearing filthy sheets off a bed and scratching up a rash on her arms. . . . Thirteen is uncommonly young for a white girl in Detroit, Miss Brook of the Detroit House of Correction said in a sad newspaper interview for the *Detroit News;* fifteen and sixteen are more likely. Eleven, twelve, thirteen are not surprising in colored . . . they are more precocious. What can we do? Taxes are rising and the tax

base is falling. The temperature rises slowly but falls rapidly. Everything is falling out the bottom, Woodward Avenue is filthy, Livernois Avenue is filthy! Scraps of paper flutter in the air like pigeons, dirt flies up and hits you right in the eye, oh Detroit is breaking up into dangerous bits of newspaper and dirt, watch out. . . .

Clarita's apartment is over a restaurant. Simon her lover emerges 22 from the cracks at dark. Mrs. Olesko, a neighbor of Clarita's an aged white wisp of a woman, doesn't complain but sniffs with contentment at Clarita's noisy life and doesn't tell the cops, hating cops, when the cops arrive. I should give fake names, more blanks, instead of telling all these secrets. I myself am a secret; I am a minor.

3. My father reads a paper at a medical convention in Los Angeles. 23 There he is, on the edge of the North American continent, when the unmarked detective put his hand so gently on my arm in the aisle of Branden's and said, "Miss, would you like to step over here for a minute?"

And where was he when Clarita put her hand on my arm, that 24 wintry dark sulphurous aching day in Detroit, in the company of closed-down barber shops, closed-down diners, closed-down movie houses, homes, windows, basements, faces . . . she put her hand on my arm and said, "Honey, are you looking for somebody down here?"

And was he home worrying about me, gone for two weeks solid, 25 when they carried me off . . . ? It took three of them to get me in the police cruiser, so they said, and they put more than their hands on my arm.

4. I work on this lesson. My English teacher is Mr. Forest, who 26 is from Michigan State. Not handsome, Mr. Forest, and his name is plain unlike Raymond Forrest's, but he is sweet and rodent-like, he has conferred with the principal and my parents, and everything is fixed . . . treat her as if nothing has happened, a new start, begin again, only sixteen years old, what a shame, how did it happen?—nothing happened, nothing could have happened, a slight physiological modification known only to a gynecologist or to Dr. Coronet. I work on my lesson. I sit in my pink room. I look around the room with my sad pink eyes. I sigh, I dawdle, I pause, I eat up time, I am limp and happy to be home, I am sixteen years old suddenly, my head hangs heavy as a pumpkin on my shoulders, and my hair has just been cut by Mr. Faye at the Crystal Salon and is said to be very becoming.

(Simon too put his hand on my arm and said, "Honey, you have 27 got to come with me," and in his six-by-six room we got to know each

other. Would I go back to Simon again? Would I lie down with him
in all that filth and craziness? Over and over again.

        a Clarita is being    28
betrayed as in front of a Cunningham Drug Store she is nervously
eyeing a colored man who may or may not have money, or a nervous
white boy of twenty with sideburns and an Appalachian look, who
may or may not have a knife hidden in his jacket pocket, or a husky
red-faced man of friendly countenance who may or may not be a member of the Vice Squad out for an early twilight walk.)

    I work on my lesson for Mr. Forest. I have filled up eleven pages.    29
Words pour out of me and won't stop. I want to tell everything . . .
what was the song Simon was always humming, and who was Simon's
friend in a very new trench coat with an old high school graduation
ring on his finger . . . ? Simon's bearded friend? When I was down
too low for him Simon kicked me out and gave me to him for three
days, I think, on Fourteenth Street in Detroit, an airy room of cold
cruel drafts with newspapers on the floor. . . . Do I really remember
that or am I piecing it together from what they told me? Did they tell
the truth? Did they know much of the truth?

## VIII. Characters

1. Wednesdays after school, at four; Saturday mornings at ten. Mother    30
drives me to Dr. Coronet. Ferns in the office, plastic or real, they look
the same. Dr. Coronet is queenly, an elegant nicotine-stained lady who
would have studied with Freud had circumstances not prevented it,
a bit of a Catholic, ready to offer you some mystery if your teeth will
ache too much without it. Highly recommended by Father! Forty dollars an hour, Father's forty dollars! Progress! Looking up! Looking better! That new haircut is so becoming, says Dr. Coronet herself, showing
how normal she is for a woman with an I.Q. of 180 and many advanced
degrees.

2. Mother. A lady in a brown suede coat. Boots of shiny black    31
material, black gloves, a black fur hat. She would be humiliated could
she know that of all the people in the world it is my ex-lover Simon
who walks most like her . . . self-conscious and unreal, listening to
distant music, a little bowlegged with craftiness. . . .

3. Father. Tying a necktie. In a hurry. On my first evening home    32

he put his hand on my arm and said, "Honey, we're going to forget all about this."

4. Simon. Outside a plane is crossing the sky, in here we're in a 33 hurry. Morning. It must be morning. The girl is half out of her mind, whimpering and vague. Simon her dear friend is wretched this morning . . . he is wretched with morning itself . . . he forces her to give him an injection with that needle she knows is filthy, she has a dread of needles and surgical instruments and the odor of things that are to be sent into the blood, thinking somehow of her father. . . . This is a bad morning, Simon says that his mind is being twisted out of shape, and so he submits to the needle which he usually scorns and bites his lip with his yellowish teeth, his face going very pale. *Ah baby!* he says in his soft mocking voice, which with all women is a mockery of love, *do it like this—Slowly—*And the girl, terrified, almost drops the precious needle but manages to turn it up to the light from the window . . . it is an extension of herself then? She can give him this gift then? *I wish you wouldn't do this to me,* she says, wise in her terror, because it seems to her that Simon's danger—in a few minutes he may be dead—is a way of pressing her against him that is more powerful than any other embrace. She has to work over his arm, the knotted corded veins of his arm, her forehead wet with perspiration as she pushes and releases the needle, staring at that mixture of liquid now stained with Simon's bright blood. . . . When the drug hits him she can feel it herself, she feels that magic that is more than any woman can give him, striking the back of his head and making his face stretch as if with the impact of a terrible sun. . . . She tries to embrace him but he pushes her aside and stumbles to his feet. *Jesus Christ,* he says. . . .

5. Princess, a Negro girl of eighteen. What is her charge? She is 34 closemouthed about it, shrewd and silent, you know that no one had to wrestle her to the sidewalk to get her in here; she came with dignity. In the recreation room she sits reading *Nancy Drew and the Jewel Box Mystery,* which inspires in her face tiny wrinkles of alarm and interest: what a face! Light brown skin, heavy shaded eyes, heavy eyelashes, a serious sinister dark brow, graceful fingers, graceful wristbones, graceful legs, lips, tongue, a sugar-sweet voice, a leggy stride more masculine than Simon's and my mother's, decked out in a dirty white blouse and dirty white slacks; vaguely nautical is Princess's style. . . . At breakfast she is in charge of clearing the table and leans over me, saying, *Honey you sure you ate enough?*

6. The girl lies sleepless, wondering. Why here, why not there? 35 Why Bloomfield Hills and not jail? Why jail and not her pink room?

Why downtown Detroit and not Sioux Drive? What is the difference? Is Simon all the difference? The girl's head is a parade of wonders. She is nearly sixteen, her breath is marvelous with wonders, not long ago she was coloring with crayons and now she is smearing the landscape with paints that won't come off and won't come off her fingers either. She says to the matron *I am not talking about anything*, not because everyone has warned her not to talk but because, because she will not talk, because she won't say anything about Simon who is her secret. And she says to the matron *I won't go home* up until that night in the lavatory when everything was changed. . . . "No, I won't go home I want to stay here," she says, listening to her own words with amazement, thinking that weeds might climb everywhere over that marvelous $180,000 house and dinosaurs might return to muddy the beige carpeting, but never never will she reconcile four o'clock in the morning in Detroit with eight o'clock breakfasts in Bloomfield Hills . . . oh, she aches still for Simon's hands and his caressing breath, though he gave her little pleasure, he took everything from her (five-dollar bills, ten-dollar bills, passed into her numb hands by men and taken out of her hands by Simon) until she herself was passed into the hands of other men, police, when Simon evidently got tired of her and her hysteria. . . . *No, I won't go home, I don't want to be bailed out*, the girl thinks as a *Stubborn and Wayward Child* (one of several charges lodged against her) and the matron understands her crazy white-rimmed eyes that are seeking out some new violence that will keep her in jail, should someone threaten to let her out. Such children try to strangle the matrons, the attendants, or one another . . . they want the locks locked forever, the doors nailed shut . . . and this girl is no different up until that night her mind is changed for her. . . .

## IX. *That Night*

Princess and Dolly, a little white girl of maybe fifteen, hardy however as a sergeant and in the House of Correction for armed robbery, corner her in the lavatory at the farthest sink and the other girls look away and file out to bed, leaving her. God how she is beaten up! Why is she beaten up? Why do they pound her, why such hatred? Princess vents all the hatred of a thousand silent Detroit winters on her body, this girl whose body belongs to me, fiercely she rides across the midwestern plains on this girl's tender bruised body . . . revenge on the oppressed minorities of America! revenge on the slaughtered Indians!

revenge on the female sex, on the male sex, revenge on Bloomfield Hills, revenge revenge. . . .

## X. Detroit

In Detroit weather weighs heavily upon everyone. The sky looms large.   37
The horizon shimmers in smoke. Downtown the buildings are impre-cise in the haze. Perpetual haze. Perpetual motion inside the haze. Across the choppy river is the city of Windsor, in Canada. Part of the continent has bunched up here and is bulging outward, at the tip of Detroit; a cold hard rain is forever falling on the expressways . . . shop-pers shop grimly, their cars are not parked in safe places, their wind-shields may be smashed and graceful ebony hands may drag them out through their shatterproof smashed windshields crying *Revenge for the Indians!* Ah, they all fear leaving Hudson's and being dragged to the very tip of the city and thrown off the parking roof of Cobo Hall, that expensive tomb, into the river. . . .

## XI. Characters We Are Forever Entwined with

1. Simon drew me into his tender rotting arms and breathed gravity   38
into me. Then I came to earth, weighted down. He said *You are such a little girl,* and he weighed me down with his delight. In the palms of his hands were teeth marks from his previous life experiences. He was thirty-five, they said. Imagine Simon in this room, in my pink room: he is about six feet tall and stoops slightly, in a feline cautious way, always thinking, always on guard, with his scuffed light suede shoes and his clothes which are anyone's clothes, slightly rumpled ordinary clothes that ordinary men might wear to not-bad jobs. Simon has fair, long hair, curly hair, spent languid curls that are like . . . exactly like the curls of wood shavings to the touch, I am trying to be exact . . . and he smells of unheated mornings and coffee and too many pills coating his tongue with a faint green-white scum. . . . Dear Simon, who would be panicked in this room and in this house (right now Billie is vacuuming next door in my parents' room; a vacuum cleaner's roar is a sign of all good things), Simon who is said to have come from a home not much different from this, years ago, fleeing all the carpeting and the polished banisters . . . Simon has a deathly face, only desperate people fall in love with it. His face is bony and cautious, the bones of his cheeks prominent as if with the rigidity of his ceaseless thinking, plotting, for he has to make money out of girls to whom

money means nothing, they're so far gone they can hardly count it, and in a sense money means nothing to him either except as a way of keeping on with his life. *Each Day's Proud Struggle*, the title of a novel we could read at jail. . . . Each day he needs a certain amount of money. He devours it. It wasn't love he uncoiled in me with his hollowed-out eyes and his courteous smile, that remnant of a prosperous past, but a dark terror that needed to press itself flat against him, or against another man . . . but he was the first, he came over to me and took my arm, a claim. We struggled on the stairs and I said, *Let me loose, you're hurting my neck, my face*, it was such a surprise that my skin hurt where he rubbed it, and afterward we lay face to face and he breathed everything into me. In the end I think he turned me in.

2. Raymond Forrest. I just read this morning that Raymond Forrest's father, the chairman of the board at _____, died of a heart attack on a plane bound for London. I would like to write Raymond Forrest a note of sympathy. I would like to thank him for not pressing charges against me one hundred years ago, saving me, being so generous . . . well, men like Raymond Forrest are generous men, not like Simon. I would like to write him a letter telling of my love, or of some other emotion that is positive and healthy. Not like Simon and his poetry, which he scrawled down when he was high and never changed a word . . . but when I try to think of something to say, it is Simon's language that comes back to me, caught in my head like a bad song, it is always Simon's language:

> There is no reality only dreams
> Your neck may get snapped when you wake
> My love is drawn to some violent end
> She keeps wanting to get away
> My love is heading downward
> And I am heading upward
> She is going to crash on the sidewalk
> And I am going to dissolve into the clouds

## XII. Events

1. Out of the hospital, bruised and saddened and converted, with Princess's grunts still tangled in my hair . . . and Father in his overcoat looking like a Prince himself, come to carry me off. Up the expressway and out north to home. Jesus Christ, but the air is thinner and cleaner here. Monumental houses. Heartbreaking sidewalks, so clean.

2. Weeping in the living room. The ceiling is two storeys high and two chandeliers hang from it. Weeping, weeping, though Billie the maid is *probably listening*. I will never leave home again. Never. Never leave home. Never leave this home again, never.  41

3. Sugar doughnuts for breakfast. The toaster is very shiny and my face is distorted in it. Is that my face?  42

4. The car is turning in the driveway. Father brings me home. Mother embraces me. Sunlight breaks in movieland patches on the roof of our traditional-contemporary home, which was designed for the famous automotive stylist whose identity, if I told you the name of the famous car he designed, you would all know, so I can't tell you because my teeth chatter at the thought of being sued . . . or having someone climb into my bedroom window with a rope to strangle me. . . . The car turns up the blacktop drive. The house opens to me like a doll's house, so lovely in the sunlight, the big living room beckons to me with its walls falling away in a delirium of joy at my return, Billie the maid is *no doubt* listening from the kitchen as I burst into tears and the hysteria Simon got so sick of. Convulsed in Father's arms, I say I will never leave again, never, why did I leave, where did I go, what happened, my mind is gone wrong, my body is one big bruise, my backbone was sucked dry, it wasn't the men who hurt me and Simon never hurt me but only those girls . . . my God, how they hurt me . . . I will never leave home again. . . . The car is perpetually turning up the drive and I am perpetually breaking down in the living room and we are perpetually taking the right exit from the expressway (Lahser Road) and the wall of the restroom is perpetually banging against my head and perpetually are Simon's hands moving across my body and adding everything up and so too are Father's hands on my shaking bruised back, far from the surface of my skin on the surface of my good blue cashmere coat (dry-cleaned for my release). . . . I weep for all the money here, for God in gold and beige carpeting, for the beauty of chandeliers and the miracle of a clean polished gleaming toaster and faucets that run both hot and cold water, and I tell them *I will never leave home, this is my home, I love everything here, I am in love with everything here. . . .*  43

I am home.  44

# Questions

1. In the title the narrator tells us that the story will be about how she "began [her] life over again." What do you imagine her later life is like?

2.  The introductory paragraph says that the story is "a revelation of the meaning of life." Is it?
3.  The introductory paragraph announces that there is "a happy ending." The last words of the story are, "I am home." Is there a happy ending? Why, or why not?
4.  Why do the girls beat up the narrator? What is the effect of the beating?
5.  Oates's story takes the fairly unusual form of "notes for an essay for an English class." What does the form convey about the girl aside from what it says explicitly?

## Arthur Hugh Clough

# The Latest Decalogue

Thou shalt have one God only; who
Would be at the expense of two?
No graven images may be
Worshiped, except the currency.
Swear not at all; for, for thy curse                          5
Thine enemy is none the worse.
At church on Sunday to attend
Will serve to keep the world thy friend.
Honor thy parents; that is, all
From whom advancement may befall.                            10
Thou shalt not kill; but need'st not strive
Officiously to keep alive.
Do not adultery commit;
Advantage rarely comes of it.
Thou shalt not steal; an empty feat.                         15

Arthur Hugh Clough (1819–1861), whose name rhymes with "rough," was born into a family of English cotton merchants. He spent 5 years of his early childhood in South Carolina, but was educated in England, where his teachers and friends, recognizing him as a gifted student and a talented poet, expected him to go on to a promising career. But Clough, deeply troubled both by doubts about the authenticity of the teachings of the Christian church and by the materialism of his age, never fulfilled those expectations.

When it's so lucrative to cheat.
Bear not false witness; let the lie
Have time on its own wings to fly.
Thou shalt not covet, but tradition
Approves all forms of competition.                    20

The sum of all is, thou shalt love,
If anybody, God above:
At any rate shall never labor
*More* than thyself to love thy neighbor.

## Questions

1. Explain the title.
2. The commandments in this poem (e.g., "Thou shalt have one God only," "Thou shalt not kill") are ancient (see page 709) and they are widely accepted as a guide to our moral life. What is new in the poem?
3. The poem was written in 1849. On the basis of this poem, how would you characterize the period? Does the poem speak to our own period also?

# 10
## SCIENCE OR PSEUDOSCIENCE?

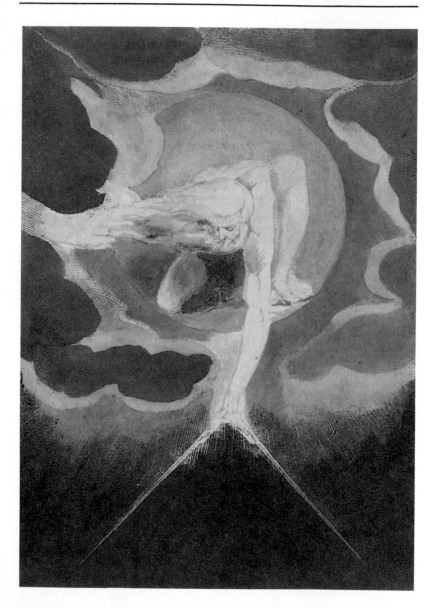

*Buzz Aldrin on the Moon*
**Neil Armstrong, 1969**

# Short Views

Nature and Nature's laws lay hid in night,
God said, "Let Newton be," and all was light.
**Alexander Pope**

Today's common sense is yesterday's science.
**Niels Bohr**

What is laid down, ordered, factual, is never enough to embrace the
whole truth: life always spills over the rim of every cup.
**Boris Pasternak**

God does not play dice with the universe.
**Albert Einstein**

$E = mc^2$
**Albert Einstein**

If science tends to thicken the crust of ice on which, as it were, we
are skating, it is all right. If it tries to find, or professes to have
found, the solid ground at the bottom of the water, it is all wrong.
**Samuel Butler**

The dangers threatening modern science cannot be averted by more
experimenting, for our complicated experiments have no longer
anything to do with nature in her own right, but with nature
charged and transformed by our own cognitive activity.
**Werner Heisenberg**

When we speak of the picture of nature in the exact science of our
age, we do not mean a picture of nature so much as a *picture of our
relationships with nature*. The old division of the world into objective
processes in space and time and the mind in which these processes
are mirrored . . . is no longer a suitable starting point for our
understanding of modern science. Science, we find, is now focused
on the network of relationships between man and nature, on the
framework which makes us as living beings dependent parts of

nature, and which we as human beings have simultaneously made the object of our thoughts and actions. Science no longer confronts nature as an objective observer, but sees itself as an actor in this interplay between man and nature. The scientific method of analysing, explaining and classifying has become conscious of its limitations, which arise out of the fact that by its intervention science alters and refashions the object of investigation. In other words, method and object can no longer be separated. *The scientific world view has ceased to be a scientific view in the true sense of the word.*
**Werner Heisenberg**

Science should leave off making pronouncements; the river of knowledge has too often turned back on itself.
**Sir James Jeans**

I wished, by treating Psychology *like* a natural science, to help her to become one.
**William James**

Sociology is the science with the greatest number of methods and the least results.
**Jules Henri Poincaré**

Sociologists . . . are the astrologers and alchemists of our twentieth century.
**Miguel de Unamuno**

Astrology fosters astronomy, Mankind *plays* its way up.
**Georg Christoph Licthenberg**

No, a thousand times no; there does not exist a category of science to which one can give the name of applied science. There are science and the applications of science, bound together as the fruit to the tree which bears it.
**Louis Pasteur**

In the fields of observation, chance favors the prepared mind.
**Louis Pasteur**

The advance of science is not comparable to the changes of a city, where old edifices are pitilessly torn down to give place to new, but

to the continuous evolution of zoological types which develop ceaselessly and end by becoming unrecognizable to the common sight, but where an expert eye finds always traces of the prior work of the past centuries.
        Jules Henri Poincaré


Anybody who has been seriously engaged in scientific work of any kind realizes that over the entrance to the gates of the temple of science are written the words: *Ye must have faith.* It is a quality which the scientist cannot dispense with.
        Max Planck


An important scientific innovation rarely makes its way by gradually winning over and converting its opponents: it rarely happens that Saul becomes Paul. What does happen is that its opponents gradually die out and that the growing generation is familiarized with the idea from the beginning.
        Max Planck


Dr. Johnson [in 1763] said it was easy to be on the negative side. . . . "I deny that Canada is taken [by the British from the French], and I can support my assertion with pretty good arguments. The French are a more numerous people than we; and it is not like that they would allow us to take it.—'But the Ministry tell us so.'—True. But the Ministry have put us to an enormous expense, and it is their interest to persuade us that we have got something for our money.—'But we are told so by thousands of men who were at the taking of it.'—Ay, but these men have still more interest in deceiving us. They don't want you should think they have gone on a fool's errand; and they don't want you should think that the French have beat them, but that they have beat the French. Now suppose you should go over and see if it is so, that would only satisfy yourself; for when you come home we will not believe you. We will say you have been bribed. . . ."
        James Boswell

Stephen W. Hawking

# Our Picture of the Universe

In order to talk about the nature of the universe and to 1
discuss questions such as whether it has a beginning or an end, you
have to be clear about what a scientific theory is. I shall take the simple-
minded view that a theory is just a model of the universe, or a restricted
part of it, and a set of rules that relate quantities in the model to observations that we make. It exists only in our minds and does not have
any other reality (whatever that might mean). A theory is a good theory
if it satisfies two requirements: It must accurately describe a large class
of observations on the basis of a model that contains only a few arbitrary elements, and it must make definite predictions about the results of future observations. For example, Aristotle's theory that everything was made out of four elements, earth, air, fire, and water, was
simple enough to qualify, but it did not make any definite predictions.
On the other hand, Newton's theory of gravity was based on an even
simpler model, in which bodies attracted each other with a force that
was proportional to a quantity called their mass and inversely proportional to the square of the distance between them. Yet it predicts
the motions of the sun, the moon, and the planets to a high degree
of accuracy.

Any physical theory is always provisional, in the sense that it is 2
only a hypothesis: you can never prove it. No matter how many times
the results of experiments agree with some theory, you can never be
sure that the next time the result will not contradict the theory. On
the other hand, you can disprove a theory by finding even a single

Stephen Hawking, born in England, is Lucasian Professor of Mathematics at
Cambridge University, a post held some three centuries ago by Isaac Newton.
The victim of Lou Gehrig's disease, for the last two decades Hawking has been
confined to a wheelchair; he speaks by means of a computer and a speech
synthesizer attached to the chair.

Hawking is often described as the most brilliant theoretical physical scientist
since Einstein. Almost all of his writings are highly technical, but he has written
one book for the general public, *A Brief History of Time*, and it is from this book
that we have drawn our selection.

observation that disagrees with the predictions of the theory. As philosopher of science Karl Popper has emphasized, a good theory is characterized by the fact that it makes a number of predictions that could in principle be disproved or falsified by observation. Each time new experiments are observed to agree with the predictions the theory survives, and our confidence in it is increased; but if ever a new observation is found to disagree, we have to abandon or modify the theory. At least that is what is supposed to happen, but you can always question the competence of the person who carried out the observation.

In practice, what often happens is that a new theory is devised  3 that is really an extension of the previous theory. For example, very accurate observations of the planet Mercury revealed a small difference between its motion and the predictions of Newton's theory of gravity. Einstein's general theory of relativity predicted a slightly different motion from Newton's theory. The fact that Einstein's predictions matched what was seen, while Newton's did not, was one of the crucial confirmations of the new theory. However, we still use Newton's theory for all practical purposes because the difference between its predictions and those of general relativity is very small in the situations that we normally deal with. (Newton's theory also has the great advantage that it is much simpler to work with than Einstein's!)

The eventual goal of science is to provide a single theory that describes the whole universe. However, the approach most scientists actually follow is to separate the problem into two parts. First, there are the laws that tell us how the universe changes with time. (If we know what the universe is like at any one time, these physical laws tell us how it will look at any later time.) Second, there is the question of the initial state of the universe. Some people feel that science should be concerned with only the first part; they regard the question of the initial situation as a matter for metaphysics or religion. They would say that God, being omnipotent, could have started the universe off any way he wanted. That may be so, but in that case he also could have made it develop in a completely arbitrary way. Yet it appears that he chose to make it evolve in a very regular way according to certain laws. It therefore seems equally reasonable to suppose that there are also laws governing the initial state.

It turns out to be very difficult to devise a theory to describe the  5 universe all in one go. Instead, we break the problem up into bits and invent a number of partial theories. Each of these partial theories describes and predicts a certain limited class of observations, neglecting the effects of other quantities, or representing them by simple sets of numbers. It may be that this approach is completely wrong. If everything in the universe depends on everything else in a fundamental way, it might be impossible to get close to a full solution by investigating parts of the problem in isolation. Nevertheless, it is certainly the way that we have made progress in the past. The classic example again is the Newtonian theory of gravity, which tell us that the gravitational force between two bodies depends only on one number associated with each body, its mass, but is otherwise independent of what the bodies are made of. Thus one does not need to have a theory of the structure and constitution of the sun and the planets in order to calculate their orbits.

Today scientists describe the universe in terms of two basic partial theories—the general theory of relativity and quantum mechanics. They are the great intellectual achievements of the first half of this century. The general theory of relativity describes the force of gravity and the large-scale structure of the universe, that is, the structure on scales from only a few miles to as large as a million million million million (1 with twenty-four zeros after it) miles, the size of the observable universe. Quantum mechanics, on the other hand, deals with phenomena on extremely small scales, such as a millionth of a millionth of an inch. Unfortunately, however, these two theories are known to be inconsistent with each other—they cannot both be correct. One of the major endeavors in physics today, and the major theme of this book, is the search for a new theory that will incorporate them both— a quantum theory of gravity. We do not yet have such a theory, and we may still be a long way from having one, but we do already know many of the properties that it must have. And we shall see, in later chapters, that we already know a fair amount about the predictions a quantum theory of gravity must make.

Now, if you believe that the universe is not arbitrary, but is governed by definite laws, you ultimately have to combine the partial theories into a complete unified theory that will describe everything in the universe. But there is a fundamental paradox in the search for such a complete unified theory. The ideas about scientific theories outlined above assume we are rational beings who are free to observe the universe as we want and to draw logical deductions from what we see. In such a scheme it is reasonable to suppose that we might progress ever closer toward the laws that govern our universe. Yet if there really is a complete unified theory, it would also presumably determine our actions. And so the theory itself would determine the outcome of our search for it! And why should it determine that we come to the right conclusions from the evidence? Might it not equally well determine that we draw the wrong conclusion? Or no conclusion at all?

The only answer that I can give to this problem is based on Darwin's principle of natural selection. The idea is that in any population of self-reproducing organisms, there will be variations in the genetic material and upbringing that different individuals have. These differences will mean that some individuals are better able than others to draw the right conclusions about the world around them and to act accordingly. These individuals will be more likely to survive and reproduce and so their pattern of behavior and thought will come to dominate. It has certainly been true in the past that what we call intelligence and scientific discovery has conveyed a survival advantage. It is not so clear that this is still the case: our scientific discoveries may well destroy us all, and even if they don't, a complete unified theory may not make much difference to our chances of survival. However, provided the universe has evolved in a regular way, we might expect that the reasoning abilities that natural selection has given us would be valid also in our search for a complete unified theory, and so would not lead us to the wrong conclusions. 8

Because the partial theories that we already have are sufficient to make accurate predictions in all but the most extreme situations, the search for the ultimate theory of the universe seems difficult to justify on practical grounds. (It is worth noting, though, that similar arguments could have been used against both relativity and quantum mechanics, and these theories have given us both nuclear energy and the microelectronics revolution!) The discovery of a complete unified theory, therefore, may not aid the survival of our species. It may not even affect our life-style. But ever since the dawn of civilization, people have not been content to see events as unconnected and inexplicable. They have craved an understanding of the underlying order in the world. Today we still yearn to know why we are here and where we came from. Humanity's deepest desire for knowledge is justification enough for our continuing quest. And our goal is nothing less than a complete description of the universe we live in. 9

# Questions

1. In the opening sentence of this excerpt Hawking says that "to talk about the nature of the universe and to discuss questions such as whether it has a beginning or an end, you have to be clear about

what a scientific theory is." What, according to Hawking, is a scientific theory? Can you explain why one must be "clear about what a scientific theory is" to discuss questions about the nature of the universe?

2. How does Hawking define a "good theory of the universe"? What examples, good and bad, does he give?

3. If a good theory must, among other things, accurately predict future observations, how can such a theory be said to exist "only in our minds and . . . not have any other reality (whatever that might mean)," as Hawking tells us in the first paragraph?

4. Why, according to Hawking (paragraph 8), would our reasoning abilities "not lead us to the wrong conclusions" in our search for a unified theory? How convinced are you by his explanation?

5. In the last two sentences of this essay Hawking suggests that our "desire for knowledge" justifies our efforts to produce "a complete description of the universe we live in." How are these efforts to be financed? Might one argue that, given pressing social problems, we cannot afford to finance the quest for a unified theory?

## Carl G. Hempel

# Scientific Inquiry
## Invention and Test

### A Case History as an Example

As a simple illustration of some important aspects of scientific inquiry   1
let us consider Semmelweis' work on childbed fever. Ignaz Semmelweis, a physician of Hungarian birth, did this work during the years from 1844 to 1848 at the Vienna General Hospital. As a member of the

Carl G. Hempel was born in 1905 in Germany, where he studied mathematics, physics, and philosophy. After receiving his doctorate, he left Germany for Belgium, and in 1937 he left Belgium for the United States, where he taught first at Yale and later at Princeton. In 1977, at the age of 72, he began yet another teaching career, this time at the University of Pittsburgh.

medical staff of the First Maternity Division in the hospital, Semmelweis was distressed to find that a large proportion of the women who were delivered of their babies in that division contracted a serious and often fatal illness known as puerperal fever or childbed fever. In 1844, as many as 260 out of 3,157 mothers in the First Division, or 8.2 per cent, died of the disease; for 1845, the death rate was 6.8 per cent, and for 1846, it was 11.4 per cent. These figures were all the more alarming because in the adjacent Second Maternity Division of the same hospital, which accommodated almost as many women as the First, the death toll from childbed fever was much lower: 2.3, 2.0, and 2.7 per cent for the same years. In a book that he wrote later on the causation and the prevention of childbed fever, Semmelweis describes his efforts to resolve the dreadful puzzle.[1]

He began by considering various explanations that were current 2 at the time; some of these he rejected out of hand as incompatible with well-established facts; others he subjected to specific tests.

One widely accepted view attributed the ravages of puerperal fever 3 to "epidemic influences", which were vaguely described as "atmospheric-cosmic-telluric changes" spreading over whole districts and causing childbed fever in women in confinement. But how, Semmelweis reasons, could such influences have plagued the First Division for years and yet spared the Second? And how could this view be reconciled with the fact that while the fever was raging in the hospital, hardly a case occurred in the city of Vienna or in its surroundings: a genuine epidemic, such as cholera, would not be so selective. Finally, Semmelweis notes that some of the women admitted to the First Division, living far from the hospital, had been overcome by labor on their way and had given birth in the street: yet despite these adverse conditions, the death rate from childbed fever among these cases of "street birth" was lower than the average for the First Division.

On another view, overcrowding was a cause of mortality in the 4 First Division. But Semmelweis points out that in fact the crowding was heavier in the Second Division, partly as a result of the desperate efforts of patients to avoid assignment to the notorious First Division.

---

[1] The story of Semmelweis' work and of the difficulties he encountered forms a fascinating page in the history of medicine. A detailed account, which includes translations and paraphrases of large portions of Semmelweis' writings, is given in W. J. Sinclair, *Semmelweis: His Life and His Doctrine* (Manchester, England: Manchester University Press, 1909). Brief quoted phrases in this chapter are taken from this work. The highlights of Semmelweis' career are recounted in the first chapter of P. de Kruif, *Men Against Death* (New York: Harcourt, Brace & World, Inc., 1932).

He also rejects two similar conjectures that were current, by noting that there were no differences between the two Divisions in regard to diet or general care of the patients.

In 1846, a commission that had been appointed to investigate the matter attributed the prevalence of illness in the First Division to injuries resulting from rough examination by the medical students, all of whom received their obstetrical training in the First Division. Semmelweis notes in refutation of this view that (a) the injuries resulting naturally from the process of birth are much more extensive than those that might be caused by rough examination; (b) the midwives who received their training in the Second Division examined their patients in much the same manner but without the same ill effects; (c) when, in response to the commission's report, the number of medical students was halved and their examinations of the women were reduced to a minimum, the mortality, after a brief decline, rose to higher levels than ever before.

Various psychological explanations were attempted. One of them noted that the First Division was so arranged that a priest bearing the last sacrament to a dying woman had to pass through five wards before reaching the sickroom beyond: the appearance of the priest, preceded by an attendant ringing a bell, was held to have a terrifying and debilitating effect upon the patients in the wards and thus to make them more likely victims of childbed fever. In the Second Division, this adverse factor was absent, since the priest had direct access to the sickroom. Semmelweis decided to test this conjecture. He persuaded the priest to come by a roundabout route and without ringing of the bell, in order to reach the sick chamber silently and unobserved. But the mortality in the First Division did not decrease.

A new idea was suggested to Semmelweis by the observation that in the First Division the women were delivered lying on their backs; in the Second Division, on their sides. Though he thought it unlikely, he decided "like a drowning man clutching at a straw", to test whether this difference in procedure was significant. He introduced the use of the lateral position in the First Division, but again, the mortality remained unaffected.

At last, early in 1847, an accident gave Semmelweis the decisive clue for his solution of the problem. A colleague of his, Kolletschka, received a puncture wound in the finger, from the scalpel of a student with whom he was performing an autopsy, and died after an agonizing illness during which he displayed the same symptoms that Semmelweis had observed in the victims of childbed fever. Although the role of microorganisms in such infections had not yet been recognized at the time, Semmelweis realized that "cadaveric matter" which the student's scalpel had introduced into Kolletschka's blood stream had caused his colleague's fatal illness. And the similarities between the course of Kolletschka's disease and that of the women in his clinic led Semmelweis to the conclusion that his patients had died of the same kind of blood poisoning: he, his colleagues, and the medical students had been the carriers of the infectious material, for he and his associates used to come to the wards directly from performing dissections in the autopsy room, and examine the women in labor after only superficially washing their hands, which often retained a characteristic foul odor.

Again, Semmelweis put his idea to a test. He reasoned that if he 9 were right, then childbed fever could be prevented by chemically destroying the infectious material adhering to the hands. He therefore issued an order requiring all medical students to wash their hands in a solution of chlorinated lime before making an examination. The mortality from childbed fever promptly began to decrease, and for the year 1848 it fell to 1.27 per cent in the First Division, compared to 1.33 in the Second.

In further support of his idea, or of his *hypothesis*, as we will also 10 say, Semmelweis notes that it accounts for the fact that the mortality in the Second Division consistently was so much lower: the patients there were attended by midwives, whose training did not include anatomical instruction by dissection of cadavers.

The hypothesis also explained the lower mortality among "street 11 births": women who arrived with babies in arms were rarely examined after admission and thus had a better chance of escaping infection.

Similarly, the hypothesis accounted for the fact that the victims of 12 childbed fever among the newborn babies were all among those whose mothers had contracted the disease during labor; for then the infection could be transmitted to the baby before birth, through the common bloodstream of mother and child, whereas this was impossible when the mother remained healthy.

Further clinical experiences soon led Semmelweis to broaden his 13 hypothesis. On one occasion, for example, he and his associates, having carefully disinfected their hands, examined first a woman in labor who was suffering from a festering cervical cancer; then they proceeded to examine twelve other women in the same room, after only routine washing without renewed disinfection. Eleven of the twelve patients died of puerperal fever. Semmelweis concluded that childbed fever can be caused not only by cadaveric material, but also by "putrid matter derived from living organisms."

## Basic Steps in Testing a Hypothesis

We have seen how, in his search for the cause of childbed fever, Sem- 14
melweis examined various hypotheses that had been suggested as possible answers. How such hypotheses are arrived at in the first place is an intriguing question which we will consider later. First, however, let us examine how a hypothesis, once proposed, is tested.

Sometimes, the procedure is quite direct. Consider the conjectures 15
that differences in crowding, or in diet, or in general care account for the difference in mortality between the two divisions. As Semmelweis points out, these conflict with readily observable facts. There are no such differences between the divisions; the hypotheses are therefore rejected as false.

But usually the test will be less simple and straightforward. Take 16
the hypothesis attributing the high mortality in the First Division to the dread evoked by the appearance of the priest with his attendant. The intensity of that dread, and especially its effect upon childbed fever, are not as directly ascertainable as are differences in crowding or in diet, and Semmelweis uses an indirect method of testing. He asks himself: Are there any readily observable effects that should occur if the hypothesis were true? And he reasons: If the hypothesis were true, then an appropriate change in the priest's procedure should be followed by a decline in fatalities. He checks this implication by a simple experiment and finds it false, and he therefore rejects the hypothesis.

Similarly, to test his conjecture about the position of the women 17
during delivery, he reasons: If this conjecture should be true, then adoption of the lateral position in the First Division will reduce the mortality. Again, the implication is shown false by his experiment, and the conjecture is discarded.

In the last two cases, the test is based on an argument to the effect 18
that if the contemplated hypothesis, say $H$, is true, then certain observable events (e.g., decline in mortality) should occur under specified circumstances (e.g., if the priest refrains from walking through the wards, or if the women are delivered in lateral position); or briefly, if $H$ is true, then so is $I$, where $I$ is a statement describing the observable occurrences to be expected. For convenience, let us say that $I$ is inferred from, or implied by, $H$; and let us call $I$ a *test implication of the hypothesis*

*H*. (We will later give a more accurate description of the relation between *I* and *H*.)

In our last two examples, experiments show the test implication 19 to be false, and the hypothesis is accordingly rejected. The reasoning that leads to the rejection may be schematized as follows:

If *H* is true, then so is *I*.

2a   But (as the evidence shows) *I* is not true.

*H* is not true.

Any argument of this form, called *modus tollens* in logic, is deductively valid; that is, if its premisses (the sentences above the horizontal line) are true, then its conclusion (the sentence below the horizontal line) is unfailingly true as well. Hence, if the premisses of (2a) are properly established, the hypothesis *H* that is being tested must indeed be rejected.

Next, let us consider the case where observation or experiment 20 bears out the test implication *I*. From his hypothesis that childbed fever is blood poisoning produced by cadaveric matter, Semmelweis infers that suitable antiseptic measures will reduce fatalities from the disease. This time, experiment shows the test implication to be true. But this favorable outcome does not conclusively prove the hypothesis true, for the underlying argument would have the form

If *H* is true, then so is *I*.

2b   (As the evidence shows) *I* is true.

*H* is true.

And this mode of reasoning, which is referred to as the *fallacy of affirming the consequent*, is deductively invalid, that is, its conclusion may be false even if its premisses are true. This is in fact illustrated by Semmelweis' own experience. The initial version of his account of childbed fever as a form of blood poisoning presented infection with cadaveric matter essentially as the one and only source of the disease; and he was right in reasoning that if this hypothesis should be true, then destruction of cadaveric particles by antiseptic washing should reduce the mortality. Furthermore, his experiment did show the test implication to be true. Hence, in this case, the premisses of (2b) were both true. Yet, his hypothesis was false, for as he later discovered, putrid material from living organisms, too, could produce childbed fever.

Thus, the favorable outcome of a test, i.e., the fact that a test im- 21 plication inferred from a hypothesis is found to be true, does not prove the hypothesis to be true. Even if many implications of a hypothesis have been borne out by careful tests, the hypothesis may still be false. The following argument still commits the fallacy of affirming the consequent:

If $H$ is true, then so are $I_1, I_2, \ldots, I_n$.

2c    (As the evidence shows) $I_1, I_2, \ldots, I_n$ are all true.

$H$ is true.

This, too, can be illustrated by reference to Semmelweis' final hypothesis in its first version. As we noted earlier, his hypothesis also yields the test implications that among cases of street births admitted to the First Division, mortality from puerperal fever should be below the average for the Division, and that infants of mothers who escape the illness do not contract childbed fever; and these implications, too, were borne out by the evidence—even though the first version of the final hypothesis was false.

But the observation that a favorable outcome of however many  22
tests does not afford conclusive proof for a hypothesis should not lead us to think that if we have subjected a hypothesis to a number of tests and all of them have had a favorable outcome, we are no better off than if we had not tested the hypothesis at all. For each of our tests might conceivably have had an unfavorable outcome and might have led to the rejection of the hypothesis. A set of favorable results obtained by testing different test implications, $I_1, I_2, \ldots, I_n$, of a hypothesis, shows that as far as these particular implications are concerned, the hypothesis has been borne out; and while this result does not afford a complete proof of the hypothesis, it provides at least some support, some partial corroboration or confirmation for it. The extent of this support will depend on various aspects of the hypothesis and of the test data.

Let us now consider another example,[2] which will also bring to  23
our attention some further aspects of scientific inquiry.

As was known at Galileo's time, and probably much earlier, a  24
simple suction pump, which draws water from a well by means of a

---

[2] The reader will find a fuller account of this example in Chap. 4 of J. B. Conant's fascinating book, *Science and Common Sense* (New Haven: Yale University Press, 1951). A letter by Torricelli setting forth his hypothesis and his test of it, and an eyewitness report on the Puy-de-Dôme experiment are reprinted in W. F. Magie, *A Source Book in Physics* (Cambridge: Harvard University Press, 1963), pp. 70–75.

piston that can be raised in the pump barrel, will lift water no higher than about 34 feet above the surface of the well. Galileo was intrigued by this limitation and suggested an explanation for it, which was, however, unsound. After Galileo's death, his pupil Torricelli advanced a new answer. He argued that the earth is surrounded by a sea of air, which, by reason of its weight exerts pressure upon the surface below, and that this pressure upon the surface of the well forces water up the pump barrel when the piston is raised. The maximum length of 34 feet for the water column in the barrel thus reflects simply the total pressure of the atmosphere upon the surface of the well.

It is evidently impossible to determine by direct inspection or observation whether this account is correct, and Torricelli tested it indirectly. He reasoned that *if* his conjecture were true, *then* the pressure of the atmosphere should also be capable of supporting a proportionately shorter column of mercury; indeed, since the specific gravity of mercury is about 14 times that of water, the length of the mercury column should be about 34/14 feet, or slightly less than 2½ feet. He checked this test implication by means of an ingeniously simple device, which was, in effect, the mercury barometer. The well of water is replaced by an open vessel containing mercury; the barrel of the suction pump is replaced by a glass tube sealed off at one end. The tube is completely filled with mercury and closed by placing the thumb tightly over the open end. It is then inverted, the open end is submerged in the mercury well, and the thumb is withdrawn; whereupon the mercury column in the tube drops until its length is about 30 inches—just as predicted by Torricelli's hypothesis. 25

A further test implication of that hypothesis was noted by Pascal, who reasoned that if the mercury in Torricelli's barometer is counterbalanced by the pressure of the air above the open mercury well, then its length should decrease with increasing altitude, since the weight of the air overhead becomes smaller. At Pascal's request, this implication was checked by his brother-in-law, Périer, who measured the length of the mercury column in the Torricelli barometer at the foot of the Puy-de-Dôme, a mountain some 4,800 feet high, and then carefully carried the apparatus to the top and repeated the measurement there while a control barometer was left at the bottom under the supervision of an assistant. Périer found the mercury column at the top of the mountain more than three inches shorter than at the bottom, whereas the length of the column in the control barometer had remained unchanged throughout the day. 26

## The Role of Induction in Scientific Inquiry

We have considered some scientific investigations in which a problem 27
was tackled by proposing tentative answers in the form of hypotheses
that were then tested by deriving from them suitable test implications
and checking these by observation or experiment.

But how are suitable hypotheses arrived at in the first place? It is 28
sometimes held that they are inferred from antecedently collected data
by means of a procedure called *inductive inference,* as contradistin-
guished from deductive inference, from which it differs in important
respects.

In a deductively valid argument, the conclusion is related to the 29
premises in such a way that if the premises are true then the conclusion cannot fail to be true as well. This requirement is satisfied, for
example, by any argument of the following general form:

If *p*, then *q*.
It is not the case that *q*.

It is not the case that *p*.

Brief reflection shows that no matter what particular statements may
stand at the places marked by the letters '*p*' and '*q*', the conclusion
will certainly be true if the premises are. In fact, our schema represents
the argument form called *modus tollens,* to which we referred earlier.

Another type of deductively valid inference is illustrated by this 30
example:

Any sodium salt, when put into the flame of a Bunsen burner,
turns the flame yellow.
This piece of rock salt is a sodium salt.

This piece of rock salt, when put into the flame of a Bunsen
burner, will turn the flame yellow.

Arguments of the latter kind are often said to lead from the general 31
(here, the premiss about all sodium salts) to the particular (a conclusion
about the particular piece of rock salt). Inductive inferences, by contrast, are sometimes described as leading from premises about particular cases to a conclusion that has the character of a general law or
principle. For example, from premises to the effect that each of the
particular samples of various sodium salts that have so far been subjected to the Bunsen flame test did turn the flame yellow, inductive
inference supposedly leads to the general conclusion that all sodium

salts, when put into the flame of a Bunsen burner, turn the flame yellow. But in this case, the truth of the premisses obviously does *not* guarantee the truth of the conclusion; for even if it is the case that all samples of sodium salts examined so far did turn the Bunsen flame yellow, it remains quite possible that new kinds of sodium salt might yet be found that do not conform to this generalization. Indeed, even some kinds of sodium salt that have already been tested with positive result might conceivably fail to satisfy the generalization under special physical conditions (such as very strong magnetic fields or the like) in which they have not yet been examined. For this reason, the premisses of an inductive inference are often said to imply the conclusion only with more or less high probability, whereas the premisses of a deductive inference imply the conclusion with certainty.

The idea that in scientific inquiry, inductive inference from antecedently collected data leads to appropriate general principles is clearly embodied in the following account of how a scientist would ideally proceed:    32

> If we try to imagine how a mind of superhuman power and reach, but normal so far as the logical processes of its thought are concerned, . . . would use the scientific method, the process would be as follows: First, all facts would be observed and recorded, *without selection* or a *priori* guess as to their relative importance. Secondly, the observed and recorded facts would be analyzed, compared, and classified, *without hypothesis or postulates* other than those necessarily involved in the logic of thought. Third, from this analysis of the facts generalizations would be inductively drawn as to the relations, classificatory or causal, between them. Fourth, further research would be deductive as well as inductive, employing inferences from previously established generalizations.[3]

This passage distinguishes four stages in an ideal scientific inquiry:    33 (1) observation and recording of all facts, (2) analysis and classification of these facts, (3) inductive derivation of generalizations from them, and (4) further testing of the generalizations. The first two of these stages are specifically assumed not to make use of any guesses or hypotheses as to how the observed facts might be interconnected; this restriction seems to have been imposed in the belief that such preconceived ideas would introduce a bias and would jeopardize the scientific objectivity of the investigation.

[3] A. B. Wolfe, "Functional Economics," in *The Trend of Economics*, ed. R. G. Tugwell (New York: Alfred A. Knopf, Inc., 1924), p. 450 (italics are quoted).

But the view expressed in the quoted passage—I will call it *the* 34
*narrow inductivist conception of scientific inquiry*—is untenable, for several
reasons. A brief survey of these can serve to amplify and to supplement
our earlier remarks on scientific procedure.

First, a scientific investigation as here envisaged could never get 35
off the ground. Even its first phase could never be carried out, for a
collection of *all* the facts would have to await the end of the world, so
to speak; and even all the facts *up to now* cannot be collected, since
there are an infinite number and variety of them. Are we to examine,
for example, all the grains of sand in all the deserts and on all the
beaches, and are we to record their shapes, their weights, their chemical composition, their distances from each other, their constantly
changing temperature, and their equally changing distance from the
center of the moon? Are we to record the floating thoughts that cross
our minds in the tedious process? The shapes of the clouds overhead,
the changing color of the sky? The construction and the trade name
of our writing equipment? Our own life histories and those of our
fellow investigators? All these, and untold other things, are, after all,
among "all the facts up to now".

Perhaps, then, all that should be required in the first phase is that 36
all the *relevant* facts be collected. But relevant to what? Though the
author does not mention this, let us suppose that the inquiry is concerned with a specified *problem*. Should we not then begin by collecting
all the facts—or better, all available data—relevant to that problem?
This notion still makes no clear sense. Semmelweis sought to solve
one specific problem, yet he collected quite different kinds of data at
different stages of his inquiry. And rightly so; for what particular sorts
of data it is reasonable to collect is not determined by the problem
under study, but by a tentative answer to it that the investigator entertains in the form of a conjecture or hypothesis. Given the conjecture
that mortality from childbed fever was increased by the terrifying appearance of the priest and his attendant with the death bell, it was
relevant to collect data on the consequences of having the priest change
his routine; but it would have been totally irrelevant to check what
would happen if doctors and students disinfected their hands before
examining their patients. With respect to Semmelweis' eventual con-
tamination hypothesis, data of the latter kind were clearly relevant,
and those of the former kind totally irrelevant.

Empirical "facts" or findings, therefore, can be qualified as logi- 37
cally relevant or irrelevant only in reference to a given hypothesis, but
not in reference to a given problem.

Suppose now that a hypothesis *H* has been advanced as a tentative    38
answer to a research problem: what kinds of data would be relevant
to *H*? Our earlier examples suggest an answer: A finding is relevant
to *H* if either its occurrence or its nonoccurrence can be inferred from
*H*. Take Torricelli's hypothesis, for example. As we saw, Pascal inferred from it that the mercury column in a barometer should grow
shorter if the barometer were carried up a mountain. Therefore, any
finding to the effect that this did indeed happen in a particular case
is relevant to the hypotheses; but so would be the finding that the
length of the mercury column had remained unchanged or that it had
decreased and then increased during the ascent, for such findings
would refute Pascal's test implication and would thus disconfirm Torricelli's hypothesis. Data of the former kind may be called positively,
or favorably, relevant to the hypothesis; those of the latter kind negatively, or unfavorably, relevant.

In sum, the maxim that data should be gathered without guidance    39
by antecedent hypotheses about the connections among the facts under
study is self-defeating, and it is certainly not followed in scientific inquiry. On the contrary, tentative hypotheses are needed to give direction to a scientific investigation. Such hypotheses determine, among
other things, what data should be collected at a given point in a scientific investigation.

It is of interest to note that social scientists trying to check a hy-    40
pothesis by reference to the vast store of facts recorded by the U.S.
Bureau of the Census, or by other data-gathering organizations, sometimes find to their disappointment that the values of some variable that
plays a central role in the hypothesis have nowhere been systematically
recorded. This remark is not, of course, intended as a criticism of data
gathering: those engaged in the process no doubt try to select facts
that might prove relevant to future hypotheses; the observation is simply meant to illustrate the impossibility of collecting "all the relevant
data" without knowledge of the hypotheses to which the data are to
have relevance.

The second stage envisaged in our quoted passage is open to sim-    41
ilar criticism. A set of empirical "facts" can be analyzed and classified
in many different ways, most of which will be unilluminating for the
purposes of a given inquiry. Semmelweis could have classified the
women in the maternity wards according to criteria such as age, place
of residence, marital status, dietary habits, and so forth; but information on these would have provided no clue to a patient's prospects
of becoming a victim of childbed fever. What Semmelweis sought were

criteria that would be significantly connected with those prospects; and for this purpose, as he eventually found, it was illuminating to single out those women who were attended by medical personnel with contaminated hands; for it was with this characteristic, or with the corresponding class of patients, that high mortality from childbed fever was associated.

Thus, if a particular way of analyzing and classifying empirical findings is to lead to an explanation of the phenomena concerned, then it must be based on hypotheses about how those phenomena are connected; without such hypotheses, analysis and classification are blind.  42

Our critical reflections on the first two stages of inquiry as envisaged in the quoted passage also undercut the notion that hypotheses are introduced only in the third stage, by inductive inference from antecedently collected data. But some further remarks on the subject should be added here.  43

Induction is sometimes conceived as a method that leads, by means of mechanically applicable rules, from observed facts to corresponding general principles. In this case, the rules of inductive inference would provide effective canons of scientific discovery; induction would be a mechanical procedure analogous to the familiar routine for the multiplication of integers, which leads, in a finite number of predetermined and mechanically performable steps, to the corresponding product. Actually, however, no such general and mechanical induction procedure is available at present; otherwise, the much studied problem of the causation of cancer, for example, would hardly have remained unsolved to this day. Nor can the discovery of such a procedure ever be expected. For—to mention one reason—scientific hypotheses and theories are usually couched in terms that do not occur at all in the description of the empirical findings on which they rest, and which they serve to explain. For example, theories about the atomic and subatomic structure of matter contain terms such as "atom," "electron," "proton," "neutron," "psi-function," etc.; yet they are based on laboratory findings about the spectra of various gases, tracks in cloud and bubble chambers, quantitative aspects of chemical reactions, and so forth—all of which can be described without the use of those "theoretical terms." Induction rules of the kind here envisaged would therefore have to provide a mechanical routine for constructing, on the basis of the given data, a hypothesis or theory stated in terms of some quite novel concepts, which are nowhere used in the description of the data themselves. Surely, no general mechanical rule of procedure can be expected to achieve this. Could there be  44 a general rule, for example, which, when applied to the data available to Galileo concerning the limited effectiveness of suction pumps, would, by a mechanical routine, produce a hypothesis based on the concept of a sea of air?

To be sure, mechanical procedures for inductively "inferring" a 45 hypothesis on the basis of given data may be specifiable for situations of special, and relatively simple, kinds. For example, if the length of a copper rod has been measured at several different temperatures, the resulting pairs of associated values for temperature and length may be represented by points in a plane coordinate system, and a curve may be drawn through them in accordance with some particular rule of curve fitting. The curve then graphically represents a general quantitative hypothesis that expresses the length of the rod as a specific function of its temperature. But note that this hypothesis contains no novel terms; it is expressible in terms of the concepts of temperature and length, which are used also in describing the data. Moreover, the choice of "associated" values of temperature and length as data already presupposes a guiding hypothesis; namely, that with each value of the temperature, exactly one value of the length of the copper rod is associated, so that its length is indeed a function of its temperature alone. The mechanical curve-fitting routine then serves only to select a particular function as the appropriate one. This point is important; for suppose that instead of a copper rod, we examine a body of nitrogen gas enclosed in a cylindrical container with a movable piston as a lid, and that we measure its volume at several different temperatures. If we were to use this procedure in an effort to obtain from our data a *general* hypothesis representing the volume of the gas as a function of its temperature, we would fail, because the volume of a gas is a function both of its temperature and of the pressure exerted upon it, so that at the same temperature, the given gas may assume different volumes.

Thus, even in these simple cases, the mechanical procedures for 46 the construction of a hypothesis do only part of the job, for they presuppose an antecedent, less specific hypothesis (i.e., that a certain physical variable is a function of one single other variable), which is not obtainable by the same procedure.

There are, then, no generally applicable "rules of induction," by 47 which hypotheses or theories can be mechanically derived or inferred from empirical data. The transition from data to theory requires creative imagination. Scientific hypotheses and theories are not *derived* from observed facts, but *invented* in order to account for them. They constitute guesses at the connections that might obtain between the phenomena under study, at uniformities and patterns that might underlie their occurrence. "Happy guesses"[4] of this kind require great ingenuity, especially if they involve a radical departure from current modes of scientific thinking, as did, for example, the theory of relativity and quantum theory. The inventive effort required in scientific research will benefit from a thorough familiarity with current knowledge in the field. A complete novice will hardly make an important scientific discovery, for the ideas that may occur to him are likely to duplicate what has been tried before or to run afoul of well-established facts or theories of which he is not aware.

Nevertheless, the ways in which fruitful scientific guesses are arrived at are very different from any process of systematic inference. The chemist Kekulé, for example, tells us that he had long been trying unsuccessfully to devise a structural formula for the benzene molecule when, one evening in 1865, he found a solution to his problem while he was dozing in front of his fireplace. Gazing into the flames, he seemed to see atoms dancing in snakelike arrays. Suddenly, one of the snakes formed a ring by seizing hold of its own tail and then whirled mockingly before him. Kekulé awoke in a flash: he had hit upon the now famous and familiar idea of representing the molecular structure of benzene by a hexagonal ring. He spent the rest of the night working out the consequences of this hypothesis.[5]

This last remark contains an important reminder concerning the objectivity of science. In his endeavor to find a solution to his problem, the scientist may give free rein to his imagination, and the course of his creative thinking may be influenced even by scientifically questionable notions. Kepler's study of planetary motion, for example, was inspired by his interest in a mystical doctrine about numbers and a

[4] This characterization was given already by William Whewell in his work *The Philosophy of the Inductive Sciences*, 2nd ed. (London: John W. Parker, 1847); II, 41. Whewell also speaks of "invention" as "part of induction" (p. 46). In the same vein, K. Popper refers to scientific hypotheses and theories as "conjectures"; see, for example, the essay "Science: Conjectures and Refutations" in his book, *Conjectures and Refutations* (New York and London: Basic Books, 1962). Indeed, A. B. Wolfe, whose narrowly inductivist conception of ideal scientific procedure was quoted earlier, stresses that "the limited human mind" has to use "a greatly modified procedure," requiring scientific imagination and the selection of data on the basis of some "working hypothesis" (p. 450 of the essay cited in note 3).
[5] Cf. the quotations from Kekulé's own report in A. Findlay, *A Hundred Years of Chemistry*, 2nd ed. (London: Gerald Duckworth & Co., 1948), p. 37; and W.I.B. Beveridge, *The Art of Scientific Investigation*, 3rd ed. (London: William Heinemann, Ltd., 1957), p. 56.

passion to demonstrate the music of the spheres. Yet, scientific objectivity is safeguarded by the principle that while hypotheses and theories may be freely invented and *proposed* in science, they can be *accepted* into the body of scientific knowledge only if they pass critical scrutiny, which includes in particular the checking of suitable test implications by careful observation or experiment.

# Questions

1. In paragraph 10 Hempel speaks of Semmelweis's "hypothesis." On the basis of the preceding paragraphs, what do you take Hempel's definition of a hypothesis to be?

2. In paragraphs 21 and 22 Hempel explains "the fallacy of affirming the consequent." State a hypothesis (you may invent as preposterous a hypothesis as you wish), and then use it in an argument in which you commit the fallacy of affirming the consequent.

3. What is the narrow inductivist conception of scientific inquiry? Suppose that a narrow inductivist of your acquaintance finds that the car he is driving comes to a surprising stop. How would he go about finding out what was wrong? How might you, in contrast, conduct a scientific inquiry into the cause of the malfunction?

4. In paragraph 36 Hempel says that "what particular sorts of data it is reasonable to collect is not determined by the problem under study, but by a tentative answer to it that the investigator entertains in the form of a conjecture or hypothesis." How does Semmelweis's experiment with the priest's routine illustrate this point? From your other reading, or from your own experience, what other example can you cite that supports his assertion?

5. In paragraph 38 Hempel defines "negatively, or unfavorably, relevant" data. If an experiment yields "negatively relevant data," should the investigators start hunting for their mistake? Or should they rejoice because now they're getting somewhere? Explain.

Thomas S. Kuhn

# The Function of Dogma
# in Scientific Research[1]

$A$t some point in his or her career every member of this    1
Symposium has, I feel sure, been exposed to the image of the scientist
as the uncommitted searcher after truth. He is the explorer of nature—
the man who rejects prejudice at the threshold of his laboratory, who
collects and examines the bare and objective facts, and whose allegiance is to such facts and to them alone. These are the characteristics
which make the testimony of scientists so valuable when advertising
proprietary products in the United States. Even for an international
audience, they should require no further elaboration. To be scientific
is, among other things, to be objective and open-minded.

Probably none of us believes that in practice the real-life scientist    2
quite succeeds in fulfilling this ideal. Personal acquaintance, the novels
of Sir Charles Snow, or a cursory reading of the history of science
provides too much counter-evidence. Though the scientific enterprise
may be open-minded, whatever this application of that phrase may
mean, the individual scientist is very often not. Whether his work is
predominantly theoretical or experimental, he usually seems to know,

[1] The ideas developed in this paper have been abstracted, in a drastically condensed
form, from the first third of my forthcoming monograph, *The Structure of Scientific
Revolutions*, which will be published during 1962 by the University of Chicago Press.
Some of them were also partially developed in an earlier essay, "The Essential
Tension: Tradition and Innovation in Scientific Research," which appeared in Calvin
W. Taylor (ed.), *The Third (1959) University of Utah Research Conference on the Iden-
tification of Creative Scientific Talent* (Salt Lake City, 1959).
    On this whole subject see also I. B. Cohen, "Orthodoxy and Scientific Progress,"
*Proceedings of the American Philosophical Society*, XCVI (1952) 505–12, and Bernard
Barber, "Resistance by Scientists to Scientific Discovery", *Science*, CX-XXIV (1961)
596–602. I am indebted to Mr. Barber for an advance copy of that helpful paper.
Above all, those concerned with the importance of quasi-dogmatic commitments
as a requisite for productive scientific research should see the works of Michael
Polanyi, particularly his *Personal Knowledge* (Chicago, 1958) and *The Logic of Liberty*
(London, 1951).

Thomas S. Kuhn, a professor of philosophy at the Massachusetts Institute of
Technology, holds a Ph.D. in physics. Among his books is *The Structure of
Scientific Revolutions*.

before his research project is even well under way, all but the most intimate details of the result which that project will achieve. If the result is quickly forthcoming, well and good. If not, he will struggle with his apparatus and with his equations until, if at all possible, they yield results which conform to the sort of pattern which he has foreseen from the start. Nor is it only through his own research that the scientist displays his firm convictions about the phenomena which nature can yield and about the ways in which these may be fitted to theory. Often the same convictions show even more clearly in his response to the work produced by others. From Galileo's reception of Kepler's research to Nägeli's reception of Mendel's, from Dalton's rejection of Gay Lussac's results to Kelvin's rejection of Maxwell's, unexpected novelties of fact and theory have characteristically been resisted and have often been rejected by many of the most creative members of the professional scientific community. The historian, at least, scarcely needs Planck to remind him that "A new scientific truth is not usually presented in a way that convinces its opponents . . . ; rather they gradually die off, and a rising generation is familiarized with the truth from the start."[2]

Familiar facts like these—and they could easily be multiplied—do not seem to bespeak an enterprise whose practitioners are notably open-minded. Can they at all be reconciled with our usual image of productive scientific research? If such a reconciliation has not seemed to present fundamental problems in the past, that is probably because resistance and preconception have usually been viewed as extraneous to science. They are, we have often been told, no more than the product of inevitable *human* limitations; a proper scientific method has no place for them; and that method is powerful enough so that no mere human idiosyncrasy can impede its success for very long. On this view, examples of a scientific *parti pris*[3] are reduced to the status of anecdotes, and it is that evaluation of their significance that this essay aims to challenge. Verisimilitude, alone, suggests that such a challenge is required. Preconception and resistance seem the rule rather than the exception in mature scientific development. Furthermore, under normal circumstances they characterize the very best and most creative research as well as the more routine. Nor can there be much question where they come from. Rather than being characteristics of the aberrant individual, they are community characteristics with deep roots in the procedures through which scientists are trained for work in their

[2] *Wissenschaftliche Selbsthiographie* (Leipzig, 1948) 22, my translation.
[3] *Parti pris*, French for preconceived opinion. (Editors' note)

profession. Strongly held convictions that are prior to research often seem to be a precondition for success in the sciences.

Obviously I am already ahead of my story, but in getting there I have perhaps indicated its principal theme. Though preconception and resistance to innovation could very easily choke off scientific progress, their omnipresence is nonetheless symptomatic of characteristics upon which the continuing vitality of research depends. Those characteristics I shall collectively call the dogmatism of mature science, and in the pages to come I shall try to make the following points about them. Scientific education inculcates what the scientific community had previously with difficulty gained—a deep commitment to a particular way of viewing the world and of practicing science in it. That commitment can be, and from time to time is, replaced by another, but it cannot be merely given up. And, while it continues to characterize the community of professional practitioners, it proves in two respects fundamental to productive research. By defining for the individual scientist both the problems available for pursuit and the nature of acceptable solutions to them, the commitment is actually constitutive of research. Normally the scientist is a puzzle-solver like the chess player, and the commitment induced by education is what provides him with the rules of the game being played in his time. In its absence he would not be a physicist, chemist, or whatever he has been trained to be.

In addition, commitment has a second and largely incompatible research role. Its very strength and the unanimity with which the professional group subscribes to it provides the individual scientist with an immensely sensitive detector of the trouble spots from which significant innovations of fact and theory are almost inevitably educed. In the sciences most discoveries of unexpected fact and all fundamental innovations of theory are responses to a prior breakdown in the rules of the previously established game. Therefore, though a quasi-dogmatic commitment is, on the one hand, a source of resistance and controversy, it is also instrumental in making the sciences the most consistently revolutionary of all human activities. One need make neither resistance nor dogma a virtue to recognize that no mature science could exist without them. Before examining further the nature and effects of scientific dogma, consider the pattern of education through which it is transmitted from one generation of practitioners to the next. Scientists are not, of course, the only professional community that acquires from education a set of standards, tools, and techniques which they later deploy in their own creative work. Yet even a cursory inspection of scientific pedagogy suggests that it is far more likely to induce professional rigidity than education in other fields, excepting, perhaps, systematic theology. Admittedly the following epitome is biased toward the American pattern, which I know best. The contrasts at which it aims must, however, be visible, if muted, in European and British education as well.

Perhaps the most striking feature of scientific education is that, to 6 an extent quite unknown in other creative fields, it is conducted through textbooks, works written especially for students. Until he is ready, or very nearly ready, to begin his own dissertation, the student of chemistry, physics, astronomy, geology, or biology is seldom either asked to attempt trial research projects or exposed to the immediate products of research done by others—to, that is, the professional communications that scientists write for their peers. Collections of "source readings" play a negligible role in *scientific* education. Nor is the science student encouraged to read the historical classics of his field—works in which he might encounter other ways of regarding the questions discussed in his text, but in which he would also meet problems, concepts and standards of solution that his future profession had long since discarded and replaced.[4] Whitehead somewhere caught this quite special feature of the sciences when he wrote, "A science that hesitates to forget its founders is lost."

An almost exclusive reliance on textbooks is not all that distin- 7 guishes scientific education. Students in other fields are, after all, also exposed to such books, though seldom beyond the second year of college and even in those early years not exclusively. But in the sciences different textbooks display different subject matters rather than, as in the humanities and many social sciences, exemplifying different approaches to a single problem field. Even books that compete for adoption in a single science course differ mainly in level and pedagogic detail, not in substance or conceptual structure. One can scarcely imagine a physicist's or chemist's saying that he had been forced to begin the education of his third-year class almost from first principles because its previous exposure to the field had been through books that consistently violated his conception of the discipline. Remarks of that sort are not by any means unprecedented in several of the social sciences. Apparently scientists agree about what it is that every student of the

---

[4] The individual sciences display some variation in these respects. Students in the newer and also in the less theoretical sciences—e.g., parts of biology, geology, and medical science—are more likely to encounter both contemporary and historical source materials than those in, say, astronomy, mathematics, or physics.

field must know. That is why, in the design of a pre-professional curriculum, they can use textbooks instead of eclectic samples of research.

Nor is the characteristic technique of textbook presentation alto- 8 gether the same in the sciences as elsewhere. Except in the occasional introductions that students seldom read, science texts make little attempt to describe the *sorts* of problems that the professional may be asked to solve or to discuss the *variety* of techniques that experience has made available for their solution. Instead, these books exhibit, from the very start, concrete problem-solutions that the profession has come to accept as paradigms, and they then ask the student, either with a pencil and paper or in the laboratory, to solve for himself problems closely modelled in method and substance upon those through which the text has led him. Only in elementary language instruction or in training a musical instrumentalist is so large or essential a use made of "finger exercises." And those are just the fields in which the object of instruction is to produce with maximum rapidity strong "mental sets" or *Einstellungen*. In the sciences, I suggest, the effect of these techniques is much the same. Though scientific development is particularly productive of consequential novelties, scientific education remains a relatively dogmatic initiation into a pre-established problem-solving tradition that the student is neither invited nor equipped to evaluate.

The pattern of systematic textbook education just described existed 9 in no place and in no science (except perhaps elementary mathematics) until the early nineteenth century. But before that date a number of the more developed sciences clearly displayed the special characteristics indicated above, and in a few cases had done so for a very long time. Where there were no textbooks there had often been universally received paradigms for the practice of individual sciences. These were scientific achievements reported in books that all the practitioners of a given field knew intimately and admired, achievements upon which they modelled their own research and which provided them with a measure of their own accomplishment. Aristotle's *Physica*, Ptolemy's *Almagest*, Newton's *Principia* and *Opticks*, Franklin's *Electricity*, Lavoisier's *Chemistry*, and Lyell's *Geology*—these works and many others all served for a time implicitly to define the legitimate problems and methods of a research field for succeeding generations of practitioners. In their day each of these books, together with others modelled closely upon them, did for its field much of what textbooks now do for these same fields and for others besides.

All of the works named above are, of course, classics of science.  10
As such their role may be thought to resemble that of the main classics
in other creative fields, for example the works of a Shakespeare, a
Rembrandt, or an Adam Smith. But by calling these works, or the
achievements which lie behind them, paradigms rather than classics,
I mean to suggest that there is something else special about them,
something which sets them apart both from some other classics of
science and from all the classics of other creative fields.

Part of this "something else" is what I shall call the exclusiveness  11
of paradigms. At any time the practitioners of a given specialty may
recognize numerous classics, some of them—like the works of Ptolemy
and Copernicus or Newton and Descartes—quite incompatible one
with the other. But that same group, if it has a paradigm at all, can
have only one. Unlike the community of artists—which can draw simultaneous inspiration from the works of, say, Rembrandt *and* Cézanne and which therefore studies both—the community of astronomers had no alternative to choosing *between* the competing models
of scientific activity supplied by Copernicus and Ptolemy. Furthermore, having made their choice, astronomers could thereafter neglect
the work which they had rejected. Since the sixteenth century there
have been only two full editions of the *Almagest*, both produced in the
nineteenth century and directed exclusively to scholars. In the mature
sciences there is no apparent function for the equivalent of an art museum or a library of classics. Scientists know when books, and even
journals, are out of date. Though they do not then destroy them, they
do, as any historian of science can testify, transfer them from the active
departmental library to desuetude in the general university depository.
Up-to-date works have taken their place, and they are all that the further progress of science requires.

This characteristic of paradigms is closely related to another, and  12
one that has a particular relevance to my selection of the term. In
receiving a paradigm the scientific community commits itself, consciously or not, to the view that the fundamental problems there resolved have, in fact, been solved once and for all. That is what Lagrange
meant when he said of Newton: "There is but one universe, and it can
happen to but one man in the world's history to be the interpreter of
its laws."[5] The example of either Aristotle or Einstein proves Lagrange

[5] Quoted in this form by S. F. Mason, *Main Currents of Scientific Thought* (New York,
1956) 254. The original, which is identical in spirit but not in words, seems to derive
from Delambre's contemporary éloge, *Memoires de . . . l'Institut. . . . année 1812*, 2nd
part (Paris, 1816) p. xlvi.

wrong, but that does not make the fact of his commitment less consequential to scientific development. Believing that what Newton had done need not be done again, Lagrange was not tempted to fundamental reinterpretations of nature. Instead, he could take up where the men who shared his Newtonian paradigm had left off, striving both for neater formulations of that paradigm and for an articulation that would bring it into closer and closer agreement with observations of nature. That sort of work is undertaken only by those who feel that the model they have chosen is entirely secure. There is nothing quite like it in the arts, and the parallels in the social sciences are at best partial. Paradigms determine a developmental pattern for the mature sciences that is unlike the one familiar in other fields.

That difference could be illustrated by comparing the development    13
of a paradigm-based science with that of, say, philosophy or literature. But the same effect can be achieved more economically by contrasting the early developmental pattern of almost any science with the pattern characteristic of the same field in its maturity. I cannot here avoid putting the point too starkly, but what I have in mind is this. Excepting in those fields which, like biochemistry, originated in the combination of existing specialties, paradigms are a relatively late acquisition in the course of scientific development. During its early years a science proceeds without them, or at least without any so unequivocal and so binding as those named illustratively above. Physical optics before Newton or the study of heat before Black and Lavoisier exemplifies the pre-paradigm developmental pattern that I shall immediately examine in the history of electricity. While it continues, until, that is, a first paradigm is reached, the development of a science resembles that of the arts and of most social sciences more closely than it resembles the pattern which astronomy, say, had already acquired in antiquity and which all the natural sciences make familiar today.

To catch the difference between pre- and post-paradigm scientific    14
development, consider a single example. In the early eighteenth century, as in the seventeenth and earlier, there were almost as many views about the nature of electricity as there were important electrical experimenters, men like Hauksbee, Gray, Desaguliers, Du Fay, Nollet, Watson, and Franklin. All their numerous concepts of electricity had something in common—they were partially derived from experiment and observation and partially from one or another version of the mechanico-corpuscular philosophy that guided all scientific research of the day. Yet these common elements gave their work no more than a family resemblance. We are forced to recognize the existence of several

competing schools and sub-schools, each deriving strength from its relation to a particular version (Cartesian or Newtonian) of the corpuscular metaphysics, and each emphasizing the particular cluster of electrical phenomena which its own theory could do most to explain. Other observations were dealt with by *ad hoc* elaborations or remained as outstanding problems for further research.[6]

One early group of electricians followed seventeenth-century practice, and thus took attraction and frictional generation as the fundamental electrical phenomena. They tended to treat repulsion as a secondary effect (in the seventeenth century it had been attributed to some sort of mechanical rebounding) and also to postpone for as long as possible both discussion and systematic research on Gray's newly discovered effect, electrical conduction. Another closely related group regarded repulsion as the fundamental effect, while still another took attraction and repulsion together to be equally elementary manifestations of electricity. Each of these groups modified its theory and research accordingly, but they then had as much difficulty as the first in accounting for any but the simplest conduction effects. Those effects provided the starting point for still a third group, one which tended to speak of electricity as a "fluid" that ran through conductors rather than as an "effluvium" that emanated from non-conductors. This group, in its turn, had difficulty reconciling its theory with a number of attractive and repulsive effects.[7]

At various times all these schools made significant contributions to the body of concepts, phenomena, and techniques from which Franklin drew the first paradigm for electrical science. Any definition of the scientist that excludes the members of these schools will exclude

---

[6] Much documentation for this account of electrical development can be retrieved from Duane Roller and Duane H. D. Roller, *The Development of the Concept of Electric Charge: Electricity from the Greeks to Coulomb* (Harvard Case Histories in Experimental Science, VIII, Cambridge, Mass., 1954) and from I. B. Cohen, *Franklin and Newton: An Inquiry into Speculative Newtonian Experimental Science and Franklin's Work in Electricity as an Example Thereof* (Philadelphia, 1956). For analytic detail I am, however, very much indebted to a still unpublished paper by my student, John L. Heilbron, who has also assisted in the preparation of the three notes that follow.

[7] This division into schools is still somewhat too simplistic. After 1720 the basic division is between the French school (Du Fay, Nollet, etc.) who base their theories on attraction-repulsion effects and the English school (Desaguliers, Watson, etc.) who concentrate on conduction effects. Each group had immense difficulty in explaining the phenomena that the other took to be basic. (See, for example, Needham's report of Lemonier's investigations, in *Philosophical Transactions*, XLIV, 1746, p. 247). Within each of these groups, and particularly the English, one can trace further subdivision depending upon whether attraction or repulsion is considered the more fundamental electrical effect.

their modern successors as well. Yet anyone surveying the development of electricity before Franklin may well conclude that, though the field's practitioners were scientists, the immediate result of their activity was something less than science. Because the body of belief he could take for granted was very small, each electrical experimenter felt forced to begin by building his field anew from its foundations. In doing so his choice of supporting observation and experiment was relatively free, for the set of standard methods and phenomena that every electrician must employ and explain was extraordinarily small. As a result, throughout the first half of the century, electrical investigations tended to circle back over the same ground again and again. New effects were repeatedly discovered, but many of them were rapidly lost again. Among those lost were many effects due to what we should now describe as inductive charging and also Du Fay's famous discovery of the two sorts of electrification. Franklin and Kinnersley were surprised when, some fifteen years later, the latter discovered that a charged ball which was repelled by rubbed glass would be attracted by rubbed sealing-wax or amber.[8] In the absence of a well-articulated and widely received theory (a desideratum which no science possesses from its very beginning and which few if any of the social sciences have achieved today), the situation could hardly have been otherwise. During the first half of the eighteenth century there was no way for electricians to distinguish consistently between electrical and non-electrical effects, between laboratory accidents and essential novelties, or between striking demonstration and experiments which revealed the essential nature of electricity.

This is the state of affairs which Franklin changed.[9] His theory     17

---

[8] Du Fay's discovery that there are two sorts of electricity and that these are mutually attractive but self-repulsive is reported and documented in great experimental detail in the fourth of his famous memoirs on electricity: "De l'Attraction & Répulsion des Corps Electriques," *Memoires de . . . l'Académie . . . de l'année* 1733 (Paris, 1735) 457–76. These memoirs were well known and widely cited, but Desaguliers seems to be the only electrician who, for almost two decades, even mentions that some charged bodies will attract each other (*Philosophical Transactions . . .* , XLII, 1741–2, pp. 140–3). For Franklin's and Kinnersley's "surprise" see I. B. Cohen (ed.), *Benjamin Franklin's Experiments: A New Edition of Franklin's Experiments and Observations on Electricity* (Cambridge, Mass., 1941) 250–5. Note also that, though Kinnersley had *produced* the effect, neither he nor Franklin seems ever to have *recognized* that two resinously charged bodies would repel each other, a phenomenon directly contrary to Franklin's theory.

[9] The change is not, of course, due to Franklin alone nor did it occur overnight. Other electricians, most notably William Watson, anticipated parts of Franklin's theory. More important, it was only after essential modifications, due principally to Aepinus, that Franklin's theory gained the general currency requisite for a par-

explained so many—though not all—of the electrical effects recognized by the various earlier schools that within a generation all electricians had been converted to some view very like it. Though it did not resolve quite all disagreements, Franklin's theory was electricity's first paradigm, and its existence gives a new tone and flavor to the electrical researches of the last decades of the eighteenth century. The end of inter-school debate ended the constant reiteration of fundamentals; confidence that they were on the right track encouraged electricians to undertake more precise, esoteric, and consuming sorts of work. Freed from concern with any and all electrical phenomena, the newly united group could pursue selected phenomena in far more detail, designing much special equipment for the task and employing it more stubbornly and systematically than electricians had ever done before. In the hands of a Cavendish, a Coulomb, or a Volta the collection of electrical facts and the articulation of electrical theory were, for the first time, highly directed activities. As a result the efficiency and effectiveness of electrical research increased immensely, providing evidence for a societal version of Francis Bacon's acute methodological dictum: "Truth emerges more readily from error than from confusion."

Obviously I exaggerate both the speed and the completeness with 18 which the transition to a paradigm occurs. But that does not make the phenomenon itself less real. The maturation of electricity as a science is not coextensive with the entire development of the field. Writers on electricity during the first four decades of the eighteenth century possessed far more information about electrical phenomena than had their sixteenth- and seventeenth-century predecessors. During the half-century after 1745 very few new sorts of electrical phenomena were added to their lists. Nevertheless, in important respects the electrical writings of the last two decades of the century seemed further removed from those of Gray, Du Fay, and even Franklin than are the writings of these early eighteenth-century electricians from those of their predecessors a hundred years before. Some time between 1740 and 1780 electricians, as a group, gained what astronomers had achieved in Antiquity, students of motion in the Middle Ages, of physical optics in the late seventeenth century, and of historical geology in the early nineteenth.

---

adigm. And even then there continued to be two formulations of the theory: the Franklin-Aepinus one-fluid form and a two-fluid form due principally to Symmer. Electricians soon reached the conclusion that no electrical test could possibly discriminate between the two theories. Until the discovery of the battery, when the choice between a one-fluid and two-fluid theory began to make an occasional difference in the design and analysis of experiments, the two were equivalent.

They had, that is, achieved a paradigm, possession of which enabled them to take the foundation of their field for granted and to push on to more concrete and recondite problems.[10] Except with the advantage of hindsight, it is hard to find another criterion that so clearly proclaims a field of science.

These remarks should begin to clarify what I take a paradigm to be. It is, in the first place, a fundamental scientific achievement and one which includes both a theory and some exemplary applications to the results of experiment and observation. More important, it is an open-ended achievement, one which leaves all sorts of research still to be done. And, finally, it is an accepted achievement in the sense that it is received by a group whose members no longer try to rival it or to create alternates for it. Instead, they attempt to extend and exploit it in a variety of ways to which I shall shortly turn. That discussion of the work that paradigms leave to be done will make both their role and the reasons for their special efficacy clearer still. But first there is one rather different point to be made about them. Though the reception of a paradigm seems historically prerequisite to the most effective sorts of scientific research, the paradigms which enhance research effectiveness need not be and usually are not permanent. On the contrary, the developmental pattern of mature science is usually from paradigm to paradigm. It differs from the pattern characteristic of the early or pre-paradigm period not by the total elimination of debate over fundamentals, but by the drastic restriction of such debate to occasional periods of paradigm change.

Ptolemy's *Almagest* was not, for example, any less a paradigm because the research tradition that descended from it had ultimately to be replaced by an incompatible one derived from the work of Copernicus and Kepler. Nor was Newton's *Opticks* less a paradigm for eighteenth-century students of light because it was later replaced by the ether-wave theory of Young and Fresnel, a paradigm which in its turn gave way to the electromagnetic displacement theory that descends from Maxwell. Undoubtedly the research work that any given paradigm permits results in lasting contributions to the body of scientific knowledge and technique, but paradigms themselves are very often swept aside and replaced by others that are quite incompatible

---

[10] Note that this first electrical paradigm was fully effective only until 1800, when the discovery of the battery and the multiplication of electrochemical effects initiated a revolution in electrical theory. Until a new paradigm emerged from that revolution, the literature of electricity, particularly in England, reverted in many respects to the tone characteristic of the first half of the eighteenth century.

with them. We can have no recourse to notions like the "truth" or "validity" of paradigms in our attempt to understand the special efficacy of the research which their reception permits.

On the contrary, the historian can often recognize that in declaring 21 an older paradigm out of date or in rejecting the approach of some one of the pre-paradigm schools a scientific community has rejected the embryo of an important scientific perception to which it would later be forced to return. But it is very far from clear that the profession delayed scientific development by doing so. Would quantum mechanics have been born sooner if nineteenth-century scientists had been more willing to admit that Newton's corpuscular view of light might still have something significant to teach them about nature? I think not, although in the arts, the humanities, and many social sciences that less doctrinaire view is very often adopted toward classic achievements of the past. Or would astronomy and dynamics have advanced more rapidly if scientists had recognized that Ptolemy and Copernicus had chosen equally legitimate means to describe the earth's position? That view was, in fact, suggested during the seventeenth century, and it has since been confirmed by relativity theory. But in the interim it was firmly rejected together with Ptolemaic astronomy, emerging again only in the very late nineteenth century when, for the first time, it had concrete relevance to unsolved problems generated by the continuing practice of non-relativistic physics. One could argue, as indeed by implication I shall, that close eighteenth- and nineteenth-century attention either to the work of Ptolemy or to the relativistic views of Descartes, Huygens, and Leibniz would have delayed rather than accelerated the revolution in physics with which the twentieth century began. Advance from paradigm to paradigm rather than through the continuing competition between recognized classics may be a functional as well as a factual characteristic of mature scientific development.

Much that has been said so far is intended to indicate that—except 22 during occasional extraordinary periods to be discussed in the last section of this paper—the practitioners of a mature scientific specialty are deeply committed to some one paradigm-based way of regarding and investigating nature. Their paradigm tells them about the sorts of entities with which the universe is populated and about the way the members of that population behave; in addition, it informs them of the questions that may legitimately be asked about nature and of the techniques that can properly be used in the search for answers to them.

In fact, a paradigm tells scientists so much that the questions it leaves for research seldom have great intrinsic interest to those outside the profession. Though educated men as a group may be fascinated to hear about the spectrum of fundamental particles or about the processes of molecular replication, their interest is usually quickly exhausted by an account of the beliefs that already underlie research on these problems. The outcome of the individual research project is indifferent to them, and their interest is unlikely to awaken again until, as with parity nonconservation, research unexpectedly leads to paradigm-change and to a consequent alteration in the beliefs which guide research. That, no doubt, is why both historians and popularizers have devoted so much of their attention to the revolutionary episodes which result in change of paradigm and have so largely neglected the sort of work that even the greatest scientists necessarily do most of the time.

My point will become clearer if I now ask what it is that the existence of a paradigm leaves for the scientific community to do. The answer—as obvious as the related existence of resistance to innovation and as often brushed under the carpet—is that scientists, given a paradigm, strive with all their might and skill to bring it into closer and closer agreement with nature. Much of their effort, particularly in the early stages of a paradigm's development, is directed to articulating the paradigm, rendering it more precise in areas where the original formulation has inevitably been vague. For example, knowing that electricity was a fluid whose individual particles act upon one another at a distance, electricians after Franklin could attempt to determine the quantitative law of force between particles of electricity. Others could seek the mutual interdependence of spark length, electroscope deflection, quantity of electricity, and conductor-configuration. These were the sorts of problems upon which Coulomb, Cavendish, and Volta worked in the last decades of the eighteenth century, and they have many parallels in the development of every other mature science. Contemporary attempts to determine the quantum mechanical forces governing the interactions of nucleons fall precisely in this same category, paradigm-articulation. 23

That sort of problem is not the only challenge which a paradigm sets for the community that embraces it. There are always many areas in which a paradigm is assumed to work but to which it has not, in fact, yet been applied. Matching the paradigm to nature in these areas often engages much of the best scientific talent in any generation. The eighteenth-century attempts to develop a Newtonian theory of vibrating strings provide one significant example, and the current work 24 on a quantum mechanical theory of solids provides another. In addition, there is always much fascinating work to be done in improving the match between a paradigm and nature in an area where at least limited agreement has already been demonstrated. Theoretical work on problems like these is illustrated by eighteenth-century research on the perturbations that cause planets to deviate from their Keplerian orbits as well as by the elaborate twentieth-century theory of the spectra of complex atoms and molecules. And accompanying all these problems and still others besides is a recurring series of instrumental hurdles. Special apparatus had to be invented and built to permit Coulomb's determination of the electrical force law. New sorts of telescopes were required for the observations that, when completed, demanded an improved Newtonian perturbation theory. The design and construction of more flexible and more powerful accelerators is a continuing desideratum in the attempt to articulate more powerful theories of nuclear forces. These are the sorts of work on which almost all scientists spend almost all of their time.[11]

Probably this epitome of normal scientific research requires no    25
elaboration in this place, but there are two points that must now be made about it. First, all of the problems mentioned above were paradigm-dependent, often in several ways. Some—for example, the derivation of perturbation terms in Newtonian planetary theory—could not even have been stated in the absence of an appropriate paradigm. With the transition from Newtonian to relativity theory a few of them became different problems and not all of these have yet been solved. Other problems—for example, the attempt to determine a law of electric forces—could be and were at least vaguely stated before the emergence of the paradigm with which they were ultimately solved. But in that older form they proved intractable. The men who described electrical attractions and repulsions in terms of effluvia attempted to measure the resulting forces by placing a charged disc at a measured distance beneath one pan of a balance. Under those circumstances no consistent or interpretable results were obtained. The prerequisite for success proved to be a paradigm that reduced electrical action to a gravity-like action between point particles at a distance. After Franklin electricians thought of electrical action in those terms; both Coulomb and Cavendish designed their apparatus accordingly. Finally, in both

---

[11] The discussion in this paragraph and the next is considerably elaborated in my paper, "The Function of Measurement in Modern Physical Science," *Isis*, LII (1961) 161–93.

these cases and in all the others as well a commitment to the paradigm was needed simply to provide adequate motivation. Who would design and build elaborate special-purpose apparatus, or who would spend months trying to solve a particular differential equation, without a quite firm guarantee that his effort, if successful, would yield the anticipated fruit?

This reference to the anticipated outcome of a research project 26 points to the second striking characteristic of what I am now calling normal, or paradigm-based, research. The scientist engaged in it does not at all fit the prevalent image of the scientist as explorer or as inventor of brand new theories which permit striking and unexpected predictions. On the contrary, in all the problems discussed above everything but the detail of the outcome was known in advance. No scientist who accepted Franklin's paradigm could doubt that there was a law of attraction between small particles of electricity, and they could reasonably suppose that it would take a simple algebraic form. Some of them had even guessed that it would prove to be an inverse square law. Nor did Newtonian astronomers and physicists doubt that Newton's laws of motion and of gravitation could ultimately be made to yield the observed motions of the moon and planets even though, for over a century, the complexity of the requisite mathematics prevented good agreements being uniformly obtained. In all these problems, as in most others that scientists undertake, the challenge is not to uncover the unknown but to obtain the known. Their fascination lies not in what success may be expected to disclose but in the difficulty of obtaining success at all. Rather than resembling exploration, normal research seems like the effort to assemble a Chinese cube whose finished outline is known from the start.

Those are the characteristics of normal research that I had in mind 27 when, at the start of this essay, I described the man engaged in it as a puzzle-solver, like the chess player. The paradigm he has acquired through prior training provides him with the rules of the game, describes the pieces with which it must be played, and indicates the nature of the required outcome. His task is to manipulate those pieces within the rules in such a way that the required outcome is produced. If he fails, as most scientists do in at least their first attacks upon any given problem, that failure speaks only to his lack of skill. It cannot call into question the rules that his paradigm has supplied, for without those rules there would have been no puzzle with which to wrestle in the first place. No wonder, then, that the problems (or puzzles) which the practitioner of a mature science normally undertakes presuppose a deep commitment to a paradigm. And how fortunate it is that that commitment is not lightly given up. Experience shows that, in almost all cases, the reiterated efforts, either of the individual or of the professional group, do at last succeed in producing within the paradigm a solution to even the most stubborn problems. That is one of the ways in which science advances. Under those circumstances can we be surprised that scientists resist paradigm-change? What they are defending is, after all, neither more nor less than the basis of their professional way of life.

By now one principal advantage of what I began by calling scientific dogmatism should be apparent. As a glance at any Baconian natural history or a survey of the pre-paradigm development of any science will show, nature is vastly too complex to be explored even approximately at random. Something must tell the scientist where to look and what to look for, and that something, though it may not last beyond his generation, is the paradigm with which his education as a scientist has supplied him. Given that paradigm and the requisite confidence in it, the scientist largely ceases to be an explorer at all, or at least to be an explorer of the unknown. Instead, he struggles to articulate and concretize the known, designing much special-purpose apparatus and many special-purpose adaptations of theory for that task. From those puzzles of design and adaptation he gets his pleasure. Unless he is extraordinarily lucky, it is upon his success with them that his reputation will depend. Inevitably the enterprise which engages him is characterized, at any one time, by drastically restricted vision. But within the region upon which vision is focused the continuing attempt to match paradigms to nature results in a knowledge and understanding of esoteric detail that could not have been achieved in any other way. From Copernicus and the problem of precession to Einstein and the photo-electric effect, the progress of science has again and again depended upon just such esoterica. One great virtue of commitment to paradigms is that it frees scientists to engage themselves with tiny puzzles.

Nevertheless, this image of scientific research as puzzle-solving or paradigm-matching must be, at the very least, thoroughly incomplete. Though the scientist may not be an explorer, scientists do again and again discover new and unexpected sorts of phenomena. Or again, though the scientist does not normally strive to invent new sorts of basic theories, such theories have repeatedly emerged from the continuing practice of research. But neither of these types of innovation would arise if the enterprise I have been calling normal science were always successful. In fact, the man engaged in puzzle-solving very often resists substantive novelty, and he does so for good reason. To him it is a change in the rules of the game and any change of rules is intrinsically subversive. That subversive element is, of course, most apparent in major theoretical innovations like those associated with the names of Copernicus, Lavoisier, or Einstein. But the discovery of an unanticipated phenomenon can have the same destructive effects, although usually on a smaller group and for a far shorter time. Once he had performed his first follow-up experiments, Roentgen's glowing screen demonstrated that previously standard cathode ray equipment was behaving in ways for which no one had made allowance. There was an unanticipated variable to be controlled; earlier researches, already on their way to becoming paradigms, would require re-evaluation; old puzzles would have to be solved again under a somewhat different set of rules. Even so readily assimilable a discovery as that of X rays can violate a paradigm that has previously guided research. It follows that, if the normal puzzle-solving activity were altogether successful, the development of science could lead to no fundamental innovations at all.

But of course normal science is not always successful, and in recognizing that fact we encounter what I take to be the second great advantage of paradigm-based research. Unlike many of the early electricians, the practitioner of a mature science knows with considerable precision what sort of result he should gain from his research. As a consequence he is in a particularly favorable position to recognize when a research problem has gone astray. Perhaps, like Galvani or Roentgen, he encounters an effect that he knows ought not to occur. Or perhaps, like Copernicus, Planck, or Einstein, he concludes that the reiterated failures of his predecessors in matching a paradigm to nature is presumptive evidence of the need to change the rules under which a match is to be sought. Or perhaps, like Franklin or Lavoisier, he decides after repeated attempts that no existing theory can be articulated to account for some newly discovered effect. In all of these ways and in others besides the practice of normal puzzle-solving science can and inevitably does lead to the isolation and recognition of anomaly. That recognition proves, I think, prerequisite for almost all discoveries of new sorts of phenomena and for all fundamental innovations in scientific theory. After a first paradigm has been achieved, a breakdown in the rules of the pre-established game is the usual prelude to significant scientific innovation.

Examine the case of discoveries first. Many of them, like Cou- 31
lomb's law or a new element to fill an empty spot in the periodic table,
present no problem. They were not "new sorts of phenomena" but
discoveries anticipated through a paradigm and achieved by expert
puzzle-solvers: That sort of discovery is a natural product of what I
have been calling normal science. But not all discoveries are of that
sort: Many could not have been anticipated by any extrapolation from
the known; in a sense they had to be made "by accident." On the other
hand the accident through which they emerged could not ordinarily
have occurred to a man just looking around. In the mature sciences
discovery demands much special equipment, both conceptual and instrumental, and that special equipment has invariably been developed
and deployed for the pursuit of the puzzles of normal research. Discovery results when that equipment fails to function as it should. Furthermore, since some sort of at least temporary failure occurs during
almost every research project, discovery results only when the failure
is particularly stubborn or striking and only when it seems to raise
questions about accepted beliefs and procedures. Established paradigms are thus often doubly prerequisite to discoveries. Without them
the project that goes astray would not have been undertaken. And
even when the project has gone astray, as most do for a while, the
paradigm can help to determine whether the failure is worth pursuing.
The usual and proper response to a failure in puzzle-solving is to blame
one's talents or one's tools and to turn next to another problem. If he
is not to waste time, the scientist must be able to discriminate essential
anomaly from mere failure.

That pattern—discovery through an anomaly that calls established 32
techniques and beliefs in doubt—has been repeated again and again
in the course of scientific development. Newton discovered the composition of white light when he was unable to reconcile measured
dispersion with that predicted by Snell's recently discovered law of
refraction.[12] The electric battery was discovered when existing detectors of static charges failed to behave as Franklin's paradigm said they
should.[13] The planet Neptune was discovered through an effort to
account for recognized anomalies in the orbit of Uranus.[14] The element

---

[12] See my "Newton's Optical Papers" in I. B. Cohen (ed.), *Isaac Newton's Papers &
Letters on Natural Philosophy* (Cambridge, Mass., 1958) 27–45.
[13] Luigi Galvani, *Commentary on the Effects of Electricity on Muscular Motion*, trans.
by M. G. Foley with notes and an introduction by I. B. Cohen (Norwalk, Conn.,
1954) 27–9.
[14] Angus Armitage, *A Century of Astronomy* (London, 1950) 111–15.

chlorine and the compound carbon monoxide emerged during attempts to reconcile Lavoisier's new chemistry with laboratory observations.[15] The so-called noble gases were the products of a long series of investigations initiated by a small but persistent anomaly in the measured density of atmospheric nitrogen.[16] The electron was posited to explain some anomalous properties of electrical conduction through gases, and its spin was suggested to account for other sorts of anomalies observed in atomic spectra.[17] Both the neutron and the neutrino provide other examples, and the list could be extended almost indefinitely.[18] In the mature sciences unexpected novelties are discovered principally after something has gone wrong.

If, however, anomaly is significant in preparing the way for new 33 discoveries, it plays a still larger role in the invention of new theories. Contrary to a prevalent, though by no means universal, belief, new theories are not invented to account for observations that have not previously been ordered by theory at all. Rather, at almost all times in the development of any advanced science, all the facts whose relevance is admitted seem either to fit existing theory well or to be in the process of conforming. Making them conform better provides many of the standard problems of normal science. And almost always committed scientists succeed in solving them. But they do not always succeed, and, when they fail repeatedly and in increasing numbers, then their sector of the scientific community encounters what I am elsewhere calling "crisis." Recognizing that something is fundamentally wrong with the theory upon which their work is based, scientists will attempt more fundamental articulations of theory than those which were admissible before. (Characteristically, at times of crisis, one encounters numerous different versions of the paradigm theory.[19]) Si-

---

[15] For chlorine see Ernst von Meyer, *A History of Chemistry from the Earliest Times to the Present Day*, trans. G. M'Gowan (London, 1891) 224–7. For carbon monoxide see Hermann Kopp, *Geschichte der Chemie* (Braunschweig, 1845) III, 294–6.

[16] William Ramsay, *The Gases of the Atmosphere: The History of their Discovery* (London, 1896) Chs. 4 and 5.

[17] J. J. Thomson, *Recollections and Reflections* (New York, 1937) 325–71; T. W. Chalmers, *Historic Researches: Chapters in the History of Physical and Chemical Discovery* (London, 1949) 187–217; and F. K. Richtmyer, E. H. Kennard and T. Lauritsen, *Introduction to Modern Physics* (5th ed., New York, 1955) 212.

[18] Ibid, pp. 466–470; and Rogers D. Rusk, *Introduction to Atomic and Nuclear Physics* (New York, 1958) 328–30.

[19] One classic example, for which see the reference cited below in the next note, is the proliferation of geocentric astronomical systems in the years before Copernicus's heliocentric reform. Another, for which see J. R. Partington and D. McKie, "Historical Studies of the Phlogiston Theory," *Annals of Science*, II (1937) 361–404, III (1938) 1–58, 337–71, and IV (1939) 113–49, is the multiplicity of "phlogiston theories"

multaneously they will often begin more nearly random experimentation within the area of difficulty, hoping to discover some effect that will suggest a way to set the situation right. Only under circumstances like these, I suggest, is a fundamental innovation in scientific theory both invented and accepted.

The state of Ptolemaic astronomy was, for example, a recognized scandal before Copernicus proposed a basic change in astronomical theory, and the preface in which Copernicus described his reasons for innovation provides a classic description of the crisis state.[20] Galileo's contributions to the study of motion took their point of departure from recognized difficulties with medieval theory, and Newton reconciled Galileo's mechanics with Copernicanism.[21] Lavoisier's new chemistry was a product of the anomalies created jointly by the proliferation of new gases and the first systematic studies of weight relations.[22] The wave theory of light was developed amid growing concern about anomalies in the relation of diffraction and polarization effects to Newton's corpuscular theory.[23] Thermodynamics, which later came to seem a superstructure for existing sciences, was established only at the price of rejecting the previously paradigmatic caloric theory.[24] Quantum mechanics was born from a variety of difficulties surrounding black-body

34

---

produced in response to the general recognition that weight is always gained on combustion and to the experimental discovery of many new gases after 1760. The same proliferation of versions of accepted theories occurred in mechanics and electromagnetism in the two decades preceding Einstein's special relativity theory. (E. T. Whittaker, *History of the Theories of Aether and Electricity*, 2nd ed., 2 vols., London 1951–53, I, Ch. 12, and II, Ch. 2. I concur in the widespread judgment that this is a very biased account of the genesis of relativity theory, but it contains just the detail necessary to make the point here at issue.)

[20] T. S. Kuhn, *The Copernican Revolution: Planetary Astronomy in the Development of Western Thought* (Cambridge, Mass., 1957) 133–40.

[21] For Galileo see Alexandre Koyré, *Études Galiléennes* (3 vols., Paris, 1939); for Newton see Kuhn, op. cit. pp. 228–60 and 289–91.

[22] For the proliferation of gases see Partington, *A Short History of Chemistry* (2nd ed., London, 1948) Ch. 6; for the role of weight relations see Henry Guerlac, "The Origin of Lavoisier's Work on Combustion," *Archives internationales d'histoire des sciences,* XII (1959) 113–35.

[23] Whittaker, *Aether and Electricity*, II, 94–109; William Whewell, *History of the Inductive Sciences* (revised ed., 3 vols., London, 1847) II, 213–71; and Kuhn, "Function of Measurement," p. 181 n.

[24] For a general account of the beginnings of thermodynamics (including much relevant bibliography) see my "Energy Conservation as an Example of Simultaneous Discovery" in Marshall Clagett (ed.), *Critical Problems in the History of Science* (Madison, Wisc., 1959) 321–56. For the special problems presented to caloric theorists by energy conservation see the Carnot papers, there cited in n. 2, and also S. P. Thompson, *The Life of William Thomson, Baron Kelvin of Largs* (2 vols., London, 1910) Ch. 6.

radiation, specific heat, and the photo-electric effect.[25] Again the list could be extended, but the point should already be clear. New theories arise from work conducted under old ones, and they do so only when something is observed to have gone wrong. Their prelude is widely recognized anomaly, and that recognition can come only to a group that knows very well what it would mean to have things go right.

Because limitations of space and time force me to stop at this point, 35 my case for dogmatism must remain schematic. I shall not here even attempt to deal with the fine structure that scientific development exhibits at all times. But there is another more positive qualification of my thesis, and it requires one closing comment. Though successful research demands a deep commitment to the status quo, innovation remains at the heart of the enterprise. Scientists are *trained* to operate as puzzle-solvers from established rules, but they are also *taught* to regard themselves as explorers and inventors who know no rules except those dictated by nature itself. The result is an acquired tension, partly within the individual and partly within the community, between professional skills on the one hand and professional ideology on the other. Almost certainly that tension and the ability to sustain it are important to science's success. Insofar as I have dealt exclusively with the dependence of research upon tradition, my discussion is inevitably one-sided. On this whole subject there is a great deal more to be said.

But to be one-sided is not necessarily to be wrong, and it may be 36 an essential preliminary to a more penetrating examination of the requisites for successful scientific life. Almost no one, perhaps no one at all, needs to be told that the vitality of science depends on the continuation of occasional tradition-shattering innovations. But the apparently contrary dependence of research upon a deep commitment to established tools and beliefs receives the very minimum of attention. I urge that it be given more. Until that is done, some of the most striking characteristics of scientific education and development will remain extraordinarily difficult to understand.

# Questions

1. In paragraph 1, Kuhn evokes "the image of the scientist as the uncommitted searcher after truth." Is this image of the scientist the one you chiefly hold in mind? In any case, where does this image

---

[25] Richtmeyer et al., *Modern Physics*, pp. 89–94, 124–32, and 409–14; Gerald Holton, *Introduction to Concepts and Theories in Physical Science* (Cambridge, Mass., 1953) 528–45.

appear? In film and television? In the classrooms of high school courses in science? In advertisements in magazines? Or where? What specific evidence can you offer?

2.  At the end of paragraph 6 Kuhn quotes the philosopher Alfred North Whitehead: "A science that hesitates to forget its founders is lost." Try restating this sentence in your own words. Explain what point of Kuhn's the quotation from Whitehead appears to support.

3.  How, according to Kuhn, do textbooks in the sciences differ from textbooks in the humanities and social sciences? Does your experience with textbooks bear out Kuhn's observations?

4.  Explain in your own words Kuhn's distinction (paragraphs 10–12) between "classics" (e.g., plays by Shakespeare, paintings by Rembrandt) and "paradigms" (e.g., Aristotle's *Physica,* Newton's *Opticks*).

5.  Explain in your own words what Kuhn means when he says (paragraph 20) that "we can have no recourse to notions like the 'truth' or 'validity' of paradigms in our attempt to understand the special efficacy of the research which their reception permits."

6.  What are the chief characteristics of a paradigm? How does a "paradigm" differ from a "theory"? If you have read Hawking's essay (page 809), compare Hawking's definition of the word "model" with Kuhn's "paradigm."

7.  What are some of the chief characteristics of Kuhn's style? (A good way to approach this topic is to take a paragraph that strikes you as typical, and then to look closely at it and to call attention to particular features, such as the kind of vocabulary, the length of sentences, the presence or absence of concrete details, of metaphors, etc.)

## Werner Heisenberg

# Science and Religion

One evening during the Solvay Conference, some of the 1
younger members stayed behind in the lounge of our hotel. This group
included Wolfgang Pauli and myself, and was soon afterward joined
by Paul Dirac. One of us said: "Einstein keeps talking about God: what
are we to make of that? It is extremely difficult to imagine that a scientist
like Einstein should have such strong ties with a religious tradition."

"Not so much Einstein as Max Planck," someone objected. "From 2
some of Planck's utterances it would seem that he sees no contradiction
between religion and science, indeed that he believes the two are perfectly compatible."

I was asked what I knew of Planck's views on the subject, and 3
what I thought myself. I had spoken to Planck on only a few occasions,
mostly about physics and not about general questions, but I was acquainted with some of Planck's close friends, who had told me a great
deal about his attitude.

"I assume," I must have replied, "that Planck considers religion 4
and science compatible because, in his view, they refer to quite distinct
facets of reality. Science deals with the objective, material world. It

---

Werner Heisenberg 1901–1976), a German physicist and one of the founders of
the quantum theory, is most widely known for the uncertainty principle. *The New
Columbia Encyclopedia* provides a good brief description: The uncertainty principle "states that it is impossible to determine with arbitrarily high accuracy both
the position and momentum (essentially velocity) of a subatomic particle like the
electron. The effect of this principle is to convert the laws of physics into statements about relative probabilities instead of absolute certainties." In 1932 Heisenberg was awarded the Nobel Prize in physics. Although most of his writings
are designed for specialists, two of his books are for the general public: *Physics
and Philosophy* and *Physics and Beyond* (our selection comes from the second
of these titles).

In the Preface to *Physics and Beyond* Heisenberg writes: "Science rests on
experiments; its results are attained through talks among those who work in it
and who consult one another about their interpretation of these experiments. . . .
The author hopes to demonstrate that science is rooted in conversation." The
persons who figure in this dialogue (Wolfgang Pauli and Paul Dirac) and the
persons they mention (Albert Einstein, Max Planck, and Niels Bohr) were all
distinguished physicists. For concise introductions to these people, check an
encyclopedia.

invites us to make accurate statements about objective reality and to grasp its interconnections. Religion, on the other hand, deals with the world of values. It considers what ought to be or what we ought to do, not what is. In science we are concerned to discover what is true or false; in religion with what is good or evil, noble or base. Science is the basis of technology, religion the basis of ethics. In short, the conflict between the two, which has been raging since the eighteenth century, seems founded on a misunderstanding, or, more precisely, on a confusion of the images and parables of religion with scientific statements. Needless to say, the result makes no sense at all. This view, which I know so well from my parents, associates the two realms with the objective and subjective aspects of the world respectively. Science is, so to speak, the manner in which we confront, in which we argue about, the objective side of reality. Religious faith, on the other hand, is the expression of the subjective decisions that help us choose the standards by which we propose to act and live. Admittedly, we generally make these decisions in accordance with the attitudes of the group to which we belong, be it our family, nation or culture. Our decisions are strongly influenced by educational and environmental factors, but in the final analysis they are subjective and hence not governed by the 'true or false' criterion. Max Planck, if I understand him rightly, has used this freedom and come down squarely on the side of the Christian tradition. His thoughts and actions, particularly as they affect his personal relationships, fit perfectly into the framework of this tradition, and no one will respect him the less for it. As far as he is concerned, therefore, the two realms—the objective and the subjective facets of the world—are quite separate, but I must confess that I myself do not feel altogether happy about this separation. I doubt whether human societies can live with so sharp a distinction between knowledge and faith."

Wolfgang shared my concern. "It's all bound to end in tears," he said. "At the dawn of religion, all the knowledge of a particular community fitted into a spiritual framework, based largely on religious values and ideas. The spiritual framework itself had to be within the grasp of the simplest member of the community, even if its parables and images conveyed no more than the vaguest hint as to their underlying values and ideas. But if he himself is to live by these values, the average man has to be convinced that the spiritual framework embraces the entire wisdom of his society. For 'believing' does not to him mean 'taking for granted,' but rather 'trusting in the guidance' of accepted values. That is why society is in such danger whenever fresh knowledge threatens to explode the old spiritual forms. The complete separation of knowledge and faith can at best be an emergency measure, afford some temporary relief. In Western culture, for instance, we may well reach the point in the not too distant future where the parables and images of the old religions will have lost their persuasive force even for the average person; when that happens, I am afraid that all the old ethics will collapse like a house of cards and that unimaginable horrors will be perpetrated. In brief, I cannot really endorse Planck's philosophy, even if it is logically valid and even though I respect the human attitudes to which it gives rise.

"Einstein's conception is closer to mine. His God is somehow in-  6 volved in the immutable laws of nature. Einstein has a feeling for the central order of things. He can detect it in the simplicity of natural laws. We may take it that he felt this simplicity very strongly and directly during his discovery of the theory of relativity. Admittedly, this is a far cry from the contents of religion. I don't believe Einstein is tied to any religious tradition, and I rather think the idea of a personal God is entirely foreign to him. But as far as he is concerned there is no split between science and religion: the central order is part of the subjective as well as the objective realm, and this strikes me as being a far better starting point."

"A starting point for what?" I asked. "If you consider man's at-  7 titude to the central order a purely personal matter, then you may agree with Einstein's view, but then you must also concede that nothing at all follows from this view."

"Perhaps it does," Wolfgang replied. "The development of science  8 during the past two centuries has certainly changed man's thinking, even outside the Christian West. Hence it matters quite a bit what physicists think. And it was precisely the idea of an objective world running its course in time and space according to strict causal laws that produced a sharp clash between science and the spiritual formulations of the various religions. If science goes beyond this strict view—and it has done just that with relativity theory and is likely to go even further with quantum theory—then the relationship between science and the contents religions try to express must change once again. Perhaps science, by revealing the existence of new relationships during the past thirty years, may have lent our thought much greater depth. The concept of complementarity, for instance, which Niels Bohr considers so crucial in the interpretation of quantum theory, was by no means unknown to philosophers, even if they did not express it so succinctly. However, its very appearance in the exact sciences has constituted a decisive change: the idea of material objects that are completely independent of the manner in which we observe them proved to be nothing but an abstract extrapolation, something that has no counterpart in nature. In Asiatic philosophy and Eastern religions we find the complementary idea of a pure subject of knowledge, one that confronts no object. This idea, too, will prove an abstract extrapolation, corresponding to no spiritual or mental reality. If we think about the wider context, we may in the future be forced to keep a middle course between these extremes, perhaps the one charted by Bohr's complementarity concept. Any science that adapts itself to this form of thinking will not only be more tolerant of the different forms of religion, but, having a wider over-all view, may also contribute to the world of values."

Paul Dirac had joined us in the meantime. He had only just turned twenty-five, and had little time for tolerance. "I don't know why we are talking about religion," he objected. "If we are honest—and scientists have to be—we must admit that religion is a jumble of false assertions, with no basis in reality. The very idea of God is a product of the human imagination. It is quite understandable why primitive people, who were so much more exposed to the overpowering forces of nature than we are today, should have personified these forces in fear and trembling. But nowadays, when we understand so many natural processes, we have no need for such solutions. I can't for the life of me see how the postulate of an Almighty God helps us in any way. What I do see is that this assumption leads to such unproductive questions as why God allows so much misery and injustice, the exploitation of the poor by the rich and all the other horrors He might have prevented. If religion is still being taught, it is by no means because its ideas still convince us, but simply because some of us want to keep the lower classes quiet. Quiet people are much easier to govern than clamorous and dissatisfied ones. They are also very much easier to exploit. Religion is a kind of opium that allows a nation to lull itself into wishful dreams and so forget the injustices that are being perpetrated against the people. Hence the close alliance between those two great political forces, the State and the Church. Both need the illusion that a kindly God rewards—in heaven if not on earth—all those who have not risen up against injustice, who have done their duty quietly and uncomplainingly. That is precisely why the honest assertion that God is a mere product of the human imagination is branded as the worst of all mortal sins."

"You are simply judging religion by its political abuses," I objected, "and since most things in this world can be abused—even the Communist ideology which you recently propounded—all such judgments are inadmissible. After all, there will always be human societies, and these must find a common language in which they can speak about life and death, and about the wider context in which their lives are set. The spiritual forms that have developed historically out of this search for a common language must have had a great persuasive force—how else could so many people have lived by them for so many centuries? Religion can't be dismissed as simply as all that. But perhaps you are drawn to another religion, such as the old Chinese, in which the idea of a personal God does not occur?"

"I dislike religious myths on principle," Paul Dirac replied, "if only    11 because the myths of the different religions contradict one another. After all, it was purely by chance that I was born in Europe and not in Asia, and that is surely no criterion for judging what is true or what I ought to believe. And I can only believe what is true. As for right action, I can deduce it by reason alone from the situation in which I find myself: I live in society with others, to whom, on principle, I must grant the same rights I claim for myself. I must simply try to strike a fair balance; no more can be asked of me. All this talk about God's will, about sin and repentance, about a world beyond by which we must direct our lives, only serves to disguise the sober truth. Belief in God merely encourages us to think that God wills us to submit to a higher force, and it is this idea which helps to preserve social structures that may have been perfectly good in their day but no longer fit the modern world. All your talk of a wider context and the like strikes me as quite unacceptable. Life, when all is said and done, is just like science: we come up against difficulties and have to solve them. And we can never solve more than one difficulty at a time; your wider context is nothing but a mental superstructure added a posteriori."

And so the discussion continued, and we were all of us surprised    12 to notice that Wolfgang was keeping so silent. He would pull a long face or smile rather maliciously from time to time, but he said nothing. In the end, we had to ask him to tell us what he thought. He seemed a little surprised and then said: "Well, our friend Dirac, too, has a religion, and its guiding principle is: 'There is no God and Dirac is His prophet.' " We all laughed, including Dirac, and this brought our evening in the hotel lounge to a close.

Some time later, probably in Copenhagen, I told Niels about our    13 conversation. He immediately jumped to the defense of the youngest member of our circle. "I consider it marvelous," he said, "that Paul should be so uncompromising in his defense of all that can be expressed in clear and logical language. He believes that what can be said at all can be said clearly—or, as Wittgenstein put it, that 'whereof one cannot speak thereof one must be silent.' Whenever Dirac sends me a manuscript, the writing is so neat and free of corrections that merely looking at it is an aesthetic pleasure. If I suggest even minor changes, Paul becomes terribly unhappy and generally changes nothing at all. His work is, in any case, quite brilliant. Recently the two of us went to an exhibition which included a glorious gray-blue seascape by Manet. In the foreground was a boat, and beside it, in the water, a dark gray spot, whose meaning was not quite clear. Dirac said, 'This spot is not admissible.' A strange way of looking at art, but he was probably quite right. In a good work of art, just as in a good piece of scientific work, every detail must be laid down quite unequivocally; there can be no room for mere accident.

"Still, religion is rather a different matter. I feel very much like   14
Dirac: the idea of a personal God is foreign to me. But we ought to remember that religion uses language in quite a different way from science. The language of religion is more closely related to the language of poetry than to the language of science. True, we are inclined to think that science deals with information about objective facts, and poetry with subjective feelings. Hence we conclude that if religion does indeed deal with objective truths, it ought to adopt the same criteria of truth as science. But I myself find the division of the world into an objective and a subjective side much too arbitrary. The fact that religions through the ages have spoken in images, parables and paradoxes means simply that there are no other ways of grasping the reality to which they refer. But that does not mean that it is not a genuine reality. And splitting this reality into an objective and a subjective side won't get us very far.

"That is why I consider those developments in physics during the   15
last decades which have shown how problematical such concepts as 'objective' and 'subjective' are, a great liberation of thought. The whole thing started with the theory of relativity. In the past, the statement that two events are simultaneous was considered an objective assertion, one that could be communicated quite simply and that was open to verification by any observer. Today we know that 'simultaneity' contains a subjective element, inasmuch as two events that appear simultaneous to an observer at rest are not necessarily simultaneous to an observer in motion. However, the relativistic description is also objective inasmuch as every observer can deduce by calculation what

the other observer will perceive or has perceived. For all that, we have come a long way from the classical ideal of objective descriptions.

"In quantum mechanics the departure from this ideal has been 16 even more radical. We can still use the objectifying language of classical physics to make statements about observable facts. For instance, we can say that a photographic plate has been blackened, or that cloud droplets have formed. But we can say nothing about the atoms themselves. And what predictions we base on such findings depend on the way we pose our experimental question, and here the observer has freedom of choice. Naturally, it still makes no difference whether the observer is a man, an animal or a piece of apparatus, but it is no longer possible to make predictions without reference to the observer or the means of observation. To that extent, every physical process may be said to have objective and subjective features. The objective world of nineteenth-century science was, as we know today, an ideal, limiting case, but not the whole reality. Admittedly, even in our future encounters with reality we shall have to distinguish between the objective and the subjective side, to make a division between the two. But the location of the separation may depend on the way things are looked at; to a certain extent it can be chosen at will. Hence I can quite understand why we cannot speak about the content of religion in an objectifying language. The fact that different religions try to express this content in quite distinct spiritual forms is no real objection. Perhaps we ought to look upon these different forms as complementary descriptions which, though they exclude one another, are needed to convey the rich possibilities flowing from man's relationship with the central order."

"If you distinguish so sharply between the languages of religion, 17 science and art," I asked, "what meaning do you attach to such apodictic statements as 'There is a living God' or 'There is an immortal soul'? What is the meaning of 'there is' in this type of language? Science, like Dirac, objects to such formulations. Let me illustrate the epistemological side of the problem by means of the following analogy:

"Mathematicians, as everyone knows, work with an imaginary 18 unit, the square root of $-1$, called $i$. We know that $i$ does not figure among the natural numbers. Nevertheless, important branches of mathematics, for instance the theory of analytical functions, are based on this imaginary unit, that is, on the fact that $\sqrt{-1}$ exists after all. Would you agree that the statement 'There is a $\sqrt{-1}$' means nothing else than 'There are important mathematical relations that are most simply represented by the introduction of the $\sqrt{-1}$ concept'? And yet these relations would exist even without it. That is precisely why this type of mathematics is so useful even in science and technology. What is decisive, for instance, in the theory of functions, is the existence of important mathematical laws governing the behavior of pairs of continuous variables. These relations are rendered more comprehensible by the introduction of the abstract concept of $\sqrt{-1}$, although that concept is not basically needed for our understanding, and although it has no counterpart among the natural numbers. An equally abstract concept is that of infinity, which also plays a very important role in modern mathematics. It, too, has no correlate, and moreover raises grave problems. In short, mathematics introduces ever higher stages of abstraction that help us attain a coherent grasp of ever wider realms. To get back to our original question, is it correct to look upon the religious 'there is' as just another, though different, attempt to reach even higher levels of abstraction? An attempt to facilitate our understanding of universal connections? After all, the connections themselves are real enough, no matter into what spiritual forms we try to fit them.''

"With respect to the epistemological side of the problem, your 19 comparison may pass,'' Bohr replied. ''But in other respects it is quite inadequate. In mathematics we can take our inner distance from the content of our statements. In the final analysis mathematics is a mental game that we can play or not play as we choose. Religion, on the other hand, deals with ourselves, with our life and death; its promises are meant to govern our actions and thus, at least indirectly, our very existence. We cannot just look at them impassively from the outside. Moreover, our attitude to religious questions cannot be separated from our attitude to society. Even if religion arose as the spiritual structure of a particular human society, it is arguable whether it has remained the strongest social molding force throughout history, or whether society, once formed, develops new spiritual structures and adapts them to its particular level of knowledge. Nowadays, the individual seems to be able to choose the spiritual framework of his thoughts and actions quite freely, and this freedom reflects the fact that the boundaries between the various cultures and societies are beginning to become more fluid. But even when an individual tries to attain the greatest possible degree of independence, he will still be swayed by the existing spiritual structures-consciously or unconsciously. For he, too, must be able to speak of life and death and the human condition to other members of the society in which he has chosen to live; he must educate his children according to the norms of that society, fit into its life. Epistemological sophistries cannot possibly help him attain these ends. Here, too, the relationship between critical thought about the spiritual content of a given religion and action based on the deliberate acceptance of that content is complementary. And such acceptance, if consciously arrived at, fills the individual with strength of purpose, helps him to overcome doubts and, if he has to suffer, provides him with the kind of solace that only a sense of being sheltered under an all-embracing roof can grant. In that sense, religion helps to make social life more harmonious; its most important task is to remind us, in the language of pictures and parables, of the wider framework within which our life is set."

"You keep referring to the individual's free choice," I said, "and 20 you compare it with the freedom with which the atomic physicist can arrange his experiments in this way or that. Now the classical physicist had no such freedom. Does that mean that the special features of modern physics have a more direct bearing on the problem of the freedom of the will? As you know, the fact that atomic processes cannot be fully determined is often used as an argument in favor of free will and divine intervention."

"I am convinced that this whole attitude is based on a simple mis- 21 understanding, or rather on the confusion of questions, which, as far as I can see, impinge on distinct though complementary ways of looking at things. If we speak of free will, we refer to a situation in which we have to make decisions. This situation and the one in which we analyze the motives of our actions or even the one in which we study physiological processes, for instance the electrochemical processes in our brain, are mutually exclusive. In other words, they are complementary, so that the question whether natural laws determine events completely or only statistically has no direct bearing on the question of free will. Naturally, our different ways of looking at things must fit together in the long run, i.e., we must be able to recognize them as noncontradictory parts of the same reality, though we cannot yet tell precisely how. When we speak of divine intervention, we quite obviously do not refer to the scientific determination of an event, but to the meaningful connection between this event and others or human thought. Now this intellectual connection is as much a part of reality as scientific causality; it would be much too crude a simplification if we ascribed it exclusively to the subjective side of reality. Once again we can learn from the analogous situation in natural science. There are well-known biological relations that we do not describe causally, but rather finalistically, that is, with respect of their ends. We have only to think of the healing process in an injured organism. The finalistic interpretation has a characteristically complementary relationship to the one based on physico-chemical or atomic laws; that is, in the one case we ask whether the process leads to the desired end, the restoration of normal conditions in the organism; in the other case we ask about the causal chain determining the molecular processes. The two descriptions are mutually exclusive, but not necessarily contradictory. We have good reason to assume that quantum-mechanical laws can be proved valid in a living organism just as they can in dead matter. For all that, a finalistic description is just as valid. I believe that if the development of atomic physics has taught us anything, it is that we must learn to think more subtly than in the past."

"We always come back to the epistemological side of religion," I  22 objected. "But Dirac's attack on religion was aimed chiefly at its ethical side. Dirac disapproves quite particularly of the dishonesty and self-deception that are far too often coupled to religious thought. But in his abhorrence he has become a fanatic defender of rationalism, and I have the feeling that rationalism is not enough."

"I think Dirac did well," Niels said, "to warn you so forcefully  23 against the dangers of self-deception and inner contradictions; but Wolfgang was equally right when he jokingly drew Dirac's attention to the extraordinary difficulty of escaping this danger entirely." Niels closed the conversation with one of those stories he liked to tell on such occasions: "One of our neighbors in Tisvilde once fixed a horseshoe over the door to his house. When a mutual acquaintance asked him, 'But are you really superstitious? Do you honestly believe that this horseshoe will bring you luck?' he replied, 'Of course not; but they say it helps even if you don't believe in it.' "

# Questions

1. What assumption about the relationship of science and religion governs the first three paragraphs?
2. In paragraph 5 Wolfgang Pauli declares, "I cannot really endorse Planck's philosophy." What, briefly stated, is Planck's philosophy as reported here? What concessions does Pauli make to it? What is Pauli's central objection?
3. From the context in which the word appears in paragraph 8, what do you take "complementarity" to mean? And why does Pauli think that the concept of complementarity may produce greater tolerance of different forms of religion?

4. We read here accounts of the religious positions of Planck, Einstein, and Dirac. Briefly restate the position of each. Which is closest to your own view, or do you find some truth in more than one?

5. What point does Heisenberg introduce by means of analogy in paragraph 18? Now that you have restated the point without benefit of the analogy, can you justify Heisenberg's use of it?

6. What is Bohr's objection to Heisenberg's position? In paragraph 19 what does Bohr mean by, "In mathematics we can take our inner distance from the content of our statements"?

7. In these pages we overhear several eminent scientists discussing religion. From their discussion, what insights do you gain into their thinking about *science*?

8. The essay ends with a humorous anecdote. Do you think this makes a good ending? Why, or why not?

## George Orwell

# What Is Science?

In last week's *Tribune*, there was an interesting letter from  1
Mr J. Stewart Cook, in which he suggested that the best way of avoiding the danger of a "scientific hierarchy" would be to see to it that every member of the general public was, as far as possible, scientifically educated. At the same time, scientists should be brought out of their isolation and encouraged to take a greater part in politics and administration.

As a general statement, I think most of us would agree with this,  2
but I notice that, as usual, Mr Cook does not define science, and merely implies in passing that it means certain exact sciences whose experi-

George Orwell (1903–1950) was the pen name adopted by Eric Blair, an Englishman born in India. Orwell was educated at Eton, in England, but in 1921 he went back to the East and served for five years as a police officer in Burma. He then returned to Europe, doing odd jobs while writing novels and stories. In 1936 he fought in the Spanish Civil War on the side of the Republicans, an experience reported in *Homage to Catalonia* (1938). His last years were spent writing in England.

ments can be made under laboratory conditions. Thus, adult education tends "to neglect scientific studies in favour of literary, economic and social subjects," economics and sociology not being regarded as branches of science, apparently. This point is of great importance. For the word science is at present used in at least two meanings, but the whole question of scientific education is obscured by the current tendency to dodge from one meaning to the other.

Science is generally taken as meaning either (a) the exact sciences, 3 such as chemistry, physics, etc., or (b) a method of thought which obtains verifiable results by reasoning logically from observed fact.

If you ask any scientist, or indeed almost any educated person, 4 "What is science?" you are likely to get an answer approximating to (b). In everyday life, however, both in speaking and in writing, when people say "science" they mean (a). Science means something that happens in a laboratory: the very word calls up a picture of graphs, test-tubes, balances, Bunsen burners, microscopes. A biologist, an astronomer, perhaps a psychologist or a mathematician, is described as a "man of science": no one would think of applying this term to a statesman, a poet, a journalist or even a philosopher. And those who tell us that the young must be scientifically educated mean, almost invariably, that they should be taught more about radioactivity, or the stars, or the physiology of their own bodies, rather than that they should be taught to think more exactly.

This confusion of meaning, which is partly deliberate, has in it a 5 great danger. Implied in the demand for more scientific education is the claim that if one has been scientifically trained one's approach to *all* subjects will be more intelligent than if one had had no such training. A scientist's political opinions, it is assumed, his opinions on sociological questions, on morals, on philosophy, perhaps even on the arts, will be more valuable than those of a layman. The world, in other words, would be a better place if the scientists were in control of it. But a "scientist," as we have just seen, means in practice a specialist in one of the exact sciences. It follows that a chemist or a physicist, as such, is politically more intelligent than a poet or a lawyer, as such. And, in fact, there are already millions of people who do believe this.

But is it really true that a "scientist," in this narrower sense, is 6 any likelier than other people to approach non-scientific problems in an objective way? There is not much reason for thinking so. Take one simple test—the ability to withstand nationalism. It is often loosely said that "Science is international," but in practice the scientific workers of all countries line up behind their own governments with fewer

scruples than are felt by the writers and the artists. The German scientific community, as a whole, made no resistance to Hitler. Hitler
may have ruined the long-term prospects of German science, but there
were still plenty of gifted men to do the necessary research on such
things as synthetic oil, jet planes, rocket projectiles and the atomic
bomb. Without them the German war machine could never have been
built up.

On the other hand, what happened to German literature when    7
the Nazis came to power? I believe no exhaustive lists have been published, but I imagine that the number of German scientists—Jews
apart—who voluntarily exiled themselves or were persecuted by the
régime was much smaller than the number of writers and journalists.
More sinister than this, a number of German scientists swallowed the
monstrosity of "racial science." You can find some of the statements
to which they set their names in Professor Brady's *The Spirit and Structure of German Fascism.*

But, in slightly different forms, it is the same picture everywhere.    8
In England, a large proportion of our leading scientists accept the structure of capitalist society, as can be seen from the comparative freedom
with which they are given knighthoods, baronetcies and even peer-
ages. Since Tennyson, no English writer worth reading—one might,
perhaps, make an exception of Sir Max Beerbohm—has been given a
title. And those English scientists who do not simply accept the *status
quo* are frequently Communists, which means that, however intellectually scrupulous they may be in their own line of work, they are ready
to be uncritical and even dishonest on certain subjects. The fact is that
a mere training in one or more of the exact sciences, even combined
with very high gifts, is no guarantee of a humane or sceptical outlook.
The physicists of half a dozen great nations, all feverishly and secretly
working away at the atomic bomb, are a demonstration of this.

But does all this mean that the general public should *not* be more    9
scientifically educated? On the contrary! All it means is that scientific
education for the masses will do little good, and probably a lot of harm,
if it simply boils down to more physics, more chemistry, more biology,
etc. to the detriment of literature and history. Its probable effect on
the average human being would be to narrow the range of his thoughts
and make him more than ever contemptuous of such knowledge as
he did not possess: and his political reactions would probably be somewhat less intelligent than those of an illiterate peasant who retained
a few historical memories and a fairly sound aesthetic sense.

Clearly, scientific education ought to mean the implanting of a    10 rational, sceptical, experimental habit of mind. It ought to mean acquiring a *method*—a method that can be used on any problem that one meets—and not simply piling up a lot of facts. Put it in those words, and the apologist of scientific education will usually agree. Press him further, ask him to particularise, and somehow it always turns out that scientific education means more attention to the exact sciences, in other words—more *facts*. The idea that science means a way of looking at the world, and not simply a body of knowledge, is in practice strongly resisted. I think sheer professional jealousy is part of the reason for this. For if science is simply a method or an attitude, so that anyone whose thought-processes are sufficiently rational can in some sense be described as a scientist—what then becomes of the enormous prestige now enjoyed by the chemist, the physicist, etc. and his claim to be somehow wiser than the rest of us?

A hundred years ago, Charles Kingsley described science as "making nasty smells in a laboratory." A year or two ago a young industrial chemist informed me, smugly, that he "could not see what was the use of poetry." So the pendulum swings to and fro, but it does not seem to me that one attitude is any better than the other. At the moment, science is on the up-grade, and so we hear, quite rightly, the claim that the masses should be scientifically educated: we do not hear, as we ought, the counter-claim that the scientists themselves would benefit by a little education. Just before writing this, I saw in an American magazine the statement that a number of British and American physicists refused from the start to do research on the atomic bomb, well knowing what use would be made of it. Here you have a group of sane men in the middle of a world of lunatics. And though no names were published, I think it would be a safe guess that all of them were people with some kind of general cultural background, some acquaintance with history or literature or the arts—in short, people whose interests were not, in the current sense of the word, purely scientific. 11

# Questions

1. By the end of paragraph 5 Orwell has developed the idea that "millions of people" believe that "a chemist or a physicist, as such, is politically more intelligent than a poet or a lawyer, as such." Do you think this assertion is true? Why? Are you among the millions who subscribe to the belief that a physical scientist's opinions on politics probably are "more intelligent" than a poet's or lawyer's

opinions on politics? If so, why do you hold this belief? If not, why not?

2.  In paragraphs 5 and 6 Orwell implies, without arguing the point, that politics is a "non-scientific" matter. Yet many colleges and universities have a department of "political science." Is such a department accurately named? Why, or why not?

3.  The fact that many physicists worked on the atomic bomb, Orwell asserts at the end of paragraph 8, is proof that a scientific education is "no guarantee of a humane or sceptical outlook." Do you agree, or do you find his reasoning faulty? Why?

4.  In paragraph 10 Orwell asserts that a "scientific education ought to mean the implanting of a rational, sceptical, experimental habit of mind. It ought to mean acquiring a *method*—a method that can be used on any problem that one meets." But if, as Orwell has already implied, politics is a non-scientific matter, why should one approach it with a scientific method? Assume that this question has been put to Orwell, and that you are Orwell. What is your (Orwell's) response? (Do *not* simply give your own response; give what you think would be Orwell's response, whether you agree with it or not.)

5.  Outline Orwell's organization, and then evaluate the organization.

6.  Consider the scientific education you have received thus far. Does it correspond to what Orwell deplores, or does it correspond to what he propses? Or both, or neither?

Isaac Asimov

# My Built-in Doubter

$O$nce I delivered myself of an oration before a small but  1
select audience of non-scientists on the topic of "What Is Science?"
speaking seriously and, I hope, intelligently.

Isaac Asimov, born in Russia in 1920, was brought to the United States at the age of three and became a naturalized citizen in 1928. Although he has taught biochemistry at Boston University and has written on Shakespeare and on the Bible, Asimov is chiefly known as a writer on scientific subjects.

Having completed the talk, there came the question period, and, 2
bless my heart, I wasn't disappointed. A charming young lady up front
waved a pretty little hand at me and asked, not a serious question on
the nature of science, but: "Dr. Asimov, do you believe in flying saucers?"

With a fixed smile on my face, I proceeded to give the answer I 3
have carefully given after every lecture I have delivered. I said, "No,
miss, I do not, and I think anyone who does is a crackpot!"

And oh, the surprise on her face!                                   4

It is taken for granted by everyone, it seems to me, that because 5
I sometimes write science fiction, I believe in flying saucers, in Atlantis,
in clairvoyance and levitation, in the prophecies of the Great Pyramid,
in astrology, in Fort's theories, and in the suggestion that Bacon wrote
Shakespeare.

No one would ever think that someone who writes fantasies for 6
pre-school children really thinks that rabbits can talk, or that a writer
of hard-boiled detective stories really thinks a man can down two
quarts of whiskey in five minutes, then make love to two girls in the
next five, or that a writer for the ladies' magazines really thinks that
virtue always triumphs and that the secretary always marries the handsome boss—but a science-fiction writer apparently *must* believe in
flying saucers.

Well, I do not.                                                     7

To be sure, I wrote a story once about flying saucers in which I 8
explained their existence very logically. I also wrote a story once in
which levitation played a part.

If I can buddy up to such notions long enough to write sober, 9
reasonable stories about them, why, then, do I reject them so definitely
in real life?

I can explain by way of a story. A good friend of mine once spent 10
quite a long time trying to persuade me of the truth and validity of
what I considered a piece of pseudo-science and bad pseudo-science
at that. I sat there listening quite stonily, and none of the cited evidence
and instances and proofs had the slightest effect on me.

Finally the gentleman said to me, with considerable annoyance, 11
"Damn it, Isaac, the trouble with you is that you have a built-in
doubter."

To which the only answer I could see my way to making was a 12
heartfelt, "Thank God."

If a scientist has one piece of temperamental equipment that is 13
essential to his job, it is that of a built-in doubter. Before he does

anything else, he must doubt. He must doubt what others tell him and what he reads in reference books, and, *most of all*, what his own experiments show him and what his own reasoning tells him.

Such doubt must, of course, exist in varying degrees. It is impossible, impractical, and useless to be a maximal doubter at all times. One cannot (and would not want to) check personally every figure or observation given in a handbook or monograph before one uses it and then proceed to check it and recheck it until one dies. *But,* if any trouble arises and nothing else seems wrong, one must be prepared to say to one's self, "Well, now, I wonder if the data I got out of the 'Real Guaranteed Authoritative Very Scientific Handbook' might not be a misprint."     14

To doubt intelligently requires, therefore, a rough appraisal of the authoritativeness of a source. It also requires a rough estimate of the nature of the statement. If you were to tell me that you had a bottle containing one pound of pure titanium oxide, I would say, "Good," and ask to borrow some if I needed it. Nor would I test it. I would accept its purity on your say-so (until further notice, anyway).     15

If you were to tell me that you had a bottle containing one pound of pure thulium oxide, I would say with considerable astonishment, "You have? Where?" Then if I had use for the stuff, I would want to run some tests on it and even run it through an ion-exchange column before I could bring myself to use it.     16

And if you told me that you had a bottle containing one pound of pure americium oxide, I would say, "You're crazy," and walk away. I'm sorry, but my time is reasonably valuable, and I do not consider that statement to have enough chance of validity even to warrant my stepping into the next room to look at the bottle.     17

What I am trying to say is that doubting is far more important to the advance of science than believing is and that, moreover, doubting is a serious business that requires extensive training to be handled properly. People without training in a particular field do not know what to doubt and what not to doubt; or, to put it conversely, what to believe and what not to believe. I am very sorry to be undemocratic, but one man's opinion is not necessarily as good as the next man's.     18

To be sure, I feel uneasy about seeming to kowtow to authority in this fashion. After all, you all know of instances where authority was wrong, dead wrong. Look at Columbus, you will say. Look at Galileo.     19

I know about them, and about others, too. As a dabbler in the history of science, I can give you horrible examples you may never     20 have heard of. I can cite the case of the German scientist, Rudolf Virchow, who, in the mid-nineteenth century was responsible for important advances in anthropology and practically founded the science of pathology. He was the first man to engage in cancer research on a scientific basis. However, he was dead set against the germ theory of disease when that was advanced by Pasteur. So were many others, but one by one the opponents abandoned doubt as evidence multiplied. Not Virchow, however. Rather than be forced to admit he was wrong and Pasteur right, Virchow quit science altogether and went into politics. How much wronger could Stubborn Authority get?

But this is a very exceptional case. Let's consider a far more normal   21
and natural example of authority in the wrong.

The example concerns a young Swedish chemical student, Svante   22
August Arrhenius, who was working for his Ph.D. in the University of Uppsala in the 1880s. He was interested in the freezing points of solutions because certain odd points arose in that connection.

If sucrose (ordinary table sugar) is dissolved in water, the freezing   23
point of the solution is somewhat lower than is that of pure water. Dissolve more sucrose and the freezing point lowers further. You can calculate how many molecules of sucrose must be dissolved per cubic centimeter of water in order to bring about a certain drop in freezing point. It turns out that this same number of molecules of glucose (grape sugar) and of many other soluble substances will bring about the same drop. It doesn't matter that a molecule of sucrose is twice as large as a molecule of glucose. What counts is the number of molecules and not their size.

But if sodium chloride (table salt) is dissolved in water, the freez-   24
ing-point drop per molecule is twice as great as normal. And this goes for certain other substances too. For instance, barium chloride, when dissolved, will bring about a freezing-point drop that is three times normal.

Arrhenius wondered if this meant that when sodium chloride was   25
dissolved, each of its molecules broke into two portions, thus creating twice as many particles as there were molecules and therefore a doubled freezing-point drop. And barium chloride might break up into three particles per molecule. Since the sodium chloride molecule is composed of a sodium atom and a chlorine atom and since the barium chloride molecule is composed of a barium atom and two chlorine atoms, the logical next step was to suppose that these particular molecules broke up into individual atoms.

Then, too, there was another interesting fact. Those substances   26 like sucrose and glucose which gave a normal freezing-point drop did not conduct an electric current in solution. Those, like sodium chloride and barium chloride, which showed abnormally high freezing-point drops, *did* do so.

Arrhenius wondered if the atoms, into which molecules broke up on solution, might not carry positive and negative electric charges. If the sodium atom carried a positive charge for instance, it would be attracted to the negative electrode. If the chlorine atom carried a negative charge, it would be attracted to the positive electrode. Each would wander off in its own direction and the net result would be that such a solution would conduct an electric current. For these charged and wandering atoms, Arrhenius adopted Faraday's name "ions" from a Greek word meaning "wanderer." 27

Furthermore, a charged atom, or ion, would not have the properties of an uncharged atom. A charged chlorine atom would not be a gas that would bubble out of solution. A charged sodium atom would not react with water to form hydrogen. It was for that reason that common salt (sodium chloride) did not show the properties of either sodium metal or chlorine gas, though it was made of those two elements. 28

In 1884 Arrhenius, then twenty-five, prepared his theories in the form of a thesis and presented it as part of his doctoral dissertation. The examining professors sat in frigid disapproval. No one had ever heard of electrically charged atoms, it was against all scientific belief of the time, and they turned on their built-in doubters. 29

However, Arrhenius argued his case so clearly and, on the single assumption of the dissolution of molecules into charged atoms, managed to explain so much so neatly, that the professors' built-in doubters did not quite reach the intensity required to flunk the young man. Instead, they passed him—with the lowest possible passing grade. 30

But then, ten years later, the negatively charged electron was discovered and the atom was found to be not the indivisible thing it had been considered but a complex assemblage of still smaller particles. Suddenly the notion of ions as charged atoms made sense. If an atom lost an electron or two, it was left with a positive charge; if it gained them, it had a negative charge. 31

Then, the decade following, the Nobel Prizes were set up and in 1903 the Nobel Prize in Chemistry was awarded to Arrhenius for that same thesis which, nineteen years earlier, had barely squeaked him through for a Ph.D. 32

Were the professors wrong? Looking back, we can see they were. 33

But in 1884 they were *not* wrong. They did exactly the right thing and they served science well. Every professor must listen to and appraise dozens of new ideas every year. He must greet each with the gradation of doubt his experience and training tells him the idea is worth.

Arrhenius's notion met with just the proper gradation of doubt. 34 It was radical enough to be held at arm's length. However, it seemed to have just enough possible merit to be worth some recognition. The professors *did* give him his Ph.D. after all. And other scientists of the time paid attention to it and thought about it. A very great one, Ostwald,[1] thought enough of it to offer Arrhenius a good job.

Then, when the appropriate evidence turned up, doubt receded 35 to minimal values and Arrhenius was greatly honored.

What better could you expect? Ought the professors to have fallen 36 all over Arrhenius and his new theory on the spot? And if so, why shouldn't they also have fallen all over forty-nine other new theories presented that year, no one of which might have seemed much more unlikely than Arrhenius's and some of which may even have appeared less unlikely?

It would have taken *longer* for the ionic theory to have become 37 established if overcredulity on the part of scientists had led them into fifty blind alleys. How many scientists would have been left to investigate Arrhenius's notions?

Scientific manpower is too limited to investigate everything that 38 occurs to everybody, and always will be too limited. The advance of science depends on scientists in general being kept firmly in the direction of maximum possible return. And the only device that will keep them turned in that direction is doubt; doubt arising from a good, healthy and active built-in doubter.

But, you might say, this misses the point. Can't one pick and 39 choose and isolate the brilliant from the imbecilic, accepting the first at once and wholeheartedly, and rejecting the rest completely? Would not such a course have saved ten years on ions without losing time on other notions?

Sure, if it could be done, but it can't. The godlike power to tell 40 the good from the bad, the useful from the useless, the true from the false, instantly and *in toto* belongs to gods and not to men.

Let me cite you Galileo as an example; Galileo, who was one of 41

---

[1] (Friedrich Wilhelm) Ostwald (1853–1932): German physical chemist and philosopher. (Editors' note)

the greatest scientific geniuses of all time, who invented modern science in fact, and who certainly experienced persecution and authoritarian enmity.

Surely, Galileo, of all people, was smart enough to know a good idea when he saw it, and revolutionary enough not to be deterred by its being radical. 42

Well, let's see. In 1632 Galileo published the crowning work of his career, *Dialogue on the Two Principal Systems of the World* which was the very book that got him into real trouble before the Inquisition. It dealt, as the title indicates, with the two principal systems; that of Ptolemy, which had the earth at the center of the universe with the planets, sun and moon going about it in complicated systems of circles within circles; and that of Copernicus which had the sun at the center and the planets, earth, and moon going about *it* in complicated systems of circles within circles. 43

Galileo did not as much as mention a *third* system, that of Kepler, which had the sun at the center but abandoned all the circles-within-circles jazz. Instead, he had the various planets traveling about the sun in ellipses, with the sun at one focus of the ellipse. It was Kepler's system that was correct and, in fact, Kepler's system has not been changed in all the time that has elapsed since. Why, then, did Galileo ignore it completely? 44

Was it that Kepler had not yet devised it? No, indeed. Kepler's views on that matter were published in 1609, twenty-seven years before Galileo's book. 45

Was it that Galileo had happened not to hear of it? Nonsense. Galileo and Kepler were in steady correspondence and were friends. When Galileo built some spare telescopes, he sent one to Kepler. When Kepler had ideas, he wrote about them to Galileo. 46

The trouble was that Kepler was still bound up with the mystical notions of the Middle Ages. He cast horoscopes for famous men, for a fee, and worked seriously and hard on astrology. He also spent time working out the exact notes formed by the various planets in creating the "music of the spheres" and pointed out that Earth's notes were mi, fa, mi, standing for misery, famine, and misery. He also devised a theory accounting for the relative distances of the planets from the Sun by nesting the five regular solids one within another and making deductions therefrom. 47

Galileo, who must have heard of all this, and who had nothing of the mystic about himself, could only conclude that Kepler, though a 48 nice guy and a bright fellow and a pleasant correspondent, was a complete nut. I am sure that Galileo heard all about the elliptical orbits and, considering the source, shrugged it off.

Well, Kepler was indeed a nut, but he happened to be luminously 49 right on occasion, too, and Galileo, of all people, couldn't pick the diamond out from among the pebbles.

Shall we sneer at Galileo for that?                                          50

Or should we rather be thankful that Galileo didn't interest himself 51 in the ellipses *and* in astrology *and* in the nesting of regular solids *and* in the music of the spheres. Might not credulity have led him into wasting his talents, to the great loss of all succeeding generations?

No, no, until some supernatural force comes to our aid and tells 52 men what is right and what wrong, men must blunder along as best they can, and only the built-in doubter of the trained scientist can offer a refuge of safety.

The very mechanism of scientific procedure, built up slowly over 53 the years, is designed to encourage doubt and to place obstacles in the way of new ideas. No person receives credit for a new idea unless he publishes it for all the world to see and criticize. It is further considered advisable to announce ideas in papers read to colleagues at public gatherings that they might blast the speaker down face to face.

Even after announcement or publication, no observation can be 54 accepted until it has been confirmed by an independent observer, and no theory is considered more than, at best, an interesting speculation until it is backed by experimental evidence that has been independently confirmed and that has withstood the rigid doubts of others in the field.

All this is nothing more than the setting up of a system of "natural 55 selection" designed to winnow the fit from the unfit in the realm of ideas, in manner analogous to the concept of Darwinian evolution. The process may be painful and tedious, as evolution itself is; but in the long run it gets results, as evolution itself does. What's more, I don't see that there can be any substitute.

Now let me make a second point. The intensity to which the built- 56 in doubter is activated is also governed by the extent to which a new observation fits into the organized structure of science. If it fits well, doubt can be small; if it fits poorly, doubt can be intensive; if it threatens to overturn the structure completely, doubt is, and should be, nearly insuperable.

The reason for this is that now, three hundred fifty years after 57 Galileo founded experimental science, the structure that has been reared, bit by bit, by a dozen generations of scientists is so firm that its complete overturning has reached the vanishing point of unlikelihood.

Nor need you point to relativity as an example of a revolution that 58 overturned science. Einstein did not overturn the structure, he merely extended, elaborated, and improved it. Einstein did not prove Newton wrong, but merely incomplete. Einstein's world system contains Newton's as a special case and one which works if the volume of space considered is not too large and if velocities involved are not too great.

In fact, I should say that since Kepler's time in astronomy, since 59 Galileo's time in physics, since Lavoisier's[2] time in chemistry, and since Darwin's time in biology no discovery or theory, however revolutionary it has seemed, has actually overturned the structure of science or any major branch of it. The structure has merely been improved and refined.

The effect is similar to the paving of a road, and its broadening 60 and the addition of clover-leaf intersections, and the installation of radar to combat speeding. None of this, please notice, is the equivalent of abandoning the road and building another in a completely new direction.

But let's consider a few concrete examples drawn from contem- 61 porary life. A team of Columbia University geologists have been exploring the configuration of the ocean bottom for years. Now they find that the mid-Atlantic ridge (a chain of mountains, running down the length of the Atlantic) has a rift in the center, a deep chasm or crack. What's more, this rift circles around Africa, sends an offshoot up into the Indian Ocean and across eastern Africa, and heads up the Pacific, skimming the California coast as it does so. It is like a big crack encircling the earth.

The observation itself can be accepted. Those involved were 62 trained and experienced specialists and confirmation is ample.

But why the rift? Recently one of the geologists, Bruce Heezen, 63 suggested that the crack may be due to the expansion of the earth.

This is certainly one possibility. If the interior were slowly ex- 64 panding, the thin crust would give and crack like an eggshell.

But why should Earth's interior expand? To do so it would have 65 to take up a looser arrangement, become less dense; the atoms would have to spread out a bit.

---

[2] (Antoine Laurent) Lavoisier (1743–1794): French chemist and physicist. (Editors' note)

Heezen suggests that one way in which all this might happen is 66
that the gravitational force of the Earth was very slowly weakening
with time. The central pressures would therefore ease up and the compressed atoms of the interior would slowly spread out.

But why should Earth's gravity decrease, unless the force of grav- 67
itation everywhere were slowly decreasing with time? Now this deserves a lot of doubt, because there is nothing in the structure of science
to suggest that the force of gravitation must decrease with time. However, it is also true that there is nothing in the structure of science to
suggest that the force of gravitation might *not* decrease with time.[3]

Or take another case. I have recently seen a news clipping con- 68
cerning an eighth-grader in South Carolina who grew four sets of bean
plants under glass jars. One set remained there always, subjected to
silence. The other three had their jars removed one hour a day in order
that they might be exposed to noise; in one case to jazz, in another to
serious music, and in a third to the raucous noises of sports-car engines. The only set of plants that grew vigorously were those exposed
to the engine noises.

The headline was: BEANS CAN HEAR—AND THEY PREFER AUTO RACING 69
NOISE TO MUSIC.

Automatically, my built-in doubter moves into high gear. Can it 70
be that the newspaper story is a hoax? This is not impossible. The
history of newspaper hoaxes is such that one could easily be convinced
that nothing in any newspaper can possibly be believed.

But let's assume the story is accurate. The next question to ask is 71
whether the youngster knew what he was doing? Was he experienced
enough to make the nature of the noise the only variable? Was there
a difference in the soil or in the water supply or in some small matter,
which he disregarded through inexperience?

Finally, even if the validity of the experiment is accepted, what 72
does it really prove? To the headline writer and undoubtedly to almost
everybody who reads the article, it will prove that plants can hear; and
that they have preferences and will refuse to grow if they feel lonely
and neglected.

This is so far against the current structure of science that my built- 73
in doubter clicks it right off and stamps it: IGNORE. Now what is an
alternative explanation that fits in reasonably well with the structure
of science? Sound is not just something to hear; it is a form of vibration.

---

[3] As a matter of fact, there have been cosmological speculations (though not, in my
opinion, very convincing ones) that involve a steady and very slow decrease in the
gravitational constant; and there is also Kapp's theory, . . . which involves decreasing gravitational force on earth, without involving the gravitational constant.

Can it be that sound vibrations stir up tiny soil particles making it easier for plants to absorb water, or putting more ions within reach by improving diffusion? May the natural noise that surrounds plants act in this fashion to promote growth? And may the engine noises have worked best on a one-hour-per-day basis because they were the loudest and produced the most vibration?

Any scientist (or eighth-grader) who feels called on to experiment  74
further, ought to try vibrations that do not produce audible sound; ultrasonic vibrations, mechanical vibrations and so on. Or he might also try to expose the plant itself to vibrations of all sorts while leaving the soil insulated; and vice versa.

Which finally brings me to flying saucers and spiritualism and the  75
like. The questions I ask myself are: What is the nature of the authorities promulgating these and other viewpoints of this sort? And How well do such observations and theories fit in with the established structure of science?

My answers are, respectively, Very poor and Very poorly.  76

Which leaves me completely unrepentant as far as my double role  77
in life is concerned. If I get a good idea involving flying saucers and am in the mood to write some science fiction, I will gladly and with delight write a flying-saucer story.

And I will continue to disbelieve in them firmly in real life.  78

And if that be schizophrenia, make the most of it.  79

# Questions

1. Asimov is an extremely popular writer. What qualities in this essay make it easy to read? What qualities might some readers find offensive?

2. In his title Asimov speaks of his "doubter" as "built-in," and in paragraph 13 he calls it a piece of "equipment." Why does he speak of his skepticism in these terms?

3. In paragraph 37 Asimov writes: "It would have taken *longer* for the ionic theory to have become established if overcredulity on the part of scientists had led them into fifty blind alleys. How many scientists would have been left to investigate Arrhenius's notions?" Do you believe Asimov adequately demonstrates this point? *Can* it be demonstrated?

4. Think of an episode in your life when your "doubter" turned out to be mistaken. (Perhaps a course that seemed pointless or useless while being taken, later, on reflection, seemed valuable.) What brought about your change of mind?

5.  If you have read Thomas Kuhn's "The Function of Dogma in Scientific Research" (page 829), indicate the respects in which Asimov and Kuhn agree and the respects in which they differ.

Bart J. Bok

# A Critical Look at Astrology

During the past ten years, we have witnessed an alarming  1
increase in the spread of astrology. This pseudoscience seems to hold
fascination especially for people of college age who are looking for firm
guideposts in the confused world of the present. It is not surprising
that people believe in astrology when most of our daily newspapers
regularly carry columns about it and when some of our universities
and junior colleges actually offer astrology courses. The public, young
and old, has the right to expect from its scientists, especially from
astronomers, clear and clarifying statements showing that astrology
lacks a firm scientific foundation.

I have spoken out publicly against astrology every ten years or so,  2
beginning in 1941 in "Scientists Look at Astrology," written with Margaret W. Mayall for the now-defunct *Scientific Monthly* (Volume 52). I
have softened a bit since my early crusading days, for I have come to
realize that astrology cannot be stopped by simple scientific argument
only. To some it seems almost a religion. All I can do is state clearly
and unequivocally that modern concepts of astronomy and space physics give no support—better said, negative support—to the tenets of
astrology.

Bart J. Bok (1906–1983) was born in the Netherlands but spent most of his adult
life in the United States, teaching astronomy at Harvard and at the University of
Arizona. One of his books, *The Milky Way*, which he wrote with his wife Priscilla,
has remained a standard work in the field for some forty years. Bok's essay on
astrology was first published in a magazine called *The Humanist*. We follow the
essay with the replies that the magazine printed in a later issue (see p. 885).

Not more than a dozen or so of my fellow astronomers have spo-     3
ken out publicly on astrology. Twice I suggested to my friends on the
Council of the American Astronomical Society that the council issue
a statement pointing out that there is no scientific foundation for astrological beliefs. Both times I was turned down, the principal argument being that it is below the dignity of a professional society to
recognize that astrological beliefs are prevalent today. To me it seems
socially and morally inexcusable for the society not to have taken a
firm stand. Astronomers as a group have obviously not provided the
guidance that the public sorely needs. Those who live in a free society
are entitled to believe in whatever causes they care to espouse. However, I have had more than half a century of day-to-day and night-to-
night contacts with the starry heavens, and it is my duty to speak up
and to state clearly that I see no evidence that the stars and planets
influence or control our personal lives and that I have found much
evidence to the contrary.

## The Origins of Astrology

Astrology had its origins in the centuries before the birth of Christ.     4
Present-day astrological concepts and techniques largely go back to the
period 100 to 200 A.D. It was only natural that early civilizations would
consider the stars and planets in the heavens as awesome evidence of
supernatural powers that could magically affect their lives. Variety was
brought into the picture by the constantly changing aspects of the heavens. No one can blame the Egyptians, the Greeks, the Arabs, or the
people of India for having established systems of astrology at times
when they were also laying the foundations for astronomy. Right up
to the days of Copernicus, Galileo, and Kepler (who was an expert
astrologer)—even to the time of Isaac Newton—there were good reasons for exploring astrology.

However, all this changed when the first measurements were     5
made of the distances to the sun, planets, and stars and when the
masses of these objects were determined. The foundations of astrology
began to crumble when we came to realize how vanishingly small are
the forces exerted by the celestial objects on things and people on
earth—and how very small are the amounts of radiation associated
with them received on earth. The only perceptible and observable effects evident to all of us are produced by the tidal forces caused by the
gravity of the moon and sun. To assume that the sun, moon, and
planets would exert special critical forces upon a baby at birth—forces

that would control the future life of the infant—seems to run counter to common sense. Radiative effects are also dubious. It is even less likely that the stars—each one a sun in its own right and several hundred thousand or more times farther from the earth than our sun—would exercise critical effects on a baby at birth. Some seasonal effects there might well be, for a baby born in northern latitudes in April faces initially a warm summer period; one born in October, a cool winter season.

Before the days of modern astronomy, it made sense to look into     6 possible justifications for astrological beliefs, but it is silly to do so now that we have a fair picture of man's place in the universe.


## Horoscopes: Their Preparation and Interpretation

Astrology claims to foretell the future by studying the positions of the     7 sun, moon, and planets in relation to the constellations of stars along the celestial zodiac at the time of the birth of the subject. This is done through the medium of the *horoscope*. Anyone with a knowledge of beginning astronomy and with an American Nautical Almanac on his desk can proceed to draw one. I have found it a not unpleasant pastime on several occasions. Some of our readers may be interested in learning a little about the technical procedures involved in the preparation of a horoscope. Figures 1 and 2, which are reproduced from the previously mentioned *Scientific Monthly* article, may help to illustrate the procedures.

For a given place on earth—the birthplace of the subject—the ce-     8 lestial sphere is drawn in the standard manner favored by teachers of college beginning-astronomy courses. We see in figure 1 that the local celestial meridian (a great circle passing through the celestial poles, the zenith, and the north and south points on the horizon) and the local celestial horizon (the great circle 90 degrees away from the zenith overhead) divide the sphere into four equal parts. The celestial sphere is further divided by cutting each of the four sections into three equal slices by great circles passing through the north and south points on the local horizon. The ecliptic, which traces the sun's annual path across the sky, is just as it would have been observed at the time and place of birth. The celestial equator at the time and place of birth is also shown, but it plays a small role in horoscope preparation, except to help in plotting the position of the sun, moon, and planets from

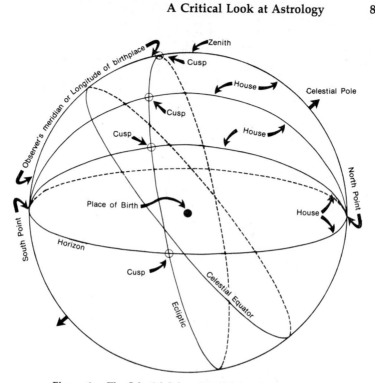

**Figure 1.** *The Celestial Sphere Divided into Twelve Parts.*

the Almanac. The intersections between the twelve great circles and the ecliptic circle mark the *cusps* of the twelve *houses*.

We are now ready to draw the horoscope for the subject at the time and place of birth. We see in figure 2 that the houses and their cusps are drawn on a graph representing the plane of the ecliptic. This is accomplished either with the aid of suitable astrological tables or by the use of some simple spherical trigonometry. The whole business can, if so desired, be prepared nicely as a program for a reasonably fast computer, all of which helps create the impression that astrology is basically scientific in nature. The houses are numbered from 1 to 12 (as shown in figure 2), with house 1 being the one that is about to rise above the local horizon. Standard tables are then used to mark the positions of the zodiacal constellations in the outer margin of the horoscope wheel. The positions of the sun, moon, and planets are shown by their symbols in the houses where they belong.

To sum up: Figure 2 shows a horoscope in which the twelve

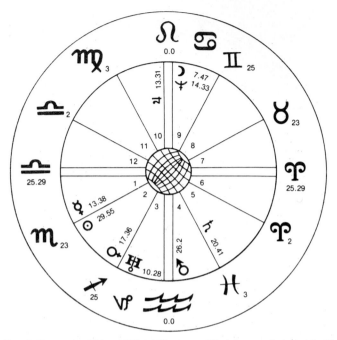

**Figure 2.**    *A Conventional Type of Natal Horoscope. The horoscope is drawn for November 23, 1907, 4 a.m. Eastern-Standard Time, latitude 40°43'N, longitude 73"58'W. The spokes of the wheel mark the limits of the houses; the zodiacal signs and the degrees mark the cusps. The position of the sun, moon, and planets are shown by their symbols.*

houses, with their cusps marked, and the positions of the zodiacal constellations and the sun, moon, and planets are drawn on the plane of the ecliptic, just as they would have been observed at the time and place of birth of the subject.

The type of horoscope shown in figure 2 is a *natal* horoscope. It becomes—according to astrologers—the all-important guide to predicting a person's future. There are other types of horoscopes in use— *judicial* and *hororary* ones, for example—but these need not concern us here.

The abracadabra begins when the astrologer starts to interpret a person's horoscope. The first and most important item is the date of birth, which makes a person an Aries if born between March 21 and April 19, a Taurus if born in the month following, and so on. The date of birth naturally fixes the sign of the zodiac in which the sun is located. It is the important fact that tells whether a person is an Aries, a Pisces, or whatever.

The next important item to note is if the moon or the sun and what    13
planets are in the first house, the one that is about to rise above the
horizon at the time and place of birth. The *ascendant* is defined as the
sign of the zodiac that is associated with the first house. It is obvious
that the time of birth must be precisely known if a proper horoscope
is to be prepared.

Third in line are the positions relative to each other of the sun,    14
moon, and planets in the various houses. The so-called *aspects* are
noted. These indicate which celestial objects are in conjunction (near
to each other in position), and which are 60, 90, 120, or 180 degrees
apart in the heavens. These aspects are important for astrological interpretation, as are the positions of the planets in the houses in which
they are found.

The astrologer can refine his interpretations to any desired ex-    15
tent—the end product becoming increasingly more expensive as further items are added.

How and by whom were these rules of analysis and interpretation    16
of horoscopes first established? They go back to antiquity, basically to
the work of Ptolemy in the second century. Ptolemy wrote two famous
books: *Almagest,* the most complete volume on the motions of the
planets published during the great days of Greek astronomy, and *Tetrabiblos,* the bible of astrology. The *Almagest* is today treated with respect and admiration by historians of science, and it is clearly one of
the great works of the past. However, no astronomer would think of
referring to it today when considering problems relating to the motions
of the planets. *Tetrabiblos* is still the standard reference guide for the
astrologer. Astronomy has been a constantly changing and advancing
science, whereas astrology has essentially stood still since the days of
Ptolemy, in spite of tremendous advances in our knowledge of the
solar system and the universe of stars and galaxies.

## A Scientist's View of Astrology

I continue to ask myself why people believe in astrology. I have asked    17
this same question of many who apparently accept its predictions,
including some of my young students in beginning-astronomy courses.
One answer is simple and straightforward: "It would be nice to know
what the future holds; so why not consult astrological predictions?"
In addition, some people feel that it is useful to have available certain
impersonal rules by which to make personal decisions. Astrology does

provide reasonably definite answers and does yield firm guidelines for personal decisions. Many people find this very comforting indeed.

Believers in astrology have a remarkable faculty for remembering 18 the times when predictions come true and ignoring the occasions when the opposite is the case. And when failure of a prediction does stare us in the face, the astrologer who made the prediction can always get out of trouble by citing the famous dictum that the stars *incline* but do not *compel*.

I have learned that many people who take astrology seriously were 19 first attracted to the field by their reading of the regular columns in the newspapers. It is deplorable that so many newspapers now print this daily nonsense. At the start the regular reading is sort of a fun game, but it often ends up as a mighty serious business. The steady and ready availability of astrological predictions can over many years have insidious influences on a person's personal judgment.

For some people astrology has become a religion. I urge them to 20 examine their beliefs with care. At best, astrology can be looked upon as a self-centered approach to religious beliefs, for it deals primarily with daily affairs and with what is best for a particular person. Astrology, when practiced as completely as possible, takes away from each of us our right and duty to make our own personal decisions.

The most complete religious approach is found in people who have 21 "experienced" astrology, who deep inside themselves "know" astrology to be true and who believe profoundly in effects of cosmic rhythms and "vibrations." I do not know how to convince these people that they are on the wrong track, and hence they will have to go their chosen ways.

Many believers in astrology speak glibly of the forces exerted by 22 the sun, moon, and planets. I should mention here that these forces— according to astrology, critically effective only at the precise moment of birth—can hardly be gravitational or radiative in nature. The known forces that the planets exert on a child at the time of birth are unbelievably small. The gravitational forces at birth produced by the doctor and nurse and by the furniture in the delivery room far outweigh the celestial forces. And the stars are so far away from the sun and earth that their gravitational, magnetic, and other effects are negligible. Radiative effects are sometimes suggested as doing the job. First of all, the walls of the delivery room shield us effectively from many known radiations. And, second, we should bear in mind that our sun is a constantly varying source of radiation, radiating at many different wavelength variations that are by themselves far in excess of the radiation received from the moon and all the planets together.

Many believers in astrology have suggested that each planet issues    23
a different variety of special, as-yet-undetected radiations or "vibrations" and that it is the interplay between these mysterious forces, or quantities, that produces strong effects of an astrological nature. If there is one thing that we have learned over the past fifty years, it is that there is apparently conclusive evidence that the sun, moon, planets, and stars are all made of the same stuff, varieties and combinations of atomic particles and molecules, all governed by uniform laws of physics. We have seen samples of the moon that are similar to rocks on earth, and as a result of our space probes we have been able to study the properties of samples from the surface of Mars. It seems inconceivable that Mars and the moon could produce mysterious waves, or vibrations, that could affect our personalities in completely different ways. It does not make sense to suppose that the various planets and the moon, all with rather similar physical properties, could manage to affect human affairs in totally dissimilar fashions.

There are many other questions that we can ask of the astrologers.    24
For example, why should the precise moment of birth be *the* critical instant in a person's life? Is the instant of conception not basically a more drastic event than the precise moment when the umbilical cord is severed? Would one not expect to find in human beings the same cumulative effects that we associate with growth and environment in plants and animals? Astrology demands the existence of totally unimaginable mechanisms of force and action.

I shall not deal here with statistical tests of astrological predictions    25
or with correlations. . . . At one time I thought seriously of becoming personally involved in statistical tests of astrological predictions, but I abandoned this plan as a waste of time unless someone could first show me that there was some sort of physical foundation for astrology.

What specifically can astronomers and scientists in related fields    26
do to make people realize that astrology is totally lacking in a proper scientific foundation? Speaking out firmly whenever the occasion demands is one way to approach the problem. This is the course that I have steadily pursued, and I hope that astronomers, young and old, will follow me on this path. I have frequently recommended that there be one or two lectures on astrology, somewhat along the lines of this essay, in each introductory astronomy course. The students should

feel free to bring their questions to the instructor. An interesting experiment has been undertaken in the Natural Science 9 course at Harvard University, in which the instructor, Michael Zeilik, is teaching a section called "Astrology—The Space Age Science?" that involves among other things a laboratory exercise in which natal horoscopes are cast.

The fact that some recent textbooks on astronomy contain sections 27 (or chapters) on astrology is a most encouraging development, as is a chapter on the subject in George Abell's book *Exploring the Universe* (third edition, 1974). I have read a similar chapter in an introductory-astronomy textbook now in preparation. Let us have more of this!

## The Psychology of Belief in Astrology

Thirty-five years ago, my good friend and colleague at Harvard University, the late Gordon W. Allport, one of the finest psychologists of 28 his day, drafted at my request a brief statement entitled "Psychologists State Their Views on Astrology." The executive council of the Society for Psychological Study of Social Issues endorsed this statement, which was publicly released, and I wish to close my present essay by reproducing it once again.

> Psychologists find no evidence that astrology is of any value what- 29 soever as an indicator of past, present, or future trends in one's personal life or in one's destiny. Nor is there the slightest ground for believing that social events can be foretold by divinations of the stars. The Society for the Psychological Study of Social Issues therefore deplores the faith of a considerable section of the American public in a magical practice that has no shred of justification in scientific fact.
>
> The principal reason why people turn to astrology and to kindred 30 superstitions is that they lack in their own lives the resources necessary to solve serious personal problems confronting them. Feeling blocked and bewildered they yield to the pleasant suggestion that a golden key is at hand—a simple solution—an ever-present help in time of trouble. This belief is more readily accepted in times of disruption and crisis when the individual's normal safeguards against gullibility are broken down. When moral habits are weakened by depression or war, bewilderment increases, self-reliance is lessened, and belief in the occult increases.
>
> Faith in astrology or in any other occult practice is harmful insofar 31 as it encourages an unwholesome flight from the persistent problems of real life. Although it is human enough to try to escape from the

effort involved in hard thinking and to evade taking responsibility for one's own acts, it does no good to turn to magic and mystery in order to escape misery. Other solutions must be found by people who suffer from the frustrations of poverty, from grief at the death of a loved one, or from fear of economic or personal insecurity.

By offering the public the horoscope as a substitute for honest 32 and sustained thinking, astrologers have been guilty of playing upon the human tendency to take easy rather than difficult paths. Astrologers have done this in spite of the fact that science has denied their claims and in spite of laws in some states forbidding the prophecies of astrology as fraudulent. It is against public interests for astrologers to spread their counsels of flight from reality.

It is unfortunate that in the minds of many people astrology is 33 confused with true science. The result of this confusion is to prevent these people from developing truly scientific habits of thought that would help them understand the natural, social, and psychological factors that are actually influencing their destinies. It is, of course, true that science itself is a long way from a final solution to the social and psychological problems that perplex mankind; but its accomplishments to date clearly indicate that men's destinies are shaped by their own actions in this world. The heavenly bodies may safely be left out of account. Our fates rest not in our stars but in ourselves.

## The Astrologers Reply

[*The Humanist*—the journal in which Bok's article first appeared—published the following replies in a later issue.]

Regarding your magazine's recent and highly publicized scurrilous at- 1 tack on astrology:

Science itself is a highly systematized, rigid series of *learned ex-* 2 *pectations* that tends to exclude that which it cannot explain. The more highly educated and degreed the scientist, the less likely he is to investigate nonconforming phenomena. . . .

Science is the New Superstition. Astrology has been known 3 for at least 4000 years. Science is about 170 years old. Which is the upstart? . . .

This high-handed, unprovoked attack on an ancient study that 4 interested men of the stature of Newton, Kepler, and Galileo sends cold shivers through the spine of anyone who believes that academic pursuits should be a free and open affair, untainted by acrimony or social pressures to desist from the process of study and learning. The chilling effect of the atmosphere of suspicion and mistrust that will be created as a result of this proclamation on the acquisition of knowledge and the determination of the validity of astrology's propositions is a move back to the time of inquisitions, the burning of books, and the hiding of outlawed knowledge from humanity. It is a step back to the Dark Ages.

R. G. Dobbins
Tempe, Ariz.

. . . The serious student of astrology does not condone the use of hor-  1
oscope columns or magazines, since the basis of these prognostications are for sun signs only. The measurable placement of the sun at the time of birth in no way determines the individual choice of career or style of life. Nor is there any relationship between that sign and day-to-day occurrences. Likewise, no astrologer who approaches his study in a rational manner lends any credence to the transit of a particular planet through a certain segment of the zodiac as the causal factor in individual behavior.

The development of astrology is based on the corresponding re-  2
lationship of cosmic forces to human behavior. The time of birth is an arbitrary standard that the astrologer will work with in order to establish a pattern of behavior related to an astronomical framework. Some astrologers do feel that the time of conception would be a more accurate moment with which to work; however, no method has yet been devised to determine that measurement with reliability. The only choice available, then, is the moment of birth, if recorded precisely. . . . In this respect, the position of the planets, sun, moon, the individual place of birth, and their relationship of angularity to one another can give a fairly accurate description of individual potential and behavior traits. The future of the individual, however, is not within the chart. . . .

Much of what has been proposed by astrologers in the past and  3
today is without foundation and should be considered "nonsense," but not until further investigation is made by those confronted with the "irrational" and the tendency to "obscurantism," so that intelligent and informed rebuttal can be made. . . .

Since we, too, take offense with the irrational, we would rather  4
promote astrology and its study as an instrument of developing a more substantial understanding of each individual and thusly creating a

higher awareness of his own potentials. The reflection of fraudulence and incompetence on the contributions of sound astrological practice will only stand in the way of greater human development and thought.

Kathleen Russo, President
Carolyn Bermingham, Vice President
Federation of Scientific Astrologers

The point you've completely overlooked in presenting "Objections to 1 Astrology" [Sept./Oct. 1975] is the possibility of an equally valid viewpoint—one not based on opinion and/or authority (as is most of astrology), but on previously unsuspected real universe data. . . .

While writing a science piece on assignment for *True* magazine in 2 1963, I became interested in the effect of weather on health and joined the American Institute of Medical Climatology. At that time the entire city of Philadelphia was engaged in a three-year study of the moon's influence and effect on rainfall. Under the aegis of the AIMC I began studying the lives of people born at the same time and place to determine whether there was an unaccountable tendency for the same sort of major events to happen to them at the same time or not. If not, then astrology could be discredited once and for all, because it based its credence entirely on the horoscope.

My initial search yielded positive results of "parallelism," which 3 were reported in magazine articles and in my book *Astrology: The Space-Age Science*. Since then, the results have been more refined and specific.

In all fairness—after publishing "Objections to Astrology"—can 4 you refuse to give equal attention to an alternate view that is backed by hard data? I note that neither Bok nor Jerome presented any new evidence or proof to back their assault, but instead relied on opinion and authority—the same mistake they're indirectly accusing the astrologers of committing.

My aim is not to defend astrology, but to present the truth as I 5 have found it. . . . If my cases of parallelism are purely anomalistic and a further study of other genetically unrelated "time twins" yields the exact opposite data, I will be just as satisfied to have it judged once and for all on the facts instead of bias or the emotional opinions of experts who know little or nothing about a subject they're condemning. I hold the same opinion about those who practice and defend astrology without ever checking the basic premise to question its validity.

I agree that astrology has never been conclusively proven on a 6 purely scientific basis, and neither has it been disproven. I'm perfectly willing to present the results of my search in Bart J. Bok's own territory:

fifty "time twins" all born at a time of the five-planet conjunction and total solar eclipse (in the zodiacal sign of Aquarius) on February 4 and 5, 1962, in Tucson, Arizona.

I suggest that the locations and identities of the families of those 7 children be given to one or two distinguished or objective observers to be investigated on their own terms. . . .

Now that *The Humanist* has acted as the catalyst of what must by 8 now be a tidal wave of reaction, pro and con, I'm sure that you—as a responsible journal—will want to examine *all* the facts, not just one set of opinions. You can be certain that before long you will receive the signatures of several thousand astrologers to back a set of arguments citing the opinion and authority of experts in *their* field.

Sooner or later, however, the facts will out. I was not prepared to 9 present my data for another eighteen months, but your action prompts me to make this premature announcement.

Joseph F. Goodavage
Whitefield, Maine

Some scientists and other equally misinformed opponents of astrology 1 assign definitions to astrology and practices to astrologers that have no foundation in fact.

A handful of scientists have proclaimed that there is no scientific 2 basis for astrology and offer as proof their opinion that vast distances from here to a star or planet precludes its exerting "gravitational or other effects." Might not astronomy also be criticized on the same basis? Does any astronomer have first-hand knowledge of a star? Has it been proven that telescopes do not distort their data during transmission? What are the "other effects" to which they so mysteriously allude? Physicists prove the existence of infinitesimal particles by their effects. Is this the special privilege of physicists or are other correlations equally valid?

The scientific basis for astrology has been neither proved nor dis- 3 proved. It has never been thoroughly and scientifically investigated.

Astrology far antedates modern science. Its tenets and beliefs are 4 based on an ancient tradition of symbolic knowledge and empirical verification. Are not the ideas and experiences of men who espoused astrology, from ancient Egypt to the Renaissance, worthy of our consideration?

Astrology is predicated on planetary and stellar correlations, not 5 on their influence. Astrologers believe in an ordered universe, which is cyclical, converging, and synchronized. The pattern of any instant of time is reflected in the angular relationships of heavenly bodies. That pattern permeates the universe, but is simultaneous, not causative. Thus, no legitimate astrologer would advise a client that celestial influences were the cause of his distress. One's reflection in a mirror causes neither a smile nor a frown.

The question of fate vs. free will is not germane in the context of 6 symbolic knowledge. A symbol, though well-defined, has within it a multitude of possibilities. The many facets of a diamond sparkle in countless ways, but a diamond is still a diamond. A human being cannot be other than a human being. Yet, within the framework of his humanness are superb possibilities. Man's free will is augmented by the awareness, nurtured by astrologers, of conditions and potentialities that are internally and externally structured. The individual is not given prescriptions of conduct that are to be followed by all men, nor is he judged by the probabilities of most. He is judged on his own individual potentials, given his own individual solutions and his own individual alternatives. The increasing interest in astrology is the result not of man's weakness but of his reaffirmation of the individual, his power and his uniqueness.

Astrologers do not and cannot predict the future. Man's free will 7 alone determines which solutions and which alternatives he will choose.

Barbara Koval
Reston, Va.

". . . Roger Elliot, astrological author and astrologer-in-residence at *TV* 1 *Times* magazine [said] 'Of course one accepts that there are a great many charlatans about. But surely scientists aren't saying that because something is hard to measure one rejects it? What about Buddhism and Christianity? What about love?'

" 'After all I'm not claiming that planets actually *influence* events. 2 I see the process as analagous to the train Departures Board at Victoria Station. It tells you what the trains are going to do, but it doesn't actually control them. Now why, precisely, the planets should fulfill this role is, indeed, a subject for speculation.'

" 'Anyway, in the last analysis, even if it emerged that astrology 3 weren't *factually* true, I think it is still valuable if it has a personal truth for the individual. I mean, the truth of, say, David Hockney or Michelangelo will always be essentially personal, won't it?' . . ." —"Mandrake," *London Sunday Telegraph*, Sept. 7, 1975.

# Questions

1.  Evaluate Bok's first three paragraphs as an opening. If you think they are effective, specify the strengths. If you think they are weak, specify the weaknesses.

2.  In paragraph 5 Bok writes:

    > To assume that the sun, moon, and planets would exert special critical forces upon a baby at birth—forces that would control the future life of the infant— seems to run counter to common sense. Radiative effects are also dubious. It is even less likely that the stars—each one a sun in its own right and several hundred thousand or more times farther from the earth than our sun—would exercise critical effects on a baby at birth.

    Do you think Bok here offers convincing objections against astrology?

3.  Why, according to Bok, do believers in astrology persist in their belief even when predictions fail to come true? Can you think of other reasons for belief in astrological predictions?

4.  In paragraph 20 Bok says that "for some people astrology has become a religion," and in paragraph 21 he says that "the most complete religious approach is found in people who have 'experienced' astrology, who deep inside themselves 'know' astrology to be true and who believe profoundly in effects of cosmic rhythms and 'vibrations.' " Is Bok in effect saying that if a person believes that the planets and stars exert an influence on behavior he or she takes astrology for a religion? Would it be equally fair, then, to say that if a person believes that genes exert an influence on behavior such a person takes biology for a religion?

5.  In paragraphs 22 and 23 Bok offers reasons for rejecting belief in astrology. How compelling do you find the reasons?

6.  We reprint some of the letters astrologers wrote in reply to Bok's essay. In your opinion, do any of the responses offer reasonable arguments against Bok's attack on astrology? If so, which ones?

Priscilla Costello

# Astrology, Science or Abracadabra?

$I$ am, I suspect, the only professional astrologer ever to 1
graduate from Wellesley College. As such, I thought it might be of
interest to Wellesley women to share my understanding of what astrology is and what I do, particularly because of the widespread public
misunderstanding of it and because of its great potential usefulness to
the counseling professions.

Most people think that it consists entirely of sun-sign newspaper 2
predictions, each valid for one-twelfth of the human race on any given
day. If this were all there were to astrology, its dismissal by the intelligent would be understandable. But newspaper-column astrology
bears about the same relation to the vastly complex discipline of astrology as magazine-ad recipes, featuring some brand's marshmallows
or condensed milk, do to gourmet cooking done by France's best chefs.
Some of the elements are superficially the same, but the ingredients
are altered for mass-market consumption and hence lack the flavour,
freshness, and originality of the genuine article.

Astrology is both an art and a science. The scientific component 3
is in the complicated mathematics and in the astronomical knowledge
necessary to erect a chart. The art is in the synthesis of a multitude of
factors and symbols into a coherent and accurate statement of their
relevance to the individual.

The scientific part of astrology demands "left brain" ability; the 4
understanding of the symbols and the perception of their *meaning*
draws on the right side of the brain. Thus the master astrologer must
be adept in *both* types of thinking. Our society is only just beginning
to appreciate right-brain thinking, feminine and intuitive as it is. A
masculine-dominant society, both literally and intellectually, accepts
the astronomy part of astrology, but not its totality, in spite of the fact
that astrology is the mother of astronomy and that for thousands of

Priscilla Costello, a teacher of English and drama in Toronto, has had a second
career as a professional astrologer. An alumna of Wellesley College, she wrote
the essay reprinted here for the Wellesley College alumnae magazine.

years the two were one. It was only during what is ironically called the Enlightenment that the celestial bodies became astronomical facts only and were divorced from any meaning other than the simple material fact of their existence.

Though almost all the great astronomers were astrologers as well  5 (Copernicus, Kepler, Galileo, and Sir Isaac Newton, in particular), after the early part of the eighteenth century, astrology fell into disrepute. Forced to go underground because the church considered it heretical, and deprived of the best scientific minds, as the astrologer-astronomers became more and more materialistic and scientifically minded, astrology fell into the hands of quacks, gypsies and hucksters. Only at the end of the last century and into this century is astrology being revived.

Astrology can be defined as the calculation and meaningful inter-  6 pretation of the positions and motions of the heavenly bodies, and their correlation with human experience. The basic tool of delineation is the horoscope, a snapshot of the planetary positions in the zodiac at the moment of the individual's birth, constructed using as coordinates the longitude and latitude of the birthplace, and the time of birth. It is difficult to explain why this correlation exists, though some scientifically minded astrologers have postulated electro-magnetic fields of influence whereby the planets affect the earth using the sun as intermediary, the specific vehicle being the solar winds.

Another scientific suggestion is that it is through the mediating  7 effect of water, as a kind of "universal solvent" that we are connected subtly to cosmic forces. But I would like to put forth another, more psychological explanation. That is Carl Jung's concept of synchronicity, which suggests that an idea, person, invention, or institution bears the stamp of the moment in which it comes into manifestation.

Jung, one of the most important theorists in psychology of this century, proposed that this principle accounted for meaningful connections between phenomena occuring simultaneously, though far apart, and having no apparent cause and effect relationship. Thus the stellar map may be meaningfully related to the life of the human being born at that moment. And, in fact, I have found it astoundingly accurate in confirming the individual's perception of life emphases, issues, and problems, as well as in encouraging the expression of talents and abilities suggested by the chart. 8

People seem to be highly aware of the areas of challenge and difficulty the chart shows in their lives, but often lacking in faith in the talents the chart also indicates. One of the important functions of an astrological counselor is to encourage the development and expression of such abilities. 9

One of the widespread misconceptions regarding astrology is that the sun, moon, and eight planetary bodies are somehow controlling the individual and, like a puppeteer pulling the puppet's strings, are manipulating the individual's actions and behavior. Such an idea is distasteful to the psychologically oriented twentieth-century mind, which prefers to deal with the issue of motives for human behavior in terms of inner needs and drives, and ascribes a great deal of free will to the individual. Given the extent to which people can be unconscious of their real goals and can be subject to emotions and moods, how free they really are may be questionable. In any case, I see the concept of "influence" or "control" from the planets as erroneous. I think that it certainly looks that way, but I do not think that that is actually what is happening. I would like to present as an explanation of "influence" from the planets the findings of the "New Physics," of which the public is generally unaware. 10

The "New Physics" is revolutionizing our perspective on apparently solid, material phenomena. It states that the observer alters what is observed simply by the act of observation. 11

So perhaps we should just admit the subjective nature of our world view, acknowledge that we *select* what we wish to believe about the world and how it operates, and be willing to investigate the awesome and unexplainable connections between "out there" where the stars and planets seem to be, and "down here," where we seem to live, 12

*In the same way that man in this diagram stands in the universe, so the universe is within man. Each is a reflection of the other, as the world's astrologers see it.*

move, and have awareness. I have always felt that either everything has meaning, even including the finer details ("the very hairs of your head are all numbered." Matthew 10:30), though our intellects may have difficulty comprehending it, or nothing has any meaning. It cannot be partial or both! I freely admit that I have chosen to believe the former, and that my studies in astrology, as well as in other fields, are attempts to understand the grand design of the whole.

Astrology provides the most complex and sophisticated psychological model yet known. Some of the multitude of factors which are used to interpret a horoscope include the eight planets, plus the sun and moon; the twelve signs of the zodiac, which are archetypes representing typical roles or approaches to life; and the twelve "houses" 13 or sectors of the wheel, each representing significant areas of experi- ence. All of these factors, let us remember, are symbols, and hence have many meanings, from the grossly obvious to the more subtle. Intense study of these symbols can enable the astrologer to "enter the reality" of the client, to understand his/her world view, and to ap- preciate his/her difficulties. As Jung said, "As the mind explores the symbol, it is led to ideas that lie beyond the grasp of reason."

Now, the nature of a symbol is that it is simultaneously a thing  14 in itself and it also represents some thing or things other than itself. What the specific symbol stands for can be a variety of things at once, or can be one thing at one time and another thing at another time. Consequently, the astrological counselor must devote much time to examining the spectrum of meanings possible for each of the astrol- ogical symbols and the variety of possible manifestations in the phys- ical world.

I believe that one can*not* specify *exactly* how the potentials of these  15 combinations of symbols have been lived out in an individual's life— and indeed it does not matter! For the psychological effect of a number of different events is likely to be similar. For example, one particular configuration suggests a father absent during childhood and youth, perhaps because he traveled frequently or perhaps because the parents divorced and the child lived with the mother, or possibly because the father either disappeared or died. Alternatively, the father might have been present, but either weak, withdrawn, or ineffective. In any of these cases, the person in question will no doubt have difficulty un- derstanding and integrating masculine qualities into the psyche. He/ she will probably have difficulty relating not only to the father, but at a later time, to other males, particularly those in positions of authority (teachers, bosses, possibly her husband). The astrologer *must* talk with the client in order to verify the specifics, but then go on to the more important task of exploring the degree to which the client is consciously resolving the problems suggested by the various "signatures" in the chart.

I feel that the purpose of a reading is to understand one's life  16 challenges and potential, to provide an opportunity for self-reflection and life evaluation, as well as to confirm one's intuitive sense of what one's life is about.

The age at which one consults an astrologer is significant too, for  17 with age usually comes greater self-knowledge and greater self-inte- gration. Thus, the potential for the client to have resolved many of the difficulties suggested by the natal chart is much greater. One can and does work out the challenges suggested by the birth map—in fact, one is *supposed* to! Astrology should *not* provide excuses for maintaining certain character traits ("I can't help it; I'm a Scorpio, and that's the way all Scorpios are!"), but the impetus to overcome the negative patterns and counter-productive behavioral traits. Rightly used, astrology puts the power firmly back into the hands of the individual, and encourages him/her to take responsibility for the way in which he/she is experiencing the world.

Now to deal with the question of prediction. The public mistakenly 18 believes that the only purpose of astrology is to predict events (those sun-sign newspaper columns again). It *is* possible to look ahead to upcoming planetary aspects to natal chart positions and speculate about the future. However, just as the exact manifestation of potentials in the horoscope is impossible to pinpoint using astrology alone, so too it is impossible to say exactly *what* will transpire and, more importantly, what the individual's *response* to it will be. To discuss future probabilities is much like giving a weather report. Yes, there is a 70 percent chance of rain tomorrow, but whether you choose to stay inside and try to avoid the rainstorm, or bravely face the elements (armed with raincoat and umbrella, having been alerted by the weatherman), is very much up to you. It is valuable as well to have a time frame for a period of profound inner or outer changes; just knowing that a period of transition will by and large be completed by, for instance, September or October, can give one the courage to face the now. But only a thorough examination of first the levels on which the individual has experienced the birth map's potentials to date in his/her life *and* his/her past responses to similar conditions can give insight into the person's more likely *future* responses. And, the more conscious one becomes of one's character, particularly one's hidden or "shadow" side, as Jung called it, the more likely that potentially difficult times will bring not challenges but rewards. So again, the outcome rests with the individual.

The most important way in which you can experience the validity 19 of astrology is through having a session with a well trained astrologer. Unfortunately, psychologically sophisticated, intelligent, and highly ethical astrological counselors are hard to find, lost as they often are amongst fortune tellers, "psychic readers," and media types who deal mostly with those sun-sign predictions. However, the presence of quacks or incompetents in the medical profession doesn't deter us from seeking competent medical advice. I would suggest the following as a guide in finding good astrological counseling.

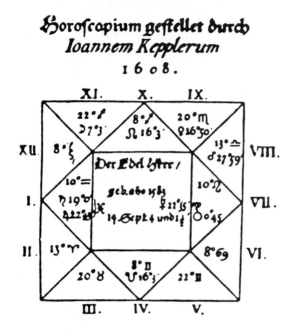

*The square horoscope was in vogue in the Middle Ages.*

First, just as you would do in searching for a doctor or a lawyer, get recommendations from friends who have experienced fine readings. Get at least two. Ask the astrologer for references or for his/her credentials. And ask *more* questions! 20

How many years has he/she studied? With whom? Does he/she have a degree? From where? What kind of psychological or spiritual background does the astrologer have? What conferences has he/she attended, and what professional organizations does he/she belong to? (Important organizations in the United States are the American Federation of Astrologers, which certifies astrologers who have passed their exams, publishes a variety of astrological writings, and holds biennial conventions; the National Council for Geocosmic Research; and the National Astrological Society.) 21

Next, I myself would be less likely to choose an astrologer who advertised in the newpapers or through the media or who participated in "psychic fairs." Finally, what is the astrologer charging? Fifty or sixty dollars an hour is the general rate, which takes into account the time the astrologer spends before the reading, computing and ana- 22

*A 16th-century woodcut of the zodiac.*

lyzing the chart, as well as the time involved in actually giving the reading. And if you are not satisfied with the reading, DON'T pay for it. It is well to bear in mind also that if the reading doesn't quite "fit," it may be due to an inaccurate birth time. Since every four minutes affects the exactness of the horoscope, establishing your time within as narrow limits as possible is crucially important.

I am often asked how *I* became an astrologer. I can't remember a    23
time when I was *not* interested in the subject, though I never dreamed while at Wellesley that I would become a professional. I did begin studying it seriously while there, but I was also exploring a number of other areas, particularly literature, mythology and Eastern religions, and astrology was pretty far down the list.

But after graduation, when I returned to Canada and embarked    24 on a teaching career, I spent enough time pursuing the elusive planets, signs, and houses to begin giving readings to friends in 1971. Not until 1979, though, did I turn professional, and by then I had begun traveling extensively to study with well-known astrologers and to attend conferences. In Toronto, I teach astrology now, and also lecture and give workshops, in addition to my principal career as an English teacher in a secondary school.

Every astrologer specializes in a certain area or areas. In my prac-   25
tice, one of the areas I concentrate on is individual counseling. Here the client's emotional, mental, and spiritual potentials and development are evaluated, as well as, in some cases, physical conditions.

Another specialty of mine is relationship counseling, usually with   26
both partners present, in which we discuss the relationship's potential and present dynamics. One especially interesting facet of this is looking at charts of an entire family, a process which is extremely helpful in clarifying issues between family members and reasons why certain people in the family are more sympathetic with some than with others within the family unit.

But these are only two applications of astrology. Since astrology,   27
far from being a simplistic system of predicting events, takes as its realm the condition of man on *every* level, one area within it focuses on the physical level particularly. Medical astrology is an examination of potentially weak organs or systems or physiological processes within the body, and the relationship between personality, stress, and disease. I would remind skeptics that Hippocrates, the father of modern medicine, said that "A physician without a knowledge of astrology cannot rightly call himself a physician."

Another division of astrology is vocational, which attempts to har-   28
monize personality and profession by matching inherent potentials or natural abilities with careers that promise a high degree of satisfaction. Mundane astrology is the application of the principle of cyclic development not only to people but also to businesses, institutions, and political entities. (Someone in politics knows more than he is telling, I suspect; otherwise why would both President Reagan and Prime Minister Pierre Elliott Trudeau of Canada refuse to give out their birth times? As well, Reagan was sworn in as governor of California at a most peculiar time: shortly after midnight. Would his astrologer have advised him that this was an auspicious time? No one will tell.)

Astrology, in sum, could play an important role in restoring the   29
psychic balance within modern man between reason and logic and faith and intuition. A conscious mind that de-emphasizes the mystery and

```
PLANET SIGN LONG   ' 4" HSE DECL  LAT  GEOCENTRIC DIS SPEED
                                       N-NODE S-NODE 29 58'19"
SUN    Vir 15°28' 4"  11  5N44  0 00
MOON   Sag 22 49 22   11 28S18  5S 3 09Ar25 09Li25  8 11°59'·>SLOW
MERC   Lib  0  4 55   11  0N23  0N28 27Le38 03Li27 13 98'14"
VENU F Vir 11 30  6   11  8N33  1N24 09Le55 21Li18 74 33
MARS E Cpr  3 26 30    1 27S 7  3S42 29Ca59 24Li27 86 28 33
JUPI   Scp  0 14 23    1 18S36  1N 2 18Ca10 27Sa46 14 10 58
SATU R Aqu 21  2 12R     15S50  1S25 27Ca05 17Cp22 70 -3 53
URAN D Leo 17 27 55   10 16N14  0N39 16Ce16 10Sa15 47 -3 24
NEPT   Tau  2 47  3R   8 10N45  1S48 11Le33 09Aq21 87 -1 1
PLUT D Tau 23 36 24R   8  4N 3 14S29 20Ca34 18Cp00  9 0-20
ASC    Lib 25  5.6     7
MC     Leo  0  1.7    10 20N 9
NODE*  Ari  8 39.8     6
PFOR   Aqu  2 26.9
VERTEX Tau 27 34.2
EASTPT Scp  4 29.0

R=RULE   D=DETRIMENT
E=EXALTED F=FALL
*=TRUE NODE
Θ> ANGLE= 97.35°

        CARD FIX MUT              MUTUAL RECEPTION
FIRE     1   2   1                MERC AND VENU
EARTH    1   2   2
AIR      1   1   0
WATER    0   1   0
```

```
      4 | 2
     ---+---
      3 | 1
```

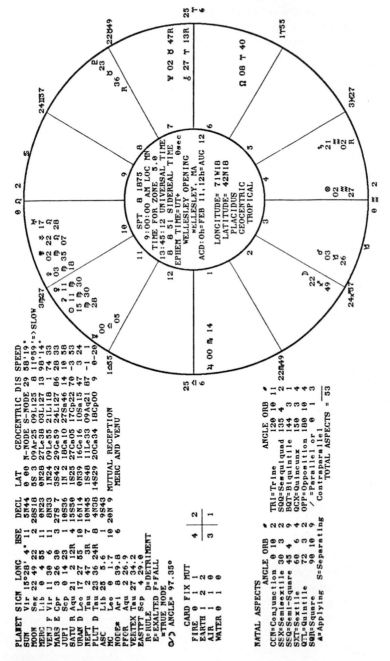

```
              SPT 8 1875
          9:00:00 AM LOC MN
          TIME FOR ZONE 5.0
       13:45:12 UNIVERSAL TIME
        EPHEM TIME=UT+ 0sec
         8 8 51 SIDEREAL TIME
          WELLESLEY OPENING
            WELLESLEY, MA
       ACD:0h=FEB 11,12h=AUG 12
          LONGITUDE= 71W18
          LATITUDE= 42N18
             PLACIDUS
            GEOCENTRIC
             TROPICAL
```

**NATAL ASPECTS**

| | ANGLE | ORB | # | | ANGLE | ORB | # |
|---|---|---|---|---|---|---|---|
| CCN=Conjunction | 0 | 10 | 11 | TRI=Trine | 120 | 10 | 11 |
| SEX=Semisextile | 30 | 3 | 2 | SQQ=Sesquiquad | 135 | 4 | 2 |
| SSQ=Semisquare | 45 | 4 | 9 | BQT=Biquintile | 144 | 3 | 1 |
| SXT=Sextile | 60 | 6 | 4 | QCX=Quincunx | 150 | 3 | 4 |
| QTL=Quintile | 72 | 3 | 2 | OPP=Opposition | 180 | 10 | 4 |
| SQR=Square | 90 | 10 | 9 | / =Parallel or | 0 | 1 | 3 |

A=Applying  S=Separating   / =Parallel   Contraparallel

TOTAL ASPECTS = 53

| | SUN | MOON | MERCURY | VENUS | MARS | JUPITER | SATURN | URANUS | NEPTUNE | PLUTO | ASC | MC |
|---|---|---|---|---|---|---|---|---|---|---|---|---|
| MOON | SQR 7 21S | | | | | | | | | | | |
| MERC | | SQR 7 16A | | | | | | | | | | |
| VENU | CON 3 58A | | | | | | | | | | | |
| MARS | | | SQR 3 22A | TRI 8 04S | | | | | | | | |
| JUPI | SSQ 0 14S | | SSX 0 09A | SSQ 3 44A | SXT 3 12S | | | | | | | |
| SATU | | SXT 1 47S | | | SSQ 2 36A | TRI 9 12S | | | | | | |
| URAN | SSX 1 60A | TRI 5 21S | SSQ 2 23A | | SQQ 0 59S | QTL 0 46S | OPP 3/34A | | | | | |
| NEPT | SQQ 2 19A | TRI 9 58A | QCX 2 42A | TRI 8 43S | TRI 0 39S | OPP 2/33A | QTL 0 15A | | | | | |
| PLUT | TRI 8 08A | QCX 0 47A | TRI 6 29S | | | | SQR 2 34S | SQR 6 08A | | | | |
| ASC | | SXT 2 16 | | SSQ 1 24 | | CON 5/09 | TRI 4 03 | | OPP 7 41 | QCX 1 29 | | |
| MC | SSQ 0 26 | BQT 1 12 | SXT 0 03 | SSQ 3 32 | | SQR 0 13 | | | SQR 2 45 | | SQR 4 56 | |
| NODE | | | OPP 8 35 | QCX 2 50 | SQR 5 13 | | SSQ 2 38 | TRI 8 48 | | SSQ 0 03 | | TRI 8 38 |

*** MID POINTS SORTED INTO ZODIACAL SEQUENCE ***

| | | | | | | | | | | |
|---|---|---|---|---|---|---|---|---|---|---|
| ♄/♇ 07♈19 | ♆/♇ 13♉12 | ♇/M 26♊49 | ♀/♇ 17♋33 | ♅ 17♌28 | ♃/M 15♍08 | ☉/♃ 07♎51 | ☽/♀ 02♏10 | ♂/♃ 01♐50 | ☽/♄ 21♑56 | ☽/♇ 08♓13 |
| ☊ 08 40 | ♄/♅ 19 15 | ☉/☊ 27 04 | ☉/♇ 19 32 | ♀/M 20 46 | ☉ 15 28 | ☽/M 11 26 | ☉/☽ 04 09 | ☉/♄ 03 15 | ♂/♄ 27 14 | ♂/♇ 13 31 |
| ☊/⚷ 17 56 | ♇ 23 36 | ♀/⚷ 04♋22 | A/⚷ 26 09 | ☉/M 22 45 | ☿/♀ 20 48 | ☿/A 12 35 | ♀/♂ 07 28 | ☿/♄ 10 34 | ♃/⚷ 28 44 | ♄/☊ 14 51 |
| ♆/☊ 20 43 | M/☊ 04♊21 | ☿/☊ 04 22 | ☿/♇ 26 51 | ♀/♅ 29 29 | ♅/A 21 17 | ☿/♃ 15 10 | ☉/♂ 09 27 | ☽ 22 49 | ☽/☊ 15♒45 | ♄/⚷ 24 08 |
| ⚷ 27 13 | ♅/☊ 13 04 | ♅/♇ 05 32 | ♆/A 28 56 | ☿/M 00♍03 | ☉/☿ 22 46 | ♂/M 16 44 | ☽/☿ 11 27 | ♄/A 23 04 | ♄ 21 02 | ♄/♆ 26 55 |
| ♆/⚷ 00♉00 | M/⚷ 13 37 | ☉/⚷ 06 21 | M 00♌02 | ☉/♅ 01 28 | ♃/♅ 23 51 | ☽/♅ 20 09 | ☿/♂ 16 46 | ♃/♄ 25 38 | ♂/☊ 21 03 | |
| ♇/☊ 01 08 | ♆/M 16 24 | ♀/♆ 07 09 | ♃/♆ 01 31 | ☿/♅ 08 46 | ☿ 00♎05 | A 25 06 | ☽/A 23 57 | ☽/♂ 28 08 | ☽/⚷ 25 01 | |
| ♆ 02 47 | ♅/⚷ 22 20 | ☉/♆ 09 08 | ♅/M 08 45 | ♀ 11 30 | ♀/A 03 18 | ♂/♅ 25 27 | ☽/♃ 26 32 | ♂ 03♑26 | ☽/♆ 27 48 | |
| ♇/⚷ 10 25 | ♀/☊ 25 05 | ☿/⚷ 13 39 | ♇/A 09 21 | A/M 12 34 | ☉/A 05 17 | ♃/A 27 40 | ♂/A 29 16 | A/☊ 16 53 | ♂/⚷ 00♓20 | |
| ♄/M 10 32 | ♅/♆ 25 07 | ☿/♆ 16 26 | ♃/♇ 11 55 | ☉/♀ 13 29 | ♀/♃ 05 52 | ♃ 00♏14 | ♀/♄ 01♐16 | ♃/☊ 19 27 | ♂/♆ 03 07 | |

JULIAN DAY # = 2406140.073056    MEAN OBLIQUITY OF ECLIPTIC = 23°27'20"    SIDEREAL AYANAMSHA (SVP) = Pic 6°59'46"

*A modern computer chart done for the time young women began arriving on the Wellesley campus: 9:00 A.M. on September 8, 1875. There is some question about the exact time of the College's establishment: when the charter was first applied for (March 17, 1870), when the charter was revised (March 7, 1873), this date, or two weeks later, when classes actually began. In any case, there are some common emphases in these charts. One is a strong emphasis on the signs Virgo/Pisces. Virgo includes the concept of service, and Pisces incorporates compassionate and unselfish giving to mankind; hence the motto of the College, "Not to be ministered unto but to minister" seems appropriate! Also, all the charts suggest enormous long-term potential to generate resources.*

wonder of life, that sees man as only matter, that entertains no purpose or progress of the soul, is dangerously imbalanced. It is no wonder that our civilization, reflecting this imbalance, continues to mistreat the environment, and creates and stockpiles such terrible weapons that their capacity to destroy boggles the imagination. Most of the deeply satisfying experiences in life—falling in love, the miracle of birth, moments of religious aspiration or awakening—have little to do with our conscious and rational side, but with the side that women instinctively understand and can respond to. And, as astrologer Stephen Arroyo comments,

> In our own individual lives, astrology can serve the purpose of guiding us through various initiations, transformations, and crucial transitions. It can provide us with that cosmic framework and meaning which infuses every major experience with deep significance. . . .

We would do well to investigate and accept any such means of restoring wholeness on the individual and on the collective level. Many find that no single established structure of religion, guidance, or healing in our society provides this balance. It may be that astrology is an important other way of gaining psychic integration, a way that confirms our deepest intuitive awareness of the roles we play in our earthly lives, and enables us to stand in awe, gazing out into the Infinite, expectant, as stars and suns wait to tell us their message.

# Questions

1. This essay appeared in the alumnae magazine of Wellesley College. Given the audience, do you think the opening sentence is effective? Would it be equally effective as the opening sentence of an introductory book on astrology? Why?

2. In paragraph 3 Costello says that astrology is "both an art and a science." If you were asked to explain this point in a few sentences, what would you say? (The question does *not* ask if you believe that astrology is an art and a science; rather, it asks what someone probably means when he or she says something is an art and a science.)

3. In the rest of the essay does Costello do much to clarify her assertion that astrology is an art and a science? Does she emphasize the art or the science, or neither? Explain.

4. In paragraph 4 Costello calls upon a distinction between "right

brain" or "feminine" and "left brain" or "masculine" thinking. Why? What is her point? Do you consider the distinction "science" or "abracadabra"? If you have read Evelyn Fox Keller's essay (page 920), what do you suppose her response would be?

5.  In paragraph 5 Costello points out that "almost all the great astronomers were astrologers as well." Whom does she name? Evaluate this argument.

6.  In paragraph 6 Costello says that "it is difficult to explain" why there is a correlation between the position of the planets at an individual's birth and the individual's later experience. Does her admission of uncertainty undermine her case? Or, paradoxically, does it increase your confidence in her?

7.  In paragraphs 11 and 12 Costello, drawing on "the New Physics," says that "we *select* what we wish to believe about the world and how it operates." If you have read Thomas Kuhn's essay (page 829), consider whether Costello's assumption and her way of proceeding are in accord with Kuhn's description of the ways in which scientists proceed.

8.  On what does Costello base her confidence in astrology? In paragraph 8 she says that she has found "the stellar map . . . astoundingly accurate in confirming the individual's perception of life emphases, issues, and problems, as well as in encouraging the expression of talents and abilities suggested by the chart." Does she support her assertion? If not, should she do so? Why?

9.  In paragraph 18 Costello says, "The more conscious one becomes of one's character, particularly one's hidden or 'shadow' side, as Jung called it, the more likely that potentially difficult times will bring not challenges but rewards." Do you think this generalization is true? If not, why not? If you think it is true, what instance can you offer from your own experience?

10. In paragraph 22 Costello advises that if you consult an astrologer—who will probably charge about fifty or sixty dollars an hour—and "you are not satisfied with the reading, DON'T pay for it." Would you offer that advice to a friend who was not satisfied with a doctor's advice, or a plumber's work, or an auto mechanic's work? To put it another way, if one were to follow Costello's advice, what action by a doctor or plumber or mechanic might one confidently predict? Is there reason to expect otherwise from an astrologer?

## J. H. Plumb

# The Stars in Their Day

$A$re you Taurus or Gemini, Pisces or Capricorn? Does your   1
eye furtively glance at the column headed "The Stars and You" and
are you relieved when you read that you could have a "speculative
benefit" or worried when you see "changeability in relationships may
pose problems"? Or does a slightly sheepish, shamefaced smile flutter
across your face as you turn hurriedly to another page in your newspaper?

I suspect it strikes few readers that the silly astrological columns   2
are the sad end of an extraordinary human enterprise stretching back
to the very dawn of history. The persistence of the belief that the movements of the stars are related to man's destiny goes back to the very
earliest days of the neolithic revolution, if not beyond. And the fact
that popular, non-elite newspapers in America, England, France, Germany, Italy, India, indeed in all non-communist countries, find it
worthwhile to publish astrological columns day in day out, indicates
the persistence of that belief. And as well as popular astrologers, high
priests of the cult still exist, dedicated astrologers, masters of intricate
calculations, who cast horoscopes and predict the fate of individuals
with the conviction of a scientist, men and women who believe as
intensely in the stars as the magicians of ancient China.

True, over the last three centuries the belief in the stars has steadily   3
weakened and the market for horoscopes dwindled. With the coming
of industrial society and the scientific revolution which has given us
an accurate knowledge of the stars, astrology has become the plaything
of the credulous and the ill-educated. But two hundred years ago its
power in the West was still strong: both Cagliostro and Casanova cast
horoscopes and interpreted the stars in order to bamboozle aristocrats,
merchants and attractive women. A further hundred years back, however, the stars were still playing a vital part in human affairs, although
historians rarely pay any attention to this aspect of seventeenth-century belief.

J[ohn] H[arold] Plumb, born in England in 1911, was professor of modern English
history at the University of Cambridge until his retirement. He also taught at
universities in the United States.

The Earl of Shaftesbury, the violent Whig who nearly toppled  4
Charles II from his throne by exploiting the hysteria of the Popish Plot
in 1678–1679, believed absolutely in astrology. John Locke, the ration-
alist philosopher, lived in his household, but made no impression it
would seem on this aspect of Shaftesbury's beliefs. A Dutch doctor
who dabbled in the occult had cast his horoscope and so, Shaftesbury
thought, foretold all that would happen to him. Nor was Shaftesbury
an isolated crank. The great German general, Wallenstein, who dominated the Thirty Years' War, took no action, military or political, without consulting the stars, and no one thought him either eccentric or
pagan.

Astrology in these centuries lived quite comfortably with Chris-  5
tianity. Many kings kept astrologers at Court and consulted them regularly. Dr. John Dee, the great Elizabethan magician, who consulted
the spirits in a polished obsidian mirror which he had somehow or
other acquired from Aztec Mexico via Spain, also used the stars to
predict the future. He created a sense of fear, but the great Elizabethans
consulted him and he died comfortably enough in his bed and not at
the stake. Magic he might practice, but even in that age, terrified as
it was by the fear of witchcraft, he survived. The stars were beyond
the Devil and his works. They belonged to the mechanism of the universe, a piece of God's handiwork: therefore good and open to interpretation. And, in this respect, Catholic and Protestant did not differ,
and a belief in astrology covered all creeds and heresies: Protestant,
Catholic, Jew and Moslem did not differ in this particular. And in this
respect, at least, they were at one with the Hindus and Chinese, and
with the remoter civilizations of the Middle East. The stars dominated
the lives of Sumerians, Akkadians, Babylonians and Egyptians.

The greatest historian of classical China, Ssŭ-ma Chi'en, gloried  6
in the title of the Grand Astrologer, possibly because the earliest archives to be kept systematically were those which dealt with astrological matters. Indeed the Chinese not only consulted the stars but
devised the most elaborate instruments to determine their precise conjunction at a precise moment of time. One of the most elaborate and
complex astronomic clocks of antiquity was built by the Chinese so
that the position of the stars, even if the heavens were cloudy, would
be known, should the empress conceive when the emperor paid a visit
to her bed, for Heaven would naturally be disclosing its hand at such
an auspicious moment, either to foretell happiness or doom.

Long before the Chinese had developed their elaborate system of  7
star-gazing, the Assyrians and Egyptians had been studying the heav-

ens just as intensely. Of all civilizations, perhaps, the Assyrian was the most addicted to astrology and no king of Babylon would act in minor, let alone major, matters without consulting them. A great reference library was built up in their palaces, so that prediction and result could be studied and referred to. By the time Babylon fell the Assyrian astrologers and divinators had reference material which dated back nearly a thousand years. The ancient Egyptians too studied the stars and believed in their benign or malevolent influence. Nor was belief in astrology derived from a single center for, without any contact with Europe, the Mayas in the Yucatán and Guatemala built huge observatories and watched the stars. From China to Peru throughout many millennia, men's lives were star-haunted and the heavens wrote in cryptic symbols the fate of nations and the destiny of men.

So those foolish columns in the newspapers have a long, long  8
history; a history heaving with portent. The stars have terrified men, made them jubilant, provided dreams of ecstasy and fear and, above all, strengthened a sense of unalterable fate, not only in the heart of the peasant and craftsman, but also in emperors and kings, priests and soldiers. It is easy, of course, to see how relevant initially the position of the stars was to all communities which depended on the soil, for changes in the constellations indicated the coming of spring or winter or foretold that rains would come in Yucatán or the Nile flood in Egypt, events which, if delayed or inadequate, could mean famine. To the peasant the sky and the seasons were in mysterious harmony, yet capable of discord. The constellations might appear and yet the rains, in spite of sacrifice and religious observance, stay away; and then for years the juxtaposition could be close. The will of the gods and the stars were interconnected but not obvious: they needed to be studied with intense and minute care, and only then could they be used safely for prediction.

But humanity's need for the stars goes deeper than the need to  9
discern the changing seasons or the coming of rain and water, deeper than the need to foretell the fate of kings, or the hopes and fears of men. There is a need in man to know and to rationalize his universe through magic and through very precise and detailed knowledge. He derives a sense of security from knowledge, whether it be the very precise and detailed knowledge of territory, of its trees and flowers and animals, such as the most primitive tribes of men acquire, or from the complexities of the modern science of physics or biology. His aim has always been both to control his environment and to banish anxiety. Man has always been, as it were, scientifically orientated even if his

earlier and more primitive sciences did not work very well. Only gradually did he learn the precise way to investigate and control (perhaps one should rather say exploit) his environment, but he put the same intellectual effort, the same passion to observe and to accumulate knowledge into his earlier attempts.

Magicians, astrologers, were but mankind's first scientists. They were men of great intelligence and keen observation, no different in quality from Newton or Rutherford and, essentially, dedicated to the same task. Many of their facts were right and beautifully observed; their pursuits led them to invent instruments of great ingenuity. What was wrong were their premises. And in the vaporings of a Katrina one sees the pathetic end of a once majestic and comprehensive study of destiny: a science which for thousands of years interpreted men's hopes and fears and which seemed to give them a chance of evading disaster and controlling their fate.

10

# Questions

1.  Plumb mentions, in the second paragraph, that newspapers in communist countries do not publish astrological columns. Why do they not?
2.  In his last sentence Plumb speaks of "the vaporings" of a modern astrologer. What are the connotations of "vaporings"? In this context, what does the name "Katrina" suggest? Do you detect male bias here?
3.  Defenders of astrology often use as arguments in its favor the persistence of belief in astrology over thousands of years and the eminent scientists known to have been astrologers. How does Plumb treat these undeniable facts?

Stephen Jay Gould

# Women's Brains

In the Prelude to *Middlemarch*, George Eliot lamented the 1
unfulfilled lives of talented women:

> Some have felt that these blundering lives are due to the inconvenient
> indefiniteness with which the Supreme Power has fashioned the na-
> tures of women: if there were one level of feminine incompetence as
> strict as the ability to count three and no more, the social lot of women
> might be treated with scientific certitude.

Eliot goes on to discount the idea of innate limitation, but while 2
she wrote in 1872, the leaders of European anthropometry were trying
to measure "with scientific certitude" the inferiority of women. Anthropometry, or measurement of the human body, is not so fashionable
a field these days, but it dominated the human sciences for much of
the nineteenth century and remained popular until intelligence testing
replaced skull measurement as a favored device for making invidious
comparisons among races, classes, and sexes. Craniometry, or measurement of the skull, commanded the most attention and respect. Its
unquestioned leader, Paul Broca (1824–80), professor of clinical surgery
at the Faculty of Medicine in Paris, gathered a school of disciples and
imitators around himself. Their work, so meticulous and apparently
irrefutable, exerted great influence and won high esteem as a jewel of
nineteenth-century science.

Broca's work seemed particularly invulnerable to refutation. Had 3
he not measured with the most scrupulous care and accuracy? (Indeed,
he had. I have the greatest respect for Broca's meticulous procedure.
His numbers are sound. But science is an inferential exercise, not a
catalog of facts. Numbers, by themselves, specify nothing. All depends
upon what you do with them.) Broca depicted himself as an apostle

Stephen Jay Gould, born in 1941, is a professor of geology at Harvard University,
where he teaches paleontology, biology, and the history of science. The essays
he has written for the magazine *Natural History* have been collected in four highly
readable books.

of objectivity, a man who bowed before facts and cast aside superstition and sentimentality. He declared that "there is no faith, however respectable, no interest, however legitimate, which must not accommodate itself to the progress of human knowledge and bend before truth." Women, like it or not, had smaller brains than men and, therefore, could not equal them in intelligence. This fact, Broca argued, may reinforce a common prejudice in male society, but it is also a scientific truth. L. Manouvrier, a black sheep in Broca's fold, rejected the inferiority of women and wrote with feeling about the burden imposed upon them by Broca's numbers:

> Women displayed their talents and their diplomas. They also invoked philosophical authorities. But they were opposed by *numbers* unknown to Condorcet or to John Stuart Mill. These numbers fell upon poor women like a sledge hammer, and they were accompanied by commentaries and sarcasms more ferocious than the most misogynist imprecations of certain church fathers. The theologians had asked if women had a soul. Several centuries later, some scientists were ready to refuse them a human intelligence.

Broca's argument rested upon two sets of data: the larger brains of men in modern societies, and a supposed increase in male superiority through time. His most extensive data came from autopsies performed personally in four Parisian hospitals. For 292 male brains, he calculated an average weight of 1,325 grams; 140 female brains averaged 1,144 grams for a difference of 181 grams, or 14 percent of the male weight. Broca understood, of course, that part of this difference could be attributed to the greater height of males. Yet he made no attempt to measure the effect of size alone and actually stated that it cannot account for the entire difference because we know, a priori, that women are not as intelligent as men (a premise that the data were supposed to test, not rest upon):

> We might ask if the small size of the female brain depends exclusively upon the small size of her body. Tiedemann has proposed this explanation. But we must not forget that women are, on the average, a little less intelligent than men, a difference which we should not exaggerate but which is, nonetheless, real. We are therefore permitted to suppose that the relatively small size of the female brain depends in part upon her physical inferiority and in part upon her intellectual inferiority.

In 1873, the year after Eliot published *Middlemarch,* Broca measured    5
the cranial capacities of prehistoric skulls from L'Homme Mort cave.
Here he found a difference of only 99.5 cubic centimeters between
males and females, while modern populations range from 129.5 to
220.7. Topinard, Broca's chief disciple, explained the increasing discrepancy through time as a result of differing evolutionary pressures
upon dominant men and passive women:

> The man who fights for two or more in the struggle for existence,
> who has all the responsibility and the cares of tomorrow, who is con-
> stantly active in combating the environment and human rivals, needs
> more brain than the woman whom he must protect and nourish, the
> sedentary woman, lacking any interior occupations, whose role is to
> raise children, love, and be passive.

In 1879, Gustave Le Bon, chief misogynist of Broca's school, used    6
these data to publish what must be the most vicious attack upon
women in modern scientific literature (no one can top Aristotle). I do
not claim his views were representative of Broca's school, but they
were published in France's most respected anthropological journal. Le
Bon concluded:

> In the most intelligent races, as among the Parisians, there are a large
> number of women whose brains are closer in size to those of gorillas
> than to the most developed male brains. This inferiority is so obvious
> that no one can contest it for a moment; only its degree is worth
> discussion. All psychologists who have studied the intelligence of
> women, as well as poets and novelists, recognize today that they
> represent the most inferior forms of human evolution and that they
> are closer to children and savages than to an adult, civilized man.
> They excel in fickleness, inconstancy, absence of thought and logic,
> and incapacity to reason. Without doubt there exist some distin-
> guished women, very superior to the average man, but they are as
> exceptional as the birth of any monstrosity, as, for example, of a gorilla
> with two heads; consequently, we may neglect them entirely.

Nor did Le Bon shrink from the social implications of his views.    7
He was horrified by the proposal of some American reformers to grant
women higher education on the same basis as men:

> A desire to give them the same education, and, as a consequence, to
> propose the same goals for them, is a dangerous chimera. . . . The
> day when, misunderstanding the interior occupations which nature

has given her, women leave the home and take part in our battles; on this day a social revolution will begin, and everything that maintains the sacred ties of the family will disappear.

Sound familiar?*

I have reexamined Broca's data, the basis for all this derivative 8 pronouncement, and I find his numbers sound but his interpretation ill-founded, to say the least. The data supporting his claim for increased difference through time can be easily dismissed. Broca based his contention on the samples from L'Homme Mort alone—only seven male and six female skulls in all. Never have so little data yielded such far ranging conclusions.

In 1888, Topinard published Broca's more extensive data on the 9 Parisian hospitals. Since Broca recorded height and age as well as brain size, we may use modern statistics to remove their effect. Brain weight decreases with age, and Broca's women were, on average, considerably older than his men. Brain weight increases with height, and his average man was almost half a foot taller than his average woman. I used multiple regression, a technique that allowed me to assess simultaneously the influence of height and age upon brain size. In an analysis of the data for women, I found that, at average male height and age, a woman's brain would weigh 1,212 grams. Correction for height and age reduces Broca's measured difference of 181 grams by more than a third, to 113 grams.

I don't know what to make of this remaining difference because 10 I cannot assess other factors known to influence brain size in a major way. Cause of death has an important effect: degenerative disease often entails a substantial diminution of brain size. (This effect is separate from the decrease attributed to age alone.) Eugene Schreider, also working with Broca's data, found that men killed in accidents had brains weighing, on average, 60 grams more than men dying of infectious diseases. The best modern data I can find (from American hospitals) records a full 100-gram difference between death by degenerative arteriosclerosis and by violence or accident. Since so many of Broca's subjects were very elderly women, we may assume that lengthy degenerative disease was more common among them than among the men.

* When I wrote this essay, I assumed that Le Bon was a marginal, if colorful, figure. I have since learned that he was a leading scientist, one of the founders of social psychology, and best known for a seminal study on crowd behavior, still cited today (*La psychologie des foules*, 1895), and for his work on unconscious motivation.

More importantly, modern students of brain size still have not 11
agreed on a proper measure for eliminating the powerful effect of body
size. Height is partly adequate, but men and women of the same height
do not share the same body build. Weight is even worse than height,
because most of its variation reflects nutrition rather than intrinsic
size—fat versus skinny exerts little influence upon the brain. Manouvrier took up this subject in the 1880s and argued that muscular
mass and force should be used. He tried to measure this elusive property in various ways and found a marked difference in favor of men,
even in men and women of the same height. When he corrected for
what he called "sexual mass," women actually came out slightly ahead
in brain size.

Thus, the corrected 113-gram difference is surely too large; the true 12
figure is probably close to zero and may as well favor women as men.
And 113 grams, by the way, is exactly the average difference between
a 5 foot 4 inch and a 6 foot 4 inch male in Broca's data. We would not
(especially us short folks) want to ascribe greater intelligence to tall
men. In short, who knows what to do with Broca's data? They certainly
don't permit any confident claim that men have bigger brains than
women.

To appreciate the social role of Broca and his school, we must 13
recognize that his statements about the brains of women do not reflect
an isolated prejudice toward a single disadvantaged group. They must
be weighed in the context of a general theory that supported contemporary social distinctions as biologically ordained. Women, blacks, and
poor people suffered the same disparagement, but women bore the
brunt of Broca's argument because he had easier access to data on
women's brains. Women were singularly denigrated but they also
stood as surrogates for other disenfranchised groups. As one of Broca's
disciples wrote in 1881: "Men of the black races have a brain scarcely
heavier than that of white women." This juxtaposition extended into
many other realms of anthropological argument, particularly to claims
that, anatomically and emotionally, both women and blacks were like
white children—and that white children, by the theory of recapitu-
lation, represented an ancestral (primitive) adult stage of human evolution. I do not regard as empty rhetoric the claim that women's
battles are for all of us.

Maria Montessori did not confine her activities to educational re- 14
form for young children. She lectured on anthropology for several
years at the University of Rome, and wrote an influential book entitled

*Pedagogical Anthropology* (English edition, 1913). Montessori was no egalitarian. She supported most of Broca's work and the theory of innate criminality proposed by her compatriot Cesare Lombroso. She measured the circumference of children's heads in her schools and inferred that the best prospects had bigger brains. But she had no use for Broca's conclusions about women. She discussed Manouvrier's work at length and made much of his tentative claim that women, after proper correction of the data, had slightly larger brains than men. Women, she concluded, were intellectually superior, but men had prevailed heretofore by dint of physical force. Since technology has abolished force as an instrument of power, the era of women may soon be upon us: "In such an epoch there will really be superior human beings, there will really be men strong in morality and in sentiment. Perhaps in this way the reign of women is approaching, when the enigma of her anthropological superiority will be deciphered. Woman was always the custodian of human sentiment, morality and honor."

This represents one possible antidote to "scientific" claims for the  15 constitutional inferiority of certain groups. One may affirm the validity of biological distinctions but argue that the data have been misinterpreted by prejudiced men with a stake in the outcome, and that disadvantaged groups are truly superior. In recent years, Elaine Morgan has followed this strategy in her *Descent of Woman*, a speculative reconstruction of human prehistory from the woman's point of view— and as farcical as more famous tall tales by and for men.

I prefer another strategy. Montessori and Morgan followed Broca's  16 philosophy to reach a more congenial conclusion. I would rather label the whole enterprise of setting a biological value upon groups for what it is: irrelevant and highly injurious. George Eliot well appreciated the special tragedy that biological labeling imposed upon members of disadvantaged groups. She expressed it for people like herself—women of extraordinary talent. I would apply it more widely—not only to those whose dreams are flouted but also to those who never realize that they may dream—but I cannot match her prose. In conclusion, then, the rest of Eliot's prelude to *Middlemarch*:

> The limits of variation are really much wider than anyone would imagine from the sameness of women's coiffure and the favorite love stories in prose and verse. Here and there a cygnet is reared uneasily among the ducklings in the brown pond, and never finds the living stream in fellowship with its own oary-footed kind. Here and there

is born a Saint Theresa, foundress of nothing, whose loving heartbeats
and sobs after an unattained goodness tremble off and are dispersed
among hindrances instead of centering in some long-recognizable
deed.

# Questions

1. In paragraph 3, what does Gould mean when he says, "But science
   is an inferential exercise, not a catalog of facts"?
2. Gould quotes (paragraph 5) Topinard's explanation for the increasing discrepancy in the size of brains. Given your own understanding
   of evolution, what do you think of Topinard's explanation?
3. In paragraph 9 Gould says, "Brain weight decreases with age." Do
   you believe this? Why? How would one establish the truth or falsity
   of the assertion?
4. In paragraph 12 Gould says, "Thus, the corrected 113-gram difference is surely too large; the true figure is probably close to zero
   and may as well favor women as men." Why "thus"? What evidence
   or what assumptions prompt Gould to say that the figure is surely
   too large?
5. In paragraph 13 Gould says, "I do not regard as empty rhetoric the
   claim that women's battles are for all of us." What does this mean?
6. Also in paragraph 13 Gould refers to the "social role of Broca and
   his school." What does he mean by that? On the basis of this essay
   (and other essays of Gould's you may have read) try to formulate
   in a sentence or two the social role of Gould.

Ruth Bleier

# Gender and
# Mathematical Ability

In the 1980s the controversy about sex-differentiated cog- 1
nitive differences rose into overnight prominence in the form of a study
that suggested to the news media that some truly new and unexpected
scientific discovery had been revealed. Days before the report in *Science,* the official journal of the largest professional science organization
in the country, the newspapers announced that Johns Hopkins researchers found that boys are "inherently" better than girls in mathematical reasoning (*New York Times,* Dec. 7, 1980). *Time* magazine carried
the story the same week the study appeared and quoted one of its
authors, Camilla Benbow, as saying that many women "can't bring
themselves to accept sexual difference in aptitude. But the difference
in math is a fact. The best way to help girls is to accept it and go from
there" (Dec. 15, 1980, p. 57). *Newsweek* of the same date asked in its
story headline, "Do Males have a Math Gene?"

The study of Camilla Benbow and Julian Stanley (1980) tested 2
about 10,000 students, mainly seventh and eighth graders who were
in the upper 3 percent of students in math ability as judged by the
College Board Scholastic Aptitude Test (SAT). The students are part
of a larger project called the Study of Mathematically Precocious Youth.
The mean score for boys in the math SAT was higher than for girls
tested during the eight years of the study, and the highest score every
year was made by a boy. It is significant that in the last two years,
1978 and 1979, however, the highest score by a boy was 790 and by a
girl, 760, the smallest and least significant difference since the beginning of the study in 1972. (It is highly doubtful that this closing math
gap reflects a change in the female *gene* pool for math.) The authors'
conclusion was: "We favor the hypothesis that sex differences in
achievement in and attitude toward mathematics result from superior

Ruth Bleier, a professor in the Neurophysiology Department and in the Women's
Studies Program at the University of Wisconsin-Madison, holds an M.D. degree.
After practicing medicine for eight years she accepted a research position at
Johns Hopkins University, and from there she went on to teach at Madison. She
is the author of *Science and Gender.*

male mathematical ability, which may in turn be related to greater male ability in spatial tasks" (p. 1264). The context of the article clearly implied a genetic sex difference.

Since up to the time of testing the girls and boys did not differ in the number of math courses taken, the authors did not seriously consider any other possible social or environmental factors, though they did suggest that their "data are consistent with numerous alternative hypotheses," which they did not explore. (It is important to note that no press reports carried that cautionary statement.) Nor did they think it important to take into account that the subjects were volunteers, despite the evidence that gifted boys are more likely to volunteer to take tests than are gifted girls (Jacklin, 1981). But as two professors of mathematics, Alice Schafer and Mary Gray, wrote in the lead editorial in *Science* five weeks after the Benbow and Stanley article appeared, in criticism of the Benbow and Stanley hypothesis, "Anyone who thinks that seventh graders are free from environmental influences can hardly be living in the real world." Who helps with the math homework, the kinds of toys and games girls and boys are given, and the expectations of parents and teachers are of critical importance. Mathematically gifted boys can confidently expect to use and be rewarded for their skills in math, science, and engineering and will thus be highly motivated to excel, but it has been well documented that, by and large, parents, school counselors, and teachers have traditionally discouraged even talented girls from seriously pursuing mathematics and science skills or, equally damagingly, simply ignored them (Beckwith and Durkin, 1980; Brophy and Good, 1970; Delefes and Jackson, 1972; Ernest, 1976; Leinhardt *et al.*, 1979). One study found that "42 percent of girls interested in careers in mathematics or science reported being discouraged by counselors from taking courses in advanced mathematics" (Haven, 1972). In addition, at an age when pressures are high to conform to expected gender roles and behaviors, many girls do not want to be seen as "unfeminine" in a culture that equates math and science skills with "masculinity." The Benbow and Stanley study and its attendant sensationalized publicity will do little to dispel what Dean Jewell Cobb of Douglass College called the "notion that proficiency in mathematics is a sex-linked characteristic which is widespread among elementary school and high school teachers, college students and young mothers" (Quoted in *Science News*, Vol. 113, p. 200, 1978).

It is only recently that efforts have been launched to educate teachers and counselors away from sex-typing and channeling. In those schools where the environment is equally challenging to both sexes, studies produce quite different results from those of Benbow and Julian. Patricia Casserly of the Educational Testing Service in Princeton has studied 20 high schools where all the teachers have science, math, or engineering backgrounds, communicate enthusiasm for math, and *expect* women to advance as well as men. In these schools, girls and boys score equally well in Advanced Placement (college level) examinations (Kolata, 1980).

It is faintly ironic that not long after the Benbow and Julian study, 5 living refutations of sex stereotyping and scientific sex delineations appeared within the same year, though they were not heralded, if noticed at all, by the popular press: 11-year-old Ruth Lawrence of England got the highest score in the mathematics entrance examinations at Oxford University's St. Hugh's College, which she was to enter in 1983 (*Ms*, June 1982); 17-year-old Laura Clark of Long Island was the only student out of 154,000 to score a perfect 800 on *both* sections (verbal and mathematical) of the Scholastic Aptitude Test (*Ms*, June 1982); for the third year in a row, a woman high school student (Reena Gordon of Brooklyn in 1982) was the winner of the National Westinghouse Science Talent Search Award (American Women in Science *Newsletter*, Vol. 11, #4, Aug.–Sept. 1982); Nina Morishige, who received her BA and MA in mathematics at 18 years of age after attending Johns Hopkins University for two years, became one of the youngest recipients ever to receive a Rhodes Scholarship to Oxford in the 78-year history of the award (*Johns Hopkins Journal*, Spring, 1982).

There are other problems with the Benbow and Stanley study or 6 with the authors' interpretation of the results. In suggesting inherent (they use the term "endogenous") superiority in mathematical reasoning in males, they overlook the substantial overlap in the distribution of scores of girls and boys; that is, among talented girls and boys, the scores are more alike than different, with a few exceptional cases. If some girls near the top are superior to most of the boys, then what does male "superiority" mean? Next, Benbow and Stanley state their belief that environmental factors affect mathematical *achievement*, whereas the SAT, which they used, measures aptitude, that is, "natural" ability. There is, however, a real question whether it is possible at all to make a distinction between achievement and aptitude; and, second, there is real doubt that the SAT is indeed capable of measuring aptitude, whatever that may be, as contrasted with achievement. A member of the Educational Testing Service of Princeton has written that "the developers of the SAT do not view it as a measure of fixed capacities," but instead, "The test is intended to measure aspects of developed ability" (Schafer and Gray, 1981). Susan Chipman of the National Institute of Education wrote that the math SAT samples "performance in a domain of learned knowledge and skill. . . . In a fundamental sense, we do not yet know what mathematical ability is . . ." (1981; see the same issue of *Science* for a number of excellent critiques of the Benbow and Stanley study in the *Letters* Section; see also Beckwith and Durkin, 1981).

Finally, Benbow and Stanley's study and conclusions stand in con-    7
tradiction to a number of other studies that fail to confirm the assumption that boys are invariably superior in mathematics achievement before the grade levels when clear socialization factors appear (Fennema and Sherman, 1977, 1978; Sherman, 1980). Following two years of intensive study of students in grades 6 through 12, Fennema and Sherman (1978) found that "when relevant factors are controlled, sex-related differences in favor of males do not appear often, and when they do, they are not large" (p. 201). Furthermore, Fennema and Sherman have not found sex differences in spatial visualization at any age. But as one might anticipate, these negative results and the innumerable other studies that show *no* differences in performance or aptitude between the sexes do not excite attention or merit headlines and national news service coverage, and many are not accepted by journals for publication.

If the Benbow and Stanley study is flawed, why, one might ask,    8
get so excited about it? It is because the message of the authors' conclusions has undoubtedly already had dire effects; it is an example of a self-perpetuating and reinforcing ideology. Teachers, counselors, and parents are told there is no particular point in encouraging seemingly talented girls because they are ultimately limited, and it tells girls directly that they should spare themselves grief and energy, even though they like math and are good at it. The study itself is likely to widen the sex-differential in performance or at least to offset the advances in confidence and achievement that have been hard-wrought by the women's movement and the more open atmosphere it has created. The predictable effects of the study and the unbridled enthusiasm of its media reception will be to confirm the comfortable stereotypes about women and men, and make it easier to keep women out of those fields that increasingly rely on sophisticated mathematical and computer knowledge—science, business, and the social sciences.

## References

Beckwith, J., and Durkin, J. Girls, boys and math. *Science for the People*, 1981, *13*, 6.

Benbow, C., and Stanley, J. Sex differences in mathematical ability: fact or artifact? *Science*, 1980, *210*, 1262–64.

Brophy, J. E., and Good, T. L. Teachers' communication of differential expectations for children's classroom performance: some behavioral data. *Journal of Educational Psychology*, 1970, *6*, 365–74.

Delefes, P., and Jackson, B. Teacher-pupil interaction as a function of location in the classroom. *Psychology in the Schools*, 1972, *9*, 119–23.

Ernest, J. *Mathematics and sex*. Santa Barbara: Mathematics Department, University of California, 1976.

Fennema, E., and Sherman, J. Sex-related differences in mathematics achievement and related factors: a further study. *Journal for Research in Mathematics Education*, 1978, *9*, 188–203.

Haven, E. W. Factors associated with the selection of advanced academic mathematical courses by girls in high school. *Research Bulletin* 72-12. Princeton: Educational Testing Service, 1972.

Jacklin, D. Methodological issues in the study of sex-related differences. *Developmental Review*, 1981, *1*, 266–273.

Kolata, G. Math and sex: are girls born with less ability? *Science*, 1980, *210*, 1234–1235.

Leinhardt, G., Seewald, A. M., and Engel, M. Learning what's taught: sex differences in instruction. *Journal of Educational Psychology*, 1979, *714*, 432–439.

Schafer, A., and Gray, M. Sex and mathematics. *Science*, 1981, *211*, 229.

Sherman, J. *Sex-related cognitive differences: an essay on theory and evidence*. Springfield: Charles Thomas, 1978.

Sherman, J. Mathematics, spatial visualization, and related factors: changes in girls and boys, grades 8–11. *Journal of Educational Psychology*, 1980, *72*, 476–482.

Sherman, J., and Fennema, E. Distribution of spatial visualization and mathematical problem solving scores: a test of Stafford's x-linked hypotheses. *Psychology of Women Quarterly*, 1978, *6*, 157–167.

## Questions

1. In her first paragraph Bleier writes of "the controversy about sex-differentiated cognitive differences." Explain (to someone who is unaware of the controversy and who has not read this article) what "sex-differentiated cognitive differences" both means and implies.

2. In paragraph 4 Bleier writes of "sex-typing and channeling." What examples does she provide? Are you aware of courses that boys are discouraged from pursuing or excelling in? Should Bleier have included examples of sex-typing and channeling for boys? Why, or why not?

3. In paragraph 5 Bleier cites examples of "living refutations of sex stereotyping and scientific sex delineations." Briefly summarize the evidence she presents. Would you agree that the evidence constitutes scientific refutation of sex stereotyping? Why, or why not?

4. What further arguments does Bleier offer in paragraphs 6 and 7? Do you find them more or less convincing than her argument in paragraph 5?

5. Have you ever been a victim of sex stereotyping, or a witness to it (in your family, for example, or in a school you attended)? To what extent does your experience support Bleier's concluding paragraph?

## Evelyn Fox Keller

# Women in Science
### An Analysis of a Social Problem

$A$re women's minds different from men's minds? In spite    1
of the women's movement, the age-old debate centering around this
question continues. We are surrounded by evidence of *de facto* differences between men's and women's intellects—in the problems that
interest them, in the ways they try to solve those problems, and in
the professions they choose. Even though it has become fashionable
to view such differences as environmental in origin, the temptation to
seek an explanation in terms of innate differences remains a powerful
one.

Evelyn Fox Keller has taught at the State University of New York at Purchase,
and at Cornell, the Massachusetts Institute of Technology, and Northeastern
University. She now teaches in the Rhetoric, Women's Studies, and History of
Science programs at the University of California, Berkeley. Among her numerous
publications is a book entitled *Reflections on Gender and Science.*

**Table I.**  *Percentage of Ph.D.'s earned by women, 1920–1970*

|  | 1920–29 | 1940–49 | 1950–59 | 1960–69 |
|---|---|---|---|---|
| Physics and Astronomy | 5.9 | 4.2 | 2.0 | 2.2 |
| Biological Sciences | 19.5 | 15.7 | 11.8 | 15.1 |
| Mathematics | 14.5 | 10.7 | 5.0 | 5.7 |
| Psychology | 29.4 | 24.1 | 14.8 | 20.7 |

*Source: National Research Council*

Perhaps the area in which this temptation is strongest is in science.    2
Even those of us who would like to argue for intellectual equality are
hard pressed to explain the extraordinarily meager representation of
women in science, particularly in the upper echelons. Some would
argue that the near absence of great women scientists demonstrates
that women don't have the minds for true scientific creativity. While
most of us would recognize the patent fallacies of this argument, it
nevertheless causes us considerable discomfort. After all, the doors of
the scientific establishment appear to have been open to women for
some time now—shouldn't we begin to see more women excelling?

In the last fifty years the institutional barriers against women in    3
science have been falling. During most of that time, the percentage of
women scientists has declined, although recent years have begun to
show an upswing (table I). Of those women who do become scientists,
few are represented in the higher academic ranks (table II). In order
to have a proper understanding of these data, it is necessary to review
the many influences that operate. I would like to argue that the convenient explanation that men's minds are intrinsically different from
women's is not only unwarranted by the evidence, but in fact reflects
a mythology that is in itself a major contribution to the phenomena
observed.

As a woman scientist, I have often pondered these questions, par-    4

**Table II.**  *Percentage representation of women, by rank, in 20 leading universities (1962)*

|  | Instructor | Assistant Professor | Associate Professor | Professor |
|---|---|---|---|---|
| Physics | 5.6 | 1.2 | 1.3 | 0.9 |
| Biological Sciences | 16.3 | 7.1 | 6.7 | 1.3 |
| Mathematics | 16.7 | 10.1 | 7.3 | 0.4 |
| Psychology | 8.3 | 10.4 | 11.1 | 2.7 |

*Source: J. B. Parrish, A. A. U. W. Journal, 55, '99*

ticularly at those times when my commitment to science seemed most precarious. Noticing that almost every other woman I had known in science had experienced similar crises of commitment, I sought to explain my ambivalence by concluding that science as a profession is not as gratifying for women as it is for men, and that the reasons for this are to be found in the intrinsic nature of women and science. Several years ago, I endeavored to find out how general my own experiences were. In studying the statistics of success and failure for women in the professions, I indeed found that women fared less well in science than in other professions, although the picture that emerged seemed fairly bleak for all of us.

I collected these data during a leave of absence I had taken to  5 accompany my husband to California. At the same time, I was also engaged in completing work I had begun the year before with a (male) colleague—work that seemed less and less compelling as the year wore on. Each week I would receive an enthusiastic telephone call from my colleague, reporting new information and responses he had received from workers he had met while delivering invited lectures on this work. At some point it occurred to me that perhaps there was a relation between my declining interest and isolation on the one hand, and his growing enthusiasm and public recognition on the other. Over the course of the year, he had received a score or more invitations to speak about this work, while I had received none. It began to dawn on me that there were far simpler explanations for both the observations I had made privately and the data I was collecting than that of intrinsic differences between the sexes.

I began to realize, for example, that had I been less isolated and  6 more rewarded, my enthusiasm would have been correspondingly greater—a recognition that has been amply corroborated by my subsequent experience. Upon further reflection, I became aware of how much my own, and other similar, attitudes are influenced by a complex interplay of subtle factors affecting us from birth on. The ways in which we rear our children, train our students, and interact with our colleagues are all so deeply imbued with our expectations and beliefs as to virtually guarantee a fulfillment of these beliefs.

How do men and women develop the characteristics we attribute  7 to them? There are clear differences between the sexes at birth, and there is even some evidence that these differences extend to the brain. Primate studies reveal marked differences in behavior between males and females—differences determined by the prenatal hormonal environment. It seems therefore quite possible that there are even intellectual differences determined prior to birth. For those inclined to believe in such predetermination, such a possibility may appear attractive. It is important to say, however, that there is to date no evidence for biologically determined differences in intelligence or cognitive styles, and that this remains true in spite of a rather considerable desire among many people to find such evidence.

An example of this interest is provided by the great enthusiasm 8 with which a recent study was met. This study purported to show that prenatal injection of progestin, a synthetic male hormone, leads to higher than average I.Q.'s in adolescent girls. Although this result was refuted by the original authors shortly after its original announcement, it nevertheless found its way into a rash of textbooks, where it remains. Similarly, there has been a great deal of interest in the measurement of differences in perceptual modes between girls and boys. Tests designed to measure the degree to which one's perception of a figure is independent of its background, or field, show that girls, by the time they enter school, are more field-dependent than boys. Field independence is positively correlated with mathematical and analytic abilities. While the results of these tests are remarkably culturally invariant (the Eskimos are a notable exception), it is important to point out both that the disparities observed are extremely small (of the order of 2 percent) and that they cannot be discerned before the age of five. While the possibility that these disparities are the result of innate differences between the sexes cannot be excluded, there is evidence relating performance on such tests to the individual's environment. What are the environmental differences that could account for such results?

We treat our sons and daughters differently from birth onward, 9 although the magnitude of our distinction is largely unconscious. A rude awakening to the extent of our differential treatment can come in those rare instances when a fallacious sex assignment is made at birth, usually as a result of ambiguous genitalia, and must be subsequently corrected. The impact of these early cues can be assessed by the fact that such reassignments are considered unduly traumatic to make after the child is eighteen months old, in spite of the fact that failure to do so dooms the child to an apparent sexual identity at odds with his or her genotype. Sex reassignments made before that time result in apparently normal development. From this and related evidence, workers in this area have concluded that gender identity appears to be established, primarily on the basis of parental treatment, by the age of eighteen months.

Children acquire the meaning of their sex identity from the models    10
before them. Their concept of female is based largely on the women
they see, as their concept of male is based on the men they see. Their
immediate perceptions are later expanded by the images they perceive
on TV, and in children's literature. It hardly need be pointed out that
both of the latter present to our children extraordinarily rigid stereotypes.

It is not surprising, then, that children, even before they enter    11
school, have acquired the belief that certain activities are male and
others female. Science is a male activity.

The tenacity of this early view is such as to resist easy change.    12
When my daughter was in nursery school, her class was asked one
day about the occupation of their fathers. I objected to this, and, as a
result, the next day the teacher asked, "Sarah, what does your mother
do?" She replied, "My mother cooks, she sews, she cleans, and she
takes care of us." "But Sarah, isn't your mother a scientist?" "Oh,
yes," said Sarah—clearly implying that this was not a very relevant
piece of information.

The explanation of her response lies not only in her need to define    13
a conventional image of her mother, but also in the reality of her direct
perceptions. Indeed it is true that, like many professional women, I
do cook, sew, clean, and take care of my children. My professional
identity is not brought into my home, although my husband's is. My
daughter, therefore, like my son, continues to view mathematics and
science as male, in spite of their information to the contrary.

While a child may be concerned with assigning sex labels only to    14
external attributes, such as clothes, mannerisms, and occupations, the
adolescent has already begun to designate internal states as male and
female. Thus, in particular, clear thinking is characterized as hard
thinking (a male image), and fuzzy thinking as soft thinking (a female
image). A girl who thinks clearly and well is told she thinks "like a
man." What are the implications of such associations for the girl who
(for whatever reasons) does transcend social expectation and finds herself interested in science? Confusion in sexual identity is the inevitable
concomitant of a self-definition at variance with the surrounding definitions of sexual norm. The girl who can take pride in "thinking like
a man" without cost to her integrity as a girl is rare indeed.

Nevertheless, a considerable number of women, for whatever rea-    15
sons, experience enough motivation and have demonstrated enough
ability to embark on professional training for a scientific career. Graduate school is a time to prove that one is, in spite of one's aspirations,

a woman, and—at one and the same time, because of one's aspirations—"more than" a woman. Social acceptability requires the former, and is considerably facilitated by the acquisition of a husband, while professional respectability requires the latter. The more exclusively male the definition of the profession, the more difficult it is to accomplish these conflicting goals.

My own experience as a graduate student of theoretical physics   16
at Harvard was extreme, but possibly illustrative. I was surrounded by incessant prophecies of failure, independent of my performance. I knew of no counter-examples to draw confidence from, and was led to believe that none existed. (Later, however, I learned that some women in theoretical physics have survived, even at Harvard.) Warned that I would ultimately despair as I came to learn how impossible my ambitions were, I did, though not for the reasons that were then implied. Having denied myself rage, depression was in fact one of the few reasonable responses to the isolation, mockery, and suspicion that I experienced, both within and without my department. Ultimately I did earn my Ph.D. from the Harvard physics department, but only after having adapted my interests and thereby removed myself from the most critical pressures—a course many women have taken before and since.

Hostility, however, was not the only response I received, and not   17
necessarily the usual response experienced by professionally ambitious young women. The necessity of proving one's femininity leaves some women particularly susceptible to another danger—that of accepting, and even seeking, sexual approbation for intellectual and academic performance. There are enough men willing, if not eager, to provide such translated affirmation as to make this a serious problem. The relation between sexuality and intellectuality is an enormously complex subject. I raise it only to point out one perhaps obvious consequence of this confusion for women. Because, unlike men, they are often dependent on sexual and intellectual affirmation from one and the same individual or group, they can never be entirely confident of what is being affirmed. Is it an "A for a Lay" or a "Lay for an A"?

Finally, the female scientist is launched. What are her prospects?   18
Many women choose this point to withdraw for a time in order to have children. Although there is a logic to this choice, it reflects a lack of awareness of the dynamics of normal professional growth. For the male scientist, the period immediately following acquisition of the Ph.D. is perhaps the most critical in his professional development. It is the time

that he has, free of all the responsibilities that will later come to plague him, to accomplish enough work to establish his reputation. Often it is a time to affiliate himself with a school of thought, to prove his own, independent worth. Although this may have been the original function of the graduate training period, it has in recent times been displaced to the postgraduate years. Awareness of this displacement, of the critical importance of these years, has not permeated to the general public, or even, for the most part, to the science student. Many women therefore take this sometimes fatal step in ignorance. After having been out of a field for a few years, they usually find it next to impossible to return to their field except in the lowest-level positions. Only when it is too late do they learn that it would have been better to have their children first, before completing the Ph.D.

I need hardly enumerate the additional practical difficulties involved in combining a scientific (or any other) career with the raising of children. While the practical drains on one's time and energy are generally recognized, perhaps it is worth pointing out that the drains on one's intellectual energy are not generally recognized by men. Only those men who have spent full time, for an extended period, caring for their children are aware of the extraordinary amount of mental space occupied by the thousand and one details and concerns that mothers routinely juggle. Many have come to the conclusion—beginning with Engels, and more recently including the Swedish government—that equality of the sexes in the work and professional force is not a realistic possibility until the sex roles in the family are radically redefined. Equality must begin at home.

Well, one might ask, what about those women in science who have no children, who never marry? Surely they are freed from all of these difficulties. Why don't they perform better?

First of all, to be freed of responsibilities towards others is not equivalent to having your own responsibilities assumed by others. Nowhere among women is to be found the counterpart of the male scientist who has a wife at home to look after his daily needs. The question, however, deserves a more serious answer, although the answer is almost painfully obvious. Our society does not have a place for unmarried women. They are among the most isolated, ostracized groups of our culture. When one thinks about the daily social and psychological pressures on the unmarried professional woman, one can hardly be surprised to discover that the data reveal that indeed, on the average, married women in science—even with children—publish more and perform better than unmarried women.

The enumeration of obstacles or handicaps faced by women in   22
science would hardly be complete without at least a reference to the
inequalities of reward and approval awarded to work done by men
and women. The personal anecdote I began with is more than an anecdote—it is evidence of a rather ubiquitous tendency, neither malicious nor necessarily even conscious, to give more public recognition
to a man's accomplishments than to a woman's accomplishments.
There are many different reasons for this—not least of which includes
the habitually lesser inclination of many women to put themselves
forward. There is also a simple, although documented, difference in
evaluation of the actual work done by men and women.

While all of the above difficulties are hardly exclusive problems of   23
women in science, the question of identity in what has been defined
as an almost exclusively male profession is more serious for women
in science than in other fields. Not only is the field defined as male
by virtue of its membership, it is also defined as male in relation to its
methodology, style of thought, indeed its goals. To the extent that
analytic thought is conceived as male thought, to the extent that we
characterize the natural sciences as the "hard" sciences, to the extent
that the procedure of science is to "attack" problems, and its goal,
since Bacon, has been to "conquer" or "master" nature, a woman in
science *must* in some way feel alien.

Traditionally, as in other similar situations, women who have suc-   24
ceeded in scientific careers have dealt with this conflict by identifying
with the "aggressor"—incorporating its values and ideals, at the cost,
inevitably, of separating themselves from their own sex. An alternative
resolution, one opted for frequently in other professions, is to attempt
to redefine one's subject so as to permit a more comfortable identification with it. It is in this way, and for this reason, that so many
professional women root themselves in subjects that are viewed by
the profession as peripheral. In science this is not easy to do, but perhaps not impossible. There is another tradition within science that is
as replete with female images as the tradition that dominates today is
replete with male images. We all know that the most creative science
requires, in addition to a hardness of mind, also fertility and receptivity. The best scientists are those who have combined the two sets
of images. It may be that a certain degree of intellectual security is
necessary in order to permit the expression of both "male" and "female" thought in science. If women have first to prove their "male"
qualifications for admission into the profession, they may never

achieve the necessary confidence to allow themselves to use their "female" abilities. What is to be done?

The central theme of my discussion is that the differential performance of men and women in science, the apparent differences between conceptual styles of men and women everywhere, are the result, not so much of innate differences between the sexes, but rather of the myth that prevails throughout our culture identifying certain kinds of thinking as male and others as female. The consequent compartmentalization of our minds is as effective as if it had been biologically, and not socially, induced.

People conform to the expectations imposed upon them in the evolution of their definition of sexual identity, thus confirming the very myth upon which these expectations are based. Such a process is not easy to change. Myths as deeply rooted and as self-affirming as this one can neither be wished nor willed away. The only hope is to chip away at it everywhere, to make enough small inroads so that future generations may ultimately grow up less hampered. Counter-measures can be effected at every stage of the process. Each may be of only limited effectiveness, but cumulatively they may permit enough women to emerge with intact, fully developed mental capacities— women who can serve as role models for future generations of students.

Specifically, we can begin by exerting a conscious effort to raise our children to less rigid stereotypes. Although the full extent to which we differentiate our treatment of our sons and daughters is hidden from us, being largely unconscious, we can, by attending to what we do, raise our consciousness of our own behavior.

We can specifically encourage and reward interests and abilities that survive social pressures. As teachers, men can consciously refrain from mixing academic with sexual approval. More generally, we can inform women students interested in science about the realities of the external difficulties they will face. It is all too easy for an individual experiencing such obstacles to internalize the responsibility for these obstacles. Specific advice can be given—for instance, to avoid interrupting a career immediately after the Ph.D. High-quality work by professional women can be sought out for recognition and encouragement in order to counteract the normal tendency to grant them less recognition. (The physicist Ernest Courant, a very wise man, responded to the news that one of his most talented students was pregnant by giving her a raise—thus enabling her to hire competent help, and, simultaneously, obligating her to continue. After four such raises, she indeed did go on to become one of the country's better mathematicians.)

Extra care can be taken not to exclude women from professional 29 interaction on any level. Finally, hiring policies must take into account the human and political realities. Women students need role models if they are to mature properly. Providing such a model is an important part of the function of a faculty member and should be considered along with scholarly performance in hiring deliberations. Similarly, marriage is a social reality, and women scientists who marry male scientists need jobs in the same area. Anti-nepotism hiring policies discriminate against women scientists, and even a neutral policy effectively does so as well. Universities might well consider pro-nepotism policies that would recognize the limitations of humans and geographical reality.

Most of the recommendations I have made require the cooperation 30 of the male scientific community to implement. Why should they? Further, one may ask, why should women even be encouraged to become scientists when the list of odds against them is so overwhelming? Is a career in science intrinsically of so much greater value than other options more available to women?

I don't believe it is. Nevertheless, our society has become more 31 and more technologically oriented. As we continue to move in this direction, as we come to attach increasing importance to scientific and technological know-how, women are threatened with a disenfranchisement possibly greater than ever before. The traditional role of the woman becomes increasingly eroded with technology and overpopulation, while the disparity between the more humanly oriented kinds of knowledge thought to be hers and the more technical kinds of knowledge operating in the real world grows larger. This disparity operates not only at the expense of the women who are thus barred from meaningful roles in society, but also at the expense of the society that has been content to relegate to women those more humanistic values we all claim to support.

Finally, myths that compartmentalize our minds by defining cer- 32 tain mental attributes as "male" and others as "female" leave us all functioning with only part of our minds. Though there may well be some innate biological differences between the sexes, there is hardly room for doubt that our preconceptions serve to exaggerate and rigidify any distinctions that might exist. These preconceptions operate as strait jackets for men and women alike. I believe that the best, most creative science, like the most creative human efforts of any kind, can only be achieved with a full, unhampered mind—if you like, an androgynous mind. Therefore, the giving up of the central myth that science is a product of male thought may well lead to a more creative, more imaginative, and, who knows, possibly even a more humanistic science.

# Questions

1. Several times in her essay Keller recounts her personal experience (as a scientist, as a parent, as a graduate student). How did you find yourself responding to these personal references? In your opinion, do they strengthen or weaken her argument?
2. What is Keller's advice to women scientists who hope to have children, and how do you evaluate this advice?
3. In paragraph 14 Keller says that "A girl who thinks clearly and well is told she 'thinks like a man.' " Have you ever heard this said—or perhaps thought it yourself? If not, do you nevertheless accept Keller's assertion about what people say?
4. In paragraph 23 Keller glances at some of the metaphors used in talking about scientific thought: "To the extent that analytic thought is conceived as male thought, to the extent that we characterize the natural sciences as the "hard" sciences, to the extent that the procedure of science is to "attack" problems, and its goal, since Bacon, has been to "conquer" or "master" nature, a woman in science *must* in some way feel alien." A reader might think that Keller here is deploring the metaphors used in discussing science because they tend to alienate women. But in the next paragraph she writes:

   We all know that the most creative science requires, in addition to a hardness of mind, also fertility and receptivity. . . . It may be that a certain degree of intellectual security is necessary in order to permit the expression of both "male" and "female" thought in science.

   What do you think Keller means by "hardness of mind"? Is she saying that this is a male quality or is she using a metaphor that a moment ago she suggested gets in the way of women in science?
5. Think for a moment about any of the previous questions. Do they require you to engage in analysis? Do they require "hardness of mind"? If so, do they resemble scientific thinking?
6. In paragraph 21 Keller speaks of "the daily social and psychological pressures on the unmarried professional woman," but she does not

amplify this point with concrete details. How might the point be amplified and supported?

7. Charlotte Perkins Gilman, in *Women and Economics* (1898), wrote, "There is no female mind. The brain is not an organ of sex. As well speak of a female liver." What do you think Evelyn Fox Keller would think of this observation?

Alfred Meyer

# Do Lie Detectors Lie? All Too Often

About the size of an attaché case and equally portable, the instrument looks fairly innocuous. Dials and knobs cluster neatly at one end, while four inked styluses rest on a roll of paper on the other. Once the tubes, cuffs, and electrodes that are its sensors emerge, however, the instrument appears more sinister, doubly so when a human subject is connected to its serpentine appurtenances. But the hardware inflicts no injury, merely records changes in some rather simple physiological responses: blood pressure, breathing, sweating. On the contrary, it is the software programmed into the instrument's keeper, a sort of wizard of truth, that is menacing. He will be well-dressed, efficient, and maddeningly neutral. In calm tones he will tell you how the instrument works and assure you that it is highly accurate. He will discuss the questions he intends to ask, switch on the instrument, and begin the questioning. Within an hour or two, he will leave, in most cases convinced that, by combining his own observations of your behavior with the readings of his instrument, he knows if you have told the truth.

Limited almost exclusively to law enforcement work and to matters of national security during its formative years in the 1940s and 1950s, the lie detector, or polygraph, today has become a common fixture in

Alfred Meyer was born in 1935. An editor and writer, he has written for the general public on a wide range of subjects.

American society, almost to an Orwellian degree. In addition to its uses in prisons, the military, police work, FBI and CIA investigations, and pretrial examinations both for the prosecution and the defense, the polygraph has also found its way into corporate America, where it is widely used for detecting white collar crime and for screening potential employees. This year, it is estimated, half a million to a million Americans, for one reason or another, will take a lie detector test. Such extravagant use takes place despite the facts that no state freely admits polygraph evidence in criminal cases (though about 25 do when both prosecution and defense agree in advance of the testing), that innocent persons often fail the polygraph test while guilty ones pass it, and that the scientific foundation of polygraph technology is, if not altogether questionable, as some critics claim, at least open to serious challenge.

Ironically, considering the procedure's inherent piety, the admin-   3 istration of the lie detector test involves a necessary touch of deception. Polygraph theory holds that physiological reactions—changes in blood pressure, rate of breathing, sweating of the palms—elicited by a set of questions will reliably betray falsehood. But it is the form and mix of questions that polygraphers claim are the key to their technique. The standard format, known as the Control Question Test, involves interspersing "relevant" questions with "control" questions. Relevant questions relate directly to the critical matter, such as, "Did you participate in the robbery of the First National Bank on September 11, 1981?" Control questions, on the other hand, are less precise, such as, "In the last 20 years, have you ever taken something that didn't belong to you?"

In the pretest interview, the polygrapher reviews all the questions   4 and frames the control questions to produce "no" answers. It is in this crucial pretest phase that the polygrapher's deception comes into play, for he wants the innocent subject to dissemble while answering the control questions during the actual test. For example, pursuing the hypothetical control question above, most people are likely to have taken something that didn't belong to them at some stage in their lives. Yet fear of embarrassment may lead the subjects to deny misdeeds and therefore to answer the control question dishonestly.

The assumption underlying the Control Question Test is that the   5 truthful subject will display a stronger physiological reaction to the control questions, whereas a deceptive subject will react more strongly to the relevant questions.

That is the heart of it. Modern lie detection relies on nothing more  6
than subtle psychological techniques, crude physiological indicators,
and skilled questioning and interpretation of the results. It resembles
nothing so much as a game of cat and mouse—often played for very
high stakes.

But does it work? The answer is, yes, sometimes. As for how  7
well—that depends on who you ask.

In a recent publication, for example, the American Polygraph As-  8
sociation cites studies that yield accuracy rates ranging from 87.2 to
96.2 percent. But such studies, conducted in the lab by criminologists
and a handful of psychologists, most of whom make their living as
polygraphers, have come under heavy attack. The chief adversary is
psychologist David Lykken of the University of Minnesota, who cites
other studies, conducted in the field, which yield far lower rates of 64
to 71 percent.

Lykken bases his criticism of lab data on several points. First, he  9
maintains that there is no "specific lie response." The polygraph
merely records general emotional arousal. It cannot distinguish anxiety
or indignation from guilt. Second—and this is his most telling point—
accuracy rates based on lab studies are flawed because they depend
on mock crimes using subjects who do not face the real life consequences of being found truthful or deceptive.

Even a stalwart of polygraphy like psychophysiologist David Ras-  10
kin of the University of Utah acknowledges the difficulty of assessing
accuracy rates in real life situations, those where people face criminal
charges. Moreover, he writes, "In a large percentage of criminal investigations, guilt or innocence is never determined conclusively."

Even in field trials, for example, where a panel of polygraph ex-  11
perts independently score the tests of people who have previously
been tried and found guilty or not guilty, one can't be sure the outcome
is accurate. Such ambiguity makes it virtually impossible to correlate
polygraph results with the truth in samples large enough to achieve
genuine statistical validity.

When it comes to verifying the truthfulness of innocent subjects,  12
both Raskin and Lykken agree that the lie detector turns up more
innocent people found guilty—false positives—than guilty people
found innocent. While Raskin believes the chances of a polygraph identifying an innocent person as lying are less than 10 percent, Lykken
believes that the chance is closer to 50 percent. He contends that it is
impossible to design control questions that will produce the same level

of responsiveness in innocent subjects as is produced by the relevant questions in guilty subjects. The discrepancy results from lack of agreement on whether to use lab or field studies as the standard.

Lykken has still other criticisms of the polygraph. He contends, 13 for example, that with some preparation it is possible to defeat the test. To illustrate, he frequently relates the experience of Floyd Fay, convicted of a murder charge—wrongfully, it was later proved—partly on the basis of a failed lie detector test. While imprisoned, Fay took an interest in polygraph technology and, after studying it, claimed to have trained fellow inmates to foil tests administered by prison officials. The inmates reportedly used such countermeasures as placing a tack in a shoe and stamping on it during the control questioning.

Raskin dismisses Fay's training efforts since they were hardly run 14 under controlled conditions. He cites the recent work of psychologist Michael Dawson in California. With the help of the late method actor Lee Strasberg, Dawson invited a large group of students from Strasberg's Actors' Studio in Hollywood to try, with all an actor's cunning control of emotions, a la Stanislavsky, to "beat the test." None did. Yet again, it was an experiment involving a mock rather than a real crime.

Clearly no one has established beyond a doubt the validity and 15 reliability of the lie detector, though many argue that it is better than any of the alternatives, such as expert testimony from psychiatrists or psychologists. Yet polygraphy is fast becoming an American obsession, one, incidentally, not shared by the British or the Europeans or, as far as we know, the Russians. America's increasing dependence on the polygraph reflects its enormous faith in the rational processes of science: Each of us can probably recall a time when our voices sounded funny as we told a fib. Surely, if we can "hear" a lie, science can detect one.

It comes as a surprise, therefore, to learn how fragile polygraphy's 16 scientific foundations are. When Raskin embarked on polygraphy research in Utah in 1970, not a single scientific laboratory had assessed the validity or reliability of the Control Question Test, by then already in wide use. Nor had a single report by a trained scientist evaluating that test appeared in the scientific literature.

Meanwhile, armed rather more with art than with science—and 17 not a little merchandising magic thrown in—the technology is spreading like wildfire, alarming even such advocates as Raskin. Though he and Lykken clash often enough in print on the scientific merits of polygraphy, there is one development that appalls both men equally:

use of polygraph tests in pre-employment screening by corporations, banks, fast-food chains, and a number of other commercial enterprises.

Such tests, according to Raskin, often are conducted hastily and haphazardly, resulting in highly questionable accuracy. They seek by vague and general questions to elicit admissions of a personal nature, thereby constituting invasion of privacy, and violate personal freedom by requiring tests that may put a job at stake. Particularly distasteful are tests given to present employees—who can hardly refuse—such as those recently used in the upper echelons of government to try to curb leaks to the media.                                                           18

For Lykken, such uses merely exacerbate an already intolerable situation. He points to the scant amount of training polygraphers receive before they qualify as technicians of truth. Perhaps as many as a dozen contemporary polygraphers do hold Ph.D. degrees, but the vast majority of the 4,000 to 8,000 practicing examiners have had no significant training in physiology or in psychology, even though lie detection demands extremely subtle—and difficult—psychophysiological interpretations. Most of the 25 or more schools that train examiners provide only an eight-week course of instruction and require two years of college for admission.                                                       19

While Raskin in his laboratory continues to attempt to make the polygraph more scientifically valid and reliable, Lykken continues to question the ground rules. Where Raskin sees the polygraph as a legitimate tool for protecting society, Lykken fears that the technology poses a greater threat to the innocent than to the guilty and, ultimately, is based on little more than an intimidating mystique that uses the language and trappings of science to sell itself to a trusting public.        20

Most law enforcement officials, however, look on the polygraph not as a technique for intimidating and imprisoning people but for screening out innocent suspects early, thus expediting the legal process. They prefer to talk about truth verification rather than lie detection. But for the present, verifying the truth appears at least as difficult as detecting a lie.                                                               21

# Questions

1. Having read the entire essay, go back and reread the first paragraph. What passages in this paragraph especially indicate the writer's attitude toward the use of lie detectors?

2. What words or phrases in paragraphs 2 and 3 are especially charged with negative connotations?
3. In paragraph 20 Meyer implies that the use of polygraphs relies chiefly on "an intimidating mystique"? What does he mean? Do you agree?
4. In paragraph 15 Meyer calls polygraphy an "American obsession." Why? How does he explain our faith in polygraphy? On the whole, do you agree with his characterization of Americans in this paragraph?
5. List Meyer's arguments against the uses of polygraphs, and then evaluate them. Do you believe that he gives convincing reasons against using polygraphs in examining persons accused of crimes? In examining applicants for jobs?
6. After reading this essay, how would you feel if a prospective employer asked you to submit to a polygraph? What course of action do you think you would follow?

Lewis Thomas

# The Hazards of Science

The code word for criticism of science and scientists these days is "hubris." Once you've said that word, you've said it all; it sums up, in a word, all of today's apprehensions and misgivings in the public mind—not just about what is perceived as the insufferable attitude of the scientists themselves but, enclosed in the same word,

1

Lewis Thomas was born in 1913 in New York, and was educated at Princeton and Harvard. A research pathologist and a medical administrator, he is now the chancellor of Memorial Sloan-Kettering Cancer Center in New York. Thomas is also the author of four books of essays, one of which won the National Book Award.

what science and technology are perceived to be doing to make this century, this near to its ending, turn out so wrong.

"Hubris" is a powerful word, containing layers of powerful meaning, derived from a very old word, but with a new life of its own, growing way beyond the limits of its original meaning. Today, it is strong enough to carry the full weight of disapproval for the cast of mind that thought up atomic fusion and fission as ways of first blowing up and later heating cities as well as the attitudes which led to strip-mining, offshore oil wells, Kepone, food additives, SSTs, and the tiny spherical particles of plastic recently discovered clogging the waters of the Sargasso Sea.

The biomedical sciences are now caught up with physical science and technology in the same kind of critical judgment, with the same pejorative word. Hubris is responsible, it is said, for the whole biological revolution. It is hubris that has given us the prospects of behavior control, psychosurgery, fetal research, heart transplants, the cloning of prominent politicians from bits of their own eminent tissue, iatrogenic disease, overpopulation, and recombinant DNA. This last, the new technology that permits the stitching of one creature's genes into the DNA of another, to make hybrids, is currently cited as the ultimate example of hubris. It is hubris for man to manufacture a hybrid on his own.

So now we are back to the first word again, from "hybrid" to "hubris," and the hidden meaning of two beings joined unnaturally together by man is somehow retained. Today's joining is straight out of Greek mythology: it is the combining of man's capacity with the special prerogative of the gods, and it is really in this sense of outrage that the word "hubris" is being used today. That is what the word has grown into, a warning, a code word, a shorthand signal from the language itself: if man starts doing things reserved for the gods, deifying himself, the outcome will be something worse for him, symbolically, than the litters of wild boars and domestic sows were for the ancient Romans.

To be charged with hubris is therefore an extremely serious matter, and not to be dealt with by murmuring things about antiscience and antiintellectualism, which is what many of us engaged in science tend to do these days. The doubts about our enterprise have their origin in the most profound kind of human anxiety. If we are right and the critics are wrong, then it has to be that the word "hubris" is being mistakenly employed, that this is not what we are up to, that there is, for the time being anyway, a fundamental misunderstanding of science.

I suppose there is one central question to be dealt with, and I am  6 not at all sure how to deal with it, although I am quite certain about my own answer to it. It is this: are there some kinds of information leading to some sorts of knowledge that human beings are really better off not having? Is there a limit to scientific inquiry not set by what is knowable but what we *ought* to be knowing? Should we stop short of learning about some things, for fear of what we, or someone, will do with the knowledge? My own answer is a flat no, but I must confess that this is an intuitive response and I am neither inclined nor trained to reason my way through it.

There has been some effort, in and out of scientific quarters, to  7 make recombinant DNA into the issue on which to settle this argument. Proponents of this line of research are accused of pure hubris, of assuming the rights of gods, of arrogance and outrage; what is more, they confess themselves to be in the business of making live hybrids with their own hands. The mayor of Cambridge and the attorney general of New York have both been advised to put a stop to it, forthwith.

It is not quite the same sort of argument, however, as the one  8 about limiting knowledge, although this is surely part of it. The knowledge is already here, and the rage of the argument is about its application in technology. Should DNA for making certain useful or interesting proteins be incorporated into *E. coli* plasmids or not? Is there a risk of inserting the wrong sort of toxins or hazardous viruses, and then having the new hybrid organisms spread beyond the laboratory? Is this a technology for creating new varieties of pathogens, and should it be stopped because of this?

If the argument is held to this level, I can see no reason why it  9 cannot be settled, by reasonable people. We have learned a great deal about the handling of dangerous microbes in the last century, although I must say that the opponents of recombinant-DNA research tend to downgrade this huge body of information. At one time or another, agents as hazardous as those of rabies, psittacosis, plague, and typhus have been dealt with by investigators in secure laboratories, with only rare instances of self-infection of the investigators themselves, and no instances at all of epidemics. It takes some high imagining to postulate the creation of brand-new pathogens so wild and voracious as to spread from equally secure laboratories to endanger human life at large, as some of the arguers are now maintaining.

But this is precisely the trouble with the recombinant-DNA prob-  10
lem: it has become an emotional issue, with too many irretrievably lost
tempers on both sides. It has lost the sound of a discussion of technological safety, and begins now to sound like something else, almost
like a religious controversy, and here it is moving toward the central
issue: are there some things in science we should not be learning
about?

There is an inevitably long list of hard questions to follow this one,  11
beginning with the one which asks whether the mayor of Cambridge
should be the one to decide, first off.

Maybe we'd be wiser, all of us, to back off before the recombinant-  12
DNA issue becomes too large to cope with. If we're going to have a
fight about it, let it be confined to the immediate issue of safety and
security, of the recombinants now under consideration, and let us by
all means have regulations and guidelines to assure the public safety
wherever these are indicated or even suggested. But if it is possible
let us stay off that question about limiting human knowledge. It is too
loaded, and we'll simply not be able to cope with it.

By this time it will have become clear that I have already taken  13
sides in the matter, and my point of view is entirely prejudiced. This
is true, but with a qualification. I am not so much in favor of recombinant-DNA research as I am opposed to the opposition to this line of
inquiry. As a longtime student of infectious-disease agents I do not
take kindly the declarations that we do not know how to keep from
catching things in laboratories, much less how to keep them from
spreading beyond the laboratory walls. I believe we learned a lot about
this sort of thing, long ago. Moreover, I regard it as a form of hubris-
in-reverse to claim that man can make deadly pathogenic microorganisms so easily. In my view, it takes a long time and a great deal of
interliving before a microbe can become a successful pathogen. Pathogenicity is, in a sense, a highly skilled trade, and only a tiny minority
of all the numberless tons of microbes on the earth has ever been
involved in it; most bacteria are busy with their own business, browsing and recycling the rest of life. Indeed, pathogenicity often seems to
me a sort of biological accident in which signals are misdirected by the
microbe or misinterpreted by the host, as in the case of endotoxin, or
in which the intimacy between host and microbe is of such long standing that a form of molecular mimicry becomes possible, as in the case
of diphtheria toxin. I do not believe that by simply putting together
new combinations of genes one can create creatures as highly skilled
and adapted for dependence as a pathogen must be, any more than I

have ever believed that microbial life from the moon or Mars could possibly make a living on this planet.

But, as I said, I'm not at all sure this is what the argument is really 14 about. Behind it is that other discussion, which I wish we would not have to become enmeshed in.

I cannot speak for the physical sciences, which have moved an 15 immense distance in this century by any standard, but it does seem to me that in the biological and medical sciences we are still far too ignorant to begin making judgments about what sorts of things we should be learning or not learning. To the contrary, we ought to be grateful for whatever snatches we can get hold of, and we ought to be out there on a much larger scale than today's, looking for more.

We should be very careful with that word "hubris," and make 16 sure it is not used when not warranted. There is a great danger in applying it to the search for knowledge. The application of knowledge is another matter, and there is hubris in plenty of our technology, but I do not believe that looking for new information about nature, at whatever level, can possibly be called unnatural. Indeed, if there is any single attribute of human beings, apart from language, which distinguishes them from all other creatures on earth, it is their insatiable, uncontrollable drive to learn things and then to exchange the information with others of the species. Learning is what we do, when you think about it. I cannot think of a human impulse more difficult to govern.

But I can imagine lots of reasons for trying to govern it. New in- 17 formation about nature is very likely, at the outset, to be upsetting to someone or other. The recombinant-DNA line of research is already upsetting, not because of the dangers now being argued about but because it is disturbing, in a fundamental way, to face the fact that the genetic machinery in control of the planet's life can be fooled around with so easily. We do not like the idea that anything so fixed and stable as a species line can be changed. The notion that genes can be taken out of one genome and inserted in another is unnerving. Classical mythology is peopled with mixed beings—part man, part animal or plant—and most of them are associated with tragic stories. Recombinant DNA is a reminder of bad dreams.

The easiest decision for society to make in terms of this kind is to 18 appoint an agency, or a commission, or a subcommittee within an agency to look into the problem and provide advice. And the easiest course for a committee to take, when confronted by any process that appears to be disturbing people or making them uncomfortable, is to recommend that it be stopped, at least for the time being.

I can easily imagine such a committee, composed of unimpeach- 19 able public figures, arriving at the decision that the time is not quite ripe for further exploration of the transplantation of genes, that we should put this off for a while, maybe until the next century, and get on with other affairs that make us less discomfited. Why not do science on something more popular, say, how to get solar energy more cheaply? Or mental health?

The trouble is, it would be very hard to stop once this line was 20 begun. There are, after all, all sorts of scientific inquiry that are not much liked by one constituency or another, and we might soon find ourselves with crowded rosters, panels, standing committees, set up in Washington for the appraisal, and then the regulation, of research. Not on grounds of the possible value and usefulness of the new knowledge, mind you, but for guarding society against scientific hubris, against the kinds of knowledge we're better off without.

It would be absolutely irresistible as a way of spending time, and 21 people would form long queues for membership. Almost anything would be fair game, certainly anything to do with genetics, anything relating to population control, or, on the other side, research on aging. Very few fields would get by, except perhaps for some, like mental health, in which nobody really expects anything much to happen, surely nothing new or disturbing.

The research areas in the greatest trouble would be those already 22 containing a sense of bewilderment and surprise, with discernible prospects of upheaving present dogmas.

It is hard to predict how science is going to turn out, and if it is 23 really good science it is impossible to predict. This is in the nature of the enterprise. If the things to be found are actually new, they are by definition unknown in advance, and there is no way of telling in advance where a really new line of inquiry will lead. You cannot make choices in this matter, selecting things you think you're going to like and shutting off the lines that make for discomfort. You either have science or you don't, and if you have it you are obliged to accept the surprising and disturbing pieces of information, even the overwhelming and upheaving ones, along with the neat and promptly useful bits. It is like that.

The only solid piece of scientific truth about which I feel totally 24 confident is that we are profoundly ignorant about nature. Indeed, I regard this as a major discovery of the past hundred years of biology. It is, in its way, an illuminating piece of news. It would have amazed the brightest minds of the eighteenth-century Enlightenment to be told by any of us how little we know, and how bewildering seems the way ahead. It is this sudden confrontation with the depth and scope of ignorance that represents the most significant contribution of twentieth-century science to the human intellect. We are, at last, facing up to it. In earlier times, we either pretended to understand how things worked or ignored the problem, or simply made up stories to fill the gaps. Now that we have begun exploring in earnest, doing serious science, we are getting glimpses of how huge the questions are, and how far from being answered. Because of this, these are hard times for the human intellect, and it is no wonder that we are depressed. It is not so bad being ignorant if you are totally ignorant; the hard thing is knowing in some detail the reality of ignorance, the worst spots and here and there the not-so-bad spots, but no true light at the end of any tunnel nor even any tunnels that can yet be trusted. Hard times, indeed.

But we are making a beginning, and there ought to be some sat-   25
isfaction, even exhilaration, in that. The method works. There are probably no questions we can think up that can't be answered, sooner or later, including even the matter of consciousness. To be sure, there may well be questions we can't think up, ever, and therefore limits to the reach of human intellect which we will never know about, but that is another matter. Within our limits, we should be able to work our way through to all our answers, if we keep at it long enough, and pay attention.

I am putting it this way, with all the presumption and confidence   26
that I can summon, in order to raise another, last question. Is this hubris? Is there something fundamentally unnatural, or intrinsically wrong, or hazardous for the species in the ambition that drives us all to reach a comprehensive understanding of nature, including ourselves? I cannot believe it. It would seem to me a more unnatural thing, and more of an offense against nature, for us to come on the same scene endowed as we are with curiosity, filled to overbrimming as we are with questions, and naturally talented as we are for the asking of clear questions, and then for us to do nothing about it or, worse, to try to suppress the questions. This is the greater danger for our species, to try to pretend that we are another kind of animal, that we do not need to satisfy our curiosity, that we can get along somehow without inquiry and exploration and experimentation, and that the human

mind can rise above its ignorance by simply asserting that there are things it has no need to know. This, to my way of thinking, is the real hubris, and it carries danger for us all.

# Questions

1. In paragraph 5 Thomas says, "If we are right and the critics are wrong, then . . . there is, for the time being anyway, a fundamental misunderstanding of science." Who are the "we" Thomas apparently addresses? Who are the "critics"? What is the "misunderstanding"? And what does Thomas seem to imply by "for the time being anyway"?

2. In paragraph 7 Thomas refers to recombinant DNA. What is recombinant DNA and why does Thomas mention it?

3. In paragraph 10 Thomas poses the question, "Are there some things in science we should not be learning about?" What is his answer? What arguments does he offer in support of his position? What means, other than arguments, does he use to persuade us to accept his arguments?

4. What is the function of "the mayor of Cambridge" in Thomas's argument? What does he or she represent?

5. How would you characterize Thomas's tone? Self-satisfied? Aggressive? Courteous? Or what? Consider, for instance, this sentence from paragraph 9: "It takes some high imagining to postulate the creation of brand-new pathogens so wild and voracious as to spread from equally secure laboratories to endanger human life at large, as some of the arguers are now maintaining." Rewrite the sentence—and one or two others of your own choice—so that the point remains essentially the same but the tone is changed, and then explain the differences.

6. It is probably fair to say that Thomas states his thesis succinctly in the second half of the first sentence of paragraph 15: ". . . it does seem to me that in the biological and medical sciences we are still far too ignorant to begin making judgments about what sorts of things we should be learning or not learning." This sentence appears midway in the essay. Is it, or something like it, needed earlier? Why, or why not?

7. In paragraph 16 Thomas says, "I do not believe that looking for new information about nature, at whatever level, can possibly be called unnatural." Is he using the word "nature" in two different senses (in the noun "nature" and the adjective "unnatural")? Is he, by appealing to "nature," opening the door to any action that anyone

wants to defend? Could one, for instance, similarly argue that rape, racial prejudice, and drug-taking are "natural" and therefore acceptable?
8. Reread Thomas's first and last paragraphs and then comment on his strategy in beginning and ending the way he does.

## Italo Calvino

# All at One Point

$T$hrough the calculations begun by Edwin P. Hubble on the galaxies' velocity of recession, we can establish the moment when all the universe's matter was concentrated in a single point, before it began to expand in space.   1

Naturally, we were all there,—*old Qfwfq said,*—where else could we have been? Nobody knew then that there could be space. Or time either: what use did we have for time, packed in there like sardines?   2

I say "packed like sardines," using a literary image: in reality there wasn't even space to pack us into. Every point of each of us coincided with every point of each of the others in a single point, which was where we all were. In fact, we didn't even bother one another, except for personality differences, because when space doesn't exist, having somebody unpleasant like Mr. Pber$^t$ Pber$^d$ underfoot all the time is the most irritating thing.   3

How many of us were there? Oh, I was never able to figure that out, not even approximately. To make a count, we would have had to move apart, at least a little, and instead we all occupied that same point. Contrary to what you might think, it wasn't the sort of situation that encourages sociability; I know, for example, that in other periods   4

---

Italo Calvino (1923–1985) was of Italian descent, but he was born in Cuba, where his father was engaged in agricultural research. Soon after his birth, the family returned to Italy, where Calvino was educated. During World War II he was a member of the Anti-Fascist Resistance; later he edited an intellectual journal and wrote stories, novels, and essays.

We print here one of the twelve fanciful stories that constitute *Cosmicomics*.

neighbors called on one another; but there, because of the fact that we were all neighbors, nobody even said good morning or good evening to anybody else.

In the end each of us associated only with a limited number of acquaintances. The ones I remember most are Mrs. Ph(i)Nk$_o$, her friend De XuaeauX, a family of immigrants by the name of Z'zu, and Mr. Pber$^t$ Pber$^d$, whom I just mentioned. There was also a cleaning woman—"maintenance staff" she was called—only one, for the whole universe, since there was so little room. To tell the truth, she had nothing to do all day long, not even dusting—inside one point not even a grain of dust can enter—so she spent all her time gossiping and complaining.

Just with the people I've already named we would have been overcrowded; but you have to add all the stuff we had to keep piled up in there: all the material that was to serve afterwards to form the universe, now dismantled and concentrated in such a way that you weren't able to tell what was later to become part of astronomy (like the nebula of Andromeda) from what was assigned to geography (the Vosges, for example) or to chemistry (like certain beryllium isotopes). And on top of that, we were always bumping against the Z'zu family's household goods: camp beds, mattresses, baskets; these Z'zus, if you weren't careful, with the excuse that they were a large family, would begin to act as if they were the only ones in the world: they even wanted to hang lines across our point to dry their washing.

But the others also had wronged the Z'zus, to begin with, by calling them "immigrants," on the pretext that, since the others had been there first, the Z'zus had come later. This was mere unfounded prejudice—that seems obvious to me—because neither before nor after existed, nor any place to immigrate from, but there were those who insisted that the concept of "immigrant" could be understood in the abstract, outside of space and time.

It was what you might call a narrow-minded attitude, our outlook at that time, very petty. The fault of the environment in which we had been reared. An attitude that, basically, has remained in all of us, mind you: it keeps cropping up even today, if two of us happen to meet—at the bus stop, in a movie house, at an international dentists' convention—and start reminiscing about the old days. We say hello—at times somebody recognizes me, at other times I recognize somebody—and we promptly start asking about this one and that one (even if each remembers only a few of those remembered by the others), and so we start in again on the old disputes, the slanders, the denigrations. Until somebody mentions Mrs. Ph(i)Nk$_o$—every conversation finally gets around to her—and then, all of a sudden, the pettiness is put aside, and we feel uplifted, filled with a blissful, generous emotion. Mrs. Ph(i)Nk$_o$, the only one that none of us has forgotten and that we all regret. Where has she ended up? I have long since stopped looking for her: Mrs. Ph(i)Nk$_o$, her bosom, her thighs, her orange dressing gown—we'll never meet her again, in this system of galaxies or in any other.

Let me make one thing clear: this theory that the universe, after    9
having reached an extremity of rarefaction, will be condensed again has never convinced me. And yet many of us are counting only on that, continually making plans for the time when we'll all be back there again. Last month, I went into the bar here on the corner and whom did I see? Mr. Pber$^t$ Pber$^d$. "What's new with you? How do you happen to be in this neighborhood?" I learned that he's the agent for a plastics firm, in Pavia. He's the same as ever, with his silver tooth, his loud suspenders. "When we go back there," he said to me, in a whisper, "the thing we have to make sure of is, this time, certain people remain out . . . You know who I mean: those Z'zus . . ."

I would have liked to answer him by saying that I've heard a num-   10
ber of people make the same remark, concluding: "You know who I mean . . . Mr. Pber$^t$ Pber$^d$ . . ."

To avoid the subject, I hastened to say: "What about Mrs.    11
Ph(i)Nk$_o$? Do you think we'll find her back there again?"

"Ah, yes . . . She, by all means . . ." he said, turning purple.    12

For all of us the hope of returning to that point means, above all,    13
the hope of being once more with Mrs. Ph(i)Nk$_o$. (This applies even to me, though I don't believe in it.) And in that bar, as always happens, we fell to talking about her, and were moved; even Mr. Pber$^t$ Pber$^d$'s unpleasantness faded, in the face of that memory.

Mrs. Ph(i)Nk$_o$'s great secret is that she never aroused any jealousy    14
among us. Or any gossip, either. The fact that she went to bed with her friend, Mr. De XuaeauX, was well known. But in a point, if there's a bed, it takes up the whole point, so it isn't a question of *going* to bed, but of *being* there, because anybody in the point is also in the bed. Consequently, it was inevitable that she should be in bed also with each of us. If she had been another person, there's no telling all the things that would have been said about her. It was the cleaning woman who always started the slander, and the others didn't have to be coaxed to imitate her. On the subject of the Z'zu family—for a change!—the horrible things we had to hear: father, daughters, brothers, sisters,

mother, aunts: nobody showed any hesitation even before the most
sinister insinuation. But with her it was different: the happiness I derived from her was the joy of being concealed, punctiform, in her, and
of protecting her, punctiform, in me; it was at the same time vicious
contemplation (thanks to the promiscuity of the punctiform convergence of us all in her) and also chastity (given her punctiform impe-
netrability). In short: what more could I ask?

And all of this, which was true of me, was true also for each of  15
the others. And for her: she contained and was contained with equal
happiness, and she welcomed us and loved and inhabited all equally.

We got along so well all together, so well that something extraor-  16
dinary was bound to happen. It was enough for her to say, at a certain
moment: "Oh, if I only had some room, how I'd like to make some
noodles for you boys!" And in that moment we all thought of the space
that her round arms would occupy, moving backward and forward
with the rolling pin over the dough, her bosom leaning over the great
mound of flour and eggs which cluttered the wide board while her
arms kneaded and kneaded, white and shiny with oil up to the elbows;
we thought of the space that the flour would occupy, and the wheat
for the flour, and the fields to raise the wheat, and the mountains from
which the water would flow to irrigate the fields, and the grazing lands
for the herds of calves that would give their meat for the sauce; of the
space it would take for the Sun to arrive with its rays, to ripen the
wheat; of the space for the Sun to condense from the clouds of stellar
gases and burn; of the quantities of stars and galaxies and galactic
masses in flight through space which would be needed to hold suspended every galaxy, every nebula, every sun, every planet, and at
the same time we thought of it, this space was inevitably being formed,
at the same time that Mrs. Ph(i)Nk$_o$ was uttering those words: ". . .
ah, what noodles, boys!" the point that contained her and all of us
was expanding in a halo of distance in light-years and light-centuries
and billions of light-millennia, and we were being hurled to the four
corners of the universe (Mr. Pber$^t$ Pber$^d$ all the way to Pavia), and she,
dissolved into I don't know what kind of energy-light-heat, she, Mrs.
Ph(i)Nk$_o$, she who in the midst of our closed, petty world had been
capable of a generous impulse, "Boys, the noodles I would make for
you!," a true outburst of general love, initiating at the same moment
the concept of space and, properly speaking, space itself, and time,
and universal gravitation, and the gravitating universe, making possible billions and billions of suns, and of planets, and fields of wheat,
and Mrs. Ph(i)Nk$_o$s, scattered through the continents of the planets,

kneading with floury, oil-shiny, generous arms, and she lost at that very moment, and we, mourning her loss.


# Questions

1. From the first line of "All at One Point" we learn that the story is being told to us by someone who heard it from "old Qfwfq," the chief narrator of the twelve stories that constitute *Cosmicomics.* What do we learn of "old Qfwfq" from this story? If you were asked to write a character sketch of him, what qualities would you mention? Can you provide a physical description?
2. How does Qfwfq characterize "the others," that is, with the exceptions of the Z'zus and Mrs. Ph(i)Nk$_o$? In what ways do the others resemble us, or people we know? What inspires Qfwfq to speak of their "closed, petty world"?
3. In paragraph 14 Qfwfq speaks, mysteriously, of the happiness of "vicious contemplation" thanks to the "punctiform convergence of us all in her [Mrs. Ph(i)Nk$_o$] and also chastity." What on earth—or wherever we are—can he mean?
4. At the beginning of the last paragraph Qfwfq tells us "something extraordinary was bound to happen." What is the extraordinary thing that happens? What causes it to happen, according to Qfwfq?
5. In what ways does Calvino's fiction make use of current scientific theories of the creation of the universe? In what ways does it evoke religious explanations of the Creation?

Richard Wilbur

# Mind

Mind in its purest play is like some bat
That beats about in caverns all alone,
Contriving by a kind of senseless wit
Not to conclude against a wall of stone.                    4

It has no need to falter or explore;
Darkly it knows what obstacles are there,
And so may weave and flitter, dip and soar
In perfect courses through the blackest air.                8

And has this simile a like perfection?
The mind is like a bat. Precisely. Save
That in the very happiest intellection
A graceful error may correct the cave.                      12

## Questions

1. If, in "Mind," the human mind is like a bat, what is like the cavern
   "it beats about in . . . all alone"? Bats are not usually alone; why
   is this bat alone?
2. What mental activities are suggested by the phrase "in its purest
   play" in line 1? In line 3, is more than one meaning of "senseless"
   possible? How are both physical and mental acts contained in line
   4?
3. In line 6 explain the pun in "darkly."
4. What change in rhythm do you detect in line 10? How is the change
   appropriate to the meaning of the line?
5. Bats have been known to change the shape of caves by brushing
   against the walls or by crashing into them. What kinds of "errors"
   are produced by "the very happiest intellection" (line 11)? In what
   sense can errors "correct the cave" in which Mind plays?

Richard Wilbur was born in 1921 in New York City. After graduating from Amherst
College and serving in the infantry in Italy and France (1943–1945), he earned
a master's degree in 1947—the year he published his first book of poems, *The
Beautiful Changes and Other Poems*. One of his later books was awarded the
Pulitzer Prize for Poetry.

# 11
## THE DEEP HEART'S CORE

*At the Lapin Agile*
**Pablo Picasso, 1905**

Private Collector

*Self-Portrait with a Palette*
**Pablo Picasso, 1906**

Philadelphia Museum of Art, A. E. Gallatin Collection

*The Sculptor and His Statue*
**Pablo Picasso, 1933**

# Short Views

The heart has its reasons which reason knows nothing of.
**Blaise Pascal**

The Masai when they were moved from their old country, north of
the railway line, to the present reserve, took with them the names
of their hills, plains, and rivers, and gave them to the hills, plains,
and rivers in the new country. It is a bewildering thing to the
traveler. The Masai were carrying their cut roots with them as a
medicine.
**Isak Dinesen,** *Out of Africa*

Man is the only animal that laughs and weeps; for he is the only
animal that is struck by the difference between what things are and
what they might have been.
**William Hazlitt**

We are not only gregarious animals, liking to be in sight of our
fellows, but we have an innate propensity to get ourselves noticed,
and noticed favorably, by our kind. No more fiendish punishment
could be devised, were such a thing physically possible, than that
one should be turned loose in society and remain absolutely
unnoticed by all the members thereof.
**William James**

My life is spent in a perpetual alternation between two rhythms, the
rhythm of attracting people for fear I may be lonely and the rhythm
of trying to get rid of them because I know that I am bored.
**C. E. M. Joad**

The eye is not satisfied with seeing, nor the ear filled with hearing.
**Ecclesiastes 1:8**

*London, December 5, 1749*

Dear Boy: Those who suppose that men in general act rationally,
because they are called rational creatures, know very little of the

world, and if they act themselves upon that supposition, will nine times in ten find themselves grossly mistaken. . . . Thus, the speculative, cloistered pedant, in his solitary cell, forms systems of things as they should be, not as they are; and writes as decisively and absurdly upon war, politics, manners, and characters, as that pedant talked, who was so kind as to instruct Hannibal in the art of war. Such closet politicians never fail to assign the deepest motives for the most trifling actions: instead of often ascribing the greatest actions to the most trifling causes, in which they would be much seldomer mistaken. They read and write of kings, heroes, and statesmen, as never doing anything but upon the deepest principles of sound policy. But those who see and observe kings, heroes, and statesmen, discover that they have headaches, indigestions, humors, and passions, just like other people; everyone of which, in their turns, determine their wills, in defiance of their reason. Had we only read in the "Life of Alexander," that he burned Persepolis, it would doubtless have been accounted for from deep policy: we should have been told, that his new conquest could not have been secured without the destruction of that capital, which would have been the constant seat of cabals, conspiracies, and revolts. But, luckily, we are informed at the same time, that this hero, this demi-god, this son and heir of Jupiter Ammon, happened to get extremely drunk with his w—e; and, by way of frolic, destroyed one of the finest cities in the world. Read men, therefore, yourself, not in books but in nature. Adopt no systems, but study them yourself. Observe their weaknesses, their passions, their humors, of all which their understanding are, nine times in ten, the dupes. You will then know that they are to be gained, influenced, or led, much oftener by little things than by great ones; and, consequently, you will no longer think those things little, which tend to such great purposes.
**Lord Chesterfield**

The changing wisdom of successive generations discards ideas, questions facts, demolishes theories. But the artist appeals to that part of our being which is not dependent on wisdom: to that in us which is a gift and not an acquisition—and, therefore, more permanently enduring. He speaks to our capacity for delight and wonder, to the sense of mystery surrounding our lives; to our sense of pity, and beauty, and pain; to the latent feeling of fellowship

with all creation—and to the subtle but invincible conviction of solidarity that knits together the loneliness of innumerable hearts, to the solidarity in dreams, in joy, in sorrow, in aspirations, in illusions, in hope, in fear, which binds men to each other, which binds together all humanity—the dead to the living and the living to the unborn.
> **Joseph Conrad**

The storyteller's own experience of men and things, whether for good or ill—not only what he has passed through himself, but even events which he has only witnessed or been told of—has moved him to an emotion so passionate that he can no longer keep it shut up in his heart. Again and again something in his own life or in that around him will seem to the writer so important that he cannot bear to let it pass into oblivion. There must never come a time, he feels, when men do not know about it.
> **Lady Murasaki,** *The Tale of Genji*

In seed time learn, in harvest teach, in winter enjoy.
Drive your cart and your plow over the bones of the dead.
The road of excess leads to the palace of wisdom.
Prudence is a rich ugly old maid courted by incapacity.
He who desires but acts not, breeds pestilence.
The cut worm forgives the plow.
Dip him in the river who loves water.
A fool sees not the same tree that a wise man sees.
He whose face gives no light, shall never become a star.
Eternity is in love with the productions of time.
The busy bee has no time for sorrow.
The hours of folly are measured by the clock; but of wisdom, no
    clock can measure.
All wholesome food is caught without a net or a trap.
Bring out number, weight, and measure in a year of dearth.
No bird soars too high, if he soars with his own wings.
A dead body revenges not injuries.
The most sublime act is to set another before you.
If the fool would persist in his folly he would become wise.
Folly is the cloak of knavery.
Shame is Pride's cloak.
> **William Blake**

Before his death, Rabbi Zusya said, "In the coming world, they will not ask me: 'Why were you not Moses?' They will ask me: 'Why were you not Zusya?' "
**Hasidic Tale**

## William Butler Yeats

# The Lake Isle of Innisfree

I will arise and go now, and go to Innisfree,
And a small cabin build there, of clay and wattles
  made:
Nine bean-rows will I have there, a hive for the honey-
  bee,
And live alone in the bee-loud glade.                              4

And I shall have some peace there, for peace comes
  dropping slow,
Dropping from the veils of the morning to where the
  cricket sings;
There midnight's all a glimmer, and noon a purple
  glow,
And evening full of the linnet's wings                             8

I will arise and go now, for always night and day
I hear lake water lapping with low sounds by the shore;
While I stand on the roadway, or on the pavements
  gray,
I hear it in the deep heart's core.                                12

---

William Butler Yeats (1865–1939), born in Ireland, became one of the leading forces both in the Irish Literary Renaissance and in English literature of the first half of the twentieth century. He wrote plays, prose fiction, and essays, but he is best known for his poetry. In 1924 he was awarded the Nobel Prize for literature. We give one of his early poems, then a comment on it from his *Autobiographies*.

## William Butler Yeats

# Remembering "The Lake Isle of Innisfree"

I had various women friends on whom I would call toward 1
five o'clock mainly to discuss my thoughts that I could not bring to a
man without meeting some competing thought, but partly because
their tea and toast saved my pennies for the bus ride home; but with
women, apart from their intimate exchanges of thought, I was timid
and abashed. I was sitting on a seat in front of the British Museum
feeding pigeons when a couple of girls sat near and began enticing my
pigeons away, laughing and whispering to one another, and I looked
straight in front of me, very indignant, and presently went into the
Museum without turning my head toward them. Since then I have
often wondered if they were pretty or merely very young. Sometimes
I told myself very adventurous love-stories with myself for hero, and
at other times I planned out a life of lonely austerity, and at other times
mixed the ideals and planned a life of lonely austerity mitigated by
periodical lapses. I had still the ambition, formed in Sligo in my teens,
of living in imitation of Thoreau on Innisfree, a little island in Lough
Gill, and when walking through Fleet Street very homesick I heard a
little tinkle of water and saw a fountain in a shop-window which balanced a little ball upon its jet, and began to remember lake water. From
the sudden remembrance came my poem *Innisfree,* my first lyric with
anything in its rhythm of my own music. I had begun to loosen rhythm
as an escape from rhetoric and from that emotion of the crowd that
rhetoric brings, but I only understood vaguely and occasionally that I
must for my special purpose use nothing but the common syntax. A
couple of years later I would not have written that first line with its
conventional archaism—"Arise and go"—nor the inversion in the last
stanza. Passing another day by the new Law Courts, a building that
I admired because it was Gothic—"It is not very good," Morris had
said, "but it is better than anything else they have got and so they
hate it"—I grew suddenly oppressed by the great weight of stone, and
thought, "There are miles and miles of stone and brick all round me,"
and presently added, "If John the Baptist or his like were to come
again and had his mind set upon it, he could make all these people
go out into some wilderness leaving their buildings empty," and that

thought, which does not seem very valuable now, so enlightened the day that it is still vivid in the memory.

## Questions

1. In his autobiographical account Yeats describes himself as "very homesick" at the time that the idea for "The Lake Isle of Innisfree" came to him. If "homesick" strikes you, as it does us, as inadequate to describe the speaker's mood in the poem, how would you describe it?
2. What other discrepancies do you find between Yeats's account of writing the poem and the poem itself? How do you explain the differences?

## E. M. Forster

# My Wood

A few years ago I wrote a book which dealt in part with the difficulties of the English in India. Feeling that they would have had no difficulties in India themselves, the Americans read the book freely. The more they read it the better it made them feel, and a cheque to the author was the result. I bought a wood with the cheque. It is not a large wood—it contains scarcely any trees, and it is intersected, blast it, by a public footpath. Still, it is the first property that I have owned, so it is right that other people should participate in my shame, and should ask themselves, in accents that will vary in horror, this very important question: What is the effect of property upon the character? Don't let's touch economics; the effect of private ownership upon the community as a whole is another question—a more important

E[dward] M[organ] Forster (1879–1970) was born in London and was graduated from King's College, Cambridge. He traveled widely and lived for a while in India, but most of his life was spent back at King's College. His best-known novel, *A Passage to India* (1926), is alluded to in the first line of the essay that we reprint.

question, perhaps, but another one. Let's keep to psychology. If you own things, what's their effect on you? What's the effect on me of my wood?

In the first place, it makes me feel heavy. Property does have this 2 effect. Property produces men of weight, and it was a man of weight who failed to get into the Kingdom of Heaven. He was not wicked, that unfortunate millionaire in the parable, he was only stout; he stuck out in front, not to mention behind, and as he wedged himself this way and that in the crystalline entrance and bruised his well-fed flanks, he saw beneath him a comparatively slim camel passing through the eye of a needle and being woven into the robe of God. The Gospels all through couple stoutness and slowness. They point out what is perfectly obvious, yet seldom realized: that if you have a lot of things you cannot move about a lot, that furniture requires dusting, dusters require servants, servants require insurance stamps, and the whole tangle of them makes you think twice before you accept an invitation to dinner or go for a bathe in the Jordan. Sometimes the Gospels proceed further and say with Tolstoy that property is sinful; they approach the difficult ground of asceticism here, where I cannot follow them. But as to the immediate effects of property on people, they just show straightforward logic. It produces men of weight. Men of weight cannot, by definition, move like the lightning from the East unto the West, and the ascent of a fourteen-stone[1] bishop into a pulpit is thus the exact antithesis of the coming of the Son of Man. My wood makes me feel heavy.

In the second place, it makes me feel it ought to be larger. 3

The other day I heard a twig snap in it. I was annoyed at first, for 4 I thought that someone was blackberrying, and depreciating the value of the undergrowth. On coming nearer, I saw it was not a man who had trodden on the twig and snapped it, but a bird, and I felt pleased. My bird. The bird was not equally pleased. Ignoring the relation between us, it took fright as soon as it saw the shape of my face, and flew straight over the boundary hedge into a field, the property of Mrs. Henessy, where it sat down with a loud squawk. It had become Mrs. Henessy's bird. Something seemed grossly amiss here, something that would not have occurred had the wood been larger. I could not afford to buy Mrs. Henessy out, I dared not murder her, and limitations of this sort beset me on every side. Ahab did not want that vineyard—he only needed it to round off his property, preparatory to plotting a

---

[1] 196-pound. (Editors' note)

new curve—and all the land around my wood has become necessary to me in order to round off the wood. A boundary protects. But—poor little thing—the boundary ought in its turn to be protected. Noises on the edge of it. Children throw stones. A little more, and then a little more, until we reach the sea. Happy Canute! Happier Alexander! And after all, why should even the world be the limit of possession? A rocket containing a Union Jack, will, it is hoped, be shortly fired at the moon. Mars. Sirius. Beyond which . . . But these immensities ended by saddening me. I could not suppose that my wood was the destined nucleus of universal dominion—it is so very small and contains no mineral wealth beyond the blackberries. Nor was I comforted when Mrs. Henessy's bird took alarm for the second time and flew clean away from us all, under the belief that it belonged to itself.

In the third place, property makes its owner feel that he ought to 5 do something to it. Yet he isn't sure what. A restlessness comes over him, a vague sense that he has a personality to express—the same sense which, without any vagueness, leads the artist to an act of creation. Sometimes I think I will cut down such trees as remain in the wood, at other times I want to fill up the gaps between them with new trees. Both impulses are pretentious and empty. They are not honest movements towards money-making or beauty. They spring from a foolish desire to express myself and from an inability to enjoy what I have got. Creation, property, enjoyment form a sinister trinity in the human mind. Creation and enjoyment are both very very good, yet they are often unattainable without a material basis, and at such moments property pushes itself in as a substitute, saying, "Accept me instead—I'm good enough for all three." It is not enough. It is, as Shakespeare said of lust, "The expense of spirit in a waste of shame": it is "Before, a joy proposed; behind, a dream." Yet we don't know how to shun it. It is forced on us by our economic system as the alternative to starvation. It is also forced on us by an internal defect in the soul, by the feeling that in property may lie the germs of self-development and of exquisite or heroic deeds. Our life on earth is, and ought to be, material and carnal. But we have not yet learned to manage our materialism and carnality properly; they are still entangled with the desire for ownership, where (in the words of Dante) "Possession is one with loss."

And this brings us to our fourth and final point: the blackberries. 6

Blackberries are not plentiful in this meagre grove, but they are 7 easily seen from the public footpath which traverses it, and all too easily gathered. Foxgloves, too—people will pull up the foxgloves, and ladies of an educational tendency even grub for toadstools to show them on the Monday in class. Other ladies, less educated, roll down the bracken in the arms of their gentlemen friends. There is paper, there are tins. Pray, does my wood belong to me or doesn't it? And, if it does, should I not own it best by allowing no one else to walk there? There is a wood near Lyme Regis, also cursed by a public foot-path, where the owner has not hesitated on this point. He has built high stone walls each side of the path, and has spanned it by bridges, so that the public circulate like termites while he gorges on the black-berries unseen. He really does own his wood, this able chap. Dives in Hell did pretty well, but the gulf dividing him from Lazarus could be traversed by vision, and nothing traverses it here.[2] And perhaps I shall come to this in time. I shall wall in and fence out until I really taste the sweets of property. Enormously stout, endlessly avaricious, pseudo-creative, intensely selfish, I shall weave upon my forehead the quadruple crown of possession until those nasty Bolshies come and take it off again and thrust me aside into the outer darkness.

# Question

Much of the strength of the essay lies in its concrete presentation of generalities. Note, for example, that the essay is called "My Wood," but we might say that the general idea of the essay is "The Effect of Property on Owners." Forster gives four effects, chiefly through concrete state-ments. Put these four effects into four general statements.

---

[2] According to Christ's parable in Luke 16:19–26, the rich man (unnamed, but tra-ditionally known as Dives) at whose gate the poor man Lazarus had begged was sent to hell, from where he could see Lazarus in heaven. (Editors' note)

## Joan Didion

# On Going Home

$I$ am home for my daughter's first birthday. By "home" I do not mean the house in Los Angeles where my husband and I and the baby live, but the place where my family is, in the Central Valley of California. It is a vital although troublesome distinction. My husband likes my family but is uneasy in their house, because once there I fall into their ways, which are difficult, oblique, deliberately inarticulate, not my husband's ways. We live in dusty houses ("D-U-S-T," he once wrote with his finger on surfaces all over the house, but no one noticed it) filled with mementos quite without value to him (what could the Canton dessert plates mean to him? how could he have known about the assay scales, why should he care if he did know?), and we appear to talk exclusively about people we know who have been committed to mental hospitals, about people we know who have been booked on drunk-driving charges, and about property, particularly about property, land, price per acre and C-2 zoning and assessments and freeway access. My brother does not understand my husband's inability to perceive the advantage in the rather common real-estate transaction known as "sale-leaseback," and my husband in turn does not understand why so many of the people he hears about in my father's house have recently been committed to mental hospitals or booked on drunk-driving charges. Nor does he understand that when we talk about sale-leasebacks and right-of-way condemnations we are talking in code about the things we like best, the yellow fields and the cottonwoods and the rivers rising and falling and the mountain roads closing when the heavy snow comes in. We miss each other's points, have another drink and regard the fire. My brother refers to my husband, in his presence, as "Joan's husband." Marriage is the classic betrayal.

Or perhaps it is not any more. Sometimes I think that those of us who are now in our thirties were born into the last generation to carry the burden of "home," to find in family life the source of all tension

Joan Didion was born in Sacramento in 1934, and she was educated at the University of California, Berkeley. She has written essays, stories, screenplays, and novels.

and drama. I had by all objective accounts a "normal" and a "happy" family situation, and yet I was almost thirty years old before I could talk to my family on the telephone without crying after I had hung up. We did not fight. Nothing was wrong. And yet some nameless anxiety colored the emotional charges between me and the place that I came from. The question of whether or not you could go home again was a very real part of the sentimental and largely literary baggage with which we left home in the fifties; I suspect that it is irrelevant to the children born of the fragmentation after World War II. A few weeks ago in a San Francisco bar I saw a pretty young girl on crystal take off her clothes and dance for the cash prize in an "amateur-topless" contest. There was no particular sense of moment about this, none of the effect of romantic degradation, of "dark journey," for which my generation strives so assiduously. What sense could that girl possibly make of, say, *Long Day's Journey into Night?* Who is beside the point?

That I am trapped in this particular irrelevancy is never more apparent to me than when I am home. Paralyzed by the neurotic lassitude engendered by meeting one's past at every turn, around every corner, inside every cupboard, I go aimlessly from room to room. I decide to meet it head-on and clean out a drawer, and I spread the contents on the bed. A bathing suit I wore the summer I was seventeen. A letter of rejection from *The Nation,* an aerial photograph of the site for a shopping center my father did not build in 1954. Three teacups hand-painted with cabbage roses and signed "E. M.," my grandmother's initials. There is no final solution for letters of rejection from *The Nation* and teacups hand-painted in 1900. Nor is there any answer to snapshots of one's grandfather as a young man on skis, surveying around Donner Pass in the year 1910. I smooth out the snapshot and look into his face, and do and do not see my own. I close the drawer, and have another cup of coffee with my mother. We get along very well, veterans of a guerrilla war we never understood.

Days pass. I see no one. I come to dread my husband's evening call, not only because he is full of news of what by now seems to me our remote life in Los Angeles, people he has seen, letters which require attention, but because he asks what I have been doing, suggests uneasily that I get out, drive to San Francisco or Berkeley. Instead I drive across the river to a family graveyard. It has been vandalized since my last visit and the monuments are broken, overturned in the dry grass. Because I once saw a rattlesnake in the grass I stay in the car and listen to a country-and-Western station. Later I drive with my father to a ranch he has in the foothills. The man who runs his cattle on it asks us to the roundup, a week from Sunday, and although I know that I will be in Los Angeles I say, in the oblique way my family talks, that I will come. Once home I mention the broken monuments in the graveyard. My mother shrugs.

I go to visit my great-aunts. A few of them think now that I am 5 my cousin, or their daughter who died young. We recall an anecdote about a relative last seen in 1948, and they ask if I still like living in New York City. I have lived in Los Angeles for three years, but I say that I do. The baby is offered a horehound drop, and I am slipped a dollar bill "to buy a treat." Questions trail off, answers are abandoned, the baby plays with the dust motes in a shaft of afternoon sun.

It is time for the baby's birthday party: a white cake, strawberry- 6 marshmallow ice cream, a bottle of champagne saved from another party. In the evening, after she has gone to sleep, I kneel beside the crib and touch her face, where it is pressed against the slats, with mine. She is an open and trusting child, unprepared for and unaccustomed to the ambushes of family life, and perhaps it is just as well that I can offer her little of that life. I would like to give her more. I would like to promise her that she will grow up with a sense of her cousins and of rivers and of her great-grandmother's teacups, would like to pledge her a picnic on a river with fried chicken and her hair uncombed, would like to give her *home* for her birthday, but we live differently now and I can promise her nothing like that. I give her a xylophone and a sundress from Madeira, and promise to tell her a funny story.

# Questions

1. Didion reveals that members of her family are difficult, inarticulate, poor housekeepers, and so forth. Do you find these revelations about her family distasteful? Would you mind seeing in print similarly unflattering things you had written about your own family? How might such revelations be justified? Are they justified in this essay?

2. Summarize the point of paragraph 2. Do you find Didion's speculations about the difference between her generation and succeeding generations meaningful? Are they accurate for your generation?

3. Do you think that growing up necessarily involves estrangement from one's family?

## C. S. Lewis

# We Have No "Right to Happiness"

"After all," said Clare, "they had a right to happiness." 1

We were discussing something that once happened in our own 2
neighborhood. Mr. A. had deserted Mrs. A. and got his divorce in
order to marry Mrs. B., who had likewise got her divorce in order to
marry Mr. A. And there was certainly no doubt that Mr. A. and Mrs.
B. were very much in love with one another. If they continued to be
in love, and if nothing went wrong with their health or their income,
they might reasonably expect to be very happy.

It was equally clear that they were not happy with their old part- 3
ners. Mrs. B. had adored her husband at the outset. But then he got
smashed up in the war. It was thought he had lost his virility, and it
was known that he had lost his job. Life with him was no longer what
Mrs. B. had bargained for. Poor Mrs. A., too. She had lost her looks—
and all her liveliness. It might be true, as some said, that she consumed
herself by bearing his children and nursing him through the long illness
that overshadowed their earlier married life.

You mustn't, by the way, imagine that A. was the sort of man 4
who nonchalantly threw a wife away like the peel of an orange he'd
sucked dry. Her suicide was a terrible shock to him. We all knew this,
for he told us so himself. "But what could I do?" he said. "A man has
a right to happiness. I had to take my one chance when it came."

I went away thinking about the concept of a "right to happiness." 5

At first this sounds to me as odd as a right to good luck. For I 6
believe—whatever one school of moralists may say—that we depend
for a very great deal of our happiness or misery on circumstances outside all human control. A right to happiness doesn't, for me, make
much more sense than a right to be six feet tall, or to have a millionaire
for your father, or to get good weather whenever you want to have a
picnic.

C[live] S[taples] Lewis (1898–1963) taught medieval and Renaissance literature
at Oxford and later at Cambridge. He wrote about literature, and he wrote fiction
(including children's books), poetry, and numerous essays and books on Christianity, from the point of view of a believer.

I can understand a right as a freedom guaranteed me by the laws  7
of the society I live in. Thus, I have a right to travel along the public
roads because society gives me that freedom; that's what we mean by
calling the roads "public." I can also understand a right as a claim
guaranteed me by the laws, and correlative to an obligation on someone else's part. If I have a right to receive £100 from you, this is another
way of saying that you have a duty to pay me £100. If the laws allow
Mr. A. to desert his wife and seduce his neighbor's wife, then, by
definition, Mr. A. has a legal right to do so, and we need bring in no
talk about "happiness."

But of course that was not what Clare meant. She meant that he  8
had not only a legal but a moral right to act as he did. In other words,
Clare is—or would be if she thought it out—a classical moralist after
the style of Thomas Aquinas, Grotius, Hooker and Locke. She believes
that behind the laws of the state there is a Natural Law.

I agree with her. I hold this conception to be basic to all civilization.  9
Without it, the actual laws of the state become an absolute, as in Hegel.
They cannot be criticized because there is no norm against which they
should be judged.

The ancestry of Clare's maxim, "They have a right to happiness,"  10
is august. In words that are cherished by all civilized men, but especially by Americans, it has been laid down that one of the rights of
man is a right to "the pursuit of happiness." And now we get to the
real point.

What did the writers of that august declaration mean?  11

It is quite certain what they did not mean. They did not mean that  12
man was entitled to pursue happiness by any and every means—including, say, murder, rape, robbery, treason and fraud. No society
could be built on such a basis.

They meant "to pursue happiness by all lawful means"; that is,  13
by all means which the Law of Nature eternally sanctions and which
the laws of the nation shall sanction.

Admittedly this seems at first to reduce their maxim to the tau-  14
tology that men (in pursuit of happiness) have a right to do whatever
they have a right to do. But tautologies, seen against their proper historical context, are not always barren tautologies. The declaration is
primarily a denial of the political principles which long governed Europe: a challenge flung down to the Austrian and Russian empires, to
England before the Reform Bills, to Bourbon France. It demands that
whatever means of pursuing happiness are lawful for any should be
lawful for all; that "man," not men of some particular caste, class,
status or religion, should be free to use them. In a century when this

is being unsaid by nation after nation and party after party, let us not call it a barren tautology.

But the question as to what means are "lawful"—what methods  15 of pursuing happiness are either morally permissible by the Law of Nature or should be declared legally permissible by the legislature of a particular nation—remains exactly where it did. And on that question I disagree with Clare. I don't think it is obvious that people have the unlimited "right to happiness" which she suggests.

For one thing, I believe that Clare, when she says "happiness,"  16 means simply and solely "sexual happiness." Partly because women like Clare never use the word "happiness" in any other sense. But also because I never heard Clare talk about the "right" to any other kind. She was rather leftist in her politics, and would have been scandalized if anyone had defended the actions of a ruthless man-eating tycoon on the ground that his happiness consisted in making money and he was pursuing his happiness. She was also a rabid teetotaler; I never heard her excuse an alcoholic because he was happy when he was drunk.

A good many of Clare's friends, and especially her female friends,  17 often felt—I've heard them say so—that their own happiness would be perceptibly increased by boxing her ears. I very much doubt if this would have brought her theory of a right to happiness into play.

Clare, in fact, is doing what the whole western world seems to  18 me to have been doing for the last forty-odd years. When I was a youngster, all the progressive people were saying, "Why all this prudery? Let us treat sex just as we treat all our other impulses." I was simple-minded enough to believe they meant what they said. I have since discovered that they meant exactly the opposite. They meant that sex was to be treated as no other impulse in our nature has ever been treated by civilized people. All the others, we admit, have to be bridled. Absolute obedience to your instinct for self-preservation is what we call cowardice; to your acquisitive impulse, avarice. Even sleep must be resisted if you're a sentry. But every unkindness and breach of faith seems to be condoned provided that the object aimed at is "four bare legs in a bed."

It is like having a morality in which stealing fruit is considered  19 wrong—unless you steal nectarines.

And if you protest against this view you are usually met with  20 chatter about the legitimacy and beauty and sanctity of "sex" and accused of harboring some Puritan prejudice against it as something disreputable or shameful. I deny the charge. Foam-born Venus . . . golden Aphrodite . . . Our Lady of Cyprus . . . I never breathed a word against you. If I object to boys who steal my nectarines, must I be supposed to disapprove of nectarines in general? Or even of boys in general? It might, you know, be stealing that I disapproved of.

The real situation is skillfully concealed by saying that the question 21 of Mr. A.'s "right" to desert his wife is one of "sexual morality." Robbing an orchard is not an offense against some special morality called "fruit morality." It is an offense against honesty. Mr. A.'s action is an offense against good faith (to solemn promises), against gratitude (toward one to whom he was deeply indebted) and against common humanity.

Our sexual impulses are thus being put in a position of prepos- 22 terous privilege. The sexual motive is taken to condone all sorts of behavior which, if it had any other end in view, would be condemned as merciless, treacherous and unjust.

Now though I see no good reason for giving sex this privilege, I 23 think I see a strong cause. It is this.

It is part of the nature of a strong erotic passion—as distinct from 24 a transient fit of appetite—that it makes more towering promises than any other emotion. No doubt all our desires make promises, but not so impressively. To be in love involves the almost irresistible conviction that one will go on being in love until one dies, and that possession of the beloved will confer, not merely frequent ecstasies, but settled, fruitful, deep-rooted, lifelong happiness. Hence *all* seems to be at stake. If we miss this chance we shall have lived in vain. At the very thought of such a doom we sink into fathomless depths of self-pity.

Unfortunately these promises are found often to be quite untrue. 25 Every experienced adult knows this to be so as regards all erotic passions (except the one he himself is feeling at the moment). We discount the world-without-end pretensions of our friends' amours easily enough. We know that such things sometimes last—and sometimes don't. And when they do last, this is not because they promised at the outset to do so. When two people achieve lasting happiness, this is not solely because they are great lovers but because they are also—I must put it crudely—good people; controlled, loyal, fairminded, mutually adaptable people.

If we establish a "right to (sexual) happiness" which supersedes 26 all the ordinary rules of behavior, we do so not because of what our passion shows itself to be in experience but because of what it professes to be while we are in the grip of it. Hence, while the bad behavior is real and works miseries and degradations, the happiness which was the object of the behavior turns out again and again to be illusory. Everyone (except Mr. A. and Mrs. B.) knows that Mr. A. in a year or so may have the same reason for deserting his new wife as for deserting his old. He will feel again that all is at stake. He will see himself again as the great lover, and his pity for himself will exclude all pity for the woman.

Two further points remain.                                               27

One is this. A society in which conjugal infidelity is tolerated must   28 always be in the long run a society adverse to women. Women, whatever a few male songs and satires may say to the contrary, are more naturally monogamous than men; it is a biological necessity. Where promiscuity prevails, they will therefore always be more often the victims than the culprits. Also, domestic happiness is more necessary to them than to us. And the quality by which they most easily hold a man, their beauty, decreases every year after they have come to maturity, but this does not happen to those qualities of personality—women don't really care twopence about our *looks*—by which we hold women. Thus in the ruthless war of promiscuity women are at a double disadvantage. They play for higher stakes and are also more likely to lose. I have no sympathy with moralists who frown at the increasing crudity of female provocativeness. These signs of desperate competition fill me with pity.

Secondly, though the "right to happiness" is chiefly claimed for   29 the sexual impulse, it seems to me impossible that the matter should stay there. The fatal principle, once allowed in that department, must sooner or later seep through our whole lives. We thus advance toward a state of society in which not only each man but every impulse in each man claims *carte blanche*. And then, though our technological skill may help us survive a little longer, our civilization will have died at heart, and will—one dare not even add "unfortunately"—be swept away.

# Questions

1.  Having read the entire essay, look back at Lewis's first five paragraphs and point out the ways in which he is not merely recounting an episode but is already conveying his attitude and seeking to persuade.

2. Lewis argues that we do not have a "right to (sexual) happiness." What *duty* or *duties* do we have, according to Lewis?
3. Evaluate Lewis's comment, in paragraph 28, on the differences between men and women.

## May Sarton

# The Rewards of Living a Solitary Life

The other day an acquaintance of mine, a gregarious and    1
charming man, told me he had found himself unexpectedly alone in New York for an hour or two between appointments. He went to the Whitney and spent the "empty" time looking at things in solitary bliss. For him it proved to be a shock nearly as great as falling in love to discover that he could enjoy himself so much alone.

What had he been afraid of, I asked myself? That, suddenly alone,    2
he would discover that he bored himself, or that there was, quite simply, no self there to meet? But having taken the plunge, he is now on the brink of adventure; he is about to be launched into his own inner space, space as immense, unexplored and sometimes frightening as outer space to the astronaut. His every perception will come to him with a new freshness and, for a time, seem startlingly original. For anyone who can see things for himself with a naked eye becomes, for a moment or two, something of a genius. With another human being present vision becomes double vision, inevitably. We are busy wondering, what does my companion see or think of this, and what do I think of it? The original impact gets lost, or diffused.

"Music I heard with you was more than music." Exactly. And    3
therefore music *itself* can only be heard alone. Solitude is the salt of personhood. It brings out the authentic flavor of every experience.

May Sarton, born in Belgium in 1912, was brought to the United States in 1916; in 1924 she became a citizen. A teacher of writing and a distinguished writer herself, she has received numerous awards for her fiction, poetry, and essays.

"Alone one is never lonely: the spirit adventures, walking/In a   4
quiet garden, in a cool house, abiding single there."

Loneliness is most acutely felt with other people, for with others,   5
even with a lover sometimes, we suffer from our differences of taste,
temperament, mood. Human intercourse often demands that we
soften the edge of perception, or withdraw at the very instant of personal truth for fear of hurting, or of being inappropriately present,
which is to say naked, in a social situation. Alone we can afford to be
wholly whatever we are, and to feel whatever we feel absolutely. That
is a great luxury!

For me the most interesting thing about a solitary life, and mine   6
has been that for the last twenty years, is that it becomes increasingly
rewarding. When I can wake up and watch the sun rise over the ocean,
as I do most days, and know that I have an entire day ahead, uninterrupted, in which to write a few pages, take a walk with my dog,
lie down in the afternoon for a long think (why does one think better
in a horizontal position?), read and listen to music, I am flooded with
happiness.

I am lonely only when I am overtired, when I have worked too   7
long without a break, when for the time being I feel empty and need
filling up. And I am lonely sometimes when I come back home after
a lecture trip, when I have seen a lot of people and talked a lot, and
am full to the brim with experience that needs to be sorted out.

Then for a little while the house feels huge and empty, and I won-   8
der where my self is hiding. It has to be recaptured slowly by watering
the plants, perhaps, and looking again at each one as though it were
a person, by feeding the two cats, by cooking a meal.

It takes a while, as I watch the surf blowing up in fountains at the   9
end of the field, but the moment comes when the world falls away,
and the self emerges again from the deep unconscious, bringing back
all I have recently experienced to be explored and slowly understood,
when I can converse again with my hidden powers, and so grow, and
so be renewed, till death do us part.

# Questions

1.  What does Sarton mean when she says: "Anyone who can see
    things for himself with a naked eye becomes, for a moment or two,
    something of a genius"? Does your own experience confirm her
    comment?

2.  Drawing on Sarton's essay, explain the distinction between being "alone" and being "lonely."
3.  What phrase in the last paragraph connects the ending with the first paragraph?

## Albert Camus

# The Myth of Sisyphus

The gods had condemned Sisyphus to ceaselessly rolling    1
a rock to the top of a mountain, whence the stone would fall back of its own weight. They had thought with some reason that there is no more dreadful punishment than futile and hopeless labor.

If one believes Homer, Sisyphus was the wisest and most prudent    2
of mortals. According to another tradition, however, he was disposed to practice the profession of highwayman. I see no contradiction in this. Opinions differ as to the reasons why he became the futile laborer of the underworld. To begin with, he is accused of a certain levity in regard to the gods. He stole their secrets. Aegina, the daughter of Aesopus, was carried off by Jupiter. The father was shocked by that disappearance and complained to Sisyphus. He, who knew of the abduction, offered to tell about it on condition that Aesopus would give water to the citadel of Corinth. To the celestial thunderbolts he preferred the benediction of water. He was punished for this in the underworld. Homer tells us also that Sisyphus had put Death in chains. Pluto could not endure the sight of his deserted, silent empire. He dispatched the god of war, who liberated Death from the hands of her conqueror.

It is said also that Sisyphus, being near to death, rashly wanted    3
to test his wife's love. He ordered her to cast his unburied body into the middle of the public square. Sisyphus woke up in the underworld.

Albert Camus (1913–1960) was born in Algeria of French parents. During World War II he was active in the French Resistance, editing an underground newspaper. After the war he published fiction, philosophic essays, and plays. In 1957 he was awarded the Nobel Prize for literature.

And there, annoyed by an obedience so contrary to human love, he obtained from Pluto permission to return to earth in order to chastise his wife. But when he had seen again the face of this world, enjoyed water and sun, warm stones and the sea, he no longer wanted to go back to the infernal darkness. Recalls, signs of anger, warnings were of no avail. Many years more he lived facing the curve of the gulf, the sparkling sea, and the smiles of earth. A decree of the gods was necessary. Mercury came and seized the impudent man by the collar and, snatching him from his joys, led him forcibly back to the underworld, where his rock was ready for him.

You have already grasped that Sisyphus is the absurd hero. He  4
*is*, as much through his passions as through his torture. His scorn of the gods, his hatred of death, and his passion for life won him that unspeakable penalty in which the whole being is exerted toward accomplishing nothing. This is the price that must be paid for the passions of this earth. Nothing is told us about Sisyphus in the underworld. Myths are made for the imagination to breathe life into them. As for this myth, one sees merely the whole effort of a body straining to raise the huge stone, to roll it and push it up a slope a hundred times over; one sees the face screwed up, the cheek tight against the stone, the shoulder bracing the clay-covered mass, the foot wedging it, the fresh start with arms outstretched, the wholly human security of two earth-clotted hands. At the very end of his long effort measured by skyless space and time without depth, the purpose is achieved. Then Sisyphus watches the stone rush down in a few moments toward that lower world whence he will have to push it up again toward the summit. He goes back down to the plain.

It is during that return, that pause, that Sisyphus interests me. A  5
face that toils so close to stones is already stone itself! I see that man going back down with a heavy yet measured step toward the torment of which he will never know the end. That hour like a breathing-space which returns as surely as his suffering, that is the hour of consciousness. At each of those moments when he leaves the heights and gradually sinks toward the lairs of the gods, he is superior to his fate. He is stronger than his rock.

If this myth is tragic, that is because its hero is conscious. Where  6
would his torture be, indeed, if at every step the hope of succeeding upheld him? The workman of today works every day in his life at the same tasks, and this fate is no less absurd. But it is tragic only at the rare moments when it becomes conscious. Sisyphus, proletarian of the gods, powerless and rebellious, knows the whole extent of his

wretched condition: it is what he thinks of during his descent. The lucidity that was to constitute his torture at the same time crowns his victory. There is no fate that cannot be surmounted by scorn.

If the descent is thus sometimes performed in sorrow, it can also take place in joy. This word is not too much. Again I fancy Sisyphus returning toward his rock, and the sorrow was in the beginning. When the images of earth cling too tightly to memory, when the call of happiness becomes too insistent, it happens that melancholy rises in man's heart: this is the rock's victory, this is the rock itself. The boundless grief is too heavy to bear. These are our nights of Gethsemane. But crushing truths perish from being acknowledged. Thus, Oedipus at the outset obeys fate without knowing it. But from the moment he knows, his tragedy begins. Yet at the same moment, blind and desperate, he realizes that the only bond linking him to the world is the cool hand of a girl. Then a tremendous remark rings out: "Despite so many ordeals, my advanced age and the nobility of my soul make me conclude that all is well." Sophocles' Oedipus, like Dostoevsky's Kirilov, thus gives the recipe for the absurd victory. Ancient wisdom confirms modern heroism. 7

One does not discover the absurd without being tempted to write a manual of happiness. "What! by such narrow ways—?" There is but one world, however. Happiness and the absurd are two sons of the same earth. They are inseparable. It would be a mistake to say that happiness necessarily springs from the absurd discovery. It happens as well that the feeling of the absurd springs from happiness. "I conclude that all is well," says Oedipus, and that remark is sacred. It echoes in the wild and limited universe of man. It teaches that all is not, has not been, exhausted. It drives out of this world a god who had come into it with dissatisfaction and a preference for futile sufferings. It makes of fate a human matter, which must be settled among men. 8

All Sisyphus' silent joy is contained therein. His fate belongs to him. His rock is his thing. Likewise, the absurd man, when he contemplates his torment, silences all the idols. In the universe suddenly restored to its silence, the myriad wondering little voices of the earth rise up. Unconscious, secret calls, invitations from all the faces, they are the necessary reverse and price of victory. There is no sun without shadow, and it is essential to know the night. The absurd man says yes and his effort will henceforth be unceasing. If there is a personal fate, there is no higher destiny, or at least there is but one which he 9 concludes is inevitable and despicable. For the rest, he knows himself to be the master of his days. At that subtle moment when man glances backward over his life, Sisyphus returning toward his rock, in that slight pivoting he contemplates that series of unrelated actions which becomes his fate, created by him, combined under his memory's eye and soon sealed by his death. Thus, convinced of the wholly human origin of all that is human, a blind man eager to see who knows that the night has no end, he is still on the go. The rock is still rolling.

I leave Sisyphus at the foot of the mountain! One always finds 10 one's burden again. But Sisyphus teaches the higher fidelity that negates the gods and raises rocks. He too concludes that all is well. This universe henceforth without a master seems to him neither sterile nor futile. Each atom of that stone, each mineral flake of that night-filled mountain, in itself forms a world. The struggle itself toward the heights is enough to fill a man's heart. One must imagine Sisyphus happy.

# Questions

1. Philosophers of the absurd hold that there is a disparity between the mind's need for coherence and the incoherence that the mind perceives in the world around it. The absurdist longs for clarity and is confronted by irrationality. It is this confrontation—not merely the irrationality of the surroundings—that makes for the absurd. How is Camus's Sisyphus an absurdist in his life on earth as well as in his life in the underworld?
2. Camus says that Sisyphus's consciousness of his torment makes him superior to the torment. Does this make sense? Camus goes even further and says that Sisyphus is happy. Presumably Camus is telling us something about how we ought to respond to life, but exactly what ought we to do?

Lewis Thomas

# Late Night Thoughts on Listening to Mahler's Ninth Symphony

I cannot listen to Mahler's Ninth Symphony with anything    1
like the old melancholy mixed with the high pleasure I used to take
from this music. There was a time, not long ago, when what I heard,
especially in the final movement, was an open acknowledgment of
death and at the same time a quiet celebration of the tranquility connected to the process. I took this music as a metaphor for reassurance,
confirming my own strong hunch that the dying of every living creature, the most natural of all experiences, has to be a peaceful experience. I rely on nature. The long passages on all the strings at the end,
as close as music can come to expressing silence itself, I used to hear
as Mahler's idea of leave-taking at its best. But always, I have heard
this music as a solitary, private listener, thinking about death.

Now I hear it differently. I cannot listen to the last movement of    2
the Mahler Ninth without the door-smashing intrusion of a huge new
thought: death everywhere, the dying of everything, the end of humanity. The easy sadness expressed with such gentleness and delicacy
by that repeated phrase on faded strings, over and over again, no
longer comes to me as old, familiar news of the cycle of living and
dying. All through the last notes my mind swarms with images of a
world in which the thermonuclear bombs have begun to explode, in
New York and San Francisco, in Moscow and Leningrad, in Paris, in
Paris, in Paris. In Oxford and Cambridge, in Edinburgh. I cannot push
away the thought of a cloud of radioactivity drifting along the Engadin,
from the Moloja Pass to Ftan, killing off the part of the earth I love
more than any other part.

I am old enough by this time to be used to the notion of dying,    3

Lewis Thomas was born in 1913 in New York, and was educated at Princeton
and Harvard. A research pathologist and a medical administrator, he is now the
chancellor of Memorial Sloan-Kettering Cancer Center in New York. Thomas is
also the author of four books of essays, one of which won the National Book
Award.

saddened by the glimpse when it has occurred but only transiently knocked down, able to regain my feet quickly at the thought of continuity, any day. I have acquired and held in affection until very recently another sideline of an idea which serves me well at dark times: the life of the earth is the same as the life of an organism: the great round being possesses a mind: the mind contains an infinite number of thoughts and memories: when I reach my time I may find myself still hanging around in some sort of midair, one of those small thoughts, drawn back into the memory of the earth: in that peculiar sense I will be alive.

Now all that has changed. I cannot think that way anymore. Not 4 while those things are still in place, aimed everywhere, ready for launching.

This is a bad enough thing for the people in my generation. We 5 can put up with it, I suppose, since we must. We are moving along anyway, like it or not. I can even set aside my private fancy about hanging around in midair.

What I cannot imagine, what I cannot put up with, the thought 6 that keeps grinding its way into my mind, making the Mahler into a hideous noise close to killing me, is what it would be like to be young. How do the young stand it? How can they keep their sanity? If I were very young, sixteen or seventeen years old, I think I would begin, perhaps very slowly and imperceptibly, to go crazy.

There is a short passage near the very end of the Mahler in which 7 the almost vanishing violins, all engaged in a sustained backward glance, are edged aside for a few bars by the cellos. Those lower notes pick up fragments from the first movement, as though prepared to begin everything all over again, and then the cellos subside and disappear, like an exhalation. I used to hear this as a wonderful few seconds of encouragement: we'll be back, we're still here, keep going, keep going.

Now, with a pamphlet in front of me on a corner of my desk, 8 published by the Congressional Office of Technology Assessment, entitled *MX Basing*, an analysis of all the alternative strategies for placement and protection of hundreds of these missiles, each capable of creating artificial suns to vaporize a hundred Hiroshimas, collectively capable of destroying the life of any continent, I cannot hear the same Mahler. Now, those cellos sound in my mind like the opening of all the hatches and the instant before ignition.

If I were sixteen or seventeen years old, I would not feel the crack- 9 ing of my own brain, but I would know for sure that the whole world was coming unhinged. I can remember with some clarity what it was like to be sixteen. I had discovered the Brahms symphonies. I knew that there was something going on in the late Beethoven quartets that I would have to figure out, and I knew that there was plenty of time ahead for all the figuring I would ever have to do. I had never heard of Mahler. I was in no hurry. I was a college sophomore and had decided that Wallace Stevens[1] and I possessed a comprehensive understanding of everything needed for a life. The years stretched away forever ahead, forever. My great-great grandfather had come from Wales, leaving his signature in the family Bible on the same page that carried, a century later, my father's signature. It never crossed my mind to wonder about the twenty-first century; it was just there, given, somewhere in the sure distance.

The man on television, Sunday midday, middle-aged and solid, 10 nice-looking chap, all the facts at his fingertips, more dependable looking than most high-school principals, is talking about civilian defense, his responsibility in Washington. It can make an enormous difference, he is saying. Instead of the outright death of eighty million American citizens in twenty minutes, he says, we can, by careful planning and practice, get that number down to only forty million, maybe even twenty. The thing to do, he says, is to evacuate the cities quickly and have everyone get under shelter in the countryside. That way we can recover, and meanwhile we will have retaliated, incinerating all of Soviet society, he says. What about radioactive fallout? he is asked. Well, he says. Anyway, he says, if the Russians know they can only destroy forty million of us instead of eighty million, this will deter them. Of course, he adds, they have the capacity to kill all two hundred and twenty million of us if they were to try real hard, but they know we can do the same to them. If the figure is only forty million this will deter them, not worth the trouble, not worth the risk. Eighty million would be another matter, we should guard ourselves against losing that many all at once, he says.

If I were sixteen or seventeen years old and had to listen to that, 11 or read things like that, I would want to give up listening and reading. I would begin thinking up new kinds of sounds, different from any music heard before, and I would be twisting and turning to rid myself of human language.

---

[1] Wallace Stevens (1879–1955) earned a law degree and became vice president of an insurance company, but he is chiefly known as a poet, and it is to his poetry that Thomas is referring. (Editor's note)

# Questions

1. What is the difference between the death spoken of in paragraph 1 and the death spoken of in paragraph 2?

2. Have you ever been told not to use the first person pronoun in your writing? If so, reread Thomas's first paragraph, or any other in this essay (except for paragraph 10), and evaluate the advice you've been given.

3. What are some of the rhetorical devices that Thomas uses in paragraph 10? Read this paragraph carefully, perhaps even aloud. In what ways does it sound different from the rest of the essay? What accounts for the differences? Vocabulary? Sentence structure? Length of sentences? Or what?

4. Note Thomas's description of a musical passage in paragraph 7. If you are in the habit of reading record jackets, or music reviews, can you find anything to equal it? Or, try yourself to describe in words the effect of a particularly moving passage of music.

5. Lewis Thomas asks, in paragraph 6, "How do the young stand it?" If you are "young," write an essay, perhaps in the form of a letter to Thomas, explaining how you stand it—or how you don't stand it. If you are no longer young (can we agree on over thirty?) write an essay—again perhaps a letter to Thomas—setting forth your response to Thomas's question.

6. If you have read Matthew Arnold's "Dover Beach" (page 983), explain in a paragraph any similarities you find in content or tone between the poem and Thomas's essay.

## Matthew Arnold

# Dover Beach

The sea is calm tonight.
The tide is full, the moon lies fair
Upon the straits;—on the French coast the light
Gleams and is gone; the cliffs of England stand,
Glimmering and vast, out in the tranquil bay.     5
Come to the window, sweet is the night-air!
Only, from the long line of spray
Where the sea meets the moon-blanched land,
Listen! you hear the grating roar
Of pebbles which the waves draw back, and fling,     10
At their return, up the high strand,[1]
Begin, and cease, and then again begin,
With tremulous cadence slow, and bring
The eternal note of sadness in.

Sophocles[2] long ago     15
Heard it on the Aegean, and it brought
Into his mind the turbid ebb and flow
Of human misery; we
Find also in the sound a thought,
Hearing it by this distant northern sea.     20

The Sea of Faith
Was once, too, at the full, and round earth's shore
Lay like the folds of a bright girdle furled.

[1] Strand: the area of the beach between tide marks. (This and other notes are the editors')
[2] Sophocles (496–406 B.C.) was a Greek tragic dramatist.

Matthew Arnold (1822–1888) was born in an English village in the valley of the Thames, but when mature he lived in a predominantly urban, industrialized world. It was, moreover, a world in which the Christianity of the previous generation seemed to Arnold no longer to accord with historical and scientific facts. In much of his writing—essays as well as poems—Arnold tries to find and enunciate values that can sustain one in an alien or at least uncertain world.

But now I only hear
Its melancholy, long, withdrawing roar,                     25
Retreating, to the breath
Of the night-wind, down the vast edges drear
And naked shingles[3] of the world.


Ah, love, let us be true
To one another! for the world, which seems              30
To lie before us like a land of dreams,
So various, so beautiful, so new,
Hath really neither joy, nor love, nor light,
Nor certitude, nor peace, nor help for pain;
And we are here as on a darkling plain                       35
Swept with confused alarms of struggle and flight,
Where ignorant armies clash by night.


# Questions

1.  At what point in the first stanza does the speaker's thought take a decided turn? In a sentence try to state the gist of the stanza, devoting the first part of the sentence to the first of Arnold's themes, and the second part to the second.
2.  Having read the entire poem—preferably several times—you may find that the first few lines take on (in the light of the rest of the poem, and especially in the light of the last stanza) suggestions that were not apparent during your first reading. If this is your experience, describe these new suggestions.
3.  To what is the sea compared in the second stanza? To what in the third stanza? Are the comparisons (metaphors) related in any ways to each other? Which is more important in the poem? What makes it more important? What new metaphor is introduced in the last stanza?
4.  In the third stanza, the Sea of Faith, we are told, "was once [like the tide] at the full," but it is now "withdrawing." Does Arnold suggest that, like the tide, Faith will return? What answer to this question does the last stanza suggest?
5.  In a letter to a friend, Arnold said that the best poetry does not awaken "a pleasing melancholy" but rather it "animates" the

---

[3] Shingles: beaches covered with pebbles.

reader. Is "Dover Beach" so weighted with "melancholy" that it cannot "animate"? Explain.

6.  Do any of Arnold's metaphors in "Dover Beach" seem particularly apt for our own times? Try to put into words, as accurately as possible, your personal response to one of the metaphors.

# 12
## ARTICLES OF FAITH

*The Creation of Adam*
**Michelangelo**

Scala/Art Resource

*The Creation of Adam (detail)*
**Michelangelo**

*Priest Kensu Achieving Enlightenment*
*While Catching a Shrimp*
**Kao, 14th Century**

Tokyo National Museum. Orion Press/Scala/Art Resource

# Short Views

A little philosophy inclineth man's mind to atheism, but depth in philosophy bringeth men's minds about to religion.
**Francis Bacon**

Religion is the opium of the people.
**Karl Marx**

If one wishes to form a true estimate of the full grandeur of religion, one must keep in mind what it undertakes to do for men. It gives them information about the source and origin of the universe, it assures them of protection and final happiness amid the changing vicissitudes of life, and it guides their thoughts and motions by means of precepts which are backed by the whole force of its authority.
**Sigmund Freud**

Religion is an attempt to get control over the sensory world, in which we are placed, by means of the wish-world, which we have developed inside us as a result of biological and psychological necessities.
**Sigmund Freud**

The language of "sonship," "brotherhood," "fellowship," "good Christian men," which pervades liturgy, prayerbooks and hymnbooks, . . . alienates women in their specific identity as women. Many women and most men are not aware of the alienation which is produced by the structures of English grammar. In pronouns and many other words, the male specific and the generic coincide. Thus when a word which is both male specific and generic is used, men naturally identify, whereas women can only identify by denying their specific identity as female.

To be sure, the image of woman is not entirely excluded from the language of Christian liturgy and theology. The church has been portrayed as a woman, referred to as "She," and discussed in feminine categories. But language applied to the church embodies sexual stereotypes and reflects and reinforces the secondary status

of women. "She" receives life, sustenance and power from "her" relation to a male Christ and is clearly subordinated to him. Women's identification with the church has not led to an elevation of their status, but rather has set the seal on their subordination.
**Carol Christ and Marilyn Collins**

To stand on one leg and prove God's existence is a very different thing from going down on one's knees and thanking him for it.
**Sören Kierkegaard**

Ethiopians have gods with snub noses and black hair; Thracians have gods with gray eyes and red hair.
**Xenophanes of Colophon**

God offers to every mind its choice between truth and repose. Take which you please; you can never have both. Between these, as a pendulum, man oscillates. He in whom the love of repose predominates will accept the first creed, the first philosophy, the first political party he meets—most likely his father's. He gets rest, commodity, reputation; but he shuts the door of truth. He in whom the love of truth predominates will keep himself aloof from all the moorings, afloat. He will abstain from dogmatism, and recognize all the opposite negations between which, as walls, his being is swung. He submits to the inconvenience of suspense and imperfect opinions, but he is a candidate for truth, as the other is not, and respects the highest law of his being.
**Ralph Waldo Emerson**

We cannot know whether we love God, although there may be strong reasons for thinking so, but there can be no doubt about whether we love our neighbor or no.
**Saint Theresa**

To the [Hebrew] biblical mind, man is above all a commanded being, a being of whom demands may be made. The central problem is not, What is being? but rather, What is required of me?
**Abraham Heschel**

The Sabbath lays down a judgment on the fundamental issues of our civilization and, specifically, demands restraint, dignity, reticence, and silent rest—not commonplace virtues. . . . The

Sabbath . . . calls into question the foundations of the life of one dimension only, asking how people can imagine that all there is is what they see just now.
                Jacob Neusner


"What," it will be questioned, "When the sun rises do you not see a round disk of fire somewhat like a guinea?" O no no, I see an Innumerable Company of the Heavenly Host crying, "Holy holy holy is the Lord God Almighty." I question not my corporeal or vegetative eye any more than I would question a window concerning sight. I look through it and not with it.
                William Blake


# A Note on the Bible

Our word "Bible" comes from *biblia*, the Greek word for "books." The Bible is a collection of many books; some of these books contain elements that go back to about a thousand years before the birth of Jesus, and some—including part of what we call the New Testament—date as recently as the middle of the second century A.D.

In the seventh century B.C. the Hebrews apparently began assembling a collection of Holy Scripture—books thought to be composed under divine inspiration, relaying the acts of God—and they continued to add works to the canon for hundreds of years. By the fifth century B.C. the Hebrew canon was almost complete, but it was not until the end of the first century A.D. that the canon reached a final form. For the earliest Christians, the Bible was the Hebrew Bible and the teachings of Jesus as they existed in oral form. But soon the Christians too established a canon of written works, consisting of the Hebrew Bible and twenty-seven books that came to be called the New Testament. (To *testify* is to give witness; the *testaments* "witnessed," or certified, God's deeds.) By calling the Hebrew Bible the Old Testament, they implied that it was in some ways superseded by the New Testament. "New Covenant" would perhaps be a better term than "New Testament," since the early Christians believed that the new material was a fulfillment of a promise found in a book of the Hebrew Bible, Jeremiah 31:31–33:

Behold, the days come said the Lord, that I will make a new covenant with the house of Israel, and with the house of Judah.

Not according to the covenant that I made with their fathers in the days that I took them by the hand to bring them out of the land of Egypt; which my covenant they brake, although I was an husband unto them, saith the Lord.

But this shall be the covenant that I will make with the house of Israel; After those days, said the Lord, I will put my law in their inward parts, and write it in their hearts; and will be their God, and they shall be my people.

The term Old Testament is still widely used, but because many Jews understandably reject the implication that the books are to be taken as anticipations of the New Testament, today there is a growing tendency to use the term Hebrew Bible.

Although parts of the Bible were translated into English as early as the eighth century A.D., the entire Bible was not translated into English until 1535. In the next decades several other translations were made, and in 1604 King James agreed that yet another translation was needed. This translation was begun in 1607, when a committee of some fifty churchmen divided into six panels. Each panel was assigned certain books of the Bible, and each member of each panel produced a translation, which was then discussed by the other members of the panel. A single, composite version of the assigned portion was then drafted, and this was read and revised by a committee of twelve—two members from each panel. Thus a final version, printed in 1611, was produced—or a nearly final version, since a few changes were made in later editions.

This translation—often said to be the only good thing ever produced by a committee—is called the King James Version, or the Authorized Version. It is widely regarded as a masterpiece, and though many later versions have been produced in English (including the Revised King James Version of 1885 and the Revised Standard Version of 1946–1957), none has had the appeal of the King James Version. It is, however, not flawless. Scholarship has made enormous strides in the understanding of Hebrew and Greek, and no one denies that the King James Version often is inaccurate. Indeed, the translators of this version were themselves aware of some scholarly problems, and in the margins of their text they sometimes gave alternative readings of the verses. Further, the English language has changed, so that expressions that were idiomatic in the seventeenth century now are archaic and sometimes misleading or even unintelligible to modern readers.

It is understandable, therefore, that new translations, based on more accurate scholarship, are produced every few decades; nevertheless, the King James Version is unrivalled as a literary masterpiece, and it is therefore the version that we give.

Italics in the translation are *not* a sign of emphasis; rather, italics were used to indicate words not in the original. Paragraph signs (¶) indicate the beginning of what the translators considered to be new paragraphs.


# A Note on Genesis

Genesis, the first book of the Hebrew Bible, gives an account of the creation of the universe and of the earth's early history. Most scholars agree that the book contains material from three traditions, which are conventionally called J, E, and P. It should be emphasized at the outset that J, E, and P are not so much three individual writers as three bodies of tradition or three composite works, even though one tends to say such things as "the J writer," or "J says."

J comes from JHVA (Jahveh), the German form of YHWH (Yahweh); J, known also as the Yahwist writer, used Yahweh as the name for God. The Yahwist material was probably compiled chiefly in the tenth century B.C., but parts of it may have been compiled earlier and other parts later. E stands for the Elohist—the writer (probably in the ninth century B.C.) who used Elohim as the word for God. P stands for the priestly writer, that is, the priest or priests who in the sixth century B.C., after the fall of Jerusalem and the destruction of the Jerusalem temple, reworked the accounts of J and E, and added material from documents preserved by priests. P was especially concerned with genealogies, precise dates, and description of rituals.

There is, of course, some disagreement about exactly which portions of the text are properly attributed to each of the three traditions, but scholars are in general agreement that, for example, P was responsible for Genesis 1:1–31 and for 2:1–4, and that J was responsible for the second half of 2:4 to 2:25. E apparently did not influence the early chapters.

# Genesis

## The Creation

*Chapter 1*

1 In the beginning God created the heaven and the earth.

2 And the earth was without form, and void; and darkness was upon the face of the deep. And the Spirit of God moved upon the face of the waters.

3 And God said, Let there be light, and there was light.

4 And God saw the light, that *it was* good: and God divided the light from the darkness.

5 And God called the light Day, and the darkness he called Night. And the evening and the morning were the first day.

6 ¶And God said, Let there be a firmament in the midst of the waters, and let it divide the waters from the waters.

7 And God made the firmament, and divided the waters which *were* under the firmament from the waters which *were* above the firmament: and it was so.

8 And God called the firmament Heaven. And the evening and the morning were the second day.

9 ¶And God said, Let the waters under the heaven be gathered together unto one place, and let the dry *land* appear: and it was so.

10 And God called the dry *land* Earth; and the gathering together of the waters called he Seas: and God saw that *it was* good.

11 And God said, Let the earth bring forth grass, the herb yielding seed, *and* the fruit tree yielding fruit after his kind, whose seed *is* in itself, upon the earth: and it was so.

12 And the earth brought forth grass, *and* herb yielding seed after his kind, and the tree yielding fruit, whose seed *was* in itself, after his kind: and God saw that *it was* good.

13 And the evening and the morning were the third day.

14 ¶And God said, Let there be lights in the firmament of the heaven to divide the day from the night; and let them be for signs, and for seasons, and for days, and years:

15 And let them be for lights in the firmament of the heaven to give light upon the earth: and it was so.

16 And God made two great lights; the greater light to rule the day, and the lesser light to rule the night: *he made* the stars also.

17 And God set them in the firmament of the heaven to give light upon the earth.

18 And to rule over the day and over the night, and to divide the light from the darkness: and God saw that *it was* good.

19 And the evening and the morning were the fourth day.

20 And God said, Let the waters bring forth abundantly the moving creature that hath life, and fowl *that* may fly above the earth in the open firmament of heaven.

21 And God created great whales, and every living creature that moveth, which the waters brought forth abundantly, after their kind, and every winged fowl after his kind: and God saw that *it was* good.

22 And God blessed them, saying, Be fruitful, and multiply, and fill the waters in the seas, and let fowl multiply in the earth.

23 And the evening and the morning were the fifth day.

24 ¶And God said, Let the earth bring forth the living creature after his kind, cattle, and creeping thing, and beast of the earth after his kind: and it was so.

25 And God made the beast of the earth after his kind, and cattle after their kind, and every thing that creepeth upon the earth after his kind: and God saw that *it was* good.

26 ¶And God said, Let us make man in our image, after our likeness: and let them have dominion over the fish of the sea, and over the fowl of the air, and over the cattle, and over all the earth, and over every creeping thing that creepeth upon the earth.

27 So God created man in his *own* image, in the image of God created he him; male and female created he them.

28 And God blessed them, and God said unto them, Be fruitful, and multiply, and replenish the earth, and subdue it: and have dominion over the fish of the sea, and over the fowl of the air, and over every living thing that moveth upon the earth.

29 ¶And God said, Behold, I have given you every herb bearing seed, which *is* upon the face of all the earth, and every tree, in the which *is* the fruit of a tree yielding seed; to you it shall be for meat.

30 And to every beast of the earth, and to every fowl of the air, and to every thing that creepeth upon the earth, wherein *there is* life, *I have given* every green herb for meat: and it was so.

31 And God saw every thing that he had made, and, behold, *it was* very good. And the evening and the morning were the sixth day.

*Chapter 2*

1 Thus the heavens and the earth were finished, and all the host of them.

2 And on the seventh day God ended his work which he had made; and he rested on the seventh day from all his work which he had made.

3 And God blessed the seventh day, and sanctified it: because that in it he had rested from all his work which God created and made.

4 ¶These *are* the generations of the heavens and of the earth when they were created, in the day that the LORD God made the earth and the heavens,

5 And every plant of the field before it was in the earth, and every herb of the field before it grew: for the LORD God had not caused it to rain upon the earth, and *there was* not a man to till the ground.

6 But there went up a mist from the earth, and watered the whole face of the ground.

7 And the LORD God formed man *of* the dust of the ground, and breathed into his nostrils the breath of life; and man became a living soul.

8 ¶And the LORD God planted a garden eastward in Eden; and there he put the man whom he had formed.

9 And out of the ground made the LORD God to grow every tree that is pleasant to the sight, and good for food; the tree of life also in the midst of the garden, and the tree of knowledge of good and evil.

10 And a river went out of Eden to water the garden; and from thence it was parted, and became into four heads.

11 The name of the first *is* Pison: that *is* it which compasseth the whole land of Havilah, where *there is* gold;

12 And the gold of that land *is* good: there *is* bdellium and the onyx stone.

13 And the name of the second river *is* Gihon: the same *is* it that compasseth the whole land of Ethiopia.

14 And the name of the third river *is* Hiddekel: that *is* it which goeth toward the east of Assyria. And the fourth river *is* Euphrates.

15 And the LORD God took the man, and put him into the garden of Eden to dress it and to keep it.

16 And the LORD God commanded the man, saying, Of every tree of the garden thou mayest freely eat:

17 But of the tree of the knowledge of good and evil, thou shalt

not eat of it: for in the day that thou eatest thereof thou shalt surely die.

18 ¶And the Lord God said, *It is* not good that the man should be alone; I will make him an help meet for him.

19 And out of the ground the Lord God formed every beast of the field, and every fowl of the air; and brought *them* unto Adam to see what he would call them: and whatsoever Adam called every living creature, that *was* the name thereof.

20 And Adam gave names to all cattle, and to the fowl of the air, and to every beast of the field; but for Adam there was not found an help meet for him.

21 And the Lord God caused a deep sleep to fall upon Adam, and he slept: and he took one of his ribs, and closed up the flesh instead thereof;

22 And the rib, which the Lord God had taken from man, made he a woman, and brought her unto the man.

23 And Adam said, This *is* now bone of my bones, and flesh of my flesh: she shall be called Woman, because she was taken out of Man.

24 Therefore shall a man leave his father and his mother, and shall cleave unto his wife: and they shall be one flesh.

25 And they were both naked, the man and his wife, and were not ashamed.

# Questions

1. In 1:6–9 God creates a "firmament," a sort of inverted bowl or other solid covering over the earth, thereby protecting the earth from water above heaven. How might belief in this kind of creation (and creator) differ in emotion or "feel," so to speak, from belief in a creation that consisted only of an airy heaven above a solid earth?
2. In 1:1–8 God creates form, light, and darkness, and He separates heaven from earth. Speaking broadly, or generally, what besides *things* does he create?
3. Many readers find that the account of the creation in 2:5–25 differs from the account in Chapter 1. Do you think, for instance, that in one account God seems somewhat more human and less transcendent than in the other? On what evidence do you base your view? Do you find some differences in the details concerning the creation? If so, what are they?

# The Fall

*Chapter 3*

1 Now the serpent was more subtil than any beast of the field which the LORD God had made. And he said unto the woman, Yea, hath God said, Ye shall not eat of every tree of the garden?

2 And the woman said unto the serpent, We may eat of the fruit of the trees of the garden:

3 But of the fruit of the tree which *is* in the midst of the garden, God hath said, Ye shall not eat of it, neither shall ye touch it, lest ye die.

4 And the serpent said unto the woman, Ye shall not surely die:

5 For God doth know that in the day ye eat thereof, then your eyes shall be opened, and ye shall be as gods, knowing good and evil.

6 And when the woman saw that the tree *was* good for food, and that it *was* pleasant to the eyes, and a tree to be desired to make *one* wise, she took of the fruit thereof, and did eat, and gave also unto her husband with her; and he did eat.

7 And the eyes of them both were opened, and they knew that they *were* naked; and they sewed fig leaves together, and made themselves aprons.

8 And they heard the voice of the LORD God walking in the garden in the cool of the day: and Adam and his wife hid themselves from the presence of the LORD God amongst the trees of the garden.

9 And the LORD God called unto Adam, and said unto him, Where *art* thou?

10 And he said, I heard thy voice in the garden, and I was afraid, because I *was* naked; and I hid myself.

11 And he said, Who told thee that thou *wast* naked? Hast thou eaten of the tree, whereof I commanded thee that thou shouldest not eat?

12 And the man said, The woman whom thou gavest *to be* with me, she gave me of the tree, and I did eat.

13 And the LORD God said unto the woman, What *is* this *that* thou hast done? And the woman said, The serpent beguiled me, and I did eat.

14 And the LORD God said unto the serpent, Because thou hast done this, thou *art* cursed above all cattle, and above every beast of the field; upón thy belly shalt thou go, and dust shalt thou eat all the days of thy life:

15 And I will put enmity between thee and the woman, and be-

tween thy seed and her seed; it shall bruise thy head, and thou shalt bruise his heel.

16 Unto the woman he said, I will greatly multiply thy sorrow and thy conception; in sorrow thou shalt bring forth children; and thy desire *shall be* to thy husband, and he shall rule over thee.

17 And unto Adam he said, Because thou hast hearkened unto the voice of thy wife, and hast eaten of the tree, of which I commanded thee, saying, Thou shalt not eat of it: cursed *is* the ground for thy sake; in sorrow shalt thou eat *of* it all the days of thy life;

18 Thorns also and thistles shall it bring forth to thee; and thou shalt eat the herb of the field;

19 In the sweat of thy face shalt thou eat bread, till thou return unto the ground; for out of it wast thou taken: for dust thou *art,* and unto dust shalt thou return.

20 And Adam called his wife's name Eve; because she was the mother of all living.

21 Unto Adam also and to his wife did the Lord God make coats of skins, and clothed them.

22 ¶And the Lord God said, Behold, the man is become as one of us, to know good and evil: and now, lest he put forth his hand, and take also of the tree of life, and eat, and live for ever:

23 Therefore the Lord God sent him forth from the garden of Eden, to till the ground from whence he was taken.

24 So he drove out the man; and he placed at the east of the garden of Eden Cherubims, and a flaming sword which turned every way, to keep the way of the tree of life.

# Questions

1. The serpent tempts the woman, but exactly why (according to 3:6) does she eat the forbidden fruit? (We are not given the reasons why the man ate, but presumably they were similar to the woman's reasons.) What is the author implying about the nature of sin?
2. In 3:5 the serpent promises the man and the woman knowledge of "good and evil." Judging from 3:7, do they gain knowledge? If so, is it the sort of knowledge they had anticipated? If not, what can be said about this knowledge?
3. The consequences of eating the forbidden fruit were, most obviously, pain (in sustaining oneself and in bearing children), expulsion from Eden, and death. But in terms of human emotions and relationships, what were the consequences?

4.   The disobedience of the man and woman, leading to their expulsion from Eden, is usually called "the Fall," a term which implies loss or diminution. Can one, however, argue that the Fall might also have had positive qualities—for instance, that it led to a creative activity impossible in Eden?

## Cain and Abel

*Chapter 4*

1 And Adam knew Eve his wife; and she conceived, and bare Cain, and said, I have gotten a man from the LORD.

2 And she again bare his brother Abel. And Abel was a keeper of sheep, but Cain was a tiller of the ground.

3 And in process of time it came to pass, that Cain brought of the fruit of the ground an offering unto the LORD.

4 And Abel, he also brought of the firstlings of his flock and of the fat thereof. And the LORD had respect unto Abel and to his offering:

5 But unto Cain and to his offering he had not respect. And Cain was very wroth, and his countenance fell.

6 And the LORD said unto Cain, Why art thou wroth? and why is thy countenance fallen?

7 If thou doest well, shalt thou not be accepted? and if thou doest not well, sin lieth at the door. And unto thee *shall be* his desire, and thou shalt rule over him.

8 And Cain talked with Abel his brother: and it came to pass, when they were in the field, that Cain rose up against Abel his brother, and slew him.

9 ¶And the LORD said unto Cain, Where *is* Abel thy brother? And he said, I know not: *Am* I my brother's keeper?

10 And he said, What hast thou done? the voice of thy brother's blood crieth unto me from the ground.

11 And now *art* thou cursed from the earth, which hath opened her mouth to receive thy brother's blood from thy hand;

12 When thou tillest the ground, it shall not henceforth yield unto thee her strength; a fugitive and a vagabond shalt thou be in the earth.

13 And Cain said unto the LORD, My punishment *is* greater than I can bear.

14 Behold, thou hast driven me out this day from the face of the earth; and from thy face shall I be hid; and I shall be a fugitive and a vagabond in the earth; and it shall come to pass, *that* every one that findeth me shall slay me.

15 And the LORD said unto him, Therefore whosoever slayeth Cain, vengeance shall be taken on him sevenfold. And the LORD set a mark upon Cain, lest any finding him should kill him.

16 ¶And Cain went out from the presence of the LORD, and dwelt in the land of Nod, on the east of Eden.

17 And Cain knew his wife; and she conceived, and bare Enoch: and he builded a city, and called the name of the city, after the name of his son, Enoch.

18 And unto Enoch was born Irad: and Irad begat Mehujael: and Mehujael begat Methusael: and Methusael begat Lamech.

19 ¶And Lamech took unto him two wives: the name of the one *was* Adah, and the name of the other Zillah.

20 And Adah bare Jabal: he was the father of such as dwell in tents, and *of such as have* cattle.

21 And his brother's name *was* Jubal: he was the father of all such as handle the harp and organ.

22 And Zillah, she also bare Tubalcain, an instructer of every artificer in brass and iron: and the sister of Tubalcain *was* Naamah. . . .

# Questions

1.  What do you make of the fact that God in 4:2–7 seems to prefer Abel to Cain, the pastoral man to the agricultural man? (Consider also that in 4:17 Cain the murderer is said to be the builder of the first city.)
2.  When Cain (4:9) asks God, "*Am* I my brother's keeper?" what is the surface meaning of his words? What deeper meaning do the words have? According to what you have read in Genesis, *are* we our brother's keeper?
3.  Is there any evidence that Cain intended to kill Abel? Even if Cain had seen a dead animal, could he have imagined that striking (or throttling?) Abel would deprive Abel of life? Let's assume that the consequences of his action were greater, and more permanent, than he anticipated. Is his action a fitting symbol or emblem of sin? Why, or why not?

## The Tower of Babel

*Chapter 11*

1 And the whole earth was of one language, and of one speech.

2 And it came to pass, as they journeyed from the east, that they found a plain in the land of Shinar; and they dwelt there.

3 And they said one to another, Go to, let us make brick, and burn them throughly. And they had brick for stone, and slime had they for morter.

4 And they said, Go to, let us build us a city and a tower, whose top *may reach* unto heaven; and let us make us a name, lest we be scattered abroad upon the face of the whole earth.

5 And the LORD came down to see the city and the tower, which the children of men builded.

6 And the LORD said, Behold, the people *is* one, and they have all one language; and this they begin to do: and now nothing will be restrained from them, which they have imagined to do.

7 Go to, let us go down, and there confound their language, that they may not understand one another's speech.

8 So the LORD scattered them abroad from thence upon the face of all the earth: and they left off to build the city.

9 Therefore is the name of it called Babel; because the LORD did there confound the language of all the earth: and from thence did the LORD scatter them abroad upon the face of all the earth. . . .

# Questions

1.  What do you take to be the aim(s) of the builders of the city and the tower (11:4)? Why is God displeased?
2.  In verse 4 the people say, "Let us make us a name." Did they succeed? If so, did they succeed in the way that they intended?
3.  What connection(s) can you make between this story and the stories of Adam and Eve and of Cain and Abel?

## The Calling of Abraham

*Chapter 12*

1 Now the LORD had said unto Abram, Get thee out of thy country, and from thy kindred, and from thy father's house, unto a land that I will shew thee:

2 And I will make of thee a great nation, and I will bless thee, and make thy name great; and thou shalt be a blessing:

3 And I will bless them that bless thee, and curse him that curseth thee: and in thee shall all families of the earth be blessed.

4 So Abram departed, as the Lord had spoken unto him; and Lot went with him: and Abram *was* seventy and five years old when he departed out of Haran.

5 And Abram took Sarai his wife, and Lot his brother's son, and all their substance that they had gathered, and the souls that they had gotten in Haran; and they went forth to go into the land of Canaan; and into the land of Canaan they came.

6 ¶And Abram passed through the land unto the place of Sichem, unto the plain of Moreh. And the Canaanite *was* then in the land.

7 And the Lord appeared unto Abram, and said, Unto thy seed will I give this land: and there builded he an altar unto the Lord, who appeared unto him.

8 And he removed from thence unto a mountain on the east of Bethel, and pitched his tent, *having* Bethel on the west, and Hai on the east: and there he builded an altar unto the Lord, and called upon the name of the Lord.

9 And Abram journeyed, going on still toward the south. . . .

## God Announces the Birth of Isaac

*Chapter 18*

1 And the Lord appeared unto him in the plains of Mamre: and he sat in the tent door in the heat of the day;

2 And he lift up his eyes and looked, and, lo, three men stood by him: and when he saw *them,* he ran to meet them from the tent door, and bowed himself toward the ground,

3 And said, My Lord, if now I have found favour in thy sight, pass not away, I pray thee, from thy servant:

4 Let a little water, I pray you, be fetched, and wash your feet, and rest yourselves under the tree:

5 And I will fetch a morsel of bread, and comfort ye your hearts; after that ye shall pass on: for therefore are ye come to your servant. And they said, So do, as thou hast said.

6 And Abraham hastened into the tent unto Sarah, and said, Make ready quickly three measures of fine meal, knead *it*, and make cakes upon the hearth.

7 And Abraham ran unto the herd, and fetcht a calf tender and good, and gave *it* unto a young man; and he hasted to dress it.

8 And he took butter, and milk, and the calf which he had dressed, and set *it* before them; and he stood by them under the tree, and they did eat.

9 ¶And they said unto him, Where *is* Sarah thy wife? And he said, Behold, in the tent.

10 And he said, I will certainly return unto thee according to the time of life; and, lo, Sarah thy wife shall have a son. And Sarah heard *it* in the tent door, which *was* behind him.

11 Now Abraham and Sarah *were* old *and* well stricken in age; *and* it ceased to be with Sarah after the manner of women.

12 Therefore Sarah laughed within herself, saying, After I am waxed old shall I have pleasure, my lord being old also?

13 And the LORD said unto Abraham, Wherefore did Sarah laugh, saying, Shall I of a surety bear a child, which am old?

14 Is any thing too hard for the LORD? At the time appointed I will return unto thee, according to the time of life, and Sarah shall have a son. . . .

## God Tests Abraham

*Chapter 22*

1 And it came to pass after these things, that God did tempt Abraham, and said unto him, Abraham: and he said, Behold, *here* I *am*.

2 And he said, Take now thy son, thine only *son* Isaac, whom thou lovest, and get thee into the land of Moriah; and offer him there for a burnt offering upon one of the mountains which I will tell thee of.

3 ¶And Abraham rose up early in the morning, and saddled his ass, and took two of his young men with him, and Isaac his son, and clave the wood for the burnt offering, and rose up, and went unto the place of which God had told him.

4 Then on the third day Abraham lifted up his eyes, and saw the place afar off.

5 And Abraham said unto his young men, Abide ye here with the ass; and I and the lad will go yonder and worship, and come again to you.

6 And Abraham took the wood of the burnt offering, and laid *it* upon Isaac his son; and he took the fire in his hand, and a knife; and they went both of them together.

7 And Isaac spake unto Abraham his father, and said, My father: and he said, Here *am* I, my son. And he said, Behold the fire and the wood: but where *is* the lamb for a burnt offering?

8 And Abraham said, My son, God will provide himself a lamb for a burnt offering: so they went both of them together.

9 And they came to the place which God had told him of; and Abraham built an altar there, and laid the wood in order, and bound Isaac his son, and laid him on the altar upon the wood.

10 And Abraham stretched forth his hand, and took the knife to slay his son.

11 And the angel of the Lord called unto him out of heaven, and said, Abraham, Abraham: and he said, Here *am* I.

12 And he said, Lay not thine hand upon the lad, neither do thou any thing unto him: for now I know that thou fearest God, seeing thou hast not withheld thy son, thine only *son* from me.

13 And Abraham lifted up his eyes, and looked, and behold behind *him* a ram caught in a thicket by his horns: and Abraham went and took the ram, and offered him up for a burnt offering in the stead of his son.

14 And Abraham called the name of that place Jehovahjireh: as it is said *to* this day, In the mount of the Lord it shall be seen.

15 ¶And the angel of the Lord called unto Abraham out of heaven the second time,

16 And said, By myself have I sworn, saith the Lord, for because thou hast done this thing, and hast not withheld thy son, thine only *son:*

17 That in blessing I will bless thee, and in multiplying I will multiply thy seed as the stars of the heaven, and as the sand which *is* upon the sea shore; and thy seed shall possess the gate of his enemies;

18 And in thy seed shall all the nations of the earth be blessed; because thou hast obeyed my voice.

19 So Abraham returned unto his young men, and they rose up and went together to Beersheba; and Abraham dwelt at Beersheba.
. . .

## Questions

1. How does 12:2, with God's promise to make Abram's name and nation great, connect with the story of the Tower of Babel, especially with 11:4 and 11:9?
2. Characterize Abraham, drawing on his response to God's command in Chapter 12.
3. The first verse of Chapter 22 tells us that God tested ("did tempt") Abraham. Suppose a reader were not given this information. That is, suppose we merely heard God call Abraham, and heard Abraham reply, "Behold, *here I am*," and then we heard the rest of the story. Would our response to the story be different? If so, why, and how?

### A Note on 2 Samuel

Two books of the Hebrew Bible are named for Samuel, the divinely inspired prophet who selected the first Hebrew king, Saul. After the deaths of Saul and three of Saul's sons in battle, David, secretly anointed by Saul at Bethlehem, became king of the twelve tribes of Israel. The two books of Samuel cover a period from about 1050 B.C. to 960 B.C.

David—warrior, musician, king, and fallible man—is one of the most beloved figures in the Hebrew Bible. As a shepherd boy armed only with a slingshot he killed the terrifying Goliath; as a musician and poet (the Psalms were attributed to him) he soothed the moody Saul and later immortalized Saul and Saul's son Jonathan in a famous poem (2 Samuel 1:17–27); as one who respected an anointed monarch he spared the life of Saul even though Saul had tried to kill him; and as king, he sought to learn Yahweh's will. Yet David's domestic life was deeply blemished, as is evident in the selection we give here, which tells of his grievous sins and of his punishments for them.

# 2 Samuel

## David and Bathsheba

*Chapter 11*

1 And it came to pass, after the year was expired, at the time when kings go forth *to battle*, that David sent Joab, and his servants with him, and all Israel; and they destroyed the children of Ammon, and besieged Rabbah. But David tarried still at Jerusalem.

2 ¶And it came to pass in an eveningtide, that David arose from off his bed, and walked upon the roof of the king's house: and from the roof he saw a woman washing herself; and the woman *was* very beautiful to look upon.

3 And David sent and enquired after the woman. And *one* said, *Is* not this Bathsheba, the daughter of Eliam, the wife of Uriah the Hittite?

4 And David sent messengers, and took her; and she came in unto him, and he lay with her; for she was purified from her uncleanness: and she returned unto her house.

5 And the woman conceived, and sent and told David, and said, I *am* with child.

6 ¶And David sent to Joab, *saying*, Send me Uriah the Hittite. And Joab sent Uriah to David.

7 And when Uriah was come unto him, David demanded *of him* how Joab did, and how the people did, and how the war prospered.

8 And David said to Uriah, Go down to thy house, and wash thy feet. And Uriah departed out of the king's house, and there followed him a mess *of meat* from the king.

9 But Uriah slept at the door of the king's house with all the servants of his lord, and went not down to his house.

10 And when they had told David, saying, Uriah went not down unto his house, David said unto Uriah, Camest thou not from *thy* journey? why *then* didst thou not go down unto thine house?

11 And Uriah said unto David, The ark, and Israel, and Judah, abide in tents; and my lord Joab, and the servants of my lord, are encamped in the open fields; shall I then go into mine house, to eat and to drink, and to lie with my wife? *as* thou livest, and *as* thy soul liveth, I will not do this thing.

12 And David said to Uriah, Tarry here to day also, and to morrow I will let thee depart. So Uriah abode in Jerusalem that day, and the morrow.

13 And when David had called him, he did eat and drink before him; and he made him drunk: and at even he went out to lie on his bed with the servants of his lord, but went not down to his house.

14 ¶And it came to pass in the morning, that David wrote a letter to Joab, and sent *it* by the hand of Uriah.

15 And he wrote in the letter, saying, Set ye Uriah in the forefront of the hottest battle, and retire ye from him, that he may be smitten, and die.

16 And it came to pass, when Joab observed the city, that he assigned Uriah unto a place where he knew that valiant men *were*.

17 And the men of the city went out, and fought with Joab: and there fell *some* of the people of the servants of David; and Uriah the Hittite died also.

18 ¶Then Joab sent and told David all the things concerning the war;

19 And charged the messenger, saying, When thou hast made an end of telling the matters of the war unto the king.

20 And if so be that the king's wrath arise, and he say unto thee, Wherefore approached ye so nigh unto the city when ye did fight? knew ye not that they would shoot from the wall?

21 Who smote Abimelech the son of Jerubbesheth? did not a woman cast a piece of a millstone upon him from the wall, that he died in Thebez? why went ye nigh the wall? then say thou, Thy servant Uriah the Hittite is dead also.

22 ¶So the messenger went, and came and shewed David all that Joab had sent him for.

23 And the messenger said unto David, Surely the men prevailed against us, and came out unto us into the field, and we were upon them even unto the entering of the gate.

24 And the shooters shot from off the wall upon thy servants; and *some* of the king's servants be dead, and thy servant Uriah the Hittite is dead also.

25 Then David said unto the messenger, Thus shalt thou say unto Joab, Let not this thing displease thee, for the sword devoureth one as well as another: make thy battle more strong against the city, and overthrow it: and encourage thou him.

26 ¶And when the wife of Uriah heard that Uriah her husband was dead, she mourned for her husband.

27 And when the mourning was past, David sent and fetched her to his house, and she became his wife, and bare him a son. But the thing that David had done displeased the LORD.

## Chapter 12

1 And the LORD sent Nathan unto David. And he came unto him, and said unto him, There were two men in one city; the one rich, and the other poor.

2 The rich *man* had exceeding many flocks and herds:

3 But the poor *man* had nothing, save one little ewe lamb, which he had bought and nourished up: and it grew up together with him, and with his children; it did eat of his own meat, and drank of his own cup, and lay in his bosom, and was unto him as a daughter.

4 And there came a traveller unto the rich man, and he spared to take of his own flock and of his own herd, to dress for the wayfaring man that was come unto him; but took the poor man's lamb, and dressed it for the man that was come to him.

5 And David's anger was greatly kindled against the man; and he said to Nathan, *As* the LORD liveth, the man that hath done this *thing* shall surely die:

6 And he shall restore the lamb fourfold, because he did this thing, and because he had no pity.

7 ¶And Nathan said to David, Thou *art* the man. Thus saith the LORD God of Israel, I anointed thee king over Israel, and I delivered thee out of the hand of Saul;

8 And I gave thee thy master's house, and thy master's wives into thy bosom, and gave thee the house of Israel and of Judah; and if *that had been* too little, I would moreover have given unto thee such and such things.

9 Wherefore hast thou despised the commandment of the LORD, to do evil in his sight? thou hast killed Uriah the Hittite with the sword, and hast taken his wife *to be* thy wife, and hast slain him with the sword of the children of Ammon.

10 Now therefore the sword shall never depart from thine house; because thou hast despised me, and hast taken the wife of Uriah the Hittite to be thy wife.

11 Thus saith the LORD, Behold, I will raise up evil against thee out of thine own house, and I will take thy wives before thine eyes,

and give *them* unto thy neighbour, and he shall lie with thy wives in the sight of this sun.

12 For thou didst *it* secretly: but I will do this thing before all Israel, and before the sun.

13 And David said unto Nathan, I have sinned against the LORD. And Nathan said unto David, The LORD also hath put away thy sin; thou shalt not die.

14 Howbeit, because by this deed thou hast given great occasion to the enemies of the LORD to blaspheme, the child also *that is* born unto thee shall surely die.

15 ¶And Nathan departed unto his house. And the LORD struck the child that Uriah's wife bare unto David, and it was very sick.

16 David therefore besought God for the child; and David fasted, and went in, and lay all night upon the earth.

17 And the elders of his house arose, *and went* to him, to raise him up from the earth: but he would not, neither did he eat bread with them.

18 And it came to pass on the seventh day, that the child died. And the servants of David feared to tell him that the child was dead: for they said, Behold, while the child was yet alive, we spake unto him, and he would not hearken unto our voice: how will he then vex himself, if we tell him that the child is dead?

19 But when David saw that his servants whispered, David perceived that the child was dead: therefore David said unto his servants, Is the child dead? And they said, He is dead.

20 Then David arose from the earth, and washed, and anointed *himself,* and changed his apparel, and came into the house of the LORD, and worshipped: then he came to his own house; and when he required, they set bread before him, and he did eat.

21 Then said his servants unto him, What thing *is* this that thou hast done? thou didst fast and weep for the child, *while it was* alive; but when the child was dead, thou didst rise and eat bread.

22 And he said, While the child was yet alive, I fasted and wept: for I said, Who can tell *whether* GOD will be gracious to me, that the child may live?

23 But now he is dead, wherefore should I fast? can I bring him back again? I shall go to him, but he shall not return to me.

24 ¶And David comforted Bathsheba his wife, and went in unto her, and lay with her: and she bare a son, and he called his name Solomon: and the LORD loved him.

25 And he sent by the hand of Nathan the prophet; and he called his name Jedidiah, because of the LORD. . . .

# Questions

1.  What impression of David do you get from the first two verses of Chapter 11? Consider especially the images that come to mind with the following phrases: "the time when kings go forth *to battle*," and "David tarried," "David arose from off his bed."
2.  In 11:3 David asks for information about the woman he saw. Judging from his actions in the next verse, how much attention does he pay to the details he learns?
3.  In 11:2 we learn that Bathsheba was "washing herself"; in 11:4 we learn that she "was purified from her uncleanness," i.e., that she had just had her period. Why does the narrator bother to give us these details about Bathsheba? What is the reader's impression of her?
4.  Why does David in 11:6 send for Uriah? In view of 11:7, what impression do you think David is trying to convey to Uriah? We are not told what Uriah reported to David, although he must have said something. What does the *absence* of the report tell us about David's interview with Uriah? Why does David cause him to get drunk (11:13)? And what does Uriah's refusal to go to his own house (11:9–13, but especially 11:11) tell us about Uriah's character? How does his character contrast with David's?
5.  Of what crimes is David guilty?
6.  Nathan's parable (in Chapter 12) of the rich man and the poor man is very brief, but it reveals a striking contrast. In your own words characterize the rich man and the poor man. How does the rich man's character (as well as his action, of course) resemble David's?
7.  Is there any evidence that Nathan is afraid to accuse David directly? If not, why does he rebuke David at first by means of a parable, rather than directly?
8.  In 12:18 the servants fear to tell David that the child is dead, but when they do convey the news (12:19) David's reaction (12:20–23) surprises them. Does his reaction make sense to you?
9.  "Solomon" (12:24) means "peace." "Jedidiah"—the name the Lord gives the child, through Nathan—means "beloved of Yahweh," i.e., beloved of the Lord. What peace has been established? Why is the child beloved of the Lord?
10. What do you think is the chief point of the story in Chapters 11 and 12? That certain acts are sinful? That even a king is not above God's law? That David acknowledged his sin? Or what?

Phyllis Trible

# Eve and Adam
## Genesis 2–3 Reread

On the whole, the Women's Liberation Movement is hos-  1
tile to the Bible, even as it claims that the Bible is hostile to women.
The Yahwist account of creation and fall in Genesis 2–3 provides a
strong proof text for that claim. Accepting centuries of (male) exegesis,
many feminists interpret this story as legitimating male supremacy and
female subordination.[1] They read to reject. My suggestion is that we
reread to understand and to appropriate. Ambiguity characterizes the
meaning of 'adham in Genesis 2–3. On the one hand, man is the first
creature formed (2:7). The Lord God puts him in the garden "to till it
and keep it," a job identified with the male (cf. 3:17–19). On the other
hand, 'adham is a generic term for humankind. In commanding 'adham
not to eat of the tree of the knowledge of good and evil, the Deity is
speaking to both the man and the woman (2:16–17). Until the differentiation of female and male (2:21–23), 'adham is basically androgynous: one creature incorporating two sexes.

Concern for sexuality, specifically for the creation of woman,  2
comes last in the story, after the making of the garden, the trees, and
the animals. Some commentators allege female subordination based
on this order of events.[2] They contrast it with Genesis 1:27 where God

[1] See inter alia, Kate Millett, Sexual Politics (New York: Doubleday, 1970), pp. 51–54;
Eva Figes, Patriarchal Attitudes (Greenwich, Conn.: Fawcett, 1970), pp. 38f; Mary
Daly, "The Courage to See," The Christian Century, September 22, 1971, p. 1110;
Sheila D. Collins, "Toward a Feminist Theology," The Christian Century, August 2,
1972, p. 798; Lilly Rivlin, "Lilith: The First Woman," Ms., December 1972, pp. 93,
114.
[2] Cf. E. Jacob, Theology of the Old Testament (New York: Harper & Bros., 1958), pp.
172f; S. H. Hooke, "Genesis," Peake's Commentary on the Bible (London: Thomas
Nelson, 1962), p. 179.

Phyllis Trible, a member of the faculty of Union Theological Seminary in New
York City, received her Ph.D. from Union Theological Seminary and Columbia
University. Trible is the author of two books, God and the Rhetoric of Sexuality
and Texts of Terror: Literary-Feminist Readings of Biblical Narratives. The essay
we reprint, originally published in 1973, has come to be regarded as a landmark
in feminist analysis of the Bible.

creates *'adham* as male and female in one act.[3] Thereby they infer that whereas the Priests recognized the equality of the sexes, the Yahwist made woman a second, subordinate, inferior sex.[4] But the last may be first, as both the biblical theologian and the literary critic know. Thus the Yahwist account moves to its climax, not its decline, in the creation of woman.[5] She is not an afterthought; she is the culmination. Genesis 1 itself supports this interpretation, for there male and female are indeed the last and truly the crown of all creatures. The last is also first where beginnings and endings are parallel. In Hebrew literature, the central concerns of a unit often appear at the beginning and the end as an *inclusio*\* device.[6] Genesis 2 evinces this structure. The creation of man first and of woman last constitutes a ring composition whereby the two creatures are parallel. In no way does the order disparage woman. Content and context augment this reading.

The context for the advent of woman is a divine judgment: "It is    3 not good that *'adham* should be alone; I will make him a helper fit for him" (2:18). The phrase needing explication is "helper fit for him." In the Old Testament the word *helper* (*'ezer*) has many usages. It can be a proper name for a male.[7] In our story, it describes the animals and the woman. In some passages, it characterizes Deity. God is the helper

---

[3] E.g., Elizabeth Cady Stanton observed that Genesis 1:26–28 "dignifies woman as an important factor in the creation, equal in power and glory with man," while Genesis 2 "makes her a mere afterthought" (*The Woman's Bible*, Part I [New York: European Publishing Company, 1895], p. 20). See also Elsie Adams and Mary Louise Briscoe, *Up Against the Wall, Mother . . .* (Beverly Hills: Glencoe Press, 1971), p. 4.

[4] Cf. Eugene H. Maly, "Genesis," *The Jerome Biblical Commentary* (Englewood Cliffs, N.J.: Prentice-Hall, 1968), p. 12: "But woman's existence, psychologically and in the social order, is dependent on man."

[5] See John L. McKenzie, "The Literary Characteristics of Gen. 2–3," *Theological Studies*, Vol. 15 (1954), p. 559; John A. Bailey, "Initiation and the Primal Woman in Gilgamesh and Genesis 2–3," *Journal of Biblical Literature*, June 1970, p. 143. Bailey writes emphatically of the remarkable importance and position of the woman in Genesis 2–3, "all the more extraordinary when one realizes that this is the only account of the creation of woman as such in ancient Near Eastern literature." He hedges, however, in seeing the themes of helper and naming (Genesis 2:18–23) as indicative of a "certain subordination" of woman to man. These reservations are unnecessary; see below. Cf. also Claus Westermann, *Genesis, Biblischer Kommentar* ¼ (Neukerchener-Vluyn: Newkirchener Verlag, 1970), p. 312.

\* *Inclusio*: a paragraph or other unit markred by the same words at the beginning and the end. (Editors' note)

[6] James Muilenburg, "Form Criticism and Beyond," *Journal of Biblical Literature,* March 1969, pp. 9f; Mitchell Dahood, "Psalm I," *The Anchor Bible* (New York: Doubleday, 1966), *passim* and esp. p. 5.

[7] See 1 Chronicles 4:4; 12:9; Nehemiah 3:19.

of Israel. As helper Yahweh creates and saves.[8] Thus 'ezer is a relational term; it designates a beneficial relationship; and it pertains to God, people, and animals. By itself, the word does not specify positions within relationships; more particularly, it does not imply inferiority. Position results from additional content or from context. Accordingly, what kind of relationship does 'ezer entail in Genesis 2:18, 20? Our answer comes in two ways: (1) The word neged, which joins 'ezer, connotes equality: a helper who is a counterpart.[9] (2) The animals are helpers, but they fail to fit 'adham. There is physical, perhaps psychic, rapport between 'adham and the animals, for Yahweh forms (yasar) them both out of the ground ('adhamah). Yet their similarity is not equality. 'Adham names them and thereby exercises power over them. No fit helper is among them. And thus the narrative moves to woman. . . . God is the helper superior to man; the animals are helpers inferior to man; woman is the helper equal to man.

Let us pursue the issue by examining the account of the creation    4
of woman ([verses] 21–22). This episode concludes the story even as the creation of man commences it. . . . The ring composition suggests an interpretation of woman and man as equals. To establish this meaning, structure and content must mesh. They do. In both episodes, Yahweh alone creates. For the last creation the Lord God "caused a deep sleep (tardemah) to fall upon the man." Man has no part in making woman; he is out of it. He exercises no control over her existence. He is neither participant nor spectator nor consultant at her birth. Like man, woman owes her life solely to God. For both of them, the origin of life is a divine mystery. Another parallel of equality is creation out of raw materials: dust for man and a rib for woman. Yahweh chooses these fragile materials and in both cases processes them before human beings happen. As Yahweh shapes dust and then breathes into it to form man, so Yahweh takes out the rib and then builds it into woman.[10] To call woman "Adam's rib" is to misread the text, which states carefully and clearly that the extracted bone required divine labor to be-

---

[8] See Psalm 121:2, 124:8; 146:5; 33:20; 115:9–11; Exodus 18:4; Deuteronomy 33:7, 26, 29.

[9] L. Koehler and W. Baumgartner, Lexicon in Veteris Testamenti Libros (Leiden: E. J. Brill, 1958), pp. 591f.

[10] The verb bnh (to build) suggests considerable labor. It is used of towns, towers, altars, and fortifications, as well as of the primeval woman (Koehler-Baumgartner, op. cit., p. 134). In Genesis 2:22, it may mean the fashioning of clay around the rib (Ruth Amiran, "Myths of the Creation of Man and the Jericho Statues," BASOR, No. 167 [October 1962], p. 24).

come female, a datum scarcely designed to bolster the male ego. More-over, to claim that the rib means inferiority or subordination is to assign the man qualities over the woman which are not in the narrative itself. Superiority, strength, aggressiveness, dominance, and power do not characterize man in Genesis 2. By contrast, he is formed from dirt; his life hangs by a breath which he does not control; and he himself remains silent and passive while the Deity plans and interprets his existence.

The rib means solidarity and equality. *'Adham* recognizes this  5 meaning in a poem:[11]

This at last is bone of bones
and flesh of my flesh.
She shall be called *'ishshah* [woman]
because she was taken out of *'ish* [man].(2:23)

The pun proclaims both the similarity and the differentiation of female and male. Before this episode the Yahwist has used only the generic term *'adham*. No exclusively male reference has appeared. Only with the specific creation of woman (*'ishshah*) occurs the first specific terms for man as male (*'ish*). In other words, sexuality is simultaneous for woman and man. The sexes are interrelated and interdependent. Man as male does not precede woman as female but happens concurrently with her. Hence, the first act in Genesis 2 is the creation of androgyny (2:7), and the last is the creation of sexuality (2:23).[12] Male embodies female, and female embodies male. The two are neither dichotomies nor duplicates. The birth of woman corresponds to the birth of man but does not copy it. Only in responding to the female does the man discover himself as male. No longer a passive creature, *'ish* comes alive in meeting *'ishshah*.

Some read into the poem a naming motif. The man names the  6 woman and thereby has power and authority over her.[13] But again

[11] See Walter Brueggemann, "Of the Same Flesh and Bone (Gen. 2:23a)," *Catholic Biblical Quarterly*, October 1970, pp. 532–42.
[12] In proposing as primary an androgynous interpretation of *'adham*, I find virtually no support from (male) biblical scholars. But my view stands as documented from the text, and I take refuge among a remnant of ancient (male) rabbis (see George Foot Moore, *Judaism* [Cambridge, Mass.: Harvard University Press, 1927]), I, 453; also Joseph Campbell, *The Hero with a Thousand Faces* (Meridian Books, The World Publishing Company, 1970), pp. 152ff., 279f.
[13] See e.g., G. von Rad, *Genesis* (Philadelphia: Westminster Press, 1961), pp. 80–82; John H. Marks, "Genesis," *The Interpreter's One-Volume Commentary on the Bible* (Nashville: Abingdon Press, 1971), p. 5; Bailey, op. cit., p. 143.

. . . reread. Neither the verb nor the noun *name* is in the poem. We find instead the verb *gara'*, to call: "She shall be called woman." Now, in the Yahwist primeval history this verb does not function as a synonym or parallel or substitute for *name*. The typical formula for naming is the verb *to call* plus the explicit object *name*. This formula applies to Deity, people, places, and animals. For example, in Genesis 4 we read:

> Cain built a city and *called* the *name* of the city after the *name* of his son Enoch. (v. 17)
> And Adam knew his wife again, and she bore a son and *called* his *name* Seth. (v. 25)
> To Seth also a son was born and he *called* his *name* Enoch. (v. 26a)
> At that time men began to *call* upon the *name* of the Lord. (v. 26b)

Genesis 2:23 has the verb *call* but does not have the object *name*. Its absence signifies the absence of a naming motif in the poem. The presence of both the verb *call* and the noun *name* in the episode of the animals strengthens the point:

> So out of the ground the Lord God formed every beast of the field and every bird of the air, and brought them to the man to see what he would *call* them; and whatever the man *called* every living creature, that was its *name*. The man gave *names* to all cattle, and to the birds of the air, and to every beast of the field. (2:19–20)

In calling the animals by name, *'adham* establishes supremacy over them and fails to find a fit helper. In calling woman, *'adham* does not name her and does find in her a counterpart. Female and male are equal sexes. Neither has authority over the other.[14]

A further observation secures the argument: *Woman* itself is not a name. It is a common noun; it is not a proper noun. It designates gender; it does not specify person. *'Adham* recognizes sexuality by the words *'ishshah* and *'ish*. This recognition is not an act of naming to assert the power of male over female. Quite the contrary. But the true skeptic is already asking: What about Genesis 3:20, where "the man called his wife's name Eve"? We must wait to consider that question. Meanwhile, the words of the ancient poem as well as their context proclaim sexuality originating in the unity of *'adham*. From this one (androgynous) creature come two (female and male). The two return

---

[14] Cf. Westermann, op. cit., pp. 316ff.

to their original unity as '*ish* and '*ishshah* become one flesh (2:24):[15] another instance of the ring composition.

Next the differences which spell harmony and equality yield to the differences of disobedience and disaster. The serpent speaks to the woman. Why to the woman and not to the man? The simplest answer is that we do not know. The Yahwist does not tell us anymore than he explains why the tree of the knowledge of good and evil was in the garden. But the silence of the text stimulates speculations, many of which only confirm the patriarchal mentality which conceived them. Cassuto identifies serpent and woman, maintaining that the cunning of the serpent is "in reality" the cunning of the woman.[16] He impugns her further by declaring that "for the very reason that a woman's imagination surpasses a man's, it was the woman who was enticed first." Though more gentle in his assessment, von Rad avers that "in the history of Yahweh religion, it has always been the women who have shown an inclination for obscure astrological cults" (a claim which he does not document).[17] Consequently, he holds that the woman "confronts the obscure allurements and mysteries that beset our limited life more directly than the man does," and then he calls her a "temptress." Paul Ricoeur says that woman "represents the point of weakness," as the entire story "gives evidence of a very masculine resentment."[18] McKenzie links the "moral weakness" of the woman with her "sexual attraction" and holds that the latter ruined both the woman and the man.[19]

But the narrative does not say any of these things. It does not sustain the judgment that woman is weaker or more cunning or more

8

9

---

[15] Verse 24 probably mirrors a matriarchal society (so Von Rad, op. cit., p. 83). If the myth were designed to support patriarchy, it is difficult to explain how this verse survived without proper alteration. Westermann contends, however, that an emphasis on matriarchy misunderstands the point of the verse, which is the total communion of woman and man (ibid., p. 317).

[16] U. Cassuto, *A Commentary on the Book of Genesis*, Part I (Jerusalem: Magnes Press, n.d.), pp. 142f.

[17] Von Rad, op. cit., pp. 87f.

[18] Ricoeur departs from the traditional interpretation of the woman when he writes: "*Eve n'est donc pas la femme en tant que 'deuxieme sexe'; toute femme et tout homme sont Adam; tout homme et toute femme sont Eve.*" But the fourth clause of his sentence obscures this complete identity of Adam and Eve: "*toute femme peche 'en Adam, tout homme est seduit 'en Eve.*" By switching from an active to a passive verb, Ricoeur makes only the woman directly responsible for both sinning and seducing. (Paul Ricoeur, Finitude et Culpabilite, II. *La Symbolique du Mal*, Aubier, Editions Montaigne [Paris; 1960]. Cf. Paul Ricoeur, *The Symbolism of Evil* [Boston: Beacon Press, 1969], p. 255).

[19] McKenzie, op. cit., p. 570.

sexual than man. Both have the same Creator, who explicitly uses the word *good* to introduce the creation of woman (2:18). Both are equal in birth. There is complete rapport, physical, psychological, sociological, and theological, between them: bone of bone and flesh of flesh. If there be moral frailty in one, it is moral frailty in two. Further, they are equal in responsibility and in judgment, in shame and in guilt, in redemption and in grace. What the narrative says about the nature of woman it also says about the nature of man.

Why does the serpent speak to the woman and not to the man? Let a female speculate. If the serpent is "more subtle" than its fellow creatures, the woman is more appealing than her husband. Throughout the myth, she is the more intelligent one, the more aggressive one, and the one with greater sensibilities.[20] Perhaps the woman elevates the animal world by conversing theologically with the serpent. At any rate, she understands the hermeneutical task. In quoting God, she interprets the prohibition ("neither shall you touch it"). The woman is both theologian and translator. She contemplates the tree, taking into account all the possibilities. The tree is good for food; it satisfies the physical drives. It pleases the eyes; it is esthetically and emotionally desirable. Above all, it is coveted as the source of wisdom (*haskîl*). Thus the woman is fully aware when she acts, her vision encompassing the gamut of life. She takes the fruit, and she eats. The initiative and the decision are hers alone. There is no consultation with her husband. She seeks neither his advice nor his permission. She acts independently.

By contrast, the man is a silent, passive, and bland recipient: "She also gave some to her husband, and he ate." The narrator makes no attempt to depict the husband as reluctant or hesitating. The man does not theologize; he does not contemplate; he does not envision the full possibilities of the occasion. His one act is belly oriented, and it is an act of quiescence, not of initiative. The man is not dominant; he is not aggressive; he is not a decision maker. Even though the prohibition not to eat of the tree appears before the female was specifically created, she knows that it applies to her. She has interpreted it, and now she struggles with the temptation to disobey. But not the man, to whom the prohibition came directly (2:16). He follows his wife without question or comment, thereby denying his own individuality. If the woman be intelligent, sensitive, and ingenious, the man is passive, brutish, and inept. These character portrayals are truly extraordinary in a cul-

10

11

[20] See Bailey, op. cit., p. 148.

ture dominated by men. I stress their contrast not to promote female chauvinism but to undercut patriarchal interpretations alien to the text.

The contrast between woman and man fades after their acts of    12 disobedience. They are one in the new knowledge of their nakedness (3:7). They are one in hearing and in hiding. They flee from the sound of the Lord God in the Garden (3:8). First to the man come questions of responsibility (3:9, 11), but the man fails to be responsible: "The woman whom Thou gavest to be with me, she gave me fruit of the tree, and I ate" (3:12). Here the man does not blame the woman; he does not say that the woman seduced him,[21] he blames the Deity. The verb which he uses for both the Deity and the woman is *ntn* (cf. 3:6). . . . This verb neither means nor implies seduction in this context or in the lexicon. Again, if the Yahwist intended to make woman the temptress, he missed a choice opportunity. The woman's response supports the point. "The serpent beguiled me, and I ate" (3:13). Only here occurs the strong verb *nsh'*, meaning to deceive, to seduce. God accepts this subject-verb combination when, immediately following the woman's accusation, Yahweh says to the serpent, "Because you have done this, cursed are you above all animals" (3:14).

Though the tempter (the serpent) is cursed,[22] the woman and the    13 man are not. But they are judged, and the judgments are commentaries on the disastrous effects of their shared disobedience. They show how terrible human life has become as it stands between creation and grace. We misread if we assume that these judgments are mandates. They describe; they do not prescribe. They protest; they do not condone. Of special concern are the words telling the woman that her husband shall rule over her (3:16). This statement is not license for male supremacy, but rather it is condemnation of that very pattern.[23] Subjugation and supremacy are perversions of creation. Through disobedience, the woman has become slave. Her initiative and her freedom vanish. The man is corrupted also, for he has become master, ruling over the one who is his God-given equal. The subordination of female to male signifies their shared sin.[24] This sin vitiates all relationships:

---

[21] See Westermann, op. cit., p. 340.

[22] For a discussion of the serpent, see Ricoeur, *The Symbolism of Evil*, op. cit., pp. 255–60.

[23] Cf. Edwin M. Good, *Irony in the Old Testament* (Philadelphia: Westminster Press, 1965), p. 84, note 4: "Is it not surprising that, in a culture where the subordination of woman to man was a virtually unquestioned social principle, the etiology of the subordination should be in the context of man's primal sin? Perhaps woman's subordination was not unquestioned in Israel." Cf. also Henricus Renckens, *Israel's Concept of the Beginning* (New York: Herder & Herder, 1964), pp. 127f.

[24] *Contra* Westermann, op. cit., p. 357.

between animals and human beings (3:15); mothers and children (3:16); husbands and wives (3:16); people and the soil (3:17–18); humanity and its work (3:19). Whereas in creation man and woman know harmony and equality, in sin they know alienation and discord. Grace makes possible a new beginning.

A further observation about these judgments: they are culturally    14 conditioned. Husband and work (childbearing) define the woman; wife and work (farming) define the man. A literal reading of the story limits both creatures and limits the story. To be faithful translators, we must recognize that women as well as men move beyond these culturally defined roles, even as the intentionality and function of the myth move beyond its original setting. Whatever forms stereotyping takes in our own culture, they are judgments upon our common sin and disobedience. The suffering and oppression we women and men know now are marks of our fall, not of our creation.

At this place of sin and judgment, "the man calls his wife's name    15 Eve" (3:20), thereby asserting his rule over her. The naming itself faults the man for corrupting a relationship of mutuality and equality. And so Yahweh evicts the primeval couple from the Garden, yet with signals of grace.[25] Interestingly, the conclusion of the story does not specify the sexes in flight. Instead the narrator resumes use of the generic and androgynous term 'adham with which the story began and thereby completes an overall ring composition (3:22–24).

Visiting the Garden of Eden in the days of the Women's Move-    16 ment, we need no longer accept the traditional exegesis of Genesis 2– 3. Rather than legitimating the patriarchal culture from which it comes, the myth places that culture under judgment. And thus it functions to liberate, not to enslave. This function we can recover and appropriate. The Yahwist narrative tells us who we are (creatures of equality and mutuality); it tells us who we have become (creatures of oppression); and so it opens possibilities for change, for a return to our true liberation under God. In other words, the story calls female and male to repent.

# Questions

1. Trible says (paragraph 2) of Genesis 2:1–23 that the story "moves to its climax, not its decline, in the creation of woman. She is not an afterthought; she is the culmination." Do you agree with her

---

[25] Von Rad, op. cit., pp. 94, 148.

interpretation? If not, on what do you base your disagreement with Trible?

2. Trible admits (paragraph 8) that "we do not know" why the serpent speaks to the woman and not to the man, but in the next two paragraphs she offers a speculation. Do you find her speculation persuasive? Why, or why not?

3. This essay is fairly technical, drawing as it does on the Hebrew text rather than simply on an English translation. Did you find the writing clear? If so, what are some of the devices by which Trible eased the reader's task? If you found the writing obscure, what are some of the sources of obscurity? For instance, does Trible fail to organize her material lucidly, or fail to define key terms, or make unexplained leaps in her argument?

Jesus

# The Sermon on the Mount [Matthew, Chapters 5, 6, and 7]

*Chapter 5*

1 And seeing the multitudes, he went up into a mountain: and when he was set, his disciples came unto him:

2 And he opened his mouth, and taught them, saying,

3 Blessed *are* the poor in spirit: for theirs is the kingdom of heaven.

4 Blessed *are* they that mourn: for they shall be comforted.

5 Blessed *are* the meek: for they shall inherit the earth.

---

The Gospel according to St. Matthew, like the Gospels according to Saints Mark and Luke, is a narrative of the life of Jesus. The word "gospel" means "good news"; in particular the good news was that God had sent Jesus into the world, and that the death of Jesus on Calvary was an act through which human beings could gain forgiveness of sins and be brought back to a normal relationship with God. The Greek book attributed to Matthew (he was one of the twelve disciples sent out by Christ to teach) was probably written in the last quarter of the first century A.D., i.e., some forty or fifty years after the Crucifixion. Tradition holds that Matthew wrote it in Palestine for Jews who had converted to Christianity.

Although the Gospels of Matthew, Mark, and Luke resemble one another in many ways, each is distinctive. For instance, in comparison with Mark, Matthew abbreviates the stories of miracles, and, on the other hand, Matthew places a greater emphasis on Jesus as a teacher. Much of the Gospel according to St. Matthew could serve as a handbook of Christian conduct. Further, in contrast to the Gospels according to Mark and Luke, the Gospel according to Matthew has been called a "Jewish Christian Gospel," partly because it quotes from the Hebrew Bible about twice as often as the others do, and partly because it places great emphasis on Jesus as the Messiah of the Hebrew Bible. It sees Jesus as having come not to destroy the Law but to fulfill it:

> Think not that I am come to destroy the law, or the prophets: I am not come to destroy, but to fulfil.
> For verily I say unto you, Till heaven and earth pass, one jot or one tittle shall in no wise pass from the law, till all be fulfilled. (5:17–18)

In the Sermon on the Mount, Jesus can be seen as the new Moses: as Moses received the Law on Mt. Sinai (Exodus 19:3), so Jesus announces the new teaching on a mountain—a new Mt. Sinai.

6 Blessed *are* they which do hunger and thirst after righteousness: for they shall be filled.

7 Blessed *are* the merciful: for they shall obtain mercy.

8 Blessed *are* the pure in heart: for they shall see God.

9 Blessed *are* the peacemakers: for they shall be called the children of God.

10 Blessed *are* they which are persecuted for righteousness' sake: for theirs is the kingdom of heaven.

11 Blessed are ye, when *men* shall revile you, and persecute *you*, and shall say all manner of evil against you falsely, for my sake.

12 Rejoice, and be exceeding glad: for great *is* your reward in heaven: for so persecuted they the prophets which were before you.

13 ¶Ye are the salt of the earth: but if the salt have lost his savour, wherewith shall it be salted? it is thenceforth good for nothing, but to be cast out, and to be trodden under foot of men.

14 Ye are the light of the world. A city that is set on an hill cannot be hid.

15 Neither do men light a candle, and put it under a bushel, but on a candlestick; and it giveth light unto all that are in the house.

16 Let your light so shine before men, that they may see your good works, and glorify your Father which is in heaven.

17 ¶Think not that I am come to destroy the law, or the prophets: I am not come to destroy, but to fulfil.

18 For verily I say unto you, Till heaven and earth pass, one jot or one tittle shall in no wise pass from the law, till all be fulfilled.

19 Whosoever therefore shall break one of these least commandments, and shall teach men so, he shall be called the least in the kingdom of heaven: but whosoever shall do and teach *them*, the same shall be called great in the kingdom of heaven.

20 For I say unto you, That except your righteousness shall exceed *the righteousness* of the scribes and Pharisees, ye shall in no case enter into the kingdom of heaven.

21 ¶Ye have heard that it was said by them of old time, Thou shalt not kill; and whosoever shall kill shall be in danger of the judgment:

22 But I say unto you, That whosoever is angry with his brother without a cause shall be in danger of the judgment: and whosoever shall say to his brother, Raca[1], shall be in danger of the council: but whosoever shall say, Thou fool, shall be in danger of hell fire.

23 Therefore if thou bring thy gift to the altar, and there rememberest that thy brother hath ought against thee;

---

[1] *Raca*: An Aramaic word, usually translated as "nitwit."

24 Leave there thy gift before the altar, and go thy way; first be reconciled to thy brother, and then come and offer thy gift.

25 Agree with thine adversary quickly, whiles thou art in the way with him; lest at any time the adversary deliver thee to the judge, and the judge deliver thee to the officer, and thou be cast into prison.

26 Verily I say unto thee, Thou shalt by no means come out thence, till thou hast paid the uttermost farthing.

27 ¶Ye have heard that it was said by them of old time, Thou shalt not commit adultery:

28 But I say unto you, That whosoever looketh on a woman to lust after her hath committed adultery with her already in his heart.

29 And if thy right eye offend thee, pluck it out, and cast *it* from thee: for it is profitable for thee that one of thy members should perish, and not *that* thy whole body should be cast into hell.

30 And if thy right hand offend thee, cut it off, and cast *it* from thee: for it is profitable for thee that one of thy members should perish, and not *that* thy whole body should be cast into hell.

31 It hath been said, Whosoever shall put away his wife, let him give her a writing of divorcement:

32 But I say unto you, That whosoever shall put away his wife, saving for the cause of fornication, causeth her to commit adultery: and whosoever shall marry her that is divorced committeth adultery.

33 ¶Again, ye have heard that it hath been said by them of old time, Thou shalt not forswear thyself, but shalt perform unto the Lord thine oaths:

34 But I say unto you, Swear not at all; neither by heaven; for it is God's throne:

35 Nor by the earth; for it is his footstool: neither by Jerusalem; for it is the city of the great King.

36 Neither shalt thou swear by thy head, because thou canst not make one hair white or black.

37 But let your communication be, Yea, yea; Nay, nay: for whatsoever is more than these cometh of evil.

38 ¶Ye have heard that it hath been said, An eye for an eye, and a tooth for a tooth:

39 But I say unto you, That ye resist not evil: but whosoever shall smite thee on thy right cheek, turn to him the other also.

40 And if any man will sue thee at the law, and take away thy coat, let him have *thy* cloke also.

41 And whosoever shall compel thee to go a mile, go with him twain.

42 Give to him that asketh thee, and from him that would borrow of thee turn not thou away.

43 ¶Ye have heard that it hath been said, Thou shalt love thy neighbour, and hate thine enemy.

44 But I say unto you, Love your enemies, bless them that curse you, do good to them that hate you, and pray for them which despitefully use you, and persecute you;

45 That ye may be the children of your Father which is in heaven: for he maketh his sun to rise on the evil and on the good, and sendeth rain on the just and on the unjust.

46 For if ye love them which love you, what reward have ye? do not even the publicans the same?

47 And if ye salute your brethren only, what do ye more *than others?* do not even the publicans so?

48 Be ye therefore perfect, even as your Father which is in heaven is perfect.

## Chapter 6

1 Take heed that ye do not your alms before men, to be seen of them: otherwise ye have no reward of your Father which is in heaven.

2 Therefore when thou doest *thine* alms, do not sound a trumpet before thee, as the hypocrites do in the synagogues and in the streets, that they may have glory of men. Verily I say unto you, They have their reward.

3 But when thou doest alms, let not thy left hand know what thy right hand doeth:

4 That thine alms may be in secret: and thy Father which seeth in secret himself shall reward thee openly.

5 ¶And when thou prayest, thou shalt not be as the hypocrites *are:* for they love to pray standing in the synagogues and in the corners of the streets, that they may be seen of men. Verily I say unto you, They have their reward.

6 But thou, when thou prayest, enter into thy closet, and when thou hast shut thy door, pray to thy Father which is in secret; and thy Father which seeth in secret shall reward thee openly.

7 But when ye pray, use not vain repetitions, as the heathen *do:* for they think that they shall be heard for their much speaking.

8 Be not ye therefore like unto them: for your Father knoweth what things ye have need of, before ye ask him.

9 After this manner therefore pray ye: Our Father which art in heaven, Hallowed be thy name.

10 Thy kingdom come. Thy will be done in earth, as *it is* in heaven.

11 Give us this day our daily bread.

12 And forgive us our debts, as we forgive our debtors.

13 And lead us not into temptation, but deliver us from evil: For thine is the kingdom, and the power, and the glory, for ever. Amen.

14 For if ye forgive men their trespasses, your heavenly Father will also forgive you:

15 But if ye forgive not men their trespasses, neither will your Father forgive your trespasses.

16 ¶Moreover when ye fast, be not, as the hypocrites, of a sad countenance: for they disfigure their faces, that they may appear unto men to fast. Verily I say unto you, They have their reward.

17 But thou, when thou fastest, anoint thine head, and wash thy face;

18 That thou appear not unto men to fast, but unto thy Father which is in secret: and thy Father, which seeth in secret, shall reward thee openly.

19 ¶Lay not up for yourselves treasures upon earth, where moth and rust doth corrupt, and where thieves break through and steal:

20 But lay up for yourselves treasures in heaven, where neither moth nor rust doth corrupt, and where thieves do not break through nor steal:

21 For where your treasure is, there will your heart be also.

22 The light of the body is the eye: if therefore thine eye be single, thy whole body shall be full of light.

23 But if thine eye be evil, thy whole body shall be full of darkness. If therefore the light that is in thee be darkness, how great *is* that darkness!

24 ¶No man can serve two masters: for either he will hate the one, and love the other; or else he will hold to the one, and despise the other. Ye cannot serve God and mammon.

25 Therefore I say unto you, Take no thought for your life, what ye shall eat, or what ye shall drink; nor yet for your body, what ye shall put on. Is not the life more than meat, and the body than raiment?

26 Behold the fowls of the air: for they sow not, neither do they reap, nor gather into barns; yet your heavenly Father feedeth them. Are ye not much better than they?

27 Which of you by taking thought can add one cubit unto his stature?

28 And why take ye thought for raiment? Consider the lilies of the field, how they grow; they toil not, neither do they spin:

29 And yet I say unto you, That even Solomon in all his glory was not arrayed like one of these.

30 Wherefore, if God so clothe the grass of the field, which to day is, and to morrow is cast into the oven, *shall he* not much more *clothe* you, O ye of little faith?

31 Therefore take no thought, saying, What shall we eat? or, What shall we drink? or, Wherewithal shall we be clothed?

32 (For after all these things do the Gentiles seek:) for your heavenly Father knoweth that ye have need of all these things.

33 But seek ye first the kingdom of God, and his righteousness; and all these things shall be added unto you.

34 Take therefore no thought for the morrow: for the morrow shall take thought for the things of itself. Sufficient unto the day *is* the evil thereof.

## Chapter 7

1 Judge not, that ye be not judged.

2 For with what judgment ye judge, ye shall be judged: and with what measure ye mete, it shall be measured to you again.

3 And why beholdest thou the mote that is in thy brother's eye, but considerest not the beam that is in thine own eye?

4 Or how wilt thou say to thy brother, Let me pull out the mote out of thine eye; and, behold, a beam *is* in thine own eye?

5 Thou hypocrite, first cast out the beam out of thine own eye; and then shalt thou see clearly to cast out the mote out of thy brother's eye.

6 ¶Give not that which is holy unto the dogs, neither cast ye your pearls before swine, lest they trample them under their feet, and turn again and rend you.

7 ¶Ask, and it shall be given you; seek, and ye shall find; knock, and it shall be opened unto you:

8 For every one that asketh receiveth; and he that seeketh findeth; and to him that knocketh it shall be opened.

9 Or what man is there of you, whom if his son ask bread, will he give him a stone?

10 Or if he ask a fish, will he give him a serpent?

11 If ye then, being evil, know how to give good gifts unto your

children, how much more shall your Father which is in heaven give good things to them that ask him?

12 Therefore all things whatsoever ye would that men should do to you, do ye even so to them: for this is the law and the prophets.

13 ¶Enter ye in at the strait gate: for wide *is* the gate, and broad *is* the way, that leadeth to destruction, and many there be which go in thereat:

14 Because strait *is* the gate, and narrow *is* the way, which leadeth unto life, and few there be that find it.

15 ¶Beware of false prophets, which come to you in sheep's clothing, but inwardly they are ravening wolves.

16 Ye shall know them by their fruits. Do men gather grapes of thorns, or figs of thistles?

17 Even so every good tree bringeth forth good fruit; but a corrupt tree bringeth forth evil fruit.

18 A good tree cannot bring forth evil fruit, neither *can* a corrupt tree bring forth good fruit.

19 Every tree that bringeth not forth good fruit is hewn down, and cast into the fire.

20 Wherefore by their fruits ye shall know them.

21 ¶Not every one that saith unto me, Lord, Lord, shall enter into the kingdom of heaven; but he that doeth the will of my Father which is in heaven.

22 Many will say to me in that day, Lord, Lord, have we not prophesied in thy name? and in thy name have cast out devils? and in thy name done many wonderful works?

23 And then will I profess unto them, I never knew you: depart from me, ye that work iniquity.

24 ¶Therefore whosoever heareth these sayings of mine, and doeth them, I will liken him unto a wise man, which built his house upon a rock:

25 And the rain descended, and the floods came, and the winds blew, and beat upon that house; and it fell not: for it was founded upon a rock.

26 And every one that heareth these sayings of mine, and doeth them not, shall be likened unto a foolish man, which built his house upon the sand:

27 And the rain descended, and the floods came, and the winds blew, and beat upon that house; and it fell: and great was the fall of it.

28 And it came to pass, when Jesus had ended these sayings, the people were astonished at his doctrine:

29 For he taught them as *one* having authority, and not as the scribes.

# Questions

1.  What do you take to be the meaning of "Ye are the salt of the earth" in 5:13? (In framing your response, consider the entire verse.)
2.  J. C. Fenton, in his valuable edition of the Gospel of St. Matthew, says of 5:21–48:

    In what sense is 5:21–48 a new law? Not in the sense that Jesus replaces one set of instructions by another set, which is more difficult to keep. His "law" is impossible, because it puts before us perfection and love which are beyond our capability. And his "law" is not a set of detailed instructions, but is reducible to one word, love. The "law" of Jesus is therefore both simpler and more demanding than the Law of the Old Testament, and by it the disciples are made entirely dependent on the mercy of God, because they are put permanently into the position of sinners who must always say *Forgive us our debts* (6:12).

    Do you agree with Fenton that the "law" here is "impossible, because it puts before us perfection and love which are beyond our capability"? And if this is true, why does Jesus not say so?
3.  Taking into account the context in 6:1–2, what do you make of verse 6:3, "But when thou doest alms, let not thy left hand know what thy right hand doeth"?
4.  In 6:3 Jesus speaks of alms. Check a dictionary to see the origin (the etymology) of the word. How does the meaning of the word tie in with the fifth Beatitude (5:7)?
5.  In 6:24 Jesus says, "Ye cannot serve God and mammon." Taking into account verses 19–23, put this idea into your own words. Do you think the point is true? Notice that in verses 25 to 34 Jesus offers a reply to disciples who might respond that they must serve mammon at least to the degree that they need food and clothing.
6.  Verse 7:3 runs thus: "And why beholdest thou the mote that is in thy brother's eye, but considerest not the beam that is in thine own eye?" Translate this bold overstatement into ordinary (literal) language.
7.  In 7:24–27 Jesus contrasts a "wise man" with a "foolish man." In the context of this chapter of the Gospel, what does he mean by wisdom, and what by folly?
8.  The Sermon on the Mount contains many astounding or even par-

adoxical statements. For instance, the assertion that those who mourn are blessed (5:4) might be said to defy common sense. Similarly, if we look about us, it is difficult to see the evidence that the meek "shall inherit the earth" (5:5). In many parts of the sermon Jesus emphasizes the novelty of his teaching, for instance by repeating "Ye have heard . . . but I say unto you." Why, however, should one accept these strange teachings? In 7:29 Matthew says that Jesus "taught them as *one* having authority." But what is the source of the authority? If (unlike Matthew) one does not believe in the divinity of Jesus, is there any reason to heed the teachings?

## C. S. Lewis

# What Christians Believe

### 1. *The Rival Conceptions of God*

I have been asked to tell you what Christians believe, and I am going to begin by telling you one thing that Christians do not need to believe. If you are a Christian you do not have to believe that all the other religions are simply wrong all through. If you are an atheist you do have to believe that the main point in all the religions of the whole world is simply one huge mistake. If you are a Christian, you are free to think that all these religions, even the queerest ones, contain at least some hint of the truth. When I was an atheist I had to try to persuade myself that most of the human race have always been wrong about the question that mattered to them most: when I became a Christian I was able to take a more liberal view. But, of course, being a Christian does mean thinking that where Christianity differs from other religions, Christianity is right and they are wrong. As in arithmetic—there

1

Clive Staples Lewis (1898–1963) taught medieval and renaissance literature at Oxford and later at Cambridge. He wrote about literature, and he wrote fiction (including children's books), poetry, and numerous essays and books on Christianity, from the point of view of a believer.

The material reprinted here was originally delivered to the British public in the early 1940s, in a series of radio addresses.

is only one right answer to a sum, and all other answers are wrong: but some of the wrong answers are much nearer being right than others.

The first big division of humanity is into the majority, who believe 2 in some kind of God or gods, and the minority who do not. On this point, Christianity lines up with the majority—lines up with ancient Greeks and Romans, modern savages, Stoics, Platonists, Hindus, Mohammedans, etc., against the modern Western European materialist.

Now I go on to the next big division. People who all believe in 3 God can be divided according to the sort of God they believe in. There are two very different ideas on this subject. One of them is the idea that He is beyond good and evil. We humans call one thing good and another thing bad. But according to some people that is merely our human point of view. These people would say that the wiser you become the less you would want to call anything good or bad, and the more clearly you would see that everything is good in one way and bad in another, and that nothing could have been different. Consequently, these people think that long before you got anywhere near the divine point of view the distinction would have disappeared altogether. We call a cancer bad, they would say, because it kills a man; but you might just as well call a successful surgeon bad because he kills a cancer. It all depends on the point of view. The other and opposite idea is that God is quite definitely "good" or "righteous," a God who takes sides, who loves love and hates hatred, who wants us to behave in one way and not in another. The first of these views—the one that thinks God beyond good and evil—is called Pantheism. It was held by the great Prussian philosopher Hegel and, as far as I can understand them, by the Hindus. The other view is held by Jews, Mohammedans and Christians.

And with this big difference between Pantheism and the Christian 4 idea of God, there usually goes another. Pantheists usually believe that God, so to speak, animates the universe as you animate your body: that the universe almost *is* God, so that if it did not exist He would not exist either, and anything you find in the universe is a part of God. The Christian idea is quite different. They think God invented and made the universe—like a man making a picture or composing a tune. A painter is not a picture, and he does not die if his picture is destroyed. You may say, "He's put a lot of himself into it," but you only mean that all its beauty and interest has come out of his head. His skill is not in the picture in the same way that it is in his head, or even in his hands. I expect you see how this difference between Pantheists and

Christians hangs together with the other one. If you do not take the distinction between good and bad very seriously, then it is easy to say that anything you find in this world is a part of God. But, of course, if you think some things really bad, and God really good, then you cannot talk like that. You must believe that God is separate from the world and that some of the things we see in it are contrary to His will. Confronted with a cancer or a slum the Pantheist can say, "If you could only see it from the divine point of view, you would realize that this also is God." The Christian replies, "Don't talk damned nonsense."[1] For Christianity is a fighting religion. It thinks God made the world— that space and time, heat and cold, and all the colors and tastes, and all the animals and vegetables, are things that God "made up out of His head" as a man makes up a story. But it also thinks that a great many things have gone wrong with the world that God made and that God insists, and insists very loudly, on our putting them right again.

And, of course, that raises a very big question. If a good God made     5 the world why has it gone wrong? And for many years I simply refused to listen to the Christian answers to this question, because I kept on feeling "whatever you say, and however clever your arguments are, isn't it much simpler and easier to say that the world was not made by any intelligent power? Aren't all your arguments simply a complicated attempt to avoid the obvious?" But then that threw me back into another difficulty.

My argument against God was that the universe seemed so cruel     6 and unjust. But how had I got this idea of *just* and *unjust?* A man does not call a line crooked unless he has some idea of a straight line. What was I comparing this universe with when I called it unjust? If the whole show was bad and senseless from A to Z, so to speak, why did I, who was supposed to be part of the show, find myself in such violent reaction against it? A man feels wet when he falls into water, because man is not a water animal: a fish would not feel wet. Of course I could have given up my idea of justice by saying it was nothing but a private idea of my own. But if I did that, then my argument against God collapsed too—for the argument depended on saying that the world was really unjust, not simply that it did not happen to please my private fancies. Thus in the very act of trying to prove that God did not exist—in other words, that the whole of reality was senseless—I found

---

[1] One listener complained of the word *damned* as frivolous swearing. But I mean exactly what I say—nonsense that is *damned* is under God's curse, and will (apart from God's grace) lead those who believe it to eternal death.

I was forced to assume that one part of reality—namely my idea of justice—was full of sense. Consequently atheism turns out to be too simple. If the whole universe has no meaning, we should never have found out that it has no meaning: just as, if there were no light in the universe and therefore no creatures with eyes, we should never know it was dark. *Dark* would be without meaning.

## 2. The Invasion

Very well then, atheism is too simple. And I will tell you another view    7 that is also too simple. It is the view I call Christianity-and-water, the view which simply says there is a good God in Heaven and everything is all right—leaving out all the difficult and terrible doctrines about sin and hell and the devil, and the redemption. Both these are boys' philosophies.

It is no good asking for a simple religion. After all, real things are    8 not simple. They look simple, but they are not. The table I am sitting at looks simple: but ask a scientist to tell you what it is really made of—all about the atoms and how the light waves rebound from them and hit my eye and what they do to the optic nerve and what it does to my brain—and, of course, you find that what we call "seeing a table" lands you in mysteries and complications which you can hardly get to the end of. A child saying a child's prayer looks simple. And if you are content to stop there, well and good. But if you are not—and the modern world usually is not—if you want to go on and ask what is really happening—then you must be prepared for something difficult. If we ask for something more than simplicity, it is silly then to complain that the something more is not simple.

Very often, however, this silly procedure is adopted by people    9 who are not silly, but who, consciously or unconsciously, want to destroy Christianity. Such people put up a version of Christianity suitable for a child of six and make that the object of their attack. When you try to explain the Christian doctrine as it is really held by an instructed adult, they then complain that you are making their heads turn round and that it is all too complicated and that if there really were a God they are sure He would have made "religion" simple, because simplicity is so beautiful, etc. You must be on your guard against these people for they will change their ground every minute and only waste your time. Notice, too, their idea of God "making religion simple": as if "religion" were something God invented, and not His statement to us of certain quite unalterable facts about His own nature.

Besides being complicated, reality, in my experience, is usually    10
odd. It is not neat, not obvious, not what you expect. For instance, when you have grasped that the earth and the other planets all go round the sun, you would naturally expect that all the planets were made to match—all at equal distances from each other, say, or distances that regularly increased, or all the same size, or else getting bigger or smaller as you go farther from the sun. In fact, you find no rhyme or reason (that we can see) about either the sizes or the distances; and some of them have one moon, one has four, one has two, some have none, and one has a ring.

Reality, in fact, is usually something you could not have guessed.    11
That is one of the reasons I believe Christianity. It is a religion you could not have guessed. If it offered us just the kind of universe we had always expected, I should feel we were making it up. But, in fact, it is not the sort of thing anyone would have made up. It has just that queer twist about it that real things have. So let us leave behind all these boys' philosophies—these oversimple answers. The problem is not simple and the answer is not going to be simpler either.

What is the problem? A universe that contains much that is ob-    12
viously bad and apparently meaningless, but containing creatures like ourselves who know that it is bad and meaningless. There are only two views that face all the facts. One is the Christian view that this is a good world that has gone wrong, but still retains the memory of what it ought to have been. The other is the view called Dualism. Dualism means the belief that there are two equal and independent powers at the back of everything, one of them good and the other bad, and that this universe is the battlefield in which they fight out an endless war. I personally think that next to Christianity Dualism is the manliest and most sensible creed on the market. But it has a catch in it.

The two powers, or spirits, or gods—the good one and the bad    13
one—are supposed to be quite independent. They both existed from all eternity. Neither of them made the other, neither of them has any more right than the other to call itself God. Each presumably thinks it is good and thinks the other bad. One of them likes hatred and cruelty, the other likes love and mercy, and each backs its own view. Now what do we mean when we call one of them the Good Power and the other the Bad Power? Either we are merely saying that we happen to prefer the one to the other—like preferring beer to cider—

or else we are saying that, whatever the two powers think about it, and whichever we humans, at the moment, happen to like, one of them is actually wrong, actually mistaken, in regarding itself as good. Now if we mean merely that we happen to prefer the first, then we must give up talking about good and evil at all. For good means what you ought to prefer quite regardless of what you happen to like at any given moment. If "being good" meant simply joining the side you happened to fancy, for no real reason, then good would not deserve to be called good. So we must mean that one of the two powers is actually wrong and the other actually right.

But the moment you say that, you are putting into the universe a    14 third thing in addition to the two Powers: some law or standard or rule of good which one of the powers conforms to and the other fails to conform to. But since the two powers are judged by this standard, then this standard, or the Being who made this standard, is farther back and higher up than either of them, and He will be the real God. In fact, what we meant by calling them good and bad turns out to be that one of them is in a right relation to the real ultimate God and the other in a wrong relation to Him.

The same point can be made in a different way. If Dualism is true,    15 then the bad Power must be a being who likes badness for its own sake. But in reality we have no experience of anyone liking badness just because it is bad. The nearest we can get to it is in cruelty. But in real life people are cruel for one of two reasons—either because they are sadists, that is, because they have a sexual perversion which makes cruelty a cause of sensual pleasure to them, or else for the sake of something they are going to get out of it—money, or power, or safety. But pleasure, money, power, and safety are all, as far as they go, good things. The badness consists in pursuing them by the wrong method, or in the wrong way, or too much. I do not mean, of course, that the people who do this are not desperately wicked. I do mean that wickedness, when you examine it, turns out to be the pursuit of some good in the wrong way. You can be good for the mere sake of goodness: you cannot be bad for the mere sake of badness. You can do a kind action when you are not feeling kind and when it gives you no pleasure, simply because kindness is right; but no one ever did a cruel action simply because cruelty is wrong—only because cruelty was pleasant or useful to him. In other words badness cannot succeed even in being bad in the same way in which goodness is good. Goodness is, so to speak, itself: badness is only spoiled goodness. And there must be something good first before it can be spoiled. We called sadism a sexual perversion; but you must first have the idea of a normal sexuality before you can talk of its being perverted: and you can see which is the perversion, because you can explain the perverted from the normal, and cannot explain the normal from the perverted. It follows that this Bad Power, who is supposed to be on an equal footing with the Good Power, and to love badness in the same way as the Good Power loves goodness, is a mere bogy. In order to be bad he must have good things to want and then to pursue in the wrong way: he must have impulses which were originally good in order to be able to pervert them. But if he is bad he cannot supply himself either with good things to desire or with good impulses to pervert. He must be getting both from the Good Power. And if so, then he is not independent. He is part of the Good Power's world: he was made either by the Good Power or by some power above them both.

Put it more simply still. To be bad, he must exist and have intelligence and will. But existence, intelligence and will are in themselves good. Therefore he must be getting them from the Good Power: even to be bad he must borrow or steal from his opponent. And do you now begin to see why Christianity has always said that the devil is a fallen angel? That is not a mere story for the children. It is a real recognition of the fact that evil is a parasite, not an original thing. The powers which enable evil to carry on are powers given it by goodness. All the things which enable a bad man to be effectively bad are in themselves good things—resolution, cleverness, good looks, existence itself. That is why Dualism, in a strict sense, will not work. 16

But I freely admit that real Christianity (as distinct from Christianity-and-water) goes much nearer to Dualism than people think. One of the things that surprised me when I first read the New Testament seriously was that it talked so much about a Dark Power in the universe—a mighty evil spirit who was held to be the Power behind death and disease, and sin. The difference is that Christianity thinks this Dark Power was created by God, and was good when he was created, and went wrong. Christianity agrees with Dualism that this universe is at war. But it does not think this is a war between independent powers. It thinks it is a civil war, a rebellion, and that we are living in a part of the universe occupied by the rebel. 17

Enemy-occupied territory—that is what this world is. Christianity is the story of how the rightful king has landed, you might say landed in disguise, and is calling us all to take part in a great campaign of sabotage. When you go to church you are really listening in to the secret wireless from our friends: that is why the enemy is so anxious 18 to prevent us from going. He does it by playing on our conceit and laziness and intellectual snobbery. I know someone will ask me, "Do you really mean, at this time of day, to reintroduce our old friend the devil—hoofs and horns and all?" Well, what the time of day has to do with it I do not know. And I am not particular about the hoofs and horns. But in other respects my answer is "Yes, I do." I do not claim to know anything about his personal appearance. If anybody really wants to know him better I would say to that person, "Don't worry. If you really want to, you will. Whether you'll like it when you do is another question."

## 3. The Shocking Alternative

Christians, then, believe that an evil power has made himself for the 19 present the Prince of this World. And, of course, that raises problems. Is this state of affairs in accordance with God's will or not? If it is, He is a strange God, you will say: and if it is not, how can anything happen contrary to the will of a being with absolute power?

But anyone who has been in authority knows how a thing can be 20 in accordance with your will in one way and not in another. It may be quite sensible for a mother to say to the children, "I'm not going to go and make you tidy the schoolroom every night. You've got to learn to keep it tidy on your own." Then she goes up one night and finds the Teddy bear and the ink and the French Grammar all lying in the grate. That is against her will. She would prefer the children to be tidy. But on the other hand, it is her will which has left the children free to be untidy. The same thing arises in any regiment, or trade union, or school. You make a thing voluntary and then half the people do not do it. That is not what you willed, but your will has made it possible.

It is probably the same in the universe. God created things which 21 had free will. That means creatures which can go either wrong or right. Some people think they can imagine a creature which was free but had no possibility of going wrong; I cannot. If a thing is free to be good it is also free to be bad. And free will is what has made evil possible. Why, then, did God give them free will? Because free will, though it makes evil possible, is also the only thing that makes possible any love or goodness or joy worth having. A world of automata—of creatures that worked like machines—would hardly be worth creating. The happiness which God designs for His higher creatures is the happiness of being freely, voluntarily united to Him and to each other in an ecstasy

of love and delight compared with which the most rapturous love between a man and a woman on this earth is mere milk and water. And
for that they must be free.

Of course God knew what would happen if they used their free-     22
dom the wrong way: apparently He thought it worth the risk. Perhaps
we feel inclined to disagree with Him. But there is a difficulty about
disagreeing with God. He is the source from which all your reasoning
power comes: you could not be right and He wrong any more than a
stream can rise higher than its own source. When you are arguing
against Him you are arguing against the very power that makes you
able to argue at all: it is like cutting off the branch you are sitting on.
If God thinks this state of war in the universe a price worth paying
for free will—that is, for making a live world in which creatures can
do real good or harm and something of real importance can happen,
instead of a toy world which only moves when He pulls the strings—
then we may take it it is worth paying.

When we have understood about free will, we shall see how silly     23
it is to ask, as somebody once asked me: "Why did God make a creature
of such rotten stuff that it went wrong?" The better stuff a creature is
made of—the cleverer and stronger and freer it is—then the better it
will be if it goes right, but also the worse it will be if it goes wrong.
A cow cannot be very good or very bad; a dog can be both better and
worse; a child better and worse still; an ordinary man, still more so;
a man of genius, still more so; a superhuman spirit best—or worst—
of all.

How did the Dark Power go wrong? Here, no doubt, we ask a     24
question to which human beings cannot give an answer with any certainty. A reasonable (and traditional) guess, based on our own experiences of going wrong, can, however, be offered. The moment you
have a self at all, there is a possibility of putting yourself first—wanting
to be the center—wanting to be God, in fact. That was the sin of Satan:
and that was the sin he taught the human race. Some people think
the fall of man had something to do with sex, but that is a mistake.
(The story in the Book of Genesis rather suggests that some corruption
in our sexual nature followed the fall and was its result, not its cause.)
What Satan put into the heads of our remote ancestors was the idea
that they could "be like gods"—could set up on their own as if they
had created themselves—be their own masters—invent some sort of
happiness for themselves outside God, apart from God. And out of
that hopeless attempt has come nearly all that we call human history—
money, poverty, ambition, war, prostitution, classes, empires, slav-

ery—the long terrible story of man trying to find something other than God which will make him happy.

The reason why it can never succeed is this. God made us: invented us as a man invents an engine. A car is made to run on gasoline, and it would not run properly on anything else. Now God designed the human machine to run on Himself. He Himself is the fuel our spirits were designed to burn, or the food our spirits were designed to feed on. There is no other. That is why it is just no good asking God to make us happy in our own way without bothering about religion. God cannot give us a happiness and peace apart from Himself, because it is not there. There is no such thing. 25

That is the key to history. Terrific energy is expended—civilizations are built up—excellent institutions devised; but each time something goes wrong. Some fatal flaw always brings the selfish and cruel people to the top and it all slides back into misery and ruin. In fact, the machine conks. It seems to start up all right and runs a few yards, and then it breaks down. They are trying to run it on the wrong juice. That is what Satan has done to us humans. 26

And what did God do? First of all He left us conscience, the sense of right and wrong: and all through history there have been people trying (some of them very hard) to obey it. None of them ever quite succeeded. Secondly, He sent the human race what I call good dreams: I mean those queer stories scattered all through the heathen religions about a god who dies and comes to life again and, by his death, has somehow given new life to men. Thirdly, He selected one particular people and spent several centuries hammering into their heads the sort of God He was—that there was only one of Him and that He cared about right conduct. Those people were the Jews, and the Old Testament gives an account of the hammering process. 27

Then comes the real shock. Among these Jews there suddenly turns up a man who goes about talking as if He was God. He claims to forgive sins. He says He has always existed. He says He is coming to judge the world at the end of time. Now let us get this clear. Among Pantheists, like the Indians, anyone might say that he was a part of God, or one with God: there would be nothing very odd about it. But this man, since He was a Jew, could not mean that kind of God. God, in their language, meant the Being outside the world Who had made it and was infinitely different from anything else. And when you have grasped that, you will see that what this man said was, quite simply, the most shocking thing that has ever been uttered by human lips. 28

One part of the claim tends to slip past us unnoticed because we 29 have heard it so often that we no longer see what it amounts to. I mean the claim to forgive sins: any sins. Now unless the speaker is God, this is really so preposterous as to be comic. We can all understand how a man forgives offenses against himself. You tread on my toe and I forgive you, you steal my money and I forgive you. But what should we make of a man, himself unrobbed and untrodden on, who announced that he forgave you for treading on other men's toes and stealing other men's money? Asinine fatuity is the kindest description we should give of his conduct. Yet this is what Jesus did. He told people that their sins were forgiven, and never waited to consult all the other people whom their sins had undoubtedly injured. He unhesitatingly behaved as if He was the party chiefly concerned, the person chiefly offended in all offenses. This makes sense only if He really was the God whose laws are broken and whose love is wounded in every sin. In the mouth of any speaker who is not God, these words would imply what I can only regard as a silliness and conceit unrivalled by any other character in history.

Yet (and this is the strange, significant thing) even His enemies, 30 when they read the Gospels, do not usually get the impression of silliness and conceit. Still less do unprejudiced readers. Christ says that He is "humble and meek" and we believe Him; not noticing that, if He were merely a man, humility and meekness are the very last characteristics we could attribute to some of His sayings.

I am trying here to prevent anyone saying the really foolish thing 31 that people often say about Him: "I'm ready to accept Jesus as a great moral teacher, but I don't accept His claim to be God." That is the one thing we must not say. A man who was merely a man and said the sort of things Jesus said would not be a great moral teacher. He would either be a lunatic—on a level with the man who says he is a poached egg—or else he would be the Devil of Hell. You must make your choice. Either this man was, and is, the Son of God: or else a madman or something worse. You can shut Him up for a fool, you can spit at Him and kill Him as a demon; or you can fall at His feet and call Him Lord and God. But let us not come with any patronizing nonsense about His being a great human teacher. He has not left that open to us. He did not intend to.

## 4. The Perfect Penitent

We are faced, then, with a frightening alternative. This man we are 32 talking about either was (and is) just what He said or else a lunatic, or something worse. Now it seems to me obvious that He was neither a lunatic nor a fiend: and consequently, however strange or terrifying or unlikely it may seem, I have to accept the view that He was and is God. God has landed on this enemy-occupied world in human form.

And now, what was the purpose of it all? What did He come to 33 do? Well, to teach, of course; but as soon as you look into the New Testament or any other Christian writing you will find they are constantly talking about something different—about His death and His coming to life again. It is obvious that Christians think the chief point of the story lies here. They think the main thing He came to earth to do was to suffer and be killed.

Now before I became a Christian I was under the impression that 34 the first thing Christians had to believe was one particular theory as to what the point of this dying was. According to that theory God wanted to punish men for having deserted and joined the Great Rebel, but Christ volunteered to be punished instead, and so God let us off. Now I admit that even this theory does not seem to me quite so immoral and so silly as it used to; but that is not the point I want to make. What I came to see later on was that neither this theory nor any other is Christianity. The central Christian belief is that Christ's death has somehow put us right with God and given us a fresh start. Theories as to how it did this are another matter. A good many different theories have been held as to how it works: what all Christians are agreed on is that it does work. I will tell you what I think it is like. All sensible people know that if you are tired and hungry a meal will do you good. But the modern theory of nourishment—all about the vitamins and proteins—is a different thing. People ate their dinners and felt better long before the theory of vitamins was ever heard of: and if the theory of vitamins is some day abandoned they will go on eating their dinners just the same. Theories about Christ's death are not Christianity: they are explanations about how it works. Christians would not all agree as to how important these theories are. My own church—the Church of England—does not lay down any one of them as the right one. The Church of Rome goes a bit further. But I think they will all agree that the thing itself is infinitely more important than any explanations that theologians have produced. I think they would probably admit that no explanation will ever be quite adequate to the reality. But . . . I am only a layman, and at this point we are getting into deep water. I can only tell you, for what it is worth, how I, personally, look at the matter.

On my view the theories are not themselves the thing you are 35 asked to accept. Many of you no doubt have read Jeans or Eddington.

What they do when they want to explain the atom, or something of that sort, is to give you a description out of which you can make a mental picture. But then they warn you that this picture is not what the scientists actually believe. What the scientists believe is a mathematical formula. The pictures are there only to help you to understand the formula. They are not really true in the way the formula is; they do not give you the real thing but only something more or less like it. They are only meant to help, and if they do not help you can drop them. The thing itself cannot be pictured, it can only be expressed mathematically. We are in the same boat here. We believe that the death of Christ is just that point in history at which something absolutely unimaginable from outside shows through into our own world. And if we cannot picture even the atoms of which our own world is built, of course we are not going to be able to picture this. Indeed, if we found that we could fully understand it, that very fact would show it was not what it professes to be—the inconceivable, the uncreated, the thing from beyond nature, striking down into nature like lightning. You may ask what good will it be to us if we do not understand it. But that is easily answered. A man can eat his dinner without understanding exactly how food nourishes him. A man can accept what Christ has done without knowing how it works; indeed, he certainly would not know how it works until he has accepted it.

We are told that Christ was killed for us, that His death has washed 36 out our sins, and that by dying He disabled death itself. That is the formula. That is Christianity. That is what has to be believed. Any theories we build up as to how Christ's death did all this are, in my view, quite secondary: mere plans or diagrams to be left alone if they do not help us, and, even if they do help us, not to be confused with the thing itself. All the same, some of these theories are worth looking at.

The one most people have heard is the one I mentioned before— 37 the one about our being let off because Christ had volunteered to bear a punishment instead of us. Now on the face of it that is a very silly theory. If God was prepared to let us off, why on earth did He not do so? And what possible point could there be in punishing an innocent person instead? None at all that I can see, if you are thinking of punishment in the police-court sense. On the other hand, if you think of a debt, there is plenty of point in a person who has some assets paying it on behalf of someone who has not. Or if you take "paying the penalty," not in the sense of being punished, but in the more general sense of "standing the racket" or "footing the bill," then, of course, it is a matter of common experience that, when one person has got himself into a hole, the trouble of getting him out usually falls on a kind friend.

Now what was the sort of "hole" man had got himself into? He 38 had tried to set up on his own, to behave as if he belonged to himself. In other words, fallen man is not simply an imperfect creature who needs improvement: he is a rebel who must lay down his arms. Laying down your arms, surrendering, saying you are sorry, realizing that you have been on the wrong track and getting ready to start life over again from the ground floor—that is the only way out of a "hole." This process of surrender—this movement full speed astern—is what Christians call repentance. Now repentance is no fun at all. It is some- thing much harder than merely eating humble pie. It means unlearning all the self-conceit and self-will that we have been training ourselves into for thousands of years. It means killing part of yourself, undergo- ing a kind of death. In fact, it needs a good man to repent. And here comes the catch. Only a bad person needs to repent: only a good person can repent perfectly. The worse you are the more you need it and the less you can do it. The only person who could do it perfectly would be a perfect person—and he would not need it.

Remember, this repentance, this willing submission to humiliation 39 and a kind of death, is not something God demands of you before He will take you back and which He could let you off if He chose: it is simply a description of what going back to Him is like. If you ask God to take you back without it, you are really asking Him to let you go back without going back. It cannot happen. Very well, then, we must go through with it. But the same badness which makes us need it, makes us unable to do it. Can we do it if God helps us? Yes, but what do we mean when we talk of God helping us? We mean God putting into us a bit of Himself, so to speak. He lends us a little of His reasoning powers and that is how we think: He puts a little of His love into us and that is how we love one another. When you teach a child writing, you hold its hand while it forms the letters: that is, it forms the letters because you are forming them. We love and reason because God loves and reasons and holds our hand while we do it. Now if we had not fallen, that would be all plain sailing. But unfortunately we now need God's help in order to do something which God, in His own nature, never does at all—to surrender, to suffer, to submit, to die. Nothing in God's nature corresponds to this process at all. So that the one road for which we now need God's leadership most of all is a road God, in His own nature, has never walked. God can share only what He has: this thing, in His own nature, He has not.

But supposing God became a man—suppose our human nature 40
which can suffer and die was amalgamated with God's nature in one
person—then that person could help us. He could surrender His will,
and suffer and die, because He was man; and He could do it perfectly
because He was God. You and I can go through this process only if
God does it in us; but God can do it only if He becomes man. Our
attempts at this dying will succeed only if we men share in God's
dying, just as our thinking can succeed only because it is a drop out
of the ocean of His intelligence: but we cannot share God's dying unless
God dies; and He cannot die except by being a man. That is the sense
in which He pays our debt, and suffers for us what He Himself need
not suffer at all.

I have heard some people complain that if Jesus was God as well 41
as man, then His sufferings and death lose all value in their eyes,
"because it must have been so easy for him." Others may (very rightly)
rebuke the ingratitude and ungraciousness of this objection; what stag-
gers me is the misunderstanding it betrays. In one sense, of course,
those who make it are right. They have even understated their own
case. The perfect submission, the perfect suffering, the perfect death
were not only easier to Jesus because He was God, but were possible
only because He was God. But surely that is a very odd reason for not
accepting them. The teacher is able to form the letters for the child
because the teacher is grown-up and knows how to write. That, of
course, makes it easier for the teacher; and only because it is easier for
him can he help the child. If it rejected him because "it's easy for
grown-ups" and waited to learn writing from another child who could
not write itself (and so had no "unfair" advantage), it would not get
on very quickly. If I am drowning in a rapid river, a man who still has
one foot on the bank may give me a hand which saves my life. Ought
I to shout back (between my gasps), "No, it's not fair! You have an
advantage! You're keeping one foot on the bank"? That advantage—
call it "unfair" if you like—is the only reason why he can be of any
use to me. To what will you look for help if you will not look to that
which is stronger than yourself?

Such is my own way of looking at what Christians call the Atone- 42
ment. But remember this is only one more picture. Do not mistake it
for the thing itself: and if it does not help you, drop it.

## 5. The Practical Conclusion

The perfect surrender and humiliation were undergone by Christ: per- 43
fect because He was God, surrender and humiliation because He was

man. Now the Christian belief is that if we somehow share the humility and suffering of Christ we shall also share in His conquest of death and find a new life after we have died and in it become perfect, and perfectly happy, creatures. This means something much more than our trying to follow His teaching. People often ask when the next step in evolution—the step to something beyond man—will happen. But in the Christian view, it has happened already. In Christ a new kind of man appeared: and the new kind of life which began in Him is to be put into us.

How is this to be done? Now, please remember how we acquired 　44 the old, ordinary kind of life. We derived it from others, from our father and mother and all our ancestors, without our consent—and by a very curious process, involving pleasure, pain, and danger. A process you would never have guessed. Most of us spend a good many years in childhood trying to guess it: and some children, when they are first told, do not believe it—and I am not sure that I blame them, for it is very odd. Now the God who arranged that process is the same God who arranges how the new kind of life—the Christ life—is to be spread. We must be prepared for it being odd too. He did not consult us when He invented sex: He has not consulted us either when He invented this.

There are three things that spread the Christ life to us: baptism, 　45 belief, and that mysterious action which different Christians call by different names—Holy Communion, the Mass, the Lord's Supper. At least, those are the three ordinary methods. I am not saying there may not be special cases where it is spread without one or more of these. I have not time to go into special cases, and I do not know enough. If you are trying in a few minutes to tell a man how to get to Edinburgh you will tell him the trains: he can, it is true, get there by boat or by a plane, but you will hardly bring that in. And I am not saying anything about which of these three things is the most essential. My Methodist friend would like me to say more about belief and less (in proportion) about the other two. But I am not going into that. Anyone who professes to teach you Christian doctrine will, in fact, tell you to use all three, and that is enough for our present purpose.

I cannot myself see why these things should be the conductors of 　46 the new kind of life. But then, if one did not happen to know, I should never have seen any connection between a particular physical pleasure and the appearance of a new human being in the world. We have to take reality as it comes to us: there is no good jabbering about what it ought to be like or what we should have expected it to be like. But

though I cannot see why it should be so, I can tell you why I believe
it is so. I have explained why I have to believe that Jesus was (and is)
God. And it seems plain as a matter of history that He taught His
followers that the new life was communicated in this way. In other
words, I believe it on His authority. Do not be scared by the word
authority. Believing things on authority only means believing them
because you have been told them by someone you think trustworthy.
Ninety-nine percent of the things you believe are believed on authority.
I believe there is such a place as New York. I have not seen it myself.
I could not prove by abstract reasoning that there must be such a place.
I believe it because reliable people have told me so. The ordinary man
believes in the Solar System, atoms, evolution, and the circulation of
the blood on authority—because the scientists say so. Every historical
statement in the world is believed on authority. None of us has seen
the Norman Conquest or the defeat of the Armada. None of us could
prove them by pure logic as you prove a thing in mathematics. We
believe them simply because people who did see them have left writings that tell us about them: in fact, on authority. A man who jibbed
at authority in other things as some people do in religion would have
to be content to know nothing all his life.

Do not think I am setting up baptism and belief and the Holy    47
Communion as things that will do instead of your own attempts to
copy Christ. Your natural life is derived from your parents; that does
not mean it will stay there if you do nothing about it. You can lose it
by neglect, or you can drive it away by committing suicide. You have
to feed it and look after it: but always remember you are not making
it, you are only keeping up a life you got from someone else. In the
same way a Christian can lose the Christ-life which has been put into
him, and he has to make efforts to keep it. But even the best Christian
that ever lived is not acting on his own steam—he is only nourishing
or protecting a life he could never have acquired by his own efforts.
And that has practical consequences. As long as the natural life is in
your body, it will do a lot towards repairing that body. Cut it, and up
to a point it will heal, as a dead body would not. A live body is not
one that never gets hurt, but one that can to some extent repair itself.
In the same way a Christian is not a man who never goes wrong, but
a man who is enabled to repent and pick himself up and begin over
again after each stumble—because the Christ-life is inside him, repairing him all the time, enabling him to repeat (in some degree) the
kind of voluntary death which Christ Himself carried out.

That is why the Christian is in a different position from other peo-    48 ple who are trying to be good. They hope, by being good, to please God if there is one; or—if they think there is not—at least they hope to deserve approval from good men. But the Christian thinks any good he does comes from the Christ-life inside him. He does not think God will love us because we are good, but that God will make us good because He loves us; just as the roof of a greenhouse does not attract the sun because it is bright, but becomes bright because the sun shines on it.

And let me make it quite clear that when Christians say the Christ-    49
life is in them, they do not mean simply something mental or moral. When they speak of being "in Christ" or of Christ being "in them," this is not simply a way of saying that they are thinking about Christ or copying Him. They mean that Christ is actually operating through them; that the whole mass of Christians are the physical organism through which Christ acts—that we are His fingers and muscles, the cells of His body. And perhaps that explains one or two things. It explains why this new life is spread not only by purely mental acts like belief, but by bodily acts like baptism and Holy Communion. It is not merely the spreading of an idea; it is more like evolution—a biological or super-biological fact. There is no good trying to be more spiritual than God. God never meant man to be a purely spiritual crea-ture. That is why He uses material things like bread and wine to put the new life into us. We may think this rather crude and unspiritual. God does not: He invented eating. He likes matter. He invented it.

Here is another thing that used to puzzle me. Is it not frightfully    50
unfair that this new life should be confined to people who have heard of Christ and been able to believe in Him? But the truth is God has not told us what His arrangements about the other people are. We do know that no man can be saved except through Christ; we do not know that only those who know Him can be saved through Him. But in the meantime, if you are worried about the people outside, the most un-reasonable thing you can do is to remain outside yourself. Christians are Christ's body, the organism through which He works. Every ad-dition to that body enables Him to do more. If you want to help those outside you must add your own little cell to the body of Christ who alone can help them. Cutting off a man's fingers would be an odd way of getting him to do more work.

Another possible objection is this. Why is God landing in this    51
enemy-occupied world in disguise and starting a sort of secret society to undermine the devil? Why is He not landing in force, invading it? Is it that He is not strong enough? Well, Christians think He is going

to land in force; we do not know when. But we can guess why He is delaying. He wants to give us the chance of joining His side freely. I do not suppose you and I would have thought much of a Frenchman who waited till the Allies were marching into Germany and then announced he was on our side. God will invade. But I wonder whether people who ask God to interfere openly and directly in our world quite realize what it will be like when He does. When that happens, it is the end of the world. When the author walks on to the stage the play is over. God is going to invade, all right: but what is the good of saying you are on His side then, when you see the whole natural universe melting away like a dream and something else—something it never entered your head to conceive—comes crashing in; something so beautiful to some of us and so terrible to others that none of us will have any choice left? For this time it will be God without disguise; something so overwhelming that it will strike either irresistible love or irresistible horror into every creature. It will be too late then to choose your side. There is no use saying you choose to lie down when it has become impossible to stand up. That will not be the time for choosing: it will be the time when we discover which side we really have chosen, whether we realized it before or not. Now, today, this moment, is our chance to choose the right side. God is holding back to give us that chance. It will not last for ever. We must take it or leave it.

# Questions

1. In paragraphs 1 and 2 Lewis argues that Christianity is a more reasonable position than atheism. How does he make this argument?
2. What is Lewis's purpose in this essay? Is it comparable to a minister's purpose in preaching a sermon? In what ways does his essay differ from a sermon?
3. Lewis says that Christians believe in an evil power, and he suggests that our world is in the midst of a civil war. "Enemy-occupied territory—that is what this world is," he says in paragraph 18. Does Lewis ask us to accept this idea literally, or metaphorically? In considering your answer to this question read the definition of "metaphor" in the glossary, and look also at paragraph 35 in Lewis's essay. Is it relevant that the talks on which this essay is based were given in the 1940s?
4. As a writer Lewis strives to be clear, and he uses examples frequently. Would you agree that he uses examples effectively? Without looking back at the essay, which example do you remember

most vividly? What point was he trying to make by it? (It's OK to look back as you answer the last part of this question!)

5.  Where does Lewis introduce the example of sex? Why does he introduce it at that point in the essay, rather than earlier?

6.  Lewis says (paragraph 11) that one reason for believing Christianity is that "it is a religion you could not have guessed." Why does he think that's a good reason? Do you agree that it is?

Bertrand Russell

# Why I Am Not a Christian

As your Chairman has told you, the subject about which    1
I am going to speak to you tonight is "Why I Am Not a Christian." Perhaps it would be as well, first of all, to try to make out what one means by the word *Christian*. It is used these days in a very loose sense by a great many people. Some people mean no more by it than a person who attempts to live a good life. In that sense I suppose there would be Christians in all sects and creeds; but I do not think that that is the proper sense of the word, if only because it would imply that all the people who are not Christians—all the Buddhists, Confucians, Mohammedans, and so on—are not trying to live a good life. I do not mean by a Christian any person who tries to live decently according

Bertrand Russell (1872–1970) was educated at Trinity College, Cambridge. He published his first book, *The Study of German Social Democracy*, in 1896; subsequent books on mathematics and on philosophy quickly established his international reputation. His pacifist opposition to World War I cost him his appointment at Trinity College, and won him a prison sentence of six months. While serving this sentence he wrote his *Introduction to Mathematical Philosophy*. In 1940 an appointment to teach at the College of the City of New York was withdrawn because of Russell's unorthodox moral views. But he was not always treated shabbily; he won numerous awards, including (in 1950) a nobel Prize. After World War II he devoted most of his energy to warning the world about the dangers of nuclear war.

"Why I Am Not a Christian" comes from a book with the same title, published in 1957.

to his lights. I think that you must have a certain amount of definite belief before you have a right to call yourself a Christian. The word does not have quite such a full-blooded meaning now as it had in the times of St. Augustine and St. Thomas Aquinas. In those days, if a man said that he was a Christian it was known what he meant. You accepted a whole collection of creeds which were set out with great precision, and every single syllable of those creeds you believed with the whole strength of your convictions.

## What Is a Christian?

Nowadays it is not quite that. We have to be a little more vague in our    2
meaning of Christianity. I think, however, that there are two different items which are quite essential to anybody calling himself a Christian. The first is one of a dogmatic nature—namely, that you must believe in God and immortality. If you do not believe in those two things, I do not think that you can properly call yourself a Christian. Then, further than that, as the name implies, you must have some kind of belief about Christ. The Mohammedans, for instance, also believe in God and in immortality, and yet they would not call themselves Christians. I think you must have at the very lowest the belief that Christ was, if not divine, at least the best and wisest of men. If you are not going to believe that much about Christ, I do not think you have any right to call yourself a Christian. Of course, there is another sense, which you find in *Whitaker's Almanack* and in geography books, where the population of the world is said to be divided into Christians, Mohammedans, Buddhists, fetish worshipers, and so on; and in that sense we are all Christians. The geography books count us all in, but that is a purely geographical sense, which I suppose we can ignore. Therefore I take it that when I tell you why I am not a Christian I have to tell you two different things: first, why I do not believe in God and in immortality; and, secondly, why I do not think that Christ was the best and wisest of men, although I grant him a very high degree of moral goodness.

But for the successful efforts of unbelievers in the past, I could not    3
take so elastic a definition of Christianity as that. As I said before, in olden days it had a much more full-blooded sense. For instance, it included the belief in hell. Belief in eternal hell-fire was an essential item of Christian belief until pretty recent times. In this country, as you know, it ceased to be an essential item because of a decision of the Privy Council, and from that decision the Archbishop of Canter-

bury and the Archbishop of York dissented; but in this country our religion is settled by Act of Parliament, and therefore the Privy Council was able to override their Graces and hell was no longer necessary to a Christian. Consequently I shall not insist that a Christian must believe in hell.

## The Existence of God

To come to this question of the existence of God: it is a large and serious question, and if I were to attempt to deal with it in any adequate manner I should have to keep you here until Kingdom Come, so that you will have to excuse me if I deal with it in a somewhat summary fashion. You know, of course, that the Catholic Church has laid it down as a dogma that the existence of God can be proved by the unaided reason. That is a somewhat curious dogma, but it is one of their dogmas. They had to introduce it because at one time the freethinkers adopted the habit of saying that there were such and such arguments which mere reason might urge against the existence of God, but of course they knew as a matter of faith that God did exist. The arguments and the reasons were set out at great length, and the Catholic Church felt that they must stop it. Therefore they laid it down that the existence of God can be proved by the unaided reason and they had to set up what they considered were arguments to prove it. There are, of course, a number of them, but I shall take only a few. 4

## The First-cause Argument

Perhaps the simplest and easiest to understand is the argument of the First Cause. (It is maintained that everything we see in this world has a cause, and as you go back in the chain of causes further and further you must come to a First Cause, and to that First Cause you give the name of God.) That argument, I suppose, does not carry very much weight nowadays, because, in the first place, cause is not quite what it used to be. The philosophers and the men of science have got going on cause, and it has not anything like the vitality it used to have; but, apart from that, you can see that the argument that there must be a First Cause is one that cannot have any validity. I may say that when I was a young man and was debating these questions very seriously in my mind, I for a long time accepted the argument of the First Cause, until one day, at the age of eighteen, I read John Stuart Mill's *Auto-biography*, and I there found this sentence: "My father taught me that 5 the question 'Who made me?' cannot be answered, since it immediately suggests the further question 'Who made God?' " That very simple sentence showed me, as I still think, the fallacy in the argument of the First Cause. If everything must have a cause, then God must have a cause. If there can be anything without a cause, it may just as well be the world as God, so that there cannot be any validity in that argument. It is exactly of the same nature as the Hindu's view, that the world rested upon an elephant and the elephant rested upon a tortoise; and when they said, "How about the tortoise?" the Indian said, "Suppose we change the subject." The argument is really no better than that. There is no reason why the world could not have come into being without a cause; nor, on the other hand, is there any reason why it should not have always existed. There is no reason to suppose that the world had a beginning at all. The idea that things must have a beginning is really due to the poverty of our imagination. Therefore, perhaps, I need not waste any more time upon the argument about the First Cause.

## The Natural-law Argument

Then there is a very common argument from natural law. That was a 6 favorite argument all through the eighteenth century, especially under the influence of Sir Isaac Newton and his cosmogony. People observed the planets going around the sun according to the law of gravitation, and they thought that God had given a behest to these planets to move in that particular fashion, and that was why they did so. That was, of course, a convenient and simple explanation that saved them the trouble of looking any further for explanations of the law of gravitation. Nowadays we explain the law of gravitation in a somewhat complicated fashion that Einstein has introduced. I do not propose to give you a lecture on the law of gravitation, as interpreted by Einstein, because that again would take some time; at any rate, you no longer have the sort of natural law that you had in the Newtonian system, where, for some reason that nobody could understand, nature behaved in a uniform fashion. We now find that a great many things we thought were natural laws are really human conventions. You know that even in the remotest depths of stellar space there are still three feet to a yard. That is, no doubt, a very remarkable fact, but you would hardly call it a law of nature. And a great many things that have been regarded as laws of nature are of that kind. On the other hand, where you can get down to any knowledge of what atoms actually do, you will find they are much less subject to law than people thought, and that the laws at which you arrive are statistical averages of just the sort that would emerge from chance. There is, as we all know, a law that if you throw dice you will get double sixes only about once in thirty-six times, and we do not regard that as evidence that the fall of the dice is regulated by design; on the contrary, if the double sixes came every time we should think that there was design. The laws of nature are of that sort as regards a great many of them. They are statistical averages such as would emerge from the laws of chance; and that makes this whole business of natural law much less impressive than it formerly was. Quite apart from that, which represents the momentary state of science that may change tomorrow, the whole idea that natural laws imply a lawgiver is due to a confusion between natural and human laws. Human laws are behests commanding you to behave a certain way, in which way you may choose to behave, or you may choose not to behave; but natural laws are a description of how things do in fact behave, and being a mere description of what they in fact do, you cannot argue that there must be somebody who told them to do that, because even supposing that there were, you are then faced with the question "Why did God issue just those natural laws and no others?" If you say that he did it simply from his own good pleasure, and without any reason, you then find that there is something which is not subject to law, and so your train of natural law is interrupted. If you say, as more orthodox theologians do, that in all the laws which God issues he had a reason for giving those laws rather than others—the reason, of course, being to create the best universe, although you would never think it to look at it—if there were a reason for the laws which God gave, then God himself was subject to law, and therefore you do not get any advantage by introducing God as an intermediary. You have really a law outside and anterior to the divine edicts, and God does not serve your purpose, because he is not the ultimate lawgiver. In short, this whole argument about natural law no longer has anything like the strength that it used to have. I am traveling on in time in my review of the arguments. The arguments that are used for the existence of God change their character as time goes on. They were at first hard intellectual arguments embodying certain quite definite fallacies. As we come to modern times they become less respectable intellectually and more and more affected by a kind of moralizing vagueness.

## The Argument from Design

The next step in this process brings us to the argument from design. 7
You all know the argument from design: everything in the world is
made just so that we can manage to live in the world, and if the world
was ever so little different, we could not manage to live in it. That is
the argument from design. It sometimes takes a rather curious form;
for instance, it is argued that rabbits have white tails in order to be
easy to shoot. I do not know how rabbits would view that application.
It is an easy argument to parody. You all know Voltaire's remark, that
obviously the nose was designed to be such as to fit spectacles. That
sort of parody has turned out to be not nearly so wide of the mark as
it might have seemed in the eighteenth century, because since the time
of Darwin we understand much better why living creatures are adapted
to their environment. It is not that their environment was made to be
suitable to them but that they grew to be suitable to it, and that is the
basis of adaptation. There is no evidence of design about it.

When you come to look into this argument from design, it is a 8
most astonishing thing that people can believe that this world, with
all the things that are in it, with all its defects, should be the best that
omnipotence and omniscience have been able to produce in millions
of years. I really cannot believe it. Do you think that, if you were
granted omnipotence and omniscience and millions of years in which
to perfect your world, you could produce nothing better than the Ku
Klux Klan or the Fascists? Moreover, if you accept the ordinary laws
of science, you have to suppose that human life and life in general on
this planet will die out in due course: it is a stage in the decay of the
solar system; at a certain stage of decay you get the sort of conditions
of temperature and so forth which are suitable to protoplasm, and there
is life for a short time in the life of the whole solar system. You see in
the moon the sort of thing to which the earth is tending—something
dead, cold, and lifeless.

I am told that that sort of view is depressing, and people will 9
sometimes tell you that if they believed that, they would not be able
to go on living. Do not believe it; it is all nonsense. Nobody really
worries much about what is going to happen millions of years hence.
Even if they think they are worrying much about that, they are really
deceiving themselves. They are worried about something much more
mundane, or it may merely be a bad digestion; but nobody is really
seriously rendered unhappy by the thought of something that is going

to happen to this world millions and millions of years hence. Therefore, although it is of course a gloomy view to suppose that life will die out—at least I suppose we may say so, although sometimes when I contemplate the things that people do with their lives I think it is almost a consolation—it is not such as to render life miserable. It merely makes you turn your attention to other things.

## The Moral Arguments for Deity

Now we reach one stage further in what I shall call the intellectual descent that the Theists have made in their argumentations, and we come to what are called the moral arguments for the existence of God. You all know, of course, that there used to be in the old days three intellectual arguments for the existence of God, all of which were disposed of by Immanuel Kant in the *Critique of Pure Reason;* but no sooner had he disposed of those arguments than he invented a new one, a moral argument, and that quite convinced him. He was like many people: in intellectual matters he was skeptical, but in moral matters he believed implicitly in the maxims that he had imbibed at his mother's knee. That illustrates what the psychoanalysts so much emphasize—the immensely stronger hold upon us that our very early associations have than those of later times.

Kant, as I say, invented a new moral argument for the existence of God, and that in varying forms was extremely popular during the nineteenth century. It has all sorts of forms. One form is to say that there would be no right or wrong unless God existed. I am not for the moment concerned with whether there is a difference between right and wrong, or whether there is not: that is another question. The point I am concerned with is that, if you are quite sure there is a difference between right and wrong, you are then in this situation: Is that difference due to God's fiat or is it not? If it is due to God's fiat, then for God himself there is no difference between right and wrong, and it is no longer a significant statement to say that God is good. If you are going to say, as theologians do, that God is good, you must then say that right and wrong have some meaning which is independent of God's fiat, because God's fiats are good and not bad independently of the mere fact that he made them. If you are going to say that, you will then have to say that it is not only through God that right and wrong came into being, but that they are in their essence logically anterior to God. You could, of course, if you liked, say that there was a superior deity who gave orders to the God who made this world, or could take up the line that some of the gnostics took up—a line which I often thought was a very plausible one—that as a matter of fact this world that we know was made by the devil at a moment when God was not looking. There is a good deal to be said for that, and I am not concerned to refute it.

## The Argument for the Remedying of Injustice

Then there is another very curious form of moral argument, which is  12
this: they say that the existence of God is required in order to bring justice into the world. In the part of this universe that we know there is great injustice, and often the good suffer, and often the wicked prosper, and one hardly knows which of those is the more annoying; but if you are going to have justice in the universe as a whole you have to suppose a future life to redress the balance of life here on earth. So they say that there must be a God, and there must be heaven and hell in order that in the long run there may be justice. That is a very curious argument. If you looked at the matter from a scientific point of view, you would say, "After all, I know only this world. I do not know about the rest of the universe, but so far as one can argue at all on probabilities one would say that probably this world is a fair sample, and if there is injustice here the odds are that there is injustice elsewhere also." Supposing you got a crate of oranges that you opened, and you found all the top layer of oranges bad, you would not argue, "The underneath ones must be good, so as to redress the balance." You would say, "Probably the whole lot is a bad consignment"; and that is really what a scientific person would argue about the universe. He would say, "Here we find in this world a great deal of injustice, and so far as that goes that is a reason for supposing that justice does not rule in the world; and therefore so far as it goes it affords a moral argument against deity and not in favor of one." Of course I know that the sort of intellectual arguments that I have been talking to you about are not what really moves people. What really moves people to believe in God is not any intellectual argument at all. Most people believe in God because they have been taught from early infancy to do it, and that is the main reason.

Then I think that the next most powerful reason is the wish for  13
safety, a sort of feeling that there is a big brother who will look after you. That plays a very profound part in influencing people's desire for a belief in God.

## The Character of Christ

I now want to say a few words upon a topic which I often think is not 14
quite sufficiently dealt with by Rationalists, and that is the question
whether Christ was the best and the wisest of men. It is generally
taken for granted that we should all agree that that was so. I do not
myself. I think that there are a good many points upon which I agree
with Christ a great deal more than the professing Christians do. I do
not know that I could go with Him all the way, but I could go with
Him much further than most professing Christians can. You will remember that He said, "Resist not evil: but whosoever shall smite thee
on thy right cheek, turn to him the other also." That is not a new
precept or a new principle. It was used by Lao-tse and Buddha some
500 or 600 years before Christ, but it is not a principle which as a matter
of fact Christians accept. I have no doubt that the present Prime Minister,[1] for instance, is a most sincere Christian, but I should not advise
any of you to go and smite him on one cheek. I think you might find
that he thought this text was intended in a figurative sense.

Then there is another point which I consider excellent. You will 15
remember that Christ said, "Judge not lest ye be judged." That principle I do not think you would find was popular in the law courts of
Christian countries. I have known in my time quite a number of judges
who were very earnest Christians, and none of them felt that they
were acting contrary to Christian principles in what they did. Then
Christ says, "Give to him that asketh of thee, and from him that would
borrow of thee turn not thou away." That is a very good principle.
Your Chairman has reminded you that we are not here to talk politics,
but I cannot help observing that the last general election was fought
on the question of how desirable it was to turn away from him that
would borrow of thee, so that one must assume that the Liberals and
Conservatives of this country are composed of people who do not agree
with the teaching of Christ, because they certainly did very emphatically turn away on that occasion.

Then there is one other maxim of Christ which I think has a great 16
deal in it, but I do not find that it is very popular among some of our
Christian friends. He says, "If thou wilt be perfect, go and sell that
which thou hast, and give to the poor." That is a very excellent maxim,
but, as I say, it is not much practiced. All these, I think, are good
maxims, although they are a little difficult to live up to. I do not profess

[1] Stanley Baldwin.

to live up to them myself; but then, after all, it is not quite the same thing as for a Christian.

## Defects in Christ's Teaching

Having granted the excellence of these maxims, I come to certain points 17 in which I do not believe that one can grant either the superlative wisdom or the superlative goodness of Christ as depicted in the Gospels; and here I may say that one is not concerned with the historical question. Historically it is quite doubtful whether Christ ever existed at all, and if He did we do not know anything about Him, so that I am not concerned with the historical question, which is a very difficult one. I am concerned with Christ as He appears in the Gospels, taking the Gospel narrative as it stands, and there one does find some things that do not seem to be very wise. For one thing, He certainly thought that His second coming would occur in clouds of glory before the death of all the people who were living at that time. There are a great many texts that prove that. He says, for instance, "Ye shall not have gone over the cities of Israel till the Son of Man be come." Then He says, "There are some standing here which shall not taste death till the Son of Man comes into His kingdom"; and there are a lot of places where it is quite clear that He believed that His second coming would happen during the lifetime of many then living. That was the belief of His earlier followers, and it was the basis of a good deal of His moral teaching. When He said, "Take no thought for the morrow," and things of that sort, it was very largely because He thought that the second coming was going to be very soon, and that all ordinary mundane affairs did not count. I have, as a matter of fact, known some Christians who did believe that the second coming was imminent. I knew a parson who frightened his congregation terribly by telling them that the second coming was very imminent indeed, but they were much consoled when they found that he was planting trees in his garden. The early Christians did really believe it, and they did abstain from such things as planting trees in their gardens, because they did accept from Christ the belief that the second coming was imminent. In that respect, clearly He was not so wise as some other people have been, and He was certainly not superlatively wise.

## The Moral Problem

Then you come to moral questions. There is one very serious defect 18 to my mind in Christ's moral character, and that is that He believed in hell. I do not myself feel that any person who is really profoundly humane can believe in everlasting punishment. Christ certainly as depicted in the Gospels did believe in everlasting punishment, and one does find repeatedly a vindictive fury against those people who would not listen to His preaching—an attitude which is not uncommon with preachers, but which does somewhat detract from superlative excellence. You do not, for instance, find that attitude in Socrates. You find him quite bland and urbane toward the people who would not listen to him; and it is, to my mind, far more worthy of a sage to take that line than to take the line of indignation. You probably all remember the sort of things that Socrates was saying when he was dying, and the sort of things that he generally did say to people who did not agree with him.

You will find that in the Gospels Christ said, "Ye serpents, ye     19 generation of vipers, how can ye escape the damnation of hell." That was said to people who did not like His preaching. It is not really to my mind quite the best tone, and there are a great many of these things about hell. There is, of course, the familiar text about the sin against the Holy Ghost: "Whosoever speaketh against the Holy Ghost it shall not be forgiven him neither in this World nor in the world to come." That text has caused an unspeakable amount of misery in the world, for all sorts of people have imagined that they have committed the sin against the Holy Ghost, and thought that it would not be forgiven them either in this world or in the world to come. I really do not think that a person with a proper degree of kindliness in his nature would have put fears and terrors of that sort into the world.

Then Christ says, "The Son of Man shall send forth His angels,     20 and they shall gather out of His kingdom all things that offend, and them which do iniquity, and shall cast them into a furnace of fire; there shall be wailing and gnashing of teeth"; and He goes on about the wailing and gnashing of teeth. It comes in one verse after another, and it is quite manifest to the reader that there is a certain pleasure in contemplating wailing and gnashing of teeth, or else it would not occur so often. Then you all, of course, remember about the sheep and the goats; how at the second coming He is going to divide the sheep from the goats, and He is going to say to the goats, "Depart from me, ye cursed, into everlasting fire." He continues, "And these shall go away into everlasting fire." Then He says again, "If thy hand offend thee, cut it off; it is better for thee to enter into life maimed, than having two hands to go into hell, into the fire that never shall be quenched; where the worm dieth not and the fire is not quenched." He repeats that again and again also. I must say that I think all this doctrine, that hell-fire is a punishment for sin, is a doctrine of cruelty. It is a doctrine that put cruelty into the world and gave the world generations of cruel torture; and the Christ of the Gospels, if you could take Him as His chroniclers represent Him, would certainly have to be considered partly responsible for that.

There are other things of less importance. There is the instance of 21 the Gadarene swine, where it certainly was not very kind to the pigs to put the devils into them and make them rush down the hill to the sea. You must remember that He was omnipotent, and He could have made the devils simply go away; but He chose to send them into the pigs. Then there is the curious story of the fig tree, which always rather puzzled me. You remember what happened about the fig tree. "He was hungry; and seeing a fig tree afar off having leaves, He came if haply He might find anything thereon; and when He came to it He found nothing but leaves, for the time of figs was not yet. And Jesus answered and said unto it: "No man eat fruit of thee hereafter for ever' . . . and Peter . . . saith unto Him: 'Master, behold the fig tree which thou cursedst is withered away.' " This is a very curious story, because it was not the right time of year for figs, and you really could not blame the tree. I cannot myself feel that either in the matter of wisdom or in the matter of virtue Christ stands quite as high as some other people known to history. I think I should put Buddha and Socrates above Him in those respects.

## The Emotional Factor

As I said before, I do not think that the real reason why people accept 22 religion has anything to do with argumentation. They accept religion on emotional grounds. One is often told that it is a very wrong thing to attack religion, because religion makes men virtuous. So I am told; I have not noticed it. You know, of course, the parody of that argument in Samuel Butler's book, *Erewhon Revisited.* You will remember that in *Erewhon* there is a certain Higgs who arrives in a remote country, and after spending some time there he escapes from that country in a balloon. Twenty years later he comes back to that country and finds a new religion in which he is worshiped under the name of the "Sun Child," and it is said that he ascended into heaven. He finds that the Feast of the Ascension is about to be celebrated, and he hears Professors Hanky and Panky say to each other that they never set eyes on the man Higgs, and they hope they never will; but they are the high priests of the religion of the Sun Child. He is very indignant, and he comes up to them, and he says, "I am going to expose all this humbug and tell the people of Erewhon that it was only I, the man Higgs, and I went up in a balloon." He was told, "You must not do that, because all the morals of this country are bound round this myth, and if they once know that you did not ascend into heaven they will all become wicked"; and so he is persuaded of that and he goes quietly away.

That is the idea—that we should all be wicked if we did not hold 23 to the Christian religion. It seems to me that the people who have held to it have been for the most part extremely wicked. You find this curious fact, that the more intense has been the religion of any period and the more profound has been the dogmatic belief, the greater has been the cruelty and the worse has been the state of affairs. In the so-called ages of faith, when men really did believe the Christian religion in all its completeness, there was the Inquisition, with its tortures; there were millions of unfortunate women burned as witches; and there was every kind of cruelty practiced upon all sorts of people in the name of religion.

You find as you look around the world that every single bit of 24 progress in humane feeling, every improvement in the criminal law, every step toward the diminution of war, every step toward better treatment of the colored races, or every mitigation of slavery, every moral progress that there has been in the world, has been consistently opposed by the organized churches of the world. I say quite deliberately that the Christian religion, as organized in its churches, has been and still is the principal enemy of moral progress in the world.

## How the Churches Have Retarded Progress

You may think that I am going too far when I say that that is still so. 25 I do not think that I am. Take one fact. You will bear with me if I mention it. It is not a pleasant fact, but the churches compel one to mention facts that are not pleasant. Supposing that in this world that we live in today an inexperienced girl is married to a syphilitic man; in that case the Catholic Church says, "This is an indissoluble sacrament. You must endure celibacy or stay together. And if you stay together, you must not use birth control to prevent the birth of syphilitic children." Nobody whose natural sympathies have not been warped by dogma, or whose moral nature was not absolutely dead to all sense of suffering, could maintain that it is right and proper that that state of things should continue.

That is only an example. There are a great many ways in which, 26 at the present moment, the church, by its insistence upon what it chooses to call morality, inflicts upon all sorts of people undeserved and unnecessary suffering. And of course, as we know, it is in its major part an opponent still of progress and of improvement in all the ways that diminish suffering in the world, because it has chosen to label as morality a certain narrow set of rules of conduct which have nothing to do with human happiness; and when you say that this or that ought to be done because it would make for human happiness, they think that has nothing to do with the matter at all. "What has human happiness to do with morals? The object of morals is not to make people happy."

## Fear, the Foundation of Religion

Religion is based, I think, primarily and mainly upon fear. It is partly 27 the terror of the unknown and partly, as I have said, the wish to feel that you have a kind of elder brother who will stand by you in all your troubles and disputes. Fear is the basis of the whole thing—fear of the mysterious, fear of defeat, fear of death. Fear is the parent of cruelty, and therefore it is no wonder if cruelty and religion have gone hand in hand. It is because fear is at the basis of those two things. In this world we can now begin a little to understand things, and a little to master them by help of science, which has forced its way step by step against the Christian religion, against the churches, and against the opposition of all the old precepts. Science can help us to get over this craven fear in which mankind has lived for so many generations. Science can teach us, and I think our own hearts can teach us, no longer to look around for imaginary supports, no longer to invent allies in the sky, but rather to look to our own efforts here below to make this world a fit place to live in, instead of the sort of place that the churches in all these centuries have made it.

## What We Must Do

We want to stand upon our own feet and look fair and square at the 28 world—its good facts, its bad facts, its beauties, and its ugliness; see the world as it is and be not afraid of it. Conquer the world by intelligence and not merely by being slavishly subdued by the terror that comes from it. The whole conception of God is a conception derived from the ancient Oriental despotisms. It is a conception quite unworthy of free men. When you hear people in church debasing themselves and saying that they are miserable sinners, and all the rest of it, it seems contemptible and not worthy of self-respecting human beings. We ought to stand up and look the world frankly in the face. We ought to make the best we can of the world, and if it is not so good as we wish, after all it will still be better than what these others have made of it in all these ages. A good world needs knowledge, kindliness, and courage; it does not need a regretful hankering after the past or a fettering of the free intelligence by the words uttered long ago by ignorant men. It needs a fearless outlook and a free intelligence. It needs hope for the future, not looking back all the time toward a past that is dead, which we trust will be far surpassed by the future that our intelligence can create.

# Questions

1. In his first paragraph Russell clears the way toward defining Christianity. Why does he find a definition necessary? How would you describe the relationship with his audience that he hopes to establish in this paragraph and the next?
2. Russell says that "there is no reason to suppose that the world had a beginning at all." Putting your own religious beliefs aside for a moment, what makes this idea difficult to grasp? Does Russell offer us any help in grasping it?
3. Russell frequently refers to time or history in constructing his argument. That is, he often uses such references as "these days," or "nowadays," or "the times of St. Augustine," or "all through the eighteenth century." What generalization does Russell draw from these references? (If you have read C. S. Lewis's essay, "What Christians Believe" (page 1033), do you recall references to time and history? Why would you not expect such references in Lewis's essay?)
4. In paragraph 8 Russell points to what he calls "defects" in the world as an argument against the existence of an omnipotent creator. (The examples of "defects" he gives are the Ku Klux Klan and the Fascists.) Anyone who wants to defend Christian faith must answer similar arguments. What answers are you familiar with? If you have read C. S. Lewis's essay (p. 1003), how does Lewis respond?
5. What answer can be given to Russell's charge (paragraph 26) that the church "inflicts upon all sorts of people undeserved and unnecessary suffering"?
6. In paragraph 27 Russell affirms his faith in science. He claims that

"science can help us to get over this craven fear in which mankind has lived for so many generations," and can help us "to make this world a fit place to live in." Do you share Russell's faith in science? Why, or why not?

William James

# Religious Faith[1]

Religion has meant many things in human history; but when from now onward I use the word I mean to use it in the supernaturalist sense, as declaring that the so-called order of nature, which constitutes this world's experience, is only one portion of the total universe, and that there stretches beyond this visible world an unseen world of which we now know nothing positive, but in its relation to which the true significance of our present mundane life consists. A man's religious faith (whatever more special items of doctrine it may involve) means for me essentially his faith in the existence of an unseen order of some kind in which the riddles of the natural order may be found explained. In the more developed religions the natural world has always been regarded as the mere scaffolding or vestibule of a truer, more eternal world, and affirmed to be a sphere of education, trial, or redemption. In these religions, one must in some fashion die to the natural life before one can enter into life eternal. The notion that this physical world of wind and water, when the sun rises and the moon sets, is absolutely and ultimately the divinely aimed-at and es-

[1] From *The Will to Believe*. (Editors' note)

William James (1842–1910), the older brother of the novelist Henry James, was one of the founders of the discipline of psychology in the United States. As he once remarked, the first lectures he ever heard on the subject were the ones he delivered in the 1870s.

James studied philosophy, science, and then medicine at Harvard University during the Civil War. In 1869–1870 he suffered extreme depression and experienced a nervous collapse, but he emerged from it with the conviction that only a belief in freedom of the will gives life meaning. This essay comes from a collection of James's essays called *The Will to Believe* (1897).

tablished thing, is one which we find only in very early religions. . . .
It is this natural religion (primitive still, in spite of the fact that poets
and men of science whose good-will exceeds their perspicacity keep
publishing it in new editions tuned to our contemporary ears) that, as
I said a while ago, has suffered definitive bankruptcy in the opinion
of a circle of persons, among whom I must count myself, and who are
growing more numerous every day. For such persons the physical
order of nature, taken simply as science knows it, cannot be held to
reveal any one harmonious spiritual intent. It is mere *weather*, as
Chauncey Wright called it, doing and undoing without end.

Now, I wish to make you feel, if I can in the short remainder of
this hour, that we have a right to believe the physical order to be only
a partial order; that we have a right to supplement it by an unseen
spiritual order which we assume on trust, if only thereby life may seem
to us better worth living again. But as such a trust will seem to some
of you sadly mystical and execrably unscientific, I must first say a word
or two to weaken the veto which you may consider that science op-
poses to our act.

There is included in human nature an ingrained naturalism and
materialism of mind which can only admit facts that are actually tangible. Of this sort of mind the entity called "science" is the idol. Fond-
ness for the word "scientist" is one of the notes by which you may
know its votaries; and its short way of killing any opinion that it disbe-
lieves in is to call it "unscientific." It must be granted that there is no
slight excuse for this. Science has made such glorious leaps in the last
three hundred years, and extended our knowledge of nature so enormously both in general and in detail; men of science, moreover, have
as a class displayed such admirable virtues—that it is no wonder if
the worshippers of science lose their head. In this very University,
accordingly, I have heard more than one teacher say that all the fundamental conceptions of truth have already been found by science,
and that the future has only the details of the picture to fill in. But the
slightest reflection on the real conditions will suffice to show how barbaric such notions are. They show such a lack of scientific imagination,
that it is hard to see how one who is actively advancing any part of
science can make a mistake so crude. Think how many absolutely new
scientific conceptions have arisen in our own generation, how many
new problems have been formulated that were never thought of before,
and then cast an eye upon the brevity of science's career. It began with
Galileo, not three hundred years ago. Four thinkers since Galileo, each
informing his successor of what discoveries his own lifetime had seen

achieved, might have passed the torch of science into our hands as we sit here in this room. Indeed, for the matter of that, an audience much smaller than the present one, an audience of some five or six score people, if each person in it could speak for his own generation, would carry us away to the black unknown of the human species, to days without a document or monument to tell their tale. Is it credible that such a mushroom knowledge, such a growth overnight as this, *can* represent more than the minutest glimpse of what the universe will really prove to be when adequately understood? No! our science is a drop, our ignorance a sea. Whatever else be certain, this at least is certain—that the world of our present natural knowledge *is* enveloped in a larger world of *some* sort of whose residual properties we at present can frame no positive idea.

Agnostic positivism,[2] of course, admits this principle theoretically     4 in the most cordial terms, but insists that we must not turn it to any practical use. We have no right, this doctrine tells us, to dream dreams, or suppose anything about the unseen part of the universe, merely because to do so may be for what we are pleased to call our highest interests. We must always wait for sensible evidence for our beliefs; and where such evidence is inaccessible we must frame no hypotheses whatever. Of course this is a safe enough position *in abstracto*. If a thinker had no stake in the unknown, no vital needs, to live or languish according to what the unseen world contained, a philosophic neutrality and refusal to believe either one way or the other would be his wisest cue. But, unfortunately, neutrality is not only inwardly difficult, it is also outwardly unrealizable, where our relations to an alternative are practical and vital. This is because, as the psychologists tell us, belief and doubt are living attitudes, and involve conduct on our part. Our only way, for example, of doubting, or refusing to believe, that a certain thing *is*, is continuing to act as if it were *not*. If, for instance, I refuse to believe that the room is getting cold, I leave the windows open and light no fire just as if it still were warm. If I doubt that you are worthy of my confidence, I keep you uninformed of all my secrets just as if you were *un*worthy of the same. If I doubt the need of insuring my house, I leave it uninsured as much as if I believed there were no need. And so if I must not believe that the world is divine, I can only express that refusal by declining ever to act distinctively as if it were so, which can only mean acting on certain critical occasions as if it were *not* so,

[2] A belief that human knowledge must be based on sense perceptions. (Editors' note)

or in an irreligious way. There are, you see, inevitable occasions in life
when inaction is a kind of action, and must count as action, and when
not to be for is to be practically against; and in all such cases strict and
consistent neutrality is an unattainable thing.

And, after all, is not this duty of neutrality where only our inner     5
interests would lead us to believe the most ridiculous of commands?
Is it not sheer dogmatic folly to say that our inner interests can have
no real connection with the forces that the hidden world may contain?
In other cases divinations based on inner interests have proved prophetic enough. Take science itself! Without an imperious inner demand
on our part for ideal logical and mathematical harmonies, we should
never have attained to proving that such harmonies lie hidden between
all the chinks and interstices of the crude natural world. Hardly a law
has been established in science, hardly a fact ascertained, which was
not first sought after, often with sweat and blood, to gratify an inner
need. Whence such needs come from we do not know: we find them
in us, and biological psychology so far only classes them with Darwin's
"accidental variations." But the inner need of believing that this world
of nature is a sign of something more spiritual and eternal than itself
is just as strong and authoritative in those who feel it, as the inner
need of uniform laws of causation ever can be in a professionally scientific head. The toil of many generations has proved the latter need
prophetic. Why *may* not the former one be prophetic, too? And if needs
of ours outrun the visible universe, why *may* not that be a sign that
an invisible universe is there? What, in short, has authority to debar
us from trusting our religious demands? Science as such assuredly has
no authority, for she can only say what is, not what is not; and the
agnostic "thou shalt not believe without coercive sensible evidence"
is simply an expression (free to any one to make) of private personal
appetite for evidence of a certain peculiar kind.

Now, when I speak of trusting our religious demands, just what     6
do I mean by "trusting"? Is the word to carry with it license to define
in detail an invisible world, and to anathematize and excommunicate
those whose trust is different? Certainly not! Our faculties of belief
were not primarily given us to make orthodoxies and heresies withal;
they were given us to live by. And to trust our religious demands
means first of all to live in the light of them, and to act as if the invisible
world which they suggest were real. It is a fact of human nature, that
men can live and die by the help of a sort of faith that goes without
a single dogma or definition. The bare assurance that this natural order
is not ultimate but a mere sign or vision, the external staging of a many-

storied universe, in which spiritual forces have the last word and are eternal—this bare assurance is to such men enough to make life seem worth living in spite of every contrary presumption suggested by its circumstances on the natural plane. Destroy this inner assurance, however, vague as it is, and all the light and radiance of existence is extinguished for these persons at a stroke. Often enough the wild-eyed look at life—the suicidal mood—will then set in.

And now the application comes directly home to you and me. Probably to almost every one of us here the most adverse life would seem well worth living, if we only could be *certain* that our bravery and patience with it were terminating and eventuating and bearing fruit somewhere in an unseen spiritual world. But granting we are not certain, does it then follow that a bare trust in such a world is a fool's paradise and lubberland, or rather that it is a living attitude in which we are free to indulge? Well, we are free to trust at our own risks anything that is not impossible, and that can bring analogies to bear in its behalf. That the world of physics is probably not absolute, all the converging multitude of arguments that make in favor of idealism tend to prove; and that our whole physical life may lie soaking in a spiritual atmosphere, a dimension of being that we at present have no organ for apprehending, is vividly suggested to us by the analogy of the life of our domestic animals. Our dogs, for example, are in our human life but not of it. They witness hourly the outward body of events whose inner meaning cannot, by any possible operation, be revealed to their intelligence—events in which they themselves often play the cardinal part. My terrier bites a teasing boy, for example, and the father demands damages. The dog may be present at every step of the negotiations, and see the money paid, without an inkling of what it all means, without a suspicion that it has anything to do with *him;* and he never *can* know in his natural dog's life. Or take another case which used greatly to impress me in my medical-student days. Consider a poor dog whom they are vivisecting in a laboratory. He lies strapped on a board and shrieking at his executioners, and to his own dark consciousness is literally in a sort of hell. He cannot see a single redeeming ray in the whole business; and yet all these diabolical-seeming events are often controlled by human intentions with which, if his poor benighted mind could only be made to catch a glimpse of them, all that is heroic in him would religiously acquiesce. Healing truth, relief to future sufferings of beast and man, are to be bought by them. It may be genuinely a process of redemption. Lying on his back on the board there he may be performing a function incalculably higher

7

than any that prosperous canine life admits of; and yet, of the whole performance, this function is the one portion that must remain absolutely beyond his ken.

Now turn from this to the life of man. In the dog's life we see the 8 world invisible to him because we live in both worlds. In human life, although we only see our world, and his within it, yet encompassing both these worlds a still wider world may be there, as unseen by us as our world is by him; and to believe in that world *may* be the most essential function that our lives in this world have to perform. But *"may* be! *may* be!" one now hears the positivist contemptuously exclaim; "what use can a scientific life have for maybes?" Well, I reply, the "scientific" life itself has much to do with maybes, and human life at large has everything to do with them. So far as man stands for anything, and is productive or originative at all, his entire vital function may be said to have to deal with maybes. Not a victory is gained, not a deed of faithfulness or courage is done, except upon a maybe; not a service, not a sally of generosity, not a scientific exploration or experiment or textbook, that may not be a mistake. It is only by risking our persons from one hour to another that we live at all. And often enough our faith beforehand in an uncertified result *is the only thing that makes the result come true.* Suppose, for instance, that you are climbing a mountain, and have worked yourself into a position from which the only escape is by a terrible leap. Have faith that you can successfully make it, and your feet are nerved to its accomplishment. But mistrust yourself, and think of all the sweet things you have heard the scientists say of *maybes,* and you will hesitate so long that, at last, all unstrung and trembling, and launching yourself in a moment of despair, you roll in the abyss. In such a case (and it belongs to an enormous class), the part of wisdom as well as of courage is to *believe what is in the line of your needs,* for only by such belief is the need fulfilled. Refuse to believe, and you shall indeed be right, for you shall irretrievably perish. But believe, and again you shall be right, for you shall save yourself. You make one or the other of two possible universes true by your trust or mistrust—both universes having been only *maybes,* in this particular, before you contributed your act.

Now, it appears to me that the question whether life is worth living 9 is subject to conditions logically much like these. It does, indeed, depend on you *the liver.* If you surrender to the nightmare view and crown the evil edifice by your own suicide, you have indeed made a picture totally black. Pessimism, completed by your act, is true beyond a doubt, so far as your world goes. Your mistrust of life has removed whatever worth your own enduring existence might have given to it; and now, throughout the whole sphere of possible influence of that existence, the mistrust has proved itself to have had divining power. But suppose, on the other hand, that instead of giving way to the nightmare view you cling to it that this world is not the *ultimatum*. Suppose you find yourself a very well-spring, as Wordsworth says, of—

> Zeal, and the virtue to exist by faith
> As soldiers live by courage; as, by strength
> Of heart, the sailor fights with roaring seas.

Suppose, however thickly evils crowd upon you, that your unconquerable subjectivity proves to be their match, and that you find a more wonderful joy than any passive pleasure can bring in trusting ever in the larger whole. Have you not now made life worth living on these terms? What sort of a thing would life really be, with your qualities ready for a tussle with it, if it only brought fair weather and gave these higher faculties of yours no scope? Please remember that optimism and pessimism are definitions of the world, and that our own reactions on the world, small as they are in bulk, are integral parts of the whole thing, and necessarily help to determine the definition. They may even be the decisive elements in determining the definition. A large mass can have its unstable equilibrium overturned by the addition of a feather's weight; a long phrase may have its sense reversed by the addition of the three letters *n-o-t*. This life *is* worth living, we can say, *since it is what we make it, from the moral point of view;* and we are determined to make it from that point of view, so far as we have anything to do with it, a success.

Now, in this description of faiths that verify themselves I have 10 assumed that our faith in an invisible order is what inspires those efforts and that patience which make this visible order good for moral men. Our faith in the seen world's goodness (goodness now meaning fitness for successful moral and religious life) has verified itself by leaning on our faith in the unseen world. But will our faith in the unseen world similarly verify itself? Who knows?

Once more it is a case of *maybe;* and once more *maybes* are the 11 essence of the situation. I confess that I do not see why the very existence of an invisible world may not in part depend on the personal response which any one of us may make to the religious appeal. God himself, in short, may draw vital strength and increase of very being from our fidelity. For my own part, I do not know what the sweat and blood and tragedy of this life mean, if they mean anything short of this. If this life be not a real fight, in which something is eternally gained for the universe by success, it is no better than a game of private theatricals from which one may withdraw at will. But it *feels* like a real fight—as if there were something really wild in the universe which we, with all our idealities and faithfulnesses, are needed to redeem; and first of all to redeem our own hearts from atheisms and fears. For such a half-wild, half-saved universe our nature is adapted. The deepest thing in our nature is this *Binnenleben*[3] (as a German doctor lately has called it), this dumb region of the heart in which we dwell alone with our willingnesses and unwillingnesses, our faiths and fears. As through the cracks and crannies of caverns those waters exude from the earth's bosom which then form the fountainheads of springs, so in these crepuscular depths of personality the sources of all our outer deeds and decisions take their rise. Here is our deepest organ of communication with the nature of things; and compared with these concrete movements of our soul all abstract statements and scientific arguments—the veto, for example, which the strict positivist pronounces upon our faith—sound to us like mere chatterings of the teeth. For here possibilities, not finished facts, are the realities with which we have actively to deal; and to quote my friend William Salter, of the Philadelphia Ethical Society, "as the essence of courage is to stake one's life on a possibility, so the essence of faith is to believe that the possibility exists."

These, then, are my last words to you: Be not afraid of life. Believe     12
that life *is* worth living, and your belief will help create the fact. The "scientific proof" that you are right may not be clear before the day of judgment (or some stage of being which that expression may serve to symbolize) is reached. But the faithful fighters of this hour, or the beings that then and there will represent them, may then turn to the faint-hearted, who here decline to go on, with words like those with which Henry IV[4] greeted the tardy Crillon after a great victory had been gained: "Hang yourself, brave Crillon! We fought at Arques, and you were not there."

[3] Interior life. (Editors' note)
[4] Henry IV of France put down a rebellion at the battle of Arques, 1589. (Editors' note)

# Questions

1. From the first two paragraphs what can you infer about James's audience? How would you characterize his relationship to the audience and the tone he establishes? Is his tone formal, or informal? Are he and his listeners on an equal footing. Does he expect that they will share most of his opinions and beliefs, or only some, or none?

2. James mentions the words "science" and "scientist" several times in his opening paragraphs, especially in paragraph 3. What is his attitude toward science? Is it mostly favorable, or critical, or mixed? How is science related to "natural religion," which he discussed in paragraph 1? And in paragraph 3, what argument (which he will further develop in paragraph 5) is suggested by the phrase "worshippers of science"?

3. In paragraph 4, what is James's argument against agnosticism? What is the *tone* of his remarks in this paragraph?

4. James frequently uses comparisons in building his argument. Read the entry on "analogy" in the Glossary, and then note the comparisons James makes that qualify as analogies. Do you find these analogies effective, or perhaps even persuasive? Is there anything about his subject matter that particularly lends itself to the use of analogy?

Will Herberg

# Religiosity and Religion

Religion is taken very seriously in present-day America, 1
in a way that would have amazed and chagrined the "advanced" thinkers of half a century ago, who were so sure that the ancient superstition
was bound to disappear very shortly in the face of the steady advance
of science and reason. Religion has not disappeared; it is probably more
pervasive today, and in many ways more influential, than it has been
for generations. The only question is: What kind of religion is it? What
is its content? What is it that Americans *believe in* when they are religious?

"The 'unknown God' of Americans seems to be faith itself."[1] What 2
Americans believe in when they are religious is . . . religion itself. Of
course, religious Americans speak of God and Christ, but what they
seem to regard as really redemptive is primarily religion, the "positive"
attitude of *believing*. It is this faith in faith, this religion that makes
religion its own object, that is the outstanding characteristic of contemporary American religiosity. Daniel Poling's formula: "I began saying in the morning two words, 'I believe'—those two words *with nothing added* . . ."[2] (emphasis not in original) may be taken as the classic
expression of this aspect of American faith.

On the social level, this faith in religion involves the conviction, 3
quite universal among Americans today, that every decent and vir-

---

[1] Reinhold Niebuhr, "Religiosity and the Christian Faith," *Christianity and Crisis,*
Vol. XIV, No. 24, January 24, 1955.
[2] Daniel A. Poling, "A Running Start to Every Day," *Parade: The Sunday Picture
Magazine,* September 19, 1954.

---

Will Herberg (1901–1977) was, in his youth, a Marxist who was active in the labor
movement in the United States. In middle age he became an anti-Communist,
and he grew increasingly interested in religion. Deeply moved by the writings
of Reinhold Niebuhr, Herberg thought of converting to Christianity, but Niebuhr
urged him to remain true to his Jewish roots. Herberg followed Niebuhr's advice,
and went on to edit a volume of writings by the Jewish philospher Martin Buber.
He also wrote two books: *Judaism and Modern Man* (1951) and *Protestant-
Catholic-Jew* (1955). A portion of this second book, a sociological study, is
reprinted here.

tuous nation is religious, that religion is the true basis of national existence and therefore presumably the one sure resource for the solution of all national problems.[3] On the level of personal life, the American faith in religion implies not only that every right-minded citizen is religious, but also that religion (or faith) is a most efficacious device for getting what one wants in life.[4] "Jesus," the Rev. Irving E. Howard assures us, "recommended faith as a technique for getting results. . . . Jesus recommended faith as a way to heal the body and to remove any of the practical problems that loom up as mountains in a man's path."[5]

As one surveys the contemporary scene, it appears that the "results" Americans want to get out of faith are primarily "peace of mind," happiness, and success in worldly achievement. Religion is valued too as a means of cultural enrichment.

Prosperity, success, and advancement in business are the obvious ends for which religion, or rather the religious attitude of "believing," is held to be useful.[6] There is ordinarily no criticism of the ends themselves in terms of the ultimate loyalties of a God-centered faith, nor

[3] At the Conference on the Spiritual Foundations of Our Democracy, held in Washington, D.C., in November 1954, Monsignor George G. Higgins, director of the social action department of the National Catholic Welfare Conference, issued a sharp warning against the widespread notion that a "return to God" on the part of the American people was in itself sufficient to solve all national problems, without the necessity of resorting to responsible and informed thinking on the "secular" level, on the level of institutions and social strategies. His warning was echoed by others at the conference.

[4] For a critique of this conception of religion, see H. Richard Niebuhr, "Utilitarian Christianity," *Christianity and Crisis,* Vol. VI, No. 12, July 8, 1946.

[5] Howard, "Random Reflections," *Christian Economics,* March 8, 1955.

[6] This is the burden of the philosophy of "positive thinking" so effectively expounded by Norman Vincent Peale, and may be documented in any of Dr. Peale's many writings. For example: "How do you practice faith? First thing every morning, before you arise, say out loud, 'I believe,' three times" (*The Power of Positive Thinking* [Prentice-Hall, 1952], p. 154). For a sharp criticism of this philosophy, see Miller, "Some Negative Thinking about Norman Vincent Peale," *The Reporter,* January 13, 1955; see also Paul Hutchinson, "Have We a 'New' Religion?" *Life,* April 11, 1955, pp. 148–157. A penetrating critique of the Peale gospel of "positive thinking" by a Catholic theologian will be found in Gustave Weigel, "Protestantism as a Catholic Concern," *Theological Studies,* Vol. XVI, No. 2, June 1955. A Jewish version of the same cult of "faith in faith" may be found in Louis Binstock, *The Power of Faith* (Prentice-Hall, 1952). Declares Rabbi Binstock: "You, like everyone else, have access to a great storehouse of dynamic power on which you can draw. . . . That storehouse is *Faith.* Not religion. Not your immortal soul. Not this House of Worship. Not God. But—FAITH" (p. 4). For a critical review of this book, see Herberg, "Faith and Idolatry," *The Pastor,* Vol. XVI, No. 3, November 1952. One of the oldest and most respectable of Protestant denominations recently ran a newspaper advertisement in which the readers were told that "there are times in life when faith alone protects" and were urged to attend church because "regular church attendance helps you build your own personal reserve of faith." Neither God nor Christ was anywhere mentioned.

is there much concern about what the religion or the faith is all about, since it is not the content of the belief but the attitude of believing that is felt to be operative.

Almost as much as worldly success, religion is expected to produce 6 a kind of spiritual euphoria, the comfortable feeling that one is all right with God. Roy Eckardt calls this the cult of "divine-human chumminess" in which God is envisioned as the "Man Upstairs," a "Friendly Neighbor," Who is always ready to give you the pat on the back you need when you happen to feel blue. "Fellowship with the Lord is, so to say, an extra emotional jag that keeps [us] happy. The 'gospel' makes [us] 'feel real good.' "[7] Again, all sense of the ambiguity and precariousness of human life, all sense of awe before the divine majesty, all sense of judgment before the divine holiness, is shut out; God is, in Jane Russell's inimitable phrase, a "livin' Doll." What relation has this kind of god to the biblical God Who confronts sinful man as an enemy before He comes out to meet repentant man as a Savior? Is this He of Whom we are told, "It is a fearful thing to fall into the hands of the living God" (Heb. 10:31)? The measure of how far contemporary American religiosity falls short of the authentic tradition of Jewish-Christian faith is to be found in the chasm that separates Jane Russell's "livin' Doll" from the living God of Scripture.

The cultural enrichment that is looked for in religion varies greatly 7 with the community, the denomination, and the outlook and status of the church members. Liturgy is valued as aesthetically and emotionally "rewarding," sermons are praised as "interesting" and "en-

[7] "The cult of the 'Man Upstairs.' A rhapsodic inquiry greets us from the TV screen and the radio: 'Have you talked to the Man Upstairs?' God is a friendly neighbor who dwells in the apartment just above. Call on him any time, especially if you are feeling a little blue. He does not get upset over your little faults. He understands. . . . Thus is the citizenry guided to divine-human chumminess. . . . Fellowship with the Lord is, so to say, an extra emotional jag that keeps him [the individual] happy. The 'gospel' makes him 'feel real good' " (Eckardt, "The New Look in American Piety," *The Christian Century*, November 17, 1954). A strong strain of this "divine-human chumminess" is to be found in certain aspects of American revivalistic religion; there, too, the gospel makes you "feel real good." "What today's cult of reassurance most lacks—and indeed disavows—is a sense of life's inevitable failures. Here is the point at which it stands in starkest contrast to the teaching of America's most searching contemporary theologian, Reinhold Niebuhr. . . . There is one central idea in his writing which . . . is validated by universal experience. This is his contention that all human effort, however noble, however achieving contains within it an element of failure. Perhaps one reason Americans say they cannot understand Niebuhr is because their minds simply will not harbor this fact that all success is dogged by failure" (Hutchinson, "Have We a 'New' Religion? *Life*, April 11, 1955, p. 148).

joyable," discussions of the world relations of the church are welcomed as "educational," even theology is approved of as "thought provoking." On another level, the "old-time religion" is cherished by certain segments of the population because it so obviously enriches their cultural life.

But, in the last analysis, it is "peace of mind" that most Americans 8 expect of religion. "Peace of mind" is today easily the most popular gospel that goes under the name of religion; in one way or another it invades and permeates all other forms of contemporary religiosity. It works in well with the drift toward other-direction characteristic of large sections of American society, since both see in adjustment the supreme good in life. What is desired, and what is promised, is the conquest of insecurity and anxiety, the overcoming of inner conflict, the shedding of guilt and fear, the translation of the self to the painless paradise of "normality" and "adjustment"! Religion, in short, is a spiritual anodyne designed to allay the pains and vexations of existence.

It is this most popular phase of contemporary American religiosity 9 that has aroused the sharpest criticism in more sophisticated theological circles. The Most Rev. Patrick A. O'Boyle, Catholic archbishop of Washington, has warned that although "at first glance piety seems to be everywhere . . ." many persons appear to be "turning to religion as they would to a benign sedative to soothe their minds and settle their nerves."[8] Liston Pope emphasizes that the approach of the "peace of mind" school is not only "very dubious on psychological grounds," but its "identification [with] the Christian religion . . . is of questionable validity."[9] Roy Eckardt describes it as "religious narcissism," in which "the individual and his psycho-spiritual state occupy the center of the religious stage" and piety is made to "concentrate on its own navel."[10] I have myself spoken of it as a philosophy that would "dehumanize man and reduce his life to the level of sub-human creation which knows neither sin nor guilt."[11] It encourages moral insensitivity

---

[8] Address at the forty-first annual meeting of the Association of American Colleges, held in Washington, January 1955, as reported in *New York Herald Tribune*, January 12, 1955.

[9] Address at the dinner meeting of the broadcasting and film commission of the National Council of Churches, New York City, March 1, 1955 (unpublished). See also Hutchinson, "Have We a 'New' Religion?" *Life*, April 11, 1955, pp. 147–148; Hutchinson calls it the "cult of reassurance."

[10] Eckardt, "The New Look in American Piety," *The Christian Century*, November 17, 1954.

[11] Herberg, *Judaism and Modern Man: An Interpretation of Jewish Religion* (Farrar, Straus, and Young, 1951), p. 29.

and social irresponsibility, and cultivates an almost lascivious preoccupation with self. The church becomes a kind of emotional service
station to relieve us of our worries: "Go to church—you'll feel better,"
"Bring your troubles to church and leave them there" (slogans on subway posters urging church attendance). On every ground, this type
of religion is poles apart from authentic Jewish-Christian spirituality
which, while it knows of the "peace that passeth understanding" as
the gift of God, promotes a "divine discontent"[12] with things as they
are and a "passionate thirst for the future,"[13] in which all things will
be renewed and restored to their right relation to God.[14]

The burden of this criticism of American religion from the point    10
of view of Jewish-Christian faith is that contemporary religion is so
naively, so innocently *man-centered*. Not God, but man—man in his
individual and corporate being—is the beginning and end of the spiritual system of much of present-day American religiosity. In this kind
of religion there is no sense of transcendence, no sense of the noth-
ingness of man and his works before a holy God; in this kind of religion
the values of life, and life itself, are not submitted to Almighty God
to judge, to shatter, and to reconstruct; on the contrary, life, and the
values of life, are given an ultimate sanction by being identified with
the divine. In this kind of religion it is not man who serves God, but
God who is mobilized and made to serve man and his purposes—
whether these purposes be economic prosperity, free enterprise, social
reform, democracy, happiness, security, or "peace of mind." God is

---

[12] "I most emphatically prefer a divine discontent to peace of mind. . . . Are you
satisfied with the state of the world? Are you content with the behavior of modern
man? Have you reached the point where soporific relaxation is the real goal, where
more than anything else you want rest and quiet and protection from stimulation?. . . . If that's what you want, count me out. . . . God pity me on the day when
I have lost my restlessness! God forgive me on the day when I'm satisfied! God
rouse me up if ever I am so dull, insensitive, lazy, complacent, phlegmatic, and
apathetic as to be at peace!" (Warren Weaver, "Peace of Mind," *The Saturday Review*,
December 11, 1954). Mr. Weaver is director of the division of natural sciences of
the Rockefeller Foundation.
[13] Ernst Renan is reported to have described the "true Israelite" as a man "torn
with discontent and possessed with a passionate thirst for the future."
[14] "We are undoubtedly in the midst of a widespread and powerful revival of religion. There is, however, a real danger of this spiritual current running up against
a steep wall of compulsive escapism and becoming a giant pool of stagnation and
futility, instead of a vital tide of constructive energy and new creative work" (Charles
W. Lowry, co-chairman of the Foundation for Religious Action, Washington, D.C.,
in a press release of the Foundation, issued June 10, 1954).

conceived as man's "omnipotent servant,"[15] faith as a sure-fire device to get what we want. The American is a religious man, and in many cases personally humble and conscientious. But religion as he understands it is not something that makes for humility or the uneasy conscience: it is something that reassures him about the essential rightness of everything American, his nation, his culture, and himself; something that validates his goals and his ideals instead of calling them into question; something that enhances his self-regard instead of challenging it; something that feeds his self-sufficiency instead of shattering it; something that offers him salvation on easy terms instead of demanding repentance and a "broken heart." Because it does all these things, his religion, however sincere and well-meant, is ultimately vitiated by a strong and pervasive idolatrous element.

# Questions

1.  Herberg several times uses the word "religiosity." How does religiosity differ from religion? What are Herberg's objections to religiosity?
2.  What evidence in the "contemporary scene" (paragraph 4) do you find to confirm Herberg's thesis, or to reject it? Look for evidence, as he does, in sermons, magazine articles, TV programs, or advertisements. Cite specific instances.
3.  Herberg writes: "Prosperity, success, and advancement in business are the obvious ends for which . . . the religious attitude of 'believing' . . . is held to be useful," and he suggests that "there is ordinarily no criticism of [these] ends" as appropriate to a "God-centered faith" (paragraph 5). Do you agree that "religiosity" has been associated with these ends? Do you agree that there is no criticism of these ends?
4.  Herberg is unhappy that many Americans simply have "faith in faith" (paragraph 2). Does William James's essay (page 1067), written long before Herberg's, provide an adequate answer to Herberg? Explain?
5.  Explain what Herberg means by "idolatrous" in his last sentence.
6.  On what points would Herberg and Steinbeck (page 1082) agree? Which article do you find more persuasive, and why?

[15] The phrase is from Jules H. Masserman, "Faith and Delusion in Psychotherapy: The Ur-Defenses of Man," *The American Journal of Psychiatry*, Vol. 110, No. 5, November 1953. For a critique of the theological aspects of Masserman's thesis, see Herberg, "Biblical Faith and Natural Religion," *Theology Today*, Vol. XI, No. 4, January 1955.

John Steinbeck

# The Sermon

Sunday morning, in a Vermont town, my last day in New   1
England, I shaved, dressed in a suit, polished my shoes, whited my
sepulcher,[1] and looked for a church to attend. Several I eliminated for
reasons I do not now remember, but on seeing a John Knox church I
drove into a side street and parked Rocinante out of sight, gave Charley
his instructions about watching the truck, and took my way with dignity to a church of blindingly white ship lap. I took my seat in the rear
of the spotless, polished place of worship. The prayers were to the
point, directing the attention of the Almighty to certain weaknesses
and undivine tendencies I know to be mine and could only suppose
were shared by others gathered there.

The service did my heart and I hope my soul some good. It had   2
been long since I had heard such an approach. It is our practice now,
at least in the large cities, to find from our psychiatric priesthood that
our sins aren't really sins at all but accidents that are set in motion by
forces beyond our control. There was no such nonsense in this church.
The minister, a man of iron with tool-steel eyes and a delivery like a
pneumatic drill, opened up with prayer and reassured us that we were
a pretty sorry lot. And he was right. We didn't amount to much to

---

[1] In the Gospel according to St. Matthew 23:27 Jesus denounces hypocritical scribes
and Pharisees, comparing them to "whited sepulchers [i.e., tombs], which indeed
appear beautiful outward, but are within full of dead men's bones, and of all uncleanness." Steinbeck's next sentence refers to Rocinante, his genial name for his
truck. Rocinante was the name of Don Quixote's horse. Literally it means "formerly
a nag."

---

John Steinbeck (1902–1968) was born in Salinas, California, and much of his
writing concerns the Salinas Valley. In 1919 he entered Stanford University but
he left without a degree. He was determined to become a writer, yet for some
ten years he had little success and supported himself by odd jobs. Between 1935
and 1939, however, he achieved fame with several important books, including
*Tortilla Flat* (1935), *In Dubious Battle* (1936), *Of Mice and Men* (1937), and *The
Grapes of Wrath* (1939).

In addition to writing novels and short stories, Steinbeck wrote some non-
fiction, notably *Travels with Charley* (1962), a record of his automobile tour—
with his poodle, Charley—of forty states. The passage we print here comes from
*Travels;* the title of the selection is our own.

start with, and due to our own tawdry efforts we had been slipping ever since. Then, having softened us up, he went into a glorious sermon, a fire-and-brimstone sermon. Having proved that we, or perhaps only I, were no damn good, he painted with cool certainty what was likely to happen to us if we didn't make some basic reorganizations for which he didn't hold out much hope. He spoke of hell as an expert, not the mush-mush hell of these soft days, but a well-stoked, white-hot hell served by technicians of the first order. This reverend brought it to a point where we could understand it, a good hard coal fire, plenty of draft, and a squad of open-hearth devils who put their hearts into their work, and their work was me. I began to feel good all over. For some years now God has been a pal to us, practicing togetherness, and that causes the same emptiness a father does playing softball with his son. But this Vermont God cared enough about me to go to a lot of trouble kicking the hell out of me. He put my sins in a new perspective. Whereas they had been small and mean and nasty and best forgotten, this minister gave them some size and bloom and dignity. I hadn't been thinking very well of myself for some years, but if my sins had this dimension there was some pride left. I wasn't a naughty child but a first rate sinner, and I was going to catch it.

I felt so revived in spirit that I put five dollars in the plate, and 3 afterward, in front of the church, shook hands warmly with the minister and as many of the congregation as I could. It gave me a lovely sense of evil-doing that lasted clear through till Tuesday. I even considered beating Charley to give him some satisfaction too, because Charley is only a little less sinful than I am. All across the country I went to church on Sundays, a different denomination every week, but nowhere did I find the quality of that Vermont preacher. He forged a religion designed to last, not predigested obsolescence.

# Questions

1. In his first sentence Steinbeck says: "Sunday morning, in a Vermont town, my last day in New England, I shaved, dressed in a suit, polished my shoes, whited my sepulcher, and looked for a church to attend." In a footnote we explain that Jesus, in the Gospel according to St. Matthew, applies the term "whited sepulchers" to hypocrites. But what is Steinbeck's tone here? Pretentious? Playful? Reverential? Savage? Or what? How does this reference prepare us for what comes later in the selection?

2.  In paragraph 2 Steinbeck says, "The service did my heart . . . good."
    Do you think he means exactly what he says? If yes, what good *did*
    it do? And do you think he means, in the final paragraph, that he
    really considered beating his dog? If he does mean—at least to
    some degree—that the service did his heart good, why not beat the
    dog?
3.  How seriously do you think Steinbeck takes religion?


Langston Hughes

# Salvation

I was saved from sin when I was going on thirteen. But    1
not really saved. It happened like this. There was a big revival at my
Auntie Reed's church. Every night for weeks there had been much
preaching, singing, praying, and shouting, and some very hardened
sinners had been brought to Christ, and the membership of the church
had grown by leaps and bounds. Then just before the revival ended,
they held a special meeting for children, "to bring the young lambs to
the fold." My aunt spoke of it for days ahead. That night I was escorted
to the front row and placed on the mourners' bench with all the other
young sinners, who had not yet been brought to Jesus.

My aunt told me that when you were saved you saw a light, and    2
something happened to you inside! And Jesus came into your life! And
God was with you from then on! She said you could see and hear and
feel Jesus in your soul. I believed her. I had heard a great many old
people say the same thing and it seemed to me they ought to know.
So I sat there calmly in the hot, crowded church, waiting for Jesus to
come to me.

Langston Hughes (1902–1967) was the first black American writer to establish
an international reputation. Enormously versatile, he wrote poems, plays, stories,
novels, children's books, filmscripts, autobiographies, and essays. Hughes also
exerted a great influence on American literature by organizing poetry readings
for black writers, and by founding three theater groups.

The preacher preached a wonderful rhythmical sermon, all moans    3
and shouts and lonely cries and dire pictures of hell, and then he sang
a song about the ninety and nine safe in the fold, but one little lamb
was left out in the cold. Then he said: "Won't you come? Won't you
come to Jesus? Young lambs, won't you come?" And he held out his
arms to all us young sinners there on the mourners' bench. And the
little girls cried. And some of them jumped up and went to Jesus right
away. But most of us just sat there.

A great many old people came and knelt around us and prayed,    4
old women with jet-black faces and braided hair, old men with work-
gnarled hands. And the church sang a song about the lower lights are
burning, some poor sinners to be saved. And the whole building
rocked with prayer and song.

Still I kept waiting to *see* Jesus.    5

Finally all the young people had gone to the altar and were saved,    6
but one boy and me. He was a rounder's son named Westley. Westley
and I were surrounded by sisters and deacons praying. It was very
hot in the church, and getting late now. Finally Westley said to me in
a whisper: "God damn! I'm tired o' sitting here. Let's get up and be
saved." So he got up and was saved.

Then I was left all alone on the mourners' bench. My aunt came    7
and knelt at my knees and cried, while prayers and songs swirled all
around me in the little church. The whole congregation prayed for me
alone, in a mighty wail of moans and voices. And I kept waiting se-
renely for Jesus, waiting, waiting—but he didn't come. I wanted to
see him, but nothing happened to me. Nothing! I wanted something
to happen to me, but nothing happened.

I heard the songs and the minister saying: "Why don't you come?    8
My dear child, why don't you come to Jesus? Jesus is waiting for you.
He wants you. Why don't you come? Sister Reed, what is this child's
name?"

"Langston," my aunt sobbed.    9

"Langston, why don't you come? Why don't you come and be    10
saved? Oh, Lamb of God! Why don't you come?"

Now it was really getting late. I began to be ashamed of myself,    11
holding everything up so long. I began to wonder what God thought
about Westley, who certainly hadn't seen Jesus either, but who was
now sitting proudly on the platform, swinging his knickerbockered
legs and grinning down at me, surrounded by deacons and old women
on their knees praying. God had not struck Westley dead for taking

his name in vain or for lying in the temple. So I decided that maybe to save further trouble, I'd better lie, too, and say that Jesus had come, and get up and be saved.

So I got up.                                                                    12

Suddenly the whole room broke into a sea of shouting, as they    13
saw me rise. Waves of rejoicing swept the place. Women leaped in the air. My aunt threw her arms around me. The minister took me by the hand and led me to the platform.

When things quieted down, in a hushed silence, punctuated by a    14
few ecstatic "Amens," all the new young lambs were blessed in the name of God. Then joyous singing filled the room.

That night, for the last time in my life but one—for I was a big    15
boy twelve years old—I cried. I cried, in bed alone, and couldn't stop. I buried my head under the quilts, but my aunt heard me. She woke up and told my uncle I was crying because the Holy Ghost had come into my life, and because I had seen Jesus. But I was really crying because I couldn't bear to tell her that I had lied, that I had deceived everybody in the church, and I hadn't seen Jesus, and that now I didn't believe there was a Jesus any more, since he didn't come to help me.

# Questions

1. Is this piece amusing, or serious, or both? Explain.
2. How would you characterize the style or voice of the first three sentences? Childlike? Sophisticated? How would you characterize the final sentence? How can you explain the change in style or tone?
3. Why does Hughes bother to tell us, in paragraph 11, that Westley was "swinging his knickerbockered legs and grinning"? Do you think that Westley, too, may have cried that night? Give your reasons.
4. Is the episode told from the point of view of someone "going on thirteen," or from the point of view of a mature man? Consult the entry on "persona" in the Glossary. One way to answer this question about point of view is to describe Hughes's persona in this essay. Does the essay strike you as in some ways "a performance"? If so, who is the audience—or who might be the ideal audience for this performance?

## A Note on Buddhism

Buddhism was founded by Siddhartha (c. 563 B.C.–c. 483 B.C.) of the princely Gautama family. This family, which lived in the part of northeast India that is now Nepal, belonged to the Shakya clan, and so Siddhartha is also called Shakyamuni, the "Wise Man of the Shakya Clan." He is also called Buddha, although "Buddha"—meaning "enlightened" or "awakened"—is a description of a condition, not a name. Anyone and everyone can become a Buddha, and much Buddhist thought holds that we are all Buddhas even though we do not know it.

At the age of twenty-nine Siddhartha vowed to save not only himself but all humanity from suffering. He left his father's palace, changed his princely robes for rags, and lived a life of asceticism, hoping to perceive a way of escaping from repeated rebirths in the cycle of existence. (Traditional Indian religion held that all actions produce fruit, good or evil. The deeds and their results are one's *karma*, and they determine the nature of the next rebirth.)

After six years, however, Siddhartha concluded that asceticism—like luxury—was not the way to perception. He abandoned a group of five monks with whom he had lived, and he wandered to Benares, where he achieved enlightenment (Sanskrit: *sambodhi*; Japanese: *satori*) or, as some prefer to call it, an "awakening" or an opening of the mind. This release of inner light or intuitive knowledge was not attained by self-castigation (e.g., by long fasts) or by scrupulous observations of rituals prescribed in sacred texts, but by meditation. Exactly what "meditation" is, however, is a topic much discussed by Buddhist sects.

The Buddha saw that the path to peace is the extinction of desires, the extinction of selfishness or of selfhood. The achievement of enlightenment is the attainment of *nirvana,* or release from the cycle of endless rebirth because all physical and psychic ties to the world are broken. Nirvana, which means something like "where no wind blows" or "without motion," is for Buddhism the real world; the illusory world that the unenlightened mistakenly believe is real is called *samsara*.

Some months after Shakyamuni became enlightened he revealed his doctrine in a sermon preached in the Deer Park near Benares. The gist of this sermon, later called "Setting in Motion the Wheel of Righteousness," is this:

1. all existence is suffering;
2. suffering is caused by craving for existence;

3. suffering can be suppressed;
4. the way to suppress suffering is to follow the eightfold path, which consists of right views, right intentions, right speech, right action, right livelihood, right effort, right mindfulness, and right concentration.

Early Buddhism, it should be noted, dispensed with the idea of divinity. Odd though it sounds, Buddhism was an atheistic religion.

Among Buddhist teachings are these:
that the phenomenal world is impermanent;
there is no permanent self, no soul (belief in a permanent self breeds attachment egotism, and a craving for existence);
good intentions are not enough;
sin is not a violation of a divine law, but is rather an act harmful to oneself or to another.

A few additional technical words in the Sermon at Benares need explanation. The Buddha is also called the *Tathagata*, which means "Thus Gone," i.e., he is one who has attained enlightenment. The *Vedas* are ancient sacred Hindu writings; a *deva* is a good spirit; the *wheel* is a common Buddhist symbol for the teachings of the Buddha. In ancient India the wheel symbolized empire, so in Buddhist thinking "to set the wheel in motion" is to engage in an expedition on behalf of the Kingdom of Righteousness.

## Gautama Buddha

# The Sermon at Benares and Parables

The five [monks] saw their old teacher approach and 1 agreed among themselves not to salute him, nor to address him as a master, but by his name only. "For," so they said, "he has broken his vow and has abandoned holiness. He is no [monk] but Gautama, and Gautama has become a man who lives in abundance and indulges in the pleasures of worldliness."

But when the Blessed One approached in a dignified manner, they involuntarily rose from their seats and greeted him in spite of their resolution. Still they called him by his name and addressed him as "friend."

When they had thus received the Blessed One, he said: "Do not call the Tathagata by his name nor address him 'friend,' for he is Buddha, the Holy One. Buddha looks equally with a kind heart on all living beings and they therefore call him 'Father.' To disrespect a father is wrong; to despise him, is sin.

"The Tathagata," Buddha continued, "does not seek salvation in austerities, but for that reason you must not think that he indulges in worldly pleasures, nor does he live in abundance. The Tathagata has found the middle path.

"Neither abstinence from fish or flesh, nor going naked, nor shaving the head, nor wearing matted hair, nor dressing in a rough garment, nor covering oneself with dirt, nor sacrificing to Agni, will cleanse a man who is not free from delusions.                                          5

"Reading the Vedas, making offerings to priests, or sacrifices to the gods, self-mortification by heat or cold, and many such penances performed for the sake of immortality, these do not cleanse the man who is not free from delusions.

"Anger, drunkenness, obstinacy, bigotry, deception, envy, self-praise, disparaging others, superciliousness, and evil intentions are rooted in delusion.

"Let me teach you, O [monks], the middle path, which keeps aloof from both extremes. By suffering, the emaciated devotee produces confusion and sickly thoughts in his mind. Mortification is not conducive even to worldly knowledge; how much less to a triumph over the senses!

"He who fills his lamp with water will not dispel the darkness, and he who tries to light a fire with rotten wood will fail.

"Mortifications are painful, vain, and profitless. And how can any      10
one be free from self by leading a wretched life if he does not succeed in quenching the fires of lust.

"All mortification is vain so long as self remains, so long as self continues to lust after either worldly or heavenly pleasures. But he in whom self has become extinct is free from lust; he will desire neither worldly nor heavenly pleasures, and the satisfaction of his natural wants will not defile him. Let him eat and drink according to the needs of the body.

"Water surrounds the lotus-flower, but does not wet its petals.

"On the other hand, sensuality of all kind is enervating. The sensual man is a slave of his passions, and pleasure-seeking is degrading and vulgar.

"But to satisfy the necessities of life is not evil. To keep the body in good health is a duty, for otherwise we shall not be able to trim the lamp of wisdom, and keep our mind strong and clear.

"This is the middle path, O [monks], that keeps aloof from both    15
extremes."

And the Blessed One spoke kindly to his disciples, pitying them for their errors, and pointing out the uselessness of their endeavors, and the ice of ill-will that chilled their hearts melted away under the gentle warmth of the Master's persuasion.

Now the Blessed One set the wheel of the most excellent law a-rolling, and he began to preach to the five [monks], opening to them the gate of immortality, and showing them the bliss of Nirvana.

And when the Blessed One began his sermon, a rapture thrilled through all the universes.

The devas left their heavenly abodes to listen to the sweetness of the truth; the saints that had parted from life crowded around the great teacher to receive the glad tidings; even the animals of the earth felt the bliss that rested upon the words of the Tathagata: and all the creatures of the host of sentient beings, gods, men, and beasts, hearing the message of deliverance, received and understood it in their own language.

Buddha said:    20

"The spokes of the wheel are the rules of pure conduct; justice is the uniformity of their length; wisdom is the tire; modesty and thoughtfulness are the hub in which the immovable axle of truth is fixed.

"He who recognizes the existence of suffering, its cause, its remedy, and its cessation has fathomed the four noble truths. He will walk in the right path.

"Right views will be the torch to light his way. Right aims will be his guide. Right words will be his dwelling-place on the road. His gait will be straight, for it is right behavior. His refreshments will be the right way of earning his livelihood. Right efforts will be his steps: right thoughts his breath; and peace will follow in his footprints."

And the Blessed One explained the instability of the ego.

"Whatsoever is originated will be dissolved again. All worry about    25
the self is vain; the ego is like a mirage, and all the tribulations that

touch it will pass away. They will vanish like a nightmare when the sleeper awakes.

"He who has awakened is freed from fear; he has become Buddha; he knows the vanity of all his cares, his ambitions, and also of his pains.

"It easily happens that a man, when taking a bath, steps upon a wet rope and imagines that it is a snake. Horror will overcome him, and he will shake from fear, anticipating in his mind all the agonies caused by the serpent's venomous bite. What a relief does this man experience when he sees that the rope is no snake. The cause of his fright lies in his error, his ignorance, his illusion. If the true nature of the rope is recognized, his tranquillity of mind will come back to him; he will feel relieved; he will be joyful and happy.

"This is the state of mind of one who has recognized that there is no self, that the cause of all his troubles, cares, and vanities is a mirage, a shadow, a dream.

"Happy is he who has overcome all selfishness; happy is he who has attained peace; happy is he who has found the truth.

"The truth is noble and sweet; the truth can deliver you from evil. 30 There is no saviour in the world except the truth.

"Have confidence in the truth, although you may not be able to comprehend it, although you may suppose its sweetness to be bitter, although you may shrink from it at first. Trust in the truth.

"The truth is best as it is. No one can alter it; neither can any one improve it. Have faith in the truth and live it.

"Errors lead astray; illusions beget miseries. They intoxicate like strong drinks; but they fade away soon and leave you sick and disgusted.

"Self is a fever; self is a transient vision, a dream; but truth is wholesome, truth is sublime, truth is everlasting. There is no immortality except in truth. For truth alone abideth forever."

And when the doctrine was propounded, the venerable Kaundi- 35 nya, the oldest one among the five [monks], discerned the truth with his mental eye, and he said: "Truly, O Buddha, our Lord, thou hast found the truth."

And the devas and saints and all the good spirits of the departed generations that had listened to the sermon of the Tathagata joyfully received the doctrine and shouted: "Truly, the Blessed One has founded the kingdom of righteousness. The Blessed One has moved the earth; he has set the wheel of Truth rolling, which by no one in the universe, be he god or man, can ever be turned back. The kingdom of Truth will be preached upon earth; it will spread; and righteousness, good-will, and peace will reign among mankind. . . ."

A foolish man, learning that the Buddha observed the principle of great love which commends the return of good for evil, came and abused him. The Buddha was silent, pitying his folly.

When the man had finished his abuse, the Buddha asked him, saying: "Son, if a man declined to accept a present made to him, to whom would it belong?" And he answered: "In that case, it would belong to the man who offered it."

"My son," said the Buddha, "thou hast railed at me, but I decline to accept thy abuse, and request thee to keep it thyself. Will it not be a source of misery to thee? As the echo belongs to the sound, and the shadow to the substance, so misery will overtake the evil-doer without fail."

The abuser made no reply, and Buddha continued: "A wicked man 40 who reproaches a virtuous one is like one who looks up and spits at heaven; the spittle soils not the heaven, but comes back and defiles his own person. The slanderer is like one who flings dust at another when the wind is contrary; the dust does but return on him who threw it. The virtuous man cannot be hurt and the misery that the other would inflict comes back on himself."

The abuser went away ashamed, but he came again and took refuge in the Buddha, the Law of Righteousness, and the Monastic Order.

And Buddha said: "All that we are is the result of what we have thought: it is founded on our thoughts, it is made up of our thoughts. If a man speaks or acts with an evil thought, pain follows him, as the wheel follows the foot of the ox that draws the carriage: If a man speaks or acts with a pure thought, happiness follows him, like a shadow that never leaves him.

"He abused me, he beat me, he defeated me, he robbed me"—in those who harbor such thoughts, hatred will never cease; in those who do not harbor such thoughts, hatred will cease. For hatred does not cease by hatred at any time: hatred ceases by love—that is an old rule.

He who lives looking for pleasures only, his senses uncontrolled, immoderate in his food, idle and weak, will certainly be overthrown by temptation, as the wind throws down a weak tree. He who lives without looking for pleasures, his senses well controlled, moderate in his food, faithful and strong, will certainly not be overthrown, any more than the wind throws down a rocky mountain. . . .

The thoughtless man, even if he can recite a large portion of the 45
law, but is not a doer of it, has no share in the priesthood, but is like
a cowherd counting the cows of others. The follower of the law, even
if he can recite only a small portion of the law, but, having forsaken
passion and hatred and foolishness, possesses true knowledge and
serenity of mind, he, caring for nothing in this world or that to come,
has indeed a share in the priesthood. . . .

As a fletcher makes straight his arrow, a wise man makes straight
his trembling and unsteady thought, which is difficult to guard, difficult to hold back. It is good to tame the mind, which is difficult to
hold in and flighty, rushing wherever it listeth; a tamed mind brings
happiness. Let the wise man guard his thoughts, for they are difficult
to perceive, very artful, and they rush wherever they list. . . .

And Punna, wishing to preach the path to enlightenment, sought
the Buddha, and the Buddha said, "But, O Punna, the men of that
country are violent, cruel and savage. When they become angry at you
and do you harm, what will you think then?"

"I shall think them truly good and kind folk, for whilst they speak
angry and insolent words, they refrain from striking or stoning me."

"They are very violent folk, Punna. What if they strike or stone
you?"

"I shall think them kind and good not to smite me with their staff 50
and sword."

"And what if they do so?"

"I shall think them kind and good indeed who free me from this
vile body with so little pain."

"Well said, Punna, well said. With your gift of patience, you may
indeed essay this task. Go, Punna, yourself saved, save others."

# Questions

1. In paragraph 2, why do you suppose the monks partly violated the
   resolution they had formed earlier? And why only partly?
2. In paragraphs 3 and 4 the Buddha speaks of himself in the third
   person. What do you make of this?
3. Why, in paragraph 7, are "anger, drunkenness," and other vices
   called "delusions."
4. The Buddha uses many metaphors, for example in paragraphs 9,
   12, and 21. Do you think these passages are effective? If you were
   abridging this sermon, would you delete them? And would you omit

paragraph 27 (the passage about the man who imagines that he has stepped on a snake)? Why, or why not would you omit such material?

5. In paragraph 39, in speaking of a "foolish man" who abused him, the Buddha says that if someone declines to accept the abuse of another person, the abuse "will . . . be a source of misery" to the abuser. Does this strike you as psychologically sound? Does your own experience confirm or contradict the point?

6. In paragraphs 47–51, *why* does the Buddha question Punna as he does?

## D. T. Suzuki

# What Is Zen?

The object of Zen training consists in making us realize  1 that Zen is our daily experience and that it is not something put in from the outside. Tennō Dōgo (T'ien-huang Tao-wu, 748–807) illustrates the point most eloquently in his treatment of a novice monk, while an unknown Japanese swordmaster demonstrates it in the more threatening manner characteristic of his profession. Tennō Dōgo's story runs as follows:

D[aisetz] T[eitaro] Suzuki (1870–1966) was one of Japan's leading writers on Zen Buddhism. He occasionally visited the United States, where he taught, lectured, and wrote. He is still regarded as the foremost interpreter of Zen Buddhism to the West.

Zen is the Japanese word for a school of Buddhism derived from China, where it was called Ch'an. In this essay Suzuki tries to explain *satori*, "enlightenment" or "awakening." The awakening is from a world of blind strivings (including those of reason and morality); the awakened being, free from a sense of the self in opposition to all other things, perceives the unity of all things. (When Suzuki was asked how it feels to have attained satori, he replied, "Just like ordinary everyday experience, except about two inches off the ground.")

Dōgo had a disciple called Sōshin (Ch'ung-hsin). When Sōshin was taken in as a novice, it was perhaps natural of him to expect lessons in Zen from his teacher the way a schoolboy is taught at school. But Dōgo gave him no special lessons on the subject, and this bewildered and disappointed Sōshin. One day he said to the master, "It is some time since I came here, but not a word has been given me regarding the essence of the Zen teaching." Dōgo replied, "Since your arrival I have ever been giving you lessons on the matter of Zen discipline."

"What kind of lesson could it have been?"

"When you bring me a cup of tea in the morning, I take it; when you serve me a meal, I accept it; when you bow to me I return it with a nod. How else do you expect to be taught in the mental discipline of Zen?"

Sōshin hung his head for a while, pondering the puzzling words of the master. The master said, "If you want to see, see right at once. When you begin to think, you miss the point."

The swordsman's story is this:

When a disciple came to a master to be disciplined in the art of sword-play, the master, who was in retirement in his mountain hut, agreed to undertake the task. The pupil was made to help him gather kindling, draw water from the nearby spring, split wood, make fires, cook rice, sweep the rooms and the garden, and generally look after his household. There was no regular or technical teaching in the art. After some time the young man became dissatisfied, for he had not come to work as servant to the old gentleman, but to learn the art of swordsmanship. So one day he approached the master and asked him to teach him. The master agreed.

The result was that the young man could not do any piece of work with any feeling of safety. For when he began to cook rice early in the morning, the master would appear and strike him from behind with a stick. When he was in the midst of his sweeping, he would be feeling the same sort of blow from somewhere, some unknown direction. He had no peace of mind, he had to be always on the *qui vive*. Some years passed before he could successfully dodge the blow from wherever it might come. But the master was not quite satisfied with him yet.

One day the master was found cooking his own vegetables over an open fire. The pupil took it into his head to avail himself of this opportunity. Taking up his big stick, he let it fall over the head of the master, who was then stooping over the cooking pan to stir its contents. But the pupil's stick was caught by the master with the cover of the pan. This opened the pupil's mind to the secrets of the art, which had hitherto been kept from him and to which he had so far been a stranger. He then, for the first time, appreciated the unparalleled kindness of the master.

The secrets of perfect swordsmanship consist in creating a certain 2 frame or structure of mentality which is made always ready to respond instantly, that is, im-mediately, to what comes from the outside. While technical training is of great importance, it is after all something artificially, consciously, calculatingly added and acquired. Unless the mind that avails itself of the technical skill somewhat attunes itself to a state of the utmost fluidity or mobility, anything acquired or superimposed lacks spontaneity of natural growth. This state prevails when the mind is awakened to a *satori*. What the swordsman aimed at was to make the disciple attain to this realization. It cannot be taught by any system specifically designed for the purpose, it must simply grow from within. The master's system was really no system in the proper sense. But there was a "natural" method in his apparent craziness, and he succeeded in awakening in his young disciple's mind something that touched off the mechanism needed for the mastery of swordsmanship.

Dōgo the Zen master did not have to be attacking his disciple all 3 the time with a stick. The swordsman's object was more definite and limited to the area of the sword, whereas Dōgo wanted to teach by getting to the source of being from which everything making up our daily experience ensues. Therefore, when Sōshin began to reflect on the remark Dōgo made to him, Dōgo told him: "No reflecting whatever. When you want to see, see im-mediately. As soon as you tarry [that is, as soon as an intellectual interpretation or mediation takes place], the whole thing goes awry." This means that, in the study of Zen, conceptualization must go, for as long as we tarry at this level we can never reach the area where Zen has its life. The door of enlightenment-experience opens by itself as one finally faces the deadlock of intellectualization.

We now can state a few things about Zen in a more or less sum- 4 mary way:

1. Zen discipline consists in attaining enlightenment (or *satori*, in 5 Japanese).

2. *Satori* finds a meaning hitherto hidden in our daily concrete 6 particular experiences, such as eating, drinking, or business of all kinds.

3. The meaning thus revealed is not something added from the  7
outside. It is in being itself, in becoming itself, in living itself. This is
called, in Japanese, a life of *kono-mama* or *sono-mama*.[1] Kono- or sono-
mama means the "isness" of a thing. Reality in its isness.

4. Some may say, "There cannot be any meaning in mere isness."  8
But this is not the view held by Zen, for according to it, isness is the
meaning. When I see into it I see it as clearly as I see myself reflected
in a mirror.

5. This is what made Hō Koji (P'ang Chü-shih), a lay disciple of  9
the eighth century, declare:

How wondrous this, how mysterious!
I carry fuel, I draw water.

The fuel-carrying or the water-drawing itself, apart from its utilitar-
ianism, is full of meaning; hence its "wonder," its "mystery."

6. Zen does not, therefore, indulge in abstraction or in concep-  10
tualization. In its verbalism it may sometimes appear that Zen does
this a great deal. But this is an error most commonly entertained by
those who do not at all know Zen.

7. *Satori* is emancipation, moral, spiritual, as well as intellectual.  11
When I am in my isness, thoroughly purged of all intellectual sedi-
ments, I have my freedom in its primary sense.

8. When the mind, now abiding in its isness—which, to use Zen  12
verbalism, is not isness—and thus free from intellectual complexities
and moralistic attachments of every description, surveys the world of
the senses in all its multiplicities, it discovers in it all sorts of values
hitherto hidden from sight. Here opens to the artist a world full of
wonders and miracles.

9. The artist's world is one of free creation, and this can come only  13
from intuitions directly and im-mediately rising from the isness of
things, unhampered by senses and intellect. He creates forms and
sounds out of formlessness and soundlessness. To this extent, the artist's world coincides with that of Zen.

10. What differentiates Zen from the arts is this: While the artists  14
have to resort to the canvas and brush or mechanical instruments or
some other mediums to express themselves, Zen has no need of things

---

[1] *Kono* is "this," *sono* "that," and *mama* means "as-it-is-ness." Kono-mama or sono-
mama thus corresponds to the Sanskrit *tathatā*, "suchness," and to the Chinese *chih-
mo* or *shih-mo*.

external, except "the body" in which the Zen-man is so to speak embodied. From the absolute point of view this is not quite correct; I say it only in concession to the worldly way of saying things. What Zen does is to delineate itself on the infinite canvas of time and space the way the flying wild geese cast their shadow on the water below without any idea of doing so, while the water reflects the geese just as naturally and unintentionally.

11. The Zen-man is an artist to the extent that, as the sculptor    15 chisels out a great figure deeply buried in a mass of inert matter, the Zen-man transforms his own life into a work of creation, which exists, as Christians might say, in the mind of God.[2]

# Questions

1. In paragraph 2 Suzuki first uses the word "im-mediately." Why does he add the hyphen? (Check a dictionary if you don't know the Latin origin of the word.)
2. Suzuki in this essay is teaching the meaning of Zen. How does he go about teaching? How successful do you find his methods?
3. In paragraph 13 Suzuki says that the artist, like the enlightened person, works from "intuition" and is "unhampered by senses and intellect." What do you understand him to mean by intuition? What value does the work of art have for the artist? Does it have the same value for us?

## A Note on Islam

Islam means, in Arabic, "submission." The Muslim submits to the will and precepts of God as they were transmitted to human beings by God's prophet Muhammad and set forth in the Quran (or Koran).

Although Muslims believe Islam is the only true faith, they also believe that the faith was revealed through prophets before Muham-

[2] After writing the above I feel somewhat uneasy lest my readers may not be able to comprehend what Zen means to us of modern time. Everything of life nowadays shows the tendency to turn into a complete routine of mechanization, leaving nothing that will demonstrate the dignity and destiny of human existence.

mad. The line of inspired prophets included Ibrahim (Abraham, regarded as the first Muslim because he was the first to submit fully to the word of God), Musa (Moses), Dawid (David), and Isa (Jesus). The full and final revelation, however, came through the last prophet, Muhammad (570?–632). He received his revelation from about 610 to the year of his death, 632, and it is now embodied in the Quran, a text which supersedes the previous revelations.

Jews and Christians thus are not regarded by Muslims as nonbelievers, since they share with Muslims the belief in one God; but they are regarded as persons who are not true believers, since they do not believe in the Quran and in Muhammad's mission.

Wilfred Cantwell Smith's essay, "Muslims," provides an admirable introduction to the faith of Islam, but a few points can be made here, by way of introduction. Islam imposes five chief obligations on the faithful. These obligations listed below are called the five pillars of Islam.

1. Testimony, or the profession of faith, through the repetition of "There is no god but God, and Muhammad is His prophet."
2. Devotional worship or prayer, five times a day—sunrise, midday, afternoon, sunset, evening—facing Mecca.
3. Payment of a religious tax, or alms. This is considered, like prayer, to be a form of worship. It implies the duty of the fortunate toward the less fortunate.
4. Fasting, during the month of Ramadan, from dawn to sunset. Believers fast (and abstain from sexual relations) in order (among other things) to remind themselves that they do not live by bread alone; to subjugate their passions and to purify their being; and to experience the pangs that the poor often feel.
5. Pilgrimage to Mecca.

## Wilfred Cantwell Smith

# Muslims

Almost any visitor to India interested in the religious life 1
of its people will note a striking difference architecturally between a
Hindu temple and a Muslim mosque. The temple is apt to be ornate,
even florid. Its involute complexity suggests that truth is much more
elaborate than one had supposed, and denies nothing, not even incongruity. Very different is the stark simplicity of the Muslim place of
worship. The mighty Imperial Mosque in Delhi, for example, is a structure whose artistic impressiveness and power come from the use of
straight lines and simple curves, splendidly graceful and yet austerely
disciplined. Certainly it is brilliantly conceived and its impact is immediate: one grasps at once the balance and dignity, the spacious reverence, the serenity of its straightforward affirmation. Its architect's
vision of the glory of God, and of man's service due to Him, is evidently
an ordered vision.

Such a point is confirmed if one has the privilege of witnessing a 2
service in such a mosque, especially at one of the great festival prayers,
where perhaps a hundred thousand people array themselves in neat
lines and bow in precise unison as token of their personal and corporate
submission to the will of God, which is definite and sure.

A similar contrast can be seen in the realm of doctrine. For a Hindu, 3
there are various systems of ideas, involute, elaborate, and always
tentative, from among which he may choose. In contrast, the Muslim
community symbolizes its belief in probably the simplest, tidiest creed
in all the world. I am sure that you have all heard it: "There is no god
but God, and Muhammad is God's apostle." The Muslims themselves
refer to this simply as "the two words," or even "the word." And
while this may be carrying compression just a trifle far, still its two
pithy clauses are, certainly, as succinct and clean as one could hope
to find.

---

Wilfred Cantwell Smith was born in Toronto in 1916, and educated at the University of Toronto and at Princeton University. After working from 1941 to 1949
with Muslims in India, he returned to Canada where he taught Islamic studies
at McGill University from 1949 to 1963. Since 1964 he has taught religion at
Harvard University.

Because of its centrality, and its neatness, this simple creed may    4
well provide us with the item for our consideration of the Muslims.
As with other religious communities, so with the Islamic, we choose
one element from out of the formal pattern of their faith, in the hope
that, exploring it, we may find that it can lead us, if not to the heart
of their religious life, at least into its precincts, and can suggest something of the richness of what lies behind. What better emblem of the
Muslim's faith, for our purposes, than this crystallized creed, which
the Muslims themselves have chosen to sum up their belief? To repeat
this creed is, formally, to become a Muslim; perhaps to understand it
is to understand a Muslim. Or let me put the point more realistically:
to begin to understand it may be to go some distance, at least, towards
understanding the position of those whose faith it typifies.

In suggesting the coherence and simplicity of the Muslim confes-    5
sion of faith, I do not wish to suggest that it is limited or lacks profundity. A mosque may be very intricately decorated—fine interlacing
arabesques and the endlessly delicate complexities of an elaborate calligraphy usually embroider the arches and the walls—yet these decorations, however ornate in themselves, are regularly held in strict
subordination to an over-all pattern that is essentially simple, so that
detail is organized into a coherent unity. Similarly in the realm of doctrine. The Muslim world has produced its philosophers and theologians, constructing elaborate systems of ideas—the names of Avicenna
and Averroes are probably the best known in the West, but there are
many others also who worked out in careful detail considerable structures of thought. And there were also meticulously elaborate systems
of law, comprehensive and ramified. But again, these were subordinate
to the higher truth, the simpler truth, of the creed.

As one gets closer to truth, one gets closer to God; and God is    6
one. He is majestic, mighty, awesome, merciful, and many other
things, but above all, for the Muslim, He is one. Every other sin, the
theologians affirm, may be forgiven man, but not that of *shirk,* polytheism, the failure to recognize that the final truth and power of the
universe is one.

Before we turn to questions of meaning, which are of course our    7
chief concern, let us note a few points about the formula as a formula.
I suppose that every effective religious symbol is not only inexhaustibly
meaningful in what it stands for, but is also in some ways intrinsically
interesting in itself. This one certainly is. We have already remarked
that it is short. It is also pungent and crisp. In the original Arabic—
the language in which it is always used, no matter what the actual

language of the people concerned, from Indonesian to African Swahili, from South Indian Malayalam to Turkish—in Arabic it is resonant and rolling, packing quite a punch. It so happens that of the fifteen syllables, about half begin with an *l* sound, or end with it, or both. This liquid alliteration, added to the rhyme, and to a very marked rhythm, is quite forceful. *Lā-'i-lā-ha-'il-lal-lāh; Mu-ham-ma-dur-ra-sū-lul-lāh.*

Then there is a calligraphic point. In the Arabic alphabet, which 8 is anyway highly decorative, it so happens that this particular set of words when written out is strikingly patterned, and lends itself to very picturesque presentation.

The formula is certainly in constant service. For example, it is whis- 9 pered in the ears of the newborn baby, so that its affirmation may be the first words that a Muslim shall hear on entering this world. And between then and its use at his funeral, he will hear it, and pronounce it, often and often and often. And apart from its ceremonial and—as it were—sacred use, it can be found in everyday affairs also. I remember a scene in India some years ago when my wife and I were one summer at a mountain resort in the Himalayas, and were out for a hike in the hills; we came upon a work-gang busy in the construction of a rude mountain road. It was, of course, all hand labor; they had crushed the stones with hammers, and were now rolling them with a large and very heavy roller. Rather in the fashion of sailors working to a sea shanty, they were rhythmically pulling this heavy roller in spurts of concerted effort: the foreman would sing out *Lā ilāha illa 'llāh,* and the rest of the gang, then, would put their shoulders to the ropes and with a heave would respond *Muhammadur rasūlu 'llāh.* This went on and on, as they continued to work, with a will and with good strong heaves. *Lā ilāha illa 'llāh* he would chant; *Muhammadur rasūlu 'llāh* would come the vigorous response. Such a scene represents, of course, a kind of living in which a split into religious and secular has not come—or has not yet come—to segment life. At a different level, of course, are the formal ceremonies in the weekly service of some of the Islamic Sufi orders, in which the initiate devotees will induce a mystic ecstasy or trance by the solemn and rhythmic repetition or incantation of the formula.

Between these two comes a religious use such as that by the 10 *mu'azzin* in his call to prayer five times a day, whose sonorous recitative from the minaret punctuates village or town life and summons the faithful to turn for a moment from their routine affairs to the life of the spirit.

I have called this creed a symbol; and in some ways it plays in 11

Muslim life a role similar to that played, for instance, for Christians by the cross. Nonetheless it is not a pictorial sign but a verbal one, and this itself is significant and appropriate. The role of linguistic form, of words, in Islamic religious life is quite special. I have already spoken of the written word—calligraphy—as a typical Muslim art form. This community has carried the decorative use of writing probably further than has any other people. And take revelation itself. In the Christian case this takes the form of a person, whereas for the Muslim it too is verbal. In the Qur'an, God makes himself and His purpose known to man in the form of words. It is altogether appropriate, then, that the chief symbol of Islam should also be verbal.

So far, I have allowed myself to follow the usual Western practice    12 of calling this two-phrase synopsis of the Muslim's faith a "creed." For to do this is not altogether misleading, though you will have seen that its place in Muslim life is only partly correlative with that of the creed for us. It is time now, however, to modify this still further. We need to see more carefully ways in which the faith of other people is expressed in patterns that do not quite correspond to our own—or even to what we expect of them.

In some ways, then, the "two words" of the Islamic assertion do    13 constitute a creed, a statement of belief, but in other ways they do not; and the Muslims do not themselves call this formula a creed. They call it, rather, a "witness." Regularly the statement is preceded by the words "I bear witness that" there is no god . . . and so on. And even when these actual terms are not employed, an idea of witnessing is involved, and can be quite basic. The Islamic has been one of the three great missionary communities in human history (along with the Buddhist and the Christian); and the idea of bearing witness to his faith is quite central to a Muslim's attitudes. His assertion is not so much an affirmation of belief, as a proclamation—of conviction. And in a subtle fashion, there is involved here a point that I rather imagine is more basic in all religious life perhaps than is usually recognized. It is this: that it is not so much that the Muslim *believes* that God is one, and Muhammad is His prophet, as it is that he takes this for granted. He presupposes it, and goes on from there. From his own point of view, one might almost say that, so far as he is concerned, he *knows* that these things are so, and what he is doing is simply announcing them, bearing witness to them.

The same kind of thing is true, I think, of all religious life. One    14 distorts a Christian's faith, for example, by saying simply that he believes Jesus Christ to be divine, to be the son of God. He would rather say that he recognizes this—these are the facts, and he has been fortunate enough to see them. In the Christian case the matter has been somewhat complicated by the use in Western languages of a single verb, *credo,* "I believe," and so on, both for intellectual belief (belief that) and for religious faith (belief in)—though men of faith have insisted that the two things are different. Anyway, I feel that true faith has already begun to crumble a bit, if it has not actually gone, as soon as people have reduced what used to be the data, the presuppositions, of their world view to a set of true-or-false propositions—I mean, when what was once the presupposed context or intellectual background for a transcending religious faith becomes rather the foreground of intellectual belief. This is one of the fundamental troubles in the modern world, and one of the fundamental problems arising from a recognition of religious diversity—that what used to be unconscious premises become, rather, scrutinized intellectualizations. At this new level the believer himself begins to wonder if he really "believes," in this new sense (and often enough finds that he actually does not).

In the Islamic case, as in the Jewish, the word of God is, funda- 15
mentally, an imperative. And even the proclamation of God's oneness is in some ways more a command, to worship Him alone, than merely an invitation to believe that He is there alone. Faith differs from belief in many ways, and goes beyond it; one way is that faith in God's oneness is a recognition of His unique and exclusive authority, and an active giving of oneself to it. Like the Christian, the classical Muslim theologian has seen faith as a commitment. He would understand at once St. James in the New Testament writing, "You believe that God is one? You do well: the devils also believe—and tremble." To a truly religious man, the question is not one merely of belief, but of doing something about it.

Having said that, however, we on the outside may still ask what 16
the presuppositions are; what belief is presumed, for those who do go on to commitment.

We find ourselves having come round, then, to the question that 17
we earlier postponed, the question of the meaning of the "two words." What does it mean to say "There is no god but God, and Muhammad is His apostle"? What does it mean, that is, to a Muslim—to someone to whom these two clauses are not merely true, but profoundly and cosmically true, are the two most important and final truths in the world, and the most crucial for man and his destiny?

Let us look at each in turn. 18

To say that there is one God, and that He alone is to be wor- 19 shipped, means at its most immediate, as it meant in pagan Arabia when it was first proclaimed, a rejection of polytheism and idolatry. When Muhammad captured Mecca in A.D. 630, and set up Islam in triumph, he gave a general amnesty to the human beings there who had resisted his cause and were now defeated, but he smashed without quarter the idols—three hundred and sixty of them, it is said—in the shrine of the Ka'bah, the figures of the pagans' gods. From that day to this, Islam has been uncompromising in its doctrine of monotheism, and its insistence on transcendence: God the Creator and Judge is Lord of all the universe, is high above all his creatures and beyond them, and beyond all their imaginings—and certainly beyond all their representations. Other deities, it asserts, are but the figments of men's wayward imagination, are unadulterated fiction; they just do not exist. Man must not bow down to them nor worship them, or look to them for help, or think about them. God is God alone; on this point Islam is emphatic, positive, and clear.

Historically, as the Islamic movement has spread, across the centuries, from Arabia through the Near East and into Central Asia and has penetrated China, into India and South-East Asia, across Africa and still today is spreading down into Africa, it has met polytheism in many forms, has attacked it and replaced it. Like the Church in the Roman Empire and Northern Europe, and later in the Americas, so Islam in large parts of the world has superseded polytheistic practice and thought with monotheistic. 20

At a subtler level, for those capable of seeing it, the doctrine has meant also at times, and certainly ought to mean, a rejection of human tyranny. God alone is to be worshipped, to be served. For the man for whom this faith is sufficiently vivid, this can mean that no earthly power, no human figure, deserves or can legitimately claim man's allegiance; and any attempt to impose a purely human yoke on man's neck is an infringement not only of human dignity but of cosmic order, and to submit to it would be sin. Admittedly there has been, especially in periods of decline, an alternative interpretation whereby God's governance of affairs is taken as determining not what ought to be but what is. This view has led to fatalism—a passive acceptance of whatever happens. Perhaps you will feel that I am intruding my own predilections here in siding with those Muslims who have taken rather the activist line, asserting God's will as something to be striven for, as was done more widely in Islam's earlier centuries, and is beginning to be done again in our own day. You will agree, in any case, that it is legitimate and proper, in interpreting other men's faith as in one's 21 own, to try to see it at its best and highest. That at least is what I am trying to do throughout these talks.

There is still a third level of meaning, which was stressed partic-    22
ularly by the Sufi mystics in the medieval period, and is beginning to get wide support today. According to this view, to worship God alone is to turn aside from false gods not only in the concrete sense of idols and religious polytheism, but also in the subtler sense of turning aside from a moral polytheism, from false values—the false gods of the heart. To pursue merely earthly goals, to value them, to give them one's allegiance and in a sense to worship them—goals such as wealth, prestige, sex, national aggrandizement, comfort, or all the other distractions and foibles of human life—this, says the sensitive Muslim conscience, like the sensitive Christian or Jewish one, is to infringe the principle of monotheism. Similarly, to look for help to purely mundane forces, to rely upon armies or clever stratagems, to trust anything that is not intrinsically good—this is to have more than one god. The affirmation that God alone is to be worshipped means, for the man of true piety and rigorous sincerity, that no other objective must claim man's effort or loyalty; he must fear no other power, honor no other prize, pursue no other goal.

I would mention, finally, one other interpretation of the "no god    23
but God" phrase, one that again has been put forward by some of the mystics. This one has not been widespread, even among these; yet I mention it because I personally find it attractive, and it shows the kind of thing that can be done. This particular view is in line with the general position taken by the mystics that the religious life is a process, a movement in faith. According to this interpretation, then, the statement that "there is no god but God" is to be taken in stages. No man, this reading suggests, can legitimately and truly say "God" who has not previously said, and meant, "no god." To arrive at true faith, one must first pass through a stage of unbelief. "There is no god": this comes first, and must be lived through in all sincerity, and all terror. A person brought up in a religious tradition must have seen through that tradition, its forms and fancies, its shams and shibboleths; he must have learned the bleakness of atheism, and have experienced its meaninglessness and eventually its dread. Only such a person is able to go on, perhaps only years later, to a faith that is without superficiality and without merely cheap and secondhand glibness. If one has said "there is no god" with the anguish of a genuine despair, one may then, with God's grace, go on to say ". . . but God," and say it with the ecstasy of genuine insight.

Let us turn, next, to the second proposition: "Muhammad is the 24 apostle of God." The first thing to grasp here is that this is a statement not about Muhammad's status but about his function. The Islamic concept of apostle, or prophet, is quite special; and one is misled if one too readily assumes that this corresponds to ideas familiar to us in the West. The underlying notion here, and it is tacitly presupposed by the formulation, is that God has something to say to mankind, and has from time to time chosen certain persons in various communities through whom to say it; the assertion here is that Muhammad was one of those persons. It too, then, is in significant degree, and even primarily, a statement about God. As the theologians worked it out, it involves the conviction that God is not essentially passive, inscrutable, content to remain transcendent; rather than from all eternity, and as part of His very nature, He is the kind of God who has something to say to mankind. What He has to say is what we would call the moral law. When He created the universe and when He created man, He did not exactly create the moral law, for this comes closer to being, rather, a part of Himself—but anyway He ordained it, or set it forth, and He created man to receive it, free and responsible to carry it out.

This is the first affirmation. The second is that He communicated 25 this moral law to mankind. He did not leave man to grope about in the dark, to discover for himself, by his own efforts, what he could. No; God Himself acted, and spoke—spoke through the mouth of the prophets and apostles, beginning with Adam, that is, from the very beginning of history. Religion is nowadays sometimes spoken of as man's search for God. On this, the Islamic position is like the Jewish and the Christian, rejecting such a view emphatically, and asserting rather that God takes the initiative. As Micah put it, in our Judeo-Christian tradition, "He hath *shown* thee, O man, what is good. . . ." Man's business in the religious life is not a quest but a response.

Thirdly, in the message that God communicated is to be found, 26 in the Muslim view, not what is true so much, though of course they do hold this, but what is *right*. The position differs from the Christian in that it is a revelation *from* God, more than *of* God. The apostle or prophet is one who conveys to men the message that God wants them to know; namely, how they should live. Accordingly, out of the message theoreticians and systematizers have extracted and constructed a law, finally elaborated in all detail and ultimately turned into a static system.

One last point, and with this I close. I said a moment ago that the 27 phrase "Muhammad is the apostle of God" is a statement not about Muhammad's status so much as about his function. Let me elaborate this just a little. The position stands over against the quite different Christian orientation, which sees the person of Christ as central and ultimate, pre-existent and divine. Muslims also posit a central and ultimate truth, pre-existent and divine, namely the Qur'an—not a person but a book, or better, what the book says. Muhammad plays in the Islamic scheme the role played in the Christian system by St. Paul or St. Peter; namely, that of an apostle who proclaims among men God's gift to them, which in the Islamic case is the scripture. In contrast to the Christian conviction, you might almost say that the Muslims' affirmation about their prophet is not a statement about Muhammad's person at all, but about the Qur'an and "what Muhammad brought." To say that he is an apostle, sent by God, is to affirm these things that we have noted, about God, and about the kind of universe that we live in, and about the human situation, and morality; and then within that framework it is to assert further that the message purveyed by Muhammad is authentic. If you believe this, then you are accepting as incumbent upon you in an ultimate moral sense the practical duties that flow from this tradition. For you are recognizing the obligation to perform them as not of human origin but of divine. Those of us for whom the content of morality is not defined in this historical source should nonetheless not allow this to obscure from us the cosmic things that those inspired from this source are saying about morality, about man, and about God.

# Questions

1. Consider the first three paragraphs as a piece of writing. Are they clear? If so, by what means did the author achieve clarity? If they are not clear, what are the causes of the obscurity?

2. In paragraph 14 Smith distinguishes between "belief in" and "belief that." Suppose a friend did not quite get Smith's point. Clarify it for this friend.

3. In paragraph 15 Smith says, "To a truly religious man, the question is not one merely of belief, but of doing something about it." (Presumably "doing something" means more than making an occasional monetary contribution to the church, and more than attending church sporadically or even regularly.) Do you think Smith is going too far here? Do you know many people who, by this stan-

dard, are "truly religious"? If so—and of course you yourself may be such a person—what do they do?

4.  In the West, Muslims (or followers of Islam) are often called Muhammadans (or Mohammedans). Why is the term "Muhammadan" offensive to Muslims? Why is the term *not* comparable to "Christian"? (Notice that Smith touches on this point in paragraph 27.)

5.  Taking the criteria set forth in the first paragraph, where a Hindu temple is contrasted with a Muslim mosque, what does a Gothic cathedral suggest, contasted with a New England Protestant church or with a southwest adobe Roman Catholic church? (You can find pictures of temples and mosques in Hugh Honour and John Fleming, *The Visual Arts;* for Hindu temples, see also Sherman E. Lee, *A History of Far Eastern Art;* for mosques, see Bernard Lewis, ed., *Islam and the Arab World;* and for Gothic cathedrals, see H. W. Janson, *History of Art.)*

## Idries Shah

# Two Islamic Tales

## 1. The Three Perceptives

There were once three Sufis, so observant and experienced in life that they were known as The Three Perceptives.

One day during their travels they encountered a camelman, who said: 'Have you seen my camel? I have lost it.'

'Was it blind in one eye?' asked the first Perceptive.

'Yes,' said the cameldriver.

'Has it one tooth missing in front?' asked the second Perceptive.

'Yes, yes,' said the cameldriver.

'Is it lame in one foot?' asked the third Perceptive.

'Yes, yes, yes,' said the cameldriver.

The three Perceptives then told the man to go back along the way they had come, and that he might hope to find it. Thinking that they had seen it, the man hurried on his way.

---

Idries Shah, born in 1924, is a leading authority on Sufi thought.

But the man did not find his camel, and he hastened to catch up with the Perceptives, hoping that they would tell him what to do.

He found them that evening, at a resting-place.

'Has your camel honey on one side and a load of corn on the other?' asked the first Perceptive.

'Yes,' said the man.

'Is there a pregnant woman mounted upon it?' asked the second Perspective.

'Yes, yes,' said the man.

'We do not know where it is,' said the third Perceptive.

The cameldriver was now convinced that the Perceptives had stolen his camel, passenger and all, and he took them to the judge, accusing them of the theft.

The Judge thought that he had made out a case, and detained the three men in custody on suspicion of theft.

A little later, the man found his camel wandering in some fields, and returning to the court, arranged for the Perceptives to be released.

The judge, who had not given them a chance to explain themselves before, asked how it was that they knew so much about the camel, since they had apparently not even seen it.

'We saw the footprints of a camel on the road,' said the first Perceptive.

'One of the tracks was faint: it must have been lame,' said the second Perceptive.

'It had stripped the bushes at only one side of the road, so it must have been blind in one eye,' said the third Perceptive.

'The leaves were shredded, which indicated the loss of a tooth,' continued the first Perceptive.

'Bees and ants, on different sides of the road, were swarming over something deposited; we saw that this was honey and corn,' said the second Perceptive.

'We found long human hair where someone had stopped and dismounted, it was a woman's,' said the third Perceptive.

'Where the person had sat down there were palm-prints, we thought from the use of the hands that the woman was probably very pregnant and had to stand up in that way,' said the first Perceptive.

'Why did you not apply for your side of the case to be heard so that you could explain yourselves?' asked the judge.

'Because we reckoned that the cameldriver would continue looking for his camel and might find it soon,' said the first Perceptive.

'He would feel generous in releasing us through his discovery,' said the second Perceptive.

'The curiosity of the Judge would prompt an enquiry,' said the third Perceptive.

'Discovering the truth by his own enquiries would be better for all than for us to claim that we had been impatiently handled,' said the first Perceptive.

'It is our experience that it is generally better for people to arrive at truth through what they take to be their own volition,' said the second Perceptive.

'It is time for us to move on, for there is work to be done,' said the third Perceptive.

And the Sufi thinkers went on their way. They are still to be found at work on the highways of the earth.

## 2. The Man, the Snake, and the Stone

One day a man who had not a care in the world was walking along a road. An unusual object to one side of him caught his eye. 'I must find out what this is,' he said to himself.

As he came up to it, he saw that it was a large, very flat stone.

'I must find out what is underneath this,' he told himself. And he lifted the stone.

No sooner had he done so than he heard a loud, hissing sound, and a huge snake came gliding out from a hole under the stone. The man dropped the stone in alarm. The snake wound itself into a coil, and said to him:

'Now I am going to kill you, for I am a venomous snake.'

'But I have released you,' said the man, 'how can you repay good with evil? Such an action would not accord with reasonable behaviour.'

'In the first place,' said the snake, 'you lifted the stone from curiosity and in ignorance of the possible consequences. How can this now suddenly become "I have released you"?'

'We must always try to return to reasonable behaviour, when we stop to think,' murmured the man.

'Return to it when you think invoking it might suit your interests,' said the snake.

'Yes,' said the man, 'I was a fool to expect reasonable behaviour from a snake.'

'From a snake, expect snake-behaviour,' said the snake. 'To a snake, snake-behaviour is what can be regarded as reasonable.'

'Now I am going to kill you,' it continued.

'Please do not kill me,' said the man, 'give me another chance. You have taught me about curiosity, reasonable behaviour and snake-behaviour. Now you would kill me before I can put this knowledge into action.'

'Very well,' said the snake, 'I shall give you another chance. I shall come along with you on your journey. We will ask the next creature whom we meet, who shall be neither a man nor a snake, to adjudicate between us.'

The man agreed, and they started on their way.

Before long they came to a flock of sheep in a field. The snake stopped, and the man cried to the sheep:

'Sheep, sheep, please save me! This snake intends to kill me. If you tell him not to do so he will spare me. Give a verdict in my favour, for I am a man, the friend of sheep.'

One of the sheep answered:

'We have been put out into this field after serving a man for many years. We have given him wool year after year, and now that we are old, tomorrow he will kill us for mutton. That is the measure of the generosity of men. Snake, kill that man!'

The snake reared up and his green eyes glittered as he said to the man: 'This is how your friends see you. I shudder to think what your enemies are like!'

'Give me one more chance,' cried the man in desperation. 'Please let us find someone else to give an opinion, so that my life may be spared.'

'I do not want to be as unreasonable as you think I am,' said the snake, 'and I will therefore continue in accordance with your pattern, and not with mine. Let us ask the next individual whom we may meet—being neither a man nor a snake—what your fate is to be.'

The man thanked the snake, and they continued on their journey.

Presently they came upon a lone horse, standing hobbled in a field. The snake addressed him:

'Horse, horse, why are you hobbled like that?'

The horse said:

'For many years I served a man. He gave me food, for which I had not asked, and he taught me to serve him. He said that this was in exchange for the food and stable. Now that I am too infirm to work, he has decided to sell me soon for horse-meat. I am hobbled because the man thinks that if I roam over this field I will eat too much of his grass.'

'Do not make this horse my judge, for God's sake!' exclaimed the man.

'According to our compact,' said the snake inexorably, 'this man and I have agreed to have our case judged by you.'

He outlined the matter, and the horse said:

'Snake, it is beyond my capabilities and not in my nature to kill a man. But I feel that you, as a snake, have no alternative but to do so if a man is in your power.'

'If you will give me just one more chance,' begged the man, 'I am sure that something will come to my aid. I have been unlucky on this journey so far, and have only come across creatures who have a grudge. Let us therefore choose some animal which has no such knowledge and hence no generalised animosity towards my kind.'

'People do not know snakes,' said the snake, 'and yet they seem to have a generalised animosity towards them. But I am willing to give you just one more chance.'

They continued their journey.

Soon they saw a fox, lying asleep under a bush beside the road. The man woke the fox gently, and said:

'Fear nothing, brother fox. My case is such-and-such, and my future depends upon your decision. The snake will give me no further chance, so only your generosity or altruism can help me.'

The fox thought for a moment, and then he said:

'I am not sure that only generosity or altruism can operate here. But I will engage myself in this matter. In order to come to a decision I must rely upon something more than hearsay. We must demonstrate as well. Come, let us return to the beginning of your journey, and examine the facts on the spot.'

They returned to where the first encounter had taken place.

'Now we will reconstruct the situation,' said the fox; 'snake, be so good as to take your place once more, in your hole under that flat stone.'

The man lifted the stone, and the snake coiled itself up in the hollow beneath it. The man let the stone fall.

The snake was now trapped again, and the fox, turning to the man, said: 'We have returned to the beginning. The snake cannot get out unless you release him. He leaves our story at this point.'

'Thank you, thank you,' said the man, his eyes full of tears.

'Thanks are not enough, brother,' said the fox; 'In addition to generosity and altruism there is the matter of my payment.'

'How can you enforce payment?' asked the man.

'Anyone who can solve the problem which I have just concluded,' said the fox, 'is well able to take care of such a detail as that. I again invite you to recompense me, from fear if not from any sense of justice. Shall we call it, in your words, being "reasonable"?'

The man said:

'Very well, come to my house and I will give you a chicken.'

They went to the man's house. The man went into his chicken-coop, and came back in a moment with a bulging sack. The fox seized it and was about to open it when the man said:

'Friend fox, do not open the sack here. I have human neighbours and they should not know that I am co-operating with a fox. They might kill you, as well as censuring me.'

'That is a reasonable thought,' said the fox; 'what do you suggest I do?'

'Do you see that clump of trees yonder?' said the man, pointing. 'Yes,' said the fox.

'You run with the sack into that cover, and you will be able to enjoy your meal unmolested.'

The fox ran off.

As soon as he reached the trees a party of hunters, whom the man knew would be there, caught him. He leaves our story here.

And the man? His future is yet to come.

# Questions

*The Three Perceptives*

1. Early in the story the first Perceptive asks if the camel is blind, but later it is the third Perceptive who explains how they knew it was blind. Similarly, the second asks if the camel lacks a tooth, but it is the first who explains how they knew this; and it is the third who asks if the camel is lame, but it is the second who cites the evidence. Why not have the first give the evidence that explains his conjecture, the second give the evidence for *his* conjecture, and the third give the evidence for *his*? Would such an arrangement in any way change the meaning of the story?

2. In paragraph 34 the third Perceptive says, "It is time for us to move on, for there is work to be done." What kind of work do you suppose he has in mind?
3. We are told that the three Perceptives are Sufis—that is, Muslim mystics. But we do not see them in ecstatic states, or in trances. What, perhaps, is the teller of the tale implying about Sufis? Or about wisdom?
4. What, in your opinion, is the chief point (or what are the chief points) of the story?

*The Man, the Snake, and the Stone*
1. At the outset we are told that the man "had not a care in the world." What, if anything, does this detail add to the story?
2. When the man addresses the sheep he says, "Sheep, sheep," and when he addresses the horse he says, "Horse, horse," but when he addresses the fox the pattern is varied to "Fear nothing, brother fox." As you know, folk tales use a good deal of repetition, for instance, the thrice-said "Someone has eaten my porridge" in "Goldilocks and the Three Bears." Why, then, is the line varied here?
3. The last line reads: "And the man? His future is yet to come." What future do you suppose the teller of the tale has in mind?


## Chewing Blackbones

# Old Man and Old Woman
### A Blackfoot Indian Myth Retold

Long, long ago, there were only two persons in the world: Old Man and Old Woman. One time when they were traveling about the earth, Old Woman said to Old Man, "Now let us come to an agree-

Nothing is known about Chewing Blackbones except that he was a Blackfoot Indian described in 1953 as "an elderly grandfather . . . [who] could tell the old tales only in the old Blackfoot language." Ella E. Clark collected this tale in 1953, and published it in her 1966 collection, *Indian Legends from the Northern Rockies*.

ment of some kind. Let us decide how the people shall live when they shall be on the earth."

"Well," replied Old Man, "I am to have the first say in everything."

"I agree with you," said Old Woman. "That is—if I may have the second say."

Then Old Man began his plans. "The women will have the duty of tanning the hides. They will rub animals' brains on the hides to make them soft and scrape them with scraping tools. All this they will do very quickly, for it will not be hard work."

"No," said Old Woman, "I will not agree to this. They must tan hides in the way you say; but it must be very hard work, so that the good workers may be found out."

"Well," said Old Man, "we will let the people have eyes and mouths, straight up and down in their faces."

"No," replied Old Woman, "let us not have them that way. We will have the eyes and mouths in the faces, as you say, but they shall be set crosswise."

"Well," said Old Man, "the people shall have ten fingers on each hand."

"Oh, no!" replied Old Woman. "That will be too many. They will be in the way. There will be four fingers and one thumb on each hand."

So the two went on until they had provided for everything in the lives of the people who were to be.

"What shall we do about life and death?" asked Old Woman. "Should the people live forever, or should they die?"

Old Woman and Old Man had difficulty agreeing about this. Finally Old Man said, "I will tell you what we will do. I will throw a buffalo chip into the water. If it floats, the people will die for four days and then come to life again; if it sinks, they will die forever."

So he threw a buffalo chip into the water, and it floated.

"No," said Old Woman, "we will not decide in that way. I will throw this rock into the water. If it floats, the people will die for four days; if it sinks, they will die forever."

Then Old Woman threw the rock into the water, and it sank to the bottom.

"There," said she. "It is better for the people to die forever. If they did not, they would not feel sorry for each other, and there would be no sympathy in the world."

"Well," said Old Man, "let it be that way."

After a time, Old Woman had a daughter, who soon became sick and died. The mother was very sorry then that they had agreed that people should die forever. "Let us have our say over again," she said.

"No," replied Old Man. "Let us not change what we have agreed upon."

And so people have died ever since.

# Questions

1. Do we think of Old Man and Old Woman as people or as gods? Explain.
2. Though briefly sketched, Old Man and Old Woman are distinct characters. What are the important differences between them?
3. The dialogue helps to characterize Old Man and Old Woman. What other function does it serve?
4. If the story ended six sentences earlier (after Old Man says: "Well . . . let it be that way"), the myth would still provide an explanation of why people die. What would be lost?

Katherine Anne Porter

# The Jilting of Granny Weatherall

She flicked her wrist neatly out of Doctor Harry's pudgy careful fingers and pulled the sheet up to her chin. The brat ought to be in knee breeches. Doctoring around the country with spectacles on his nose! "Get along now, take your schoolbooks and go. There's nothing wrong with me."

Doctor Harry spread a warm paw like a cushion on her forehead where the forked green vein danced and made her eyelids twitch. "Now, now, be a good girl, and we'll have you up in no time."

"That's no way to speak to a woman nearly eighty years old just because she's down. I'd have you respect your elders, young man."

"Well, Missy, excuse me." Doctor Harry patted her cheek. "But I've got to warn you, haven't I? You're a marvel, but you must be careful or you're going to be good and sorry."

"Don't tell me what I'm going to be. I'm on my feet now, morally speaking. It's Cornelia. I had to go to bed to get rid of her."

Her bones felt loose, and floated around in her skin, and Doctor Harry floated like a balloon around the foot of the bed. He floated and pulled down his waistcoat and swung his glasses on a cord. "Well, stay where you are, it certainly can't hurt you."

Katherine Anne Porter (1890–1980) had the curious habit of inventing details in her life, but it is true that she was born in a log cabin in Indian Creek, Texas, that she was originally named Callie Russell Porter, that her mother died when the child was two years old, and that Callie was brought up by her maternal grandmother in Kyle, Texas. Apparently, the family was conscious of former wealth and position in Louisiana and Kentucky, for Callie was sent to convent schools, where, in her words, she received a "strangely useless and ornamental education." When she was sixteen she left school, married (and soon divorced), and worked as a reporter, first in Texas and later in Denver and Chicago. She moved around a good deal, both within the United States and abroad: she lived for a while in Mexico, Belgium, Switzerland, France, and Germany.

Even as a child she was interested in writing, but she did not publish her first story until she was thirty-three. She wrote essays and one novel (*Ship of Fools*), but she is best known for her stories. Porter's *Collected Stories* won the Pulitzer Prize and the National Book Award in 1965.

"Get along and doctor your sick," said Granny Weatherall. "Leave a well woman alone. I'll call for you when I want you. . . . Where were you forty years ago when I pulled through milk-leg and double pneumonia? You weren't even born. Don't let Cornelia lead you on," she shouted, because Doctor Harry appeared to float up to the ceiling and out. "I pay my own bills, and I don't throw my money away on nonsense!"

She meant to wave good-by, but it was too much trouble. Her eyes closed of themselves, it was like a dark curtain drawn around the bed. The pillow rose and floated under her, pleasant as a hammock in a light wind. She listened to the leaves rustling outside the window. No, somebody was swishing newspapers: no, Cornelia and Doctor Harry were whispering together. She leaped broad awake, thinking they whispered in her ear.

"She was never like this, *never* like this!" "Well, what can we expect?" "Yes, eighty years old. . . ."

Well, and what if she was? She still had ears. It was like Cornelia to whisper around doors. She always kept things secret in such a public way. She was always being tactful and kind. Cornelia was dutiful; that was the trouble with her. Dutiful and good: "So good and dutiful," said Granny, "and I'd like to spank her." She saw herself spanking Cornelia and making a fine job of it.

"What'd you say, Mother?"

Granny felt her face tying up in hard knots.

"Can't a body think, I'd like to know?"

"I thought you might want something."

"I do. I want a lot of things. First off, go away and don't whisper."

She lay and drowsed, hoping in her sleep that the children would keep out and let her rest a minute. It had been a long day. Not that she was tired. It was always pleasant to snatch a minute now and then. There was always so much to be done, let me see: tomorrow.

Tomorrow was far away and there was nothing to trouble about. Things were finished somehow when the time came; thank God there was always a little margin over for peace: then a person could spread out the plan of life and tuck in the edges orderly. It was good to have everything clean and folded away, with the hair brushes and tonic bottles sitting straight on the white embroidered linen: the day started without fuss and the pantry shelves laid out with rows of jelly glasses and brown jugs and white stone-china jars with blue whirligigs and words painted on them: coffee, tea, sugar, ginger, cinnamon, allspice: and the bronze clock with the lion on top nicely dusted off. The dust

that lion could collect in twenty-four hours! The box in the attic with
all those letters tied up, she'd have to go through that tomorrow. All
those letters—George's letters and John's letters and her letters to them
both—lying around for the children to find afterwards made her uneasy. Yes, that would be tomorrow's business. No use to let them know
how silly she had been once.

While she was rummaging around she found death in her mind
and it felt clammy and unfamiliar. She had spent so much time preparing for death there was no need for bringing it up again. Let it take
care of itself now. When she was sixty she had felt very old, finished,
and went around making farewell trips to see her children and grandchildren, with a secret in her mind: This is the very last of your mother,
children! Then she made her will and came down with a long fever.
That was all just a notion like a lot of other things, but it was lucky
too, for she had once for all got over the idea of dying for a long time.
Now she couldn't be worried. She hoped she had better sense now.
Her father had lived to be one hundred and two years old and had
drunk a noggin of strong hot toddy on his last birthday. He told the
reporters it was his daily habit, and he owed his long life to that. He
had made quite a scandal and was very pleased about it. She believed
she'd just plague Cornelia a little.

"Cornelia! Cornelia!" No footsteps, but a sudden hand on her
cheek. "Bless you, where have you been?"

"Here, Mother."

"Well, Cornelia, I want a noggin of hot toddy."

"Are you cold, darling?"

"I'm chilly, Cornelia. Lying in bed stops the circulation. I must
have told you that a thousand times."

Well, she could just hear Cornelia telling her husband that Mother
was getting a little childish and they'd have to humor her. The thing
that most annoyed her was that Cornelia thought she was deaf, dumb,
and blind. Little hasty glances and tiny gestures tossed around her
and over her head saying, "Don't cross her, let her have her way, she's
eighty years old," and she sitting there as if she lived in a thin glass
cage. Sometimes Granny almost made up her mind to pack up and
move back to her own house where nobody could remind her every
minute that she was old. Wait, wait, Cornelia, till your own children
whisper behind your back!

In her day she had kept a better house and had got more work
done. She wasn't too old yet for Lydia to be driving eighty miles for
advice when one of the children jumped the track, and Jimmy still

dropped in and talked things over: "Now, Mammy, you've a good business head, I want to know what you think of this? . . ." Old Cornelia couldn't change the furniture around without asking. Little things, little things! They had been so sweet when they were little. Granny wished the old days were back again with the children young and everything to be done over. It had been a hard pull, but not too much for her. When she thought of all the food she had cooked, and all the clothes she had cut and sewed, and all the gardens she had made—well, the children showed it. There they were, made out of her, and they couldn't get away from that. Sometimes she wanted to see John again and point to them and say, Well, I didn't do so badly, did I? But that would have to wait. That was for tomorrow. She used to think of him as a man, but now all the children were older than their father, and he would be a child beside her if she saw him now. It seemed strange and there was something wrong in the idea. Why, he couldn't possibly recognize her. She had fenced in a hundred acres once, digging the post holes herself and clamping the wires with just a negro boy to help. That changed a woman. John would be looking for a young woman with the peaked Spanish comb in her hair and the painted fan. Digging post holes changed a woman. Riding country roads in the winter when women had their babies was another thing: sitting up nights with sick horses and sick negroes and sick children and hardly ever losing one. John, I hardly ever lost one of them! John would see that in a minute, that would be something he could understand, she wouldn't have to explain anything!

It made her feel like rolling up her sleeves and putting the whole place to rights again. No matter if Cornelia was determined to be everywhere at once, there were a great many things left undone on this place. She would start tomorrow and do them. It was good to be strong enough for everything, even if all you made melted and changed and slipped under your hands, so that by the time you finished you almost forgot what you were working for. What was it I set out to do? she asked herself intently, but she could not remember. A fog rose over the valley, she saw it marching across the creek swallowing the trees and moving up the hill like an army of ghosts. Soon it would be at the near edge of the orchard, and then it was time to go in and light the lamps. Come in, children, don't stay out in the night air.

Lighting the lamps had been beautiful. The children huddled up to her and breathed like little calves waiting at the bars in the twilight. Their eyes followed the match and watched the flame rise and settle in a blue curve, then they moved away from her. The lamp was lit, they didn't have to be scared and hang on to mother any more. Never, never, never more. God, for all my life I thank Thee. Without Thee, my God, I could never have done it. Hail, Mary, full of grace.

I want you to pick all the fruit this year and see that nothing is wasted. There's always someone who can use it. Don't let good things rot for want of using. You waste life when you waste good food. Don't let things get lost. It's bitter to lose things. Now, don't let me get to thinking, not when I am tired and taking a little nap before supper. . . .

The pillow rose about her shoulders and pressed against her heart and the memory was being squeezed out of it: oh, push down the pillow, somebody: it would smother her if she tried to hold it. Such a fresh breeze blowing and such a green day with no threats in it. But he had not come, just the same. What does a woman do when she has put on the white veil and set out the white cake for a man and he doesn't come? She tried to remember. No, I swear he never harmed me but in that. He never harmed me but in that . . . and what if he did? There was the day, the day, but a whirl of dark smoke rose and covered it, crept up and over into the bright field where everything was planted so carefully in orderly rows. That was hell, she knew hell when she saw it. For sixty years she had prayed against remembering him and against losing her soul in the deep pit of hell, and now the two things were mingled in one and the thought of him was a smoky cloud from hell that moved and crept in her head when she had just got rid of Doctor Harry and was trying to rest a minute. Wounded vanity, Ellen, said a sharp voice in the top of her mind. Don't let your wounded vanity get the upper hand of you. Plenty of girls get jilted. You were jilted, weren't you? Then stand up to it. Her eyelids wavered and let in streamers of blue-gray light like tissue paper over her eyes. She must get up and pull the shades down or she'd never sleep. She was in bed again and the shades were not down. How could that happen? Better turn over, hide from the light, sleeping in the light gave you nightmares. "Mother, how do you feel now?" and a stinging wetness on her forehead. But I don't like having my face washed in cold water!

Hapsy? George? Lydia? Jimmy? No, Cornelia, and her features were swollen and full of little puddles. "They're coming, darling, they'll all be here soon." Go wash your face, child, you look funny.

Instead of obeying, Cornelia knelt down and put her head on the pillow. She seemed to be talking but there was no sound. "Well, are you tongue-tied? Whose birthday is it? Are you going to give a party?"

Cornelia's mouth moved urgently in strange shapes. "Don't do that, you bother me, daughter."

"Oh, no, Mother. Oh, no. . . ."

Nonsense. It was strange about children. They disputed your every word. "No what, Cornelia?"

"Here's Doctor Harry."

"I won't see that boy again. He just left five minutes ago."

"That was this morning, Mother. It's night now. Here's the nurse."

"This is Doctor Harry, Mrs. Weatherall. I never saw you look so young and happy!"

"Ah, I'll never be young again—but I'd be happy if they'd let me lie in peace and get rested."

She thought she spoke up loudly, but no one answered. A warm weight on her forehead, a warm bracelet on her wrist, and a breeze went on whispering, trying to tell her something. A shuffle of leaves in the everlasting hand of God. He blew on them and they danced and rattled. "Mother, don't mind, we're going to give you a little hypodermic." "Look here, daughter, how do ants get in this bed? I saw sugar ants yesterday." Did you send for Hapsy too?

It was Hapsy she really wanted. She had to go a long way back through a great many rooms to find Hapsy standing with a baby on her arm. She seemed to herself to be Hapsy also, and the baby on Hapsy's arm was Hapsy and himself and herself, all at once, and there was no surprise in the meeting. Then Hapsy melted from within and turned flimsy as gray gauze and the baby was a gauzy shadow, and Hapsy came up close and said, "I thought you'd never come," and looked at her very searchingly and said, "You haven't changed a bit!" They leaned forward to kiss, when Cornelia began whispering from a long way off, "Oh, is there anything you want to tell me? Is there anything I can do for you?"

Yes, she had changed her mind after sixty years and she would like to see George. I want you to find George. Find him and be sure to tell him I forgot him. I want him to know I had my husband just the same and my children and my house like any other woman. A good house too and a good husband that I loved and fine children out of him. Better than I hoped for even. Tell him I was given back everything he took away and more. Oh, no, oh, God, no, there was something else besides the house and the man and the children. Oh, surely they were not all? What was it? Something not given back. . . . Her breath crowded down under her ribs and grew into a monstrous frightening shape with cutting edges; it bored up into her head, and the agony was unbelievable: Yes, John, get the doctor now, no more talk, my time has come.

When this one was born it should be the last. The last. It should have been born first, for it was the one she had truly wanted. Everything came in good time. Nothing left out, left over. She was strong, in three days she would be as well as ever. Better. A woman needed milk in her to have her full health.

"Mother, do you hear me?"

"I've been telling you—"

"Mother, Father Connolly's here."

"I went to Holy Communion only last week. Tell him I'm not so sinful as all that."

"Father just wants to speak to you."

He could speak as much as he pleased. It was like him to drop in and inquire about her soul as if it were a teething baby, and then stay on for a cup of tea and a round of cards and gossip. He always had a funny story of some sort, usually about an Irishman who made his little mistakes and confessed them, and the point lay in some absurd thing he would blurt out in the confessional showing his struggles between native piety and original sin. Granny felt easy about her soul. Cornelia, where are your manners? Give Father Connolly a chair. She had her secret comfortable understanding with a few favorite saints who cleared a straight road to God for her. All as surely signed and sealed as the papers for the new Forty Acres. Forever . . . heirs and assigns forever. Since the day the wedding cake was not cut, but thrown out and wasted. The whole bottom dropped out of the world, and there she was blind and sweating with nothing under her feet and the walls falling away. His hand had caught her under the breast, she had not fallen, there was the freshly polished floor with the green rug on it, just as before. He had cursed like a sailor's parrot and said, "I'll kill him for you." Don't lay a hand on him, for my sake leave something to God. "Now, Ellen, you must believe what I tell you. . . ."

So there was nothing, nothing to worry about any more, except sometimes in the night one of the children screamed in a nightmare, and they both hustled out shaking and hunting for the matches and calling, "There, wait a minute, here we are!" John, get the doctor now, Hapsy's time has come. But there was Hapsy standing by the bed in a white cap. "Cornelia, tell Hapsy to take off her cap. I can't see her plain."

Her eyes opened very wide and the room stood out like a picture she had seen somewhere. Dark colors with the shadows rising towards the ceiling in long angles. The tall black dresser gleamed with nothing on it but John's picture, enlarged from a little one, with John's eyes very black when they should have been blue. You never saw him, so how do you know how he looked? But the man insisted the copy was perfect, it was very rich and handsome. For a picture, yes, but it's not my husband. The table by the bed had a linen cover and a candle and a crucifix. The light was blue from Cornelia's silk lampshades. No sort of light at all, just frippery. You had to live forty years with kerosene lamps to appreciate honest electricity. She felt very strong and she saw Doctor Harry with a rosy nimbus around him.

"You look like a saint, Doctor Harry, and I vow that's as near as you'll ever come to it."

"She's saying something."

"I heard you, Cornelia. What's all this carrying on?"

"Father Connolly's saying—"

Cornelia's voice staggered and bumped like a cart in a bad road. It rounded corners and turned back again and arrived nowhere. Granny stepped up in the cart very lightly and reached for the reins, but a man sat beside her and she knew him by his hands, driving the cart. She did not look in his face, for she knew without seeing, but looked instead down the road where the trees leaned over and bowed to each other and a thousand birds were singing a Mass. She felt like singing too, but she put her hand in the bosom of her dress and pulled out a rosary, and Father Connolly murmured Latin in a very solemn voice and tickled her feet. My God, will you stop that nonsense? I'm a married woman. What if he did run away and leave me to face the priest by myself? I found another a whole world better. I wouldn't have exchanged my husband for anybody except St. Michael himself, and you may tell him that for me with a thank you in the bargain.

Light flashed on her closed eyelids, and a deep roaring shook her. Cornelia, is that lightning? I hear thunder. There's going to be a storm. Close all the windows. Call the children in. . . . "Mother, here we are, all of us." "Is that you, Hapsy?" "Oh, no, I'm Lydia. We drove as fast as we could." Their faces drifted above her, drifted away. The rosary fell out of her hands and Lydia put it back. Jimmy tried to help, their hands fumbled together, and Granny closed two fingers around Jimmy's thumb. Beads wouldn't do, it must be something alive. She was so amazed her thoughts ran round and round. So, my dear Lord, this is my death and I wasn't even thinking about it. My children have come to see me die. But I can't, it's not time. Oh, I always hated surprises. I wanted to give Cornelia the amethyst set—Cornelia, you're to have the amethyst set, but Hapsy's to wear it when she wants, and, Doctor Harry, do shut up. Nobody sent for you. Oh, my dear Lord, do wait a minute. I meant to do something about the Forty Acres, Jimmy doesn't need it and Lydia will later on, with that worthless husband of hers. I meant to finish the altar cloth and send six bottles of wine to Sister Borgia for her dyspepsia. I want to send six bottles of wine to Sister Borgia, Father Connolly, now don't let me forget.

Cornelia's voice made short turns and tilted over and crashed. "Oh, Mother, oh, Mother, oh, Mother. . . ."

"I'm not going, Cornelia. I'm taken by surprise. I can't go."

You'll see Hapsy again. What about her? "I thought you'd never come." Granny made a long journey outward, looking for Hapsy. What if I don't find her? What then? Her heart sank down and down, there was no bottom to death, she couldn't come to the end of it. The blue light from Cornelia's lampshade drew into a tiny point in the center of her brain, it flickered and winked like an eye, quietly it fluttered and dwindled. Granny lay curled down within herself, amazed and watchful, staring at the point of light that was herself; her body was now only a deeper mass of shadow in an endless darkness and this darkness would curl around the light and swallow it up, God, give a sign!

For the second time there was no sign. Again no bridegroom and the priest in the house. She could not remember any other sorrow because this grief wiped them all away. Oh, no, there's nothing more cruel than this—I'll never forgive it. She stretched herself with a deep breath and blew out the light.

# Questions

1.  Who is Hapsy? What do we know about her? *How* do we know these things?
2.  How would you describe Granny Weatherall? In what ways does her name suit her?
3.  The final paragraph begins: "For the second time there was no sign." What happened the first time? What is happening now? How are the two events linked? (The paragraph alludes to Christ's parable of the bridegroom, in Matthew 25:1–13. If you are unfamiliar with the parable, read it in the Gospel according to St. Matthew.)
4.  What do you think happens in the last line of the story?

## Gerard Manley Hopkins

# God's Grandeur

The world is charged with the grandeur of God.
  It will flame out, like shining from shook foil;
  It gathers to a greatness, like the ooze of oil
Crushed. Why do men then now not reck[1] his rod?        4

Generations have trod, have trod, have trod;
  And all is seared with trade; bleared, smeared with toil;
  And wears man's smudge and shares man's smell: the soil
Is bare now, nor can foot feel, being shod.        8

And for all this, nature is never spent;
  There lives the dearest freshness deep down things;
And though the last lights off the black West went
  Oh, morning, at the brown brink eastward, springs—    12
Because the Holy Ghost over the bent
  World broods with warm breast and with ah! bright wings

## Questions

1. Hopkins, a Roman Catholic priest, lived in England during the last decades of the nineteenth century—that is, in an industrialized society. Where in the poem do you find him commenting on his setting? Circle the words in the poem that can refer both to England's physical appearance and to the sinful condition of human beings.
2. What is the speaker's tone in the first three and a half lines (through "Crushed")? In the rest of line 4? In lines 5–8? Is the second part of the sonnet (the next six lines) more unified in tone or less?

---

Gerard Manley Hopkins (1844–1889) was born in London of a prosperous family. He was educated at Oxford, where he became increasingly interested in the High Church wing of the Anglican Church and then in Roman Catholicism. In 1866 Hopkins converted to Roman Catholicism, and in 1868 he became a Jesuit priest. For the rest of his life he served as a parish priest (chiefly in the slums of London) and as a teacher. He wrote poetry and showed it to a few friends, but his work did not become widely known until 1918, twenty-nine years after his death, when his literary executor gave the material to a publisher.

---

[1] Heed. (Editors' note)

# APPENDIX A

## Reading (and Writing About) Pictures

Let's begin by talking about pictures that most of us would agree are "art"—paintings and drawings rather than photographs, though we shall go on to argue that most of what we say from the outset is also true of photography.

Until the twentieth century most pictures were representational, showing gods and goddesses and kings and saints and landscapes and dishes of fruit; but they were also expressive, revealing the artist's feelings toward the subject, the artist's (or society's) particular vision. An object is seen, but not only with the eye; the mind interprets it, and when the object ends up on canvas, it has been shaped by an idea. As the painter Degas said, "The artist does not draw what he sees, but what he must make others see." Van Gogh put it thus, when he heard that a painter complained that his figures were distorted:

> I don't want them to be "correct." Real artists paint things not as they are, in a dry analytical way, but as *they* feel them. I adore Michelangelo's figures, though the legs are too long and the hips and backsides too large. What I most want to do is to make these incorrectnesses, deviations, remodelings, or adjustments of reality something that may be "untrue" but is at the same time more true than literal truth.

The proportion of (on the one hand) accurate optical representation to (on the other hand) distortion introduced by the expression of an idea of course varies from age to age and from painter to painter, but even in periods when individuality was not highly valued we may speak of an expressive content; the expression is that of the age. After all, it is entirely possible that innumerable nameless and almost indistinguishable twelfth-century painters expressed their religious ideals while working comfortably within the established traditions of medieval art. In twelfth-century art Christ is regularly shown seated on the heavens with the earth as a footstool; he holds the Bible in his left hand and gives a benediction with his right hand. The pose and setting, and even the rendering of stylized details, are traditional; the difference between one rendition and another is chiefly a matter of the painter's technical competence. But all the renditions, similar though they are, may express what the artists wanted to express about Christ. Don't we often express ourselves in thoroughly traditional ways? We applaud at the end of a performance that has impressed us; we feel no need to find a personal way (throwing white mice into the air?) of expressing our pleasure and approval. We are content to express ourselves in the traditional way.

The artist of course often works within bounds that severely limit personal expression. If a court painter, obliged to represent the splendor of his king, did not share the king's opinions, he might very well have had to suppress his feelings. Then again, he might have been able to smuggle something subversive into his painting, so that the royal sitter might see the painting as the image of kingliness, though the painter and the perceptive viewer saw it as the image of arrogance. A painter might even, with a splendid painting and a sitter endowed with taste, persuade the king that arrogance was more interesting and attractive than kingliness.

Even artists working under tight control, then, may—and do—endow their paintings with a life beyond optical representation of the apparent subject. In ordinary language we recognize that a painting is not simply *of* something but *by* someone; we may say, "That's a painting of a Dutch merchant," but more often we say, "That's a painting by Rembrandt," or, more tellingly, "Look at that Rembrandt." For when we look at the picture we experience Rembrandt—his way of seeing—quite as much as a merchant-sitter.

Although many of the world's greatest artists have had to please their royal or ecclesiastical or bourgeois patrons by representing certain subjects in certain ways, we know that often another subject lies on the canvas: the paintings give visible form to the artist's mind. A picture, then, is a sort of utterance, an "outterance," a sending out of attitudes, an outer report of feelings. The picture conveys meaning (as well as phenomena) in visual form, and it may intensify or newly shape the spectator's perception of any aspect of life.

Speaking metaphorically, we can say that this meaning is conveyed in the *language* of painting. Just as a succession of short sentences "says" something different from a succession of long ones (probably if it doesn't convey mere childishness it tells of tight-lipped assurance, authority, or at least self-restraint), so too a picture with short, choppy, angular lines will "say" something different from a picture with gentle curves, even though the object represented (let's say a woman sitting at a table) is about the same. Similarly, a painting with a rough surface built up with vigorous or agitated brushstrokes will not say the same thing as a painting with a smooth polished surface that gives no evidence of the brush. And a soft pencil drawing on pale gray paper will say something different from a pen drawing made with a broad nib on bright white paper; at the very least, the medium and the subdued contrast of one are "quieter" or "less active" than the other.

What are some of the basic things to look for in understanding the language of pictures? One can begin almost anywhere, but let's begin with the relationship among the parts:

Do the figures share the space evenly, or does one figure overpower another, taking most of the space or the light?

Are the figures harmoniously related, perhaps by a similar stance or shared action, or are they opposed, perhaps by diagonals thrusting at each other? (Speaking generally, diagonals may suggest instability, except when they form a triangle resting on its base. Horizontal lines suggest stability, as do vertical lines when connected by a horizontal line. Circular lines are often associated with motion, and sometimes—especially by men—with the female body and with fertility. These simple formulas, however, must be applied cautiously, for they are not always appropriate.)

In a landscape, what is the relation between humans and nature? Are the figures at ease in nature, or are they dwarfed by it? Are they earthbound, beneath the horizon, or (because the viewpoint is low) do they stand out against the horizon and perhaps seem in touch with the heavens, or at least with open air? If there are woods, are these woods threatening or are they an inviting place of refuge? If there is a clearing, is the clearing a vulnerable place or is it a place of refuge from threatening woods? Do the natural objects in the landscape somehow reflect the emotions of the figures in it?

If the picture is a portrait, how do the furnishings and the background and the angle of the head or the posture of the head and body (as well, of course, as the facial expression) contribute to our sense of the person portrayed?

What is the effect of light in the picture? Does it produce sharp contrasts, brightly illuminating some parts and throwing others into darkness, or does it, by means of gentle gradations, unify most or all of the parts? Does the light seem theatrical or natural, disturbing or comforting? If the picture is in color, is the color realistic or is it expressive, or both?

We believe that you can stimulate responses by asking yourself two kinds of questions:

1. *What is this doing?* Why is this figure here and not there, why is this tree so brightly illuminated, why are shadows omitted, why is this seated figure leaning forward like that?
2. *Why do I have this response?* Why do I find this figure pathetic, this landscape oppressive, this child revoltingly sentimental but that child fascinating?

The first of these questions, "What is this doing?," requires you to identify yourself with the artist, wondering perhaps whether pen is better than pencil for this drawing, or watercolor better than oil paint for this painting. The second question, "Why do I have this response?," requires you to trust your feelings. If you are amused or repelled or unnerved or soothed, assume that these responses are appropriate and follow them up, at least until further study of the work provides other responses.

Let's turn to a specific painting, Velázquez's *The Water Seller*, painted about 1620. Velázquez painted it while he lived in Seville, but the precise locale and the time are unimportant, because even if we didn't realize until now that in the seventeenth century people required the services of a water carrier, the picture tells us so. Velázquez reproduces appearances with careful fidelity to nature. But what is Velázquez saying, and how does he say it?

We'll begin with the largest figure, the old man who, in full light, dominates the center of the picture and who seems to stand closest to us, his hand on the great jar that appears easily within our reach. His clothes are tattered, but he has immense dignity, partly because he seems almost a central pillar, partly because his hand rests assuredly on the big globular vessel of life-sustaining water, partly because his facial expression is serious, and partly because we see his face in profile. If we think of the profile of Lincoln on a penny, of Jefferson on a nickel, of Roosevelt on a dime, of Washington on a quarter or in the painting *Washington Crossing the Delaware*, we notice that a face in profile is in no immediate relation to us. It stares off, ignoring us, looking at something that exists only in the flat world of the picture plane. Because a profile avoids contact with the space or world between the picture and the viewer, it usually strikes us as independent, even aloof. If a profile has a personality or inner life, it is probably not jovial or confiding or anguished; it is probably solemn, poised, self-sufficient. And there is another important thing about a profile: it can be very interesting, for we are attracted to, say, that high forehead, long nose, downturned mouth. The line that defines the profile is sharply arresting, in a way that the lines of a frontal view usually are not.

*The Water Seller*
**Diego Velázquez, c. 1620**

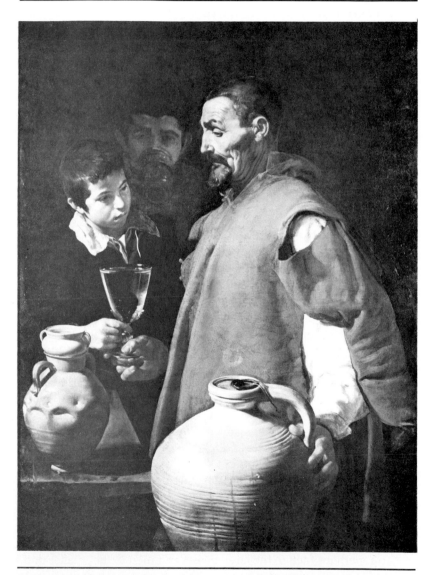

In any case, if we ask ourselves which figure in Velázquez's painting is the center of interest, the answer must be evident. But the other
figures are not mere contrasts to set off the water carrier. The old water
seller is giving a glass to a boy, and we notice that between the two
figures, to the rear, is a third person, apparently older than the boy
and younger than the old man. And so we have the ages of man: youth,
maturity, old age. The man in the middle, whose glass is tipped in
front of his face, has already drunk substantially—even in this frozen
action he is in mid-career, so to speak—but the boy is about to receive
a full glass, for his life is all ahead of him. The figure in the middle,
mostly obscured, although the least important, is not unimportant; he
is represented because Velázquez wants more than the obvious contrast of youth and age. The painter, however, concentrates his vision
on the old man passing the life-sustaining water to the young man.
We see the renewal of life.

And what of the vessels, so prominent in the picture? Of course
they belong in the picture; a water seller must have a jar of water, and
his customers must have jars or glasses to receive the water. These
vessels are handsome ones, interesting shapes beautifully painted.
Still, realism would have been satisfied with a glass and perhaps the
top of the large pot. The painter must have had not only a perceptive
eye for things of the real world, but an idea for a picture. (This is not
to say that an artist's idea precedes visual stimulus. Quite the reverse:
almost surely the artist first sees something, something he feels he
wants to capture and to show to others, and this initial perception
stimulates whatever idea he develops. Velázquez perhaps was first
moved by the face of the water carrier, or by the way the old man
poured water into a glass, or even by the gleaming droplets on the
shoulder of a great earthenware jar; this, he may have felt, glows with
such an inner life that it must be recorded for others to see, forever.
Perhaps with some such thought the picture began, but it did not stop
there.) Velázquez's utensils, beautiful though they are in themselves,
contribute to the whole picture and take their fullest life from the whole
picture. What do they contribute?

For one thing, although the three figures are closely bound by
their physical positions and (even more important) by participating in
a unified action, the vessels help to bring them still closer to one another, for our eye makes a sort of wheeling motion as it goes from one
bright patch to another, from the water carrier's face to his shoulder
and arm, perhaps then to the large vessel and then to the smaller one,
then to the boy's illuminated hand and up along the glass to the boy's

face, and finally to the shadowy face of the man in the middle. But there may be more. What is the effect of that great bulging jar at the bottom of the canvas? Why should earthenware receive so much space and be painted so much more illusionistically than the rather flat face of the mature man drinking from the glass?

Our own response—and the picture has long exerted a spell on us—is that this vessel, the thing nearest to us, almost bulging into the space we occupy, and made of the substance to which we return, is given prominence and exerts it appeal because it contains not only the stuff that sustains life but the stuff out of which life came. First, water; then, nourished by water, life. In fact, impressive though the figures are, it seems to us that it is to this pregnant jar with unseen precious contents that the eye (or at least the mind's eye) returns after it surveys the figures.

After we have admired the astounding technical skill that can render people and objects so convincingly and interestingly, what can we say about the meaning of the picture? The painter, in pictorial language, perhaps is saying something like this. Our lives may seem poor battered things, as the water carrier's torn smock and wrinkled face indicate, but a source whose bottom we cannot see has given us the gift of life, and we can live with dignity and nourish succeeding generations.

Of course Velázquez probably never said anything like this in words, but he did say it in paint. Our summary is crudely put and takes no account of the sheer sensuous appeal of the lines and colors (mostly earthy colors), but anything that we say about a great picture is crude compared with the richness of the picture itself. We realize too that our commentary has come close to turning the picture into an allegory. We hope that we have not quite said that the three men stand for three parts of a life span, that the water stands for life, that the rip in the carrier's sleeve stands for the hardships of this world. When we look at this painting, we never forget that it is a representation of men engaged in a specific commonplace action. Still, the more we respond to this representation, the more we feel that it adds up to something; and the more we feel that the whole is greater than the sum of its parts, the more we want to account for its mysterious appeal. By asking ourselves questions and trying to answer them, we may heighten our understanding of the picture and of life.

We have banged this picture around a good deal, but it can withstand anything we do to it, and we want to spend another minute on it, setting forth what we might write if we were asked to write a paragraph about it, perhaps as a caption in a picture-book or a label on a museum wall. Up to now we have tried to show, in some detail, how we came to our understanding of the picture, but of course in writing, a finished piece one does not reproduce all the byways of thought. Here is what we would say.

> Velázquez's *The Water Seller* was painted in Seville, and doubtless it represents a common enough sight, people receiving the carrier's services. But we sense more than mere realism here, more than an optically convincing report of what happened at a particular moment. Velázquez has turned the disorder of daily experience into a pattern and a meaning. We see three people closely joined; an old man of enormous gravity (despite his tattered appearance) hands a glassful of water to a youth; between them, and between them in years, too, a mature man drinks a glass, and so we see a cycle of life, a cycle reinforced as our eyes move from the great water jar in the foreground up to the glass, to the boy's attentive face, across the adult's face to the water seller's solemn profile, and down again to the jar that is the source of nourishment for all ages.

In 1839, more than two hundred years after Velázquez painted *The Water Seller*, Louis Jacques Mandé Daguerre made public the daguerreotype, an early photographic process. "From this moment," the painter Paul Delaroche is supposed to have said, "painting is dead." This remark implies, of course, that painting seeks to render external appearances and that it cannot compete with a camera. But another and far greater painter of the period took a different view. Honoré Daumier said that photography describes everything and explains nothing. The implication is that photography offers optical realism but cannot offer the idea, the vision, which a work of art embodies. Daumier's statement, it turned out, was as inadequate as Delaroche's, as we shall try to show in a capsule historical analysis of photography.

In the middle of the nineteenth century, after a few years of intoxication with machines that could produce a permanent image that was neither drawn nor painted, photographers began to divide into two schools, which we can call *pictorialists* and *reporters*. (Of course we are simplifying; the labels are overstatements, and some photographers occupied a middle ground, or shifted allegiance from one school to the other.) The pictorialists had artistic ambitions. They posed their subjects carefully into compositions resembling those of the old master painters, and they often used religious or literary motifs, as painting had done. Julia Margaret Cameron (1815–1879) pressed her friends and

servants to dress up like King Arthur's knights so that she might photograph scenes from Tennyson's *Idylls of the King,* or she arranged a
woman and children into a composition that she called "Madonna with
Children." She also did portrait photography, and although it might
at first be thought that this at least was tied to reportage, her subjects
were such notables as Tennyson, Browning, Longfellow, and Darwin,
and she did not at all wish to present them as ordinary men caught
in some trivial act of daily living:

> When I have had such men before my camera my whole soul has
> endeavored to do its duty towards them in recording faithfully the
> greatness of the inner as well as the features of the outer man. The
> photograph thus taken has been almost the embodiment of a prayer.

Moreover, because early photography required a long exposure during
which the subject could not move, almost all the pictures of people—
even of ordinary people, say a man supposedly sawing wood or a
middle-class family dining—have a studied, posed, pictorial effect.

In Julia Cameron's time, however, other photographers (we are
calling them reporters) specialized in a technique that was supposed
to be the mere reproduction of anything the eye might see. Many of
these concentrated on exotic sights—the Nile, American Indians,
Greek architecture. The idea was that the folks back home could see
exactly what these strange places and people looked like. These photographs were documents, it was claimed, showing what you would
see if you were able to take the long, expensive, arduous trip. Supposedly, the photograph offered the facts—not the Ideal Truth of the
pictorialists but the truth of the fleeting moment. This tradition of recording the passing scene was fostered by technical developments that
greatly decreased the time required for the exposure, allowing shots
of moving objects; the development of easily portable cameras, too,
was essential to the documentary or reportorial tradition. The result
was photo-journalism, which implicitly offers the facts without comment, and also the run-of-the-mill snapshot, which tells us what Aunt
Julie looks like, standing on the porch of her new house.

Still speaking broadly, we can say that the pictorialists usually
emphasize an obviously studied composition; they often use a soft
focus to suppress details, they alter the negative by underdeveloping
or by overdeveloping it, and they print their pictures (often retouched)
on warm, soft, matte (dully finished) paper. On the other hand, the
reporters value pictures with seemingly unplanned compositions (a

figure cut at the side, or the top of a head cut off); they also prefer a sharp focus and prints on cold, hard, glossy paper. The effect, they might claim, is that of the moment, not that of the ages; truth, not beauty.

Now, a newspaper photograph or an amateur's snapshot does not in fact record the object-as-it-really-is. It records what you would see if you had only one eye and stood at a particular place at a particular time of day, and if what you saw was printed on a particular kind of paper. Besides, except for a few pictures taken in desperation—a picture of a parade taken by a photographer who, unable to see over the heads of a crowd, simply holds the camera as high as he can and snaps at random—the pictures of the reporters (and we include the amateur who takes snapshots) are, like those of the pictorialists, at least somewhat composed. After all, one backs up a little, shifts the lens to the right a bit, bends the knees, waits for someone to get out of the way, or, conversely, waits for a dog to come along and sniff the garbage. A Victorian reportorial photographer went up in a balloon so that he could get an interesting shot of the entrance to a cave in India, and today there is scarcely a serious photographer who has not gone to great pains to get a shot that seems "natural," "inevitable," "spontaneous." There is, of course, a visible difference between pictures at either extreme, but most of the reporters as well as the pictorialists will have to say with the late Minor White, "I don't take pictures, I make them."

What we said about reading paintings, then, applies to reading photographs too, whether they are conspicuously pictorial or allegedly reportorial. The relationships between one object and another (of one figure to another, or figures to background) are revealing, and so too is the angle of vision. And the focus—soft, or precise and hard—and the degree of contrast—gentle gradations suggesting harmony, or unity, or sharp contrasts of black and white suggesting dislocations or conflict or at least harshness—contribute to the meaning of a photograph. Because photographers make these and many other choices, they might agree with the painter Cézanne, who said that pictures are "the means of making the public feel what we feel ourselves."

Let's look at a photograph from Robert Frank's book, *The Americans* (1969), "Drugstore—Detroit." If he had to choose from our categories, Frank would unhesitatingly call himself a reporter, so his photograph will be a severe but fair test of a method of analysis derived from studying painting.

As we look at Frank's photograph, here are some of the things

©Robert Frank, from *The Americans,* 1958. Courtesy Pace MacGill Gallery

we see. (We see them partly because we have asked ourselves questions, as suggested on pages 1131–1132.)

1.  A line of crowded people. Possibly the seating really is ample, but the angle from which the picture was taken gives us the impression that the eaters are crowded.
2.  Most of these people, though in an eating place, are in fact waiting, not eating. Each is waiting by himself. Although there is a crowd, no one seems to be conversing with a neighbor. It's a lonely crowd. Those who are not staring blankly are looking curiously at the photographer, but even the unusual experience of seeing a photographer taking a picture at a lunch counter does not seem to break through to most of the men here.
3.  The counter serves a useful purpose in the eatery, but in the picture it gives the effect of a barrier, separating all the customers (white males) from the women (apparently black) who serve them. Moreover, the angle from which the picture was taken (relatively high) produces a swift foreshortening; the rear of the picture seems eerily tilted up, giving a slightly surrealistic effect.
4.  A good deal of machinery (apparently mini-jukeboxes) is evident along the counter, further dehumanizing the place.
5.  Advertisements for Orange Whip, Orange Whip, Orange Whip, hang over the heads of the customers, almost threateningly. If the man in the foreground is indeed drinking Orange Whip, he shows no sign of enjoying it.

If we were to write a short paragraph on this picture, then, trying to report not only what it says but also *how* it says it, we might write:

> Robert Frank's photograph shows us people at mealtime, but this occasion is not a time of relaxed and friendly renewal of body or of spirit. The picture shows clutter, machine after machine, boredom, and isolation. Men sit, for the most part not dining but staring into space, each avoiding eye-contact with his neighbor, and separated by a counter from the women who serve them. Apparently not even two of the dozen or so are friends with a word to exchange. In the foreground, perhaps submitting to the aggressive advertisements for Orange Whip that dangle overhead, a man sips a beverage. He shows no sign of pleasure. The steep perspective unsettles us as we look at

this picture of people who seem almost as dehumanized as the counter they sit at.

The Chinese aphorism says that a picture is worth a thousand words; but sometimes it takes that many words (well, a couple of dozen, anyway) to bring the picture home to us.

# APPENDIX B

## A Writer's Glossary

**analogy.** An analogy (from the Greek *analogos*, proportionate, resembling) is a kind of comparison. Normally an analogy compares substantially different kinds of things and reports several points of resemblance. A comparison of one city with another ("New York is like Chicago in several ways") does not involve an analogy because the two things are not substantially different. And a comparison giving only one resemblance is usually not considered an analogy ("Some people, like olives, are an acquired taste"). But if we claim that a state is like a human body, and we find in the state equivalents for the brain, heart, and limbs, we are offering an analogy. Similarly, one might construct an analogy between feeding the body with food and supplying the mind with ideas: the diet must be balanced, taken at approximately regular intervals, in proper amounts, and digested. An analogy may be useful in explaining the unfamiliar by comparing it to the familiar ("The heart is like a pump . . ."), but of course the things compared are different, and the points of resemblance can go only so far. For this reason, analogies cannot prove anything, though they are sometimes offered as proof.

**analysis.** Examination of the parts and their relation to the whole. For a brief example, see the paragraph on page 1136 analyzing Velázquez's painting, *The Water Seller*.

**argument.** Discourse in which some statements are offered as *reasons* for other statements. Argument, then, like emotional appeal and wit, is a form of persuasion, but argument seeks to persuade by appealing to reason. (See *deduction*, pages 1143–1144.)

**audience.** The writer's imagined readers. An essay on inflation written for the general public—say, for readers of *Newsweek*—will assume less specialized knowledge than will an essay written for professional economists—say, the readers of *Journal of Economic History*. In general, the imagined audience in a composition course is *not* the instructor (though in fact the instructor may be the only reader of the essay); the imagined audience usually is the class, or, to put it a little differently, someone rather like the writer but without the writer's specialized knowledge of the topic.

**cliché.**   Literally, a *cliché* was originally (in French) a stereotype or an electrotype plate for printing; in English the word has come to mean an oft-repeated expression such as "a sight for sore eyes," "a heart-warming experience," "the acid test," "a meaningful relationship," "last but not least." Because these expressions implicitly claim to be impressive or forceful, they can be distinguished from such unpretentious common expressions as "good morning," "thank you," and "see you tomorrow." Clichés in fact are not impressive or forceful; they strike the hearer as tired, vague, and unimaginative.

**compare/contrast.**   Strictly speaking, to compare is to examine in order to show similarities. (It comes from the Latin *comparare*, "to pair," "to match.") To contrast is to set into opposition in order to show differences. (It comes from the Latin *contra*, "against," and *stare*, "to stand.") But in ordinary usage a comparison may include not only similarities but also differences. (For a particular kind of comparison, emphasizing similarities, see *analogy*.) In comparing and contrasting, a writer usually means not simply to list similarities or differences but to reveal something clearly, by calling attention either to its resemblances to something we might not think it resembles, or to its differences from something we might think it does resemble.

**connotation.**   The associations that cluster around a word. "Mother" has connotations that "female parent" does not have, yet both words have the same denotation or explicit meaning.

**convention.**   An agreed-on usage. Beginning each sentence with a capital letter is a convention.

**deduction.**   Deduction is the process of reasoning from premises to a logical conclusion. Here is the classic example: "All men are mortal" (the major premise); "Socrates is a man" (the minor premise); "therefore Socrates is mortal" (the conclusion). Such an argument, which takes two truths and joins them to produce a third truth, is called a syllogism (from Greek for "a reckoning together"). Deduction (Latin for "lead down from") moves from a general statement to a specific application; it is, therefore, the opposite of induction (page 1147), which moves from specific instances to a general conclusion.

   Notice that if a premise of a syllogism is not true, one can reason logically yet can come to a false conclusion. Example: "All teachers are members of a union"; "Jones is a teacher"; "therefore Jones is a member of a union." Although the process of reasoning is correct here, the major premise is false and so the conclusion is worthless—Jones may or may not be a member of the union.

Another point: some arguments superficially appear logical but are not. Let's take this attempt at a syllogism: "All teachers of Spanish know that in Spanish *hoy* means 'today' " (major premise); "John knows that in Spanish *hoy* means 'today' " (minor premise); "therefore John is a teacher of Spanish" (conclusion). Both of the premises are correct, but the conclusion does not follow. What's wrong? Valid deduction requires that the subject or condition of the major premise (in this case, teachers of Spanish) appear also in the minor premise, but here it does not. The minor premise should be "John is a teacher of Spanish," and the valid conclusion, of course, would be "therefore John knows that *hoy* means 'today.' "

**denotation.**    The explicit meaning of a word, as given in a dictionary, without its associations. "Daytime serial" and "soap opera" have the same denotation, though "daytime serial" probably has a more favorable connotation (see *connotation*).

**description.**    Discourse that aims chiefly at producing a sensory response (usually a mental image) to, for example, a person, object, scene, taste, smell, and so on. A descriptive essay, or passage in an essay, uses concrete words (words that denote observable qualities such as "hair" and "stickiness") and it uses specific language (words such as "basketball" rather than "game," and "steak, potatoes, and salad" rather than "hearty meal").

**diction.**    Choice of words. Examples: between "car," "auto," and "automobile," between "lie" and "falsehood," between "can't" and "cannot."

**euphemism.**    An expression such as "passed away" for "died," used to avoid realities that the writer finds unpleasant. Thus, oppressive governments "relocate people" (instead of putting them in concentration camps).

**evaluation.**    Whereas an interpretation seeks to explain the meaning, an evaluation judges worth. After we interpret a difficult piece of writing we may evaluate it as not worth the effort.

**explication.**    An attempt to reveal the meaning by calling attention to implications, such as the connotations of words and the tone conveyed by the brevity or length of a sentence. Unlike a paraphrase, which is a rewording or rephrasing in order to set forth the gist of the meaning, an explication is a commentary that makes explicit what is implicit. If we paraphrased the beginning of the Gettysburg Address (page 607), we might turn "Four score and seven years ago our fathers brought forth" into "Eighty-seven years ago our ancestors established," or some such statement. In an explication, however, we would mention that "four score" evokes the language of the Bible, and that the biblical echo helps to establish the solemnity and holiness of the occasion. In an explication we would also mention that "fathers" initiates a chain of images of birth, continued in "conceived in liberty," "any nation so conceived," and "a new birth." (See Highet's explication of the Gettysburg Address, page 608.)

**exposition.**    An expository essay is chiefly concerned with giving information—how to register for classes, the causes of the French Revolution, or the tenets of Zen Buddhism. The writer of exposition must, of course, have a point of view (an attitude or a thesis), but because exposition—unlike persuasion—does not assume that the reader's opinion differs from the writer's, the point of view in exposition often is implicit rather than explicit.

**general** and **specific** (or **particular**).    A general word refers to a class or group; a specific (particular) word refers to a member of the class or group. Example: "vehicle" is general compared with "automobile" or with "motorcycle." But "general" and "specific" are relative. "Vehicle" is general when compared to "automobile," but "vehicle" is specific when compared to "machine," for "machine" refers to a class or group that includes not only vehicles but clocks, typewriters, and dynamos. Similarly, although "automobile" is specific in comparison with "vehicle," "automobile" is general in comparison with "Volkswagen" or "sportscar."

**generalization.**    A statement relating to every member of a class or category, or, more loosely, to most members of a class or category. Example: "Students from Medford High are well prepared." Compare: (1) "Janet Kuo is well prepared" (a report of a specific condition); (2) "Students from Medford High are well prepared" (a low-level generalization, because it is limited to one school); (3) "Students today are well prepared" (a high-level generalization, covering many people in many places).

**imagery** and **symbolism.**    When we read "rose," we may more or less call to mind a picture of a rose, or perhaps we are reminded of the odor or texture of a rose. Whatever in a piece of writing appeals to any of our senses (including sensations of heat and pressure as well as of sight, smell, taste, touch, sound) is an image. In short, images are the sensory content of a work, whether literal (the roses discussed in an essay on rose-growing) or figurative (a comparison, in a poem, of a girl to a rose). It is usually easy to notice images in literature, particularly in poems, which often include comparisons such as "I wandered lonely as a cloud," "a fiery eye," and "seems he a dove? His feathers are but borrowed." In literature, imagery (again, literal as well as figurative) plays a large part in communicating the meaning of the work. For instance, in *Romeo and Juliet* abundant imagery of light and dark reenforces the conflict between life and death. Juliet especially is associated with light (Romeo says, "What light through yonder window breaks? It is the east and Juliet is the sun"), and at the end of the play, when the lovers have died, we are told that the morning is dark: "The sun for sorrow will not show his head."

If we turn from imaginative literature to the essay, we find, of course, that descriptive essays are rich in images. But other kinds of essays, too, may make use of imagery—and not only by literal references to real people or things. Such essays may use figures of speech, as Thoreau does when he says that the imagination as well as the body should "both sit down at the same table." The imagination, after all, does not literally sit down at a table—but Thoreau personifies the imagination, seeing it as no less concrete than the body.

The distinction between an image and a symbol is partly a matter of emphasis and partly a matter of a view of reality. If an image is so insisted on that we feel that the writer sees it as highly significant in itself and also as a way of representing something else, we can call it a symbol. In Henry James's words, symbolism is the presentation "of objects casting . . . far behind them a shadow more curious . . . than the apparent figure." A symbol is what it is, and yet it is also much more. We may feel that a passage about the railroad, emphasizing its steel tracks and its steel cars, its speed and its noise, may be not only about the railroad but also about industrialism and, even further, about an entire way of life—a way of thinking and feeling—that came into being in the nineteenth century.

A symbol, then, is an image so loaded with significance that it is not simply literal, and it does not simply stand as a figure for something else; it is both itself *and* something else that it richly suggests, a kind of manifestation of something too complex or too elusive to be otherwise revealed. In a symbol, Thomas Carlyle wrote, "the Infinite is made to blend with the Finite, to stand visible, and as it were, attainable there." Still, having said all of this, one must add that the distinction between image and symbol is not sharp, and usage allows us even to say such things as, "The imagery of light symbolizes love," meaning that the imagery stands for or represents or is in part about love.

**induction.**   Reasoning from the particular to the general, or drawing a conclusion about all members of a class from a study of some members of the class. Every elephant I have seen is grayish, so by induction (from Latin, "lead into," "lead up to") I conclude that all elephants are grayish. Another example: I have met ten graduates of Vassar College and all are females, so I conclude that all Vassar graduates are females. This conclusion, however, happens to be incorrect; a few years ago Vassar began to admit males, and so although male graduates are few they do exist. Induction is valid only if the sample is representative.

Because one can rarely be certain that it *is* representative, induced conclusions are usually open to doubt. Still, we live our lives largely by induction; we have dinner with a friend, we walk the dog, we write home for money—all because these actions have produced certain results in the past and we assume that actions of the same sort will produce results consistent with our earlier findings. Nelson Algren's excellent advice must have been arrived at inductively: "Never eat at a place called Mom's, and never play cards with a man called Doc."

**interpretation.**   An explanation of the meaning. If we see someone clench his fist and tighten his mouth, we may interpret these signs as revealing anger. When we say that in the New Testament the passage alluding to the separation of sheep from goats is to be understood as referring to the saved and the damned, we are offering an interpretation.

**irony.**   In *verbal irony*, the meaning of the words intentionally contradicts the literal meaning, as in "that's not a very good idea," where the intended meaning is "that's a terrible idea."

Irony, in distinction from sarcasm, employs at least some degree of wit or wryness. Sarcasm reveals contempt obviously and heavily, usually by asserting the opposite of what is meant: "You're a great guy" (if said sarcastically) means "It's awful of you to do this to me." Notice that the example of irony we began with was at least a trifle more ingenious than this sarcastic remark, for the sarcasm here simply is the opposite of what is meant, whereas our example of verbal irony is not quite the opposite. The opposite of "that's not a very good idea" is "that is a very good idea," but clearly (in our example) the speaker's meaning is something else. Put it this way: sarcasm is irony at its crudest, and finer irony commonly uses overstatement or especially understatement, rather than a simple opposite. (For a brief discussion of the use of irony in satire, see the entry on satire, pages 1150–1151.)

If the speaker's words have an *un*intentional double meaning, the irony may be called *dramatic irony:* a character, about to go to bed, says, "I think I'll have a sound sleep," and dies in her sleep. Similarly, an action can turn dramatically ironic: a character seeks to help a friend and unintentionally harms her. Finally, a situation can be ironic: thirsty sailors are surrounded by water that cannot be drunk.

All these meanings of irony are held together, then, by the sense of a somewhat bitter contrast.

**jargon.**   Technical language used inappropriately or inexactly. "Viable" means "able to survive." To speak of "a viable building" is to use jargon. "A primary factor in my participation in the dance" is jargon if what is meant is "I dance because. . . ."

**metaphor.**   Words have literal meanings: a lemon is a yellow, egg-shaped citrus fruit; to drown is to suffocate in water or other fluid. But words can also have metaphoric meanings: we can call an unsatisfactory automobile a lemon, and we can say that we are drowning in paperwork. Metaphoric language is literally absurd; if we heed only the denotation it is clearly untrue, for an automobile cannot be a kind of citrus fruit, and we cannot drown in paperwork. (Even if the paper literally suffocated someone, the death could not be called a drowning.) Metaphor, then, uses not the denotation of the word but the associations, the connotations. Because we know that the speaker is not crazy, we turn from the literal meaning (which is clearly untrue) to the association.

**myth.**   (1) A traditional story dealing with supernatural beings or with heroes, often accounting for why things are as they are. Myths tell of the creation of the world, the creation of man, the changes of the season, the achievements of heroes. A Zulu myth, for example, explains that rain is the tears of a god weeping for a beloved slain bird. *Mythology* is a system or group of such stories, and so we speak of Zulu mythology, or Greek mythology, or Norse mythology. (2) Mark Schorer, in *William Blake*, defines myth as "a large controlling image that gives philosophic meaning to the facts of ordinary life. . . . All real convictions involve a mythology. . . . Wars may be described as the clash of mythologies." In this sense, then, a myth is not a traditional story we do not believe, but any idea, true or false, to which people subscribe. Thus, one can speak of the "myth" of democracy or of communism.

**narration.**   Discourse that recounts a real or a fictional happening. An anecdote is a narrative, and so is a history of the decline and fall of the Roman Empire. Narration may, of course, include substantial exposition ("four possible motives must be considered") and description ("the horse was an old gray mare"), but the emphasis is on a sequence of happenings ("and then she says to me, . . .").

**parable.**   A parable is a short narrative from which a moral or a lesson can be drawn. Christ's tale of the prodigal son (page 730) is told in order to reveal the blindness of the Pharisees who blame Christ for receiving sinners. A parable may, but need not, be an allegory wherein, say, each character stands for an abstraction that otherwise would be hard to grasp. Usually the parable lacks the *detailed* correspondence of an allegory.

**paradox.**   An apparent self-contradiction, such as "He was happiest when miserable."

**paraphrase.**   A rewording of a passage, usually in order to clarify the meaning. A paraphrase is a sort of translating within the same language; it can help to make clear the gist of the passage. But one must recognize the truth of Robert Frost's charge that when one paraphrases a line of good writing one puts it "in other and worse English." Paraphrase should not be confused with *explication,* pages 1144–1145.

**parody.**   A parody (from the Greek "counter song") seeks to amuse by imitating the style—the diction, the sentence structure—of another work, but normally the parody substitutes a very different subject. Thus, it might use tough-guy Hemingway talk to describe not a bullfighter but a butterfly catcher. Often a parody of a writer's style is a good-natured criticism of it.

**persona.**   The writer or speaker in a role adopted for a specific audience. When Abraham Lincoln wrote or spoke, he sometimes did so in the persona of commander in chief of the Union army, but at other times he did so in the persona of the simple man from Springfield, Illinois. The persona is a mask put on for a performance (*persona* is the Latin word for mask). If mask suggests insincerity, we should remember that whenever we speak or write we do so in a specific role—as friend, or parent, or teacher, or applicant for a job, or whatever. Although Lincoln was a husband, a father, a politician, a president, and many other things, when he wrote a letter or speech he might write solely as one of these; in a letter to his son, the persona (or, we might say, personality) is that of father, not that of commander in chief. The distinction between the writer (who necessarily fills many roles) and the persona who writes or speaks a work is especially useful in talking about satire, because the satirist often invents a mouthpiece very different from himself. The satirist—say, Jonathan Swift—may be strongly opposed to a view, but his persona (his invented essayist) may favor the view; the reader must perceive that the real writer is ridiculing the invented essayist.

**persuasion.**     Discourse that seeks to change a reader's mind. Persuasion usually assumes that the writer and the reader do not agree, or do not fully agree, at the outset. Persuasion may use logical argument (appeal to reason), but it may also try to win the reader over by other means—by appeal to the emotions, by wit, by geniality.

**rhetoric.**     Although in much contemporary usage the word's meaning has sadly decayed to "inflated talk or writing," it can still mean "the study of elements such as content, structure, and cadence in writing or in speech." In short, in the best sense rhetoric is the study of the art of communicating with words.

**satire.**     A work ridiculing identifiable objects in real life, meant to arouse in the reader contempt for its object. Satire is sometimes distinguished from comedy in that comedy aims simply to evoke amusement, whereas satire aims to bring about moral reform by ridicule. According to Alexander Pope, satire "heals with morals what it hurts with wit." Satire sometimes uses invective (direct abuse), but if the invective is to entertain the reader it must be witty, as in a piling up of ingenious accusations. Invective, however, is probably less common in satire than is irony, a device in which the tone somehow contradicts the words. For instance, a speaker may seem to praise ("well, that's certainly an original idea that you have"), but we perceive that he is ridiculing a crackpot idea. Or the satirist may invent a naive speaker (a persona) who praises, but the praise is really dispraise because a simpleton offers it; the persona is sincere but the writer is ironic and satiric. Or, adopting another strategy, the writer may use an apparently naive persona to represent the voice of reason; the persona dispassionately describes actions that we take for granted (a political campaign), and through this simple, accurate, rational description we see the irrationality of our behavior. (For further comments on irony, see pages 1147–1148.)

**style.** A distinctive way of expression. If we see a picture of a man sitting on a chair, we may say that it looks like a drawing for a comic book, or we may say that it looks like a drawing by Rembrandt or Van Gogh or Andrew Wyeth. We have come to recognize certain ways of expression—independent of the content—as characteristic of certain minds. The content, it can be said, is the same—a man sitting in a chair—but the creator's way of expressing the content is individual.

Similarly, "Four score and seven years ago" and "Eighty-seven years ago" are the same in content; but the styles differ, because "Four score and seven years ago" distinctively reflects a mind familiar with the Bible and an orator speaking solemnly. Many people (we include ourselves) believe that the content is *not* the same if the expression is not the same. The "content" of "Four score and seven years ago" includes suggestions of the Bible and of God-fearing people not present in "eighty-seven years ago." In this view, a difference in style is a difference in content and therefore a difference in meaning. Surely it is true that in the work of the most competent writers, those who make every word count, one cannot separate style and content.

Let C. S. Lewis have the next-to-last word: "The way for a person to develop a style is (a) to know exactly what he wants to say, and (b) to be sure he is saying exactly that. The reader, we must remember, does not start by knowing what we mean. If our words are ambiguous, our meaning will escape him. I sometimes think that writing is like driving sheep down a road. If there is any gate open to the left or the right the readers will most certainly go into it." And let the Austrian writer Karl Kraus have the last word: "There are two kinds of writers, those who are and those who aren't. With the first, content and form belong together like soul and body; with the second, they match each other like body and clothes."

**summary.** The word "summary" is related to "sum," to the total something adds up to. (The Greeks and Romans counted upward, and wrote the total at the top.) A summary is a condensation or abridgment briefly giving the reader the gist of a longer work. Here are a few principles that govern summaries:

1.  A summary is much briefer than the original. It is *not* a paraphrase—a word-by-word translation of someone's words into your own—for a paraphrase is usually at least as long as the original, whereas a summary is rarely longer than one-fourth the original, and may even be much briefer, perhaps giving in a sentence or two an entire essay.

2.  A summary usually achieves its brevity by omitting almost all the concrete details of the original, presenting only the sum that the details add up to.

3.  A summary is accurate; it has no value if it misrepresents the point of the original.

4.  The writer of a summary need not make the points in the same order as that of the original. In fact, a reader is occasionally driven to write a summary because the original author does not present the argument in an orderly sequence; the summary is an attempt to disengage the author's argument from the confusing presentation.

5.  A summary normally is written in the present tense, because the writer assumes that although the author *wrote* the piece last year or a hundred years ago, the piece speaks to us today. (In other words, the summary is explicitly or implicitly prefaced by "He says," and all that follows is in the present tense.

6.  Because a summary is openly based on someone else's views, not your own, you need not use quotation marks around any words that you take from the original.

Here is a summary of this entry on "summary":

> A summary is a condensation or abridgment. These are some characteristics: (1) it is rarely more than one-fourth as long as the original; (2) its brevity is usually achieved by leaving out most of the concrete details of the original; (3) it is accurate; (4) it may rearrange the organization of the original, especially if a rearrangement will make things clearer; (5) it normally is in the present tense; (6) quoted words need not be enclosed in quotation marks.

**thesis.**   The writer's position or attitude; the proposition advanced.

**thesis statement.**   A sentence or two summarizing the writer's position or attitude. An essay may or may not have an explicit thesis statement. (See page 14.)

**tone.**   The prevailing spirit of an utterance. The tone may be angry or bitter or joyful or solemn, or expressive of any similar mood or emotion. Tone usually reflects the writer's attitude toward the subject, the audience, and the self. (For further comments on tone, see pages 2–3.)

# ACKNOWLEDGMENTS

Bart J. Bok. "A Critical Look at Astrology." This article first appeared in *The Humanist* issue of September/October 1975 and is reprinted by permission.

"The Astrologers Reply." These letters first appeared in *The Humanist* issue of November/December 1975 and are reprinted by permission.

Ian Buruma. "Work as a Form of Beauty" from Mildred Friedman, ed., *Tokyo: Form and Spirit* (Minneapolis: Walker Art Center, 1986). Reprinted by permission.

"All at one Point" from *Cosmi-Comics* by Italo Calvino, English translation copyright © 1968 by Harcourt Brace Jovanovich, Inc. and Jonathan Cape Limited, reprinted by permission of Harcourt Brace Jovanovich, Inc.

Italo Calvino. "The Aquatic Uncle" from *Cosmi-Comics* by Italo Calvino, copyright © 1965 by Guilio Einuaudi Editore SpA, Torino, English translation copyright © 1968 by Harcourt Brace Jovanovich, Inc. and Jonathan Cape Ltd., reprinted by permission of Harcourt Brace Jovanovich, Inc. and Jonathan Cape Ltd.

Albert Camus. "The Myth of Sisyphus." From *The Myth of Sisyphs and Other Essays*, by Albert Camus, translated by Justin O'Brien. Copyright © 1955 by Alfred A. Knopf, Inc. Reprinted by permission of the publisher.

Stephen Chapman. "The Prisoner's Dilemma" from *The New Republic*, 8 March 1980. Reprinted by permission of *The New Republic*, © 1980, The New Republic Inc.

Chewing Blackbones. "Old Man and Old Woman" from *Indian Legends from the Northern Rockies*, by Ella E. Clark. Copyright © 1966 by the University of Oklahoma Press. Reprinted by permission.

Robert Coles. "Student Volunteers, Academic Credit," *The New York Times*, 30 April 1988. Copyright © 1988 by The New York Times Company. Reprinted by permission.

Lewis Coser. "The Family." From Lewis A. Coser, *Sociology Through Literature*, © 1963, pp. 250–251. Reprinted by permission of Prentice-Hall, Inc., Englewood Cliffs, New Jersey.

Priscilla Costello. "Astrology: Science or Abracadabra?" Reprinted by permission from *Wellesley Alumnae Magazine*, Spring 1983.

Laura Cunningham. "The Girls' Room" from *The New York Times*, 10 September 1981. Reprinted by permission of William Morris Agency, Inc., on behalf of the author.

Joan Didion. "On Going Home" from *Slouching Towards Bethlehem* by Joan Didion. Copyright © 1967, 1968 by Joan Didion. Reprinted by permission of Farrar, Straus and Giroux, Inc.

Excerpt on p. 225 from pp. 21–22 of *Measuring Growth in English* by Paul Diederich. © 1974 by the National Council of Teachers of English. Reprinted by permission.

Barbara Erhenreich. "The 'Playboy' Man and the American Family" from *Ms.*, June 1983. Reprinted by permission of the author.

Barbara Ehrenreich. "A Step Back to the Workhouse?" from *Ms.*, November 1979. Reprinted by permission of the author.

Letters sent to *Ms.* Magazine in response to "A Step Back to the Workhouse?" and published in the February 1988 issue. Reprinted by permission of the authors.

Barbara Ehrenreich and Annette Fuentes, "Life on the Global Assembly Line" from *Ms.*, June 1981. Reprinted by permission of the authors.

Joseph Epstein. "Obsessed by Sport." Reprinted by permission of Georges Borchardt, Inc. for the author. Copyright © 1976 by Joseph Epstein. Originally appeared in *Harper's* Magazine.

Joyce Carol Oates. "How I Contemplated the World From the Detroit House of Correction and Began My Life Over Again." Reprinted from *The Wheel of Love and Other Stories* by Joyce Carol Oates, by permission of the publisher, Vanguard Press, Inc. Copyright © 1970, 1969, 1968, 1967, 1966, 1965 by Joyce Carol Oates.

George Orwell. "Politics and the English Language," copyright 1946 by Sonia Brownell Orwell, renewed 1974 by Sonia Orwell, reprinted from *Shooting an Elephant and Other Essays* by George Orwell by permission of Harcourt Brace Jovanovich, Inc., the estate of the late Sonia Brownell Orwell, and Martin Secker & Warburg Ltd.

George Orwell. "Shooting an Elephant" from *Shooting an Elephant and Other Essays* by George Orwell, copyright 1950 by Sonia Brownell Orwell, renewed 1978 by Sonia Pitt-Rivers, reprinted by permission of Harcourt Brace Jovanovich, Inc., the estate of the late Sonia Brownell Orwell, and Martin Secker & Warburg Ltd.

George Orwell. "What Is Science?" from *Collected Essays, Journalism and Letters of George Orwell: In Front of Your Nose, 1945–1950, IV,* edited by Sonia Orwell and Ian Angus, copyright 1968 by Sonia Brownell Orwell, reprinted by permission of Harcourt Brace Jovanovich, Inc., the estate of the late Sonia Brownell Orwell, and Martin Secker & Warburg Ltd.

Noel Perrin. "A Part-time Marriage," *The New York Times* (Magazine), 9 September 1984. Copyright © 1984 by The New York Times Company. Reprinted by permission.

J. H. Plumb. "The Dying Family" and "The Stars in Their Day" from *In the Light of History* by J. H. Plumb, published by Houghton Mifflin Company and Penguin Books Ltd. Copyright © 1972 by J. H. Plumb. Reprinted by permission of Sir John Plumb.

Katherine Anne Porter. "The Jilting of Granny Weatherall" from *Flowering Judas and Other Stories* by Katherine Anne Porter, copyright 1930, 1958 by Katherine Anne Porter, reprinted by permission of Harcourt Brace Jovanovich, Inc.

Neil Postman. "Order in the Classroom," (original title, "Teaching as a Conserving Activity") excerpted from the book *Teaching as a Conserving Activity* by Neil Postman. Copyright © 1979 by Neil Postman. Reprinted by permission of Delacorte Press, a division of Bantam, Doubleday, Dell Publishing Group, Inc.

Paul Robinson. "TV Can't Educate" from *The New Republic*, 12 August 1978. Reprinted by permission of *The New Republic*, © 1974, The New Republic, Inc.

Theodore Roethke. "Child on Top of a Greenhouse," copyright 1946 by Editorial Publications, Inc., and "My Papa's Waltz," copyright 1942 by Hearst Magazines, Inc., from *The Collected Poems of Theodore Roethke*. Reprinted by permission of Doubleday, a division of Bantam, Doubleday, Dell Publishing Group, Inc.

Thomas P. Rohlen. Reprinted by permission of the *Harvard Business Review*. "From the Manager's Bookshelf: Why Japanese Education Works" by Thomas P. Rohlen (September/October 1987). Copyright © 1987 by the President and Fellows of Harvard College.

Bertrand Russell. "Why I Am Not a Christian." from *Why I Am Not a Christian and Other Essays* by Bertrand Russell. Copyright © 1957, 1985, by Allen & Unwin. Reprinted by permission of Simon & Schuster, Inc., and Unwin Hyman Ltd.

Bertrand Russell. "Work." Reprinted from *The Conquest of Happiness* by Bertrand Russell, with the permission of Liveright Publishing Corporation and Unwin Hyman Ltd. Copyright 1930 by Horace Liveright, Inc. Copyright renewed 1958 by Bertrand Russell.

Excerpt on p. 33 reprinted from *The Conquest of Happiness* by Bertrand Russell, with the permission of Liveright Publishing Corporation and Unwin Hyman Ltd. Copyright 1930 by Horace Liveright, Inc. Copyright renewed 1958 by Bertrand Russell.

May Sarton. "The Rewards of Living a Solitary Life," *The New York Times*, 6 April 1974. Copyright © 1974 by The New York Times Company. Reprinted by permission.

Lionel Tiger. "Omnigamy: The New Kinship System." Reprinted by permission of International Creative Management, Inc. Copyright © 1978 by Lionel Tiger. Originally appeared in *Psychology Today* magazine.

Phyllis Trible. "Eve and Adam: Genesis 2–3 Reread," *Andover Newton Quarterly* 13, March 1973. Reprinted by permission of the publisher and the author.

John Updike. "A & P." Copyright © 1962 by John Updike. Reprinted from *Pigeon Feathers and Other Stories* by John Updike, by permission of Alfred A. Knopf, Inc.

Excerpt on p. 151 from *Assorted Prose*, by John Updike, reprinted by permission of Alfred A. Knopf, Inc. Copyright © 1964 by John Updike. First appeared in *The New Yorker*.

Excerpt on p. 228 from *In My Own Way*, by Alan Watts, reprinted by permission of Pantheon Books, a Division of Random House, Inc. Copyright © 1972 by Alan Watts.

E. B. White. "The Door" from *Poems & Sketches of E. B. White*. Copyright 1939, 1967 by E. B. White. Originally appeared in *The New Yorker*. By permission of Harper & Row, Publishers.

E. B. White. "Education." From pp. 52–54 in "Education—March 1939" in *One Man's Meat* by E. B. White. Copyright 1939, 1967 by E. B. White. By permission of Harper & Row, Publishers.

Merry White. "Japanese Education: How Do They Do It?" Reprinted with permission of the author from *The Public Interest*, No. 76 (Summer 1984), pp. 87–101. © 1984 by National Affairs, Inc.

Richard Wilbur. "Mind" from *Things of This World* by Richard Wilbur, copyright © 1956, 1984 by Richard Wilbur, reprinted by permission of Harcourt Brace Jovanovich, Inc.

Williams Carlos Williams. "The Poor" from William Carlos Williams, *Collected Poems, Volume I: 1909–1939*. Copyright 1938 by New Directions Publishing Corporation. Reprinted by permission of New Directions Publishing Corporation.

Marrie Winn. "The End of Play" from *Children Without Childhood* by Marie Winn. Copyright © 1981, 1983 by Marie Winn. Reprinted by permission of Pantheon Books, a Division of Random House, Inc.

Virginia Woolf. "Professions for Women" from *The Death of the Moth and Other Essays* by Virginia Woolf, copyright 1942 by Harcourt Brace Jovanovich, Inc., renewed 1970 by Marjorie T. Parsons, Executrix, reprinted by permission of Harcourt Brace Jovanovich, Inc., the estate of Virginia Woolf, and The Hogarth Press.

Wu-tsu Fa-yen. "Zen and the Art of Burglary" from Daisetz T. Suzuki, *Zen and Japanese Culture*, Bollingen Series 44. Copyright © 1959 by Princeton University Press. Reprinted with permission of Princeton University Press.

W. B. Yeats. "The Lake Isle of Innisfree" from *Collected Poems* by W. B. Yeats. Copyright 1906 by Macmillan Publishing Company, renewed 1934 by William Butler Yeats. Reprinted by permission of A. P. Watt Ltd. on behalf of Michael B. Yeats and Macmillan London Ltd.

W. B. Yeats. "Remembering 'The Lake Isle of Innisfree'" excerpted from W. B. Yeats, *Autobiography*. Copyright 1916, 1935 by Macmillan Publishing Company; renewed 1944, 1963 by Bertha Georgie Yeats. Reprinted by permission of Macmillan Publishing Company and A. P. Watt Ltd. on behalf of Michael B. Yeats and Macmillan London Ltd.

# Index

# To the Student

Part of our job as educational publishers is to try to improve the textbooks we publish. Thus, when revising a book, we take into account the experience of both instructors and students with the previous edition. At some time your instructor will be asked to comment extensively on *The Little, Brown Reader*, Fifth Edition, but right now we want to hear from you. After all, though your instructor assigned this book, you are the one who paid for it.

Please help us by completing this questionnaire and returning it to College English Developmental Group, Scott, Foresman and Company, 1900 East Lake Avenue, Glenview, Illinois 60025.

School _____ Course title _____

Instructor's Name _____

Please rate the selections:

|  | Liked best | | | | Liked least | Didn't read |
|---|---|---|---|---|---|---|
| **1. READING (AND WRITING ABOUT) ESSAYS** | | | | | | |
| George Orwell, Shooting an Elephant | 5 | 4 | 3 | 2 | 1 | |
| | | | | | | |
| **2. ALL IN THE FAMILY** | | | | | | |
| Lewis Coser, The Family | 5 | 4 | 3 | 2 | 1 | \_\_ |
| J. H. Plumb, The Dying Family | 5 | 4 | 3 | 2 | 1 | \_\_ |
| Judy Syfers, Why I Want a Wife | 5 | 4 | 3 | 2 | 1 | \_\_ |
| Julie Matthaei, Political Economy and Family Policy | 5 | 4 | 3 | 2 | 1 | \_\_ |
| Jonda McFarlane, The Meaning of Marriage | 5 | 4 | 3 | 2 | 1 | \_\_ |
| Richard John Neuhaus, Renting Women, Buying Babies and Class Struggle | 5 | 4 | 3 | 2 | 1 | \_\_ |
| Lionel Tiger, Omnigamy: The New Kinship System | 5 | 4 | 3 | 2 | 1 | \_\_ |
| B. Aisha Lemu, In Defense of Polygamy | 5 | 4 | 3 | 2 | 1 | \_\_ |

|  | Liked best | | | | Liked least | Didn't read |
|---|---|---|---|---|---|---|
| Barbara Ehrenreich, The "Playboy" Man and the American Family | 5 | 4 | 3 | 2 | 1 | — |
| Noel Perrin, A Part-time Marriage | 5 | 4 | 3 | 2 | 1 | — |
| Jane Howard, All Happy Clans Are Alike: In Search of the Good Family | 5 | 4 | 3 | 2 | 1 | — |
| Laura Cunningham, The Girls' Room | 5 | 4 | 3 | 2 | 1 | — |
| Black Elk, High Horse's Courting | 5 | 4 | 3 | 2 | 1 | — |
| Anonymous, Confessions of an Erstwhile Child | 5 | 4 | 3 | 2 | 1 | — |
| Jonathan Swift, A Modest Proposal | 5 | 4 | 3 | 2 | 1 | — |
| Peter Singer, Animal Liberation | 5 | 4 | 3 | 2 | 1 | — |
| Jamaica Kincaid, Girl | 5 | 4 | 3 | 2 | 1 | — |
| Italo Calvino, The Aquatic Uncle | 5 | 4 | 3 | 2 | 1 | — |
| Theodore Roethke, My Papa's Waltz | 5 | 4 | 3 | 2 | 1 | — |

## 3. FOOD, CLOTHING, SHELTER

|  | Liked best | | | | Liked least | Didn't read |
|---|---|---|---|---|---|---|
| Roger B. Swain, Firewood | 5 | 4 | 3 | 2 | 1 | — |
| Peter Farb & George Armelagos, The Patterns of Eating | 5 | 4 | 3 | 2 | 1 | — |
| Michael J. Arlen, Ode to Thanksgiving | 5 | 4 | 3 | 2 | 1 | — |
| Paul Goldberger, Quick! Before It Crumbles! | 5 | 4 | 3 | 2 | 1 | — |
| Henry David Thoreau, As for Clothing | 5 | 4 | 3 | 2 | 1 | — |
| Melvin Konner, Kick Off Your Heels | 5 | 4 | 3 | 2 | 1 | — |
| Garrison Keillor, Something from the Sixties | 5 | 4 | 3 | 2 | 1 | — |
| Robert Sommer, Hard Architecture | 5 | 4 | 3 | 2 | 1 | — |
| John Steinbeck, Mobile Homes | 5 | 4 | 3 | 2 | 1 | — |
| Jane Jacobs, A Good Neighborhood | 5 | 4 | 3 | 2 | 1 | — |
| E. B. White, The Door | 5 | 4 | 3 | 2 | 1 | — |
| William Carlos Williams, The Poor | 5 | 4 | 3 | 2 | 1 | — |

## 4. TEACHING AND LEARNING

|  | Liked best | | | | Liked least | Didn't read |
|---|---|---|---|---|---|---|
| Plato, The Myth of the Cave | 5 | 4 | 3 | 2 | 1 | — |
| Ernesto Galarza, Growing into Manhood | 5 | 4 | 3 | 2 | 1 | — |
| E. B. White, Education | 5 | 4 | 3 | 2 | 1 | — |
| Maya Angelou, Graduation | 5 | 4 | 3 | 2 | 1 | — |
| Pauline Kael, High School and Other Forms of Madness | 5 | 4 | 3 | 2 | 1 | — |
| Nathan Glazer, Some Very Modest Proposals for the Improvement of American Education | 5 | 4 | 3 | 2 | 1 | — |

|  | *Liked best* |  |  |  | *Liked least* | *Didn't read* |
|---|---|---|---|---|---|---|
| Neil Postman, Order in the Classroom | 5 | 4 | 3 | 2 | 1 | __ |
| Merry White, Japanese Education: How Do They Do It? | 5 | 4 | 3 | 2 | 1 | __ |
| Theodore Sizer, Principal's Questions | 5 | 4 | 3 | 2 | 1 | __ |
| Robert Coles, Student Volunteers, Academic Credit | 5 | 4 | 3 | 2 | 1 | __ |
| John Holt, The Right to Control One's Learning | 5 | 4 | 3 | 2 | 1 | __ |
| Paul Goodman, A Proposal to Abolish Grading | 5 | 4 | 3 | 2 | 1 | __ |
| Mary Field Belenky, Blythe McVicker Clinchy, Nancy Rule Goldberger, and Jill Mattuck Tarule, Toward an Education for Women | 5 | 4 | 3 | 2 | 1 | __ |
| Paul Robinson, TV Can't Educate | 5 | 4 | 3 | 2 | 1 | __ |
| Patricia Nelson Limerick, The Phenomenon of Phantom Students: Diagnosis and Treatment | 5 | 4 | 3 | 2 | 1 | __ |
| Toni Cade Bambara, The Lesson | 5 | 4 | 3 | 2 | 1 | __ |
| Wu-tsu Fa-yen, Zen and the Art of Burglary | 5 | 4 | 3 | 2 | 1 | __ |

## 5. WORK AND PLAY

|  | *Liked best* |  |  |  | *Liked least* | *Didn't read* |
|---|---|---|---|---|---|---|
| Bertrand Russell, Work | 5 | 4 | 3 | 2 | 1 | __ |
| W. H. Auden, Work, Labor, and Play | 5 | 4 | 3 | 2 | 1 | __ |
| Malcolm X, The Shoeshine Boy | 5 | 4 | 3 | 2 | 1 | __ |
| Studs Terkel, Three Workers | 5 | 4 | 3 | 2 | 1 | __ |
| Virginia Woolf, Professions for Women | 5 | 4 | 3 | 2 | 1 | __ |
| Gloria Steinem, The Importance of Work | 5 | 4 | 3 | 2 | 1 | __ |
| Charles Krauthammer, The Just Wage: From Bad to Worth | 5 | 4 | 3 | 2 | 1 | __ |
| Barbara R. Bergmann, Pay Equity— How to Argue Back | 5 | 4 | 3 | 2 | 1 | __ |
| Lester C. Thurow, Why Women Are Paid Less Than Men | 5 | 4 | 3 | 2 | 1 | __ |
| Barbara Ehrenreich, A Step Back to the Workhouse? | 5 | 4 | 3 | 2 | 1 | __ |
| Ian Buruma, Work as a Form of Beauty | 5 | 4 | 3 | 2 | 1 | __ |
| Sir Thomas More, Work and Play in Utopia | 5 | 4 | 3 | 2 | 1 | __ |
| Marie Winn, The End of Play | 5 | 4 | 3 | 2 | 1 | __ |
| Black Elk, War Games | 5 | 4 | 3 | 2 | 1 | __ |

| | Liked best | | | | Liked least | Didn't read |
|---|---|---|---|---|---|---|
| Joseph Epstein, Obsessed with Sport | 5 | 4 | 3 | 2 | 1 | — |
| John Updike, A & P | 5 | 4 | 3 | 2 | 1 | — |
| Theodore Roethke, Child on Top of a Greenhouse | 5 | 4 | 3 | 2 | 1 | — |

## 6. OPEN FOR BUSINESS

| | Liked best | | | | Liked least | Didn't read |
|---|---|---|---|---|---|---|
| Alexis de Toqueville, That Aristocracy May Be Engendered by Manufactures | 5 | 4 | 3 | 2 | 1 | — |
| W. H. Auden, The Almighty Dollar | 5 | 4 | 3 | 2 | 1 | — |
| Elbert Hubbard, A Message to Garcia | 5 | 4 | 3 | 2 | 1 | — |
| Alexandra Armstrong, Starting a Business | 5 | 4 | 3 | 2 | 1 | — |
| Thomas P. Rohlen, For the Manager's Bookshelf: Why Japanese Education Works | 5 | 4 | 3 | 2 | 1 | — |
| Robert W. Keidel, A New Game for Managers to Play | 5 | 4 | 3 | 2 | 1 | — |
| Warren Bennis, Time to Hang Up the Old Sports Clichés | 5 | 4 | 3 | 2 | 1 | — |
| Milton Friedman, The Social Responsibility of Business Is to Increase Its Profits | 5 | 4 | 3 | 2 | 1 | — |
| Barbara Ehrenreich and Annette Fuentes, Life on the Global Assembly Line | 5 | 4 | 3 | 2 | 1 | — |
| Bowen H. McCoy, The Parable of the Sadhu | 5 | 4 | 3 | 2 | 1 | — |
| John S. Fielden, "What Do You Mean You Don't Like My Style" | 5 | 4 | 3 | 2 | 1 | — |
| Sherwood Andersen, The Egg | 5 | 4 | 3 | 2 | 1 | — |

## 7. MESSAGES

| | Liked best | | | | Liked least | Didn't read |
|---|---|---|---|---|---|---|
| Edward T. Hall, Proxemics in the Arab World | 5 | 4 | 3 | 2 | 1 | — |
| Keith H. Basso, "Stalking with Stories": Names, Places, and Moral Narratives Among the Western Apache | 5 | 4 | 3 | 2 | 1 | — |
| C. S. Lewis, Xmas and Christmas | 5 | 4 | 3 | 2 | 1 | — |
| Abraham Lincoln, Address at the Dedication of the Gettysburg National Cemetery | 5 | 4 | 3 | 2 | 1 | — |
| Gilbert Highet, The Gettysburg Address | 5 | 4 | 3 | 2 | 1 | — |
| George Orwell, Politics and the English Language | 5 | 4 | 3 | 2 | 1 | — |

| | Liked best | | | | Liked least | Didn't read |
|---|---|---|---|---|---|---|

Robin Lakoff, You Are What You
Say    5   4   3   2   1   ___

Barbara Lawrence, Four-Letter Words
Can Hurt You    5   4   3   2   1   ___

Stevie Smith, Not Waving but
Drowning    5   4   3   2   1   ___

## 8. NETWORKS

Patricia Spacks, What Have 60
Million Readers Found in Nancy
Drew?    5   4   3   2   1   ___

Richard Hawley, Television and
Adolescents: A Teacher's View    5   4   3   2   1   ___

Tipper Gore, Curbing the
Sexploitation Industry    5   4   3   2   1   ___

Marya Mannes, Television
Advertising: The Splitting Image    5   4   3   2   1   ___

Dolores Hayden, Advertisements,
Pornography, and Public Space    5   4   3   2   1   ___

X. J. Kennedy, Who Killed King
Kong?    5   4   3   2   1   ___

Ursula K. Le Guin, American SF and
The Other    5   4   3   2   1   ___

Stephen King, Why We Crave
Horror Movies    5   4   3   2   1   ___

Woody Allen, The Colorization of
Films Insults Artists and Society    5   4   3   2   1   ___

Stanley Milgram, Confessions of a
News Addict    5   4   3   2   1   ___

James Thurber, The Secret Life of
Walter Mitty    5   4   3   2   1   ___

## 9. LAW AND ORDER

Martin Luther King, Jr., Nonviolent
Resistance    5   4   3   2   1   ___

Plato, Crito    5   4   3   2   1   ___

Luke, John, and an Anonymous
Japanese, Four Short Narratives    5   4   3   2   1   ___

Thomas Jefferson, The Declaration of
Independence    5   4   3   2   1   ___

Rosika Schwimmer, Court Record of
Petition for Naturalization    5   4   3   2   1   ___

Pierce Butler, Opinion of the
Supreme Court, in *The United
States of America, Petitioner*, v.
*Rosika Schwimmer*    5   4   3   2   1   ___

| | Liked best | | | | Liked least | Didn't read |
|---|---|---|---|---|---|---|
| Oliver Wendell Holmes, Dissent in the Rosika Schwimmer Case | 5 | 4 | 3 | 2 | 1 | ___ |
| Byron R. White, Opinion of the Supreme Court, in *New Jersey* v. *T.L.O.* [On the Right to Search Students] | 5 | 4 | 3 | 2 | 1 | ___ |
| John Paul Stevens, Dissent in the Case of *New Jersey* v. *T.L.O.* | 5 | 4 | 3 | 2 | 1 | ___ |
| Edward I. Koch, Death and Justice: How Capital Punishment Affirms Life | 5 | 4 | 3 | 2 | 1 | ___ |
| Henry Schwarzschild, In Opposition to Death Penalty Legislation | 5 | 4 | 3 | 2 | 1 | ___ |
| Stephen Chapman, The Prisoner's Dilemma | 5 | 4 | 3 | 2 | 1 | ___ |
| Joyce Carol Oates, How I Contemplated the World from the Detroit House of Correction and Began My Life Over Again | 5 | 4 | 3 | 2 | 1 | ___ |
| Arthur Hugh Clough, The Latest Decalogue | 5 | 4 | 3 | 2 | 1 | ___ |

## 10. SCIENCE OR PSEUDOSCIENCE?

| | Liked best | | | | Liked least | Didn't read |
|---|---|---|---|---|---|---|
| Stephen W. Hawking, Our Picture of the Universe | 5 | 4 | 3 | 2 | 1 | ___ |
| Carl G. Hempel, Scientific Inquiry: Invention and Test | 5 | 4 | 3 | 2 | 1 | ___ |
| Thomas S. Kuhn, The Function of Dogma in Scientific Research | 5 | 4 | 3 | 2 | 1 | ___ |
| Werner Heisenberg, Science and Religion | 5 | 4 | 3 | 2 | 1 | ___ |
| George Orwell, What Is Science? | 5 | 4 | 3 | 2 | 1 | ___ |
| Isaac Asimov, My Built-in Doubter | 5 | 4 | 3 | 2 | 1 | ___ |
| Bart J. Bok, A Critical Look at Astrology | 5 | 4 | 3 | 2 | 1 | ___ |
| The Astrologers Reply (Five Letters) | 5 | 4 | 3 | 2 | 1 | ___ |
| Priscilla Costello, Astrology, Science or Abracadabra? | 5 | 4 | 3 | 2 | 1 | ___ |
| J. H. Plumb, The Stars in Their Day | 5 | 4 | 3 | 2 | 1 | ___ |
| Stephen Jay Gould, Women's Brains | 5 | 4 | 3 | 2 | 1 | ___ |
| Ruth Bleier, Gender and Mathematical Ability | 5 | 4 | 3 | 2 | 1 | ___ |
| Evelyn Fox Keller, Women in Science: An Analysis of a Social Problem | 5 | 4 | 3 | 2 | 1 | ___ |
| Alfred Meyer, Do Lie Detectors Lie? | 5 | 4 | 3 | 2 | 1 | ___ |
| Lewis Thomas, The Hazards of Science | 5 | 4 | 3 | 2 | 1 | ___ |

| | Liked best | | | | Liked least | Didn't read |
|---|---|---|---|---|---|---|
| Italo Calvino, All at One Point | 5 | 4 | 3 | 2 | 1 | —— |
| Richard Wilbur, Mind | 5 | 4 | 3 | 2 | 1 | —— |

## 11. THE DEEP HEART'S CORE

| | Liked best | | | | Liked least | Didn't read |
|---|---|---|---|---|---|---|
| William Butler Yeats, The Lake Isle of Innisfree | 5 | 4 | 3 | 2 | 1 | —— |
| William Butler Yeats, Remembering "The Lake Isle of Innisfree" | 5 | 4 | 3 | 2 | 1 | —— |
| E. M. Forster, My Wood | 5 | 4 | 3 | 2 | 1 | —— |
| Joan Didion, On Going Home | 5 | 4 | 3 | 2 | 1 | —— |
| C. S. Lewis, We Have No "Right to Happiness" | 5 | 4 | 3 | 2 | 1 | —— |
| May Sarton, The Rewards of Living a Solitary Life | 5 | 4 | 3 | 2 | 1 | —— |
| Albert Camus, The Myth of Sisyphus | 5 | 4 | 3 | 2 | 1 | —— |
| Lewis Thomas, Late Night Thoughts on Listening to Mahler's Ninth Symphony | 5 | 4 | 3 | 2 | 1 | —— |
| Matthew Arnold, Dover Beach | 5 | 4 | 3 | 2 | 1 | —— |

## 12. ARTICLES OF FAITH

| | Liked best | | | | Liked least | Didn't read |
|---|---|---|---|---|---|---|
| Genesis 1–2 (The Creation) | 5 | 4 | 3 | 2 | 1 | —— |
| Genesis 3 (The Fall) | 5 | 4 | 3 | 2 | 1 | —— |
| Genesis 4 (Cain and Abel) | 5 | 4 | 3 | 2 | 1 | —— |
| Genesis 11 (The Tower of Babel) | 5 | 4 | 3 | 2 | 1 | —— |
| Genesis 12, 18, 22 (The Calling of Abraham, and Abraham and Isaac) | 5 | 4 | 3 | 2 | 1 | —— |
| 2 Samuel 11–12 (David and Bathsheba) | 5 | 4 | 3 | 2 | 1 | —— |
| Phyllis Trible, Eve and Adam: Genesis 2–3 Reread | 5 | 4 | 3 | 2 | 1 | —— |
| Jesus, The Sermon on the Mount | 5 | 4 | 3 | 2 | 1 | —— |
| C. S. Lewis, What Christians Believe | 5 | 4 | 3 | 2 | 1 | —— |
| Bertrand Russell, Why I Am Not a Christian | 5 | 4 | 3 | 2 | 1 | —— |
| William James, Religious Faith | 5 | 4 | 3 | 2 | 1 | —— |
| Will Herberg, Religiosity and Religion | 5 | 4 | 3 | 2 | 1 | —— |
| John Steinbeck, The Preacher | 5 | 4 | 3 | 2 | 1 | —— |
| Langston Hughes, Salvation | 5 | 4 | 3 | 2 | 1 | —— |
| Gautama Buddha, The Sermon at Benares and Parables | 5 | 4 | 3 | 2 | 1 | —— |
| Daisetz Teitaro Suzuki, What Is Zen? | 5 | 4 | 3 | 2 | 1 | —— |
| Wilfred Cantwell Smith, Muslims | 5 | 4 | 3 | 2 | 1 | —— |
| Idries Shah, Two Islamic Tales | 5 | 4 | 3 | 2 | 1 | —— |
| Chewing Blackbones, Old Man and Old Woman | 5 | 4 | 3 | 2 | 1 | —— |

|  | Liked best |  |  |  | Liked least | Didn't read |
|---|---|---|---|---|---|---|
| Katherine Anne Porter, The Jilting of Granny Weatherall | 5 | 4 | 3 | 2 | 1 | — |
| Gerard Manley Hopkins, God's Grandeur | 5 | 4 | 3 | 2 | 1 | — |
| Appendix A: Reading (and Writing About) Pictures | 5 | 4 | 3 | 2 | 1 | — |
| Appendix B: A Writer's Glossary | 5 | 4 | 3 | 2 | 1 | — |

What did you think of the *Short Views*? Did you discuss them in class?

_____

_____

Did you like the idea of discussing and writing about pictures?

_____

Please add any comments or suggestions on how we might improve this book.

_____

_____

_____

_____

Your Name _____ Date _____

Mailing address _____

May we quote you either in promotion for this book or in future publishing ventures?

Yes _____ No _____

Thank you.